COLLECTING TOYS NO. 6

by Richard O'Brien

A COLLECTOR'S
IDENTIFICATION & VALUE GUIDE

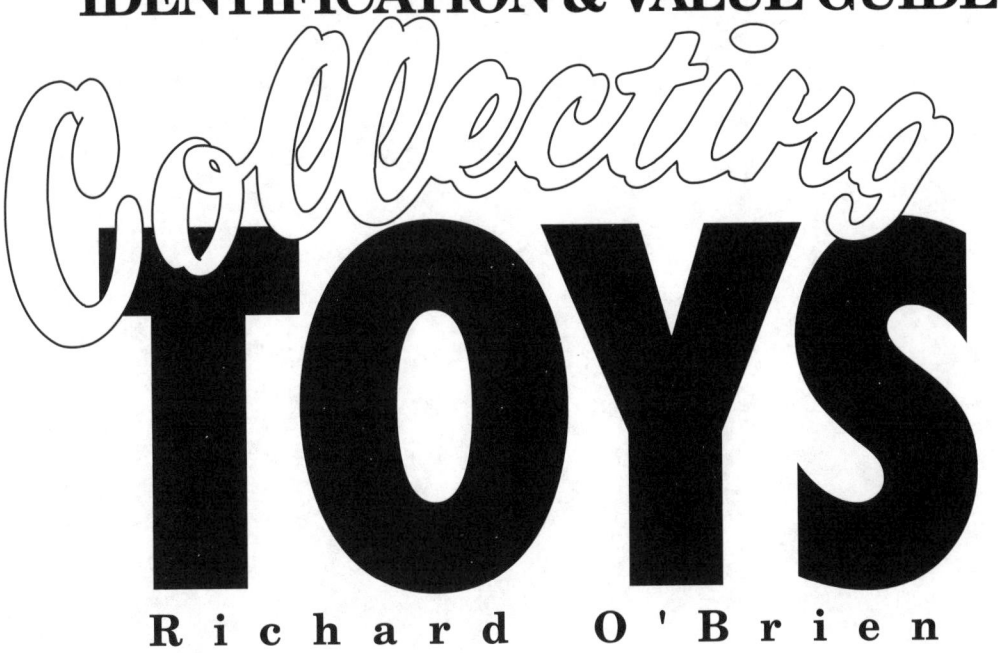

Collecting
TOYS

Richard O'Brien

BOOKS AMERICANA
INC.

ISBN 0-89689-094-5

To Fred Maxwell

Who, at the age of 84,

plopped himself into a car in Virginia

and drove all the way to Kansas to research old

toy companies of the 1920s and 1930s.

The results are in this book,

including the history of the formerly unknown

(though their toys were) C.A.W.

TABLE OF CONTENTS

...continued

ACKNOWLEDGMENTS

One of the benefits of doing this book is all the collectors it puts me in touch with. This edition they were more numerous than ever, and once again I found myself thoroughly impressed and grateful for their generosity and willingness to do what I know is very hard work.

So thanks to all. To Jim Harmon, who once again was just as prompt and just as expert. To Barbara and Jonathan Newman for their usual stellar job. To that whirlwind of aid Don Hultzman for handling not only his own section but pitching in prodigiously in a number of other areas.

Blossom Abell, having revamped Schoenhut in the last edition, demonstrated her perfectionism by doing it again, this time so spectacularly that it's been handed a section of its own. Perry Eichor came through handsomely again, and also flung in some extra help in other areas. No-Faster-Man-With-A-Deadline, otherwise known as Dick MacNary, kept his shining reputation unblemished. Even without needing a penny stuck in his slot and a lever pushed, Bill Bertoia did it again on mechanical banks.

Charles W. Best was back again, once more with camera in hand, and James Schleyer weighed in for the first time with an acute rundown on Western-style guns. Another adept with a camera, Ron Smith kept us all up to date on his specialty, as did the energetic and enterprising Dave Leopard on all of his.

Pez and Figure Kits are big: David Welch weighed in with a masterful survey of both fields. Also in the full-steam-ahead bracket is action figures, and Barry Goodman on G.I. Joe, Gary J. Linden on Hartland, and Jim Main on just about everything else really charged in and took over.

Joe and Sharon Freed once again did it all on Courtland-Walt Reach, and the redoubtable Fred Maxwell continued his relentless attack on the rapidly diminishing mysteries of lead alloy vehicles and aircraft.

Photos are a prime part of this book. So whether for a single shot or a slew, I'm as grateful as can be to the following: Bob West, Gary Franson, Perry Eichor, Fred Maxwell, Lawrence Scripps Wilkinson and Barbara Niman of the Detroit Toy Museum's Wilkinson Collection, Sotheby's New York, Max Heiss, Calvin L. Chaussee, Chic Gast, James Apthorpe, Islyn Thomas (catalogs), Barry Goodman, Gary J. Linden, Rex & Richard Gray, Charles W. Best, Charles D. Richards, Lloyd W. Ralston, James S. Maxwell/Virginia Caputo, Blossom Abell (aided by Jim & Patsy Carlson), Thomas G. Nefos of the Federal Shipping Network, Christie's East, Don Hultzman & Ron Chojnacki, Phillips, Ed Hyers, Brad Krewson, Don Coviello, Bruce Bergstrom of Artman Originals, Stan Alekna, Mark S. Brumback, Dave Leopard, Ron Smith, Scott Smiles, Ron Fink, Dick MacNary, Joe & Sharon Freed, James Schleyer, John Wright Co., Gail Seeley, K. Warren Mitchell, Barry

Koester, Mary Ann Kennedy, Jack Matthews, David Welch, Donn Fagans - Farrant Assoc., Heinz Mueller of Continental Hobby House, Orville C. Britton, John M. Ianuzzi, Craig A. Clark (plus much information on lead alloy vehicles), William G. Floyd, Rodney A. Heesacker, Ferd Zegel, Ed Poole, R.F. Sapita, Gerald F. Slack, Joe Higgins and Larry Giancola, who contributed information as well.

Finally, thanks all over again to all of those who've contributed in the past, to anyone I've forgotten (did I do it *again*?), to my agent Al Zuckerman and to Books Americana publisher Dan Alexander for his continuing courtesy, friendliness and professionalism.

INTRODUCTION

When I began work on this edition, there were two concerns in the toy-collecting community. The first was the economy, and the second was a shop that opened in New York in 1990 which asked stunningly high prices, prices that seemed to threaten the foundation of the hobby.

Seven months later, as I put the finishing touches to this book, and even though the recession remains, the furrowed brows have smoothed. Although there has been some stasis in the highest-priced regions of collectible toys, basically the hobby has remained very healthy, with prices continuing their upward climb, and more and more toys being judged collectible. As for the second concern, collectors agree there was no effect whatever (the shop has since closed).

One thing hasn't changed. As always, it should be stressed that when it comes to prices, this book is a **guide**. It is **not** the absolute last word on the price of a toy. Nothing could be. Prices may inflate or deflate in the months it takes to publish a book. And even on the same day a toy can vary in price, depending on the dealer, the buyer, the geographical area in which it's being sold, and whether it's being offered in the first moments of a toy show or in the last, draggy minutes, when the dealer finds himself having to pack up all that stuff again. Employed by itself, "Collecting Toys" should at least prevent very serious mistakes being made. Used with the assistance of a few current prices found on lists or on dealer tables, it can get the prospective buyer or seller much nearer to the current (always fuzzily defined) market price.

CONDITION OF A TOY
AND ITS RELATION TO PRICE

CONDITION CODE:

C6 - Good. Evident overall wear, well-played with, but acceptable to many collectors

C8 - Very Good Minor wear overall, very clean

C10 - Mint (like new)

Note: Mint in Box commands a higher price. Condition below C6 brings considerably lower prices

---

There have been some changes made in this edition. Because a book can contain only so many pages before it begins to fall apart, and there was much I wished to add, I've eliminated all but the most significant toy soldier companies. Making this decision easy was the knowledge that I'd be able to go directly from working on this book to the second edition of "Collecting Toy Soldiers", since that book's first edition has sold out.

Despite that considerable cut, the addition of a number of toys has raised the count from something over 12,000 listings in the last book to a bit over 14,000 in this.

Finally, for those who wish to consider this field as an investment, and it can be a good one, it should be stressed that mint or near-mint condition provides considerably more financial safety than any of the other conditions, as this is the only condition sure to attract all collectors and dealers of any particular toy.

Richard O'Brien
September, 1992

VEHICLES
(Also see Tin Wind-Up)

Average mint price of vehicles in the last edition was $363.85; this edition
it is $488.23, an increase of 34%.

CAST IRON AUTOMOTIVE TOYS
by C.B.C. Lee

The manufacture of cast iron toys began shortly after the Civil War and had about reached its zenith by the beginning of the twentieth century. The first toy automobiles began to appear soon after their real life prototypes began chugging along the horse-carriage roads, by which time some of the great 19th century toy makers had already gone out of business. Among those that continued into the automotive era were Hubley, Dent, Wilkins, and Kenton. During the first three decades of this century, others came to the forefront, such as Arcade, Kilgore, A. C. Williams, and Champion. Others also made toy cars and trucks in smaller numbers or for a short period of time, such as Grey Iron, Freidag, and North and Judd. Many of these firms made no identifying marks on their toys, and it has only been in recent years that many very familiar toys have been correctly attributed, as catalogues, patents, and old advertisements have gradually come to light. Probably the greatest American toymaker of all was Ives, but this firm is thought to have made only one toy car, a clockwork-driven horseless carriage runabout with figure, measuring 6½" long and 6" to the top of the jockey-cap on the driver.

Value does not have much relationship to either age or size, however, having more to do with scarcity, complexity and nicety of design, detail, and "desirability". As with anything else in a free market, it is simply the rule of supply and demand.

Demand and "desirability" are affected by a number of factors. One of these is nostalgia.

As a general guide to factors affecting desirability, there are a few broad easy clues, however. Accuracy of scale and proportion, the use of many different cast parts, cast-in or decal logos and details, hand-painting (by the original maker, but NOT by some later child or collector!!), etc. all enhance the value. In most cases, a 4-inch roadster with a separate chassis, separate nickel-plated radiator and headlights, and a separate cast figure will be worth much more than a two-piece one with the halves riveted together.

Values are very volatile, both up and down, and may be badly obsolete even by the time this is printed. The lawyers long ago defined the "fair market value" as that price paid by a (knowledgeable) willing buyer to a (knowledgeable) willing seller.

A WORD OF CAUTION!!!

In recent years several American makers have begun to make cast-iron or brass copies of old toys, and more recently many more have been coming in from Taiwan and perhaps other sources. These are marketed as decorator pieces, and sell quite cheaply. Many unscrupulous dealers are using these pieces to cheat unwary new collectors. They usually rust them hurriedly - and sometimes make other modifications of tip-off parts (axles or screws) to fool the uninitiated. The Makers, "IRON ART", "UTEXIQUAL" and others here and abroad are running an honest enough business, but the dishonest dealers are using the products to turn a quick profit at the expense of naive buyers.

The fakes are usually easy to spot once one has gained a little experience. They are usually held together by a long screw, which is threaded all the way up to the hub, as are standard stove bolts in your local hardware store (only a few genuinely old toys are assembled with a screw rather than a long peaned rivet, and the few screws used often had only about 1/4-inch threaded at the tip (the Hubley Packard is an important exception). Modern axles are usually a hollow rolled piece of sheet-metal, much like a long shear-pin, though a few are rods with threaded ends and sheetmetal acorn nuts. The castings themselves are the most dependable give-away, but require a little experience; a blindman could tell in an instant. The old castings are thinner, lighter, and smoother, the modern ones being gritty, thick and coarse of detail.

CLINT SEELEY (8/28/27—3/6/84), a New England doctor, used the pen-name C.B.C. LEE when writing about toys, which he did prolifically. He contributed to books and magazines not only in this country but also in England, France, Italy, New Zealand, Australia and Japan and was in touch with collectors on five continents. His extensive research on the subject, and his generosity in sharing what he'd learned, will keep his name alive as long as interest remains in the hobby he so loved.

TOOTSIETOYS, DIE-CAST AND SLUSH

by C.B.C. Lee

Die-casting was an outgrowth of the invention of the Linotype machine, introduced at the Columbian Exposition at Chicago in 1893. A trade-journal publisher in that city named Samuel Dowst began to adapt the type-casting machine to making small promotional miniatures, collar buttons, and so on related to the Laundry Journal he also published. By the turn of the century, however, the die-casting business had become his principal business, and he was producing a myriad of small party favors, candy premiums, political items and penny jewelry. Amongst these were several charms and miniatures of automotive, trains, and aircraft. By 1911, he produced a small 47 mm. limousine with free-turning wheels. By 1914 a 77 mm. Ford touring car was marketed, and a matching pick-up truck was made two years later. All three of these stayed in the catalogue until the late 20s, and the truck as late as 1932. In 1922 a line of doll furniture was developed, and was trade-named Tootsietoy after the daughter of the company's president at that time, Tootsie Dowst. The name later was used to identify nearly all of the toys the company sold. However, it continued to make items for other buyers, and still makes the metal marker pieces used in the deluxe Monopoly game. Tootsietoys continue to be made today, the present name of the Company being the Strombecker Corporation.

As with other collectibles, the value of obsolete toys today is not greatly related to age. The oldest Tootsietoys were made in such large numbers and for so long a period that they are not hard to find today. Others, some of which were unpopular in their day, were not sold in great numbers and are rare today. The 1932 Funnies series of six pieces drawn from the contemporary comic strips is an example of this. These were made in a boxed set of 6, having cams on the axles, which imparted action to the figures as the toy was pushed along the floor, and having details and figures hand-painted in up to seven different colors. This boxed set sold for $1.00. The six pieces were also made in simpler non-action versions with simple paint and sold for 10¢ each. For reasons hard to understand today, these toys were not popular. Consequently they are very hard to find, and are more valuable. Some of the individual pieces must have been better liked by their owners and were played to death or lost, making them even scarcer. So, though all were made in about equal numbers, some are rarer than others. Uncle Walt Wallet in a roadster is the most valuable. Uncle Willie and Mamie in a boat is at the other end, worth about half as much.

In regular production cars, LaSalles and a sort of pseudo-Lincoln have the greatest value, while other Fords, Yellow Cabs, and early Mack trucks are about one-third of that. A 1925 delivery truck, often called "Federal" by collectors, was made in stock versions having legends on the side panels saying: MILK, MARKET, LAUNDRY, GROCERY, BAKERY, and FLORIST. Their rarity is in about that order, MILK being worth the least. This same line of small trucks were also made in small numbers with custom private liveries, and over a dozen such versions with store names on the sides are presently known to exist. There were probably more. These, too vary in value according to scarcity, the most common being HORSCHSCHILD KOHN & CO. One which had the J.C. Penney logo is worth twice that, and a few might find a buyer at even higher prices.

Other manufacturers also made die-cast toys, and a few of these are desirable enough to have some value. Barclay made a small series of separate body/chassis vehicles in the late 1930s, and a west coast firm, TIP-TOP Toys, which are of fair value. So are a few of the finer die-cast Manoils and ERIEs. Many others are in little demand, such as JANE FRANCIS, GOODIE, METAL MASTERS and IT'S A BEAUT.

Slush casting was a process simple enough to be done in tiny factories, and even in home-industries during the depression. A few large manufacturers made toys in this way, most notably Barclay, Manoil, Savoye, Kansas Toy and Novelty, and others, but many were made by anonymous and small unidentifiable and local operations, using molds made and marketed by a few firms. Many slush-cast toys are of very little value today, but there are exceptions. Foremost among these were dealer promotional replicas of real cars, made by Banthrico and National Products. Other very accurate and detailed slush models, similar in size and scale to the contemporary Tootsietoys, can be valuable, most notable among these being certain nicely cast models of the Reo Victoria, Packard, Chrysler Imperial, Cord coupe, late 20s, Buick and Model A Ford; these, and others made with an extra moldpart resulting in detailed radiator grilles, were made by the Lincoln White Metal Works. Other small accurate replicas, with the names cast on the door sides, were made by Tommy Toy.

As with other toys, condition is very important. The values quoted here are for those in like-new condition. Paintwear can drop the value to half, and broken or missing parts can drop it to nearly nothing. Repairing can occasionally partially rescue an exceptionally rare piece, but more often depresses the value. Reproductions are beginning to appear on the market, and will also tend to depress the values of the real thing. As with anything else in a free market, cost is largely a matter of supply and demand, both of which can wax and wane cyclically. Let the buyer beware.

RUBBER TOY VEHICLES

by Dave Leopard

For about 20 years (roughly 1935-1955), American kids enjoyed playing with rubber toys and Moms were told that these toys would not mar the furniture or floors. Then, almost as suddenly as they came on the market, they disappeared again, but left a rich legacy for toy collectors.

The Auburn Rubber Company of Auburn, Indiana was not the first to introduce rubber toys to the American market but they were no doubt the largest and had the greatest impact on the toy field. After introducing some toy soldiers in 1935, Auburn brought out its first vehicle in 1936 - a beautiful coffin-nosed Cord sedan. Today, the Auburn Cord is one of the most highly prized rubber toys and is seldom seen offered for sale. Auburn followed the Cord with a wealth of vehicles, including trucks, farm tractors and implements, motorcycles, racers, fire engines, military vehicles, aircraft, ships, and trains. In all, I have catalogued about 90 different varieties of Auburn rubber vehicles and I'm sure there are more than that. To my knowledge, 1952 was Auburn's last year of marketing rubber toys exclusively. The 1953 Auburn catalog contained a vinyl motorcycle, which I believe was their first vinyl toy. By 1955, their toy line was mostly vinyl with a few rubber varieties hanging on. The 1956 catalog is exclusively vinyl, except for two rubber fire engines, which were no doubt the last rubber toys to be marketed by Auburn. Auburn continued in the toy business in Auburn, Indiana and later in Deming, New Mexico until they went out of business in 1969.

The Sun Rubber Company of Barberton, Ohio was the second largest producer of rubber toys and, like Auburn, produced a full line of toys, in addition to vehicles, including dolls, balls, and baby squeak toys. I have catalogs that confirm Sun's line of rubber toy vehicles, beginning in 1936 and ending in 1955, which pretty well puts them on the same course with Auburn - about 20 years of rubber toys. The Sun 1936 catalog contains a good selection of cars, trucks, and racers. In later years, they added a few airplanes and military vehicles but unlike Auburn never produced any motorcycles, ships, or trains. Among the most famous of the Sun Rubber vehicles are the Walt Disney characters, Mickey Mouse and Donald Duck driving a tractor, firetruck, roadster, or airplane. The Disney tractor and firetruck are the only examples of each produced by Sun. By 1955, Sun's catalog line largely consisted of athletic balls, with the the Disney toys included as the only vehicle toys. Sun existed as a company until 1974 but they did not manufacture rubber toy vehicles past 1955. I have catalogued 32 varieties of Sun Rubber toy vehicles, which I believe accounts for all of the toys they made.

Auburn and Sun made the vast majority of rubber toys we see today but there were a significant number of rubber toys made by other companies, mostly prior to World War II. Several companies from the rubber industry produced some rubber toy vehicles, including Firestone, Seiberling, Barr, and Rainbow. All of the Rainbow, Barr, and Seiberling toys appear to have been made in 1935-1936, or at least based on real cars from those years. All of the Seiberling or Barr toys I have seen are 1935 Fords. The Firestone toys include a 1935 Ford, a 1936 Ford, and a 1939 Mercury. Rainbows are mostly based on a 1935 Oldsmobile. Some of these toys were mass-marketed via dimestores, just like Auburn and Sun toys were, but some were sold (or given away?) at expositions and exhibits. All of the Firestone toys seem to be marked with some significant event being celebrated, like the Texas Centennial in 1936. I have catalogued only 14 varieties of toys produced by these four companies.

Many rubber toys were produced as "promotionals" for the automobile industry and are not marked to indicate who manufactured them. A number of Chrysler, DeSoto, Dodge, and Plymouth vehicles were produced during the mid-thirties as promotionals and are highly prized as collectibles.

A few rubber vehicles were produced as very inexpensive toys, perhaps sold in sets, and can take the form of either a solid rubber or hollow vehicle. These toys often had the wheels molded in, so they could not turn. Some of these solid rubber toys are two-dimensional and are referred to as "flat" toys. Although they were originally sold as cheap toys, they are actively sought by collectors and constitute a small but important segment of the field.

DAVE LEOPARD is a retired Air Force Colonel, now employed by the State of South Carolina Budget and Control Board, Division of Human Resource Management. Dave is a collector of small, American made toy cars and trucks and is an authority on rubber toys. He currently writes the "Little Wheels" column monthly for "U.S. Toy Collector Magazine" and is engaged in research for his own book on rubber toy vehicles.

A.C. WILLIAMS (*see Williams, A.C.*)

ACME

Acme seems to have produced only two toy vehicles, both in clockwork; a 1903 curved-dash Oldsmobile roadster and a delivery truck with a pressed-steel canopied roof. In 1905 Jacob Lauth, the owner of the Chicago firm, turned to production of the real thing, under the name Lauth-Juergens Co.

	C6	C8	C10
Acme Curved Dash Olds, 11" long, clockwork, circa 1905.	$500	$750	$1000

ACME Curved Dash Olds, 11" long. Courtesy Wilkinson Collection, Detroit Antique Toy Museum.

ACME

Many Acme vehicles are exactly like Thomas Toys. The reason is that New York's Ben Shapiro was a financial partner in Thomas Toys, and Thomas Toys' Islyn Thomas made up toys for Shapiro at his request, with the Acme imprint substituted for that of Thomas. Acme was located at 121 East 24th Street in Manhattan.

	C6	C8	C10
Acme No. 138 Airline Limousine, plastic, 4" long	5.00	7.50	10.00
"Aerocar PT 560 Made in U.S.A. Plas-Tex", 7½", plastic	30	45	60

ALL AMERICAN TOY COMPANY

All American was founded by Clay Steinke in Salem, Oregon about 1948. It continued till 1955, with its location the Jorgenson Building on Ferry Street. At its peak it employed 42 people and in its existence sold a total of 26,000 toys. Their most popular toy was the Timber Toter, despite its formidable 1950 price of twenty dollars. Bill Hellie purchased the defunct company; molds, dies, parts. All American now sells parts and is producing new limited editions (see Leading Collectors and Dealers).

	C6	C8	C10
All American C-5 Cattle Liner, 38" long	150	225	315

A page from an ALL AMERICAN TOY COMPANY catalog.

All American CL-8 Cargo Liner, 38" long	220	330	460
All American D-3 Dyna-Dump, 20" long	220	330	450
All American HD-6 Play-Loader, 11" long	No Price Found		
All American Play-Dozer, 9" long	No Price Found		
All American HH-9 Heavy Hauler, 38" long	250	375	550
All American L-2 Timber Toter, with logs, 38" extended length	200	300	400
All American LJ-4 Timber Toter, Jr., 20" long, with lumber	No Price Found		
All American MS Midget Skagit, 18" long, battery-powered	225	338	450
All American S-1 Scoop-A-Veyor, 16" long	No Price Found		
All-Nu "Field Kitchen," approx. 2 1/2 long, "Made in USA," slush lead	No Price Found		
All-Nu Searchlight, approx. 2¾" long, "Made in USA", slush lead	No Price Found		
All-Nu Sound Detector, approx. 2¾" long, "Made In USA", slush lead	No Price Found		
All-Nu Tank "USA", 3" long, "Made in USA", slush lead	No Price Found		
American National Army Truck, Mack "Giant," 26½" long	500	750	1000

	C6	C8	C10
American National "Juvenile Auto" dump truck pedal car, red and yellow tin, 57" long	1500	2250	3000
American National Packard Coupe, 30" long, 1920s, steerable front wheels	900	1400	2000

	C6	C8	C10
American National Velie, child's pedal car, circa 1918	1000	1400	2000
Animate Toy "Baby Tractor", friction, "patented June 20, 1916"	90	135	180

ALL-NU Searchlight, "Field Kitchen", Tank, Sound Detector. (Head of soldier missing on Field Kitchen.) Photo by Bill Kaufman. Courtesy Evelyn Besser.

ANIMATE TOY "Baby Tractor", circa 1916. Courtesy Good Old Days Store. Photo by Bill Kaufman.

ARCADE MANUFACTURING COMPANY
A Brief History
by C.B.C. Lee
(based on information from Dave Davison)

In 1869 a foundry in Freeport, IL. was organized as a two-man partnership under the name of Novelty Iron and Brass Foundry, but was dissolved in 1885, when a new, larger factory was incorporated under the name of Arcade Manufacturing Co. It made industrial castings and household items, but no toys. After a disastrous fire in 1892 and management changes in 1893, toys began to appear in its catalogue, and by the early 1900's the line had become so extensive that a 50-page catalogue was issued showing a large line of notions and novelties, small stoves, banks and a few trains, including a unique pile-driver. But it was not until an enterprising young lawyer married the daughter of one of the officers and joined the firm in 1919 that the firm rapidly became one of the major makers of cast iron toys. Struck by the large number of Yellow Cabs in the streets of Chicago (my reference doesn't say he was hit or injured by them), the young man approached the Yellow Cab Company with a novel proposition: in return for the sole right to make toy replicas of the cab, the Yellow Cab Company would have the exclusive right to use the toy in its advertising. Success was instantaneous.

Arcade went on to duplicate this pattern with miniature Buicks, Chevrolets, Ford cars, McCormack-Deering and Harvester farm equipment, and several makes of trucks and buses. Arcade's slogan "They look real" was well justified by its products. In the booming 1920s the company's sales swelled so much that a new and larger plant was built in 1927. Two years later, the stock market crash heralded the great depression, and hard times hit the small car business just as it did the large ones. Cheap competition and dwindling demand for toys costing more than a dime had brought the company to the brink of bankruptcy by 1933. But, once again, the enterprising management gave the firm new life with an exclusive arrangement to provide souvenir replicas of the fairground buses made by G.M.C. for the Chicago Century of Progress. The depression caused a cheapening of quality, but World War II gave the firm business in military material. After the war, the company returned to making industrial and household hardware and a few toys, but cheaper toys of die-cast zamac, plastic, rubber and lithographed tin eclipsed the costlier cast iron toys. In 1946 the firm was sold to Rockwell Manufacturing Co. of Pittsburgh. Death and retirement soon finished the change of the old firm, and it followed its guiding directors into oblivion when Rockwell moved to Alabama.

Though the source is gone, the toys live on in collections across the land. Arcade is a prestigious name in cast iron automotive toys exceeded by none and approached by very few of its old competitors. No serious collection of cast iron toy cars, trucks, buses, or farm and construction equipment can pretend to be representative without its inclusion.

ARCADE
(The year noted is the year the toy was introduced)

ARCADE AR4. Courtesy Dick & Nancy Dice.

ARCADE AR10. Courtesy Mapes Auctioneers & Appraisers.

	C6	C8	C10
(AR1)A.C.F. Bus, 1927, 11½" long 1500		2500	3700
(AR2)Allis-Chalmers Tractor and Trailer,1936, No. 2650, 13" long total length 125		200	275
(AR3)Allis-Chalmers Tractor and Dump Trailer, 1937, No. 2657, 12¾" long with trailer................80		120	160
(AR3A)Allis-Chalmers Tractor and Dump Trailer, 1937, No. 2660, 8¼" long .125		188	250
(AR4)Allis-Chalmers Tractor Trailer, 1937, No. 2650, 13" long with trailer 200		300	400
(AR5)Allis-Chalmers "WC" Tractor, 1941, 7¾" long 200		300	400
(AR6)Ambulance, 1932, No. 187, 7¾" long ....No Price Found			
(AR7)Ambulance, 1932, No. 188, 6" long .No Price Found			
(AR8)Ambulance, 1936, 4" long, (white-painted version of No. 2620X Chevrolet Panel Delivery Truck, ...No Price Found			
(AR9)Anthony Dump Truck, 1927, 8⅛" long 1500		2500	3600
(AR10)Austin Autocrat Road Roller, 1928, No. 291, 7" long...........300		450	600
(AR11)Austin Delivery Truck, 1932, No. 173, 3¾" long.........50		75	100

	C6	C8	C10
(AR12)Austin Racer, 1932, No. 175X, 3¾"long 40		60	80
(AR13)Austin Roadster, 1932, No. 174, 3¾" long ......No Price Found			
(AR14)Austin "Roll-A-Plane" ......No Price Found			
(AR15)Austin Stake Truck, 1932, No. 176X, 3¾" long......150		225	300
(AR16)Austin Wrecker, 1932, No. 177X, 3¾" long......150		225	300
(AR17)Avery Tractor, 1923, 4½" long, stack, no hood 30		45	60
(AR18)Avery Tractor, 1926, 4½" long, has hood, no stack......125		188	250
(AR19)Borden's Milk Bottle Truck, 1936, 6¼" long, No. 2640X......1000		1500	2500
(AR20)Brinks Express Truck, 1932, 11¾" long......3000		5000	7500
(AR21)Buick Coupe, 1927, 8½" long ...1800		3000	4500
(AR22)Buick Sedan, 1927, 8½" long.. .2500		4000	7000
(AR23)Bus, Double-Decker, 1929, No. 316X, 8½" long......450		675	900
(AR24)Bus, Double-Decker, 1936, No. 317, "Chicago Motor Coach" stamp, 8¼" long......450		675	900
(AR25)Car Carrier, 1931, No. 238, 24½" long, cargo has four 25-cent cars or three 50-cent cars. 800		1400	2000
(AR26)Car Carrier, 1932, No. 296, carries either 2 No. 114 Ford sedans and one 113X Ford Coupe, or one No. 213 Ford Stake Truck and one each of the others 800		1400	2000
(AR27)Car Transport, 1937, No. 3107, came with 2 No. 1501 sedans. No. 1502 stake truck and No. 1503 wrecker.18½" long......800		1400	2000
(AR28)Car Transport, 1937, No. 2977, holds 2 sedans, 2 trucks, 12¼" long ...No Price Found			

ARCADE AR17. Photo by Orville C. Britton.

ARCADE AR21. Courtesy Phillips New York.

ARCADE AR23. Courtesy Phillips New York.

ARCADE AR22. Courtesy James S. Maxwell / Virginia Caputo. Photo by Virginia Caputo.

ARCADE Buicks and Chevrolets: on top are Chevy 1924 coupe and 1928 sedan and coupe. The latter were later made with double-striping around the waistline, rarer and more valuable. Bottom row, the famous Arcade Buicks, Sedan and 4-passenger coupe. Photo by C.B.C. Lee.

ARCADE made other brands of cars and trucks; Top,1922 Dodge coupe; 1931 Reo Royale coupe 9 1/4"; Mack high-lift coal truck, one of a very large range of various trucks; bottom: Yellow panel truck; White panel delivery; International-Harvester panel truck; each of these vans was issued in various private liveries, the best known being the I-H Hathaway Bakery, which was done in versions using either decal transfers or colored rubber stamping. Photo by C.B.C. Lee.

	C6	C8	C10
(AR29)Carry Car Truck and Trailer Set, 1934, No. 2970, 14¼" long, carries Austin coupe, delivery and stake ......No Price Found			
(AR30)Caterpillar Tractor, 1930, No. 271, 7½" long 700		1200	1600
(AR31)Caterpillar Tractor, 1931, No. 269X, 6⅞" long.................... 500		800	1100
(AR31A)Caterpillar Tractor, 1931, No. 268X 5⅝" long................ 400		600	800
(AR32)Caterpillar Tractor, 1931, No. 267X, 3⅞" long..................... 50		75	100
(AR33)Caterpillar Tractor, 1931, No. 266X, 3" long...................... 50		75	100
(AR34)Caterpillar Tractor, 1936, No. 270Y, later 2700Y, 7¾" long... 700		1100	1500
(AR35)Century of Progress Bus, 1933, No. 3200, later No. 3250 (1934), 14½" long 350		525	700
(AR36)Century of Progress Bus, 1933, No. 3210, 12" long......................... 250		375	500
(AR37)Century of Progress Bus, 1933, No. 3220, 10½" long..................... 175		263	350
(AR38)Century of Progress Bus, 1933, No. 3230, 7⅝" long..................... 130		195	260
(AR38A)Century of Progress Bus, 1933, approx 5½" long, won't pivot or detach ....No Price Found			

	C6	C8	C10
(AR39)Checker Cab, 1923, 9" long, paint variation of No. 1 Yellow Cab 700		1100	1500
(AR40)Checker Cab, 1932, No. 157, 9¼" long (came with and without "Checker" on visor) ....No Price Found			
(AR41)Chevrolet Coupe, 1929, No. 121X, 8¼" long..................... 1100		1650	2200
(AR42)Chevrolet Coupe, 1934, rumble seat, No. 1150X, 4⅜" long............. 60		90	120
(AR43)Chevrolet Panel Delivery Truck, 1936, No. 2620X, 4" long .. 125		188	250

ARCADE AR37. *Courtesy Mapes Auctioneers & Appraisers.*

ARCADE AR41. *Courtesy James S. Maxwell / Virginia Caputo. Photo by Virginia Caputo.*

ARCADE AR46. *Courtesy Lloyd W. Ralston Auctions.*

ARCADE AR64. *Courtesy Ed Hyers Antique Toys.*

	C6	C8	C10
(AR44)Chevrolet Sedan, 1929, No. 122X, 1929, 8¼" long............800		1200	1800
(AR45)Chevrolet Sedan, 1934, No. 1170X, 4¼ long......................50		75	100
(AR46)Chevrolet Stake truck, 1925, 9" long..............................1200		2000	3000
(AR47)Chevrolet Stake Truck, 1936, No. 2610, 4¼" long..........................No Price Found			
(AR48)Chevrolet Superior Roadster, 1925, 7" long.................................750		1125	1500
(AR49)Chevrolet Superior Sedan, 1925, 7" long..............................No Price Found			
(AR50)Chevrolet Superior touring Car, 1925, 7" long............................1000		1700	2400
(AR51)Chevrolet Utility Coupe, 1925, 7" long.............................. 700		1100	1400
(AR52)Chevrolet Wrecker Truck, 1936, No. 2630X, 4¼" long..........150		225	300
(AR53)"Chief' Fire Chief Coupe, 1934, No. 1230, 6¾" long.................No Price Found			
(AR54)"Chief' Fire Chief Coupe, 1934, No. 1240, 5" long....................No Price Found			
(AR55)"Coast To Coast GMC" Transcontinental Bus, 1937, No. 4378X, 9" long......................450		675	900
(AR56)Corn Harvester, 1939, No. 702, 6½" long...............................200		300	400
(AR57)Corn Harvester, 1939, No. 4180, 5" long.............................. 150		225	300

	C6	C8	C10
(AR58)Corn Planter, 1939, 4½" long....62		93	125
(AR59)Coupe, "1922" on spare tire, 9" long ....No Price Found			
(AR60)Coupe, like above, no 1922 date on spare 1500		2250	3000
(AR61)Coupe, 1932, No. 109, 6" long, .no Arcade markings, rumble seat opens.175		263	350
(AR62)Deluxe Sedan, 1941, No. 1590X, same as Yellow Cab No. 1590Y, but with top lights and sun roof ground off. 8½" long 350		525	700
(AR63)DeSoto Sedan, 1936, No. 1460X, 4" long...................... .150		225	200
(AR64)Double Decker Bus, 1939, No. 3180, 8" long..............................475		715	950
(AR65)Dump Truck, 1936, No. 2320, 4½" long 50		75	100
(AR66)Dump Truck, 1941, No. 3910X, 7" long................................No Price Found			
(AR67)Dump Truck Trailer, 1931, No. 234, 12⅞" long.....................1200		2000	3000
(AR68)Dump Wagon, 1923, 7" long, driver, no cab 225		338	450
(AR69)Express Truck, 1929, No. 207X, 8" long................................No Price Found			
(AR70)Express Truck, 1929, No. 209X, 6" long................................No Price Found			
(AR71)Express Truck, 1929, No. 214X, 5" long................................No Price Found			

ARCADE AR72. Courtesy Good Old Days Store. Photo by Bill Kaufman.

	C6	C8	C10
(AR72)Fageol Bus, 1925, 12''' long	500	750	1000
(AR73)Fageol Bus, 12½" long	500	750	1000
(AR74)Fageol Bus, 8" long	250	375	500
(AR74A)Fageol Bus, 5" long	180	270	360
(AR75)Farm Mower, 1939, No. 4210X, 4" long	60	90	120
(AR76)Farmall "A" Tractor, 1941, No. 7050, 7½" long	1000	1700	2500
(AR77)Farmall "M" Tractor, 1941, No. 7070, 7¼" long	300	450	600
(AR78)Farmall Tractor, 1929, No. 279, 6" long	350	525	700
(AR79)Fire Engine, 1923, pumper, 7½" long	No Price Found		
(AR80)Fire Engine, 1936, No. 1740, pumper, 9" long	200	300	400
(AR81)Fire Engine, 1936, No. 1810, 6¼" long	No Price Found		
(AR82)Fire Engine, 1936, No. 2340, 4½" long	90	135	180
(AR83)Fire Engine, 1941, No. 6990, 13½" long	900	1350	1800

	C6	C8	C10
(AR84)Fire Ladder Truck, 1936, No. 1820, 7" long	200	300	400
(AR85)Fire Trailer Truck, 1934, No. 1940, ladder truck, 16¼" long	500	750	1000
(AR86)Ford Carry Car Truck and Trailer, 1934, No. 2400	No Price Found		
(AR87)Ford Coupe,1923, 6" long	150	225	300
(AR88)Ford Coupe, 1924, 6½" long	150	225	300
(AR89)Ford Coupe, 1934, No. 1610X, 6¾" long, rumble seat opens	175	263	350
(AR90)Ford Coupe, 1930s, No. 1190X, 4¾" long	100	150	200
(AR91)Ford Dump Truck, 1929, No. 219X, 7½" long	200	300	400
(AR92)Ford Express Truck, 1929, No. 210X, 8¼" long	No Price Found		
(AR93)Ford Fordor Sedan, 1924, 6½" long, removable chauffeur	450	675	900
(AR94)Ford Sedan, 1923, 6½ long	350	525	700
(AR95)Ford Sedan, 1934, No. 1620X, 6⅞" long	No Price Found		
(AR96)Ford Sedan, 1934, "Century of Progress", 6⅞" long	No Price Found		
(AR97)Ford Sedan, 1930's No. 1200, 4¾" long	125	188	250
(AR97A)Ford Sedan, 1934, "Century of Progress", 4¾" long	No Price Found		
(AR98)Ford Sedan with Trailer, 1937, No.1970, 12" long (trailer 5½" long)	1000	1500	2200
(AR99)Ford Stake Truck, 1925, 8¾" long	No Price Found		

ARCADE AR68. Driver in photo may be wrong. Courtesy Sotheby's New York..

ARCADE AR73. Courtesy Lloyd W. Ralston Autions.

ARCADE AR85. Courtesy Mapes Auctioneers & Appraisers.

ARCADE, Top to Bottom: AR96, AR97A. Photo by John M. Ianuzzi.

ARCADE AR94. Courtesy Ed Hyers Antique Toys.

ARCADE AR96. Courtesy Chic Gast.

ARCADE AR110. Courtesy Mapes Auctioneers.

	C6	C8	C10
(AR100)Ford Stake Truck, 1927, 9" long	No Price Found		
(AR101)Ford Stake Truck, 1934, No. 2010X 4¾" long	No Price Found		
(AR102)Ford Touring Car, 1923, 6½"long	275	363	550
(AR103)Ford Touring Car Bank, 1923, 6½" long	450	675	900
(AR104)Ford Tractor and Plow, 1941, No.7220, tractor 6½" long, overall length 8¾"	225	338	450
(AR105)Ford Truck, 1923, 8½" long	No Price Found		
(AR106)Ford Wrecker, 1929, No. 215, 8¼" length to end of hoist	1200	2000	2800
(AR107)Ford Wrecker, 1930, No. 218, 4½" long	125	188	250
(AR108)Fordson Tractor, 1923, 5⅜" long	250	375	500
(AR109)Fordson Tractor, 1928, No. 274, 4¾" long	112	168	225
(AR110)Fordson Tractor, 1928, 3⅞" long, No. 273	50	75	100
(AR111) Fordson Tractor, 1934, rubber wheels, No.2730X, 3½" long,	75	112	150
(AR112)Greyhound Cruiser Coach bus, 1941, No. 4400, 9⅛" long	200	300	400

	C6	C8	C10
(AR113)"Greyhound Lines" Bus, 1937, No. 3850 SP, 7¾" long	350	525	700
(AR114)"Greyhound Lines Great Lakes Exposition", 936, No. 437, 11" long	800	1200	1600
(AR115)"Greyhound Lines Great Lakes Exposition", 1936, No. 436, 6¾" long	450	675	900
(AR116)Greyhound Super Coach, 1937, No. 4380, 9" long	450	675	900
(AR117)"Ice" Truck, circa 1941, No. 1933, 6¾" long	300	450	600
(AR118)International Delivery Truck, 1932, No. 226, 9¾" long	1000	1500	2000
(AR119)International Delivery Truck, 1936, No. 3020 9½" long	No Price Found		
(AR120)International Dump Truck, 1931, No. 236-0, 10¾" long	1200	1800	2400
(AR121)International Dump Truck, 1936, No. 3030, 10½" long	No Price Found		
(AR122)International Dump Truck, 1937, No. 3710, 9½" long	No Price Found		
(AR123)International Dump Truck, 1940, No. 1670, chassis and dump box are steel, 11⅝" long	600	900	1200
(AR124)International Dump Truck, 1941, No. 7100, 11⅛" long	600	900	1200
(AR125)International Harvester Company Public Utility Truck, 1932, No. 197, 11¼" long	No Price Found		
(AR126)International Pickup Truck, 1941, No. 7000, 9½" long	1000	1500	2000
(AR127)International Stake Truck, 1931, No. 237-0, 12" long	750	1125	1500
(AR128)International Stake Truck, 1936, No. 3090, 12" long	700	1100	1600
(AR129)International Stake Truck, 1937, No. 2600, 9½" long	No Price Found		

ARCADE AR143. Courtesy Phillips New York.

ARCADE AR151. Courtesy Mapes Auctioneers & Appraisers.

ARCADE AR155. Courtesy James S. Maxwell/Virginia Caputo. Photo by Virginia Caputo.

ARCADE AR153. Courtesy Sotheby's New York.

ARCADE AR161. Courtesy Ed Hyers Antique Toys.

ARCADE AR156. Courtesy Perry R. Eichor.

*ARCADE
Top, Left to Right: AR171, AR112,
Second Row, Left to Right: AR116,
AR37. Third Row, Left to Right: AR36,
AR172. Bottom Row, Left to Right:
AR173, AR38. Courtesy Sotheby's New
York.*

	C6	C8	C10
(AR130)International Stake Truck, 1941, No. 7090, 11½" long	600	900	1200
(AR131)International Wrecker, 1940, No. 1650, 13" long, wrecker crane body and crane are steel	400	600	800
(AR132)Ladder Truck, 1936, No. 1700, length with ladders 12½" long	450	675	900
(AR133)Ladder Truck, 1936, No. 2350, 4¾" long	75	112	150
(AR134)"Mack" Bus, 1929, No. 318, 13¼" long	2000	3500	6000
(AR135)Mack Cement Mixer, 1931, 6 ¹¹⁄₁₆" long, drum revolves	No Price Found		
(AR136)Mack Chemical Truck, 1928, fire engine No. 245R, 15" long,, has ladders	400	600	800
(AR137)Mack Chemical Truck, 1929, fire ladder truck, 15" long	400	600	800
(AR138)Mack Chemical Truck, 1929, fire engine with ladders, 10" long	No Price Found		
(AR139)Mack Dump Truck, 1925, 12" long	1000	1500	2000
(AR140)Mack Dump Truck, 1929, No. 248X, 8½" long	1200	2000	3000
(AR141)Mack High Dump Truck, 1931, No. 244X, 12⅜" long	750	1125	1500
(AR142)Mack High Dump Truck, 1931, No. 259X, 8½" long	1000	1500	2000
(AR143)Mack Fire Apparatus Truck, 1929, No. 242, 21" long, ladder truck	800	1200	1600
(AR144)Mack Hoist Truck, 1932, No. 198, body 8" long	No Price Found		
(AR145)Mack Ice Truck, 1930, No. 257, 7" long	250	375	500
(AR146)Mack Ice Truck, 1931, No. 226, 8½" long	300	450	600
(AR147)Mack Ice Truck, 1932, No. 257, 10¾", with driver, glass "ice" and tongs	400	600	800
(AR148)Mack Side Dump Truck, 1932, No. 1960, 9" long	No Price Found		
(AR149)Mack Stake Truck, 1929, 12" long, No. 246X	No Price Found		
(AR150)Mack Stake Truck, 1929, 8¾" long, No. 253	125	188	250
(AR151)Mack Tank Truck, 1925, 13¼" long	1000	1500	2000
(AR152)Mack Tank Truck, 1925, 13¼" long, "American Gasoline"	1200	1850	2500
(AR153)Mack Tank Truck, 1925, 13¼" long, "Lubrite"	1100	1800	2800
(AR154)Mack Tank Truck, 1930, No. 241, sheet metal tank, "Gasoline", "Mack", 13" long	1000	1600	2650
(AR155)Mack Wrecker, No. 255, 1930, 12½" long	1500	2800	4500
(AR156)McCormick-Deering Farmall Tractor, 1937, 6¼" long	300	450	600
(AR157)McCormick-Deering Thresher, 1927, 12" long	425	636	850
(AR158)McCormick-Deering Thresher, 1930, 9½" long	300	450	600
(AR159)McCormick-Deering Tractor, 1925, 7¼" long	250	375	500
(AR160)Milk Truck, 1931, No. 256, 13⅝" long box, is wood	No Price Found		
(AR161)Model A Coupe, 1928, No. 116X, 5" long, rumble seat	500	850	1200
(AR162)Model A Coupe, 1928, No. 106, 6¾" long, rumble seat	500	750	1000
(AR163)Model A Coupe, 1928, No. 113X, 4⅛" long	125	188	250
(AR164)Model A Fordor, 1928, No. 207, 6¾" long	375	525	750
(AR165)Model A Tudor, 1928, No. 108, 6¾" long	500	750	1000
(AR166)Model T Stake Truck, 1927, 9" long	200	300	400
(AR167)Model T Stake Truck, 1927, 5¾" long	130	195	260
(AR168)Model T Wrecker, 1927, 11" long	800	1300	2000
(AR169)Nash Wrecker, 1936, 4½" long	250	375	500
(AR170)National Trailways Bus, 1937, No. 3870, 9¼" long	450	675	900
(AR171)New York World's Fair Bus, 1939, No. 3780, 10½" long	600	900	1200
(AR172)New York World's Fair Bus, 1939, No. 3770, 8½" long	450	675	900
(AR173)New York World's Fair Bus, 1939, No. 3750, 7" long	600	950	1300
(AR174)New York World's Fair Tractor-Train, 1939, No. 7270, tractor and one car, tractor 3¼" long, car 4¼" long	200	300	400
(AR175)New York World's Fair Tractor-Train, 1939, No. 7290, same as above with three cars	300	450	600
(AR176)Oliver Plow, 1923, 6½" long	250	375	500
(AR177)Oliver Plow, 1941, No. 4230X, 6¼" long	125	188	250
(AR178)Oliver Superior Spreader, No. 7140, 1941, 10¼" long	No Price Found		

ARCADE AR162. Courtesy Ed Hyers Antique Toys.

ARCADE AR197. CourtesyPhillips New York.

ARCADE AR198. Courtesy James S. Maxwell/Virginia Caputo. Photo by Virginia Caputo.

ARCADE AR208. Courtesy James S. Maxwell/Virginia Caputo. Photo by Virginia Caputo.

	C6	C8	C10
(AR179)Oliver Tractor, 1937, No. 356, 7½" long 225		338	450
(AR180)Oliver Tractor, 1941, No. 3560, 7½" long 75		112	150
(AR181)"Plymouth" Coupe, 1934, No. 1340X, 4½" long 100		150	200
(AR182)"Plymouth" Sedan, 1934, No. 1330X, 4¾" long........350		600	900
(AR183)"Plymouth" Stake Truck, 1934, No. 1840X, 4¾" long........No Price Found			
(AR184)"Plymouth" Wrecker, 1934, No. 1830X, 4¾" long 125		188	250
(AR185)Pontiac Sedan, 1934, No. 1350X, 4¼" long 125		180	250
(AR186)Pontiac Sedan, 1935, 6½" long 500		750	1000
(AR187)Pontiac Stake Truck, 1935, No. 2390X, 6¼" long........No Price Found			
(AR188)Pontiac Stake Truck, 1936, 2780X, 4¼" long........No Price Found			
(AR189)Pontiac Wrecker, 1936, No. 2000X, 4¼" long........125		188	250
(AR190)Racer,1923, 7¾" long ....No Price Found			
(AR191)Racer, Bullet Racer, 1931, No. 139X, 7⅝" long........175		263	350
(AR192)Racer,1931, No. 138X, 6¾" long ....No Price Found			
(AR193)Racer,1932, No. 140X, 10½" long ....No Price Found			

	C6	C8	C10
(AR194)Racer,1932, No. l37X, 5⅝" long 125		188	250
(AR195)Racer, 1937, No 1440X, 8" long ....No Price Found			
(AR196)Racer, 1937, No. 1457 , 5¾" long 100		150	200
(AR197)Red Baby Dump Truck. 1923. No. 2. 10⅜" long........500		750	1000
(AR198)Red BabyTruck, 1923, No. l, 10¾" long........700		1100	1500
(AR199)Red Baby "Weaver" Wrecker, 1929, 12" long 800		1200	1600
(AR200)Reo Coupe, 1931, No. 1247, 9⅜" long 3500		6000	9000
(AR201)Reo Coupe, 1931, smaller size ..300		450	600
(AR202)Sand Loading Shovel, 1932, No. 298 (later No. 299) 600		900	1200
(AR203)Scraper, 1929, No. 287, 8¼" long 42		63	85
(AR204)Sedan, 1937, No. 1501X, 4¾" long 100		150	200
(AR205)Sedan and Trailer, 1937, No. 1497X, car 5⅝" long, trailer 2½" long 200		300	400
(AR206)Side Dump Trailer, 1932, No. 290, 7" long, fastens to trucks or tractors ....No Price Found			
(AR207)"Silver Arrow", 1934, 7¼" long 175		263	350

ARCADE AR218.

	C6	C8	C10
(AR208)Stake Trailer Truck, 1931, No. 233, 11⁵/₁₆" long	1500	2400	3500
(AR209)Stake Truck, 1929, No. 208X, 6" long	175	263	350
(AR210)Stake Truck, 1929, No. 213X, 5" long	No Price Found		
(AR211)Stake Truck, 1932, No. 208, 6" long, no Arcade markings	No Price Found		
(AR212)Stake Truck, 1937, No. 1502X, 4¼" long	No Price Found		
(AR213)Steam Shovel, 1932, No. 292 Industrial Derrick, body 6" long	750	1125	1500
(AR214)Tandem Disc Harrow, 1939, No. 704, 6¾" long	60	90	120
(AR215)Tank, Army, 1937, No. 400, 8" long	300	500	700
(AR216)Tank, Army, 1941, No. 3960, 4" long, shoots	175	263	350
(AR217)Texas Centennial Bus, 1936 10¾" long (*Extremely Rare*)	No Price Found		
(AR218)"Trac-Tractor", International Harvester, 1937, No. 277, 8¼" long	800	1300	1800
(AR219)Trac Tractor, 1941, No. 7120, 7½" long	No Price Found		
(AR220)Tractor, 1923, "W&K" (Whitehead & Kales), body 5¾" long	No Price Found		
(AR221)Tractor, 1937, No. 359, 5½" long	No Price Found		

	C6	C8	C10
(AR222)Tractor, 1941, No. 7200, 6½" long	No Price Found		
(AR223)Tractor, 1941, No. 4060X, 6¼" long, black rubber wheels	No Price Found		
(AR224)Tractor, 1941, No. 7341X, 6¼" long, wood wheels	No Price Found		
(AR225)Tractor, 1941, No. 7321X, 4¼" long	No Price Found		
(AR226)Tractor, 1941, No. 7260X, 3⅛" long, wooden wheels	No Price Found		
(AR227)Tractor, 1941, No. 7240X, 3⅛" long, rubber wheels	No Price Found		
(AR228)Tractor and Dump Trailer, 1941, No. 7300, 15½" long	No Price Found		
(AR229)Trailer, farm, 1929, No. 286, 6⅜" long	40	60	80
(AR230)Trailer, farm, 1929, No. 288, 4⅝" long	35	52	70
(AR231)Trailer, farm, 1929, No. 289, 3¾" long	30	45	60
(AR232)Transport Trailer Truck, 1934, No. 1800, 7½" long	900	1400	1900
(AR233)W&K Truck Trailer, 1923, 8½" long	No Price Found		
(AR234)Two-Wheeled Jack, 1932, No. 216, 5½" long	30	45	60
(AR235)White Bus No. 319, 1928, 13¼" long	2000	3200	4500
(AR236)White Delivery Truck, 1929, No. 252X, 8¼" long	1200	2000	3000
(AR237)White Delivery Van, 1929, No. 251,13½" long	1500	2800	4500
(AR238)White Dump Truck, 1929, No. 249, 11½" long	1700	3000	5000
(AR239)White Dump Truck, 1931, No. 258X, 13½" long	No Price Found		
(AR240)White Tank Truck, 1931, No. 254X, 14⅛" long, "Gasoline"	1000	1500	2000
(AR241)Wrecker, 1929, No. 217, 1928, body 8" long	425	638	850

ARCADE AR236. Courtesy James S. Maxwell/Virginia Caputo. Photo by Virginia Caputo.

ARCADE AR237. Courtesy James S. Maxwell/Virginia Caputo. Photo by Virginia Caputo.

ARCADE AR249. Courtesy Sotheby's New York.

ARCADE AR250. Courtesy Wilkinson Collection, Detroit Antique Toy Museum.

ARCADE AR259. Side-mounted tire, original tires missing. Courtesy James S. Maxwell/Virginia Caputo. Photo by Virginia Caputo.

ARCADE AR259. Courtesy Phillips New York.

	C6	C8	C10
(AR242)Wrecker, 1932, No. 225, no Arcade markings	200	300	400
(AR243)Wrecker, 1934, No. 2020X, 7" long	200	300	400
(AR244)Wrecker, 1937, No. 1493X, 6½" long	150	225	300
(AR245)Wrecker, 1937, No. 1503X, 4¾" long	100	150	200
(AR246)Wrecker, 1941, No. 3900X, 8½" long	150	225	300
(AR247)Yellow Baby Wrecker, 1929, 12" long	No Price Found		
(AR248)Yellow Cab, 1922, No .1, 9¼" long	600	900	1200
(AR249)Yellow Cab, 1923, No. 2, 8" long	600 ✓	900	1200
(AR250)Yellow Cab, 1927, No. 1, 9" long	600	900	1200
(AR251)Yellow Cab, 1927, No. 05, 8½" long	425	638	850
(AR252)Yellow Cab, 1927, No. 2, 8" long	425 ✓	638	850
(AR253)Yellow Cab, 1927, No. 3, 5¼" long	700	1050	1400
(AR254)Yellow Cab, 1934 Ford Sedan, 6⅞" long	750	1125	1500

	C6	C8	C10
(AR255)Yellow Cab, 1936, No. 1580Y, 8¼" long	1500	2500	3500
(AR256)Yellow Cab, 1941, No. 1590Y, 8½" long	550	825	1100
(AR257)Yellow Cab Bank, 1923, 8" long	1000	1500	2200
(AR258)Yellow Cab Bank, 1927	750	1125	1500
(AR259)Yellow Cab Panel Delivery Truck, 1925, 8¼" long, with driver	1200	2000	2800
(AR260)Yellow Coach Double-Decker bus, 1925, 14" long	2000	3500	5500
(AR261)Yellow Parlor Coach Bus, 1926, 13" long	1000	1600	2400
(AR262)Yellow Parlor Coach Bus, 1926, 9½" long	800	1250	1800

ARCADE "Yellow Cab," 9" long, ca. 1928, no driver. Courtesy Mapes Auctioneers & Appraisers.

AUBURN RUBBER

This company also manufactured rubber tires for other companies, including
Wyandotte. The following list and its codings were compiled by David Leopard.
Vehicles are broken down by types.

AUBURN AA01. Photo by Max Heiss.

AUBURN AA03. Photo by Dave Leopard.

	C6	C8	C10
AA01 '36 Cord, four door coffin-nose sedan 6" long ....No Price Found			
AA02 '37 Olds, 4 door sedan, 4½" long 15		18	22
AA03 '38 Olds, 4 door sedan, 5¾" long 20		25	30
AA04 '40 Olds, 4 door sedan, open fenders, 6" long.................20		25	30
AA05 '40 Olds, 4 door sedan, fender skirts, 6" long.................20		25	30
AA06 '48 Buick, 2 door sedanette, fastback, 7¼" long 30		35	40
AA07 '39 Buick, Y Job Experimental Roadster, 9¾" long ....No Price Found			
AA08 '35 Ford Coupe, 4" long.............20		25	30
AA09 '35 Ford 2 door slantback sedan, 4" long 20		25	30
AA10 '50 Cadillac, 4 door sedan, 7¼" long ....No Price Found			
AA11 '50 Cadillac, 4 door sedan, 5¾" long ....No Price Found			
AA12 '39 Plymouth, 2 door trunkback sedan, 4¼" long 15		18	22
AA13 '46 Lincoln convertible, 2 door, square headlights, 4½" long...........15		18	22
AA14 '46 Lincoln convertible, 2 door, round headlights, 4½" long...........15		18	22

AUBURN, Left to Right: AA05, AA04. Photo by Dave Leopard.

	C6	C8	C10
AA15 Late 40's Futuristic Sedan, fin down back, 5" long 15		18	22
AT01 '37 International cabover stake truck, 5⅜" long 20		25	30
AT01A '37 Same as above, "U.S. Army" decal, khaki 20		25	30
AT02 Same as above with rounded bumper, minor variations 20		25	30
AT03 '37 International cabover stake truck, 4¼" long 15		18	22
AT03A Same as above, khaki.................15		18	22
AT04 Same as above with rounded bumper, minor variations 15		18	22
AT05 '37 International cabover stake truck, 3¾" long 15		18	22
AT06 Same as above with rounded bumper, minor variations 15		18	22
AT07 '37 International cabover stake truck, milk version, 4¼" long ....No Price Found			
AT08 '37 International cabover stake truck, ambulance version ....No Price Found			
AT09 Cab-Forward box truck, smooth sides, futuristic, 5½" long...............15		18	22
AT10 Cabover box truck, smooth sides, futuristic, 4-⅛" long...............15		18	22
AT11 '47 Chevy Cab Forward Box Truck, 5¾" long 15		18	22
AT12 c. '50 Pickup truck open fenders, 4½" long.................15		18	22
AT13 c. '50 Pickup truck, fender skirts, 4½" long.................15		18	22
AT14 '38 GMC "Carry Car" Auto Transport, 11½" long 40		50	75
AT15 '38 GMC Cab/Open Squared-off Trailer, 9" long.................30		40	50

AUBURN AA12. Photo by Dave Leopard.

AUBURN, Left to Right: AA13, AA14. Photo by Dave Leopard.

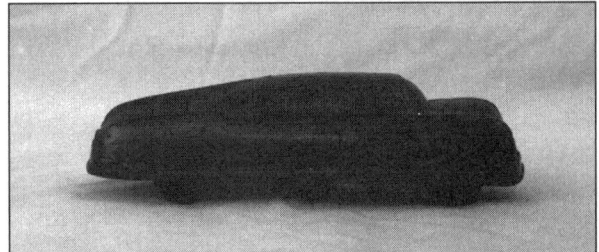

AUBURN AA15. Photo by Dave Leopard.

AUBURN AT01A. Photo by Ed Poole.

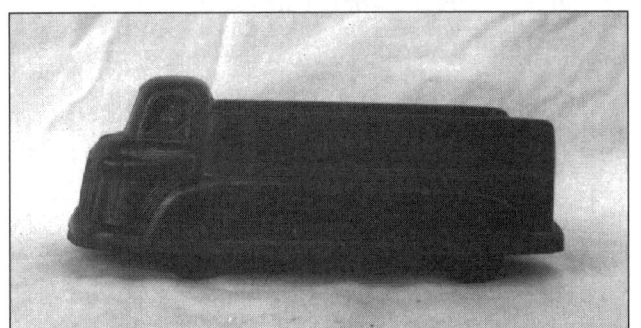

AUBURN AT09. Photo by Dave Leopard.

AUBURN AT11. Photo by Dave Leopard.

	C6	C8	C10
AT16 Updated Carry Car Transport, cab changed, trailer same, 11¾" long	No Price Found		
AT17 '35 Ford Stake Body Truck, 4¾" long	No Price Found		
AE01 Ahrens-Fox Fire Engine, 5½" long	No Price Found		
AE02 c. 40s Fire Engine, hose and ladders, 7¾" long	25	30	35
AE03 c. 40s Pumper, boiler, 7¾" long	25	30	35
AE04 c. 40s Fire Engine, ladders, no hose, 7¾" long	25	30	35
AR01 Open racer, V-6, high fin, 10½" long	40	50	65
AR02 Open racer, V-6, low fin, 10½" long	35	45	55
AR03 Open racer, short, tapered tail, large tires, 10½" long	40	50	65
AR04 Open racer, short, boat tail 6½" long	35	45	55
AR05 Open racer, boat tail, 4¾" long	20	27	35

	C6	C8	C10
AR06 Open racer, small fin, 6¼" long	20	27	35
AR07 Open racer short, boat tail, early, 6½" long	30	40	50
AR08 Open racer, no fenders, low fin, long back, 5¼" long	15	20	25
AR09 Open racer, boat tail, no side pipes, 4¾" long	30	35	40
AR10 Open racer, midget type, early, 5" long	40	50	60
AF01 Farm Tractor, John Deere "A", 5" long	20	25	30
AF02 Farm Tractor, John Deere, 4¼" long	20	25	30
AF03 Farm Tractor, Minneapolis-Moline "Z", 4" long	20	25	30
AF04 Farm Tractor, Minneapolis-Moline "R", early style, 7½" long	40	50	60
AF05 Farm Tractor, Minneapolis, Moline "R", later style, 7¼" long	40	50	60
AF06 Farm Tractor, Oliver Row Crop "70", 8" long	40	50	60

	C6	C8	C10
AF07 Farm Tractor, Oliver Row Crop "70", 6½" long	40	50	60
AF08 Farm Tractor, McCormick-Deering IH Farmall "M", 4" long	20	25	30
AF09 Farm Tractor, Graham-Bradley, 4¼" long	25	30	35
AI01 Trailer, 2 wheel, Graham-Bradley, 5¾" long	15	20	25
AI02 Trailer, 4 wheel, Graham-Bradley, 4¾" long	15	20	25
AI03 Harvester, open top, 5½" long	15	20	25
AI04 Manure Spreader, David Bradley, 4¾" long	10	15	20
AI05 Reliable Front-Lift Seeder, 5" long	10	15	20
AI06 Plow Seeder, 3½" long	No Price Found		
AI07 Side-Cutter Sickle Bar Mower, David Bradley, 3¾" long	No Price Found		
AI08 Two Furrow Plow, David Bradley, 4¾" long	10	15	20
AI09 Cultipacker (Disc Harrows?), David Bradley, 4⅜" long	10	15	20
AI10 Harrow, 4½" long	No Price Found		
AI11 Disc Harrows, 4½" long	15	20	25

	C6	C8	C10
AI12 Plow with riding farmer	No Price Found		
AM01 Tank, Marmon-Harrington, 4½" long	25	30	35
AM02 Tank, Marmon-Harrington, 3¼" long	15	20	25
AM03 Tractor and Cannon, 11½" long, olive green	No Price Found		
"Austin", cast iron, early 1930s	50	75	100
Austin Racer, 4" cast iron	20	30	40
"Austin" stakebody, 3¾" long, 1920s, cast iron	100	150	200
Auto Express 546, 6" long with drivers and barrels	250	375	500
Auto Express 546, 7" long, cast iron	125	187	250
Auto, raked cab, cast iron, early 1930s, approx. 4" long	70	105	140
Auto Trailer, 12½" long, carries three cars, all two-door, circa 1932	80	120	160
Auto Trailer, 1920s, 22" long, with coupe, two-door sedan, and four-door sedan on trailer	240	360	480
Auto with house trailer, late 1930s, cast iron, 13½"	400	600	800

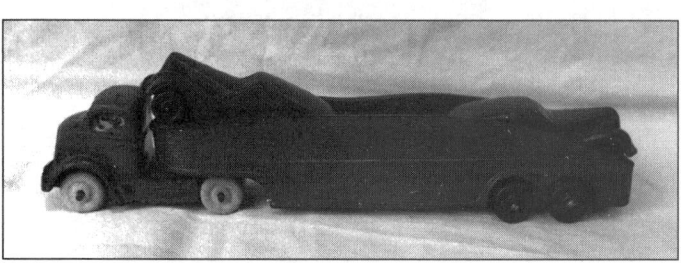

AUBURN AT14. Photo by Dave Leopard.

AUBURN AA06. Photo by Dave Leopard.

AUBURN AE02. Photo by Dave Leopard.

AUBURN AR03. Photo by Dave Leopard.

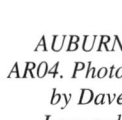

AUBURN AR04. Photo by Dave Leopard.

AUBURN AF05. Photo by Dave Leopard.

18

BANNER

Banner was begun by Emanuel M. Pressner (8/4/99-1/1/74) and Bernard Schiller[SP] in 1945 or 1946 at 150 Bruckner Blvd. in the Bronx, New York. Pressner had been a toy importer before the war. When the war cut off imports, he went to work for Columbia Protektosite, which, among other things, cast Beton's plastic toy soldiers. (Though his family has no recollection of this, in 1942 Pressner was noted in a toy trade magazine as being secretary of Beton.) Schiller was eventually edged out. Banner moved to 80 Beckwith Avenue in Paterson, New Jersey in 1950, where it remained. The firm's original toys seem to have been small plastic cars and trucks, with the leading items for years being tea sets and metalicized plastic forks, knives and spoons. Other items included

plastic sand molds. The stamped steel Banner used was made up of "off-falls" - the blanks formed when holes were cut in steel to allow for car windows and television tubes.

The company, which at its peak periods had as many as 200 employees, went into Chapter 11 bankruptcy in 1965, came out of it, and then was sold in 1967 to Tal-Cap, a toy conglomerate in Minnesota. During its heyday, Banner produced at least tens of thousands of toys a week, according to former vice-president Joseph Stern. Banner got its name, according to Stern, because Pressner (his father-in-law) wanted a company with a name "high up in the alphabet".

	C6	C8	C10
Banner American Express Truck, tin, 11" long	300	450	600
Banner American Express van,	47	70	94
Banner Dodge, 1950, 4", plastic	5.00	7.50	10.00
Banner Dump Truck, Ford. plastic	10	15	20
Banner Garbage Truck, Ford, plastic, 1954, 4"	5.00	7.50	10.00
Banner International Harvester Metro 1950 van, plastic, 4"	5.00	7.50	10.00
Banner Jewel Tea van	175	263	350
Banner LaFrance Fire Truck, plastic, 4", 1950	5.00	7.50	10.00
Banner North American Van Lines Truck & Trailer, 15" long	65	97.50	130

	C6	C8	C10
Banner Service Station (cardboard) with 3 plastic trucks, circa late 40s - early 50s	19	27	38
Banner Stake Truck, GMC, 4" plastic	5.00	7.50	10.00
Banner Station Wagon, 1948 Oldsmobile, plastic, 4"	5.00	7.50	10.00
Banner Tanker, plastic, 7" long	15	22	30
Banner "Toy Truck" van, 9" long	45	68	90
Banner Tractor, Wheelhorse, 3" plastic	5.00	7.50	10.00
Banner Wonder Bread Truck, circa 1950s 11" long, tin litho	80	120	160

BARCLAY VEHICLES

Barclay vehicles can be roughly dated by their tires. The earliest are metal. About 1934 rubber tires on wooden hubs were introduced. About 1936 nail axles began to replace the wooden hubs. Black tires are post War (after 1945).

A number of unmarked vehicles were in possession of late Barclay-All Nu designer Frank Krupp. Most of these were too early to have been All-Nu and were checked with

four early Barclay employees. The number of Xs in parenthesis after the toy's description indicate how many thought it had been Barclay. However, it is possible, since these are based on memories of several decades, that not all are Barclay. An X? indicates the employee believed it was Barclay but was not sure. Those not marked with Xs have been identified in other ways.

	C6	C8	C10
(BV 1) Ambulance, No. 194, 3½" long, small cross	20	30	40
(BV 2) Ambulance, No. 194, 3½" long, large cross	20	30	40
(BV 3) Ambulance No. 50, 5" long	25	38	50
(BV 4) No. 151 Army Truck with Gun, 2¾" long	15	22	30
(BV 5) No. 151 Army Truck with Anti-Aircraft Gun, 2½" long	12	18	25

	C6	C8	C10
(BV 6) No. 152 Armored Army Truck, 2⅞" long	9	13	18
(BV7) No. 197 Army tank truck, circa 1935-36, 3⅛" long	15	22	30
(BV 8) Army Car with two silver bullhorns, approx. 2½" long (this may be the same as BV 86)	22	33	44
(BV 9) Army Tractor (Minneapolis-Moline "Jeep"), 2¾" long	14	21	28

Barclay BV8. Photo by Stan Alekna.

Barclay Left to Right: BV12, BV13. Photo by Craig A Clark.

Barclay, Left to Right: BV80, BV10, BV26, BV 59. Photo by Bill Kaufman. Courtesy Evelyn Besser.

Barclay, Top, Left to Right: BV60, BV63, BV25, BV 28, BV71; Bottom. Left to Right: BV37, BV61, BV55, BV24. Photo by Bill Kaufman. Courtesy George Buhler.

Barclay, Left to Right: BV54, BV30, BV81. Photo by Bill Kaufman. Courtesy Evelyn Besser.

Barclay, Left to Right: BV65, BV52. Photo by Bill Kaufman. Courtesy Evelyn Besser.

Barclay, Top, Left to Right: BV11, BV49, BV14, BV13; Bottom. Left to Right: BV82, sedan for BV61 set, BV47. Photo by Bill Kaufman. Courtesy George Buhler.

Barclay, Left to Right: BV32, BV33, BV41. Photo by Bill Kaufman. Courtesy Evelyn Besser.

	C6	C8	C10
(BV 10) Austin Coupe, circa 1931, 2" long, No. 43	22	33	45
(BV 11) No. 330 Auto Transport Set, 4½" long, 2 50's cars	30	45	60
(BV 12) "Beer" truck, circa 1940, No. 376, 4" long, wood barrels	17	26	35
(BV 13) Beer Truck No. 377, with barrels	17	26	35
(BV 14) Bus, futuristic, "Made U.S.A.", 3" long	15	22	30
(BV 15) Cannon Car, 3 5/16" long, gunner low	13	19	26
(BV 16) No. 198, Anti-Aircraft Gun Truck, in 1931 Barclay catalog, 3⅛" long	17	25	34
(BV 17) Cannon Car, 3¼" long, slight casting differences from headlight			

	C6	C8	C10
version	17	25	34
(BV 18) Cannon Car, battery-powered headlight, 3½" long, in 1935 catalog	80	130	225
(BV 19) No. 48 Anti-Aircraft Gun Truck, 4" long, one man	17	26	35
(BV 20) No. 48, Anti-Aircraft Gun Truck, 4" long, two men	16	24	32
(BV 21) Cannon Truck, 4" long, with moveable cannon	20	30	40
(BV 22)		(Unused)	
(BV 23) Chrysler Airflow, 4" long, circa 1936	15	22	30
(BV 24) "Coast to Coast" diecast bus, 2⅞" long, "Barclay Toy," two-piece, No. 405	37	56	75

Barclay, BV34 (tire in photo not correct). Photo by James Apthorpe.

Barclay BV51. Photo by Craig A Clark.

Barclay, Top, Left to Right:BV15, BV6, BV4, BV9,; Middle, Left to Right:BV56, BV19, BV20; Bottom Left to Right: BV16, BV18, BV17. Photo by Ed Poole

Barclay, Top, Left to Right:BV57, BV21 cannon missing, BV39; Middle, Left to Right:BV67, BV66, BV70; Bottom Left to Right: BV68, BV5, BV69, cannon 4" long, Post WWII. Photo by Ed Poole

Barclay, Top, Left to Right:Howitzer, 4 wheels, loop hitch horozontal, Howitzer, 4 wheels, loop hitch vertical, BV78 with wire hitch, BV78 with peg hitch; Bottom Left to Right: BV7, BV77, peg hitch, BV77, wire hitch, BV76, no hitch. Photo by Ed Poole

Barclay BV83.Photo by Ed Poole

Barclay BV45. Courtesy Toy Soldier Review.

In 1984, 45 plaster castings retained by Barclay's chief of maintenance when he cleaned out the shut-down factory in 1971 were shown to the author in the course of his research. Included were soldiers, Disney figures, vehicles and an autogiro, many never produced. Some of the toys in this photo may now identify previously unmarked vehicles as being made by Barclay.

	C6	C8	C10
(BV 25) Coupe, 1930s, "Made in U.S.A.", 3" long	15	22	30
(BV 26) Coupe, 2½" long, circa 1935 XXX	15	22	30
(BV 27) Coupe, 1934, 4¼" long, XXX	40	60	80
(BV 28) Coupe, 2-piece, 1930s, 2⅞" long, "Barclay Toy"	32	48	65
(BV 29) (Unused)			
(BV 30) Coupe, 1934, 4¼" long XXX	40	60	80
(BV 31) *No. 40 Cord Front Drive Coupe*, circa 1931, 3⅝" long	20	30	40
(BV 32) *No. 302 Streamline Car*, circa 1936, 3⅛" long?	25	38	50
(BV 33) "Delivery" Truck, No. 309, 2 15/16" long, XXX	14	21	28
(BV 34) Double Decker Bus, 4"	35	52	70
(BV 35) (Unused)			
(BV 36) (Unused)			
(BV 37) "Express" stake truck, 1930s, 2 15/16" long	22	33	45
(BV 38) Fire Engine No. 390?, moveable ladder, circa,1950s	15	22	30
(BV 39) Field Kitchen, 2¼" long	9	13	18
(BV 40) Fire Engine, 2 firemen, black metal wheels, 1930s, No. 41, 2¾"	12	18	25
(BV 41) Fire Engine, 4" long, French-looking (Barclay often copied foreign toys), XXX	15	22	30
(BV 42) Ford, 1931, 2¼"	15	22	30
(BV 43) "Golden Arrow Racer", 4½" long, X?X	20	30	40
(BV 44) Mack Pick Up Truck, 3½"	15	22	30
(BV 45) "Milk & Cream" truck, stamped *No. 377*, 3⅝" long, white rubber tires	35	52	70
(BV 45A) Milk Truck No. 377, 3⅝" long, black rubber tires	22	33	45
(BV 46) Motorcycle with flat rider, full-dimensional sidecar, *No. 55*, 2¾"	25	38	50
(BV 47) "Oil-Fuel" truck, No. 308, circa 1936, 3⁹/₁₆" long	12	18	25
(BV 48) "Parcel Delivery", 3⅝" long, slush lead, *No. 45* circa 1931	65	98	130
(BV 49) "Police" Car *No. 317*, slush mold, approx. 3⅝" long, circa 1930s (Radio Police), 1939 Packard	22	33	45
(BV 49A) Police Car No. 317, diecast, 3⅝" long	15	22	30
(BV 50) Race Car, 3"	12	18	24
(BV 51) Racer, 5½", closed cockpit	17	26	35
(BV 52) Racer, closed cockpit, 7" long circa 1939	30	45	60
(BV 53) Racer, No. 53, early slush lead, 1920s-30s, approx. 2" long	12	18	24
(BV 54) Racer, two passengers, 4¼" long, XXX	25	38	50
(BV 55) Racer with tail fin, "Made U.S.A.", 3½" long	17	25	35
(BV 56) Renault Tank, circa 1937, No. 47, 4" long	20	30	40
(BV 57) Searchlight Truck, white rubber tires, circa 1940, 4 1/16" long	87	130	175
(BV 57A) Searchlight Truck, second version	87	130	175
(BV 58) Sedan, 4 door, approx. 5" long, maybe Chrysler, circa 1936	17	26	35
(BV 59) Sedan, two door, 3⅛" long, rubber wheels, circa 1935, XX	17	26	35
(BV 60) Sedan, two-piece, No. 401 2-door, 1930s, "Barclay Toy", diecast, 2⅞" long	32	48	65
(BV 61) Sedan and "Tourist Trailer", Made in U.S.A.," 1930s, 6½" long	35	52	70
(BV 62) Silver Arrow Race Car, 5½"	22	33	45
(BV 63) Station Wagon, No. 404, diecast, 1930s, 2-piece, "Barclay Toy", 2¹⁵/₁₆" long	37	55	75
(BV 64) Steam-Roller, 3¼" long, traction type, slush lead with tin roof No. 44, (Circa 1931)	30	45	60
(BV 65) No. 363 Large Streamline Racer, in 1935 catalog, 6⅞" long	25	38	50
(BV 66) Tank "4562", one man in turret, 3⅞" long	17	26	35
(BV 67) Tank "4562", two men in turret, 3⅞" long	17	25	35
(BV 68) Tank T41, 4½" long	12	18	25
(BV 69) Tank, 2⅝" long, man in turret, diecast, black rubber tires	12	18	25
(BV 70) Tank 2¼" long (based on US M2 light tank)	15	22	30
(BV 71) Taxi, 3¼" long, circa 1940s, slush	12	18	25
(BV 71A) Taxi, No. 318, diecast, 3¼" long	11	16	22
(BV 72) Tractor, approx. 2⅝" long, caterpillar type, slush lead, XX	17	26	35
(BV 73) (Unused)			
(BV 74) Trailer Truck variously"Railway			

Barclay BV85.

Barclay BV90A. Photo by Perry R. Eichor.

	C6	C8	C10
Express", or with MovingCompany name, circa 1950s ...5	8	10
(BV 75) Transport Set No. 330, 2 cars, 1960s, 4½" long ...30	45	60
(BV 76) No. 204 U.S. Army Truck, 2½" long, no hitch, red wood hubs ..7	11	15
(BV 77) "U.S. Army" truck, white rubber wheels, 2½" long, wire or peg hitch...10	15	20
(BV 78) Truck "U.S. Motor Unit", circa 1940, white rubber tires, came 3 ways; no hitch, wire hitch, peg hitch, 3¼" long ...17	26	35
(BV 79) Wheel-A-Rific speedway track, two lead racers, black rubber wheels, 10' of plastic track, soldfor $1.00 circa 1970 ...6	9	12
(BV 80) No. 46 Wrecker, 3½" circa 1931.17	26	35
(BV 81) Wrecker, 3 $^{15}/_{16}$" long, circa 1934, XXX ...17	26	35

	C6	C8	C10
(BV 82) Wrecker, two-piece, No. 403, diecast 1930s, "Barclay Toy", 2⅞" long ...37	56	75
(BV 83) Cannon Truck, moveable cannon, 4" long...37	56	75
(BV 84) Milk truck in shape of bottle, No. 567...40	60	80
(BV 85) "Milk" Van truck, 2⅞" long, bottle on side ...17	26	35
(BV 86) Officer's car, 2½" long with megaphone on top ...22	33	44
(BV 87) Side dump, approx. 1½" long ..2	3	5
(BV 88) Convertible with vactioners 17	26	35
(BV 89) 100/4 Build & Paint Auto Set, 6 vehicles, parts, paints, 1930s ....No Price Found		
(BV 89A) No. 5004 Build and Paint Auto Set, circa 1934...........No Price Found		
(BV 90) 2004 Build & Paint Set, truck, coupe, sedan, parts, paints, early ...200	300	400
(BV 90A) 2004 Build & Paint Set, same number only 2 vehicles............No Price Found		
(BV 91) "U.S. Mail" truck, 1960s, approx. 2"...4	6	8
(BV 92) Moving Truck, circa 1960s, approx. 2"...4	6	8
(BV 93) Log Truck, circa 1960s, approx. 2"...4	6	8
(BV 94) Dump Truck, circa 1960s, approx. 2"...4	6	8
(BV 95) Racing Car, circa 1968, approx.. 2" ...4	6	8
(BV 96) "Police" Car (like BV86 and BV97), approx. 2" long...4	6	8
(BV 97) "Chief" police car (like BV86 and BV 96), approx. 2" long...4	6	8
(BV 98) Vintage Car, approx. 2" long....3	4.50	6
(BV 99) Oil Truck, circa 1960s, approx. 2" long...4	6	8

BV90, showing from Top to Bottom: BV140, BV145, BV144A. Photo by Roger Sanders.

Barclay, Left to Right:BV92, BV93, BV94, BV87. Courtesy Toy Soldier Review.

Barclay, Left to Right:BV95, BV96, BV97, BV98. Courtesy Toy Soldier Review.

Barclay, Left to Right:BV99, BV100, BV101, BV102. Courtesy Toy Soldier Review.

Barclay BV107. Courtesy Toy Soldier Review.

Barclay BV137A. Photo by Craig A. Clark.

Barclay BV151. Photo by Craig A. Clark.

	C6	C8	C10
(BV 100) Pepsi-Cola Truck, 1960s, approx. 2" long	5	8	10
(BV 101) Racing car, circa 1968, no fenders, approx. 2" long	3	4	6
(BV 102) Volkswagen, 1960s, approx. 2 " long	3	4	6
(BV 103) U.S. Army truck, circa 1968, approx. 2" long	6	9	12
(BV 104) Hospital Truck, circa 1968, approx. 2" long	6	9	12
(BV 105) Army truck, open bed, circa 1968, approx. 2" long	6	9	12
(BV 106) Army oil truck, circa 1968, approx. 2" long	6	9	12
(BV 107) Double Transport Set No. 44, 4½" long, four cars on upper and lower racks, 1960s, hinged for unloading	15	22	30
(BV 108) Two-door Sedan, 1960s, 1⅝" long	3	4	6

	C6	C8	C10
(BV 109) No. 203 Tractor, 2⅛" long, peg hitch	11	16	22
(BV 110) Open coupe with driver in cap, early 30s	15	22	30
(BV 111) "Esso Gas" truck, 1930s, 5" long	20	30	40
(BV 112) No. 361 Streamline Large Coupe	17	26	35
(BV 113) 1935 DeSoto Airflow, 5 3/16" long	17	26	35
(BV 114) Car Carrier, two small cars, early 1930s	25	38	50
(BV 115) No. 371 Racing Car, large, 1930s, 4¼" long	16	24	32
(BV 116) No. 7 Tractor, circa late 20s-early 30s	15	22	30
(BV 117) No. 1105 (or 1705) "Towing Service" truck, large	20	30	40
(BV 118) 1929 Buick Sedan?, 3" long	15	22	30

Barclay BV27 - BV110.

Barclay BV125.

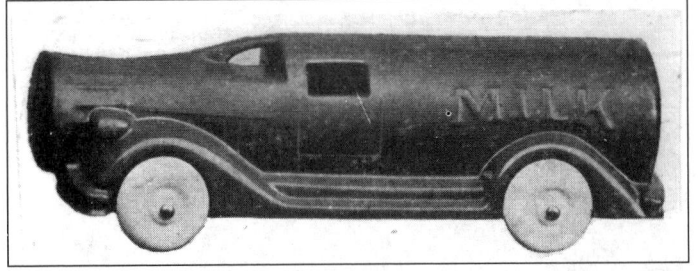

Barclay BV84.

Barclay BV126.

Barclay BV117.

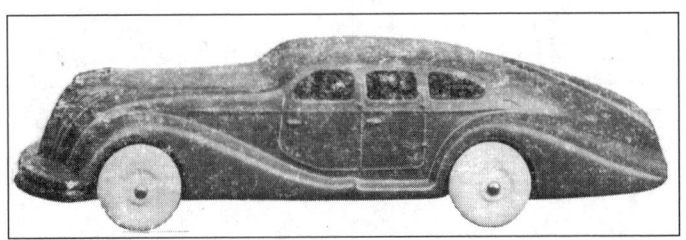

Barclay BV127

Barclay BV137.

Barclay BV116.

Barclay BV128.

Barclay BV118.

	C6	C8	C10
(BV 119) No. 312 "Towing" truck, in 1936 catalog, 3⅜" long	17	26	35
(BV 120) No. 306 Racer, in 1936 catalog	15	22	30
(BV 121) No. 303 Streamline Racer, 4⅜" long	15	22	30
(BV 122) No. 208 Hook and Ladder, in 1935 catalog, 3" long	16	24	32
(BV 123) No. 301 Coupe Streamline, 3¼" long	12	18	25
(BV 124) No. 207 Stake Truck, in 1935 catalog, 3⅛" long	17	26	35
(BV 125) No. 362 Streamline Sedan Large, in 1935 catalog	15	22	30
(BV 126) No. 368 Fire Truck, 1930s, "Fire Dept. No. 99" 5¾" long	20	30	40

	C6	C8	C10
(BV 127) No. 1703 1935 Chrysler Airflow sedan, large	17	26	35
(BV 128) No. 42 small tractor, in 1931 magazine, 2-3/16" long	12	18	25
(BV 129) No. 39 New Imperial Chrysler Coupe, circa 1931	15	22	30
(BV 130) No. 5 Racer, in 1931 magazine, Golden Arrow	15	22	30
(BV 131) No. 206 Delivery Truck "Bakery Fine Cake Pies", circa 1934, 3⅛" long	20	30	40
(BV 132) No. 51 Coupe, circa 1931, 2-3/16" long	12	18	25
(BV 133) No. 210 Fire Truck, circa 1934, 3⅛" long	12	18	25
(BV 134) No. 209 Fire Engine, circa 1934, 3⅛" long	12	18	25

Barclay BV152. Photo by Craig A. Clark

Barclay BV155. Photo by Craig A. Clark

Barclay BV153.
Photo by Dave Leopard.

	C6	C8	C10
(BV 135) No. 311 Sedan, circa 1936 12		18	25
(BV 136) No. 309 "Delivery" truck, circa 1936, 3½" long........................12		18	25
(BV 137) No. 50 Fire Truck, circa 1931, 2⅜" long 22		33	45
(BV 137A) Like BV137, but with gold hydraulics on both sides, wood hubs, rubber tires, 2 7/16" long.........No Price Found			
(BV 138) No. 56 Double-Decker Bus, circa 1931, 3¼" long........................22		33	45
(BV 139) No. 58 Auburn Speedster, circa 1931............................17		26	35
(BV 140) Sedan, circa 1934 15		22	30
(BV 141) No. 205 Tow Car, in 1935 catalog, 3 1/16" long......................20		30	40
(BV 142) No. 338 Contractor Set, tractor, two hoppers, 1930s, approx. 6¼" long (has hole hitch for wire, unlike BV109's peg hitch) ....No Price Found			
(BV 143) Large Streamline Coupe, 1930s......................................15		22	30
(BV 144) "Gasoline" Truck, small, circa 1931, 2 5/16" long, 3 tank top 12		18	25
(BV 144A) Gas Truck, circa 1935, 200 series?, 4 tank top, 3" long..............17		26	35
(BV 145) Coupe, cast rear tire, circa 1935, 200 series?, 3⅛" long............17		26	35
(BV 146) Coupe, removable spare tire, in 1935 catalog, 4½" long...............25		38	50
(BV 147) Dump Truck, spring action, ratchet, in 1935 catalog, 4" long 20		30	40

	C6	C8	C10
(BV 148) Sport Coupe, 2⅞" long, removable spare tire, in 1935 catalog..25		38	50
(BV 149) Racing Car, large, raised exhaust pipe, driver, in 1935 catalog	17	26	35
(BV 150) Race Car, open, driver, 4" long..70		105	140
(BV 151) Stake Truck, 4⅜" long, in 1935 catalog...............................25		38	50
(BV 152) 2-car Transport set, approx. 4¾" long 42		63	85
(BV 153) 4-car Transport set, 10¼" long, open-cab Mack truck, 4 2½" cars, in 1935 catalog ....No Price Found			
(BV 154) Roadster, 4½" long, open, driver, dummy spare tire on each side, in 1935 catalog ....No Price Found			
(BV 155) Streamline Coupe, 5" long, in 1937 catalog..............................No Price Found			
(BV 156) "White Horse" van, approx. 3" long (some have sticker reading "Welcome I.C.M.A. compliments the White Motor Co.") 62		93	125

Barclay, Left to Right: BV148, BV147. Photo by Fred Maxwell

Barclay BV121.

Barclay BV122.

Barclay BV142.

*Barclay
BV138.*

Barclay BV129.

Barclay BV123.

Barclay BV141.

Barclay BV135.

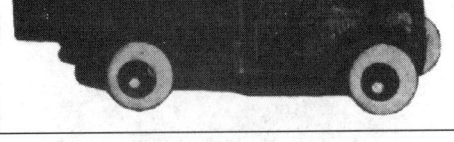

Barclay BV124.

Barclay BV132.

Barclay BV131.

Barclay BV143.

Barclay BV139.

Barclay BV130.

Barclay BV136.

*Barclay
BV144a.*

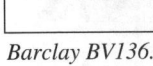

Barclay BV144.

Barclay BV133.

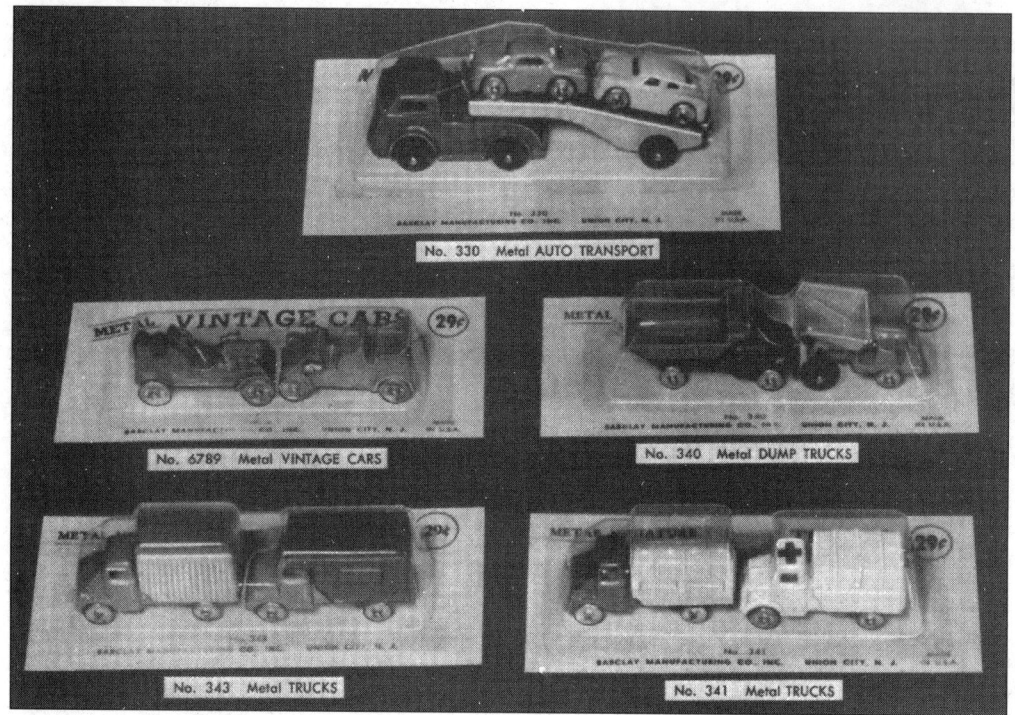

No. 330 Metal AUTO TRANSPORT

No. 6789 Metal VINTAGE CARS

No. 340 Metal DUMP TRUCKS

No. 343 Metal TRUCKS

No. 341 Metal TRUCKS

Barclay Blister pack sets, circa 1968. The No. 330 Auto Transport (BV75) is worth about $35 in mint. The others are worth about $20 in mint. Courtesy Toy soldier review.

Barclay's trucks in "Bottle" blister packs sell for about $15 in mint. Photo from the Barclay files. Courtesy Toy soldier review.

Barclay BV79. Courtesy Toy soldier review.

Barclay, Top, Left to Right: BV53, BV71, BV49; BV87, BV74; Bottom Left to Right: BV46, BV4, BV6, BV68.

Barclay, Left to Right: BV31, BV48, BV43.

28

325 TRAILER TRUCK

339 MINIATURE AUTOS

349 MINIATURE FOREIGN CARS

347 SPORTS CARS

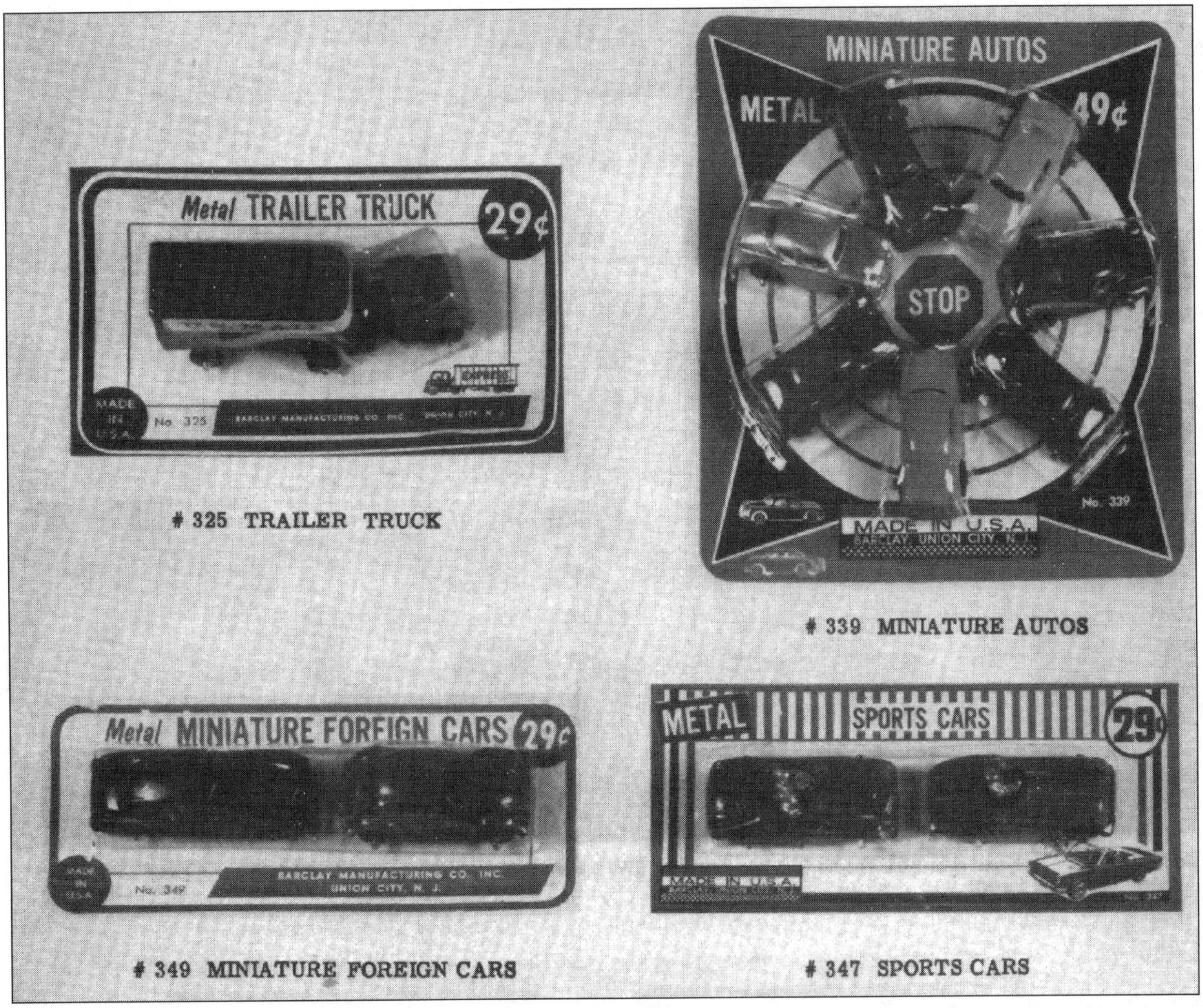

BARR RUBBER

Barr Rubber was located in Sandusky, Ohio. The following list, with its codings, was compiled by Dave Leopard. Vehicles are broken down by type.

BARR BA01. Photo by Dave Leopard.

	C6	C8	C10
BA01 '35 Ford Coupe, 4" long	25	30	35
BA02 '35 Ford 2 door slantback sedan, 4" long	25	30	35
BT01 '35 Ford Stake Body Truck, 4¾" long	25	30	35
BT02 '35 Ford Panel Truck/Ambulance, 4¼" long	25	30	35

BARR RUBBER ad from the November 1935 Playthings magazine. Courtesy Playthings.

29

BEAUT MFG. CO.

Beaut Mfg. Co., North Bergen, New Jersey, was founded in 1946 by Eugene Buhler and Irving Reader, former machinist and salesman, respectively, for Barclay Mfg. Co. The company put out five toys: a taxicab, a police car, a fire engine, a sedan and a child's wagon. The company was successful at first, employing ten people, and selling to Woolworth's and many overseas buyers. It ceased its toy-making activities (it continued until 1982 as a general machine shop) around 1950, because of competition from plastic toys.

BEAUT "Police" car (left) and "Taxi". Photo by Bill Kaufman. Courtesy George Buhler.

	C6	C8	C10		C6	C8	C10
BEAUT Fire Engine	7	11	15	BEAUT Sedan, approx. 3¾"	7	11	15
BEAUT "Police" car, approx. 3¾"	7	11	15	BEAUT "Taxi", approx. 3¾"	7	11	15

BEST TOY & NOVELTY FACTORY

By Fred Maxwell, Slushmold Contributing Editor and Margaret Rice
With the assistance of members of the Best family,
Perry Eichor, Kenneth Nudson and Ferd Zegel.

John M. Best, Sr., who founded Best Toy in Manhattan, Kansas, was an entrepreneur who stuck his neck out. Only senior citizens can understand how low our economy was in the 1930s, so starting a new business after watching other toy companies fail successively tells us something about John Best, and something about the perennial appeal of good toys. To Best, the molding of potmetal toys must have seemed a good risk for a second income as he was a printer who worked with metal alloys. And he probably had been following the ups and downs of "those TOYS with the NUMBERS" for he had lived in Clifton, the home of Kansas Toy Company.

It was started as a family hobby for his children, relatives, friends and neighbors according to Minnie Nelson, his daughter. Other employees we know of were John Best Jr. and his family, and Conrad Morsch, a molder. For a "hobby" it grew into a respectable business, supplying toy distributors and dime stores; for the toys are readily found in today's toy markets. After several years of operation it was sold to Ralstoy, a Ralston, Nebraska company, in 1939.

At this point we are not certain when Best started or what "number" in the series was his first molding. Although contradictory, evidence from family members suggests purchase of the assets of a Clifton toy company occurred about 1933. Nor do we know whether he introduced any new patterns, although with his experience it is likely that he did. If he did not create, but only reproduced from old molds, then there is still a mystery-maker out there who also continued the Kansas Toy tradition. Regardless, it was an important chapter in the story of those wandering molds. (See history of Kansas Toy in this book).

Of great assistance was a donation from Dee Buchanan, Mrs. Nelson's granddaughter, of a faded copy of a Best Toy brochure. It appears to be a pre-publication printer's mockup, and undated; but its 42 illustrations (some shown here) were adequate to identify most of the Best and many of the Kansas toys in collections. With no paper trail to guide us previously, this was indeed a find. So with the publication of the 5th Edition much of the hearsay errors and confusion of this family of toys was eliminated. Many thanks to all who helped and continue to help.

(O'Brien: Dee Buchanan, great granddaughter of John Best Sr., also contributed a history in 1988 that may be of interest to readers: "About 55 years ago, John Milner Best Sr. and his wife Roseanna, purchased a company from Kansas Toy & Novelty Company* located in Vining*, Kansas - actually a suburb of Clifton. (*This is not confirmed by our Clifton sources). The Bests owned a newspaper, printing plant and book-bindery in Manhattan, Kansas. They moved the toy company to a building in back of their home at 530 Fremont Street, Manhattan,. The family, in-laws and friends all worked making the lead cars produced by the toy company and were shipping them all over the world. There were also farm implements, tractors, airplanes, buses and trains as well as all types of cars. One of the Bests' grandchildren, Rosemary, remembers the Toy Factory well, as when she was about three years old and was playing about the factory she fell into one of the lead-melting pots head first. Very fortunately the lead was not hot - so she just had a bad bruise on her head; whereas if the lead had been hot and melted it would indeed have been a tragedy".)

Best Toy reproductions can usually be distinguished from those of earlier makes in the "numbers" dynasty if they have white rubber wheels or are embossed "Made in USA". However, some of their toys used the metal wheels (MW) of the Kansas Toy originals, or the later wood hubs with rubber tires (WHRT). In their first years the larger Best toys had realistic hard-rubber disk wheels, sometimes

painted with black "tires". The soft-rubber white "balloon" wheel, often out of scale, was a Best standard. It is also possible that Best modified or rebuilt his molds to create variations.

Best molded a great number of designs. In order to reduce redundancy in this book we list them here but will not describe them in detail if they are adequately covered in Kansas Toy or Ralstoy lists. The following numbered toys and some unnumbered duplicates were found: #6, 10, 14, 17, 20, 25, 26, 27, 31, 32, 34, 35, 36, 37, 39, 40, 41, 42, 43, 45, 46, 47, 49, 51, 54, 55, 57, 58, 59, 60, 67, 70, 71, 72, 74, 76, 77, 78, 79, 80, 81. Higher numbered are described and illustrated.

BEST'S three different wheels, Top Row: BEV4, BEV7, BEV9a; Middle Row: BEV1, BEV8; Bottom Row: BEV11, BEV14. Courtesy of Fred Maxwell.

	C6	C8	C10
BEV1 Racer, "85", 4". Record car w/ large square fin, driver, HO, VG, 12 exhaust ports, WHRT	10	15	20
BEV2 Sedan, "86", 4". Lincoln ? 2 dr. fastback, slant grille w/grid pattern, HL, divided w/s, read wheel skirts	No Price Found		
BEV3 Sedan, "87". Brewster?	No Price Found		
BEV4 Sedan, "90", 3½". 2 dr. airflow, hood reaches front bumper w/no grille, 4 OW, hard rubber wheels	No Price Found		
BEV5 Sedan, "91", 3½". Cadillac ? 2 dr. airflow, high style vee grille, faired front fenders	No Price Found		
BEV6 Coupe, "92", 3¾". Dodge?, chopped top, Brewster-like heart shaped grille, HO, long stream-lined front fenders	No Price Found		
BEV7 Coupe, "93", 3⅝". Cadillac ?, streamlined, hood similar to #91, grid pattern grille, 2 OW, hard rubber wheels. (see illustration of #96)	16	24	32

	C6	C8	C10
BEV8 Large Sedan, "94", 4½". 2 dr. airflow, similar to #90, 4 OW, taxi lamp on roof	No Price Found		
BEV9a Sedan, "95", 3½". 2 dr. airflow similar to #94, with 3 headlamps, 4 OW, trunk, hard rubber wheels. Chrysler-Briggs show car ?	No Price Found		
BEV9b Sedan, "95", 3½". Same as above with "Police Dept." shield on doors. Centered headlamp may be a siren. Other version have "Police" painted on roof	10	15	20
BEV10 Coupe, "96", 3½". Apparently same car as #93. Were both produced?	No Price Found		
BEV11 Large racer, "97", 4½". Bluebird record car, driver, large fin, 12 exhaust ports, hard rubber wheels, faired	10	15	20
BEV12 Coupe, "98"	No Price Found		
BEV13 Coupe, "99", 4". Pontiac ?, streamlined, HO, rearmount	No Price Found		
BEV14 Sedan, "100", 4". Pontiac, stream-lined, 2 dr., HO, HG, 4 OW, trunk	No Price Found		

BEST TOY Tanker: BEV15, BEV16. Photo courtesy of Perry Eichor.

BEV15 Cab Unit, "101", 3¼". Inter-national ? sleeper cab, slanted grille, HO, 2 OW ......No Price Found

BEV16 Oil Transport, "No. 102", 4". Streamlined "Gasoline" semi-trailer to #101, 4 tanks, 4 storage

(BEV 14) No. 100 - 4" long

(BEV 13) No. 99 - 4" long

(BEV 2) No. 86 - 4" long

(BEV 10) No. 96 - 3½" long

(BEV 5) No. 91 - 3½" long

(BEV 9a) No. 95 - 3½" long

(BEV 6) No. 92 - 3¾" long

(BEV 4) No. 90 - 3½" long

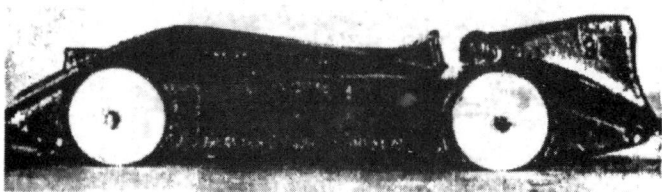

(BEV 11) No. 97 - 4½" long

(BEV 1) No. 85 - 4" long

No. 81 - 4½" long

No. 26 - 4" long

No. 76 - 4¼" long

No. 10 - Medium Racer

32

Box from a BEST TOYS Farm Set. All the Toys illustrated are from molds believed to have originated with Kansas Toys. Photo by Perry Eichor. Courtesy Fred Maxwell.

Box from a BEST TOYS Set. The drawings on the boxtop offer good representations of BEST vehicles and cannon. All or most of the toys shown appear to have originated with Kansas Toy & Novelty. Courtesy Margaret Rice & Fred Maxwell.

	C6	C8	C10
compartments. Total length of cab-trailer - 6¾"..................No Price Found			
BEV17 ? Sedan, no #, 3⅞". DeSoto ? Airflow 2 door, HO, VG, HL, 4 OW, divided open windshield, bottom pan, Best ?..................No Price Found			
Big Bang carbide armored car, cast iron, 9½" long..............	100	150	200
Big Bang motor tank, 9" long, circa 1933.	60	90	120
Big Boy: See Kelmet			
Boattail Speedster, cast iron, 5" long, blue with nickel wheels, driver, circa 1920s..............	100	150	200
Brinks truck bank, aluminum, 8" long..............	55	82	110

BUDDY "L"

Buddy "L": Buddy "L" toys were first manufactured by the Moline Pressed Steel Company, Moline, Illinois, in 1921, and were named after the son of the owner, Fred Lundahl. Lundahl had started the company about eight years earlier, manufacturing auto and truck parts (fenders, etc.). The toys were originally made as special items for his son, but as Buddy Lundahl's playmates began to clamor for similar toys of their own and their fathers began asking Lundahl senior to make duplicate toys for their sons, Lundahl went into the toy business. Buddy "L" toys were large, typically 21 to 24 or more inches long for trucks and fire engines. Construction was of very heavy steel, strong enough to support a man's weight. These were made until the early 1930s, when the line was modified and lighterweight materials were employed.

Before this time, Fred Lundahl had died, having already lost control of the company. The company has changed names several times, being known as the Buddy "L" Corp., Buddy "L" Toy Co., etc., in recent years dropping the quotes around the L. Continuing to make toys till the present day, the company even put out a few wooden toys during World War II, when its main plant made nothing but war-related items. The early Buddy "L" trains are also popular, and tend to be worth even more than the vehicles. Buddy "L" material from the pre-1932 period is almost indestructible and as a consequence, 50% of the pieces found are either very rusty or have been repainted at some point. The basic metal seems to hold up forever, but repainting and rust drops the price well below "good".

33

Following is a list of pre-1932 Buddy "L" toys compiled by Thomas W. Sefton.

Large Trucks

	C6	C8	C10
Buddy L 200 Express Truck 1921-31 ...1000	1500	2000
Buddy L 201 Dump Truck (Ratchet) 1921-30. 450	675	900
Buddy L 201A Hydraulic Dump Truck 1926-31.......................450	675	900
Buddy L 202 Coal Truck 1926-31.......1100	1650	2200
Buddy L 202A Sand & Gravel Truck 1926-31 850	1150	1450
Buddy L 203 Stake Truck 1921-24, 1926-28 650	975	1250
Buddy L 203A Lumber Truck 1925-30...900	1350	1800
Buddy L 203B Baggage Truck 1929-31 1500	2300	3200
Buddy L 204 Moving Van 1924-30......600	950	1400
Buddy L 204A Railway Express 1926-31..1000	1600	2200
Buddy L 206, 206B Street Sprinkler Truck 1924-31...............................1000	1500	2000
Buddy L 206A Oil Truck 1925-30 1000	1600	2200
Buddy L 207 Ice Truck 1926-31 1200	1900	2600
Buddy L 208 Coach 1928-31 (Lt. Green Motorbus)...........................1200	1800	2400
Buddy L 209 Auto Wrecker 1928-31 (Tow Truck).......................1500	2200	3000

Fire Trucks

	C6	C8	C10
Buddy L 205 Hook & Ladder 1924-31 1100	1700	2300
Buddy L 205A Pumper 1925-30 900	1400	1900
Buddy L 205AB (Working) Pumper 1930-31 475	825	1450
Buddy L 205B Aerial Ladder 1926-30 600	900	1200
Buddy L 205C Insurance Patrol 1926-30. ...450	800	1000
Buddy L 205D Water Tower Truck (Working) 1930-31 500	950	1500

Model T Series

	C6	C8	C10
Buddy L 210 Flivver Truck 1925-30....600	900	1200
Buddy L 210A Flivver Roadster 1925-27 550	850	1150
Buddy L 210B Flivver Coupe 1925-30 ...750	1125	1500
Buddy L 211 Ford Dump Cart 1926-30...850	1200	1700
Buddy L 211A Ford Dump Truck 1926-30 750	1125	1500
Buddy L 212 Ford Express Truck 1929-30 1000	1500	2000
Buddy L 212A One-Ton Ford Delivery Truck 1929-30.................600	1100	1850

Construction Equipment

	C6	C8	C10
Buddy L 220 Steam Shovel 1921-31 ...150	275	375
Buddy L 220A Heavy Steam Shovel 1929-30 500	800	1100

BUDDY L, No. 202, Coal Truck. Courtesy Mapes Auctioneers, Vestal, N.Y.

BUDDY L, No. 201, Ratchet Dump. Courtesy Mapes Auctioneers.

BUDDY L, No. 205, Hook and Ladder. Courtesy Mapes Auctioneers.

BUDDY L, Model T 210A Flivver Roadster. Courtesy Wilkinson Collection, Detroit Antique Toy Museum.

BUDDY L, No. 204-A, Railway Express Truck.

BUDDY L, No. 205, Fire Truck.

BUDDY L, No. 205-AB, Pumping Fire Engine.

BUDDY L, No. 205-B, Hydraulic Aerial Truck.

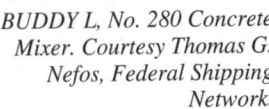
BUDDY L, No. 300, Sand Screener.

BUDDY L, No. 280 Concrete Mixer. Courtesy Thomas G. Nefos, Federal Shipping Network.

	C6	C8	C10
Buddy L 220AB Heavy Shovel (on Treads) 1929-30	450	700	950
Buddy L 230 Sand Loader 1925-31	500	750	1000
Buddy L 240 Small Derrick 1922-31	275	363	550
Buddy L 241 Large Derrick 1922-31	350	562	700
Buddy L 250 Overhead Crane 1924-27	750	1125	1500
Buddy L 250A Traveling Crane 1928-30	750	1125	1500
Buddy L 260 Pile Driver 1926-28	800	1200	1600
Buddy L 270 Dredge (Clamshell) 1926-30	1000	1700	2400
Buddy L 270A Tractor Dredge (on Treads) 1929-30	1000	1700	2400
Buddy L 280 Concrete Mixer 1926-30	300	450	700
Buddy L 280A Mixer (on Treads) 1929-31	400	600	800
Buddy L 290 Road Roller 1929-31	1200	1800	2400
Buddy L 300 Sand Screener 1929-30	1000	1500	2000
Buddy L 350 Hoisting Tower 1929-31	1000	1500	2000
Buddy L 360 Aerial Tramway 1929-30	1000	1500	2000
Buddy L 400 Trencher 1928-31	500	700	1300

End listing by Thomas W. Sefton

Buddy L 1932 on

	C6	C8	C10
Buddy L "Allied Van Lines" moving van No. 366, 31" long	250	375	500

	C6	C8	C10
Buddy L "Army Signal Corps" Truck, 1941-42, 12" long	120	175	260
Buddy L Army Tank, wood, 1943, 13" long	85	130	175
Buddy L Army Transport, 27" with towed cannon, 6-spoke wheels	135	200	270
Buddy L "Army Truck 21", circa 1940, cloth top	120	180	240
Buddy L Army Truck No. 506, 20½" long	125	195	250
Buddy L Army Truck, wood	110	165	225
Buddy L Automatic Tail-Gate Loader with steering handle	150	225	300
Buddy L Baggage Truck No. 11, 26½" long, 1933	225	385	500
Buddy L Baggage Truck No. 41	65	98	130
Buddy L "Big Show Circus" truck, wood, 1947, No. 484, 25½" long	No Price Found		
Buddy L City Baggage Dray No. 439, 1934, 19" long	110	165	220
Buddy L City Baggage Dray No. 839, 1939, 20¾" long	125	188	250
Buddy L Coca Cola Truck, wooden, 19" long, circa WWII, only 3 known, worth $4200 in mint 1984.			
Buddy L Coca Cola Truck, 15" long, post WWII	100	150	200

BUDDY L, No. 484, "Big Show Circus" truck, wood, 1947. Photo by William G. Floyd.

BUDDY L, No. 483, Fire Chief's Car with Siren, wood, 1947. Photo by William G. Floyd.

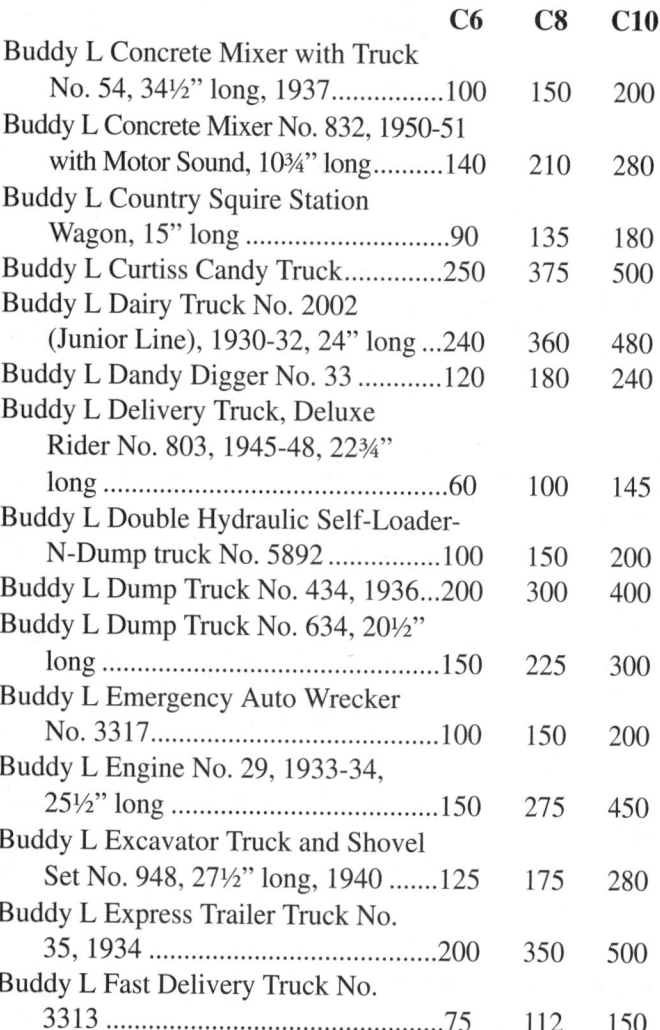

BUDDY L, No. 5892 Double Hydraulic Self-Loader-N-Dump Truck. Courtesy Thomas G. Nefos, Federal Shipping Network.

BUDDY L, No. 5429, Merry-Go-Round. Courtesy Thomas G. Nefos, Federal Shipping Network.

	C6	C8	C10
Buddy L Concrete Mixer with Truck No. 54, 34½" long, 1937.............100		150	200
Buddy L Concrete Mixer No. 832, 1950-51 with Motor Sound, 10¾" long..........140		210	280
Buddy L Country Squire Station Wagon, 15" long 90		135	180
Buddy L Curtiss Candy Truck..............250		375	500
Buddy L Dairy Truck No. 2002 (Junior Line), 1930-32, 24" long ...240		360	480
Buddy L Dandy Digger No. 33 120		180	240
Buddy L Delivery Truck, Deluxe Rider No. 803, 1945-48, 22¾" long............60		100	145
Buddy L Double Hydraulic Self-Loader-N-Dump truck No. 5892 100		150	200
Buddy L Dump Truck No. 434, 1936...200		300	400
Buddy L Dump Truck No. 634, 20½" long 150		225	300
Buddy L Emergency Auto Wrecker No. 3317..............100		150	200
Buddy L Engine No. 29, 1933-34, 25½" long 150		275	450
Buddy L Excavator Truck and Shovel Set No. 948, 27½" long, 1940 125		175	280
Buddy L Express Trailer Truck No. 35, 1934 200		350	500
Buddy L Fast Delivery Truck No. 3313 75		112	150

	C6	C8	C10
Buddy L "Fast Freight", 20" long 85		127	170
Buddy L Fire Chief's Car with Siren No. 483, wood, 1947, 19½" long......No Price Found			
Buddy L Fire Ladder Truck, semi, rounded trailer fenders, 1960 115		172	230
Buddy L Greyhound Bus, winds up, 16" long..............225		350	550
Buddy L Greyhound Bus with Bell No. 481, wooden, 18½" long.........250		375	500
Buddy L Hose Truck No. 38, 1933, 21¾" long 150		240	325
Buddy L Hook and Ladder Truck No. 859, wooden, 21½" long................125		200	275
Buddy L Hydraulic Aerial Truck No. 27, 1933-34, 40" long with ladders down................500		750	1100
Buddy L Hydraulic Dump Truck No. 10, 24¾" long, 1933-34 130		195	260
Buddy L Ice Truck No. 12, 1933-34, 26½" long 200		350	460
Buddy L International Delivery Truck No. 51, 1935, 24½" long............200		300	400
Buddy L Merry-Go-Round Truck No. 5429 90		135	180
Buddy L Mister Buddy Ice Cream Van 100		150	210
Buddy L "Railway Express" truck No. 480, wooden, 1947, 16¼" long.........No Price Found			
Buddy L Repair-It, 24" long................125		188	250

BUDDY L, "Repair-It" (1953). Courtesy Mapes Auctioneers.

BUDDY L, No. 711, "Scarab". Courtesy Heinz Mueller, Continental Hobby House.

BUDDY L, No. 803, Deluxe Rider Delivery Truck. Courtesy Joe and Sharon Freed.

BUDDY L, "Wrigley's Spearmint" Railway Express Truck, 1935. Courtesy Rodney A. Heesacker.

	C6	C8	C10
Buddy L Ride N Dump Truck	60	90	120
Buddy L "Riding Academy" No. 5455 truck, with 3 horses	112	168	225
Buddy L Robotoy Dump Truck with driver, operates on remote control	700	1050	1400
Buddy L Sand & Gravel Truck No. 3312	75	112	150
Buddy L Scarab No. 211, no wind-up mechanism	No Price Found		
Buddy L Scarab No. 711, winds up	90	135	180
Buddy L Service Truck, 1953	75	112	150
Buddy L "Shell" truck, 13½" long	55	82	110
Buddy L Siren Pull-n-Ride	120	180	240
Buddy L Steam Shovel and International Truck No. 16, 1937, 29½" long, 13½" high	110	165	225
Buddy L Steam Shovel, Mechanical, No. 30, 1935, 17½" long, 13½" high	200	325	450
Buddy L Steam Shovel on Treads (Junior Line) No. 2005, 1930-32, 24" long	150	275	400
Buddy L Tank Truck No. 438, 19¼" long, 1935	200	325	480

	C6	C8	C10
Buddy L Tank Truck No. 938, 21½" long, 1941	200	325	450
Buddy L "Texaco" tanker, 25" long, promo sold at gas stations	90	135	180
Buddy L Traveling Zoo, post WWII	40	60	80
Buddy L Utility Delivery Truck No. 946, 25" long, 1941-42	90	130	185
Buddy L Victory Jeep and Cannon, wood	100	150	200
Buddy L Water Tower No. 28, 1936	800	1250	1800
Buddy L Wrecker No. 13, 31" long, 1933	1000	1700	3000
Buddy L Wrecker No. 37, 1933, 24" long	150	250	400
Buddy L Wrecker No. W37, 25¼" long, 1939	90	145	200
Buddy L Wrecker No. 437, 1934, 24" long	200	325	450
Buddy L Wrecker No. 503, 1940, 19¼" long, 1941-42	90	135	225
Buddy L No. 647, 1949, 26¼" long	110	165	200
Buddy L Wrecker No. 813, 1938, 32" long	80	140	200
Buddy L Wrecker, Emergency Towing Rider No. 903, 1949, 33" long	70	115	150

	C6	C8	C10
Buddy L Wrecker No. 903, 33" long, 1950, "Buddy L Emergency Towing"	100	160	225
Buddy L Wrecker No. 937, 1939, 25¼" long	130	180	285
Buddy L Wrecker No. 937, 1941-42 version, 25" long	50	95	135
Buddy L "Wrigley's Spearmint"			

	C6	C8	C10
Railway Express Truck No. 835, 25" long, 1938	400	700	1000
Buddy L "Wrigley's Spearmint" Railway Express truck, 1935, headlights light up, 23⅛" long	350	550	850
Buddy L "Wrigley's Spearmint Railway Express Agency" truck No. 953, 1940	400	700	1000

BUS, 1930's 15½" long, aluminum. Courtesy James S. Maxwell/Virginia Caputo. Photo by Virginia Caputo.

	C6	C8	C10
Buffalo Toys Silver Bullet Racer, 26" long	100	150	200
Buick, 1947, plastic, 5⅜" long	2	3	5
Bus, 1930s, 15½" long, aluminum	2000	3500	6000
Bus, late 1920s, 23½" long, six side windows	150	225	300
Bus, cast iron, approx. 3½" long, A.C. Williams?	20	30	40
Bus, cast iron, 4" long	20	30	40

	C6	C8	C10
Bus, cast iron, 4½" long, five side windows, circa 1928	100	150	200
Bus, cast iron, 4¾" long, circa 1920s	75	112	150
Bus, cast iron, with driver, rubber tires, 13" long	500	750	1000
Bus, double-decker, cast iron, four figures, 8" long	200	300	400
Bus, cast iron, double-decker, 9½" long	400	600	800

C. A. W. NOVELTY COMPANY
Another Kansas Slushmolder Revaled

By Fred Maxwell, Slushmold Contributing Editor and Ferd Zegel
With the assistance of the Clay Center Historical Society, Gary Franson, Arlan and Gerry Conrad.

It is remarkable indeed that collectors had not found this fine company until 1990. Charles A. Wood not only ran a substantial operation but he made some of the finest replica toys in the slushmold industry. Chic Gast, a collector, was perceptive when he wrote of unidentified toys as "orphans"; this company may have been the most invisible of those orphan companies. Ironically, Wood had one of the longest histories of the slushmold industry. Founded about 1925, his company was active until about 1940 when

lead casting came to a halt with WWII.

Wood's line was heavy with miniature airplanes for he was a pilot, an aviation mechanic and an air enthusiast. (for these toys, see Aircraft Section, this book) It was even reported he flew his toys to Eastern markets; this could have been true under special circumstances only, for in its best years (over 60 employees and 2 million toys) the company output would have been too large to "ship by air".

All of Wood's output showed artistry, ingenuity and meticuluous craftmanship. All his toys are smooth, crisp, detailed moldings; with extra touches such as open windshields and 2 or 3 colors per toy. The early production had metal disk wheels with painted black "tires", or metal-spoked. When you find trucks with open, V-shaped, divided windshields, drivers inside cabs and trimotored aircraft with the outboard engines mounted on the landing gear struts you wonder how he did it for the 5c price. Perhaps Wood explained it, for he once told a reporter that it sometimes took 3 or 4 years to make a mold. The molds are also works of art-of the machinists art. This tells us something about his pride in his work; and also that toy-making was not his primary occupation at the time.

Charles Wood was born about 1891. He had lived and worked in Topeka and in nearby Clifton before coming to Clay Center. He was perhaps better known for his civic boosterism, good works and social life. After he had helped establish the local airport he built and operated his own aircraft maintenance hangar. A master machinist, he made all his toy molds, production tools and toy parts, even plastic wheels.

Although researching this slush industry for 20 years, I had only heard rumors of a "small molder in Clay Center, Kansas". Then, a few years ago, I found this nice little monoplane with initials "CAW" under a tailplane. I put the pressure on my Kansas friends with the happy result that eventually I saw a nice mint collection owned by a realative of Wood's and also a few pieces and some paper memorabilia in their Historical Society Museum. What a pleasant surprise!

Although we do not yet have a complete list, we have identified some of those "orphans" and some never heard of. Wood made airplanes, autos, novelties and trucks. Some of these have been well known to collectors, although unidentified "orphans". A very few of Wood's toys have been attributed to other companies by experienced sources. We hope these confusions will eventually be settled. Clearly, this company and its toys deserve to be more fully known. It would be appreciated if readers contribute further information, photos or leads.

Note: The accompanying (partial) sales sheet of C & H Mfg. Co. was issued circa 1936. All evidence suggests C & H was a distributor, and that this sheet covered only C.A.W. toys. The following list includes additional vehicles made by Wood.

C.A.W., CWV2. Courtesy Gary Franson.

C.A.W., CWV3. Courtesy Gary Franson.

C.A.W., CWV12b. Courtesy Gary Franson.

C.A.W., CWV8. Courtesy Gary Franson.

C.A.W., CWV9. Courtesy Gary Franson.

C.A.W., CWV12c. Courtesy Gary Franson.

C.A.W., CWV13. Courtesy Gary Franson.

C.A.W., CWV11b. Courtesy Gary Franson.

TOYS THAT SELL THEMSELVES

Modern Metal Toys that Sell the Year Around, Realistic in Every
Detail. Finished in Bright Colors with the Best of Lacquers

No. 25 AIR DRIVE COACH
Length 3⅞ in. He'ght 1⅜ in. Weight per
gro. 33 lbs. Retails for 10c.

Price per doz. ....

No. 32. DE SOTO SEDAN
Length 3⅞ in. Height 1⅜ in. Weight per
gro. 32 lbs. Retails for 10c.
Price per doz. ....

No. 30 STREAMLINE COUPE
Length 3 in. Height 1 in. Weight per gro.
19 lbs. Retails at 5c.

Price per doz. ....

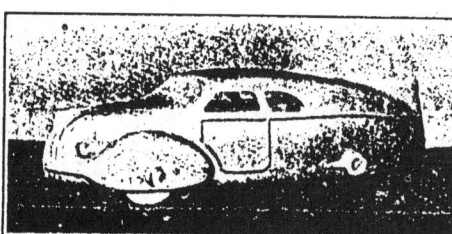

No. 33 WONDER SPECIAL
Length 3⅜ in. Height 1 in. Weight per gro
19 lbs. Retails for 5c.

Price per doz. ....

No. 31. MARVEL RACER
Length 3⅝ in. Height 1 3-16 in. Weight
per gro. 20 lbs. Retails at 5c.

Price per doz. ....

No. 38 NEW DESIGN RACER
Length 3⅜ in. Height 1¼ in. Weight per
gro. 20 lbs. Retails for 5c.

No. 39
TRANSPARENT WINDSHIELD RACER
Length 3 in. Height 1 in. Weight per gro.
15 lbs. Retails for 5c.

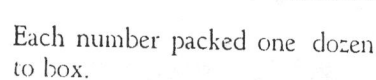

Each number packed one dozen
to box.

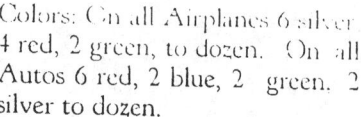

Colors: On all Airplanes 6 silver
4 red, 2 green, to dozen. On all
Autos 6 red, 2 blue, 2 green. 2
silver to dozen.

Rubber Wheels on All Autos
Plastic Wheels on Airplanes Except No. 29

TERMS: 2% Ten Days, Net 30
Days. Prices are f. o. b. St. Louis,
Mo.

C & H Mfg. Co.

1610 So. Florissant Rd.

ST. LOUIS, MO.

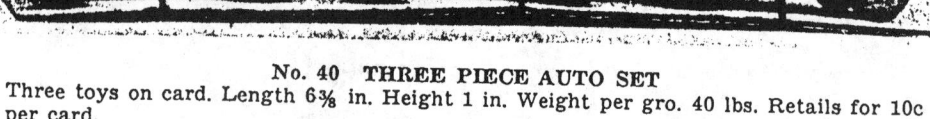

No. 40 THREE PIECE AUTO SET
Three toys on card. Length 6⅜ in. Height 1 in. Weight per gro. 40 lbs. Retails for 10c
per card.

Price per doz. ....

What is certainly a flyer of C.A.W. toys. Courtesy Fred Maxwell.

Left to Right:
C.A.W. CWV 4, CWV 1.
Courtesy Fred Maxwell.

C.A.W.CWV 5b (no rear/propellor). Courtesy of Gary Franson.

C.A.W. CWV 6. Courtesy of Gary Franson.

C.A.W. CWV 12a. Courtesy of Gary Franson.

line art C.A.W. Toys; Top to Bottom: CWV 5, CWV 4. Drawings by Deb Eccles.

CONDITION CODE

C6 - **Good. Evident overall wear, well-played with, but acceptable to many collectors**

C8 - **Very Good minor wear overall, very clean**

C10 - **Mint (like new)**

Note: Mint in box commands a higher price.
Condition below C6 brings considerably lower prices

39 B

C.A.W., CWV14. Courtesy Gary Franson.

C.A.W., CWV7. Courtesy Gary Franson.

C.A.W., CWV10. Courtesy Gary Franson.

	C6	C8	C10

CWV1 Sport Roadster, no #, 3½".
Open Packard, driver w/cap (gilt or silver), no windshield (w/s), horizontal grille (hg), vertical louvers (vl), no headlamps, rearmount (rm), metal disk wheels (mdw)......................20   30   40

CWV2 Sport Roadster, no #, 3½".
Similar to above, Buick?, no w/s, plain grille, vl, rm, right sidemount (sm), mdw, (also spoked version (msw). 22   33   44

CWV3 Overland Bus, no #, 3¾". Fageol? Yellow Line? tour bus, hg, no head-lamps, 12 windows,shallow "observer deck", mdw, left sm. 12   18   24

CWV4 Fuel Tanker, no #, 3¾".
Ford? truck, cab w/driver inside, no w/s, hg, 3 tanks, hose compart., msw....................................20   30   40

CWV5 Air Drive Coach, #25, 3⅞".
Blimp-like bus w/fin and rear propeller drive. (b. Also a version molded w/o prop.) 12 open windows (ow), white rubber wheels (wrw) with unique fitted hubs which cap hidden axles ....No Price Found

CWV6 Streamline Coupe, #30, 3".
Airflow, V-pattern grille, hood ornament (ho), 4 ow, small rear fin, small winged design on rear-wheel skirts, mdw also wrw. Bottom pan goes over rear axle, not under. 16   24   32

CWV7 Wonder Special, #33, 3⅜".
Airflow coupe, 3 wheeled companion to #30 above, vg, 4 ow, wrw, front wheel skirts. Pan goes over front axle. 16   24   32

CWV8 Marvel Racer, #31, 3⅝".
Streamlined FWD Indy type, driver, torpedo tail with very small fin, V-grille pattern, 8 exhaust ports, alum. wheels.

Also found in a modern bubble-pack, w/lucent hard plastic wheels, "Woodchuck Industries Metal Toys, Clay Center, Ks." This name may have been a new idea, part of a recent market test......................No Price Found

CWV9 Desoto Sedan, #32, 3⅞".
Airflow, divided windshield, b ow, hl, vg, ho, wrw.........................No Price Found

CWV10 New Design Racer #38, 3⅜". Streamlined coupe, rounded tail, 2 oval open windows show driver, hood ornament loop (stringpull?), wrw w/hubs..............................No Price Found

CWV11 Transparent Windshield Racer, #39, 3". Indy FWD 2 man racer, v-shaped vg, dual exhausts, boattail, unique hub-tires as in #25 (also wrw). (Not complete if divided plastic windshield is missing (fragile) ....No Price Found

CWV12 Three Piece Auto Set, #40, as follows:
a. Midget coupe racer, no #, 2 1/16". Hg, hl, divided open w/s, 2 ow, 2 colored body, mdw, head-lamps and cowl ventilators! ....No Price Found
b. Midget racer, no #, 2⅛". Gilt driver, vl, hg, mdw. (easily confused w/ Barclay #53).....................................No Price Found
c. Austin Bantam, no #, 2". 2 dr. sedanette, 5 ow, hl, plain grille, rm, mdw. (Easily confused with other makers' Bantams). ....No Price Found

CWV13 Dump Truck, no #, 3⅛".
Ford ?, hinged dump body, divided open w/s, 2 ow, hg, mdw .....No Price Found

CWV14 Tank Truck, no #, 3 3/16".
Ford ?, 3 fuel tanks, otherwise matching above. Unusual 2 pc. body connected by rear axle ....No Price Found

	C6	C8	C10
"C2 to C Co." semi-trailer, cast iron steel wheels, small 30		45	60
Cabriolet with rumble seat, cast iron, cicra 1920s 200		300	400
Cadillac, plastic, 8" long 20		30	40
"Cannonball Express" child's pedal car, red painted, 37" long 500		750	1000
Car, cast iron, 1½" long, maybe			

	C6	C8	C10
Cracker Jack. Possibly smallest cast iron car 50		75	100
Car, cast iron, 4" long 75		112	150
Car, cast iron, with people, 3" long 35		52	70
Caterpillar tractor, cast iron, red, with driver, chain treads 150		225	300
Century of Progress cast iron Greyhound bus, 11" detachable trailer 175		262	350

CHAMPION

The Champion Hardware Co., though in business from 1883-1954, produced toys only from 1930-36, as a Depression stopgap. As might be expected from a hardware firm, its toys were cast iron. During its toy years the Geneva, Ohio outfit was headed by C. I. Chamberlin.

	C6	C8	C10
Champion Coupe, Reo type, 7½" long 400		600	800
Champion Gas and Motor Oil truck, 8" long, cast iron, circa 1930s 225		338	450
Champion four-casting nickeled radiator car, approx. 4" long 175		262	350
Champion Mack Dump, 7" long, circa 1930s 375		563	750
Champion Mack Stake truck, 4½" long, circa 1930 90		135	180
Champion Mack Stake Truck, 7½" long 350		525	700
"Champion" motorcycle and rider, 4½" long 40		60	80

	C6	C8	C10
Champion Motorcycle, 6" long 135		198	270
Champion Motorcycle, 7¼" long 100		150	200
Champion Panel Delivery 750		1300	1800
Champion policeman on motorcycle, 7" long, rubber tires 112		168	225
Champion Race Car, 2 riders, 5½" 125		188	250
Champion Race car, 6" long, cast iron, detachable driver 100		150	200
Champion Race car, 9" long, circa 1930s 150		225	300
"Champion" Wrecker, 7½" long, cast iron 140		210	280

CHAMPION, Mack Dump, 7" long. Courtesy Wilkinson Collection, Detroit Antique Toy Museum.

"CHAMPION", policeman on motorcycle. Courtesy Mapes Auctioneers & Appraisers.

	C6	C8	C10
Checker Cab, circa 1920s, with driver, thin white rubber tires, with rear tire 1000	1500	2000
Chein Army Truck, cannon on back, 8½" long, tin, early 75	111	150
Chein Army Truck, open bed, 8½" long, tin, early 75	111	150
Chein Hercules Motor Express, tin litho, 19½" long, Mack 600	900	1200
Chein Hercules Roadster 350	525	700
Chein Hercules Wrecker Truck, 20" long 425	638	850
Chein "Junior Oil Tank" truck, 8½" long, 1920s 62	93	125
Chein Mack Tanker Truck, 19" long, circa 1928 200	300	400
Chein Roadster, tin litho, circa 1925, 8½" long 125	188	250
Chein "Royal Blue Line Coast to Coast Service" 600	900	1200
Chein Touring Car, tin litho, 7" long 250	375	500
Chrysler Airflow, heavy sheet metal with wind-up motor. Tin grill, headlights and bumper, wooden wheels, 4" long 150	225	300
Chrysler Airflow, cast iron, 4½" long, 1930s 40	60	80
Chrysler Airflow, pressed steel, 6" long, circa 1937 50	75	100
Circus Band Wagon, plays record and moves, 17" long, comic musicians on top, circa 1922 1000	1500	2000
"City Fire Dept. Truck", 1930, pressed steel, rubber tires, 26" long 450	675	900
Clark friction auto, produced in 1894, 10½" long, wood, iron and tin 800	1300	2000
Clark friction auto, circa 1901, wood body coverd with steel 700	1200	1500
Cleveland Toy Racer, aluminum, steel wheels, circa 1935, 13" long 175	262	350
Converse Auto with fringe on top, 3-seat, 1905, painted, pressed steel, clockwork, rubber tires 600	900	1200
Converse Fire Engine ladder truck, bell, wooden headlight, 10", 1915 .. 1250	1875	2500
Converse Pick-Up Truck, very early, open cab 500	750	1000
Converse Touring Auto, 1910, pressed steel, canvas roof 900	1350	1800
Converse Transitional Taxi, clockwork, 10½" long 525	770	1050
Convertible, futuristic, 1930s, with large streamlined fenders, black		

CHEIN Hercules Motor Express. Courtesy Wilkinson Collection, Detroit Antique Toy Musuem

CHEIN Mack Tanker Truck, 19" long, circa 1928. Courtesy Phillips, New York.

CHEIN Roadster, tin litho, circa 1925, 8½" long, Courtesy Mapes Auctioneers & Appraisers.

	C6	C8	C10
wooden wheels, heavy pressed steel, large size 75	112	150
Cor-Cor Airflow windup, electric lights 1000	1500	2000
Cor-Cor Bus, 23" long 300	450	600
Cor-Cor dump truck, dumps back or side to side, 23" long 375	563	750
Cor-Cor Graham Paige sedan, 20" long, electric 800	1200	1650
Cor-Cor Van, painted metal, circa 1928, 23" long 250	380	525

CONVERSE, Transitional Taxi, 10½" long. Courtesy Sotheby's, New York.

CLARK Friction Auto, produced in 1894, 10½ long, wood, iron and tin. Photo by Joe and Sharon Freed.

"City Fire Dept. Truck"', 1930, 26" long. Courtesy Lloyd W. Ralston Auctions.

CLEVELAND TOY racer, aluminum, 13" long. Courtesy Mapes Auctioneers & Appraisers.

	C6	C8	C10
Coupe, tin friction, 17½" long	40	60	80
Coupe with rumble seat, tin, 1920s, 5" long	30	45	60

COURTLAND (WALT REACH)
NON-POWERED VEHICLES

List by Joe and Sharon Freed

	C6	C8	C10
600 Courtland Open Van tractor-trailer L-13", W-3", H-3¼" 1946 retail price 49 cents	45	60	85
610 Courtland Side dump tractor-trailer, L-13", W-3", H-3¼", 1946 retail price 49 cents	35	50	75
620 Courtland Log Truck tractor-trailer. L-13", W-3", H-3¼", 1946 retail price 59 cents	45	60	85
700 Courtland Side dump tractor-trailer. L-13", W-3", H-3¼", 1946 retail price 49 cents	45	60	85
900 Courtland Ice Cream Truck. L-9" W-3", H-2¾" 1946 retail price 39 cents	65	80	125
900 Courtland Moving and Storage Truck. L-9", W-3", H-2¾", 1946 retail price 39 cents	70	90	135

	C6	C8	C10
900 Courtland Fire Patrol No. 2 Truck, L-9", W-3", H-2¾", 1946 retail price 39 cents	65	80	125
900 Courtland Express and Hauling Truck. L-9", W-3", H-2¾", 1946 retail price 39 cents	65	80	125
1050 Courtland Logging Camp Train Set. L-26¾", W-3", H-3¼", 1946 retail price $1.79			No Price Found
1060 Courtland Trailer Truck Parade. L-13", W-3", H-3¼", 1946 retail price $1.79			No Price Found
1070 Courtland Big 4 Truck Parade. The four 900 L-9½", W-3¼", H-3", 1946 retail price $1.79			No Price Found
1200 Courtland Side Dump tractor-trailer. L-13", W-3", H-3¼"	65	80	125

Courtland tractor-trailer. Same tractor as No. 2000 except marked, "Loft-Fresh Candies." However, it is unknown what type trailer as only the tractor has been located. No reference to Courtland or Walt Reach Toys but unquestionably a Courtland ....No Price Found

COURTLAND Non-Powered VehicleTractor-Trailer. Same tractor as No.2000 except marked "Loft-Fresh Candies". Photo courtesy Joe and Sharon Freed.

COURTLAND Non-Powered Vehicle No. 620 Log Truck. Photo courtesy Joe and Sharon Freed.

COURTLAND (WALT REACH) FRICTION-POWERED VEHICLES

List by Joe and Sharon Freed

	C6	C8	C10
3875 Courtland Mechanical "Gulf" Gasoline tractor-trailer L-13", W-3", H-3¼"..................100		145	185
4000 Courtland Woody Sedan, Red & Tan, L-7¼", W-3¼", H-2¾".......60		80	110
4000 Courtland Woody Sedan, Blue & Tan, L-7¼", W-3¼", H-2¾", Note: This is one of only four Courtland styled toys stamped "A Walt Reach Toy by Courtland Toy Co. Phila. Pa. Made in U.S.A." The only known Courtland-styled toys marked with the Courtland Toy Company, Philadelphia stamping is this No. 4000 sedan, a non-powered "Fire Chief" car, a private garage similar to No. 9075 and a mechanical parking meter bank......50		75	100

	C6	C8	C10
4060 Courtland Space Rocket Patrol Car. L-7¼", W-3¼", H-2¾", 1952 retail price 98 cents.................90		125	160
7500 Courtland Mechanical State Police Car with siren. L-7¼", W-3¼", H-2¾"................................50		70	90
7500 Courtland Mechanical Fire Chief Car with siren. L-7¼", W-3¼", H-2¾" 50		70	90
XXXX Courtland Dump Truck w/dual rear wheels, L-10½", W-3", H-3⅜" 75		105	135
7600 Courtland FBI Riot Squad Car. L-7¼", W-3¼", H-2¾"...................50		70	90
XXXX Courtland "Pop-Up" Ladder Fire Truck. L-13", W-3", H-3¼" ...75		105	135
XXXX Courtland Mechanical Military Gun Car. L-7½", W-3¼", H-2½", painted gun shield..75		105	135
XXXX Variation of above, lithographed gunshield....................75		105	135

COURTLAND Friction-Powered Vehicle No.3875. Photo courtesy Mapes Auctioneers.

COURTLAND Friction-Powered Vehicle No.4000, Fire Chief Car, red and white, with red plastic bubble on hood. Photo courtesy Joe and Sharon Freed.

COURTLAND Friction-Powered Vehicle No.XXXX, "Pop-up" Ladder Fire Truck. Photo courtesy Joe and Sharon Freed.

COURTLAND Friction-Powered Vehicle No.XXXX, Mechanical Military Gun Car, variation with litho gun shield. Photo courtesy Joe and Sharon Freed.

COURTLAND Friction-Powered Vehicle No.XXXX, Dump Truck with dual rear wheels. Photo courtesy Joe and Sharon Freed.

CRAFTOYS

By Fred Maxwell and Ron Eccles

Craftoy. a small Omaha, Nebraska firm, had a brief career casting slushmold vehicles before the War's need for lead brought the potmetal era to a long halt. We have discovered little more about the company than the accompanying sales sheet. It acquired some of the assets when Ralstoy was reorganizing about 1940.

For those readers accustomed to identifying by "those numbers", note: #92 sedan has the same number as a Best Toy coupe but they are not the same car. #100 racer is obviously not the same as Best #100 sedan. Older molds were also used for #78 mixer, #81 racer and #102 gasoline

semitanker. #101 fire truck, #103 Speed car, #104 oil truck and #105 station wagon possible come from Ralstoy. The ancestry of Kansas toy is evident in #17 tractor and the freight train set. The designs of the RR coal car, stock car and tank car are recent or new. Thus we come to the end of the line as "those toys with the numbers" roll into history. These catalog numbers may or may not be found on the toys.

Black rubber wheels are seen to be characteristic of this line, but they are not exclusive with Craftoy.

	C6	C8	C10
Craftoy Tractor, "17", 2½". "Fordson", "Made in USA" farm tractor, driver, rear wheels larger, visible engine.....8	12	16
Craftoy Freight Train, "3600", 16½". Locomotive, 0-6-4, 4½", "KT&N RR"; cars 3¼"; caboose 2¾". "Made in USA". Value of indiv. cars.6	9	12
Craftoy Cement Mixer, "78", 3¾". 2 open windows, "Made in USA". 8	12	16
Craftoy Racer, "81", 4½". Miller FWD Indy racer, "Made in USA"...10	15	20
Craftoy Sedan, #92, 4". Streamlined 2 door sedan, 4 open windows, screen pattern grille..........................No Price Found		
Craftoy Racer #100, 4¼". Indy type, driver, removable tin hood, rounded nose. ....No Price Found		

	C6	C8	C10
Craftoy ? Racer, no #, 3¾". Indy type, driver, removable tin hood, slanted nose.......................................No Price Found		
Craftoy Fire Truck, #101, 4½". Hose truck or insurance patrol, 4 open windows....No Price Found		
Craftoy Tanker, "102", 6¾". 1938 International K-line ?, "gasoline" semi-trailer, 2 open windows............No Price Found		
Craftoy Speed Car, #103, 4¼". Streamlined closed racer, body trimmed in fantasy streamlines.........No Price Found		
Craftoy Oil Truck, #104, 3¾". 1938 International ?, COE, "gas", "oil" tanker. 2 open windows ....No Price Found		
Craftoy Station Wagon, #105, 3¾". Streamlined, 4 open windows...........No Price Found		

DAYTON FRICTION WORKS

Dayton was owned by D.P. Clark of Dayton, Ohio. Clark's wood and metal "Hill Climber" friction toys were his best known. Clark was in business from 1898, and his company was one of the first to use a friction motor, which is activated by moving the toy by hand against a surface and then releasing it. William Schieble, who joined the company in the early 1900s, left in 1909 and formed the Schieble Toy and Novelty Company, using the "Hill Climber" name, which he felt was legally his, while Clark continued to use it, despite Schieble's lawsuits. Thus the parentage of some "Hill Climbers" is uncertain.

	C6	C8	C10
Dayton Coal and Ice Truck, tin friction circa 1920......150		225	300
Dayton Coupe, 12", 1928, pressed steel...125		187	250
Dayton Coupe, 12½" long, circa 1920 600		900	1200
Dayton "Dayton Friction", pressed steel, rubber tires, 1920s, 14¼" long........ ..250		375	500
Dayton Dump Truck.....................375		563	750
Dayton Fire Ladder Truck, 18" long 185		278	370
Dayton Fire Pumper, 1920 100		150	200
Dayton Ladder Truck, 1920s...............200		300	400

	C6	C8	C10
Dayton open touring car, dated 1909, friction motor, driver......................250		375	500
Dayton touring car, 13½" long, friction motor 440		660	880
Dayton touring car, 13½" long, unpowered.....................................350		525	700
Delivery truck, 3½" long, cast iron.......60		90	120
Delivery Truck, 10½" long, with driver, friction 100		150	200
Delivery Truck, "Packard", 28" long steel.400		600	800

DENT HARDWARE COMPANY

Dent, of Fullerton, Pennsylvania, was in business from 1895-1973. Henry H. Dent, with four partners, was the owner. Cast iron toys seem to have first emerged in 1898. Dent is known for particularly fine castings in its vehicles.

It was also one of the first manufacturers to try (with little success) aluminum toys (in the 1920s). Toys seem to have been phased out during the hard times of the Depression.

	C6	C8	C10
Dent "American Oil Co.", cast iron truck, approx. 10½" long 750		1125	1500
Dent bus, cast iron, 6¼" long 375		563	750
Dent Coast to Coast Bus, 7½" long......125		187	250
Dent "Coast to Coast" bus, circa 1925, 15" long 750		1000	1500
Dent Coupe, 5" long 125		188	250
Dent "Express J & B" stakebed truck, 14½", 1915, driver 500		800	1100
Dent fire truck, cast iron, 7" long.........150		225	300
Dent fire ladder truck, 8½" long, with driver.............................450		675	900
Dent fire truck with ladder and men, cast iron, 18" long..........................900		1350	1800
Dent hose reeler with men, cast iron, large 500		750	1000
Dent "Interurban" bus, cast iron, 9" long.250		375	500
Dent La Salle, approx. 4" long.............200		300	400
Dent Ladder truck, 10" long, two drivers 250		375	500
Dent Mack Dump Truck, 4½" circa 1925, iron wheels...........................55		82	110
Dent Model T two door sedan, iron wheels, circa 1925......................125		187	250

	C6	C8	C10
Dent "Patrol", 6½" long, circa 1920s...125		187	250
Dent "Police Patrol", 8¾" long 750		1125	1500
Dent "Public Service" Bus, circa 1926, 13½" long 1800		3000	4500
Dent Sedan, 7½" long, spare tire, has stop and go light, full bumpers on front...................................900		1350	1800
Dent Steam Roller, cast iron, 6" long....45		68	90
Dent Touring Car........................500		7500	1000
Dent Yellow Cab, approx. 7¾" long 900		1400	1900
"Dept. of Street Cleaning" dump truck, 10½" long, circa 1935 50		75	100

DENT "Police Patrol", approx. 8¾" long. Courtesy Phillips New York.

DINKY

Dinky toys were first made in England in 1932 under the name "Modeled Miniatures", later "Meccano Miniatures", and in 1934, "Dinky", which in England means "fetching".

	C6	C8	C10		C6	C8	C10
Dinky 14c Coventry Fork Lift	30	45	60	Dinky 135 Triumph 2000	17	26	35
Dinky 23H Ferrari racer	17	26	35	Dinky 137 Plymouth, 1963	17	26	35
Dinky 25C Flat Truck	75	112	150	Dinky 151 Austin Devon	17	26	35
Dinky 27f 1948 Plymouth Station				Dinky 154 Ford Taurus	17	26	35
Wagon	60	90	120	Dinky 157 Jaguar XK120	40	60	80
Dinky 29C Double Decker Bus	75	112	150	Dinky 168 Ford Escort	7	11	15
Dinky 30r Fordson Truck	17	26	35	Dinky 172 Studebaker Land Cruiser	70	105	140
Dinky 32c/576 Panhard Esso	100	150	200	Dinky 174 Hudson Hornet Sedan	32	48	65
Dinky 34 Royal Mail Van	32	48	65	Dinky 181 Volkswagen MBD	75	112	150
Dinky 36b Bentley	40	60	80	Dinky 200 Matra 630	17	26	35
Dinky 36c Humber, 1936	30	45	60	Dinky 201 Plymouth Rally, 1976	17	26	35
Dinky 36d Rover	75	112	150	Dinky 207 Triumph TR7 Leyland	17	26	35
Dinky 38c Lagonda	30	45	60	Dinky 227 Beach Buggy	17	26	35
Dinky 38d Alvis	30	45	60	Dinky 241 Austin taxi	17	26	35
Dinky 39c Lincoln Zephyr	150	225	300	Dinky 252 1968 Pontiac	22	33	45
Dinky 40a Riley 4DS	60	90	120	Dinky 254 Taxi	25	38	50
Dinky 45 Vauxhall Victor	15	22	30	Dinky 261 Telephone Van	40	60	80
Dinky 97 Euclid Truck	11	16	22	Dinky 267 Dodge Fire Rescue	37	56	75
Dinky 106 Thunderbird 2 space	40	60	80	Dinky 267 Bedford Dump	9	13	18
Dinky 112 Triumph Purdey	17	26	35	Dinky 308 Leyland Tractor	17	26	35
Dinky 130 Ford Corsair	17	26	35	Dinky 344 Estate Car	20	30	40
Dinky 134 Triumph Vitesse	17	26	35				

DINKY, Left to Right: 157 Jaguar KX120 Coupe, 334 Estate Car. Courtesy Phillips New York.

DINKY, Left to Right: 174 Hudson Hornet Sedan, 172 Studebaker Land Cruiser. Courtesy Phillips New York.

DOEPKE "MODEL TOYS"

by Ray Funk
(See also Miscellaneous)

Doepke "Model Toys" advertised their toys as outlasting all others 3 to 1. The company's full title was the "Charles Wm. Doepke Mfg. Co., Inc." of Rossmoyne, Ohio. Each toy was an authorized replica of the actual thing and the decals and coloring were exactly as upon the real equipment or trucks, with the exception of the manufacturer having his own, in this case "Model Toys."

At the end of the Second World War, the Doepke Corp. hit the market with five models, first in a line of heavy duty metal operating replicas, employing metal tread or authentic miniature tires, either Goodyear or Firestone, with authentic tread and name and tire sizes, exactly as on the real tires. This, to the best of my knowledge, has never been done so perfectly, even in the model kits of today.

RAY FUNK is a leading collector and authority on trains and other toys, as well as a collector and authority on comic books and western literature.

These toys all had rubber smoke stacks, and received the approval of Parents Magazine, P.T.A., Boy's Life Magazine, and all other experts and advocates of good toys at that period. The first five numbers were 2000, 2001, 2002, 2006, 2007. Why not 3, 4 and 5, I cannot say. Perhaps Doepke had toys planned for these numbers that fell through. Following is a list of the Doepke vehicles.

No. 2000, Wooldridge H.D. earth hauler, bright yellow, four huge tires, 25" long, and weighing 10 lbs. The actual manufacturer's address is listed as Sunnyvale, Calif. I'm sure most of you have seen the John Wayne movie, "The Fighting Seabees", which used several of these, along with caterpillar bulldozers and road graders. These Wooldridge's caught my eye with their maneuvering ability, and could traverse the roughest terrain easily. Two long doors, the length of the bottom of the dirt-hauling area, could be released to deposit a load. Price was $14.75 new in 1945.

No. 2001, Barber-Greene high-capacity bucket loader, 13" high, 10 lbs., dark green, all steel and rolling on steel tread, was designed as a toy to load earth haulers. Handcrank operated, operated exactly as the real thing. Price $14.75.

No. 2002, Jaeger concrete mixer, bright yellow, 15" long, 8 lbs. on four wheels, steerable via draw bar (all model toys steered exactly like the real thing), though perhaps the best-detailed, was the poorest selling toy, as although you could, it wasn't feasible to really mix concrete in them, due to small amount received versus cleaning time. This toy was priced at $10.75 to $13.75.

No. 2006, Adams diesel road grader, dark orange, 26" long, 14 lbs., all six wheels, three axles, and blade adjustable to all angles, exactly like the real thing, steerable via steering wheel, priced at $14.75.

No. 2007, Unit Mobile Crane, dark orange, 11½" long, 19½" boom, eight lbs. and eight ounces, adjustable side jacks, steered via a drawbar, with block and tackle, and removable operating clam shell as standard accessory. Priced at $14.75.

No number 2008, as the next year, No. 2009 was released and No. 2000 dropped. No 2009 was a Euclid earth-hauler truck, with uncoupling four-wheel tractor to use to tow other toys. 27" long, 11 lbs., Euclid green, or light road-grader orange, the trailer dumped in the same way as the Wooldridge. Priced $14.75.

No. 2010, American-LaFrance pumper fire truck, 18" long, 7 lbs., bright red with chrome trim, ladder, bell, fire extinguisher, hoses and nozzle, a reservoir that held water for hand-operated pressure pump. A beautiful toy at $16.75.

No 2011, Heiliner earth scraper, 29" long, 13 lbs., bright dark red, loaded and dumped and operated on four wheels as the Wooldridge did. Priced at $16.75.

No. 2012, Caterpillar D6 tractor and bulldozer, caterpillar yellow, 15" long, 7 lbs., with real bulldozer treads for sharp realistic turning (removable only by using punch and hammer to remove connecting pin from between two of the pads) and adjustable bulldozer blade, plus heavy draw bar. Truly a beautiful toy at $13.75. Diesel motor was cast metal.

No. 2013 eliminated and replaced No. 2001. No. 2013, Barber-Green mobile high-capacity bucket loader, 22" long, 12" high, 10 lbs., buckets on chains and rubber conveyor belt, adjustable and steered by steering wheel, priced at $19.75.

No. 2014, American La-France aerial ladder truck, 23" long, 42" extended ladder height, 11 lbs., bright red and chrome, bell, red light, adjustable side jacks, single unit truck steered by steering wheel, priced at $20.75.

Doepke "Model Toys" were doomed to extinction by lower-priced, lighter-constructed imitators of lesser quality, some of which were started in the 1920s, and others that came into being in the 1950s, several of which are still around today, but none ever containing, before or after, the heavy-duty constructed realism and operating qualities as had the one and only "Model Toys".

Of the Doepke Model Toys that were mass produced, several had variations in their basic construction from time to time. Usually these changes were an elimination of the more intricate operating procedures, and had little or no effect on the toy's overall outward appearance.

In Antique Toy World, Philip Sayer wrote a two part article on the Doepke Co., and featured pictures of nearly all toys manufactured by the firm. The ones that were produced in such limited numbers (only one to a few), are mentioned and often times described. Also listed are nearly all of the slight changes in the mass produced toys, though I could not (perhaps overlooked it) find mention of the change in the D-6 Caterpillar. The first models to hit the market have the front axles held tightly forward by springs, so when being pushed forward and they strike a solid object to climb over, there is some give to absorb the shock and protect the tract pads. Later models eliminated this and opted for simple axle wells as in the rear wheels. Had I not had both types, this slight change would have easily gone unnoticed.

It would seem that the Doepke Co. would accept orders to make model toys of the real thing for the actual producers, and the toys with the most allure, playability, and feasible mass production design, and greatest entertainment to be provided to the child that received one, would be mass produced. Of the others that would not withstand rough handling by young hands, or because of cost and time required to produce them, there were only one to a few produced as previously mentioned. This is no doubt the explanation for the number gaps between the marketed items.

Among the scarcer articles produced, were even a few automobiles, avidly sought after by collectors that have delved into this company's past history to any depth. Of these, perhaps there were catalogs or brochures about them, though all I have seen are the ones dealing with the mass produced toys I have listed.

An ad for DOEPKE Model Toys. Photo by Bill Kaufman. Courtesy Ray Funk.

DOEPKE Catalog illustration of Model No. 2012. Photo by Bill Kaufman. Courtesy Ray Funk.

DOEPKE No.2000 Wooldridge. Courtesy Ray Funk.

DOEPKE No.2001, Barber-Greene high capacity bucket loader. Courtesy Ray Funk.

DOEPKE No.2007, Unit Mobile Crane. Courtesy Ray Funk.

Dump Truck, steel wind-up, 4½" long. Courtesy James S. Maxwell/Virgina Caputo. Photo by Virginia Caputo.

DOEPKE No.2018 Jaguar. Courtesy Ray Funk.

DOEPKE No.2012, Caterpillar D6's. Courtesy Ray Funk.

	C6	C8	C10
Doepke No. 2000 Wooldridge H.D. Earth Hauler, 25" long 140	210	280
Doepke No. 2001 Barber-Greene high capacity bucket loader, 13" high....225	338	450
Doepke No. 2002 Jaeger Concrete Mixer, 15" long 300	450	600
Doepke No. 2006 Adams Diesel Road Grader, 26" long.........................90	135	180
Doepke No. 2007 Unit Mobile Crane, 11½" long..............................120	180	240
Doepke No. 2008 American La France Aerial Ladder Truck...........200	300	400
Doepke No. 2009 Euclid Earth Hauler Truck, 27" long 150	225	300
Doepke No. 2020 American-La France pumper fire truck, 18" long 190	275	380
Doepke No. 2011 Heiliner Earth Scraper, 29" long 210	315	420
Doepke No. 2012 Caterpillar D6 tractor and bulldozer, 15" long 212	318	425
Doepke No. 2013 Barber-Green mobile high-capacity bucket loader 22" long.............................250	375	525
Doepke No. 2014 American-La France aerial ladder fire truck, 23" long 200	300	400
Doepke No. 2015 Clark Airport Tractor and Baggage Trailers.........400	600	900

	C6	C8	C10
Doepke No. 2015 MG, 1954, 15" long...225	338	450
Doepke No. 2018 Jaguar, 1955 325	488	650
Doepke No. 2023 Searchlight Truck, 1955 700	1050	1400
Drudge "Hyster" lumber carrier 175	263	350
Dump Truck, 4½" long, cast iron, "2205"..90	135	180
Dump Truck, tin, 5¾" long, wooden wheels 20	30	40
Dump Truck, 6" long, pressed steel, circa 1939......................................50	75	100
Dump Truck, 7" long, cast iron, driver 90	135	180
Dump Truck (Beck), steers via horn on top of cab, late 1940s, large 60	90	120
Dump Truck, steel windup, 4½" long 5	8	10

DUNWELL

Dunwell was the trade name given to its toys by Metal Products Co. of Clifton, New Jersey. Its trucks seem to have been sold circa 1953 - 1958. Their line resembles Tonka's rather closely, and is rare.

	C6	C8	C10
Dunwell Auto Transport........................162	243	325
Dunwell "Grain Hauler".........................200	300	400
Dunwell Log Truck 85	128	170
Dunwell "Red Star Express Lines" truck 300	450	600
Dunwell "Snowcrop" Refrigerator Semi .280	420	560
Dunwell "Steel Carrier Co." semi 220	330	440

DYNA-MODEL PRODUCTS COMPANY
(Dyna-Mo)
by Fred Maxwell

Dyna-Model Products Co., 93 South Street, Oyster Bay, Long Island, New York, may have pioneered the scale models industry dominating today's markets with their "Dyna-Mo" brand of HO toys to be used in train layouts. They are rather high quality pot-metal toys, identified by their method of assembling body parts, clamping axles between small posts and the standardized appearance of the undersides of the whole line.

Probably produced in the 1930's, and perhaps in the post-war era, the toys were made by a coarse diecasting process. The earlier vintage cars were made into two to five parts, exclusive of wheels and axles, to be pinned, clamped or glued together: body, frame, steering wheel, top and windshield. Some were packaged as kits, with instructions printed on the box: "Pinch ends of axel (their spelling) after installing wheels" (R-26). The toys were factory painted in as many as 4 colors per toy.

	C6	C8	C10
D1 Dyna "R-26 HO Surrey, 35c": 1¾". Horseless carriage, tiller steering, 3 colors, 3 pc. body, kit 4	6	8
D2 Dyna Touring Car: 2" Antique Stanley Steamer, open tonneau, rt. hand steering, 4 colors, 4 pc 4	6	8
D3 Dyna Speedster: 2". Antique Mercer, rt. hand steering, 4 colors, 3 pc 4	6	8

	C6	C8	C10
D4 Dyna Roadster: 1⅞". Antique Buick? Open, rt. hand steering, 4 pcs., 3 colors 4	6	8
D5 Dyna Touring Car: 1⅞". Antique. Realistic folded top attachable with hinge pins, left hand steering, 5 pcs., 2 colors..................4	6	8

DYNA-MODEL, Top, Left to Right: D1, Ford T Roadster, 1⅞", D7, D3, Franklin steam touring 2⅛". Middle, Left to Right: D5, D6, D9, D10, D8. Bottom, Left to Right: D11, Cadillac sedan 2", D23, D16. Photo by Fred Maxwell.

DYNA-MODEL, Top, Left to Right: D14, D20?, D12, Cadillac 2-door sedan, 2⅜". Middle, Left to Right: D15, D18, D21. Bottom, Left to Right: D22, D23, D24. Photo by Fred Maxwell.

	C6	C8	C10
D6 Dyna "R-61 HO Model T Ford 1914 touring with top 60c": 1⅝". One piece body, top up, 3 colors. "Cut plastic windshield to fit, darken edges with ink or paint and glue top and windshield in place, in slots provided."	4	6	8
D7 Dyna Touring car: 1¾". 1914 Ford, top down cast in one-piece body, glued windshield, 3 colors	4	6	8
D8 Dyna Roadster: 2". 1920's Packard convertible, top down, rumble seat, one piece body, glued windshield, spoked wheels, 3 colors	6	9	12
D9 Dyna Roadster: 2". Packard, same as above, top up, 3 colors	6	9	12
D10 Dyna Touring: 2". Packard, same as above, top down, 3 colors	6	9	12
D11 Dyna Roadster: 2". Model A Ford? Top down, open rumble seat, disc wheels, one piece body, unpainted	2	3	4
D12 Dyna Sedan: 2". Buick sedan, 1930's. Open windshield and windows. 2 colors	4	6	8
D13 Dyna "R-68 HO Buick convertible 55c": 2⅜". Late 1930's. Open, 2 dr. sedan, top down, one piece body, solid cast windshield, disk wheels	6	9	12
D14 Dyna Sedan: 2⅜", Buick 2 dr. airflow, open windshield and windows	6	9	12
D15 Dyna Taxi: 2⅜". Buick sedan, late 1930's. Open windshield and windows, 2 colors	6	9	12
D16 Dyna Convertible, 2⅜". Cadillac 2 dr. sedan, late 1930's	6	9	12

	C6	C8	C10
D17 Dyna Sedan: 2⅜". Cadillac 2 dr. sedan, open windshield and windows, incl. rear, late 1930's	6	9	12
D18 Dyna Taxi: 2⅜". Cadillac sedan, late 1930's, open windshield and windows including rear, 2 colors	6	9	12
D19 Dyna Sedan: 2⅜". Pontiac 4 dr. airflow, open windshield and windows incl rear	6	9	12
D20 Dyna Limousine: 2½". Cadillac, late 1930's, open windows as above	6	9	12
D21 Dyna Delivery Van: 2⅜". Pontiac, late 1930's, open windshield and door windows	4	6	8
D22 Dyna Pickup Truck: 2½". GMC?, late 1930's, open windows, spoked wheels, 2 piece, 3 colors	4	6	8
D23 Dyna Wrecker: 2¾", GMC?, late 1930's, open windows, 3 piece, 4 colors	6	9	12
D24 Dyna Dump Truck: 2¾". Open windows, hinged body with realistic load of coal. 3 pieces, 2 colors, dual rear wheels	8	12	16
D25 Dyna Pickup Truck: 2". GMC?, 1930's, one piece, open windows, one color	4	6	8
D26 Dyna Pickup Truck: 2". Mack? "US Army", Air Corps star decals, late 1930's, 2 pc. body, 2 colors	4	6	8
D27 Dyna Truck: 2". Mack? Same chassis as above, but tarpaulin covered, 2 pc. body	4	6	8

	C6	C8	C10
Eldon Corvette, 14" long	40	60	80
Eldon Road Race slot car set, 1965	32	48	65

ERIE
(*Parker White Metal*)
Listing by Dave Leopard

According to James Apthorpe, Erie toys were made by Parker White Metal Company, which apparently began in Erie, Pennsylvania, but moved to Fairview (West of Erie), Pa. in the early 1960s. However, according to company officials he contacted, the firm made toys only prior to World War II. It printed no catalogs.

ERIE Sedan, two-door. Photo by James Apthorpe.

	C6	C8	C10
EV01 Lincoln Zephyr sedan, 1936, 5½" long, painted	40	50	60
EV02 Lincoln Zephyr sedan, 1936, 5½" long, plated	45	55	65
EV03 Lincoln Zephyr sedan, 1936, 3½" long, painted	25	30	35
EV04 Lincoln Zephyr sedan, 1936, 3½" long, plated	30	35	40
EV05 Packard Roadster, 1936, 6" long, painted	40	50	60
EV06 Packard Roadster, 1936, 6" long, plated	45	55	65
EV07 Packard Roadster, 1936, 3½" long, painted	25	30	35
EV08 Packard Roadster, 1936, 3½" long, plated	30	35	40
EV09 Ford Pickup Truck, 1935, low sides, 5" long, painted	40	50	60
EV10 Ford Pickup Truck, 1935, low sides, 5" long, plated	45	55	65
EV11 Ford Pickup Truck, 1935, high sides, 5" long, large rear window	40	50	60
EV12 Ford Pickup Truck, 1935, high sides, 5" long, small rear window ...	40	50	60
EV13 Ford Ice Truck, 1935, "Pure Ice Co.", 5" long	50	60	70
EV14 Ford Tow Truck, 1935, "Servel Body", 5" long	50	60	70
EV15 Cabover truck, c. 1937, no tail gate, 3¼" long	20	25	30
EV16 Cabover truck, c. 1937, tailgate, updated, 3¼" long	20	25	30

	C6	C8	C10
EV17 Tow Truck, c. 1939, no chassis, 4¼" long	30	35	40
EV18 Sedan, c. 1939, futuristic, fin on trunk, no chassis, 4¼" long	30	35	40
EV19 Coupe, c. 1939, futuristic, no chassis, 4¼" long	30	35	40
EV20 Sedan, c. 1939, sharknose, no chassis, 4¼" long	30	35	40

ERTL

Ertl was begun by Fred Ertl Sr. in 1945, working out of his Dubuque, Iowa home. As business expanded, the firm moved to Dyersville. Ertl had learned about using sand molds in his native Germany, and very early in the company's history began working directly from the original blueprints to make his toy tractors, trucks and other wheeled toys. Ertl's specialty is farm toys, with rights obtained from such manufacturers as International Harvester and John Deere. Today Ertl is the largest manufacturer of toy farm equipment in the world, and in addition makes a number of other toys, such as cars, trucks and airplanes.

ERTL Ford 4000 Tractor (FOR26A). Courtesy Wilkerson Collection, Detroit Antique Toy Museum.

	C6	C8	C10
Ertl AC 12-B Track Loader Bulldozer .	125	188	250
Ertl Allied Moving Van	28	42	56
Ertl Bell Telephone Van	12	18	25
Ertl Firetruck No. 9, 22" long	15	22	30
Ertl Firetruck No. 9 with Fire Chief's car .	20	30	40
Ertl Ford 4000 Tractor (for 26A) 10½" long	45	68	90
Ertl Harvester, first Ertl	175	262	350
Ertl International Harvester btm. plow ..	12	18	25
Ertl IH TD-25 toplites bulldozer	175	263	350
Ertl IH Payloader	45	68	90
Ertl IHC Scout Pickup Truck	17	26	35
Ertl Lodestar Dump Truck	90	135	180
Ertl Lodestar Grain/Cattle stack truck ...	87	131	175
Ertl Mary Kay Cosmetics trailer truck ..	42	63	85
Ertl Sears Trailer Truck	30	45	60
Ertl Shell Tanker, 20" long	27	41	55
Ertl Spreader with metal beater	20	30	40
Ertl Star Dump Truck	60	90	120

FALLOWS TOYS, Frederick & Henry, Horseless Carriage with driver, 8" long. Courtesy Wilkinson Collection, Detroit Antique Toy Museum.

Fire Pumper, Cast Iron, 5" long, Circa 1935. Courtesy Mapes Auctioneers & Appraisers.

	C6	C8	C10
Ertl Tractor, No. 656	10	15	20
Ertl Velveeta Trailer Truck, 22" long	32	48	65
Ertl "White" cabover	250	375	500
Fallows Toys, Frederick & Henry, Horseless Carriage with driver, 8" long, cast iron and tin, circa 1905	900	1350	1800
Farm truck, "Speed," with driver, 7" cast iron	150	225	300
Fire Engine "9608" die cast, 6" long, Post-War	35	52	70
Fire Engine Pumper, friction, gear shift lever, with drivers	200	300	400
Fire Pumper, 5" long, cast iron, circa 1935	65	97	130
Fire Pumper, approx. 6½" long, cast iron	100	150	200
Fire Pumper, 8" long, cast iron	85	112	170
Fire Pumper, 11" long, cast iron	125	187	250
Fire Truck, cast iron, 7" long	70	105	140
Fire Truck, friction, with driver, metal and wood, pat. Nov. 2, 1897	600	900	1200
Fire Truck, pressed steel friction toy 10½" long, early with driver	350	525	700

FIRESTONE

The following list, with its codings, was compiled by David Leopard.

	C6	C8	C10
FA01 '39 Mercury fastback 4 door sedan, 4¾" long	40	50	60
FA02 '35 Ford 2 door humpback sedan, 4⅞" long	40	50	60
FA03 '36 Ford 2 door humpback sedan, 4⅞" long	40	50	60
Ford coupe, 4" long, 1924	80	120	160
Ford coupe, blue, chrome wheels, 5" long	80	120	160

Fire Pumper, cast iron, 11" long. Photo by Bill Kaufman. Courtesy Good old Days Store.

	C6	C8	C10
Ford coupe, cast iron, black, chrome wheels, circa 1920s, 5" long	80	120	160
"Fordson" tractor with driver, cast iron, 5¾" long	140	210	280
Fordson tractor with hay rake, cast iron, 1930s	150	225	300
Friction car, cast iron and wood, with figures	125	187	250
Friction car, 7¼", 1910	900	1350	1800
Friction toy with two riders, 1897	150	225	300
GMC "Greyhound Lines" cast iron bus, 7½" long, circa 1934	200	300	400

FIRESTONE FA-03 (both) with original box. Photo by Ron Smith.

GIRARD Fire Chief Siren Coupe. Photo by Bill Kaufman.

GIRARD Touring Bus. Courtesy Mapes Auctioneers & Appraisers.

GIFTCRAFT, TA01. Photo by Dave Leopard.

GREY IRON "Midget" Vehicles, approx. 1½" long. Photo by Stan Alekna.

	C6	C8	C10
"Gasoline" truck, circa late 30s, red, approx. 2¾" long, slush	10	15	20
Gibbs "Gibbs No. 701" truck	150	250	350
Giftcraft (possibly only the distributor) TA01 Fastback Sedan, circa 1946 Nash, solid rubber, 4" long	15	20	25

GIRARD

	C6	C8	C10
Girard Coupe, 14" long, battery operated headlights	410	615	820
Girard Fire Chief Car, 15" long	175	263	350
Girard "Fire Chief Siren Coupe," 14½" long	275	413	550
Girard Fire truck, 12" long, 1920s	125	188	250
Girard Pump Truck, battery operated, headlights, 10" long	100	150	200
Girard Roadster, 14½" long, electrified	212	318	425
Girard Side Dump, 11½" long	165	248	330
Girard Stake Truck, 10", electric headlights	112	168	225
Girard Tank Truck, 11½" long, wood wheels	92	138	185
Girard Touring Bus, painted tin, circa 1920, 12" long	150	225	300
Girard Truck with Trailer, 1930s, 17"	100	150	200
Goodee Cadillac Convertible, 1957?, 3" long	6	9	12

GREY IRON

	C6	C8	C10
Grey Iron, Convertible Midget, 1½" long	20	30	40
Grey Iron, Coupe Midget, 1½" long	20	30	40

	C6	C8	C10
Grey Iron, Delivery Truck, Midget, 1½" long	20	30	40
Grey Iron, Racer, Midget, 1½" long	20	30	40
Grey Iron, Sedan, Airflow Type, Midget, 1½" long	20	30	40
Grey Iron, Sedan, Older, Midget, 1½" long	20	30	40
Grey Iron Sedan, 1927, 9" long	1000	1500	2000
"Guided Missile Unit No. 10" truck, tin litho, circa 1960	60	90	120
Hafner "Auto Express Co." truck, 8½" long, steel clockwork	450	675	900
Hafner Curved Dash Olds circa 1903, pressed steel, clockwork, 10" long	400	600	800
Hafner Roundabout with upholstered driver's seat, steel clockwork, 7" long	450	675	900
Hafner Touring Car, 10" long, pressed steel, clockwork	750	1125	1500
Happy Sam driving wood truck, circa 1920s, 8" long	80	120	160

HAFNER curved dash Olds, circa 1903. Courtesy Sotheby's New York.

HAFNER, Left to Right: "Auto Express Co.", Roundabout with upholstered driver's seat. Courtesy Sotheby's New York.

HILLCLIMBER Horseless Carriage, woman driver, 7" long. Courtesy Mapes Auctioners & Appraisers.

HAFNER Touring Car, 10" long. Courtesy Sotheby's New York.

HESS

Promotional vehicles, all of them plastic, are turned out annually for Hess Service Stations in limited editions available to the public through the Christmas season. Hess' headquarters are in Woodbridge, NJ, under the name Amerada Hess. Virtually all collector sales are mint in the box, thus the pricing here.

	MIB
1964 B-Model Mack Tanker	1200
1967 Split Window, Velvet Bottom Box	1150
1968 Tanker Truck	225
1970 Pumper Fire Truck	400
1972 Split Window Tanker	185
1975 Box Trailer	220
1976 Box Trailer w/Barrels	200
1977 Tank Truck - Large Label	175
1978 Tank Truck - Small Label	155
1980 Training Van	150
1982 "First Hess Truck"	65
1983 "First Hess Truck", bank	65
1984 Tank Truck Bank	55
1985 Tanker Truck	40
1986 Ladder, Fire Truck, red	65
1987 "18 Wheeler" Truck w/Barrels	45
1988 Race Car Transporter	45
1989 Ladder Fire Truck w/Siren, white	35
1990 Tanker Truck w/Horn	25

	C6	C8	C10
Hillclimber "Ambulance", 10½" long, very early	500	800	1100
Hillclimber Armored Truck, 11" long, pressed steel friction	150	225	300
Hillclimber Auto, woman driver, friction, very early, 6" long	500	750	1000
Hillclimber hook and ladder wagon, painted pressed steel friction, driver, 20" long	200	300	400
Hillclimber Horseless Carriage, woman driver, cast iron and wood, very early, 7" long	400	600	800
Hillclimber Racer with track, 7½" long	375	525	750
Hillclimber Touring car, 11" long	85	127	170
Hiller Comet race car, "3", fuel-powered, circa 1940-42	350	525	700
Hoge Fire chief car, 15" long	550	825	1100
"Holmes Coal Co." pressed steel delivery truck, 17½" long	40	600	800
Hook and ladder, aluminum, with driver, 13" long	100	150	200
Hook and ladder truck, tin friction, 21" long	100	150	200
Hose Wagon, 1897, two riders, friction toy	125	187	250

HESS 1967 Split Window. Courtesy Thomas G. Nefos, Federal Shipping Network.

HESS 1970 Red Pumper Fire Truck. Courtesy Thomas G. Nefos, Federal Shipping Network.

"Holmes Coal Co.". Courtesy Sotheby's New York.

HESS 1976 Box Trailer. Courtesy Thomas G. Nefos, Federal Shipping Network.

HESS 1982 "First Hess Truck". Courtesy Thomas G. Nefos, Federal Shipping Network.

HILLER, Comet Race Car "3". Photo by William G. Floyd.

HESS 1989 Ladder Fire Truck. Courtesy Thomas G. Nefos, Federal Shipping Network.

HUBLEY

The Hubley manufacturing company was founded at least as early as 1892 by John Hubley, and made iron toys from the start at its plant in Lancaster, Pennsylvania. All toys at the beginning were cast iron, and some early toys included coal ranges, circus wagons and mechanical banks. Hubley's cast iron toys were popular almost from the start, and have long been collector's items, as they were well-made and attractive. By 1940, however, the cast iron toy, due to the increased cost of freight and foreign competition, was slowly becoming a thing of the past. At this time, when Hubley was the largest producer of cast iron toys and cap pistols in the world, it began to introduce die cast zinc alloy toys. During the Second World War, Hubley was 98% engaged in war production, turning out over five million M-74 bomb fuses, which the Hubley engineers played a large part in developing. Since the war, Hubley manufactures die cast toys and plastic toys exclusively. In 1952, Hubley manufactured 9,763,610 toys and 11,184,878 cap pistols, about ten times the amount of toys and pistols they produced in 1930, but with a line of toys 80% smaller than in 1930. It is the combination of the relative scarcity (and multiplicity) of the older toys, plus the preference by collectors for cast iron over die cast zinc alloy and plastic toys that makes the pre-World War II toys the most attractive to collectors. Hubley was acquired by Gabriel Industries in late 1965, and puts out holster sets, cap pistols, vehicles, hobby kits and a number of other toys.

	C6	C8	C10
Hubley Air Compress Truck, 7" long, circa 1950s	37	56	75
Hubley Army Motor Truck No. 807 with driver, 15" long	1000	1500	2000
Hubley Auto, 6½"	80	120	160
Hubley Auto, 9", 1922, Chevy?	400	600	800
Hubley Auto carrier, 10" long, with three cars and one pickup truck, circa 1939	550	825	1100
Hubley Auto Express, 9" long, cast iron	900	1350	1800
Hubley Avery tractor, 4¾" long, very early	120	180	240
Hubley auto circa 1950s, black plastic wheels, die cast	12	18	25
Hubley Bell Telephone Truck, 3¾" long	90	135	180
Hubley Bell Telephone, 5¼"	300	450	600
Hubley "Bell Telephone", 12" long, with tools	60	90	120
Hubley Bell Telephone truck, 12½" long, 1940s	175	263	350
Hubley Bell Telephone truck, 10" long, 1931, with derrick and windlass, auger, trailer with 10" pole, three digging tools, and two loose ladders	800	1200	1600
Hubley "Bell Telephone", 13" long, just ladders as equipment	250	375	500
Hubley Bell Telephone Truck, 9" long, implements	400	600	800
Hubley Bell Telephone, 24" long, post WWII	132	198	265
Hubley Black & White cab, 1920s	1200	2000	3000
Hubley "Borden's Milk Cream", deluxe version, 7½" long, rubber tires, clicker	1250	1875	2500
Hubley "Borden's Milk Cream", standard version	1000	1500	2000
Hubley Bulldozer, die-cast, front scoop, circa 1950, 10¼" long, rubber treads	50	75	105
Hubley bus, (futuristic type), 3½", circa 1935	25	37	50
Hubley bus, 5½", circa 1938, rubber wheels	90	135	180
Hubley bus, 8" long, 1930s	60	90	120
Hubley Bus, 9" long, diecast, circa 1950s	20	30	40
Hubley Cadillac, 7" die cast	16	24	32
Hubley 2278 car and 2279 house trailer, circa 1939	150	225	300
Hubley Caterpillar Tractor, 3¼" long, driver in cab	100	150	200
Hubley Caterpillar Tractor, 9" long	62	93	125
Hubley Cattle Truck, post war	45	68	90
Hubley Cement Mixer, 18" long	400	600	800
Hubley Champion Stake Truck, 8½" long, 1930s, white rubber tires	140	210	280

HUBLEY, Bell Telephone, 24" long, postwar. Courtesy Thomas G. Nefos, Federal Shipping Network.

HUBLEY, Caterpillar, 3¼" long. Courtesy Mapes Auctioneers & Appraisers.

HUBLEY, Dump Truck, Mack, 1930's, 6 tires, 10¾" long. Driver missing in photo. Courtesy James S. Maxwell/Virginia Caputo. Photo by Virginia Caputo.

HUBLEY, "5 Ton Truck". Courtesy Sotheby's New York.

	C6	C8	C10
Hubley Chemical Truck with ladders, 13" long	200	300	400
Hubley Chevrolet 1932 Coupe, kit	30	45	60
Hubley Chevrolet 1932 Phaeton Kit, 1960s	25	38	50
Hubley Chevrolet 1932 Roadster Kit, 1960s	25	38	50
Hubley Chrysler airflow, 4½" long, take-apart body	100	150	200
Hubley Chrysler Airflow, 6¾" long, take-apart body	350	525	750
Hubley Chrysler Airflow, 8" long, electrified, white rubber tires on wood hubs	600	900	1200
Hubley Chrysler Airflow racing car, circa 1938	100	150	200
Hubley Coal Truck, cast iron, with driver, 16¾"	1200	1800	2500
Hubley "Coast to Coast" bus, cast iron, 1927, 13" long	450	675	900
Hubley Corvette	200	300	400
Hubley Coupe, 1933 Ford	90	135	180
Hubley Coupe roadster, rumble seat, 11" long, rubber tires	125	187	250
Hubley Crash Car, three-wheel motorcycle, chrome wheels	100	150	200
Hubley Crash Car, circa 1937, 4¾" long, white rubber tires	115	172	230
Hubley Digger, Mack, General, 10" long	362	548	725
Hubley Duesenberg Town Car, 9" build-it model	37	56	75
Hubley Dump Truck, 5½"	50	75	100
Hubley Dump Truck, circa 1938, 7½" long	1000	1600	2400
Hubley Dump Truck, Mack, 1930s, 6 tires, 10¾" long	100	1800	2800
Hubley "Elgin, The" Street Sweeper, 8" long, cast iron, 1931	3500	5000	7500
Hubley Fire Engine Pumper, circa 1920, 12½" long, cast iron, black rubber tires, driver, boiler-tender	350	525	700
Hubley Fire Engine pumper, early, No. 504	350	525	700
Hubley Fire Engine No. 526, 10½" long, circa 1936	175	263	350
Hubley Fire Engine, die cast, white rubber tires with wooden rims, circa 1941	40	60	80
Hubley Fire Ladder Truck, 8½", early	250	375	500
Hubley Fire Ladder Truck, 19½" long	500	750	1000
Hubley Fire Truck with searchlight, white rubber tires with wooden rims	55	82	110
Hubley Fire Truck, 5"	60	90	120
Hubley "5 Ton Truck", 17" long, 8 wooden barrels, circa 1920	725	1088	1450
Hubley Ford Coupe, 1936	40	60	80
Hubley Ford Model A Coupe Kit, 1960s	27	41	55
Hubley Ford Model A Phaeton Kit, 1960s	32	48	64
Hubley Ford Model A Pickup Kit, 1960s	30	45	60
Hubley Ford Model A Station Wagon Kit, 1960s	30	45	60
Hubley Ford Model A Town Car Kit, 1960s	30	45	60
Hubley Ford Model A Victoria Kit, 1960s	25	38	50
Hubley Fordson Front-End Loader, cast iron, circa early 1930s	1000	1700	2500
Hubley Hook & Ladder No. 463	28	42	56
Hubley Hook & Ladder Truck, 19½" long, cast iron	200	300	400
Hubley Huber Road Roller, 8" long	312	468	625
Hubley Huber Road Roller, 13" long	2500	3850	5000
Hubley Huber Road Roller, 15" long	3000	4500	6000
Hubley "Jaeger" Cement Mixer	475	712	950
Hubley Jaguar Roadster, 9", 1950s	55	82	110
Hubley Kiddietoy No. 432 MGTD Roadster, 6" long	110	165	220
Hubley Kiddietoy No. 510 series Dump Truck	125	188	250
Hubley Kiddietoy No. 457 Racer, 6½" long, diecast, rubber tires	27	41	55
Hubley Kiddietoy, "Patrol" stake truck, circa 1937	27	41	55
Hubley Ladder Truck circa late 1930s, 5"	45	67	90
Hubley Ladder Truck, terraplane front, 1930s, 6" long	70	105	140
Hubley Ladder Truck, 10" long, 1930s	60	90	120
Hubley Ladder Truck, 13½" circa 1940	200	300	400
Hubley Life Saver Truck, circa 1930, hole in rear is large enough to hold pack of Life Savers	125	187	250
Hubley Life Saver Truck, small hole in rear, can't hold Life Savers	400	600	800
Hubley Limousine, 7" long, six-door, 1920s	160	240	320
Hubley Lincoln Zephyr, 7¼" long	200	300	400
Hubley Lincoln Zephyr and House Trailer, cast iron, 14" long overall	400	600	800

HUBLEY, Motorcycle, Harley-Davidson, with policeman, 1930's, approx. 6½" long, swivel head, wheels and color variation. Courtesy Wilkinson Collection, Detroit Antique Toy Museum.

HUBLEY, Motorcycle, Parcel Post delivery. Courtesy Sotheby's New York.

HUBLEY, Huber Road Roller, 8" long.. Courtesy Mapes Auctioneers & Appraisers.

HUBLEY, Motorcycle, "U.S. Air Mail". Courtesy Sotheby's New York.

	C6	C8	C10
Hubley Log Truck No. 469	70	105	140
Hubley Log Truck with five chained logs, black rubber tires, die-cast, approx. 19" long	70	105	140
Hubley Low Boy truck, trailer, tractor	225	338	450
Hubley Mack Dump Truck, 11½" long, with driver	900	1400	2200
Hubley Mack Truck Steam Shovel-Digger, circa 1920, nickel wheels and scoop, 7" long	450	675	920
Hubley "Merchants Delivery" 1920s, approx. 6" long	No Price Found		
Hubley MG, large	55	82	110
Hubley MG, small	20	30	40
Hubley "Milk Cream" truck, 1930s, cast iron, 3½" long, white rubber tires	200	300	400
Hubley Monarch tractor, 5½" long	600	900	1200
Hubley Motor Express tractor and trailer, black rubber tires, 500 series, approx. 19" long	132	198	265
Hubley 2287 "Motor Express" truck and trailer, 8" long	80	120	160
Hubley Motorcycle, Armored, with side car and removable riders, 9" long	1000	1500	2000
Hubley Motorcycle, 4" long, early, with side car, 2 civilian riders	75	112	150

	C6	C8	C10
Hubley Motorcycle, 6" has light in front and place for battery	100	150	200
Hubley Motorcycle and rider, 4"	125	188	250
Hubley Motorcycle, "Harley David-son", Civilian Rider	500	750	1000
Hubley Motorcycle, Harley-Davidson, with policeman, 1930s, 6½" long, swivel head, small wheels near feet	425	638	850
Hubley Motorcycle, Harley Davidson, with policeman, white rubber wheels, 6" long	110	165	220
Hubley Motorcycle, Harley Davidson, with side car and rider	820	1230	1640
Hubley Motorcycle Hill Climber, 1936, 6¾" long, No. 649	250	375	500
Hubley Motorcycle Hill Climber, approx. 9" long, No. 11756-X	No Price Found		
Hubley Motorcycle, Indian 9½" long, policeman rider, nickel-plated cylinder	925	1388	1850
Hubley Motorcycle, Kiddietoy, plastic, 5" long	15	22	30
Hubley Motorcycle policeman with side-car 4" long, 1920s	125	188	250
Hubley Motorcycle policeman with sidecar, 5" long	70	105	140

HUBLEY, Motorcycle with side car, battery-operated headlight, cop driver, passenger. Courtesy Sotheby's New York.

HUBLEY, Motorcycle, Harley Davidson with side car and rider. Courtesy Sotheby's New York.

HUBLEY, Motorcycle with side car. Courtesy Sotheby's New York..

HUBLEY, Motorcycle, 6", has light in front and place for battery. Courtesy Sotheby's New York.

Left to Right: HUBLEY, "Merchants Delivery", ARCADE, Ambulance, "City Ambulance", 6" long. Courtesy Chic Gast.

	C6	C8	C10
Hubley Motorcycle with detachable cop, 4¼" long, cast iron, "Made USA", circa mid 1930s	50	75	100
Hubley Motorcycle, policeman rider, 5", circa 1936	35	52	70
Hubley Motorcycle with policeman, 1920s, 5" long	70	105	140
Hubley Motorcycle w/Sidecar, battery-operated headlight, cop driver, passenger, 8" long	1200	1800	2500
Hubley Motorcycle with side car, 8½" long, No. 46-F, two demountable policemen, 1936	750	1125	1500
Hubley Motorcycle, two-cylinder Indian, with side car, no riders	600	900	1200
Hubley Motorcycle "Traffic Car", approx. 8½" long, four-cylinder Indian with stake sides on two-wheel cart	1000	1500	2000

	C6	C8	C10
Hubley Motorcycle, Parcel Post delivery, with two-wheel cart	1000	1500	2000
Hubley Motorcycle, four-cylinder P.D.Q. delivery	400	600	800
Hubley Motorcycle, three-wheel with stake sides, rider, chrome wheels	90	135	180
Hubley Motorcycle, "U.S. Air Mail", 9" long	600	900	1200
Hubley Motorized Steam Pumper, 4" long, circa 1930s	50	75	100
Hubley Nite Coach, 3½" long, metal wheels, went on "Nu-Car" carrier, 1930s	30	45	60
Hubley "Nucar Transport" with trailer 17" long, 4 cars	500	750	1000
Hubley Packard, 15 parts, 1929, 11" long	5000	7500	10,000
Hubley Packard, 1930 "Phaeton" Kit	37	52	75

	C6	C8	C10
Hubley Packard Roadster Kit	47	70	95
Hubley "Panama" Digger, approx. 3½" long (hard to find)	300	450	600
Hubley "Panama" digger, 9½" long	800	1200	1650
Hubley "Panama" digger, Mack, 13" long	1100	1650	2200
Hubley Parcel Post motorcycle and sidecar, Harley Davidson	4000	6000	8000
Hubley "Patrol," 15½" long, driver, policeman	1400	2100	2800
Hubley Pipe Truck No. 803, 9½" long, c. 1950s	35	52	70
Hubley Power Shovel, 14"	87	130	175
Hubley Pumper, circa late 1930s	100	150	200
Hubley Pumper, terraplane front, 1930s, 6¼" long	100	150	200
Hubley Racer, "1790", 5" long approx.	100	150	200
Hubley Racer, 5½" long, 1930s, 2 passengers	125	188	250
Hubley Racer, 6½" long, plastic	44	66	88
Hubley Racer, driver, 7" long	230	345	460
Hubley Racer, 2241, 7½" long, 1930s	45	68	90
Hubley Racer No. 5, early wheels	1250	1875	2500
Hubley Racer No. 5, painted and nickeled iron and aluminum, 9½" long, raise hood-see motor	1250	1875	2500

	C6	C8	C10
Hubley Racer 629, 1936 6¾" long	112	168	225
Hubley Racer "No. 1", 8" long	400	600	800
Hubley Racer, driver, rubber tires, 8" long	125	188	250
Hubley Racer, die-cast, black rubber tires, 4" long	25	38	50
Hubley Racer, animated exhaust stacks, 8" long, driver	500	750	1000
Hubley "Railway Express" Truck, 5" long, rubber tires	100	150	200
Hubley Road Grader, 12"	50	75	100
Hubley Road Roller, late 1920s, 8" long, driver	300	450	600
Hubley Road Scraper No. 481	45	67	90
Hubley Sedan, 1920, cast iron, 7" long	100	150	200
Hubley Sedan, 1928, cast iron, 7" long	125	187	250
Hubley Sedan, circa 1938, 2-door, 3½", looks like Ford, rubber wheels	60	90	120
Hubley Service Car, 4¼" long	60	90	120
Hubley Service Car, 5" cast iron, including wheels, 1930s	200	300	400
Hubley 726 Shovel Truck, 10" long, circa 1930			No Price Found

HUBLEY "Elgin, The" Street Sweeper, 8" long. Courtesy Chic Gast.

HUBLEY, Motorcycle "Traffic Car". Courtesy Continental Hobby House.

HUBLEY, Racer "1790". Photo by Bill Kaufman.

HUBLEY, Stake bed truck. 7" long. Courtesy Mapes Auctioneers & Appraisers.

HUBLEY, Nite Coach, 3½" long, metal wheels, went on "Nu-Car" carrier, 1930's. Courtesy Chic Gast.

HUBLEY, "Railway Express" truck, 5" long. Courtesy Mapes Auctioneers & Appraisers.

HUBLEY, "Panama" digger, 13" long. Courtesy Joe and Sharon Freed.

	C6	C8	C10
Hubley Sport Car No. 485 70	105	140
Hubley Stake Truck, circa late 1930s ...150	225	300
Hubley No. 614 Stake Truck, circa 1930s 75	112	150
Hubley Stake Bed Truck, cast iron, 3½ long 30	45	60
Hubley Stake bed truck, 7" long 200	300	400
Hubley Stake Truck with trailer - No. 927. Two pieces, 21" long 40	60	80
Hubley No. 452 stake-type truck, black rubber tires, circa post WWII 40	60	80
Hubley Station Wagon, circa 1940s, 1950s 75	112	150
Hubley Steam Roller, 5" 150	225	300
Hubley Steam Shovel, "General", 9" long, rubber tires on hubs 400	600	800
Hubley Steam Shovel, "General", 15" long 425	637	850
Hubley Studebaker Roadster, frame and body separate 300	450	600
Hubley Studebaker Touring car, cast iron 325	518	650
Hubley Telephone Truck, plastic 25	38	50
Hubley Touring Auto, 1915, 9½" long, cast iron, chauffeur and rider 750	1125	1500
Hubley Tow Truck, 8¾" long, cast iron, circa 1930s 125	190	250
Hubley T-Bird 60	90	120

	C6	C8	C10
Hubley Tractor No. 472 50	75	100
Hubley Tractor, Ford 6000 80	120	160
Hubley Tractor, steam boiler in front, 4¾" long, circa early 1920s 125	187	250
Hubley Tractor, 5", 1930s 90	135	180
Hubley Tractor Loader No. 501, 11" long, 1950s 87	131	175
Hubley Tractor Trailer and Road Scraper No. 506 100	150	200
Hubley Trailer Truck, circa 1936-38 ...100	150	200
Hubley Transitional Fire Patrol, 12" cast iron, driver, firemen, 1920 1000	1500	2000
"Hubley U.S.A." Airflow type, circa 1937, approx. 3½" long 20	30	40
Hubley Wrecker, chrome wheels, Service Car 45	68	90
Hubley Wrecker, 3½" 30	45	60
Hubley Wrecker, 4½", rubber wheels, 1930 70	105	140
Hubley Wrecker, 4¾" 70	105	140
Hubley Wrecker, 6", circa 1940, white wheels on large hubs 100	150	200
Hubley Wrecking Truck, 1930, cast iron, rubber tires, 7½" long 150	225	300
Hubley Yellow Cab, 8" 300	450	600
"Ice" Stake Truck, circa 1940, streamlined fenders, pressed steel ...60	90	120
Ice Cream Truck, cast iron, 8" long ...300	450	600

	C6	C8	C10
Ideal American la France Fire Truck 75	112	150
Ideal Atomic Cannon, 13" long............125	188	250
Ideal Barracuda coupe, 1964, plastic, 4"........................7	11	15
Ideal Cadillac, four door, 1948, plastic, 4" 20	30	35
Ideal Car Trailer, circa 1945, plastic, 3".........................20	30	35
Ideal Car Trailer, plastic, 4 cars, 27" long 35	52	70
Ideal Corvette 40	60	80
Ideal Mercedes Sedan, 9" long, plastic 30	40	52
Ideal Pickup Truck, American, 1948, 4" plastic 20	30	35
Ideal Pickup Truck, Ford, 1940, 4" plastic 20	30	35
Ideal Semi, 12" long.....................30	40	48
Ideal "Television Repair" truck 40	60	80
Ideal Tow Truck, 17" long, plastic and metal................100	150	200
Ideal Tractor, 1948, plastic, 4" long 15	20	25
International Diesel Crawler, Product Miniature, Inc., 11", plastic with black rubber treads, 1950s 300	450	600
Irwin Dream Car convertible, 16", metal................165	248	330
Irwin Ford Sunliner, 9" plastic friction .50	75	100
Irwin Ice Cream Truck, plastic..............50	75	100
Irwin Jaguar Roadster, 6" 35	52	70
Ives horseless carriage runabout, 6½" long, 6" high to the top of jockey cap on driver.....................2500	3750	5000
Ives steamer, cast iron, 19½" long, two drivers 500	750	1000
Jaeger Cement Mixer, cast iron..........475	712	950

JAEGER cement mixer. Courtesy Mapes Auctioneers & Appraisers.

JANE FRANCIS TOYS
(Information and listing from Dave Leopard.)
These toys seem to have been made in Pittsburgh, Pa. during the early post-WWII period. All of their vehicles were diecast.

	C6	C8	C10
JF01 Pickup truck, 6½" long.................20	25	30
JF02 Pickup truck, 5" long, NO. 347 15	20	25
JF03 Pickup truck, 5" long, No. 447 15	20	25
JF04 Tow truck, 5" long, No. 447 25	30	35
JF05 Gulf truck, tin cover, 5" long, No. 447..................25	30	35
JF06 Sedan, fastback, futuristic, 6½" long 20	25	30
JF07 Sedan, fastback, futuristic, 6½" long, with windup motor.................25	30	35
Jeep, glass candy container, 4" long 20	30	40
"Jeepster", rubber tires, 14¼" long 20	30	40
Jones Tank, throwing flame, flame touching hull 40	60	80
Jones Tank, throwing flame, flame not touching hull 45	67	90
Jones Tank, throwing flame, "No. 25" ..60	90	120
Jones Tank, "22" on side 50	75	100
Jones & Bixler, "Express J&B" truck, 15½" long.....................900	1350	1800

JONES & BIXLER, "Express J&B" truck. Courtesy Sotheby's New York.

THE JUDY COMPANY
History and listings by Dave Leopard
The Judy Company of Minneapolis, Minnesota made educational toys, including a farm set called "Happy's Farm Family" (patented in 1945), which included a solid rubber car, pickup truck, and tractor, along with human and animal figures.

	C6	C8	C10
JA01 Sedan, 2 dimensional, (part of set), solid rubber, 5¼" long.............15	20	25
JT01 Pickup Truck, 2 dimensional (part of set), solid rubber, 5¼" long.............15	20	25
JF01 Farm tractor, 2 dimensional (part of set), solid rubber, 3½" long.............15	20	25

KANSAS TOY & NOVELTY COMPANY

By Fred Maxwell, Slushmold Contributing Editor and Bob Condray
With the assistance of Lorene Sorell, L. D. Morgison
and the Clifton Historical Society

Arthur Haynes, an auto mechanic, started molding toys in his Clifton, Kansas shed for local stores in 1923. With clever hands and an artist's eye, he charmed his friends and local townspeople with his bright-colored toys. He made his patterns from advertising pictures, from local vehicles and probably from other makes of toys, such as Tootsietoy. He made his own production tools. His range was diverse, for he made miniatures of aircraft and autos then making international and national news, farm equipment and even a zeppelin; also a few animals, novelties and charms.

This was a town enterprise from the beginning. Jess Foster, the News editor, helped with alloy mixtures; Mr. Hadsell, the Union Pacific agent (see #38, an early promotional?), suggested they send samples to Woolworth's in New York. Clayton D. Young, a traveling salesman, saw the toys, joined the company and built a profitable business with the chain stores, including Kress, Kresge and Sears-Roebuck; and became a partner. At its peak of international sales in the late 1920s they employed as many as 65 in two shifts during the Xmas order season.

They were young people who had grown up together, a happy gang who joked and sang at their work. This informality was reflected in the local name, "the Hoopie Factory". Two or three of their early toys, #26 and #33, were stripdowns - hoopies - probably raced locally. Whether "Whoopee", tractor toy #48, was a local spelling of this or whether it celebrated a fat, cheering order, is not known. Certainly a lot of happy whoopee-e-e-s must have floated from hoopie-land.

Teamwork there must have been, for a molder, according to Ernest Istas, could produce 2000 toys a day. Helen Istas was the secretary; Bill Haynes was another molder, showing the family nature of the work force, with its clippers (trimmers), painters, clampers (axles) and boxers. "Butch" Morgison, one of our sources, was each of these during his long career with the company. Haynes believed that he invented hollow-casting of metal toys, so he must have started with solid toys. One day he dropped his full mold, spilling its hot metal. To his delight he had a perfect, hollow auto toy, with promise of savings of metal and shipping costs.

Those "numbers" embossed on the toys may enhance realism on aircraft, racers, taxis and trains. On classic autos they mar irritate adults although they couldn't have bothered the kids who eagerly collected them. The earliest Kansas toys were not numbered so it may have filled a need. It may have become a convenience between salesman and certain buyers when discussing orders without a catalog.

Although neither the first Kansas Toy nor the last have been firmly identified, we have made great progress. But now that those numbers are better understood, what other clues should dealers and collectors rely on? If it has metal wheels and a number under #75 it is most likely KT&N, although a few pieces made by later owners had metal wheels. Look for simulated wire wheels and spoke wheels; the reverse sides of these are disks; tractor wheels are open spoked. These simulated wheels are exclusive with KT&N, but regular disk wheels were standard throughout the industry. Many of these toys had stringpull loops or knobs in the handcrank position. Bottom pans are not found; they were introduced by later owners. "Made in USA" labels were a late 1930s regulation. KT&N often issued the same design in two or three scales (5c, 10c & 15c ?)

Generally the style of the prototype will aid in dating; they may commemorate an event such as world speed records (#46). Toy experts will recognize the herd instinct which prompted makers to issue popular toys simultaneously. The first pieces were said to be unpainted; if so, few have survived. The first finish used was Egyptian (a U.S. brand name) lacquer, a japanning which applied thinly gave the toys a glittery look. Toys with this finish have been found up to #66. Later they used enamel in all colors including gold. The bodies usually had single colors with "tires" simulated in black. All rules have exceptions; in this case the towed farm implements, #61 to #65 made out of several moving parts. My harrow is in red, green and blue; disks and wheel spokes are unpainted but the rims are orange. A whimsical touch for such a down-to-earth toy.

During its good years KT&N created more designs and produced more toys than any in the industry, save Barclay. Mr. Young left the company in the late 1920s and retired in Kansas City. Whether it was the loss of his assets or the onset of the Depression, the company was in trouble by 1930. George Hoeffer (sp?) reorganized the company and moved the factory down the road, but this effort lasted only a few months. A happy era had come to an end for Clifton.

Fred Maxwell, collector and occasional author, has been collecting antique aircraft and vehicle toys for 25 years. This retirement hobby was started from scratch, for his lead soldiers were missing when he returned home from college. He founded Capital Miniature Auto Collectors Club 20 years ago to promote interest in the Central Atlantic states. He felt challenged by the lack of public knowledge and the ambiguity of that orphan category: Pot Metal or Slushmold Toys.

Transitional Era - Following those Numbers

Where were those Hobo molds? During this period the molds and some of the employees too, were wandering but we don't know under whose roof they were producing. Hardly surprising, for during the 1930s the U.S. was full of wanderers, hoping to find a roof and a job. We called some of them "hobos".

This story is included here because the number series started by KTN will always be associated with its creator. It is not surprising that the series continued unbroken because the migrating assets included Ernest and Helen Istas and others with all their know-how. Today, the true story is elusive or contradictory and may continue so. To the average collector the real makers may not matter, for style, condition and supply may be more important in setting market value. For the serious collector I have included details and clues to maker and vintage lest much of it be lost to history.

Some believe that after Hoeffer failed in 1931 there was a second reorganization in Clifton. If this version sticks then the numbers from #75 to at least #85 were Clifton toys. Other insiders say that the assets moved to Ralston, Ne., but the Ralston historian, herself a Ralstoy ex-employee, says that the toy factory started in 1939. Next, it is said, the assets moved to Springfield, Mo. (a vague story with no evidence yet), and from there to Manhattan, Ks. and the

Best Toy Co. John Best, Sr. had lived in Clifton earlier and probably had been following those Hobo molds. The transitional era numbers may have gone as high as #102, for we have been unable to determine whether Best Toy created new patterns or just reproduced from old molds, or both.

Starting with #75 the new issues used wooden wheels, or hubs, and white rubber tires, a style popularized by Tootsietoy in 1932. This ended the era of metal wheels, although a few pieces, particularly farm toys, continued with metal wheels until 1940. Parallel with these wood wheels was another style, a white hard-rubber disk wheel, often found with black painted "tires". These have been found on numbers from #59 to #97 on both new toys and repros. They may have been used on early Best toy production. Also during this area we find two-colored toy bodies, such as gilt grilles and trunks, or different-colored tops. Since these are rare, they may have been sales samples.

The transitional era included some of Best Toy. For this history see the Best section earlier in this book.

The following list has been carefully prepared but it is probably not yet complete. All cast numbers and labels are shown in quotes, i.e. "48".

For collectors who find variations useful, the following abbreviations are used:

HRDW	white hard rubber disk wheels		**OW**	open windows
HG	horizontal grille pattern		**RM**	rearmount spare
HL	horizontal hood louvers		**SW**	sidemount spare
HO	hood ornament, cap or motometer		**SP**	stringpull knob or loop, in front
LI	landau irons, on convertibles		**T**	trunk, external
			UV	unnumbered version
MDW	metal disk wheels		**VG**	vertical grille
MDSW	metal solid spoke wheels		**VL**	vertical hood louvers
MSW	metal open spoke wheels		**WS or W/S** - windshield	
MWW	metal simul. "wire" wheels		**WV**	windshield visor
			WHRT	wood hubs, rubber tires

	C6	C8	C10
KTV1 Midget racer, no #, 3". No driver, torpedo tail, HO, SP, VL, HG, ⅝" MDW w/ simulated lug nuts, lacquer finish. Some say this was their first toy; some say first had non-moveable wheels or was a large racer	20	30	40

	C6	C8	C10
KTV2 Midget racer, no #, 3". Same as above, with driver, plain MDW, lacquer. Easily confused with another maker's copy. See #31 and #67	14	21	28
KTV3 Large Indy racer, no #, 6". Driver, boattail, HO, MDW, lacquer		No Price Found	

KANSAS TOY Racers, Left to Right, Top Row: KTV1, KTV2; Middle Row: KTV14, KTV24, KTV52; Bottom Row: KTV35, KTV25. Photo courtesy Fred Maxwell.

KANSAS TOY Autos, Left to Right, Top Row: KTV4, KTV5; Middle Row: KTV7, KTV7; Bottom Row: KTV26, KTV26, KTV43. Photo courtesy Fred Maxwell.

	C6	C8	C10
KTV4 Coupe, no #, 3⅛". Crude, slant roof, shallow rear body, no fenders, hood similar to first racer above, lacquer. First "hoopie" or stripdown made?			No Price Found
KTV5 Sedan, no #, 3⅜". Crude limousine or stretch taxi, 6 windows, louvered rear quarters, HO, VL,HG, T, SP, large MDW, lacquer			No Price Found
KTV6 Coupe, no #, 2⅞". Convertible, LI, VL, HG, WV, SP, MDSW, lacquer	30	45	60
KTV7 Coupe, "8", 3⅛". Convertible, LI, VL, HG, WV, SP, RM, MWW, no HO, no headlamps, enamel finish. Also UVs with "Chrysler", headlamps and HO; or with MDSW	20	30	40
KTV8 Coupe, "8", 3⅛". Trunk convertible, T, HO, VG, SM, MDW			No Price Found

Note: #8 is the lowest numbered vehicle found. Its realistic, high quality signals the ending of a novice toymaker's experimental phase. The five coupes above have the same 1924 Chrysler hood and nice details like landau irons and kickplates, but not all had headlamps. The basic body expanded into this series of coupes, #14 roadsters, and sedans (all (?) unnumbered), lacquered or enameled, with 3 types of wheels: MDW, MDSW, and MWW. They were unnamed or named: Chrysler, Cadillac, Chevrolet. Any Fords out there? The large coupe, KTV9, is a scale-up of #8. Only 3 of these large pieces are known: the racer KTV3, John Deere tractor KTV19, and a mail-plane.

KTV9 Large coupe, no #, 5".
    Chrysler convertible, MWW

	C6	C8	C10
and 2 golf club doors. Larger version of #8			No Price Found
KTV10 Sedan, no #, 2⅞". "Chevrolet", 6 windows, LI, WV, VL, SP, RM, MWW	16	24	32
KTV11 Sedan, no #, 3¼". "Chevrolet", as above, HG, HO, MSW			No Price Found
KTV12 Overland bus, "9", 3½". "Fageol", solid windows			No Price Found
KTV13 Overland bus, no #, 3½". "Fageol", 9 male passengers, driver and "baggage" cast on windows, HG, RM, MDW. Also an UV w/various family passengers on windows, also w/comic characters (Kansas Toy?)	26	39	52
KTV14 Indy racer, "10", 3⅛ ". Driver, boattail, exhaust right, VL,HG, HO, SP, MSW or MWW. Also UV	6	9	12
KTV15 Roadster, "14", 3⅛". Open "Chrysler", solid W/S, plain grille, HO, VL, SP, RM, MDSW	18	27	36
KTV16 Roadster, no #, 3⅛". Same as above, HG, 2 golfclub doors			No Price Found
KTV17 Farm tractor, "17", 2⅞". "Fordson", driver, HG, crank, no tow hook, large 1¼" and ¾" MDW with 4 holes in disks. Also found with same size 6 spoke wheels. See #57			No Price Found

KANSAS TOY Bus, KTV12. Photo courtesy Fred Maxwell.

KANSAS TOY Farm Vehicles; Left to Right, Top Row: KTV17, KTV17; Middle Row: KTV23, KTV21; Bottom Row: KTV23, KTV17. Photo courtesy Fred Maxwell.

KANSAS TOY Commercial Vehicles; Left to Right, Top Row: KTV20, KTV33; Middle Row: KTV34, KTV36; Bottom Row: KTV38, KTV41. Photo courtesy Fred Maxwell.

	C6	C8	C10
KTV18 Farm tractor, no #, 2⅝". Same basic body as above, "Fordson" on radiator and crankcase, VG and towhook, with smaller, plain MDW	No Price Found		
KTV19 Large farm tractor, no #, 4⅞". Deere Model D. A finely crafted replica in 2 colors, steering shaft, fly wheel, belt drive wheel, rear fenders, large 2" and 1" 12-spoke wheels	No Price Found		
KTV20 Truck, "20", 3⅛″. Ford?, solid w/s, 2 OW, 3 tanks, VL, HG, rear faucet, MWW. Versions w/and w/o driver. Also an UV	16	24	32
KTV21 Steam tractor, "25", 3". "Case", crew of 2, tow loop, large front, small rear MSW and flywheel. See #71. Also an UV with no name	20	30	40
KTV22 Racer, "26", 4". "Bearcat" stripdown, long hood, motometer, 3 intakes, driver, open frame, left exhaust. See #33	No Price Found		
KTV23 Separator-thresher, "27", 3". Tow hook, auto-type MSW (not tractor rims), lacquer or enamel. Also UV. See #72	15	23	30
KTV24 Midget racer, "31", 2⅛". Driver, torpedo tail, VL, HG, HO, MWW, lacquer. Also UV. See #67	12	15	18
KTV25 Racer, "33", 3". "Bearcat" stripdown, smaller version of #26 above	No Price Found		

	C6	C8	C10
KTV26 Coupe, "35", 2¼". Convertible,LI, VL, HG, HO, RM, MWW. Also an UV	No Price Found		
KTV27 Locomotive-tender, "36", 4⅜". "KT & N RR" 6 MSW, 4 MDW, 0-6-4	7	10	14
KTV28 "Pullman" car, "37", 3½". "KT & N RR", 4 MDW	No Price Found		
KTV29 Box car, "38", 3¼". "KT & N RR", Union Pacific			

KANSAS TOY Vehicles; Left to Right, Top Row: KTV16, KTV15; Second Row: KTV14, KTV25; Third Row: KTV33, KTV35, Bottom Row: KTV36, KTV58. Photo courtesy Fred Maxwell.

shield (an early promotional?),
4 MDW ....No Price Found

KTV30 Tank car, "39", 3⅛".
"KT & N RR", ladder, filler, MDW.....No Price Found

KTV31 Caboose, "40", 2¾".
"KT & N RR", stack. brakeman's
cab, MDS ....No Price Found

KTV32 Stock car, "41", "KT & N RR",
MDW ....No Price Found

KTV33 Dump truck, "42", 3½". Ford ?,
driver, no cab, diamond emblem
on hinged body, VL, HG, SP,
MWW 30   45   60

KTV34 Steam road roller, "43", 3¼".
Driver, SP, boiler, wooden rollers ...10   15   20

KTV35 Racer. "46", 2⅞". 1929 Golden
Arrow record car, driver, large tail
fin, MWW 12   18   24

KTV36 Warehouse tractor, "48", 3".
"Caterpillar", "Whoopee", driver, VL,
HG, HO, SP, tow loop, MWW.
Also an UV 18   27   36

KTV37 Tour bus, "49", 2⅜". 1928
Pickwick COE "Nite Coach", HG,
SP, MDW duals. Also an UV.
See #59.............................No Price Found

KTV38 Pickup truck, "51", 2¾". Ford
w/cab, VL, HG, tow loop, MDW,
lacquer. Also an UV ....No Price Found

KTV39 Roadster, "54", 2⅜".
Buick, driver w/cap, rumble seat,
T, plain hood and grille, no head-
lamps, SM, MWW. Also an UV.
See #77.............................10   15   20

KTV40 Roadster, "54", 2¼". Same
as above, no trunk ....No Price Found

KTV41 Truck-semi, "55", 4". Ford,
stake trailer, VL, HG, MDW ....No Price Found

KTV42 Farm tractor, "57", 1¾". Ford-
son, driver, SP, MDW rear, MSW
front. Smaller version of #17.
Also an UV ....No Price Found

KTV43 Sedanette, "58", 2¼". Austin
Bantam, unique fighting cock on
door panels, 4 OW, HL, VG, RM,
MWW ....No Price Found

KTV44 Tour bus, "59", 3⅜". 1928
Pickwick COE double-deck night-
coach, screen grille. Larger version
of #49 above. Also an UV with
dual wheels ....No Price Found

KTV45 Sedan, "60", 3½". 1930 Reo
Royale ? or Chrysler 2 dr. brougham,
plain hood, vee-VG, square rear deck,
MDW, MDWSM. Also an UV with
MWW and MWWSM...................24   36   48

*Note: The following is a unique towed farm set with
several hinged or moving parts, each a different color and
large 1¼" spoked tractor wheels.*

KTV46 Planter, "KTN No. 61", 4".
V-blade plough with seed hopper.
4 piece incl. wheels and 3 colors ......No Price Found

KTV47 Disc harrow, "62", 4". 8
discs on same 1⅝" wide frame
as #61. 13 pieces, incl. discs and
wheels, 4 colors....................No Price Found

KTV48 Plough, "63", 4". Single
blade on same shaft as #61 ....No Price Found

KTV49 Dirt tumble, "64", 4".
Adjustable dumping scoop, 1½"
wide on same frame as #62. 6
pieces, 4 colors.....................20   30   40

*KANSAS TOY AND NOVELTY,
KTV34. Photo by R.F. Sapita.*

*KANSAS TOY, Left to Right: KTV22, mid
1930's, KTV25, 1920's. Photo by Perry
Eichor.*

KANSAS TOY, Left to Right: KTV17, KTV47, KTV46. Photo by Chic Gast.

KANSAS TOY Towed Implements; Left to Right, Top Row: KTV46, KTV49; Bottom Row: KTV47, KTV50. Photo Courtesy Fred Maxwell.

KANSAS TOY , KTTV64. Photo by Craig A. Clark.

	C6	C8	C10
KTV50 Dirt scraper, "65", 3⅝". Blade, 1⅞," adjustable, on same frame as #62	No Price Found		
KTV51 Coupe, "66", 3½". Streamlined 3-wheeler, 6 OW, MWW, lacquer	No Price Found		
KTV52 Midget racer, "67" 1½". Driver, torpedo-tail, VL, HG, HO, MDW. Smaller version of #31. Also an UV	No Price Found		
KTV53 Fire engine, "70", 2¼". Seagrave ? pumper, driver, VL, HG, MDW	No Price Found		
KTV54 Steam tractor, "71", 2½". Crew of 2, tow-loop. Small version of #25	10	15	20
KTV55 Separator-thresher, "72", 2+". Tow hook for #71	No Price Found		
KTV56 Army tank, "74", 2¼". "US Army" WWI type, high turret, large front, small rear wheels. OD color	No Price Found		
KTV57 Racer, no #, 1". Miniature solid-cast version of #10, moving wheels, charm loop on nose	No Price Found		

KANSAS TOY TRANSITIONAL VEHICLES

	C6	C8	C10
KTTV58 Tractor, "48", 3". "Caterpillar", "Whoopee" same as KTV36 except ¾" grooved metal wheels with rubber track	No Price Found		

	C6	C8	C10
KTTV59 Tour bus, no #, 3⅜". Pickwick COE, a more streamlined version of #59 above, with 8 open windows	No Price Found		
KTTV60 ? Fire engine, no #, 3¼". Pumper, 2 firemen w/old style helmets, hose reel, HG, MDW. Kansas?	12	18	24
KTTV61 Army tank, "74", 2¼". "US Army", 2 gun turret, OD color. A different tank than #74 above	No Price Found		
KTTV62 Coupe, "75", 4¼". Graham like (Tootsietoy) VG, SM, T, WHRT, 1933 issue	No Price Found		
KTTV63 Racer, "76", 4¼". Auburn speedster, low driver, headrest fairing, SP, HG, slanted louvers, large oval fin, kickplates, HWRW or WHRT	20	30	40
KTTV64 Roadster, "77", 4". Open sport Duesenberg, W/S down, driver, VG, slanted lourvers, SM, T, WHRT	16	24	32
KTTV65 Concrete mixer, "78", 3¾". Truck with water tank & mixing barrel, VG, HL, WHRT. Found both with and w/o a bottom pan. Sometimes called a fuel tanker	No Price Found		
KTTV66 Sedan, "79", 4¼". 2 door, Graham like, 4 OW, VG, HL, RM, WHRT w/ 5 removable tires. Found both with and w/o a bottom pan	14	21	28
KTTV67 Coupe, "80", 3½". Convertible, top up, LI, 2 OW, VG, T, MWW w/ MWW SM	20	30	40
KTTV68 Coupe, "80", 3½". Same as above except HRDW w/MDW SM. (a different casting re sidemounts)	No Price Found		
KTTV69 Racer, "81", 4⅜". Miller FWD, driver, 8 cyl., right exhaust, HG, WHRT. 1933 issue	No Price Found		

KANSAS TOY Vehicles with Wood Hubs; Left to Right, Top Row: KTTV64, KTTV65; Bottom Row: KTTV66, KT&N?#85. Photo courtesy Fred Maxwell.

KANSAS TOY Autos with Hard Rubber Wheels; Left to Right, Top Row: KTTV59, KTV45; Middle Row: KTTV63; Bottom Row: KTTV67, KTTV72. Photo courtesy Fred Maxwell.

	C6	C8	C10
KTTV70 Sedan, "82", 4". Pierce Arrow Silver Arrow fastback, 6 OW, HRDW. Also an UV ....No Price Found			
KTTV71 Indy racer, "83", 4⅝". FWD type, driver, VG, HL, right exhaust, WHRT ....No Price Found			
KTTV72 Sedan, "84", 3⅝". Desoto? airflow, 4 OW, HO, HG, HL, HRDW. 1934 issue	20	30	40

Note: Although not yet certain when the hobo molds changed hands, the higher numbers are described and illustrated under Best Toy and Ralstoy.

KELMET, No.501, White Dump Truck, "Big Boy". Courtesy Joe and Sharon Freed.

	C6	C8	C10
Kelmet Aerial Ladder Truck.................	750	1125	1500
Kelmet No. 501, White Dump Truck, 25" long..........................	400	700	1000
Kelmet White Fire Truck (ladder).......	1400	2100	2800

KENTON

KENTON "Army Motor Truck 807", incorrect driver in photo. Courtesy Sotheby's New York.

KENTON Ambulance, 7" long, cast iron, driver incorrect. Courtesy Sotheby's New York.

	C6	C8	C10
Kenton Ambulance, 7" long, cast iron .	750	1300	1700
Kenton "Army Motortruck 807", 14" long, cast iron..................	600	950	1300
Kenton Auto, 6" long, cast iron...........	1200	1800	2400
Kenton Boat-tail cut-down speedster, 1910, 7" long.................	120	180	240
Kenton Buckeye Ditcher	700	1050	1400

	C6	C8	C10
Kenton Bus, Double-Decker, 6" long, 1920s............................	400	600	800
Kenton Bus, Double Decker, 1920, 7¼" long	1100	1650	2200
Kenton Bus, double-decker, 9½" long	1000	1500	2000
Kenton Bus, 8" long, cast iron	340	510	680
Kenton Bus, 1920s, 10¾" long	375	525	750

KENTON Buckeye Ditcher, 12½" long. Courtesy Sotheby's New York.

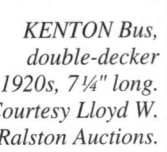

KENTON Bus, double-decker 1920s, 7¼" long. Courtesy Lloyd W. Ralston Auctions.

KENTON Bus, double-decker, 9½" long. Courtesy Phillips New York.

KENTON Touring Car, open, driver and passenger, 8½" long (air-cooled Franklin). Courtesy Sotheby's New York.

	C6	C8	C10
Kenton Cement Mixer, rubber wheels, marked "Jaeger", 7" long, cast iron...200	300	400
Kenton Cattle Truck, 8" long, cast iron, circa 1938 150	225	300
Kenton Cement Mixer.........................400	600	800
Kenton Circus Truck, 10" long 1300	2000	2700
Kenton "Coal" dump truck, 8½" long..140	210	280
Kenton "Coast-to-Coast" bus 350	525	700
Kenton "Contractors" Dump Wagon, cast iron..................................250	375	500
Kenton Coupe, 5" long.....................230	345	460
Kenton Dump Truck, 6" long...............337	505	675
Kenton Emergency Truck, circa 1930s, black rubber tires, takes batteries for headlights and spotlight.180	270	360
Kenton Fire Apparatus Truck...............400	600	800
Kenton Fire Pump truck, early with driver, approx. 10" long 325	488	650
Kenton Fire Pumper, 14½" long, 1920s ..800	1200	1600
Kenton Fire Pumper, 18" long, circa 1920, has gong 350	525	700
Kenton Fire Truck, 15"long with pumper 400	600	800
Kenton Franklin, air-cooled, 8½" long ...1300	1950	2600
Kenton "Hose" truck, approx. 6¾" long, open cab, circa 1920s, green, driver, rider, hose, ladders.............350	525	700
Kenton Ice Truck, tongs and glass ice, 7½' 300	450	600

	C6	C8	C10
Kenton Jaeger cement mixer, 6½" long, iron wheels............................300	450	600
Kenton Jaeger cement mixer,8" long ..1000	1500	2000
Kenton Jaeger "Mixer", cast iron cement truck, 9" long...................500	750	1000
Kenton Ladder Truck, approx. 7½" long, cast iron.................................200	300	400
Kenton Ladder Truck, pressed steel ladders, 16" long 300	450	600
Kenton Ladder Truck, 17¼" long 300	450	600
Kenton Overland Circus cage truck with driver, 7½" long.....................300	450	600
Kenton Overland Circus with lion, 9" long 900	1350	1800

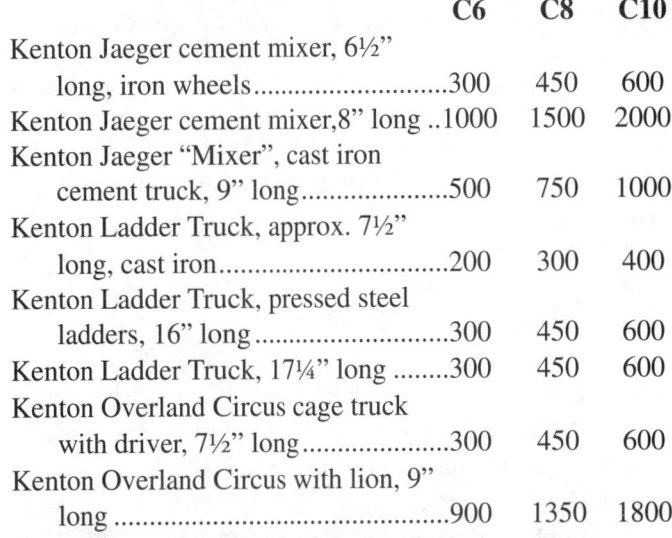

KENTON Fire Pumper, 18" long, has gong. Courtesy Mapes Auctioneers & Appraisers.

KENTON Ladder Truck, pressed steel ladders, 16" long. Courtesy Lloyd W. Ralston Auctions..

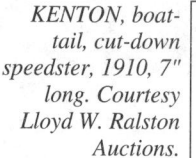

KENTON, boat-tail, cut-down speedster, 1910, 7" long. Courtesy Lloyd W. Ralston Auctions.

KENTON Sedan, 7" long, late 30s. Courtesy Lloyd W. Ralston Auctioneers.

KENTON Tow Auto, 1920s, 9½" long. Courtesy Lloyd W. Ralston Auctions.

KENTON "Jaeger" Cement Mixer Truck, 8" long. Courtesy HAKE'S Americana & Collectibles.

KENTON Steam Shovel. Courtesy Mapes Auctioneers & Appraisers.

	C6	C8	C10
Kenton Patrol Wagon, marked "Patrol" on side, circa 1920s-1930s	325	500	650
Kenton Phaeton touring car, 12"	350	562	700
Kenton "Pickwick Nite Coach", 14" long, cast iron	1900	2750	3800
Kenton Pontiac, approx. 4" long	150	225	300
Kenton Racer, 7½" long, early	240	360	480
Kenton Racer, 9" long, early, cast iron	700	1050	1400
Kenton Road Grader, cast iron, 7½" long, rubber tires, nickel-plated moveable blade	200	300	400
Kenton Runabout Auto, 5" long, 1900	350	525	700
Kenton Runabout Auto, cast iron, 7" long, resembles a 1910 Franklin, has driver	700	1050	1400

	C6	C8	C10
Kenton Sedan, 4" long	110	165	225
Kenton Sedan, 7" long, late 1930s, rubber tires, take apart body	1400	2100	2800
Kenton "Speed" stake truck, circa 1927, 5½" long	50	75	100
Kenton Sprinkler Truck, early, 8"	300	450	600
Kenton Stake Truck, 6" long	337	405	675
Kenton Steam Roller, "Gallon Master", 6½" long	150	225	300
Kenton Steam Shovel, Marion, 7¼"long	600	900	1200
Kenton Tank, cast iron, 2½" long	80	120	160
Kenton Touring Car, open, driver and passenger, 8½" long	650	975	1300
Kenton Tow Auto, 1920s, 9½" long	1600	2400	3200
Kenton Yellow Cab, 1950s, 6⅜" long	300	450	600

KEYSTONE

Keystone, of Boston, Massachusetts, had an odd assortment of products; movie projectors, steel trucks, wooden boats and pressed wood forts and garages. Founded in June, 1922 or 1923 by Chester Rimmer and Arthur Jackson, it was first located in a small shop in Malden, Mass. under the name Jacrim, using parts of partners' last names. Rimmer retired in 1958 and sold out to various companies. Address in Boston was 288 A Street. All numbers and descriptions in bold type are Keystone's own.

KEYSTONE "Moving Van Long Distance Hauling". Courtesy Mapes Auctioneers & Appraisers.

KEYSTONE No.?, "Dugan Brothers" "ridem" truck. Courtesy Joe and Sharon Freed.

KEYSTONE, Packard Pump Truck 26" long. Courtesy PB Eighty-Four, New York.

KEYSTONE No.43, American Railway Express.

	C6	C8	C10
Keystone No. ? "Dugan Brothers" "ridem" truck	250	375	525
Keystone **No. 41 Dump Truck**, 26½" long	500	750	1000
Keystone **No. 43 American Railway Express**, 26" long	750	1125	1500
Keystone **No. 44 Truck Loader**, 17¾" high	200	300	400
Keystone **No. 45 U.S. Mail Truck**, 26" long	600	1100	1575
Keystone **No. 46 Steam Shovel**, 26" long when arm is extended	250	375	500
Keystone **No. 47 Steam Shovel**, 34½" long when arm is extended	175	545	500
Keystone **No. 48 U.S. Army Truck**, 26" long	400	700	1000
Keystone **No. 49 Fire Truck**, 27½" long..	600	1000	1480
Keystone **No. 51 Police Patrol**, 27½" long	1400	2100	2800
Keystone **No. 52 Fire Truck**, 27½" long	700	1050	1400
Keystone **No. 53 Sprinkler Truck**, tank 12" long	800	1200	1600
Keystone **No. 54 Koaster Truck**, with skids, hoist cable, windlass, 26" long when skids retracted	800	1350	1825
Keystone **No. 55 Koaster Truck**, without skids and windlass	1000	1500	2000

	C6	C8	C10
Keystone **No. 56 Water Pump Tower**, 29" long	700	1050	1450
Keystone **No. 57 Chemical Pump Engine**, 27½" long	800	1150	1575
Keystone **No. 58 Moving Van**, 26" long	600	1200	1750
Keystone No. 60 Riding Steam roller	250	375	500
Keystone **No. 62 Hydraulic Dump Truck**, 26" long	300	650	975
Keystone **No. 73 Ambulance**, military, 27" long	1250	1875	2500
Keystone **No. 78 Wrecking Car**, 27" long	475	713	950
Keystone **79 Aerial Ladder**, 30½" long	900	1350	1800
Keystone No. ?? Greyhound Bus windup	800	1200	1600
Keystone No. ?? Ladder Truck, 24" long	225	338	450
Keystone No. ?? Plastic Sedan, 4½" long, circa 1950, hood lifts, gas tank fills & drains	14	18	22
Keystone No. ?? Steam Roller, red and black, air pressure whistle, brass bell, 20" long	400	600	800
Keystone No.?? "World's Greatest Circus" Truck, 26" long, circa 1930s	1500	2250	3000

KEYSTONE, No.51, Police Patrol. Photo by Calvin L. Chaussee.

KEYSTONE, No.58, Moving Van. Courtesy Joe and Sharon Freed.

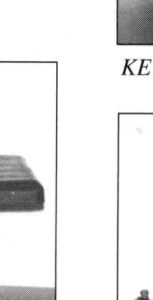

KEYSTONE, No.55. Courtesy Joe and Sharon Freed.

KEYSTONE, No.49 Fire Truck. Photo by Calvin L. Chaussee.

KILGORE

Kilgore, of Westerville, Ohio, appears to have begun toymaking in the 1920s. Its toys were cast iron and low-priced, with cap pistols its most popular line. But it also did well with a number of attractive trucks, fire engines and cars, as well as scattered aircraft and ships. Some subsidiary manufacturing was done in Lancaster, Pennsylvania and Canada. In 1937 Kilgore began making plastic cars, trucks, planes and buses, and later added plastic cap pistols, placing it among the first (if not the first) companies to produce plastic toys. Kilgore remained in business until at least 1978. The first owner, a Mr. Kilgore, sold out in 1921.

KILGORE, "Fire Chief" sedan, plastic. Photo by Dave Leopard.

KILGORE, Pontiac, 10" long. Courtesy Sotheby's New York.

	C6	C8	C10
Kilgore Arctic Ice Cream Truck, 8" long.	700	1050	1400
Kilgore "Arctic Ice Cream" truck, 9" long	500	750	1000
Kilgore Auto, "LF 1300A", with driver	180	270	360
Kilgore Bus, plastic, advertised in 1937, 4"	10	12	15
Kilgore Convertible with Rumble Seat, 7" long, early 1930s, with driver	160	240	320

	C6	C8	C10
Kilgore Coupe, streamlined, plastic, 4", advertised in 1939	15	20	25
Kilgore Dump Truck, cast iron, circa 1934, 5¾" long	160	240	320
Kilgore Dump Truck, 7" long, 1930s	180	270	360
Kilgore Dump Truck, 8½" long, cast iron, circa 1934	1200	1800	2500
Kilgore "Express" Truck, plastic, 4", advertised in 1937	15	20	25

KILGORE, Coupe, streamlined, plastic. Photo by Dave Leopard.

KILGORE, Arctic Ice Cream Truck.

	C6	C8	C10
Kilgore "Fire Chief" sedan, plastic, 4" advertised in 1937	15	20	25
Kilgore Livestock Truck, 7" long, 1930s	700	1050	1400
Kilgore Livestock Truck, 9" long	500	750	1000
Kilgore Motorcycle, 4" long, single rider	80	120	160
Kilgore Motorcycle, 4¼," long double rider	100	150	200
Kilgore Packard Luxury Sedan, 8¼", take-apart body	800	1200	1600
Kilgore Pierce-Arrow Roadster, 6⅛" take-apart body	250	375	500

	C6	C8	C10
Kilgore Police Car, plastic, 4" long, 1937	15	20	25
Kilgore Pontiac, 10" long, cast iron, 1930	2500	4000	5500
Kilgore Roadster, 6" long, driver, rumble seat	230	345	460
Kilgore Sedan, 3¼" long	70	105	140
Kilgore Stutz Roadster, 13 parts	500	750	1000
Kilgore "Taxi", plastic, 4", advertised in 1937	15	20	25
Kilgore "Toy Town Delivery" truck, 6⅛" long	200	300	400

KINGSBURY

Kingsbury had its origins in 1886 in Keene, New Hampshire. Its owner was Harry T. Kingsbury, who bought the Wilkins Toy Company, apparently not changing that firm's name till after World War One. Steel and spring motors characterize Kingsbury's toys, with cars, fire engines, farm equipment and racing cars its primary output. Kingsbury is still in business, but seems to have given up toy production in 1942.

KINGSBURY Golden Arrow Racer, 20" long. Courtesy Wilkinson Collection, Detroit Antique Toy Museum.

KINGSBURY Phaeton Auto, 1900, 9½" long. Courtesy Lloyd W. Ralston Auctions.

	C6	C8	C10
Kingsbury Aerial Ladder Truck, pressed steel windup circa 1941, 24" long, ladder rises automatically to height of 38 inches when the truck runs into any obstruction, fireman on ladder climbs up and down by turning crank at base of ladder, early version new in 1905	175	263	350

	C6	C8	C10
Kingsbury Airflow, circa 1934, pressed steel, rubber tires, 14" long	400	600	800
Kingsbury Airflow, clockwork, 14" long	300	450	650
Kingsbury Auto, very early, 9¾" long, steel windup	350	525	700
Kingsbury Bluebird Racer	800	1300	2000

	C6	C8	C10
Kingsbury Brougham Sedan, 13" long, pressed steel windup	450	675	900
Kingsbury Bus, 18" long, pressed steel	400	600	800
Kingsbury Cannon Truck, very early, 11" long, clockwork	135	205	270
Kingsbury Cannon Truck circa 1939, 15" windup	600	950	1300
Kingsbury Caterpillar, 8½" long, wind-up	150	225	300
Kingsbury Cattle Truck, 19" long, 1930s	90	135	180
Kingsbury DeSoto, 14½" long, pressed steel windup, circa 1938	75	112	150
Kingsbury Dump Truck, tin, driver, 10" long	225	337	450
Kingsbury Dump Truck, early 30s, 16" long, clockwork	350	525	700
Kingsbury "Fire Chief" coupe, 1930s, 14" long	550	825	1100
Kingsbury Fire Pumper, 11" long, very early, clockwork iron and steel	450	675	900
Kingsbury Fire Pumper, 1920s, 23" long	1000	1500	2100
Kingsbury Fire Truck, 18" long	150	225	300
Kingsbury Ford Sedan & House Trailer, 1937, 23" long, pressed steel	400	600	800
Kingsbury Golden Arrow Racer, 20" long, pressed steel windup	800	1250	1700
Kingsbury Greyhound Bus, windup	250	375	500
Kingsbury Ladder Truck, steel, driver, 22"	150	225	300
Kingsbury ladder wagon fire truck, tin, rubber tires, 23½" long	75	112	150
Kingsbury Phaeton Auto, 1900, rubber slip tires, 9½" long	750	1125	1500
Kingsbury Rack Truck, 16" long, pressed steel windup	350	525	700
Kingsbury Roadster, 13" long, electric headlights, spring motor, luggage rack	1100	1650	2200
Kingsbury Sedan, two-door, with trailer, 22½" long, 1930s, clockwork	175	262	350

	C6	C8	C10
Kingsbury Sunbeam Racer, sheetmetal, red with rubber tires on steel wheels, clockwork motor, 19" long	650	975	1300
Kingsbury Tractor, mechanical, 8" with driver	250	375	500
Kingsbury Tractor and cart, tin, with iron driver, white rubber wheels, circa 1930s	110	165	220
Kingsbury Transit Truck, 1930s, 19" long	140	210	290
Kingsbury Truck with C Cap, 10" long, tin	175	262	350
Kingsbury Wind-Up Car, curved dash, driver, 9" long	225	337	450
Kingsbury Wrecker, 13" long, pressed steel, windup	250	375	500
Kingston Producers, Kokomo, Indiana, Electricar, 15" long, the Red Arrow, 1930s	100	150	200

KNAPP, "Electric Automobile", circa 1903. Courtesy Sotheby's New York.

	C6	C8	C10
Knapp "Electric Automobile" circa 1903, pressed steel, 11" long, battery-activated	1500	2400	4000
Ladder Truck, driver front and rear, cast iron, 5" long	45	67.50	90
Ladder Truck approx. 14" long, battery operated lights, wind-up	150	225	300
Laketoy "John Wanamaker" delivery van, 10½" long, wooden	180	270	360

LANSING SLIK-TOYS

(Listing and history by Dave Leopard)

Lansing Slik-Toys were made in Lansing, Iowa and sometimes bear the name "Kipp", in addition to the "Lansing" and "Slik-Toy" trademarks. Most Slik-Toys are made of aluminum in a single casting but some were made of hard plastic. The company made many farm and construction toys but the list below is confined to cars and trucks. All Slik-Toys I have seen bear a 4 digit number beginning with "9". If a toy bears such a number, even if it has no other markings, it is almost surely a Slik-Toy.

LAPIN Sedan, 6 side windows. Photo by Dave Leopard.

LAPIN Coupe, plastic 1939 Hudson? Photo by Dave Leopard.

	C6	C8	C10
Stakebody truck, 11" long, No. 9500 25		30	40
Sedan, fastback, 7" long, No. 9600 20		25	30
Sedan, fastback, 7" long, No. 9600,			
taxi version.....................................25		30	35
Pickup truck, 7" long, No. 9601 20		25	30
Open Stake Truck, 7" long, No. 9602 ...20		25	30
Tank truck, 7" long, No. 9603 20		25	30
Sedan, 4 door, 6" long, No. 9604 15		20	25
Pickup truck, 6" long, No. 9605.............15		20	25
Firetruck, 6" long, No. 9606..................15		20	25
Tank truck, 6" long, No. 9607 15		20	25
Tractor/trailer rig (milk tanker), 8"			
long, No. 9610 20		25	30
Tractor/trailer rig (grain trailer), 8"			
long, No. 9611.............................20		25	30
Tractor/trailer rig (flatbed trailer), 8"			
long, No. 9613 20		25	30

	C6	C8	C10
Tractor/trailer rig (log trailer), 8"			
long, No. unknown..........................20		25	30
Wrecker, 5" long, No. 9617...................15		20	25
Firetruck, 3½" long, No. 9700 15		20	25
Roadster, 3½" long, No. 9701 15		20	25
Pickup truck, 4" long, plastic, No. 9703..15		20	25
End Slik-Toy			
Lapin Cadillac, 1948, 4 doors, 6" long....5		7.50	10
Lapin Coupe, plastic, 1939 Hudson?.....10		12	15
Lapin Sedan, six side windows, plastic,			
1939 Hudson ?................................10		12	15
Lapin Stake Truck, Chevrolet, plastic,			
1947, 4"...5		7.5	10
Lincoln Toys (Windsor, Ontario,			
Canada) Dump Truck, 7" long........25		38	50
Lincoln Toys "Sand Truck", dump,			
14" long...50		75	100

LINCOLN WHITE METAL WORKS
By Fred Maxwell, Slushmold Contributing Editor and Perry Eichor

This Lincoln, Nebraska firm has long been a mysterious pre-war maker of slushmold "orphan toys", so-called when we cannot identify a collectible toy. One might think that with other major lines fairly well documented we could identify Lincoln toys by a process of elimination, but there were too many small makers and homecasters to rely on this. This obscurity is surprising, for Clayton E. Stevenson, the founder, made interesting designs with high quality casting in high volume for a long period - 9 years during the 1930s. What we know came from a Xmas story in the Nebraska State Journal of December 20, 1931 and a good article in the Antique Toy World of January 1984.

Stevenson was born in 1896 and raised in Axtell, Kansas. He was an auto mechanic who was associated with Western Diecasting Co. and Kansas Toy & Novelty Co. for several years in the 1920s. He may also have been familiar with C.A.W. Novelty Co. for his style and quality is closer to Charles Wood toys than Kansas toys. He, and his wife, Esther, moved to Lincoln in 1931 and started making toys in his home at 1250 Dakota St. For a new business, he had a rapid rise. In his first season he made "800,000 toys

in three months". He was manager, purchaser, worker and salesman.

As his business grew - "30,000 toys a day and 27 to 30 laborers" at one time - he moved to a larger facility at 2204 Y street. In 1935 he was listed at 3433 J street. The toys were sold to Woolworth, Kress, Kresge and Schwartz Paper Co. stores, as well as all over the country, especially California and New York, and even abroad.

The factory was sold in 1940, after 9 years of production, due to shortages of lead and rubber and the rising costs of labor - all due to expansion of war production. (We were not told who bought what, although a few clues point to nearby Ralstoy. Although 1940 is the date given by a family member, I did not find the business listed in Lincoln directories after 1937.)

A variety of toys were made, "tiny airplanes, midget racers, larger speed cars - about 6 inches long - brilliant sedans, small coupes, tri-motor plane models and miniature sawmills. They range in size from 3 to 7 inches in length." "Mr. Stevenson, who does the modeling, uses pictures of planes and cars shown in magazines. For his midget racer he used a picture of a Miller Special. His sedan is a replica of the front-drive Cord. His coupe is a Nash model. His trimotor plane is taken from a photo of a Ford product." This in 1931; other patterns were issued later. Early toys used metal wheels and tin propellers and had neat patterned bottom-pans we use as clues. Later toys had rubber wheels. The list below is incomplete; we were dependent on the few toys we have found. Can anyone help with more data?

LINCOLN WHITE METAL, LWV1, mid 1930s - Other ?. Photo by Perry Eichor.

LINCOLN WHITE METAL, Top: LWV2, Bottom: LWV3. Photo by Perry Eichor.

LINCOLN WHITE METAL, LWV8. Photo by Perry Eichor.

LINCOLN WHITE METAL, Top: LWV10, Bottom: LWV11. Photo by Perry Eichor.

	C6	C8	C10

LWV1 Indy Racer, 5⅛". Miller FWD Special, driver, rounded grille, horizontal cooling fins alongside hood, torpedo tail ....No Price Found

LWV2 Speed Car, 6". Bluebird record car, driver, V-8 engine with intake ports, triangular fin with wing design embossed............................No Price Found

LWV3 Speed Car, 4". Bluebird, smaller version of above................................No Price Found

LWV4 ? Speed car, 4⅜". A V-12 version of Bluebird with triangular fin. Lincoln?....................................No Price Found

LWV5 ? Sedan, 3½". Pierce-Arrow Silver Arrow, vertical vee-grille, headlamps and front fenders faired, 6 open windows (OW), divided windshield (W?S), plain pan. Lincoln? ....No Price Found

LWV6 Sedan, 3¾". 2 door Chrysler or DeSoto airflow, hood ornament (HO), divided open W/S, horizontal louvers (HL), plain pan.....................No Price Found

	C6	C8	C10

LWV7 ? Sedan, 3⅞". 2 door Pontiac, HO, grid pattern grille, HL, 4 OW, trunk....................No Price Found

LWV8 "Wrecker", 3½". High style with chopped top, Graham-like grille, 2 OW, fenders faired bumper to bumper, solid crane with grid pattern and hook, patterned pan "Made in USA"................................No Price Found

LWV9 fire engine, 3¾". Pumper with fireman on rear step, Graham-like grille, fenders faired bumper to bumper, patterned pan "Made in USA"...................................No Price Found

LWV10 Tanker truck, 3¾". COE, 2 OW, 6 tanks, 8 compartments, patterned pan "Made in USA".........................No Price Found

LWV11 Railcar, 4½". Streamlined "UNION PACIFIC" and shield symbol, 2 OW in cab, 18 OW in passenger section, hidden rubber wheels, patterned pan "Made in USA"................................No Price Found

LINDSTROM

The Lindstrom Tool & Toy Company made windups of light pressed steel as well as tin. It was located in Bridgeport, Ct., and began making toy cars about 1913. It seems to have ceased production sometime in the 1940s.

	C6	C8	C10
Lindstrom Lumber Truck no. 160, steerable front wheels, tin, with driver, 10" long	125	187	250
Lindstrom Steam Roller No. 181, mechanical, 12" long	50	75	100
Lionel Electric Racing Automobile set	1500	2250	3000
Log Truck (Beck), steers via horn on top of cab, late 1940s, large	60	90	120
Lumar: See Marx			
Lupor Ambulance	50	75	100
Lupor Fire Chief car	55	82	110
Lupor Police Car, 1949 Ford	50	75	100

M & L TOY CO. INC

M&L was incorporated October 21, 1947. It was located on Paterson Plank Road in Union City, New Jersey and got its name from the Father & son who owned it, Morris and Louis (last name unknown). The company may have begun in 1946, and lasted till at least 1948. It made vehicles, trains, "jeweled swords", and plastic horns. Most or all of its vehicles seem to have been sold unpainted and with plastic wheels. The alloy used in the vehicles was more than 99% zinc, with a smidgen of aluminum added. Most or all of their toys were copies. There were about thirty employees.

	C6	C8	C10
M&L (1) Racer, 2¾" long	10	15	20
M&L (2) Cabin Racer	12	18	25
Mack Dump Truck, cast iron, 12" long	120	180	240
Mack Dump truck, cast iron, 1930s	75	112	150
"Mack" Ladder Truck, 18" long, cast iron	300	450	600
Mack Stake Truck, cast iron, 7" long	70	105	140

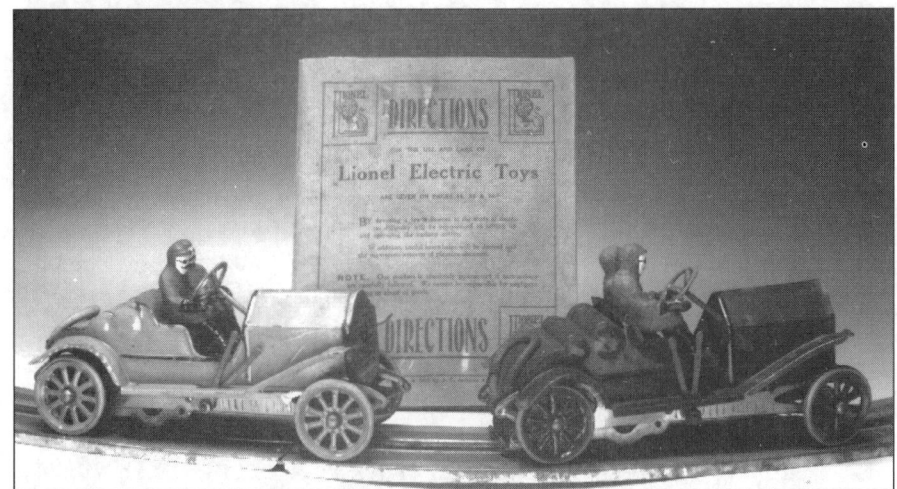

LIONEL Electric Racing Automobile set. Courtesy Sotheby's New York.

M&L (1) Racer. Photo by Craig A. Clark.

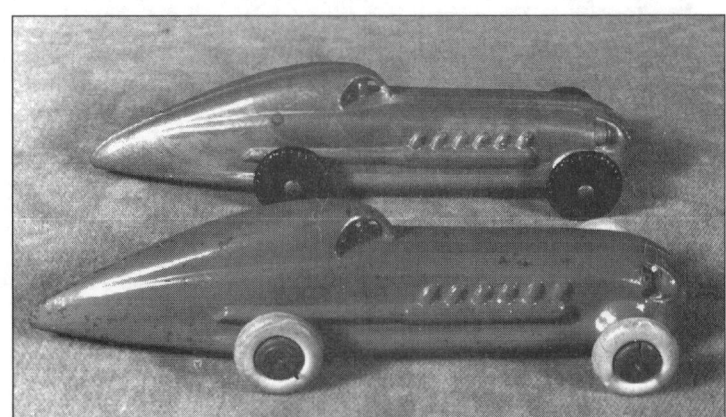

M&L (2), Top: Cabin Racer, cast headlamps; Bottom: Barclay Prototype, rhinestone headlamps missing. Photo by Perry Eichor.

MACK Stake Truck, cast iron, 7" long. Courtesy Mapes Auctioneers & Appraisers.

MACK Dump Truck, Cast iron, 1930s. Courtesy Mapes Auctioneers & Appraisers.

MANOIL, Top Left to Right: 713, 716, P-7 and Bottom Left to Right: 714, P-10, P-11. P-9. Courtesy Marjorie and Peter Ruben.

MANOIL

List compiled by Terry Sells, Numbers and words in bold are Manoil's
own description. 701-706 began production in 1934.

	C6	C8	C10
Manoil **700 Sedan**, futuristic	45	68	90
Manoil **701 Sedan**, futuristic	45	68	90
Manoil **702 Coupe**, futuristic	45	68	90
Manoil **703 Wrecker**, futuristic	45	68	90
Manoil **704 Roadster**, futuristic, Pat. No. 95791	45	68	90
Manoil **705 Sedan**, futuristic, Pat. No. 95792	45	68	90
Manoil **706 Rocket**, futuristic bus-like vehicle, Pat. No. 95793	60	90	120
Manoil **70 Soup Kitchen**, large number	9	13	18
Manoil **70A Soup Kitchen**, small number	9	13	19
Manoil **71 Shell Carrier with Soldier On Shell Box**, has loop	11	16	22
Manoil **71A** Same as above, no loop	10	15	20
Manoil **72 Water Wagon**, large number	10	15	20
Manoil **72A** Same as above, small number	9	13	18
Manoil **72B** No number	9	13	18

	C6	C8	C10
Manoil **73 Tractor**, loop front	11	16	22
Manoil **73A Tractor**, plain front	11	16	22
Manoil **74 Armored Car with Anti-Tank Gun**	17	26	35
Manoil **75 Armored Car with Anti-Aircraft Gun**	27	41	55
Manoil 75A Armored Car with Siren, siren cast separately	25	38	50
Manoil **75A Armored Car with Siren**, siren cast with vehicle	32	48	65
Manoil **95 Tank**	8	12	17
Manoil **96 Large Shell on Truck**	9	13	18
Manoil **97 Pontoon on Wheels**	18	27	36
Manoil **98 Torpedo on Wheels**	10	15	20
Manoil **103 Gasoline Truck**	10	15	20
Manoil **104 Chemical Truck**	12	18	24
Manoil **105** Five Barrel Gun on Wheels	11	16	22
Manoil **(MC5) Tank**, composition	12	18	25

Manoil Post War Vehicles

	C6	C8	C10
Manoil **707 Sedan**	25	38	50
Manoil **708 Roadster**, horizontal radiator	17	26	35
Manoil **708A Roadster**, vertical radiator	25	38	50

MANOIL 69 Cannon, metal wheels, wood wheels, wood wheels variant. MANOIL Vehicles, Left to Right; Top: 70, 71; Middle: 71 with variant on wheel support, 72, 73 with front tow loop, 74; Bottom: 75, 75A with siren cast separately, 75A siren cast integrally. Photo by Ed Poole.

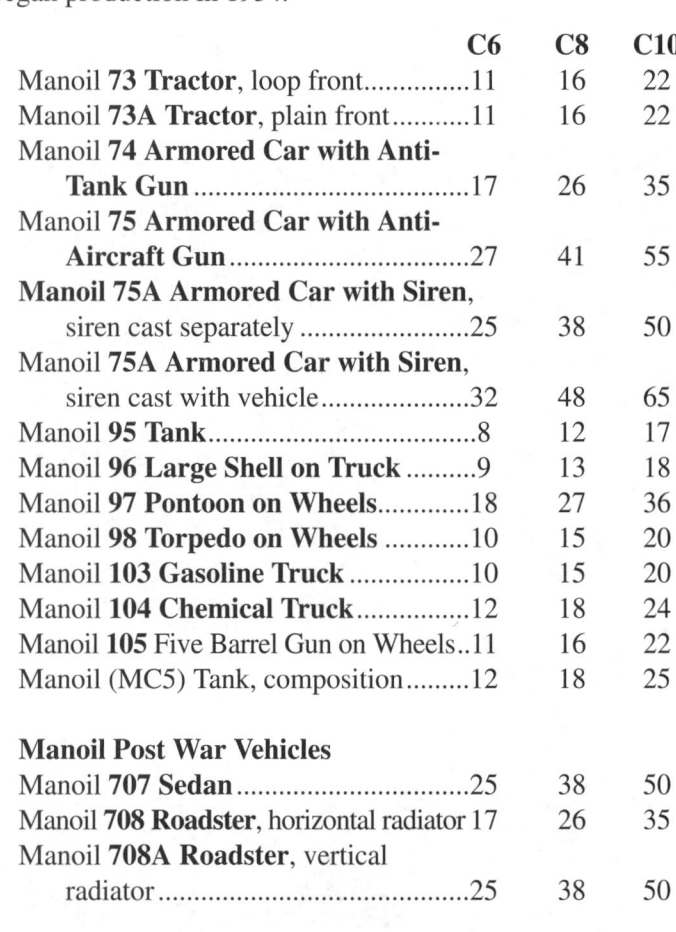

MANOIL Vehicles and "Metal Action Cannon" No.200, Left to Right; Top: 95, 96, 97, 98; Bottom: 103, 104, 105, 200. Photo by Ed Poole.

	C6	C8	C10
Manoil **709 Fire Engine**	15	22	30
Manoil **710 Oil Tanker**	12	18	25
Manoil **711 Aerial Ladder**	No Price Found		
Manoil **712 Pumper**	No Price Found		
Manoil **713 Bus**	12	18	24
Manoil **714 Towing Truck**	10	15	20
Manoil **715 Commercial Truck**	10	15	20
Manoil **716 Sedan**	10	15	20
Manoil **717 Hard Top Convertible**	12	18	24
Manoil **718 Convertible**	10	15	20
Manoil **719 Sport Car**	10	15	20

	C6	C8	C10
Manoil **720 Ranch Wagon**	10	15	20
Manoil Plastic Vehicles			
Manoil **P-7 Roadster**	2.50	3.75	5.00
Manoil **P-8 Sedan**	2.50	3.75	5.00
Manoil **P-9 Pick-Up**	2.50	3.75	5.00
Manoil **P-10 Towing Truck**	2.50	3.75	5.00
Manoil **P-11 Road Scraper**	2.50	3.75	5.00
Manoil **P-12 Tractor**	2.50	3.75	5.00
Manoil **P-13 Dump Cart**	2.50	3.75	5.00

End Manoil

MANOIL, Left to Right; Top: 705, 708 early, 708 later; Bottom: 707, 710, 709. Courtesy Marjorie and Peter Ruben. Photo by Norbert Schachter.

MANOIL, Top: 712 Pumper; Bottom: 711 Aerial Ladder. Courtesy Marjorie and Peter Ruben. Photo by Norbert Schachter.

MARX

	C6	C8	C10
Marx Air Force truck, "Air Defense Group", ridem toy, 32" long, No. 3290	125	188	250
Marx Air Force Truck, canvas top, 20" long	105	158	210
Marx Ambulance No. 8500, approx. 14" long, 1930s	240	360	480
Marx Ambulance No. 8600, approx. 14" long, 1930s	240	360	480
Marx "American Railroad Express Agency Inc.", early 1930s, open cab, 7"	120	180	240
Marx American Truck Co. No. 65 moving truck, friction	65	98	130
Marx Army Corps of Engineers, 20", canvas top	125	188	250
Marx Army Jeep with Searchlight Trailer, steel	120	180	240
Marx Army Staff Car, 9", plastic friction	25	38	50
Marx Auto Transport, 1950s with Tin Litho cars (2 of them), 34" long	125	188	250
Marx "Auto Transwalk" No. T-50447B, 1930s truck with three cars	175	263	350

	C6	C8	C10
Marx Big Boss Car Carrier, 42" long	80	120	160
Marx "Big Shot" Cannon Truck, plastic, 22" long, fires cap-loaded missile	52	76	105
Marx "Chief-Fire Dept. No. 1", "Friction Drive", circa 1948	45	68	90
Marx "City Sanitation Dept. Help Keep Your City Clean", circa 1940, 12¾" long	37	56	75
Marx Coal Truck, electric motor & lights, early	190	275	380
Marx "Cloverdale Farms" milk truck	200	300	400
Marx Coca Cola Truck, Linemar, 3" long, tin friction	50	75	100
Marx Coca Cola truck, 20" long, sprite decal, stamped steel, late 1940s to early 1950s	120	180	240
Marx Convertible Roadster, 1930s, nickel plated tin, 11" long	200	300	400
Marx Cord Convertible, 11" long	250	375	400
Marx Corvette Coupe, plastic friction, 8" long	40	60	80
Marx "Deluxe Delivery" truck	32	48	65

MARX "City Sanitation Dept. Help Keep Your City Clean". Photo by Calvin L. Chaussee.

MARX Tricky Taxi. Photo by William G. Floyd.

MARX Coca-Cola Truck, 20" long. Courtesy Richard MacNary.

MARX "Deluxe Delivery" Truck. Courtesy Thomas G. Nefos, Federal Shipping Network.

	C6	C8	C10
Marx Dump Truck, 17" long, No. 695B	65	98	130
Marx Dump Truck, two-color, No. T751, circa 1930s	62	93	125
Marx No. 1084 Dump Truck	30	45	60
Marx Easter Stake Truck, 10½" long, 1938	190	275	380
Marx "Electrically Lighted Truck and Trailer Set" No. T-5715, circa 1930s, 15" long	150	225	300
Marx Falcoln with plastic bubble top, black rubber tires	165	248	330
Marx "Fanny Farmer" candy truck, plastic	35	52	70
Marx Fire Truck, friction, 25" long	225	338	450
Marx Fix-All Convertible and Wrecker (set)	100	150	200
Marx Fix-It Jaguar, 12" long, plastic	100	150	200
Marx G-man Pursuit car, No. 7000, 15" long, 1930s	200	300	400
Marx Gang Buster Car No. 7200, approx. 14" long, 1930s	550	825	1100
Marx "Gravel" truck, 13" long	90	135	180
Marx "Gravel" truck, 9" long	50	75	100
Marx Grocery Truck, 1950s, 14½" long	62	93	125
Marx Guided Missile Truck No. 4488	60	90	120
Marx "Heavy Gauge Tractor" No. 926	100	150	200

	C6	C8	C10
Marx "High-Boy Climbing Tractor" No. 950, 10½" long	60	90	120
Marx Hi-way Express Truck	150	225	300
Marx Hydraulic Dump	80	120	160
Marx Jeep, 11" long	55	82	110
Marx Lazy-Dazy Dairy Farm Pick-Up Truck and Trailer, 22" long	40	60	80
Marx Livestock Truck	100	150	200
Marx Lonesome Pine trailer and convertible sedan, 1930s, 19" long	200	300	400
Marx "Lumar Contractors" 962 dump truck	110	165	220
Marx "Lumar Contractors" Steam Shovel	34	51	68
Marx Lumar Contractors Crane	120	180	240
Marx Lumar Power Grader	55	82	110
Marx Lumar Scoop-A-Dump	40	60	80
Marx M.D. War Dept. Ambulance, 1930s	180	270	360
Marx No. 1016 Machinery Moving Truck	100	150	200
Marx "Mammoth Truck Train, No. T-50-12345, circa 1930s, truck with five trailers	175	262	350
Marx Marcrest Dairy stake truck	67	100	135
Marx "Motor Market"	75	112	150
Marx Mystery Taxi, circa 1930s, press down to operate	80	120	165

MARX Power Grader. Courtesy Continental Hobby House.

	C6	C8	C10
Marx Navy Jeep No. 1078	65	97	130
Marx Navy Jeep with Searchlight Trailer	100	150	200
Marx Nutty Mad cars, friction, 4" long, circa 1965, each	70	105	140
Marx Panel Wagon	40	60	80
Marx Pepsi-Cola Truck, 11" long, 1950s	30	45	60
Marx "Pet Shop Delivery", 1950s, 10" long	50	75	100
Marx Pickup Truck	50	75	100
Marx "Power Grader" No. 1759, black or white wheels, 17½" long	55	82	110
Marx Pure Milk Dairy Truck with glass bottles, pressed steel, tin wheels, circa 1940	100	150	200
Marx REA Express Truck No. 1021	125	187	250
Marx Road Grader, heavy-duty	25	38	50
Marx Rocker Dump No. 1752, 17½" long	60	90	120
Marx "Sand & Gravel" dump truck, 10" long, 1940s	50	75	100
Marx Searchlight Truck	70	105	140
Marx "Sinclair" fuel truck, steel	165	248	330
Marx Side Dump Truck, four-color No. T-475, circa 1940	60	90	120
Marx Side Dump Truck and Trailer, No. T-4045, circa 1930s	100	150	200
Marx "Siren Fire Chief", circa 1930, "F.D. 1st Batt.", 15" long	150	225	300

	C6	C8	C10
Marx Siren Police Car No. 8300, 1930s, approx. 14" long	250	375	500
Marx "Sparkling Hot Rod Racer", 1950s plastic wind-up, 8" long	37	52	75
Marx Sports Coupe, 1930s, 15"	125	187	250
Marx Stake-type truck, 3-color, No. E-271, circa 1941	50	75	100
Marx No. 1008 Stake Truck	50	75	100
Marx "Tricky Taxi", friction, 4½" long	125	188	250
Marx "U.S. Mail" truck, 14" long	200	300	400
Marx "USA 41573147" Army Truck, circa 1952, 13¾" long	62	93	125
Marx Willys Jeep, steel, circa 1938, 12" long, hood opens, windshield folds down	20	30	40
Marx Willys Jeep and trailer, circa 1940s	125	188	250
Marx Willys Jeepster, plastic windup	75	112	150
Marx Wrecker Truck No. T-16, circa 1930s	150	225	300
Marx Wrecker Truck, 1920s, 10" long	100	150	200
Mattel Hot Wheels Chapparal 26 No. 6256	15	22	30
Mattel Hot Wheels Daredevil Loop pak, 1968	8	12	15
Mattel Hot Wheels Ford Coupe No. 6253	15	22	30
Mattel Hot Wheels Jetthreat 11 No. 8235	4	6	9
Mattel Hot Wheels Poison Pinto No. 9240	4	6	9
Mattel Hotwheels Silhouette No. 6209	15	22	30
Mattel Hotwheels Trestle Aces Pak, 1968	7	11	15
McCormick-Deering Spreader, "Made in USA", steel, 10½" long, black rubber, 1950s	60	90	120

METAL CAST PRODUCTS COMPANY

By Fred Maxwell, Slushmold Contributing Editor

Metal Cast Products, an outgrowth in 1929 of a venerable toy soldier company, S. Sachs, made hand-operated slushcasting molds for small businesses and hobbyists, what some have called the homecasting industry. Since identical molds were sold to many franchisees we cannot identify the actual makers unless they engraved their names on their products. One who did was Fred Green Toys, whose name is found prominently on their toys.

Metal Cast offered full support services to its franchisees, including marketing, printing, publishing and parts.

A variety of wheels may be found on its vehicles: metal disk wheels, metal spoke wheels, wood wheels w/rubber tires, and white or black rubber wheels.

We see many homecast lead soldiers and novelties, but the production of toy vehicles has not left much of a mark. Perhaps it was the Great Depression, perhaps it was the lack of identity; demand today seems weak. However, collectors of the unusual should find many collectibles; most of those I have seen were well designed and professionally finished.

	C6	C8	C10
Metal Cast Van Truck, #01-02, 6". COE cab, semi-trailer moving van. Trailer also found in a "FRED GREEN" version ....No Price Found			
Metal Cast Tank Truck, #01-03, 6". Same COE cab, semi-fuel tanker. My version is 5¾", "FRED GREEN TOYS" "Made in USA:"	4	6	8
Metal Cast Open Rack Truck, #01-04, 6". COE cab, stake semi-trailer	8	12	16
Metal Cast War Tank, #08, 4". Early heavy Sherman tank	33	49	66
Metal Cast Cadillac Sedan, #40, 5¼". 2 door ....No Price Found			
Metal Cast Packard Convertible, #41, 5¼". 2 door, top down	10	15	20

	C6	C8	C10
Metal Cast Dump Truck, #42, 5¼". COE chassis, dump body mechanism..No Price Found			
Metal Cast Streamline Sedan, #60, 4". De Soto ? Airflow, 8 open windows, spoke wheels, rubber tires	10	15	20
Metal Cast Fire Engine, #61, 4½". Hook and ladder truck, crew of 2	6	10	14
Metal Cast Racer, #62, 4½". Bluebird type record car, driver ....No Price Found			
Metal Cast Coupe, #63. Convertible, 2 open windows, sidemounts, trunk.....No Price Found			
Metal Cast Truck, #64, 4¼", Dodge? stake-body, 1920s 2 OW ....No Price Found			
Metal Cast Fire Engine, #65, 4". Steam pumper w/watercannon, driver ....No Price Found			
Metal Cast Fire Engine, no #, 3⅞". Similar to #65 without water-cannon ..	6	10	14

METAL CAST PRODUCTS, Top: Greyhound bus, MCP #62; Middle: Limousine, MCP #40, MCP 60; Bottom: MCP #64. Photo by Perry Eichor.

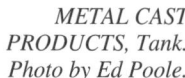

METAL CAST PRODUCTS, Top: MCP #01-02; Middle: MCP #01-03; Bottom: MCP #40. Photo by Perry Eichor.

METAL CAST PRODUCTS, Tank. Photo by Ed Poole.

METAL MASTERS

(listing by Dave Leopard)

	C6	C8	C10
MM01 Roadster, c. 1938, 7" long	20	25	30
MM02 Bus, c. 1938, 7¼" long	20	25	30
MM03 Pickup truck, c. 1938, 7" long ...	20	25	30
MM04 Firetruck version of pickup, c. 1938, 7" long..............................	25	30	35
MM05 Tow Truck version of pickup, c. 1938, 7" long..............................	25	30	35
MM06 Jeep, c. 1947, 5½" long	10	15	20
MM07 Station Wagon, c. 1940, 8½" long	35	40	45
MM08 Station Wagon, c. 1940, 8½" long, windup motor......................	40	45	50

	C6	C8	C10
MM09 Station Wagon, c. 1940, 8½" long, ambulance version	40	45	50
MM10 Tow Truck, c. 1940, 10" long, "ABC Towing Service"	35	40	45
MM11 Tow Truck, c. 1940, 10" long, windup motor................................	40	45	50
MM12 Firetruck, c. 1940, 10" long, removable ladders	40	45	50
MM13 Firetruck, c. 1940, 10" long, ladders, windup motors..................	45	50	55

METALCRAFT

Metalcraft, of St. Louis, Missouri, began producing its pressed steel trucks in 1928. About a million were sold, most as "advertising toys". In 1937, defeated by the Depression, Metalcraft shuttered.

	C6	C8	C10
Metalcraft "Bordens Milk" truck 225		338	450
Metalcraft "Bunte Candies" 12" truck 175		262	350
Metalcraft Coca Cola Truck, 11" long, pressed steel, rubber tires, circa late 20s-early 30s, 10 bottles in rack, "Every Bottle Sterilized" 500		750	1100
Metalcraft Coca Cola Truck, 10 bottles, 10½" long, 1930s 450		675	950
Metalcraft Coca Cola Truck, 12" long, 10 bottles, late 1930s, long nose, stamped metal 450		675	900
Metalcraft Coca Cola Truck, circa 1928, with bottles in racks 500		750	1000
Metalcraft CW Coffee Dump Truck, 10¾" long 350		525	700
Metalcraft CW Coffee wrecker 300		450	600
Metalcraft Delivery Truck Van, 11" long, steel 200		300	400
Metalcraft "Goodrich Silvertone Tires" wrecker, with 3 spare tires 200		300	400
Metalcraft "Heinz" truck, circa 1932 "Baked Beans, Bottled Vinegar", "Rice Flakes", 12" long 300		450	600
Metalcraft "Kroger Food Express", 11" long.....................................160		240	320
Metalcraft "Krug Bakery" truck...........450		675	935
Metalcraft "Machinery Hauling"..............No Price Found			
Metalcraft "Meadow Gold Butter" truck 13" long, battery lights 300		450	600
Metalcraft "Shell Motor Oil" truck 500		750	1000
Metalcraft "St. Louis" truck, 11" long, circa 1930......................................250		375	500
Metalcraft Steam Shovel 55		82	110
Metalcraft "Sunshine Biscuits" truck ...350		525	700
Metalcraft "Towing & Repairs" 135		205	275
Metalcraft "Werks Tag Soap" truck 270		405	540
Metalcraft "White King Delivery" truck 12" long 250		375	500

METALCRAFT Coca-Cola Truck, 11" long. Courtesy Wilkinson Collection, Detroit Antique Toy Museum.

MINIATURE VEHICLE CASTINGS INC.

Though these appear to be toys from the 1930s, they were first produced in 1985. The models were carved and cast by owner Robert E. Wagner. Made of diecast lead from silicone molds, they were sold for $21 apiece, and at least 3500 have been sold. Some are beginning to appear at toy shops and on dealer lists. 21 different types were made, among them a 1937 Ford Sedan, a 1937 Studebaker coupe and a 1936 Plymouth Sedan. The average length is about 4½", and the N.J. firm's name is visible (sometimes dimly) on a piece of tin soldered to the bottom. The toys today seem to sell at about their original price.

	C6	C8	C10
Model T Ford, tin 100		150	200
Motorcycle "Cop", 3¾" long, cast iron...40		60	80
Motorcycle, cast iron, white rubber tires, 3" long..................................30		45	60
Motorcycle, Harley-Davidson, rider, 6" long 175		263	350
Motorcycle, Harley-Davidson, cast iron, 9" long, cop rider..................400		600	800
Motorcycle with sidecar, policeman rider, 4" long, cast iron 60		90	120
"Moxie" Horse car (based on the actual promotional vehicle) tin litho, 8" long 750		1125	1500

METALCRAFT Coca-Cola Truck, late 1930s, 12" long. Courtesy Richard L. MacNary.

METALCRAFT, Left to Right: Coca-Cola truck, "Heinz" truck. Courtesy Phillips New York.

MINIATURE VEHICLE CASTINGS, INC. cars. Courtesy Robert E. Wagner.

"Moxie" Horse Car. Courtesy Sotheby's New York.

NEFF-MOON TOY COMPANY

Neff-Moon, of Sandusky, Ohio was owned by William Moon and Charles Neff. Production of their pressed steel toys began in 1923, with the firm, which seems to have been located above a grocery, apparently an early victim of the Depression.

	C6	C8	C10
Neff-Moon Groceries Van	175	262.5	350
Neff-Moon Tow Truck, 16", circa 1925	200	300	400
Nonpareil Ambulance	30	45	60
Nonpareil Dry Goods	30	45	60
Nonpareil Police Patrol	30	45	60
Nonpareil Toyville Express	30	45	60

NORTH & JUDD

Research by collector C.B.C. Lee suggests that this company, located at the time in New Britain, Connecticut, made cast iron toys for only one year, probably 1930, for S.H. Kress. Their original designs appear to have been marked with the company's name, but their companies for the most part are unmarked. The company is still in business, making quality hardware.

	C6	C8	C10
Austin Convertible, open top, marked "North & Judd"			No Price Found
Austin Sedan, two-door, marked "North & Judd"			No Price Found
Bus, looks like Dent, 4.667" long			No Price Found
Ford Model A Coupe, looks like Arcade, length of left cab 1.528", has driver in window, trunk at rear			No Price Found
Ford Model T stake truck, like Arcade's, but marked "Anchor Truck Co." (an anchor is North & Judd's trademark)			No Price Found
Motorcycle cop, like Hubley's "Cop", separate nickeled driver is held by mushrooms at front of handle-bars and on driver's feet			No Price Found
Semi-Trailer Stake Truck, marked "North & Judd"			No Price Found
Tractor, looks like Arcade, but has nickeled driver, 2.988" long			No Price Found

NYLINT

The Nylint Tool and Manufacturing Company was formed in 1937 by Bernard C. Klint and David Nyberg (thus its name) in Rockford, Illinois. Toy production began in the spring of 1946. Since 1950, the firm has concentrated on the production of heavy duty scale reproductions, in steel, of earth-moving equipment and over-the-road trucks. The following list was compiled by Calvin L. Chaussee, showing the period each group of toys was introduced.

NY-LINT No.1600 Payloader, 1949. Courtesy Continental Hobby House.

NY-LINT (1952-53) No.1300 Tournarocker. Courtesy Thomas G. Nefos, Federal Shipping Network.

NY-LINT 1960-61, No. 4100, U-Haul Truck. Courtesy Thomas G. Nefos, Federal Shipping Network.

NY-LINT, 1949, No. 2200 Michigan Shovel. Courtesy Continental Hobby House.

	C6	C8	C10
1947 Nylint Fork Lift 67	100	135
1949			
Nylint No. 100 Amazing Car (Turns-Parks-Corners), 13¾" Long...........175	263	350
Nylint No. 800 Scootcycle (windup), 7¼" long 175	263	350
Nylint No. 1000 Deliverall (windup), 10" long..........................110	165	220
Nylint No. 1100 Elgin Street Sweeper (windup), 8¼" long........................100	150	200
Nylint No. 1200 Pump Mobile (wind-up), 8⅝" long 120	180	240
Nylint No. 1400 Roadgrader, 19¼" long 100	150	200
Nylint No. 1600 Payloader, 18" long ...100	150	200
Nylint No. 2000 Speed Swing, 19".......90	135	180
Nylint No. 2100 Tournadozer, 20" long 85	128	170
Nylint No. 2200 Michigan Shovel, 31½" long 137	205	275
Nylint No. 2400 Electric Cannon, 22½" long 140	210	280
Nylint No. 2500 Telescoping Crane, 27" 90	135	180
Nylint No. 2600 Missile Launcher, 31½" 200	300	400
Nylint No. 2700 Uranium Hauler, 22½" long 210	315	420
Nylint No. 2800 Guided Missile Carrier, 15½" long 55	82	110
Nylint No. 2900 Junior Jack Hammer, 19½"........................75	112	150
1952-52-52			
Nylint No. 1300 Tourna Rocker, 18" 50	75	100
Nylint No. 1500 Tournahopper, 22½"...92	138	185

	C6	C8	C10
Nylint No. 1700 Tourna Hauler, 30¼" long 90	135	180
Nylint No. 1800 Traveloader, 30" long 162	243	325
Nylint No. 1900 Tourna Tractor-Dozer, 14¾" 95	142	190
1956-59			
Nylint No. 2500 Telescoping Crane, 35¾" 160	240	320
Nylint No. 2600 Missile Launcher 50	75	100
Nylint No. 2800 Guided Missile Carrier 50	75	100
Nylint No. 3000 Grader-Loader, 23¾" 160	240	320
Nylint No. 3100 Payloader Tractor-Shovel, 17⅝" 80	120	160
Nylint No. 3200 Power and Light Lineman Truck, 35¾" 160	240	320
Nylint No. 3300 Power and Light Truck, Posthole Digger, 35¾" long 180	270	360
Nylint No. 3400 Highway Emergency Truck, 18⅝" long 85	128	170
Nylint No. 3500 Count Down Rocket Launcher, 21" 75	112	150
Nylint No. 3600 Ford Rapid Delivery, 18¼" long 90	135	180
Nylint No. 3700 Street Sprinkler Truck, 18" long 90	135	180
Nylint No. 3800 Ford Sales and Service, 13⅝" long 70	105	140
Nylint No. 3900 Ford Platform Tilt Truck, 15¾" 87	131	175
Nylint No. 4000 Ford Speedway Truck with Racer, 24¾".................120	180	240

	C6	C8	C10
1960-61			
Nylint No. 4100 U-Haul Truck and Trailer, 22" long	87	131	175
Nylint No. 4200 Bulldozer, 14" long	37	56	75
Nylint No. 4400 Camper on Pickup, 13½" long	60	90	120
Nylint No. 4600 Construction 4 Wheel Platform Dump, 15¾" long	100	150	200
Nylint No. 4700 Happy Acres truck with Horses, 14"	100	150	200
Nylint No. 48-4900 (2) U-Haul Trailers, 3 piece set, 33¼" long	150	225	300
1962			
Nylint No. 5000 Dump Truck w/ Cement Mixer, 20½" long	70	105	140
Nylint No. 5100 Dump Truck, 13½" long	37	56	75
Nylint No. 5200 Pickup Truck (Econoline), 11¼" long	35	52	70
Nylint No. 5300 Custom Camper on above, 12½" long	45	68	90
Nylint No. 5400 Custom Camper on above with boat, 23½" long	150	225	300
Nylint No. 5500 Pepsi Truck, 16½" long	144	216	288
1963			
Nylint No. 5800 Ford Econoline Van, 12" long	47	71	95
Nylint No. 6000 American Oil Emergency Truck, 11¼" long	70	105	140
Nylint No. 6200 Kennel Truck with dogs, 11½" long	52	78	105
Nylint No. 6300 Horse Van, 23½" long	40	60	80
1964			
Nylint No. 6600 Mobile Home, Semi Type, 30" long	100	150	200
Nylint No. 6700 Ambulance, 12" long	90	135	180
Nylint No. 6800 Jalopy, 9⅝" long	32	48	65
Nylint No. 6900 Airport Courtesy Van, 12" long	160	240	320
Nylint No. 7100 Fun on Farm Econoline Truck, 11¼" long, 29 pieces	190	285	380
1965			
Nylint No. ???? Race Team V. Racer, 21"	120	180	240
Nylint No. 1100 Digger Power Shovel, 27" long	80	120	160
Nylint No. 1200 Lawn and Garden Service Truck, 20" long, 12 piece set	170	255	340

	C6	C8	C10
Nylint No. 6100 Hydraulic Dump Truck, 13½" long	55	82	110
Nylint No. 6801 Jalopy w/Top, 9⅝" long	50	75	100
Nylint No. 7300 Army Ambulance, 12" long	66	99	132
Nylint No. 7900 Road Grader, 15" long	36	54	72
Nylint No. 8000 Pony Farm Van, 11¼" long, 7 piece set	100	150	200
Nylint No. 8100 Suburban Fire Pumper, 12½" long	85	128	170
Nylint No. 8200 Bronco, 12½" long	32	48	65

OHIO Armored Car, C. WWI, 7¼" long. Courtesy Lloyd W. Ralston Auctions.

OHIO Delivery Truck, 1920s, 12" long. Courtesy Lloyd W. Ralston Auctions.

	C6	C8	C10
Nylint No. 8300 Texaco Service Van, 12" long	85	128	170
Ohio Armored Car, circa WW I, friction, 7¼" long	225	337	450
Ohio Coupe, 2-door, 17" long pressed steel	150	225	300
Ohio Delivery Truck, 1920s, painted pressed steel, friction, 12" long	350	525	700
Ohio Fire Ladder Truck, 13½" long, 1920s	200	300	400

OHIO Fire Truck, 19½" long, 1910. Courtesy Lloyd W. Ralston Auctions.

OHIO Roadster, 18" long, 1920s. Courtesy Lloyd W. Ralston Auctions.

	C6	C8	C10
Ohio Fire Patrol, 9¾" long, pressed steel, cast iron, wood, very early ...500	750	1000
Ohio Fire Truck, 10½" long, pressed steel, cast iron, wood, very early ..1200	1800	2400
Ohio Fire Truck, 19½", friction 250	375	500
Ohio Pickup Truck, 13" long, 1920s, friction..............125	187	250
Ohio Roadster, 7½" long, cast iron and wood, friction, very early..............350	525	700
Ohio Roadster, 13" long, 1920s............175	262	350
Ohio Roadster, 18" long, 1920s, friction, pressed steel 400	600	800
Ohio Touring Auto, friction.................100	150	200
Ohio Truck, "1909", 10½" long, friction.............450	675	900
Ohlsson & Rice, midget race car, aluminum body, rubber tires, circa 1940s.................200	300	400
Oil and Gas Truck, cast iron, 8" long.200	300	400
Oil Truck, circa 1936, pressed steel 10¾" long 100	150	200
Packard Van Truck, 27" long, screen side, pressed steel..........500	750	1000
"Patrol" Motorcycle and rider, circa 1940, 6¼" long, cast iron..............100	150	200
"Patrol" stake truck, Wyandotte? pressed steel, 4⅞" long 40	60	80
Pedal Car, American National "Big Boy" Dump Truck.......................6000	10,000	22,000
Pedal Car, "American National Company Toledo Ohio, USA", sheet metal and wooden, dashboard with dials, rubber tread on wheels, 46" long....................1000	1500	2000
Pedal Car, "AMF", Hook and Ladder, late 1970s 90	135	180
Pedal Car, Boycraft, 1925, open coupe2000	3500	6000
Pedal Car, circa 1905, chain driver, wooden spoke wheels 1250	1875	2500
Pedal Car, Cadillac, circa 1915 Toledo Metal Wheel Co. lithographed dashboard..............500	750	1000

	C6	C8	C10
Pedal Car, Cadillac, early, 40½" long ..800	1200	1600
Pedal Car, Chrysler Airflow 500	750	1000
Pedal Car, DeSoto, 1939 1250	1875	2500
Pedal Car, Essex, 1927 1100	1650	2200
Pedal Car, Fire Truck, Mack, Steel-Craft 2500	4000	7000
Pedal Car, "Ford, 1896", Tubular frame with wire wheels, sheet metal seat with wooden back rest and steering lever, plate under seat has diagram of motor, 39" long 1000	1500	2000
Pedal Car, "Ford", 1937, painted steel.....750	1125	1500
Pedal Car, Garton "Hot Rod" 410	615	825
Pedal Car, Gendron "Skippy", 1940....1200	2200	3500
Pedal Car, Hudson, wood and steel, folding windshield, tilt-up steering wheel 400	600	800

"Patrol" Motorcycle and rider, circa 1940. 6¼" long, cast iron.

PEDAL CAR, Cadillac, early, 40¼" long. Courtesy James S. Maxwell/Virginia Caputo. Photo by Virginia Caputo.

PEDAL CAR, "Ford". Courtesy Mapes Auctioneers & Appraisers.

	C6	C8	C10
Pedal Car, Kidillac circa 1950s	450	675	900
Pedal Car, Lincoln 1921, Toledo	2500	5000	7500
Pedal Car, Lincoln, 1937	1250	1875	2500
Pedal Car, Mercer Raceabout, 1920	2000	3000	4000
Pedal Car, Nash Sideway, 34" long, 1920s	1000	1500	2000
Pedal Car, Murray "Earth Mover"	250	375	500
Pedal Car, Open Coupe, 1920s or early 1930s, Gendron, 36" long	1200	1800	2400
Pedal Car, Packard Dual Cowl Phaeton, 6' long, American National	3000	4500	6000
Pedal Car, Packard Roadster, 1920s, American National, 45" long	3000	5500	8000
Pedal Car, "Packard", early, wire wheels	300	450	600
Pedal Car, "Pioneer" race car, metal and wood	700	1050	1400
Pedal Car, steelcraft Auburn streamliner	3000	5500	8000
Pedal Car, Steelcraft Buick, late 1920s, 36" long	4000	7000	12,000
Pedal Car, steelcraft Chrysler Airflow	2000	3500	5500
Pedal Car, Steelcraft Jewett open coupe, 55" long	2500	5000	7500
Pedal Car, Terraplane, 1934	1500	2250	3000
Pedal Car, Winner, circa 1906	1000	1500	2000
Pickup Truck, cast iron, 3½" long, 1920s, white rubber tires on wooden wheels	40	60	80
Pickup Truck, cast iron, 4" long	80	120	160
Pickup Truck, 7¼" long, cast iron, 1920s	125	187	250
Pickup Truck, tin friction toy, 19" long, 1920s	200	300	400
Pickup Truck, tin or pressed steel, circa 1937-38, 6", wood wheels	40	60	80
Playboy Dump Truck 22" long, tan	150	225	300
Playboy "Intercity Bus", 23½" long, cream color	300	450	600

PYRO

Pyron began in 1939 in Pyron Park, Union City, New Jersey. The owner was William Lester. At its height, the company had 400 employees.

	C6	C8	C10
Pyro Race Car, 4" long	18	24	30
Pyro Range Patrol Truck	6	8	10
Pyro "U.S. Army" Truck	6	8	10
Pyro "U.S.M.C." Truck	6	8	10
Pyro "U.S. Navy" Truck	6	8	10
Race Car, cast iron, 9"	125	187	250
Racer "Parker Special," simple body of heavy steel with steel wheels, 11" long	75	112	150
Race Car, friction, with driver, circa 1925	150	225	300
Race Car, 8" long, circa 1918	150	225	300
Racer, 7½" pressed steel with driver, white rubber tires, rubberband and gear powered	17	26	35
Racing Car, cast iron, 5½" long, with figure	90	135	180
Racing Car, cast iron, with driver, full figure, spiked wheels, early 1920s	75	112	150
Racing Car, cast iron, 7¼"	250	375	500
Racing Set, 1930s, 3 tin racing cars, small tin garage	125	187	250
"Railway Express" truck, cast iron, early 1930s, 5" long	110	165	220

RAINBOW

The following list, with its codings, was compiled by David Leopard. Vehicles are broken down by types.

	C6	C8	C10
RA01 `35 Oldsmobile Coupe, 3¾"long	30	40	50
RA02 `35 Oldsmobile 4 door sedan, 3¼" long	30	40	50
RA03 `35 Oldsmobile 4 door sedan, 5" long	34	45	55
RT01 `35 Studebaker (?) stake side pickup, 5¼" long	35	45	55
RR01 Open Racer, tapered tail, 4" long	No Price Found		

Racing Car, cast iron, 5½" long, with figure. Courtesy Wilkinson Collection, Detroit Antique Toy Museum.

RALSTOY

(Ralston Toy and Novelty Company)

By Fred Maxwell, Slushmold Contributing Editor and Ferd Zegel
with Assistance of Alice Shooter and the Ralston Archives

Ralston Toy & Novelty Co. was founded in July 1939 to manufacture slushmold toys and novelties. It was formed by Dr. Felix Despecher, former mayor of Ralston, Nebraska, A.M. Erickson and Henry C. Nestor to acquire the assets of Best Toy Co. of Manhattan, Kansas and the surviving molds of Kansas Toy Co. of Clifton, Kansas. These assets included the temporary services of John M. Best, his molder Conrad Morsch and about 140 molds from these pioneering slushmold vehicle toy companies. The new enterprise was located in a building formerly occupied by the American Legion at 7632 Burlington St. This continued a low-cost toy line familiar to collectors since Kansas Toy was founded in 1923.

With the death of its founder, Dr. Despecher, about a year later the young company was forced into reorganization. Paul Massey, a lawyer, reorganized the company but had to give up production of potmetals soon thereafter due to the war's need for lead. To survive he turned to making wooden toys, including a replica of the famous Army Jeep of which about 2 million copies were sold through the Dime Stores, mainly Woolworth and Kresge. Other wooden toys included an Army tank, a Navy PT boat and a (rumored) DUKW amphibious landing craft. These toys

were completely made in Ralston except for Jeep wheels which were made in Omaha by the blind. When war-time labor became short handicapped workers were hired.

After the war the company turned to diecasting toys and novelties. As the business expanded it moved to 5707 So. 77th St., where it is today producing a well-known line of promotional trucks under Art Massey. But the post-war history is for other researchers.

By now the history of those migrating molds "with the numbers" is getting confusing. Although market values will depend on other factors than the actual makers we will mention some clues to assist collectors. Ralstoy did label a few of its toys. They liked bottom pans, introduced by Best to increase rigidity of these fragile toys; this provided a surface to emboss "Ralstoy" and "Made in USA". Military olive drab colors reflected the growing war consciousness. Wheels are not a good clue, even when the latest fad, black rubber wheels, were used.

Ralstoy probably reproduced many pieces from their acquired molds, but there is no practical way to know who made them when they are not labeled. (See Best Toy Co. and Kansas Toy Co. in this book.) The toys described below are mostly new issues.

RALSTOY, RAV11. Photo by Ed Poole.

RALSTOY, Sedan RAV12. Photo courtesy by Fred Maxwell.

	C6	C8	C10
RAV1 Dump Truck, "42", 3⅜". International ? COE, 2 open windows (OW), hinged tin dump body. Different casting than Kansas Toy dump truck #42	No Price Found		
RAV2 Tractor, "48", 3". "Caterpillar" tractor, "Whoopee", driver in different color, grooved wood ¾" wheels with rubber tracks on Kansas Toy body	No Price Found		
RAV3 Army tank, "74", 2¼". "US Army", 2 gun turret. Entirely different tank than Kansas Toy #74	13	20	26

	C6	C8	C10
RAV4 Tanker truck, "No. 102", 6¾". "Ralstoy" International ? sleeper cab, 3⅜", 2 OW, vertical grille with "Gasoline" semi-trailer, "No. 102", 4", 4 tanks, 4 storage compartments	14	21	28
RAV5 Large transporter, 9". "Ralstoy" cab unit in RAV4 above, steel semi-trailer with #74 tank, #34 muzzle loading cannon and #32 aircraft, olive drab color. Not known if Ralstoy issued them as a set. (Some stamped "No. 108", some No. 101)	20	45	60

RALSTOY, Left to Right; Top: RAV5 - Transporter with tank #74, Cannon #34, Aircraft #32 ?; Middle: RAV6 - Anti-aircraft unit, RAV8 - Railway? cannon, Bottom: RAV7 - Tank #107, Cannon. Photo by Ed Poole.

RALSTOY, Left to Right; Top: RAV4, Middle: RAV2a, RAV2b, metal wheels, Bottom: Ralstoy field gun. Photo courtesy of Perry Eichor.

	C6	C8	C10
RAV6 Large gun truck, 5⅝". "US Army Anti-aircraft Unit", 3 axle carrier, AA gun, searchlight and crew of 3 28	42	56
RAV7 Army tank, "107", 3⅛". "US Army", wood grooved ¾" track-laying wheels, 2 gun turret, larger version of #74 above. Also version w/black rubber wheels 13	20	26
RAV8 Railway ? gun, "108", 3¼". Version of #23 muzzle-loading cannon on wheeled platform with hook and loop connectors. Perhaps addition to #3600 toy train..............12	18	25
RAV10 Army Jeep. Wooden, WWII issue 20	30	40
RAV11 Army tank. Wooden, "USA W356", "Ralstoy" on bottom, WWII issue 37	56	75
RAV12 Large sedan, "2R", 5⅝". Diecast, Cadillac ?, "Ralstoy", "Made in USA", 4 open vent windows, divided open windshield, 3 open rear windows, long fenders, rear-wheel skirts, bumper guards, black rubber wheels. Early postwar issue? ....No Price Found
Ralstoy Ford Tractor, 1948, with trailer, 9" overall..30	45	60
Ralstoy Mayflower Moving Van 30	45	60
Rehrberger "David" Moving Van, circa 1924, 7¼" long 1500	2500	3000
Remco Bulldog Tank............................25	37	50
Remco Flying Dutchman Antique Car ..32	48	65

RENWAL

The Renwal Manufacturing Company, founded in 1939 by either Irving Rosenblum or Irving Lawner (accounts vary), seems to have begun as a manufacturer of a glass knife. A plastic knife replaced it, and probably led to the manufacture of plastic toys. Toy production began about 1945. When the firm went out of business circa the 1970s, the tooling was sold to Chein, which in turn sold it to Revell.

	C6	C8	C10
Renwal Cadillac Hardtop Convertible, 5½" 15	20	25
Renwal Cement Truck, 1940s, 6½" 25	38	50
Renwal Fire Ladder Truck, plastic 25	38	50
Renwal Gasoline Truck No. 49, plastic 32	48	65
Renwal Hardtop Convertible, 1940s, 6½" 20	30	40
Renwal Pickup Truck, diecast, black rubber tires, approx. 7" long 30	45	60
Renwal Speed King racer, 6½" long 40	60	80
Renwal TV Truck No. 260, with camera, mike, working spotlight, 18" long ..75	112	150
Renwal Visible Auto Chassis 225	338	450
Republic Roadster, 1920s, 10" long 350	525	700
Republic Taxi Cab with driver, sheet-metal, friction motor, circa 1926....200	300	400
Reuhl Caterpillar D-7 300	450	600
Reuhl Cedar Rapids Rock Crusher.......600	900	1200
Revell Plumber's Truck, plastic, 10" long 45	68	90
Richmond Dump Truck 55	82	110
Road Grader, 7½" long, cast iron, rubber wheels 100	150	200
Roadster, cast iron, early, driver, 7" long 125	187	250
Roadster, pressed steel, circa 1936, rumble seat 60	90	120

	C6	C8	C10
Roadster Tow Truck, cast iron, 5" long	60	90	120
"Rocket Launcher" truck, "U.S.A.F.", friction, pressed steel and plastic, circa 1960	60	90	120

RUBBER VEHICLES
Unknown Manufacturers

The following list, with its codings, was compiled by Dave Leopard. Vehicles are broken down by types.

	C6	C8	C10
UA01 '35 Ford 2 door slantback sedan, 4" long (Auburn?)	25	30	35
UA02 '35 Ford Coupe, 4" long (Auburn)?	25	30	35
UA03 '35 Ford 2 door slantback sedan, 4" long (Sieberling?)	25	30	35
UA04 `'35 Ford Coupe, 4" long (Sieberling?)	25	30	35
UA05 `'35 Pontiac 2 door slantback sedan, 4" long (Rainbow?)	30	40	50
UA06 `'35 DeSoto 4 door Airflow Sedan, 5" long	30	40	50
UA07 `'35 Chrysler 4 door Airflow Sedan, rear spare, 4¾" long, ad on roof	No Price Found		
UA08 `'35 Chrysler 2 door Airflow Sedan, 5⅛" long	30	40	50

	C6	C8	C10
UA09 `'36 Plymouth 4 door trunkback sedan, 4⅞" long	No Price Found		
UA10 `'37 Plymouth 4 door trunkback sedan, 4⅞" long	No Price Found		
UA11 `'46 Nash, 2 door Fastback Sedan, hollow, molded tires, 4" long	12	15	20
UA12 c. `'36 LaFayette (?) Sedan, fastback, solid, w/tires, 4" long	25	30	35
UA13 `'35 Ford 2 door slantback sedan, 5" long	No Price Found		
UT01 `'35 Ford Stake Truck, 4¾" long (Sieberling?)	25	30	35
UT02 `'35 Ford Stake Truck, Army version with canvas cover, 4¾" long (Sieberling?)	35	45	55
UT03 `'35 Ford Panel Truck or Ambulance (Paint variations), 4¼" long (Sieberling?)	25	30	35
UT04 `'34 Dodge Rack Truck, 4⅞" long	No Price Found		
UR01 Open Racer, left side Header pipes, solid rubber, 3½" long	No Price Found		
UR02 Open Racer, V-8, solid, large tires on wood hubs, 4" long	No Price Found		
UR03 Open Racer, solid, rubber tires on wood hubs, 6"	No Price Found		
Saunders Fire Truck	50	75	100
Saunders Police Car	27	41	55
Saunders Sedan	32	48	65

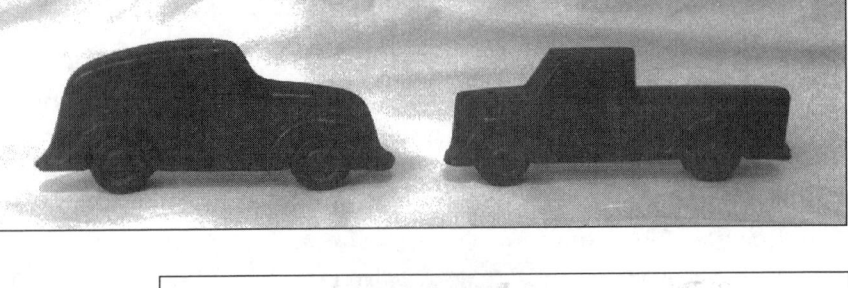

RUBBER VEHICLES, Left to Right; UA14, UT05.

RUBBER VEHICLES UA11. Photo by Dave Leopard.

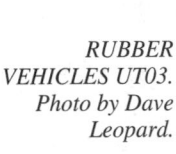

RUBBER VEHICLES UT03. Photo by Dave Leopard.

RUBBER VEHICLES, Left to Right; UA02, UT01. Photo by Dave Leopard.

SAVOYE PEWTER TOY COMPANY

Savoye was incorporated August 1930. In 1931 Savoye Pewter Toy Co., manufacturer of "pewter toys" (pewter was often the word used for lead alloy or potmetal) was listed in a directory at 69 Paterson Plank Road in North Bergen, New Jersey, with six male and three female employees. The names of the owners may have been Selma and Joseph Wigh. In 1934 at the same address the workforce was seven males and two females. Slushmold toys were probably their only product. Savoye was in the 1936 phonebook, and out of the February, 1937 directory.

Collectors identify vehicle toys as Savoye if they have a somewhat coarse appearance, heavy slushmold body and white rubber tires on oversized red wooden hubs that are smooth on the outside surface (no axle showing); but whether this is simply lore is not known at present. The son of one of the owners of Tommy Toy Co. thinks some Savoye-looking vehicles were made by Tommy Toy. If so, it's possible Savoye sold its molds to nearby Tommy Toy.

The following was contributed by Fred Maxwell, one of our principal slushmold researchers.

Those big red hubs and rubber tires are consistent with industry styles of the early 1930s, but the style of some of the vehicles is from an earlier era (see SA17 & SA19 whose metal wheels suggest an earlier beginning of the Savoye-Tommy Toy-Barclay dynasty).

SAVOYE, Left to Right; Top: SA1, SA2; Middle: SA7, SA3; Bottom: SA9. Photo by Fred Maxwell.

SAVOYE, Left to Right; Top: SA10, SA15; Middle: SA7, SA6; Bottom: SA14, SA12. Photo by Fred Maxwell.

	C6	C8	C10
SA1 Roadster, 3½". Driver, open rumble seat, silver vertical grille, (VG, reminiscent of Tootsietoy Graham), vertical louvers (VL)			No Price Found
SA2 Roadster, 3½". Similar to above; different casting			No Price Found
SA3 Coupe, 3⅜". 2 open windows (OW), silver VG, (Graham like), VL	20	30	40
SA4 ? Coupe, 3⅜". Similar to above (Savoye or copy ?). Slanted louvers, fantasy grille and large black rubber wheels (original ?)	14	21	28
SA5 Van, 3¼". "Milk Grade A", 2 OW, sidemounts (SM)	20	30	40
SA6 Van, 4". "Police Patrol", policeman on rear step, 6 OW, gilt trim, SM	24	36	48
SA7 Bus, 4¾". Heavy 5th Ave. sightseeing bus, open overhanging upper deck, 12 OW, gilt or silver trim	30	45	60

	C6	C8	C10
SA8 Bus, 3⅜". Cross-country bus, partial upper deck, 12 OW, rearmount spare.	20	30	40
SA9 Bus, 7½". Tour bus; Mack cab, 3½", 2 OW; "Motor Coach", 5¼", dual-axle semi-trailer, 12 OW, gilt trim			No Price Found
SA10 Truck, 4⅜". Heavy "Beer Truck", 6 wood barrels set in cast depressions	40	60	80
SA11 Truck, 4½". Stake body	12	18	24
SA12 Truck, 5¾". Stake body, hinged tailgate w/chains			No Price Found
SA13 Truck, c. 4". Tow truck, SA3 - like coupe cab, chain & hook on crane			No Price Found
SA14 Truck, 5¾". Heavy tow truck, oversized crane, wire hook			No Price Found
SA15 Fire truck, 4¼". Driver and steersman w/high style gilt helmets, bell on hood, 2 ladders (glued on), oversized wheel wells, oversized tires			No Price Found

SAVOYE, SA13. Photo by Craig A. Clark.

SCHIEBLE Roadster, 18¼" long. Courtesy Joe and Sharon Freed.

SAVOYE, SA22. Photo by Perry R. Eichor.

SCHIEBLE Racer, team, 12" long. Courtesy Wilkinson Collection, Detroit Toy Museum.

	C6	C8	C10

SA16 Fire truck, 3¾". Driver & fireman
w/ high style gilt helmets, 2 detachable
ladders on high rack, oversized
wheel wells, oversized tires ....No Price Found

SA17 ? Fire Engine,3¾". Steam pumper,
driver & fireman w/high style gilt
helmets, large 10-spoke metal wheels.
An early Savoye ? in the style of the
fire trucks above; large wheels would
explain over-sized wheel wells in
SA15 & SA16 above........................No Price Found

SA18 Tractor, 2¾". Caterpillar?
tractor w/stack................................10   15   20

SA19 ? Tractor, 3". Same as above w/
large 10 spoke metal wheels. An
early Savoye? (same casting as
Tommy Toy but longer wheelbase
than Barclay #7)............................No Price Found

SA20 Tank car set, 10¼". Tow cab
shorter version of SA13, 3¼";
2 tank cars 3½", "Oil" "Cap.
80000" (RR type). Not know
whether Savoye sold these as a
set; no known Savoye train, either....40   60   80

SA21 Gun Truck, 3¼". Army, driver
& gunner. (Angular rear deck
distinguishes it from similar gun
trucks) ....No Price Found

SA22 Pickup truck................................20   30   40

(See the Aircraft Section for a blimp and a monoplane. Since we are still finding additions to our 5th Edition list, this list is probably still incomplete. Any help will be appreciated.)

SCHIEBLE TOY AND NOVELTY

Schieble, located in Dayton, Ohio, was formed in 1909 when William Schieble, former partner with D.P. Clark in the firm of that name, bought it out (Clark then formed the Dayton Friction Works, continuing to use Schieble's patents as well as the Hillclimber name, and protracted lawsuits followed).

	C6	C8	C10
Schieble Racer, team, 12" long, circa 1910, steel windup	200	300	400
Schieble Roadster, 18¼" long, spare tire on back	350	525	700
Schieble Sedan, 17" long	200	300	400
Schoenhut "Every Boy Auto Build 5 in 1 Toy" wood set to build, boxed	45	67	90

SEIBERLING RUBBER

Compiled by Dave Leopard

	C6	C8	C10
GA01 ``'35 Ford 2 door slantback sedan, 5" long	30	40	50
GA02 ``'35 Ford 2 door slantback sedan, 4" long	25	30	35

SEIBERLING GA01. Photo by Dave Leopard.

SMITTY TOYS

by Ray Funk

A line of large cast metal and aluminum toy trucks hit the market in 1945, the Smith-Miller "Smitty Toys", "Famous Trucks in Miniature", produced in Santa Monica, California. These trucks were doomed from the beginning as they were entering a highly competitive market, one that had toy producers of trucks dating back to the 30s and earlier, such as Buddy "L", Structo, Marx, Hubley, and in 46 Ny-lint, Tonka in early 50s, and in the mid-1950s, Eldon plastics. However, despite the heavy competition, they fought to stay on the market for a full ten years, into 1955, outclassing virtually all toy trucks before and after, by far, although the last year they changed their profile from Mack Trucks to Auto-Car diesels, with opening doors and steering wheels that actually steered like the real thing. Their first trucks had two different classes, expensive replicas, and, still not cheap, though not actually true replicas, of a smaller type of truck of no name that looked to be a half-breed Ford. I will list the cheaper line first.

No. 401 Tow Truck, 15" long, No. 402 Dump Truck 11½" long, No. 403 Scoop Dump, 14" long (same dump with scoop), all complete cast, cast wheels and rubber tires.

The larger scale models were cast and aluminum, such as No. 404 Lumber Truck (six wheels), 19" long, $10.75; No. 404T Lumber Trailer, 17" long, $6.95; No. 405 Silver Streak, 28" long (14 wheels) six wheel tractor and eight wheel bogey'd heavy duty grain trailer, $15.95; No. 406 Bekins Van, 29" long, six wheel tractor and four-wheel trailer (single axle); No. 407 Searchlight Truck, long (six wheel) based frame 18½" long with platform that has diesel motor (to hold batteries) and huge searchlight, at $16.95; No. 408 Blue Diamond ten wheel huge dump truck, last double set of duals bogey'd, 18½" long, $17.95; No. 409 Pacific Intermountain Express (P.I.E.) six wheel tractor semi with eight wheel bogey'd aluminum trailer, 29" long, $19.75, No. 410 Aerial Ladder semi, six wheel tractor and four wheel single axle trailer, 36" long, ladder extends to 48" high, $27.95. By 1950 some mid-West stores had the aerial ladder priced at $37.50, and various of the others higher-priced.

Later, various modifications were produced, one a straight Box bed truck, using the searchlight truck with metal box and rear double doors. Then yet another variation was the box truck employing the eight wheel bogey set-up, and the log trailer base with a same box to make a ten wheel straight truck and eight wheel trailer, as there were many on the California highways. Then the long base tractor (ten-wheeler) with bogey on rear eight wheels, hooked to Silver Streak and P.I.E. trailers, and yet other variations such as the P.I.E. eight wheel trailer minus top and raising rear door, as high-side grain hauler, and finally a long refrigeration trailer with small side door, all using ten-wheel tractors.

At the same time the company was putting the smaller wheels on the P.I. E. and Silver Streak trailers, and using the small six-wheeled cast "Half-Breeds" tractors, priced at lower competitive prices.

Their first Mack trucks were of the older 1940s types with running boards, old-type fenders and raised separate headlights, and all had fuel tanks, the later Mack trucks being 1954 Macks with air horn on top. (These were produced for just one year.)

The final year saw a complete change, Smith dropping out and Ironson coming in, changing the name to M.I.C. toys, Miller-Ironson Corporation, and to the best of my knowledge they produced only four different, all cast trucks, and though no truck company name, definitely Auto-Car diesels. One was a heavy-duty tow truck as tows large semis, a flat bed with removable side racks, and turn-down hydraulically lowering tailgate (up and down), door handles that worked to open doors, seat, steering wheel and front wheel which were steered like on the "model toy" fire trucks and others of the "model toy" line, the last, fire truck #410 with Mack Tractor, I cannot say, as I only have the cab and no catalog or advertisement of this toy.

Honorable mention must be made, before closing, that one company in Minnesota, owned by Teamsters President Beck's son (in the late 1940s) put out a huge cast metal truck, mostly loggers and dumpers, which steered via a horn on top of the cab, and two, Wyandotte put out in 1950, a very realistic cab over semi six wheel tractor of cast and eight wheel bogey'd long aluminum trailer, with beautifully realistic cast center replica wheels and rubber tires. The fifth wheel on the tractor was operational to couple and uncouple from the trailer, and though of no name, the cast tractor was finely detailed, fuel tanks and all. The Wyandotte sold at $10 while the aforementioned, name unknown, and very short-lived trucks, sold at $20 each, a much too high price for the 1940s. All are now gone, but live on in the minds of those who played with them. There were a few minor variations of the Smith-Miller which I did not mention, and no doubt possibly some on all items that I do not know about, nor have catalogs depicting. Any added information would be appreciated.

Evidence via photographs, etc., has unearthed the fact that there are more in this toy truck line than I had listed.

An early Smitty truck is an all pot metal truck, mostly painted as an armored bank truck with square box and locking doors.

I received a picture of a tanker, using the small bastard six wheel tractor, and trailer having the dual-tandem setup. As by the pictures there did not seem to be any spare room in the wheel wells, I must assume that this was only produced with the small wheels and tractor. It is bright yellow, and has "SHELL" on the trailer.

Still yet another produced in the early years, a cattle hauling truck. This one was large as the largest S.M. and had the large early Mack with long frame. I have found this truck, minus wheels, so I can only assume that it was produced as many others with similar tractor frames as an 18 and also 14 wheeler. The enclosed trailer features double doors on the rear with latch, slotted vented sides and truck was same yellow as tanker, other than frame and fenders (all actually one piece on the early 'Macks') were gloss black, making an eye catching toy, colorwise. Eventually I hope to restore this item and have it pictured for your enjoyment.

How many different trucks, or variations Smitty produced, I have no idea, as I begin to suspect that like Doepke, at times they too made up a one, or few of a kind.

(NOTE: New versions of SMITTY vehicles, using original and new parts, are currently being produced — See Leading Collectors and Dealers)

SMITTY "Bank of America" Armored Truck. Courtesy Good Old Days Store.

SMITTY GMC Coca-Cola Truck. Courtesy R.L. MacNary.

SMITTY Catalog illustraions of Models 402, 401. Photo by Bill Kaufman. Courtesy Ray Funk.

SMITTY Catalog illustraions of Models 406, 405. Photo by Bill Kaufman. Courtesy Ray Funk.

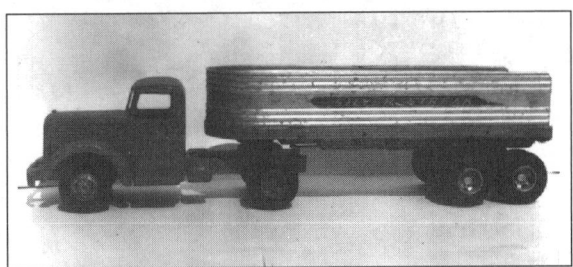

SMITTY No. 405, Silver Streak. Photo by Ray Funk.

SMITTY MIC Tow Truck, "Official Tow Car". Photo by Ray Funk.

	C6	C8	C10
Smitty (Smith-Miller) No. 201-L Lumber Truck, 60 boards, 6 wheel, 14" long	275	413	550
Smitty No. 202-M Material Truck, 3 barrels, 3 cases, 18 boards, 4 wheels, 14" long	210	315	420
Smitty No. 203-H Heinz Grocery Truck, 6 wheels, 14" long	237	355	475
Smitty No. 204-A Arden Milk Truck, 12 milk cans, 4 cases, 4 wheels, 14" long	150	250	325
Smitty No. 205-P Oil Truck, 4 drums, 6 wheels, 14" long	130	195	260
Smitty No. 206-C Coca-Cola Truck, 16 Coca-Cola cases, 4 wheels, 14" long	450	675	900
Smitty No. 208-B Bekins Vanliner, 14 wheels, 22½" long	1000	1500	2000
Smitty No. 209-T Timber Giant, 3 logs, 14 wheels, 23½" long	150	225	300
Smitty No. 210-S Stake Truck, 14 wheels, 23½" long	250	375	500
Smitty No. 211-L Sunkist Special, 14 wheels, 23½" long	150	250	375
Smitty No. 212-R Red Ball, 14 wheels, 23½" long	150	250	375
Smitty No. 301-W GMC Wrecker, 4 wheeler	125	188	250
Smitty No. 302-M GMC Materials Truck, 4 barrels, 3 timbers	200	300	400
Smitty No. 303-R GMC Rack Truck, 6 wheels	150	225	310
Smitty No. 304-K GMC Kraft Foods, 4 wheels	350	525	700
Smitty No. 305-T GMC Triton Oil, 3 drums	150	225	300
Smitty No. 306-C GMC Coca-Cola, 4 wheels, 16 Coke cases	300	480	625
Smitty No. 307-L GMC Redwood Logger Tractor-Trailer, 3 logs	120	190	250
Smitty No. 308-V GMC Lyon Van Tractor-Trailer, 14 wheels,	275	410	550
Smiyyt No. 309-S GMC Super Cargo Tractor-Trailer, 14 wheels, ten barrels	200	300	400
Smitty No. 310-H GMC Hi-Way Freighter Tractor-Trailer, 14 wheels.	150	225	310
Smitty No. 311-E GMC Silver Streak Express Tractor Trailer, 14 wheels	150	250	350
Smitty No. 312-P GMC Pacific Inter-mountain Express ("P.I.E.") Tractor-Trailer	375	525	750
Smitty No. 401 Tow Truck, 15" long	125	188	250

SMITTY Box Truck with Box Trailer, ten wheeler. Courtesy Ray Funk.

	C6	C8	C10
Smitty No. 402 Dump Truck, 11½" long	150	225	300
Smitty No. 403 Scoop Dump, 14" long	110	165	225
Smitty No. 404 Lumber Truck, 19" long	250	375	500
Smitty No. 404T Lumber Trailer, 17" long	150	225	310
Smitty No. 405 Silver Streak 6-wheel tractor, 28" long	170	255	340
Smitty No. 406 Bekins Van, 29" long, six-wheel tractor and four-wheel trailer	275	410	550
Smitty No. 407 Searchlight Truck, 18½" long, "Hollywood Filmad"	150	225	300
Smitty No. 408 Blue Diamond 10-wheel dump truck, 18½" long	225	395	500
Smitty No. 409 Pacific Intermountain Express (P.I.E.) six-wheel tractor semi with eight wheel aluminum trailer, 29" long	180	270	360
Smitty No. 410 Aerial Ladder semi, six-wheel tractor and four-wheel trailer, 36" long, "SMFD"	450	675	900
Smitty No. 401-W GMC Wrecker, 6 wheels	200	300	400
Smitty No. 402-M GMC Material Truck, 4 barrels, 2 timbers	175	263	350
Smitty No. 403-R GMC Rack Truck, 6 wheels	125	188	250
Smitty No. 404-B GMC Bank of America, lock and key, 4 wheels	210	315	420
Smitty No. 405-T GMC Triton Oil, 6 wheels, 3 drums	125	188	250
Smitty No. 406-L GMC Lumber Tractor-Trailer, 14 wheels, eight timbers	140	210	280
Smitty No. 407-V GMC Lyon Van Tractor-Trailer, 10 wheels	250	375	525
Smitty No. 408-H GMC Machinery Hauler, 13 wheels	150	225	335

	C6	C8	C10
Smitty No. 409-G GMC Mobilgas Tanker, 14 wheels, 2 hoses.............250		375	500
Smitty No. 410-F GMC Transcontinental Tractor-Trailer, 14 wheels...165		255	370
Smitty No. 411-E GMC Silver Streak Tractor-Trailer, 14 wheels.............170		270	390
Smitty No.412-P GMC P.I.E. 14 wheels..200		300	400
Smitty "B" Mack "Associated Truck Lines," 14 wheels.....................No Price Found			
Smitty "B" Mack Bekins Van, 10 wheel..350		600	800
Smitty "B" Back Blue Diamond Dump, 10 wheels 300		500	650
Smitty "B" Mack Jr. Fire Truck, warning light, battery-operated, 4 wheel............300		550	700
Smitty "B" Mack Lumber Truck, 6 wheels, 9 timbers 200		320	450
Smitty "B" Mack Lumber Truck & Trailer, 12 wheels, 18 timbers........750		1350	1800
Smitty "B" Mack Orange Dump, 10 wheels 275		440	600
Smitty "B" Mack P.I.E., 14 wheels 320		475	680
Smitty "B" Mack P.I.E., 18 wheels 320		475	680
Smitty "B" Mack Searchlight, 6 wheels, battery powered light........350		550	750
Smitty "B" Mack Silver Streak, 14 wheels 350		550	750
Smitty "B" Mack "Watson Bros." 18 wheels 325		500	700
Smitty "Bank of America" Armored Truck, No. 602B, 14½" long 200		300	425
Smitty Chevy Bekins Van, 14 wheels, plain tires, hubcaps 250		375	500
Smitty Chevy Coca-Cola, 4 wheels, plain tires, early 400		700	1000
Smitty Chevy Flatbed Tractor-Trailer, 14 wheels, unpainted wood trailer, plain tires, hubcaps, early 150		250	350

	C6	C8	C10
Smitty Chevy Milk Truck, 4 wheels, plain tires, hubcaps, early 180		300	400
Smitty Ford Bekins Van, 14 wheeler, plain tires, hubs. Earliest Smitty? .180		300	400
Smitty Ford Coca-Cola, 4 wheels, wood soda cases, early...................450		750	1000
Smitty GMC Be Mac 14 wheel T-Trailer.................................165		250	370
Smitty GMC Coca-Cola Truck, 24 plastic bottles in 6 cases, 4 wheels 125		188	250
Smitty GMC "Drive-O" Steerable Dump, 6 wheels, cable with hand control 160		265	365
Smitty GMC "Furniture Mart" Pick-Up, 4 wheels 150		225	310
Smitty GMC Heinz Grocery Truck 180		300	400
Smitty GMC Machinery Hauler, 10 wheels 150		250	335
Smitty GMC Marshall Field & Company Tractor-Trailer, 10 wheel T-Trailer.................................225		350	460
Smitty GMC Peoples First National Bank and Trust Company armored truck; lock and key 225		385	500
Smitty GMC Rexall Drug, 4 wheels 225		375	480
Smitty GMC Searchlight Truck, "Hollywood Film Ad" with trailer...........................255		385	575
Smitty GMC Silver Streak, 14 wheels .150		225	300
Smitty GMC Triton Oil, 3 drums 140		210	290
Smitty GMC U.S. Treasury Truck armored truck, with lock and key ..200		300	400
Smitty "L" Mack Aerial Ladder, "SMFD", 8 wheels 400		650	900
Smitty "L" Mack Army Materials Truck, 3 barrels, 2 boards, 1 large crate, 1 small, 10 wheel 400		650	900

SMITTY Catalog illustrations of models 407. 403, 409. Photo by Bill Kaufman. Courtesy Ray Funk.

SMITTY Catalog illustrations of model 410. Photo by Bill Kaufman. Courtesy Ray Funk.

"Star Brand Shoes Are Better" racing car. Courtesy Sotheby's New York.

	C6	C8	C10
Smitty "L" Mack Army Personnel Carrier, 10 wheels 400		600	825
Smitty "L" Mack Bekins Van, all white, 10 wheels 800		1700	2000
Smitty "L" Mack Blue Diamond Dump, 10 wheels 450		750	1100
Smitty "L" Mack International Paper Co., 10 wheels.......................300		450	650
Smitty "L" Mack Lyon Van, 6 wheels..450		750	1000
Smitty "L" Mack Material Truck, 2 barrels, 6 timbers, 6 wheels 325		500	700
Smitty "L" Mack Merchandise Van, 6 wheels 250		400	550
Smitty "L" Mack Merchandise Van & Trailer, 12 wheels.....................275		440	600
Smitty "L" Mack Mobil Tandem Tanker, 12 wheels 300		500	700
Smitty "L" Mack Orange Hydraulic Dump, 10 wheels 350		550	800
Smitty "L" Mack Orange Material Truck, 10 wheels, 3 barrels, 2 boards, one large crate, one small..300		450	650
Smitty "L" Mack Orange Utility Truck, 4 wheels 325		550	775
Smitty "L" Mack P.I.E., 14 wheel 300		450	600
Smitty "L" Mack "Sibley's" Van, 6 wheels (rare) 400		650	900

	C6	C8	C10
Smitty "L" Mack Tandem Timber, 6 wheel, 18 or 24 timbers (varies) 400		650	900
Smitty "L" Mack Telephone Truck, 6 wheels 300		455	625
Smitty "L" Mack West Coast Transport, 6 wheel 300		450	600
Smitty MIC Aerial Ladder 300		455	625
Smitty MIC "Fruehauf Road Star" tractor-trailer, 14 wheels 250		385	550
Smitty MIC House Trailer....................350		650	800
Smitty MIC Hydraulic Dump, 10 wheels 400		700	950
Smitty MIC Life-O-Matic, 6 wheels, 2 barrels.....................................400		650	900
Smitty MIC Lincoln Capri (for MIC House Trailer), steerable...............375		600	850
Smitty MIC Lumber Truck, 6 wheels, 9 timbers 350		575	800
Smitty MIC P.I.E. Tractor-Trailer, 14 wheels 375		600	850
Smitty MIC "Teamsters" Hydraulic Dump, 10 wheels 375		600	850
Smitty MIC "Teamsters" Tow Truck, 6 wheels ....No Price Found			
Smitty MIC "Teamsters" Tractor-Trailer, 14 wheels.........................350		550	800
Smitty MIC Town Truck, "Official Tow Car," 6 wheels.......................225		375	500
Smitty MIC Tow Truck, 6 wheels, un-painted, polished 225		375	500
Smitty MIC Tractor-Trailer, polished aluminum trailer, no decals, 14 wheels 375		600	850
Sonny Army Truck "U.S.A. 1120" 300		500	680
Sonny Dump, 26" long........................800		1300	1800
Sonny Moving Van...............................900		1450	2000
Sonny Parcel Post Van........................700		1150	1600

SONNY "US 1120' Artillery Truck, 26" long. Courtesy Joe Freed.

SONNY "USA 1120" Anti-Aircraft Truck, 24" long. Courtesy Joe and Sharon Freed.

STEELCRAFT "U.S." Mail. Photo by Calvin L. Chaussee.

STEELCRAFT Fire Truck, approx. 25" long.

STEELCRAFT Steam Shovel.

	C6	C8	C10
Sonny "USA 1120" Anti-Aircraft Truck ...700	700	1100	1550
Sonny "US 1120" Artillery Truck, 26" long...700	700	1100	1550
"Star Brand Shoes Are Better", racing car "The Winner", tin litho, 8½" long...1200	1200	1900	2800
Steam Pumper, "Boston," with lamp, cast iron wheels, 15½" long...2500	2500	3750	5000
Steam Pumper fire truck, cast iron, 5" ..25	25	37	50
Steam Pumper truck, cast iron, hard rubber wheels, driver, 12" long...150	150	225	300
Steam Pumper, tin and wooden chain and friction drive with driver, "National," 10" ...200	200	300	400
Steam Pumper, tin and wooden friction drive, 11" long...70	70	105	140
Steam Roller, steam-engine powered..200	200	300	450
Steam Roller, cast iron, 4¾" long, circa early 1930s ...75	75	112	150
Steam Shovel, "Sand Digger," 28" long.150	150	225	300
Steelcraft Army Truck, Mack, circa 1930, 22" long...800	800	1300	1800
Steelcraft "City Delivery" truck ...450	450	675	900

	C6	C8	C10
Steelcraft "City Milk Co.", 18" long....400	400	600	800
Steelcraft Coca-Cola Truck, 12 bottles on side...400	400	600	800
Steelcraft "Cream Crest" truck...375	375	563	750
Steelcraft Dump Truck, Airflow...1750	1750	2625	3500
Steelcraft Dump Truck, Mack ...1100	1100	1650	2200
Steelcraft Fire Truck, 25" long...750	750	1100	1500
Steelcraft "Fro-Joy" Ice Cream Truck, circa 1930s ...350	350	525	700
Steelcraft GMC Scissor Dump Truck...500	500	750	1000
Steelcraft Inter City Bus. 24" ...450	450	675	900
Steelcraft Little Jim Fire Truck ...600	600	900	1200
Steelcraft Model T Roadster pedal car, 50" long, Lic. #65-287 ...450	450	675	900
Steelcraft Railway Express Truck, 26" long ...450	450	675	900
Steelcraft Road Roller, 16" long ...150	150	225	300
Steelcraft Shell Motor Oil truck with oil barrels ...300	300	450	600
Steelcraft Steam Shovel...175	175	263	350
Steelcraft Tank truck, sheet metal, 25½" long ...160	160	240	320
Steelcraft "U.S. Mail," 27¼" long, circa 1928...1150	1150	1725	2300

STRUCTO

Structo, of Freeport, Illinois, was founded in 1908 by three men: brothers Louis and Edward Strohacker and C.C. Thompson. They initially manufactured Erector Construction Kits, and about 1919 they started making toy vehicles. In 1935 J.G. Cokey bought a majority of the business, and when he died in 1975, the toy patents and designs were taken over by the Ertl Company. (Numbered Structos are found at the end of this listing.)

	C6	C8	C10
Structo Army Ambulance No. 416, 17" long...175	175	263	350
Structo Army Truck with canvas top, 21" long...155	155	233	310

	C6	C8	C10
Structo Army Van, 17½" long, pressed steel and canvas, No. 415 ...170	170	255	340
Structo Bearcat Racer, 12¼" long, clockwork ...350	350	525	700

STRUCTO Tank, 11" long, No. 48. Courtesy Mapes Auctioneers & Appraisers.

	C6	C8	C10
Structo Camper with cloth top, 12"…….50	75	100
Structo Cement Mixer, 20" long, circa 1950s……………………………80	120	160
Structo Coupe, convertible, circa 1920s.160	240	320
Structo Caterpillar Tractor with Trailer, heavy spring clockwork motor, steel treads, No. 46 …………250	375	500
Structo Communications Center truck, 21" long……………………………70	105	140
Structo Delivery Truck, tin electric lights…………………………………150	225	300
Structo Dump Truck, early, Mack type….750	1125	1500
Structo Fire Dept. Emergency Patrol Truck, red bubble light, 12" long 1950s…………………………………50	75	100
Structo Garbage Truck, 21" long………..45	68	90
Structo Gasoline Truck No. 912, 1950s, 13" long…………………………………75	112	150
Structo Guided Missile Launcher, No. 906 with plastic launcher, missiles of wood and vinyl, 13" long ………..70	105	140
Structo Guided Missile Launching Truck, truck metal, missiles, etc., plastic, rubber tires………………….50	75	100
Structo Ladder Truck, 1950s ………..85	128	170
Structo Machinery Hauler …………….37	56	75
Structo Moving Van, 16" long, open cab, circa 1929, No. 427 …………..175	265	350

	C6	C8	C10
Structo Packard Dump Truck, No. 405, circa 1930, 18" long………………….700	1050	1400
Structo Pick Up Truck, 13" …………….70	105	140
Structo Police Patrol Truck, 17" long, No. 426……………………………….300	450	600
Structo Renault Tank, clockwork, green with red turret………………….260	390	520
Structo Roadster, 16" long, 1920s, clockwork…………………………….400	600	800
Structo Sand Loader, 12" high, circa 1928 …………………………………32	48	65
Structo "Sanitation Dept." garbage truck …………………………………120	180	240
Structo Searchlight Truck, truck metal, light and generator plastic, uses batteries, has rubber tires ……..62	93	125
Structo Steam Shovel, 14" x 11"………150	225	300
Structo Steam Shovel, 16"……………100	150	200

STRUCTO Dump Truck, early, Mack type. Courtesy Joe and Sharon Freed.

	C6	C8	C10
Structo Steam Shovel, 21" x 18"...........37	56	75
Structo "Structo Telephone Co.", 12" long, circa 1948...............67	101	135
Structo Tank, 11" long, #48................250	375	500
Structo Tank, olive drab with orange turret, ten metal wheels, 12½" long .300	450	600
Structo Toyland Oil Co.........................175	263	350
Structo Toyland Tow Truck....................30	45	60

Structo Tractor 8½" long with cast iron driver, early, caterpillar type...250 375 500

Structo Truck Assortment No. 317: Dump truck, blue, Stake truck, Lumber truck. Each 9" long, 3½" wide, 3½" tall. Heavy gauge metal, rubber wheels, original box folds to form garage. 1920s. Price per set 150 225 300

Structo U.S. Mail Delivery Truck, 17" long, No. 428 ....250 375 500

Structo Whippet Tank, 12" long, heavy spring clockwork motor enameled green, red and black, may read "Patented 1920," on sale in 1929, No. 48...........................200 300 400

Structo Wrecker, "Toyland Garage"......40 60 80

Structo No. 601 Motor Express stake truck, early 1950s...........................110 175 230

Structo No. 603 Package Delivery, early 1950s.....................................60 90 120

Structo No. 605 Shovel Dump, early 1950s..150 225 300

Structo No. 607 Machinery Truck, early 1950s.....................................170 255 340

Structo No. 609 Barrel Truck, early 1950s .60 90 120

Structo No. 700 Transport Trailer, early 1950s......................................150 225 300

Structo No. 702 Steel Cargo Trailer, early to mid-1950s 300 450 600

Structo No. 704 Overland Freight Trailer, early 1950s 140 210 280

Structo No. 704 Grain Trailer, early and mid-1950s (replaced Freight Trailer) 100 150 200

Structo No. 706 Auto Transport Trailer, sold 1953-54, with cars 125 188 250

Structo No. 708 Cattle Trailer 75 112 150

Structo No. 811 Barrel Truck wind-up, early 1950s..............................600 900 1200

Structo No. 822 Wrecker Truck, wind-up, early-mid 1950s................55 82 110

Structo 844 Hi-Lift Dump, wind-up, early 1950s......................................140 210 280

Structo 866 Gasoline Truck, wind-up, early 1950s......................................260 390 520

	C6	C8	C10
Sturdi Built Logging Truck.................325	510	650

Sturditoy Ambulance, 26" long, open cab, circa 1929 ....140 210 280

Sturditoy American Railway Express Truck, circa 1920s.........................1000 2200 3500

Sturditoy Dump Truck, 1920s, 25" long 450 675 900

Sturditoy Dump Truck, 1920s, 26½" long 800 1200 1600

Sturditoy Pumper, 26" long, circa 1930 ....1000 1500 2000

Sturditoy Traveling Store 1000 1500 2000

Sturditoy U.S. Mail Screenside Truck....900 1350 1800

Sturditoy Water Tower..........................1100 1650 2200

SUN RUBBER

Sun Rubber of Barberton, Ohio was founded in 1923. Toymaking started in 1924 and autos were introduced in April, 1935. Owner was Tom W. Smith Jr.

	C6	C8	C10
SA01 Coupe, external exhaust pipes, from 1936, 4" long, No. 515...........15	20	25
SA02 `'34 Desoto Airflow, four door sedan, 4" long No. 500....................15	20	25
SA03 `'40 Dodge, 4 door sedan, 4½" long No. 12001 15	20	25
SA04 circa 1936 "Teardrop" Sedan, 5½" long, No. 1010 (1936)............15	20	25
SA05 Art Deco Housetrailer, fits SA04, 4⅜" long, No. 1025 ....No Price Found		
SA06 Town Car, Brewster type limo, exposed driver, 5⅜" long, No. 1015 20	25	30

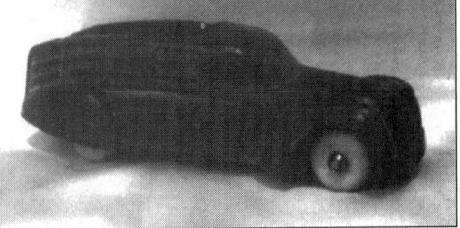

SUN ST01. Photo by Dave Leopard.

SUN ST02. Photo by Dave Leopard.

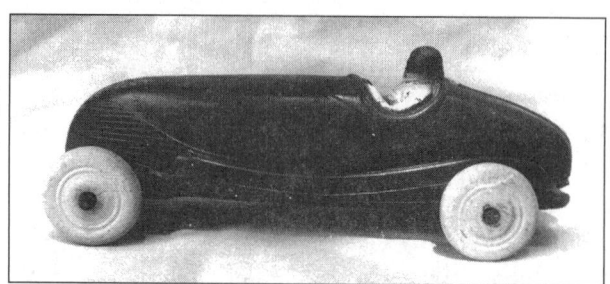

SUN SR03. Photo by Dave Leopard.

SUN SA04. Photo by Dave Leopard.

SUN SA07. Photo by Dave Leopard.

SUN ST03. Photo by Dave Leopard.

SUN ST07. Photo by Dave Leopard.

SUN both SR01. Photo by Dave Leopard.

SUN ST04 and ST05. Photo by Dave Leopard.

SUN ST08. Photo by Dave Leopard.

	C6	C8	C10
SA07 Station Wagon, woody, mid-30s, 3¾" long, No. 12007	15	20	25
ST01 Pickup Truck, stake sides, streamlined, 4½" long, No. 510	15	20	25
ST02 Open Truck, stake sides, streamlined (White?), 5¼" long No. 1005	20	25	30
ST03 Tractor/trailer, one-piece, 3 axles, futuristic, 5⅛" long, No. 12013	20	25	30
ST04 Open Truck, futuristic, 4½" long, No. 12003	15	20	25
ST05 Open "Master" truck, futuristic, 5⅝" long, No. 12111	20	25	30
ST06 Open "Master" truck, futuristic, 6⅝" long, No. 12011	No Price Found		
ST07 ``'36 White Bus, streamlined, 4¼" long, No. 520 (1936)	15	20	25

	C6	C8	C10
ST08 Ambulance, c. late 1930s, 3¾" long, No. 12006	15	20	25
SR01 Open racer, 2 drivers, 4⅜" long, No. 505 (1936)	15	20	25
SR02 Open racer, full fenders on rear, 6½" long, No. 1000 (1936)	20	25	30
SR03 Open racer, boat tail, "Super" racer, 6¾" long, No. 12012	20	25	30
SM01 Tank, revolving turret and gunner, 6" long, No. 12015 (1946)	25	30	35
SM02 Scout Car, 4 gunners, 6¾" long, No. 12014 (1946)	25	30	35
Texaco Tank Truck, 24" long	35	52	70
Thimble Drome Racer	125	188	250
Thimble Drome Racer with engine	250	375	500

THOMAS TOYS

Thomas Toys was founded by Islyn Thomas in 1944. Located from first to last at 80 Clinton Street, Newark, New Jersey, at its peak it had 350 employees. The company's first toys were plastic jeeps, planes and vinyl dolls. In 1960 Thomas sold the firm to Banner.

	C6	C8	C10
Thomas Toys No. 133 Buick Torpedo Sedan, plastic, 11" long	6	8	10
Thomas Toys Harley Davidson with removable rider, 3"	30	40	50
Thomas Toys Jet Car, No. 457	6	8	10
Thomas Toys No. 140 Loudspeaker Van, plastic, 4" long	6	8	10
Thomas Toys Wrecker, 4½" long	16	22	28

THOMAS TOYS No.457 Jet Car. Courtesy Islyn Thomas.

TIP TOP TOY CO.

The Tip Top Toy Co. was located in San Francisco, and produced slush cast vehicles through most of the 1920s and 30s. The firm embossed its name inside some of its toys, but not all. (List by C.B.C. Lee and Craig A. Clark)

These are a rare make of toy, evidently manufactured through most of the twenties and thirties in San Francisco by the Tip Top Toy Co. Photo by C.B.C. Lee.

	C6	C8	C10
Tip Top Coupe, 1923 Dodge, 3⅛" long	16	24	32
Tip Top Tanker, marked "Gasoline", 3½" long	No Price Found		
Tip Top Tow Truck, 3 5/16" long,	16	24	32
with trailer, 5¼" overall	No Price Found		
Tip Top Pick-up truck with tailgate, 3 3/16" long	No Price Found		
Tip Top Bus, 3⅜" long	No Price Found		
Tip Top Coupe, 3 3/16" long	No Price Found		
Tip Top Coupe 1935 Hupmobile, 3¼" long	No Price Found		
with trailer	No Price Found		
Tip Top Small tanker, 2 11/16" long	No Price Found		
Tip Top Small tanker with bumpers	No Price Found		

	C6	C8	C10
Tip Top "Parcel Delivery" panel truck, 2⅛" long	No Price Found		
Tip Top Small coupe, 2⅛" long	No Price Found		
Tip Top Studebaker Sedan, 1935, 2 9/16" long	No Price Found		
Tip Top Stake truck, four or six wheels, 5 5/16" long	No Price Found		
Tip Top Airflow, smaller	No Price Found		
Tip Top Airflow, larger	No Price Found		

TOLEDO METAL WHEEL COMPANY
("Blue Streak")

The Toledo Metal Wheel Company was located in Toledo, Ohio during at least the early and late 1920s. It manufactured a large range of pedal cars as well as toy trucks. Its trade name for its products was "Blue Streak."

	C6	C8	C10
Toledo No. 45 "Bull Dog" Truck, 26" long, open cab	500	1000	1500
Toledo No. 46 "Bull Dog" Dump Truck, 26½" long	600	1000	1475
Toledo No. 47 "Bull Dog" Sprinkler Truck, 27½" long	600	1100	1510
Toledo No. 48 "Bull Dog" Moving Van, 26" long	550	1050	1550
Toledo No. 50 "Bull Dog" Coal Truck, 25" long	800	1350	1875
Toledo Fire Pumper Pedal Car, red-painted, 59" long	1250	1875	2500

TOMMY TOY

The following vehicles have been identified by Charles E. Weldon Jr., son of one of the owners of Tommy Toy. He is sure these are Tommy Toy, but admits there is always a chance he could be mistaken on some. Certainly the Cannon Truck, aside from the hubs, looks just like Barclay's, which was produced in the same years. Some others resemble Metal Cast, Savoye and other companies'

vehicles. However, since slush molds did tend to change hands, production of a vehicle by one company would not preclude later manufacture of the same toy by another company. American Alloy is known to have produced copies of Tommy Toy's soldiers using new molds. The only vehicle known to bear the Tommy Toy trademark is the 810 Cord.

	C6	C8	C10
TTV1 Aerial Ladder Truck (like Savoye), late 20s type 20		30	40
TTV2 Airflow type auto (like Kansas Toy), circa 1935 32		48	65
TTV3 "Ambulance," late 20s-early 30s type...........16		24	32
TTV4 "Beer Truck" with wooden barrels, late 1930s 14		21	28
TTV5 Cannon Truck, mid-30s (like Barclay; Barclay's had wooden hubs)...........17		25	34
TTV6 Convertible no driver, mid-late 30s .8		12	16
TTV7 Convertible with driver, mid-late 30s, 1935 Oldsmobile 10		15	20
TTV8 Cord, 810 (1935)...........40		60	80
TTV9 "Delivery Deluxe" delivery truck (like Savoye), late 30s 18		27	36

	C6	C8	C10
TTV10 Double-Decker Bus, closed top, early 30s...........16		24	32
TTV11 Double-Decker Bus, open top, extended hood (like Savoye), late 1920s...........35		52	70
TTV12 Double-Decker Bus, open top, no hood (like Barclay), late 1930s...........16		24	32
TTV13 Dump Truck, late 1930s (resembles Kansas Toy, Best Toy, Manhattan Toys) 16		24	32
TTV14 "General Trucking," late 30s 12		18	25
TTV15 Ladder Truck, mid 30s...........20		30	40
TTV16 "Milk" truck, late 1930s 20		30	40
TTV17 "Milk Truck," grilled window circa late 1930s 20		30	40

TOMMY TOY, Left to Right, Top: TTV27, TTV28; Bottom: TTV2, TTV30, TTV32. Photo by Bill Kaufman. Courtesy Charles E. Weldon Jr.

TOMMY TOY, Left to Right, Top: TTV18, TTV17, TTV14, TTV 16; Bottom: TTV10, TTV11, TTV12. Photo by Bill Kaufman. Courtesy Charles E. Weldon Jr.

TOMMY TOY, Left to Right, Top: TTV20, TTV5, TTV7, TTV21; Bottom: TTV4, TTV18, TTV6. Photo by Bill Kaufman. Courtesy Charles E. Weldon Jr.

TOMMY TOY, Left to Right, Top: TTV31, TTV33, TTV13; Bottom: TTV9, TTV29, TTV30. Photo by Bill Kaufman. Courtesy Charles E. Weldon Jr.

TOMMY TOY TTV8. Courtesy C.B.C. Lee.

	C6	C8	C10
TTV18 "Milk Truck," smooth window, circa late 30s	20	30	40
TTV19 "Motorcoach," mid-30s (like Savoye)	No Price Found		
TTV20 "Oil" tanker, "Cap 80000" (like Metal Cast, which has different capacity number), 1930s, attaches to Tommy Toy Towing Car Coupe	8	12	16

	C6	C8	C10
TTV21 "Packard," coupe, mid-30s	17	26	35
TTV22 "Police Patrol," open windows, late 20s-early 30s type	40	60	80
TTV23 "Police Patrol," solid windows, late 20s-early 30s type	35	52	70
TTV24 Pumper, mid 1930s	12	18	25
TTV25 Pumper, large, red hubs, late 30s	11	16	22
TTV26 Pumper, small, late 30s	8	12	16
TTV27 Racing Car, large, circa mid-30s	16	24	32
TTV28 Racing Car, small, circa mid-30s	12	18	25
TTV29 Sedan, four-door, circa 1935	17	26	35
TTV30 Sedan towing "Tourist" trailer, circa 1936-37	20	30	40
TTV31 Towing Car Coupe (like Savoye), early 30s type	16	24	32
TTV32 Tractor	12	18	25
TTV33 Wrecker, late 1930s	10	15	20

TONKA

Tonka was incorporated in Mound, Minnesota, in September, 1946. The firm had secured the tooling for a steam shovel and crane and clam from Streator Industries, which had unsuccessfully introduced those toys at the Toy Fair in February, 1946. Tonka, which means "great" in Sioux-French, was located on the banks of Lake Minnetonka (and is now situated in Minnetonka itself). In 1948, Tonka introduced a lift fork with trailer, and in 1949 premiered its line of trucks, including a dump and wrecker. The firm had originally been incorporated as Mound Metal Crafts, with a line of tie racks and garden tools. Most of the following list was compiled by Calvin L. Chaussee, grouping the toys by period.

	C6	C8	C10
1947			
Tonka No. 50 Steam Shovel, 20¾" long	110	165	220
Tonka No. 150 Crane and Clam, 24" long	175	263	350
Tonka Coca-Cola Truck ('47 or '48 special order of 100 for a bottler)	400	600	800
1948			
Tonka No. 200 Lift Truck and Cart	100	150	200
1949			
Tonka No. 100 Steam Shovel Deluxe, 22" long	No Price Found		
Tonka No. 120 Tractor and Carry-All Trailer with No. 50 Steam Shovel	155	283	310
Tonka No. 125 Tractor & Carry-All Trailer with No. 100 Steam Shovel	No Price Found		
Tonka No. 130 Tractor-Carry-All Trailer, 30½" long	80	120	160
Tonka No. 140 Transport Van, 22¼" long	250	375	500

	C6	C8	C10
Tonka No. 170 Tractor & Carry-All Trailer with No. 150 Crane & Clam	200	300	400
Tonka No. 180 Dump Truck, 12" long	52	78	105
Tonka No. 190 Loading Tractor, 10½" long	No Price Found		
Tonka No. 250 Wrecker Truck, 12½" long	120	180	240
1951 *(1950 almost identical to 1949 line with minor color and decal changes.)*			
Tonka No. 145 Street Carrier Semi, 22" long	125	188	250
Tonka No. 175 Utility Hauler, 12" long	75	112	150
Tonka No. 400 Allied Van Semi, 23H" long	160	240	320
1952			
Tonka No. 500 Livestock Hauler Semi, 22¼" long	135	200	270
Tonka No. 550 Grain Hauler Semi, 22¼" long	120	180	240

TONKA No. 750. Courtesy Lloyd W. Ralson Auctions.

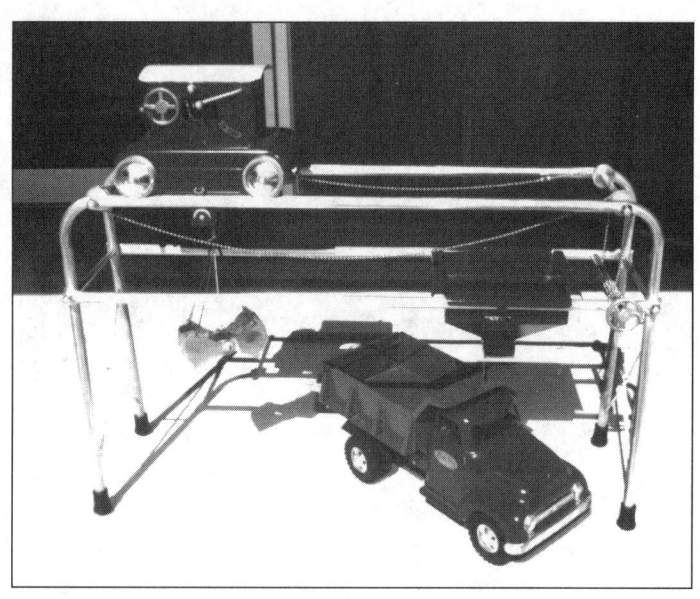

TONKA, 1956, No. 992, Aerial Sand Loader Set. Courtesy Thomas G. Nefos, Federal Shipping Network.

	C6	C8	C10
1953			
Tonka No. 575 Logger semi, 22¼" long	100	150	200
Tonka No. 600 Road Grader, 17" long	45	68	90
Tonka No. 650 Green Giant Transport Semi, 22¼" long	125	188	250
Tonka No. 675 Trailer Fleet Set, two tractors (five interchangeable trailers), per set	387	580	775
1954 (*Newer Style Trucks - Rounded Fenders*)			
Tonka No. 580 Pickup Truck	67	100	135
Tonka No. 700 Aerial Ladder Semi Fire Truck, 32½" long	175	263	350
Tonka No. 725 Minute Maid Delivery Van, 14½" long	260	390	520
Tonka No. 725 Star Kist Van, 14½" long	210	315	420
Tonka No. 750 Carnation Milk Step Van, 11¾" long (rare)	165	248	330
Tonka No. 750 Parcel Delivery Van, 11¾" long	190	285	380
Tonka No. 775 Road Builder Set - 5 pc. set - Road Grader (Semi T&T - Crane and Dump Truck)	350	525	700
1955			
Tonka No. 725 Minute Maid Orange Juice Van	160	240	320
Tonka No. 750 Carnation Milk Delivery Van	150	225	300
Tonka No. No. 880 Pick Up Truck	125	188	250
Tonka No. No. 0850 Lumber Truck, 6 wheel	125	188	250
Tonka No. 0860 Stake Truck, 6 wheel	62	93	125
1956			
Tonka No. 990 Suburban Pumper, 17" long	200	300	400
Tonka No. 991 Farm Stake Truck, 13" long	80	120	160
Tonka No. 992 Aerial Sand Loader Set, Loader and Dump Truck	175	263	350
Tonka No. 994 Sand Loader Set, Loader and Dump Truck	137	206	275

	C6	C8	C10
Tonka No. 996 Wrecker (white color), 12" long	120	180	240
Tonka No. 998 Lumber Truck, 18¾" long	112	168	225
Tonka Fire Dept. Set - Aerial Ladder Semi, Rescue Squad Van and Pumper	450	675	900
Tonka State Highway Department Set - Road Grader Dump Truck, Side Dump Hydraulic Truck, Pickup Truck and six Highway Signs and 2 Road Barriers	400	600	800
1957			
Tonka Big Mike Dual Hydraulic Dump Truck, 14" long	120	180	240
Tonka Gasoline Truck, 15" long (rare)	250	375	500
Tonka Parcel Delivery Van, 12" long	125	188	250
Tonka Pickup w/Box Trailer, 20½" long	100	150	200
Tonka Pickup w/Stake Trailer, 20½" long	112	168	225
Tonka Stock Rack Truck with Animals, 16¼" long	175	263	350
Tonka 3 in 1 Hiway Service Truck, w/2 snowblades, 13" long	200	300	400
Tonka Thunderbird Express Semi, 24" long	300	450	600
1958 Next Generation Cars			
Tonka No. 34 Deluxe Sportsman w/Boat Trailer, 22¾" long	150	225	300
Tonka No. 35 Farm Stake w/Horse Trailer, 21¾" long	75	112	150
Tonka No. 39 Nationwide Moving Semi, 24¼" long	250	375	500
Tonka Sportsman Pickup w/topper, 12¾" long	60	90	120

	C6	C8	C10
1959			
Tonka No. 14 Dragline, 20" long 55	83	110
Tonka No. 30 Tandem Platform Stake w/Trailer, 28¼" long......................140	210	280
Tonka No. 36 Tandem Air Express w/Trailer, 24¾" long......................270	405	540
Tonka No. 41 Boat Transport Semi, 5 pc., 38" long..........................85	128	170
Tonka No. 42 Hydraulic Land Rover, big tires, 15" long.........................112	168	225
Tonka No. 44 Dragline and Semi Trailer, 3 pc., 26¼" long 115	171	230
Tonka B-203 Sanitary Service Truck, 22¾" long 250	375	500
Tonka No. 01 Service Truck, 12¾" long ..55	82	110
Tonka No. 05 Sportsman w/topper and Boat, 12¾" long.............................110	165	220
1960			
Tonka No. 100 Bulldozer, 8⅞" long......50	75	100
Tonka No. 105 Rescue Squad Van, 13¾" long 100	150	200
Tonka No. 110 Fisherman Pickup, 14" long..65	98	130
Tonka No. 115 Power Boom Loader, 18½" long 150	225	300
Tonka No. 120 Cement Mixer Truck, 15½" long 60	90	120
Tonka No. 125 Bulldozer and Low boy Semi, 3 pc., 26¼" long 137	206	275
1961			
Tonka No. 105 Golf Club Tractor, 12½" long 70	105	140
Tonka No. 116 Dump Truck and Sand loader, 23¼" long...................80	120	160

	C6	C8	C10
Tonka No. 136 Houseboat Set with Truck, 29" long 200	300	400
Tonka No. 142 Mobile Clam on Truck, 27¼" long 100	150	200
Tonka No. 145 Tanker Semi, 28" long .165	248	330
1962			
Tonka No. 201 Servi-Car, 9⅛" long......32	48	65
Tonka No. 249 Jeep Universal, 9¾" long 40	60	80
Tonka No. 250 Airport Tractor, 8⅝" long 60	90	120
Tonka No. 250 Jeep Surrey, Stripe Top, 10½" long 48	72	95
Tonka No. 301 Utility Dump Scooter, 12½" long 75	112	150
Tonka No. 402 Bulldozer Loader, 11½" long...40	60	80
Tonka No. 410 Jet Delivery, 14" long ..100	150	200
Tonka No. 420 Luggage Service - Tractor and Trailer, 16⅝"...............100	150	200
1963			
Tonka No. 251 Military Jeep, 10½" long 30	45	60
Tonka No. 422 Backhoe on Truck, 17½" long 125	188	250
Tonka No. 425 Jeep Pumper, 10¾" long 80	120	160
Tonka No. 524 Bulldozer w/Packer, 18¼" long 200	300	400
Tonka No. 530 Truck w/Camper, 14½" long 50	75	100
Tonka No. 534 Trencher, 18¼" long 32	48	65
Tonka No. 640 Ramp Hoist Flat Bed, 19¼" long 715	263	350

TONKA, 1956, No. 994, Sand Loader. Courtesy Thomas G. Nefos, Federal Shipping Network.

TONKA, Dump Truck. Courtesy Thomas G. Nefos, Federal Shipping Network.

	C6	C8	C10
1964			
Tonka No. 375 Jeep Wrecker, 11" long	37	56	75
Tonka No. 384 Jeep w/Box Trailer, 19⅜" long	65	98	130
Tonka No. 720 Terminal Train, 33⅜" long, 4 pc	105	158	210
1964 *(Two series of toys introduced. Smaller versions first, Junior Size follows:)*			
Tonka No. 50 Pickup (Jeep style), 9½" long	32	48	65
Tonka No. 56 Stake Truck, 9½" long	35	52	70

	C6	C8	C10
Tonka No. 68 Wrecker, 9½" long	29	44	58
Tonka No. 70 Camper, 9½" long	75	112	150
Tonka No. 60 Dump, 9½" long	25	38	50
Tonka No. 76 Road Grader, Open, 10¾" long	27	41	55
Tonka No. 77 Cement Mixer, 9" long	32	48	65
Tonka No. 86 Van, Semi, 16" long	36	54	72
Tonka No. No. 90 Livestock Semi, 16" long	32	48	64
Tonka No. 96 Car Carrier Semi, 18½" long	45	68	90

TOOTSIE TOY
(Compiled by C.B.C. Lee)

TOOTSIETOY Funnies No. 5101, 5106. Courtesy Christie's East.

TOOTSIETOY No. 04638.
Courtesy Phillips New York.

	C6	C8	C10
Tootsietoy 4528 Limousine circa 1910, in 1911-1928 catalogs	15	22	30
Tootsietoy 4570 Ford, Model T, open tourer, 1914, in catalog 1915-1926	37	56	75
Tootsietoy 4610 Ford Model T pick-up truck, 1914, in catalog 1919-1932	34	51	68
Tootsietoy 4629 (Yellow Cab) sedan, 1921, in catalog 1923-1933	17	26	35
Tootsietoy 4630 (Federal) "Grocery" delivery van, 1921, in catalog 1924-1933	45	67	90
Tootsietoy 4631 (Federal) "Bakery" delivery van, 1921, in catalog 1924-1933	70	105	140

	C6	C8	C10
Tootsietoy 4632 (Federal) "Market" delivery van, 1921, in catalog 1924-1933	40	60	80
Tootsietoy 4633 (Federal) "Laundry" delivery van, 1921, in catalog 1924-1933	40	60	80
Tootsietoy 4634 (Federal) "Milk" delivery van, 1921, in catalog 1924-1933	30	45	60
Tootsietoy 4635 (Federal) "Florist" delivery van, 1921, in catalog 1924-1933	100	150	200
Tootsietoy 4636 coupe, 1921, in catalog 1924-1933	35	52	70
Tootsietoy 4638 Mack stake truck, 1922, in catalog, 1925-1933	30	45	60

	C6	C8	C10
Tootsietoy 4639 Mack coal truck, 1922, in catalog 1925-1933 35		52	70
Tootsietoy 4641 closed tourer, 1924, in catalog 1925-1933............................47		71	95
Tootsietoy 4642 cannon, in catalog 1931-1941 6		9	12
Tootsietoy 4643 Mack AA Gun Truck, 1922, in catalog 1931-1941 .25		38	50
Tootsietoy 4644 Mack searchlight truck, 1922, in catalog 1931-1941 ..27		41	55
Tootsietoy 4645 Mack "US Mail - Airmail Service," 1922, in catalog 1931-1933 40		60	80
Tootsietoy 4646 Caterpillar tractor, in catalog 1931-1939............................12		18	25
Tootsietoy 4647 (Renault) tank, 1915, in catalog, 1931-1941 22		33	45
Tootsietoy 4648 steamroller, in catalog 1931-1934 100		150	200
Tootsietoy 4651 (Fageol) safety coach, circa 1927, in catalog 1927-1933....50		75	100
Tootsietoy 4652 Fire Engine - hook and ladder, in catalog 1927-1933....75		112	150
Tootsietoy 4653 Fire Engine - water tower, in catalog 1927-1933 40		60	80
Tootsietoy 4654 Farm Tractor, in catalog 1927-1932............................25		37	50
Tootsietoy 4655 Ford, Model A Coupe, 1928, in catalog 1928 -1933 30		45	60
Tootsietoy 4656 (Buick) coupe in tinplate garage, 1930, in catalog 1931-1932 ...90		135	180
Tootsietoy 4657 (Buick) sedan in tinplate garage, 1930, in catalog 1931-1932 90		135	180
Tootsietoy 4658 Mack insurance patrol in garage, in catalog 1931-1932......90		135	180
Tootsietoy 4665 Ford Model A Sedan ..30		45	60
Tootsietoy 4666 Bluebird I Daytona record car, 1927, in catalog 1932-1941 22		33	45
Tootsietoy 4670 Mack tractor and two semi-trailers, 1927, "A&P", "American Express," in catalog 1929-1932 125		188	250
Tootsietoy 4680 "Overland Bus Lines," in catalog 1929-1933..........70		105	140

Left to Right: TOOTSIETOY Moon Mullins Police Patrol Car, TOOTSIETOY Uncle Willie and Mamie in Boat, TOOTSIETOY Kayo Ice Truck. Courtesy PB Eighty-Four, New York..

Left to Right: TOOTSIETOY Herbie & Smitty motorcycle and sidecar, TOOTSIETOY Andy Gump in Roadster. Courtesy PB Eighty-Four, New York..

	C6	C8	C10
Tootsietoy 23 racer with driver, in catalog 1927-1933............................40		60	80
Tootsietoy 190 Mack auto transport (3 Buicks), 1922 in catalog 1931-1933 125		187	250
Tootsietoy 190 Mack auto transport (4 Buicks) 1922, in catalog 1933-1936..100		150	200
Tootsietoy 191 Contractors set, 1932, tractor, 3 tipper trailers...................175		263	350
Tootsietoy 5101 Funnies Set, "Andy Gump" roadster, in catalog 1932-1933, standard version..........290		435	580
Tootsietoy 5102 Funnies Set, "Uncle Walt" roadster, in catalog 1932-1933, standard version 412		618	825
Tootsietoy 5103 Funnies Set, "Smitty" motorcycle with sidecar, in catalog 1932-1933, standard version..........275		363	550
Tootsietoy 5104 Funnies Set, "Moon Mullins" police wagon, in catalog 1932-1933, standard version..........350		525	700
Tootsietoy 5105 Funnies Set, "Kayo" ice wagon, in catalog 1932-1933, standard version 350		525	700
Tootsietoy 5106 Funnies Set, "Uncle Willie" rowboat in catalog 1932-1933, standard version..........250		375	500
Tootsietoy 6001 Buick Roadster, 1926, in catalog 1927-1933 35		52	70
Tootsietoy 6002 Buick coupe, 1926, in catalog 1927-1933............................30		45	60

TOOTSIE TOY, Left to Right; 4670, 4680, 4651, 4634. Courtesy Phillips New York.

TOOTSIETOY, Left to Right; 4665, 5655, unnumbered "U.S. Mail" (sold only in sets), 0716 "Doodlebug". Courtesy Phillips New York.

	C6	C8	C10
Tootsietoy 6003 Buick Brougham, 1926, in catalog 1927-1933	30	45	60
Tootsietoy 6004 Buick sedan, 1926, in catalog 1927-1933	30	45	60
Tootsietoy 6005 Buick closed touring car, 1926, in catalog 1927-1933	35	52	70
Tootsietoy 6006 Buick screenside panel delivery, 1926, in catalog 1927-1933	50	75	100
Tootsietoy 6101 Cadillac roadster, 1926, in catalog 1927-1933	40	80	120
Tootsietoy 6102 Cadillac coupe, 1926, in catalog 1927-1933	40	80	120
Tootsietoy 6103 Cadillac Brougham, 1926, in catalog 1927-1933	40	80	120
Tootsietoy 6104 Cadillac Sedan, 1926 in catalog 1927-1933	40	80	120
Tootsietoy 6105 Cadillac closed Touring car, 1926, in catalog 1927-1933	75	112	150
Tootsietoy 6106 Cadillac Panel Delivery van, 1926, in catalog 1927-1933	27	41	55
Tootsietoy 6201 Chevrolet Roadster, 1926, in catalog 1927-1933	40	60	80
Tootsietoy 6202 Chevrolet Coupe, 1926, in catalog 1927-1933	40	60	80

	C6	C8	C10
Tootsietoy 6203 Brougham, 1926, in catalog 1927-1933	40	60	80
Tootsietoy 6204 Chevrolet Sedan, 1926, in catalog, 1927-1933	40	60	80
Tootsietoy 6205 Chevrolet closed touring car, 1926, in catalog 1927-1933	100	150	200
Tootsietoy 6206 Chevrolet panel delivery van, 1926, in catalog 1927-1933	40	60	80
Tootsietoy 6301 Oldsmobile Roadster, 1926, in catalog 1927-1933	40	60	80
Tootsietoy 6302 Oldsmobile Coupe, 1926, in catalog 1927-1933	40	60	80
Tootsietoy 6303 Oldsmobile Brougham, 1926, in catalog 1927-1933	40	60	80
Tootsietoy 6304 Oldsmobile Sedan, 1926, in catalog 1927-1933	40	60	80
Tootsietoy 6305 Oldsmobile closed touring car, 1926, in catalog 1927-1933	75	112	150-
Tootsietoy 6306 Oldsmobile panel delivery van, 1926, in catalog 1927-1933	40	60	80
Tootsietoy 6-01 Roadster, 1926, in catalog 1933 only	75	112	150

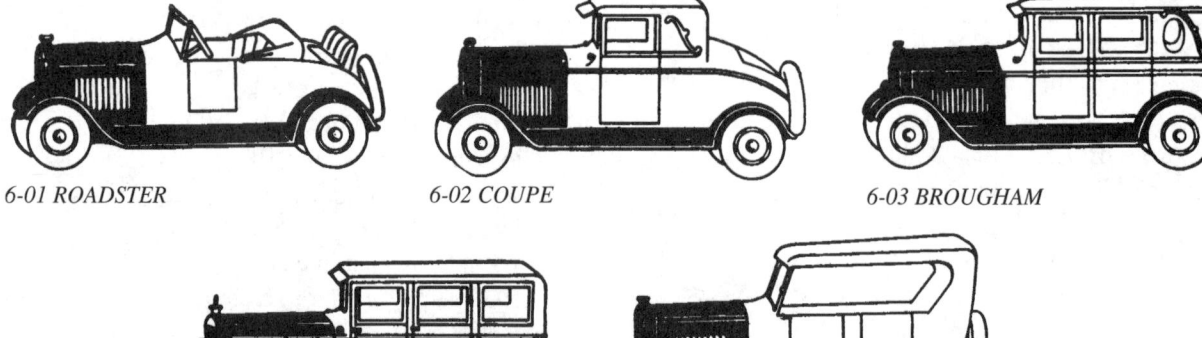

6-01 ROADSTER

6-02 COUPE

6-03 BROUGHAM

6-04 SEDAN

6-05 TOURING CAR

6-06 DELIVERY TRUCK

No, 4652 HOOK AND LADDER

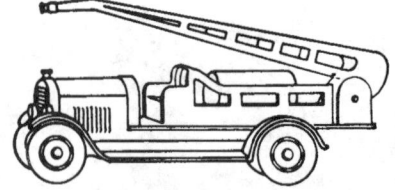

No, 4652 WATER TOWER

	C6	C8	C10
Tootsietoy 6-02 Coupe, 1926, in catalog 1933 only	75	112	150
Tootsietoy 6-03 Brougham, 1926, in catalog 1933 only	75	112	150
Tootsietoy 6-04 Sedan, 1926, in catalog 1933 only	75	112	150
Tootsietoy 6-05 Closed Touring Car, 1926, in catalog 1933 only	110	165	220
Tootsietoy 6-06 Panel Delivery Van, 1926, in catalog 1933 only	75	112	150
Tootsietoy , unnumbered, Ford Model A Van marked "U.S. Mail," sold only in sets	45	67	90
Tootsietoy 4654 Farm Tractor made in special version for Army Field Battery Set No. 5071, with cannons	65	97	130
Tootsietoy Box Trailer and road-scraper raker, sold only in boxed set Farm Tractor No. 7003	135	200	270
Tootsietoy 6665 Ford Model A Sedan, 1928, in catalog 1929-1933	27	41	55
Tootsietoy 101 Buick Coupe (see no. 4656), 1930, in catalog 1932-1934	15	22	30
Tootsietoy 102 Buick Roadster, 1930, in catalog 1932-1934	15	22	30
Tootsietoy 103 Buick Sedan (see no. 4657) 1930, in catalog 1932-1934	15	22	30
Tootsietoy 104 Mack Insurance Patrol (see 4658) in catalog 1932-1934	20	30	40
Tootsietoy 105 Mack tank truck, in catalog 1932-1934	30	45	60
Tootsietoy 108 Caterpillar Tractor, in catalog 1932-1934	12	18	24

	C6	C8	C10
Tootsietoy 109 Ford? Stake pick-up truck, in catalog 1932-1934	25	37	50
Tootsietoy 110 Bluebird I Daytona record car, 1927, in catalog 1932-1934	20	30	40

In the 1933 catalog, rubber tires were introduced, and many earlier models became available with optional rubber tires. Their catalog number was then preceded by the digit "0" so that the "Yellow Cab" with rubber tires, for example, was designated as 04629. New models with rubber tires only were also shown with a prefix of "0", so that the 1932 Macks, Grahams, etc., are thus listed below. However, all "0" prefixes were dropped in the 1937 and later catalogs. Also in the 1933 catalog, use of the new alloy (Zamac) was announced. Earlier models had been of lead and lead alloys. Some lead contamination in later castings resulted in the deterioration of the zamac. Lead-free zamac endures well.

	C6	C8	C10
Tootsietoy 0191 Mack dumper train, 3 carts, 1932 in catalog 1933-1941	125	188	250
Tootsietoy 0192 Mack "Tootsietoy Dairy" train semi-trailer plus two full trailers, 1932, in catalog 1933-1941	115	172	230
Tootsietoy 0198 Mack car transport(three Fords), 1932, in catalog 1935-1941	125	188	250
Tootsietoy 0801 Mack "Express" stake semi-trailer, 1932, in catalog 1933-1941	25	38	50
Tootsietoy 0802 Mack "Domaco" tank semi-trailer, 1932, in catalog 1933-1939	50	75	100

TOOTSIETOY 0802. Photo by Bill Kaufman. Courtesy Good Old Days Store.

TOOTSIETOY 0805. Photo by Bill Kaufman. Courtesy Good Old Days Store.

TOOTSIETOY 0192. Courtesy Phillips New York.

TOOTSIETOY 0806. Courtesy Phillips New York.

	C6	C8	C10
Tootsietoy 0803 Mack "Long Distance Hauling," cargo van, semi-trailer, 1932, in catalog 1933-1936, tin top ..60		90	120
Tootsietoy 0804 "City Fuel Co.," lo-wheel truck, 1932, in catalog 1933-1935 60		90	120
Tootsietoy 0804 "City Fuel," four wheels only, in catalog 1936-1938 ...75		112	150
Tootsietoy 0805 Mack "Tootsietoy Dairy" semi-trailer truck, 1932, in catalog 1933-1939...........................60		90	120
Tootsietoy 0806 Graham Wrecker, 1932, in catalog 1933-1939 50		75	100
Tootsietoy 0807 delivery motorcycle (adapted from 5103), in catalog 1933-34 65		97	130
Tootsietoy 0808 Graham "Tootsietoy Dairy" van, 1932 in catalog 1933-1938 100		150	200
Tootsietoy Graham "Commercial Tire & Supply Co." delivery van, was sold only in sets. 05300 set is shown in 1935 catalog 125		188	250
Tootsietoy 0809 Graham ambulance, 1932, in catalog 1935-1941 20		30	40
Tootsietoy 0810 Mack "Railway Express Co." van (with Wrigley's ad), 1932, in catalog 1935-1939 70		105	140

The larger 1932 Macks were first issued in two-piece castings and dual wheels. In 1936 they were issued as one-piece castings with single rear wheels, worth about $20 less in mint. The tractor for the dumper train was never cast in the later one-piece (set 0191), and the car transport (0198) was never issued in the earlier two-piece casting. Tootsietoy Graham Series: There were several minor changes in chassis castings. Initially, there were none without spare tire on either the sides or rear. The "convertible" coupes and sedans listed below are castings identical to the non-convertible coupe and sedan, but painted two-toned with tan top. The same applies to the later 1934 Fords and 1935 LaSalles.

	C6	C8	C10
Tootsietoy 0511 Graham Roadster, five wheel, 1932, in catalog 1933-1935 60		90	120
Tootsietoy 0512 Graham Coupe, five-wheel, 1932, in catalog 1933-1935 90		135	185
Tootsietoy 0513 Graham Sedan, five-wheel, 1932, in catalog 1933-1935...95		142	190
Tootsietoy 0514 Graham Convertible coupe, five-wheel, 1932, in catalog 1933-1935 40		60	80
Tootsietoy 0515 Graham Convertible sedan, five-wheel, 1932, in catalog 1933-1935 40		60	80
Tootsietoy 0516 Graham Town Car, five-wheel, 1932, in catalog 1933-1935 45		67	90
Tootsietoy 0611 Graham Roadster, six-wheel, 1932, in catalog 1933-1935...50		75	100
Tootsietoy 0612 Graham coupe, six-wheel, 1932, in catalog 1933-1935...40		60	80
Tootsietoy 0613 Graham Sedan, six-wheel, 1932, in catalog 1933-1935.....55		82	110
Tootsietoy 0614 Graham Convertible Coupe, six-wheel, 1932, in catalog 1933-1935 45		67	90
Tootsietoy 0615 Graham Convertible sedan, six-wheel, 1932, in catalog 1933-1935 112		168	225
Tootsietoy 0616 Graham Town Car, six-wheel, 1932, in catalog 1933-1935 45		67	90
Tootsietoy (number not known) Graham Roadster, four-wheel, 1932..62.5		93	125

	C6	C8	C10
Tootsietoy (number not known) Graham Coupe, four-wheel, 1932, in catalog 1935?-1939 (Build-A-Car)	40	60	80
Tootsietoy (number not known) Graham Sedan, four-wheel, 1932, in catalog 1935?-1939 (Build-A-Car)	90	135	180
Tootsietoy 0712 LaSalle Coupe, 1935, in catalog 1936-1938	110	165	220
Tootsietoy 0713 LaSalle Sedan, 1935, in catalog 1936-1938	100	150	200
Tootsietoy 0714 LaSalle Convertible Coupe, 1935, in catalog 1936 only	110	165	220
Tootsietoy 0715 LaSalle Convertible Sedan, 1935, in catalog 1936 only	110	165	220
Tootsietoy 0716 (Briggs Lincoln) prototype "Doodlebug" 1933, in catalog 1936-1937	45	67	90
Tootsietoy 6015 Lincoln (only the grille is accurate, the rest of the body being the same as the Briggs prototype, which was never publicly sold) Zephyr, 1936, in catalog 1937-1939	125	187	250
Tootsietoy 6016 Lincoln Wrecker, 1936, in catalog 1937-1938	175	262	350

Tootsietoy Ford Series

The coupe and sedan in single color and convertible versions and the wrecker were issued in 1935 as 1934 Fords, having a separate grill-piece like the Grahams, the rubber tires mounted on metal hubs. The following year they were recast in one piece as 1935 Fords with slight changes also to the hood louvers and fender skirts and fitted with solid rubber wheels. The roadster, pick-up truck, etc., were not in the 1934 series. *C.B.C. Lee*

	C6	C8	C10
Tootsietoy 0111 Ford V-8 sedan, 1934, in catalog 1935 only	23	35	46
Tootsietoy 0111 Ford V-8 sedan, 1935, in catalog 1936-1939	24	36	48
Tootsietoy 0112 Ford V-8 coupe, 1934, in catalog 1935 only	35	52	70
Tootsietoy 0112 Ford V-8 coupe, 1935, in catalog 1936-1939	27	41	54
Tootsietoy 0113 Ford V-8 wrecker, 1934, in catalog 1935 only	40	60	80
Tootsietoy 0113 Ford V-8 wrecker, 1935, in catalog 1936-1941	22	33	45
Tootsietoy 0114 Ford V-8 convertible coupe, 1934, in catalog 1935 only	40	60	80
Tootsietoy 0115 Ford V-8 convertible sedan, 1934, in catalog 1935 only	40	60	80

	C6	C8	C10
Tootsietoy 0116 Ford V-8 Roadster, 1935, in catalog 1936-1939	22	33	45
Tootsietoy 0117 Zephyr railcar, in catalog 1935-1936	37	56	75
Tootsietoy 0118 DeSoto Airflow sedan, 1935, in catalog 1935-1939	30	45	60
Tootsietoy 0120 Oil Tank Truck, in catalog 1936-1039	17	26	35
Tootsietoy 0121 Ford pick-up truck, 1935, in catalog 1936-1939	21	31	42
Tootsietoy 0123 Ford "Special Delivery" van, 1936, in catalog 1937-1939	32	48	65

This "camelback" van was also issued in several custom liveries by use of a tin-plate insert on the side panels. *C.B.C. Lee*

	C6	C8	C10
Tootsietoy 180 set, Lincoln Zephyr and Roamer house-trailer issued in 1938 with clockwork motor, in 1939 without motor, 1936, in catalog 1938-1939	250	375	500
Tootsietoy 187 Mack car transport (up-tilted), 1932, in catalog 1941	125	188	250
Tootsietoy 4634 Army supply truck (adapted from 1042), in catalog 1939-1941	50	75	100
Tootsietoy 4635 Armored Car, in catalog from 1939 to at least 1941	20	30	40
Tootsietoy 1006 "Standard" oil truck, in catalog from 1939 to at least 1941	25	38	50
Tootsietoy 1007 "Sinclair" oil truck, in catalog from 1939 to at least 1941	30	45	60
Tootsietoy 1008 "Texaco" oil truck, in catalog from 1939 to at least 1941	30	45	60
Tootsietoy 1009 "Shell" oil truck, in catalog from 1939 to at least 1941	25	38	50
Tootsietoy 1010 "Wrigley" box van, in catalog from 1940 to at least 1941	31	46	62
Tootsietoy 1011 Farm tractor, in catalog 1941	40	60	80
Tootsietoy 1016 (Auburn) roadster "torpedo", 1934, in catalog 1936 to at least 1941	27	41	55
Tootsietoy 1017 torpedo coupe, in catalog from 1936 to at least 1941	30	45	60
Tootsietoy 1018 torpedo sedan, in catalog from 1936 to at least 1941	35	52	70
Tootsietoy 1019 pick-up truck in catalog from 1936 to at least 1941	20	30	40
Tootsietoy Greyhound bus (see 1045), in catalog 1941	30	45	60

	C6	C8	C10
Tootsietoy (no number known) Trans-america bus, in set only, in 1941 catalog	42	63	85
Tootsietoy 1027 wrecker, in catalog 1938-1941	22	33	45
Tootsietoy 1040 hook & ladder, in catalog 1937-1941	82	123	165
Tootsietoy 1041 hose car, in catalog 1937-1941	82	123	165
Tootsietoy 1042 Insurance Patrol with open rear, in catalog 1937-1938	25	38	50
Tootsietoy 1042 Insurance patrol with single rear ladder and rear fireman in catalog 1939-1941	35	52	70
Tootsietoy 1043 Ford and small house trailer, 1935, in catalog 1937-1941	60	90	120
Tootsietoy 1044 Roamer house-trailer (see 180 set), in catalog 1937 only	80	120	160
Tootsietoy 1045 Greyhound deluxe bus, 1935, in catalog 1937 to at least 1941	60	90	120
Tootsietoy 1046 station wagon, circa 1939, in catalog 1940 to at least 1941	30	45	60
Tootsietoy 230 (LaSalle) sedan, circa 1939, in catalog 1940 to at least 1941	17	26	35
Tootsietoy 231 coupe, circa 1939, in catalog 1940 to at least 1941	18	27	36
Tootsietoy 232 open touring car, circa 1939, in catalog from 1940 to at least 1941	17	26	35
Tootsietoy 233 boat-tail roadster, circa 1939, in catalog from 1940 to at least 1941	22	33	45
Tootsietoy 234 box van, in catalog from 1940 to at least 1941	16	24	32
Tootsietoy 235 oil tank truck, in catalog from 1940 to at least 1941	13	19	27
Tootsietoy 236 fire engine, hook & ladder, in catalog from 1940 to at least 1941	25	38	50
Tootsietoy 237 fire engine, insurance patrol, in catalog from 1940 to at least 1941	12	18	25
Tootsietoy 238 Fire Engine Hose Wagon, in catalog from 1940 to at least 1941	22	33	45
Tootsietoy 239 station wagon, circa 1939, in catalog from 1940 to at least 1941	22	33	45

Tootsietoy 260 Paramount Air-N-Lite taxi "Yellow," 261 Paramount Air-N-Lite taxi "Checker", 262 fire engine and 263 hook & Ladder were a "Giant Series," shown in 1941 catalog but never released. *End of List by C.B.C. Lee*

Post-War Tootsietoys

	C6	C8	C10
American LaFrance Pumper, 3", 1954	14	21	28
Austin-Healy 100-6 4-passenger roadster, 1956, 6"	27	41	55
Austin-Healy 100-6, 1955, 9"	No Price Found		
Buick Century Estate Wagon, 1954, 6"	27	41	55
Buick LeSabre Experimental Roadster, 1951, 6"	31	46	62
Buick Roadmaster 4-door sedan, 1949, 6"	37	56	75
Buick special experimental coupe, 1954, 6"	26	39	52
Buick Special Fastback, 1947, 4"	20	30	40
Buick Super Estate station wagon, 1948, 6"	95	148	190
Buick Y Experimental Roadster, 4", 1938 (postwar release)	30	45	60
Cadillac 60 special 4-door sedan, 1948, 6"	20	30	40
Cadillac 62 4-door sedan, 6", 1954	22	33	45
Caterpillar Bulldozer, 1956, 6"	25	38	50
Same as above, with blade	30	45	60
Caterpillar Scraper 1956, 6"	21	31	42
Chevrolet Ambulance, 1950	15	22	30
Chevrolet Bel Air four-door sedan, 3", 1955	13	20	26
Chevrolet Cameo Pickup, 4", 1956	25	38	50
Chevrolet Coupe, 1947	25	38	50
Chevrolet Deluxe Panel Truck, 1950, 4"	12	18	25
Same as above, as Army Ambulance	20	30	40
Chevrolet Deluxe Panel Truck, 1950, 3", civilian	12	18	25
Chevrolet El Camino camper truck with boat atop, 1960, 6"	No Price Found		
Chevrolet El Camino pickup truck, 1960, 6"	15	22	31
Chevrolet Fleetline 2-door sedan, 1950 fastback, 3"	15	22	30
Chevrolet Semi with Gooseneck Trailer, 6", 1959	No Price Found		
Chrysler New Yorker 4-door sedan, 1953, 6"	18	27	36
Chrysler 300 2-door hardtop, 1955, 6"	12	18	25
Chrysler Thunderbolt experimental roadster, 1942, (postwar), 6"	35	52	70
Chrysler Windsor convertible, 1941 (released postwar), 4"	22	33	45
Chrysler Windsor convertible, 1950, 6"	12	18	24
Chrysler Windsor convertible, 1960, 4"	12	18	24

TOOTSIETOY Jeep CJ3, 3", 1950. Photo by Ed Poole.

	C6	C8	C10
Corvette Roadster, 1954-55, 4"	12	18	25
Dodge D100 Panel Truck, 6", 1956	32	48	65
Dodge Pickup Truck, 1950, 4"	12	18	25
Ferrari Racer, 6", 1956	9	13	18
Ford B Hot Rod, 1931 (made 1960), 3"	9	13	18
Ford C600 Oil Tanker, 1956, 3"	20	30	40
Ford C600 Truck, 1962, 6"	11	16	22
Ford Country Sedan Station Wagon, 6", 1959	17	26	35
Ford Country Sedan Station Wagon, 1960, 3"	12	18	25
Ford Country Sedan Station Wagon, 1962, 6"	25	38	50
Ford Custom Convertible, 3", 1949	12	18	24
Ford Custom 4-door sedan, 1949, 3"	11	16	22
Ford Customline V-8 2-door sedan, 3", 1955	11	16	22
Ford Econoline Pickup, 1962, 6"	11	16	22
Ford F1 Pickup, 1949, 3"	8	12	16
Ford F6 Oil Tanker, 1949, 6"	18	27	36
Ford F6 Oil Tanker, 4", 1949	10	15	20
Ford F6 Stake Truck, 4", 1949 (no stakes, looks like long pickup)	9	13	18
Ford F100 Styleside Pickup, 3", with rear window, 1957	11	16	22
Ford F100 Styleside Pickup, 3" without rear window	11	16	22
Ford F-600 Army Gun Truck, 6", 1956	22	33	45
Ford F-600 Stake Truck with tin cover, 1955, 6"	25	38	50
Ford Fairlane 500 convertible, 1957, 3"	12	18	24
Ford Falcon, two-door sedan, 1960, 3"	7	11	15
Ford Farm Tractor, 1956, 6"	57	85	115
Ford LTD 2-door hardtop, 4", 1960 (last metal Tootsietoy)	9	13	18
Ford Mainline four-door sedan, 1952, 3"	15	22	30
Ford Ranch Wagon, 1954, 4"	22	33	45
Ford Ranch Wagon, 1954, 3"	16	24	32
Ford Special Deluxe convertible, 1940 (sold 1960), 6"	10	15	20
Ford V-8 Hot Rod, 1940 (made 1960), 6"	15	22	30

	C6	C8	C10
GMC 3571 Greyhound Bus, 1948, 6"	26	39	52
GMC Greyhound Scenicruiser Bus, 1957, 6"	20	30	40
Hook and Ladder Truck, No. 1040 (postwar release), 4"	15	22	30
Hose Car No. 1041 (postwar), 4"	25	38	50
International K1 panel truck, 1941, 4" (postwar release)	27	41	54
International K-11 Oil Tanker, 1946, 6"	26	39	52
International Metro Van, 1960, 6"	30	45	60
International RC 180, 1955, 6", gooseneck Army version with launcher	10	15	20
Same as above, gooseneck	27	41	55
Same as above, grain trailer	10	15	20
Same as above, oil	35	52	70
Same as above, moving van	12	18	24
Same as above, boat transport	No Price Found		
Same as above, car transport	75	112	150
Jaguar type D 1957, 3"	12	18	24
Jaguar XK 120 roadster, 3", 1954	11	16	22
Jaguar XK 140 coupe, 1956, 6"	14	21	28
Jeep, CJ3, Army version, 4", 1950	12	18	25
Same as above, civilian version	7	11	14
Same as above, 3", Army	6	9	12
Same as above, 3", Civilian	10	15	20
Jeep CJ5, 1960, 6"	8	12	16
Same as above, Army version	10	15	20
Same as above, snowplow version	No Price Found		
Jeepster, 1947, 3"	15	22	30
Kaiser Sedan, 6", 1947	22	33	45
Lancia Racer, 1956, 6"	7	11	15
Lincoln Capri 2-door hardtop, 1952, 6"	37	55	75
Mack B Line, 1955, 6", Cement Mixer	22	33	45
Same as above, Hook and Ladder	25	38	50
Same as above, Moving	10	15	20
Same as above, Log	No Price Found		
Mack B Line, 1955, 6", Oil	26	39	52
Same as above, Open Stake	30	45	60
Same as above, Pipe	No Price Found		
Mack L-Line Dump, 1947, 6"	21	31	42
Mack L-Line Fire Pumper, 6", 1947	21	31	42
Mack L-Line with fire trailer (ladder), 1947, 6"	27	41	55
Mack L-Line Truck, 6", 1947, Log	No Price Found		
Same as above, Moving Van	8	12	16
Same as above, Pipe	No Price Found		
Same as above, Stake, closed side	10	15	20
Same as above, stake trailer	20	30	40
Same as above, "Tootsietoys Coast to Coast" trailer truck	10	15	20
Same as above, Tow	20	30	40
Mercedes 190SL Coupe, 1956, 6"	22	33	45

117

	C6	C8	C10
Mercedes 300SL Gullwing Coupe, 1955, 9"..............No Price Found			
Mercury custom sedan, four-door, 1952, 4"............15		22	30
Mercury Fire Chief car, 1949, 4"..........18		27	36
Mercury Sedan, four-door, 1949, 4"......22		33	45
Metro Van, HO series...........................20		30	40
MG TF Roadster, 6", 1954...................17		25	34
Same as above, 3"...............................17		25	35
Nash Metropolitan Convertible, 3", 1954.............14		21	28
Offenhauser Hill Climber Racer, 1947, 3"............9		13	18
Oldsmobile 88 convertible, 4", 1949.....11		16	22
Oldsmobile Dynamic 88 convertible, 6", 1959............14		21	28
Oldsmobile 98 Holiday 2-door hard-top, 1955, army version, 4"..............15		22	30
Same as above, civilian version 18		27	36
Packard Patrician 4-door sedan, 1956, 6"............19		28	38
Plymouth Belvedere 2-door hardtop, 1957, 3"............7		10	14
Plymouth Special Deluxe 4-door Sedan, 3", 1950.............13		20	26
Pontiac Chieftain Deluxe Coupe Sedan, 4", 1950..............15		22	30
Pontiac Chieftain Fire Chief Coupe Sedan, 4"..............22		33	45
Pontiac Safari Station Wagon, 2-door, 1955, 9"............10		15	20
Pontiac Star Chief 4-door sedan, 1959, 4"............12		18	25
Porsche Spyder Roadster, 1956, 6".......26		39	52
Rambler Super Cross-Country 6-cylinder station wagon, 4", 1960.19		29	38
School Bus, HO series..........................12		18	25
Studebaker Champion Coupe, 1947, 3" 40		60	80
Studebaker Lark customer convertible, 3", 1960............10		15	20
Thunderbird Coupe, 4", 1955................12		18	25
Thunderbird Coupe, 3", 1955................9		13	18
Triumph TR3 Roadster, 3", 1956..........10		15	20
Twin Coach Bus, 1950, 3"....................21		31	42
Volkswagen 113 Beetle, 1960, 6"..........12		18	24
Same as above, 3"...............................5		8	10
White Army Half Track, 1941 (postwar), 4"...............15		22	30

End Tootsietoy

Tow Truck, cast iron, 6" long. Courtesy Mapes Auctioneers & Appraisers.

	C6	C8	C10
Tow truck, cast iron, 6" long................70		105	140
Tow truck, cast iron, 7½", rubber wheels.125		187	250
Trailer Truck "C to C C Co.," circa 1929, approx. 6¾" long 45		67	90
Traveleer Land Coach Traveler, Trailer Co., L.A., 1927...................180		270	360
Truck, open back, 4¼" long, cast iron, wheels marked "Hamilton Corhart"...35		52	70
Truck cab with interchangeable flat bed and tank, sheet metal with wooden wheels, 10¾"....................16		24	32
Turner Bulldog Mack closed cab dump truck, red and green steel, 23" long..............400		600	800
Turner Car Hauler 425		638	850
Turner Dump, friction, 15½" long, circa early 1930s 240		360	480
Turner Dump 22" long, C-Cab.............400		600	800
Turner Dump, 26" long 800		1200	1600
Turner Fire Engine Pumper, 15" long ..550		825	1100
Turner Hook and Ladder, 15" long, circa 1930s............225		338	450
Turner Lincoln Sedan, 26" long 1950		2925	3900
Turner "Overland Bus", pressed steel .....No Price Found			
Turner Packard Roadster, 16½" long, 1920s.............900		1350	1800
Turner Packard (?) Roadster, 26" long, friction...................900		1350	1800
Turner Speedster, 1920s, 17" long, circa late 1920s, early 1930s..........500		750	1000
Turner Steam Shovel 150		225	300
Turner Tow Truck................................250		375	500
Turner Water Truck with Copper tank..150		225	300
"U.S. Army Shooting Tank," 6" wood, pre WW II, 6" long, metal action....22		33	45
U.S.A.W. No. 60118 half-track, black wooden wheels, die-cast, approx. 4¾".10		15	20

WILKINS Hook and Ladder open truck, steel, windup motor, 9¾" long. Courtesy Phillips New York.

Choicer small cast iron pieces include: Top Row; A.C. Williams 1934 Ford (series included coupe and sedan); A.C.W. 1936 Ford (series includes coupe, sedan, roadster and panel truck and in a simpler single-piece casting only three, omitting the roadster); A.C.W. generic take-apart (series included coupe, sedan and stake truck). Bottom row shows Arcade 1933 Nash (coupe and sedan); Arcade 1935 Ford (sedan and stake truck); Dent 1935 LaSalle (sedan, coupe, roadster, pick-up truck, wrecker and panel truck). Photo by C.B.C. Lee.

Weeden Auto, live steam, early. Courtesy Sotheby's New York.

	C6	C8	C10
Vindex Coast to Coast Bus, cast iron, circa 1930, 12" long	1250	1875	2500
Vindex Hay Loader	1600	2400	3200
Vindex "P&H" power shovel, cast iron, 12" (17" extended), wheels in caterpillar base, handle revolves rig	2000	3000	4000
Vindex Pick-Up Truck, cast iron, 7½" long	300	450	600
Vindex Racer, cast iron, "2" 11½" long, circa 1920s	1500	2500	3800
Wannatoy Cadillac, 9" long, plastic	7	11	15
Wannatoy Convertible, 6" long	7	11	14
Wannatoy Delivery truck, 4" long	3	4	6
Wannatoy Tank Truck, 5" long	2	3	5
Weeden Auto, live steam, 8¾" early	1500	3000	4500
Weeden Steam Fire Pumper	1200	2000	3000
Weeden Steam Road Roller, 1920s, 7" long, brass, tin, cast iron, steam toy fired by alcohol	250	375	500
Weeden Steam Tractor, 9"	250	375	500
Wilkins Aerial Ladder Truck, 1910, 18" windup	500	750	1000
Wilkins Fire Engine, circa 1900, with driver, steam boiler	125	188	250
Wilkins Hook and Ladder open truck, steel, wind-up motor, 9¼" long	150	225	300
Wilkins, Olds, 1904, curved dash, wind-up, 10"	400	600	800
Wilkins Truck, open cab, 11" long, very early, clockwork	450	675	900

A.C. WILLIAMS

A.C. Williams was founded in 1886 when Adam Clark Williams (1/22/1848-6/15/32) bought the J.W. Williams Company from his father. After a fire the firm was moved in 1893 from Chagrin Falls, Ohio to Ravenna. Toy production began about this time. Small cast iron toys were Williams' specialty, with banks, cars and aircraft predominant. A.C. Williams retired in 1919, but the firm continued to make toys until 1938, after which it continued in business in a non-toys capacity. Williams marked few, if any, of its toys. Two clues to an A.C. Williams toy are turned steel hubs and starred axle peens.

	C6	C8	C10
Williams Car Carrier, with three Austins, 1920	700	1050	1400
Williams Coupe, 3" long, 2-piece body, 1936	70	105	140
Williams Coupe, rumble seat, side mounts, 1930, cast iron, rubber tires, 6¾" long	175	262	350
Williams Delivery Van, 8"	350	525	700
Williams four-casting nickeled radiator car, approx. 4" long	75	112	150
Williams Laundry Truck, 8" long	400	600	800
Williams Lincoln Touring Car, 7" long	150	225	300
Williams Mack Gas Tank Truck, 3¾" long	45	68	90
Williams Mack Gas Tank Truck, 5⅛" long	65	98	130

WILLIAMS Sedan, 6½" long. Courtesy Phillips New York.

	C6	C8	C10
Williams Mack Gas Tank Truck, 7¼" long 112	168	225
Williams Mack Stake Truck, 3½" long .45	68	90
Williams Mack Stake Truck, 4¼" long .90	135	180
Williams Mack Stake Truck, 5⅛" long 112	170	225
Williams Mack Stake Truck, 7" long ...150	225	300
Williams Mack Stake Truck, 8½" long 200	300	400
Williams Mack Truck, 3½" long 45	68	90
Williams Mack Truck, 4¾" long 55	82	110
Williams Mack Truck, 6¾" long 100	150	200
Williams Model T Coupe, 6" long 125	187	250
Williams Racer, boat-tailed, 6½" long .175	262	350
Williams Sedan, circa 1930, cast iron, 6½" long, streamlined rear fender .225	337	450
Williams Sedan, 6¾"long, circa 1931, cast iron, interchangeable body 170	255	340
Williams Stake Truck 7" long, circa 1931, interchangeable body 170	225	340
Williams Steamroller, 5½", 1930s.........75	112	150
Williams Studebaker, circa 1933-34, approx. 4" long, two tone sedan 110	165	220
Williams Tank, 4" long.........................67	101	135
Williams Touring Car, 9½" long, cast iron 450	675	900
Willys Knight, cast iron, 8" long, 1920s, with driver 120	180	240
Winross Roadway Express 40	60	80
Winross Sunoco truck.........................22	33	45
Wolverine Car & Trailer, 27" long, press down to operate 75	112	150
Wolverine "Mystery Car," press down to make car move, circa 1938 100	150	200
Wolverine Speeding Bus "5 Via Main St." tin litho, driver and occupants, 14" long, "19302," press down on rear to move 50	75	100
Wolverine Taxi, 13" long, tin 100	150	200
Wolverine "White Mustang" dump truck, 14" long..............................50	75	100
Wood Commodities Corp. Army Jeep and Cannon, 23" long 62	93	125

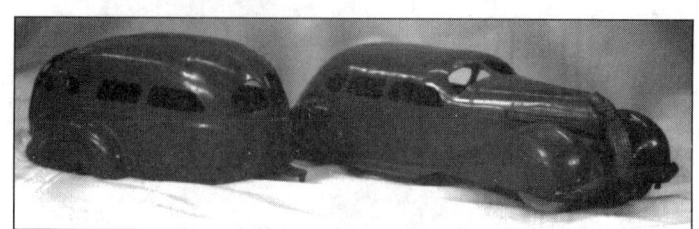

WYANDOTTE LaSalle Sedan with trailer. Photo by Calvin L. Chaussee.

WYANDOTTE
(ALL METAL PRODUCTS COMPANY)

Wyandotte seems to have been formed in the early 1920s, with pistols and rifles its main product. But by 1935 the Wyandotte, Michigan firm became best known for its simply built, streamlined, art deco steel cars and trucks, almost all of them employing wooden wheels. During WW II it made clips for the M-1 rifle, and after the war moved to Piqua, Ohio. In an attempt to diversify, it bought the Hafner trains line, but went out of business in 1956. Wyandotte's heavy gauge steel toys with baked enamel finish also included aircraft, doll buggies, musical toys, wagons and games.

	C6	C8	C10
Wyandotte Ambulance, 11¼" long, swinging rear door, No. 340...........112	168	225
Wyandotte Army Truck, 10" long, steel with wood wheels 45	68	90
Wyandotte Army Truck, 22" long 100	150	200
Wyandotte Auto Transport, circa 1950s ..75	112	200
Wyandotte Bank Truck, 6½" long.........45	68	90
Wyandotte boattail racer, 8½" long, steel, red with white rubber tires, electric headlamps...........................64	96	128
Wyandotte Car Carrier, early 1930s 80	120	160
Wyandotte Car Carrier, late, 22" long ...50	75	100
Wyandotte Circus Truck, 10¾" long 110	165	220
Wyandotte Circus Truck, No. 503, 11" long 400	600	800
Wyandotte Circus Truck with Trailer, 19" long.....................................250	375	500
Wyandotte City Delivery Truck, circa 1940 117	175	235
Wyandotte Coffin Nose Cord, 13" long, pressed steel, rubber tires......325	488	650
Wyandotte Coffin Nose Cord, Fire Dept. version, red...........................475	715	950
Wyandotte Convertible (Open) Roadster, 10" long, 1930s..............110	165	220
Wyandotte Coupe, 2-door, about 1930, 6"..35	52	70
Wyandotte Coupe, 6", circa 1940..........25	38	50
Wyandotte Coupe, 7½" long, 1930s......50	75	100
Wyandotte Coupe, 8" long, with rumble seat, early 1930s...........................80	120	160

WYANDOTTE Circus Truck, 10¾".

WYANDOTTE Oil Tanker, 1930s.. Photo by Calvin L. Chaussee.

WYANDOTTE Side Dump, 1930s, 20" long. Photo by Calvin L. Chaussee.

	C6	C8	C10
Wyandotte Coupe, circa 1935, red with white rubber tires, electric headlights, 8½" long	60	90	120
Wyandotte Dairy Truck, 1930s, 12" long	100	150	200
Wyandotte "Deluxe Delivery" truck, 11" long, circa 1936	100	150	200
Wyandotte Dump Truck No. 122	45	67	90
Wyandotte Dump Truck No. 124	50	75	100
Wyandotte Dump Truck, 6", 1930s	150	225	300
Wyandotte Dump Truck, pressed steel, approx. 6½" long, circa 1940	40	60	80
Wyandotte Dump Truck, steel, 7" long, circa 1937	35	52	70
Wyandotte Dump Truck, 12"	50	75	100
Wyandotte Dump Truck, circa mid-1930s, 15" long, white rubber tires	80	120	160
Wyandotte Dump Truck, 1930s, 12H" long	60	90	120
Wyandotte Dump w/Sand Loader, circa 1941	300	450	600
Wyandotte Dump w/Scoop, post war	50	75	100
Wyandotte "Express" trailer truck, tin wheels	75	112	150
Wyandotte Fire Truck, 12", with ladder, ringing bell, 1939	100	150	200
Wyandotte "Grey Van," late, 24" long	112	168	225
Wyandotte Hydraulic Dump Truck, rear and side tip, 20" long	90	135	180

	C6	C8	C10
Wyandotte Ice Truck, marked "ICE" on sides, circa 1940, No. 348	55	82	110
Wyandotte LaSalle Sedan, 1930s	240	360	480
Wyandotte LaSalle Sedan w/trailer, 25½" long, 1930s	300	450	600
Wyandotte "Lazy Daisy Farms" truck	150	225	300
Wyandotte "Medical Corps" open truck, ca. 1939, 12" long	125	188	250
Wyandotte Motor Express Trailer Truck, circa 1950s	70	105	140
Wyandotte "Official AAA Service Car", 1930s, 12" long	150	225	300
Wyandotte Oil Tanker, 1930s	150	225	300
Wyandotte Pickup Truck, 6" long, circa late 1930s	30	45	60
Wyandotte "Pickway Pastures" Livestock truck	160	240	320
Wyandotte Race Car, 8½" long, pressed steel, rubber tires, circa 1937	85	128	170
Wyandotte Railway Express Truck, 12" long, circa 1939	222	333	445
Wyandotte School Bus, 1930s, 24" long	100	150	200
Wyandotte Sedan, 4" long, circa 1940	35	52	70
Wyandotte Sedan, 6", circa 1940	30	45	60

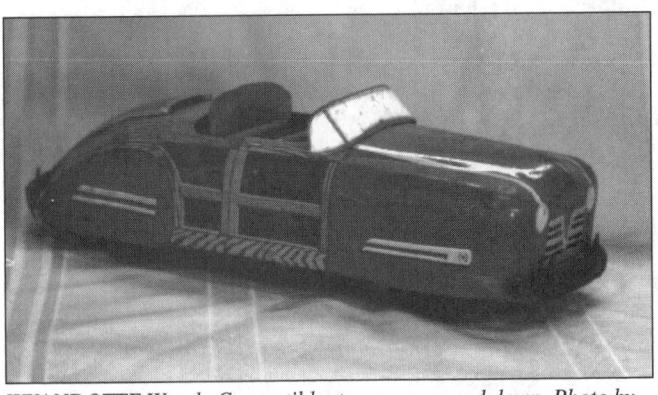

WYANDOTTE Woody Convertible, top goes up and down. Photo by Calvin L. Chaussee.

WYANDOTTE Stake Truck, 10" long, battery-operated headlights. Courtesy Mapes Auctioneers & Appraisers.

WYANDOTTE "Wyandotte Truck Lines" stake van. Photo by Calvin L. Chaussee.

	C6	C8	C10
Wyandotte Semi, Grey Lines, cast wheels	100	150	200
Wyandotte Semi-Trailer Stake Truck "Valley Farms Livestock Produce" 2-piece, 8½" long, 1940s	100	150	200
Wyandotte Side Dump, 1930s, 20" long	45	68	90
Wyandotte Stake Truck, 5½" long, rubber wheels	27	41	55
Wyandotte Stake Truck about 1930, 6¾"	27	41	55
Wyandotte Stake Truck 1930s, 7½", white rubber wheels	37	56	75
Wyandotte Stake Truck, 1931, 9¾" long, No. 325	125	188	250
Wyandotte Stake Truck, 10" long, battery-operated headlights	100	150	200

	C6	C8	C10
Wyandotte Stake Truck, 12" long, circa 1930s	75	112	150
Wyandotte Stake Truck, 15" long, 1930s	125	188	250
Wyandotte Stake Truck, 20"	65	98	130
Wyandotte Station Wagon, Cadillac, 1941, Woody model, 21" long, metal, No. 1007	150	225	300
Wyandotte Steam Shovel	55	82	110
Wyandotte Sunshine Dairy Truck, 12"	60	90	120
Wyandotte Tow Truck, late	55	82	110
Wyandotte Town & Country Chrysler convertible, 1940s, 12" long	125	188	250
Wyandotte "Toytown Delivery", 21" long, 1941	150	225	300
Wyandotte "Toytown Estate" Station Wagon	250	375	500
Wyandotte "Toytown Ice Co.", circa 1941	200	300	400
Wyandotte Trailer Truck, plastic cab	65	98	130
Wyandotte Trailer truck, 1950, extruded aluminum trailer	100	150	200
Wyandotte "Valley Farms", 8½" long	100	150	200
Wyandotte Woody Convertible, 12" long, top converts	115	172	230
Wyandotte Wrecker, 1930s, wooden wheels, 10" long	41	62	82
Wyandotte "Wyandotte Truck Lines" stake van	80	120	160
Wyandotte "Wyandottey," pressed steel two-door sedan, sweeping long fenders, circa WW II black plastic wheels	30	45	60

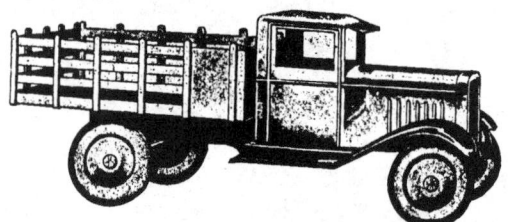

A Wyandotte ad from December, 1931, in Toys and Novelties magazine.

MATCHBOX

Matchbox began in London, England, with the partnership of longtime friends Leslie and Rodney Smith, who in 1947 combined portions of their first names to form Lesney Products. Business began in a former pub, and consisted of industrial zinc diecastings. Toys were added as a sideline, and in 1952 England's Woolworth's encouraged the Smiths to expand their toys line. In 1953 the I-75 series began, and in 1954 the firm began using the Matchbox name. Sales to Japan began in 1958, and to the U.S. in 1959. Lesney was acquired by Universal holdings (since 1986 known as Matchbox Toys) in 1982. In 1987 Matchbox, of Moonachie, New Jersey, was one of the top three toy car makers, selling 77 million vehicles. Matchboxes are modeled to a one-sixty-fourth scale. (Moses Kohnstadt was the firm's first agent and sold the toys under his own label, Moko, using portions of his name. Lesney later acquired Moko.) The C10 prices are for **unboxed** Matchbox.

Different versions of MATCHBOX boxes. Courtesy Gary Linden.

	C6	C8	C10
No. 1 Diesel Road Roller, 1953	12	18	25
No. 1 Aveling Barford Road Roller, 1964	15	23	30
No. 1 Mercedes Benz Lorry, 1968	4	6	8
No. 1 Mod Rod, 1971	5	7.50	10
No. 1 Dodge Challenger, 1976	3	5	7
No. 2 Dumper, 1953	12	18	25
No. 2 Muir-Hill Dumper, 1962	6	9	12
No. 2 Mercedes Trailer, 1968	4	6	8
No. 2 Hot Rod Jeep, 1971	3	4.50	6
No. 2 Hovercraft, 1976	4.50	6.75	9
No. 3 Cement Mixer, 1953	17	26	35
No. 3 Bedford Ton Tipper, 1961	4	6	8

	C6	C8	C10
No. 3 Mercedes Benz Ambulance, 1968	6	9	12
No. 3 Monteverdi Hai, 1973	4.50	6.75	9
No. 3 Porsche Turbo, 1978	4	6	8
No. 4 Tractor, 1954	25	38	50
No. 4 Triumph Motorcycle and sidecar, 1959	12	23	30
No. 4 Stake Truck, 1967	3	4.50	6
No. 4 Gruesome Twosome, 1971	3	4.50	6
No. 4 Pontiac Firebird, 1976	3	4.50	6
No. 4 '57 Chevy, 1981	2.50	3.75	5
No. 5 London Bus, 1954	15	23	30
No. 5 Lotus Europea Sports Car, 1969	10	15	20
No. 5 Seafire, 1976	2	3	4
No. 5 U.S. Mail Truck, 1981	2	3	4
No. 6 Quarry Truck, 1955	12	18	25
No. 6 Euclid 10-wheel Quarry, 1964	12	18	25
No. 6 Ford Pick-Up, 1969	6	9	12
No. 6 Mercedes Tourer, 1974	4	6	8
No. 7 Horse Drawn Milk Cart, 1955	35	53	70
No. 7 Ford Anglia, 1961	12	18	25
No. 7 Ford Refuse Truck, 1967	5	7.50	10
No. 7 Hairy Hustler, 1971	4.50	6.75	9

MATCHBOX No. 7 Horse-drawn Milk Cart. Courtesy Gary Linden.

MATCHBOX No. 9 Merryweather Marquis Fire Truck. Courtesy Gary Linden.

MATCHBOX No. 12 Land Rover. Courtesy Gary Linden.

MATCHBOX No. 14 Bedford Lomas Ambulance. Courtesy Gary Linden.

	C6	C8	C10
No. 7 VW Golf, 1976	3	4.50	6
No. 8 Caterpillar Tractor, 1955	15	22	30
No. 8 Ford Mustang Fastback, 1966	6	10	13
No. 8 Wildcat Dragster, 1971	6	9	12
No. 8 De Tomaso Pantera, 1975	6	9	12
No. 9 Dennis Fire Engine, 1955	25	38	50
No. 9 Merryweather Marquis Fire Engine, 1959	8	12	16
No. 9 Boat & Trailer, 1967	4	6	8
No. 9 Javelin, 1972	4.50	6.75	9
No. 9 Ford Escort RS2000, 1978	2.50	3.75	5
No. 10 Mechanical Horse & Trailer, 1955	30	45	60
No. 10 Sugar Container Truck, 1961	12	18	25
No. 10 Pipe Truck, 1967	10	15	20
No. 10 Piston Popper, 1973	4.50	6.75	9
No. 10 Plymouth 'Gran Fury' Police Car, 1980	2	3	4
No. 11 Petrol Tanker (Esso decal), 1955	15	22	30
No. 11 Jumbo Crane (Taylor), 1964	6	9	12
No. 11 Scaffolding Truck (Mercedes), 1969	4.50	6.75	9
No. 11 Flying Bug, 1972	4.50	6.75	9
No. 11 Car Transporter, 1977	4	6	8
No. 12 Land Rover, 1953	10	15	20
No. 12 Safari Land Rover, 1965	8	12	16
No. 12 Setra Coach, 1971	7.50	11	15
No. 12 Big Bull, 1975	4.50	6.75	9
No. 12 Citroen CX, 1981	4.50	6.75	9
No. 13 Bedford Wreck Truck, 1955	15	22	30
No. 13 Thames Wreck Truck (MB Garages), 1959	20	30	40
No. 13 Dodge Wreck Truck (BP Label), 1961	11	16	22

	C6	C8	C10
No. 13 Baja Buggy, 1971	4.50	6.75	9
No. 13 Snorkel Fire Engine, 1977	2	3	4
No. 14 Daimler Ambulance, 1955	10	15	20
No. 14 Bedford Lomas Ambulance, 1962	7	11	15
No. 14 Iso Grifo Sports Car, 1968	5	8	11
No. 14 Mini Ha Ha, 1975	6	9	12
No. 15 Prime Mover, 1955	20	30	40
No. 15 Dennis Refuse Truck, 1963	10	15	20
No. 15 Volkswagen 1500 Saloon, 1968	6	9	13
No. 15 Fork Lift Truck, 1972	3.50	5.25	7
No. 16 Low-Loading Trailer, 6 wheels, 1955	14	21	28
No. 16 Low-Loading Trailer, 8 wheels, 1955	14	21	28

MATCHBOX "Home Stores" building, 3" long.. Courtesy Gary Linden.

MATCHBOX No. 19 MGA, Sports Car. Courtesy Gary Linden.

	C6	C8	C10
No. 16 Scammel Mountaineer Dump with Plow, 1961 10	15	20
No. 16 Case Tractor Bulldozer, 1969 6	9	13
No. 16 Badger, 1974 ....4.50	6.75	9
No. 16 Pontiac, 1981 2	3	4
No. 17 Bedford Removal Van, 1955 15	22	30
No. 17 Austin Taxi, 1960 20	30	40
No. 17 8-Wheel Tipper "Hover-ingham", 1964............................5	7.50	10
No. 17 Horse Box "Ergomatic Cab", 1969 4	6	8
No. 17 Londoner, 1973 ....4.50	6.75	9
No. 18 Caterpillar Bulldozer, 1955 14	21	28
No. 18 Field Car, 1969 4	6	8
No. 18 Hondarora, 1975 ....4.50	6.75	9
No. 19 MG Midget Sports Car, 1955 17	27	35
No. 19 MGA Sports Car, 1959.............12	18	25
No. 19 Aston-Martin F.I., 1961 20	30	40
No. 19 Lotus Racing Car, 1965 ....3.50	5.25	7
No. 19 Road Dragster, 1971.................3.50	5.25	7
No. 19 Cement Truck, 1976 3	4.50	6
No. 20 E.R.F. Lorry Truck, 1955...........20	30	40
No. 20 Taxi Cab (Chevrolet Impala), 1965 5	8	11
No. 20 Lamborghini Marzel, 1969 ......4.50	6.75	9
No. 20 Police Patrol, 1975 ....2.50	3.75	5
No. 21 Long Distance Coach "London To Glasgow", 1955 20	30	40
No. 21 Commer Milk Truck, 1961 12	18	24
No. 21 Foden Concrete Truck, 1969 6	9	13
No. 21 Road Roller, 1973 ....4.50	6.75	9
No. 22 Vauxhall Cresta, 1955...............17	26	35
No. 22 Pontiac 'Grand Prix' Sports Coupe, 1964 ....7.50	11.25	15
No. 22 Freeman Inter City Com-muter, 1970............................4.50	6.75	9

	C6	C8	C10
No. 22 Blaze Buster, 1975.......................2	3	4
No. 23 Caravan Trailer, 1956...............3.50	5.25	7
No. 23 House Trailer Caravan, 1967.....12	18	24
No. 23 Volkswagen Camper, 1970.......3.50	5.25	7
No. 23 Atlas, 1975.................................3	4.50	6
No. 24 Excavator, 1956 11	16.50	22
No. 24 Rolls Royce Silver Shadow, 1967......................................3.50	5.25	7
No. 24 Team 'Matchbox', 1973 3	4.50	6
No. 24 Diesel Shunter, 1979...................2	3	4
No. 25 Bedford 'Dunlop' Van, 1956.....25	38	50
No. 25 Volkswagen 1200 Sedan, 1958 25	38	50
No. 25 B.P. Tanker, 1960.......................14	21	28
No. 25 Ford Cortina G.T., 1968...........3.50	5.25	7
No. 25 Mod Tractor, 1972 3	4.50	6

MATCHBOX No. 28 Bedford Compressor Truck. Courtesy Gary Linden.

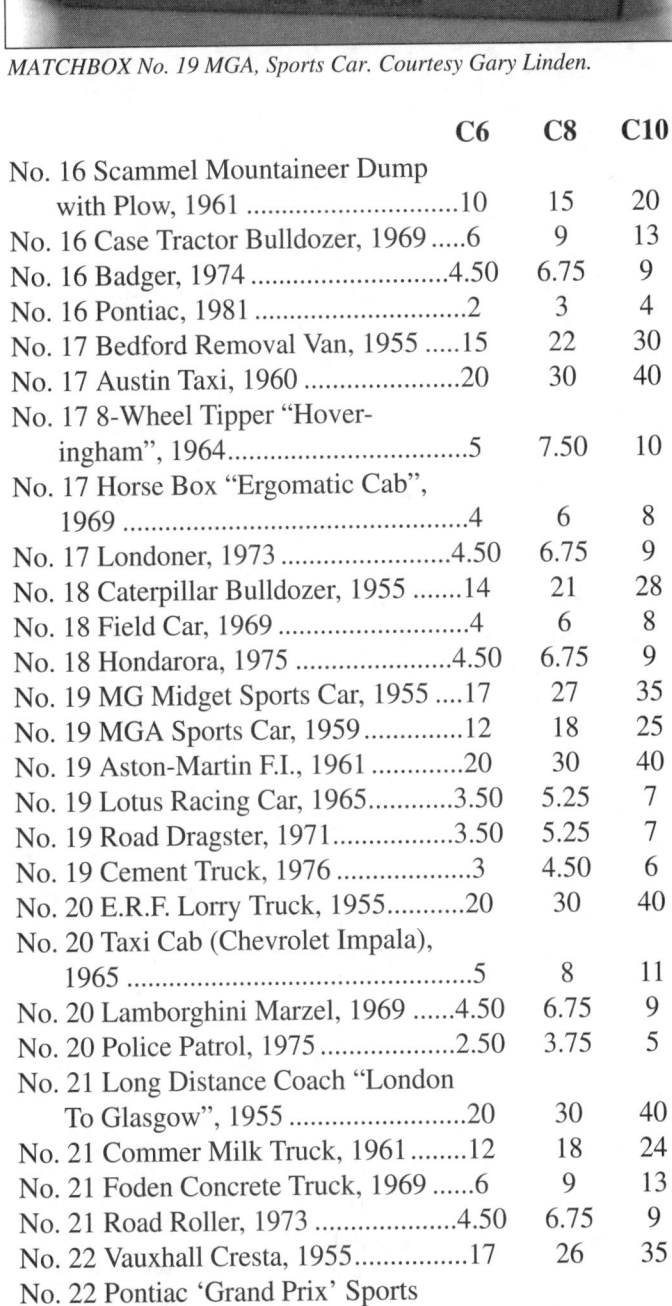

MATCHBOX No. 37 Coca-Cola Truck. Courtesy Gary Linden.

MATCHBOX No. 36 Lambretta Motorcycle with sidecar. Courtesy Gary Linden.

	C6	C8	C10
No. 25 Flat Car & Container, 1979 3	4.50	6
No. 26 Ready Mix Concrete Truck, 1956 12	18	24
No. 26 G.M.C. Tipper Truck, 1968 4	6	8
No. 26 Big Banger, 1972 3	4.50	6
No. 26 Site Dumper, 1976 ....2.50	3.75	5
No. 27 Bedford Low Loader, 1956 17	27	35
No. 27 Cadillac Sedan, 1960 30	45	60
No. 27 Mercedes Benz, 230SL, 1965 ..4.50	6.75	9
No. 27 Lamborghini Countach, 1974 ..3.50	5.25	7
No. 28 Bedford Compressor Truck, 1956 ..16	24	32
No. 28 Thames Compressor Truck, 1959 .10	15	20
No. 28 Mark Ten Jaguar, 1964 15	23	30
No. 28 Mack Dump Truck, 1968 ....3.50	5.25	7
No. 28 Stoat, 1974 ....2.50	3.75	5
No. 28 Lincoln Continental, 1980 ....4.50	6.75	9
No. 29 Bedford Milk Delivery Van, 1956 ..12	18	25
No. 29 Austin A55 Cambridge, 1961 15	22	30

	C6	C8	C10
No. 29 Fire Pumper Truck, 1965 6	7	12
No. 29 Racing Mini, 1971 3	4.50	6
No. 29 Shovel Nose Tractor, 1976 ......2.50	3.75	5
No. 30 Ford Prefect with Towbar, 1956 17	25	35
No. 30 German Crane Truck, 1961 16	24	32
No. 30 Favin Crane, 8 wheel, 1965 7	11	15
No. 30 Beach Buggy, 1971 ....2.50	3.75	5
No. 30 Swamp Rat, 1977 ....2.50	3.75	5
No. 30 Articulated Truck, 1981 2	3	4
No. 31 Ford Customline Station Wagon, 1956 20	30	40
No. 31 Ford Fairlane Station Wagon, 1959 20	30	40
No. 31 Lincoln Continental, 1964 5	8	10
No. 31 Volks Dragon, 1971 ....4.50	6.75	9
No. 31 Caravan, 1977 ....2.50	3.75	5
No. 32 Jaguar XK 140 Coupe, 1956 20	30	40
No. 32 Leyland Tanker, 1968 6	9	12
No. 32 Excavator, 1981 10	15	20
No. 33 Ford Zodiac MKII, 1956 20	30	40
No. 33 Ford Zephyr 6 MKIII, 1963 14	21	28
No. 33 Lamborghini Muira P400, 1969 ..4.50	6.75	9
No. 33 Datsun 126X, 1973 ....3.50	5.25	7
No. 33 Police Motorcyclist, 1977 2	3	4
No. 34 Volkswagen Microvan 'Matchbox' Express, 1956 20	30	40
No. 34 Volkswagen Camper, 1961 8	12	17
No. 34 Formula 1 Racing Car, 1971 4	6	8
No. 34 Vantastic, 1976 ....2.50	3.75	5
No. 34 Chevy Pro Stocker, 1981 2	3	4
No. 35 Marschall Horse Box, 1956 35	52	70
No. 35 Sno-Trac Tractor, 1961 8	12	16
No. 35 Merryweather Marquis Fire Engine, 1970 4	6	8
No. 35 Fandango, 1975 ....4.50	6.75	9
No. 36 Austin A50 with Towbar, 1956 .15	22	30
No. 36 Lambretta & Sidecar, 1960 30	45	60

MATCHBOX No. 38 Darrier Refuse Collector. Courtesy Gary Linden.

MATCHBOX No. 46 Morris Minor 1000. Courtesy Gary Linden.

MATCHBOX No. 47 Trojan "Brooke Bond Tea" van. Courtesy Gary Linden.

	C6	C8	C10
No. 36 Opel Diplomat, 1966	4	6	8
No. 36 Hot Rod Draguar, 1971	4.50	6.75	9
No. 36 Formula 5000, 1975	3	4.50	6
No. 36 Refuse Truck, 1981	2.50	3.75	5
No. 37 Coca-Cola Truck, 1956	24	36	48
No. 37 Cattle Truck (Dodge), 1967	4.50	6.75	9
No. 37 Soopa Coopa, 1973	4.50	6.75	9
No. 37 Skip Truck, 1976	2	3	4
No. 38 Darrier Refuse Collector	15	22	30
No. 38 Vauxhall Estate, 1963	10	15	20
No. 38 Honda Motorcycle with Trailer, 1968	6	9	12
No. 38 Stingeroo, 1973	4.50	6.75	9
No. 38 Armored Jeep, 1976	2.50	3.75	5
No. 38 Camper, 1981	2	3	4
No. 39 Ford Zodiac Convertible, 1956	15	22	30
No. 39 Pontiac Convertible, 1962	20	30	40
No. 39 Ford Tractor, 1967	5	8	11
No. 39 Clipper, 1973	4.50	6.75	9
No. 39 Rolls-Royce Silver Shadow MKII	3.50	5.25	7
No. 40 Bedford 7 Ton Tipper, 1956	15	23	30
No. 40 Hay Trailer, 1967	2.50	5.25	7
No. 40 Leyland 'Royal Tiger' Coach/Long Distance, 1961	9	14	18
No. 40 Guildsman, 1971	4.50	6.75	9
No. 40 Horse Box, 1977	2.50	3.75	5
No. 41 'D' Type Jaguar Racing Car, 1956	60	90	120
No. 41 Ford G.T. 40 (Sports Racer), 1965	7	10	14
No. 41 Siva Spyder, 1972	4.50	6.75	9
No. 41 Ambulance, 1978	2.50	3.75	5
No. 42 Bedford 'Evening News' Van, 1956	22	33	45
No. 42 Studebaker Lark Wagonaire, 1965	9	13	18
No. 42 Iron Fairy Crane, 1969	4.50	6.75	9

	C6	C8	C10
No. 42 Tyre Fryer, 1972	4	6	8
No. 42 Container Truck, 1977	4	6	8
No. 43 Hillman Minx, 1957	25	38	50
No. 43 Aveling-Barford Shovel, 1962	6	9	12
No. 43 Pony Trailer, 1968	6	9	12
No. 43 Dragon Wheels, 1972	3.50	5.25	7
No. 43 Steam Loco, 1978	2	3	4
No. 44 Rolls-Royce Silver Cloud, 1957	12	18	24
No. 44 Refrigerator Truck, GMC, 1967	3.50	5.25	7
No. 44 Boss Mustang, 1972	2	3	4
No. 44 Passenger Coach, 1978	2	3	4
No. 45 Vauxhall Victor, 1957	12	18	25
No. 45 Ford Corsair with Green Boat, 1959	6	9	12
No. 45 Ford Group Six, 1970	4.50	6.75	9
No. 45 BMW, 1976	4.50	6.75	9
No. 46 Morris Minor 1000, 1957	25	38	50
No. 46 Pickfords Removal Van, 1960	11	16	22
No. 46 Mercedes-Benz 300SE, 1968	6	9	12

MATCHBOX No. 49 Army Half Track MK III. Courtesy Gary Linden.

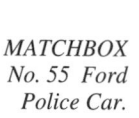

MATCHBOX No. 54 Army Saracen Personnel Carrier.

MATCHBOX No. 55 Ford Police Car.

	C6	C8	C10
No. 46 Stretcha Fetcha, 1972 ....2.50	3.75	5
No. 46 Ford Tractor, 1978 ....3.50	5.25	7
No. 47 Trojan 'Brooke Bond' Van, 1957 ..22	33	45
No. 47 Neilson Ice Cream Van, 1963 10	15	20
No. 47 Daf Tipper Container Truck, 1968 .4	6	8
No. 47 Beach Hopper, 1973 ....4.50	6.75	9
No. 47 Pannier Loco, 1980 ....1.50	2.25	3
No. 48 Sports Boat & Trailer, 1957 17	25	35
No. 48 Dodge Dumper Truck, 1967 4	6	8
No. 48 Pi-Eyed Piper, 1973 3	4.50	6
No. 48 Sambron Jack Lift, 1977 2	3	4
No. 49 Army Half Track MKIII, 1958 ..13	21	27
No. 49 Mercedes Unimog Truck, 1967 ....4.50	6.75	9
No. 49 Chop Suey, 1973 ....4.50	6.75	9
No. 49 Crane Truck, 1976 ....1.50	2.25	3

	C6	C8	C10
No. 50 Commer Pick-up Truck, 1958 ...16	24	32
No. 50 John Deere-Lanz Tractor, 1963 ..8	12	16
No. 50 Ford Kennel Truck, 1969 7	11	14
No. 50 Articulated Truck, 1973 3	4.50	6
No. 50 Harley Davidson Motorcycle, 1981 2	3	4
No. 51 Albion Truck 'Portland Cement', 1958 ....12.50	18.75	25
No. 51 Tipping Farm Trailer, 1963 5	7.50	10
No. 51 8 Wheel Tipper Truck, 1969 4	6	8
No. 51 Citroen SM, 1972 4	6	8
No. 51 Combine Harvester, 1979 ....2.50	3.75	5
No. 52 Maserati 4 CLT, 1958 25	38	50
No. 52 BRM Racing Car, 1965 4	6	8
No. 52 Dodge Charger MKIII, 1970 ....3.50	5.25	7
No. 52 Police Launch, 1976 2	3	4
No. 53 Aston-Martin DB2/4, 1959 7	10	14
No. 53 Mercedes-Benz 220SE, 1968 10	15	20
No. 53 Ford Zodiac MKIV, 1968 6	9	12

MATCHBOX No. 56 Fiat 1500.

MATCHBOX No. 59 Ford "Singer" Van. Courtesy Gary Linden.

MATCHBOX No. 60 Morris Omnitruck J-2 Pick-up. Courtesy Gary Linden.

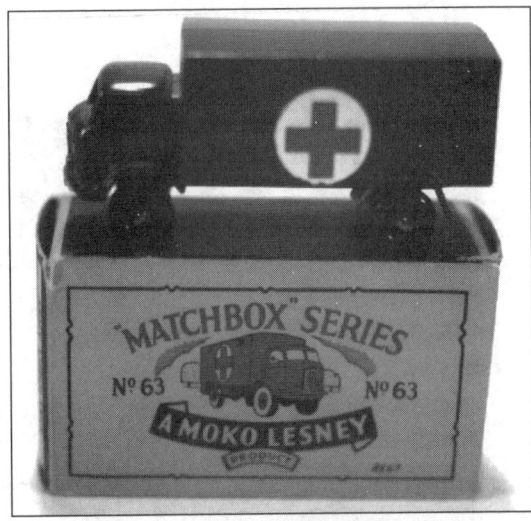

MATCHBOX No. 63 Army Ambulance. Courtesy Gary Linden.

MATCHBOX Garage, 3" long, metal, with early tow truck. Courtesy Gary Linden.

MATCHBOX No. 64 Scammell Army Wreck Truck. Courtesy Gary Linden.

MATCHBOX No. 68 Army Austin MK II Radio Truck. Courtesy Gary Linden.

MATCHBOX No. 69 Commer 30 CWT. Van "Nestle's". Courtesy Gary Linden.

MATCHBOX No. 73 R..A.F. 10 Ton Pressure Refueler Tanker. Courtesy Gary Linden.

	C6	C8	C10
No. 53 Tanzara, 1972	3	4.50	6
No. 53 C.J. 6 Jeep, 1977	2	3	4
No. 54 Army Saracen Personnel Carrier, 1959	7	11	14
No. 54 Cadillac Ambulance, 1965	11	16	22
No. 54 Ford Capri, 1971	4	6	8
No. 54 Personnel Carrier, 1976	2.50	3.75	5
No. 54 Mobile Home, 1981	2	3	4
No. 55 D.U.K.W. (Army Amphibian), 1959	18	27	36
No. 55 Ford Police Car, 1963	45	68	90
No. 55 Mercury Parkland Police Car, 1969	10	15	20
No. 55 Mercury Police Car (Station Wagon), 1970	5	8	10
No. 55 Hell Raiser, 1975	2.50	3.75	5
No. 55 Ford Cortina, 1980	5	7.50	10
No. 56 London Trolley Bus, 1959	17	27	35
No. 56 Fiat 1500, 1965	5	7.50	10
No. 56 BMC 1800 Pininfarina, 1970	4.50	6.75	9
No. 56 Hi Trailer, 1975	3	4.50	6
No. 56 Mercedes 450SEL, 1980	2	3	4
No. 57 Wolseley 1500, 1959	12	18	25
No. 57 Chevrolet Impala, 1966	15	22	30
No. 57 Eccles Caravan, 1970	5	7.50	10
No. 57 Wild Life Truck, 1973	4.50	6.75	9
No. 58 British European Airways Coach, 1959	12	18	25
No. 58 Drott Excavator, 1963	12	18	25
No. 58 Daf Girder Truck, 1968	4	6	8
No. 58 Woosh-N-Push, 1972	4.50	6.75	9
No. 58 Faun Dumper, 1976	3	4.50	6
No. 59 Ford 'Singer,' Van, 1959	32	48	65
No. 59 Ford Fairlane Fire Car, 1964	7	11	15
No. 59 Fire Chief Car, 1966	65	88	130
No. 59 Planet Scout, 1975	10	15	20
No. 59 Porsche 928, 1981	2.50	3.75	5
No. 60 Morris Omnitruck J2 Pick-up	11	16	22
No. 60 Truck with Site Office, 1967	4	6	8
No. 60 Lotus Super Seven, 1971	4	6	8
No. 60 Holden Pick-Up, 1977	4	6	8
No. 61 Military Scout Car (Ferret), 1959	11	16	22
No. 61 Alvis Stalwart, 1967	5	7.50	10
No. 61 Blue Shark, 1971	2.50	3.75	5
No. 61 Wreck Truck, 1978	2.50	3.75	5
No. 62 General Army Lorry, 1959	10	15	20
No. 62 TV Service Van, 1964	10	15	20
No. 62 Mercury Cougar, 1969	5	8	10
No. 62 Rat Rod Dragster, 1971	4	6	8
No. 62 Renault 17TL, 1974	3.50	5.25	7
No. 62 Chevrolet Corvette, 1980	2	3	4
No. 63 Army Ambulance, 1959	20	30	40
No. 63 Airport Fire Fighting Crash Tender, 1964	12	18	25
No. 63 Dodge Crane Truck, 1968	4	6	8
No. 63 Freeway Gas Tanker, 1973	4.50	6.75	9
No. 64 Scammell Army Wreck Truck, 1959	16	24	32
No. 64 MG 1100, 1966	4	6	9
No. 64 Slingshot Dragster, 1971	3	4.50	6
No. 64 Fire Chief Car, 1976	2	3	4
No. 64 Caterpillar Tractor, 1981	2.50	3.75	5
No. 65 Jaguar 3.4 Litre Saloon, 1959	8	12	16
No. 65 Claas Combine Harvester, 1968	3	4.50	6
No. 65 Saab Sonnet, 1973	3	4.50	6
No. 65 Airport Coach, 1977	2	3	4
No. 66 Citroen DS19, 1959	12	18	25
No. 66 Harley Davidson Motorcycle & Sidecar, 1963	35	52	70
No. 66 Greyhound Bus, 1967	15	22	30
No. 66 Mazda RX500, 1972	4.50	6.75	9
No. 66 Ford Transit, 1977	5	7.50	10
No. 67 'Saladin' Armored Car, 1959	16	24	32
No. 67 Volkswagen 1600 T.L., 1968	4.50	6.75	9
No. 67 Hot Rocker, 1973	2.50	3.75	5
No. 67 Datsun 260Z, 1978	2	3	4
No. 68 Army Austin MKII Radio Truck, 1959	7	11	15
No. 68 Mercedes Coach, 1965	8	12	16
No. 68 Porsche 910, 1970	4.50	6.75	9
No. 68 Cosmobile, 1975	10	15	20
No. 68 Chevrolet Van, 1980	12	18	24
No. 69 Commer 30 Cwt. Van 'Nestles', 1959	20	30	40
No. 69 Hatra Tractor Shovel, 1965	7	11	14

MATCHBOX Y-5 Talbot Van. Courtesy Gary Linden.

MATCHBOX Y-12 1912 Model T Ford. Courtesy Gary Linden.

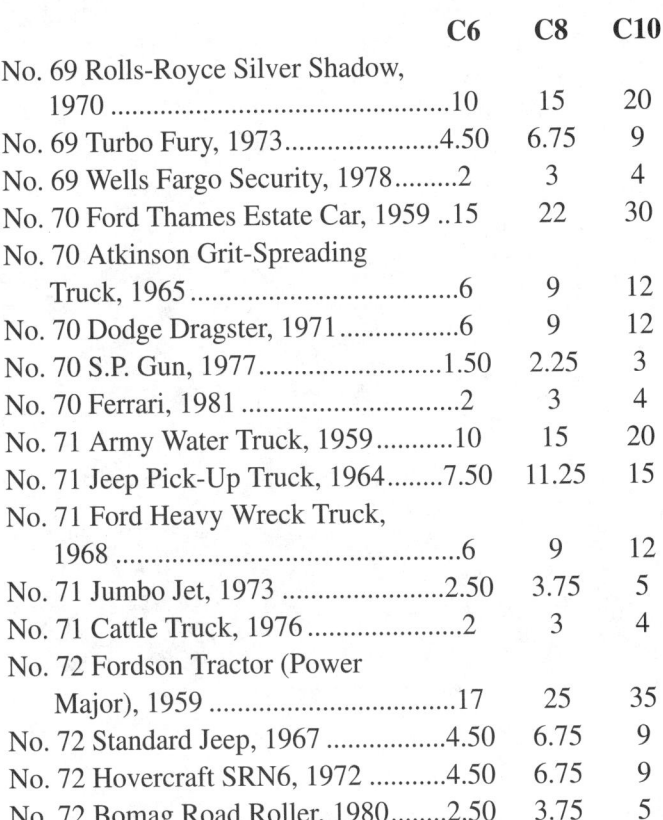

MATCHBOX Y-6 1913 Cadillac. Courtesy Gary Linden.

MATCHBOX Y-14 1931 Stutz Bearcat. Courtesy Gary Linden.

	C6	C8	C10
No. 69 Rolls-Royce Silver Shadow, 1970	10	15	20
No. 69 Turbo Fury, 1973	4.50	6.75	9
No. 69 Wells Fargo Security, 1978	2	3	4
No. 70 Ford Thames Estate Car, 1959	15	22	30
No. 70 Atkinson Grit-Spreading Truck, 1965	6	9	12
No. 70 Dodge Dragster, 1971	6	9	12
No. 70 S.P. Gun, 1977	1.50	2.25	3
No. 70 Ferrari, 1981	2	3	4
No. 71 Army Water Truck, 1959	10	15	20
No. 71 Jeep Pick-Up Truck, 1964	7.50	11.25	15
No. 71 Ford Heavy Wreck Truck, 1968	6	9	12
No. 71 Jumbo Jet, 1973	2.50	3.75	5
No. 71 Cattle Truck, 1976	2	3	4
No. 72 Fordson Tractor (Power Major), 1959	17	25	35
No. 72 Standard Jeep, 1967	4.50	6.75	9
No. 72 Hovercraft SRN6, 1972	4.50	6.75	9
No. 72 Bomag Road Roller, 1980	2.50	3.75	5

	C6	C8	C10
No. 73 RAF 10-Ton Pressure Refueler Tanker, 1959	17	25	35
No. 73 Ferrari Racing Car, 1963	14	21	28
No. 73 Mercury Station Wagon (Commuter), 1969	3.50	5.25	7
No. 73 Weasel, 1974	2	3	4
No. 73 Model 'A' Ford, 1981	2	3	4
No. 74 Mobile Refreshment Bar (Canteen), 1959	20	30	40
No. 74 Daimler Bus, 1966	9	13	18
No. 74 Toe Joe, 1972	2	3	4
No. 74 Cougar Villager, 1978	2.50	3.75	5
No. 75 Ford Thunderbird, 1959	38	56	75
No. 75 Ferrari Berlinetta, 1965	8	12	16
No. 75 Alfa Carabo, 1971	4.50	6.75	9
No. 75 Helicopter, 1976	2	3	4

Matchbox 'Models of Yesteryear'
(With Year of Introduction)

	C6	C8	C10
Y-1 1925 Allchin 7 N.H.P. Traction Engine, 1955	30	45	60
Y-1 1911 Model 'T' Ford, 1964	10	15	20

	C6	C8	C10
Y-1 1936 Jaguar SS100, 1977 12	18	25
Y-2 1911 'B' Type London Bus, 1955 ..40	60	80
Y-2 1911 Renault 2-Seater, 1963...........5	8	11
Y-2 Prince Henry Vauxhall, 1970...........8	12	16
Y-3 1907 London 'E' Class Tramcar, 1955 45	68	90
Y-3 1910 Benz Limousine, 1965...........8	12	16
Y-3 1934 Riley MPH, 1972.................7	10	14
Y-4 Sentinel Steam Wagon, 1955..........37	56	75
Y-4 1905 Shank-Mason Horse-Drawn Fire Engine, 1960....................75	112	150
Y-4 1909 Opel Coupe, 1966...........10	15	20
Y-4 1930 Dusenberg Model J, 1976......15	22	30
Y-5 1929 LeMans Bentley, 1955...........37	53	75
Y-5 1929 Supercharged 4:1/2 Litre Bentley, 1960....................12	18	24
Y-5 1907 Peugeot, 1968 14	21	28
Y-5 1927 Talbot Van, 1978....................15	22	30
Y-6 1916 A.E.C. "Y" type Lorry Truck, 1955.....................22	33	45
Y-6 1926 Type "35" Bugatti, 1961........15	22	30
Y-6 1913 Cadillac, 1967.........................20	30	40
Y-6 1920 Rolls-Royce Fire Engine, 1978.15	22	30
Y-7 1914 4-Ton Leyland, 1955..........27	41	55
Y-7 1913 Mercer Raceabout Sportcar, 1961 20	30	40
Y-7 1912 Rolls-Royce, 1967 17	26	35
Y-8 1926 Morris Cowley "Bullnose", 1955 50	75	100
Y-8 1914 Sunbeam Motorcycle with Sidecar, 1962....................20	30	40
Y-8 1914 Stutz Roadster, 1968..............10	15	20
Y-8 1945 MC TC Sports Car, 1978......4.50	6.75	9
Y-9 1924 Fowler "Big Lion" Showman Engine, 1955 40	60	80
Y-9 1912 Simplex, 1967.........................20	30	40
Y-10 1908 Grand Prix Mercedes Racing Car, 1957....................30	45	60
Y-10 1928 Mercedes-Benz 36/220, 1963 20	30	40
Y-10 1906 Rolls-Royce Silver Cloud, 1968 8	12	16
Y-11 1920 Aveling & Porter Steam Roller, 1957....................30	45	60
Y-11 1912 Packard Landaulet, 1963 12	18	25
Y-11 1938 Lagonda Drophead Coupe, 1972 12	18	25
Y-12 1899 Horse-Bus (London), 1957..60	90	120
Y-12 1909 Thomas Flyabout, 1967 12	18	24
Y-12 1912 Model "T" Ford, 1979 10	15	20
Y-13 1862 American 4-4-0 Locomotive 25	38	50
Y-13 1911 Daimler, 1965 10	15	20
Y-13 1918 Crossley Truck, 1972...........17	26	35
Y-14 1903 "Duke of Connaught" Locomotive, 1957 65	98	130
Y-14 1911 Maxwell Roadster, 1965 15	22	30
Y-14 1931 Stutz Bearcat, 1972...............6	9	12
Y-15 1907 Rolls-Royce "Silver Ghost", 1960 15	22	30
Y-15 1930 Packard Victoria, 1969 6	9	12
Y-16 1904 Spyker Veteran Automobile, 1961 18	27	36
Y-16 1928 Mercedes SS, 1971 6	9	12
Y-17 1938 Hispano Suiza, 1972.............8	12	16
Y-18 1937 Cord 812, 1979...................4.50	6.75	9
Y-19 1935 Auburn 851, 1980................2	3	4
Y-20 1938 Mercedes 540K, 1981 ....4.50	6.75	9
Y-21 1929 Woody Wagon, 1981.........4.50	6.75	9

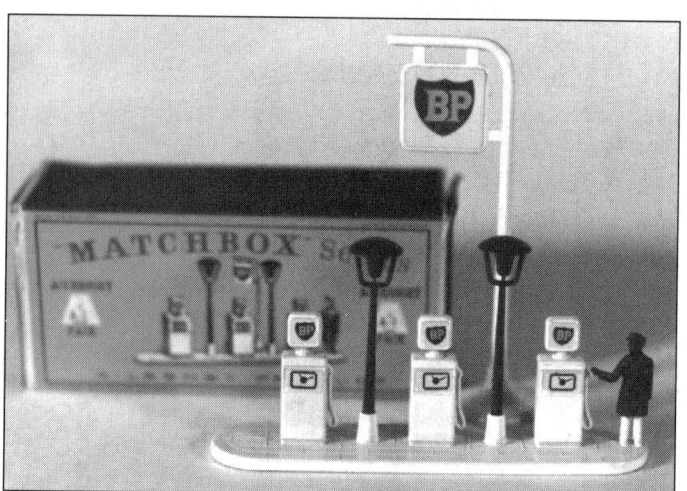

MATCHBOX Accessory Pack A-1 BP Gas Pump and BP sign, with box. Courtesy Gary Linden.

Box cover for MATCHBOX service station. Courtesy Gary Linden.

JAPANESE (ETC.) TIN CARS

by Ron Smith

The average mint price of these toys was $260.95 in the last edition, rising to $335.98 in this, an increase of 29%.

Tin toy cars have been manufactured since the first horseless carriages roamed the streets of the United States and Europe. They ranged in size and price from the tiny one-inch penny toy to the 28" Eldorado which sold at the ten dollar mark. Although there are German, Spanish and French toy cars listed here, our concentration will be the 1950's Golden Era of Japanese tin toy cars. These examples enjoy much popularity today and prices have been raised by the limitlessness of some people's insanity. Keep one thing foremost in your mind when trying to sell a toy at the mint listed price; the person who paid that price already has one.

Ron Smith has always loved toy cars and planes. He can still show you his first Dinky Toy bought for him in 1940 by his aunt in Fred Harvey's Toy Store inside Cleveland's Terminal Tower Building. Born and raised in Shaker Heights, Ohio, Ron served in the United States Navy, attended John Carroll University, and for the last 14 years has been employed by Arrow Distributing of Solon, Ohio as Vice President of Sales. He has collected die cast cars, trucks and planes, cast iron toys, plastic promotional cars and, for the last 10 years, specialized in tin plate cars and planes. Ron lives in Solon, Ohio with his wife Joan and their two cats, Trouble and Bogart.

No.	Year	Model	Manufacturer	Power	Size	C6	C8	C10
J1	1960s	Aston-Martin DB5 (James Bond)	Gilbert	Friction	11½"	50	100	200
J2	1960s	Aston-Martin DB6	Asahi Toy Co.	Friction	11"	100	200	400
J2A	1959	Austin Healey 100 Six Coupe	Bandai	Friction,	8"	40	80	150
J2B	1959	Austin Healey 100 Six Convertible	Bandai	Friction	8"	40	80	150
J3	1953	Buick	Marusan	Friction	7"	75	125	250
J4	1954	Buick Station Wagon	Unknown	Battery	8"	75	150	200
J5	1955	Buick Roadmaster	Yoshiya	Friction	11"	125	175	400
J6	1958	Buick Century	Yonezawa	Friction	12"	300	500	900
J7	1958	Buick Century	Bandai	Friction	8"	80	110	130
J8	1959	Buick	TN.	Friction	11"	90	150	300
J9	1959	Buick	Ichiko	Friction	12"	100	275	350
J10	1960	Buick	Ichiko	Friction	17½"	150	250	600
J11	1961	Buick	T.N.	Friction	11"	50	100	175
J12	1961	Buick Emergency Car	T.N.	Friction	14"	50	95	125
J13	1963	Buick Wildcat	Ichiko	Friction	15"	125	250	400
J14	1966	Buick Le Sabre	Asahi Toy Co.	Friction	19"	100	150	275
J15	1968	Buick Sportswagon	Asakusa	Friction	15"	100	150	200
J16	1950	BMW 600 Isetta	Bandai	Friction	9"	150	200	250
J17	1950	BMW Isetta (three wheels)	Bandai	Friction	6½"	75	125	150
J18	1950	Cadillac	Marusan	Friction	11"	300	500	700
J19	1950	Cadillac	Marusan	Battery	11"	400	600	900
J20	1952	Cadillac	Alps	Friction	11½"	200	300	600
J21	1952	Cadillac	T.N.	Battery	13"	75	150	350
J22	1954	Cadillac	Gama	Friction	12"	200	300	500
J23	1954	Cadillac	Joustra	Battery	12"	200	300	500
J24	1959	Cadillac Sedan	Bandai	Friction	12"	75	100	200
J25	1959	Cadillac Convertible	Bandai	Friction	12"	75	100	200
J26	1960s	Cadillac	Bandai	Friction	17"	125	175	375
J27	1960	Cadillac	Yonezawa	Friction	18"	150	200	350
J28	1961	Cadillac 60	Unknown	Friction	9"	95	125	150
J29	1961	Cadillac Fleetwood	SSS	Friction	17½"	150	300	500

J1

J2

J5

J6

J7

J8

J13

J18

J20

All Photos by Ron Smith.

No.	Year	Model	Manufacturer	Power	Size	C6	C8	C10
J30	1962	Cadillac	Yonezawa	Friction	22"	100	250	350
J31	1963	Cadillac	Bandai	Friction	17"	125	200	350
J32	1965	Cadillac	Asahi Toy C.	Friction	17"	100	200	300
J33	1965	Cadillac	Ichiko	Friction	22"	300	400	600
J34	1967	Cadillac	K.O.	Friction	10½"	100	150	300
J35	1967	Cadillac	Unknown	Friction	10¾"	75	100	125
J36	1967	Cadillac El Dorado	Ichiko	Friction	28"	200	400	700
J37	1953	Chevrolet Corvette	Bandai	Friction	7"	75	100	150
J38	1958	Chevrolet Corvette	Yonezawa	Friction	9½"	200	300	500
J39	1962	Chevrolet Corvette	Bandai	Friction	8"	50	75	100
J40	1965	Chevrolet Corvette	Bandai	Friction	8"	65	90	125
J41	1964	Chevrolet Corvette	Ichida	Battery	12"	150	225	350
J42	1968	Chevrolet Corvette	Taiyo	Battery	9½"	35	50	75
J43	1960s	Chevrolet Corvair	Bandai	Friction	8"	50	65	90
J44	1963	Chevrolet Corvair	Ichiko	Friction	9"	50	65	95
J45	1967	Chevrolet Camaro	Taiyo	Friction	9½"	10	20	30
J46	1967	Chevrolet Camaro	T.N.	Friction	14"	150	250	400
J47	1967	Chevrolet Camaro	Modern Toys	Friction	11"	25	50	75
J48	1971	Chevrolet Camaro Rusher	Taiyo	Battery	9½"	10	20	35
J49	1954	Chevrolet	Marusan	Friction	11"	300	400	700
J50	1955	Chevrolet	Marusan	Battery	10¾"	300	500	800
J51	1956	Chevrolet Station Wagon	Bandai	Friction	9½"	75	125	175
J52	1956	Chevrolet Pick Up	Bandai	Friction	9½"	75	125	175
J53	1956	Chevrolet Convertible	Bandai	Friction	9½"	100	150	225

J24

J25

J29

J31

J34

J37

All Photos by Ron Smith.

No.	Year	Model	Manufacturer	Power	Size	C6	C8	C10
J54	1958	Chevrolet Red Cross Ambulance	Bandai	Friction	8"	20	30	50
J55	1958	Chevrolet Pick Up Truck	Bandai	Friction	8"	50	65	90
J56	1958	Chevrolet Convertible	Bandai	Friction	8"	60	90	125
J57	1958	Chevrolet Station Wagon	Bandai	Friction	8"	50	60	85
J58	1958	Chevrolet Sedan	Bandai	Friction	8"	75	100	125
J59	1959	Chevrolet Sedan/Convertible	SY	Friction	11½"	200	300	500
J60	1960	Chevrolet	Marusan	Friction	11½"	200	300	500
J61	1959	Chevrolet Wagon	SY	Friction	12"	60	90	115
J62	1961	Chevrolet Impala Sedan	Bandai	Friction	11"	100	150	300
J63	1961	Chevrolet Impala Convertible	Bandai	Friction	11"	100	150	300
J64	1962	Chevrolet Secret Agent	Unknown	Battery	14"	50	75	125
J65	1962	Chevrolet	Unknown	Friction	11"	125	250	350
J66	1963	Chevrolet Impala	Unknown	Friction	18"	150	225	375
J67	1960	Citroen DS 19 Convertible	Bandai	Friction	12"	100	150	300
J68	1960	Citroen DS 19 Sedan	Bandai	Friction	12"	100	150	300
J69	1960	Citroen ID 19 Station Wagon	Bandai	Friction	12"	100	150	300
J70	1950	Chrysler	Guntherman	Friction	11"	100	200	500
J71	1955	Chrysler	Yonezawa	Friction	8"	100	200	300
J72	1957	Chrysler New Yorker	Alps	Friction	14"	500	700	1000+
J73	1958	Chrysler	Unknown	Battery	13"	200	300	600
J74	1959	Chrysler Imperial convertible	Bandai	Friction	8"	75	90	125
J75	1959	Chrysler Imperial Sedan	Bandai	Friction	8"	75	90	125
J76	1960	Chrysler Valiant	Bandai	Friction	8"	20	45	65
J77	1962	Chrysler Imperial	Asahi Toy. Co.	Friction	16"	500	700	1000+
J78	1960	DKW 1000 Convertible	Bandai	Friction	8"	90	125	200
J79	1960s	Datsun Bluebird 1200	Bandai	Friction	8"	60	75	125
J80	1950s	Divco Dugans Bakery Truck	Unknown, Japan	Friction	7½"	300	400	600
J81	1930s	Desoto	Masudaya	Friction	8"	300	400	800
J82	1958	Dodge Sedan	T.N.	Friction	11"	300	400	600
J83	1959	Dodge Truck	Unknown	Friction	24"	350	500	800
J84	1959	Dodge Pick Up	Unknown	Friction	18½"	350	500	800
J85	1968	Dodge Yellow Cab	T.N.	Friction	12"	90	125	175
J86	1958	Edsel Convertible/Sedan	Haji	Friction	10½"	300	400	800
J87	1958	Edsel Wagon	Haji	Friction	10½"	200	300	400

J38

J41

J46

J42

J48

J49

J50

Photo Abensur. J57

J59

J60

J62

All Photos unless marked otherwise, are by Ron Smith.

J63

J64

J65

All Photos by Ron Smith.

No.	Year	Model	Manufacturer	Power	Size	C6	C8	C10
J88	1958	Edsel Ambulance	Haji	Friction	11"	200	250	300
J89	1958	Edsel Station Wagon	T.N.	Friction	11"	150	200	300
J90	1958	Edsel H.T.	Asahi	Friction	10¾"	300	400	600
J91	1958	Edsel H.T.	Toy Nomura	Friction	8½"	100	150	250
J92	1958	Edsel	Yonezawa	Friction	10½"	300	400	600
J93	1949	Ford Sedan	Guntherman	Wind Up	11"	150	300	400
J94	1951	Ford Sedan	Guntherman	Wind Up	11"	150	300	400
J95	1950	Ford Good Humor Ice Cream Truck	KTS, Japan	Friction	10¾"	150	250	350
J96	1955	Ford Pick Up	Bandai	Friction	12"	150	250	300
J97	1955	Ford Station Wagon	Bandai	Friction	12"	150	250	300
J98	1955	Ford Ambulance	Bandai	Friction	12"	150	250	300
J99	1955	Ford Panel Truck	Bandai	Friction	12"	300	500	700
J100	1955	Ford Convertible	Bandai	Friction	12"	300	500	700
J101	1956	Ford H.T.	Yonezawa	Friction	12"	300	500	800
J102	1956	Ford Convertible	Haji	Friction	11½"	400	600	1000
J103	1956	Ford Sedan	Marusan	Friction	13"	500	800	1000
J104	1956	Ford Wagon	Nomura	Friction	10½"	100	150	300
J105	Ford	Fairlane Sedan	Ichiko	Friction	10"	100	200	300
J106	1957	Ford H.T	T.N.	Friction	12"	100	200	300
J107	1957	Ford Sedan/Con./Wagon/Pick Up	Joustra	Friction	12"	200	250	300
J108	1957	Ford Sedan/Conv./Wagon/Pick Up	Bandai	Friction	12"	200	250	300
J109	1957	Ford Station Wagon	Nomura	Friction	7½"	60	80	100
J110	1958	Ford Retractable Top	K. Japan	Friction	10"	70	90	150
J111	1958	Ford Retractable Top	T.N.	Battery	11"	100	125	175
J112	1958	Ford Country Squire Station Wagon	Bandai	Friction	8"	60	80	100
J113	1958	Ford Fairlane H.T./Conv.	Bandai	Friction	8"	60	80	100
J114	1958	Ford Fairlane H.T./Conv.	Sankei Gangu	Friciton	9"	90	115	125
J115	1959	Ford Fairlane Skyliner	Sankei Gangu	Friction	9"	90	115	125
J116	1950	Ford Station Wagon	T.N.	Friction	12"	100	150	200
J117	1959	Ford Retractable	T.N.	Friction	11"	100	150	200
J118	1960s	Ford Falcon	Bandai	Friction	8"	20	30	50
J119	1960	Ford	Haji	Friction	11"	125	150	250
J120	1961	Ford Country Sedan	Bandai	Friction	10½"	125	150	250
J121	1962	Ford Country Sedan	Asahi	Friction	12"	200	250	400
J122	1964	Ford H.T.	Ichiko	Friction	13"	125	150	200
J123	1964	Ford H.T.	Rico	Friction	17"	200	400	600
J124	1964	Ford Convertible	Rico	Friction	17"	200	400	600
J125	1965	Ford Galaxie H.T.	MT	Friction	11"	125	150	250
J126	1968	Ford Torino	S.T.	Friction	16"	200	250	400
J127	1956	Ford Thunderbird	T.N.	Friction	11"	275	325	375
J128	1956	Ford Thunderbird H.T. Clear Top	T.N.	Friction	11"	275	325	375
J129	1956	Ford Thunderbird	T.N.	Battery	11"	275	350	400
J130	1959	Ford Thunderbird Sedan	Bandai	Friction	8"	50	60	80

J71

J73

J72 *Photo Bruce Sterling.*

J77

J86

J86

All Photos, unless marked otherwise, are by Ron Smith.

J87

J93

J96

J99

J100

J103 *Photo Bruce Sterling.*

J102

J106

J107

All Photos by Ron Smith.

No.	Year	Model	Manufacturer	Power	Size	C6	C8	C10
J131	1959	Ford Thunderbird Convertible	Bandai	Friction	8"	50	60	80
J132	1961	Ford Thunderbird Retractable	Yonezawa	Battery	11"	90	120	150
J133	1962	Ford Thunderbird Retractable	Yonezawa	Battery	11"	90	120	150
J134	1963	Ford Thunderbird Retractable	Yonezawa	Battery	11"	90	120	150
J135	1964	Ford Thunderbird Convertible	Asahi	Friction	12½"	150	200	400
J136	1964	Ford Thunderbird H.T.	Asahi	Friction	12"	150	200	400
J137	1964	Ford Thunderbird	Ichiko	Friction	16"	100	200	400
J138	1965	Ford Thunderbird H.T.	Bandai	Friction	10¾"	60	85	125
J139	1965	Ford Mustang F.B.	Bandai	Friction	11"	45	65	90
J140	1965	Ford Mustang H.T./Conv.	Bandai	Fric/Bat	11"	75	125	150
J141	1965	Ford Mustang (FBI)	Bandai	Friction	11"	75	100	125
J142	1965	Ford Mustang Convertible	Yonezawa	Battery	13½"	90	125	200
J143	1966	Ford Mustang F.B.	T.N.	Friction	17"	100	175	250
J144	1967	Ford Mustang	Bandai	Battery	13"	45	65	100
J145	1960s	Ford Taunus 17M Convertible	Bandai	Friction	8"	30	40	60
J146	1960s	Ford GT	Bandai	Battery	10"	65	85	125
J147	1957	Ferrari 250 G. Convertible	A.T.C.	Friction	9½"	100	250	400
J148	1958	Ferrari	Bandai	Battery	11"	90	150	300
J149	1960	Ferrari Super America Coupe	Bandai	Friction	12"	100	200	300
J150	1960s	Ferrari Super America Convertible	Bandai	Friction	12"	100	200	300
J151	1960s	Fiat 600 Sedan	Bandai	Friction	8"	50	65	95
J152	1950s	International Cement Mixer	SSS	Friction	19"	275	300	400
J153	1950s	International Grain Hauler	SSS	Friction	23"	275	300	400
J154	1960	Jaguar XK150 H.T. Conv.	Bandai	Friction	9½"	75	125	200
J155	1960s	Jaguar XKE Convertible	T.T.	Friction	10½"	95	125	175
J156	1960s	Jaguar XKE Coupe	Lendolet Auto	Friction	10½"	75	100	125
J157	1960s	Jaguar XK140	Bandai	Friction	9½"	40	60	90
J158	1960s	Jaguar XKE	Bandai	Battery	10"	90	125	200
J159	1960s	Jaguar 3.4 Sedan	Bandai	Friction	8"	50	60	100
J160	1960s	Jaguar 3.4 Convertible	Bandai	Friction	8"	50	60	100
J161	1965	Jaguar XKE 120	Alps	Friction	6½"	90	150	350
J162	1954	Lincoln	Unknown	Friction	12"	175	275	375
J163	1955	Lincoln Sedan	Yonezawa	Friction	12"	250	325	500
J164	1956	Lincoln Continental Mark II	Linemar	Friction	12"	400	600	1000
J165	1956	Lincoln	Ichiko	Friction	16½"	150	250	375
J166	1959	Lincoln Continental Mark III Conv.	Bandai	Friction	12"	90	150	200
J167	1959	Lincoln Continental Mark III Sedan	Bandai	Friction	12"	90	150	200
J168	1960	Lincoln H.T./Convertible	Yonezawa	Friction	11"	100	150	300
J169	1964	Lincoln	Unknown	Friction	10½"	90	175	275
J170	1950s	Lotus Elite	Bandai	Friction	8½"	25	35	45
J171	1960s	Land Rover "88" Station Wagon	Bandai	Friction	8"	30	40	60
J172	1950s	Mercedes Limousine	Tipp & Co.	Friction	14"	500	800	1000
J173	1950s	Mercedes Benz Racer	Line Mar	Friction	9½"	95	150	185
J174	1950s	Mercedes Benz Racer W196	Marusan	Battery	10"	150	200	250

J116

J117

J119

J120

J121

J122

J125

J126

J129

J134

J136

J137

J138

J140

J164

J166

J168

J177

All Photos by Ron Smith.

No.	Year	Model	Manufacturer	Power	Size	C6	C8	C10
J175	1960s	Mercedes	Ichiko	Friction	12½"	115	155	185
J176	1960s	Mercedes Benz 219 Sedan	Bandai	Friction	8"	50	80	100
J177	1960s	Mercedes Benz 219 Convertible	Bandai	Friction	8"	50	80	100
J178	1960s	Mercedes Benz 230 SL	Modern Toys	Battery	15"	175	210	250
J179	1960s	Mercedes Benz 230 SL	Alps	Battery	10"	65	75	95
J180	1960s	Mercedes Benz 230 SL	Yanoman	Battery	14½"	125	155	185
J181	1960s	Mercedes Benz 250 SE	Ichiko	Battery	13"	110	140	185
J182	1960s	Mercedes Benz 250 S	Daiya	Friction	14"	110	155	175
J183	1950s	Mercedes Benz 300 SL	T.N.	Battery	11"	125	150	200
J184	1950s	Mercedes Benz 300 SL	KS	Battery	7"	45	65	85
J185	1950s	Mercedes Benz 300 SL	Dist. Cragstan	Battery	9"	65	95	125
J186	1950s	Mercedes Benz 300 SL	Bandai	Friction	8"	65	95	125
J187	1957	Mercedes Benz 300 SL	Marusan	Friction	8½"	150	250	325
J188	1960s	Mercedes Benz 600	Unknown	Friction	10"	95	125	175
J189	1960s	Mercedes Benz Taxi	Bandai	Battery	10"	75	100	125
J190	1962	Mercedes Benz	SSS	Battery	12"	200	250	350
J191	1970	Mercedes Benz	Ichiko	Friction	24"	125	150	200
J192	1954	Mercury H.T.	Rock Valley Toys	Battery	9½"	100	125	150
J193	1956	Mercury H.T	Alps	Friction	9½"	400	500	800
J194	1958	Mercury Station Wagon	Bandai	Friction	8"	60	80	100
J195	1958	Mercury H.T.	Yonezawa	Friction	11½"	250	325	400
J196	1967	Mercury Cougar H.T.	Taiyo	Battery	10"	25	45	65
J197	1967	Mercury Cougar H.T	Asakusa Toys	Friction	15"	175	225	275
J198	1952	MG TF	Unknown	Friction	8½"	50	75	95
J199	1954	MG TD	SSS	Friction	6½"	35	65	85
J200	1955	MG TF	Bandai	Friction	8"	95	125	150
J201	1957	MGA	A.T.C.	Friction	10"	175	250	400
J202	1960s	MG Magnette Mark III Sedan	Bandai	Friction	8"	95	125	150
J203	1960s	MG Magnette Mark III Convertible	Bandai	Friction	8"	95	125	150
J204	1960s	Messerschmitt 4 Wheels Convert.	Bandai	Friction	8"	200	250	300
J205	1960s	Messerschmitt 4 Wheels Sedan	Bandai	Friction	8"	200	250	300
J206	1950s	Nash	MSK	Battery	8"	40	70	90
J207	1956	Nash Ambassador	Sankei Gangu	Friction	8"	100	125	150
J207A	1952	Oldsmobile	Y	Friction	11"	150	350	500
J208	1956	Oldsmobile Sedan	Ichiko/Kanto	Friction	10½"	200	400	600
J209	1956	Oldsmobile Super 88 Sedan	Masudaya	Friction	16"	300	400	600
J210	1958	Oldsmobile Sedan	A.T.C.	Friction	12"	200	300	400
J211	1958	Oldsmobile Super 88 Sedan	A.T.C.	Friction	13"	250	325	425
J212	1958	Oldsmobile Sedan	Y	Friction	16"	300	400	700
J213	1959	Oldsmobile Sedan	Ichiko	Friction	12½"	75	125	175
J214	1961	Oldsmobile Convertible	Yonezawa	Friction	12"	75	125	175
J215	1966	Oldsmobile Toronado	Bandai	Battery	11"	65	110	150
J216	1968	Oldsmobile Toronado	Ichiko	Friction	17½"	300	400	500
J217	1950s	Opel Sedan	Yonezawa	Battery	11½"	70	90	125
J218	1954	Pontiac Star Chief	Asahi	Friction	11"	250	350	450
J218A	1954	Pontiac	Minister	Friction	11"	New Issue		15
J219	1967	Pontiac Firebird	Akasura	Friction	15½"	90	150	275
J220	1967	Pontiac Firebird	Bandai	Friction	10"	30	55	75
J221	1967	Pontiac Firebird (w/wipers)	Bandai	Battery	9½"	40	55	75
J222	1953	Packard Convertible/Sedan	Alps	Friction	16"	500	800	1500
J223	1957	Packard Hawk Convertible	Schuco	Battery	10¾"	300	400	500
J224	1956	Plymouth H.T.	Unknown	Friction	8½"	200	400	600
J225	1956	Plymouth H.T	Alps	Battery	12"	300	400	600
J226	1957	Plymouth Fury H.T	Y	Friction	11½"	300	400	600

J193

J195

J197

J208

J209

J210

J207A

J218A

All Photos by Ron Smith.

J215

J219

J222

J223

J224

J225

J227

J232

J235

J236

J237

J240

J242

J243

J252

J260

J265

J276

J265A

J278A

All Photos by Ron Smith.

No.	Year	Model	Manufacturer	Power	Size	C6	C8	C10
J227	1958	Plymouth Fury	Bandai	Friction	8"	75	90	150
J228	1959	Plymouth Hardtop	A.T.C.	Friction	10½"	200	400	600
J229	1959	Plymouth Convertible	A.T.C.	Friction	10½"	250	400	600
J230	1961	Plymouth Sedan	Ichiko	Friction	12"	125	250	350
J231	1961	Plymouth Station Wagon	Ichiko	Friction	12"	125	165	195
J232	1961	Plymouth T.V. Car	Ichiko	Battery	12"	125	175	250
J233	1964	Plymouth Fury H.T.	Kusama	Friction	10"	60	80	100
J234	1960	Porsche 911	Bandai	Battery	10"	65	95	125
J235	1950s	Porsche Speedster	Distler	Battery	10½"	350	400	600
J236	1960	Rolls Royce "Silver Coupe" Conv.	Bandai	Friction	12"	100	150	300
J237	1960s	Rolls Royce "Silver Coupe" Sedan	Bandai	Friction	12"	100	150	250
J238	1960s	Rolls Royce (with Electric Lights)	Bandai	Battery	12"	100	200	400
J239	1960	Rolls Royce	T.N.	Friction	10½"	175	250	375
J240	1960s	Rambler Rebel Station Wagon	Bandai	Friction	12"	50	85	125
J241	1960	Renault	Bandai	Friction	7½"	95	150	200
J242	1960s	Studebaker Avanti	Bandai	Friction	8"	125	175	300
J243	1954	Studebaker	Yoshiya	Friction	9"	150	200	300
J244	1960s	Saab 93 B	Bandai	Friction	7"	50	70	90
J245	1960s	Subaru 360	Bandai	Friction	7"	75	100	125
J246	1960s	Triumph TR-3 Convertible	Bandai	Friction	8"	50	75	150
J247	1960s	Triumph TR-3 Coupe	Bandai	Friction	8"	50	75	150
J248	1960s	Toyopet Crown	Bandai	Friction	9"	40	50	75
J249	1960s	Toyota	Ichiko	Friciton	16"	150	275	325
J250	1967	Toyota 2000 GT	A.T.C.	Friction	15"	150	275	325
J251	1960s	Vespa	Bandai	Friction	9"	50	75	125
J252	1960	VW Karmann-Ghia	Bandai	Friction	7"	100	150	250
J253	1960s	Volkswagen Bus	A.T.C.	Friction	12"	125	175	350
J254	1960s	Volkswagen Pick Up Truck	Bandai	Friction	8"	50	60	75
J255	1960s	Volkswagen Bus	Bandai	Friction	8"	50	60	75
J256	1960s	Volkswagen Bus	Bandai	Bat/Fric	9½"	75	125	175
J257	1950s	Volkswagen Bus	Tipp & Co.	Battery	9"	250	375	450
J258	1950s	Volkswagen Convertible	T.N.	Friction	9½"	100	150	225
J259	1960s	Volkswagen Convertible	Bandai	Battery	7½"	50	70	90
J260	1960s	Volkswagen Convertible	Bandai	Battery	11"	110	145	185
J261	1960s	Volkswagen Convertible	Taiyo	Battery	10½"	25	45	90
J262	1960s,	Volkswagen	Bandai	Friction	8"	25	40	60
J263	1960s	Volkswagen	Bandai	Battery	10½"	25	50	75
J264	1960s	Volkswagen	Bandai	Battery	11"	25	50	75
J265	1960s	Volkswagen with/without Sun Roof	Bandai	Friction	15"	60	90	125
J265A	1950s	Volvo	Sweden	Wind Up	11"	600	700	1800
J266	1960s	Willys Jeep FC-150 Pick Up	T.N. Toy Nomura	Friction	11"	50	75	95
J267	1950s	Zuendapp Janus	Bandai	Friction	8"	125	150	200
J268	1950s	Mazda Auto Tricycle K 360	Bandai	Friction	6"	75	100	200
J269	1950	Daihatsu Midget	Kokyu Shokai	Friction	5"	75	100	200
J270	1950s	Daihatsu Midget	Yonezawa	Friction	7"	75	100	200
J271	1950s	Mitsubishi Auto Tricycle Leo	Bandai	Friction	5"	75	100	200
J272	1950s	Mitsubishi Auto Tricycle	Bandai	Friction	11"	100	150	300
J273	1950s	Orient Auto Tricycle	Yonezawa	Friction	9"	75	100	200
J274	1950s	Mazda Auto Tricycle	Bandai	Friction	8"	75	100	200
J275	1950s	Daihatsu Auto Tricycle	Nomura	Friction	11"	100	150	300
J276	1950s	Buick Futuristic Le Sabre	Yonezawa	Friction	7½"	100	200	400
J277	1963	Corvair Bertone	Bandai	Battery	12"	75	150	200
J278	1950s	Dream Car Buick Phantom	Tipp & Co.	Friction	12"	300	400	600

J284

J289

J287

J290

J286

J291

J288

All Photos by Ron Smith.

145

No.	Year	Model	Manufacturer	Power	Size	C6	C8	C10
J278A	-	Dream Car	Y	Friction	17"	600	800	1500
J279	1960s	Dream Car Firebird III	Alps	Friction	11"	100	200	300
J280	1960	Ford Gyron	Ichida	Battery	11"	75	100	150
J281	1956	GM's Gas Turbine Powered Firebird II	Ashahi	Friction	8½"	100	200	500
J282	1950s	Pontiac Dream Car	Mitsubishi	Friction	10"	100	200	500
J283	1950s	Atom Jet Car	Y	Friction	30"	300	500	1000
J284	1950s	Atom Car	Yonezawa	Friction	17"	200	400	800
J285	1950s	Record Racer NSU	Bandai	Friction	18"	100	150	200
J286	1950s	Agajanian Racer No. 98	Y	Friction	18"	500	800	2000
J287	1950s	Champion's Racer No. 98	Y	Friction	18"	500	800	1500
J288	1950	Champion Racer No. 42	Gem	Friction	18"	500	750	1200
J289	1950	Champion Racer No. 15	German	Friction	18"	500	750	1200
J290	-	Electrospecial #21	Y	Battery	10"	300	500	700
J291	-	Midget Special#6	Y	Friction	7"	300	500	700

JAPANESE TIN AIRPLANES

by Ron Smith

The average mint price of these toys was $224.03 in the last edition,
rising to $441.93 in this, edition an increase of 97%.

No.	Type	Manufacturer	Power	Wingspan	C6	C8	C10
A1	Cessna	T.N.	Friction	25"	100	200	400
A2	Jenny Biplane	S&E	Friction	14½"	100	150	200
A3	Jenny Biplane	S&E	Friction	14½"	100	150	200
A4	Bristol Bulldog	S&E	Friction	14½"	80	150	225
A5	Cessna	W. Ger	Friction	12"	50	80	150
A6	Ford	T.N.	Friction	15"	60	90	175
A7	Jenny Biplane	Haji	Friction	11½"	40	60	90
A8	Ryan Spirit of St. Louis	HTC	Friction	12"	75	125	200
A9	U.N. Hospital Plane	HTC	Friction	12"	70	120	210
A10	WWII Fighter	Japan	Friction	14½"	80	150	250
A11	Constellation	Ingap	Friction	15"	100	200	400
A12	F3F Biplane	Cragstan	Battery	11½"	100	200	400
A13	Bluebird Seaplane	S&E	Friction	13"	50	80	150
A14	B 50	Bandai	Friction	7½"	40	60	90
A15	Sky Bird "Spirit of St. Louis"	Bandai	Friction	9"	50	80	120
A16	Spitfire	HTC	Friction	10"	80	150	200
A17	P-51 Mustang	HTC	Friction	10"	90	160	250
A18	P-47 Thunderbolt	HTC	Friction	10"	80	150	200
A19	Zero	Japan	Friction	15½"		New Issue	75
A20	De Havilland Comet	Rico	Wind Up	13"	100	150	350
A21	WWII Fighter	Spain	Wind Up	8½"	100	200	300
A22	F-80	Bandai	Friction	7½"	40	70	100
A23	Disney Comic Plane	Linemar	Friction	10"	100	150	300
A24	WWII Fighter	Spain	Wind Up	9"	100	150	300
A25	WWII Tri-Motor	Spain	Wind Up	9"	100	150	300
A26	Hospital Plane	Tekno	-	14"	300	500	800
A27	German Biplane	Tipp	Bat/WU	20"	500	800	1800
A28	Construction	England?	-	22"	125	175	400
A29	30s German	Tipp	Wind Up	16"	500	800	2200
A30	Fiat CR-42	Ingap	Wind Up	10"	500	700	800
A31	Stuka	Dux	-	12"	200	400	600

A1

A2

A3

A4

A5

A6

A7

A8

A9

A10

*All Photos by
Ron Smith.*

147

A11

A12

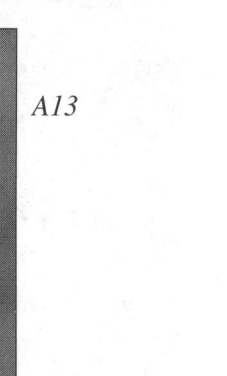

A13

A14

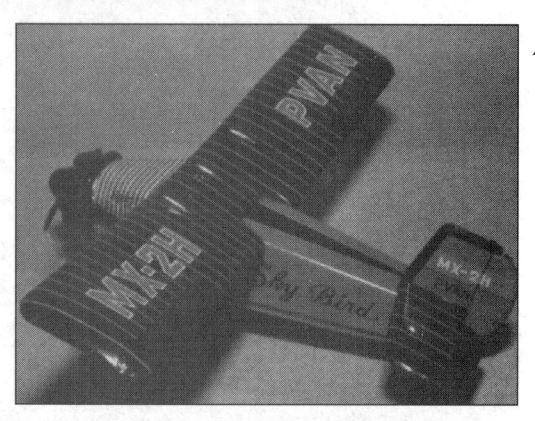

A15

A17

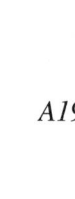

A18

A19

A20

A21

*All Photos by
Ron Smith.*

148

No.	Type	Manufacturer	Power	Wingspan	C6	C8	C10
A32	Hein	Banda	Friction	14"	200	350	500
A33	Zero	Nomura	Friction	14"	150	275	350
A34	Zero	Nomura	Friction	14"	150	275	350
A35	Lockheed Sirus	Japan	Friction	13"	400	600	900
A36	Farman	Japan	Friction	10"	500	800	1200
A37	American Airlines DC-7	Japan	Battery	24"	200	400	500
A38	American Airlines Electra	Linemar	Battery	20"	200	400	500
A39	American Airlines Boing 727	Y	Battery	16"	125	175	225
A40	Boeing 707	Japan	Battery	18"	200	300	400
A41	Boeing Stratocruiser	T.N.	Friction	20"	300	400	600
A42	Comet Jetliner	Y	Friction	19"	200	300	400
A43	Eastern Constellation	MSK	Friction	7½"	100	150	200
A44	Eastern Constellation	Hadson	Friction	12"	200	350	450
A45	Eastern DC7	Bandai	Friction	17½"	300	400	600
A46	Presidents Plane	Japan	Battery	20"	275	350	500
A47	PanAm DC7	TN	Friction	17"	300	600	800
A48	PanAm Stato Clipper	Japan	Friction	14"	225	300	450
A49	PanAm Jet Clipper	Linemar	Battery	18"	200	300	425
A50	Northwest DC7	Y	Friction	10"	100	150	225
A51	Northwest Orient	Y	Battery	24"	300	500	650
A52	Northwest DC7	Asahi	Friction	19"	300	600	900
A53	TWA Constellation	Y	Friction	12"	200	300	400
A54	TWA DC4	Linemar	Friction	19"	150	350	475
A55	TWA DC2	Japan	Wind Up	10"	175	300	425
A56	United DC7 Mainliner	TN	Battery	19"	150	275	350
A57	United DC7	Japan	Friction	23"	125	250	400
A58	B-29	Y	Friction	19"	150	300	475
A59	B-36	Y	Friction	26"	300	600	900
A60	B-45 Tornado	Bandai	Friction	16"	100	150	250
A61	B-47 USAF	Daiya	Friction	12"	150	225	325
A62	B-50 USAF	Y	Battery	19"	200	300	400
A63	B-50 superfortress	TCP	Friction	15"	200	300	400
A64	C-120 Pack Plane	Japan	Friction	16"	250	500	750
A65	C-124 Globemaster	Y	Friction	20"	250	600	800
A66	F-84 Airforce	Linemar	Battery	13"	100	150	200
A67	F-86 Airforce	J	Friction	10"	75	125	175
A68	F-94C Starfire	Y	Friction	18"	150	300	450
A69	F-102 USAF	HTS	Friction	11"	125	150	225
A70	F-104 Lockheed	Y	Friction	16"	125	150	175

A22 Photo by Ron Smith.

A23 Photo by Ron Smith.

A24

A25

All Photos, unless marked otherwise, are by Ron Smith.

A26

A27

A28

A29

A30

A32 *Photo Tanaka.*

A33 *Photo Tanaka.*

A34 *Photo Tanaka.*

A35 *Photo Tanaka.*

A36
*Courtesy
Sotheby's.*

ANIMAL-DRAWN

The average mint price in this section in the last edition was $1244.89,
with the average mint price in this edition $1332.82, an increase of 1%. (Left out of this averaging is
the price paid for the George Brown "Charles".)

In this category, the toys generally commanding the highest prices are horse-drawn cast iron pieces. One reason for the eye-opening prices is that horse-drawn cast iron toys have considerable value apart from their lure as toys. There is an air of genuine Americana about them and they are likely to attract the interest of many who otherwise pay no attention to toys (decorators figure largely in this area.)

Since prices are often so high, reproductions, whether honest or dishonest, can be a problem. Things to look for

when a reproduction is suspected include a rougher surface than an old toy would have (recastings are invariably rougher), uneven fit of pieces, a blurring of details, and "aging" that doesn't have the patina of age. Since at least one company, John Wright (formerly Grey Iron), is still manufacturing turn-of-the-century horse-drawn vehicles, some of them from the original molds, it is wise to become familiar with the field before investing heavily.

Carpenter Doctor's Cart. Courtesy Ed Hyers Antique Toys.

ALL-NU Trotter. Photo by Bill Kaufman Courtesy Evelyn Besser.

	C6	C8	C10
"Alderney Dairy" Milk Truck two-horse wood and lithographed paper	175	263	350
All-Nu Trotter, lead alloy, 1941, approx. 4" long	22	34	45

ALTHOF, BERGMANN

Althof, Bergmann began in 1867, when L. Althof teamed with the brothers Bergmann, forming a jobbing firm (the brothers were already jobbers). In 1874 the New York company received two patents, one for a bell toy with three soldiers. In addition to bell and animal-drawn toys, they made (or jobbed out) toy furniture, banks, hoop and clockwork toys.

	C6	C8	C10
Althof, Bergmann "Express" Wagon pull toy, tin with iron wheels 26"	3000	5000	8000
Althof, Bergmann "Fruits and Vegetables", 17½" long	5000	7500	10,000

ALTHOF, BERGMANN "Fruits and Vegetables". Courtesy Ed Hyers Antique Toys.

ALTHOF, BERGMANN "Milk Wagon", 13" long, tin. Courtesy Sotheby's New York.

	C6	C8	C10
Althof, Bergmann Milk Cart, "Pure Milk," 14" long, c. 1880	500	750	1000
Althof, Bergmann "Milk Wagon," 13" long, tin	600	900	1200

ARCADE
(ALL ARCADE TOYS ARE CAST IRON)

	C6	C8	C10
Arcade Bakery wagon, 13"	300	450	600
Arcade "Big Six Circus & Wild West" wagon, 14½" long, (see Movies-"Tom Mix Big Six Circus," appears to be the same except for name)	225	338	450
Arcade Cart, wicker, horse, driver, cast iron	100	150	200
Arcade Coal car with horse	150	225	300
Arcade Contractors Dump Wagon, 14" long, horse team, driver	250	375	500
Arcade "Contractors Dump Wagon," 13¼" two-horse, driver, 1930s	100	150	200
Arcade Farm Wagon, two-horse driver	250	338	500
Arcade McCormick-Deering Plow	175	263	350

ALTHOF, BERGMANN "Express" Wagon, 26" long. Courtesy Sotheby's New York.. Courtesy Ed Hyers Antique Toys.

ARCADE "Contractors Dump Wagon". Courtesy Mapes Auctioneers & Appraisers.

BARCLAY Coach and two, Driver, no outrider. Photo by K. Warren Mitchell.

	C6	C8	C10
Arcade McCormick Deering Farm Wagon, two-horse	400	600	800
Arcade McCormick Deering manure spreader, with team of horses	450	675	900
Arcade Sulky plow, one horse,10½"	150	250	350
Bakery Wagon, one horse, 13" long cast iron	100	200	300
Barclay "Animal Cage" circus wagon, circa 1930s, lead and tin, approx. 9⅞" long, slush lead	30	45	60
Barclay Coach and Four, approx. 10¼" long, slush lead, circa 1930s	30	45	60
Barclay Coach and Two, driver, no outrider	30	45	60
Barclay Covered Wagon with Oxen, under 6½" long, 1930s, "1849"	27	38	55
"Barnum and Bailey" circus cage, elephant drawn, 1930, painted, stained and litho wood, 35" long	400	600	800

"Barnum and Bailey" Circus Cage, 35" long. Courtesy Lloyd W. Ralston Auctions.

ARCADE McCormick Deering Spreader.

BARCLAY Coach and Four, approx. 10¼" long. Photo by Bill Kaufman. Courtesy Evelyn Besser.

BLISS

Bliss was founded about 1832 by Rufus Bliss. Toymaking may not have begun till the late 1860s or early 1870s in its Rehoboth, Mass., plant. But by 1871 its toys were being advertised. Most were made of wood and the range was wide; from dollhouses to trains, Noah's arks and ships. In 1883 Bliss made what might have been the first toy telephone set. The brilliant color lithography of Bliss's toys has made many of them prime collectibles.

	C6	C8	C10
Bliss Cinderella coach, 1890, paper litho on wood, 26" long, 2 horses, 4 coachmen, lift off roof, blocks inside tell Cinderella story	1000	3500	5500
Bliss Fire Hook and Ladder, 29" long, 2 firemen, 2 horses	2000	3000	4000
Bliss fire Hook and Ladder, 31" long, paper litho on wood	1500	2500	4000
Bliss Pansy 4 horse stagecoach, 1890, paper litho on wood, 31", long	1000	1500	2500
"Borden's Farm Products," wood, horse-drawn wagon pull-toy with articulated legs	1000	1500	2000
Bread Wagon "Bread and Cakes" with driver, tin horse, 12½"	350	525	700
Brewery Wagon, cast iron and pressed steel, two horse with driver, 20½" long	350	525	700
Brownie on Elephant-drawn cart, cast iron	400	700	1000
Buckboard, cast iron, 14" long, one horse and driver	200	300	400
Buggy and Horse, tin	300	450	600
Buggy, pressed steel, cast iron wheels and horse	40	60	80

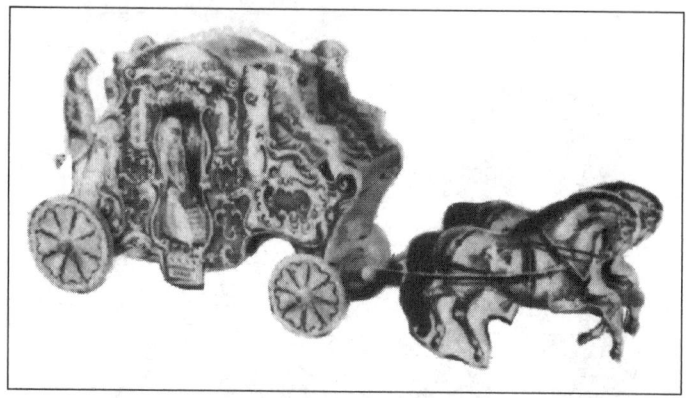

BLISS Cinderella Coach. 1890. Courtesy Lloyd W. Ralston Auctions.

BLISS Pansy 4-horse stagecoach, 1890. Courtesy Lloyd W. Ralston Auctions.

Buggy and Horse, tin. Courtesy Sotheby's New York.

BLISS Fire Hook & Ladder, 2-horse, approx 30" long. Courtesy Wilkinson Collection, Detroit Antique Toy Museum.

	C6	C8	C10
Buggy with driver, cast iron, 6½" long	70	105	140

CARPENTER

Carpenter (Francis W.) of Harrison and Port Chester New York, was in business from 1844-1925. Malleable iron was its trademark; malleable iron being a type that has a bit of give, making it less fragile. Its two predominant lines were horse-drawn toys and trains.

	C6	C8	C10
Carpenter Cart, animated, pat. 1883, cast iron	150	225	300
Carpenter Cart, two-horse, 12" long	250	375	500
Carpenter Cart, two-wheel, one horse, no driver, pat. 1882	250	400	500
Carpenter Coal Cart, iron	2000	3000	4000
Carpenter Delivery Wagon, Pat. 1881, 12" long	200	300	400
Carpenter Doctor's Cart	400	600	800
Carpenter Dump Cart, one-horse 12" long	400	600	800
Carpenter Dump Cart, 2-horse	350	600	800
Carpenter Fire Patrol, cast iron, 2-horse, driver and 3 figures, 1885, 16½" long	900	1400	1900
Carpenter Fire Wagon, one horse, one fireman	350	500	750
Carpenter Hook and Ladder, two-horse, two firemen in standard helmets, early	800	1200	1600

	C6	C8	C10
Carpenter Hook and Ladder, cast iron, 2-horse with driver and rear man, ladders, circa 1883-1890, 26½" long	700	1050	1401
Carpenter Horse and Carriage, 1880 painted cast iron, 14" long	750	1000	1500
Carpenter Horse Cart, cast iron, c. 1880, 14½" long, one horse, two men	800	1200	1600
Carpenter Ox Cart, 2 oxen, cast iron, circa 1880-1903, 11" long	400	600	800
Carpenter Pumper, two-horse 18" long No. 33	750	1125	1500
Carpenter Tally Ho, 27½" long, 4-horse, cast iron, seven festive riders in coach	4000	9500	12,000
Carpenter Wagon, two-horse, 10" long	550	850	1300
Carriage, cast iron, one-horse, 7½" long, Doctors Cart	400	600	800
Carriage, metal and wood, one-horse, malleable iron horse with articulated legs and tail, carriage made of wood	300	450	600
Cart, bull-pulled, cast iron two-wheeled cart	100	150	200
Cart, cast iron lion, two wheels, 8" long	125	188	250
Cart, one-horse, cast iron, 9" long	50	75	100

CARPENTER, Left to Right: Cart, two-horse, 12" long, Dump Cart, one-horse, 12" long (driver not correct in photo). Courtesy Sotheby's New York.

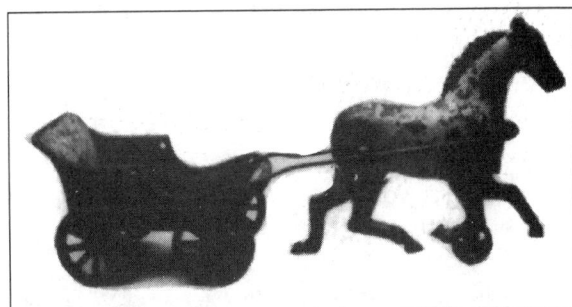

CARPENTER Horse and Carriage, 1880, 14" long. Courtesy Lloyd W. Ralston Auctions.

CARPENTER "Tally-Ho", approx, 27½" long. Courtesy Sotheby's New York.

CARPENTER Fire Patrol, cast iron, 2-horse (one figure in photo missing). Courtesy Sotheby's New York.

Cart one Horse, tin 15" long. Courtesy Lloyd W. Ralston Auctions.

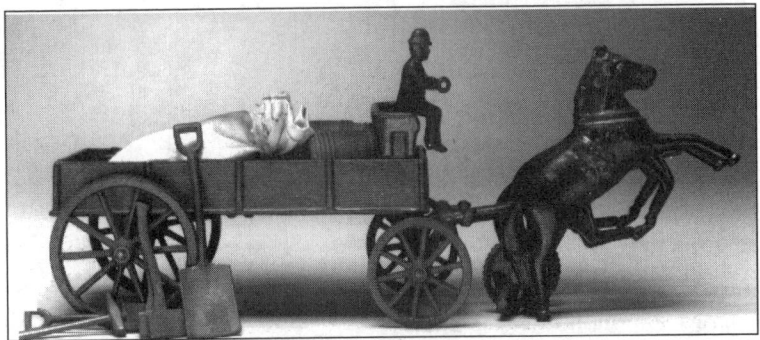

CARPENTER Wagon, two-horse, 16" long (driver in photo replaced). Courtesy Sotheby's New York.

DENT Hook and Ladder, 1915, 14" long. Courtesy Lloyd W. Ralston Auctions.

Chariot with Clown, Camel-Drawn. Courtesy James S. Maxwell/Virginia Caputo. Photo by Virginia Caputo.

DENT Hose Reel, three-horse. Courtesy Sotheby's New York.

DENT Pumper, 1915, 14½" long. Courtesy Lloyd W. Ralston Auctions.

	C6	C8	C10
Cart, one horse 8" long, early tin..........125	188	250
Cart, one horse, painted tin, 1890, 15" long 250	500	750
Cart with driver and buffalo, 7½" long, cast iron..................400	600	800
Cart with cast iron woman and prancing horse, 10¼" long..................500	750	1200
Cart with elephant, cast iron, 7" long...125	188	250
Cart, stake sides, 1-horse, 7" long, early cast iron..................150	225	300
Chariot drawn by tin horse, highly decorated, 13½" long....................125	187	250
Chariot with clown, camel-drawn, cast iron..................1000	1600	2400
Chein "Dispatch" Wagon, 1-horse, 11½" long..................90	135	180
Chief's Wagon, cast iron "Chief," one horse, circa 1915-1920, 12" long...150	225	300
"Chief" fire chief wagon, cast iron, one-horse 15½" long..................200	300	400
Circus Wagon, iron and tin, two horses, lion cage, 9" long...............200	300	400
Circus Wagon, cast iron and wood, containing carved wood bear, 13" long ..250	337	500
"City Sprinkler" 8¼" long, cast iron.....No Price Found		
Coal Wagon, cast iron, small 50	75	100
"Coal" Wagon, cast iron with driver and coal shovel, 9¼" long..............150	225	300
Conestoga Wagon, cast iron, with cloth cover and two horses, 12½"...50	75	100
Conestoga Wagon lithographed walking horses, iron wheels, 18" long...140	210	280
Confectionary Wagon, early 1-horse ..500	750	1000
Courtland Circus Parade No. 300, "Monkeys" on side..................75	100	150
Courtland Circus Parade No. 400, "African Lions" on side 75	100	150
Courtland Circus Parade No. 500, "Circus Band" on side (all Circus Parades 11⅝" long)......................100	150	200

	C6	C8	C10
Courtland Easter Rabbit pulling van, 11⅝" long, No. 200........................50	75	100
Covered Wagon, 13" long, cast iron, cloth top, one horse, driver 170	255	340
Covered Wagon, tin, driver and horse, Indian head lithographed on side 4060	80	
Dent buckboard, rider, one horse, very early, primitive looking..................125	188	250
Dent Cart, horse and driver, 10" long...125	188	250
Dent Cart, lady driver, horse, 11" long 150	225	300
Dent Cart, mule, driver......................250	375	500
Dent Contractors Dump Wagon, two horse, 15" long..................150	225	300
Dent Coupe, one horse, driver, 9¾".....125.	188	250
Dent Dump Cart, black man, mule.......300	450	600
Dent Fire Engine Pumper, silver with white horses, two horse, 21" long..400	750	1000
Dent Fire Engine steam pumper, three horses, 21" long 400	750	1200
Dent Fire Hook & Ladder, 27" long....1200	1800	2400
Dent Fire Patrol, 15½" long, 3-horse, firemen figures................................400	1000	2000
Dent Fire "Patrol", circa 1905, 3-horse, 22" long, cast iron, driver, 6 riders 600	1200	2500
Dent Fire Pumper, circa 1908, 15½" long 3-horse, driver, paint and nickel plate......................................250	400	750
Dent Fire Snorkle Wagon, 3-horse, driver..300	450	600
Dent Hansom Cab, 14" long, cast iron, circa 1905, lady passenger, driver..300	500	850
Dent No. 57 Hansom Cab, two-wheeled, one horse........................175	262	350
Dent Hook and Ladder, three-horse, extra large 500	1000	1500
Dent Hook and Ladder, painted cast iron, 1915, 14" long, mechanized horses 250	400	800

Doctor's Cart, cast iron, 11" long. Courtesy Sotheby's New York.

A tin dog cart circa 1875. The ten inch-long toy's maker is unknown.

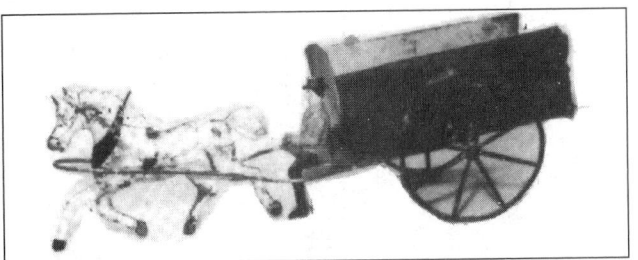

Dumpcart, "Hard and Soft Coal - Coke and Kindlings". Courtesy Lloyd W. Ralston Auctions.

	C6	C8	C10
Dent Hose Reel, three-horse, 24", 10" horse, figures 600	100	1800
Dent Horse and Cart, cart is tin 150	225	300
Dent Horse and Cart, low sides, all cast iron 125	188	250
Dent "Ice" wagon, two horse, 12" 100	200	300
Dent "Ice" wagon, one horse, 14" long 300	500	750
Dent "Ice" Wagon, cast iron, black horse pulling yellow and orange ice wagon, with driver, circa 1910, 15½" long 600	800	1200
Dent Ladder Wagon, 1890, 43½" long, 4-horse, may be longest cast iron toy made 3000	4500	6500
Dent Ox Wagon, 2 oxen, driver, 16" long, cast iron..................................250	500	600
Dent Ox Cart, stake sides, one ox 125	188	250
Dent Police Patrol, three horses, driver and four patrolmen, 21" long 500	1000	1500
Dent Pony Cart No. 20, has driver, team of horses, stake sides on cart ..125	187	250
Dent Pumper, painted cast iron, 1915, 14½" long, moving horses 300	450	600
Dent Road Cart, 1-horse, driver in top hat, 2 seats, 16" long 450	675	900
Dent small truck wagon, stake sides 200	300	400
Dent one horse truck wagon, stake sides, with driver, 16" long 200	300	400
Dent Sulky with jockey 150	225	300
Dent Surrey, horse has wheel attached to one leg.....................................200	300	400
Doctors Cart, cast iron, 11" long 850	1450	2000
Dog Cart (baby carriage), black cloth top, 5½" long, tin 75	112	150
Dog Cart, tin, 10" long, circa 1875 400	600	800
Donkey and Cart, cast iron, with driver...250	375	500
Donkey and Cart, tin, 8" long, iron star wheels.....................................300	450	600
Donkey and Cart, tin, 8½" long 250	375	500

	C6	C8	C10
Dray, cast iron, one horse, black horse pulling yellow dray 200	300	400
Dray Wagon, cast iron, driver and two horses, 18" long 250	375	500
"Dry Goods" cloth and wood two-horse drawn wagon pull-toy circa 1860, 26" long............................400	600	800
Dump Cart, "Hard and Soft Coal-Coke and Kindlings," tin, 19" long...500	750	100
"Dump Cart," horse pulling cart pull toy, 7¾" long..................................80	120	160
Dump Truck, cast iron and tin, one horse 200	300	400

JAMES FALLOWS

James Fallows was a foreman at the very early American tin toy company, Francis, Field and Francis. In 1874 he formed James Fallows & Company in Philadelphia. His toys were often marked "IXL" which may have stood for "I excel." Most of Fallows' toys were tin, though often with cast iron wheels. Papier mache was another prime material, in a toy line that was made up of over 200 items.

	C6	C8	C10
Fallows Cart, tin, 12" long 500	750	1000
Fallows Cart and Horse, painted tin, 1870, 8½" long 100	200	400
Fallows covered Wagon painted tin, litho paper scenes on sides, 12" long 800	1000	1500
Fallows "Dump Cart," 1-horse, 16" long, tin, circa 1890 600	1000	1200
Fallows "Fancy Goods and Toys," 21" long...1750	2625	3500
Fallows "Fine Groceries" delivery wagon, 7½" long...........................1250	1875	2500
Fallows Fire Pumper, 18" long, two horse, very early..........................5000	8500	10,000
Fallows Fire Pumper, 24" long, tin, very early 5000	10,000	15,000
Fallows Horse and Carriage, 1890, American painted and stenciled tin, 12½" long 500	750	1000

"Fire Patrol", cast iron, two horse, three fireman and driver, 20½" long, circa 1890. Courtesy Phillips New York.

FALLOWS Streetcar, "4th Avenue". Courtesy Ed Hyers Antique Toys.

FALLOWS Horse and Carriage, 1890, 12½" long. Courtesy Lloyd W. Ralston Auctions.

FALLOWS Covered Wagon, 12" long. Courtesy Lloyd W. Ralston Auctions.

FALLOWS "Pure Milk" wagon, 12½" long. Courtesy Lloyd W. Ralston Auctions.

	C6	C8	C10
Fallows "Pure Milk" wagon, 1895, painted and stenciled tin, 12½" long	800	1200	2000
Fallows Streetcar, "4th Avenue," one-horse tin	500	750	1000
Fallows Streetcar, 9" long	400	600	900
Fallows Streetcar, 10" long, two horse	350	500	800
Fallows Wagon and Donkey, cast iron, 10½" long	175	263	350
Farm Wagon, cast iron, two horse, 10"	200	300	400
Farm Wagon, cast iron, 14" long, two unusual horses, with driver	250	375	500
Farm Wagon, cast iron, large heavy horses, body wood, 25½" long	300	450	600
Farm Wagon, tin, with horse, 10½" long	40	60	80
"Fine Groceries," tin wagon, two horses, 14" long	400	600	800
Fire Hose Reel, cast iron, horse-drawn, 6"	150	225	300
"Fire Patrol" cast iron three horse wagon contains two firemen and driver, 17" long	900	1350	1800
"Fire Patrol" three-horse, 18¾" long, driver, riders	1000	1500	2000
"Fire Patrol" cast iron, two horse, three firemen, driver, circa 1910, 19" long	1250	1875	2500
"Fire Patrol," cast iron, two-horse, three firemen, one driver, 20½" long, circa 1890	500	750	1000

	C6	C8	C10
Fire Pumper, cast iron, three horse, 11¼"	.500	750	1000
Fire Pumper, cast iron, two horse with driver, 13" long	600	900	1200
Fire Pumper, cast iron, three horse, 14½" long	650	975	1300
Fire Pumper, cast iron, two horse, driver, 19¾" long	500	750	1000
Fire Pumper, circa 1910, cast iron, three horse, 17½" long	500	750	1000
Fire Pumper, cast iron, three horse with driver, fireman, circa 1910, 18¼" long	600	900	1200
Francis, Field and Francis Doctor's Buggy, one-horse, 14" long, tin, circa 1860	No Price Found		

GEORGE BROWN

In 1856, George W. Brown, with Chauncey Goodrich, founded George W. Brown and Company, toymakers. Brown, an innovator, introduced the American clockwork toy (he'd spent 11 years in the clockmaking business). He invented many of his toys' mechanisms and may also have designed all or most of his toys. Brown worked primarily in tin. jobbing some of the work out to companies like Clinton, Connecticut's Union Manufacturing Company. Necessarily simple because of the material and manufacturing techniques employed, Browns's toys made up for it with brilliant hand-painted color and stenciling. Tops, rattles, flutes, wagons, fire engines, swords, trains and toy buckets were among the many items put out by the firm. The company merged with Stevens in 1868 and was dissolved in 1880.

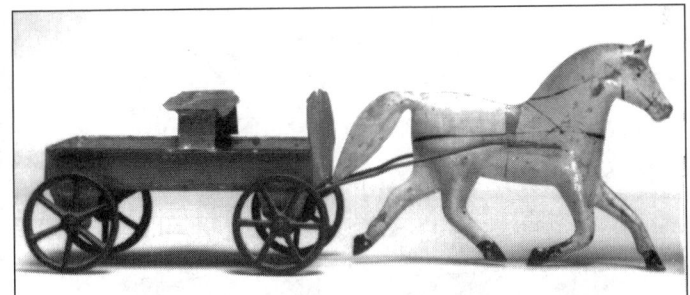

GEORGE BROWN "Express" Wagon, 10½" long. Courtesy Sotheby's New York.

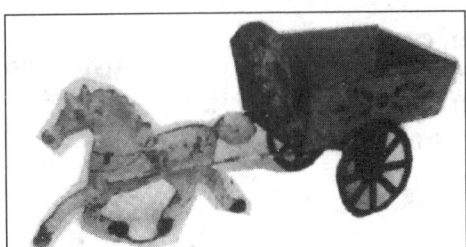

GEORGE BROWN Cart and Horse, 1880, 7½" long. Courtesy Lloyd W. Ralston Auctions.

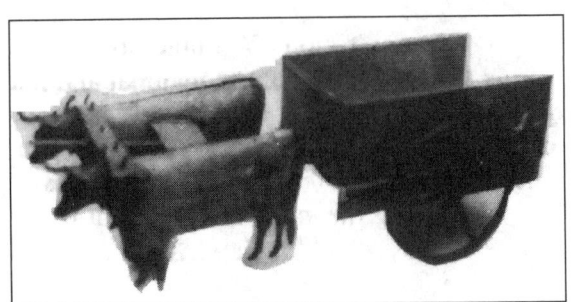

GEORGE BROWN Ox Cart, 9" long. Courtesy Lloyd W. Ralston Auctions.

GEORGE BROWN Dump Cart, 1885, 8¼" long. Courtesy Lloyd W. Ralston Auctions.

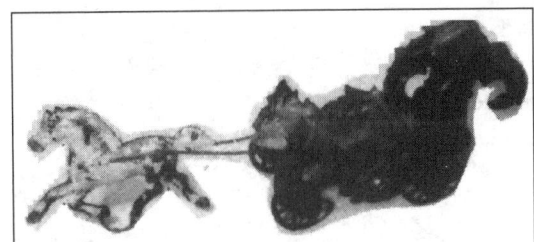

GEORGE BROWN Eagle Chariot. Courtesy Lloyd W. Ralston Auctions.

	C6	C8	C10
George Brown Cab, driver, one-horse, 8½" long	560	840	1120
George Brown Cart and Horse, 1880, painted and stenciled tin, 7½" long	200	300	500
George Brown "Charles" hose reel, circa 1870, 15" long, tin, auctioned in 1991 for $231,000			
George Brown Delivery Cart, 12" long	1100	1800	2600
George Brown Doctor's Buggy, 14" long, tin, and cast iron	650	975	1300
George Brown Dump Cart, painted tin, 1885, 8¼" long	100	150	200
George Brown Dump Cart, 1880, 13" long, tin, back gate lifts out for dumping	150	225	300
George Brown "Eagle Chariot," painted tin, 1870, 11" long	500	1000	2500
George Brown "Express" Wagon, 10½" long, tin wtth iron wheels	300	450	600
George Brown "Fine Groceries" Cart and horse	1250	1875	2500
George Brown gig, tin, 9" long	150	225	300
George Brown gig, tin, 10" long, 1-horse	150	225	300
George Brown Goat Cart. 7" long	300	450	600
George Brown Horse Cart, 1870, tin 11½" long	125	188	250
George Brown Ox Cart, 1880, painted tin, 9" long	500	1000	2000
George Brown Peddle Wagon, tin, circa 1880, 20" long, two wheeled horses, driver, awning	1000	2500	5000

	C6	C8	C10
George Brown Rockaway, passsenger cart, 2-horse, 13" long	1850	2500	4500
George Brown Sulky, 8¾" long	250	375	500
George Brown Yankee Notions Peddler Wagon, 16½" long	3000	7000	10,000

GIBBS

Gibbs Manufacturing Company of Canton, Ohio began turning out toys in 1896 (after previously, from about 1830, manufacturing wooden barrels and tubs and metal plows). The company's first toy was a political giveaway for William McKinley. (McKinley was from Canton.) It was a spring-operated top, and variations of it remained in the firm's catalogs till 1969, when it stopped making toys. Most Gibbs toys were wood or tin, with much use made of lithographed paper for decoration. Many of Gibbs' playthings were of the push and pull variety. Lewis Gibbs was the original owner.

	C6	C8	C10
Gibbs No. 6 Pony Chariot	150	225	300
Gibbs No. 14 "Delivery 14"	150	225	300
Gibbs "No. 27 U.S. Mail" Cart	200	300	400
Gibbs No. 40 English Pony Cart	100	150	200
Gibbs No. 50 Gray Beauty Pacers	150	225	300
Gibbs No. 53 "Pony Circus" Wagon	200	300	400
Gibbs No. 56 "Yankee" Dump Cart	250	375	500
Gibbs No. 57 "Gypsy Wagon"	250	375	500
Gibbs Cart and Horse, paper litho on wood, 13" long	150	225	300
Gibbs "Groceries The Great Atlantic and Pacific Tea Co." mule-drawn cart, 12"	350	500	1000

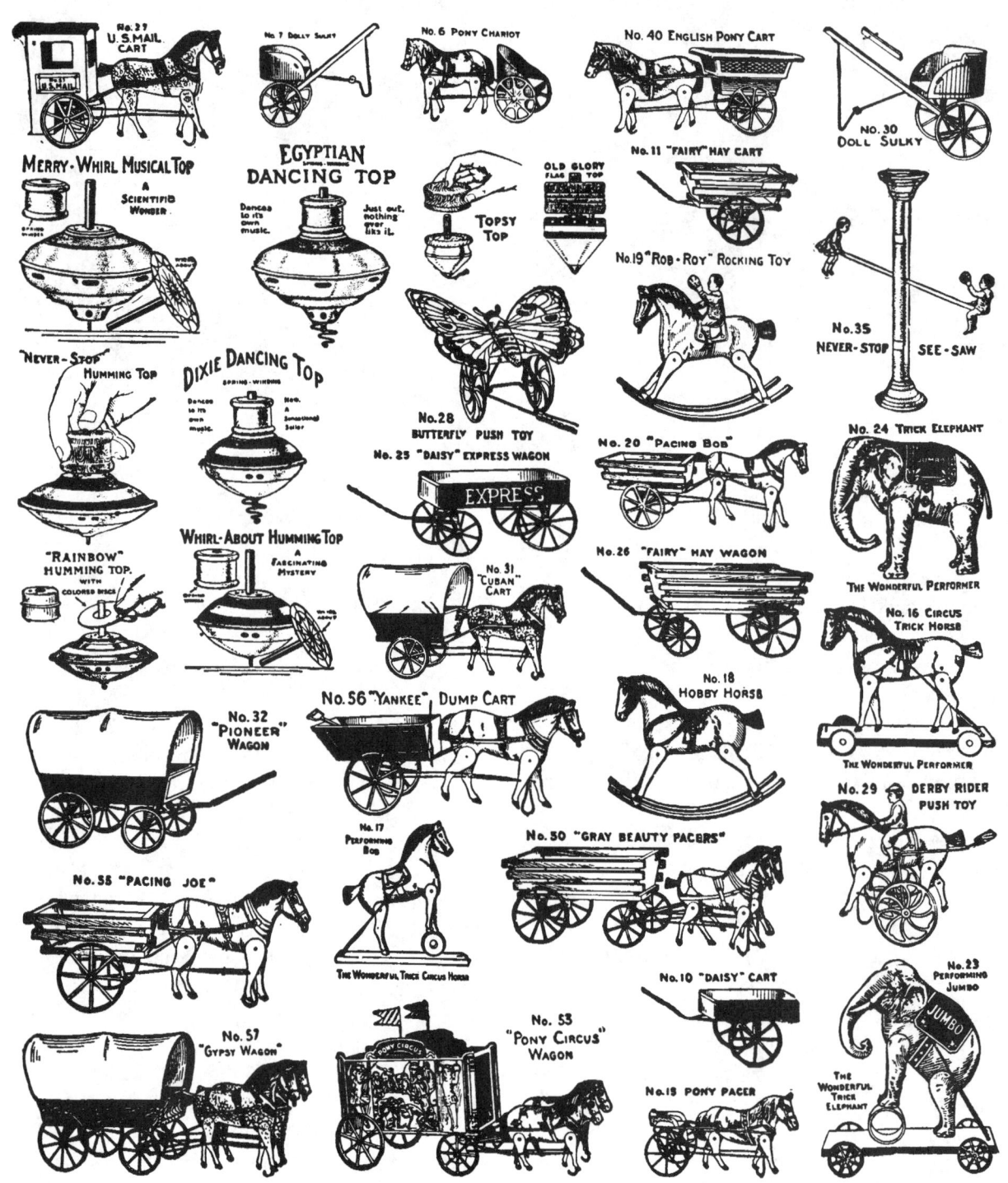

GIBBS No. 50 "Gray Beauty Pacers". Courtesy Lloyd W. Ralston Auctions.

"Golden Pasture Farm Products, Milk and Cream". Courtesy Lloyd W. Ralston Auctions.

GIBBS "U.S. Mail No. 27", 12" long. Courtesy Wilkinson Collection, Detroit Antique Toy Museum.

	C6	C8	C10
Gibbs Tea Co. Mule Cart	350	500	1000
Girard Wagon, 2 tin horses, stake sides	125	188	250
Goat Cart, 7½" long, iron goat and wheels, tin cart	100	150	200
Goat Cart, 10½" long, tin early	150	225	300
"Golden Pasture Farm Products, Milk & Cream" 1915, horse-drawn milk wagon, steering mechanism for child to ride, painted and stenciled wood, 30" long	500	750	1000
Grass Cutter, two horse, driver, two-wheeled cart, cast iron	1000	1500	2000
Hansom Cab, cast iron, no horse or figures	1500	2250	3000
Hansom Cab, 8" long	150	225	300
Hansom Cab with driver, cast iron, 9½" long	120	188	250
Hansom Cab, 9¾" long, cast iron, with driver	250	375	500
Hansom Cab, one horse, driver, 10" long, cast iron	250	375	500

HARRIS

Harris Toy Company of Toledo, Ohio seems to have begun production of cast iron toys during the late 1880s. The firm, which also jobbed for Dent, Hubley and Wilkins, stopped making toys in 1913.

	C6	C8	C10
Harris Brownie Shell Cart, 1903, cast iron	225	338	450
Harris Cart, mule driver, 10" long	250	500	750
Harris, Gloomy Gus standing in tin cart pulled by iron horse, 7½" long	200	350	500

	C6	C8	C10
Harris goat Cart, shell-type, 5" long, cast iron, driver	100	250	350
Harris Goat Cart, two goats, cast iron, driver	1000	2500	3000
Harris Hook and Ladder, 3 horse, cast iron, 19" long	140	210	280
Harris Transfer Wagon, 1903, 18½" long 3-horse	400	650	850
Harris Wagon, mule, 12" long	300	450	600
"Hood's Milk," Rich Toys, wood and tin, horse-drawn wagon pull-toy	37.50	56.25	75.00
Hook and Ladder, cast iron, tin and wood, two-horse with driver and three ladders. 16½" long	150	225	300
Hook and Ladder, cast iron and tin, three horse, two firemen, ladders, 21" long	175	263	350
Hook and Ladder, cast iron, two-horse, 22¾" long	1000	1650	2000
Hook and Ladder, cast iron, three-horse, with driver, 25" long	500	750	1000
Hook and Ladder truck, cast iron, three-horse, 25½" long	600	900	1200
Hook and Ladder truck, cast iron, three-horse, two drivers, four ladders, circa 1910-1914, 31¼" long	1000	1500	2000
Hook and Ladder, pressed steel and iron, figures, ladders, unusual hanging horses	250	375	500
Hook and Ladder, three horses, 27½" long, driver	750	1125	1500
Hook and Ladder, wood ladder with figurines, three-horse, 29½" long	750	1125	1500

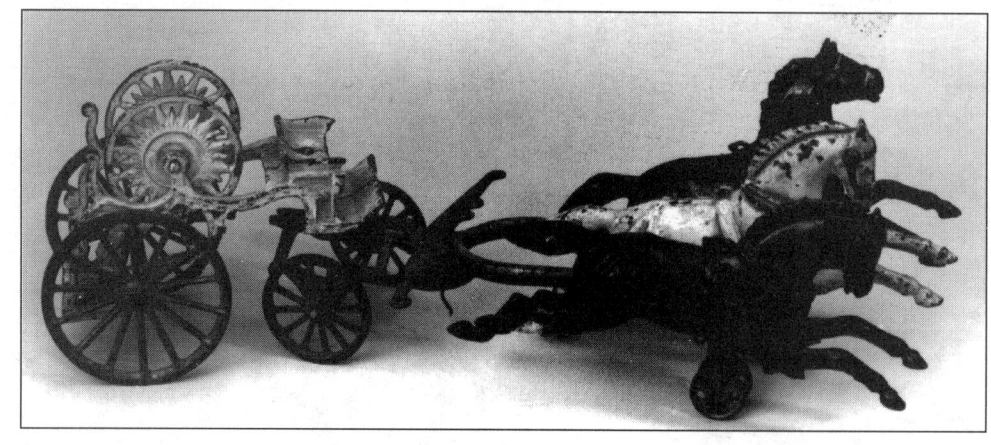

HOSE REEL, cast iron, 3-horse, 19" long. Courtesy Mapes Auctioneers & Appraisers.

	C6	C8	C10
Horse and Cart, lithograph paper on wooden horse, tin cart	150	225	300
Horse pulling two wheel cart, tin	400	600	800
Horse with open carriage and driver in top hat, tin 5½" long	150	225	300
Hose Reel, cast iron, one horse with driver, 11" long	1000	1650	2500
Hose Reel;, cast iron, one horse with driver, 12" long	1000	1650	2500
Hose Reel Wagon, cast iron with driver and cord fire hose, one horse, 12½" long	500	750	1000
Hose Reel, early, two-horse, cast iron, 14½" long, with figure	500	750	1000
Hose Reel, cast iron, 19" long, 3-horse, circa 1910"	600	900	1200
Hose Reel, Wagon, cast iron, driver, 2-horses, man standing on rear bumper, 21" long	750	1125	1500
Hose Reel, cast iron, circa 1910-1914, 3-horse with driver and fireman, 21' long	1000	1500	2000
Hose Reel, early, cast iron, unusual horse	500	750	1000
Hose Wagon, cast iron, two firemen, 3-horse and bell, 21½" long	750	1125	1500
Hubley Brake, four-seated, 4-horse, 8 articulated passengers, 28" long	5000	10,000	12,000
Hubley Brake, 3-seated, 18" long, 2 plumed horses, cast iron	3000	8500	10,000

	C6	C8	C10
Hubley Brake, 2-seated, 16½" long, driver, 3 women passengers	2500	5000	7500
Hubley Brake, 2-seat, 16" long	1600	2700	4000
Hubley Brougham, 16" long, cast iron and nickeled, horse and driver	300	1000	1500
Hubley Brougham, top-hatted driver, 1-horse, 17" long	300	900	1500
Hubley Cab, 14" long	300	500	700
Hubley Cane Wagon, 15" long	600	900	1200
Hubley Cart, 5½" long, driver	150	225	300
Hubley Cart, 8" long, horse and driver	175	263	350
Hubley Cart, wood, iron wheels, iron horse, 10½" long, 1910	175	263	350
Hubley Chariot, cast iron, 8¾"	500	750	1000
Hubley Chariot, 9½" long, 2-horse, driver	600	900	1200
Hubley Chariot with Clown, early, cast iron, three horse, 12½" long	800	1200	1600
Hubley Chariot, Roman, with driver, 3-horse	350	550	800
Hubley Coal Wagon, 16" long, 2-horse	350	550	800
Hubley Coal Wagon, 9" long, mule	250	375	500
Hubley "Dray" 22" long	300	500	700
Hubley Dray Barrel Wagon with barrels, barrel ramp, driver, two-horse	1000	1600	2400

HUBLEY Brake, four-seated, 4-horse, 8 articulated passengers. Courtesy Sotheby's New York.

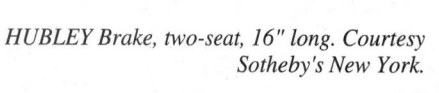

HUBLEY Brake, two-seat, 16" long. Courtesy Sotheby's New York.

HUBLEY Cab, 14" long. Courtesy Sotheby's New York.

HUBLEY Coal Wagon, 16" long, two-horse. Courtesy Sotheby's New York.

HUBLEY Chariot with clown, early, cast iron, three-horse, 12½" long. Courtesy Ed Hyers Antique Toys.

HUBLEY "Royal Circus" Calliope, 12¾" (medium). Courtesy Ed Hyers Antique Toys.

HUBLEY "Dray", 22" long (driver and horses in photo wrong). Courtesy Sotheby's New York.

HUBLEY Hose Tower Wagon, circa 1915, 28" long. Courtesy Sotheby's New York.

HUBLEY "Ice" Wagon, one-horse, 15" long. Courtesy Sotheby's New York.

HUBLEY "Ice" Wagon, 9½" long, 1920's. Courtesy Lloyd W. Ralston Auctions.

163

	C6	C8	C10
Hubley Eagle Milk Wagon, 12" long ...300	750	1000	
Hubley Essex Trap, 13" long, 1890, cast iron, driver and horse..............500	1500	2500	
Hubley Expandable Wagon with wood bed, 26" long, cast iron, 2-horse driver..................750	1125	1500	
Hubley Farm Wagon, 12½" long, 1-horse, circa 1915, cast iron.........400	600	800	
Hubley Fire Patrol, 13" long, driver, four riders, all in standard helmets.500	750	1000	
Hubley Fire Patrol, 21", driver, 4 firemen, prancing horse team.........700	1100	1500	
Hubley fire pumper, cast iron, two horses with driver, crica 1910, 14" long.......200	400	600	
Hubley fire pumper, cast iron, two horse, white-painted, circa 1906-1910, 19" long 750	1125	1500	
Hubley fire pumper, two horse, cast iron, with driver and two firemen, 20" long..............750	1125	1500	
Hubley fire pumper, three-horse, with driver, circa 1906-1910, 20½" long ..800	1200	1600	
Hubley fire pumper, two horses, cast iron, with American Eagle, circa 1905-1910, 21" long 500	1000	1500	
Hubley Gig, lady driver, 15" long, horse drawn.....................350	650	950	
Hubley Hansom Cab, driver cast in window, horse 300	500	750	
Hubley Hook and Ladder, three-horse, two firemen, two wooden ladders, circa 1906-1910, 27¾" long 400	700	1200	
Hubley Hook and Ladder, 2-horse, 28" long, cast iron.....................700	1200	1650	
Hubley hook and ladder wagon, three-horse, 33" long with eagle and shield on side 1200	2000	3000	
Hubley Hose reel, cast iron, three-horse with driver, circa 1906,19"long 750	1200	1700	
Hubley Hose Tower Wagon, circa 1915, 28" long..................800	1300	1800	
Hubley "Ice Wagon," 1920s, 9½" long ...125	188	250	
Hubley "Ice Wagon," 14" long, 1910, cast iron, driver, horse, paint and nickel plate.....................400	850	1200	
Hubley "Ice" Wagon, one-horse, 15" long............................400	650	900	
Hubley "Ice" Wagon, 15" long, 2-horse, cast iron....................550	900	1300	
Hubley "Ice" Wagon, 15½" long, 2-horse, cast iron, black horses pulling green wagon, with driver, circa 1906.....................600	1000	1500	
Hubley "Ice" Wagon, 16½" long, driver, 2-horse.....................750	1125	1500	
Hubley Landau Carriage, 1905, painted cast iron, 16½" long.........1400	2100	2800	
Hubley Log Wagon, 15" long, two oxen, driver, circa 1905 600	1000	1300	
Hubley Log Wagon, 19" long, horse 300	500	750	
Hubley Monkey Trapeze circus mirror van, 12½" long.....................500	1000	1500	
Hubley Phaeton, one-horse..................1200	2000	3000	
Hubley "Police Patrol," 13" long, driver, 3 riders, early 500	750	1000	
Hubley "Police Patrol", 21" long, driver, six cops 1000	1600	2200	
Hubley Revolving Monkey Cage, auctioned for $30,000 in 1988			
Hubley Roman Chariot, three small horses 425	637.50	850	
Hubley Roman Chariot, three large horses 600	900	1200	
Hubley Royal Circus, animals, driver, 2 horses, 15" long 500	1000	1200	
Hubley Royal Circus Bandwagon, 22" long, 4-horse, 7 riders, cast iron....1000	2000	3000	
Hubley Royal Circus Bandwagon, circa 1920, 22½" long, cast iron, 2 horses, 7 riders 1800	2900	4000	
Hubley "Royal Circus" Band Wagon, 30" long, 8 musicians and driver, 1920s.....................1500	2250	3000	
Hubley Royal Circus Bear Wagon, 15" long, cast iron.....................350	550	800	
Hubley "Royal Circus" Calliope, 12¾" (medium).....................600	900	1200	
Hubley "Royal Circus" Clown on Trapeze van, 16½" long, 1920, oval-mirrored sides 1500	2500	3500	
Hubley "Royal Circus" Farmer Van, 1920, 16" long, head revolves and disappears in top of wagon as toy pulled 2000	3000	4000	
Hubley "Royal Circus" Giraffe Cage with large and small giraffes, driver, 1920, 27" long 4200	7700	12,500	
Hubley Royal Circus Lion Cage, 9" long 300	500	750	
Hubley "Royal Circus" Lion Wagon, 15¾" long with rare grey horses and wagon 900	1350	1800	
Hubley Royal Circus Polar Bear Cage, 1920s, 11¾" long 550	850	1450	
Hubley Royal Circus Rhino Wagon, 16" long.....................1000	2000	3000	

HUBLEY Landau Carriage, 1905, 16½" long. Courtesy Lloyd W. Ralston Auctions.

HUBLEY Log Wagon, 15" long, two oxen, driver. Courtesy Ed Hyers Antique Toys.

HUBLEY "Police Patrol", 21" long. Courtesy Sotheby's New York.

HUBLEY Sleigh, one horse, 15" long. Courtesy Lloyd W. Ralston Auctions.

HUBLEY "Royal Circus" Lion Wagon, 15¾" long with rare grey horses and wagon. Courtesy Ed Hyers Antique Toys.

HUBLEY Sleigh, two horse, 15" long. Courtesy Lloyd W. Ralston Auctions.

HUBLEY Sleigh, one horse, 14½" long. Courtesy Lloyd W. Ralston Auctions.

HUBLEY Brake, Left to Right: 2-seated and 3-seated. Courtesy Sotheby's New York.

HUBLEY Royal Circus Bear Wagon, 15" long. Courtesy Sotheby's New York.

HUBLEY Left to Right: Royal Circus Bandwagon, 30" long, Revolving Monkey Cage (extremely rare). Courtesy Sotheby's New York.

HUBLEY "Royal Circus" Bandwagon, 22" long, 4-horse, 7 riders (driver in photo incorrect. Courtesy Sotheby's New York.

HUBLEY "Royal Circus" Farmer Van. Courtesy James S. Maxwell/Virginia Caputo. Photo by Virginia Caputo.

HUBLEY "Royal Circus" Rhino Wagon. Courtesy James S. Maxwell/Virginia Caputo. Photo by Virginia Caputo.

HUBLEY Stanhope Gig. Courtesy Sotheby's New York.

HUBLEY "Royal Circus", Left to Right: Rhino Wagon, Tiger Wagon. Courtesy Sotheby's New York.

HUBLEY Santa Claus sleigh, 16" long. Courtesy Sotheby's New York.

IDEAL "Patrol", cast iron fire patrol, 21" long. Courtesy Sotheby's New York.

	C6	C8	C10
Hubley "Royal Circus" Tiger Wagon Cage, 1920, 16" long, driver, 2 tigers 350	750	1000
Hubley Santa Claus Sleigh, 16" long, 1910, 2 reindeer, cast iron.............600	1000	1500
Hubley Santa Claus, Sleigh, 17" long, early 500	1000	1500
Hubley Shell Cart and Horse, 7", 1905.250	375	500
Hubley Sleigh, one-horse, painted cast iron, 1910, 14½" long 500	750	1000
Hubley Sleigh, one-horse, woman with movable arms, 14¾", early 600	950	1400
Hubley Sleigh, one horse, 1900, painted cast iron, nickel plated, 15" long.....................250	375	500
Hubley Sleigh, 2 horse, 1910, painted and nickel plated cast iron, 15" long..........250	375	500
Hubley Spring Wagon, horse, driver, cast iron.......................200	300	400
Hubley Stanhope Gig, cast iron, 11½" long .200	300	400
Hubley Sulky, 8½" long 150	225	300
Hubley Surrey, clockwork, 1894, 9" long cast iron, brass works, five colors 500	1000	1500
Hubley Surrey, 2-horse, woman driver, 13¾" long........................750	1125	1500

	C6	C8	C10
Hubley Surrey, 18" long, 2-horse, driver..400	600	800
Hubley Surrey, tin and cast iron, two-seat with driver and woman passenger, two horse 600	900	1200
Hubley Surrey, two-seat, 13¾" long, driver, woman passenger, two horse 600	900	1200
Hubley Trotter, 1900, 8¾" long, cast iron, horse and driver 200	300	400
Hubley Trotter Gig, lady driver, 11" long 150	225	300
Hubley Wagon, 12" long, horse, cast iron..150	225	300
Hull & Stafford Dump Cart 700	1000	1600
Hull & Stafford Express Wagon...........350	550	750
Hull & Stafford Wagon, 9" long..........800	1400	2000
Ice Cart, tin horse-drawn......................200	300	400
"Ice" Wagon, one horse, 12", cast iron...500	750	1000
Ice Wagon, cast iron, two-horse, 12" long 600	900	1200
Ideal Fire Pumper, 2-horse, 20½" long, cast iron, 2 riders.............250	500	750
"Ideal Fire Department" 30" long, 3-horse, cast iron.....................500	1000	1500
Ideal "Patrol" cast iron fire patrol, 21" long.........................1000	1700	2500

IVES

Ives is one of the fabled companies in American toy history. It was founded by Riley Ives as a metal stamping shop by at least the late 1850s. About 1865 the company made tin whistles for New York Rubber's squeak toys. This seems to have led to Ives' first true toys, hot air playthings, which were put in motion by the hot air from stoves, lanterns, etc. These were first sold in 1868. Son

Edward Ives joined about 1860. Edward's son, Harry, took over the reins in 1895. He was ousted in 1929, and the firm was dissolved in 1932. During its heyday, which lasted about 40 years, the firm put out a deluge of toys of every type, with quality its watchword. Toymaking was carried on from about 1870 till the end in Bridgeport, Connecticut.

	C6	C8	C10
Ives "Adams Express", 21" long, two-horse 700	1200	1700
Ives Bandwagon, 31½" long, 9 passenger, cast iron 2500	4000	6000
Ives Caisson, 21" long, driver, cannon, two-horse 900	1450	2000
Ives "Chief Fire Dept.", 14½" long......400	700	1000
Ives Coal Dump Cart, donkey, black driver.................500	750	1000
Ives Coal Dump Wagon, donkey, black driver 375	562.50	750
Ives Doctor's Cart, two wheels, 10¼" .400	600	1000
Ives dog pulling stake cart....................200	300	400
Ives Donkey Cart, one of 4 walking animal toys by Ives, circa 1890, 15" long, cast iron.......................750	1500	2500

	C6	C8	C10
Ives Dray Wagon, stake sides...............300	500	700
Ives "Fast Mail" wagon, 17" long, cast iron, walking horses................750	2000	3500
Ives "Fire Patrol," 19" long, circa 1890, 1 horse, 5 riders, driver 1500	2500	4000
Ives Fire Patrol, 20½" long, 2-horse, driver, 6 firemen, cast iron, circa 1880-1910..................800	1600	3000
Ives Fire Pumper, 2 horse, 13" long 400	650	900
Ives Gig, 1890s, driver with top hat, 5½" long 500	750	1000
Ives Hansom Cab with walking horse, oversized 4500	6500	10,000
Ives Hook and Ladder, Phoenix, circa 1890, 28" long.................1500	2400	3600

	C6	C8	C10
Ives Hook and Ladder, circa 1890, 29" long, 2 horse, 2 riders, cast iron 1000	1700	2500
Ives Hook and Ladder, 34" long, cast iron, two-horse, driver 1200	2000	2800
Ives Horse Cart, 1870, 10" long, tin.....600	950	1400
Ives Horse Cart, 1883, 17½" long, 2 horse..750	1200	2500
Ives Hose reel, cast iron, one horse, driver, "Phoenix," circa 1880-1910, 15" long1600	2400	3200
Ives Hose Reel Wagon, one horse, driver, 16" long 750	1125	1500
Ives Ice Wagon with mules, 1896........600	950	1400
Ives Ox Cart, 2 oxen............................800	1300	1800
Ives "Patrol" fire wagon, 22" long 750	1125	1500
Ives Phoenix Pumper, circa 1890, 19" long, cast iron, rarest of Ives pumpers (clockwork) 1500	2400	3800

	C6	C8	C10
Ives Police Patrol Wagon, 1890s, 20½" long, 6 patrolmen, driver 3000	1000	2000	
Ives Pumper, 23" long 2000	3200	4500
Ives Sleigh pulled by walking horse, auctioned in December, 1990 for $25,300			
Ives Stake Wagon, two donkeys, 15½" long 400	600	800
Ives Steam Pumper, two-horse, 20½" .4000	6000	8000
Ives Walking Horse, pull toy, late 19th century, horse which walks by means of wheel mechanism under it, pulling a two-wheeled cart.........................1800	2800	4000
Ives and Blakeslee Fire Pumper, 1893, 25" long, cast iron, largest cast iron pumper made by Ives 1500	3000	5500
Jones & Bixler Uncle Sam Chariot, cast iron, 11½" long.......................550	900	1300

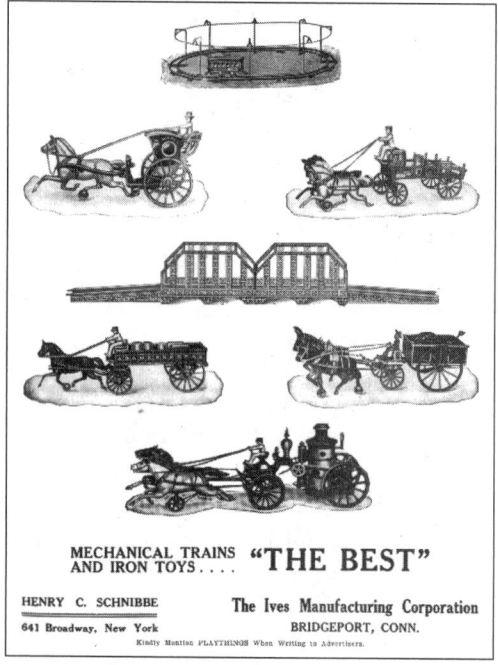

IVES toys from November, 1908. Courtesy Playthings Magazine.

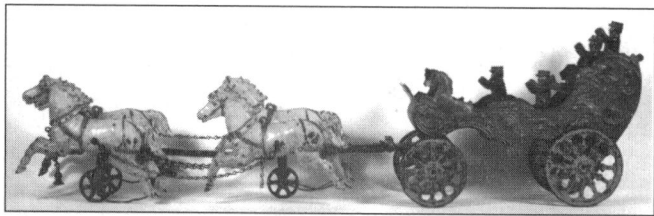

IVES Bandwagon, 31½" long, 5 figures missing in photo. Courtesy James S. Maxwell/Virginia Caputo. Photo by Virginia Caputo.

IVES "Fire Patrol", 20½" long. Courtesy Sotheby's New York.

IVES Dray Wagon, stake sides, 17" long. Courtesy Sotheby's New York.

IVES "Chief Fire Dept.", 14½" long (driver in photo incorrect.). Courtesy Sotheby's New York.

IVES Coal Dump Wagon. Courtesy Sotheby's New York.

IVES Hook and Ladder, 34" long. Courtesy Sotheby's New York.

IVES Hook and Ladder, circa 1890, 29" long. Courtesy Sotheby's New York.

IVES Hose Reel Wagon, one horse, driver, 16" long. Courtesy Sotheby's New York.

IVES "Patrol" fire wagon, 22" long. Courtesy Sotheby's New York.

IVES Stake Wagon, two donkeys, 15½" long. Courtesy Sotheby's New York.

IVES Phoenix Pumper (clockwork). Courtesy Sotheby's New York.

IVES Hook and Ladder, Phoenix. Courtesy Sotheby's New York.

JONES & BIXLER Uncle Sam chariot. Courtesy Sotheby's New York.

KENTON

Kenton Lock Manufacturing Co. was incorporated in May, 1890, in Kenton, Ohio. In November of 1894, it became the Kenton Hardware Manufacturing Company, and around this period, began producing toys. It ceased production of horse-drawn toys in the early 1920s (except for a 1930s beer wagon), but in 1939 introduced a completely new line of horse-drawn pieces, running through 1954.

	C6	C8	C10
Kenton Bakery Wagon, marked "Bakery," 1941	250	375	500
Kenton Band Wagon, musicians, driver, rider on horse	150	225	300
Kenton Boar Cart, 8" long, circa 1910, cast iron, Egyptian driver	350	500	750
Kenton Cabriolet, painted cast iron, 2nd series made into 1950s, 15" long	250	400	600
Kenton Cement Mixer, driver, horse, 14" long	350	750	1000
Kenton Chariot, 6" long, cast iron	150	225	300
Kenton Chariot, 7½" long with comic driver, 1910, cast iron	250	375	500

	C6	C8	C10
Kenton Chariot, 3-horse, cast iron	600	900	1200
Kenton "Chief" wagon, one-horse, driver, 12¼" long	500	800	1500
Kenton Circus Cage Wagon, two horses, two riders, driver, animal in cage	350	700	1000
Kenton "Coal" cart, donkey pulling, black driver	250	375	500
Kenton Contractor's Wagon, with black driver, 15½"	400	600	800
Kenton covered wagon, cast iron, two-horse	500	750	1000
Kenton Delivery Cart, donkey, cast iron	150	225	300

KENTON Hook and Ladder, 30" long. Courtesy Sotheby's New York.

KENTON Log Wagon, 15" long. Courtesy Sotheby's New York.

KENTON "Milk" Wagon. Courtesy Sotheby's New York.

KENTON Overland Circus, Left to Right: Band Wagon, Bear Wagon. Courtesy Sotheby's New York.

KENTON "Overland Circus" Calliope Wagon. Courtesy Sotheby's New York.

KENTON Spider Phaeton, 11½" long. Courtesy Sotheby's New York.

	C6	C8	C10
Kenton Delivery Wagon No. 5 with driver and 2 horses	400	600	800
Kenton Dog Cart, 7" long, greyhound pulling dog riding	250	375	500
Kenton Dray, 13¼" long	100	150	200
Kenton Dray, cast iron, two horse, black and white horses pulling green dray, with driver, 13½" long	300	450	600
Kenton Dray No. 5 painted cast iron, 1930, 14½" long	200	300	400
Kenton Dray Wagon with horse and driver, cast iron, 14¾"	200	300	400
Kenton Dray, cast iron, two-horse, two dark horses pulling a green cart, with driver, 14¾" long	200	300	400
Kenton Dump Cart, mule	125	187.50	250
Kenton Dump Wagon, 10¼" long, early 1900s	150	225	300
Kenton Dump Wagon, two-horses, lever releases bottom wagon	250	375	550
Kenton Egyptian Cart, elephant-drawn	300	450	600
Kenton Express Wagon, horse, driver, cast iron	225	337.50	450

	C6	C8	C10
Kenton Express Wagon, 11" long	225	337.50	450
Kenton Farm Wagon, 14" long, driver, 1 horse	300	500	700
Kenton Farm Wagon, two horse, cast iron, 14½" with figure	500	750	1100
Kenton Farm Wagon, 15" long, driver, 1 horse, early	300	450	600
Kenton Farm Wagon, two horse, 15" with driver	500	750	1000
Kenton Fire Ladder Wagon, front driver only, 12" long	150	225	300
Kenton Fire Ladder Wagon, horsedrawn, 17" long, drivers front and rear	135	202.50	270
Kenton Fire Pumper, 20" long, 2 horse, driver	175	262.50	350
Kenton Fire Pumper, cast iron, 26½" long, horses 11" long	250	375	500
Kenton Fire Wagon, 23" long, 2 horse, driver, equipment, bell, wagon nickel-plated	200	300	400
Kenton goat cart, 7", figure with large ears	250	375	500
Kenton gravel wagon, 13" with two horses	150	225	300

	C6	C8	C10
Kenton Hansom Cab, lady rider, driver in top hat, cast iron 700	1050	1400
Kenton Hansom Cab, 10" long, one horse, top-hatted driver 1000	1500	2000
Kenton Hansom Cab, 12" long.............500	750	1000
Kenton Hansom cab, 15½" long, figures, horse.................................300	500	700
Kenton Hook and Ladder Wagon, 20" long, 2 horse, driver 250	375	500
Kenton Hook and Ladder Wagon, 20" long, nickel-plated, 2-horse, driver 200	300	400
Kenton Hook and Ladder, 16" long, 3-horse, cast iron...........................300	450	650
Kenton Hook and Ladder, wagon, three horses, 17" long 250	375	500
Kenton Hook and Ladder, cast iron, three-horse, circa 1910, 19" long...150	225	300
Kenton Hook and Ladder, 1915, painted cast iron, ladders, 26" long....300	450	600
Kenton Hook and Ladder, 30" long 1400	2200	3200
Kenton Hose Reel, 1920, painted cast iron, 13½" long 500	750	1000
Kenton Hose Reel, cast iron, 14½" long, circa 1905, two-horse............600	900	1200
Kenton "Ice" wagon, 15" long, 2-horse, driver, 1920s, cast iron.....250	375	500
Kenton landau, cast iron, white horse pulling green carriage with driver, circa 1910, 15" long 600	900	1200
Kenton Log Wagon, one horse with driver, 14½" long 450	675	900

	C6	C8	C10
Kenton Log Wagon, 15" long, black man, 2 oxen, early 1900s, cast iron 400	650	900
Kenton "Milk" Wagon, with horse and driver 150	250	350
Kenton Overland Circus Band Wagon, six musicians and driver, 15" long 500	850	1200
Kenton "Overland Circus" Bear Wagon, cast iron, two-horse with driver, cage containing cast iron bears, 13" long, 1940s 200	325	450
Kenton, "Overland Circus" Calliope Wagon 300	500	700
Kenton "Overland Circus", cast iron, 2-horse with driver, cage containing cloth bear, 14" long 500	750	1000
Kenton Ox Cart, 5" long, cast iron.......100	150	200
Kenton Ox Cart, 7" 110	165	220
Kenton Ox Cart, 12½" long 150	225	300
Kenton Ox Wagon, two oxen, 18" long...400	600	800
Kenton "Patrol" No. 526, 2-horse, driver, riders, 17" long 650	1100	1500
Kenton Plantation Cart, 1910, 10" long, black driver, mule 225	337.50	450
Kenon "Polar Ice" wagon, 2-donkey ...500	750	1000
Kenton Police Patrol with mule team, 16"..500	750	1000
Kenton Pumper, 3 horses, 18".............400	600	800
Kenton Rabbit, 5" long, pulling cart with two wheels and seat, cast iron...200	300	500
Kenton Rhino Cart, 8" long................100	200	30

KENTON Plantation Cart, 1910. Courtesy Mapes Auctioneers & Appraisers.

KENTON Hose Reel, 1920, 13½" long. Courtesy Lloyd W. Ralston Auctions.

KENTON Hook & Ladder, 1915, 26" long. Courtesy Lloyd W. Ralston Auctions.

KENTON Dray No. 5, 14½" long. Courtesy Lloyd W. Ralston Auctions.

	C6	C8	C10
Kenton Sand and Gravel dump wagon, 15" long, driver, 2 horses ..225		350	500
Kenton "Sand and Gravel" dump wagon, 10" long, driver, 2 horses ..200		300	400
Kenton Spider Phaeton, 11½" long, cast iron ..850		1350	2000
Kenton Stake Wagon, two horse, 15" long, driver with reins ..200		300	400
Kenton Sulky, driver cast to sulky, 6" long ..75		112.50	150
Kenton Sulky, two-wheel race cart with jockey and horse, 6" ..75		112.50	150
Kenton Sulky and driver, cast iron, 7" long ..250		375	500
Kenton Surrey, two-horse, cast iron with driver and passenger, 12½" ..150		225	300
Kenton Surrey with fringe top, driver and passenger, two-horse (circa 1943?), 13" long ..200		300	400
Kenton Surrey, one horse, approx. 1940, 16" long ..150		225	300
Kenton team of horses with log and black driver ..500		750	1000
Kenton Transfer Wagon, 2-horse, driver ..650		975	1300
Kenton 3.2 Beer Delivery Wagon, 14½" long, 1930s, cast iron, 2-horse, driver, 10 wooden kegs ..350		525	700
Kenton Victoria Cab and horse, cast iron, with driver and woman, 15½" long ..200		300	400
Kenton No. 3, one-horse wagon, with driver, 15" long ..125		187.50	250
Kenton No. 5 wagon, one horse, 15" long ..125		187.50	250
Kenton wagon with driver, two-horse, 10¼" long ..100		150	200
Kingsbury Dray, 2-horse, cast iron, 20¼" ..300		450	600
Kingsbury Hook & Ladder, 25½" long, 3-horse, 2 riders, rubber covers on wheels, cast iron and pressed steel ..400		600	800
Kingsbury Hook and Ladder, 2-horse, driver, 3 ladders, 27" long ..600		900	1200

	C6	C8	C10
Kingsbury Ladder Truck, 13", 1900, cast iron, tin and wood ..300		450	600
"The Klondike Ice Co., New York" tin ice wagon, two-horse, 17½" long ..350		525	700
Kyser & Rex Santa Claus in sleigh, cast iron and steel, auctioned in 1990 for $2970			
Ladder Wagon, cast iron, two ladders and three galloping horses, 13½ " long ..150		225	300
Ladder Wagon, cast iron, with two horses, three sections of ladder, bell, 25½" long ..250		375	500
Ladder Wagon, cast iron with two drivers, four sections of ladder and three horses, Dart type, 30½" long ..200		300	400
Lancaster Hook and Ladder, two-horse cast iron, 25" long ..150		225	300
Lancaster Hook and Ladder, cast iron, 28" long, two horses, two drivers ..200		300	400
Lancaster Hook and Ladder, 28" long, iron, three horse, two drivers ..250		375	500
Lancaster Hubley No. 58 Surrey, no driver ..75		112.50	150
Lancaster Hubley No. 174, surrey with one seat, driver, horse ..150		225	300
Landau, four-horse, 24" with driver ..300		450	600
Lehmann "Africa" tin friction toy, ostrich pulling cart ..400		600	800
Lehmann "Duo" Rooster pulling egg cast with a rabbit perched on top, tin friction ..800		1200	1600
Lincoln Logs No. 30 Covered Wagon Set ..62.50		93.75	125
Log Wagon, cast iron with driver and two oxen, 15¼" long ..450		675	900
Mail Cart, tin, horse-drawn ..100		150	250
Marx Covered Wagon, tin litho, 9" long, friction ..60		90	120
Marx Parcel Wagon with 2-horse team .55		83	110

LEHMANN "Africa". Courtesy Sotheby's New York.

Milk Wagon, tin, 13" long (Merriam?). Courtesy Sotheby's New York.

MASON & PARKER Buckboard, one-horse, 31" long. Courtesy Lloyd W. Ralston Auctions.

MASON & PARKER Cart and Horse, 13" long. Courtesy Lloyd W. Ralston Auctions.

	C6	C8	C10
Mason & Parker, buckboard, one-horse, 1910, pressed painted steel, 31" long.	500	750	1000
Mason & Parker Cart & Horse, 1910, painted pressed steel, 13" long, mechanical action from axle	500	750	1000
McCormick Deering farm wagon, two-horse, 12½" long, cast iron	125	187.50	250
Merriam, cab and horse, 1880, painted and stenciled tin, 8½" long	1000	1500	2000
Merriam Wagon and Horse, American painted & stenciled tin, 1890, 19½" long	2500	3375	5000
Mess Cart, WW I-type, tin, two horse drawn, painted	100	150	200
Milk Wagon, goat-drawn, possibly George Brown, painted tin, 6" long	150	225	300
"Milk" wagon, driver and one horse, 12¾" long	100	150	200
Milk Wagon, tin, 13" long, Merriam ?	500	800	1200
Mower, two horses and driver, cast iron, 10" long	150	225	300
"National Express" wagon, tin litho, horse, 15" long	250	375	500
Omnibus, "People's" tin, with two horses, driver, circa 1880s-1890s	4000	6000	8000
Ox Cart, cast iron, 5" long, with ox	90	135	180
Ox Cart, cast iron, 11½" long	250	337.50	500
"**Pansy**" Stage Coach, Reed, 28" long, 4 horse, driver, lithographed alphabet blocks	1000	1500	2000

	C6	C8	C10
Phaeton, one-horse with driver, 16" long	450	700	1000
Plow, one horse, cast iron, 10¾"	150	225	300
Police Patrol Wagon, cast iron, 11½" long, figures and driver, one horse.	100	150	200
"Police Patrol," cast iron, one-horse, 12"	150	225	300
"Police Patrol" wagon, cast iron, with driver and five policemen and two horses, 15"	1700	2800	4000

PRATT & LETCHWORTH

Pratt and Letchworth was in business from about 1880 into the 1890s. The Buffalo, New York firm sold its toys under the name Buffalo Toy Works. Iron and steel were its main materials, and all of its most prominent toys seem to have been horse-drawn.

	C6	C8	C10
Pratt & Letchworth Artillery, 34" long, circa 1890, cast iron, hand-painted, 4-horse caisson, cannon, 4 riders, one auctioned in late 1990 for $19,250			
"Pratt & Letchworth" Cart, 10" long	150	225	300
Pratt & Letchworth Chief's Wagon	1100	1650	2200
Pratt & Letchworth Double Surrey, 15" long	450	750	1100
Pratt & Letchworth Dray, one horse, cast iron and wood, 1890, 12" long	250	500	750

MERRIAM Wagon & Horse, 1890, 19½" long. Courtesy Lloyd W. Ralston Auctions.

MERRIAM Cab & Horse, 1880, 8½" long. Courtesy Lloyd W. Ralston Auctions.

PRATT & LETCHWORTH Artillery. Courtesy Sotheby's New York.

PRATT & LETCHWORTH four-seat Brake, 28" long. Courtesy Sotheby's New York.

PRATT & LETCHWORTH, Top to Bottom: Hansom Cab circa 1892, Double Surrey, 15" long. Courtesy Sotheby's New York.

PRATT & LETCHWORTH Surrey, 15" long. Courtesy Sotheby's New York.

	C6	C8	C10
Pratt & Letchworth four-seat Brake, four horse, driver, 7 passengers, 28" long	2500	4000	6000
Pratt & Letchworth Gig, cast iron and pressed steel, 10½" long, seven colors, one horse, one rider	400	600	800
Pratt & Letchworth Hansom Cab, circa 1892, cast iron, 13" long	400	600	800
Pratt & Letchworth Hay Cart, 10½" long	500	750	1000
Pratt & Letchworth Hose Reel, small, one-horse, driver in standard helmet	900	1350	1800
Pratt & Letchworth Hose Reel, one horse, 14¼"	900	1350	1800
Pratt & Letchworth Pumper, two horse	1750	2625	3500
Pratt & Letchworth Sulky, 8½" long	400	650	900
Pratt & Letchworth Surrey, 15" long	500	850	1200
Pratt & Letchworth-Welker & Crosby Dray, 14½" long, one-horse, driver	500	850	1500
Produce Wagon, painted tin, one horse, George Brown?, 12½" long	350	525	700

	C6	C8	C10
Pull Toy, tin, horse and cart, iron wheels, 11" long	250	375	500
Pull Toy, horse and covered delivery wagon, tin, 5¼" long	150	225	300
Pull Toy, horse and wagon, two wheels, tin, 9¼" long	125	187.50	250
Pull Toy, horse-drawn carriage, tin, 12" long.	150	225	300
Pull Toy, horse pulling water wagon, tin, iron wheels, 6¾" long	350	525	700
Pull Toy, horse pulling water, wagon, tin, iron wheels, 7¼" long	125	187.50	250
Pumper, 15½" long, driver part of casting, 2-horse, early	200	300	400
Pumper, cast iron, with driver and two horses	325	500	750
Pumper, cast iron, three horses with figure, 13" long	120	180	240
Reed "Band Chariot", 28½" long, 14 bandsmen	800	1200	2000
Rich Toys "Borden's Golden Crest" wooden dairy cart, 18" long	50	80	120
Rich Toys "Budweiser" Beer wagon	300	500	800
Rich Toys "Rich's City Dairy"	125	188	250
Rich Toys Streetcar No. 59, 2-horse 20" long, c. 1925	600	900	1200

*Produce Wagon, painted tin, one-horse (George Brown?).
Courtesy Sotheby's New York.*

*RICH TOYS NO.59 Streetcar, two-horse, 20" long.
Courtesy Wilkinson Collection, Detroit Antique Toy
Museum.*

*SHIMER "Choice Family Groceries Tea, Coffee & Spices".
Courtesy Sotheby's New York.*

*SHIMER "Patrol", animated, black prisoner. Courtesy James S. Maxwell/Virginia
Caputo. Photo by Virginia Caputo.*

	C6	C8	C10
"**Sand and Gravel**," wagon with driver, cast iron, 9½" long	150	225	300
Sand and Gravel Wagon, cast iron, 10" long, two horses	150	225	300
Sand and Gravel Wagon, single horse with driver, cast iron, 10½" long	175	262.50	350
"Sand and Gravel" Wagon, cast iron, driver, two-horse, 14¾" long	100	150	200
"Sand and Gravel" Wagon, with driver and two horses, cast iron, 15"	150	225	300
Santa and Sleigh, cast iron, 16x7"	500	750	1000
Santa Claus in wooden sleigh pulled by reindeer, 25" long, Santa composition, reindeer plush with cast pewter antlers, early	1500	2250	3000
Santa Claus, reindeer pulling sled, two reindeer pulling white sled containing black-painted Santa Claus	500	800	1200
Sheep, cast iron, pulling two-wheeled tin wagon, 8" long	125	200	300
"**Sheffield Farms Company**," wooden horse-drawn milk wagon, horse has articulated legs, 21" long	250	400	650
Shimer "Choice Family Groceries Tea, Coffee & Spices," 12½" long	500	800	1200
Shimer "Patrol," animated, cast iron, 21" long, black prisoner, 5 cops	3500	6500	9000
Shimer Surrey, woman driver	375	562.50	750

	C6	C8	C10
Spring Wagon, cast iron with driver, horse, 11"	150	225	300
Spring Wagon, cast iron, driver, one horse, 14½" long	150	250	350
Spring Wagon, driver and two horses, cast iron, 14½" long	150	275	400
Spring Wagon, driver and two horses, miniature pick, shovel, sledge-hammer, 14¼" long, cast iron	600	900	1200
Spring Wagon, cast iron, two horses, 15"	150	225	300
Stagecoach with cowboy driver and two horses, 11" long, cast iron	130	195	260
Stagecoach, 6-horse, 27" long, cast iron	60	90	120
Stake Bed Wagon, cast iron, one horse, 14¾"	400	700	1000
"**Stanley**" surrey with driver, lady passenger, two-horse, 14¾" long	110	165	220
Steam Pumper with stationary driver, two horses, cast iron, 9¼" long	100	150	250
Steam Pumper, cast iron, stationary driver, three horses, 10½" long	150	225	300
Steam Pumper, cast iron, 15" long with stationary driver and two horses	500	750	1000
Steam Pumper, cast iron, two horses, stationary driver, 15¼" long	800	1350	2000
Steam Pumper, cast iron, driver, three horses, bell, 17½" long	600	900	1200

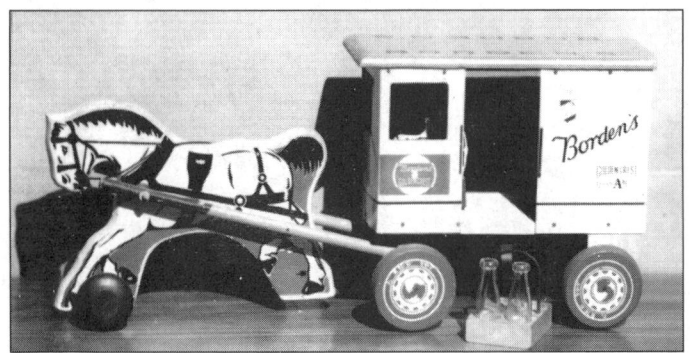

RICH TOYS "Borden's Golden Crest" wooden dairy cart. Courtesy Joe and Sharon Freed.

Santa Claus in wooden sleigh pulled by reindeer, 25" long. Photo courtesy Garth's Auctions Inc.

STEVENS Black Man in cart whipping mule. 9" long. Courtesy Lloyd W. Ralston Auctions.

STEVENS Donkey Cart. Courtesy Sotheby's New York.

	C6	C8	C10
Steam Pumper, two-horse, cast iron with driver, 18" long 600		1000	1500
Steam Pumper, cast iron, driver and two horses, 20½" long 600		900	1500
Steam Pumper, cast iron, three horses and bell, 21¼" high 500		750	1000
Steamer with driver, two horses, 17" long 600		900	1500
Stevens Black Man in cart whipping mule, painted cast iron, mechanical, 1890, 9" 400		600	900
Stevens Donkey Cart, cast iron, 8" long ..300		500	700
Sulky, cast iron, horse and rider, cart mounted with four bells, 6½" 200		300	400
Sulky, cast iron, with driver, 7¼" long.....150		225	300
Sulky, cast iron, with driver, circa 1890s, 8½" long 250		400	550
Sulky, cast iron, with rider, 8¾" 100		150	200
Sulky Rig, horse and driver pull toy, comic style, 10" long, 8" high, 1¼" thick 100		150	200
Surrey, cast iron, two-horse, 13" long.150		225	300
"Teddy Bear" enclosed cart, painted litho tin, 1915, 9" long 600		900	1200
Transfer Wagon, cast iron, two-horse, driver 400		600	800

	C6	C8	C10
"Transfer Wagon", three horses and driver, cast iron, wagon bolted to team, 19" long 400		650	850
"Transfer" Wagon, cast iron, driver and two horses, 19½" long 400		600	800
"Trotter, jockey and horse", cast iron, 6" long 150		225	300
Uncle Sam Eagle Head Chariot, two horse, cast iron 3000		5000	8000
"United States Transfer Co. No. 7," wood wagon with cast iron wheels, 2 stuffed horses, 31" long 300		450	600

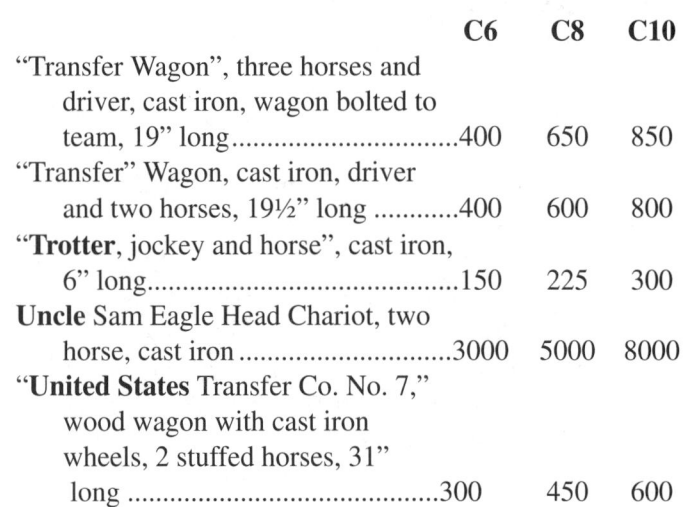

Uncle Sam Eagle Head Chariot, two-horse. Courtesy James S. Maxwell/Virginia Caputo. Photo by Virginia Caputo.

	C6	C8	C10
U.S. Mail Wagon, tin, two-horse, 17" long	500	750	1000
Wagon, two-wheeled, with driver, cast iron, 7¼"	100	150	200
Wagon, cast iron, mule, driver, two-wheeled wagon, 9½" long	350	525	700
Wagon, two-seater, cast iron, one horse	150	225	300
Walking Horse and Sulky Cart, horse			

	C6	C8	C10
of wood, moving legs and cart of tin, wheels cast iron, 7" long	250	375	500
Water Tower with three horses, cast iron and pressed steel, 43" long, horse 11" long	1000	1500	2000
Welker & Crosby Hose Reel, 13½" long	1200	2000	2900
Welker & Crosby Ox Cart, two oxen, black driver	600	900	1200

WILKINS TOY COMPANY

Wilkins, of Keene, New Hampshire, was begun by James S. Wilkins as the Triumph Wringer Company. But the tiny model Wilkins produced to promote his product proved so intriguing to prospective customers and their children that requests for them poured in. The real thing was quickly forgotten as Wilkins turned to toymaking. Its toys were generally cast iron and steel. The firm was acquired in 1894 by Kingsbury, which is still in business, though now as a tool and die maker.

	C6	C8	C10
Wilkins Aerial Fire Wagon, 43" long, cast iron, 3-horse, driver	1200	1800	2400
Wilkins Artillery, 10" long, circa 1895, 2-horse, rider on caisson, seat top lifts off, cannon	1000	1500	2000
Wilkins Buckboard, cast iron	120	180	240
Wilkins Caisson, horse-drawn, 18" long	700	1050	1400
Wilkins Cane Wagon, mule, driver, 11" long	300	450	600
Wilkins Carriage, driver in derby, 1-horse, passenger	1000	1500	2000
Wilkins Cart, animated, 6"	250	375	500
Wilkins Cart and Horse, 10" long	450	700	1000
Wilkins Cart and Horse, 12" long, driver	750	1200	1600
Wilkins Chariot, 7" long, four-horse	180	270	360
Wilkins (?) Chariot, woman driver, 3-horse, cast iron, 10½" long	400	600	800
Wilkins "City Truck," cast iron, two-horse with driver	1000	1500	2000
Wilkins "Coal and Wood" wagon	750	1125	1500
Wilkins Delivery Wagon, 21" long, driver, prancing horse team	600	900	1200
Wilkins Doctor's Cart	325	487.50	650
Wilkins Dog Cart, 7½" long, 1890, cast iron	150	225	300
Wilkins Dog Cart, 10½" long, circa 1890, cast iron, large St. Bernard-type dog, rider in cap	750	1200	1600
Wilkins Donkey Cart, 13¼" long	500	750	1000
Wilkins Dray, 15" long, cast iron	400	600	800
Wilkins, Dray, 16" long, 2-horse, cast iron	325	500	700

	C6	C8	C10
Wilkins Dray, 17½" long, two mules, driver	600	900	1200
Wilkins Dray, cast iron and tin barrel, drawn by two horses, driver in derby hat, circa 1910, 20½"	300	450	600
Wilkins Fire Chief buggy, one horse with rider, 12" long	650	1050	1500
Wilkins Fire Chief Engine Pumper, two horses, 19" long	500	750	1000
Wilkins Fire Hose Reel, 10½" long	350	550	750
Wilkins Fire Ladder Truck, cast iron, 20" long, 3-horse, circa 1910, two firemen	400	600	800
Wilkins Fire Patrol, 20" long, 6 firemen, 3 horses	1700	2700	3650
Wilkins Fire Patrol Wagon, four firemen in wagon, 12" long	250	375	500
Wilkins Fire Patrol, 2-horse, 2 men, cast iron	200	300	400
Wilkins Fire Pumper, 20" long, 2-horse, driver	600	900	1200
Wilkins Gentleman's Cart, 1900, 10" long, gentleman driver, white horse	300	450	600
Wilkins Gig, fancy, and driver, 10" long	150	225	300
Wilkins "Groceries" wagon, one-horse, 13½" long, circa 1900	200	300	400
Wilkins Hansom Cab, cast iron	150	225	300
Wilkins Hook and Ladder, 24" long	500	750	1000
Wilkins Hook and Ladder, 27" long, prancing team, cast iron	750	1125	1500
Wilkins Hook and Ladder, two-horse, horses sit on pegs, has ladders, figures	1000	1500	2000

WILKINS (?) Chariot, Woman Driver. Courtesy Sotheby's New York.

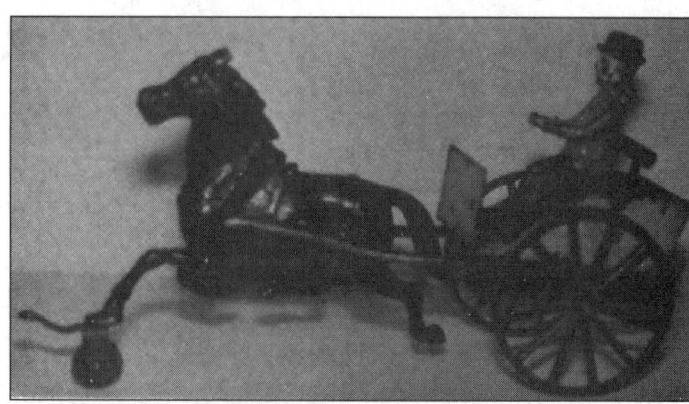

WILKINS Doctor 's Cart. Courtesy Ed Hyers.

WILKINS Dray, cast iron and tin barrel. Courtesy Sotheby's New York.

WILKINS Ox Cart, cast iron. Courtesy Sotheby's New York.

WILKINS Hose Reel, two horse, two firemen in standard helmets. Courtesy Ed Hyers Antique Toys.

WILKINS Fire Ladder Truck, cast iron, 3-horse, 20" long, circa 1910. Courtesy Mapes Auctioneers & Appraisers.

WILKINS Pumper, two horses, two firemen. Courtesy Ed Hyers Antique Toys.

WILKINS Hook And Ladder, two horses, two firemen. Courtesy Ed Hyers Antique Toys.

	C6	C8	C10		C6	C8	C10
Wilkins Hook and Ladder, two horse, two firemen	1000	1500	2000	Wilkins Pony Cart, 7½" long, one horse, driver	400	600	800
Wilkins Hose Reel, two horse, two firemen in standard helmets	750	1125	1500	Wilkins Pumper, two-horse, two firemen	1100	1650	2200
Wilkins Hose Reel, 18" long, circa 1890, 1-horse, cast iron	1000	1500	2000	Wilkins Spring Wagon, driver, horses	300	450	600
Wilkins Huckster's Wagon, two-horse, driver	900	1350	1800	Wilkins Stake Wagon, 1907	625	937.50	1250
Wilkins Ice Wagon, horse, tin and cast iron, 10" long	150	225	300	Wilkins Steam Engine, two-horse, with driver, 17" long	600	900	1300
Wilkins Landau	2000	3000	4000	Wilkins Streetcar, "Broadway Car Line 75," horse-drawn	700	1100	1400
Wilkins Ox Cart, cast iron	300	500	700	Wilkins Streetcar, "Consolidated Street RR 712," 14" long, cast iron	1000	1700	2500
Wilkins Phaeton, driver in top hat, gray pony	450	750	1100	Wilkins Transfer Wagon, tin and cast iron, 15" long	500	850	1200
Wilkins Phaeton, woman driver, 16" long, late 1800s	500	750	1000	Wilkins Wagon, driver, mule, 9" long	300	450	600
Wilkins Plantation Cart, 1910, cast iron and pressed steel, tilt dump, 11" long	400	600	800	Wilkins "Worlds Fair Street RR 372," 15" long, one horse, 6 passenger, cast iron	500	850	1200
Wilkins Plow, one horse, driver, 10½" long	1500	2400	3200	Williams Sulky, 8" long, circa 1920, cast iron	150	225	300
Wilkins Police Patrol, 20" long, driver, 6 policemen, 2 horse, 1911	1700	2700	3750	Wolverine Sulky Racer, plastic	38	53	75

WILKINS Streetcar, "Broadway Car Line 75", horse-drawn
Courtesy Mapes Auctioneers & Appraisers.

WILKINS Aerial Fire Wagon, cast iron, 43" long. Circa 1895, and believed to be the largest cast iron toy made during the 19th century. Courtesy Phillips New York.

WILKINS, Top to Bottom: "World's Fair Street R.R. 372", Transfer Wagon,
tin and cast iron, both 15" long. Courtesy Sotheby's New York.

WILKINS Streetcar, "Consolidated Street RR 712".
Courtesy Wilkinson Collection, Detroit Antique Toy Museum.

MECHANICAL BANKS

by Bill S. Bertoia

The average mint price in this category in the last edition was $7383.91 and in this edition it is $8185.41, an increase of 11%.

After trains, Mechanical Banks are perhaps the most avidly pursued of all the toys cataloged in this book, and the most collectible remain those which were produced in cast iron from around 1870 to 1908, over three hundred different types being producing during that period. One factor that adds to their interest is that many were manufactured with an eye to adult trade as well as to that of children (the "Tammany" bank, for instance). As a result, prices are high, and have been so long before any of the other toys in this book were thought of as collector's items. With prices of this sort, the problem of counterfeiting arises, and care is urged in the purchase of any high-priced bank. Briefly, counterfeits tend to be rougher, to fit together less smoothly, and to not have the patina or "look" of age.

Bill S. Bertoia is a recognized authority in the field of antique toys and banks. As an avid toy and bank collector, he is a member of the Antique Toy Club of America, the Mechanical Bank Collectors of America and the Still Bank Collectors of America. As an active Antiques Dealer Specialist in the field, he handled and appraised the largest collections to have been offered for sale including the Perelman Antique Toy Museum, The Atlanta Toy Museum, The Hegarty Mechanical Bank Collection, The Barenholtz Toy Collection and most recently the largest toy collection ever sold: The Acevedo Toy Collection. He is married to Jeanne Bertoia, the author of the *Doorstop* book. They have two young children who are starting to share their interest in collecting. They reside in Vineland, New Jersey.

	C6	C8	C10
Acrobat Bank, 5" high	1500	3500	6000
Alligator In Trough patented 1867	10,000	20,000	35,000
Always Did Despise A Mule, black jockey on mule, 1879, 10" long	300	700	1200
Always Did Despise A Mule, black on bench being kicked by mule, 1897	450	1000	1900
American Bank sewing machine	3000	6000	10,000
Artillery Bank, Union officer with mortar firing at fort, 1877	650	1100	2100
Astronaut's Bank - gold moon with rocket on stand, has rings showing orbit of space capsule, ring has astronauts' names: "Shepard, Grissom, Glenn, Carpenter, Schirra, Cooper," little plane up side of rocket shoots money into moon, 11" high, pot metal	25	38	50
Atlas Bank	1000	1750	3000
Bad Accident, Mule and black on two-wheeled car, 1887	850	1500	2500
Bear Hugging Tree	150	400	600
Bill E. Grin	200	700	1200
Bird On Roof	500	1200	2500
Book of Knowledge Reproduction of Original Banks, circa 1950; Artillery Bank; Bulldog Bank; Creedmore; Eagle and Eagles; Jonah & Whale; Magician; Man and Pig; Man Milking Cow; Teddy and the Bear; Trick Dog, Trick Pony, Tree Trunk and Buffalo. *(Note - original markings sometimes filed away from bottom and sold as originals).* Price per each	60	90	125

	C6	C8	C10
Boy On Trapeze	850	1500	2500
Boy Robbing Nest	450	1000	2200
Boy Scout	2000	3500	6000
Boys Stealing Watermelons	750	1500	2500
Bread Winner	6000	10,000	15,000
Bull & Bear, brass model	1000	1750	2500
Bulldog Savings Bank	1750	2500	3500
Bulldog, c. 1887, Judd	300	450	600
"Butting" Buffalo	1250	2500	4000
Butting Goat In Tree Stump, c. 1887, Judd	600	900	1200
Calamity, patented August 29, 1905, J&E Stevens Co., three football players	2500	6000	10,000
Cat and Mouse Bank	750	2000	3500
Charlie McCarthy, sitting with legs crossed on top of trunk, drop coin in back and mouth moves, pot metal, copyright 1938, 5¾" high	75	125	200
Chein Monkey, seated, tips hat when coin dropped in, tin litho, 5" high	25	37.50	50
Chief Big Moon, Indian in teepee, etc. 1899	750	1250	2250
Chimpanzee	1500	2200	3500
Chinese Reclining, 1882	1800	2800	4000
Circus Ticket Taker	350	700	1000
Clown & Harlequin, auctioned for $90,000 in 1988			
Clown on Bar, auctioned for $45,000 in 1988			
Clown On Globe, 1873	500	1000	1500
Columbus	200	400	600
Confectionery	3000	6000	10,000
Cow Kicking cow kicks over boy	2000	4500	8000
Creedmore Bank, man firing into tree, 1877, 10" long	200	500	750

181

ALWAYS DID DESPISE A MULE. Courtesy PB Eighty-Four, New York.

ALWAYS DID DESPISE A MULE. Courtesy Sotheby's New York.

ARTILLERY. Courtesy Sotheby's New York.

ALLIGATOR IN TROUGH. Courtesy Sotheby's New York.

ACROBAT. Courtesy PB Eighty-Four, NY.

BIRD ON ROOF. Courtesy Sotheby's New York.

BOY ON TRAPEZE. Courtesy Sotheby's New York.

CREEDMORE. Courtesy Sotheby's New York.

BULLDOG SAVINGS. Courtesy PB Eighty-Four, NY.

BUFFALO, BUCKING. Courtesy Sotheby's New York.

BOY SCOUT. Courtesy Sotheby's New York.

BREAD WINNER. Courtesy Sotheby's New York.

BULLDOG, dog swallows coin. Courtesy Sotheby's New York.

CAT AND MOUSE - CAT BALANCING.
Courtesy Phillips New York.

COW KICKING. Courtesy Sotheby's New York.

DARKY AND CABIN. Courtesy Sotheby's New York.

DINAH. Courtesy Sotheby's New York.

DENTIST. Courtesy PB Eighty-Four, NY.

DOG ON TURNTABLE. Courtesy PB Eighty-Four, NY.

GIANT. Courtesy Sotheby's New York.

JONAH AND THE WHALE. Courtesy Garth's Auction Inc.

CLOWN ON GLOBE Courtesy PB Eighty-Four, New York.

CHIEF BIG MOON. Courtesy PB Eighty-Four, New York.

HOME. Courtesy Sotheby's New York.

FORTUNE TELLER. Courtesy PB Eighty-Four, New York.

ELEPHANT AND CLOWNS. Courtesy Sotheby's New York.

A Full-color ad card for the bank listed here as Eagle and Eaglets. This sold at auction in late 1990 for $200. Courtesy James S. Maxwell/Virginia Caputo. Photo by Virginia Caputo.

	C6	C8	C10
Crowing Rooster...................500	750	1000
Dapper Dan......................200	400	600
Darktown Battery, black pitcher and		
catcher, 1888 600	1200	2000
Darky Football, auctioned for $245,000 in 1988		
Darky and Cabin, 1885.................200	400	600
Dentist Bank, white dentist working		
on black patient, 1880................2500	4000	7500
Dinah, bust of black woman, 6½".......150	350	500
Dog Charges Boy, bronze finish.........400	700	1000
Dog On Turntable, Judd Mfg. Co........150	300	450
Dog Standing.......................150	350	500
Eagle and Eaglets, 1883 300	600	900
Elephant, late cast iron, Hubley..........100	175	250
Elephant, Three Star, cast iron, trunk		
flips up to catch coin, 5" high........150	300	450
Elephant And Clowns.................500	1000	1500
Elephant and Howdah, 1920 250	500	750
Elephant Howdah, circa 1934, Hubley.375	563	750
Ferris Wheel, Hubley/Bauer..............1000	2000	3000
Fortune Teller patented February 19,		
1901, safe, complete with roll of		
fortunes 400	600	800
The Forty-Niner, donkey moves ears		
and tail..........................100	225	400
Freedman, auctioned for $250,00.00 in 1988		
Frog and Snake In Pond lithographed		
tin mechanical bank in the form		
of a snake striking at a frog which		
opens its mouth to receive the		
coin...........................3000	4500	6500
Frog, Goat And Old Man 1200	2500	4000
Frog On Arched Track, auctioned for $35,000.00 in 1988		
Frog On Lattice, Stevens, 1870s 150	350	600
Frog On Rock, Kilgore Mfg. Co. 200	350	550
Frog On Stump, 1872..................200	400	600
Frogs, two, J&E Stevens 600	900	1200
Gem, Dog and building................200	350	500
Giant, giant holding a club..............10,000	15,000	20,000
Girl Skipping Rope, with key 7500	12,500	18,000
Globe Savings Fund Bank...............250	375	500
Guessing Bank......................1500	2500	3500
Hall's Excelsior Bank, monkey cashier.100	350	500
Hall's Lilliput, 1875 200	350	500
Hen And Chick, circa 1901, Stevens...1200	1800	2400
Hen Setting, J&E Stevens 650	975	1300
Hindu, 1882, Kyser & Rex...............1000	1500	2000
Home building with two pillars, teller		
at window, tin....................100	200	300
Hometown Battery, 1940s 200	300	500
Horse Race 4500	7500	10,000
Humpty Dumpty....................250	650	1000
Independence Hall....................150	325	500
Indian Shooting Bear, 1888 600	1000	1500

	C6	C8	C10
Initiating Bank First Degree 3500	6500	10,000
Jolly Nigger, bust.....................100	250	400
Jolly Nigger, high hat, 8" high 150	350	600
Jolly Nigger, moves ears 75	112.50	150
Jonah And The Whale, cast iron		
(Jonah in boat) 900	1250	2000
Jonah And Whale (Jonah emerges)....15,000	22,000	30,000
Jumbo On Platform 800	1150	1500
Katzenjammer Kids...................1500	3500	6000
"Keep 'Em Flying" dime register, tin2537.50	50	
Kick Inn lithographed paper and wood		
mechanical bank, Presto, a mule		
standing in front of a small building..250	375	450
King Aqua, auctioned for $95,00 in 1988		
Leap Frog Bank, two boys, tree, 1891....750	1500	2000
Liberty Bell.........................200	350	500
Lighthouse Bank, 1891.................300	500	750
Lion And Monkeys...................200	400	650
Lion Hunter 2000	3000	4500
Little Jocko........................150	225	300
Little Joe..........................150	225	300
Locomotive........................300	600	900
Magic.............................250	700	1000
Magician Bank, 1882 1500	4000	6500
Mama Katzenjammer And The Kids,		
5¾"..........................3200	5000	6500
Mammy Feeding Child.................2000	3250	5500
Mason And Hod Carrier, 1887 2500	4000	6500
Merry Go Round, semi-mechanical 100	175	250
Meyers No. 84, Jumbo Elephant 100	250	350
Money Box Bank, hand-carved on		
wood base, 10¼"..................800	1200	1600
Monkey And Coconut 500	1100	1600
Mosque 400	800	1200
Mule Bucking Black man riding a		
mule 500	750	1000
Mule Entering Barn 300	600	900
National Bank.......................1500	3500	5000
Naughty Girl Bank, modern 25	50	75
New Creedmore Meyer no.54 200	300	400
New Bank, cast iron, circa 1875, brass		
policeman in building, 4½" long ...200	350	500
North Pole, J&E Stevens Co., Eskimos		
and dog sled 7000	10,000	15,000
Novelty Bank, house-like bank, 1873 ..250	500	750
Organ Bank, monkey and revolving		
cat and dog, 7¼" high 250	500	750
Organ Bank, monkey only.............150	250	400
Organ Boy And Girl, patented June		
13, 1882, monkey flanked by boy		
and girl holding tambourine..........350	700	1000
Organ Grinder And Bear 2000	3000	5500
Organ Grinder And Monkey, 1929.......150	225	350

FROGS, TWO. Courtesy Sotheby's New York.

HEN SETTING. Courtesy Sotheby's New York.

GEM. Courtesy Sotheby's New York.

OWL, turns head. Courtesy PB Eighty-Four, New York.

KICK INN. Courtesy Sotheby's New York.

HUMPTY DUMPTY. Photo Courtesy PB Eighty-Four, New York.

MAGIC. Courtesy Sotheby's New York.

LEAP-FROG BANK. Courtesy Sotheby's New York.

MONKEY AND COCONUT. Courtesy Sotheby's New York.

MAGICIAN. Courtesy Sotheby's New York.

INDIAN SHOOTING BEAR. Courtesy Sotheby's New York.

MULE BUCKING. Courtesy Sotheby's New York.

MULE ENTERING BARN. Courtesy Sotheby's New York.

LION AND MONKEYS. Courtesy Sotheby's New York.

	C6	C8	C10
Owl, slot in back, cast iron	225	337.50	450
Owl, slot in head	150	300	500
Owl, turns head, cast iron	200	350	500
Paddy And His Pig	750	1250	2500
Panorama, building	2000	3500	5000
Patronize The Blind Man And His Dog, patented February 19, 1878, J&E Stevens Co.	1500	3000	4500
Pegleg Beggar	500	1000	1500
Pelican, cast iron, "boy thumbs nose"	500	1000	1500
Perfection Registering	4500	7000	10,000
Piano, circa 1900, E.M. Roche	250	500	750
Picture Gallery	4500	6000	8500
Pig, Bismarck	1500	3000	4500
Pig In High Chair	250	375	500
Preacher In Pulpit	30,000	40,000	50,000
Presto, shape of building	150	250	400
Presto-Mouse On Roof lithographed paper on wood	7500	12,000	17,500
Professor Pug Frog's Great Bicycle Feat	2500	4500	6500
Pump, Bucket	300	700	1000
Punch & Judy, Shepherd Hardware, Buffalo, NY, circa 1890	400	800	1200
Rabbit, tall	300	500	800
Rabbit, small, circular base	200	400	600
Rabbit In Cabbage patch	175	300	450
Red Riding Hood	10,000	15,000	20,000
Roller Skating	15,000	22,000	30,000
Rooster	200	300	450
Santa Claus At Chimney	750	1000	2000
See Him Frisk, auctioned for $55,000 in 1988			
Shoot The Chute	12,500	17,500	25,000
Speaking Dog Bank, J.E. Stevens, pat. 1885	500	1000	1500
Springing Cat, lead alloy, sold for $23,100 in 1991			
Squirrel And Tree Stump	500	850	1200
Standing Bear	100	165	220

	C6	C8	C10
Strato Bank, pot metal, rocket and planet, 8" long, 1950s	10	15	25
Stump Speaker, cast iron	800	1200	2000
Tabby	150	350	600
Tammany Bank, 1875, 5¾" high	100	250	400
Tank And Cannon, 1916	200	300	400
Teddy And The Bear, man firing at bear in tree, 1907	600	950	1400
Telephone	150	300	450
3-Star Elephant, brass	150	300	450
Trick Dog, clown with hoop, dog and barrel, 1888 version, has six part base	300	550	850
Trick Dog, clown with hoop, dark dog and dark barrel, 1929	150	225	300
Trick Pony	400	650	900
Turtle Bank, auctioned for $30,000 in 1988			
Two Frogs (see Frogs, Two)			
U.S. Building, circa 1878, boy and dog in windows, Stevens?	3100	4650	6200
U.S. And Spain	3000	4000	5000
Uncle Remus	2500	3500	5500
Uncle Sam, bust	300	450	600
Uncle Sam, has umbrella in left hand, 1886	1200	2000	3000
Uncle Tom, with lapels and one star	200	350	500
Uncle Tom, with lapels, one star, brass base	600	900	1200
United States Bank, Stevens	650	975	1300
Watchdog Safe	150	300	450
Weeden's Plantation, tin	800	1500	2200
William Tell, 1896	300	500	750
Wireless Bank, 1913	100	250	450
Woodpecker	1500	2800	4000
World's Fair	500	650	850
Zoo	400	700	950

PIANO. Courtesy Sotheby's New York.

NOVELTY. Courtesy Sotheby's New York.

"Professor Pug Frog's Great Bicycle Feat". Courtesy Sotheby's New York.

NEW BANK. Courtesy
Sotheby's New York.

HORSE RACE. Courtesy PB
Eighty-Four, New York.

PEGLEG BEGGAR.
Courtesy Sotheby's New
York.

ORGAN GRINDER AND MONKEY. Courtesy
Sotheby's New York.

LION HUNTER. Courtesy PB Eighty-Four, New
York.

ORGAN BANK, Monkey
only. Courtesy Sotheby's
New York.

MASON AND HOD-CARRIER. Courtesy PB
Eighty-Four, New York.

PRESTO. Courtesy
Sotheby's New York.

PIG IN HIGH CHAIR. Courtesy
Sotheby's New York.

TRICK DOG. Courtesy Sotheby's
New York.

PUNCH AND JUDY. Courtesy PB
Eighty-Four, New York.

UNCLE REMUS. Courtesy Sotheby's New
York.

DARKTOWN BATTERY. Courtesy PB Eighty-
Four, New York.

SANTA CLAUS
AT THE
CHIMNEY.
Courtesy PB
Eighty-Four, NY.

187

PICTURE GALLERY. Courtesy Sotheby's New York.

TEDDY AND THE BEAR. Courtesy PB Eighty-Four, NY.

WILLIAM TELL. Courtesy PB Eighty-Four, NY.

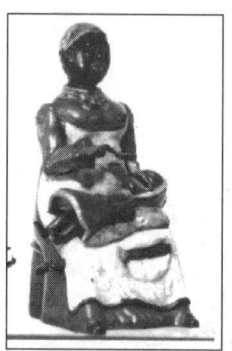

MAMMY FEEDING CHILD. Courtesy Sotheby's New York.

GIRL SKIPPING ROPE. Courtesy PB Eighty-Four, NY.

STUMP SPEAKER. Courtesy PB Eighty-Four, NY.

TRICK PONY. Courtesy PB Eighty-Four, NY.

ROLLER SKATING. Courtesy Sotheby's New York.

RED RIDING HOOD. Courtesy Sotheby's New York.

PADDY AND HIS PIG. Courtesy Garth's Auctions Inc.

ZOO. Courtesy Sotheby's New York.

FROG ON LATTICE. Courtesy PB Eighty-Four, NY.

SPEAKING DOG. Courtesy PB Eighty-Four, NY.

PAPER TOYS

(See also Premiums, Comic Character)
The average price for a mint paper toy in the last edition was $47.64,
and in this edition it is $55.33, an increase of 16%.

AMERICAN PAPER TOYS

by Barbara and Jonathan Newman

The prices of paper toys have stabilized somewhat since the last edition but celebrity paper dolls of the 40's and WW. II military theme materials continue to show larger increases. There is a continuing availability of new models from around the world and an increased availability of some interesting East European paper toys.

This subject of paper toys is so vast that it continues to receive only superficial treatment even in books limited to just that medium. Some brief introduction, nevertheless, should be attempted. They have been called cut-outs, punch outs and press outs. By whatever name, forts, planes, trains, paper dolls and much much more have been produced in paper. What adult does not have some memories (usually fond, often frustrating) of crisp booklets, shiny boxes, or just complicated sheets of paper and cardboard toys?

Throughout the period from the end of the last century to the period after World War II, paper was, if not king, certainly close to the throne. It was, in many ways, the plastic of its day. Every subject matter found in toys can be found in its own version in paper or cardboard.

No collector of military toys or toy soldiers can be unfamiliar with the whole world of paper soldiers, even though they were never quite as popular in this country as in Europe, where paper soldiers were born almost 200 years ago. American companies by the turn of the century were turning out paper toys by the thousands. The most popular was easily the McLoughlin Bros. Company which started out with paper toys in 1857 in New York City and was eventually bought out by Milton Bradley and moved to Springfield, Massachusetts in 1920. Their products included beautifully lithographed covered boxed sets of cardboard figures on wooden stands, or for the young boy with less resources, over a hundred different sheets of American and foreign armies to be cut out and mounted on little wooden stands.

During this same general time period, centered around the 10 years from 1895 to 1905, almost every major newspaper in the country (at least those big city ones with large Sunday editions) had Sunday "Art Supplements" which varied their "give away" fare from Armies or Navies of the world to historical panoramas illustrating our history, from political figures and personalities of the day to cut-out dolls of celebrities with vast wardrobes of clothes. Even the "Globe Quadruple Perfecting Press" itself was offered as a cut-out to construct a complete diorama as the Boston Sunday Globe's offering of August 6, 1896.

Paper houses and villages, a great favorite with little girls of the day, were sold by a wide variety of companies. The earlier ones included the ubiquitous McLoughlin Bros. and Milton Bradley (yes, they're still around) and more recent ones were World War II era giants in the field, Built-Rite and Megow.

In fact, while there was no shortage in the 20's and 30's, it's WW II that was really the Golden Age of paper toys in this country. The reason is obvious and the lack of any alternative material to paper caused the king of toy companies, Lionel, to produce as its only offering in the war, a complete train set in die-cut cardboard. Who would have thought such a poor substitute in 1943 would be a sought after and valuable rarity today? If you have one in mint condition you've got a real gem in both the world of toy trains and paper toys.

During these war years every conceivable type of toy, usually given a wartime, patriotic theme, was available. Punchout cardboard sets of "Rap-A-Jap", "Sink The Axis", "Camouflage Defense Force", books of punch out Naval Craft by Rigby, etc. were the birthday, Christmas or other presents of the forties and early fifties. A whole range of Built-Rite forts, trenches, troops and doll houses are among our own fond memories. Celebrity paper dolls were at their zenith and, except for some vague awareness of the war and being forced to go to school against our wills, Barbara and Jonathan were having a great time playing.

The list and illustrations could go on and on and someday perhaps a reasonably definitive book will be written. For the meantime, just settle for a brief taste in words and pictures to either jog your own memory or kindle an interest in a lifetime passion for paper toys.

For those of you that already have a passion or develop one, there are now quite a few books on the subject of paper dolls, a good general book on paper toys and at least two real specialty books are expected out shortly; one on Paper Soldiers by Edward Ryan and one on World War II era paper toys by John Matthews.

ARMY NURSE AND DOCTOR PAPER DOLLS. Photo by Jonathan Newman. Courtesy Barbara and Jonathan Newman.

ARMY AMBULANCE BUILD FOR VICTORY ACTION ON ROLLING WHEELS. Photo by Jonathan Newman. Courtesy Barbara and Jonathan Newman.

ALL-NU Cardboard soldiers, No.111, 109, 106, 108. Photo by Jonathan Newman. Courtesy Barbara and Jonathan Newman.

	C6	C8	C10
Air-Hostess, 1947, Saalfield 2546	30	40	50
Alice Faye, 1941, Merrill 4800	135	200	225
All-Nu decal sheet of soldiers, meant to be attached to heavy cardboard backing, circa 1942, by Frank Krupp	60	75	100
All-Nu soldiers, 5" high on heavy cardboard, circa 1942-3			
100 Officer marching with sabre	3.00	4.50	6.00
101 Marching, slope arms, WWI helmet	3.00	4.50	6.00
102 Bugler, campaign cap	3.00	4.50	6.00
103 Signalman, WW I helmet	3.00	4.50	6.00
104 Officer kneeling with binoculars	3.00	4.50	6.00
105 Kneeling, firing rifle with WW I helmet	3.00	4.50	6.00
106 Throwing grenade, WW I helmet	3.00	4.50	6.00
107 Fixed bayonet, WW I helmet	3.00	4.50	6.00
108 Charging with gas mask, WW I helmet	3.00	4.50	6.00
109 Charging with rifle, port arms, WW I helmet	3.00	4.50	6.00
110 Seated machine gunner, WW I helmet	3.00	4.50	6.00
111 Flag-bearer, WW I helmet	3.00	4.50	6.00
112 General McArthur	5.00	8.00	12.00
113 Nurse	3.00	4.50	6.00
114 2 Men carrying wounded soldier on stretcher, WW II helmets	3.00	4.50	6.00
115 2 Men firing rifles from prone position, WW II helmets	3.00	4.50	6.00
116 Soldier on wireless radio	3.00	4.50	6.00
117 3 Soldiers w/rifles leaving boat, WW II helmets	3.00	4.50	6.00
118 2 Paratroopers, one w/tommy gun, WW II helmets	3.00	4.50	6.00

	C6	C8	C10
119 Ski trooper	3.00	4.50	6.00
120 Soldier advancing w/rifle, WW II helmet	3.00	4.50	6.00
150 3 Men in jeep, WW I helmets	3.00	4.50	6.00
151 5-man team with cannon, WW I helmets	3.00	4.50	6.00
152 2 men manning wheeled AA gun, WW I helmets	3.00	4.50	6.00
153 Tank with 3 men	3.00	4.50	6.00
154 Ambulance	3.00	4.50	6.00
155 Truck w/soldiers in rear, WW II helmets	3.00	4.50	6.00
All-Nu boxed set of 24 of the above solders	No Price Found		
American Beauties, Paper Dolls, circa 1942, Reuben Lilja & Co., No. 917	15	20	25
American Beauty Paper Dolls with dresses worn by White House First Ladies 1789-1951, Merrill No. 154815, 1951	20	30	40
American Defense Battles Punch-out Book by George Trimmer, Merrill No. 3430, 1940	65	80	90
American Family Paper-Doll Book "Costumes for all the family from 1610 to now," Grinnel No. C1002	45	60	75
Amos & Andy - Cutout cardboard of just Andy, 8½" high, stand-up	4	6	8
Animal Paper Dolls to Dress, 1950, Saalfield 2598, Bear, Monkey, Pig, Kitten	12	15	20
Animals to Paint, 1910, Saalfield	10	15	22
Ann Blythe, 1952 Merrill No. 2250-25	40	75	90

	C6	C8	C10
Army Air Forces Aircraft Identification Silhouette Model - Feb. 1943, 1/72 scale of Japanese fighter Najajima T-97, A.N.F. 7x11 envelope 14	18	25
Army Ambulance, circa 1942, Handi-Kraft..25	35	40
Army Cut Outs, 1937, Saalfield No. 245 ..50	60	75
Army Nurse and Doctor Paper Dolls, 1942, Merrill 3425 40	50	75
Around the World with Bob and Barbara, 1946, Children's Press No.3000 10	15	20
Assemble 9 Model Warplanes, 4 Model Tanks, 1941, Fawcett Publications, Lowe......50	65	80
Ava Gardner, 1949, 1952 Whitman No. 119215......60	75	90
Baby Brother by Queen Holden, 1929, Whitman 920......80	100	125
Baby First Step, 1965 (Mattel), Whitman No. 1997......8	12	15
Babyland 1955, Merrill No. 3642 45	50	70
Baby Pat 1963 Whitman No. 2072......6	8	10
Baby Sitter Paper Dolls, Lowe No.945.....30	35	40
Barbara Britton Paper Dolls with Magic Stay-On Costumes, 1954, Saalfield 5190, Boxed Set......45	55	60
Barbie and Ken 1962 Whitman No. 4797, 7"x12" boxed set 10.00	15.00	20.00
Barbie and Skipper 1964 Whitman No. 1957, Yachting outfits......10.00	15.00	18.00
Barbie Boutique 1973, Whitman No. 1954 ..10	15	18
Beautiful Paper Dolls by Betty Campbell, 1941, Saalfield No. 242, has some of same paper dolls as Little Miss America Paper Dolls 50	60	75
Belle of the Ball Paper Dolls, 1948, Saalfield 2702 25	32	40
Betsy McCall, 1971, Whitman No. 4744 10	12	15
Betsy McCall around the world Paper Dolls, circa 1962 12	15	20
Betsy McCall Dress 'N Play Paper Dolls, 1963, Standard / Toycraft /McCall No. 802 12"x18" boxed set 14	18	22
Betsy Ross and Her Friends - 1963, Platt and Munk No. 224B, 7"x11" boxed set 12	15	20
Betty and Joan, 1941, 1945, Whitman No. 1015, Joan also appears in Mary and Joan, Lois and Joan 30	35	40
Betty Bonnett - Her Family and Friends by Sheila Young, George W. Jacobs & Co., Phila 1915. Each series with 6 sheets and folder. First series......125	150	180
Second series......100	145	175

Left, ALICE FAYE. Right, AMERICAN DEFENSE BATTLES PUNCH-OUT BOOK. Photo by Jonathan A. Newman. Courtesy Barbara and Jonathan Newman.

	C6	C8	C10
Third series 100	145	175
Betty Grable, 1951, Merrill No. 1558 ...60	75	95
Betty Sue - A Cut Out Doll - circa 1940 No. 1010......15	20	25
The Beverly Hillbillies - Jed, Jethro, Granny and Elly May, Whitman No. 1955, 1964......25	30	35
Big-Girl Paper Dolls, 1940, McLoughlin Bros. No. 707, actually Milton Bradley......18	20	25
Big Invasion Punch-Out Book, 1964, Whitman No. 1936, Punchout of beach landing 18	24	30
Bild-A-Set Constructor Kit No.85 boxed, Erector-type set of cardboard......18	20	25
Binson-Freeman Pre Flight Trainer, cockpit and how to fly course 75	113	150
Birthday Party Stand-Up Cut-Out Dolls, 1944, National Syndicate Displays, Inc., 20 boys and girls.....35	42	50
Blue Bonnet Paper Dolls by Florence Salter, Merrill No. 3444, 1942......30	35	40
Blue Feather and Silver Cloud, 1940s, Abbott No. 1356, Indian dolls 35	45	50
Boarding School Dolls and Clothes, 1942, Merrill No. 3492 40	45	55
Bob Hope and Dorothy Lamour, 1942, Whitman No. 976......175	200	225
Bobby Socks Cut Out Dolls designed by Doris Lane Butler, 1945, Whitman No. 988......40	50	60
Bombers by Schomburg, Whitman no. 961, 1943, B017, B-25, B-24, Douglas A-20A, Short "Stirling"....60	75	100
Book of Airplanes, A, Whitman No. 923, 1930 15	20	25
Book of Paper Doll Cut-Outs, The, 1927, Saalfield No. 2051 40	60	75

BOB HOPE & DOROTHY
LAMOUR CUT-OUT BOOK.
*Photo by Jonathan Newman.
Courtesy Barbara and
Jonathan Newman.*

*BETTY BONNET HER
FAMILY AND FRIENDS
(Second Series). Photo by
Jonathan Newman.
Courtesy Barbara and
Jonathan Newman.*

*BIRTHDAY PARTY STAND-UP CUT-OUT DOLLS.
Photo by Jonathan Newman.. Courtesy Barbara and
Jonathan Newman.*

	C6	C8	C10
The Brady Bunch, 1973, Whitman No. 1976	10	15	20
Brenda Lee, 1964, No. 4360 De Journette, 6½"x10" boxed set, includes toy phonograph and records	40	45	50
Brenda Lee Teenage Celebrity, 1961, Lowe No. 2785	15	20	25

*BILD-A-SET CONSTRUCTOR KIT. Photo by Jonathan Newman..
Courtesy Barbara and Jonathan Newman.*

	C6	C8	C10
Bridal Party, 1950, Whitman No. 1187, five dolls	15	20	25
Bride and Groom, 1949, Merrill No. 3443	50	65	75
Bride and Groom, 1949, Merrill No. 1555	50	65	75
Bride and Groom Military Wedding Party, 1941, Merrill No. 3411, 16 dolls	80	90	100
Bride Doll Cut-Out Book, 1940s, Samuel Lowe No. 1043	20	25	30
Brother and Sister Statuette Dolls, 1950, Whitman 1182-15, two heavy cardboard 7½" dolls	15	20	25
Buffy Paper Dolls ("Family Affair") 1968, Whitman No. 1955	15	20	25
Buffy and Jody, 1970, ("Family Affair"), Whitman 4764, Two magic dolls with Stay-On wardrobes	15	20	25

BUILT-RITE

Built-Rite began in 1922 as a manufacturer of cardboard boxes. Somewhere along the line, at least as early as 1934, it began to produce cardboard construction toys. Judging by its catalogs, it sold its last fort (25A) in 1954. Its last few construction sets, three train accessories sets, made their last appearance in the 1956 catalog until 1963-64 when the No. 1033 Doll House and No. 1027 Stock Farm appeared. All construction sets were out from 1967-68 on. In 1978 Built-Rite added plastic playsets No. 6002 Fort Laredo and No. 6001 Starship Counterforce Action Playset. It dropped the Built-Rite name for Warren in 1976, and continues to make card games, games and puzzles under that name. Its greatest period of success was probably enjoyed during and just prior to WWII.

	C6	C8	C10
No. 1 Toy Soldiers, WW I helmets, per each	1.50	2.25	3.00
No. 2 Toy Trench	20	35	40
No. 7 Private Garage, brick	30	40	50
No. 7 Army Plane Hangar	40	45	55

	C6	C8	C10
No. 8 House, brick	65	75	85
No. 9 House, stucco and brick	65	75	85
No. 10 House, two story, brick and shingle	65	75	85
No. 14 "Front Line" Trench and Soldier set, with trench, 6 WW II soldiers	30	40	45

BUILT-RITE, No.20, Army Battery Set. Photo by Ed Poole.

BUILT-RITE, AirportNo.26. Photo by Jonathan A. Newman. Courtesy Barbara and Jonathan Nenman.

BUILT-RITE, Fort No.25, with Barclay soldiers. Photo by Ed Poole.

	C6	C8	C10
No. 15 Commercial Garage	65	70	80
No. 16 Fort, no ramp	65	70	80
No. 17 Service Station	65	70	80
No. 18 Airport	60	65	75
No. 19 Railroad Station	50	60	70
No. 20 Railroad Tunnel	8	15	20
No. 20 Army Battery Set	80	100	125
No. 22 Army Outpost	40	50	60
No. 25 Fort, one ramp	80	100	120
No. 25A 26-piece Fort and Soldier set same fort as 25, WW II soldiers, 2 sandbag foxholes and fiberboard pistol, sold through 1954	90	125	150
No. 26 United Airlines Airport Hangar	55	65	75
No. 27 Barn with Animals	25	35	45
No. 28 Garage and Super Service Station	65	75	85
No. 29 Three Cart Set	25	35	45
No. 33 Lokdwood Dolls, late 1940s, paper dolls	18	25	40
No. 33 House, Tudor type	65	75	85
No. 34 House, two story	65	75	85
No. 35 Modern Doll House	65	75	85
No. 36 House	65	75	85
No. 36F 3-Room Furnished Doll House	65	75	85
No. 37 Farm Machinery Set	25	35	45
No. 45 Living Room Furniture	45	55	65
No. 46 Dining Room Furniture	45	55	65
No. 47 Bedroom Furniture	45	55	65
No. 48 Bathroom Furniture	45	55	65
No. 49 Kitchen Furniture	45	55	65
No. 50 Army Raiders' Victory Unit, 28 pieces, truck, tank, AA gun, jeep, semitrack truck, 20 soldiers, WW II	65	75	85

	C6	C8	C10
No. 55 5 Miniature cardboard houses	30	55	60
No. 56 5 Miniature buildings, church, school, RR station, firehouse, drugstore	30	55	60
No. 57M 8 Piece Farm Set	25	35	45
No. 60 Navy Battle Fleet and Coast Artillery Gun	20	45	60
No. 66 3-piece Kitchen	No Price Found		
No. 75 Living room Furniture	45	55	65
No. 76 Dining Room Furniture	45	55	65
No. 77 Bedroom Furniture	45	55	65
No. 77 American Ranger Fighters, 8 vehicles, WW II soldiers	65	75	85
No. 78 Kitchen Furniture	45	55	65
No. 83 Weapons Carrier	No Price Found		
No. 84 Armored Car	No Price Found		
No. 100A Fortress, circa 1938, two ramps	110	135	150
No. 105 Farm Set with 20 plastic animals	30	40	50
No. 111 Railroad Accessory Set	20	25	35
No. 112 American Fighters - includes 100A fortress with soldiers, cannons, etc., 55 pieces, no flag on tower	100	125	150
No. 115 Doll House, Garage Set (with car)	65	75	85
No. 119 Farm Set	40	50	60
No. 120 Five Room Suburban Doll House	65	75	85
No. 127 Large Barn with Animals	25	35	45
No. 128 Miniature Village and Scenery Set	25	35	45
No. 148 Train Accessory Set	25	35	45
No. 156 Miniature Houses and Buildings	55	65	70

BUILT-RITE, No.22, "Army Outpost". Courtesy John D. (Jack) Matthews.

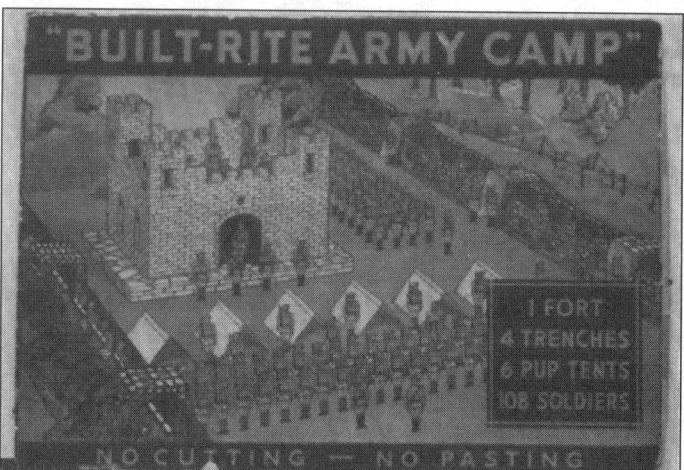

BUILT-RITE, Fort No.16. Courtesy John D. (Jack) Matthews.

CAMOUFLAGE DEFENSE FORCE

	C6	C8	C10
No. 178 Train Accessory Set.................25	35	45
No. 201 26 Piece Guardsman Set, 2 trenches, artillery base, cannon, pistol, WW II soldiers.....................70	80	90
No. 202 Train Scenery (28 pieces, Terminal, Scenery, etc.) 45	65	75
No. 204F Furnished Country Estate 55	65	75
No. 210 Railroad Station and Accessories 25	35	45
No. 212 Station and Railroad Accessories..25	40	50
No. 245 Miniature Village.....................25	35	45
No. 252 Fort Set, 26 pcs, No. 25 Fort, post-war 90	125	150
No. 298 Train Accessory Set.................25	35	45
No. 300 Stock and Grain Glenator 25	35	45
No. 375 Station and Railroad Set 25	35	45
No. 415 House, circa 1943, 13"x20" boxed set with 19" house and garage, 27 pieces of furniture, sedan, baby buggy, shrubbery, etc. .75	90	100
No. 459 5 Rooms of Toy Furniture 25	35	45
No. 460 Pocket Size Series of Miniatures Paperdoll Set.................15	20	24
No. 498 Train Accessary Set.................25	35	45
No. 566 Village..................................40	50	60
No. 1001 Modern Stock Farm..............45	55	75
No. 1027 Stock Farm..........................45	55	75
No. 1033 Doll House...........................45	55	65
No. 1422 Fort and Soldiers (94 pieces, 2-ramp fort)...............................100	135	150
No. 2050 Country Estate, house, bushes, dog, cat, baby buggy 65	75	90
Built-Rite Ranch, over 180 pieces........150	185	200

	C6	C8	C10
Camouflage Defense Force Airplane, soldiers, anti-aircraft guns all hidden within farm buildings. Heavy cardboard. Jay Line Manufacturing Co., 431, boxed. Circa 1943.....................................55	75	90
Career Girls with Cloth-Like Clothes, 1944, Whitman No. 937 by Doris Lane Butler 20	30	40
Charmin' Chatty, 1964, Whitman No. 1959 8	12	15
Charming Paper Dolls, circa 1960, Saalfield No. 1357 6	10	12
Cheerleader - Teen age Doll, 1950? Stephens Publishing Co., No. 182, Mary and Elaine and four pages of clothes...6	12	15
Children From Other Lands, 1961, Whitman, No. 2089, 8 cut-out dolls and native costumes 9	15	18
Children In The Shoe, 1949, Merrill No. 1562...35	40	50
Cinderella Steps Out, Lowe No. 1242 .15	20	25
Circus Day - 1946 by Art Tanchon, Stephens Printing No. 135, Animals, clown, circus cages and wagons 10	15	18

*CLAUDETTE COLBERT PAPER DOLLS.
Photo by Jonathan A. Newman. Courtesy
Barbara and Jonathan Newman.*

*COLLEGE STYLE PAPER DOLLS. Photo
by Jonathan A. Newman. Courtesy
Barbara and Jonathan Newman.*

*CUT-OUT PUPPIES AND KITTENS.
Photo by Jonathan A. Newman. Courtesy
Barbara and Jonathan Newman.*

	C6	C8	C10
Circus Paper Dolls, 1952, No. 2610, Saalfield	6	10	12
Claire McCardell - designer of the American look, 1956, Whitman No. 2067	45	55	65
Claudette Colbert, 1943, Saalfield No. 2451	150	175	200
Cloth-Like Clothes For 3 Cute Girls, 1949, Whitman No. 1178:15, Flocked clothes	20	30	40
Clothes Make A Lady, 1941, Lowe No. 1029	20	30	40
Coke Crowd, The, 1946, Merrill No. 3445, 8 teens, costumes	50	65	75
College Style Paper Dolls, 1941, Merrill 3400	50	65	75
Colorgraphic Statue-ettes, 1943, 3-Dimensional and stand-up paper dolls of Marine, Soldier, Sailor, Nurse, WAAC, WAVE, boxed	25	35	45
Comet Model Airplane Co. Die Cut Glider, 5½x8" sheet containing die cut U.S. Army fighter printed in 1942 by the Comet Model Airplane Co.	6	10	12
Commando Machine Gun 1940s. Thin cardboard cut-out makes model over 25" long	10	15	20
Connie Francis, 1963, Whitman No. 1956	40	50	60
Coronation Cut-Out Model Book	45	55	60
Coronation Glitter Model Book	25	35	40

	C6	C8	C10
Coronation Paper Dolls and Coloring Book, 1953, Saalfield No. 4450, 10½x15" book. Queen Elizabeth, Prince Philip, young Prince Charles and Princess Ann	65	75	90
Cowboy and Cowgirl Cut-Outs, 1950, Merrill No. 3449	30	35	45

CUT AND STICK

CIRCUS DAY Cut-Out Book. Photo by Jonathan A. Newman. Courtesy Barbara and Jonathan Newman.

DOUBLE WEDDING 15 PAPER DOLLS. Photo by Jonathan A. Newman. Courtesy Barbara and Jonathan Newman.

DENISON'S CREPE PAPER DOLL OUTFIT No. 36. Photo by Jonathan A. Newman. Courtesy Barbara and Jonathan Newman.

	C6	C8	C10
Cowboy Cutouts Circa 1930s, Platt and Munk 25		30	40
Cowboys and Indians Cutouts, 1937, Saalfield 50		55	60
Cowgirl Jill and Cowboy Joe, Merrill, No. 3459 25		35	45
The **Cradle** Crowd, 1948, Four doll babies with cloth-like clothes, Whitman No. 1173 50		65	75
Cut and Stick - Our Army and Navy in Action, Merrill No. 4835, 1942 ..30		40	50
Cut-Me Out Paper Dolls, 1940s, Abbott No. 1358 15		20	25
Cut-Out Dolls, Puppies and Kittens, Whitman No. 931, 1939 55		75	90
Cut-Out Dolls with Paints and Clothes to Color, by Avis Mac, Whitman No. 983, circa 1930s 11x18" book with four 17" children and 16 pages of clothing and sheet of paints 50		70	75
Cyd Charisse 1956, Whitman No. 2084 ..45		55	70
Dancing Dolls with famous costumes, Merrill No. 3448, 1954, ballet dancers 35		45	55
Davy Crockett Punch Out Book, 1955, No. 1943 45		60	75
Deanna Durbin, 1940, Merrill No. 3480 175		200	225
Debs and Sub Debs Paper Doll Book, 1941, No. 2361 Saalfield, 20 Punchouts 30		40	50
Decalco-Litho Co. Paper Dolls Sheets. Circa 1920s, 8x10½" sheets, 1. Woman and girl and 9 outfits. 2. Woman and girl and 10 outfits. 3. Two women and 7 outfits. Price per sheet 10		15	20

	C6	C8	C10
Dennison's Crepe Paper Doll Outfit No. 36 70		90	125
Dennison's Dolls and Dresses No. 37, circa 1930 70		90	125
Diane and Daphne The Round About Dolls Book, 1937, No. 545 McLoughlin Bros. Large cut-outs by Campbell 45		60	75
Diana Lynn Paper Dolls, 1953, Saalfield, 157910 45		55	65
Dick the Sailor, circa 1942, Samuel Lowe No. L1074 25		35	45
Disneyland Park Punch Out, 1960, No. 175 30		40	45
Dodie From My Three Sons TV Series, 1971, Artcraft No. 5115, Dodie and Dolly 20		25	35
Dolls From Storyland by Vivian Robbins, 1948, Merrill 1554 30		40	50
Dolls That Walk - "They Walk - They Dance - They Play," designed by Emily Sprague Wurl, Whitman No. 977, 1939, two identical girls and two identical boys 60		70	80
Donna Reed Paper Dolls, 1960, Saalfield/Artcraft No. 5197, 9x12" boxed set 45		55	65
Doris Day, 1952, Whitman No. 210325 ...45		55	65
Dorothy Provine, 1962, Whitman No. 1964 .35		40	50
Double Date Cut-Out Dolls by Elinee Fon Vaughan, 1949, Whitman No. 962 35		40	50
Double Wedding, 1939, Merrill 3472 65		85	100
Down On The Farm, 1940s, Lowe 1056 ..18		25	30
Dr. Kildare and Nurse Susan, early 1960s, Lowe No. 2740 20		30	40
Dress-Up Doll Book, The, 1953 Treasure Books No. T-167 10		15	20

FAIRY FOLK CUT-OUT PAPER DOLLS, Little Bo-Peep. Photo by Jonathan A. Newman. Courtesy Barbara and Jonathan Newman.

GRACE KELLY 2 CUT-OUT DOLLS AND CLOTHES. Photo by Jonathan A. Newman. Courtesy Barbara and Jonathan Newman.

GLENN MILLER MARION HUTTON TURNABOUT DOLL BOOK. Photo by Jonathan A. Newman. Courtesy Barbara and Jonathan Newman.

	C6	C8	C10
Dress Up For The New York World's Fair by Judy and Barry Martin, Spertus No. 700, 1963......8		12	15
Dress-Up Paper Doll Cut-Outs 1947, Reuben Lilja & Co.......15		20	25
Drum Major and Majorette Paper Dolls, 1941, Merrill No. 3415......45		55	65
8 Ages of Judy, The, by Fern Bisil Peat, 1941, Lowe L1025, Judy as baby and ages 1-7......60		75	85
Elizabeth Taylor, 1950, Whitman No. 973-10......65		75	85
Eskimo Cut Outs by Milo Winter, 1939, Whitman 1054......20		30	40
Esther Williams, 1950, Merrill 1563, 3 dolls......60		75	85
Eve Arden Paper Dolls, 1953, Saalfield 158510......50		55	65
Evelyn Rudy - Little Star of Screen and Television, 1958, Saalfield No.1745..30		40	45
Fabulous High Fashion Models, 1958, Bonnie Brooks/Child Craft No. 2776......8		12	15
Fairy Folk Cut-Out Paper Dolls by Margaret Carlson, Still & Edwards Co., Inc., 1920s......12		20	25
Family Princess Paper Dolls, 1958, Merrill No. 1548......45		55	65
Family Affair, 1968, Whitman No. 4767......20		25	30
Family of Paper Dolls, 1947, Saalfield 2564......20		30	40

	C6	C8	C10
Family of Paper Dolls by Queen Holden, Whitman No. 991, Mother, Father, Nurse, 6 kids......80		100	125
Farm Cut-Outs by Milo Winter, 1938, Whitman No. 1054, 6½x10½", six pages of heavy paper cut-outs...20		30	40
The **Fashion** Book of The Round About Dolls, 1936, McLoughlin Bros. Over an inch thick, eight stand-up dolls plus scissors and pack of paper dolls clothes in package by Betty Campbell......50		60	75
Fashion Cut-Outs with Sturdibilt Dolls, 1940s, Lowe No. 1243......15		20	30
Fifteen ABC Blocks to Play and Learn, 1933, Whitman No. 976, book containing 15 die-cut blocks to put together. Illustrations of nursery rhymes, alphabet letters, animals and numbers on each block......15		20	30
Fire Fighters in Action, Saalfield, 1938......20		45	50
Fire House P-18 by Megow, 1945, Brick firehouse. boxed set......20		25	30
Five Little Peppers, Little Women and Annie Lauries, 1941, Lowe L1030, 3-book set......50		60	75
The **Flying** Nun, 1968, 1969, Artcraft No. 4417......20		25	30
Four Sisters Paper Dolls, 1943, Saalfield No. 269......18		20	25

HOUSE FOR SALE. Photo by Jonathan A. Newman. Courtesy Barbara and Jonathan Newman.

LITTLE MARY MIXUP AND HER FRIEND PEGGY. Photo by Jonathan A. Newman. Courtesy Barbara and Jonathan Newman.

	C6	C8	C10
Fourteen Dogs To Cut Out and Stand Up, Copyright 1930, Whitman, No. 935, 12 pages of dogs, cardboard punchouts ...20		30	45
French Infantry - Milton Bradley? circa 1915, approx. 6" high. Single figure, each cardboard...2		4	5
Frontier Fort, 1952, Merrill No.257225...12		18	25
Fun Farm, Reed and Associates...6		10	12
Gene Autry Melody Ranch Cut-Out Dolls, 1950, Whitman No. 990-10..50		65	75
Gene Autry Ranch cut-out book, 1940, Merrill ...65		75	85
Gene Autry Ranch cut-out book, 1953 ...45		55	65
Gigi Perreau Paper Dolls, 1951, Saalfield 1542 ...35		45	50
Gigi Perreau, 1951, Saalfield No. 2605 35		45	50
Girl Friend - Boy Friend Paper Dolls, 1955, Saalfield, No. 1605 ...12		18	20
Girl Friends paper dolls, 1944, Whitman No. 974...20		25	30
Girl Pilots of the Ferry Command, 1943, Merrill 4852 ...75		85	95
Girls In Uniform Paper Dolls Book, circa 1942 No. L1048 ...55		65	75
Glamour Parade Cut-Out Dolls, Stephens Publishing Co., No. 184, 1950s? Four models and four pages of clothes...8		10	14
Glenn Miller, Marion Hutton Turnabout Doll Book, 1942, Lowe No. 21041...120		140	170
Gloria Jean Paper Doll Cut-Outs, 1940, Saalfield No. 1661 ...60		75	90

	C6	C8	C10
Gone With The Wind, 1940, Merrill No. 3404, 18 dolls...325		350	400
Gone With The Wind, 1940, Merrill, 3405, 5 dolls...300		350	400
Good Neighbor Paper Dolls, 1944, Saalfield No. 2487 ...12		20	25
Grace Kelly 2 Cut-Out Dolls and Clothes No. 2049 Whitman, 1955 ..55		60	75
Grace Kelly, 1956, Whitman No. 2069 ...50		55	70
Gulliver's Travels No. 1261 cut-outs, 1939, Saalfield ...50		60	70
Hair-Do Dolls by Queen Holden, 1948, Whitman 991...80		90	110
Harry The Soldier, 1941, Samuel Lowe. No. L1074 ...30		35	40
Hayley Mills, "The Moonspinners," 1964, Whitman No. 1960...40		45	50
Heavy Cruiser "This Is The Navy," circa 1943, Skyline Mfg. Co. ...20		25	30
Hedy Lamarr Paper Dolls, Saalfield 1555	100	120	150
Hee Haw, 1971, Artcraft No. 5139...20		25	30
Heidi and Peter, circa 1970, Saalfield No. 1355...10		12	15
Here Comes The Bride, 1952, Whitman No. 118915...20		25	30
Here's The Bride, 1953, Whitman No. 2109 ...20		25	28
High School Girls, 1948, Merrill No. 1551 ...50		55	65
Historical Dolls To Cut Out And Dress, 1961, Platt & Munk No. 226B, 7"x11" boxed set. Mother, father, and two children of heavy cardboard, plus outfits...12		18	20
Holiday Paper Dolls, 1950s, Saalfield No. 1742...6		10	12
Hollywood Fashion Dolls 1939, Saalfield No. 397, 12 male and female dolls, clothes ...35		45	55

JAUNTY JUNIORS. Photo by Jonathan A. Newman. Courtesy Barbara and Jonathan Newman.

JUNE BRIDE. Photo by Jonathan A. Newman. Courtesy Barbara and Jonathan Newman.

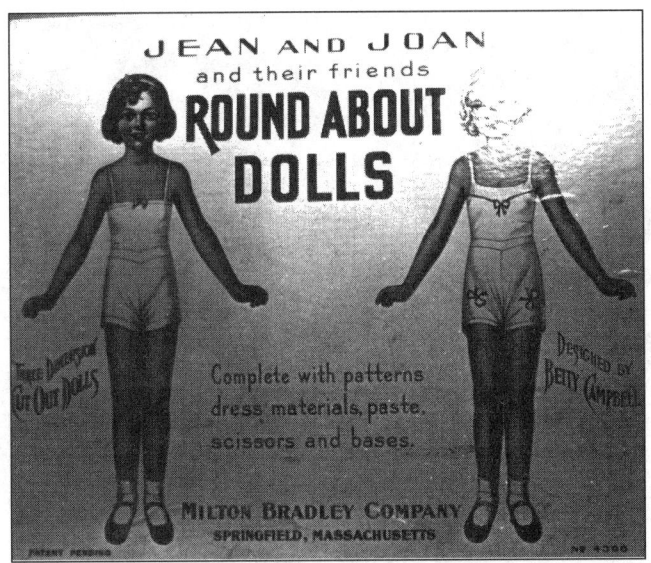

JEAN AND JOAN AND THEIR ROUND ABOUT DOLLS. *Photo by Jonathan A. Newman. Courtesy Barbara and Jonathan Newman.*

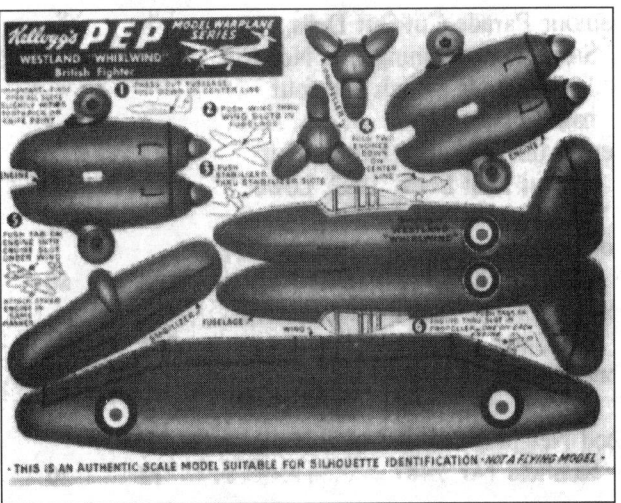

KELLOGG'S PEP WARPLANE, CARDBOARD, CIRCA 1944. *Courtesy HAKE'S Americana & Collectibles.*

	C6	C8	C10
Hollywood Fashions, 1949, Saalfield No. 1535	20	35	50
Hour of Charm Paper Dolls, 1943, women musicians, Saalfield No. 2481	70	80	90
House For Sale, 1962, Lowe No. 9042	30	35	40
House That Jack Built, circa 1895, Bliss, R.I. Paper litho, house and story's characters with stands	400	500	600
Howdy Doody Puppet Show Punch-out Book Copyright 1952, Whitman No. 211129, Punchout cardboard puppets may be controlled by strings. Includes Howdy, Bluster, Inspector, Dilly Dally, Clarabell and Flubadub	50	55	65
Howdy Doody Sticker Fun, copyright 1951, Whitman No. 219525	25	30	35
Howdy Doody Sticker Fun, copyright 1953, Whitman No. 215825	25	30	35
Howdy Doody Sticker Fun Circus, copyright 1955, Whitman No. 2165	25	30	35
I Love Lucy - Lucille Ball and Desi Arnaz, 1953, Whitman No. 2101	55	65	75
Jack and Jill, 1962, Merrill No. 1561, 6 dolls and clothes from storyland	15	20	25
Jane Russell, 1955, Saalfield No. 2611	35	65	75
Janet Leigh Cutouts and Coloring Books, 1953, Merrill No. 2554	55	65	70
Janet Leigh, 1958, Abbott No. 1805	45	50	60
Jaunty Juniors, 1946, No. 903	20	25	30

	C6	C8	C10
Jean and Joan And Their Friends, Round About Dolls designed by Betty Campbell, 1934, boxed set, Milton Bradley No. 4396	75	85	100
Jeanette MacDonald, 1941, Merrill 3640	175	200	225
Jimmy & Jane Visit Gene Autry At Melody Ranch, 1951, Whitman No. 118415	55	60	65
Joan's Wedding by Florence Sarah Winship, clothes designed by Ruth M. Ruhman, 1942, Whitman No. 990	40	45	50
Judy and Jack, Peg & Bill Cut-Out Dolls by Pelagie Doane, 1940, Lowe No. L1024	30	40	45
"Julia" - Diahann Carroll, Julia, Corey, Marie and Earl J. Waggedorn, 1968, Artcraft No. 5140	25	30	35
Julia with Julia, Earl J. Waggedorn and Corey, 1969, Saalfield	25	30	35
June Allyson, 1950, 1952, Whitman No. 119015	40	50	60
June Allyson, 1953, Whitman 1173:15	40	50	60
June Bride by Art Tanchon, 1946, Stephens No. 136	15	20	25
Junior Bombardier, 1953, Einson & Freeman Co. No. 202	20	25	30
Junior Prom by Newman, 1942, Lowe 1042	35	40	45
Karen Goes To College! 1955, Merrill No. 1564	20	30	35
Kiddieland Village circa 1935, Whitman No. 2004, 11½"x15" boxed set, nine buildings and 65 cut-out figures	60	75	90

KIDDIELAND VILLAGE. Photo by Jonathan A. Newman. Courtesy Barbara and Jonathan Newman.

LITTLE FOLKS' FRIENDS. Photo by Jonathan A. Newman. Courtesy Barbara and Jonathan Newman.

LUCILLE BALL, DESI ARNAZ CUT-OUT DOLLS WITH LITTLE RICKY. Photo by Jonathan A. Newman. Courtesy Barbara and Jonathan Newman.

THE LETTIE LANE PAPER FAMILY. Photo by Jonathan A. Newman. Courtesy Barbara and Jonathan Newman.

LITTLE FRIENDS FROM HISTORY. Photo by Jonathan A. Newman. Courtesy Barbara and Jonathan Newman.

LOTS OF LITTLE PAPER DOLLS. Photo by Jonathan A. Newman. Courtesy Barbara and Jonathan Newman.

	C6	C8	C10
Lucille Ball, Desi Arnaz Cut-Out Dolls With Little Ricky, 1953, Whitman 2116:25 50	55	60
Lucille Ball Paper Dolls, 1944, Saalfield 2475 60	75	90
Madame Hattie Fashions, 1940s, Reuben Lilja 908..........25	35	40
Magic Mary, 1955, Milton Bradley No. 4010-1, 10½"x10½" boxed set, complete with magnetic doll and strips to put on clothes 10	15	18
Make Your Own Battle Set Mechanized Force, 1942, Electric Corporation of America 30	35	40
Margaret O'Brien Paper Dolls, Whitman 96410 100	120	150
Marge and Gower Champion, 1959, Whitman..........40	55	65
Martha Hyer Paper Dolls, 1958, Saalfield 4423 35	45	50
Mary and Joan, 1941, 1945, Whitman		

	C6	C8	C10
No. 1015 (Joan also appears in Lois & Joan and Betty & Joan)..........25	35	40
Mary Belle Cut Out Doll by Fern Bisel Peat, Saalfield No. 2100, four separate sheets, 17" doll with three sheets of clothes, 1934 50	60	70
Mary Jane - A Cut Out Doll, by Florence Winship, 1939, 1941, Whitman No. 1010 with suitcase for accessories 40	50	60
Mary Lee - A Cut Out Doll Whitman No. 1010, circa 1939 40	45	50
Mary Martin, 1942, Saalfield 2427 150	175	200
Mary of the WACS - A Young American, by Hilda Miloche and Wilma Kane, Whitman No. 1012, 1943 40	50	60
Mary Poppins, 1973, Whitman No.1977 ..20	25	28
Marybelle Mercer's Front and Back Dolls With Wrap-Around Dresses by Queen Holden No. 978 75	90	100

MCLOUGHLIN BROS. OF BROOKLYN, NEW YORK

McLoughlin Brothers was the largest American producer of paper soldiers, and one of the earliest in the paper doll field. The firm, which traced its founding to 1828, began producing paper dolls at least as early as 1857. Among the other paper toys it sold were dollhouse furniture, toy theaters with actors and scenery, and blocks. The company was sold in 1920 to Milton Bradley.

	C6	C8	C10
McLoughlin Bros., circa 1884, mounted U.S. Cavalry, Hussar type, charging, several different poses. Price per figure 2.75	3	3.50
McLoughlin Bros. Infantry soldiers, printed 1857, price per each $5, complete set $200-250		
McLoughlin Bros., Infantry circa 1875, price per each 3	4	5
McLoughlin Bros., Zouaves, 1884, price per each 2.75	3.50	4.50
McLoughlin Bros. Brass Bank, 1890, price per each 3.50	4.50	5.50
McLoughlin Bros. Grenadiers, 1890, price per each 3	3.50	4
McLoughlin Bros. Paper Dolls 1860-1890, price per cut set, $50 and up; uncut $100 and up, depending on title, date, etc.		
McLoughlin Bros. 100 Soldiers on Parade circa 1898..........300	350	400
McLoughlin Bros. 100 Soldiers on Parade, second set, circa 1898 300	350	400
McLoughlin Bros. 260 series, circa 1889-1895;		
c. U.S. Regulars, spiked helmet, each...2.25	2.75	3d. D.

	C6	C8	C10
d. U.S. Infantry 2.25	2.75	3
e. Mounted U.S. Cavalry, hussar. type, charging 2.25	2.75	3
f. West Point Cadets 2.25	2.75	3
g. U.S. Regulars..........2.25	2.75	3
h. U.S. Infantry 2.25	2.75	3
i. Bandsmen, various instruments, each..........2.75	3	3.50
j. Navy - USS Boston 2.25	2.75	3
k. Grenadier Guards, each 2.25	2.75	3
l. Annapolis Cadets, each 2.25	2.75	3
McLoughlin Bros. Printed 1898, sailor 5¼" high, landing party for USS Texas 4	5	6
McLoughlin Bros. U.S. Infantry from Spanish-American War circa 1898. Approx. 6" high on wooden blocks. Price per figure 4	5	6
McLoughlin Bros. Circa 1898, small glossy series, 4½" high, West Point Cadets. Price per figure 4	5	6
McLoughlin Bros. Circa 1898, glossy series, g. U.S. Regulars, full dress, 5" high..........4	5	6

McLOUGHLIN BROS. 100 SOLDIERS ON PARADE. Photo by Jonathan A. Newman. Courtesy Barbara and Jonathan Newman.

McLOUGHLIN BROS. THE NEW PRETTY VILLAGE. Photo by Jonathan A. Newman. Courtesy Barbara and Jonathan Newman.

McLOUGHLIN BROS., Building from New Pretty Village. Photo by Jonathan A. Newman. Courtesy Barbara and Jonathan Newman.

	C6	C8	C10
McLoughlin Bros. circa 1898, British Infantry red coats, spiked helmets, 6" high on small wooden blocks. Price per figure...........4	5	6
McLoughlin Bros. circa 1898, U.S. Zouaves, Civil War era, blue coats, red baggy trousers, 6" high on small wooden blocks...........4	5	6
McLoughlin Bros. "02" series, circa 1904-1910 a. British Highlanders b. U.S. Zouaves c. U.S. Continentals d. U.S. Navy e. U.S. Infantry in Campaign Uniforms (Spanish American War) h. American Indians, kneeling and standing i. West Point Cadets. Price per figure...........2	2.50	3
McLoughlin Bros. Same as above g. West Point Cadets (round base), circa 1915..2	2.50	3
McLoughlin Bros. No. 0103 Dutch Paper Doll, boy of the Village of		

	C6	C8	C10
Vollendam. Circa 1910, 10½x10½" sheet.15	22	25
McLoughlin Bros. Circa 1915. Boy Scouts holding rifles across chests...4	5	6
McLoughlin Bros. Series No. 4026 10½x10½" Paper soldiers on sheet, seven soldiers plus officer (5½" high) in field uniform. Circa 1916. 1. Belgium 2. France 3. Italy 4. Britain. Price per sheet.......20	30	40
McLoughlin Bros. New Folding Doll House, 1897, boxed set, cardboard with lithographed paper.................350	425	500
McLoughlin Bros. New Pretty Village - Church set 1897...........90	120	140
McLoughlin Bros. New Pretty Village School Set, 1897...........90	120	140
McLoughlin Bros. New Pretty Village, individual bldgs...........12	15	18
Me and Mimi, 1957, A Bonnie Story Book Doll, 6"x8" in the style of the Little Golden Books. A Doll and Her Dolly Story Book, plus dolls and their dresses.................12	20	25
Mexican Cut Outs by Milo Winter, 1938, Whitman 1054, six pages of people, animals, houses, etc. 20	30	40
Mickey and Minnie Paper Dolls, 1930s 2 10" figures with clothes.....90	150	175
Model Airplanes, Samuel Lowe No.1069, 1941, WW II airplanes, International.40	65	75
Model Battleship by Reed, circa 1945, 7x10".................12	18	20
Model Flat-Top by Reed, circa 1945.....12	18	20
Model Tanks, Samuel Lowe No.1065, 1941.45	65	70
Model Tanks Construction Set, boxed set, 1942, Lowe No. 1267 45	65	70

ONE HUNDRED SOLDIERS PUNCH-OUT BOOK, 1943, WHITMAN 999. Courtesy John D. (Jack) Matthews.

MODEL TANKS CONSTRUCTION KIT. Photo by Jonathan A. Newman. Courtesy Barbara and Jonathan Newman.

MAYBELLE MERCER'S FRONT AND BACK DOLLS. Photo by Jonathan A. Newman. Courtesy Barbara and Jonathan Newman.

Make Your Own Battle Set Mechanized Force. Photo by Jonathan A. Newman. Courtesy Barbara and Jonathan Newman.

MODEL WAR PLANES CONSTRUCTION KIT. Photo by Jonathan A. Newman. Courtesy Barbara and Jonathan Newman.

	C6	C8	C10
Model War Planes Construction Set, boxed set, 1942, Lowe No. 1266 45		65	70
Modern Miss in Paper Dolls, 1942, by Van Swearingen, Saalfield 2397 30		40	45
Molly Bee, 1962, Whitman No. 2091 ...12		20	25
Mommy and Me, 1954, Whitman No. 977:10 12		15	18
Mother and Daughter by Patrie Winston, Grinnel Lithographic No. C-1005, 15" mother, 11" daughter, 2 Scotties, 1940 30		45	50
Mouseketeer Cut Outs, 1957, Whitman No. 1974...............................35		45	50
Movie Starlets, 1946, Whitman No. 960, Gail Russell, Diana Lynn, Olga San Juan, Marjorie Reynolds, Joan Caulfield 60		75	90

	C6	C8	C10
Movie Starlets Paper Dolls, circa 1949, Stephens Publishing Co. No.178. Four dolls - Miss Premier, Miss Stardust, Miss Hollywood, Miss Preview and four pages of costumes ..20		25	28
Mrs. Beasley Paper Doll Book, 1970 ("Family Affair" TV show) Whitman No. 1973.................................10		12	15
My Fair Lady, 1965, Ottenheimer Publishers No. 2960-2, by Evon Hartman 30		35	40
My Paper Doll's Sewing Kit, 1940, by Margot Voight, Grinnell C-1018.....22		40	45
My Twin Babies With Older Brother and Sister, 1940, Whitman 970.......40		45	50
My Very First Paper Doll Book, 1957, A Bonnie Book No. 4732, Samuel Lowe 6		10	12

ON GUARD A PUNCH OUT BOOK. Photo by Jonathan A. Newman. Courtesy Barbara and Jonathan Newman.

NEW SHIRLEY TEMPLE IN PAPER DOLLS. Photo by Jonathan A. Newman. Courtesy Barbara and Jonathan Newman.

OUR SOLDIERS CUT-OUT ARMY UNIFORMS. Photo by Jonathan A. Newman. Courtesy Barbara and Jonathan Newman.

OUR HAPPY FAMILY CUT-OUT SHEETS. Photo by Jonathan A. Newman. Courtesy Barbara and Jonathan Newman.

	C6	C8	C10
Nancy and Her Dolls With Seven Busy Days of Fun, 1944, Saalfield No. 2478	20	40	45
Nanny And The Professor, 1971, Art-craft No. 5114	15	25	30
Natalie Wood Paper Dolls, 1958, Whitman	90	120	150
National Velvet, 1961, Whitman No. 1958	20	30	35
Navy Scouts Paper Doll Book, 1942, Merrill No. 3428	65	75	90
New Shirley Temple In Paper Dolls, The, 1942, Saalfield No. 2425	120	150	175
New York World's Fair Make A Model, 1963, by Ottenheimer. Spertus No. 600-50. Includes Unisphere, Swiss Ride, N.Y. Port Authority, Heliport, etc.	15	20	25
Night Before Christmas With Cutouts Whitman No. 948	15	20	25
19 Farmyard Animals To Cut Out And Stand Up - Copyright 1930, Whitman No. 935, 12 pages	30	35	40
Oklahoma With Shirley Jones and Gordon MacRae, 1956, Whitman No. 1954	45	55	65

	C6	C8	C10
On Guard, 1942, Lowe No. L535	35	45	50
One Hundred Soldiers Punchout Book, 1943, Whitman 999	50	55	60
Our Happy Family Cut-Out Sheets, 1928, Sam's Gabriel Sons Co. No. D141	65	75	90
Our New Home, 1930, story by Susan S. Popper, pictures by Helen E. Ohrenschall, Sam'l Gabriel Sons, hardcover book, 6 pages of rooms, 6 gummed pages of people, furniture, etc.	80	100	125
Our Nurse Nancy - A Young American, by Hilda Miloche and Wilma Kane, 1943, cutouts, Whitman No. 1012	45	50	55
Our Sailor Bob, 10" doll with uniforms, Whitman, circa 1943	30	35	40
Our Soldier Jim, 1943, Whitman No. 3980, designed by Hilda Miloche and Wilma Kane, 10½" standup doll with uniforms	30	35	40
Our Soldiers Cut Out Army Uniforms by Nat Falk, Dell, 1941, 4 cutout dolls and several uniforms	50	55	65
Our Wave Joan - A Young American, by Hilda Miloche and Wilma Kane, 1943, Whitman No. 1012	40	45	50
Outdoor Paper Dolls, 1941, Saalfield No. 1958, fourteen dolls and four pages of clothes	12	15	18
Over 80 Turn-About, Stand-Up Sailors, 1943, Lowe No. 141	30	45	50
Over 80 Turn-About Stand-Up Soldiers, 1943, Lowe No. 140	30	45	50
Paper Doll Family And Their House by Florence and Margaret Hoopes, 1934, Saalfield No. 4125	60	70	75
Paper Doll Family And Their Trailer, Merrill No. 3436, 1938	70	80	90
Paper Doll "Joan" and Paper Doll "Bobby" by Queen Holden, 1928, Whitman 907	80	90	100
Paper Doll Outfit, American Toy Works No. 102, boxed set	50	60	75
Paper Doll Playmates, 1940, Saalfield No. 154, nurse, 19 children, costumes, toys	38	45	48
Paper Dolls From Mother Goose, 1957, Saalfield No. 2758, Mary, Bo-Peep, Boy Blue, Bobbie Shaftoe, Miss Muffett, Jack Horner	12	15	18

PAPER DOLL FAMILY AND THEIR TRAILER. Photo by Jonathan A. Newman. Courtesy Barbara and Jonathan Newman.

PAPER DOLL OUTFIT DRESSES AND HATS. Photo by Jonathan A. Newman. Courtesy Barbara and Jonathan Newman.

PILOT AND STEWARDESS AIRLINER PAPER DOLLS.

Photos by Jonathan A. Newman. Courtesy Barbara and Jonathan Newman.

PLAYHOUSE PAPER DOLLS by Doris and Marion Henderson.

PAPER DOLLS TO CUT OUT AND PAINT.

PAPER DOLLS JULIA MARIE.

Photos by Jonathan A. Newman. Courtesy Barbara and Jonathan Newman.

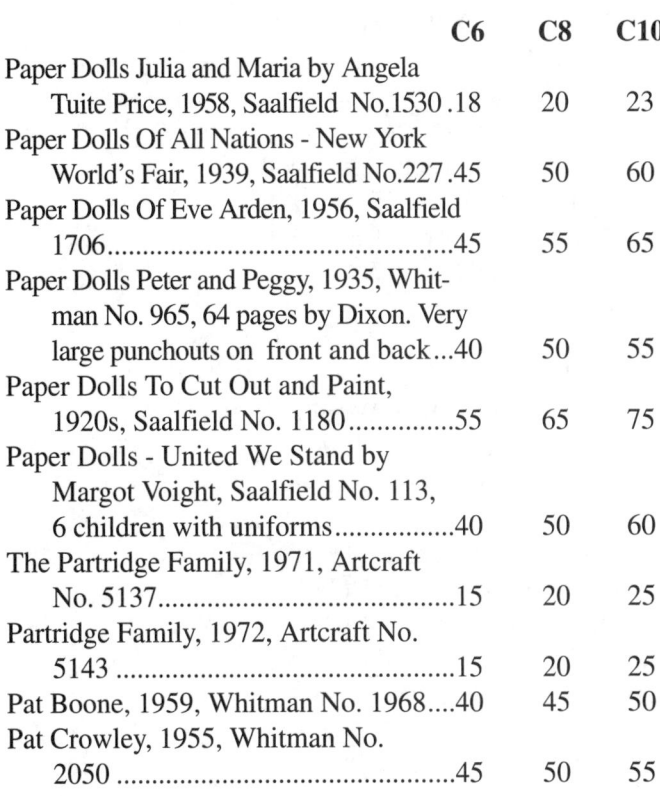

PLAYHOUSE PAPER DOLLS. Photo by Jonathan A. Newman. Courtesy Barbara and Jonathan Newman.

PLAYHOUSE PAPER DOLLS. Photo by Jonathan A. Newman. Courtesy Barbara and Jonathan Newman.

PAPER DOLLS OF ALL NATIONS NEW YORK WORLD'S FAIR, 1939. Photo by Jonathan A. Newman. Courtesy Barbara and Jonathan Newman.

	C6	C8	C10
Paper Dolls Julia and Maria by Angela Tuite Price, 1958, Saalfield No.1530 .18		20	23
Paper Dolls Of All Nations - New York World's Fair, 1939, Saalfield No.227 .45		50	60
Paper Dolls Of Eve Arden, 1956, Saalfield 1706...45		55	65
Paper Dolls Peter and Peggy, 1935, Whitman No. 965, 64 pages by Dixon. Very large punchouts on front and back...40		50	55
Paper Dolls To Cut Out and Paint, 1920s, Saalfield No. 1180...............55		65	75
Paper Dolls - United We Stand by Margot Voight, Saalfield No. 113, 6 children with uniforms.................40		50	60
The Partridge Family, 1971, Artcraft No. 5137....................................15		20	25
Partridge Family, 1972, Artcraft No. 5143 15		20	25
Pat Boone, 1959, Whitman No. 1968....40		45	50
Pat Crowley, 1955, Whitman No. 2050 45		50	55

	C6	C8	C10
Patience And Prudence, 1958, Lowe No. 2736 (Popular singers of the 1950s)..12		15	18
Patsy, 1946, Children's Press, No. 30002, Patsy, dog, doghouse, etc. 20		25	30
Patsy A Wooden Doll With Dresses (actually a 10" standup cardboard doll with wood backing) circa 1938, Whitman 3037.......................35		40	45

	C6	C8	C10
Patsy Ann And Her Trunk Full of Clothes by Queen Holden, 1939, Whitman No. 992	80	90	100
Patti Page 1958 book of paper dolls	45	50	55
Patty's Party Paper Dolls, circa 1950, Stephens Publishing Co. No. 175	10	12	15
Pert And Pretty, 1948, Merrill No. 1552	40	45	50
Peter And Peggy, 1950, Whitman No. 99210	10	12	15
Peter And Peggy, Jerry And Joan Paper Dolls by Rachel Taft Dixon, 1935, Whitman No. 985	55	65	75
Photo Fashions, 1953, Whitman No. 973	8	10	12
Pig Tails, 1949, Merrill No. 344410	35	45	50
Pilot And Stewardess Paper Doll Book No. 3423, 1941, Merrill	40	45	50
The Pink Wedding, 1952, Merrill No. 1559	50	55	65
Piper Laurie, 1953, Merrill No. 2551	40	45	50
Playhouse Dolls 1949, Stephens Publishing Co. No. 1965. Four dolls and four pages of clothes	10	12	15
Playhouse Paper Dolls designed by Doris and Marion Henderson, Lowe No. 1028, 1941	25	30	35
Playhouse Paper Dolls, 1947, Saalfield No. 381	15	20	25
Playmates, 1952, Whitman No. 99510	10	12	15
Playthings To Cut Out And Stand Up, circa 1935, Whitman No. 934. Contains ventriloquist's dummy, floating ships, general's hat, lantern, animals, other moving toys	25	30	35
Play Time, 1952, Whitman 210525	8	10	12
Playtime Pals, 1946, Lowe No. 1045	12	15	18
Polly Patchwork And Her Friends by Pelagie Doane, 1941, Lowe No. 1024	30	35	40
Polyanna Cut-Out Dolls, 1941, Whitman 995	50	55	65
Popular Paper Dolls, 1942, Saalfield No. 1973	20	25	30
Portrait Girls With Cloth-Like Clothes, 1947, designed by Hilda Miloche and Wilma Kane, Whitman No. 1170	30	35	40
Power Models Cut Out Dolls Book, 1942, Whitman No. 981, six dolls	30	40	45
Pressed Board Dolls And Their Dresses, boxed set, Lowe No. 1942	25	30	35
Pre-Teen Paper Dolls circa 1960s, Saalfield No. 1366	8	10	12
Prince And Princess Paper Dolls, 1949, Saalfield No. 2706	18	20	25
Prom Time, 1962, Whitman No. 2084, 2 dolls and party clothes	8	10	12
Queen Holden! Queen Holden! Betty and Bob, 1952, 12½" high children, Whitman 99110	50	55	60
Queen Holden! Queen Holden! Hair-Do Dolls, 1948, 3 dolls, clothes and 31 different hair-dos, Whitman No. 991	75	80	90
Quiz Kids Paper Dolls, 1942, Saalfield 2430	90	100	125
Raggedy Ann and Andy, 1953, by Ethel Hays, Saalfield 2719	16	24	32
Raggedy Ann And Andy Paper Dolls, 1944, Saalfield No. 2719-15	45	50	55
Raggedy Ann And Andy Paper Dolls, 1944, Saalfield No. 2741 by Ethel Hays	40	45	50
Raggedy Ann And Andy, 1968, Whitman No. 4740	15	18	20
"Rap-A-Jap," circa 1943, Woodburn Mfg. No. C1	50	60	70
Ready Cut Village, 1930s, no mfg. listed	55	75	90
Ricky Nelson paper dolls, 1959	30	40	45
Riders Of The West Paper Dolls, 1950, Saalfield No. 2716-15	12	15	18
Rigby's Book of Model Ships, 1953	75	85	90
Rigby's Easy To Build Models Of Fighting Planes	80	90	110

RIGBY'S Book of Model Ships. Courtesy Mapes Auctioneers & Appraisers.

"Rap-A-Jap". Courtesy Jack Matthews.

	C6	C8	C10
Rigby's Easier To Build Models Of Naval Craft, 24 models of warships, 27 pages, 11½"x 14", designed by Wallace Rigby, 1944, includes Battleship North Carolina, aircraft carrier, cruiser, destroyer, etc.	90	110	135
Rigby Flying Models of Jet and Rocket Planes, ten planes, 1949, Garden City Books	70	80	90
Rigby's Model Book of Flying Clippers, 11"x14" book designed by Wallace Rigby, two scale models of Douglas DC-Jet Clipper and Douglas DC-7C, 1947	60	70	80
Rigby's Model Sports Cars of the World, 1954, includes 18" "sports-racer," Chevette, Jaguar, Mercedes-Benz, etc.	60	70	80
Robin Hood And Maid Marian, 1950s, Saalfield, No. 1761, paper dolls	15	20	25
Rock Hudson paper Dolls, 1957, Whitman No. 2087	35	40	45
Rosemary Clooney, Samuel Lowe No. 1256	40	45	55
Rosemary Clooney, 1958, Samuel Lowe No. 2487	40	45	55
Rowan & Martin's Laugh-In Punch Out Paper Doll Book, 1969, Saalfield No. 1325, Rowan, Martin, Jo Ann Worley, Arte Johnson, Judy Carne and Goldie Hawn	25	30	35
Roy Rogers and Dale Evans, 1950, Whitman No. 1186	45	55	60
Roy Rogers and Dale Evans, 1954, Whitman No. 1950	45	55	60

	C6	C8	C10
Roy Rogers Cut Out Dolls, 1948, Whitman No. 995	50	60	65
Roy Rogers Sticker Fun Book, 1953, No. 2161	15	20	25
Royalty Cut-Out Books: A Procession of the Knight of the Garter	55	60	65
Royalty Cut-Out Books: Trooping The Colour	55	60	65
Ruth Newton's Cut Out Dolls and Animals "with over 80 pieces to cut out and play with," 1934, 11"x17"	55	65	75
Sally Ann A Cut Out Doll, circa 1940, Whitman No. 1010	30	35	40
Sally's Silver Skates, 1956, Merrill No. 1549	40	45	50
Sally The Standing Doll, 1940s, Lowe No. 1042	35	45	48
Sandra And Sue Statuette Dolls And Their Clothes, by Lee Lunzer, 1948, Whitman No. 1180	30	35	40
Sandra Dee, 1959, boxed, two dolls and 34 costume pieces, Saalfield No. 5511	40	50	55
Sandy and Sue, 1963, Whitman No. 1956.	10	15	18
School Girl Paper Dolls, 1942, Saalfield No. 2400	25	30	35
Scissors Bird Paper Dolls, 1946, Stephens No. 137	10	15	18
Service Kit Of America's Armed Forces - On Land - On Sea - In The Air, 1942, Lowe No. 265	40	50	55
6 Good Little Dolls, no date, Stephens Publishing Co. No. 183	8	10	12
6 Movie Starlets, 1942, Anne Nagel, Peggy Moran, Jane Frazee, Anne Gwynne, Helen Parrish, Ann Gillis	135	150	175
Sharp Shooters, circa 1915, Milton Bradley No. 4103, boxed set with two sets of five cardboard soldier and one officer on stands	75	90	125
Skating Party Paper Doll Book, 1941, No. 2328, Saalfield, 17 punchouts	30	35	40
Skating Stars, 1954, Whitman No. 2105	12	15	18
Smart Paper Dolls, 1940, Saalfield No. 1935	30	45	48
Smash The Axis, 1943, Electric Corp. of America	35	50	55
Snow White And The Seven Dwarfs Paper Dolls, 1938, 12"x17", Whitman No. 970	100	125	150
Snow White And The Seven Dwarfs, circa 1970, Whitman No. 1998	12	15	18

SERVICE KIT OF AMERICA'S ARMED FORCES ON LAND ON SEA AND IN THE AIR. Photo by Jonathan A. Newman. Courtesy Barbara and Jonathan Newman.

SHARPSHOOTERS, box and contents. Photo by Jonathan A. Newman. Courtesy Barbara and Jonathan Newman.

SOLDIERS FIVE WITH PISTOL. Photo by Jonathan A. Newman. Courtesy Barbara and Jonathan Newman.

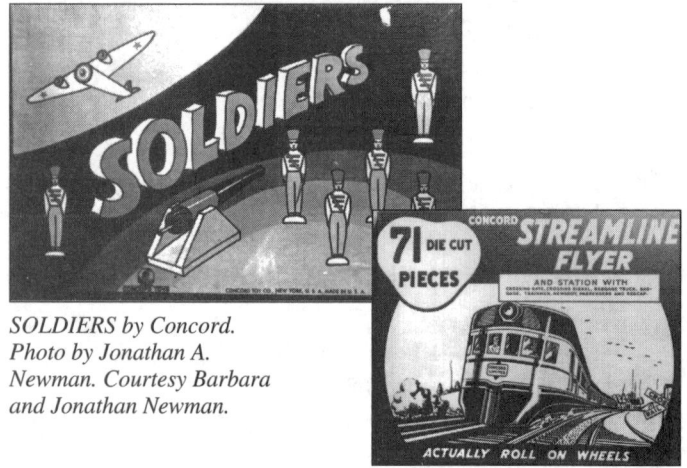

SOLDIERS by Concord. Photo by Jonathan A. Newman. Courtesy Barbara and Jonathan Newman.

STREAMLINE FLYER. Photo by Jonathan A. Newman. Courtesy Barbara and Jonathan Newman.

	C6	C8	C10
Soldiers, circa 1940, Concord toy Co. boxed set contains 9 press-out soldiers, 3½" each, wooden cannon and ammunition	50	60	75
Soldier Set by J. Pressman and Co., Inc., New York. No. 1551, circa 1940, contains five cardboard soldiers, 4½" high and marbles	30	40	50
Soldiers, cardboard, approx. 6" high on wooden blocks, Navy, both officer and sailors circa 1920. Price per single figure	3	4	4.50
Soldiers, cardboard, approx. 6" high on wooden blocks. Sailor, U.S.	3	4	4.50
Soldiers, cardboard, approx. 6" high on wooden blocks. U.S. Infantry in campaign hats, mounted. Price per single figure	3	4	4.50

	C6	C8	C10
Soldiers, cardboard approx. 6" high on wooden blocks, West Point Cadets	3	4	4.50
Soldiers Five, circa 1920, boxed set, Milton Bradley No. 4395, five cardboard soldiers, pistol	80	100	125
Soldiers On Parade, early, Milton Bradley No. 4518, set of 10	50	80	90
Spaceport, U.S.A. 1953, Whitman	10	12	15
Sports Time, 1952, Whitman No. 210525	6	10	12
Square Dance Paper Dolls, 1950, Saalfield No. 2717	12	15	18
Square Dance Paper Dolls, by J. Voelz, Lowe 968-10	12	15	18
Stage Door Canteen, 1943, Saalfield 2468	60	75	90
Stand-Up Dolls, Honey and Bunny, Merrill No. 3403, 1936	60	75	90

208

SALLY THE STANDING
DOLL.

STATUETTE DOLLS AND
THEIR CLOTHES.

Photos by Jonathan A. Newman. Courtesy Barbara and Jonathan Newman.

	C6	C8	C10
Statuette Dolls, 1943, Whitman No. 992, Two women	25	35	40
Statuette Dolls And Their Clothes, 1942, Whitman No. 998	25	35	40
Statuette Dolls And Their Clothes, 1946, Whitman No. 986, Two girls and a boy	25	35	30
Stencils Large and Small by Roy Best, circa 1935, No. 954 (Whitman?) folder of 30 animals to punch out and use as stencils. Comes with tiny box of crayons	12	20	25
Stock Farm Set, circa 1944, Concern No. 123, boxed 1200 die-cut pieces, including house, barn, silo, chicken house, tractor, etc.	40	50	60
The Story of Cinderella, A Fold-A-Way Toy Book designed by Will Pente. Circa 1925, Reilly & Britton Co.	18	25	30
Streamline Flyer, 10¾"x13½" boxed set, Concord Toy Co., No. 122, circa 1940. Contains engine, station, crossing gates, crossing signal, baggage truck, baggage and people	40	50	60
Style Shop Paper Dolls, 1943, Saalfield No. 1516	18	25	30
Sub-Deb Paper Dolls by Irving Nurick, 1941, Merrill No. 3408, 12 teenage boys and girls dolls, clothes	35	45	48
Sue And Tom Cut-Out Dolls Book, The 1946, Lowe No. 149	15	20	25
Sunbonnet Sue, 1951, Whitman No. 2062-29	12	15	18
Sunshine Cut-Outs, Sports Series, Spring, by M&F Hoopes, 1926, 4-part foldout, Stoll & Edwards Co.	70	80	90

	C6	C8	C10
Susan Dey As Laurie ("Partridge Family" TV show), 1972, Artcraft, Fashions by Kate Greenaway	16	20	25
Sweetheart Paper Dolls, 1943, Saalfield No. 2458	30	40	45
Sweetie Pie Twins, 1949, Stephens Publishing Co. No. 166, Jane and Jean	12	15	18
Swing-A-Plane by J.L. Schilling Co., Model of a Flying Tiger, 1944, flies on string	10	15	18
Tammy, 1963, A Little Golden Story Book with paper dolls to cut out and dress. Illustrated by Ada Salvi	12	15	18
Tarzan Of The Apes, 1933 figure set	30	50	55
Teen Gal Cut Out Dolls, 1943, by Hilda Miloche and William Kane, Whitman No. 980	35	40	45
Teen Town, 1949, Merrill No. 3443	35	45	48
That Girl - Marlo Thomas, 1967, Saalfield No. 1351	20	25	30
That Girl - Marlo Thomas, 1967, Saalfield No. 1379	20	25	30
They Stand Up, by Avis Mac, 1939, Whitman No. 932, 13"x18" with five children	65	75	90
30 Toy Soldiers, circa 1943, Whitman No. 2950	35	50	60
This Is Bunny One Of The Five Cut-Out Dolly Sisters, 1939	35	45	50
This Is Dotty One Of The Five Cut-Out Dolly Sisters, Whitman, 1939	35	45	50
This Is Magic One Of The Five Cut-Out Dolly Sisters, Whitman, 1939	35	45	50
This Is Patsy, One Of The Five Cut-Out Dolly Sisters, Whitman, 1939	35	45	50
This Is Peggy One Of The Five Cut-Out Dolly Sisters, Whitman No. 1002, 1939	35	45	50

STAND-UP DOLLS HONEY
AND BUNNY.

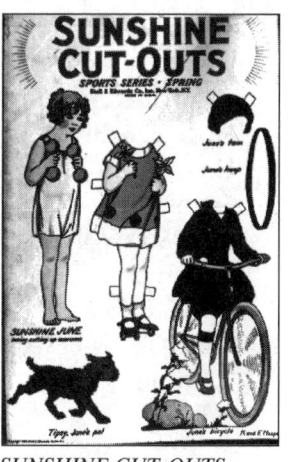

SUNSHINE CUT-OUTS
SPORTS SERIES, SPRING.

Photos by Jonathan A. Newman. Courtesy Barbara and Jonathan Newman.

Left: *THIS IS BUNNY, ONE OF THE FIVE CUT-OUT DOLLY SISTERS, Right: THIS IS PATSY, ONE OF THE FIVE CUT-OUT DOLLY SISTERS. Photo by Jonathan A. Newman. Courtesy Barbara and Jonathan Newman.*

	C6	C8	C10
This Is The Navy No. 500A Skyline Mfg., Destroyer and PT Boat, circa 1942	20	25	30
This Is The Navy No. 501 circa 1942, Skyline Mfg., Heavy Cruiser	20	25	30
Three Bears Cut Out Book, Copyright 1939, Whitman No. 1020, Goldilocks and 3 Bears	40	50	55
Three Flying Models of Famous Allied Fighting Planes by Judd Reed, 9"x12", contains Hell Cat, Spitfire and Stormovik planes. Included is "American Ace Spotter," with turning dial of 48 3-view silhouettes of 16 planes in little windows, 1944	30	35	40
Three Little Girls Who Grew And Grew And This Is How They Grew, 1945, Whitman No. 99410	25	35	40
Three Little Girls Who Grew And Grew And This Is How They Grew, with cloth-like clothes, flocked, 1945, Whitman No. 1176	25	35	40
Three little Pigs Cut Out Book, Copyright 1939, Whitman No. 1020, Pigs and Big Bad Wolf	40	50	55
Three Sweet Baby Dolls To Cut Out And Dress, 1954, Whitman No. 975	12	15	18
Thrilltown Railroad, 1943, Reed, Pullman Passenger Set	60	80	90
Tiny Chatty Twins Paper Dolls, 1963, Whitman No. 1985	10	12	15
Toby Tyler Circus Playbook Punch Out, 1959, No. 1936	25	35	40
Tom Corbett Space Cadet Punch Out Book, 1952, Saalfield No. 4304, 14" long, 10½" wide	30	40	45

	C6	C8	C10
Tom The Aviator, circa 1942, Samuel Lowe No. L1074	20	30	40
Toni Hair-Do Cut-Out Dolls, Lowe No. 1284, 1950	35	48	55
Top Notch Paper Dolls, 1948, Saalfield No. 1504	20	28	35
Toy Models: Warplane and Tank Punchout, 1941, Fawcett Publications, Lowe	45	50	65
Toy Town, 1916, series of 50 different buildings by American Color Type Co. boxed set	75	100	125
Transfer Pictures, Copyright 1939, Whitman No. 1085, 100 decalcomanias	7.50	11.25	15
Treasure Hour Puppet Book, No. 4, 1968, Murray Sales and Service, The Rustlers of Rocky Ranch, a play of cowboys and Indians in five scenes. Cut-out section makes model theatre	15	20	25
Tricia, 1969, Artcraft No. 4248	20	25	30
Tricia Paper Dolls, 1970, Saalfield No. 1248, White House tour game, White House stand-up doll of Tricia Nixon and costumes	20	30	35
Trudy Phillips And Her Crowd, 1954, Whitman No. 2104	15	20	25
Tuesday Weld Paper Dolls, 1960, Saalfield No. 5112 boxed two dolls and 58 costume pieces	30	40	45
Turnabouts Dolls Book, The, 1940s, Lowe No. 1048, dolls printed front view on each side	35	45	48
TV Star Time Paper Dolls, circa 1950s, Abbott No. 1367	12	15	18
TV Tap Stars Paper Dolls, Lowe 99010	12	15	18
22 Animals To Cut Out And Stand Up, copyright 1930, Whitman, No. 935, rabbits, bears, owls, squirrels, etc.	25	35	45
Twiggy Paper Doll, 1967, Whitman No. 1999, with "plastilon" Twiggy dress for small girls	25	30	35
Tyrone Power & Linda Darnell, 1941, Merrill No. 3438	155	180	200
Umbrella Girls, 1956, Merrill No. 2562, wrap-around dresses	45	50	55
Uncle Sam's Little Helpers Paper Dolls by Ann Kovach, 1943, Saalfield 2450	35	42	45
United States Soldiers, 1942, Samuel Lowe No. L1063	45	50	55
U.S. Commandos Book, 1943, Lowe No. 1089	40	50	60

TONI HAIR-DO CUT-OUT DOLLS. Photo by Jonathan A. Newman. Courtesy Barbara and Jonathan Newman.

	C6	C8	C10
U.S. Infantry - Spanish American War, approx. 6" high soldier on small wooden block	3	4	4.50
Victory Girls - Arlene The Airline Hostess, circa 1940s, Lowe	45	55	60
Victory Punch-Out Tanks, Soldiers, Sailors, Planes circa 1943, Lowe No. 848	45	55	60
Victory Volunteers, 1942, dolls with uniforms by Merlin, Merrill No. 3424	55	75	90
Virginia Mayo, 1957, Saalfield, No. 4422	45	50	55
WACS and WAVES, 1943, Whitman No. 985	55	70	75
Walking Paper Doll Family No. 1074, Saalfield 1934	55	70	75
Walt Disney's Babes in Toyland, 1961, Golden Punch-Out Book No. 10363	20	30	35
Walt Disney's Jane and Michael From Mary Poppins, 1963, Watkins/Strathmore 1892-6	20	25	30
Walt Disney's Let's Build Disneyland, 1957, Whitman No. 1986, forms sets for Adventureland, Frontierland, Tomorrowland and Fantasyland	15	25	30
Walt Disney's Mary Poppins, 1964, Whitman No. 1982	25	30	35
Walt Disney Match and Patch Sticker Fun, 1953, Whitman, Mickey Mouse, Donald Duck, Pluto, Goofy, etc.	10	15	18

	C6	C8	C10
Walt Disney Presents Hayley Mills in That Darn Cat, 1965, Whitman No. 1955	25	30	35
Walt Disney Sticker Fun Book, 1951, Whitman	6	10	12
Walt Disney Sticker Fun With Peter Pan, 1952, Whitman	6	10	12
War Between The States, 1959, Golden Press No. GF152	40	50	55
War Plane Cut Outs, 1943, 10"x14", heavy stock, 8 different scale models	30	30	35
Wedding Paper Dolls, 1970, Whitman No. 1970	10	12	15
We're A Family Cut-Out Dolls, 1954, Whitman No. 1181	10	18	20
White House Party Dresses, 1961, Merrill No. 1550	30	35	40
Whitman No. 1146, little 3½"x7½" paper doll books, copyright 1939. A Nancy and Tommy. B. Ann and Arthur. C. Kitty and Billy. D. Muriel and David. E. Cynthia and Bobby. F. Judy and Dick	45	60	65
Whitman Paper Doll Book, 1933, No. 3059, four dolls, ten sheets of clothes in folder	25	35	40
Winnie's New Wardrobe by Geraldine Cline, 1939, McLoughlin Bros. No. 555	25	30	35
Young Patriot Invasion Set, circa 1944, Colorgraphic No. 500, contains destroyer, amphibian tractor, tank, jeep, antitank, gun, bomber and dive bomber, 10½"x13" boxed set	60	75	80
Young Patriot - Learn To Know Your Army, 1943, Colorgraphic No. 350, tank, howitzer, jeep, antitank gun, bomber, fighter and soldiers. Guns shoot, bombs drop, etc.	60	75	80
Young Pariot - Learn To Know Your Navy, 1943, Colorgraphic construction set No. 360, 10"x14" boxed set includes battleship, destroyer, aircraft carrier, mosquito boat, submarine, planes, depth charges, etc., with moveable parts	60	75	80
Ziegfeld Girl paper dolls, No. "1", 1941, Merrill No. 3466	170	190	225
Zoo Cut Outs by Milo Winter, 1938, Whitman No. 1054, six pages of heavy cut-out animals	20	30	40

TIN WIND-UP

(See also Movie, Comic Character, Disney)

The average mint price for tin wind-ups in the last edition was $346.22, and in this volume averages $480.05, an increase of 39%.

Unlike most toys in this book, tin wind-ups do not "feel" particularly good in the hand, and depend more on the lure of motion and colorful lithography. Esthetically the most appealing, perhaps, are those of Lehmann, a Germany company which also patented a number of its toys in the United States, and which holds a strong attraction for a large number of collectors.

	C6	C8	C10
A.C. Gilbert delivery truck, open, circa 1915	300	450	600
Aircraft Carrier, circa post WW II, tin litho, approx. 15" long, Japan	90	135	180
"Aircraft Carrier X53," with five jet planes, tin litho, circa 1950s	75	112	150

ANIMATE TOY CO.

In 1918 this firm was located at East 17th Street in New York City, and its president was L.T. Savage. By 1931 it had moved to 30 North 15th Street in East Orange, New Jersey, and employed ten men and forty women. In 1934 the president-vice president was George V. Turnbull and the secretary-treasurer was George H. Webb. Five men and eleven women made up the work force.

	C6	C8	C10
Animate Toy "U.S. Baby Tank," pat. 6/20/16, 2½" long, new in 1918	25	38	50
Animate Toy "Climbing Tractor," 9" long, 1929	90	135	180
Automatic Toy Co. "Auto Speedway," circa 1930	55	83	110
Automatic Toy Co. Cross-Over Trolley Set	70	105	140
Automatic Toy Co., "Dizzy Liz", No. 180, 1940s, 5" long	40	60	80
Automatic Toy Co. "Jungle Pete" No. 175, 15" long	55	83	110
Automatic Toy Co. "Mysterious Alpine Express," 1940s, 20" long, 14" wide, 2" high	70	105	140

	C6	C8	C10
Automatic Toy Co. "Rocket Space Ship," No. 305, 8½" long, sparks, 1940s	55	83	110
Automatic Toy Co., "Space Shooting Range," 1950s, 15" long	150	225	300
Automatic Toy Co. Speedway, 1930s, with 2 race cars, garage	87	130	175
Automotive Toy Co., "Magic Crossroads" track, 2 wind-up cars, circa 1950	80	120	160
Baby L Racing Boat, 1930, 11" long, Lindstrom	100	150	200
"Barnum & Bailey," c. 1935, elephant pulling a four-wheeled cart loaded with a collapsible cage containing a camel, a monkey, a lion and a giraffe, each mounted on four wheels	150	225	300
Biplane, very early, Wright Bros.-like paper propellor blades, 6" long	400	600	800
Bird in Cage, 3½" high, German	60	90	120
Bird with flapping wings, 1930s, 6½" long, German	75	112	150
Black boy eating watermelon with dog biting his backside, 6½" high, Occ. Japan	280	370	560
Boy on St. Bernard on rocker, 6¾" long	200	300	400
Buffalo Bill, hand-painted, hand-soldered, German, 1910	400	600	800
Buffalo Toys, "Aero Speeders," 1920s, carousel with 3 planes, screw-rod spring drive, 10" tall	140	210	280

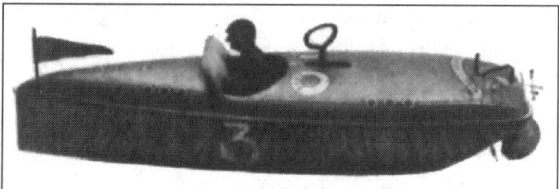

Baby L. Racing Boat, 11" long. Courtesy Lloyd W. Ralston Auctions.

AUTOMATIC TOY COMPANY. Auto Speedway. Photo by Don Hultzman.

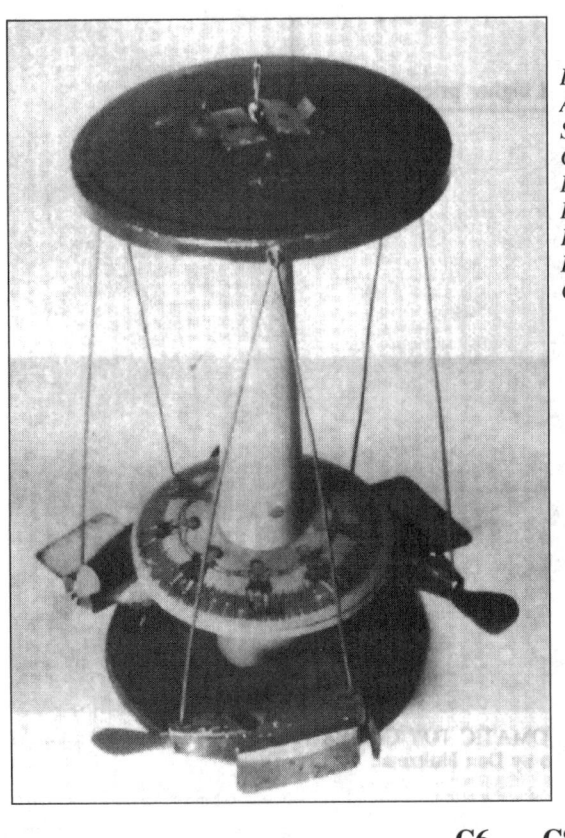

Buffalo Toy Aero-Speeders. Courtesy Don Hultzman. Photo by Ron Chojnacki.

Caterpillar Tractor, "1916". Photo by Bill Kaufman.. Courtesy Good Old Days Store.

	C6	C8	C10
Cat pushing cage with two mice, 8¼" long	280	420	560
Caterpillar Tractor, "1916," rubber treads, tin wind-up, probably by Woodhaven Metal Stamping Co., Brooklyn, NY	142	214	285

CHEIN

Chein (pronounced "chain") was founded in 1903 by Julius Chein. The New Jersey company specialized in lithographed metal toys, the majority of them mechanical. In 1918 it was located at 310 Passaic Avenue, Harrison, New Jersey, with 250 employees. In 1934 it had 55 male and 92 female workers. In a 1946-47 directory it listed 148 male and 132 female employees. Chein made toys until 1979, and is still in business today in Burlington, New Jersey.

	C6	C8	C10
Chein Alligator with native on its back	130	195	260
Chein "Army Drummer," 1930s, plunger-activated, 7" high	120	180	240
Chein Barnacle Bill, looks like Popeye, 1930s	300	450	600
Chein "Barnacle Bill in a Barrel," 1930s, 7" high	300	450	600
Chein "Barnacle Bill the Sailor," punching a bag, 7½"	750	1125	1500
Chein Bass Drummer (like Chein Drummer Boy, but drum vertical)	150	225	300
Chein Bear with hat, pants, shirt, bow-tie, circa 1938	35	52	70
Chein "Ski-Boy," 8" long, 1930s	150	225	300
Chein Cabin Cruiser, 1940s, 9" long	15	22	30
Chein chick, brightly colored clothes and polka dot bowtie, 4" high	30	45	60
Chein Chicken pulling wheelbarrow, 6x3½", 1930s	30	45	60
Chein "Clown in Barrel," 1930s, 8" high	275	313	550

	C6	C8	C10
Buffalo Toys, "Aero-Zeps," 3 zeppelins fly on carousel, 9" high	150	225	300
Buffalo Toys, "Bumper Ride", 1930s, 10" long	50	75	100
Buffalo Toys, Dodgem Car, 1930s, 10" long	80	120	160
Buffalo Toys, "T-zer", 1925, 6" high, (screw drive)	180	240	360
"Cable Car" 1950s, Technofix Co., 16" long with two 2" tin cars	150	225	300
"The Crackling Hen of Paradise," 8" long, turn side handle and hen cackles; patented	60	90	120
"Cakewalk Dancers," short black man dancing with tall, heavy black woman	400	600	800
"Candy" cart driven by monkey in cap, also marked "candy," circa 1950s	80	120	160
Carousel with four biplanes and pilots, paper vanes, flag finial, 17" high, 1920s, German	1200	1800	2400
Carousel with four double horse and riders that alternate with four women in cars, velvet top with ball fringe, flag finial, 17" high	1600	2400	3200
Carousel with four men in canoes, propellers with paper vanes, 11" high	1400	2100	2800
Carter "Pan-Gee The Funny Dancer," 1920, 10" high	300	450	600

CHEIN "Barnacle Bill in a Barrel". Courtesy PB Eighty-Four, New York.

CHEIN Duck. Courtesy Scott Smiles.

CHEIN Drummer Boy. Courtesy Scott Smiles. Photo by Mike Adams.

CHEIN Marine, hand on belt. Courtesy Scott Smiles. Photo by Mike Adams.

CHEIN "Ferris Wheel" 1930's. Courtesy Scott Smiles.

CHEIN Mechanical Frog Man. Photo by Don Hultzman.

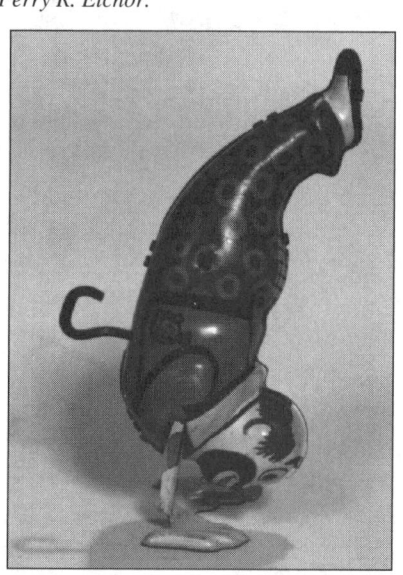

CHEIN Mechanical Aquaplane, 7½" wingspan. Courtesy Perry R. Eichor.

CHEIN Bear with Hat. Courtesy Scott Smiles.

CHEIN Penguin. Courtesy Scott Smiles. Photo by Mike Adams.

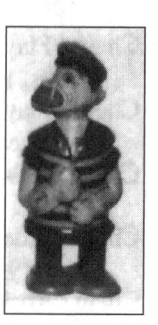

CHEIN Barnacle Bill. Courtesy PB Eighty-Four, New York.

CHEIN Handstand Clown. Courtesy Scott Smiles.

	C6	C8	C10
Chein Clown with umbrella	100	150	200
Chein "Dan-Dee Dump Truck"	200	300	400
Chein "Doughboy," 1920s, 6" high	150	225	300
Chein "Drummer Boy," 9" high, with shako, circa 1930s	75	112	150
Chein duck, 4" high, waddles, 1930	30	45	60
Chein duck, long-beaked, in orange sailor suit, not Donald Duck, but similar. Waddles, 6" high	60	90	120
Chein "Ferris Wheel," 16½" high, 6 compartments, ringing bell, 1930s	190	275	380
Chein "Greyhound" bus	70	105	140
Chein Handstand Clown, 1940s, 6" high	60	90	120
Chein "Indian in Headdress," 1930s, 5½" high	90	135	180
Chein "Jumping Rabbit", 1925, 5" long	130	195	260
Chein Marine, hand on belt, 1950s, 6" high	100	150	200
Chein "Mark I" Cabin Cruiser, 8½" long, 1957	30	45	60
Chein "Mechanical Aquaplane" No. 39, boat-like pontoons, 1932, 8½" long, 7½" wingspan, no insignia	125	188	250
Chein "Mechanical Aquaplane," post WW II insignia	160	240	320
Chein "Mechanical Aquaplane,' pre-WWII insignia	200	300	400
Chein "Mechanical Fish," 1940s, 11" long	25	38	50
Chein "Mechanical Frog Man," 1950s, 11" long	80	120	160
Chein "Mechanical Rocket Ride" No. 400, 1950s, 18" high	500	750	1000
Chein "Musical Aero Swing," 1940s, 10" high	200	300	400
Chein Pan-Am clipper, 11" wing span, 1930s, pontoons	387	582	775
Chein Pelican, 1950s, 4" high	150	225	300
Chein Penguin in tuxedo type jacket, circa 1940	22	33	45
Chein Pig, 4½" high, 1940s	37	56	75
Chein "Playland Merry-Go-Round," 1930s, 9½" high	300	450	600

	C6	C8	C10
Chein "Playland Whip" No. 340, 4 bump cars, driver's head wobbles	400	600	800
Chein Rabbit in shirt and pants, circa 1938	35	52	70
Chein "Racer #3," 1920s, 6½" long	120	180	240
Chein "Rocket Ride" No. 400, 18" high, base 11" diameter, 4 rockets	600	900	1200
Chein "Roller Coaster," includes 2 cars, circa 1938	200	300	400
Chein "Roller Coaster," 1950s, includes 2 cars	150	225	300
Chein "Santa Elf," 1920s, 6" high	200	300	400
Chein "Ski Boy", No. 157, 1940s, 7¾" long, 5¼" tall	100	150	200
Chein "Space Ride" No. 205, 1950s, 10" high	450	675	900
Chein "Space Ride", 1940s, 9" high,, lever action	600	900	1200
Chein "Spirit of St. Louis" Airplane, 1930s, 8" long, 8" wingspan	200	300	400
Chein Taxi, 7" long, 1920s	175	263	350
Chein Toy Town Helicopter, 13" long, 1950s	55	83	110
Chein Turtle with Native on back	120	180	240
Chein "U.S. Army Sergeant" No. 153, 1950s, 5½" high	40	60	80
Chicken pulling chick in cart, 7½" long, Wyandotte	40	60	80
Circus-type Trainer, baton in hand, revolves, with rooster on each side, 3½" long, musical, German	100	150	200
Clown in Donkey Cart, 7½" long	60	90	120
Clown in Hoop, 6½" high, Japan	150	225	300
Clown Musicians, four, on a pedestal, musical, 8" high	200	300	400
"Clown on Scooter", 1915, Tipp Co., 6" tall	200	300	400
"Coney Island" 1950s, Technofix Co., 1950s, 14"x21" base and two 3" cars	100	150	200

CHEIN "Roller Coaster" 1930's. Courtesy Don Hultzman. Photo by Ron Chojnacki.

CHEIN "Roller Coaster" 1950's. Courtesy Don Hultzman. Photo by Ron Chojnacki.

COURTLAND MFG. CO.
WALT REACH

(History based on information from Joe and Sharon Freed)

Walter Reach, owner of Courtland, had a burning desire to be known as the second Louis Marx. Also functioning as designer, he began production in 1944 with two die-cut cardboard toys (a rabbit and cart and horse and cart). Reach turned to tin litho toys after the war, a number of them non-wind-ups. At its height, Courtland, located first in Camden, New Jersey, and later in Philadelphia, had 600 workers and in 1947 its sales exceeded 1.5 million. But success was short-lived, and the firm lasted just seven years.

Courtland Toys Listing by Joe and Sharon Freed

	C6	C8	C10
No. 15 Mechanical Lawn Mower, 8¼" wide, 24" high, 3" wheels. 1950 retail price 79¢ 1951 retail- 98¢ 20	30	45
No. 20 Mechanical Lawn Mower, 11¼" wide, 29" high, 5" wheels, 1950 retail- $1.29; 1951 retail -$1.49 25	35	50
No. 21 Mechanical Lawn Mower, 12" wide, 29" high, 5" wheels, 1951 retail - $2.98 30	45	70
No.25 Mechanical Power Lawn Mower, 12" wide, 29" high, 5¾" wheels, 1951, retail $2.98 50	70	90
No. 200 Easter Rabbit and Trailer, 11⅝" long, 3" wide, 3½" high, 1946 retail - 49¢ ...15	20	25
No. 300 Circus Elephant and "Monkeys" Cart, 11⅝" high, 3" wide, 3½" high, 1946 retail - 49¢ ...45	70	100
No. 400 Circus Elephant and "African Lions" Cart, 11⅝" long, 3" wide, 3½" high, 1946 retail - 49¢ 45	70	100
No. 500 Circus Elephant and "Circus Band" Cart, 11⅝" long, 3" wide, 3½" high, 1946 retail - 49¢ 60	85	125
No. 1070 Mechanical Big 4 Truck Parade, 9" long, 3" wide, 2¾" high, 1947 retail - $3.39 ....No Price Found		
No. 1200 Mechanical Trailer - Truck 13" long, 3" wide, 3¼" high, 1947 retail - $1.00.65	80	125
No. 1300 Mechanical Ice Cream Truck, 9" long, 3" wide, 2¾" high, retail 79¢ 75	90	135
No. 1300 Mechanical Moving and Storage Truck, 9" long, 3" wide, 2¾" high, 1947 retail - 79¢ 90	115	145
Same as above, with No. 130 lithographed on the sides of the truck bed 90	115	145

	C6	C8	C10
No. 1300 Mechanical Fire Patrol No. 2 Truck, 9" long, 3" wide, 2¾" high, 1947 retail - 79¢ 75	90	135
No. 1300 Mechanical Express and Hauling Truck, 9" long, 3" wide, 2¾" high, 1947 retail - 79¢ 75	90	135
No. 1400 Mechanical "Automatic Ladder" Fire Truck, 9" long, 3" wide, 2¾" high, 1947 retail - $1.00 80	100	140
No. 1500 Mechanical Road Roller Truck, 9" long, 3" wide , 3¼" high ...100	145	175
No. 1600 Mechanical Dump Truck, 7" long, 3" wide, 2¾" high 45	60	85
No. 2000 Mechanical "ESSO" Gasoline tractor-trailer, 13" long, 3" wide, 3¼ "high.......85	100	145
No. 2000 Mechanical Gasoline tractor-trailer, 13" long,, 3" wide, 3¼" high...75	90	135
No. 2050 Mechanical Milk tractor-trailer, 13" long, 3" wide, 3¼" high, "American Dairies" 85	100	145

NOTE: 1951 catalog shows Milk trailer markings that read the same as above except 'Approved' is used in place of the words ' Vitamin D.' This variation is not known to have been produced.

	C6	C8	C10
No. 2100 Mechanical Hook and Ladder tractor-trailer, 13" long, 3" wide, 3¼" high.....75	90	135
No. 2150 Mechanical Emergency Rescue Squad tractor-trailer, 13", 3" wide, 3¼" high....85	100	145
No. 2200 Mechanical Logging tractor-trailer, 13" long, 3" wide, 3¼" high ...85	100	145
No. 2300 Mechanical Open Van tractor-trailer, 13" long, 3" wide, 3¼" high.....75	90	135
No. 2350 Mechanical Open Van tractor-trailer, 13" long, 3" wide, 3¼" high ...85	100	145
No. 2375 Mechanical Heavy Duty Sand and Gravel tractor-trailer, 13" long, 3" wide, 3¼" high 70	90	125
No. 2400 Mechanical Trailer Tow Truck, 13" long, 3" wide, 3¼" high..........85	100	145

COURTLAND Motor Guaranteed for Life No. 2000 Mechanical Gasoline Tractor-Trailer (packed in individual boxes all with motor guarantee certificate). Courtesy Joe and Sharon Freed.

COURTLAND Motor Guaranteed for Life No. 2050 Mechanical Milk Tractor-Trailer. Courtesy Joe and Sharon Freed.

COURTLAND Motor Guaranteed for Life No. 2200 Mechanical Logging Tractor-Trailer. Courtesy Joe and Sharon Freed.

	C6	C8	C10
No. 2600 Mechanical Freight Haulers tractor-trailer, 13" long, 3" high, 3¼" wide.....85	85	100	145
No. 2700 Mechanical Side Tipper tractor-trailer, 13" long, 3" high, 3¼" wide.....85	85	100	145
No. 2800 Assortment consists of 2 No. 2000 Gasoline Trucks, 2 No. 2050 Milk Trucks, 2 No. 2200 Log Trucks, 2 No. 2350 Open Van Trucks, 2 No. 2600 Freight Hauler Trucks and 2 No. 2700 Side Tipper Trucks - Wholesale Assortment Only....No Price Found			
No. 3000 Mechanical Road Roller Truck, 9" long, 3" wide, 3¼" high.100	100	150	200
No. 3100 Mechanical Dump Truck, 7" long, 3" wide, 3¼" high.....45	45	60	85
No. 3200 Mechanical Stake Bed Truck, 7" long, 3" wide, 3¼" high.....45	45	60	85
No. 3800 Assortment consists of 6 No. 3200 Stake Bed Trucks and 6 No. 3100 Dump trucks. Wholesale Assortment Only....No Price Found			
XXXX Courtland Mechanical Side Tipper Tractor-trailer, "Black Diamond Coal Company - 340", L-13", H-3", W-3¼"..90	90	115	150

	C6	C8	C10
No. 4000 City Meat Market Delivery Sedan, 7¼" long, 3¼" wide, 2¾" high.....45	45	75	100
No. 4000 Modern Bakery Delivery Sedan, 7¼" long, 3¼" wide, 2¾" high.....45	45	74	100
No. 4000 Fire Chief Car, 7¼" long, 3¼" wide, 2¾" high, red & white...45	45	75	100
Same as above, all red.....55	55	85	115
No. 4000 Checker Cab Car, 7¼" long, 3¼" wide, 2¾" high, green and yellow.....55	55	85	115
Same as above, green and white.....60	60	90	125
No. 4500 Express Service Pick-up, 7¼" long, 3¼" wide, 2¾" high.....45	45	75	100
No. 4500 Country Produce Pick-up, 7¼" long, 3¼" wide, 2¾" high.....45	45	75	100
No. 4500 Modern Decorators Pick-up, 7¼" long, 3¼" wide, 2¾" high.....45	45	75	100
No. 5000 Mechanical Operating No. 51 Crane Truck 13" long, 3⅝" wide, 5" high.....70	70	100	135
No. 5100 Mechanical "Black Diamond" Coal Truck, 10½" long, 3" wide, 3⅜" high.....65	65	95	130
No. 5200 Mechanical No. 51 Steam Shovel, 15½" long, 3¾" wide, 9½" high.....50	50	70	90

COURTLAND Motor Guaranteed for Life No. 2100 Mechanical Hook & Ladder Tractor-Trailer. Courtesy Joe and Sharon Freed.

COURTLAND Motor Guaranteed for Life No. 2150 Mechanical Emergency Rescue Squad. Courtesy Joe and Sharon Freed.

COURTLAND No. 3000 Mechanical Road Roller Truck. Courtesy Joe and Sharon Freed.

COURTLAND No. 6050 Mechanical Farm Tractor. Courtesy Continental Hobby House.

COURTLAND "Motor Guaranteed For Life" No. 5100 "Black Diamond" Coal Truck. Courtesy Joe and Sharon Freed.

COURTLAND 5300. Photo by Joe Freed.

COURTLAND No. 4000 Checker Cab Car. Courtesy Joe and Sharon Freed.

COURTLAND No. 4000 City Meat Market Delivery Sedan. Courtesy Joe and Sharon Freed.

XXXX COURTLAND Mechanical Side Tipper Tractor-Trailer, "Black Diamond Coal Company 340". Courtesy Joe and Sharon Freed.

XXXX COURTLAND Motor Guaranteed For Life No. 6500 Mechanical Ice Cream Scooter. Courtesy Joe and Sharon Freed.

	C6	C8	C10
No. 5300 Mechanical Combination Steam Shovel carried by low-boy tractor-trailer, 15½" long, 3⅞" wide, 10½" high......100	150	200
No. 5800 Assortment consists of 3 No. 2300 Aluminum Open Van Trucks, 3 No. 2150 Emergency Rescue Squad Trucks, 3 No. 2375 Sand and Gravel Trucks and 3 No. 2400 Towing Service Trucks - Wholesale Assortment Only ....No Price Found		
No. 6000 Mechanical Farm Tractor w/scraper, rear tires are large rubber and front are small rubber tires 8¾" long, 4¾" wide, 4½" high.................60	80	100
No. 6050 Mechanical Farm Tractor w/o scraper. Rear tires are large rubber and front are small rubber tires, 7½" long, 4¾" wide, 4½" high.................45	65	85
No. 6075 Mechanical Farm Tractor w/o scraper, rear tires are large tin litho while the front are small rubber tires, 7½" long, 4¾" wide, 4½" high.......75	100	135
No. 6100 Mechanical Caterpillar Tractor with rubber treads, 6" long, 3" wide, 4½" high...............85	110	150
No. 6500 Mechanical Ice Cream Scooter, 6½" long, 3" wide, 4½" high............100	165	225
No. 7000 Mechanical Fire Chief Car with siren, 7¼" long, 3¼" wide, 2¾" high 50	70	90
No. 7500 Mechanical State Police Car with siren, 7¼" long, 3¼" wide, 2¾" high 50	70	90

No. 7500 Mechanical Parking Meter and Bank, Base 6"x 6", 24½" high.
NOTE: This is one of only four Courtland toys stamped "A Walt Reach Toy by Courtland Toy Co., Phila. Pa. Made in U.S.A." The only known Courtland styled toys marked with the Courtland Toy Company, Philadelphia stamping is this mechanical parking meter bank, a No. 4000 sedan, a non-power "Fire Chief" car, a private and a garage similar to No. 9075..... ...65   75   100

| No. 8000 Mechanical "Rocking R Ranch" See-Saw, 17¾ "long, 2⅛" wide, 6" high.....,.................20 | 30 | 40 |
| No. 8500 Mechanical Chromed Trimmed Tow Truck, 8" long, 3¼" wide, 3½" high, tow boom shows detail ....75 | 85 | 125 |

	C6	C8	C10
No. 8500 Mechanical Chromed Trimmed Tow Truck, 8" long, 3¼" wide, 3½" high, tow boom is solid color 75	85	125

End Courtland

Dancing dogs, two, and a boy with whip 200	300	400
Dancing horse, two small bells on top of bridle, 7½" high.......................100	150	200
Ferris Wheel carrying eight gondolas, the gondolas containing a total of 16 small bisque dolls, 33½" high..1200	1800	2400
Ferris Wheel, carved with figures and music box, 17" 400	600	800
Freight Cart pulled by man in cap, with luggage on cart, circa 1940.....60	90	120
Gama "Komical Walking Cat," circa 1929, 7" high...........................150	225	300

GIRARD "Flasho The Mechanical Grinder".
Courtesy Scott Smiles. Photo by Mike Adams.

GIRARD

Girard Model Works was founded in Girard, Pennsylvania in 1906 by C.G. Wood. Originally it made patterns, models and special machinery, with Wood's son Frank joining the firm a few years after its inception. In 1918 they began making toys for "a large firm in New York" (otherwise unidentified), and in 1920 began making them under their own name, originally as "Wood's Mechanical Toys". By 1931 the firm had a thousand employees, with Louis Marx by then associated with Girard. During the Depression he took over the firm. The last Girard toys seem to have been produced in 1975, though the firm remained in business until 1980. Many of Marx's and Girard's toys are interchangeable.

Girard Air Mail Biplane, 3-engine 600	900	1200

"Ham and Sam" maker unknown, piano player and dancer. Courtesy Ed Hyers Antique Toys.

GIRARD Railroad Handcar. Courtesy Mapes Auctioneers & Appraisers.

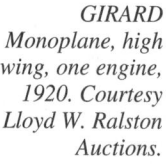

GIRARD Monoplane, high wing, one engine, 1920. Courtesy Lloyd W. Ralston Auctions.

IVES Destroyer, "3009". Courtesy PB Eighty-Four, New York.

IVES Tugboat "King". Courtesy PB Eighty-Four, New York.

INGAP Mouse Car. Courtesy Christie's East.

	C6	C8	C10
Girard "Bi-Wing Monoplane", 1918, 12" long, 14" wingspan (Wood's)	150	225	300
Girard bus with driver, 12½" long	150	225	300
Girard Coolie & Pushcart	140	210	280
Girard "Farm Boy Walking," 1920, 6" long, (with shovel and rake) (Wood's)	450	675	900
Girard "Fire Chief" siren coupe, 1930s, 14" long	350	525	700
Girard "Flasho The Mechanical Grinder," 1920s	100	150	200
Girard "Goble, The Gobbling Goose"	120	180	240

	C6	C8	C10
Girard Man pushing wheelbarrow, 5½"	150	225	300
Girard Monoplane, high wing, one engine, 1921-22, 13" long	350	525	700
Girard Railroad Handcar	70	105	140
Girard "Spirit of St. Louis", 9"	400	600	800
Girard "Tri Motor Air Lines", 1920s	175	263	350
Girard "U.S. Marines" monoplane	No Price Found		
"Grand Prix", 1950's, Technofix Co., 20" long with three 3" tin cars	80	120	160
"Ham and Sam", 1950s, Linemar, 4x5" base, 6" high	450	675	900

	C6	C8	C10
"Ham and Sam," maker unknown, piano player and dancer	450	675	900
Hansom Cab, horse moves backward and forward as wheels rotate, driver atop cab, 5¾" long	100	150	200
Hy Line car, ultra-streamlined two-door coupe type, circa 1938	100	150	200
Hy-Lo, Buffalo Toys Ferris Wheel, 14½" high	150	225	300
Indian, like cigar store Indian, circa 1937	70	105	140
Ingap Mouse Car, 6" long, Halian, eccentric wheels, arms extend	1650	2475	3300
Ives "Destroyer" "3009," 1923, painted, 9" long	400	600	800
Ives Submarine, 10½" long	300	450	600
Ives Tugboat "King"	150	225	300
Katz Toys, "Coney Island", 1930s, 18" long-roller coaster with eight-passenger car and four monoplanes on pylon	400	600	800
Katz Toys NY "The Question Mark" airplane, 18" wingspan, high-wing, two motor	200	300	400
Kellerman "Armored Vehicle," 1930s, 4" long	55	88	110
Kingsbury Ambulance, 7"	200	300	400
Kingsbury Artillery Launcher	75	112	150
Kingsbury Biplane, circa 1925, single engine, rubber wheels, 16" long	300	450	600
Kingsbury "Bi-Wing Airplane", 1918, 16" long - 17" wingspan (with cast iron pilot)	500	750	1000
Kingsbury Borden's Milk Truck	250	375	500
Kingsbury Convertible with rumble seat, electric headlamps, hard rubber wheels, 12½" long	150	225	300
Kingsbury fireman's ladder truck, hard rubber wheels, driver, 23½" long	150	225	300
Kingsbury Monoplane, high wing, single engine, wind-up wheels and spins prop via rubber band, 1930s, 11" long	250	375	500
Kingsbury Roadster, electric headlamps, 12½" long	250	375	500
Kingsbury Station Wagon, 1920s	150	225	300
Kingsbury "Streetcar," 1930s, No. 782, 9" long	150	225	300
Kingsbury "Transatlantic Air-Go-Round"	250	375	500
Lehmann "Adam the Porter," 1920s, 9" high	825	1238	1650
Lehmann "Aha" delivery van, 5½" long, 1920s	550	825	1100
Lehmann "Ajax" Warrior with two clubs	1050	1575	2100

	C6	C8	C10
Lehmann "Alabama Coon Jigger"	400	600	800
Lehmann "Also"	275	363	550
Lehmann "Am Pol," Amundsen driving, figure behind with umbrella, map of North Pole	1800	2700	3750
Lehmann "Anxious Bride," chauffeur on tricycle, woman in car	2400	3600	4900
Lehmann Autobus	1200	1800	2400
Lehmann Baker & Sweep	2500	3750	5000
Lehmann Balky Mule, 1930s, 7½" long	325	488	650
Lehmann "Bucking Bronco, Wild West," 6½" long	600	900	1200
Lehmann "Climbing Miller," cardboard blades	340	510	680
Lehmann "Climbing Monkey," (Tom 385), 9" long, 1920s	150	225	300
Lehmann "Crawling Beetle, The", 1900s, 4" long	175	263	350
Lehmann Crocodile, circa 1905	350	525	700
Lehmann "Dancing Sailor," 1920s, 7½" high	550	825	1100
Lehmann "Daredevil" Zebra Cart	450	675	900
Lehmann "Duo"	800	1200	1600
Lehmann "Echo Motorcycle" No. 725, 1907, 9" long	1000	1500	2000
Lehmann "EHE & Co.," open trunk	550	825	1100
Lehmann EPL II dirigible	750	1125	1500
Lehmann "Express," porter pulling cart, circa 1927, 6" long	350	525	700
Lehmann "Galop" zebra cart	200	300	400
Lehmann "Going to the Fair"	1900	2800	3900
Lehmann Heavy Swell, dude-it-up man	2000	3000	4000
Lehmann "Ito" sedan, 1920s, 6½" long	1300	2000	2600
Lehmann "Kadi", two Chinese carrying chest	500	750	1000
Lehmann "Lehmann's Autobus 590"	1200	1800	2400
Lehmann "Li La," early car with two excited women passengers, driver in top hat and dog with turning head, 5½" long	1000	1500	2000
Lehmann "Lo Li", clown and ring master	5000	8000	12,000
Lehmann "Lu-Lu" bird	100	150	200
Lehmann "Masuyama," coolie pulling rickshaw	1100	1650	2200
Lehmann "Mikado Family," 1920s, 6½" long	1800	2700	3600
Lehmann "Motor Car Kutsche," 1897, 5½" long	750	1125	1500
Lehmann "Motor Coach," 1920s, 5½" long	400	600	800
Lehmann "Naughty Boy"	600	900	1200

LEHMANN Alabama Coon Jigger.

LEHMANN Dancing Sailor. Courtesy Christie's East.

LEHMANN "Kadi". Courtesy Sotheby's New York.

LEHMANN Masuyama. Courtesy Mapes Auctioneers & Appraisers.

LEHMANN, Top to Bottom: "Uhu", "Lehmann's Autobus 590". Courtesy Sotheby's New York.

LEHMANN, Left to Right: "Naughty Boy", "Quack-Quack", "Onkel". Courtesy Sotheby's New York.

LEHMANN, Left to Right: "Li La", "Zig Zag", "Tut Tut". Courtesy Sotheby's New York.

LEHMANN, Left to Right: Stubborn Donkey, EPL-II Dirigible, "Motor Coach", "Bucking Bronco, Wild West". Courtesy Sotheby's New York.

LEHMANN, Left to Right: "Express", "Paddy Pig". Courtesy Sotheby's New York.

LEHMANN Ito. Courtesy Christie's East.

LEWCO See-Saw Circus with box. Courtesy Scott Smiles. Photo by Mike Adams.

LINDSTROM toys 1930's, Sweeping Mammy, Betty, Mammy (Shakos). Courtesy Don Hultzman.

	C6	C8	C10
Lehmann "Na-Ob," man driving horse cart, wheels marked with elf, 6" long 400	600	800
Lehmann "New Century Cycle", 1907, 5" long...............1250	1875	2500
Lehmann "Nu-Nu" No. 733, rickshaw with puller and rider, circa 1913, 4½" long 550	825	1100
Lehmann "Oh My," 10" high 420	630	840
Lehmann "OHO" patented 1903 325	510	650
Lehmann "Onkel"...............400	600	800
Lehmann "Paak-Paak" ducklings in cart pulled by duck...............300	450	600
Lehmann "Paddy Pig" c. 1912, 6" long 700	1050	1400
Lehmann "Pao Pao" peacock, 10" long ...250	375	500
Lehmann "Performing Sea Lion, The" 1900s, 7" long 175	263	350
Lehmann "Power Carriage" 360	540	720
Lehmann "Quack-Quack," mother duck pulling cart with three small ducks 300	450	600
Lehmann "Rad-Cycle," 5" long circa 1927...............650	975	1300
Lehmann "Rollo Chair"...............1200	1800	2400
Lehmann Stubborn Donkey, clown in donkey cart, 7½" long...............350	525	700
Lehmann Tap Tap, man pushing wheelbarrow...............280	420	560
Lehmann "Terra" 1500	2250	3000
Lehmann "Tom" climbing monkey, 8" long 140	210	280
Lehmann "Tut-Tut," man in car with horn, 6¾" long 1000	1500	2000
Lehmann "Uhu" amphibious car...............1800	2700	3600
Lehmann "Walking Down Broadway" strolling couple 2000	3000	4000
Lehmann Walking Sailor, 7½" high 500	750	1000
Lehmann Wild West 250	375	500

	C6	C8	C10
Lehmann "Zig Zag" patented 1903, 5" long 1125	1688	2250
Lehmann "Zikra" No.752, 1920s, 7" long .900	1350	1800
Lehmann "Zulu," black man in cart pulled by ostrich...............750	1125	1500
Lewco "See-Saw Circus", 1940s, 6½" high.100	150	200
Limousine, license plate "N.Y. 1918" litho, approx. 6" long 200	300	400
Lindstrom Bird 80	120	160
Lindstrom "Betty," 1930s, 8" tall, shako walker 90	135	180
Lindstrom Bumper Car, 6½" long...............100	150	200
Lindstrom Dancing Dutch Boy, 1930s, 8" high...............125	188	250
Lindstrom "Dancing Lassie," 8" tall, shako, 1930s...............100	150	200
Lindstrom "Delfine 7" motorboat, circa 1930...............175	263	350
Lindstrom "Johnny The Dancing Clown" No. 122, 1930s, 8" tall 150	225	300
Lindstrom "Katrinka", 1930s, 8" tall ...100	150	200
Lindstrom "Lindstrom's Ferry Boat," approx. 8¼", litho 100	150	200
Lindstrom "Lindstrom Flyer," 14" long...100	150	200
Lindstrom, "Mammy," 1930s, 8" tall, shako walker 200	300	400
Lindstrom "Miss America" speedboat .120	180	240
Lindstrom "Parcel Post No. 2" truck....200	300	400
Lindstrom Racing Car, 1930s...............90	135	180
Lindstrom "Skeeter Bug", 1930s, (bumper car) 7" long...............120	180	240
Lindstrom Speedboat, circa 1950, 18½" long 150	225	300
Lindstrom "Sweeping Betty" 125	188	250
Lindstrom "Sweeping Mammy," No.1750, 1930s, 8" tall, shako walker while sweeping 150	225	300
Lupor Metal Products N.Y. Racer No. 8, 1930s 30	45	60

LOUIS MARX

By the 1950s, Louis Marx was the largest manufacturer of toys in the world; six large factories in the U.S., and ownership of interest in factories in seven other countries. Marx, born in Brooklyn in 1896, was working for "Toy King" Ferdinand Strauss when he was in his teens, and by the age of twenty his energy and enterprise had made him a director of that company. A falling out with Strauss persuaded him to go into business for himself, and in 1921 he and his brother began making their own toys, including some adaptations of items by the now-defunct Strauss. Marx's watchword seems to have been quality at the lowest possible price, and he was such a favorite with toy buyers that he had virtually no need for salesmen or advertising. Although Marx made virtually every type of toy with the exception of dolls, his tin wind-up toys are probably the most favored by toy collectors. Marx, in April, 1972, sold his company to the Quaker Oats Company, who in 1976 sold it to Europe's largest toy manufacturer, Dunbee-Combex-Marx. The company went into bankruptcy in 1980. Louis Marx died in 1982 at the age of 85. In 1982 American Plastics bought much of the Marx assets and in 1990 began producing toys from the original molds. In the first Marx break-up, certain rights and molds were retained in Mexico, and these continue.

	C6	C8	C10
"Acrobatic Marvel", 1930s, monkey on 13" spring and 7½" rocking base ...100	150	200
Air Mail Biplane, 1930, 4-engine........300	450	600
Air Mail Monoplane, 1930, 2-engine...165	248	330
Airplane, U.S. Army No. 6, 2-engine, no guns, 18" wingspan..................137	205	275
Airplane No. 90, light fuselage 100	150	200
Airplane No. 90, medium fuselage.......100	150	200
Alligator...65	98	130
"Ambulance" with siren, 1930s, 14½" long.190	285	380
Ambulance, "M.D. War Dept.," 1930s 450	675	900
"American Tractor" with implements, 1920s, 10" long..............................180	270	360
Armored Trucking Co. 110	165	220
"Army Dive Bomber" No. 482............137	205	275
Army Staff Car, 1930s, litho steel 200	300	400
"Army Staff Car," W-601158, with flasher and siren, 11" long, 1940s..225	338	450
Army Truck, 10" long, cloth cover, 1930s.425	638	850
"Automatic Fire House," 1950s, Fire Chief Car, 7½" long, Volunteer Fire Dept. Garage, 19" long 110	165	220

	C6	C8	C10
"Automatic Reversing Road Roller", 1925, 9" long.................................200	300	400
Balky Mule, pre-war............................100	150	200
"Balky Mule," 1950s, 8" long...............70	105	140
"Bear Cyclist," 1930s, 6 long.............120	180	240
"Beat It" The Komikal Kop," 1930s 250	375	500
"Be Bop -The Jivin' Jigger," 1948, 10" high.160	240	320
"Bi-Wing Airplane," 1930s, 18" wingspan250	375	500
"Big Parade," moving vehicles, soldiers, tin airplane, etc., 1929, 24" long....600	900	1200
"Big Silver," Mack Dump Truck..........250	375	500
Big Three Aerial Acrobats, 1920 200	300	400
Big Lizzie car, early 1930s, 7¼" long..150	225	300
Bomber, four engine, 18" wingspan, ca. 1941.200	300	400
Bomber, four engine, 18" wingspan, camouflaged, circa 1940 200	300	400
Bomber, two engine, 18" wingspan 200	300	400
Boy on Trapeze.....................................100	150	200
Bulldozer Climbing Tractor, caterpillar type, circa 1950s, 10½" long 110	165	220
Bumper Auto , streamlined, circa 1939, large bumpers, front and rear.........120	180	240

MARX Acrobatic Marvel. Photo by Don Hultzman

MARX Balky Mule, post-war, with box. Courtesy Scott Smiles. Photo by Mike Adams.

MARX 'Ambulance" with siren. Courtesy Mapes Auctioneers & Appraisers.

MARX Bulldozer Climbing Tractor. Courtesy Continental Hobby House

MARX "Busy Bridge". Courtesy PB Eighty-Four New York.

MARX Coo-Coo Car. Photo by Don Hultzman.

MARX "Flipo the Jumping Dog". Courtesy Mapes Auctioneers

MARX "Butter & Egg Man". Courtesy Scott Smiles. Photo by Mike Adams.

MARX "Big Silver" Mack dump truck. Courtesy Ed Hyers Antique Toys.

	C6	C8	C10
"Busy Bridge," vehicles on bridge, 1935.	375	562	750
"Busy Delivery" (black Pinocchio), 1930s, 9" long, 8" high	450	675	900
"Busy Miners," 1930s, 16½" long, includes 2¼" tin litho miner's car	95	142	190
"Busy Parking Station", 1930s, 17" long with 2" tin race car	150	225	300
"Butter & Egg Man," 1930s, 8" high	300	450	600
Cadillac Roadster, 13" long, trunk with tools on luggage carrier, 1930	200	300	400
"Careful Johnnie," 1950s, 5½" long	100	150	200
Cat with ball in front, two wheels in back, circa 1938	85	128	170
Caterpillar Climbing Tractor, Ca. 1950s, 10" long	90	135	180

	C6	C8	C10
"Charleston Trio," one black adult, dog, black kid dancer, 1921	600	900	1200
Chicken Snatcher, black holding chicken, dog biting at the seat of his pants, circa 1927	900	1350	1800
Climbing Tractor, sparkling, 1960s, 8½" long.	110	165	220
Climbing, Fighting Tank"	100	150	200
"Coast Defense," circular, with three cannon, revolving airplane, 1929	350	525	700
"Coke Coal City Coal Co." truck	250	375	500
"Construction" tractor	325	488	650
"Coo Coo Car," 1920s, 7½" long	300	450	600
"Cowboy Rider," circa 1941, cowboy with lariat on dapple or black horse	200	300	400
Crazy Dora nodder head (also "Dan")	105	158	210
"Cross-Country Flyer", Zeppelin and Airplane, 1920s, fly around 18" hangar tower	200	300	400
"Dan Dipsy Car", 1950s, 5½" long (plastic nodder)	90	135	180

MARX Cat with Ball. Courtesy Scott Smiles. Photo by Mike Adams.

MARX Charleston Trio, one adult, child, dog. Courtesy Ed Hyers Antique Toys.

	C6	C8	C10
"Flipo the Jumping Dog, See Me Jump," on hind legs, circa 1940, 3½x4"	90	135	180
"Flying Fortress 2905" sparkling aeroplane, 1940s, 4 engines	225	338	450
"Flying Helicopter Skyport," 1950s, 12x9"	100	150	200
"Funny Face," new in 1928	400	600	800
"Funny Flivver" circa 1925	300	450	600
G-Man Pursuit Car, 1930s	250	375	500
"George the Drummer Boy," 1930s, 9" tall with moving eyes	100	150	200
"George the Drummer Boy," 1930s, 9" tall with stationary eyes, No. 881	75	112	150
"Giant King Racer," circa 1930s, "711"	110	165	220
Giant Reversing Tractor Truck with tools, "Hauling," 14" long, circa 1950s	100	150	200
Golden Pecking Goose, 9½" long, dated July 8, 1924, hops along, pecking at ground	90	135	180
"Hee-Haw" balky mule, 1929, 10¾" long, six-color litho, goes backward, forward and rears, farmer and his dog on seat and 5 milk cans in cart	150	225	300
Highboy Climbing Tractor, circa 1950s, 10½" long	100	150	200
Highboy Tractor, sparkles, circa 1950s, 10" long	100	150	200
"Honeymoon Express," old-fashioned train on circular track, 1927	160	240	320
"Honeymoon Express," circa late 1930s	110	165	220
"Honeymoon Express," circa 1940, circling train and plane, 9⅜" diameter	132	198	265
"Honeymoon Express," streamlined train on circular track, 1947, 9⅜" diameter	90	135	180
"Hoppo The Waltzing Monkey With Cymbals", 1930s, 9½" high	150	225	300
"Ice Man"	300	450	600
Jalopy Pickup Truck, 7"	80	120	160
"Jazzbo Jim," 1920s, 9" high	300	450	600
"Joy-Rider," 1929, 8" long, College Boy driver with bag, wording on car "goes backward, forward, circles and rears" head moves	200	300	400
Jumpin-' Jeep, circa WW II, 6"	100	150	200
"King Racer," 1930s, 8½" long	450	675	900

	C6	C8	C10
"Dapper Dan Coon Jigger," 1910	260	390	520
Dare Devil Flyer, new in 1928	400	600	800
"Daredevil Motor Drome," 1930s, 5½" high, 9" diameter, 2" windup car	100	150	200
"Deluxe Delivery Truck", 1950s, 11" long	100	150	200
"Dipsy Doodle Bug" Dodge 'em cars (Dan or Dora), 6" high	250	375	500
Donkey pulling cart, with rider, 1950s, 10" long	110	165	220
"Dora Dipsy Car", 1950s, 5½" long (plastic nodder)	90	135	180
"Dottie the Driver," 1950s, 6½" long	80	120	160
Doughboy Tank, two side turrets, with top turret, 9¼" long, 1930, soldier with gun pops out	110	165	220
"Driver Training Car", 1950s, 6" long	50	75	100
"Drive-UR-Self Car", 1950s, 11" long	300	450	600
Dump Truck, 13" long	187	280	375
"Fireman Joe," 8" tall, ladder 24" high, 1930s	75	112	150
"1st Batt. F.D. Chief's Car," 16", siren, battery headlights	110	165	220
"Firewater Boat," 1920, 9" long	350	525	700

MARX Fireman on Ladder. Courtesy Scott Smiles.

MARX G-Man Pursuit Car. Courtesy Gary Linden

MARX "Honeymoon Express" circa late 1930s. Courtesy Phillips New York.

MARX George the Drummer Boy with moving eyes. Courtesy Scott Smiles. Photo by Mike Adams.

MARX Highboy Climbing Tractor. Photo by Don Hultzman.

MARX "Merrymakers" without marquee. Courtesy Phillips New York.

MARX Motorcycle Policeman with side-car, "Police", "3". Courtesy Phillips New York.

MARX Mystic Motorcycle. Courtesy Scott Smiles. Photo by Mike Adams.

MARX "Midget Special". Courtesy Scott Smiles.

MARX Piggy. Courtesy Scott Smiles. Photo by Mike Adams.

MARX "Midget Climbing, Fighting Tank". Courtesy K. Warren Mitchell.

MARX "P.D." Police motorcycle w/sidecar. Courtesy Gary Linden.

MARX 'Old Jalopy" large and small. Courtesy Ed Hyers Antique Toys.

MARX "Rex Race Car". Courtesy Thomas G. Nefos, Federal Shipping Network.

MARX "Tom Tom Jungle Boy." Photo by Ed Hyers Antique Toys.

MARX "Royal Van Co.". Courtesy Mapes Auctioneers & Appraisers.

MARX Ride 'Em Cowboy. Photo by Don Hultzman.

MARX "Rocket Fighter". Courtesy Don Hultzman. Photo by Ron Chojnacki.

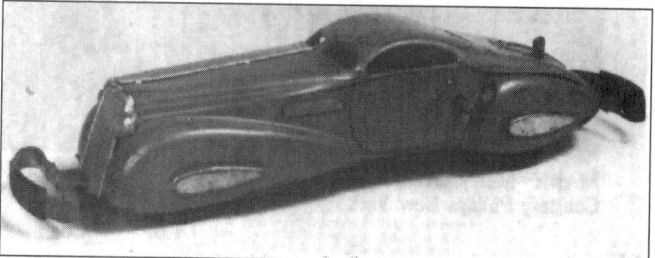

MARX "Reversible Coupe, The Marvel Car". Courtesy Mapes Auctioneers & Appraisers.

	C6	C8	C10
"Let The Drummer Boy Play," 1930s, 8½" high	350	525	700
"Limping Lizzie" car	200	300	400
"Looping Plane," No. 182	90	135	180
"Looping Plane," No. 382	90	135	180
Lucky Stunt Flyer	200	300	400
"Mack Dump Truck", 1930s, (City Coal Co.) 13" long	350	525	700
"Main Street," moving vehicles, traffic cop, etc., 1929	350	525	700
"Mammy's Boy", 1930s, 11" tall	400	600	800
"Mechanical Airplane," new in 1928	200	300	400
"Mechanical Roadster", 1950s, 11" long	70	105	140
"Mechanical Speedway Racer"	60	90	120
Mechanical Station Wagon	125	188	250
"Mechanical Taxi Cab", 1950s, 11" long	80	120	160
"Mechanical Tractor," 6" long, ca. 1930s	110	165	220
"Mechanical Tractor with Earth Grader," 21½" long, circa 1950s	120	180	240
Merrymakers, four mice, three in band, one a dancer, 1929, with marquee	800	1200	1600
Same as above without marquee	700	1050	1400
"Midget Climbing Fighting Tank," approx. 5½" long, circa 1935, Pat. No. 1,334,539	60	90	120
Midget Climbing Tractor, 5½" long, circa 1950	60	90	120
"Midget Racer", 1950s, 6" long, plastic	50	75	100
"Midget Special," race car - driver in old headgear and goggles, 5" long, No. 2 racer, 1930s	65	98	130
"Midget Special" race car driver in old headgear and goggles, 5" long No. 7 racer, 1930s	65	98	130
Minstrel figure, 11" high	160	240	320
"Monkey Cyclist," 1930s	80	120	160
"Moon Creature," 1950s, 5½" high (Japan)	90	135	180
Motorcycle Policeman with side-car "Police," "3" license plate reads "102D", approx. 8" long, 5¾" high, circa 1940	220	330	440
"Motorcycle Trooper," 1935	160	240	320
"Mountain Climber," 1960s (Japan), 32" long, 4" car	80	120	160
"Mysterious Kitty Kat," 1950s, 8" long	90	135	180
"Mystery Police Cycle," 1930s, 4½" long	110	165	220
Mystery Tunnel	60	90	120
"Mystic Motorcycle," circa 1930s	90	135	180
"New Flivver," 1920s, 7" long	312	418	625

	C6	C8	C10
"New Rocket Racer", 1930s, 16" long	200	300	400
"New York," circular, with train, new in 1928, 9½" diameter, tin airplane	500	750	1000
Nodding Goose	70	105	140
"North American Van Lines Inc. Long Distance Moving" truck	125	188	250
"Old Jalopy"	100	150	200
"Old Jalopy," small, 1950s, Linemar	75	112	150
"P.D." Motorcyclist, "Pat. 2001625," approx. 4" long	120	180	240
"P.D." Police motorcycle w/side car, wood wheels, on-off lever, 1930s, 3½" long	100	150	200
"Parade Drummer," 1930s, "Let the Drummer Boy Play While You Swing and Sway"	300	450	600
"Parcel Post U.S. Mail," 8½" long, early	225	238	450
Peter Rabbit, eccentric car	300	450	600
"Piggy"	40	60	80
"Pinched" roadster, motorcycle cop in circular track, circa 1927, 9½"x9½"	550	825	1100
"Play-Away-Piano," 1930s, 9x9", with songbook	60	90	120
"Police Patrol," motorcycle with sidecar, 1935	150	225	300
Police Precinct Police Patrol armored truck, 10½" long, circa early 1930s	2000	3000	4000
"Police Siren Motorcycle," 1930s, 8" long	175	263	250
"Power Snap Caterpillar Climbing Tractor," 1950s, 8" long	80	120	160
"Prone WW I Soldier," 1925, 8" long	90	135	180
Racer No. 2, 1930s, 5" long	44	66	88
Racer No. 3, 1930s, 5" long	44	66	88
Racer No. 5, 1930s, 5" long	44	66	88
Racing Car, 12" litho, circa 1940, two-man team	110	165	220
Racing Car, "12", litho, plastic driver, circa 1950	112	168	225
Racing Car, "27", litho, plastic driver circa 1950	150	225	300
"Range Rider," 1940s, 8½" high	125	188	250
"Range Rider," 1940s, 10½" high on rocker base	150	225	300
"Red Cap" Porter	500	750	1000
Renfrew Tank	175	263	350
"Reversible Coupe" "The Marvel Car," circa 1938	180	270	360
Reversing Road Roller	100	150	200

MARX "Sparkling Climbing Fighting Tank", cannon recoils. Courtesy Charles D. Richards.

MARX Sparkling Tank, 4" long. Courtesy Continental Hobby House.

MARX "Subway Express", Chein "Boy Skier". Courtesy Don Hultzman. Photo by Ron Chojnacki.

MARX "Speed Boy Delivery". Courtesy Don Hultzman. Photo by Ron Chojnacki.

	C6	C8	C10
Scenic Express Train Set, circa 1950s...90		135	180
"Sheriff Sam & His Whoopee Car," 1950s, 6" long 180		270	360
"Sheriff Sam & His Whoopee Car," 1960s, 6" long 100		150	200
"Single Track Speedway," 1938, 8 track sections, 4" long windup car..............60		90	120
"Sky Hawk" airport tower, two planes, tower 7½" high, No. 333 ...200		300	400
Skybird Flyer, new circa 1927.............200		300	400
"Skyscraper Go-Round," 1930s, 13½" high, monoplane, Zeppelin 400		600	800
Smoky Sam, the Wild Fireman 150		225	300
Soldier, prone, firing rifle, WWI helmet..80		120	160
"Space Mobile" 1960s (Japan), 32" long, 3 sections, 4" long car 120		180	240
"Space Satellite with Launching Station," 1950s, 9"x12" base and plastic accessories 50		75	100

	C6	C8	C10
Reversing Tank, 1930s 65		98	130
"Reversing Tractor".............................125		188	250
"Rex" race car, 1920s 162		243	325
"Rex Mars Planet Patrol", 1950s, 9½" long, pastel colors 180		270	360
"Ride 'Em Cowboy" 90		135	180
"Ring-A-Ling Circus," early ringmaster and circus animals........500		750	1000
Road Roller, 8½" long, circa 1930, has driver, company 125		188	250
"Rocket Fighter" circa 1950s, complete with tail fin and sparking mechanism.300		450	600
Rocket Racer, 1930s 225		338	450
"Rodeo Joe," 1933................................155		233	310
"Roll Over Plane," circa 1920s 175		263	350
"Rookie Cop," with siren, 1930s, 8½" long150		225	300
Rookie Pilot, 7" long, No.77, circa 1940 .400		600	800
Rooster Pulling Wagon, 1930s 60		90	120
Royal Bus Line, 10" long.....................100		150	200
"Royal Coupe", 1920s, 9" long............400		600	800
"Royal Van Co." "We Haul Anywhere," 9" long..180		270	360
"Running Scottie," 1940s, 5½" long.....80		120	160
"Sam, The Gardner", 1950s, 8" tall, (includes 6 plastic tools) 110		165	220
"Sand and Gravel Truck - Builders Supply Co.," 1920................................100		150	200

MARX "Toyland's Farm Products.

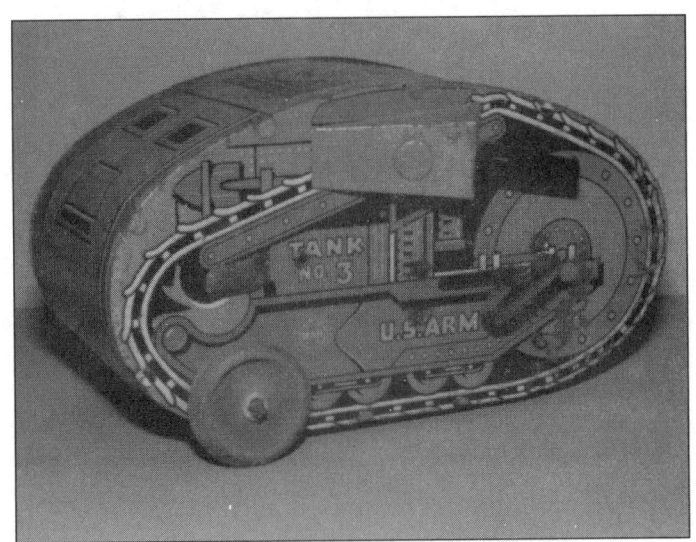

MARX Turnover Tank No. 3. Photo by Max Heiss.

	C6	C8	C10
"Sparkling Climbing Fighting Tank," cannon recoils	175	263	350
"Sparkling Climbing Tank," 1939	60	90	120
Sparkling Climbing Tractor, 8½" long, circa 1950s	62	93	125
"Sparkling Climbing Tractor and Trailer," 16" long, circa 1950s	130	195	260
Sparkling Heavy Duty Bulldog Tractor with Road Scraper, circa 1950s, 11" long	125	188	250
"Sparkling Luxury Liner," 1950s, 14" long	80	120	160
Sparkling Soldier Motorcycle, circa 1940	200	300	400
Sparkling Rocket Ship	300	450	600

	C6	C8	C10
Sparkling Super Power Tank, circa 1950s, 9½" long	110	165	220
Sparkling Tank, 4" long	100	150	200
"Sparkling Tractor," tractor with plow blade, 1939	120	180	240
Sparkling Tractor and Trailer Set, "Marbrook Farms," circa 1950s, 21" long	75	112	150
Sparkling Turn Over Tank	40	60	80
Sparkling Warship, 14" long (same as U.S.S. Washington)	135	205	275
"Speed Boy Delivery," (Motorcycle delivery), 1930s, 9¾" long, battery operated lights	250	375	500
Same as above, no lights	220	330	440
Speedway coupe, battery to be inserted for headlights, 8" long	300	450	600
"Spic and Span, the Hams What Am," drummer and dancer, 1924	1100	1650	2200
"Spic Coon Drummer," 1924, 8½" high	475	713	950
"Streamline Speedway," 1938 (tin figure 8 track, 2 windup cars, 31" long	70	105	140
Streamlined Coupe	160	240	320
"Subway Express," with plastic tunnel, 1950s, 9⅜" diameter	90	135	180
"Super Streamline Racer," 1950s, 17" long	120	180	240
"Tidy Tim" Streetcleaner, pushing wagon, 1933, 7½" high, 8½" long	475	713	950
"Tom Tom Jungle Boy	75	112	150

MARX "Whoopee Car", "Yale-Princeton" pennants on wheels. Courtesy Mapes Auctioneers.

	C6	C8	C10
"Toto Acrobat", 1930s, 12" high	100	150	200
"Tower Aeroplane," 1940s, 7½" high, two 3" tin airplanes	125	188	250
"Toyland Farm Products," 1930s, milk wagon, 10½" long	150	225	300
"Toytown Dairy," horsedrawn cart, 10½" long, 1930s	90	135	180
Tractor, early 1940s	50	75	100
Tractor and Trailer set, 1930s, similar to climbing tractor set, but with rounded and radiator front and copper finish metal. Tin plow attaches to front, silver metal trailer attaches to rear; has tin, copper finish and "balloon" tires	150	225	300
Tractor and Trailer, 16½" long, circa 1950s	110	165	220
"Trans-Atlantic Zeppelin," 1930s, 10" long, rear propeller	200	300	400
"Tricky Motorcycle," 1930s, 4¼" long, non-fail action	125	188	250
"Tricky Taxi," 1940s, 4½" long	55	82	110
Trolley, headlight, bell, 9" long	170	225	340
"Tumbling Monkey," 1930s, 5" high, on two chairs	70	105	140
"Tumbling Monkey on Trapeze", 6" high, 1920s	75	112	150
Turn Over Tank No. 3	75	112	150
"TWA - U.S. Mail - 990", 5", circa 1941	125	188	250
"U.S. Army" bomber, post-War, 1940s, two-engine	180	270	360
"U.S. Army Fighter Plane," 1940, 8" wingspan	200	300	400
"U.S. Mail" truck, 9½" long	200	300	400
"U.S. Mail - TWA Biplane", 1930s, 15" long - 18" wingspan	350	525	700

	C6	C8	C10
"U.S.S. Washington" Battleship	137	206	275
"Uncle Wiggily, He Goes A Ridin'," 1935	*See Comic Character*		
Vacationland Express	62	93	125
Wacky Taxi	75	112	150
Walking Clancy	400	600	800
Walking Drummer Boy, "Let The Drummer Boy Play While You Swing and Sway," circa 1939	300	450	600
Wee Scottie, 5" long	100	150	200
Whoopee Car, laughing cows on wheels, driver looks like cowboy, 1929	225	338	450
Whoopee Car, "Yale-Princeton" pennants on wheels	275	413	550
"Whoopee Car with Flappers," 7½" long	300	450	600
"Wonder Cyclist", 1930s, 9" high	200	300	400
Xylophonist, 5"	100	150	200
"Yellow Cab - LMN 52", 1940s, 6½" long	80	120	160
Zeppelin, 10" long	162	243	325
"Zeppelin", 1925, 11" long, (propeller on front)	150	225	300
Zeppelin, 27" long, 1930s	200	300	400
Zeppelin TransAtlantic, 10" long	162	243	325
"Zippo, The Climbing Monkey", 1930s, 9½" long	90	135	180

End Marx

MARX Wee Scottie. Courtesy Scott Smiles. Photo by Mike Adams.

MARX "U.S. Mail" truck, 9½" long. Courtesy Phillips New York.

MARX Zippo the Climbing Monkey. Photo by Ron Chojnacki. Courtesy Don Hultzman.

OHIO ART Automatic Airport. Photo by Ron Chojnacki. Courtesy Don Hultzman.

	C6	C8	C10
"**Mike** Mallard The Climbing Fireman", 1950s, Linemar Co., 13¾" high (ladder), with 4½" long tin duck	150	225	300
"**Movie** Man" Touring Car, rare	2000	3000	4000
Newsboy, "Extra" with cap and bell, circa 1940s	110	165	220

OHIO ART

	C6	C8	C10
Ohio Art "Automatic Airport", 1940s, 9" high	90	135	180
Ohio Art Boat, 14" long	80	120	160
Ohio Art "Circus Shooting Gallery," 1950s, 12" high, 17" long	30	45	60
Ohio Art "Coast Guard Seaplane," 1950s, 10" wingspan	50	75	100
Ohio Art "Commando Joe", 1950s, 8" long	70	105	140
Ohio Art "Giant Ride Ferris Wheel," 1950s, 16" high	150	225	300
Ohio Art Hot Job Floatplane	100	150	200
Ohio Art "Injun Chief," 1950s, 8" long	60	90	120
Ohio Art "Jungle Eyes Shooting Gallery," 1950s, 18" long, 14" high	50	75	100

	C6	C8	C10
Ohio Art "Mechanical Sea Plane"	90	135	180
Ohio Art "Switch and Dump Train", 1950s, 28" long	100	150	200
Ohio Art "Traffic Control," 1950s, tin wind-up cars, 3½ " long, base 19x13"	40	60	80
Ori-O Tailspin 4" puppy	10	15	20
Orkin Coast Guard Cutter, 25" long	350	525	700
Pecking Bird, 5½" long, 1927	20	30	40
Pecking Chicken, 5½" high, 1927	40	60	80
"**PT 10**," tin litho PT boat, circa 1941	60	90	120
Ranger Steel Products, Roslyn Heights, NY Billiard Table, two players, 14" long	175	263	350
Ranger Steel Products Cross Country Turnpike, 26x14"	60	90	120
Roadster, orange and green	80	120	160
Santa Claus in red cloth suit and holding Christmas tree, 5½" high, (Occupied Japan)	200	300	400
Santa Claus with green sleigh, Christmas tree, presents and white celluloid reindeer, bell, sleigh on three wheels, 8½" long (Occupied Japan)	220	330	440

SCHUCO

by Don Hultzman

Schuco was founded in 1912 by Heinrich Muller and Herr Schreyer which was later called Schreyer and Co. and adopted the name "Schuco" as its trademark. Schuco toys are noted for their ingenious mechanisms, and were produced in the 1930s-1950s, and marked either "Germany" or "U.S. Zone - Germany". Other markings are reissues.

OHIO ART Giant Ride Ferris Wheel. Photo by Don Hultzman.

SCHUCO Examico 4001. Photo by Ron Chojnacki. Courtesy Don Hultzman.

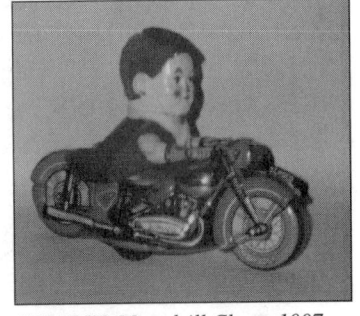

SCHUCO Motodrill Clown 1007. Photo by Don Hultzman.

SCHUCO Micro Racer 1040. Photo by Don Hultzman.

	C6	C8	C10
"Akustico 2002," 1940s, 5½" long 80	120	160
"Anno 2000", 1940s, 5½" long.............80	120	160
"Cadillac DeVille Convertible 5505", 1960s, 11" long, plastic...................80	120	160
"Combinato 4003", 1950s, 7½" long, with windup horn 120	180	240
"Curvo 1000", 1950s, 5" long..............130	195	260
"Dalli 1011", 1950s, 6½" long, tin car & plastic driver 80	120	160
"Electro Radiant 5600", 1950s, 16" long, 19" wingspan, battery operated 400	600	800
"Electro Record 5555", 1950s, 11" long, battery op. plastic...................50	75	100
"Elektro Ingenico 5311", 1950s, 8½" long, remote control.......................220	330	440
"Examico 4001", 1950s, 6" long, 5 speed BMW 120	180	240
"Fex 1111", 1950s, 6" long 60	90	120
"Gas Station 3054", 1950s, 8" long 60	90	120
"Grand Prix Racer 1070", 1950s, 6" long 90	135	180
"Hegi-Fipsi 110", 1950; airplane (glider) kit....................................70	105	140
"Jaguar 1250", 1940s, 5½" long 160	240	320
"Kommando Anno 2000", 1940s, 5½" long 100	150	200
"Lasto 3042", 1950s, 4½" long truck....60	90	120
"Magico Auto 2008", 1950s, 5½" long, responds to blowing..............140	210	280
"Magico Car and Garage", 1950s, 6" long..120	180	240
"Mercedes 190SL, 2095", 1950s, 8" long..150	225	300
"Mercedes TYP SSK 1928", 1950s, 4" long..100	150	200
"Mercer Auto 1225", 1950s, 7½" long.....90	135	180
"Micro-Jet 1030" -Thunderjet, 1950s, 5½" long - 5" wingspan 80	120	160
"Micro-Jet 1031", -Magister 170R, 1950s, 5½" long - 5" wingspan 80	120	160
"Micro-Jet 1032" - Super Sabre F 100, 1950s, 5½" long - 5" wingspan 80	120	160
"Micro-Jet 1033" - Douglas F4 D-1, 1950s, 5½" long - 5" wingspan 80	120	160
"Micro Racer 101", 1950s, 3½" long, Porsche style 90	135	180
"Micro Racer 102", 1950s, 3½" long, Indy style...................................90	135	180
"Micro Racer 104", 1950s, 3½" long, Indy style...................................90	135	180
"Micro Racer 1036", 1950s, 4½" long 100	150	200
"Micro Racer 1040", 1950s, 4" long 100	150	200

	C6	C8	C10
"Micro Racer 1041", 1950s, 4" long....100	150	200
"Micro Racer 1042", 1950s, 4" long....100	150	200
"Micro Racer 1043", 1950s, 4" long....100	150	200
"Micro Racer '57 Ford 1045", 1950s, 4" long..80	120	160
"Micro Racer Apha Romeo 1048", 1950s, 4" long.............................90	135	180
"Micro Racer Go Kart 1035", 1950s, 4" long..100	150	200
"Micro Racer Hotrod 1036", 1950s, 4" long..80	120	160
"Micro Racer - Mercedes Benz 1038", 1950s, 4" long.............................90	135	180
"Micro Racer - Mercedes Benz 1044", 1950s, 4" long...........................110	165	220
"Micro Racer Mercer 1036/1", 1950s, 4" long..100	150	200
"Micro Racer Porsche 1047", 1950s, 4" long...110	165	220
"Micro Racer Rally 1034", 1950s, 10'6" long - 8 three lane tracks.......60	90	120
"Micro Racer Stake Truck 1049", 1950s, 4" long.............................90	135	180
"Micro Racer Volkswagen 1046", 1950s, 4" long.............................90	135	180
"Micro Racer Volkswagen Polizei 1039", 1950s, 4" long.............................100	150	200
"Mikifex 922", 1950s, 3½" long, non-fall action mouse.....................40	60	80
"Mirakocar 1001", 1950s, 4½" long, non-fall action 80	120	160
"Mirakomot 1012", 1950s, 5¼" long, non-fall action 300	450	600
"Monkey Car", 1930s, 6" long, orange-black, smiling monkey.......1400	2100	2800
"Motodrill 1006", 1950s, 5" long, circular action 250	375	500
"Motodrill Clown 1007", 1950s, 5" long, composition head.................400	600	800
"Mystery Car 1010", 1950s, 5½" long, non-fall action..............................90	135	180
"Racing Boat 1015" 1950s, 5" long, non-fall action..............................90	135	180
"Radio 4012", 1950s, 6" long, musical car 200	300	400
"Solisto", Clown Drummer, 1950s, 4¼" tall 90	135	180
"Solisto", Clown Fiddler, 1950s, 4¼" tall 90	135	180
"Solisto", Clown Flutist, 1950s, 4¼" tall 120	180	240
"Solisto", Clown Juggler, 1950s, 4½" tall 140	210	280

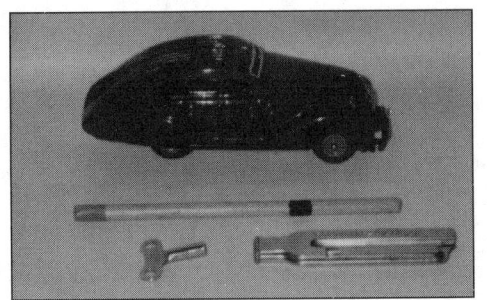

SCHUCO Magico Auto 2008. Photo by Don Hultzman.

SCHUCO, Left to Right: Solisto Clown Drummer, Clown Juggler, Clown Fiddler. Photo by Don Hultzman.

SCHUCO, Left to Right: Solisto Monkey Drummer, Monkey Lifter, Monkey Fiddler. Photo by Don Hultzman.

SCHUCO Studio Racer 1050. Photo by Don Hultzman.

	C6	C8	C10
"Solisto", Monkey Drummer, 1950s, 4½" tall	90	135	180
"Solisto", Monkey Fiddler, 1950s, 4½" tall	90	135	180
"Solisto", Monkey Flutist, 1950s, 4½" tall	120	180	240
"Solisto", Monkey Lifter, 1950s, 4½" tall, lifts pig or bear	150	225	300
"Sonny 2005", 1950s, 5¼" long,, mouse with balloon in BMW	200	300	400
"Station Car 3118", 1950s, 4½" long	60	90	120
"Studio Racer 1050", 1950s, 5½" long, includes tools	120	180	240
"Submarine 3007", 1950s, 12" long, tin and plastic	70	105	140
"Synchromatic 5700", 1950s, 11" long - resembles Packard Hawk	500	750	1000
"Telesteering 3000 Limo", 1950s, 4" long	50	75	100
"Varianto 3010", 1950s, tin cars are 4½ " long, two car playset	100	150	200
"Varianto 3010 Super", 1950s, service station with two 4½" tin cars	170	225	340
"Varianto 3041 Limo", 1950s, 4" long	50	75	100
"Varianto 3064", 1950s, 8" long, all plastic	30	45	60
"Varianto Box 3010/30", (tin garage and 3041 Limo, 1950s, 4½" long	110	165	220
"Varianto Bus 3044", 1950s, 4" long	60	90	120

	C6	C8	C10
"Varianto Electro 3112", 1950s, 4" long truck	60	90	120
"Varianto Electro 3112u", 1950s, 4½" long truck	60	90	120

End Schuco

	C6	C8	C10
Selrite, "Home Run King", 1930s, 4"x6" base with 5" tall hitter	400	600	800

"Skidoodle", Nifty. Photo Courtesy PB Eighty-Four.

	C6	C8	C10
"**Skidoodle**," Nifty, circa 1920, family in odd-looking car	2250	3375	4500
Speedboat, "G.E. 200", tin litho, circa 1930	80	120	160
Spinning Globe, tin litho, two tin planes circling it, circa 1930	200	300	400
"**Spirit** of America" airplane PNX211, NY to Paris litho on wings	200	300	400
Steam Roller, circa 1925	100	150	200

STRAUSS

Ferdinand Strauss was an immigrant from Alsace. He began as a toy importer in the early 1900s, and by 1914 had four New York toy shops. When war disrupted imports of toys, he began manufacturing them. In 1918 he was located in East Rutherford, New Jersey, with fifty employees. Eventually Strauss was known as "The Founder of the Mechanical Toy Industry in America." Strauss seems to have been wholly or partially out of business in the late 1920s, and then resumed turning out wind-ups and other toys until at least 1941-42. He is also famous for having given employment to the very young Louis Marx.

	C6	C8	C10
"Alabama Coon Jigger," 9¾"	410	615	820
"Alabama Coon Jigger - Tombo" 1918, 10½" high, 3"x5" base	400	600	800
"Aluminum Flying Airship" - LA 1O17, 1930s, 9" long	160	240	320
Big Show Circus Truck	900	1350	1800

	C6	C8	C10
"Big Trixo," climbing monkey, 10" long	150	225	300
Billiards Player	300	450	600
Black Porter Pulling wheelbarrow, 6¼"	180	270	360
"Bus Deluxe," 1920s, 12" long	600	900	1200
Check-A-Cab	450	675	900
"Chicago Zeppelin," 1930s, 9" long	400	600	800
Circus Wagon, containing lion and tamer, 8½" long, no engine compartment	420	630	840
Circus Wagon, 10" long, has engine compartment	500	750	1000
"Dandy Jim", "copyright 1921"	250	375	500
"Dizzie Lizzie"	160	240	320
"Ham and Sam The Minstrel Team," piano player and banjoist, 1921, 6½" long	500	750	1000
"Haul Away Truck" No. 22, dump body	240	360	480

STRAUSS "Alabama Coon Jigger". Courtesy Mapes Auctioneers & Appraisers.

STRAUSS Circus Wagon, containing lion and tamer. Courtesy Sotheby's New York.

STRAUSS Hooligans Hack. Courtesy Mapes Auctioneers & Appraisers.

STRAUSS, Top Left: Jackee the Hornpipe, Top Right: Leaping Lena, Middle Right: Knockout Prize Fighters, Bottom: Billiards Player. Courtesy PB Eighty-Four, New York.

STRAUSS Interstate Double-Decker Bus, 10½" long.
Courtesy Lloyd W. Ralston Auctions.

STRAUSS "Jenny the Balky Mule". Courtesy Scott Smiles.

STRAUSS Rollo Chair.

STRAUSS "Santee Claus". Courtesy Sotheby's New York.

	C6	C8	C10
Hooligans Hack	300	450	600
Interstate Double Decker Bus, 1920	600	900	1200
"Jackee The Horn Pipe Dancer," 8½" long , No. 51	500	750	1000
"Jazzbo Jim The Dancer on the Roof," 1910, 10" high	300	450	600
"Jenny the Balky Mule," 10" long, six-color litho, goes backward, forward and rears, farmer holding extended tin grain pail from his seat in front of mule's face to keep him moving vegetables in cart, No. 55	200	300	400
Jocko the Golfer	337	506	675
Knock-Out Prize Fighters, ca. 1910, 7" high, No. 52	450	675	900
"Kraka Jack Car," 1920s, 5½" long	150	225	300
"Leaping Lena"	200	300	400
"Long Haulage Truck"	350	525	700
"Mailplane"	300	450	600
"Miami Sea Sled," 1920s, 10" long with 4" dinghy attached	250	375	500
Monkey driving 3-wheel cart pulled by bulldog, 1930s, 4½" high	280	420	560

	C6	C8	C10
"Old Jalopy, The", 4 college kids	100	150	200
"Play Golf", 1920s, 7"x12" base with 5" high golfer	375	525	750
"Red-Cap Porter," porter pushing a large trunk	300	450	600
"Red Star Van"	400	600	800
Rollo Chair, black man pushing boardwalk chair, "Stock, DRGM, December 6, 1921"	600	900	1200
"Santee Claus", 1921, in sleigh, 6" high, 2 reindeer	800	1200	1600
"Speedwagon"	200	300	400
"Tip Tip" man with wheelbarrow	500	750	1000
"Tip Top Porter," No. 40, 1920s, 6" long	150	225	300
Tippy Canoe	150	225	300
"Tom Twist", 1920s, 8½" tall	300	450	600
"Travel Chiks" chickens on railroad car	300	450	600
"Trikauto," No. 53	200	300	400
"What's It?" Car, No. 53, 1925, 9½" long	700	1050	1400
"Yell-o Taxi"	400	600	800

End Strauss

237

	C6	C8	C10
Structo red and black painted tin wind-up automobile, 15" long	80	120	160
Structo Racer, early 1920s	140	210	280
Structo Steam Shovel, large size, rubber wheels, early	80	120	160
Structo Toyland Garage Truck	120	180	240
"**Super** Rocket Racer," tin litho, 1940s?	200	300	400
Sweetie Pie Boat, Lindstrom, 1920s	80	120	160
"**Tip** Top Toy Airplane," high wing, single engine, "Giant Flyer No. 200," 1930s, 23" long, 19½" wingspan	400	600	800
Tom Turkey, "B&S", 6" long, turkey struts, tail spreads, then moves up and down, German			
"**Tobaggon**", 1950s, Technofix Co., 14"x 21" base and two 3½" tin cars	90	135	180
Tom Turkey, "B&S", 6" long, turkey struts, tail spreads, then moves up and down, German	180	270	360

TPS

by Don Hultzman

"TPS" is the trademark of Toplay, Ltd., founded in 1956 and is noted for its most unusual and unique mechanical toys. A Japanese Company.

TPS: Pop Eye Pete and Comical Clara. Photo by Don Hultzman.

	C6	C8	C10
"Animal Barber Shop", 1950s, 5" high	180	270	360
"Animals Playland", 1950s, 9¼" long	100	150	200
"Ball Playing Giraffe", 1950s, 8½" tall	100	150	200
"Basketball Monkey", 1950s, 7½" tall	150	225	300
"Bear Golfer", 1950s, 7½" long - assembled	150	225	300
"Bouncing Doll Ball", 1950s, 5¼" high	100	150	200
"Busy Choo Choo", 1950s, 5½"x 9¼" base with 2¼" tin locomotive	70	105	140
"Busy Mouse", 1950s, 6"x 9" base with 3¼" tin mouse	70	105	140

	C6	C8	C10
"Calypso Joe", 1950s, 6" tall	200	300	400
"Candy Loving Canine", 1950s, 5½" high	90	135	180
"Champ On Ice", 1950s, 10" long	500	750	1000
"Circus Cyclist", 1950s, 6½" tall	150	225	300
"Circus Parade", 1950s, 11½" long	200	300	400
"Climbing Panda", 1970s, 6" high - all plastic	20	30	40
"Climbing Pirate", 1950s, 6" long (string climber)	100	150	200
"Climbo The Climbing Clown", 1950s, 6" long, (string climber)	120	180	240
"Clown Jalopy Cycle", 1950s, 11" long, friction	180	270	360
"Clown Making Lion Jump Through Flaming Hoop", 1950s, 5" high	100	150	200
"Clown on Rollerskates", 1950s, 5¾" tall	150	225	300
"Clown Trainer and His Dog", 1950s, 6" high	100	150	200
"Comical Clara", 1950s, 5½" tall	350	525	700
"Coney Island Scooter", 1950s, 10" square with 2½" tin bumper car	150	225	300
"Dreamland Airport", 1950s, 6½"x12" base with 3½" tin helicopter	90	135	180
"Fishing Bear", 1950s, 7½" high	100	150	200
"Fishing Monkey On Whale", 1950s, 9" long	300	450	600
"Gay 90's Cyclist", 1950s, 7" high	120	180	240
"Girl Feeding Chickens", 1950s, 6" tall - 5" long	100	150	200
"Happy Caterpillar", 1950s, 13" long	80	120	160
"Happy Hippo", 1950s, 5½" long	250	375	500
"Happy Skaters" - (bear), 1950s, 6½" tall	150	225	300
"Happy Skaters" - (Monkey), 1950s, 5½" tall	250	375	500
"Happy Skaters" - (Rabbit), 1950s, 5½" tall	250	375	500
"Happy The Violinist", 1950s, 9" tall	120	180	240
"Juggling Clown", 1950s, 8½" tall	200	300	400
"Lady Bug Family Parade", 1950s, 12" long	80	120	160
"Magic Choo Choo", 1950s, 5½"x 9¼" base with 2¼" tin locomotive	70	105	140
"Magic Cross Road", 1950s, 5½"x 9¼" base with 2¼" tin locomotive	70	105	140
"Magic Tunnel", 1950s, 6"x 9" base with 2" tin "Dreamland Bus"	70	105	140
"Mama Kangaroo With Playful Baby In Her Pouch", 1950s, 6" tall	100	150	200

	C6	C8	C10
"Midget Lady Bug", 1950s, 7½" tall	60	90	120
"Missle Robot", 1960s, 6" high	80	120	160
"Monkey Basketball Player, 1950s, 7" high	150	225	300
"Monkey Golfer", 1950s, 7½" long - assembled	150	225	300
"Monkey On Whale", 1950s, 4" long - 3¾" high	200	300	400
"Mountain Climber", 1950s, 6½" long (string climber)	100	150	200
"Mouse Race Cat", 1950s, 10"x 10" base	70	105	140
"Pango Pango", 1950s, 6" tall	120	180	240
"Performing Seal and Monkey With Fish", 1950s, 4½" tall	150	225	300
"Playland Scooter", 1950s, 6"x 9" base with 2" long tin car	60	90	120
"Pop Eye Pete", 1950s, 5½" tall	350	525	700
"Popeye Skater", 1950s, (Linemar), 6½" tall	500	750	1000

	C6	C8	C10
"Skating Chef", 1950s, 6" tall	150	225	300
"Skating Chef" - Black, 1950s, 6" tall	250	375	500
"Skip Rope Animals", 1950s, 8" long	110	165	220
"Skippy The Tricky Cyclist", 1950s, 6" tall	100	150	200
"Suzy Bouncing Ball", 1950s, 5½" tall	90	135	180
"Tricycle Tot", 1950s, 5" high	100	150	200
"Wagon Fantasyland", 1950s, 11" long	150	225	300
End TPS			
Trolley, horse-drawn, German	150	225	300
Two rotating blimps and two cars, with passengers, that spin and rotate, 11¼" high, German	600	900	1200
"2001 Circus" 1930, 8" long	450	675	900
Train Set 1930s, three pieces, 20" long, wooden wheels	150	225	300
"U.S.A. Army" d-105 truck, 10½" long	100	150	200

UNIQUE ART MFG. CO.

Unique Art Mfg. Co. was in business from 1916, when it introduced its Merry Juggler and Charlie Chaplin. In 1931 it was located at Waverly and Peshine Avenues in Newark, New Jersey. Its president was Wm. Marbe, and there were 28 male employees (no females listed). In 1934 employees numbered 110 male and 165 female (same address). In a 1946-47 directory the address was 200 Waverly Avenue, Newark and the president was Samuel Burger (this last name may be incorrect; the handwriting in my notes is hard to read). Employees were equally divided: 125 male and 125 female. Unique was still manufacturing toys, mainly wind-ups, in 1952. Little else is known about the company, except that at some date, Louis Marx bought it.

	C6	C8	C10
Unique Artie the Clown in his Crazy Car	250	375	500
Unique "Bombo the Monk," two-piece, tree 9½" high, monkey 5½" long, 1930s	112	180	225
Unique "Capitol Hill Racer," 1930s, 17½" long with 2" tin racing car	100	150	200
Unique "Casey the Cop" early	600	900	1200
Unique "Dandy Jim" dancer, 1921	600	900	1200

UNIQUE "Kiddy Cyclist". Courtesy Scott Smiles.

UNIQUE Artie the Clown in his Crazy Car. Courtesy Don Hultzman. Photo Ron Chojnacki.

UNIQUE "Bombo the Monk". Courtesy Scott Smiles.

UNIQUE Rodeo Joe Whoopie Car. Courtesy Mapes Auctioneers & Appraisers.

UNIQUE Jazzbo Jim - "The Dancer on the Roof". Courtesy Sotheby's New York.

UNIQUE "G.I. Joe and the K-9 Pups". Courtesy Scott Smiles.

UNIQUE Flying Circus. Photo by Don Hultzman.

UNIQUE G.I. Joe and his Jouncing Jeep. Courtesy Scott Smiles, photo Mike Adams.

S.S. Wolverine Oceanliner.

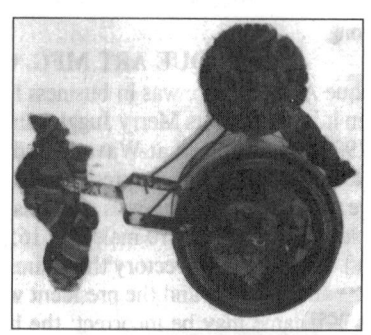

Left to Right: UNIQUE Sky Rangers, Marx Skybird Flyer. Courtesy Phillips, New York.

Walking Man, carring red top hat over his head, head revolves to reveal three different faces. Photo courtesy PB Eighty-Four.

Top: "2001" Circus. Bottom: UNIQUE Krazy Kar, 1940. Courtesy Lloyd W. Ralston Auctions.

240

	C6	C8	C10
Unique "Daredevil Motor Cop," 8½" long, 1940s	200	300	400
Unique Flying Circus, elephant supports flying plane and flying clown	600	900	1200
Unique "G.I. Joe and His Jouncing Jeep," post WW II, 7"	112	168	225
Unique "G.I. Joe and the K-9 Pups," circa 1941, 9" high	140	210	280
Unique "Gertie the Galloping Goose," 9½" long, 1930s	150	225	300
Unique "Hee Haw" donkey pulling milk cart, 10" long	125	188	250
Unique Art, "Hillbilly Express," 1930s, 18" long, 3 pcs. and 3¼" tin locomotive	150	225	300
Unique Hobo Train, 8½" long, 1920s, dog biting pants of hobo atop train	160	240	320
Unique "Jazzbo Jim" dancer, new in 1921	250	375	500
Unique "Jazzbo Jim - The Dancer on the Roof," 1920s, 10" high, base 5x3x3"	250	375	500
Unique "Kid-Go-Round," Plastic horsemen and boat	80	120	160
Unique Art "Kiddy Cyclist," 1930s, 8¾" tall, steers figure 8 pattern and rings bell	150	225	300
Unique Krazy Kar, new in 1921	210	315	420
Unique "Lincoln Tunnel," moving vehicles, cop, 1935, 24" long	200	300	400
Unique "Motorcycle Cop," 1930s, 9" long	120	180	240
Unique Musical Sail-Way Carousel with 3 kids in spinning plastic boats, 9" tall	180	270	360
Unique Pecking Goose, Witch and Cat	250	375	500
Unique Rodeo Joe Crazy Car	175	263	350
Unique "Rollover Motorcycle Cop," 1935	200	300	400
Unique "Sky Rangers" plane and zeppelin revolving from tower, 1933	190	285	380

End Unique

	C6	C8	C10
Walking Man, carrying red top hat over his head, head revolves to reveal 3 different faces	450	675	900
Wilkins Roadster, early with driver, 9" long	300	450	600
Wilkins Auto, early, woman driver, 9" long	290	425	580
Wolverine Acrobat	110	165	220
Wolverine "Acrobatic Monkeys" No. 810, 1930s, 10" diameter base	200	300	400
Wolverine "Autolift", 1930s, 10¼" high, includes 2½" tin car and four sections of track	150	225	300
Wolverine "Drummer Boy," 14" high	130	195	260
Wolverine "Drum Major," No. 27, patent 1892546, 1930s, 13¼" tall on circular 4¼" base	125	188	250
Wolverine "Drum Major," No. 27, pat. 1892546, 1930s, 13⅝" tall on rectangular 4½ x 6½" base	200	300	400
Wolverine Farm Wagon, 1950s, 10" long - plastic	50	75	100
Wolverine Jet Roller, Coaster and small car, 21" long extended	100	150	200
Wolverine "Loop-A-Loop," 1930s, 19" long, includes small car No. 30	125	188	250
Wolverine Luxury Liner	70	105	140
Wolverine "Mechanical Man on the Flying Trapeze," 1930s, 8½" high	100	150	200
Wolverine "Merry-Go-Round," 1930s, 11" diameter, 12" high, includes four tin-litho flags, No. 31	175	263	350
Wolverine, "Neck & Neck," 1940s, 36" long - Horse racing game	80	120	160
Wolverine Pontiac Mystery Car	100	150	200
Wolverine "S.S. Wolverine," 14½" long	110	165	220
Wolverine "Sandy Andy Circus," dancing toy	150	225	300
Wolverine "Sunny Andy" Tank, 14" long	100	150	200
Wolverine "Zilotone" with six interchangeable records, 1930s	400	600	800
"The Wonder Cyclist" boy on tricycle, circa 1930, 8¾" high	200	300	400
Woodhaven "Robot Bus with the Mechanical Brain," 1940s, 13½" long	80	120	160
Woodhaven Tractor, 1916	112	168	225
World on base, wind-up plane circles it, German	100	150	200
Wyandotte Carnival, 16x11"	250	375	500
Wyandotte Carousel, 5¼" high	130	195	260
Wyandotte Duck pulling tin Easter cart, 15" long, litho, wooden wheels	75	112	150
Wyandotte "Hoky-Poky" handcar with 2 clowns	160	240	320
Wyandotte "Man On The Flying Trapeze", 1930s, 9" high	150	225	300
Wyandotte "Red Ranger Ride 'Em Cowboy," circa 1930s, rocker base, No. 515, 6½" high	150	225	300

BATTERY-OPERATED TOYS

by Don Hultzman

The average mint price of Battery toys in the last edition was $198.28; this edition it is $348.45, an increase of 76%.

During the years preceding World War II, the Japanese toy industry was content with making cheap imitations of American and European toys, mostly out of recycled tin cans. Immediately after the war and through the 1960's, the Japanese came into their own with a new and different dimension in the toy world—the battery-operated toy.

Previously, early US. and European toy makers used batteries in their toys to add realism to their boats, cars, trains and airplanes by adding flashlight bulbs where headlights, spotlights, tail-lights and navigation lights were required. Later, batteries were used to power horns, buzzers and electromagnets as well as lights, but these early mechanical toys still depended on a spring or small flywheel to function as a mechanical toy should. There was just so much these early toys could do until the Japanese toy revolution opened up a whole new area with their clever automatons.

Starting in 1946, the Japanese toy makers began to replace the wind-up clockwork mechanisms and friction-drive mechanical toys with mini-electric motors powered by one or more batteries. These small electric motors could run much longer than the spring powered or friction drive mechanisms and with this advantage, the Japanese toy makers designed and manufactured the most ingenious and complicated automatons imaginable. There were able to simulate just about every conceivable type of human-animal motions and behavioral actions. This ingenuity carried over into a multitude of different types of novelty toys. Just how many different types of automata and vehicles were manufactured is unknown, but a conservative estimate would be around the 1200 mark. Multiply this figure by the thousands and it was no wonder that Japan held the title of the leading toy maker for the next 20 years. About 95% of the battery-operated toys came from Japan during this period while the U.S. and other countries manufactured the remaining 5% of these toys.

Since most of the Japanese production was destined for the U.S. and European market, international distributorships were organized for the marketing of these thousands of toys. Cragstan, Linemar and Rosko were some of the largest distributors on an international scale, but a few American toy makers hopped on the band wagon in marketing these toys under their brand names, such as Marx, Ideal, Hubley and Daisy (the BB gun people). Therefore many of the trademarks stamped on Japanese battery-operated toys are not necessarily that of the original manufacturer, but of the distributor or marketer. Many Japanese toy shops and factories manufactured,

assembled and sold their products through a central factory which in turn was under contract to an international marketer. As a result it is very difficult to pinpoint a specific designer or manufacturer of any battery-operated toy.

Some of the early Japanese toy makers such as the Masutoku Toy Factory (later Masudaya Toy Co.), founded in 1924 (which uses the "M-T" of "Modern Toy" trademark) and the Nomura Toys, Ltd., founded in 1923 (which uses the "T-N" trademark), are probably a couple of the original designers and manufacturers of many of the hundreds of different automations exported from Japan. "Alps", the trademark of the Alps Shoji, Ltd., (Alps Toy Midzuno Co.), founded in 1948 and "SAN", the mark of the Marusan Co., founded in 1946, can also be accountable for the creation of many original battery toys. In fact, Marusan Co., and Bandai, founded in 1950, as well as the Taijo Kogyo Co., founded in 1959, can be credited with some of the most spectacular scale model, battery-operated cars ever made in the batt-op category. "ATC", (Asahi Toy Co., founded in 1950), "T.P.S." (Toplay Ltd., founded in 1956), and "Haji", (founded in 1951), of the Mansei Toy Co., have their trademark on many more toys. The alphabet soup continues with many other toy companies using only a single letter to letters like "K", "S", "J", "KO", "Y", and "S&E", etc. Why only letters is a mystery, unless they represent many subsidiaries of the parent company. Besides being clever, the Japanese have left toy collectors very confused, but this is a small disadvantage compared to the fun of collecting battery-operated toys.

After peaking in the late 60's, the Japanese tin toy production began to decline due to increased labor costs, increased safety restrictions, inflation and competition from the cheaper die-cast and plastic toy makers. Many of the original toy companies either folded or diversified into the electronic field, using the IC-microchip the same way they used the mini-electric motor to develop new electronic products. It seems that presently, Japan has relinquished its toy monopoly to China, Hong Kong, Korea and Taiwan, in favor of its automotive and electronic industry. The battery operated toys now coming from these countries consist mostly of plastic, are higher priced, lack quality and are presently not very collectable. There is no comparison to the beauty of these toys with those from Japan. Tin and plastic just have never been compatible in a quality toy and this tends to "turn off" most serious toy collectors.

It is generally agreed upon by battery-operated toy collectors that the period of the 40's-60's should be considered as the "Golden Age of the Battery Operated Toy". During this 20 year period, most of the quality toy companies were founded and the most desirable and beautiful toys were produced. They were high in quality, most complex, and the detail and lithography most fascinating. These are the ones most sought after and in demand today. Prices of these toys are generally increasing as they become more scarce, and more and more toy collectors are beginning to focus on their desirability and are willing to pay as much for them as they have for many of the early classical tin wind-ups. Top prices go for the most complex toys, comic character, space, robots, scale-model cars, Blacks, and the older and earlier figurals.

The "Ball Playing Bear" is a good example of one of the first batt-op toys of the late 40's. As in most early toys, it uses one D-cell; is made of tin and celluloid, and has six actions going on and is very difficult to find complete with accessories.

Although tens of thousands of battery-operated toys were in circulation during this period, it is a rarity and a thrill to find one in mint condition, with original box, as the mortality rate of these toys was extremely high. Corrosion from leaking batteries left in them by their absent-minded owners took a high toll as well as deterioration of rubber parts due to age. (Rubber hoses of the water-drinkers and the rubber bellows of the bubble blowers were classic victims of aging and hardening of the rubber.) Rust was inevitable with the wet-toys that depended on water or bubble solutions to perform. Lubricants dried out or stiffened, rendering the toy inoperable, wires frequently worked loose or broke and electrical contacts corroded. Accidents, abuse, tampering and interfering with the toy while it was going through its cycle added enormously to the mortality rate. Reversing battery polarity by not following instructions burned out and ruined many a fine toy. Like a precision watch, the more complex the toy, the more delicate the mechanism and the more susceptible it becomes to damage due to negligence and abuse, such as physically interfering with the actions of the toy, and stopping it before it completes its cycle will damage the many levers and gears inside the toy, making it useless. Many toys require accessory parts to perform correctly and these were often lost, such as bowls for the bubble-blowers, trays, balls, umbrellas, discs, flags, clothes, etc. Top prices usually go for the complete toys with no parts missing.

The original box for battery-operated toys is extremely important, probably more so than other mechanical toys, because the instructions were often printed on the box lid. Also a picture or illustration of the toy showing any accessory parts the toy might need as well as the correct battery insertion was noted, if not on the actual toy's battery compartment. Finally, the name of the toy, if not lithographed on the toy itself, was printed on the box and very often, the name of the toy was nowhere near the actual appearance of the toy. Many times the name of the toy was given for its function rather than what it was supposed to be and since many toys did not have their identity stamped on them, the box lid was the only means of identifying the toy. The toy listing that follows are names of toys actually identified from their original boxes or the toy itself. Therefore the original box usually adds to the value of the toy.

The value of a battery-operated toy depends not only on its scarcity, desirability and condition. but also on the number of actions taking place during its performance cycle. These toys are classified as MAJOR or MINOR toys. Major action toys will have **three or more** actions taking place while performing, and will command top price, whereas minor action toys have only one or two actions and will have a correspondingly lower price. The actions of a major or minor toy include all the individual movements taking place during one cycle and include any lights, sounds or smoke effects. Also the major battery toys must have all actions functioning and in proper sequence. There should be no missing parts and the toy itself should be constructed mostly of tin, about 85-90%, and the rest plastic or vinyl such as heads, limbs, accessories, etc. Usually the more plastic, the lower the value of the toy, regardless of condition.

The following list of battery-operated toys are, for the most part, major action toys, and include, if known, the manufacturer or distributor derived from the box or lithographed on the toy itself. A "?" indicates that the name of this toy has not been verified by the author. Also the circa or year, if known, will follow, along with the most obvious or helpful dimensions and any special notes if necessary. The prices are the average market prices based on supply and demand, and not on "auction ' or "will pay anything for this toy" price. Geographic area is another factor in their pricing and these were based on the going prices in the midwestern states.

A "RARE" toy is one that is difficult to find on the open market because: 1. It had a limited production, or; 2. It is of such a fragile nature that it is difficult to find complete or in operating condition, or; 3. They are so popular and highly collectible that they exist only in private collections.

DON HULTZMAN confesses he has always been a collector of toys, but didn't really get serious about the hobby until ten or so years ago, not

only collecting but also repairing them. Born and raised in Cleveland, Ohio, he received a masters degree in Guidance and Administration at Kent State, and is currently employed by the Parma City School System as a school Counselor. He does free-lance writing as a science consultant to the encyclopedia department of World Publishing Co. and lives in Brunswick Hills, Ohio. Many of his tin wind-up toys can be seen in the 1983 MGM movie "A Christmas Story".

	C6	C8	C10
"**A-B-C** Fairy Train," 1950s, M-T Co., 14½" long, one pc., four actions 80	120	160
"**Accordion** Bear," 1950s, "Y" Co., 10½" tall, six actions 220	330	440
"**Accordion** Bear," 1950s, MST Co. (Flare Toy), 9¼" high, five actions 120	180	240
"**Accordion** Player Bunny," 1950s, Alps Co., 12" tall, 9" long, six actions 200	300	400
"**Accordion** Player Hobo With Baby Monkey Playing Cymbals," 1950s, Alps Co., six actions 240	360	480
"**Acrobat** Clown," 1960s, 9" tall, Y-M Co., minor toy 60	90	120
"**Acro** Chimp Porter," 1960s, Y-M Co., 8½" tall, minor toy 50	75	100
"**Acrobat** Robot," 1970s, S-H Co., 4½" tall, three actions 40	60	80
"**Air** Cargo Prop-Jet Airplane - Seaboard World Airlines," 1960's, Marx Co., 12" long, 14½" wingspan, five actions...............200	300	400
"**Air** Control Tower," 1960s, Bandai Co., 11" high, 37" span (extended), four actions (includes detachable airplane and helicopter.................220	330	440
"**Air** Defense Pom-Pom Gun," 1950s, Linemar Co., 14" long, five actions......120	180	240
"**Air** Taxi Helicopter" 1960s, Haji Co., three actions 40	60	80
"**Aircraft** Carrier" - with multi-actions, 1950's, Marx Co., six actions, 20" long..........................300	450	600
"**Aircraft** Carrier - Forrestal, 1950's, Linemar, 13¾" long, three actions, (includes detachable plastic airplane)........................150	225	300
"**Aircraft** Carrier," 1950s, Marx Co., 20" long, eight actions 200	300	400
"**Airport** Saucer," 1960s, MT Co., 8" diameter, four actions..........80	120	160
"**Airport** Saucer", 1960's, S-T Co., four actions , 9" diameter 100	150	200
"**All** Stars Mr. Baseball Jr.", 1950's, K Co., three actions, RARE, (includes 8 plastic balls) 250	375	500
"**Alley** - The Exciting New Roaring Stalking Alligator," 1960s, Marx Co., 17½" long, five actions 150	225	300
"**American** Airlines - 4 Prop Airliner," 1960's, Waco Co., 12" long, 16½" wingspan, four actions 120	180	240

	C6	C8	C10
"**American** Airlines DC-7" (with automatic turnover propellers), ca.1950s, Linemar, 7 action, 19" wingspan.................200	300	400
"**American** Airlines Airliner DC-7," Multiaction," 1960s, Yonezawa Co., 21" long 23½" wingspan, seven actions 195	285	380
"**American** Airlines Airliner DC-7," 1960s, Linemar Co., 17½" long, 19" wingspan, seven actions..........200	300	400
"American Airlines Electra," 1950s, Linemar Co., 18" long, 19½" wingspan 200	300	400
"American Airlines Flagship Caroline" 1950s, Linemar Co., 18" long, 19½" wingspan, three actions.................190	285	380
"**American** Circus Television Truck" 1950's, Exelo Co., 9¼" long, six actions, RARE, (includes detachable metal antenna)..............400	600	800
"**Amphibian** Navy Patrol Plane" with Flashing Lights, 1950s, Alps Co., 13" long - 15" wing-span, five actions, RARE...............900	1350	1800
"**Amtrak** Locomotive" 1960s, ST Co., 16" long, minor toy 60	90	120
"**Andy** Gard - Brink's Armored Car-Bank," 1950s, General Molds & Plastics Corp. 6¾" long, minor toy 40	60	80
"**Andy** Gard Combat Knight No. 143," 1960s, General Molds & Plastic Corp., 10¼" high, three actions, includes lance, stanchion, 3 plastic rings and helmet plume 50	75	100
"**Animated** Santa on Rotating Globe," 1950s, HTC Co., 15" high, five actions 220	330	440
"**Animated** Squirrel," 1950s, S&E Co., 8½" tall, eight actions, rare.............100	150	200
"**Answer** Game Machine" robot, 1960s, Ichida Co., 14½" tall, educational toy, eight actions.........300	450	600
"**Anti-Aircraft** Jeep," 1950s, "K" Co., 9½" long, five actions.....................90	135	180
"**Anti-Aircraft** Jeep", 1950s, T-N Co., 11" long, six actions, (includes detachable tin radar antenna).........250	375	500
"**Anti-Aircraft** Unit No. 1," 1950s, Linemar Co., 12½" long, three electrical actions and three manual actions 150	225	300
"**Antique** Gooney Car," 1960s, Alps Co., 9" long, four actions.................60	90	120

244

Accordion Bear. Photo by Don Hultzman.

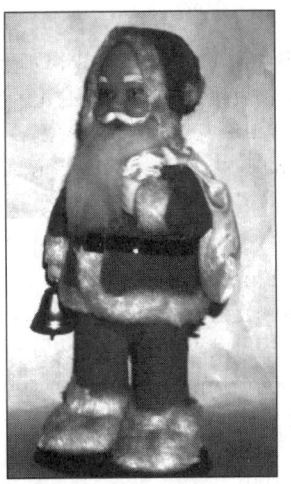

Automated Santa. Photo by Don Hultzman.

Air Defense Pom-Pom Gun. Photo by Don Hultzman.

Antique Gooney Car. Photo by Don Hultzman.

American Airlines Electra.. Photo by Don Hultzman.

Arthur A-Go-Go. Photo by Don Hultzman.

Accordion Player Hobo with Baby Monkey Playing Cymbals. Photo by Don Hultzman.

American Circus Television Truck. Photo by Don Hultzman.

Acrobat Robot. Photo by Don Hultzman.

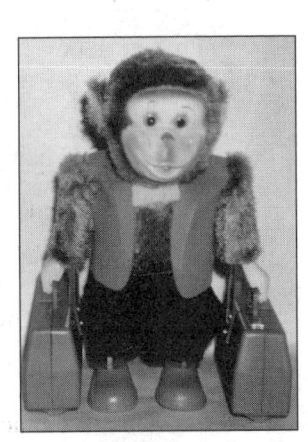

Acro Chimp Porter. Photo by Don Hultzman.

Air Control Tower. Photo by Don Hultzman.

245

	C6	C8	C10

"Apollo II-American Eagle Lunar Module", 1960s, DSK Co., 10" high, seven actions, (includes detachable plastic antenna) 150   225   300

"Apollo Lunar Module," 1970s, DSK Co., 6" high, four actions, mostly plastic 100   150   200

"Apollo Spacecraft", 1960s, M-T Co., 10" long, four actions, (includes detachable astronaut) 200   300   400

"Apollo Space Ship USA-NASA", 1960s, M-T Co., 9" long, four actions 60   90   120

"Apollo Super Space Capsule," 1960s, S-H Co., 9" high, five actions 90   135   180

"Apollo-X Moon challenger," rocket, 1960s, T-N Co., 16" long, six actions 120   180   240

"Armored Attack Set," 1960s, Marx Co., jeep 6¼" long and tank 5¼" long, plus 15 2" plastic figures 140   210   280

"Army Radio Jeep - J1490," 1950s, Linemar Co, 7¼" long, four actions 80   120   160

"Army Helicopter" - Huey by Bell, 1960s, T-N Co., six actions, 10½" long 70   105   140

"Arthur A-Go-Go," 1960s, Alps Co., 10" high, six actions, (includes detachable cymbals and drum set) .140   210   280

"Astro Captain", 1960s, Daiya Co., 6½" tall, three actions, RARE 300   450   600

"Astro Dog," 1960s, "Y" Co., 11" high, 2 cycles, five actions (looks like Snoopy) 90   135   180

"Astro Dog," 1960s, Y-M Co., 11" tall, three actions 90   135   180

"Astrobase" (motorized), 1960s, Ideal Co., 20" high, six actions 140   210   280

"Atom Motorcycle", 1950s, M-T Co., five actions, 11¾" long 400   600   800

"Atom Rocket 7", vehicle with fins, 1950s, M-T Co., 9½" long, four actions 120   180   240

"Atomic Boat", 1950s, Famus Co., minor toy, 15" long 150   225   300

"Atomic Fighter" robot, 1950s, S-H Co., 11" tall, five actions 90   135   180

"Atomic Rocket X-1800", 1960s, M-T Co., three actions, 9" long 150   225   300

"Attacking Martian Robot," 1950s, S-H Co., 11½" tall, 7 actions - two cycles 120   180   240

"Auto-Top Ferrari Convertible", 1960s, Bandai Co., three actions, 11" long ..450   675   900

"Automatic Toll Gate", 1955, Sears, 16"x17" base, six actions, (includes 8" tin Valiant) 150   225   300

"Automated Santa," ca. 1960s, Santa Creations Co., 3 actions, 10¼" tall 100   150   200

"B-58 Hustler Jet", 1950s, Marx Co., four actions, 21" long, 12" wing-span 450   675   900

"Ball Blowing Clown," 1950s, T-N Co., 11" tall, three actions with ball 160   240   320

"Ball Playing Bear," 1940s, no marking, 10½" tall, six actions, includes five celluloid balls and one umbrella, rare 200   300   400

"Ball Playing Dog," 1950s, Linemar Co., 9" high, three actions 120   180   240

"Balloon Blowing Monkey," 1950s, Alps Co., 11⅛" tall, five actions with balloon 100   150   200

"Balloon Blowing Teddy Bear," 1950s, Alps Co., 11⅛" tall, six actions with balloon 100   150   200

"Balloon Vendor," 1960s, Y Co., 12" tall, four actions, includes four plastic balloons and tin tray 120   180   240

"Baragon", 1960s, Bullmark Co., three actions, 10" tall 290   435   580

"Barber Bear," 1950s, T-N Co., (Linemar) 9½" tall, five actions 200   300   400

"Barking Boxer Dog," 1950s, Marx, 7" long, minor toy 40   60   80

"Barking Dog," 1950s, STS Co., 7" long, 7" high, four actions, two cycles 50   75   100

"Barking Spaniel Dog," 1950s, Marx, 7" long, minor toy 40   60   80

"Barney Bear Drummer," 1950s, Alps Co., 11" tall, five actions, resembles "Steiff" bear 120   180   240

"Barnyard Rooster," 1950s, Marx, 10" high, five actions 90   135   180

"Bartender," 1960s, T-N Co., 11½" tall, six actions 30   45   60

"Batmobile," 1972 National Periodical Publications, ASC Co., 12" long, three actions 170   255   340

"Battery Locomotive No. 123," 1950s, T-N Co., 10" long, three actions 30   45   60

"Bear Chef" (Cutey Cook), 1960s, "Y" Co., 9½" tall, five actions, (includes chef hat and tin litho egg) ...140   210   280

Aircraft Carrier. Photo by Don Hultzman.

Aircraft Carrier - Forrestal. Photo by Don Hultzman.

Alley ... Alligator. Photo by Don Hultzman.

Amphibian Navy Patrol Plane. Photo by Ron Chojnacki. Courtesy Don Hultzman.

Atomic Boat. Photo by Don Hultzman.

Atom Motorcycle. Photo by Don Hultzman.

Armored Attack Set. Photo by Don Hultzman.

Astro Dog. Photo by Don Hultzman.

Anti-Aircraft Jeep. Photo by Don Hultzman.

Bartender. Photo by Bill Kaufman. Courtesy Good Old Days.

Big Wheel Coca-Cola Truck. Photo by Don Hultzman.

Bubble Blowing Popeye. Photo by Don Hultzman.

Busy Secretary. Photo by Don Hultzman.

Barking Spaniel Dog, Sleeping Baby Bear, Barking Boxer Dog, Pap Bear - Smoking.

Ball Blowing Clown, Sammy Wong-the Tea Totaler, Nutty Nibs.

Ball Playing Dog. Photo by Don Hultzman.

Baragon. Photo by Don Hultzman.

Frankie the Rollerskating Monkey, Buttons - Puppy with a Brain, Jocko - the Drinking Monkey, Blushing Willie. Courtesy Don Hultzman. Photo by Ron Chojnacki.

Barber Bear. Photo by Don Hultzman.

Bear Target Game. Photo by Don Hultzman.

Big John - The Indian Chief. Photo by Don Hultzman.

Batmobile. Photo by Don Hultzman.

Bongo Player. Photo by Don Hultzman.

Bowling Bank. Photo by Don Hultzman.

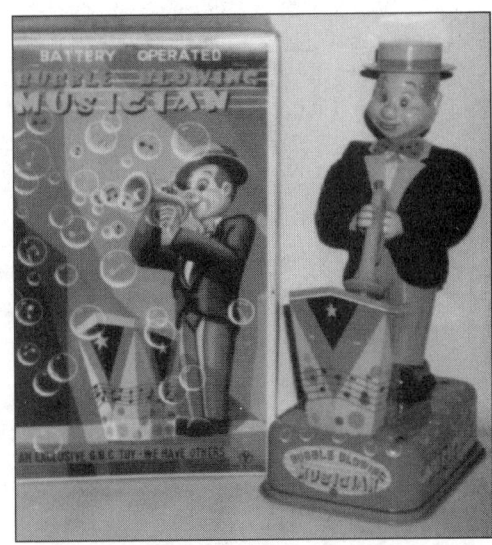

Bubble Blowing Musician. Photo by Don Hultzman.

Bubble Blowing Kangaroo. Photo by Don Hultzman.

Brewster the Rooster. Photo by Don Hultzman.

Black Smithy Bear. Photo by Ron Chojnacki. Courtesy Don Hultzman.

	C6	C8	C10
"Bear Target Game," 1950s, M-T Co., 8¾" high and 4"x5" base (includes gun, rubber tipped darts, detachable drum), four actions.......200	300	400
"Bear - the Cashier," 1950s, M-T Co., 7½" high, five actions...................190	285	380
"Bear the Magician", 1950s, MTS Co., nine actions, 12½" tall, RARE.......300	450	600
"Begging Puppy," 1960s, "Y" Co., 9" long, six actions 40	60	80
"Bengali - The Exciting New Growling, Prowling Tiger," 1961, Marx Co., Linemar Div., 18½" long from nose to end of tail, 2 cycles, three actions...90	135	180
"Betty Bruin - Cashier," 1950s, Linemar, 9" tall, six actions ....*See Suzy-Cashier Bear*		
"Beauty Parlor Bear," 1950s, S&E Co., 9½" high, seven actions, rare ...400	600	800
"Big Dipper", 1960s, Technofix Co., minor toy, 21" long - 11" high, (includes three tin cars)....................90	135	180
"Big Hunter - Automatic Gun," 1950s, Tada Co., 21" long - extended, three actions 50	75	100
"Big John," 1960s, Alps Co., 12" high, three actions 60	90	120
"Big John - The Indian Chief," ca. 1960s, T-N Co., 5 actions, 12½" tall 90	135	180
"Big Loo - Your Friend From The Moon," 1960s, Marx Co., 38" tall, twelve actions, includes balls, darts, compass, etc. 1000	1500	2000
"Big Max Robot," 1958, Remco Co., 8" long, 7" tall, four actions............90	135	180
"Big Ring Circus Truck," 1950s, M-T Co., 13" long, three actions............120	180	240
"Big Shot Cadillac," 1950s, T-N Co., 10" long, four actions, Rare 190	285	380
"Big Wheel Coca Cola Truck," 1970s, Taiyo Co., three actions 60	90	120
"Big Wheel Family Camper," 1970s, 10" long, three actions 60	90	120
"Big Wheel Ice Cream Truck", 1970's 10" long, three actions 60	90	120
"Biller Train No. 573," 1950s, T-N Co., 13" long, includes rubber cable track and two hopper cars, a minor toy - Rare 80	120	160
"Billy Blastoff Space Scout," Eldon Co., 1960s, 4 actions, 16" long.......80	120	160
"Billy the Kid Sheriff," 1950s, "Y" Co., 10½" tall, 2 cycles, four actions 180	270	360
"Bimbo the Clown," 1950s, Alps Co.,		

	C6	C8	C10
9¼" tall, three actions, (includes detachable hat) 200	300	400
"Bingo Clown," 1950s, T-N Co., 13" tall, three actions 150	225	300
"Bird Watching Bear" (?), 1950s, M-T Co., 10" tall, three actions - Rare...300	450	600
"Blacksmith Bear," 1950s, A-1 Co., 9½" tall, six actions 180	270	360
"Black Smithy Bear," 1950s, T-N Co., 9" high, four actions, RARE..........180	270	360
"Blink-A-Gear-Robot," 1960s, S-H Co., 14½" tall, five actions 400	600	800
"Blinky-the-Clown," 1950s, no marking, 10½" tall, five actions, includes multicolor paper hat 200	300	400
"Blow-Up-Ball Locomotive," 1950s, M-T Co., 9½" long, minor toy, includes celluloid ball 80	120	160
"Blushing Willie," 1960s, Y Co., 10" tall, four actions 50	75	100
"Bobby Drinking Bear," 1950s, Y Co., 10" tall, six actions........................140	210	280
"Bobby the Drumming Bear," 1950s, Alps Co., 10" tall, four actions 190	285	380
"Boeing 727 Jet Liner," 1960s, Y Co., 17½" long, 16¼" wingspan, three actions......140	210	280
"Boeing 727 Jet Plane," 1960s, M-T Co., 12½" long, 10⅜" wingspan, three actions 150	225	300
"Bomber Pilot," 1960s, K-O Co., 10½" long, 9" wingspan, six actions 120	180	240
"Bongo, Drumming Monkey," 1960s, Alps Co., 9½" high, three actions, includes plastic hat..........................80	120	160
"Bongo Player," 1960s, Alps Co., 10" tall, four actions 80	120	160
"Bowling Bank," 1960s, M.B. Daniel & Co., 10" long, three actions 90	135	180
"Brave Eagle," 1950s, T-N Co., 5 actions, 11" tall 90	135	180
"Brave Eagle", 1960s, TN Co., 12" tall, Four Actions 80	120	160
"Breakfast Chef," 1960s, K Co., 8¼" tall, minor toy (includes plastic egg and coffee maker)....................70	105	140
"Brewster the Rooster," 1950s, Marx Co., 9½" high, five actions 120	180	240
"Bristol Bulldog Airplane," T-360, S&E Co., lights, prop spins, stop & go, noise, 4 actions, 12" long, 14½" wingspan 160	240	320

Cabin Cruiser with Outboard Motor. Photo by Don Hultzman.

Caterpillar Tank M-1. Photo by Don Hultzman.

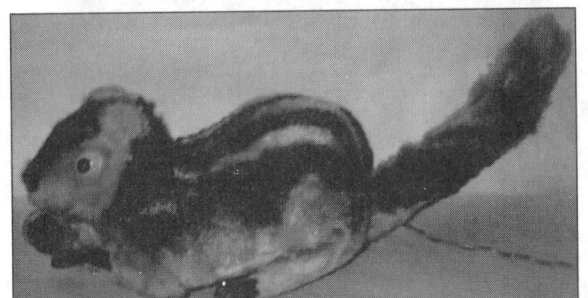

Chippy the Chipmunk. Photo by Don Hultzman.

Circus Jet. Photo by Don Hultzman.

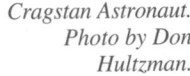

Bunny - The Magician. Photo by Don Hultzman.

Clown & Monkey Car. Photo by Don Hultzman.

Captain Blushwell. Photo by Don Hultzman.

Clancy the Great, Ideal. Photo by Ron Chojnacki. Courtesy Don Hultzman.

Cragstan Astronaut. Photo by Don Hultzman.

Clown & Lion. Photo by Don Hultzman.

251

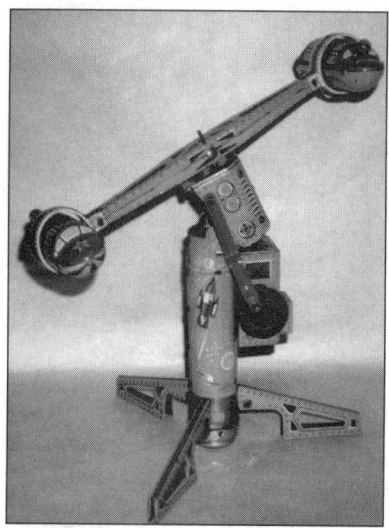

Coney Island Rocket Ride. Photo by Don Hultzman.

Cragstan Roulette - A Gambling Man. Photo by Don Hultzman.

Drinking Dog. Photo by Don Hultzman.

Coca Cola Dispenser Bank. Photo by Don Hultzman.

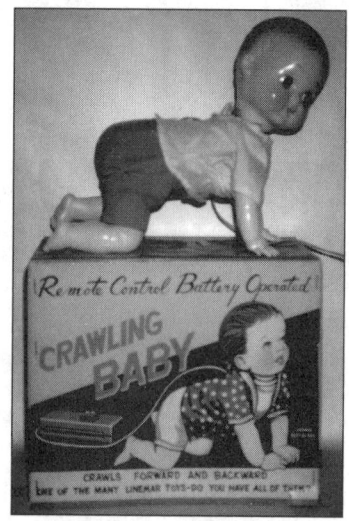

Crawling Baby. Photo by Don Hultzman.

Drum Monkey. Photo by Don Hultzman.

Electro Train Transcontinental. Photo by Don Hultzman.

Electric Vibraphone. Photo by Don Hultzman.

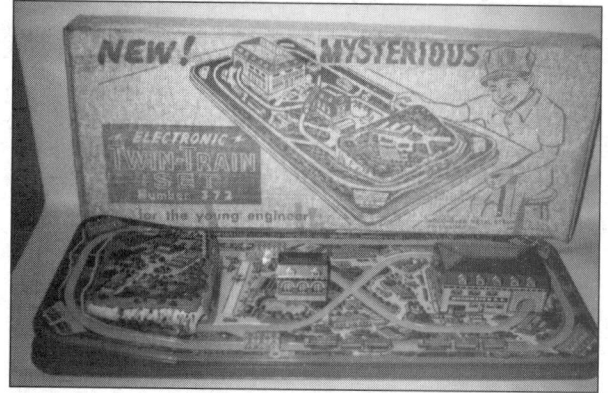

Electronic Twin Train Set - Woodhaven Co.. Photo by Don Hultzman.

Crazy Car. Photo by Don Hultzman.

Electronic Periscope (Nautilus) Firing Range. Photo by Don Hultzman.

252

	C6	C8	C10

"**Broadway** Trolley," 1950s, M-T Co., 10½" long, four actions - two cycles..*See "Tinkling Trolley"*

"**Bruno** the Accordion Bear," 1950s, "Y" Co., 10½" tall, five actions.....120 180 240

"**Bubble** Blowing Bear," 1950s, M-T Co., 9½" high, 4"x5" base, four actions ...140 210 280

"Bubble Blowing Boil Over Car," 1950s, M-T Co., three actions, 10" long 90 135 180

"Bubble Blowing Boy," 1950s, "Y" Co., 7" high, four actions 100 200 300

"Bubble Blowing Bunny," 1950s, "Y" Co., 7" high, four actions 90 135 180

"Bubble Blowing Dog," 1950s, "Y" Co., 8" high, three actions...............90 135 180

"Bubble Blowing Kangaroo," 1950s, M-T Co., 9" high (base to tip of ears), three actions - RARE 200 300 400

"Bubble Blowing Lion," 1950s, M-T Co., 7½" high, 3½"x 7" base, four actions 90 135 180

"Bubble Blowing Musician," 1950s, "Y" Co., 11" tall, three actions 130 195 260

"Bubble Blowing Monkey," 1950s, Alps Co., 10" tall, four actions, includes plastic bowl for bubble solution................................90 135 180

"Bubble Blowing Popeye," 1950s, Linemar Co., 11¾" tall, five actions 800 1200 1600

"Bubble Blowing Washing Bear," 1950s, Y Co., 8" high, three actions, (includes plastic washtub)................................160 240 320

"**Bubbling** Bull," 1950s, Linemar Co., 6½" long, 8" high, five actions (Plastic bowl) 80 120 160

"**Bulldozer**," 1950s, T-N Co., 7½" long, five actions......................60 80 120

"Bulldozer," 1950s, M-T Co., 11" long, six actions 70 105 140

"**Bunny** The Cashier," 1950s, M-T Co., five actions, 7½" high...................120 180 240

"Bunny The Magician," 1950s, Alps Co., 14½" tall, five actions, (includes card-ribbon apparatus for card trick).........190 285 380

"**Burger** Chef," 1950s, "Y" Co., 9" tall, eight actions (includes chef's hat and tin-litho hamburger) 100 150 200

"**Busy** Bizzy Friendly Bug," 1950s, M-T Co., 6¼" long, three actions 60 90 120

"Busy Housekeeper, The," 1950s, Alps Co., 8½" tall, four actions..............160 240 320

"Busy Housekeeper, The" (bunny) 1950s, Alps Co., 10" tall, four actions..........140 210 280

"Busy Robot," ca. 1960s, S-H Co., 4

actions, includes plastic wheelbarrow, 11" high................................200 300 400

"Busy Secretary," 1950s, Linemar Co., 7½" high, 7¼" long, seven actions ...150 225 300

"Busy Shoe Shining Bear," 1950s, Alps Co., 10" high, five actions.....120 180 240

"**Butt** Stompin' Ashtray," 1977, Poynter Prod., 7¼" high, four actions (includes tin manhole cover, ashtray insert and 4½" high plastic shoe)......................40 60 80

"**Buttons**-Puppy With A Brain," also called "Buttons The Push Button Pup," 1960s, Marx, 12" high, 8 actions 180 270 360

"**B-Z** Porter" Baggage truck, 1950s, M-T Co., 7½" long, 6½" high, minor toy, includes three pcs. of luggage (tin)..............................140 210 280

"B-Z Rabbit," ca. 1950s, M-T Co., 4 actions, 7" long 60 90 120

"B-Z Vendor" - ice cream cart, 1950s, M-T Co., three actions, 7½" long, RARE .400 600 800

"**Cabin** Cruiser," ca. 1950s, SGK Co., 3 actions, 21½" long 180 270 360

"Cabin Cruiser With Outboard Motor," 1950s, Linemar Co., 12" long, minor toy...............................100 150 200

"**Cable** Train," 1940s, T-N Co., 12" long, four pc. set, minor toy............80 120 160

"**Cadillac**" car, 1949, Ashai Toy Co., 10" long, three actions 140 210 280

"**Calypso** Joe," 1950s, Linemar, 11" tall, four actions - RARE 200 300 400

"**Candy** Vending Machine Bank," 1950s, Wonderful Toy Co., 9" high, five actions - RARE..............600 900 1200

"**Capitol** Airlines Viscount 321," 1950s, Linemar, 11" long, 14" wingspan, four actions 160 240 320

"**Cappy** the Baggage Porter Dog," 1960s, Alps Co., 12" high, 11" long, four actions...90 135 180

"**Captain** Blushwell," 1960s, "Y" Co., 11" tall, six actions.........................80 120 160

"Captain Hook," 1950s, Marusan Co., 10¾" high, three actions, (includes tin sword and felt hat) RARE 800 1200 1600

"**Caterpillar**," 1950s, Alps Co., 16" long, three actions 90 135 180

"Caterpillar Tank M-1", 1950s, M-T Co., five actions, 8½" long, 11" long with barrel extended 150 225 300

"**Central** Choo Choo," 1960s, M-T Co., 15" long, three actions.............30 45 60

	C6	C8	C10
"Champion Weight Lifter," 1960s, Y-M Co., 10" tall, five actions............90		135	180
"Chaparral 2F," car, 1960s, Alps Co., 11" long, five actions 80		120	160
"Charlie the Drumming Clown," 1950s, Alps Co., six actions (includes detachable drum and cymbals), 9½" tall 140		210	280
"Charlie Weaver," 1962, T-N Co., 12" tall, six actions......................40		60	80
"Change Man Robot"-Astronaut, 1960s, S-H Co., four actions 13¼" tall, RARE 4000		6000	8000
"Charm the Cobra," 1960s, Alps Co., 6" high, three actions 90		135	180
"Chee Chee Chihuahua," 1960s, Mego Co., 8" high, five actions 30		45	60
"Chef Cook," 1960s, Y Co., 11½" tall with hat on, five actions (includes tin litho egg and hat) 140		210	280
"Chemical Fire Engine," 1950s, HTC Co., 10" long, four actions.............100		150	200
"Chief Robotman," 1950s, K.O. Co., 12" tall, four actions......................400		600	800
"Chimp and Pup Rail Car," 1950s, T-N Co., 8" high, four actions.........90		135	180
"Chimp With Xylophone," 1970s, Y Co., 12" long, 8" high, minor toy (includes 4 records and hammer)....80		120	160
"Chimpy the Drumming Monkey," 1950s, Alps Co., 9" high, six actions, includes detachable drum and cymbals 70		105	140
"Chippy the Chipmunk," 1950s, Alps Co., 12" long, (nosetip to tail tip), four actions 80		120	160
"Christmas Time," 1950s Murusan Co., 10" high, 7" base diameter, three actions - RARE 300		450	600
"Cindy the Meowing Cat," 1950s, Tomiyama Co., 12" high, (nosetip to tail tip), 2 cycles, four actions.....50		75	100
"Cine Bear," 1950s, Linemar Co., 11" tall, five actions 320		480	640
"Circus Elephant With Blowing Ball and Parasol," 1950s, T-N Co., 9¾" high, three actions (includes celluloid ball and tin litho umbrella), rare 150		225	300
"Circus Fire Engine," 1960s, M-T Co., 11" long, four actions......................120		180	240
"Circus Jet," 1950s, T-N Co., three actions, 9" high assembled, Jet 6¼" long 90		135	180
"Circus Lion," 1950s, Rock Valley Toy Co., (Via), 11" high, four actions, includes whip and flannel carpet with levers (2 cycles) 190		285	380
"Clancy The Great," 1960s, Ideal Toy Co., three actions, 19½" tall without hat, (includes plastic hat and test coin)......................100		150	200
"Climbing Donald Duck On His Friction Fire Engine," 1950s, Linemar Co., four actions, 12" long......................300		450	600
"Climbing Fireman," 1950s, TPS Co., 24" high assembled, five actions (includes 3 tin ladder sections) 190		285	380
"Climbing Fireman" (remote control), 1950s, T.P.S., 28" high assembled, five actions 210		315	420
"Climbing Linesman," 1950s, T.P.S. Co., 24" high when assembled, three actions, (includes 3 tin pole sections) Rare......................200		300	400
"Clown Circus Car," 1960s, M-T Co., 8½" long, 9" high, five actions 120		180	240
"Clown and Lion", 1960s, M-T Co., four actions, 11¾" high from base to top of tree 240		360	480
"Clown and Monkey Car," 1960s, M-T Co., 10¼" long, 8" high, three actions 160		240	320
"Clown on Unicycle," 1960s, M-T Co., 10½" high, three actions 190		285	380
"Clown with Lion," 1950s, T-N Co., 12" high, four actions (includes spiral apparatus) 200		300	400
"Clowns Bank, The," 1940s, unmarked, 10" high, minor toy (all plastic)......80		120	160
"Clown-The-Magician No. 40244," 1950s, Alps Co., 12" tall, six actions includes card-ribbon apparatus for card trick 200		300	400
"Coca-Cola Dispenser - Bank," 1950s, Linemar Co., minor toy, 9½" tall, (includes four plastic Coke glasses and rubber stopper)............450		675	900
"Cock-A-Doodle-Doo Rooster," 1950s, Mikuni Co., 8" high, four actions ...80		120	160
"Colonel Hap Hazard" Robot, 1968, Marx Co., 11¼" tall, four actions ..300		450	600
"Combi-O-Mixer," 1950s, Excelo Co., (mixer-blender), 9" long, 9" high, minor toy......................30		45	60
"Comic Hungry Bug," VW auto, 1970s, Tora (S-T) Co., 7¾" long, five actions......................30		45	60
"Comic Musical Car," 1960s, T-N Co., four actions, 6" long, 8½" tall.........60		90	120

	C6	C8	C10
"Comic Road Grader," 1950s, Bandai Co., 9" long, four actions	60	90	120
"Comic Road Roller," 1960s, Bandai Co., four actions, 9" long	60	90	120
"Coney Island Penny Machine," 1950s, Remco Co., 13" high, minor toy, (includes plastic prizes)	90	135	180
"Coney Island Rocket Ride," 1950s, Alps Co., 13½" high, four actions	250	375	500
"Continental Blue Locomotive," 1960s, M-T Co., 12½" long, 4 actions	20	30	40
"Corvair Bertone," 1970s, Bandai Co., four actions, 12" long	40	60	80
"Cowboy Riding Horse," 1950s, T-N Co., 7" high, three actions	60	90	120
"Cragstan Astronaut," 1950s, Daiya Co., 14" tall, four actions	400	600	800
"Cragstan Beep Beep Greyhound Bus," 1950s, Cragstan Co., 20" long, three actions	110	165	220
"Cragstan Biplane," 7F7, U.S. Navy, 1950s, T-N Co., 9½" long, 11½" wingspan, four actions	180	270	360
"Cragstan Biplane-7F18," 1950s, T-N Co., 12" long, 14⅜" wingspan, five actions	180	270	360
"Cragstan Crapshooter," 1950s, Y Co., 9½" tall, four actions, includes pair of small dice	90	135	180
"Cragstan Crapshooting Monkey," 1950s, Alps Co., 9" tall, three actions, includes pair of small dice	70	105	140
"Cragstan Dishwasher - Automatic," 1960s, Alps Co., 9" high, (includes 24 pc. dish set, 2 dish baskets and metal tray), minor toy	40	60	80
"Cragstan Firebird III", 1950s, Alps Co., three actions, 11½" long	400	600	800
"Cragstan Flying Plane - With Pylon Tower," 1950s, minor toy, plane 8" long, 9½" wingspan, tower 26" high	110	165	220
"Cragstan Great Astronaut, 1960s, Alps Co., 14" tall, five actions	500	750	1000
"Cragstan's Mr. Robot," 1960s, Y Co., 10½" tall, four actions	300	450	600
"Cragstan Mother Goose," 1960s, Y Co., 8¼" high, six actions	80	120	160
"Cragstan One-Arm Bandit," 1960s, Y Co., 6¼" high, three actions, includes 3"x3¼" sign	90	135	180

	C6	C8	C10
"Cragstan Peanut Vendor," 1950s, T-N Co., 8" tall, five actions (includes felt hat)	180	270	360
"Cragstan Playboy," 1960s, Cragstan Co., 13" high, five actions	90	135	180
"Cragstan Roulette - A Gambling Man," 1960s, Y Co., 9" tall, five actions, (includes steel ball, chips, tin table, game sheet)	140	210	280
"Cragstan Satellite," 1950s, Cragstan Co., 8" diameter, 5½" high	90	135	180
"Cragstan Smoking Jet Plane - U.S.A.F." 1950s, T-N Co., 11½" long, 7½" wingspan, four actions	120	180	240
"Cragstan Talking Robot," 1960s, Y Co., 10½" tall, three actions	320	480	720
"Cragstan Telly Bear," 1950s, S&E Co., 8" high, six actions	140	210	280
"Cragstan Tootin'-Chuggin' Locomotive," 1950s, Cragstan Co., 24" long, three actions (longest single piece battery toy made)	60	90	120
"Cragstan Tugboat," 1950s, San Co., 12¾" long, three actions	80	120	160
"Cragstan Vertol 1107 Helicopter," 1950s, T-N Co., 13½" long, four actions, includes rotors	100	150	200
"Cragstan Western Locomotive," 1950s, Cragstan Co., 12" long, four actions	60	90	120
"Cragstan's Two Gun Sheriff," 1950s, Y Co., 9½" tall, five actions (includes tin hat)	120	180	240
"Crane Tractor," 1950s, SKK Co., 7½" long, 11½" high extended	70	105	140
"Crawling Baby," 1940s, Linemar Co., 11" long, 8½" high, minor toy	50	75	100
"Crazy Car," 1950s, Marusan Co., five actions, 9" long	60	90	120
"Cry-Baby-In-Buggy" (?), 1950s, T-N Co., 11¾" long, 7" high, minor toy, includes plastic baby bottle to activate switch	60	90	120
"Cycling Daddy," 1960s, Bandai Co., 10" high, four actions	90	135	180
"Cyclist Clown," 1950s, K Co., seven actions, 7" high	190	285	380
"Cyclist Clown," 1950s, M-T Co., 6½" high, six actions	200	300	400
"Cyclist Clown," 1950s, Alps Co., 9" high, five actions	210	305	420
"Cymbal Playing Turnover Monkey, 1960s, T-N Co., 8" tall, three actions	40	60	80

Cragstan "Tootin-Chuggin Locomotive", Greyhound Bus Scenicruiser.

Fire Command Car. Photo by Don Hultzman.

Cragstan Biplane 7F18. Photo by Don Hultzman.

Fighter Airplane. Photo by Don Hultzman.

Dynamic Fighter Robot. Photo by Don Hultzman.

Excavator Robot. Photo by Don Hultzman.

Charlie Weaver. Photo by Bill Kaufman. Courtesy Good Old Days.

Flashy Jim Robot. Photo by Don Hultzman.

Farm Truck. Photo by Don Hultzman.

Farm Truck. Photo by Don Hultzman.

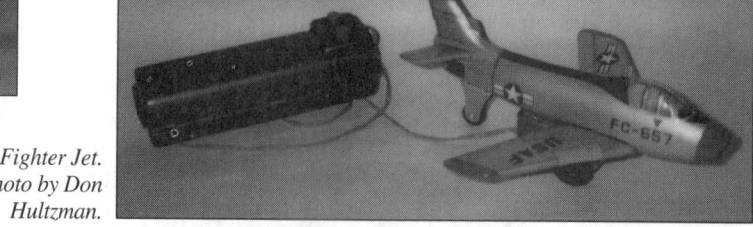

Fighter Jet. Photo by Don Hultzman.

	C6	C8	C10

"Daisy - The Jolly Drumming Duck,"
1950s, Alps Co., 9" high, seven
actions, (includes detachable drum
and cymbals, rare 120 180 240

"Dalmation One-Man Band No. 90262,"
1950s, Alps Co., 9" high, six actions,
includes cymbals and stand............110 165 220

"Dancing Merry Chimp," 1960s,
Kuramochi Co., (C-K), 11" tall,
five actions 80 120 160

"Dancing Sweethearts," 1950s, T-N
Co., 7" tall, minor toy 90 135 180

"Dandy-The Happy Drumming Pup,"
1950s, Alps Co., 8½" high, six actions,
(includes detachable drum and
cymbals) 100 150 200

"Dapper Jigger Dancer," 1950s, Haji
Co., 12" tall, minor toy 90 135 180

"Dennis The Menace" (Playing London
Bridge), 1950s, Rosko, 9" high, 3
actions, includes xylophone............100 150 200

"Dentist Bear," 1950s, S&E Co., 9½"
tall, 6¾"x4¼" base, seven
actions, includes detachable head ..250 375 500

"Desert Patrol Jeep," 1960s, M-T Co.,
11" long, four actions, includes
turret gunner......................90 135 180

"Destroyer 206" boat, 1950s, Y Co.,
14" long, six actions, includes
detachable antenna and five depth
charges 110 165 220

"Diesel Locomotive," 1950s, Cragstan
Co., minor toy, 16½" long 30 45 60

"Dino Robot," 1960s, S-H Co., 11"
tall, five actions......................400 600 800

"Disney Acrobats" (Mickey, Donald &
Pluto), 1950s, Linemar Co., 9"
high, minor toys 400 600 800

"Disney Fire Engine", 1950s, Linemar
Co., 11" long, four actions 440 660 880

"Disneyland Fire Engine," 1950s, Linemar
Co., 18" long, five actions 300 450 600

"Docking Rocket," 1960s, Daiya Co.,
16" long, 24" extended, six actions,
(includes plastic radar antenna).........100 150 200

"Dog Family", 1960s, Alps Co., 11"
long, four actions 30 45 60

"Dog Sled," T-N Co., 14" long, four
actions - RARE, 1950s...................200 300 400

"Dolly Dressmaker," 1950s, T-N Co.,
7" high, ten actions, includes cloth
sample ("Dolly Seamstress" on
box) Rare......................140 210 280

"Donald Duck," 1960s, Linemar Co.,
8" tall, four actions............190 285 380

"Donald Duck Locomotive," 1970s,
M-T Co., three actions, 9" long 140 210 280

"Donald Duck Trolley," 1960s, M-T
Co., 11" high, three actions............160 240 320

"Douglas C-124 Globe Master," ca.
1950s, Yonezawa Co., 8 actions,
20½" wingspan, 18" long 300 450 600

"Douglas DC-9TWA Jet Plane" 1960s,
T-N Co., four actions, 14" long,
17" wingspan 70 105 140

"Doxie The Dog," 1950s, Linemar
Co., 9" long, five actions 20 30 40

"Dozo-The-Steaming Clown," 1960s,
T-N Co., Rosko toys, 10" tall,
five actions 160 240 320

"Dream Boat Hot Rod," ca. 1950s, M-
T Co. (?), 4 actions, 7" long............90 135 180

"Drill," 1950s, Linemar Co., 6" long,
includes attachments, minor toy 20 30 40

"Drinker's Savings Bank," 1960s,
Illfelder Co., 9" high, minor toy 80 120 160

"Drinking Captain," 1960s, S&E Co.,
12" tall, six actions..........................90 135 180

"Drinking Dog," 1950s, Y Co., four
actions............80 120 160

"Drinking-Licking Cat," 1950s, T-N
Co., 10" high, 4"x4" base, six
actions 90 135 180

"Drum Bear," ca. 1950s, Alps Co., 5
actions, walks, lights, beats drum,
noise, 7¾" tall 100 150 200

"Drum Monkey," 1970s, Yada Co., 8"
high, three actions 40 60 80

"Drummer Bear," 1950s, Alps Co.,
10" tall, six actions..........................140 210 280

"Drumming Mickey Mouse," 1950s,
Linemar, 10" tall, four actions,
Rare 700 1050 1400

"Drumming Polar Bear," 1960s, Alps
Co., 12" tall, three actions..............80 120 160

"Ducky Duckling," 1960s, Alps Co.,
8" high, four actions........................40 60 80

"Dump Truck No. 7343," 1960s, T-N
Co., 10¼" long, seven actions 60 90 120

"Dynamic Fighter Robot," 1960s, Junior
Toy Co., 10" tall, five actions 60 90 120

"Earthman-Astronaut", 1950s, T-N Co.,
five actions, 9½" tall, RARE 900 1300 1800

"El Toro-Cragstan Bullfighter," 1950s,
T-N Co., 9½" long, four actions,
includes detachable tin matador.....100 150 200

	C6	C8	C10
"Electric Powered TV and Radio Station," 1950s, Marx, 30" long, three actions	80	120	160
"Electric Remote Control Robot," 1950s, M-T Co., 7½" tall, four actions, Rare	400	600	800
"Electric Robot," 1950s, Marx, 14½" tall, five actions, Rare	300	450	600
"Electric School Bus," 1950s, M-T Co., 9½" long, minor toy	70	105	140
"Electric Vibraphone," 1950s, T-N Co., 7½" long, 5½" high, three actions	60	90	120
"Electro Special Racer," 1950s, Yonezawa Co., 10" long, three actions	90	135	180
"Electro Toy Racer," 1950s, Yonezawa Co., three actions, 10" long	1000	1500	2000
"Electro Train Transcontinental," 1950s, "M" Co., 20½" long, (3 pcs.) three actions	70	105	140
"Electronic Countdown," 1959, Ideal Toy Co., 24" long, six actions	60	90	120
"Electronic Fighter Jet 4800," 1950s, 19" long, eleven actions	120	180	240
"Electronic Fire House," 1940s, Banner Co., 7" square, minor toy (includes plastic fire engine)	70	105	140
"Electronic Periscope (Nautilus) Firing Range," 1950s, Cragstan, 11" high on tripod, three actions	80	120	160
"Electronic Twin Train Set #372," 1950s, Woodhaven Metal Stamping Co., minor toy, 28" long - 11" wide, (include two 3 pc. trains)	100	150	200
"Engine Robot," 1960s, S-H Co., 9½" tall, four actions	60	90	120
"Excavator Robot," 1960s, S-H Co., 10" tall, four actions	180	270	360
"Expert Motor Cyclist," 1950s, MT Co., 12" long, five actions	600	900	1200
"F-14-A Navy Jet Fighter," 1960s, T-N Co., six actions, 13" long, 13" wingspan	200	300	400
"F-101A Voodoo Fighter," 1960s, K-O Co., minor toy, 15" long, 14" wingspan	100	150	200
"FS-059-Fighter Plane", (Jet with prop), 1950s, T-N Co., five actions, 11" long, 13" wingspan	170	255	340
"Fairyland Loco," (Locomotive), 1950s, Daiya Co., 9" long, four actions	60	90	120
"Farm Truck", 1960s, Alps Co., 11" long, three actions	110	165	220

	C6	C8	C10
"Farm Truck," 1950s, T-N Co., five actions, 9" long	100	150	200
"F.D. Fire Engine," 1960s, Y-M Co., 10" long, 12" high when ladder is extended, four actions	90	135	180
"Feeding Bird Watcher," 1950s, Linemar, 9" high, five action, (includes detachable tin branch and bird), Rare	240	360	480
"Ferris Wheel Truck," ca. 1950s, Linemar Co. (?) 4 actions, 11" long	140	210	280
"Fido - The Xylophone Player," ca. 1950s, Alps Co., body sways, head turns, arms activate lights, sound, 6 actions, 8¾" high, includes detachable xylophone	120	180	240
"Fighter," (airplane), 1960s, K-O Co., 10½" long, 9" wingspan, six actions	140	210	280
"Fighter Airplane," ca. 1960s, Marx Co., 4 actions, 7" wingspan	60	90	120
"Fighter Jet" ca. 1960s, Marx Co., 4 actions, 7" wingspan	60	90	120
"Fighting Bull," 1960s, Alps Co., 9½" long, five actions	60	90	120
"Fighting Bull," 1970s, Rock Valley Tech Co., 12" long, nose to tail tip, four actions, two cycles	70	105	140
"Fighting Robot," 1970s, S-H Co., four actions, 10" tall, (all plastic)	50	75	100
"Fighting Spaceman," 1960s S-H Co., 12" tall, five actions	140	210	280
"Fire Boat," 1950s, M-T Co., 15" long, five actions	70	105	140
"Fire Chief No. 8 Car," 1960s, Y Co., 11¼" long, three actions	80	120	160
"Fire Chief Mystery Action Car," 1960s, T-N Co., 9¾" long, four actions	110	165	220
"Fire Command Car," 1950s, T-N Co., five actions	170	255	340
"Fire Engine," 1950s, Marusan Co., four actions, 9" long	100	150	200
"Fire Engine," 1950s, T-N Co., (Electro Toy), three actions, 9" long - ladder extends 13"	140	210	280
"Fire Engine," 1950s, Y Co., 12" long, ladder extends 16", six actions	80	120	160
"Fire Engine," ca. 1950s, S-H Co., 3 actions, 8" long	80	120	160
"Fire Patrol Boat," 1950s, KKS Co., 12" long, three actions	90	135	180
"Firebird Racer," 1950s, Tomiyama Co., four actions, 14¼" long	300	450	600

"Mod Monster, Blushing Frankenstein", Hootin' Haunted House, Frankenstein Monster.

Flintstone Yacht. Photo by Don Hultzman.

B-Z Porter, Cragstan "Tugboat", Goodtime Charlie, Picnic Bunny.

The Floating Satellite Target Game. Photo by Don Hultzman.

Maxwell Coffee Loving Bear, Bird WatchingBear, Cragstan Peanut Vendor.

Fork Lift Truck. Photo by Don Hultzman.

Gear Robot. Photo by Don Hultzman.

Go-Kart, M-T Co.. Photo by Don Hultzman.

Bulldozer, Shaking Old-Timer Car, Tractor.

Foto Finish. Photo by Don Hultzman.

Fruit Juice Counter. Photo by Don Hultzman.

Treasure Chest Bank, Santa Bank, Hole-In-One Bank, Poverty Pup Bank.

Drinking Captain, Hi Jinks of the Circus, Cragstan "Playboy"

Flower Watering Pup, Rock 'N Roll Monkey, Barney Bear Drummer.

Silver Mountain Express, Spirit of 1776.

Hamburger Chef.

Chimpy, Drumming Monkey, Happy Santa One-Man Band, Fred Flintstone's Bedrock Band, Dalmation One-Man Band.

Greyhound Bus.

Grandpa Bear.

Happy Singing Bird in Cage, Cragstan-One Arm Bandit, Comic Hungry Bug, Mag-oo.

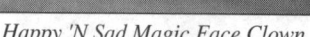

Happy 'N Sad Magic Face Clown.

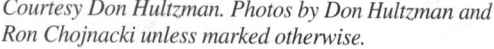

Courtesy Don Hultzman. Photos by Don Hultzman and Ron Chojnacki unless marked otherwise.

Green Caterpillar.

	C6	C8	C10

"**Fire** Tricycle," 1950s, T-N Co., 9½" long, four actions 180 270 360

"**Fishing** Bear," (also Fishing Panda Bear, Polar Bear, Forest Bear), 1950s, Alps Co., 10" high, six actions, (includes detachable pond, tin fish) 120 180 240

"**Fishing** Bears-Bank," 1950s, Wonderful Toy Co., 9½" tall, six actions, Rare 140 210 280

"**Flashing** Jet-FC-657 Airplane-U.S.A.F. 7452," 1950s, Marx Co., 7" long, 6" wingspan, four actions 80 120 160

"**Flashy** Jim" 1950's, S.N.K. Co. (Ace), Minor toy, 7¾" tall, RARE............1100 1650 2200

"**Flashy** Ray Space Gun," 1950's, T-N Co., 18½" long, minor toy 50 75 100

"**Flintstone** Yacht", 1961 Remco Co., 17" long 100 150 200

"**Floating** Satellite Target Game," 1960's, 8½" high, (includes tin gun, rubber tipped darts & celluloid ball) 100 150 200

"**Flutter B**irds," 1950s, Alps Co., 26½" high when assembled, six actions, includes detachable pulley assembly, Rare 200 300 400

"**Flying** Dutchman-PH-KLM Airliner," 1950s, T-N co., 11" long,, 14" wingspan, five actions....................100 150 200

"**Flying** Jet Plane-Boeing 747P,'" 1960s, J Toy Co., 13" long, 12" wingspan, five actions....................90 135 180

"**Flying** Platform", 1950's, Cragstan Co., four actions, 5½" diameter-9" high, (includes detachable tin soldier) -RARE 400 600 800

"**Flying** Tiger Airplane," 1960s, Marx Co., 7" long, 7" wingspan, four actions (remote control) 60 90 120

"**Ford** Model T," 1950s, Nihonkogei Co., 10¼" long, four actions (includes detachable tin roof) 60 90 120

"**Ford** Mustang 2"x 2," 1960s, Wenmac-AMF Co., four actions, 16" long......................60 90 120

"**Ford** Skyliner" 1950s, T-N Co., four actions, 9" long 100 150 200

"**4** Prop Airplane," 1960s, Waco Co., 17" long, 16¼" wingspan, four actions 140 210 280

"**Fork** Lift Truck," 1960s, M-T Co., 10¼" high, Minor Toy 60 90 120

"**Foto** Finish"-Racehorse, 1950's, M-T Co., minor toy, 12" long 90 135 180

"**Frankenstein**" (tin), 1950s, Marx Co., (Japan), 12" tall, five actions (remote control), rare 700 1050 1400

"**Frankenstein** Monster," 1960s, T-N Co., 14" tall, six actions 140 210 280

"**Frankie**-The Rollerskating Monkey," 1950s, Alps Co., 12" tall 100 150 200

"**Fred** Flintstone on Dino", 1961, Marx Co., (Japan) eight actions, 22" long......................300 450 600

"**Fred** Flintstone Bedrock Band," 1962, Alps Co., 9½" high, four actions 250 375 500

""**Friendly** Jocko-My Favorite Pet," 1950s, Alps Co., 8" high, five actions (includes detachable cymbals, plastic cup)....................120 180 240

"**Fruit** Juice Counter," 1960s, "K" Co., 8" long, 8" high, three actions (includes plastic barrel, lid, glasses and tin tray) 90 135 180

"**Funland** Cup Ride," 1960s, Sonsco Co., 7" tall, 6"x 6" base, three actions, includes 6" umbrella..........90 135 180

Galloping Cowboy Savings Bank," 1950s, Y Co., (Cragstan), 8" high, 6½" long, minor toy..............160 240 320

"**Gama** Mercedes Benx 220 SE Sedan," 1960s, Mignon Co., 9" long, three actions 140 210 280

"**Gear** Robot" 1960s, "Y" Co., 10" tall, four actions 240 360 480

"**Gino**-Neapolitan Ballon Blower," 1960s, Tomiyama Co., (Rosko), 10" tall, five actions, includes bubble solution plastic tray 90 135 180

"**Girl** With Baby Carriage," 1960s, T-N Co., 8" high, three actions 80 120 160

"**Go-Go** Girl," (bar toy), 1969 Poynter Prod. Co., 15¼" tall, minor toy (risque toy - PG rated) 30 45 60

"**Go Kart**," 1960s, M-T Co., 6½" long, minor toy (includes control wire with steering key) 80 120 160

"**Go Kart**," 1950s, Rosko Co., 10" long, three actions, includes detachable head..............................90 135 180

"**Godzilla**," 1960s, Bullmark Co., five actions, 10½" tall....................300 450 600

"**Godzilla** Monster," 1970s, Marusan Co., 11½" tall, three actions............70 105 140

Puzzled Puppy, Shutter Bug, Popcorn Vendor.

Military Police Car, Desert Patrol Jeep.

Teddy the Rhythmical Drummer, Major Tooty, McGregor, Cycling Daddy.

Happy Naughty Chimp. Photo by Don Hultzman.

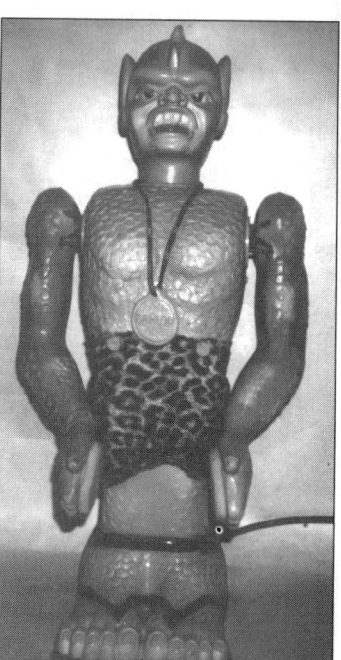

The Great Garloo.

Fighting Spaceman.

Fishing Bear, three variations

Courtesy Don Hultzman. Photos by Don Hultzman and Ron Chojnacki unless marked otherwise.

Fighter. Photo by Don Hultzman.

Highway Skill Driving.

262

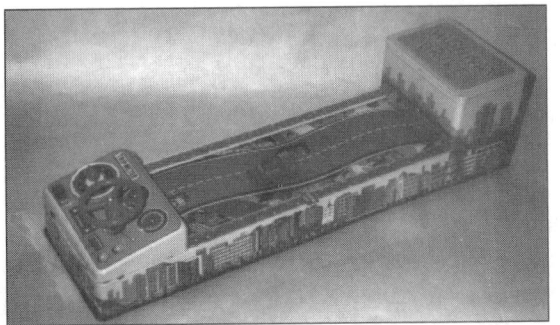

Highway Drive.

Roaring Gorilla, Mighty Kong, Dancing Merry Chimp.

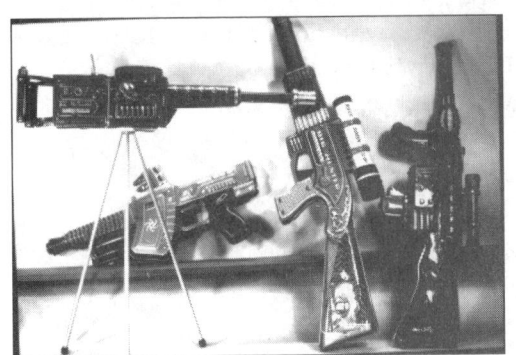

Heavy Machine Gun.

Railroad Handcar, Winner-25-Rocket, Biller Train No.573.

Balloon Vendor, Miss Friday, Sam the Shaving Man, Gino the Neapolitan Balloon Blower.

Hoop Zing Girl.

Ray Gun, Universal Machine Gun, Big Hunter Automatic Gun, Flashy-Ray Gun.

Hy-Que Monkey.

Jolly Bear the Drummer Boy.

Jolly Daddy.

Jolly Bambino.

Hiller Hornet Helicopter

Courtesy Don Hultzman. Photos by Don Hultzman and Ron Chojnacki unless marked otherwise.

263

	C6	C8	C10
"**Golden** Locomotive," 1950s, Nihonkogei Co., 10½" long, minor toy ...30		45	60
"**Golden** Gear Robot", 1960's, S-H Co., five actions, 9" tall ...240		360	480
"**Golden** Roto Robot," 1960s, S-H Co., 8½" tall, five actions ...90		135	180
"**Gomora** Monster", 1960's Bullmark Co., four actions, 8" tall, (includes plastic missles) ...110		165	220
"**Gorilla**", 1950s T-N Co., five actions 9¼" tall (white or brown) ...180		270	360
"**Go-Stop Benz Racer**", 1950s, Marusan Co., three actions, 11" long ...150		225	300
"**Good** Time Charlie," 1960s M-T Co., 12" tall, seven actions ...90		135	180
"**Grace** Ocean Liner", 1950s, M-T Co., three actions, 15"long ...250		375	500
"**Grandpa** Bear," (rocking chair),1950s, Alps co., 9" tall, five actions ...140		210	280
"**Grand-Pa** Car," 1950s, Y Co., 9" long, four actions ...50		75	100
"**Grandpa** Panda Bear", 1950's, M-T Co., five actions, 9" tall ...120		180	240
"**Great** Garloo, The", 1960s, Marx Co., 23" tall, seven actions, (includes chain and medallion) ...300		450	600
"**Green** Caterpillar", 1950's Daiva Co., three actions, 19½" long ...150		225	300
"**Greyhound** Bus", 1950s, KKK. Co., minor toy, 7¼" long ...90		135	180
"**Greyhound** Bus-Scenicruiser," 1950s, I.Y. Metal Toy Co., 16" long, three actions ...90		135	180
"**Greyhound** Bus with Headlights," 1950s, Linemar co., 10¼" long, three actions ...100		150	200
"**Grumman** F9F Navy Jet"-Cougar, 1950's, K Co., three actions, 11½" long, 10¼"wingspan ...150		225	300
"**Guided** Missile Launcher," 1950s, Irco Co., 8" long, 3" tall, 5" wide, three actions (includes plastic missiles) ...100		150	200
"**Gypsy** Fortune Teller", 1950's, Ichida Co., five actions,12" high with hat, 5¾"x 7" base, (includes: 20 fortune cards) ...400		600	800
"**H-O** Gauge Electric Train set wtih Real Smoke", 1960's, Amico Co., 23" long- total length, 17 pc. set ...60		90	120
"**Hamburger** Chef," 1960s, K Co., 8" long, 8" high, three actions, (in-			

	C6	C8	C10
cludes tin frying pan, hamburger, plastic bottles) ...100		150	200
"**Handy** Hank Mystery Tractor," 1950s, T-N Co., 9" long, four actions ...40		60	80
"**Happy** Band Trios," 1970s, M-T Co., 12" high, seven actions ...90		135	180
"**Happy** Clown Car," 1960s, Y Co., 6½" long, three actions ...70		105	140
"**Happy** Clown Theater," (with Pinocchio-like puppet), 1950s, Y Co., 10" tall, three actions ...120		180	240
"**Happy** Fiddler Clown, The"1950s, Alps Co., 9½" high, four actions, includes tin litho violin, ...210		315	420
"**Happy** Miner," 1960s, Bandai Co., 11" tall, three actions ...100		150	200
"**Happy** Naughty Chimp," 1960s, Daishin Co., 9½" high, assembled, four actions ...40		60	80
"**Happy**'n Sad Magic Face Clown," 1960s Y Co., 10" tall, five actions ...100		150	240
"**Happy**'N' Sad Face Cymbal Clown," 1960s, Y Co., 10"tall, five actions ...120		180	200
"**Happy** Plane", 1960s, TPS Co., three actions, 9"long, 10½" wingspan ...100		150	200
"**Happy** Santa", 1960s, "Z" Co., 11" tall, three actions ...100		150	200
"**Happy** Santa" (Walking), 1950s, Alps Co., 11" tall, five actions ...140		210	280
"**Happy** Santa-One Man Band," 1950s, Alps Co., 9" high, six actions, includes cymbals and stand ...120		180	240
"**Happy** Singing Bird," 1950s, M-T Co., 9" high, bird 3" long, 5⅝" dia. base, three actions ...60		90	120
"**Happy** the Clown Puppet Show", (with Pinocchio-like puppet), 1960's, Y Co., 10" tall, three actions ...180		270	360
"**Happy** Tractor," 1960s, Daiya Co., 8" long, four actions ...30		45	60
"**Harbor**-Queen Boat", 1950's, M-T Co., 12" long, minor toy ...150		225	300
"**Hasty** Chimp," 1960s Y Co., 9" high, four actions ...40		60	80
Haunted House Mystery Bank", 1960s, (Disneyland promotion), Brumberger Co., 7⅝" high, four actions, ...100		150	200
"**Heavy** Machine Gun," 1950s, T-N Co., 24" long, 13" high on tripod, four actions (includes detachable tripod and plastic ammo belt) ...120		180	240

	C6	C8	C10

"Hi Bouncer Moon Scout" robot, 1968, Marx Co., 11¼" tall, five actions, includes five plastic balls, Rare 400 600 800

"High Jinks of the Circus," 1950s, T-N Co., 14" high, extends to 29", six actions 120 180 240

"Highway Drive," 1950s, T-N Co., 15½" long, three actions (includes tin magnetic car) 50 75 100

"Highway Patrol Police Special, 1960's, Y Co., five actions, 11½" long 90 135 180

"Highway Patrol Jeep," 1950s, Daiya Co., 10" long, four actions.............60 90 120

"Highway Skill Driving," 1960s, K Co., 13" long, three actions.............60 90 120

"Hiller Hornet Helicopter," 1950s, Alps Co., 12¼" long, 15" 2-pc. metal rotor, four actions 100 150 200

"Hippo Chef" (Cuty Cook) 1960s, Y Co., 10" tall, five actions (includes chef hat and tin litho egg) 110 165 220

"Hobo Clown With Accordion" (with cymbal playing monkey), 1950's, Alps Co., six actions, 10½" high ...200 300 400

"Hole-In-One Bank," 1960s, no marking, 8½" long x 3½" wide, minor toy, includes marked test coin and golfer 60 90 120

"Holiday Sink-Stove Combination," 1950s, T-N Co., 9" high, minor toy includes 3 pc. pan set 40 60 80

"Hoop Zing Girl," 1950s, Linemar Co., 11½" tall, minor toy 120 180 240

"Hoopy-the Fishing Duck," 1950s, Alps Co., 10" high, seven actions (includes magnetic fish and detachable 'pond') 160 240 320

"Hootin' Hollow Haunted House," 1960s, Marx, 11" high, eight actions, Rare.........................400 600 800

"Hooty the Happy Owl," 1960s, Alps Co., 9" tall, six actions..................70 105 140

"Hot Rod" car, 1950s, T-N Co., 10" long, minor toy...........................160 240 320

"Hot Rod Custom 'T' Ford", 1960s, Alps Co., four actions, 10½" long 180 270 360

"Hot Rod Limousine", 1960's Alps Co., four actions, 10½" long..........180 270 360

"Hungry Cat," 1960s, Linemar Co., 9" high, seven actions (includes tin tray and plastic fish).....................300 450 600

"Hungry Hound Dog," 1950s, Y Co., 9½" high, six actions 120 180 240

"Hungry Sheep," 1950s, M-T Co., 9" long, three actions, 2 cycles 100 150 200

"Hy Que Monkey," 1960s, T-N Co., 17" tall, six actions......................150 225 300

"Hysterical Robot, The," (a.k.a. 'Hysterical Harry and Happy Harry'), 1960s, S-H Co., 13½" tall, seven actions 140 210 280

"Ice Cream Loving Bear" (?), 1950s, M-T Co., 9½" high, three actions, rare 200 300 400

"Ice Cream Truck," 1960s, Bandai Co., 10½" long, five actions 90 135 180

"Indian Joe," 1960s, Alps Co., 12" tall, four actions 60 90 120

"Indian Signal Choo Choo," 1960s, Kanto Toys Co., 9½" long, four actions 60 90 120

"Interceptor," target game, 1950s, S&E Co., 13" high, 16" wingspan, four actions 120 180 240

"Interplanetary Rocket", 1960s, Y Co., 14¾" tall, five actions 100 150 200

"JDN 7673 Sedan-4 door", 1920's, Distler Co., minor toy and one of the earliest battery operated toys, 14" long, Rare 400 600 800

"James Bond's Aston-Martin"......*see "007 Aston Martin"*

"James Bond-007 Car-M101," 1960s, Daiya Co., 11" long, seven actions, includes ejectable driver....................*see "M101 Aston Martin"*

"Jeep-USA," 1950s, TKK Co., 12½" long, a minor toy 60 90 120

"Jeep No. 10560," 1950s, Cragstan, 5½" long, a minor action toy 60 90 120

"Jet Airport with 4 Jet Airplanes," 1960s, Turnpike Lines (Sears), 12½" long, seven actions 140 210 280

"Jet Plane Base," 1950's, Y Co., 7¼" x 11" base, plane 9" long, 7" wingspan, seven actions (includes crank) 220 330 440

"Jig-Saw-Matic," 1950s, Z Co., 7¼" high, 4½" x 8½", a minor action toy 40 60 80

"Jo-Jo the Flipping Monkey", 1970s, T-N Co., (Illfelder), 10" high, minor toy..................................40 60 80

Jolly Pianist

Tank (M-4), Tank (X-3), Tank (M-103).

Jolly Santa on Snow.

Jumbo - The Bubble Blowing Elephant.

King Size Fire Engine

Kissing Couple

Lambo

Leo - The Growling Pet Lion with Magic Face Change.

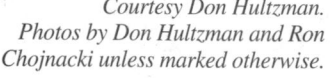

Knight In Armor Target game.

*Courtesy Don Hultzman.
Photos by Don Hultzman and Ron Chojnacki unless marked otherwise.*

Lion.

James Bond's Aston-Martin.

266

	C6	C8	C10

"Jocko the Drinking Monkey," 1950s, Linemar, 11" tall, four actions, includes top hat ....80 / 120 / 160

"John's Farm Truck," 1950s, T-N Co., 9" long, seven actions ....90 / 135 / 180

"Jolly Bambino," 1950s, Alps Co., 9" high, five actions, includes candy pieces, ...180 / 270 / 360

"Jolly Bear Peanut Vendor, The" 1950s, T-N Co., five actions, 8" high (includes: felt hat) ....200 / 300 / 400

"Jolly Bear the Drummer Boy," 1950s, K Co., 7" tall, five actions ....70 / 105 / 140

"Jolly Daddy", 1950's, Marusan Co., four actions, 8¾" tall ....160 / 240 / 320

"Jolly Drummer Chimpy," 1950s, Alps Co., 9" high, 6 actions, includes cymbals and stand ....70 / 105 / 140

"Jolly Drumming Bear," 1950s, T-N Co., 7" tall, four actions ....60 / 90 / 120

Jolly Penguin," 1950's, T-N Co., 7" tall, five actions ....60 / 90 / 120

"Jolly Pianist," 1950s, Marusan Co., 8" high, five actions ....100 / 150 / 200

"Jolly Santa on Snow," 1950s, Alps Co., 12½" tall, four actions, two cycles (includes tin skis) ....150 / 225 / 300

"Josie The Walking Cow," 1950s, Daiya Co., 14" long, 8½" high, seven actions, two cycles ....100 / 150 / 200

"Journey Pup," ca. 1950s, S&E Co., Four actions, remote control, 7½" long ....40 / 60 / 80

"Jumbo The Bubble Blowing Elephant," 1950s Y Co., 7¼" high, three actions, includes plastic bowl for bubble solution ....60 / 90 / 120

"Jungle Jumbo," 1950s, B.C. Co., 9" high, five actions ....90 / 135 / 180

"Jungle Trio," 1950s, Linemar, 8" high, eight actions, includes tin litho whistle, ...300 / 450 / 600

"Jupiter Robot," 1950s, Yonezawa Co., 12¾" tall, four actions............150 / 225 / 300

"Jupiter Rocket Launching Pad," 1960s, T-N Co., 8½" long, 7" high ....190 / 285 / 380

"K-55 Electric Tractor", ca. 1950s, M-T Co., 3 actions, 7" long ....60 / 90 / 120

"King Flying Saucer," 1960s, K.O. Co., 7½" diameter, three actions ....60 / 90 / 120

"King Size Fire Engine", 1960's, Bandai Co., three actions, 12½" long ....150 / 225 / 300

"Kissing Couple," 1950s, Ichida Co., 10¾" long, five actions.................150 / 225 / 300

"Kitchen-ette Stove and Sink," 1940s, no marking, 6½" long x 6¾" high, a minor toy, includes kitchen utensils and side tray and stoppers ....40 / 60 / 80

"Knight In Armor", 1950's, M-T Co., five actions, 10" tall, RARE ....1100 / 1650 / 2200

"Knight in Armor Target Game," 1950s, M-T Co., 12" tall, three actions (includes crossbow and rubber tipped darts) ....120 / 180 / 240

"Knitting Grandma," 1950s, T-N Co., 8½" tall, three actions ....100 / 150 / 200

"Kooky-Spooky Whistling Tree," 1950s, Marx Co., 14¼" tall, six actions, (two color schemes) Rare ....500 / 750 / 1000

"Ladder Fire Engine", 1950s, Linemar Co., five actions, 13" long.................................170 / 255 / 340

"Lady Pup Tending Her Garden," 1950s, Cragstan Co., 8" high, five actions ....140 / 210 / 280

"Lambo" - With Magnetic Trunk and Light, 1950s, Alps Co., seven actions, 16" long with trailer, (includes two tin logs and trailer), Rare ....210 / 315 / 420

"Laughing Clown Robot," 1960s, S-H Co., 14" tall, seven actions ....160 / 240 / 320

"Lectric Revolver," 1950s, Daisy Mfg. Co., 11½" long, three actions..........30 / 45 / 60

"Leo-The Growling Pet Lion With Magic Face-Change," 1970s, Toyiyama Co., 9" long, 2 cycles, three actions ....80 / 120 / 160

"Light House," 1950s, Alps Co., 8½" high, 6¾" x 6¾" base, five actions (includes detachable spin-ball tower) Rare ....300 / 450 / 600

"Lighted Freight Train," 1950s, Y Co., four actions, 25½" long, five pcs., 8 section track........................60 / 90 / 120

"Lighted Space Vehicle wtih Floating Satellite," 1960s, M-T Co., 8½" long, three actions (includes cell ball) ....140 / 210 / 280

"Linda Lee Laundromat," washing machine, 1940s, T-N Co., 6½" high, a minor toy ....20 / 30 / 40

Bongo Monkey, Chef Cook, Cola Drinking Bear.

Happy Fiddler Clown, Roarin' Jungle Lion, Mama Dog Feeding Hungry Baby Dog.

Patrol Helicopter, Cragstan Biplane, T360 Monoplane.

Western Badman-Red Gulch Bar, Drinker's Savings Bank.

Happy the Clown Puppet Show Drummer Mickey Mouse, Clown the Magician.

Jet Plane Base

Linemar Music Hall

Smoking Grandpa in Rocking Chair, Rocking Chair Bear, Mama Bear & Hungry Baby Bear, Pop Drinking Bear.

Happy Plane T.P.S. Co., 3 actions, mint price $200.

Courtesy Don Hultzman. Photos by Don Hultzman and Ron Chojnacki unless marked otherwise.

Jungle Trio.

Loop the Loop Clown.

	C6	C8	C10
"**Linemar** Music Hall", 1950's, Linemar Co., four actions, 8" high-7¾"x 5½" base	200	300	400
"**Lion**," 1950s, Linemar, 9" long, four actions	70	105	140
"**Lion** Target Game," 1950s, M-T Co., 7½" high, four actions (includes dart gun and darts)	110	165	220
"**Locomotive**-Continental Blue," 1970s, 13" long, four actions, M-T Co.	30	45	60
"**Loop** The Loop Clown", 1960s, T-N Co., minor toy, 10" high	60	90	120
"**Looping** Airplane," ca. 1960s, "Y" Co., Sears (distribution), minor toy, 14½" high, airplane 5" long	30	45	60
"**Looping** Space Tank", 1960's, Daiya Co., five actions, 8" long	250	375	500
"**Los** Walky-Son" 1960s, Geyper Co., 11½" high, 15" wide, includes detachable rifles and baton	120	180	240
"**Lost** in Space Robot," 1966, Remco Co., 13" tall, three actions	200	300	400
"**Love**-Beetle-Volks," 1960s, K.O. Co., 10" long, three actions	60	90	120
"**Lucky** Crane," 1950s, M-T Co., 8½" high, five actions (includes tin prizes) RARE	200	300	400
"**Lucky** Locomotive," 1950s, Marusan Co., four actions, 8" long	40	60	80
"**Lucky** Seven -Dice Throwing Monkey," 1960s, Alps Co., 11½" tall, five actions (includes plastic straw hat, five dice, two game sheets, twenty chips)	90	135	180
"**Lufthansa** Jet Airplane," 1960s, GAMA Co., 19½" long, 18½" wingspan, three actions	110	165	220
"**Lunar** Captain", 1960's, T-N Co., 13½" long extended, five actions	110	165	220
"**Lunar** Loop/Swing and Orbiting Action," 1960s, Daiya Co., 14" high, 12" diameter hoop, three actions	90	135	180
"**M-101** Aston Martin Secret Ejector Car," 1960s, Daiya Co., 11" long, six actions, (includes ejectable passenger)	140	210	280
"**Mac** the Turtle," 1960's , "Y" Co., 8" high, five actions	90	135	180
"**Magic** Action Bulldozer," 1950's, T-N Co., 9½" long, three actions	90	135	180
"**Magic** Color Moon Express," 1960s, S-H Co., 13" long, four actions	60	90	120
"**Magic** Man Clown", 1950s, Marusan Co., five actions, 11" tall	260	390	520
"**Magic** Snowman," 1950's, M-T Co., (Santa Creations) 11¼" tall, four actions, (includes detachable tin broom, plastic pipe and styro ball).	130	195	260
"**Magnet** Rail Moon Orbiter," 1960s, "Y" Co., 14" high, 12" diameter,minor toy.	60	90	120
"**Mainstreet**", 1950's, Linemar Co., three actions, 19½" long	180	270	360
"**Major** Tooty," 1960s, Alps Co., (R.F.), 14" tall, three actions, includes drum and hat	90	135	180
"**Make** Up Bear", 1960s, M-T Co., four actions, 9" high, Rare	280	420	560
"**Mambo**-the Jolly Drumming Elephant," 1950s, Alps Co., 9½" high, six actions, includes cymbals and stand	100	150	200
"**Man** in Space - Astronaut," 1960s, Alps Co., 6" tall, a minor action toy	80	120	160
"**Mars** Explorer," Robot, 1950s, S-H Co., 9½" tall, seven actions	200	300	400
"**Mars** Explorer"-Astronaut, 1960's, S-H Co., six actions 10" tall	250	375	500
"**Mars** King Robot No. 12101," 1960s, S-H Co., 9½" tall, four actions	210	315	420
"**Marshall** Wild Bill," 1950s, Y Co., 10½" tall, four actions, 2 cycles, includes tin cowboy hat	180	270	360
"**Martian** Robot," 1970s, SJM Co., 12" tall, four actions	60	90	120
"**Marvelous** Car", T-Bird, 1956, T-N Co., three Actions, 11" long	250	375	500
"**Marvelous** Fire Engine, 1960s, "Y" Co., 11" long, four actions	40	60	80
"**Marvelous** Mike," 1950s, Saunders Co., 17" long, four actions	120	180	240
"**Maxwell** Coffee-Loving Bear," 1960s, T-N Co., 10" tall, five actions	100	150	200
"**McGregor**," 1960s, T-N Co., 12" tall when standing, six actions	90	135	180
"**Mechanic Robot**," 1960s, "Y" Co., 12" tall, five actions	120	180	240
"**Mechanized Robot, The**," ('Robby') 1950's, T-N Co., 13½" tall, fouractions, Rare	600	900	1200
"**Mercury** Explorer," 1960's, T.P.S. Co., 8" long, five actions	120	180	240
"**Mercury** X-1 Space Saucer," 1960s, "Y" Co., 8" diameter, four actions	60	90	120
"**Merry** Christmas"-Santa In His Rockin' Chair, 1950s, Alps Co., three actions, 21" tall assembled, (includes detachable tree and stocking) RARE	500	750	1000

Lucky Seven - Dice Throwing Monkey.

Magic Man Clown.

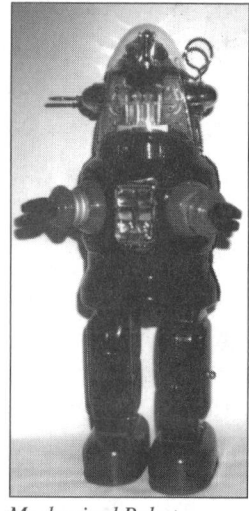

Mechanized Robot (Robbie).

Mainstreet.

Marshal Wild Bill.

Marvelous Mike.

Marvelous Fire Engine.

Mischievous Monkey.

Mickey Mouse Locomotive.

Military Command Car.

Mighty Mike, the Barbell lifter.

*Courtesy Don Hultzman.
Photos by
Don Hultzman and
Ron Chojnacki
unless marked otherwise.*

270

	C6	C8	C10
"Merry Ice Cream Truck", 1960s, Bandai Co., 10½" long, five actions ..80	120	160
"**Mexicali** Pete-Drum Player," 1960s, Alps Co., 10½" high, three actions 60	90	120
"**Mickey** Mouse and Donald Duck Fire Engine," 1960s, M-T Co., 16" long, three actions 180	270	360
"Mickey Mouse Locomotive," 1960's, M-T Co., six actions, 9" long.........190	285	380
"Mickey Mouse Melody Railroad," 1960's, Frankonia Co., minor toy, 6¾" long (handcar), (includes 4 circular rails with xylophone bars), RARE..................800	1200	1600
"Mickey Mouse on Handcar," 1960s, M-T Co., 9¾" long, 7¾" high, three actions 200	300	400
"Mickey Mouse Sand Buggy," 1960s, M-T Co., 11" long, four actions.....140	210	280
"Mickey Mouse Trolley," 1960s, M-T Co., 11" high, three actions............140	210	280
"Mickey the Magician," 1960s, Linemar, 10" tall, four actions, includes tin rabbit, Rare 800	1200	1600
"**Mighty** Mike the Barbell Lifter Bear," 1950s, "K" Co., 10½" tall, four actions 120	180	240
"Mighty Kong," 1950s, Marx, 11" tall, five actions.............................160	240	320
"Mighty Robot," 1960s, K-O Co., 11½" tall, four actions...................1000	1500	2000
"**Military** Air Defense Truck", 1950's, Linemar Co., four actions, 15¼" long 90	135	180
"Military Command Car", 1950's, T-N Co., five actions, 11" long 150	225	300
"Military Jet Plane," 1960s, Marx Co., 16" long, 14" wingspan, three actions 90	135	180
"Military Police Car," 1950s, Linemar, 8½" long, six actions 90	135	180
"**Million** Bus", 1950s, KKK Co., three actions, 12" long, RARE..............1250	1875	2500
"**Mimi** Poodle with Bone," 1950s, T-N Co., 11" long, 10" high, five actions, two cycles, (includes plastic bone)............................40	60	80
"**Mischievous** Monkey," 1950s, M-T Co., 18" tall, six actions, includes tree and monkey............................200	300	400
Mischievous Monkey with Bulldog," 1950s, T-N Co., 12" high, four actions 220	330	440

	C6	C8	C10
"**Miss** Friday- The Typist," 1950s, T-N Co., 8" tall, six actions, removable head...120	180	240
"**Missile** Robot-Mr. 45," M-T Co., 17½" tall, five actions.....................80	120	160
"**Mr.** Atom - The Electronic Walking Robot," 1950s, Advance Doll & Toy Co., 17" tall, six actions..........500	750	1000
"Mr. Atomic" robot, 1950s, Cragstan, 11" tall, three actions, rare 2500	3750	5000
"Mr. Baseball Junior," 1950s, T-N Co., 7" high, three actions 200	300	400
"Mr. Chief" Robot, 1950s, K-O Co., 12" tall, four actions......................400	600	800
"Mr. Fox, the Magician - With the Magical Disappearing Rabbit," 1960s, Y Co., 9" tall, five actions, includes plastic rabbit 240	360	480
"Mr. Hustler Robot," 1960s, Taiyo Co., 11" tall, six actions 160	240	320
"Mr. MacPooch"-Taking A Walk And Smoking His Pipe, 1950's, SAN Co., four actions, 8" tall 110	165	220
"Mr. Magoo Car," 1961, Hubley Co., 9" long, five actions, includes cloth roof top........................140	210	280
"Mr. Mercury" Type I (all tin), 1960s, Marx Co., 13" tall, seven actions...400	600	800
"Mr. Mercury" Type II (lighted), 1960s, Marx Co., seven actions 400	600	800
"Mr. Robot" - The Mechanical Brain, 1950s, Alps Co., three actions, 8" tall, RARE................................600	900	1200
"Mr. Strong Pup - Weight Lifting Dog", 1950s, "K" Co., 9" tall, five actions ..100	150	200
Mr. Traffic Policeman," 1950s, A-I Co., 14" tall, 6"x6" base, four actions 180	270	360
"Mr. Zerox," 1960s, S-H Co., 9½" tall, four actions 140	210	280
"**Mix-ette** Mixer," 1940s, KDP Co., 9" high when assembled, a minor toy, includes mixer stand and bowl 20	30	40
"**Mobile** Satellite Tracking Station", 1960's, Y Co., six actions, 9" long, (includes detachable antenna) Rare 400	600	800
"Mobile Space T.V. Unit With Trailer," 1960's T-N Co., six actions, RARE ..500	750	1000
"**Mod** Monster - Blushing Frankenstein," 1960s, T-N Co., 13¼" tall, five actions 150	225	300
Modern Robot," 1950s, Yoshiya Co., four actions, 12" tall, RARE ..450	675	900
"**Monkee**-Mobile," 1967, ASC Co. (Aoshin Co.) minor toy, 12" long ..280	420	560

Light House.

Lucky Crane with Box.

Magic Snowman.

"Lost in Space" Robot.

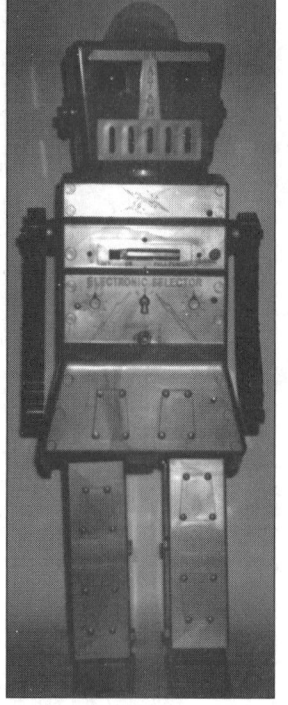

Mr. Atom - Robot.

M-101 Aston-Martin Secret Ejector Car.

Mr. Robot

Mobile Satellite Tracking System.

Mickey Mouse on Handcar.

Moon Patrol Space Rover.

Courtesy Don Hultzman. Photos by Don Hultzman and Ron Chojnacki unless marked otherwise.

272

Moon Globe Orbiter.

Musical Showboat.

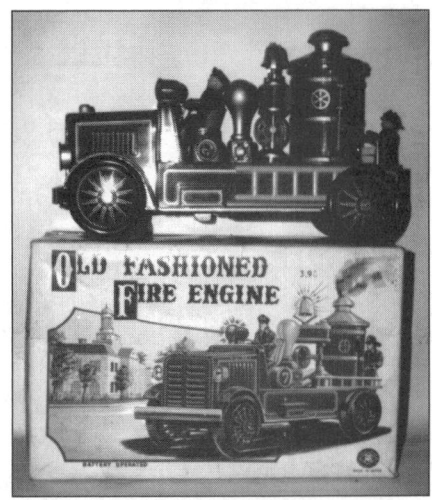

Old Fashioned Fire Engine.

"Ol' MacDonald's Farm Truck". Courtesy
Mapes Auctioneers & Appraisers.

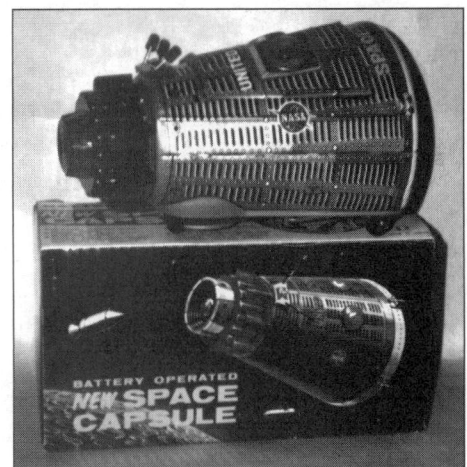

New Space Capsule.

Mystery Police Car.

Warpath Indian, Nutty Mad Indian, Indian Joe.

Papa Bear - Reading & Drinking
In his Old Rocking Chair.

Tank (M-81), Tank (M-35), Tank (M-56), Tank (M-197).

Nautilus SSN 571 Submarine.

Monkee-
Mobile

*Courtesy Don Hultzman. Photos by Don Hultzman and
Ron Chojnacki unless marked otherwise.*

273

	C6	C8	C10
"**Monkey** Artist," 1950s, Alps Co., 8" high, five actions	180	240	360
"**Monkey** Handcar," 1950s, T-N Co., 7" high, three actions	60	90	120
"**Monkey** On A Picnic," 1950s, Alps Co., 9½" high seven actions	150	225	300
"**Monorail** Rocket Ship," 1950s, Linemar Co., 10" long with supports and rail rods, minor toy	140	210	280
"**Monster** Robot," 1970s, S-H Co., three actions, 10" tall	50	75	100
"**Moon** Astronaut," 1950s, Daiya Co., 9" tall, four actions	500	750	1000
"Moon Explorer" Robot, 1960s, Bandai Co., 17½" tall (feet to antenna top), five actions, rare	600	900	1200
"**Moon** Explorer," Vehicle, 1960s, Gakken Co., five actions, 11" long	150	225	300
"**Moon** Express," Magic Color, 1950's, TPS Co., 12" long, three actions	120	180	240
"**Moon** Globe Orbiter," ca. 1960s, "Y" Co., (Mego) 3 actions, rocket orbits globe, noise, lights, 10½" high	70	105	140
"**Moon** Orbiter," 1960s, Y Co., minor toy, 4" long, includes 6 sections of track and trestles	90	135	180
"**Moon** Patrol Space Rover," 1960s, Gakken Toy Co., 11½" long, five actions	140	210	280
"**Moon** Rocket," 1950s, Y Co., 15¼" long, three actions. Rare	400	600	800
"**Moon** Traveler - Apollo Z," 1960s, T-N Co., 12" long, 15" extended, five actions	120	180	240
"**Mother** Bear-Sitting and Knitting In Her Old Rocking Chair," 1950s, M-T Co., 9½" high, four actions	170	255	340
"**Motorcycle** Cop", 1950s, Daiya Co., 10½" long, 8¼" high, five actions	200	300	400
"**Mountain** Cable Car," 1950s, Cragstan Co., 9" long, minor toy, includes cable	60	90	120
"**Movieland** Drive-In Theater," 1959, Remco Co., 14" long, minor toy (includes 6 small cars ad cards, filmstrips)	100	150	200
"**Multi** Action Electra Jet - KLM Royal Dutch Airlines PH-DSF," 1960's T-N Co., 14" long, 17" wingspan, three actions	90	135	180
"**Mumbo** Jumbo," (Hawaiian drummer,) 1960s, Alps Co., 9¾" high, three actions	80	120	160
"**Musical** Bank Organ Grinder & Monkey," 1950s, HTC Co., 8" tall, four actions, includes test coin and detachable celluloid monkey, Rare	300	450	600
"**Musical** Bear" (Drum and cymbals), 1950s, Linemar Co., 10" tall, six actions (including detachable tin horn)	140	210	280
"**Musical** Bulldog Playing Piano," 1950s, SAN Co., 8½" tall, 6"x 9" base, four actions, Rare	600	900	1200
"**Musical** Cadillac Car", 1950s, Irco Co., 9" long, minor toy	300	450	600
"**Musical** Clown" (New Adventures of Clown), 1960s, T-N Co., 9" tall, three actions	140	210	280
"**Musical** Comic Jumping Jeep," 1970s, M-T Co., 12" long, six actions	60	90	120
"**Musical** Drummer Robot," 1950s, T-N Co., 8¼" tall, three actions, RARE	4000	6000	8000
"Musical Jackal," 1950s, Linemar Co., 10" tall, six actions	150	225	300
"**Musical** Jolly Chimp," 1960s, C-K Co., 10½"high, five actions, two cycles	30	45	60
"**Musical** Marching Bear," 1950s, Alps Co., four actions, 11" tall, (includes detachable tin horn)	120	180	240
"**Musical** Showboat," 1960s, Gakken Toy Co., 13" long, minor toy, (Includes two detachable smokestacks)	60	90	120
"**My** Fair Dancer," 1950s, Haji Co., 10½" tall, minor toy	90	135	180
"**Mystery** Fire Chief Car No. 81", 1950s, Sanshin Co., 9¼" long, three actions	100	150	200
"**Mystery** Plane," 1950s, T-N Co., four actions, 10" long, 10½"wingspan	120	180	240
"**Mystery** Police Car," 1960s, T-N Co., 9¾" long, 6" wide, 4" high, three actions	100	150	200
"**NAR** Television Truck," 1950s, Linemar Co., 12" long, four actions (includes six strip film inserts)	280	420	560
"**NBC** Television Truck", 1950s, Linemar Co., five actions, 9" long	240	360	480

Tootsietoy Funnies sets, numbers 5101 - 5106 (Vehicles). Courtesy Christies East.

Structo Packard Dump Truck, No. 405 (Vehicles). Courtesy Joe and Sharon Freed.

Schoenhut "Every Boy Auto Build 5 in 1 Toy" (Vehicles). MacNary Collection. Photo: RLM.

Tootsietoy's Funnies Set (Vehicles). Clinton B. Seeley Collection. Courtesy Gail Seeley.

Steelcraft Inter-City Bus (Vehicles). Courtesy Joe and Sharon Freed.

Schieble Roadster, 18¼" long, spare tire on back (Vehicles). Courtesy Joe and Sharon Freed.

Top: Manoil No. 701 Sedan; Bottom, Left to Right: Barclay BV63 Station Wagon, Manoil No. 702 Coupe. Courtesy Chic Gast.

Barclay BV18 Cannon Car, battery powered headlight. This toy was advertised in a 1935 Butler Bros. catalog. Photo by Max Heiss.

Buddy L Emergency Auto Wrecker. Courtesy Thomas G. Nefos, Federal Shipping Network.

Tonka from 1962; its No. 420 Luggage Service - Tractor and Trailer. Courtesy Thomas G. Nefos, Federal Shipping Network.

Nylint's new in 1964 No. 6600 Mobile Home. Courtesy Thomas G. Nefos, Federal Shipping Network.

A14 B50 by Bandai (Japanese Tin). Photo by Ron Smith

A27 German Biplane (Japanese Tin). Photo by Ron Smith.

A16 Spitfire by HTC (Japanese Tin). Photo by Ron Smith.

A19 Zero by unknown manufacturer (Japanese Tin). Photo by Ron Smith.

A23 Disney Comic Plane by Linemar (Japanese Tin). Photo by Ron Smith.

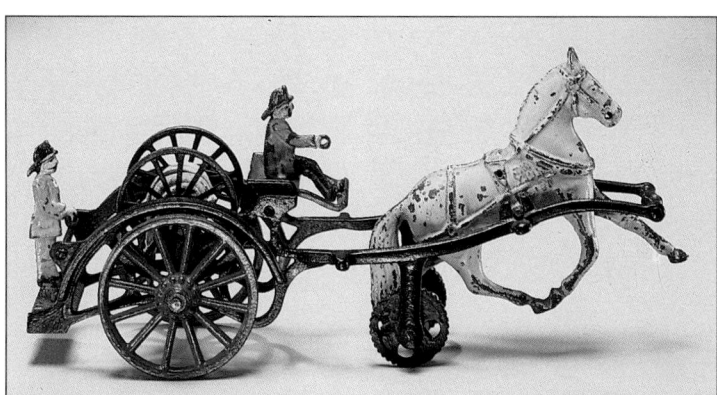

Carpenter Hose Cart, cast iron, circa 1880 (Animal-Drawn). Courtesy Sotheby's New York.

Hillclimber Horseless Carriage, woman driver. Photo Courtesy Mark S. Brumback.

Ives Phoenix Pumper (Animal-Drawn). Courtesy Sotheby's New York.

Gibbs No. 53 "Pony Circus" wagon. (Animal-Drawn). Courtesy Wilkinson Collection, Detroit Antique Toy Museum.

Hubley Roman Chariot, three large horses (Animal-Drawn). Courtesy Sotheby's New York.

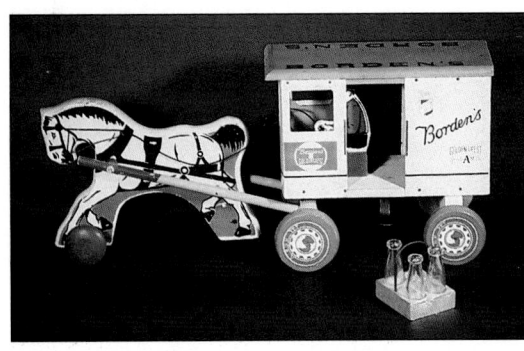

Rich Toys "Borden's Golden Crest" wooden dairy cart (Animal-Drawn). Courtesy Joe and Sharon Freed.

Rich Toys "Budweiser" Beer Wagon. Courtesy Joe and Sharon Freed.

Springing Cat (Mechanical Banks). Courtesy Sotheby's New York.

Tammany Bank (Mechanical Banks). Courtesy Wilkinson Collection - Detroit Antique Toy Museum.

All-Nu paper Soldiers, circa 1942 (Paper).

Uncle Sam, umbrella (Mechanical Banks). Courtesy Wilkinson Collection - Detroit Antique Toy Museum.

Marx "Main Street" (Tin Wind-Up). Courtesy Don Hultzman. Photo by Ron Chojnacki.

Unique Hobo Train, 1920s (Tin Wind-Up). MacNary Collection. Photo: RLM.

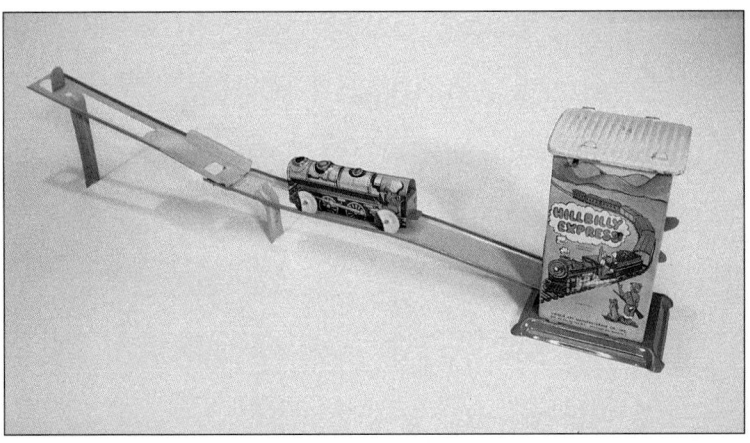

Unique Art "Hillbilly Express," Tin Wind-Up, #515. MacNary Collection. Photo: RLM.

Lehmann Tut Tut (Tin Wind-Up). Courtesy Christie's East.

Marx Whoopee Car, laughing cows on wheels (Tin Wind-Up). Courtesy Don Hultzman. Photo by Ron Chojnacki.

Marx "Balky Mule," post WWII (Tin Wind-Up). Courtesy Don Hultzman. Photo by Ron Chojnacki.

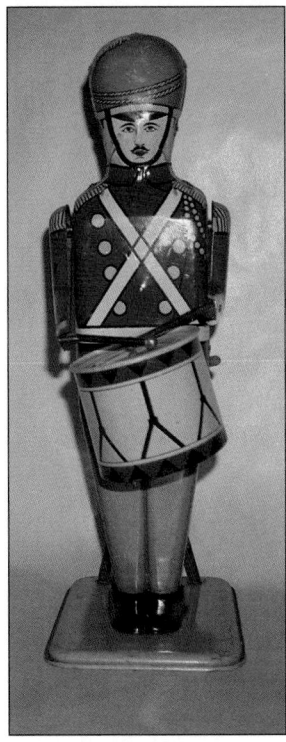

Wolverine "Drum Major" No. 27 (Tin Wind-Up). Courtesy Don Hultzman. Photo by Ron Chojnacki.

Marx Sparkling Soldier Motorcycle (Tin Wind-Up). Courtesy Don Hultzman. Photo by Ron Chojnacki.

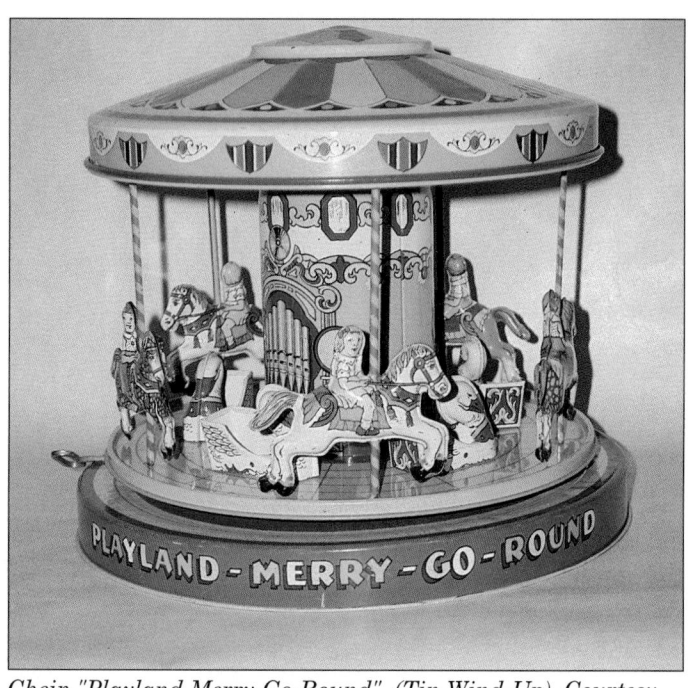

Chein "Playland Merry-Go-Round" (Tin Wind-Up). Courtesy Don Hultzman. Photo by Ron Chojnacki.

Marx "Honeymoon Express," 1920s, Tin Wind-Up. Courtesy Don Hultzman. Photo by Ron Chojnacki

Marx "New York" (Tin Wind-Up). Courtesy Wilkinson Collection, Detroit Antique Toy Museum.

Wolverine "Zilotone" Tin Wind-Up. Courtesy Don Hultzman. Photo by Ron Chojnacki.

Chein Alligator with native on its back (Tin Wind-Up). Courtesy Joe and Sharon Freed.

Marx "Big Parade" (Tin Wind-Up). Courtesy Don Hultzman.

Ohio Art "Jungle Eyes Shooting Gallery" (Tin Wind-Up). Courtesy Don Hultzman. Photo by Ron Chojnacki.

Mechanized Robot (Battery-Operated). Courtesy Sotheby's New York.

Marx Doughboy Tank (Tin Wind-Up), circa 1920s. Courtesy Don Hultzman. Photo by Don Hultzman.

Marx "Jumpin' Jeep" (Tin Wind-Up). Courtesy Don Hultzman. Photo by Ron Chojnacki.

Marx "U.S.S. Washington" Tin Wind-Up. Courtesy Don Hultzman. Photo by Ron Chojnacki.

Marx "Old Jalopy" (Tin Wind-Up). Courtesy Don Hultzman. Photo by Ron Chojnacki.

Marx "Speed Boy Delivery" (Tin Wind-Up). Courtesy Joe and Sharon Freed.

Katz Toys, NY "The Red Arrow" No. 137 single engine plane (Aircraft). Courtesy Joe and Sharon Freed.

Barclay podfoot soldiers in red, 1950s. MacNary Collection. Photo: RLM.

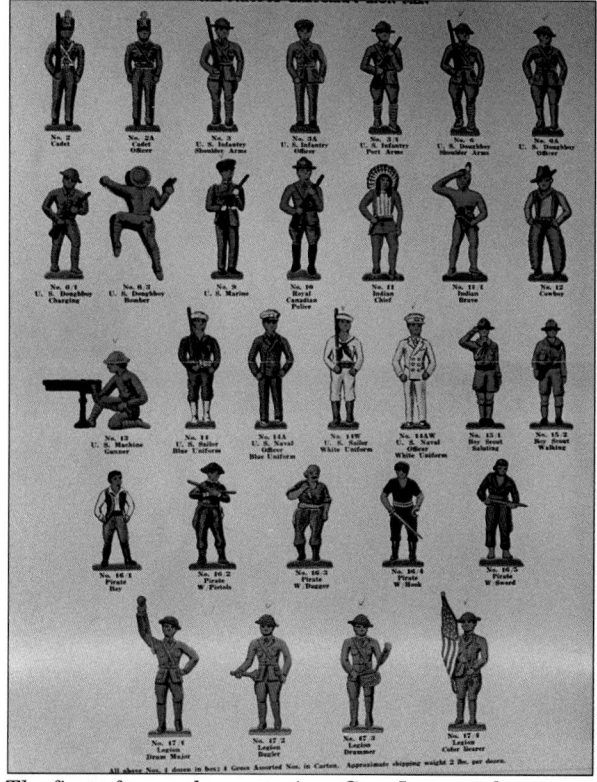

The first of two color pages in a Grey Iron catalog hand-stamped "April 20, 1936". Courtesy John Wright Co.

Hartland No. 801 Lone Ranger (newer) (Action Figures). Photo by Gary J. Linden.

Jack Armstrong paper airplane models (#6 Japanese "Nakajima (Oscar) and #5 American "Hellcat", Wheaties Premiums. MacNary Collection. Photo: RLM.

Dick Tracy Squad Car No. 1, Marx, 11" long (Comic Character). Courtesy Thomas G. Nefos, Federal Shipping Network.

Hi-Way Henry (Comic Character). Courtesy Sotheby's New York.

"Li'l Abner and his Dogpatch Band". Photo Courtesy Scott Smiles.

Buck Rogers Rocket Police Patrol (Comic Character). Courtesy Don Hultzman. Photo by Ron Chojnacki.

Flash Gordon Rocket Fighter (Comic Character). Courtesy Don Hultzman. Photo by Ron Chojnacki.

Jaymar comic toys, maximum height 5" (Comic Character). Courtesy Christie's East.

Toonerville Trolley - Dent, cast iron (Comic). Courtesy Don Hultzman. Photo by Ron Chojnacki.

Left to Right: Henry and his Brother, Henry's Mahout on Donkey, Henry on Trapeze (Comic Character). Courtesy Christie's East.

Popeye & Olive Oyl Jiggers (Comic Character). Courtesy Don Hultzman. Photo by Ron Chojnacki.

Katzenjammer Kids, Mama spanking kid (Comic Character). Courtesy Christie's East.

Popeye in a Rowboat, 1935, Hoge (Comic Character). Courtesy Christie's East.

Uncle Wiggily, Marx Crazy Car (Comic Character). Courtesy Don Hultzman. Photo by Ron Chojnacki.

Lone Ranger, 1938, Marx wind-up (on "Range Rider" rocker base), 10½" high (Movies, Radio, Television). Courtesy Don Hultzman. Photo by Ron Chojnacki.

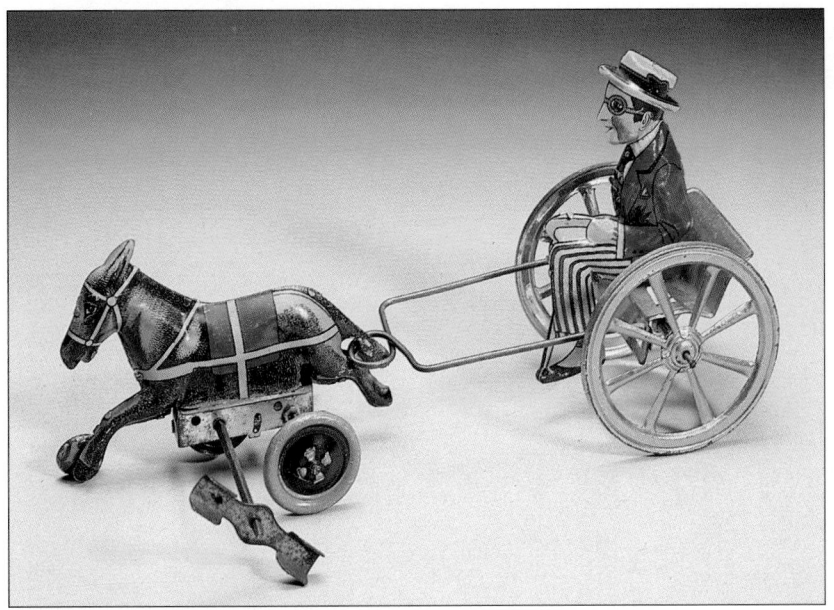

Harold Lloyd Donkey Cart, tin litho, Spanish (Movies, Radio, Television). Courtesy Christies East.

Andy tin wind-up (Movies, Radio, Television). Courtesy Don Hultzman. Photo by Ron Chojnacki.

Joe Penner tin wind-up (Movies, Radio, Television). Courtesy Don Hultzman. Photo by Ron Chojnacki.

Amos & Andy Fresh Air Taxi (Movies, Radio, Television). Courtesy Don Hultzman. Photo by Ron Chojnacki.

Cecil Sea Serpent, stuffed talking doll, Mattel. Photo by Brad Krewson.

Beany Doll, talks, 17" high, Mattel (Movies, Radio, Television). Photo by Brad Krewson.

Roy Rogers "Ranch Lantern" (Movies, Radio, Television). Courtesy Don Hultzman. Photo by Ron Chojnacki.

Mickey & Minnie Mouse Playland (Disney). Courtesy Christie's East.

Pinocchio "Walking Pinocchio". Courtesy Ed Hyers Antique Toys.

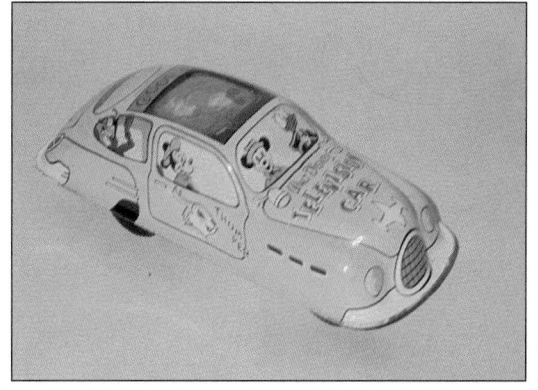

Walt Disney Television Car (Disney). Courtesy Don Hultzman. Photo by Ron Chojnacki.

Pecos Bill, Marx wind-up, plastic (Disney). Photo by Don Hultzman.

"Roy Rogers," Hubley, 1941, 8" long. Photo by Charles W. Best

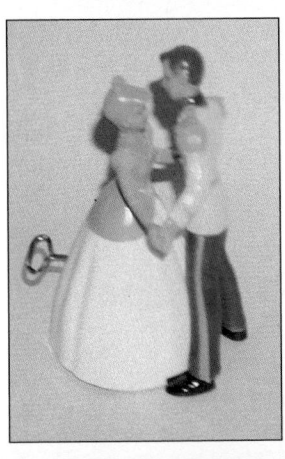

Cinderella and Prince - Dancing, No. 7000. Courtesy Don Hultzman. Photo by Ron Chojnacki.

"G-Man Automatic," Marx (Guns). Courtesy Don Hultzman. Photo by Ron Chojnacki.

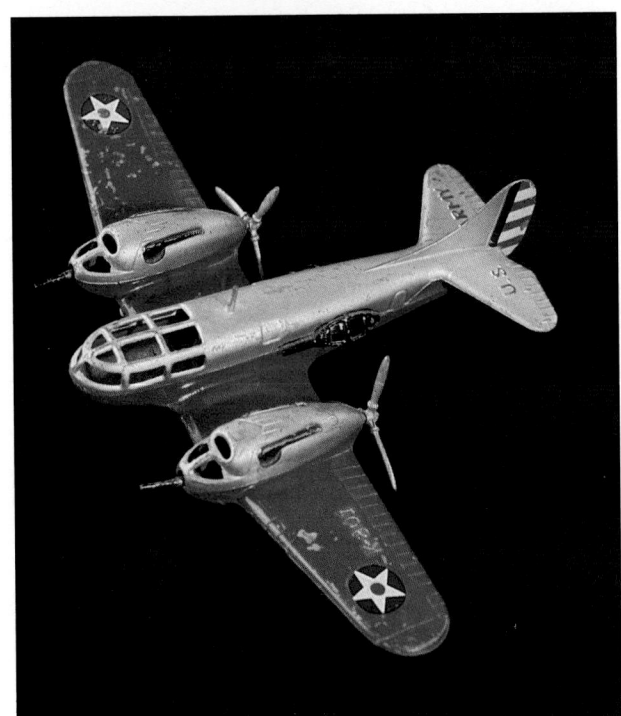

Hubley H2 Bell Airacuda. Photo by Perry R. Eichor.

Marx "Skycruiser Stratoliner 700" with Manoil Hostess M61. Photo by Ron Fink.

Various Tootsietoy boxes for its aircraft sold in the 1930s and 1940s. Photo by Perry R. Eichor.

Four versions of Tootsietoy's 119 Army Plane, originally issued in 1936 and representing the Northrup C-19. Photo by Perry R. Eichor.

Schoenhut: A majority of the pieces from Teddy Roosevelt's Adventures in Africa. Photo by Blossom Abell.

Argo Aircraft Carrier, 36″ long. Missing are the airplanes and signal flags, but the empty midsection is how the toy was sold in 1955. The sailors are by Manoil. Photo by Ron Fink.

Ives Fire Engine House (Miscellaneous) and Ives Fire Pumper, 2-horse, 13" long. Courtesy Sotheby's New York.

Dancers, black, Automatic Toy Works, Ives Judge, clockwork, circa 1880 (Miscellaneous). Courtesy Sotheby's New York.

Ives Walking Horse, 10" long, circa 1890s (Miscellaneous). Courtesy Sotheby's New York.

Left to Right: Fanny Brice (Baby Snooks), Mortimer Snerd, 13" high, both by Ideal. Courtesy Wilkinson Collection, Detroit Antique Toy Museum.

Ives Crawling Baby, on its original box (Miscellaneous).
Courtesy Wilkinson Collection, Detroit Antique Toy Museum.

Wolverine "Post Office" (Miscellaneous). Courtesy Don Hultzman. Photo by Ron Chojnacki.

Crandall "Crandall's District School" (Miscellaneous). Courtesy Wilkinson Collection, Detroit Antique Toy Museum.

Keystone "Keystone Fire Department" (Miscellaneous) and Hubley Ladder Truck. Photo by Ron Fink.

	C6	C8	C10
"**Neptune** Tugboat," 1950s, M-T Co., 15" long, 7" high, four actions	70	105	140
"**New** Astronaut" Robot, 1970s, S-H Co., 9½" tall, six actions	70	105	140
"**New** Bell Ringer Choo Choo", locomotive, 1960s, M-T Co., 10" long, three actions	40	60	80
"**New** Space Capsule", 1960s, S-H Co., six actions, 9" long	110	165	220
"**News** Service Car," 1960s, TPS Co., 10" long, four actions	120	180	240
"**Non**-Stop Robot," 1960s, M-T Co., 15" tall, three actions, Rare	600	900	1200
"**Nutty** Mad Indian," 1960s, Marx, 12" tall, four actions	80	120	160
"**Nutty** Mads Car" (Drincar), 1960s, Marx Co., 9¼"long, three actions	140	210	280
"**Nutty** Nibs," 1950s, Linemar, 11½" tall, a minor action toy, includes litho bowl of nuts and steel ball, Rare	500	750	1000
"**007** Aston Martin," 1966, Gilbert Co., 11½" long, eight actions, (includes ejectable passenger)	170	255	340
"**007** Secret Agent's Car," (Impala), 1960s, Spesco Co., (Joy Toy), 15" long, five actions	170	255	340
"**Ol**' Macdonald's Farm Truck", 1960's, Frankonia, four actions (includes plastic pig, cow and chicken)	100	150	200
"**Ol**' Sleepy Head Rip," 1950s, "Y" Co., 9" long, seven actions,	140	210	280
"**Old** Fashioned Fire Engine," 1950's, M-T Co., four actions, 12½" long	100	150	200
"**Old** Fashioned Car," 1950s, S-H Co., 10" long, four actions	40	60	80
"**Old** Fashioned Telephone Bear," (?) 1950s, M-T Co., 9½" high, four actions	100	150	200
"**Old** Ford Touring Car," 1950s, Z Co., 10" long, four actions	40	60	80
"**Old** Time Automobile," 1950s, "Y" Co., 8¾" long, three actions (includes detachable tin litho driver and steering wheel)	80	120	160
"**Old** Timer," Car, 1950s, Cragstan Co., 9" long-three actions	90	135	180
"**Oldtimer** Automoball," 1950s, M-T Co., 10" long, three actions, includes celluloid ball	80	120	160
"**Oldtimer** Sunday Driver," 1960's, Daiya Co., 9" long, four actions	60	90	120
"**Overland** Choo Choo Express" locomotive, 1950s, M-T Co., 14" long, a minor action toy	20	30	40
"**Overland** Stage Coach," 1960s, Ichida Co., 18" long, four actions	100	150	200
"**P-51** Mustang Shooting Fighter Plane", 1950's, T-N Co., minor toy, 9" long, 9" wingspan	80	120	160
"**Pacific** Piping Express Locomotive," 1960s, Kanto Toy Co., 14" long, four actions	30	45	60
"**Pan** Am Sky Taxi-Helicopter," 1960s, Haji Co., 3 actions, 11" long	50	75	100
"**Pan** American World Airways 'Seven Seas' DC-7," 1950s, T-N Co., 15" long, 19" wingspan, five actions	140	210	280
"**Panda** Bear," 1970s, M-T Co., (Masudaya Co.), 10" long, four actions, mostly plastic	30	45	60
"**Papa** Bear - Reading & Drinking in his Old Rocking Chair," 1950s, M-T Co., four actions, 10" high	120	180	240
"**Passenger** Bus," 1950s, "Y" Co.,16" long, four actions	230	345	560
"**Pat** O'Neill," 1960s, T-N Co., 12" tall, standing, six actions	110	165	220
"**Pat** The Dog", 1950s, NGS Co., 9½" long, five actions, two cycles	30	45	60
"**Pat** the Roaring Elephant," 1950s, "Y" Co., 9" long with attached baby elephant, four actions	110	165	220
"**Patrol** Auto-Tricycle," 1960s, T-N Co., 19" long, 7½" high, four actions	150	225	300
"**Patrol** Helicopter No. 7", 1960s, Bandai Co., 11" long, four actions	60	90	120
"**P.D.** No. 5 - Police Patrol Car," (Buick),1960s, Asakusa Toy Co., 11½" long, three actions	80	120	160
"**Penguin** on Tricycle," 1950s, T-N Co., 6½" high, three actions	90	135	180
"**Pepi**-Tumbling Monkey," 1960s, Yanoman Toy Co., 9½" high, minor toy	40	60	80
"**Peppermint** Twist Doll," 1950s, Haji Co., 12" tall, minor toy	150	225	300
"**Peppy** Puppy," 1950s, "Y" Co., 8" long, 6½" high, seven actions, two cycles, (includes tin litho bone)	50	75	100
"**Pet** Turtle," 1960s, Alps Co., 7" long, four actions, two cycles	70	105	140

	C6	C8	C10
"**Pete** the Space Man," 1960's, Bandai Co., 5" tall, minor action (Walking Mate Series)	50	75	100
"**Peter** The Drumming Rabbit," 1950s, Alps Co., (VIA-Cragstan), 13" tall, five actions	140	210	280
"**Phillips** '66' Power Yacht, 1950's, unmarked, minor toy, 18" long, (includes plastic parts for yacht and dock)	90	135	180
"**Pick-Up** Truck," T-N Co., 10" long, four actions	80	120	160
"**Picnic** Bear," 1950s, (with Coke, Pepsi and generic logo) Alps Co., 10" high, five actions	80	120	160
"**Picnic** Bunny," 1950s, Alps Co., 10" tall, four actions	90	135	180
"**Picnic** Monkey," 1950s, Alps Co., 4 actions, 10" high	70	105	140
"**Picnic** Poodle," 1950s, STS Co., 7" long, 7" high, four actions, two cycles	30	45	60
"**Piggy** Barbecue," 1950s, Y Co., 9½" tall, five actions, includes chef's hat and tin litho fried egg	130	195	260
"**Piggy** Cook," 1950s, Y Co., 9½" tall, 4"x 6" base, five actions, includes chef's hat and tin litho fried egg	140	210	280
"**Pinkee** the Farmer," 1950s, M-T Co., 9½" long, seven actions	100	150	200
"**Pinky** The Clown," 1950s, Rock Valley Toy Co., (Via) 10¼" tall, five actions, (includes tin litho propeller-ball on nose) Rare	180	270	360
"**Pinocchio** Playing London Bridge," 1962, T-N Co., (Rosko), 10" tall, three actions, includes xylophone	120	180	240
"**Pioneer** Covered Wagon," 1960s, Ichida Co., 14½" long, four actions (includes detachable canopy and driver)	110	165	220
"**Pipie** the Whale," 1950s, Alps Co., 12" long, minor toy	70	105	140
"**Piston** Action Bulldozer," 1960s, Linemar Co., 7½" long, two cycles	70	105	140
"**Piston** Action Robot", 1950's, T-N Co., three actions, 8¼" tall, resembles "Robbie"	900	1350	1800
"**Piston** Head Robot", 1960's, S-H Co., three actions, 10" tall	150	225	300
"**Piston** Robot," 1960s, S-H Co., 10½" tall, four action	110	165	220

	C6	C8	C10
"**Pistol** Pete," 1950s, Marusan Co., 5 actions, 10¼" high, includes tin hat	150	225	300
"**Planet** Explorer," 1950's, S-H Co., four actions, 9" long	120	180	240
"**Planet** Rover," wheeled tank, 1960s, J Co., 9" long, 6½" high, six actions	120	180	240
"**Planet** 'Y' Space Station," 1960's, T-N Co., three actions, 9" diameter	140	210	280
"**Playful** Pup in Shoe," 1960s, "Y" Co., 10" long, three actions	40	60	80
"**Playful** Puppy," 1950s, M-T Co., 7⅜" long, 5" high, four actions	100	150	200
"**Pluto**," 1960s, Linemar Co., 10" long, five actions	190	285	380
"**Polar** Bear," 1970s, Alps Co., 8" long, three actions	40	60	80
"**Police** Auto Cycle," 1960s, (motorcycle and plastic driver), Bandai Co., five actions. Remote Control	150	225	300
"**Police** Motorcycle," 1950s, M-T Co., 11¾" long, seven actions	180	270	360
"**Police** No. 5" Police Car, 1950's, T-N Co., four actions, 9½" long	90	135	180
"**Police** Patrol Jeep," 1960's T-N Co., 4 actions, lights, bump & go, noise, smoke, 9¼" long	90	135	180
"**Pom Pom** Tank", 1950's, S&E Co., 12" long, five actions	160	240	320
"**Popcorn** Eating Bear," 1950s, M-T Co., 9" high, five actions	100	150	200
"**Popcorn** Vendor," No. 4035, 1960s, S&E Co., 8" high, 7" long, six actions, includes litho umbrella	200	300	400
"**Popcorn** Vendor Truck," 1960s, T-N Co., 9" long, three actions	120	180	240
"**Popeye** and Rowboat With Moving Oars," 1950's, Linemar Co., three actions, 10" long. RARE	5000	7500	10000
"**Porsche** With Visible Engine," 1964, Bandai Co., 10" long, three actions	80	120	160
"**Poverty** Pup," bank, 1966, Poynter Products Co., 6" long, 4¼" high, three actions	60	90	120
"**Power** Shovel," 1950s, Alps Co., 15" long, extended, six actions	90	135	180
"**Pretty** Peggy Parrot," 1950s, T-N Co., 11" long, six actions	230	345	460
"**Princess** the French Poodle," 1950s, no markings, 9" long, 8" high, five actions	40	60	80

Pat O'Neill.

"Old Timer" Car, Cragstan. Courtesy Mapes Actioneers & Appraisers.

Pistol Pete.

Cragstan "Crapshooter", Tumbles the Bear, Overland Stage Coach.

Peppermint Twist Doll.

Piston Robot.

Piston Action Robot (Robbie).

Pioneer Covered Wagon.

Pinky The Clown, Circus Elephant, Tom & Jerry Handcar (Tom).

Puffy Morris, Piggy Cook, Cragstan "Crapshooting Monkey".

Courtesy Don Hultzman. Photos by Don Hultzman and Ron Chojnacki unless marked otherwise.

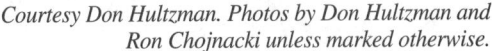

	C6	C8	C10
"**Professor** Owl," 1950s, E-T Co., 8" high, five actions, includes two discs..150	225	300
"**Project** Yankee Doodle," 1959, Remco Co., 15" long, six actions (includes plastic missiles, rockets & accessories) 60	90	120
"**Puffy** Morris," 1960s, Y Co., 10" tall, five actions, uses real cigarette...........90	135	180
"**Puzzled** Puppy," 1950s, M-T Co., 7½" long, 5" high, five actions 100	150	200
"**Queen** of the Sea," 1950's, M-T Co., four actions, 21½" long (includes detachable antenna and flag) 300	450	600
"**RCA**-NBC Mobile Color T.V. Truck," 1950s, Yonezawa Co., 9" long, four actions 300	450	600
"**R.R.** Line Locomotive," 1950's, Marx, 6½" long, four actions..........40	60	80
"**R-35** Robot," 1950's, M-T Co., 7½" tall, five actions..............................400	600	800
"**Racecar** #25", 1950's, Alps Co., three actions, 9" long, RARE.........800	1200	1600
"**Radar** Jeep", 1950's, T-N Co., 11" long, four actions 150	225	300
"**Radar** Robot," 1960s, T-N Co., 9" tall, three actions, remote robot-face control box 600	900	1200
"Radar Robot", 1970s, S-H Co., 12" tall five actions......................................70	105	140
"**Radar** Scope Space Scout", 1960s, S-H Co., three actions, 9¼" tall 120	180	240
"**Radio** Rex," 1920's, Elmwood Button Co., 5"x7" dog house, minor toy (includes cell. dog)..........................70	105	140
"**Railroad** Hand Car," 1950's, KDP Co., 8" long, a minor toy, includes rubber track 90	135	180
"**Railway** Yard - Shuttle Train," 1950's, ATC Co., 8" long, track 28" long, three actions, includes locomotive boxcar and track...........80	120	160
"**Ranger** Robot," 1950's Daiya Co., six actions, 11" tall.........................400	600	800
"**Ray** Gun," machine gun, 1950s, T-N Co., 17½" long, three actions, includes tripod....................................40	60	80
"**Reading** Bear," 1950's, Alps Co., 9" tall, five actions.............................100	150	200
"**Reversible** Diesel Electric Tractor," 1950s, Marx Co., minor toy...........50	75	100
"**Ricki**- The Begging Poodle," 1950s, Rock Valley Toys (VIA), 9" long, 8" high, 5 actions 30	45	60

	C6	C8	C10
"**Riverboat**," 1950s, Marusan Co., 12¾" long, three actions (includes detachable tin smokestack..............110	165	220
"**River** Queen Sidewheeler," 1950s, M-T Co., 13½" long, three actions 100	150	200
"**Road** Construction Roller," 1950s, Daiya Co., 8½" long, four actions ..60	90	120
"**Road Grader**," 1960s, T-N Co., 12" long, three actions 50	75	100
"**Road Roller**," 1950s, M-T Co., 9" long, four actions 60	90	120
"**Roaring** Gorilla," (white gorilla),1950s, T-N Co., 9¼" tall, five actions .... *see "Gorilla"*
"**Roaring** Gorilla Shooting Gallery," 1950s, M-T Co., 9½" tall, three actions (includes fold-out target box, tin gun, plastic darts)..............200	300	400
"**Roarin'** Jungle Lion," (?) 1950s, Marx Co., 16" long, nose to tail tip, four actions, 2 cycles 140	210	280
"**Robbie** Robot," 1950s, Yonezawa Co., 13" tall, five actions ....*see "Mechanized Robot"*
"**Robby** Space Patrol," 1950's, T-N Co., 12½" long, five actions, RARE.......2000	3000	4000
"**Robert** the Robot," 1950s, Ideal Toy Co., 14" tall, three actions..............120	180	240
"Robert the Robot Mechanical Bulldozer," 1950's, Ideal Toy Co., 9" long, four actions, RARE..........300	450	600
"**Robot**", 1950's, Y Co., minor toy, 6" tall, RARE................................600	900	1200
"**Robot**," 1960s, Y Co., 10½" tall, three actions 400	600	800
"**Robot 2500**," 1970s, Durham In-dustries, 10½" tall, four actions 60	90	120
"**Robotank** TR-2", 1960s, T-N Co., four actions, 5" high........140	210	280
"**Robotank-Z** Space Robot," 1960s, T-N Co., 10¼" high, five actions ...300	450	600
"Rock 'N' Roll Hotrod", (Dreamboat), 1950s, T-N Co., three actions, 7" long .100	150	200
"**Rock** 'N' Roll Monkey, 1950s, Rosko Co., 13" tall, five actions, includes plastic hat (2 variations)................140	210	280
"**Rocket** Express"-Rocket Ship Monorail, 1950s, Linemar Co., three actions, 10" long (20 pc. rail & girder set).............70	105	140
"**Rocket** Launching Pad," 1950s, "Y" Co., 8½" high, five actions (in-cludes tin litho satellite and rocket) ..140	210	280
"**Rocking** Chair Bear," (?) 1950s, M-T Co., 10" high, five actions 90	135	180

	C6	C8	C10
"Rocking Santa," 1950s, Alps Co., 10" high, four actions, Rare...................300	450	600
"**Roller** Skater," 1950s, Alps Co., minor toy, 12" tall 90	135	180
"**Rollerskating** Clown," 1950s, T.P.S. Co., 6" tall, minor toy, RARE.......300	450	600
"**Romance** Car M-841," 1950s, "M" Co., 8" long, three actions...............80	120	160
"**Rootbeer** Counter," 1960s, "K" Co., 8" long, 8" high, three actions (includes plastic barrel & glasses & tin tray)....100	150	200
"**Rosko** Robot," (blue), 1950's, Rosko Co., five actions, 13" tall, RARE.....1000	1500	2000
"**Rotate**-O-Matic Super Astronaut," 1960's, S-H Co., 11½" tall, six actions, two cycles 90	135	180
"**Rover** The Poodle Bell Ringer," 1960's, Alps Co., three actions-2 cycles, 10½" tall 60	90	120
"**Roy** Roger Western Telephone," Ideal Co., 1950s, 3 actions, 9" high.............80	120	160
"**Royal** Cub In Buggy," (pushed by Mama Bear), 1940s, S&E Co., 8" long, 8" high, six actions 120	180	240
"**Rudy** the Robot," 1968, Remco Co., 16¼" tall, four actions 110	165	220
"**SSN-571** Submarine"-Nautilus, 1950s, Marusan Co., minor toy, 16" long, (rudder extended) 110	165	220
"SSN-S71 Submarine", Skate, 1950s, Marusan Co., minor toy, 16" long (rudder extended) 110	165	220
"**Sam** the Shaving Man," 1960s, Plaything Toy Co., 11½" tall, seven actions, includes metal mirror 120	180	240
"**Sammy** Wong- The Tea Totaler," 1950s, T-N Co., 10" tall, four actions 140	210	280
"**Santa** Bank," 1960, HTC Co., (Trim a Tree), 11" high, four actions 150	225	300
"**Santa** Claus - Bellringer," 1950s, Santa Creations Co., 13" tall, five actions 80	120	160
"**Santa** Claus," No. M-750 (Sitting on House), 1950's, H.T.C. Co., 8" high, four actions 90	135	180
"**Santa** Claus on Handcar," 1960s, M-T Co., 10" high, three actions 90	135	180
"**Santa** Claus on Scooter," 1960s, M-T Co., 10" high, four actions.............90	135	180
"**Santa** Claus - Stands & Sits," 1960s, T-N Co., 10" tall, six actions..........90	135	180
"**Santa** Copter," 1960s, M-T Co., 8½" long, three actions 70	105	140
"**Santa** in Rocker," 1950s, Alps Co., 21" high, from base to tree top, four actions (includes detachable tree and stocking) rare................*see "Merry Christmas"*		
"**Santa** Claus Phone Bank," 1950s, S&E Co., 7 actions, 8" high, includes remote 4¾" high payphone RARE ...300	450	600
"Santa Sled", 1950s, T-N Co., 14" long, four actions 200	300	400
"**Santa** the Bellringer," 1950s, Chase Import Co., 7" high, minor toy (electro-magnet activated & Blinker bulb) Rare............100	150	200
"**Santa** Fe Diesel"-Battery Cable Train With Headlight, 1950s, T-N Co., minor toy, 13½" long, (2 pc. hookup) 70	105	140
"**Satellite** Interceptor"-Target set, 1950s, Linemar Co., minor toy (2 pc. set with 6½" long gun-telescope, 5" high blower and 2 plastic darts and styro ball)......200	300	400
"**Satellite** Target Game," 1960s, S-H Co., 8" high, 10½" wide, minor toy (includes celluloid ball and special gun) 100	150	200
"**Saxophone** Playing Monkey," 1950s, Alps Co., 9½" high, four actions ...120	180	240
"**School** Bus," 1950s, Cragstan, 20½" long, a minor toy 50	75	100
"**Sea** Bear #7 Racing Boat," 1950's, Bandai Co., minor toy 10" long......60	90	120
"**Seascape** Tugboat," 1950's, Marx Co., three actions, 6½" long 30	45	60
"**Secret** Service Action Car," (Green Hornet" motif), 1960s, ASC Co., 11" long, four actions 200	300	400
"**Serpent** Charmer," 1950s, Linemar Co., 7" high, four actions 200	300	400
"**Shaggy** The Friendly Pup," 1960s, Alps Co., 8" long, three actions......30	45	60
"**Shaking** Classic Car," 1960s, T-N Co. 7" long, four actions 50	75	100
"Shaking Old-Timer Car No. 2511-1", 1960s, T-N Co., 9" long, four actions, includes plastic driver........60	90	120
"**Shark**-U-Control Racing Car," 1961, Remco Ind. Inc., 19" long, all plastic, minor toy 80	120	160
"**Sheriff** Car," 1950's, T-N Co., four actions, 10" long.....................80	120	160
"**Shoe** Maker Bear," 1960s, T-N Co., 8½" high, three actions 110	165	220

Circus Lion.

Peter the Drummer Rabbit, Picnic Bear, Bunny the Magician.

Police Auto Cycle.

Cragstan "Schoolbus", Cragstan "Western Locomotive", New Bell Ringer Choo-Choo.

Police No. 5.

Pretty Peggy Parrot.

Mickey The Magician.

Mr. Fox the Magician-blowing magic bubbles, Professor Owl, Mr. Fox the Magician with the Magical Disappearing Rabbit.

Bubble Lion, Wild West Rodeo, Cragstan "Bullfighter".

Courtesy Don Hultzman. Photos by Don Hultzman and Ron Chojnacki unless marked otherwise.

Queen of the Sea.

Trumpet Playing Monkey, Monkey On A Picnic, Busy Housekeeper.

"Nutty Mads Car"

Power Shovel.

Police Motorcycle.

"Ol' Sleepy Head Rip", 1950's.

New Astronaut.

Musical Bulldog.

Playful Puppy.

Courtesy Don Hultzman. Photos by Don Hultzman and Ron Chojnacki unless marked otherwise.

Funland Cup Ride, Big Shot Cadillac.

Animated Squirrel, Cock-A-Doodle-Doo Rooster, Josie-the-Cow, Sparky-the-Seal.

Old Fashioned Telephone Bear, Cragstan Telly Bear, V.I.P. the Busy Boss, Telephone Bear.

Broadway Trolley, Battery Locomotive No. 123, A-B-C Fairy Train, Smoking Pop Locomotive-the General.

Roaring Gorilla Shooting Gallery.

Tom & Jerry Choo-Choo, Old Timer Automoball.

River Boat.

Root Beer Counter.

Robert The Robot Mechanical Bulldozer, Rare, Value $400 in mint.

Royal Cub in Buggy, Cry-Baby-In-Buggy.

Courtesy Don Hultzman. Photos by Don Hultzman and Ron Chojnacki unless marked otherwise.

	C6	C8	C10
"Shoe-Shaking Dog," 1950s, M-T Co., 8" long, 6" tall, five actions 30		45	60
"Shoe Shine Bear," 1950s, T-N Co., 9" tall, five actions 120		180	240
"Shoe Shine Joe," 1950s, Alps Co., 11" high, six actions....................130		195	260
"Shoe Shine Monkey," 1950s, T-N Co., 9" high, five actions 130		195	260
"Shooting Bear," 1950s, SAN Co., 10" tall, six actions.........................160		240	320
"Shooting Gorilla," 1950s, M-T Co., 12" high, four actions, includes gun and darts, Rare 160		240	320
"Shutterbug," photographer, 1950s, T-N Co., 9" tall, five actions 400		600	800
"Shuttling Freight Train," 1950's, Cragstan Co., six actions, 51" long-assembled (includes locomotive, lumber car, 4pc. of track, platform, logs)................................110		165	220
"Shuttling Train and Freight Yard," 1950s, Alps Co., 11" long, track 51" long, four actions, includes locomotive, baggage car, two platforms, litho luggage 120		180	240
"Sight Seeing Bus," 1960s, Bandai Co., 14½" long, four actions..........100		150	200
"Sight Seeing Bus", 1950s, Yonezawza Co., minor toy, 9" long 140		210	280
"Sikorsky Rescue Army Helicopter," 1950's, Alps Co., four actions,11" long 70		105	140
"Silver Bell Choo Choo," 1950s, Kanto Co., 12" long, three actions..30		45	60
"Silver Mountain Express Locomotive," 1960's, M-T Co., four actions, 15¾" long.......................................30		45	60
"Silver Mountain Locomotive," 1950s, M-T Co., 16" long, three actions 30		45	60
"Silver Ray Secret Weapon Space Scout," 1960's, S-H Co., six actions, 9" tall, RARE.................................750		1075	1500
"Silver Streak Locomotive No. 6682," 1950s, M-T Co., 16" long, four actions...30		45	60
"Singing Bird In Cage," 1950s, T-N Co., 9" high, 4"x 6" rectangular base., four actions 90		135	180
"Siren Fire Car," 1950's, M-T Co., 9" long, four actions 120		180	240
"Siren Patrol Car," 1960's, M-T Co., four actions, 12½" long 70		105	140

	C6	C8	C10
"Siren Patrol Motorcycle," 1960's, M-T Co., three actions, 12" long ...190		285	380
"Skating Circus Clown," 1950's, TPS Co., minor toy, 6" tall, RARE..400		600	800
"Skiing Santa," 1960s, M-T Co., 12" tall, four actions, (includes tin skis) ..150		225	300
"Skipping Monkey," 1960s, T-N Co., 9½" tall, minor toy 40		60	80
"Sky Patrol Flying Saucer," 1950s, K-O Co., 7½" diameter, seven actions, includes detachable antenna..90		135	180
"Sky Patrol"-Space Cruiser, 1950's, T-N Co., five actions, 13" long......150		225	300
"Sky Taxi-Panam-Boeing Vertol 107" 1970s, Haji Co., 12¾" long, three actions, includes 2 detachable rotors 90		135	180
"Slalom Game," 1960's, T-N Co., minor toy, 15¼" long (includes plastic skier)..................................100		150	200
"Sleeping Baby Bear," 1950s, Linemar, 9" long, six actions, includes detachable Alarm Clock.................200		300	400
"Sleeping Pup," 1960s, Alps Co., 9" long, five actions......................50		75	100
"Slurpy Pup," 1960s, T-N Co., 6½" long, 4" high, four actions...............50		75	100
"Smilex Deluxe Coffee Set," 1950s, Y Co., 12" high assembled, minor toy includes four sets of cups, saucers and spoons-plastic 60		90	120
"Smoky Bear," 1950's, SAN Co., four actions, 9" tall (includes detachable tin hat-Pioneer) 200		300	400
"Smoky Bill on Old Fashioned Car," 1960s, T-N Co., 9" long, four actions 100		150	200
"Smokey the Bear Jeep," 1950s, M-T Co., 10" long, four actions 220		330	440
"Smoking Bulldozer," 1960s, WKC Co., 9" long, four actions 70		105	140
"Smoking Bunny," 1950s, SAN Co., 10½" tall, four actions 90		135	180
"Smoking Elephant," 1950s, Marusan Co., 8¾" tall, four actions..............110		165	220
"Smoking Grandpa," (in Rocking Chair,) 1950s, SAN Co., 8" tall, four actions (Type I-eyes open) 150		225	300
"Smoking Grandpa," (in Rocking Chair) 1950s, SAN Co., 8" tall, four actions (Type II-eyes closed)..160		240	320

R-35 Robot.

Radar Scope Space Scout.

Santa Pay-Phone Bank.

Radio Rex. Unlike listing, this was made by John Hugo Co. of New Haven, Conn., with a last patent date of 1922. Auctioned with box in generally fine condition in late 1990 for $198. Courtesy James S. Maxwell/Virginia Caputo. Photo by Virginia Caputo.

Rocket Express -, Monorail.

Rabbits And The Carriage.

"Rotate-O-Matic Super Astronaut, with box. Courtesy James S. Maxwell/ Virginia Caputo. Photo by Virginia Caputo.

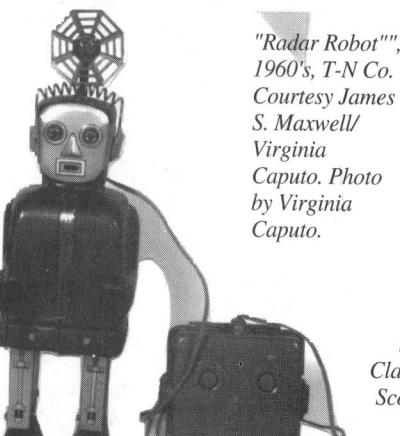

"Radar Robot"", 1960's, T-N Co. Courtesy James S. Maxwell/ Virginia Caputo. Photo by Virginia Caputo.

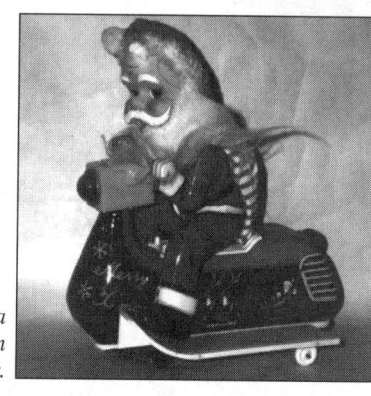

Santa Claus on Scooter.

Sneezing Bear.

Courtesy Don Hultzman. Photos by Don Hultzman and Ron Chojnacki unless marked otherwise.

	C6	C8	C10
"Smoking Jet Plane," 1950s, T-N Co., 12" long, 11" wingspan, four actions	120	180	240
"Smoking Pop Locomotive-the General," 1950s, SAN Co., 10¼" long, four actions	50	75	100
"Smoking Popeye," 1950s, Linemar, 9" tall, five actions, rare	600	900	1200
"Smoking Robot," 1960s, M-T Co., 10" tall, four actions (all plastic)	60	90	120
"Smoking Spaceman," 1950s, Linemar Co., 12" tall, six actions, Rare	800	1200	1600
"Smoking U.S.A.F Jet," 1950s, T-N Co., 13" long, 12" wingspan, four actions	120	180	240
"Smoking Volkswagen," 1960s, Aoshin Co., 10½" long, four actions	50	75	100
"Smoking PaPa Bear," 1950s, SAN Co., 8" tall, four actions	90	135	180
"Smoky Joe-Fancy Mobile," 1960s, T-N Co., 4 actions, smokes, lights, bump & go, noise, 9" long	80	120	160
"Snake Charmer (And Casey the Trained Cobra)" 1950s, Linemar Co., 8" high, four actions	200	300	400
"Snappy the Dragon," 1960s, T-N Co., 30" long, six actions, rare	800	1200	1600
"Sneezing Bear," 1950s, Linemar Co., 9" high, five actions	180	270	360
"Snoopie the Non-Fall Dog," 1960s, Amico Co., 8" long, three actions	40	60	80
"Snoopy Sniffer," 1960's, M-T Co., four actions, 8" long	40	60	80
"Somersaulting Pup With Bark,"1960's, T-N Co., four actions, 2 cycles, 9" long	40	60	80
"Sonicon Space Rocket," 1960's, M-T Co., minor toy, 13" long	100	150	200
"Space Capsule," 1960s, M-T Co., 10" long, four actions, includes styrofoam saucer and astronaut	90	135	180
"Space Capsule-5", 1960's, M-T Co., four actions, 10½" long	150	225	300
"Space Commando-Spaceman," 1960s, M-T Co., 7¾" tall, four actions	500	750	1000
"Space Commando"-Space Station , 1960s, T-N Co., 10" diameter, four actions	100	150	200
"Space Explorer #1041, 1960s, Yonezawa Co., 7¾" high, extends to 11½" high, six actions, rare	600	900	1200
"Space Explorer Ship" 1950s, M-T Co., six actions, 11" diameter, (saucer)	80	120	160

	C6	C8	C10
"Space Fighter," Robot, 1970s, S-H Co., 9"tall, six actions	60	90	120
"Space Frontier Saturn 5 Rocket," 1960s, K-Y co., (Yoskino Toy Co.,) 18" long, six actions	100	150	200
"Space Patrol Car," 1950s, T-N Co., four actions, 9½" long	300	450	600
"Space Patrol Car,"-With Lighting guns-1950s, Linemar Co., 9" long, three actions	450	675	900
"Space Patrol Robot," 1950s, S-H Co., 11" tall, six actions	120	180	240
"Space Patrol Rocket," 1970s, M-T Co., 11" long, three actions	50	75	100
"Space Patrol- Snoopy," 1960s, M-T Co., 11" long, four actions	90	135	180
"Space Patrol Tank," 1950's, Cragstan Co., five actions, 9" long (includes detachable tin jet plane)	100	150	200
"Space Patrol 3 Saucer," 1950s, K-O Co., 7½" diameter, five actions	90	135	180
"Space Patrol Vehicle," 1950s, K Co., 9" long, four actions	100	150	200
"Space Patrol Vehicle," 1960s, M-T Co., 9½" long, three actions	90	135	180
"Space Pioneer"-Vehicle, 1960's, M-T Co., three actions, 12" long	100	200	300
"Space Robot Trooper," 1950s, K-O Co., 7½" tall, three actions, Rare	400	600	800
"Space Robot (X-70)", 1960s, T-N Co., 12" tall, five actions, rare	500	750	1000
"Space Robot Car," 1950s, Yonezawza Co., six actions, 9¼" long, RARE	1000	1500	2000
"Space Rocket-Blue Eagle," 1950s, Masuya Toy Co., 15" long, (tail to probe tip)	120	180	240
"Space Rocket-Solar X," 1960s T-N Co., 15½" tall, five actions	110	165	220
"Space Scooter," 1960s,, M-T Co., 10½" high, 8" long, three actions	100	150	200
"Space Scooter," -Snoopy or Astro-Dog, 1960s, M-T Co., three actions, 8" long	80	120	160
"Space Ship," 1950s, I.Y. Co., 9½" diameter, four actions	180	270	360
"Space Ship," 1970s, M-T Co., 9" long, three actions	90	135	180
"Space Ship X-5," 1970s, M-T Co., 8" diameter, four actions	60	90	120
"Space Ship X-8," 1960s, Tada Co., 8" long, four actions	100	150	200
"Space Station," 1950s, T-N Co., 9" diameter, four actions	100	150	200

Teddy-Go-Cart, Mambo-the Jolly Drumming
Elephant.

F.D. Fire Engine, Fire Engine, Fire Chief Mystery Action Car,
Police Motorcycle Cop.

"Talking Parrot"

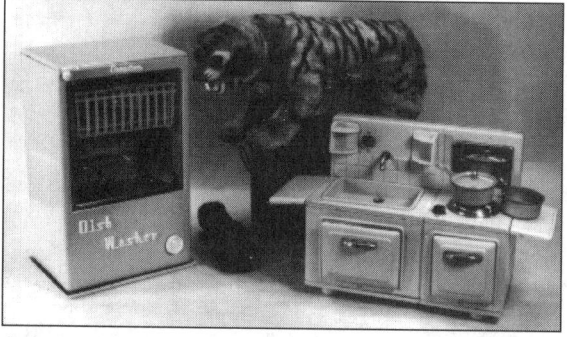

Cragstan Automatic Dishwasher, Bengali Tiger, Holiday
Sink/Stove Combination.

The Big Parade.

Champion Weight Lifter.

Tom and Jerry Car.

Smoking Robot.

"Talking Robot".

"Susie the Cashier Bear".

Courtesy Don Hultzman. Photos by Don Hultzman and
Ron Chojnacki unless marked otherwise.

Santa Claus - Bellringer.

Santa Fe Diesel.

Shooting Bear.

U.S. Air Force Smoking Jet.

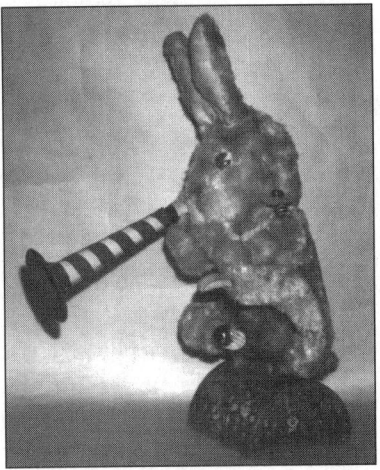

Trumpet Playing Bunny

Satellite Interceptor

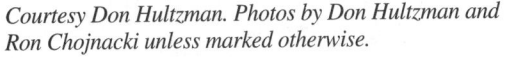

Shoe Shine Joe.

Musical Jolly Chimp, Grand-Pa Car, Circus Fire Engine.

Mix-ette Mixer, Wash-O-Matic Washing Machine, Jig-Saw-Matic Jigsaw, Kitchen Stove & Sink.

Courtesy Don Hultzman. Photos by Don Hultzman and Ron Chojnacki unless marked otherwise.

Sikorsky Rescue Army Helicopter.

	C6	C8	C10
"Space Station," 1950s, S-H Co., 11¾" diameter, five actions	500	750	1000
"Space Tank," 1960s, K-O Co., 6" long, four actions "Robbie Type"	800	1200	1600
"Space Tank," 1950s, Daiya Co., 8" long, four actions	100	150	200
"Space Tank-M41," 1950s, M-T Co., 9" long, four actions (includes detachable plastic antenna)	90	135	180
"Spaceman," Robot, 1950s, Linemar, 7½" tall, three actions	260	390	520
"Spaceman," Robot, 1950s, T-N Co., 9¼" tall, four actions	300	450	600
"Spad XIII S-7 Stunt Biplane," 1960s, T.P.S. Co., 9" long, 10⅜" wingspan, three actions	110	165	220
"Spanking Bear," 1950s, Linemar Co., 9" high, six actions	140	210	280
"Sparking Burp Gun," 1950's, Mark Co., three actions, 24" long	40	60	80
"Sparkling Mike The Robot," 1950s, Ace Co., 7½" tall, three actions, rare	500	750	1000
"Sparky Savings Bank," 1930s, Byron Co., 4"long, 4½" high doghouse, minor toy (electo magnet action-includes 4" long compo dog)	60	80	120
"Sparky the Seal," 1950s, M-T Co., 6" high, 7" long, four actions, two cycles, includes celluoid ball	80	120	160
"Spirit of 1776," locomotive No. 4406, 1976, M-T Co., 15¾" long, five actions	30	45	60
"Sports Car Race Set," 1960's, TPS Co., Minor toy, 8"X14" base, includes 4 plastic racecars	80	120	160
"Star Strider" Robot, 1980s, S-H Co., six actions, 12" tall	110	165	220
"Steam Roller (Road Roller), 1950s, T-N Co., (Rosko), 12" long with trailer, four actions	80	120	160
"Steam Roller," 1950s, "Y" Co., 8" long, four actions (includes tin trailer)	100	150	200
"Steerable Tank," 1950s, Linemar Co., 9" long, 5 actions	50	75	100
"Strange Explorer," 1960s, DSK Co., 7½" long, four actions	100	150	200
"Strato Jet U.S.A.F.," 1950s, T-N Co., 13" long, 14" wingspan, three actions	120	180	240
"Strutting My Fair Dancer," (Dancing Sailor Girl), 1950s, Haji Co., 12" tall, (two pieces) a minor toy	90	135	180

	C6	C8	C10
"Struttin' Sam," 1950s, Haji Co., 10½" tall, minor jigger toy	200	300	400
"Sunbeam Jeep No. 1," 1940s, 10" long, unmarked, three actions	90	135	180
"Sunday Driver," 1950s, M-T Co., 10" long, four actions (includes detachable driver)	60	90	120
"Super Astronaut," Robot, 1960s, S-H Co., 11½" tall, five actions, two cycles	110	165	220
"Super Astronaut Robot," 1960s, SJM Co., 12" tall, four actions	150	225	300
"Super Giant Robot, 1960s, S-H Co., 15½" tall, six actions	120	180	240
"Super Jet," 1950s, T-N Co., three actions, 12" long, 8" wingspan	250	375	500
"Super Space Capsule," 1960s, S-H Co., 9" high, four actions	100	150	200
"Super Space Commander," 1960s, S-H Co., 10" tall, three actions	60	90	120
"Superman Tank," 1950s, Linemar Co., 10¼" long, three actions rare	600	900	1200
"Surrey Jeep," 1960s, T-N Co., 11" long, three actions	80	120	160'
"Susie the Cashier Bear," 1950s, Linemar Co., 9" high, six actions	280	420	560
"Suzy-Q Automatic Ironer," 1950s, GW Co., 7" high, four actions	90	135	180
"Suzette the Eating Monkey," 1950s, Linemar Co., 8¾" high, 7"x 5" base, five actions (includes tin litho steak) RARE	260	390	520
"Swingtail Airplane Flying Tigers," 1960s, Marx Co., 19½" long, 21" wingspan, seven actions	200	300	400
"Swing Tail Cargo Plane-Flying Tiger," 1960s, T-N Co., five actions, 14" long-14" wingspan	300	450	600
"Switchboard Operator" (?) 1950s, Linemar, 7½" high, four actions, rare	260	390	520
"Swivel-O-Matic Astronaut" robot, 1960s, S-H Co., 11½"tall, five actions, 2 cycles	60	90	120
"T 360 Monoplane," 1950s, S&E Co., 12" long, 14½" wingspan, four actions		*see "Bristol Bulldog Airplane"*	
"Talking Parrot," 1950s, T-N Co., 18" high, six actions (called "Pete")	200	300	400
"Talking Police Car-Mystery Action," 1960s, Y Co., 14" long, three actions	60	90	120

Sky Patrol.

Slalom Game.

Smoking Popeye.

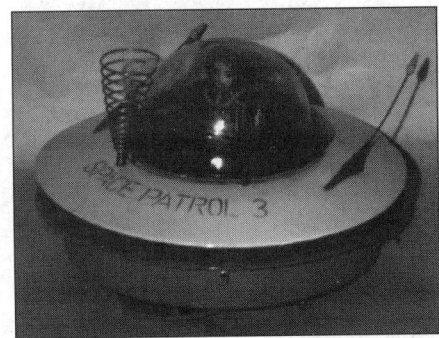

Space Patrol 3 Saucer.

Space Capsule - 5.

Somersaulting Pup.

Smoky Bear.

Thunder Jet Boat.

Space ExplorerShip X-7.

Star Strider.

Space Pioneer.

Courtesy Don Hultzman. Photos by Don Hultzman and Ron Chojnacki unless marked otherwise.

Teddy Bear Swing.

Strutting Sam.

The Playing Monkey.

Telephone Bunny - Ringing And Talking in his Old Rocking Chair.

Television Spaceman.

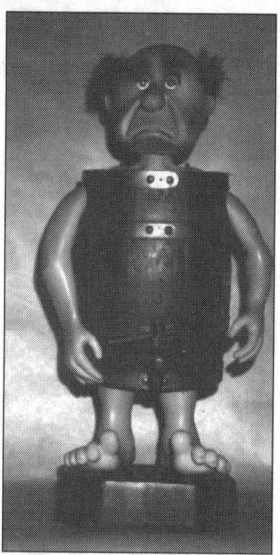

The Loser.

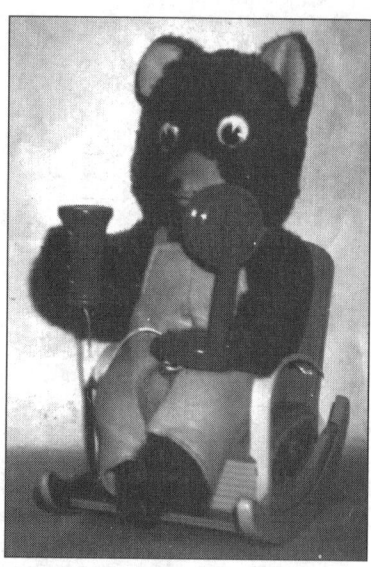

Telephone Bear - Ringing and Talking In His Old Rocking Chair.

Tom and Jerry Handcars.

Tric-Cycling Clown.

Tom Tom Indian.

Sunday Driver.

Courtesy Don Hultzman. Photos by Don Hultzman and Ron Chojnacki unless marked otherwise.

	C6	C8	C10
"Talking Robot," 1960s, Yonezawa Co., three actions, 10¾" tall, rare ..600	600	900	1200
"**Tank** M-4 Combat Tank," 1960s, Taiyo Co., 11½" long, 13" with gun barrel extended, five actions 60	60	90	120
"Tank M-35," 1950s, HTC Co., 8" long, three actions 100	100	150	200
"Tank M-41," 1970s, J Co., 8¼" long, four actions 100	100	150	200
"Tank M-48-T," 1960s, T-N Co., 8¼" long, four actions 80	80	120	160
"Tank M-56," 1940s, M-T Co., 7½" long, wheel drive, seven actions 90	90	135	180
"Tank M-81," 1960s, M-T Co., 8½" long, seven actions 90	90	135	180
"Tank M-103," 1950s, M-T Co., 7" long, three actions 80	80	120	160
"Tank M-107-US Army," 1950s, Y Co., 6" long, four actions, includes four missiles 100	100	150	200
"Tank M-X," 1950s, T-N Co., 8½" long, five actions..........60	60	90	120
"Tank T-5," 1950's, T-N Co., 8½" long, three actions, includes detachable radar antenna 100	100	150	200
"Tank 392-U.S. Tank Division," 1950's, Marx Co., three actions, 9½" long 60	60	90	120
"Tank X-3" (explorer defense), 1950s, Cragstan Co., 7¾"long, five actions, includes six cartridge shells..........120	120	180	240
"Tank X-75," 1950's, M-T Co., 9" long, three actions, includes tin gun and darts..........100	100	150	200
"Tank-Daisymatic No 64 Rapid Fire Tank," 1960s , Daisy Mfg. Co., 8" long, four actions 100	100	150	200
"Tank-Daisy-Matic No. 80," 1965, Daisy Mfg. Co., 8½" long, five actions, includes darts 90	90	135	180
"Tank Robot," 1960s, S-H Co., five actions, 10" tall 250	250	375	500
"**Tarzan**," 1966, Marusan Co., (Banner), four actions, 13" tall, rare 500	500	750	1000
"Taxi," (yellow cab), 1950s, Linemar Co., 7½" long, five actions 60	60	90	120
"Taxi Cab," 1950s, "Y" Co., 8½" long, five actions..........60	60	90	120
"Taxi Cab," 1960's, Y Co., four actions, 9" long..........70	70	105	140
"**Teddy** Bear Circus Acrobat," 1950's, Tomiyana Co., three actions, 15" high (includes detachable bear flyer). Rare.400	400	600	800

	C6	C8	C10
"Teddy Bear Swing," 1950s, T-N Co.,three actions, two cycles, 17" high, (includes four wire supports and tin sign)..........200	200	300	400
"Teddy-Go-Kart," 1960s, Alps Co., 10½" long, four actions 80	80	120	160
"Teddy the Artist," 1950's, Y Co., 8½" high, 5¼"x 7" base, 3 actions, includes removable tray and 9 patterns..........180	180	270	360
"Teddy the Boxing Bear," 1950s, "Y" Co., 9" tall, five actions 120	120	180	240
"Teddy the Rhythmical Drummer," 1960s, Alps Co., 11" tall, three actions 80	80	120	160
"**Telephone** Bear," 1950s, Linemar, 7½" high, six actions 140	140	210	280
"Telephone Bear - Ringing and Talking In His Old Rocking Chair," 1950s, M-T Co., 10" high, four actions.....190	190	285	380
"Telephone Bunny-Ringing and Talking In His Old Rocking Chair," 1950s, M-T Co., 10" high, four actions.....140	140	210	280
"**Television** Spaceman," 1960s, Alps Co., 14½" high to tip of antenna, six actions 400	400	600	800
"Television Truck," 1950s, Linemar Co., 11" long, three actions..........200	200	300	400
"**The** Big Parade," 1963, Marx Co., 11½" tall, 15" wide, four actions (includes detachable gun and baton)..........120	120	180	240
"The Loser," (Bar Toy), ca. 1971, Poynter Prod. Co., 3 actions, 13" high 30	30	45	60
"The Rabbits and Carriage," 1950's, S&E Co., four actions, 10" tall (should have tin Butterfly)..........150	150	225	300
"The Playing Monkey", 1950s, S&E Co(Ahi Brand), six actions, 10" tall, includes detachable hat and tin yo yo..........150	150	225	300
"**Thunder** Jet Boat," 1950s, Bandai Co., 9¾" long, three actions 130	130	195	260
"**Tin** Man" Robot, 1960s, Remco Industries, Inc., 21" tall, all plastic, four actions 100	100	150	200
"**Tinkling** Trolley," 1950's, M-T Co., four actions, two cycle, 10½" long, includes two plastic cowcatchers...100	100	150	200
"**Tiny** Jeep," 1950's, WACO Co., 4¼" long, minor action 20	20	30	40
"Tiny Tank," 1950's WACO Co., 4¼" long, minor action 20	20	30	40
"**Tom** and Jerry Car," 1960s, Rico Co., (Spain) 13" long, three actions, rare ..400	400	600	800

Turn-O-Matic Gun Jeep.

Twin Coupled Tramcars.

U.S. Army Machine Gunner. Photo by Don Hultzman. Collection of Beau Cassity.

Walking Bear with Xylophone.

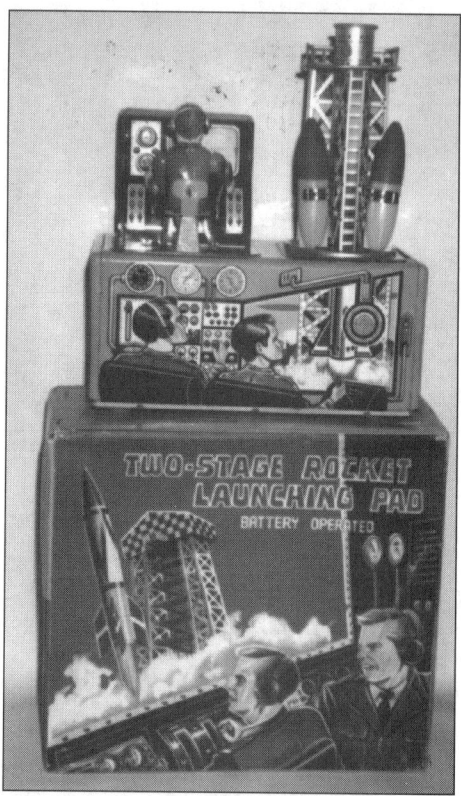

Two Stage Rocket Launching Pad.

Worried Mother Duck & Baby.

Winner of the West.

Twin Racing Cars.

Courtesy Don Hultzman. Photos by Don Hultzman and Ron Chojnacki unless marked otherwise.

	C6	C8	C10
"Tom and Jerry Choo Choo," 1960s, M-T Co., 10¼" long, five actions	120	180	240
"Tom and Jerry Handcar- Jerry," 1960s, M-T Co., 7¾" high, 7¾" long, three actions	130	195	260
"Tom and Jerry Handcar- Tom," 1960s, M-T Co., 9¾" high, 7¾" long, three actions	130	195	260
"Tom and Jerry Helicopter," 1960s, M-T Co., 9½" long, three actions	100	150	200
"Tom and Jerry Highway Patrol," 1960s, M-T Co., 8" long, three actions	110	165	220
"Tom and Jerry Jumping Jeep," 1960s, M-T Co., 9" long, three actions	120	180	240
"Tom-Tom Indian," 1961, Y Co., 10½" tall, four actions	80	120	160
"Topo Gigio Playing the Xylophone," 1960s, T-N Co., three actions	260	440	520
"Torpedo Boat-PT 107," 1950s, Linemar 11½" long, three actions	100	150	200
"Tractor," 1950s, Showa Co., 7½" long, four actions, includes litho tin figure (driver)	50	75	100
"Tractor," 1960s, Y Co., 6" long, three actions	50	75	100
"Tractor On Platform," 1950's, T-N Co., tractor 9" long, trailer 7" long, minor toy	80	120	160
"Train Robot," 1950's, M-T Co., four actions, 15½" tall, rare	1500	2250	3000
"Traveler Bear," 1950s, Linemar Co., 8" high, three actions	80	120	160
"Treasure Chest" Bank, 1960s, Illfelder Co., 11" tall, five actions, two cycles, risque toy- pg rated	70	105	140
"Tric-cycling Clown," 1960s, M-T Co., five actions, 12" high	250	375	500
"Tricky Dog House," No. 673, 1960s, Y Co., 6¾" high, 7¼" long, 6¾" wide, four actions	60	90	120
"Trumpet Playing Bunny," 1950s, Alps Co., 10" high, four actions	140	210	280
"Trumpet Playing Monkey," 1950s, Alps Co., 9" high, four actions, includes tin horn	150	225	300
"Tubby the Turtle," 1950s, Y Co., 7" long, three actions	50	75	100
"Tugboat," 1950s, Marx, 6½" long, a minor toy	50	75	100
"Tugboat," 1950s, Marusan Co., 3 actions, 13½" long	110	165	220

	C6	C8	C10
"Tumbles the Bear," 1960s, Y-M Co., (Yanoman), 8½" tall, minor toy, includes porter's hat	80	120	160
"Turn Signal Robot," 1960s, T-N Co., 11" tall, five actions (Auto Accessory)	160	240	320
"Turn-O-Matic Gun Jeep," 1960s, T-N Co., 10" long, five Actions	90	135	180
"Turntable Xylophone Melody Train," 1960s, Cragstan Co., 29½" long assembled, three actions	40	60	80
"TWA Multiaction DC-7C Airliner," 1960s, Yonezawa Co., 22½" long, 23¼" wingspan, seven actions	200	300	400
"Twin Coupled Tram Cars," 1950s, K Co., minor toy, 11½" long (two cars)	100	150	200
"Twin Racing Cars," 1950s, Alps Co., three actions, 7" long-10" long with coupling rod)	400	600	800
"Twirly Whirly," 1950's, Alps Co., four actions, 13½" high	300	450	600
"Twist Dancer" (Let's Twist), 1960s, no mfr. mark, minor toy, 15" high	90	135	180
"Two Stage Rocket Launching Pad," 1950s, T-N Co., 7" long, 4" wide, 8" high, three actions (includes 2 plastic-rubber rockets)	200	300	400
"UFO-X05," 1970s, M-T Co., 7½" diameter, three actions	50	75	100
"Union Mountain Cable Lines," Monorail set, 1950s, T-N Co., car 8" long, 16 pc. oval track, 22"x 32", minor toy	70	105	140
"United DC7 Mainliner," 1950s, Yonezawa Co., 14" wingspan, five actions	200	300	400
"United Mainliner Stratocruiser," 1950s, Linemar, 19½" long, 13" wingspan, four actions	190	285	380
"United States Ocean Liner," 1950s, Linemar Co., 14" long, three actions	160	240	320
"United States Ocean Liner," 1950s, Y Co., three actions, 18½" long	300	450	600
"Universal Machine Gun," 1950s, T-N Co., 14¾" long, three actions	60	90	120
"USA-NASA Apollo Space Ship, 1960s, M-T Co., 9" long, four actions	140	210	280
"Usa-NASA Gemini Space Capsule," 1960s, M-T Co., 9"long, four actions (includes detachable astronaut)	120	180	240
"U.S. Army Machine Gunner," 1960s, unmarked, 10" long, 4 actions	80	120	160
"U.S. Air Force Military Airlift Command Jet," 1960s, T-N Co., 14" wingspan, 4 actions	120	180	240

	C6	C8	C10
"U.S. Air Force Smoking Jet No. 75029," 1950s, (rare) T-N Co., 12" wingspan, 3 actions, smokes, engine noise, bump & go 150	225	300
"U.S. Navy Pom Pom Gun," 1950s, Remco Co., 20" long, four actions..60	90	120
"U.S. Royal Tire-Mechanical Toy" (Ferris Wheel) souvenir for 1964-65 N.Y. World's Fair (now permanently located at Uniroyal Co. on rt.. 94, west of Detroit), includes plastic figures, minor toy, 10" high, Ideal.................110	165	220
"Video Robot," 1960s, S-H Co., 10" tall, three actions 80	120	160
"V.I.P the Busy Boss," 1950s, S&E Co., 8" high, six actions 200	300	400
"Visible Ford Mustang," 1960s, Bandai Co., 10" long, four actions 80	120	160
"Vision Robot," 1960s, S-H Co., 11¾" tall, five actions 140	210	280
"Voice Control Astronaut Base," 1969, Remco Co., 19" long, four actions (includes plastic missiles and phonograph records) 90	135	180
"Volkswagen Convertible," 1950's, T-N Co., three actions, 9¾" long ...250	375	500
"Volkswagen-Elektrik," 1950s, Mignon Co., 8½" long, three actions 60	90	120
"Volkswagen No. 7653," 1960s, Bandai Co., 10" long, three actions.......70	105	140
"Volkswagen With Visible Engine," 1960s, K.O. Co., 7" long, three actions........60	90	120
"Volkswagen with Visible Engine No. 4049," 1960s, Bandai Co., 8" long, three actions 80	120	160
"Wagon Master," 1960s, M-T Co., 18" long, four actions....................100	150	200
"Walking Bear with Xylophone," 1950s, Linemar Co., 10" high, seven actions .180	270	360
"Walking Elephant," 1950s, Linemar Co., 8½" long, three actions 80	120	160
"Walking 'Esso' Tiger," 1950s, Marx Co., 11½" tall, four actions............200	300	400
"Walking Itchy Dog," 1950s, Alps Co., 9" long, five actions 50	75	100
"Walky-Son" (Los), 1960s, rare, Geyper Co., 4 actions, 11½" high, includes detachable guns and baton ....*see "Los Walky Son"*		
"Warpath Indian," 1950s, Alps Co., 12" tall, three actions...................80	120	160
"Wash-O -Matic" washing machine, 1940s, T-N Co., 5¾" high, 4¼" diameter, a minor toy, includes lid..30	45	60

	C6	C8	C10
"Water Spouting Whale with Flopping Tail," 1950s, KKS Co., 13" long, minor toy..100	150	200
"Western Badman," (Red Gulch Bar), 1960s, M-T Co., 9¾" high, eight actions, includes 3 plastic bottles and 2 plastic glasses, rare...............260	390	520
"Western Express," Locomotive, 1960s, Kanto Toy Co., 14" long, four actions .40	60	80
"Western Locomotive," 1950s, M-T Co., 10½" long, four actions...........40	60	80
"Western Special Locomotive," 1950s, M-T Co., 12" long, five actions 40	60	80
"Wheel-A-Gear" Robot, 1960s, Taiyo Co., 14" tall, five actions 200	300	400
"WHOH-Skyway Patrol Helicopter," 1950s, M-T Co., 18" long, four actions............70	105	140
"Whirlybird Helicopter," 1960s, Remco Co., 25" long, three actions 60	90	120
"Whistling Showboat," 1950s, M-T Co., 14" long, three actions............100	150	200
"Wild West Rodeo," 1950s, Linemar, 6½" long, 8" high, five actions, includes plastic bowl for bubble solution.........90	135	180
"Windy the Elephant" 1950s, T-N Co., 9¾" high, 3 actions, includes celluloid ball and tin litho umbrella...120	180	240
"Winner-23," Rocket, 1950s, KDP Co., (Excelo), 5½" long, minor action, includes rubber track......................110	165	220
"Winner of the West"-Overland Stagecoach with Four Galloping Horses, 1950s, Alps Co., four actions, 18" long...........200	300	400
"Winston the Barking Bulldog," 1950s, Tomiyama Co., three actions, two cycles, 10" long...............................70	105	140
"Worried Mother Duck and Baby", 1950s, T-N Co., 11" long, 7" high, three actions 90	135	180
"X-7 Space Explorer Ship," 1960s, M-T Co., 7" diameter, four actions 70	105	140
"X-70 Robot," 1960s, T-N Co., 12¼" tall, five actions, Rare 500	750	1000
"X-1800 Space Vehicle," 1960s, M-T Co., 9" long, five actions (includes detachable plastic antenna) 140	210	280
"X-F 160 Jet Airplane," 1960s, K-O Co., 8" wingspan.............................80	120	160
"Yeti the Abominable Snowman," 1960s, Marx, 12" tall, four actions 220	330	440
"Yo-Yo Clown," 1960s, Alps Co., 9" high, three actions (includes plastic yo-yo)..110	165	220
"Yo-Yo Monkey," 1960s, Alps Co., 9" tall, three actions (includes plastic yo-yo)..120	180	240

	C6	C8	C10
"Yo-Yo Monkey," 1960s, Y-M Co., 12" tall, spring extension to 32", minor	90	135	180
"Yum Yum Kitty," 1950s, Alps Co., 9½" high, five actions	180	270	320
"Zero Fighter Plane," 1950s, Bandai Co., 12½" long, 15" wingspan, three actions	160	240	320

	C6	C8	C10
"Zoom Motorboat," 1950s, K Co., 12" long, three actions	80	120	160
"Zoomer the Robot," 1950s, T-N Co., 8" tall, three actions	220	330	440

Walky-Son (los). Photo by Don Hultzman.

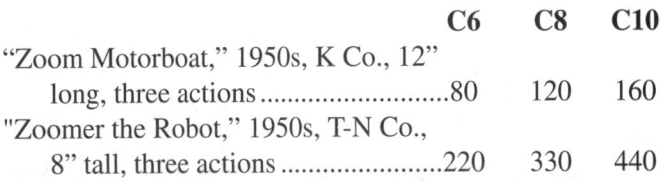

Smoking Popeye. Courtesy Christie's East.

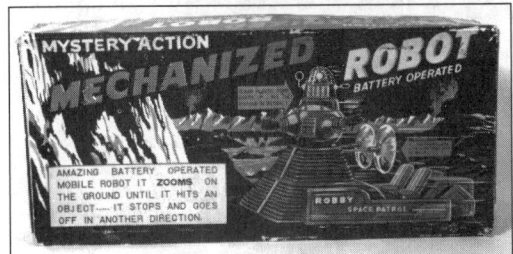

"Mechanized Robot" (Robby). This toy was auctioned, with box, in late 1990 in near-mint condition for $27,830. Courtesy James S. Maxwell/Virginia Caputo. Photo by Virginia caputo.

Mechanized Robot. Courtesy Christie's East.

Big Loo. Courtesy Christie's East.

Superman Tank, Linemar. Courtesy Christie's East.

Tubby The Turtle. Photo by Don Hultzman.

SOLDIERS

The average price in the last edition of American dimestore soldiers listed here was $39.49 and in this edition it is $45.29, an increase of 15%.

CONDITION OF A TOY SOLDIER AND ITS RELATION TO PRICE

The price of a toy soldier depends not only on its desirability, but on its condition. "Mint" means just that; the condition in which it was originally issued - perfect, regardless of age, not the slightest blemish. Needless to say this is a fairly rare state of affairs, but enough soldiers exist in mint condition to make it an employable term. Many people, hoping to dispose of toys, are tempted to term them "mint" when they are really "near mint", "very good" or sometimes even just "good". Inevitably this can result in unhappiness all around, and not infrequently, in a canceled sale.

"Very Good" indicates a soldier which has obviously seen use; with signs of wear and aging, but with most of its paint remaining and in general having a freshness to its appearance that makes it seem attractive and collectible to all but the most discriminating.

"Good" signals a soldier that has seen considerable wear, but has at least one half to one third of its original paint, and is basically sound. A collector will collect it, but will often not be wholly satisfied with it as an example of his collection, and thus prices are well below that which the same item in mint can command.

Condition below good results in another drastic drop in price, and figures with missing parts, although otherwise in excellent condition, will usually fall into this lower-priced category. At present, a BARCLAY soldier minus its tin helmet (signaled by a large round hole in the top of its head) is worth about half of what it would otherwise bring. Rust, even small spots of it on the cast iron soldiers, can seriously lower their price, as can repainting of any of the soldiers. "Near-Mint," "Fine," "Very Fine" and similar terms often found in sellers' descriptions, denote conditions between Mint and Very Good, and are priced accordingly.

The key to grading is to avoid wishful thinking. Grading can sometimes be a problem for the uninitiated, but common sense will usually prevail, and when possible a consultation with an expert in the field can often clear up lingering doubts. A toy in its original box is worth up to 10 to 20% more if the box is in mint condition, with the price dropping as condition lessens.

BARCLAY

(See Vehicles, Animal-Drawn, Aircraft and Miscellaneous)

Barclay Mfg. Co. was the largest manufacturer of toy soldiers in the U.S. prior to World War II, selling millions of figures annually. The company, named after Barclay Street in West Hoboken, New Jersey, (now 10th Street in Union City) began in 1924 or late 1923, owned by an elderly Frenchman, Leon Donze (1865-66-1950) and by Michael Levy (c. 1895-10/9/64), who became affiliated by buying a partnership. Levy eventually took over the company (around 1932) and it was he who turned it into a major one. From about five employees in 1924, the company expanded to a pre-War peak of 400 workers, and moved several times as it was forced to expand. Barclay's soldiers came in four styles prior to World War II. The first, which were probably produced almost from Barclay's beginning, were small, with the mounted figures having moving arms. The second, approximately 3¼" high, with a separate tin helmet, seem to have begun production in 1935, and were designed and sculpted by Barclay employee Frank Krupp. This figure (the tin helmet was subcontracted) was rather stiff and is known by collectors as "short stride" because its marching figures' feet were close together. The third style, again by Krupp, also had a separate tin helmet, was more realistic, and is known as "long stride." These were on sale as early as 1937. In 1937 or 1938, a clip was designed to hold on the tin helmets, as the formerly glued-on helmets frequently came off, and drew complaints from the chain stores such as Woolworth's, which sold Barclay toys. The fourth style, introduced about 1939-1940, when Barclay moved from slush casting to die casting its soldiers, was by free-lance artist Olive Kooken (1904-1964), and is known as "cast helmet", as the soldiers featured helmets that were an integral part of the figure. Barclay's soldiers were made of antimonial lead, consisting of about 13% antimony and the rest lead. When slush-molding was done, only one mold was made of each single figure. The lead would be poured into the mold, rocked, and immediately poured out, those providing a hollow figure. Later, the die-cast molds produced a number of the same figures at the same time. During the Second World War BARCLAY laid off all but four of its employees, and did sub-contract work. It was never as successful after the war, and finally closed down in 1971, by this time employing only 50-75 people. Although BARCLAY assigned numbers to its figures from the beginning for its own records, many of the soldiers themselves bore no numbers. Figures listed with a question mark after the number are based on the memory of longtime BARCLAY employee George Fall, whose memory, judged against known BARCLAY numbers, is quite accurate, but not infallible. All short stride BARCLAYS have separate helmets.

BAC

BAD

Pre - 1934

*(All **bold words** and numbers are **Barclay's Own Description**)*

	C6	C8	C10
(Ba) 87? Mounted Officer, moving arm holding sword, on rearing horse	25	38	50
(Baa) 87? Same as above on cantering horse	25	38	50
(Bb) 87? Mounted Officer, moving arm holding bugle, on rearing horse	25	38	50
(Bba) 87? Same as above, on cantering horse	25	38	50
(Bc) 87? Mounted Officer, moving arm holding pistol on cantering horse	32	48	64
(Bd) 88? Mounted Cowboy with lasso	No Price Found		
(Be) 89? Mounted Indian, moving arm holding rifle	40	60	80
(BeA) Same as above, holding pistol	40	60	80
(Bf) 90? Mounted Cowboy with pistol	40	60	80
(BfA) 90? Mounted Cowboy with moving arm, holding rifle (horse's tail missing in photo)	35	53	70
(Bfa) Indian Chief on foot, 54mm high, blue and red-striped headdress, may look like Ideal I-14	No Price Found		

Top Row Left to Right: Ba, Baa, Bb, Bba. Bottom Row Left to Right: Bc, Be, Bg, Bh. Photo by Ed Poole. Courtesy Tony Salamone.

	C6	C8	C10
(Bfb) Indian brave on foot, 54 mm high, carrying rifle across stomach	No Price Found		
(Bg) 186? Cavalryman mounted, 2¾" high, no moving parts, modeled on French toy soldier, circa late 1920s-early 30s	11	16	22
(Bh) **486 Cavalryman**, approx. 2¼" high, circa early 30s, no moving parts	10	15	21
(Bi) Baseball fielder, approx. 1⅞" high, circa 1920s	42	63	85
(Bj) Baseball pitcher, circa 1920s	42	63	85
(Bk) Baseball batter, circa 1920s	42	63	85
(Bl) Mounted Indian on rearing horse	15	23	30
(Bm) **200 Jockey on Horse**	17	25	34
(Bn) **No. 87 Officer on Horse**, smaller size, circa 1931 (4 known)	No Price Found		

1934 and After

	C6	C8	C10
(BA) Paint Your Own Army Set No. 2003, circa 1934, boxed	125	188	250
(BAa) Paint Your Own Army Set No. 2003, larger size than above, same toys, with compartment for one more toy. Only 1 known	No Price Found		
(BAC) **89 Indian on Horse** (on catalog sheet with Ethiopians)	17	26	35
(BAD) **90 Cowboy on Horse** (on catalog sheet with Ethiopians)	17	26	35
(B1) **89 Indian on Horse**	12	18	24

Left to Right: Bi, Bk, Bj.

Left to right: B1, BfA.

Top Row, Left to Right: B1, B2, B2A. Bottom Row, Left to Right: B3, B3A, B4. Photo by Ed Poole.

Top Row, Left to Right: B5, B6, B7, B9, B10, B11, B12. Bottom Row, Left to Right: B13, B14, B15, B16, B17, B18, B19. Photo by Bill Kaufman.

Left to Right: B2C, B2B, B225, B227. Photo by Don Pielin.

	C6	C8	C10
(B1a) **89 Indian on Horse** two feathers (earlier)............22		33	44
(B2) **90 Cowboy on Horse** 12		18	24
(B2A) **90 Cowboy on Horse** variation, thinner bullets in gunbelt, saddle not as long..............12		18	25
(B2AA) **90 Cowboy on Horse**, variation, no bullets in gunbelt ....No Price Found			
(B2AAA) **100 Masked Rider on Horse** (may not have been produced; in the order sheet the figure faces forward)....No Price Found			
(B2B) 100? Masked rider on Horse, horse's tail down..............21		32	42
(B2C) 100? Masked rider on Horse, horse's tail up..............18		27	36
(B3) 87? Mounted, in grey cap, intermediate size..............37		53	75
(B3A) **87 Officer on Horse**, in cap, khaki or grey, larger black, grey or brown horse..............14		21	28
(B4) 87? Mounted in colored jacket and cap, may be Chinese or Japanese (horse's tail missing in photo)..........19		28	38
(B5) **701 Flagbearer**, tin helmet, short stride..............11		17	22
(B6) **701 Flagbearer**, tin helmet, long stride..............7		11	15
(B7) **701 Flagbearer**, cast helmet..........8		12	16
(B8) **701** Flagbearer, Cuban flag variation painted for 10 Woolworth's in Cuba, cast helmet or pot helmet ....No Price Found			

	C6	C8	C10
(B9) **701 Machine-Gunner**, kneeling, short stride..............7		11	15
(B10) **702 Machine-Gunner**, kneeling, long stride..............9		14	18
(B11) **702** Machine-Gunner, kneeling, cast helmet..............10		15	20
(B12) **703 Sniper**, kneeling, firing short stride..............7		11	14
(B12A) 703 Sniper, kneeling, firing, short stride, shorter rifle, in front of fingers fat portion of gun and thin portion of barrel about equal length..............9		14	18
(B13) **703 Sniper**, kneeling, firing, long stride, tin helmet..............10		15	20
(B14) **704 Soldier on Parade**, shoulder arms, short stride..............7		11	15
(B15) **704 Soldier on Parade**, shoulder arms, long stride, tin helmet..............8		13	17
(B16) **705 Soldier at Attention** (actually port arms)..............11		16	21
(B17) **705** Soldier at Attention (actually port arms), cast helmet..............10		15	20
(B18) **706 Soldier**, charging, short stride ...7		11	15
(B18a) Same as above, with shorter rifle, sling around hand, one known .....No Price Found			
(B19) **706** Tall, tin helmet, solid puttees ..300		450	600
(B20) **706** Soldier, charging, tin helmet, long stride..............50		75	100
(B21) **706** Soldier, charging, cast helmet...11		17	22
(B22) **707** At Attention, cast helmet 9		14	19
(B23) **708 Officer** with sword, short stride..............12		18	24
(B24) **723 Marine Officer**, same as above, in blue..............14		21	28
(B25) **708 Officer**, with sword, tin helmet, long stride..............9		14	18

	C6	C8	C10
(B25a) 708 Officer with sword, tin helmet, long stride, no chest strap...60	90	120
(B25b) 723 Marine Officer with sword, tin helmet, long stride, no chest strap, in blue..............60	90	120
(B26) **723 Marine Officer**, with sword, tin helmet, long stride 17	26	35
(B27) **708** Officer with sword, cast helmet.............25	38	50
(B28) **708** Marine Officer with sword, cast helmet 27	40	55
(B29) **709 Bugler**, short stride 12	18	24
(B30) **709 Bugler**, long stride, tin helmet ..8	12	16
(B31) **710 Drummer** short stride..........9	14	18
(B32) **710 Drummer** long stride, tin helmet..............9	14	18
(B33) **711 Drum Major**, short stride 11	17	22
(B34) **711** Drum Major, long stride, tin helmet..............12	18	24
(B35) **743 West Point Officer**, short stride..............8	12	16
(B36) **718 West Point Cadet**, with rifle, short stride 10	15	20
(B37) Same as above but painted as wooden soldier, only three known ..300	450	600
((B37a) Same as B36, with line-and-dot eyes, white pants, white gloves.........10	15	20
(B38) **718 West Point Cadet**, long stride..8	12	16
(B39) **724 Ethiopian Soldier**, circa 1935-36...........100	150	200
(B40) **725 Ethiopian Officer**, circa 1935-36...........105	158	210
(B41) **727 Italian Officer**, circa 1935-36...90	135	180
(B42) **726 Italian Soldier**, circa 1935-36...........120	180	240
(B43) Japanese, charging with rifle, circa 1937............55	83	110
(B44) Japanese Officer, circa 1937 (this is the original Ethiopian officer, painted as a Japanese)....................110	165	220
(B45) Chinese or Mongolian Officer in steel helmet, circa 1937 125	188	250
(B46) Chinese or Mongolian Rifleman circa 1937,pronounced right breast pocket..........90	135	180
(B46a) Same as above, narrower face, faint right breast pocket 60	90	120
(B47) **717 Indian Brave**, rifle across waist.7	11	15
(B48) **716 Indian Chief**.....................7	11	14
(B49) **719 Sailor White Uniform**, marching, short stride 10	15	20
(B50) **720 Sailor Blue Uniform**, like above...........11	16	22

B1a

	C6	C8	C10
(B51) **719** Sailor White Uniform, long stride, bell bottoms...........7	11	14
(B51a) 720 Sailor in Blue Uniform, long stride, bell bottoms.................12	18	25
(B52) **719 Sailor in White Uniform**, in puttees 7	11	14
(B52a) **720 Sailor Blue Uniform**, in puttees 8	12	16
(B53) **756 Sailor, Flagbearer**, long stride.................11	17	22
(B54) **721 Naval Officer**, short stride, tin top to cap 45	68	90
(B55) **721 Naval Officer,** short stride ...11	17	23
(B55a) 721 Naval Officer, same as above, in blue.................100	150	200
(B56) **721 Naval Officer**, long stride 8	12	16
(B57) **722 Marine**, short stride, tin top to cap....................45	68	90
(B58) **722 Marine**, short stride 11	17	22
(B59) 722 Marine, long stride 8	12	16
(B59a) 722 Marine, long stride, white cap (probably post-War) 17	26	34
(B60) **757 Sailor with Signal Flag**s 12	18	24
(B60a) **757 Sailor with Signal Flags,** flat underbase, minor variations in cap ...13	19	27
(B61) **728 Machine Gunner Lying Flat** ..8	12	16
(B62) **728** Machine Gunner Lying Flat, cast helmet 12	18	24
(B63) **728** Machine Gunner Lying Flat, cast helmet, lip of base extends under gun barrel 7	11	15
(B64) **750 Soldier, Crawling**................10	15	21
(B65) **730 Soldier Signal Man with Flag**.10	15	21
(B66) **731 Soldier Pigeon Dispatche**r...9	14	18
(B67) **732 Soldier Telephone Operator** 7	11	15
(B68) **733 Soldier Bullet Feeder** (actually a shell)..............7	11	14

Left to Right: B46, B46a. Variations noticed by Gordon Gee on Barclay B46. The Figure at left has a wider face and a right breast pocket and appears to be less common. Photo by Gordon Gee.

Top Row, Left to Right: B20, B21, B22, B23, B24, B25, B25a, B26, B27, B28. Bottom Row, Left to Right: B29, B30, B31, B32, B33, B34, B35, B36, B37. Photo by Bill Kaufman.

	C6	C8	C10
(B69) **734 Soldier Ammunition Carrier**...8	12	16
(B70) **735 Soldier Range Finder** 7	11	15
(B71) **736 Soldier Sentry** 7	11	15
(B72) **737 Soldier Charging Machine Gunner**, tin helmet 6	9	13
(B73) **737** Soldier Charging Machine gunner, cast helmet 13	20	26
(B74) **738 Soldier Bomb Thrower** 7	11	15
(B75) **738** Soldier Bomb Thrower, tall, tin helmet, solid puttees ....No Price Found
(B76) **738** Soldier Bomb Thrower, rifle off ground, tin helmet 11	17	22
(B77) **738** Soldier Bomb Terhrow, rifle off ground, cast helmet 10	15	21
(B78) **739 Soldier Fifer** 10	15	20
(B79) **740 Soldier French Horn** 8	12	17
(B79a) Machine Gunner, seated, cast helmet, bandage-type puttees 13	20	27
(B80) **741 Aviator** 8	12	17
(B81) **745 Navy Doctor,** in white, flat underbase 9	13	18
(B81a) **746 Army Doctor,** in brown, flat underbase 9	13	18
(B81A&B) **746** Doctor, as above, in- verted base 11	17	22
(B82) **767 Nurse,** kneeling....................11	17	22
(B83) **744 Nurse,** hand on hip................7	11	15
(B83a) Same as above in blue 50	75	100
(B84) **751 Soldier, Sharpshooter,** prone position................................10	15	20
(B85) **762 Wounded,** sitting, arm in sling.....................................9	14	19
(B86) **707 Sharpshooter**, standing, fir- ing, short stride 9	13	18

	C6	C8	C10
(B87) **747 Sharpshooter,** standing, fir- ing, long stride 8	12	16
(B88) **747** Sharpshooter, standing, fir- ing cast helmet 9	14	18
(B89) **748 Soldier, Running** with rifle, tin helmet 8	12	16
(B90) **748** Soldier, Running, with rifle, cast helmet 11	16	22
(B91) **749 Soldier, Gas Mask,** charging with rifle.......................................8	12	16
(B92) **749** Soldier, Gas Mask, charging with rifle cast helmet.....................13	20	26
(B93) 310 Army Motorcyclist...............20	30	40
(B93a) **310 Cop** on motorcycle.............20	30	40
(B93b) 310 Motorcyclist, head higher ..20	30	40
(B93c) 310 Cop on motorcycle, head lower 20	30	40
(B93d) 310 Motorcyclist, larger, mark- ings on cycle, like B93A and B93B, but cruder 25	38	50
(B93A) **310** Army Motorcyclist, post- War, dot eyes or none at all, larger, motor variation.....................25	38	50
(B93B) **310** Cop on Motorcycle, post- War, dot eyes, or none at all, larger, Motor variation 22	33	45
(B94) **715 Cowboy** with tin hat brim.....5	8	11
(B95) **752 Cowboy with lasso**...............7	11	14
(B95A) 752 Masked Cowboy with lasso..8	12	16
(B95a) 752 Cowboy with lasso, Post- WW II version, lasso goes directly through hands..............................7	11	14
(B96) **753 Cowboy With Two Guns,** pointing one 8	12	16

	C6	C8	C10
(B97) **754 Indian Chief**, tomahawk and shield............5	8	10
(B97a) Same as above, flat base, some with fatter lags 5	8	10
(B98) **755 Indian, Bow and Arrow** 5	8	10
(B99) **756 Indian Chief,** long headdress, may only have been produced post-WW II............36	54	72
(B100) **757 Indian Brave,** standing with bow and arrow, may only have been produced post WW II........11	16	22
(B101) **758 Camera Man,** kneeling, tin helmet............15	23	30
(B102) **759 Soldier, Stretcher Bearer,** open hand............36	54	72
(B102a) **759** Soldier, Stretcher Bearer, closed hand 8	12	16
(B103) **760 Surgeon,** with stethoscope.10	15	21
(B104) **761** Lying wounded, tin helmet..7	11	14
(B105) **763 Raiding,** in crouch, in helmet .8	12	16
(B106) **767 Advance,** raised rifle, tin helmet.11	17	23
(B107) **765 Bayoneting,** although no bayonet, thrusting with gun muzzle; tin helmet............20	30	40
(B107a) **756** Bayoneting, same as above, no bayonet, cast helmet 80	120	160

	C6	C8	C10
(B108) **766 Clubbing** with rifle, tin helmet.20	30	40
(B109) **766** Clubbing with rifle, cast helmet............45	68	90
(B110) **769 Cook** holding roast............13	20	26
(B110a) 769 Cook egg-timer............35	52	70
(B111) **771 Peeling Potatoes** 11	16	22
(B112) Soldier eating 17	27	35
(B113) 729 Soldier with Binoculars, long binoculars............9	14	18
(B114) **729 Soldier with Binoculars,** short binoculars............40	60	80
(B115) **760 Soldier Sitting Position** 13	20	27
(B116) **776 Officer Reading Orders** ...10	15	20
(B117) **774** Soldier with AA gun, tin helmet............9	14	18
(B118) **774** Soldier with AA gun, cast helmet 9	14	18
(B119) **775** Wounded on crutches 10	16	21
(B120) **776** Standing at searchlight, smooth lens, elevation wheel 50	75	100
(B120a) **776** Standing at searchlight, smooth lens, no elevation wheel 50	75	100
(B121) **776** Standing at searchlight, ridges along base (this and following have ridged lenses) 17	25	34

Top Row, Left to Right: B38, B39, B40, B42, B41, B43, B44. Bottom Row, Left to Right: B45, B46, B47, B48, B49, B51, B52. Photo by Bill Kaufman.

Left to Right: B12, B12a. Photo by K. Warren Mitchell.

Top Row, Left to Right: B64, B65, B66, B67, B68, B69. Bottom Row, Left to Right:B70, B71, B72, B73, B74, B75, B76. Photo by Bill Kaufman.

Top Row, Left to Right: B53, B60, B54, B55, B56, B57, B58, B59. Bottom Row, Left to Right: B61, B62, B63.

Top Row, Left to Right: B77, B78, B79, B79a, B80, B81a, B81, B82, B83.. Bottom Row, Left to Right: B84, B85, B86, B87, B88.

Top Row, Left to Right: B89, B90, B91, B92, B93. Bottom Row, Left to Right: B94, B95, B96, B97, B98, B99, B100. Photo by Bill Kaufman.

Top Row, Left to Right: B101, B102, B102a, B103, B104, B105, B106. Bottom Row, Left to Right: B107, B107a, B108, B109, B110, B111, B112, B107a. Courtesy Jeff Maund.

Top Row, Left to Right: B113, B114, B115, B116, B117, B118. Bottom Row, Left to Right: B119, B120, B121, B122, B124. Above photos by Bill Kaufman.

	C6	C8	C10
(B122) **776** Standing at searchlight, smooth base connected to searchlight, no elevation wheel 16		24	32
(B123) **776** Standing at searchlight, low seat, not connected to searchlight 11		16	22
(B124) **776** Standing at searchlight, high seat, two rivets in front of left foot 14		21	28
(B125) **776** Standing at searchlight, high seat, no rivets in front of left foot 14		21	28
(B126) **777** Marching with pack, tin helmet..............8		12	16
(B127) **777** Marching with pack, cast helmet.7		11	14
(B128) **778** Officer with gas mask, cast helmet..............10		15	20
(B129) **779** Firing from behind wall, cast helmet 30		45	60
(B130) **780** Falling with rifle, cast helmet .16		24	32
(B131) **781** Digging, cast helmet 22		33	45
(B132) **782** Leaning out, with field phone, antenna, cast helmet 31		46	62
(B133) **783** Crouching with binoculars, cast helmet 16		24	32
(B134) **784** Parachutist landing............10		15	20

	C6	C8	C10
(B135) **785** Skier in white, cast helmet, 1940, with separate metal skis. (Meant to be Finn) 12		19	25
(B136) **785** Skier in white, no skis.........9		14	18
(B137) **785** Skier in brown, no skis.......26		39	52
(B138) 785 Skier in red, meant to be Russian, may not have been produced (listed based on memory) ....No Price Found			
(B139) **787** Diver with axe 350		525	700
(B140) **788** Marching with slung rifle, cast helmet 7		11	14
(B141) **789** Soldier with AA gun, cast helmet, sitting.................10		16	21
(B142) **790** Two soldiers on raft, cast helmet................30		45	60
(B143) **791** Two-man rocket team.........11		17	22
(B144) **792** Mechanic with airplane engine, prop spins, brace on back of engine bulges 17		26	34
(B144a) Same as above, brace on back of engine doesn't bulge) 17		26	34
(B145) Soldier kneeling with anti-tank gun, cast helmet 12		19	25
(B146) **960 Surgeon and Soldier** 50		75	100

Top Row, Left to Right: B18a, B120a, B120, B177, B179, B180. Bottom Row, Left to Right: B181, B190, B191, B192, B193. Photo by Don Pielin.

Top Row, Left to Right: B131, B132, B133, B134, B135, B140, B141. Bottom Row, Left to Right: B142, B143, B144, B145, B146. Photo by Bill Kaufman.

Top Row, Left to Right: B123, B125, B126, B127. Bottom Row, Left to Right: B128, B129, B130. Photo by Bill Kaufman.

B139. Photo by Ed Poole.

	C6	C8	C10
(B147) **951 Soldier Wireless Operator** ..15		23	31
(B148) **952 Soldier, Dispatcher with Dog** 21		32	42
(B149) **953** American Legionnaire in overseas cap, tall, made for 1937 Legion convention in New York, 12 known color combinations........120		180	240
(B150) 954? American Legionnaire flag-bearer, tall, cloth flag, made in 1937, as above, five known 300		450	600
(B151) **961 At Typewriter,** with typewriter and table 30		45	60
(B151A) **770 At Mess,** typist alone, apparently meant to sit at mess table 6		10	13
(B152) **374 Army Motorcycle,** with side-car..30		45	60
(B153) **45** Two-man machine-gun car...21		32	42
(B154) **714 Pirate** 7		12	15
(B155) **713 Knigh**t with pennant 7		12	15
(B156) **712 Knight** with shield 6		9	12
(B157) **610 Woman Passenger,** with dog ..6		9	10
(B158) **611 Man Passenger**, overcoat over arm 5		8	10
(B159) **614 Red Cap** with bags 6		10	13

	C6	C8	C10
(B160) **613 Porter,** with whisk broom...6		9	12
(B161) **612 Conductor** 6		10	13
(B162) **615 Engineer** 5		8	11
(B163) **616 Boy** 5		8	11
(B164) **617 Girl**......................................5		8	10
(B165) **618 Elderly Woman**.................6		9	12
(B166) **619 Old Man** 7		11	14
(B167) **620** Minister walking 25		38	50
(B168) **621** Minister holding hat...........9		14	18\
(B169) **621** Newsboy 6		9	12
(B170) **622** Shoeshine boy 6		9	12
(B171) **623** Detective with pistol 62		94	125
(B172) **624** Burglar 39		60	78
(B173) **625 Bride** 10		15	20
(B174) **626 Groom** 10		15	20
(B175) **627** Girl in Rocker....................8		12	16
(B176) **628** Boy Skater..........................5		7	11
(B177) **629** Girl Skater 5		7	11
(B178) **630 1/2 Man and Woman on Park Bench** 13		20	27
(B179) Seated man and woman in winter coats................................10		15	20
(B180) **635 Man Speed Skater** 6		10	13
(B181) **636 Girl Figure Skater** 6		10	13
(B182) **801 Boy Scout Hiking**..............18		27	36
(B183) **802 Boy Scout Saluting** 15		23	31
(**B184**) **803 Boy Scout Signaling** 17		26	35
(B185) **804 Boy Scout Cooking** 22		34	45
(B186) **850 Policeman,** arm raised 8		12	16
(B186a) 850 Policeman, figure eight base...8		12	16
(B187) **851 Fireman,** with axe 11		16	21
(187a) Fireman with axe, flat under-base..12		19	25
(B188) **852 Fireman** (with hose)..........14		21	28
(B189) **853** Mailman 7		11	14
(B190) **495 Man on skis**......................8		13	17
(B191) **496 Girl on skis**......................8		13	17
(B192) **497 Man on Sled** 7		12	15

Top Row, Left to Right: B147, B148, B149, B150, B151. Bottom Row, Left to Right: B152, B153, B154, B155, B156. Photo by Bill Kaufman.

Top Row, Left to Right: B157, B158, B159, B160, B161, B162, B163, B164. Bottom Row, Left to Right: B165, B166, B167, B168, B169, B170, B171, B172. Photo by Bill Kaufman.

	C6	C8	C10
(B193) **498 Girl on Sled** 7	12	15
(B194) **499 Santa Claus on Sled**..........19	29	38
(B195) **500 Santa Claus on Skis**..........23	35	46
(B195a) **500 Santa Claus on Skis,** no skis or poles and no holes for them..........27	41	55
(B196) Santa Claus with holly sprig 30	45	60
(B197) Santa Claus seated, bag of toys at side, made to ride in sleigh 100	150	200
(B198) **510 One Horse Open Sleigh** (Sleigh, horse, seated man and woman).25	38	50
(B199) **530 Man Pulling Children on Sled**.25	38	50
(B200) **535 Young Man putting Skates on Girl Sitting on Bench**...50	75	100

Post World War II

	C6	C8	C10
(B201) **701** Flagbearer, pot helmet........11	17	22
(B202) 703? Kneeling, firing rifle..........17	26	35
(B203) **705** Port Arms 12	19	25
(B204) **707** Order Arms 11	16	22
(B205) 708 Officer with Sword..............10	15	20
(B206) **728** Prone Machine Gunner 9	14	18
(B207) 737 Tommy-gunner.......................9	14	9
(B208) **747** Standing Firing Rifle..........13	20	26
(B209) 774 AA Gunner 7	12	15

Top Row, Left to Right: B173, B174, B175, B176, B178, B182, B183, B184, B185. Bottom Row, Left to Right: B186, B187, B188, B189. Photo by Bill Kaufman.

	C6	C8	C10
(B210) 777 Marching at Slope 10	16	21
(B211) **788** Marching, rifle slung 11	16	22
(B212) **789** AA gunner 10	15	20
(B212a) Cowboy, two pistols, one in air...26	39	52
(B213) Drum Major..............................27	41	55
(B214) Drummer 22	33	45
(B215) Bugler......................................19	28	38
(B215A) Bugler, buttons run down front of uniform 22	34	45
(B216) Clarinetist................................22	34	45
(B217) Tubist......................................25	38	50
(B218) Sailor, white 17	26	35
(B218a) **720 Blue Sailor**......................17	26	35

BARCLAY POD FOOT SERIES
Circa 1950s to 1971

Most podfoot soldiers came in khaki and later, green.

	C6	C8	C10
(B219) **81 Two soldier Crew at Radar Equipment** 11	17	23
(B220) **82 Three Soldier Crew at Range Finder** 12	19	25
(B221) **83 Two Soldier Crew at Searchlight** 10	15	20
(B222) **84 Two soldier Crew at Mobile Cannon** 10	15	20
(B223) **85 Two Soldier Crew at A.A. Gun**.12	18	24
(B224) **187 Officer on Horse** (pot helmet)...37	53	75
(B225) **188 Cowboy on Horse** (lasso)..11	16	22
(B226) **189 Indian on Horse** 10	16	21
(B227) **190 Cowboy with Pistol on Horse**...8	12	16
(B228) **800 Black Knight w/Sword & Shield** 11	17	23
(B229) **801 Knight w/Red & Blue Shield & Sword** 15	23	30
(B230) **802 Knight w/Orange & Black Shield & Sword** 7	11	14
(B231) **803 Knight w/Red & Green Shield & Sword** 10	15	20
(B232) **901 Soldier Flag Bearer** 6	10	13

Top Row, Left to Right: B194, B195, B196, B197. Bottom B198. Photo by Don Pielin..

Top Row, Left to Right: B199, B200, B205. Bottom Row, Left to Right: B225, B227, B226. Photo by Don Pielin.

Top Row, Left to Right: B201, B202, B203, B204, B206. Bottom Row, Left to Right: B207, B208, B209, B210, B211, B212. Photo by Ed Poole.

Top Row, Left to Right: B219, B220, B221. Bottom Row, Left to Right: B222, B223. Photo by Ed Poole.

Left to Right: B213, B214, B215, B216, B217. Photo by Ed Poole.

Top Row, Left to Right: B224, B232, B233, B234, B235, B236. Bottom Row, Left to Right: B237, B218, B238, B239, B240, B241. Photo by Ed Poole.

Top Row, Left to Right: B228, B231, B230, B229, B247, B248, B250, B249, B251. Bottom Row, Left to Right: B252, B253, B254, B263, B265, B266, B267, B268, B269, B270. Photo by Dan Pielin.

	C6	C8	C10
(B232A) Same as above, in red (not shown).30	45	60
(B233) **903 Soldier Sniper** (kneeling)...6	9	12
(B233A) 903 same as above, in red (not shown)....20	30	40
(B234) **906 Soldier Charging** 6	10	13
(B234A) Same as above, in red (not shown).16	24	32
(B235) **908 Soldier Officer** 5	8	10
(B235A) Same as above, in blue.........32	48	64
(B235B) Same as above, in red...........15	23	30
(B236) **909 Soldier Bugler** 5	8	11
(B236A) Same as above, in red (not shown).17	27	35
(B237) **919 Sailor White Uniform** 5	8	10
(B238) **920 Sailor Blue Uniform** 7	11	15
(B239) **922 Marine** 7	11	14
(B240) **928 Soldier Machine Gunner Lying Flat**..............................5	8	10
(B240A) Same as above, in red...........18	27	36
(B241) **929 Soldier w/Pistol, Crawling** ..14	21	28
B(241A) Same as above, in red.............37	53	75
(B242) **937 Soldier, Charging Machine Gunner** (holding tommy gun).........7	11	14
(B242A) Same as above, in red...........18	27	36
(B243) **938 Soldier Bomb Thrower** 5	8	11
(B243A) Same as above,, in red...........16	24	32
(B244) **941 Aviator**............................6	9	12
(B244A) Same as above, in red...........18	27	36
(B245) **947 Soldier Marksman**............5	8	10
(B245A) Same as above, in red...........14	21	28
(B246) **948 Soldier Running**...............6	9	12
(B247) **950 Cowboy w/Pistol Shooting**....6	9	12
(B248) **951 Cowboy w/Rifle** 6	9	12
(B249) **952 Cowboy w/Lasso**...............4	6	8
(B250) **953 Cowboy w/Pistol** (upraised)...4	7	9
(B251) **954 Cowboy w/Shield & Tomahawk** 4	7	9
(B252) **955 Indian w/Rifle**..................4	7	9
(B253) **956 Indian w/Knife & Spear** ...5	8	10
(B254) **957 Indian w/Bow & Arrow** 5	8	10
(B255) **960 Soldier, Wounded, w/Crutches**..............................11	17	23
(B255A) Same as above, in red...........30	45	60
(B256) **961 Soldier, Wounded Head & Arm**......................................9	14	18
(B256A) Same as above, in red (not shown).24	36	48
(B257) **962 Nurse** 15	23	31
(B258) **974 Soldier, Anti-Aircraft Gunner**..................................6	9	12
(B258A) Same as above, in red...........20	30	40
(B259) **977 Soldier Under Marching Orders** (marching) 5	8	10
(B259A) Same as above, in red (not shown).15	23	30
(B260) **988 Soldier, Marching w/Gun on Back** (Gun slung over shoulder) 5	8	10
(B260A) Same as above, in red............15	23	30

	C6	C8	C10
(B261) **990 Soldier w/Bazooka**............6	10	13
(B261A) Same as above, in red............18	27	36
(B262) **991 Soldier Flame Thrower**....5	8	11
(B262A) 991, same as above, in red 14	21	28
"Midi" Size (Smaller Than Pod Foot)			
(B263) **200** Flame Thrower..................30	45	60
(B264) Bugler....................................30	45	60
(B265) Officer with binoculars 30	45	60
(B266) Talking on Field Phone 30	45	60
(B267) Advancing with Rifle................30	45	60
(B268) Marching, slung rifle................30	45	60
(B269) Firing Bazooka.........................30	45	60
(B270) Firing Tommygun 30	45	60
(B270A) Walking Forward, rifle at side, pointing down........................30	45	60
(B271) Cowboy with Rifle 6	9	12
(B272) Cowboy with Pistol 6	9	12
(B273) Indian with Hatchet....................6	9	12
(B274) Indian with Rifle 6	9	12
(B275) **350 Policeman**........................4	7	9
(B276) **351 Man**................................4	7	9
(B277) **352 Woman** 4	7	9
(B278) **353 Conductor**.......................4	7	9
(B279) **354 Redcap**............................4	7	9
(B280) **355 Oiler**...............................4	7	9
(B281) **356 Brakeman**........................4	7	9
(B282) **357 Engineer**.........................4	7	9
(B283) **358 Porter**.............................4	7	9
(B284) **359 Dining Steward**...............4	7	9
(B285) **360 Hobo** 4	7	9
(B286) **361 Newsboy** 4	7	9
(B287) **362 Mailman** 4	7	9
(B288) **363 Fireman**...........................4	7	9
(B289) **366 Peg Legged Gateman** 6	9	12
(B290) **369 Woman Carrying Baby**.....4	7	9
(B291) **370 Little Boy**........................3	5	7
(B292) **371 Little Girl**........................3	5	7
(B293) **372 Bride** 5	8	10
(B294) **373 Groom** 5	8	10
(B295) Woman with dog 6	9	12

Top Row, Left to Right: B271, B272, B273, B274, All others are 300 series. Photo by Don Pielin.

Left to Right: B242, B243, B244, B245, B246, B255, B256, B257. Photo by Ed Poole.

Left to Right: B258, B259, B260, B261, B262. Photo by Ed Poole.

MANOIL

(See also Vehicles, Aircraft, Ships and Miscellaneous)

Manoil began production of toy soldiers in 1935. It was in business as early as 1927 under the name Jack Manoil, turning out metal lamps and novelties at 34 West Houston Street in New York City. The company changed its name to Man-O-Lamp Corporation on July 11, 1928, and was owned by Maurice Manoil (12/4/1893-9/15/74) and Jack Manoil (1/29/02-9/1/55), two brothers who had emigrated from Rumania in the early 1900s. The final name-change to Manoil Manufacturing Co., Inc. took place on July 7, 1934.

The two brother were essentially partners, with Maurice handling the business end of the operation and Jack, who oversaw the creative area, working closely with Walter Baetz (1894-1978), who sculpted all the company's toys.

Manoil advanced firmly into toy-making in 1934, with seven vehicles, and moved to other addresses as it grew, leaving Manhattan in 1937 for Brooklyn, and then in June, 1940, moving to Waverly, New York (which afforded excellent shipping by rail), employing 225 people at its peak.

With the oneset of World War II, Manoil shut down, but then resumed production of soldiers in a fine-grained composition form (employing sulfur) in January, 1944. Brittle, the pieces were ultimately unsuccessful, and their manufacture ended by the end of the year.

After the Second World War, the company introduced several new lines of soldiers, (also containing some of its pre-War soldiers and its appealing Happy Farm series), but they were no longer distributed as widely.

Manoil's soldiers have a distinctive jauntiness to them, at times veering on caricature, the latter trait becoming more pronounced as the years wore on. In 1953 the firm moved to a smaller location in Waverly, changing its name to Jack Manoil Specialty Company, but went out of business shortly after Jack's death. Baetz and Jack Manoil were both keenly interested in the company's soldiers and would work late into the night as they collaborated on ideas for them. One of Baetz's continuing concerns was to design the molds so that there was no structural weakness in the soldiers as a result of air bubbles. For this reason, many of Manoil's soldiers were redesigned a number of times, sometimes with subtle and sometimes with broad variations.

Unlike Barclay, Manoil also produced plastic toys, selling millions of vehicles and airplanes in its later years. Models of Manoil and Barclay soldiers are being reproduced (see Leading Collectors and Dealers), hollow-cast from the original molds. **All bold words and numbers are Manoil's own description.**

Top Row, Left to Right: M1, M2, M3, M4, M5, M6, M7, M8, M9, M10. Bottom Row, Left to Right: M11, M12, M13, M14, M15, M16, M17. Photo by Bill Kaufman.

M23. Photo by Ed Poole.

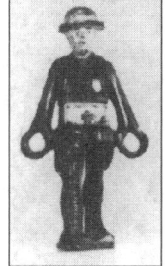

M58a. Photo by Don Pielin.

M38b. Photo by Norbert Schachter. Courtesy Peter & Marjorie Ruben.

	C6	C8	C10
(M1) **7 Flag Bearer,** hollow base version.	37	56	75
(M2) **7 Flag Bearer,** second version	10	16	21
(M3) **7 Flag Bearer**	10	15	20

	C6	C8	C10
(M4) **8 Parade,** hollow base version	20	30	40
(M5) **8 Parade,** stocky version	8	12	16
(M6) **8 Parade,** campaign cap straight			

Left to Right; Top: M18, M19, M20; Bottom: M21, M22, M23, M24, M25, M26, M27a, M27. Photo by Bill Kaufman.

Left to Right; Top: M28, M29, M30, M31, M32, M35, M36; Bottom: M37, M38, M38a, M39, M40, M41. Photo by Bill Kaufman.

	C6	C8	C10
on head	20	30	40
(M7) **8 Parade,** number on back	32	48	64
(M8) **8 Parade,** fifth version	8	12	16
(M9) **9 Officer,** hollow base version	37	56	75
(M10) **9 Officer,** second version	9	14	18
(M11) **10 Bugler,** hollow base version	30	45	60
(M12) **10 Bugler,** second version	9	14	18
(M13) **11 Drummer,** hollow base version	27	40	54
(M14) **11 Drummer,** stocky version	12	19	25
(M15) **11 Drummer,** vertical drum	17	26	35
(M16) **12 Machine Gunner (Prone),** grass on base	11	16	22
(M17) **12 Machine Gunner (Prone),** flat base, no grass	12	18	24
(M18) **12 Machine Gunner** (Prone), spaces under body	25	38	50
(M19) **12 Machine Gunner** (Prone), no aperture between hands and gun	12	18	24
(M20) **12 Machine Gunner** (Prone), no aperture, pack on back	9	14	18
(M21) **13 Cadet,** hollow base, no buckle on belt	22	33	44
(M22) **13 Cadet,** second version	9	14	18
(M23) **14 Sailor,** hollow base	22	33	44
(M23a) Same as above, in blue	25	38	50
(M24) **Sailor,** second version	8	12	16
(M25) **15 Marine,** hollow base	32	49	65
(M26) **15 Marine,** second version	8	12	16
(M27) **16 Ensign**	9	14	18
(M27a) **16 Ensign,** hollow base	32	49	65
(M28) **17 Signal Man,** hollow base version	20	30	40
(M29) **17 Signal Man,** second version	18	27	36
(M30) **18 Cowboy,** hollow base version	20	30	40
(M31) **18 Cowboy,** second version	9	14	18
(M32) **18A Cowboy With Hands Up**	10	15	20

	C6	C8	C10
(M33) **18A Cowboy With Hands Up** (subtle variation)	10	15	20
(M34) **20 Doctor** (same as 20K, but in white)	11	16	22
(M35) **20K Doctor** (khaki)	16	24	32
(M36) **21 Nurse**	8	12	16
(M36a) **21 Nurse,** no hem in skirt, shorter, etc.	14	21	28
(M37) **Indian** with hatchet	75	113	150
(M38) **22 Indian** with knives	7	12	15
(M38aa) **22 Indian,** with knives, same as above, minor difference in hairline may be casting flaw	No Price Found		
(M38a) **22 Indian,** with knives, right toes off base	10	15	20
(M38b) **22 Indian,** with knives, sarong-like garment, only three known	No Price Found		
(M39) **23 Machine Gunner Sitting,** seated on four pillows, bullets feed from ammo box	11	17	23
(M40) **23 Machine Gunner Sitting,** markings under base	11	17	23
(M41) **Machine Gunner Sitting,** squarer-looking, markings near right leg	11	16	22

Left to Right; Top: M42, M43, M44, M45, M46, M47; Bottom: M48, M49, M50, M51, M52, M53. Photo by Bill Kaufman.

Left to Right; Top: M55, M56, M57, M58, M59, M60, M61; Bottom: M62, M63, M64, M65, M66, M67. Photo by Bill Kaufman.

Left to Right: M36a, M36. Photo by K. Warren Mitchell.

Left to Right; Top: M68, M69, M70, M71; Bottom: M72, M73, M74, M75, M75b, M76, M77. Photo by Bill Kaufman.

	C6	C8	C10
(M42) **24 Cannon Loader** 7	12	15
(M43) **25 Sniper (kneeling)** hollow base, (may not be Manoil).............40	60	80
(M44) **25 Sniper (kneeling)** folding rifle 150	225	300
(M45) **25 Sniper (kneeling)** short thin rifle 9	14	18
(M46) **25 Sniper (kneeling)** longer, thicker rifle 10	15	20
(M47) **26 Sniper,** folding rifle 130	195	260
(M48) **26 Sniper** 9	14	18
(M48a) **26 Sniper,** shorter rifle, angle different on underside of rifle 10	15	20
(M49) **27 Tommy Gunner,** bloated version.....................................15	23	30
(M50) **27 Tommy Gunner,** second version.....................................10	15	20
(M51) **28 Observer** 9	14	18
(M52) **29 Wounded Soldier (Walking)** ...9	14	18
(M53) **30 Wounded Soldier (Lying)** 8	12	16
(M54) **30 Wounded Soldier (Lying)** number on back, shorter head 9	14	18
(M55) **31 Bomb Thrower,** three grenades in pouch....................8	12	17
(M56) **31 Bomb Thrower,** two grenades in pouch....................9	13	18
(M57) **32 Stretcher Carrier,** no medical kit...........................8	12	16

	C6	C8	C10
(M58) **32 Stretcher Carrier,** medical kit ..9	14	19
(M58a) **32 Stretcher Carrier,** medical kit, number on back, buttons on uniform, different pockets and collar from above 45	68	90
(M59) **33 Sitting Soldier** 20	30	40
(M60) **34 Aviator**.................................10	15	20
(M61) **35 Hostess,** in white 35	53	70
As above, in green.........................30	45	60
(M61a) **35 Hostess in Khaki**.................No Price Found
(M62) **36 Soldier With Bayonet Charging** 17	26	35
(M63) **37 Soldier with Gun Charging** ..22	33	44
(M64) **38 Soldier With Gun Butting** ..22	33	45
(M65) **39 Soldier With Bayonet Jabbing** 25	38	50
(M66) **40 Soldier (Kneeling With Bayonet)** 31	47	62
(M67) **41 Soldier (Crouching With Hand Grenade)** 30	45	60
(M68) **42 Field Doctor (Crawling)** 30	45	60
(M69) **43 Officer (Lying Down - Shooting Revolver)** 27	41	54
(M70) **44 Crawling Scout With Gun,** left leg high when right leg on ground (only three known).............90	135	180
(M71) **44 Crawling Scout With Gun,** left leg lower 27	41	54
(M72) **45 Observer (With Periscope)** .12	19	25
(M73) **46 Anti-Aircraft Gunner,** barrel of gun drops below arm 8	13	17
(M74) **46 Anti-Aircraft Gunner,** barrel of gun ends at arm 10	16	21
(M75) **47 Anti-Aircraft Searchlight** ...10	15	20
(M75a) **47** like above, with tin lens 55	83	110
(M75b) **47** like M75, number on back, helmet looks as if it was adapted to look like WW II helmet 11	17	22

Left to Right; Top: M79, M80, M81; Bottom: M82, M83, M84, M85, M86. Photo by Bill Kaufman.

Left to Right; Top: M87, M88, M89, M90, M91, M92; Bottom: M93, M94, M95, M96, M97, M98, M99, M100. Photo by Bill Kaufman.

Left to Right; Top: M101, M102, M103, M104, M105, M106; Bottom: M107, M108, M109, M110, M111. Photo by Bill Kaufman.

	C6	C8	C10
(M76) **48 Navy Gunner**	11	17	23
(M77) **49 Policeman**	8	12	17
(M78) **49 Policeman,** slightly larger	8	12	17
(M79) **50 Bicycle Dispatch Rider**	13	20	26
(M80) **51 Motorized Machine Gunner**	21	32	42
(M81) **52 Motorcycle Rider,** number over rear wheel, grass base	15	23	30
(M81a) **52** Same as above, motor variation	No Price Found		
(M82) **52 Motorcycle Rider**	20	30	40
(M83) **53 Sitting Soldier Without Gun**	17	26	35

	C6	C8	C10
(M84) **54 Sitting Soldier Eating**	23	35	46
(M85) **55 Sitting Soldier At Table With Phone & Map**	17	26	34
(M86) **56 Paymaster**	92	138	185
(M87) **57 Camouflage Sharpshooter Lying Down**	13	20	26
(M88) **58 Parachute Jumper**	10	15	20
(M89) **59 Soldier Writing Letter**	32	49	65
(M89a) Same as M89, foot not curled up, pencil is flat, helmet rounder, fuller	No Price Found		
(M90) **60 Cook's Helper With Ladle,** normal helmet	21	32	42
(M91) **60 Cook's Helper with Ladle,** helmet looks as if it was adapted to look like WW II helmet	60	90	120
(M92) **61 Soldier With Camera**	31	46	62
(M92a) **Soldier With Camera,** thinner arm	31	46	62
(M93) **62 Soldier With Gas Mask & Gun**	10	15	20
(M94) **63 Soldier With Gas Mask With Flare Pistol**	11	17	22
(M95) **64 Soldier Playing Banjo**	50	75	100
(M96) **65 Deep Sea Diver**	15	23	30
(M97) **65 Deep Sea Diver** with "65" on chest	10	15	20
(M98) **66 Soldier With Gun on Parade with Overseas Cap**	22	34	45
(M99) **67 Soldier With Gun and Pack Marching**	9	14	18
(M100) **68 Soldier Boxing**	37	53	75
(M101) **77 Lineman & Telephone Pole,** pole comes with two different-shaped bases, oval or diagonal	43	65	86
(M102) **78 Anti-Tank Gun,** round shield, 4 variations based on Vickers 2.95 mountain gun	15	23	30
(M103) **78 Anti-Tank Gun,** squared shield	15	23	30
(M103a) **78 Anti-Tank Gun,** angled shield	No Price Found		
(M104) **78 Anti-Tank Gun,** wooden wheels	30	45	60
(M105) **79 Soldier marching with gun slung at angle**	87	130	175
(M106) **80 Anti-Aircraft Machine Gunner**	9	14	18
(M107) **81 Machine Gunner and Helper,** aperture between hand and machine gun	16	24	32
(M108) **81 Machine Gunner and Helper,** no aperture	12	19	25

Left to Right: M112a, M113, M114, M115, M116, M117, M118. Photo by Bill Kaufman.

Left to Right; Top: M125, M126, M127; Bottom: M128, M129-M131. Photo by Bill Kaufman..

Left to Right: M132, M133, M134, M135, M137, M138, M139. Photo by Don Pielin.

Left to Right: M119, M120, M121, M122, M123, M124. Photo by Bill Kaufman.

	C6	C8	C10
(M109) **82 Anti-Aircraft With Range Finder** 12	19	25
(M110) **83 Soldier Trench Mortar** 12	19	25
(M111) **84 Soldier With Shell** 14	21	28
(M112) **85 Aviator Holding Bomb** 13	20	26
(M112a) **Aviator Holding Bomb,** hand variation.................................13	20	26
(M113) **86 Aviator Mechanic With Propeller,** away from head 250	375	500
(M114) **86 Aviator Mechanic With Propeller,** orange prop, flat lower hand 44	66	88
(M114a) **86 Silver prop** 60	90	120
(M114b) **86 Orange prop, curved lower hand** 44	66	88
(M115) 87 Aviator carrying bomb sight 20	30	40
(M115a) 87 Aviator carrying bomb sight, smaller base ....No Price Found		
(M116) **88 Radio Operator Standing** .27	41	55
(M117) **89 Radio Operator (Lying Down)** 17	26	35
(M118) **90 Soldier Digging Trench** 22	33	45
(M119) **91 Soldier With Barbed Wire,** wide-faced version 20	30	40
(M120) **91 Soldier With Barbed Wire** ..17	26	35
(M121) **92 Fire Fighter** in white..........37	53	75
(M121a) **92 Fire Fighter** in gray..........75	113	150
(M122) **93 Soldier on Guard Duty** ....55`	83	110
(M123) **94 Soldier Running With Cannon** marked "Manoil USA," "1" cannon slants to right when looked at from above 19	28	38

	C6	C8	C10
(M123a) **94 Soldier Running With Cannon,** no markings, cannon straight from above, face narrower 19	28	38
(M124) **94 Soldier Running With Cannon,** wood wheels, thin face 25	38	50
(M125) **99 Finn with Skis**...................40	60	80
(M126) **100 Finn Machine Gunner** 25	38	50
(M127) **101 Soldier Jumping With Chute** 50	75	100
(M127a) **101 Soldier Jumping With Chute,** foot variation, number in different place.................................No Price Found		
(M128) **102 Soldier Jumping With Machine Gun** 33	49	66

HAPPY FARM SERIES

According to the late Peter Ruben, a great number of color varieties and shades in this series exist, many of which can be related to the women who did the detail painting, and the season, as represented by 41/2 with long and short sleeve dresses. A number of Happy Farm figures were produced circa 1960 for the Smithsonian Museum, solid-cast with a patina or black finish.

	C6	C8	C10
(M129) **41/1 Bench**...............................4	7	9
(M130) **41/2 Girl** 4	7	9
(M131) **41/3 Young Man** 4	7	9
(M132) **41/4 Man Carrying Sack on Back** 10	15	20
(M133) **41/5 Farmer Pitching Sheaves** ...10	16	21

Left to Right; Top: M141, M142, M143, M144, M145, M146; Bottom: M147, M148, M149, M150, M151, M154. Photo by Don Pielin.

Left to Right; Top: M152, M153, M155, M156, M157, M158, M159, M160, M161; Bottom: M162, M163, M164, M165, M166, M167, M168, M169. Photo by Don Pielin.

Left to Right; Top Middle: M173; Bottom: M170, M171, M172, M174, M175, M176. Photo by Ed Poole.

Left to Right; Top: M177, M178, M179, M180, M181, M182; Bottom: M183, M184, M185, M186. Photo by Ed Poole.

Left to Right; Top: M187, M188, M189, M190, M191, M192, M193; Bottom: M194, M195, M196, M197. Photo by Ed Poole.

	C6	C8	C10
(M134) **41/6 Farmer Sharpening Scythe**	10	16	21
(M135) **41/7 Blacksmith Making Horseshoes**	12	19	25
(M136) **41/8 Farmer Cutting With Scythe**	11	17	22
(M137) **41/9 Farmer Cutting Corn**	12	18	24
(M138) **41/10 Farmer Sowing Grain**	10	15	20
(M139) **41/11 Man Carrying Sheaves Under Arm**	10	15	20
(M140) **41/12 Scarecrow With Top Hat**	12	19	25
(M141) **41/13 Farmer Carrying Pumpkin**	10	15	20

	C6	C8	C10
(M142) **41/12 Darky Eating Watermelon**	37	53	75
(M143) **41/15 Scarecrow With Straw Hat**	10	16	21
(M144) **41/16 Watchman Blowing Out Lantern**	11	17	23
(M145) **41/17 Hod Carrier With Bricks**	15	23	30
(M146) **41/18 Man Chopping Wood**	11	17	23
(M147) **41/19 Mason Laying Bricks**	19	28	38
(M148) **41/20 Man Dumping Wheel Barrow**	11	17	23
(M149) **41/21 Old Man Fixing Shoe**	16	25	33
(M150) **41/22 Blacksmith With Wheel**	12	18	24
(M151) **41/23 Carpenter Carrying Door**	18	27	36
(M152) **41/24 Hound**	8	13	17
(M153) **41/25 Carpenter Sawing Lumber**	12	18	24
(M154) **41/26 Carpenter With Square**	22	33	45
(M155) **41/27 Shepherd With Flute**	26	39	52
(M156) **41/28 Lady With Pie**	14	21	29
(M157) **41/29 Lady With Child**	15	23	30
(M158) **41/30 School Teacher**	18	27	36
(M159) **41/31 Girl Watering Flowers**	9	14	18

Left to Right; Top: M198, M199, M200, M201; Bottom: M202, M203, M204, M205, M206. Photo by Ed Poole.

	C6	C8	C10
(M160) **41/32 Woman Lifting Hen From Nest**	12	18	24
(M161) **41/33 Woman With Butter Churn**	11	16	22
(M162) **41/34 Woman Laying Out Wash On Grass**	14	21	28
(M163) **41/35 Woman Sweeping With Broom**	13	20	26
(M164) **41/36 Man Juggling Barrel**	15	23	30
(M164a) As above, in khaki	28	42	56
(M165) **41/37 Man Planting Tree**	20	31	41
(M166) **41/38 Girl Picking Berries**	26	39	52
(M167) **41/39 Farmer At Water Pump**	11	16	22
(M168) **41/40 Boy Carrying Wood**	12	18	24
(M169) **41/41 Stacks of Sheaves**	8	12	16
(M169) **41/41/ Haystack** is a rare variant, easily distinguished by the bottle and jug by its side	No Price Found		
(M169a) Boxed Happy Farm Set (10 pieces) mint with box, no standard contents	180	275	360

End Happy Farm Listing

MANOIL COMPOSITION

(MC1) Prone machine-gunner	25.00	37.50	50.00
(MC2) Seated machine-gunner	24	36	48
(MC3) Motorcyclist	24	36	48
(MC3A) Motorcyclist, mirror variation of above	24	36	48
(MC4) Firing camouflaged AA gun	24	36	48

POST-WAR

M170 through M176 were the first new Post WWII series, and were produced only for a limited time. On a trial basis early production was also sold unpainted.

	C6	C8	C10
(M170) Flag Bearer (thin), circa late 1945	13	20	26
(M171) Parade (thin), circa late 1945	16	24	33
(M172) Tommy Gunner (thin, circa late 1945)	14	21	28
(M173) Machine Gunner Sitting (thin), circa late 1945	30	45	60
(M174) Machine Gunner Lying (thin), circa late 1945	50	75	100
(M175) Sniper (thin), circa late 1945	27	41	54
(M176) **45/6** Parade (thin), circa late 1945	14	21	28
(M177) **45/7 Flag Bearer**	17	26	35
(M178) **45/8 Parade**	10	15	20
(M179) **45/9 Combat**	12	19	25
(M180) **45/10 At Attention** (present arms)	16	24	32
(M181) **45/11 Sniper**	17	26	34
(M182) **45/12 Tommy Gunner**	13	20	27
(M183) **45/13 Soldier With Bazooka Cannon** (some marked "45/18")	15	23	30
(M184) **45/14 Soldier With Shell For Bazooka** (some marked "46/14")	15	23	30
(M185) **45/15 General** (some "46/15")	77	112	155
(M186) **45/16 Mine Detector** (some "46/16")	19	28	39
(M187) **521** Flag Bearer, all 500s, circa 1950	13	20	27
(M188) **522** Parade	13	20	27
(M189) **523** Soldier in poncho	19	28	39
(M190) **524** Combat	15	23	31
(M191) **525** Aviator Holding Bomb	15	23	30
(M194) **528** Soldier with bazooka	12	18	24
(M195) **529** Motorcycle rider	24	36	48
(M196) **530** Machine gunner (lying)	16	24	32
(M192) **526** Observer	18	27	36
(M193) **527** Aircraft Spotter	19	29	38
(M197) **531** Machine gunner sitting	15	23	30
(M198) **532** Sniper (Kneeling)	16	24	32
(M199) **533** Soldier with gas mask with flare pistol	21	31	42
(M200) **534** Sniper	17	27	35
(M201) **535** Soldier throwing hand grenade	24	36	48
(M202) **536** Anti-Aircraft gunner	18	28	37
(M203) **537** Soldier with tommy gun	20	30	40
(M204) **538** Soldier firing up	18	28	37
(M205) **539** Stretcher bearer	55	83	110
(M206) **540** Wounded Soldier (lying)	57	86	115

MY RANCH CORRAL SERIES

	C6	C8	C10
(M207) **C-23 Cowboy Rider**	5	8	10
(M208) **C-24 Cowgirl Rider**	5	8	10
(M209) **C-29 Mounted Cowboy**	27	41	55
(M210) **C-30 Mounted Cowboy Shooting**	24	36	48
(M211 C2 Ranch fence, gate	37	53	75
(M212) C12 Blanket over Fence Section	16	24	32

Left to Right: M207, M208, M209, M210. Photo by Don Pielin.

Left to Right: M213, M215, M214, M218, M216, M212.

	C6	C8	C10
(M213) C18 Small Calf	6	9	13
(M214) C20 Bull, head turned	7	11	15
(M215) C19 Cow feeding	6	9	12
(M216) C28 Short Cactus	7	11	15
(M217) C14 Brahma Bull	8	12	16
(M218) C26 Large Cactus	13	20	26

	C6	C8	C10
(M219) C1 Fence	4	7	9
(M220) C25 Small Horse	12	19	25
(M221) Horse for Mounted Cowboy	10	15	20
(M222) Horse for Mounted Cowgirl	11	17	22
(M223) Small Gate	15	23	30
(M224) Large Gate	14	21	28

GREY IRON

Grey Iron made the only 3¼" cast iron soldiers. The company began in 1840 as the Brady Machine Shop in Mount Joy, Pennsylvania, where it has remained to this day, and in 1881 was organized as the Grey Iron Casting Company, Limited. As early as 1903 it was manufacturing toy banks and stoves, cap pistols, wheeled toys and trains, as well as a number of non-toy items. On August 14, 1917, the company was granted two patents for their 40 mm solid cast iron Grey Klip Armies, which they then manufactured through 1941, the last of the series emerging in1938 as "Uncle Sam's Defenders", painted khaki rather than nickel-plated, as the earlier versions had been. The soldiers were not successful at first, but with the advent of a new distributor, the company was swamped with orders, and in January, 1933, introduced a new line of thirty-five different cast iron soldiers, in an approximately 3" size (four Revolutionary War soldiers; an infantryman, a foot officer, a flagbearer and a mounted officer, may have been introduced earlier, as they are numbered lower, but were not part of the 1933 announcement).

The figures tended to be slight, and while apparently successful, were superseded in July 1936 by Grey's "Iron Men" series, a slightly larger, more robust model, which continued to be sold until World War II ended all toy production. Designers for the soldiers were at least two; Edward Musser and Samuel S. Schmidt. The soldiers were hand-poured and then painted on an assembly-line basis, and at least initially were sold for a dime, while their competitors charged a nickel. Grey is still in business today as the John Wright division of Donsco, and has recently been producing, on an erratic basis, some unpainted soldiers from its old molds. Some years ago, the author saw, at a Pennsylvania flea market, some crude, cast iron Continental Soldiers, about 2½" high, which he believes may be early Grey Iron, but none have surfaced since, and there is no evidence that Grey made them. However, they would be valuable to serious collectors, and in mint would probably bring about $40 apiece. **All bold words and numbers are Grey Iron's own description.**

GREYKLIP ARMIES

	C6	C8	C10
(GA) **Set 1/Company A,** at attention, consists of bugler, officer, flagbearer, drummer, rifleman, price per each	2	3	4
(GB) **Set 2/Company B,** marching, consists of bugler, officer, flagbearer, drummer, rifleman, price per each	2.50	3.75	5
(GC) **Set 3/Company C,** charging, consists of bugler, officer, flag-bearer, drummer, rifleman, pricer per each	2.50	3.75	5
(GD) **Set 4/Troop D,** consists of four mounted troopers, one mounted officer, troopers all look alike, pricer per each	4	6	8
(GE) **Set 5/Battery E,** two-piece set, leb by officer from Troop D, second piece is a gun limber with four horses, several attached soldiers, price for second piece	6	9	12
(GF) **Set 6/Battery F,** consists of shell stack, loader bending, loader standing, gunner, cannon, price per each, shells double	3.50	5.25	7

Very rare Grey Iron set No. F114 "American Family on the Farm" boxed set. Traded in 1987 for estimated value of $325. Barn is part of set. Courtesy K. Warren Mitchell.

GREY IRON (GD) Set 4, Troop D. Courtesy Karl Zipple.

GREY IRON (GA) Set 1, Company A. Courtesy Karl Zipple.

GREY IRON (GE) Set 5, Battery E. Courtesy Don Pielin.

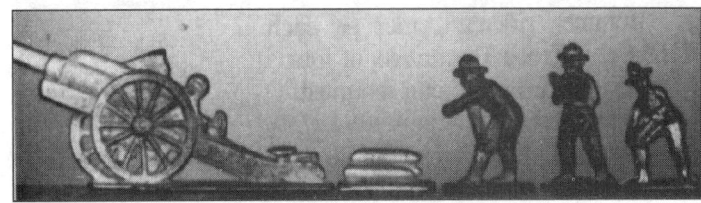

GREY IRON (GF) Set 6, Battery F. Courtesy Don Pielin.

GREY IRON (GB) Set 2, Company B. Courtesy Karl Zipple.

GREY IRON (GG) Set 5, Aviation Corps. Courtesy Karl Zipple.

GREY IRON (GC) Set 3, Company C. Courtesy Karl Zipple.

GREY IRON (GH) Uncle Sam's Defenders. Courtesy Karl Zipple.

	C6	C8	C10

(GG) Set 5/Aviator Corps, consists of
pilot (two of the same figure in
set) and plane with detachable
wing. Price for set 70 105 140

(GH) **Uncle Sam's Defenders,** consists
of charging rifleman, machine
gunner, charging officer, rifleman
at attention, flagbearer, officer
saluting, price per each (double
the price on saluting officer and
flagbearer) 6 9 12

End Greyklip Armies

(G1) **1 Colonial Soldier** 11 17 23
(G2) **1A Colonial Foot Officer**............12 19 25
(G3) **1B Colonial Color-Bearer** 175 263 350
(G3a) 1B Colonial Color-Bearer, 1950s
version, with rifle barrel drilled
out for flag..25 38 50
(G4) **1MA Colonial Mounted Officer** ..20 30 40
(G5) **2 Cadet,** early version 7 11 15
(G6) **2 Cadet**..11 17 22
(G7) **2A Cadet Officer,** early 9 14 18
(G8) **2A Cadet Officer** 12 19 25
(G9) **3 U.S. Infantry, Shoulder Arms,**
early..8 12 16
(G10) **3 U.S. Infantry, Shoulder Arms** .7 11 15
(G10a) Same as above, no tie..................No Price Found
(G11) **3/1 U.S. Infantry, Port Arms**....10 15 21
(G12) **3A U.S. Infantry Officer,** early .8 12 16
(G13) **3A U.S. Infantry Officer** 7 11 15
(G14) **3AP Traffic Officer** (same as
above, in blue)................................11 17 22
(G15) **3AR Red Cross Officer** (same
as above, with armband) 17 26 35
(G16) **4 U.S. Infantry, Port Arms,** early ...8 12 16
(G17) **4A U.S. Doughboy Officer With**
Field Glasses 11 17 22
(G18) **4/1 U.S. Doughboy Signaling** ...12 19 25
(G19) **4/2 U.S. Doughboy Combat**
Trooper...12 18 24
(G20) **4/3 U.S. Doughboy With Range**
Finder 40 60 80
(G21) **4/4 U.S. Doughboy Ammunition**
Carrier...42 63 85
(G22) **4/5 U.S. Doughboy Sharpshooter** .12 18 24
(G23) **4/6 U.S. Doughboy With**
Bayonet...11 17 22
(G24) **5 U.S. Infantry, Charging,** early7 11 15
(G25) **6 U.S. Doughboy, Port Arms,**
early..8 13 17
(G26) **6 U.S. Doughboy, Shoulder Arms** 5 8 11
(G27) **6A U.S. Doughboy Officer,**
early..9 14 18

*Left to Right; Top: G1, G2, G3, G3a, G4, G5, G6, G7, G8; Bottom: G9,
G10, G11, G12, G13, G15, G16, G17, G18. Photo by Ed Poole.*

*Left to Right; Top: G19, G20, G21, G22, G23, G24, G25; Bottom:
G26, G27, G28, G29, G30, G31, G32, G33. Photo by Bill Kaufman.*

*Left to Right; Top: G34, G35, G37, G38, G39, G40, G41; Bottom:
G42, G45, G46, G47, G48, G49, G50. Photo by Bill Kaufman.*

	C6	C8	C10

(G28) **6A U.S. Doughboy Officer** 7 11 15
(G29) **6/1 U.S .Doughboy Charging** 7 11 14
(G30) **6/2 U.S. Doughboy Sentry** 11 17 22
(G31) **6/3 U.S. Doughboy Bomber,**
crawling...8 13 17
(G32) **6/4 U.S. Doughboy Grenade**
Thrower.......................................15 23 30
(G33) **7 U.S. Doughboy Charging,** early .6 10 13

Left to Right; Top: G51, G52, G53, G54, G55, G56, G57; Bottom: G58, G59, G60, G61, G62.

Left to Right; Top: G64, G65, G66, G68, G69, G71, G72, G73, G74, G75; Bottom: G76, G77, G78, G79, G80, G81, G82, G83, G84. Photo by Bill Kaufman.

Left to Right; Top: G85, G86, G87, G88, G89, G90, G91, G92; Bottom: G93, G94, G95, G96, G97, G98.

Left to Right: G99, G100, G101, G102, G103, G104, G105. Photo by Bill Kaufman.

	C6	C8	C10
(G34) **8M U.S. Cavalryman,** early......17	25	34
(G35) **8M U.S. Cavalryman**................15	23	30
(G36) **8M U.S. Cavalry Color Bearer With Silk Flag** (not shown, same as G34) ....No Price Found		
(G37) **8MA U.S. Cavalry Officer,** early..18	28	37
(G38) **8MA U.S. Cavalry Officer** 17	26	35
(G39) **9 U.S. Marine,** early 6	10	13
(G40) **9 U.S. Marine** 8	12	16
(G42) **10 Royal Canadian Police,** early11	17	22
(G42) **10 Royal Canadian Police** 16	24	32
(G43) **10M Royal Canadian Mounted Police** (same as G34) 21	31	42
(G44) **10M Royal Canadian Mounted Police** (same as G35) 22	33	45
(G45) **11 Indian,** with hatchet, early 7	11	14
(G46) **11 Indian Chief,** with knife 8	13	17
(G47) **11/1 Indian Brave,** shielding eyes................................11	17	22
(G48) **11/2 Chief Attacking,** upraised tomahawk 50	75	100
(G49) **11M Indian Mounted,** early......17	25	34
(G50) **11M Indian Mounted,** lying on horse 37	53	75
(G51)**11/1M Indian Scout, Mounted,** firing pistol rearward..................100	150	200
(G52) **12 Cowboy,** early 6	9	13
(G53) **12 Cowboy** 6	9	13
(G54) **12/1/Hold-Up Man** 10	15	20
(G55) **12/2 Cowboy With Lasso,** with lasso price is 50.00 in mint.............18	27	36
(G56) **12/3 Bandit,** surrendering 45	68	90
(G57) **12M Cowboy Mounted,** early...22	33	44
(G58) **12M Cowboy Mounted**..............27	41	55
(G59) **12/1M Masked Cowboy Mounted** 110	165	220
(G60) **13 U.S. Machine Gunner,** early .7	11	14
(G61) **13 U.S. Machine Gunner**...........7	11	14
(G62) **13/1 U.S. Machine Gunner**........8	13	17
(G63) **14 U.S. Sailor,** in blue, early 8	13	17

	C6	C8	C10
(G64) **14 U.S. Sailor,** in white, early 7	11	15
(G65) **14 U.S. Sailor,** in blue 7	11	15
(G66) **14W U.S. Sailor,** in white 7	11	15
(G67) **14A U.S. Naval Officer,** early, in blue................................8	12	16
(G68) **14AW U.S. Naval Officer,** early, in white...............................8	13	17
(G69) **14A U.S. Naval Officer,** in blue .7	11	14

Left to Right: G106, G107. Courtesy Hank Anton.

	C6	C8	C10
(G102) Greek Evzone	60	90	120
(G103) **75 Radio Set, Operator and Aerial**	75`	113	150
(G103A) **75 Radio Set, Operator only**	48	73	95
(G104) **D26 Nurse and Wounded Soldier**	105	158	210
(G105) **D27 Doughboy Supporting Wounded Soldier**	125	188	250
*(G106) U.S. Cavalryman, probably Grey Iron, like G34, but horses's head and left leg up	70	105	140
*(G107) U.S. Cavalry Officer, Probably Grey Iron, like G87, but horse's head and left leg up	60	90	120

*These may not have been produced by Grey Iron, but instead by Distinctive Products, Inc.

	C6	C8	C10
(G108) **6AF Foreign Legion Officer**	14	21	28
(G109) **6F Foreign Legion - Shoulder Arms**	14	21	28
(G110) **6/1F Foreign Legion Charging**	14	21	28
(G111) **6/3 Foreign Legion Bomber**	19	27	38
(G112) **13F Foreign Legion Machine Gunner**	14	21	28
(G113) **8A/F Foreign Legion Cavalry Officer**	27	41	55
(G114) **8/F Foreign Legion Cavalryman**	27	21	55
(G115) Foreign Legion Stretcher Bearer, only one known	No	Price	Found

AMERICAN FAMILY SERIES
(approximately 2¼ high)

The American Family Travels

	C6	C8	C10
T-1 **Man in traveling suit**	5	8	10
T-2 **Woman in traveling costume**	5	8	10
T-3 **Boy in traveling suit**	6	9	12
T-4 **Girl in traveling suit**	6	9	12
T-5 **Conductor**	5	8	10
T-6 **Engineer**	5	8	10
T-7 **Porter**	6	9	12
T-8 **Policeman**	5	8	10
T-9 **Postman**	5	8	10
T-10 **Newsboy**	6	9	12
T-11 **Preacher**	6	10	13
T-12 **Old Colored Man - sitting**	8	12	16
T-13 **Seat**	4	6	8

The American Family on the Farm

	C6	C8	C10
F-1 **Farmer**	4.50	6.75	9
F-2 **Farmer's Wife**	4.50	6.75	9
F-3 **Girl**	5	7.50	10
F-4 **Hired Man digging**	5	7.50	10
F-5 **Horse**	3.50	5.25	7
F-6 **Cow**	3.50	5.25	7

	C6	C8	C10
(G70) **14AW U.S. Naval Officer** in white	6	10	13
(G71) **14/1W U.S. Sailor Signalman**	14	21	28
(G72) **15/1 Boy Scout Saluting,** early	9	14	19
(G73) **15/2 Boy Scout Walking,** early	8	13	17
(G74) **16/1 Pirate Boy** (all pirates circa 1935, were also sold as a Treasure Island set, with either tent or treasure chest included, pirates meant to represent Jim, Captain Flint, Long John, Blind Pew, Billie Bones)	12	18	24
(G75) **16/2 Pirate Chief**	10	15	20
(G76) **16/3 Pirate With Dagger**	11	17	22
(G77) **16/4 Pirate With Hook**	10	15	20
(G78) **16/5 Pirate With Sword**	9	14	18
(G79) **17/1 Legion Drum Major,** early	21	32	42
(G80) **17/1 Legion Drum Major**	10	15	20
(G81) **17/2 Legion Bugler,** early	7	11	15
(G82) **17/2 Legion Bugler**	8	12	16
(G83) **17/3 Legion Drummer,** early	9	14	18
(G84) **17/3 Legion Drummer**	7	11	15
(G85) **17/4 Legion Color Bearer**	7	11	15
(G86) **18/1 Ethiopian Tribesman,** circa 1936	26	39	53
(G87) **18/2 Ethiopian Chief**	28	43	57
(G88) **18/3 Ethiopian Soldier, Shoulder Arms**	19	28	38
(G89) **18/3A Ethiopian Officer**	25	38	50
(G90) **18/5 Ethiopian Soldier, Charging**	30	45	60
(G91) Italian or English Desert Infantryman	125	188	250
(G92) Italian or English Desert Officer	85	128	170
(G93) **19 Knight In Armor**	8	12	16
(G94) **20 Red Cross Doctor**	15	23	30
(G95) **21 Stretcher Bearer**	20	30	40
(G96) **22 Stretcher With Patient**	14	21	28
(G97) **22/1/Wounded Sitting**	48	72	96
(G98) **22/2 Wounded On Crutches**	20	30	40
(G99) **23 Red Cross Nurse**	12	18	24
(G100) **25 Aviator** (24 is non-soldier)	19	29	39
(G101) Ski Trooper, circa 1940, with skis four times the noted price	12	18	25

Left to Right; Top: T1, T2, T3, T4, T5, T6, T7, T8, T9, T10, T11, T12, T13; Bottom: F1, F2, F3, F4, F11, F7, F9, F8, F12, F7, F6, F5. Photo by Don Pielin.

Left to Right; Top: B1, B2, B3, B4, B5, B6, B7, B8, B9, B11, B10, B12; Bottom: H1 to H11. Photo courtesy Don Pielin.

	C6	C8	C10
F-7 Calf	3.50	5.25	7
F-8 Pig	3.50	5.25	7
F-9 Sheep	3.50	5.25	7
F-10 Goat	3.50	5.25	7
F-11 Goose	3.50	5.25	7
F-12 Dog	3.50	5.25	7
F-13 Gate with Post	10	15	20
F-14 Fence	7	11	14

THE AMERICAN FAMILY AT HOME

	C6	C8	C10
H-1 Man with watering can	5	8	11
H-2 Woman with basket	7	11	14
H-3 Boy flying kite	8	12	16
H-4 Girl skipping rope	10	15	20
H-5 Old man sitting	3.50	5.25	7
H-6 Old woman sitting	4	6	8
H-7 Colored cook	9	13.50	18
H-8 Colored man digging	16	24	32
H-9 Garageman	5	7.50	10
H-10 Delivery Boy	5	7.50	10
H-11 Milkman	6	9	12
H-12 Dog	3.50	5.25	7
H-13 Lawn Seat	4	6	8

THE AMERICAN FAMILY ON THE BEACH

	C6	C8	C10
B-1 Man in bathing suit	10	15	20
B-2 Woman in bathing suit	10	15	20
B-3 Boy in summer suit	6	9	12
B-4 Girl in slacks	9	13.50	18

	C6	C8	C10
B-5 Old Man Sitting	3.50	5.25	7
B-6 Boy with Life Preserver	9	13.50	18
B-7 Girl with Sand Pail	9	13.50	18
B-8 Boy with Ball	9	13.50	18
B-9 Girl Catching Ball	8	12	16
B-10 Life Guard	11	16	22
B-11 Life Guard's Chair	12	18	24
B-12 Life Boat	12	18	24
B-13 Bench	4	6	8
B-14 Cabana	No Price Found		

THE AMERICAN FAMILY ON THE RANCH

	C6	C8	C10
R-1 Cowboy with lasso	9	14	18
R-2 Cowboy Rider	19	28	38
R-3 Cowboy squatting	8	12	16
R-4 Boy in CowboySuit	8	12	16
R-5 Girl in Riding Suit	7	11	15
R-6 Cowgirl Rider	11	16	22
R-7 Stallion	8	12	16
R-8 Bucking Bronco	10	15	20
R-9 Colt	6	9	12
R-10 Burro	7	11	15
R-11 Calf	5	8	11
R-15 Rooster and Chickens	4	6	8
R-16 Three Ducks	5	8	10

THE CHAMPIONS ON THE DIAMOND

M69 Fielder in Position, appox 1½" high.....................No Price Found

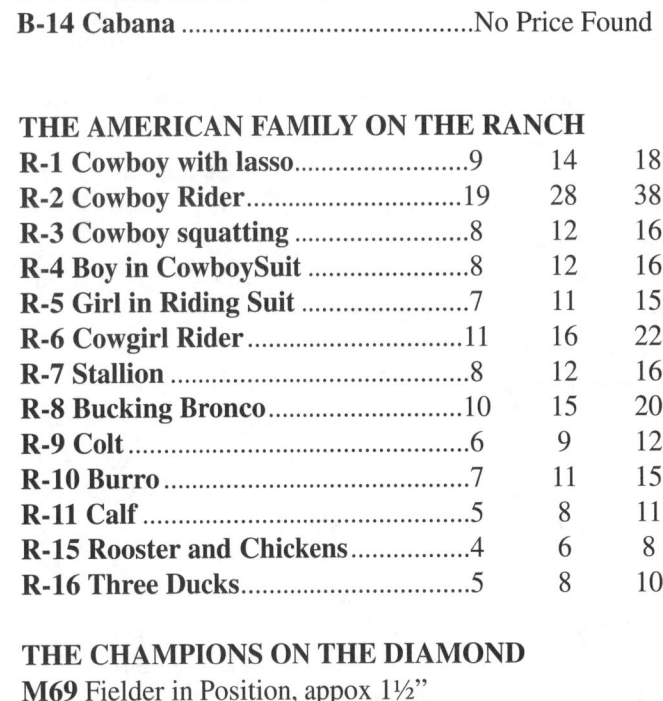

Left to Right: R1, R3, R6/R7, R10, R11, R2/R8, R5, R4, R9. Photo by Don Pielin.

AUBURN RUBBER

Although AUBURN (also Aub-Rub'r) was founded in 1913, in Auburn, Indiana, as the Double Fabric Tire Corporation, making auto tubes and tires for Model T Fords, etc., it didn't produce its first toy until 1935, with five soldiers. The prototype was a Palace Guard, which AUBURN President and chief stockholder A.L. Murray had obtained in England. The model was taken to a local pattern-maker who made patterns from it, and then the company made the original molds from lead and molded sample toys for Murray. These samples were next taken to an artist and decorated per Murray's instructions. Presented to buyers, they immediately caught on. The soldiers were molded in 24" rubber presses, each containing forty to sixty soldiers, with cure time approximately 6-12 minutes. The soldiers, once trimmed, were dipped in a base laquer (advertised as "pure vegetable dyes") and then sent down a decorating conveyor, where as many as 24 women, using small camel hair brushes, added finishing touches, painting the faces, shoes, belts, buttons, medals, and finally eyes. After drying, each was wrapped individually in waxed paper and packed three dozen to a chip-board carton and twelve dozen to a corrugated carton for shipment. Design of the soldiers was credited to Edward McCandlish, a free-lance artist. The soldiers sold well from the beginning, with approximately 200 of the 400 AUBURN employees (AUBURN consistently made non-toy products as well) involved in them and other toys on a two-shift basis. Shortly after the first soldiers were introduced, animals and wheeled vehicles, the first a Cord automobile, were marketed, all successfully. AUBURN produced no soldiers during the war, and few after, though it continued to make toys in great quantity (70,000 wheeled items a day in 1962, for example). In 1960 the toys portion of AUBURN was purchased by the town of Deming, New Mexico, where it remained until it went out of business in 1969. AUBURN'S soldiers, all approximately the standard 3¼" length, went through three stages. The first were frail-looking, with long, thin bodies; the second, which emerged as early as September, 1938 , were stockier and larger-headed, and the third, introduced in 1941, were more well-proportioned and realistic. Unlike its competitors, AUBURN produced no cowboys, Indians, sailors or civilians, except for baseball and football players and two farm workers. AUBURN's infantry came in colors other than brown. The blue were meant to represent U.S. Marines. The white also were sold as Marines. It is thought that some Auburn Ethiopians remain to be discovered. Still elusive is the A35 running pilot, known to have been sold, but with none currently known to be in any collection.

*(All **bold words** and numbers are **Auburn's own description**)*

	C6	C8	C10
(A1) **1200 Infantry Private**	6	10	13
(A2) **200 U.S. Infantry Private**	5	8	11
(A3) **1202 Infantry Bugler**	9	14	18
(A4) **202 Bugler, U.S. Infantry**	9	14	18
(A5) **Foreign Legion**, also **White Guard** officer, **No. 220**	11	17	22
(A6) **214 & 218 Foreign Legion Private** .	10	15	20
(A7) Ethiopian with shield and rifle	60	90	120
(A7a) Ethiopian bugler .... No Price Found			
(A7b) Ethipian with rifle and shield, in robes	50	75	100
(A8) Officer, early	7	11	14
(A9) **204 U.S. Infantry Officer**	7	11	14
(A10) **1238 Charging Soldier**	22	34	44
(A11) **238 Charging Soldier** with tommy gun	7	11	15
(A12) **232 Officer on Horse**	18	27	36
(A13) **230 Machine Gunner**	7	11	15
(A14) **224 Red Cross Doctor**	17	26	35
(A14a) Army Doctor, Khaki uniform ..... No Price Found			
(A15) **226 Red Cross Nurse** white or khaki uniform	17	26	35
(A16) **206 Stretcher Bearer**	15	23	30
(A17) **208 Wounded Soldier**	17	26	35

A14a. Photo by Ron Steiner.

Rough sketch from memory going back 40 years of A35. Note no box in hand, head tilted up toward left, left hand forward. None known.

Auburn A19a. Courtesy John Stetson.

Left to Right; Top: A1, A2, A3, A4, A5, A6, A7, A7a, A8, A9; Bottom: A10, A11, A12, A13, A14, A15, A16. Photo by Bill Kaufman.

Left to Right; Top: A34, A36, A37, A38, A39; Bottom: A40, A41. A42, A43, A44, A45, A46. Photo by Bill Kaufman.

Left to Right; Top: A17, A18, A19, A20; Bottom: A21, A22, A23, A24. Photo by Bill Kaufman.

Left to Right; Top: A25, A26, A27, A28, A29; Bottom: A30, A31, A32, A33. Photo by Bill Kaufman.

	C6	C8	C10
(A18) **216 Observer With Binoculars**	7	11	15
(A19) **236 Signalman**	30	45	60
(A19a) **Signalman**, early smaller size, only three known	100	150	200

	C6	C8	C10
(A20) **222 Sniper**, crawling, rifle over shoulder	36	54	72
(A21) **234 Bomb Thorwer**	12	18	24
(A22) **242 Anti-Aircraft Gun**	15	23	30
(A23) **1546 Motorcycle Cop**, blue or khaki as soldier	25	38	50
(A24) **240 Motorcycle Soldiers,** with sidecar	25	38	50
(A25) **Aircraft Defender**	15	23	30
(A26) **Color Bearer**	22	33	44
(A27) **Marching Soldier**	9	14	18
(A28) **Firing Soldier**	22	33	44
(A29) **272 Plane Shooter**	18	27	36
(A30) **Sound Detector**	17	25	34
(A31) **Searchlight**	18	27	37
(A32) **296 Trench Mortar**	16	24	32
(A33) **Tank Defender**	24	36	48
(A34) **Tank Soldier,** running with box	17	26	35
(A35) Pilot running, looking skyward, in pilot helmet and goggles	No Price Found		
(A36) **Motor Scout**	20	30	40
(A37) **258 Baserunner**	13	20	26
(A38) **252 Batter**	20	30	41
(A39) **256 Fielder or Baseman**	14	21	29
(A40) **250 Pitcher**	21	31	42
(A41) **254 Catcher**	17	25	34
(A42) **268 Carrier** football player	17	26	35
(A43) **264 Center** football player	16	24	32
(A44) **262 Backfieldman,** football player	15	23	30
(A45) **260 Lineman,** football player	16	24	32
(A46) **266 Passer,** football player	21	32	42
(A47) Motorcycle Cop, large 5" high	25	38	50
(A48) Cowboy, large, on wheeled horse	30	45	60

JONES

Jones' 3¼" hollow lead soldiers probably began in the late 1930s, apparently cutting off in September, 1941. Sculpting was by a Polish immigrant, Henry Kasselowski, who also designed the toy soldiers for Lincoln Log until the 1950s, when England's Crescent took over the Lincoln Log line. Jones was owned by J. Edward Jones, who operated under a number of company names from 1930 into the 1960s, among them Miniature Products, Metal Miniatures, Metal Arts, Military Miniatures, World Miniatures and the Visual History Association. It is now known that the prone German (J3) was made directly over Barclay B61, Kasselowski removing the tin helmet, shaping a German helmet of red wax, then making a plaster cast of the entire figure, from which a bronze mold was made. Many, and perhaps all, of the Jones soldiers were also painted in gray, as "enemy". In 1982, research disclosed that Jones, under the company name of Metal Arts, produced an entirely different set of 3" lead figures from 1929-1931.

	C6	C8	C10
(J1) German, kneeling with rifle 102	53	205
(J1a) Same as above, short rifle 110	165	220
(J2) German, charging with rifle...........95	143	190
(J3) German, prone machine gunner.....70	105	140
(J4) Observer with binoculars and rifle...37	53	75
(J5) Wire-cutter, prone 225	338	450
(J6) Soldier with rifle, gassed or shot in neck 175	263	350
(J7) Stretcher-bearer............................50	75	100
(J8) Kneeling with AA Gun 40	60	80
(J9) Charging, port arms 125	188	250
(J10) Firing machine gun on stump 40	60	80
(J10a) Same as above, No. 1 on pocket 100	150	200
(J11) Grenade thrower, no weapons......55	83	110
(J12) Seated with rifle 38	53	76
(J13) Officer in greatcoat, pointing, holding pistol...........110	165	220
(J14) Prone with rifle, trunk upraised ...75	113	150
(J15) Prone, firing double-barreled machine gun 50	75	100
(J16) Kneeling, firing anti-tank gun......40	60	80
(J16a) Same as above with barrel brace, "23" on wheel 50	75	100
(J17) Cook with chef's hat, frying pan 30	45	60
(J18) Ammunition Carrier.....................200	300	400
(J19) Motorcyclist with machine gun mounted on motorcycle...........70	105	140
(J20) Flagbearer (similar to Barclay B7)...........90	135	180
(J21) Kneeling with searchlight 37	53	75
(J21a) Kneeling with searchlight, "27" "Made in USA" on sides of stanchion 50	75	100
(J22) Seated with phone.........................45	68	90
(J23) Kneeling, firing rifle, no stand.....62	93	125
(J23a) Same as above, shorter rifle 70	105	140
(J24) Prone, body arched, firing machine gun 60	90	120

	C6	C8	C10
(J25) Bugler 82	123	165
(J26) Soldier with gas mask, plunging rifle down, slightly smaller in size ..112	169	225
(J27) Nurse with bag, like Barclay B82 ..40	60	80
(J28) Doctor with bag, like Barclay B81 (in khaki, add $45 in mint) 40	60	80
(J29) Standing, firing rifle.....................45	68	90
(J30) Wounded supine, like Manoil M53...45	68	90
(J31) Cowboy on rearing horse, firing backward 130	195	260
(J32) Marching with rifle 57	85	115
(J33) Cowboy kneeling 30	45	60
(J33A) Cowboy kneeling, with base, one known...............................No Price Found		

Left to Right: J18, J26, J16a, J27, J28, J29. Photo by Don Pielin.

Left to Right; Top: J22, J12, J5; Bottom: J2, J1, J3. Photo by Ed Poole.

	C6	C8	C10
(J34) Indian on Rearing Horse	50	75	100
(J35) Indian with Bow (may resemble Beton's)	No Price Found		
(J36) Tramp	7	11	15
(J37) Farmer	6	9	13

	C6	C8	C10
(J38) Farmer's Wife	6	9	13
(J39) Cowboy on Prancing Horse, similar to Barclay B2	No Price Found		
(J40) Knight with shield, flat underbase	No Price Found		
(J41) Knight with pennant, flat underbase	No Price Found		

Left to Right; Top: J4, J7, J8, J10, J13, J14; Bottom: J16, J19, J20, J23, J30. Photo by Norbert Schachter.

Left to Right; Top: J4, J7, J8, J10, J13, J16, J14, J17; Bottom: J19, J20, J21a, J23, J30, J32, J33, J34. Photo by Bill Kaufman.

Left to Right; Top: J24, J15; Bottom: J21, J6, J11, J9. Photo by Ed Poole.

Left to Right: J25, J17, J31, J39, J33. Photo by Don Pielin.

Top: Jones Animals; Left to Right; Bottom: J37, J38, J36, Jones Animals. Photo by Don Pielin

J23a. Photo by Ron Eccles.

Left to Right: J40, J41. Photo by Don Pielin.

MARX PLAYSETS

These sets, with plastic figures and metal buildings, were produced from the late 1940s through 1976, and have become increasingly popular in the past few years. The following list is not complete, but simply a compilation of those sets that appeared for sale recently. 90% of the sculpture was by Joe Ferriot of Ferriot Bros., of Akron, Ohio.

Mint with the Playsets means a boxed set that hasn't been opened, or if opened, the building hasn't been put together, and all the parts are in their original paper bags. Very Good signals that the building has been put together, that all parts are there, and that everything is in excellent condition. In Good, the building shows wear, and some parts are missing.

	C6	C8	C10
Alamo No. 3442 225	338	450
Alamo, Walt Disney Official Davy Crockett at the, No. 3544 425	638	850
Atomic Cape Canaveral Missile Base..200	300	400
Babyland Nursery 175	263	350
Bar-M Ranch.....................................45	68	90
Battle of the Alamo, Sears No. 7959091 225	338	450
Battle of the Blue and Gray No. 4762..450	675	900
Battle of the Little Big Horn 200	300	400
Battleground No. 4202 30	45	60
Battleground No. 4754 250	375	500
Battleground No. 4756 125	188	250
Ben Hur No. 4696 1250	1875	2500
Blue and Gray, circa 1961, No. 4528...350	525	700
Cape Canaveral No. 4528 175	263	350
Charge of the Light Brigade.................225	338	450
Daniel Boone Frontier.........................400	600	800
Fort Apache No. 3681 125	188	250
Fort Apache No. 3686 125	188	250
Fort Apache No. 4202 125	188	250
Fort Dearborn No. 3510 190	285	380
Freight Trucking Terminal No. 5422 ...185	280	375
Galaxy Command No. 4206 35	52	70
Knight and Viking Set No. 4733..........175	263	350
Lone Ranger Ranch Set, Series 500........ *See Movies*		

	C6	C8	C10
Lone Ranger Rodeo, no number, figures early, no bases, has Lone Ranger on Foot.............................. *See Movies*		
Medieval Castle No. 4700....................200	300	400
Medieval Castle No. 4710....................125	188	250
Modern Farm Set 100	150	200
Modern Service Station No. 3471.........90	135	180
Navarone No. 3412 92	138	185
Operation Moonbase No. 4654 250	375	500
Prehistoric No. 3398 110	165	220
Prehistoric Animals No. 3399..............125	188	250
Prince Valiant No. 4706 ....*See Comic Character*		
Rifleman Ranch .... *See Movies*		
Rin Tin Tin of Fort Apache.................... *See Movies*		
Roy Rogers Western Town No. 4258...500	750	1000
Sons of Liberty....................................175	263	350
Stagecoach No. 3814 47	72	95
Super Circus No. 4319 175	263	350
Tales of Wells Fargo No. 4264............1000	1500	2000
Trucking Terminal No. 5422.................225	338	450
Tom Corbett 450	675	900
U.S. Armed Forces Training Center No. 4120.......................................200	300	400
Western Ranch Set No. 3954 100	150	200
White House of the United States with 36 Presidential figures (Sears Heritage) .30	45	60

Marx Castle Fort.

Marx Castle/Fort Box.

BRITAINS

The most collected of all toy soldiers are those manufactured by Englands' Britains Ltd. The firm was originally owned by William Britain, and in 1893 he introduced a hollow, three-dimensional lead soldier which was to revolutionize the toy soldier industry, and turn Britains into the largest toy soldier manufacturer in the world. **Prices include the box.**

BRITAINS No. 153 Prussian Hussars. Courtesy Christie's East.

BRITAINS No. 167 Turkish Infantry. Courtesy Christie's East.

BRITAINS No. 191 Turcos. Courtesy Christie's East.

Britains Boxed Sets

Set No.

	C6	C8	C10
1 The Life Guards - walking with tin swords, 1893 version may be first set of British hollow lead soldiers made	175	263	350
1953 version	80	120	160
2 Horse Guards - mounted with Aigulettes, 1953 version	105	153	210
8 Queen's Own Fourth Hussars, 1953 version	100	150	200
11 Black Watch - charging with piper, 1950 issue, 6 pcs.	65	98	130
12 Prince Albert's Own Eleventh Hussars - with carbines, 1930 issue	150	225	300
13 Third Hussars - Fred Whisstock label, officer on prancing horse	325	488	650
15 Prince Louise's Argyll & Sutherland Highlanders running	125	188	250

	C6	C8	C10
16 East Kent Regiment (The Buffs)	150	225	300
17 Somerset Light Infantry	80	120	160
19 West Indian Regiment	350	525	700
24 Queen's Royal Ninth Lancers, 1935	90	135	180
27 Infantry Band, 1955 issue	200	300	400
28 Mountain Artillery, 1950 issue	225	338	450
30 Drums and Bugles of the Line - 1908 - 1912	75	113	150
32 Scots Greys, 1950 issue	90	135	180
33 Sixteenth Lancers - officer turned to face troops, 1950 issue	100	150	200
35 Royal Marines, slope	100	150	200
36 Sussex Regiment, slope, 1950 issue	75	113	150
37 Coldstream Guard Band, 1950 issue	225	338	450
39 Royal Horse Artillery, 1950 issue	350	525	700
43 Second Life Guards - full gallop, 1930s painting	175	263	350
44 Second Dragoon Guards, 1935 issue	140	210	280

BRITAINS No. 199 Motor Machine Gun Corps (soldier missing on 3rd motorcycle).
Courtesy Phillips New York.

	C6	C8	C10
47 Indian Army cavalry - 1936 issue 80	120	160
48 Egyptian Camel Corps, 1960 issue.....150	225	300
66 Thirteenth Duke of Connaught's Own Bombay Lancers, 1950 issue...75	113	150
68 Fourth Bombay Grenadiers, 1935 ...200	300	400
74 Royal Welsh Fusiliers - with goat mascot, officer, 1960 issue.............80	120	160
76 Middlesex Regiment - at the slope...75	113	150
77 Gordon Highlanders - at slope with piper, postwar issue 75	113	150
79 Royal Navy Landing Party, 1960 issue................................275	413	550
80 Royal Navy Whitejackets at trail 112	168	225
82 Scots Guards Pioneers - with axes, flag bearer 100	150	200
94 Twenty-first Lancers with steel helmets 400	600	800
98 King's Royal Rifle Corps - green uniforms, red facings, 1930 issue..200	300	400
100 Empress of Indian's Twenty-first Lancers 275	413	550
101 Life Guards mounted band in State Dress, 1960 issue...................375	563	750
105 Imperial Yeomanry, 1901 issue.....250	375	500
109 Dublin Fusiliers...........................150	225	300
112 Seaforth Highlanders - at slope, 1940......................................125	188	250
114 Queen's Own Cameron Highlanders - marching, 1930 issue................................175	263	350
115 Egyptian Lancers, 1950 issue.........75	113	150
117 Egyptian Infantry at attention, 1958..135	203	270
119 Gloucestershire Regiment firing ...200	300	400
120 Coldstream Guards kneeling firing - officer with binoculars, 1950 issue......................................75	113	150
122 The Black Watch - firing..............150	225	300
123 The Bikanir Camel Corps - with wire tails...300	450	600

	C6	C8	C10
127 Seventh Dragoon Guards - at trot....160	240	320
134 Japanese Infantry - Charging 200	300	400
136 Russian Cossack Cavalry 1935 issue...100	150	200
138 French Cuirassiers...........................90	135	180
141 French Infantry of the Line - light blue greatcoats, red trousers..........125	188	250
142 French Zouaves - charging, post-War 75	113	150
144 Royal Field Artillery 800	1200	1600
145 The Royal Army Medical Corps - horsedrawn ambulance.................200	300	400
145A Royal Army Medical Corps - horse and wagon, khaki.................300	450	600
146 Army Service Corps Wagon - two horse team and crew.....................150	225	300
146A Royal Army Service Corps - active service wagon 275	413	550
147 Zulu Warriors 110	165	220
150 North American Indians - on foot..62	93	125
152 North American Indians - mounted, with rifles and tomahawks 50	75	100
153 Prussian Hussars - Types of the German Army 400	600	800
154 Prussian Infantry - marching, 1908...275	413	550
156 Royal Irish Regiment 125	188	250
157 Highlanders, firing 150	225	300
160 Territorial Infantry, 1915 issue......160	240	320
164 Bedouin Arabs of the Desert - mounted with scimitars and jezails .100	150	200
167 Turkish Infantry 150	225	300
169 Italian Bersaglieri, 1958 issue.......100	150	200
178 Austrian - Hungarian Foot Guards 150	225	300
182 Eleventh Hussars - dismounted with horses, 1950 issue 90	135	180
183 Cowboys on foot - early painting...80	120	160

	C6	C8	C10
187 Bedouin Arabs - on foot 70	105	140
189 Belgian Infantry 130	195	260
191 French Turcos 120	180	240
192 French Infantry of the Line - with shrapnel proof helmets 120	180	240
195 Infantry of the Line - with shrapnel proof helmets, officer with baton 125	188	250
196 Greek Evzones marching, 1950 issue 100	150	200
197 Gurkhas at the trail 125	188	250
199 Motorcycle Machine Gun Corps - with side car and detachable operator 150	225	300
201 Officers of the General Staff - mounted, Fred Whisstock label 175	263	350
202 Togoland Warriors - with bows and arrows 100	150	200
203 Royal Engineers' Pontoon Section 450	675	900
205 Coldstream Guards at Present 100	150	200
207 Officers and Petty Officers 150	225	300
212 Royals Scots - with piper at slope, 5 pcs. 85	128	170
213 Highland Light Infantry - at slope 275	413	550
214 Royal Canadian Mounted Police - marching in winter coats 200	300	400
216 Argentine Infantry - at slope 150	225	300
221 Uruguayan Cadets 225	338	450
224 Bedouin Arabs - mounted and dismounted and on camels, Fred Whisstock label, 11 pcs. 237	355	475
225 Kings African Rifles - at slope 100	150	200
227 U.S. WW I Doughboys - with campaign hats 112	168	225
228 U.S. Marines - winter dress 85	128	170
240 Royal Air Force - 1925, light blue uniforms 160	240	320
258 WW I British Infantry - Fred Whisstock label, with gas masks ...125	188	250
299 West Point Cadets - in summer clothes 75	113	150
312 Grenadier Guards in greatcoats, 1955 issue 80	120	160
320 Royal Medical Corps 90	135	180
329 Scots Guards Sentry Box and Sentry 30	45	60
400 The Life Guards - in winter cloaks 90	135	180
429 Scots Guards and Life Guards in overcoats and cloaks 200	300	400
432 German Infantry, 1960 issue 75	113	150
1201 Royal Artillery Gun - 5½" long ...27	42	55
1203 Tank of the Royal Tank Corps 90	135	180

	C6	C8	C10
1250 Royal Tank Corps 160	240	320
1253 U.S. Navy, white jackets 100	150	200
1257 Yeoman of the Guard (Beefeaters) - with governor 150	225	300
1263 Royal Artillery Gun - thin wheels 3¾" 18	27	36
1265 18" Howitzer for Garrison work - 3 shell cases 105	158	210
1283 Grenadier Guards 65	98	130
1291 Band of Royal Marines 220	330	440
1292 Royal Artillery Gun 25	38	50
1301 U.S. Military Band, khaki 175	163	350
1307 16th Century Knights - in full armor, mounted and on foot 90	135	180
1318 Machine Gunners 60	90	120
1323 Royal Fusiliers, Seaforth Highlanders, Royal Sussex Regiment with 23 pcs. 250	375	500
1330 Royal Engineers General Service Wagon galloping 200	300	400
1333B Life Guard, winter cape, white horse, Picture Pack box, 1 pc. 30	45	60
1334 Army Truck, metal wheels 100	150	200
1335 Army Truck - six wheels, 1955 issue 110	165	220
1337B Royal Horse Guard, trumpeter with grey horse in Picture Pack box 30	45	60
1343 Royal Horse Guards - mounted with cloaks 125	188	250
1432 Army Tender, with driver 110	165	220
1433 Army Tender split windshield and driver, caterpillar treads 100	150	200
1435 Italian Infantry, khaki green uniforms, 1955 issue 100	150	200
1436 Italian Infantry, foreign service dress, 1936 210	315	420
1437 Italian Carabinieri, 1958 issue 140	210	280
1448 Army Staff Car - twin windshields, 1955 issue 160	240	320
1470 George VI Coronation Coach 162	243	325
1475 Display Box, Beefeaters, Outriders, Footmen of the Royal Household 175	263	350
1512 Army Ambulance, Post War 135	200	270
1515 Coldstream Guards - at slope 75	113	150
1518 British Infantry of the Line, "1815" 175	263	350
1519 Waterloo Highlanders, "1815" 165	248	330
1542 New Zealand Infantry 110	165	220
1544 Australian Infantry 237	355	475
1554 Royal Canadian Police on foot, summer dress 85	128	170

	C6	C8	C10
1603 Republic of Ireland Infantry - marching, 1939 peak caps	180	270	360
1612 Gas Mask Infantry, service dress, bomb throwers	100	150	200
1614 Gas Mask Infantry Digging - assorted positions, 24 pcs.	118	177	235
1631 The Governor General's Horse Guards	95	143	190
1637 Governor-General's Horse and Foot Guards with officers	130	195	260
1638 Sound Locator	32	48	65
1639 Range Finder with operator, post war painting	24	36	48
1641 Underslung Heavy Duty Truck - 18 wheels, driver, white metal wheels	180	270	360
1711 French Foreign Legion - mounted officers and troops at slope	112	168	225
1715 Two-pound Light Anti-Aircraft Gun brass fixings	22	34	45
1717 AA two-pounder on mobile screw jack chassis	50	75	100
1720 Band of Royal Scot Greys - mounted	210	315	420
1722 Drums and Pipes of the Scot Guard	500	750	1000
1725 4.5" Howitzer	15	23	30
1726 Regulation Type Limber-rubber tires	12	19	25
1728 Predictor and Operator	22	33	44
1729 Height Finder and Operator	20	30	40
1730 The Royal Artillery	100	150	200
1731 Spotter and Chair	20	30	40
1759 Air Raid Precautions National Service Stretcher Party	150	225	300
1791 Royal Corps of Signals - dispatch riders	70	105	140
1855 Miniature Barrage Truck with winch and balloon	115	173	230
1858 British Infantry	90	135	180
1859 Sentry Box with Sentry at ease - steel helmet	55	83	110
1876 Bren Gun Carrier	30	45	60
1877 Beetle Truck with Driver	50	75	100
1893 Indian Army Service Corps - includes mule	125	188	250
1898 WW I British Infantry - Tommy Funners	62	93	125
1901 Cape Town Highlanders	110	165	220
2010 Airborne Regiment - "Red Devils" marching with red berets	100	150	200
2019 Danish Livgarde	140	210	280
2021 U.S. Military Police, "Snowdrops"	90	135	180
2022 Swiss Papal Guards	180	270	360
2026 25-Pounder Howitzer	12	18	24
2027 Red Army Guards in overcoats	87	131	175
2029 The Life Guards - mounted and on foot, 1953	70	105	140
2030 Australian Infantry - 1948, blue ceremonial dress	150	225	300
2035 Swedish Lifeguards - ceremonial dress	100	150	200
2037 Ski Trooper, 1 pc.	82	123	165
2041 Trailer - universal clockwork unit with keys	55	83	110
2044 U.S. Air Corps, 1949 blue uniform, marching	75	113	150
2046 Arab Display, 12 pcs.	175	263	350
2051 Uruguayan Military School Cadets	140	210	280
2055 Confederate Cavalry	82	123	165
2056 Union Cavalry	90	135	180
2059 Union Infantry	65	98	130
2060 Confederate Infantry	65	98	130
2062 Seaforth Highlanders, 1953, with pipers	150	225	300
2063 Argyll and Sutherland Highlanders, firing	75	113	150
2064 155 mm Gun	60	90	120
2065 Her Majesty the Queen, mounted	37	56	75
2067 Sovereign's Standard & Escort	225	338	450
2075 Seventh Hussars - 1953	125	188	250
2076 Prince of Wales' 12th Royal Lancers	110	165	220
2078 Irish Guards - At "Present Arms"	125	188	250
2079 The Royal Company of Archers, 14 pcs.	325	487	650
2091 Glouchestershire Regiment at the slope	100	150	200
2094 Open State Landau - duke of Edinburgh	200	300	400
2095 French Foreign Legion in Action	170	255	340
2102 Austin Champ jeep - detachable hood	90	135	180
2106 18" Heavy Howitzer on Tractor Wheels - 2 shell cases	50	75	100
2148 The Fort Henry Guard with goat mascot	70	105	140
2152 Waterloo Gunners	55	83	110
9158 Fort Henry Guards - with goat	70	105	140

ACTION FIGURES

Though there had previously been similar toys, it was Hasbro's G.I. Joe which truly created the category of the Action Figure.

Don Levine, the Director of Development for Hasbro, conceived the idea of G.I. Joe while standing outside a Manhattan art supply shop in February, 1963. A licensing agent had suggested a military toy based on a t.v. series, "The Lieutenant." Levine had discarded the idea of a tie-in because the series was for adults, but the thought was in his mind as he looked at an artist's manikin in the shop window. The idea of a boy's soldier with movable parts came to him.

Sam Speers, who worked under Levine, came up with the engineering for G.I. Joe, both the mechanical and esthetic inventions (for which he received many patents), which included devising a way that enabled the toy to stand on its own (unlike artists' manikins) in various positions and while holding weapons or bearing equipment. Speers also thought of the added touch of the facial scar (the 11½" height was because the Barbie doll was that tall and a great success).

Noted artist Phil Kraczkowski sculpted the head, which was **not** a composite of 23 Medal of Honor winners, despite ad claims to that effect, and though Speers designed the parts and how they should go together, Walter Hansen and Norman Jacques did the sculpting of the body. It wasn't an easy sell to the Hasbro executives for Levine and Speers, but after the first year's enormous success, Levine was upped to Vice President and Speers moved up to Levine's job as Director of Development.

(Note: after the Hasbro-G.I. Joe listing, all Action Figures are listed alphabetically by company.)

ADDITIONAL G.I. JOE INFORMATION
by Barry Goodman

G.I. Joe first entered the U.S. market in 1964. The 11½" doll would undergo several changes during its eleven-year life span, 1964-75. The first dolls, 1964-69, had painted hair and were based primarily upon military uniforms of World War II. In 1965, Hasbro added six foreigners to the series (Japanese, German, French, Australian, Russian, British). These were distinctly different in appearance. An easy way of knowing if you have a foreigner is that the scar found on the GI is not present.

In 1965, Hasbro introduced a black G.I. Joe, which today is one of the most sought-after .

In 1967, Hasbro introduced its "Vietnam series" outfits, which were pulled off the market very quickly due to the negative response to the Vietnam war raging in southeast Asia. Thus these uniforms (green and tan airborne M.P., Air Security set and Marine Jungle Fighter) are the most sought after and scarcest. This was the year that also produced the extremely scarce nurse doll.

Protests about the war continued, so in 1969 Hasbro dropped the military line and substituted the "adventurer series". G.I. Joe was transformed from a military doll to an adventure doll. In 1970 G.I. Joe received flock hair and then a flocked moustache and beard. Furthermore, the "adventurer" line was dropped and the "Adventure Team" line substituted. The theme of this line was that G.I. Joe would fight nature and the elements, rather than other men.

In 1972, G.I. Joe was given a "kung-fu" grip. The same year, the oil embargo created havoc because oil-based plastic became prohibitively expensive. Because of this, in 1973 Hasbro changed the basic composition of the plastic, which created a much more fragile doll that by 1975 children had totally lost interest in.

Most collectors concentrate on the 1964-9 dolls. Hasbro consulted military manuals to create the most realistic and authentic boys' doll ever made.

Barry James Goodman is a Leading collector and authority on G.I. Joe dolls and 1960s character figures. As an active toy dealer, he has been able to amass one of the largest collections od G.I. Joes.

ACTION SOLDIER (Revised listings by Barry Goodman)	C6	C8	C10
7000 - GI Joe 5 Star Jeep, 106mm Rocket Launcher, ¼ ton trailer, tripod mounted searchlight and four 106mm shells	50	100	150

	C6	C8	C10
7100 - "Let's Go Joe" board game	15	22	40
7500 - GI Joe Action Soldier	35	50	65
7501 - Combat Set A			
Field jacket	5	10	15

1965 Catalog Illustrations.

	C6	C8	C10
M-1 rifle	5	10	15
Bayonet	5	10	15
Cartridge belt	5	10	15
Six hand grenades	5	10	15
Price for 7501 Set	35	50	60
7502 - Combat Set B - back pack, canteen and cover, entrenching tool and cover, mess kit, utensils and single pouch cartridge belt, each individually	5	10	15
Price for 7502 Set	35	50	60
7503 - Combat Fatigue Shirt	5	8	12
7504 - Combat Fatigue Pants	5	8	12
7505 - Combat Field Jacket	8	15	20
7506 - Combat Field Pack - entrenching tool and cover	10	20	30
7507 - Combat Helmet, camouflage netting and foliage	10	20	25
7508 - Army Sandbags Set	5	10	12.50
7509 - Canteen with cover and mess kit, utensils	5	10	15
7510 - M-1 Rifle with bayonet and cartridge belt with six grenades	20	30	40
7511 - Camouflage Netting with poles and foliage	5	10	15
7512 - Bivouac Set A - zipped sleeping bag, M-1 Rifle, bayonet, cartridge belt, canteen with cover, and mess kit with utensils, individually	5	10	15
7513 - Bivouac Set B - tent, stakes, poles, foliage, camouflage netting, entrenching tool with cover	10	15	25

	C6	C8	C10
.30 cal. tripod mounted machine gun, ammo box	10	15	25
7514 - 30 cal. tripod mounted machine gun, ammo box	10	15	25
7515 - Zippered Sleeping Bag	10	15	25
7517 - Command Post Set - Rain Poncho, .45 pistol w/belt and holster, field radio, field phone, wire roll, map and map case, individually	5	10	15
7518 - .45 Pistol, holster, belt	5	10	15
ammo pouch	5	10	15
six grenades	5	10	15
cloth hat	5	10	15
Price for 7518 Set	25	45	80
7519 Rain Poncho	5	10	15
7520 - Field Phone, Field Radio, Wire Spool, Map Case and map, individually	5	10	15
7521 - Military Police Set - "Ike" Jacket, trousers, ascot, white belt, nightstick, .45 pistol, holster, armband and duffel bag, stem gun	35	50	60
7522 - Jungle Fighter Set - belt, entrenching tool, mess kit, utensils, canteen, cover, machete, sheath and Jungle knife	35	50	70
7523 - Duffel bag	5	10	15
7524 - MP Uniform	250	350	500
7524 - "Ike" Jacket, ascot and MP armband	15	25	35
7525 - "Ike" Trousers	5	10	15
7526 - MP Helmet, black	50	100	150

	C6	C8	C10

7526 - MP Helmet, white belt, .45 pistol, holster and nightstick 20   30   40

7527 - Ski patrol helmet, winter white cartridge belt, winter white M-1 rifle and six grenades 20   30   40

7528 - Bazooka and two shells..............10   20   30

7529 - Snow Shoes, pick axe, climbing rope and sun goggles.......................15   20   25

7530 - Mountain Troops Set - Snow shoes, winter white belt, winter white field pack, pick axe, climbing rope and four grenades..............20   30   40

7531 - Ski Patrol Set - two-piece white parka, gloves, boots, skis, poles and sun goggles..............................20   40   60

7532 - Special Forces Set - uniform, beret, bazooka, two shells and four grenades...................................25   50   100

7533 - Beret, M-16 rifle and field radio 25   50   75

7536 - Green Beret Set - G.I. Joe action soldier dressed in special forces uniform, M-16 rifle, .45 pistol, belt, holster, six grenades and field radio 75   150   250

7537 - West Point Cadet Set - parade uniform, cap, feather, sword, scabbard, M-1 rifle and dress shoes.......75   150   240

7538 - Heavy Weapons Set - 81 mm mortar, 3 shells, M-60 machine gun, tripod, ammo belt, bullet proof vest, bullet belt and 2 grenades 40   75   100

7590 - GI Joe talking action soldier 75   100   125

8000 - Official GI Joe footlocker 10   15   30

8030 - GI Joe desert patrol jeep w/.50 cal. tripod mounted machine gun, radio antenna and GI Joe desert trooper...200   500   800

ACTION SAILOR

7600 - GI Joe Action Sailor...................50   75   90

7601 - Sea Rescue Set A - inflatable raft, oar, sea anchor, tow line, flare gun, knife, scabbard and first aid kit, individually 5   10   15

7602 - Frogman Set - three pc. black scuba set, swim fins, face mask, oxygen tanks, depth gauge, knife, scabbard and depth charges 50   100   150

7603 - Black scuba suit jacket and hood 15   50   100

7604 - Black scuba suit pants 7.50   25   35

7605 - Swim fins, face mask, knife, scabbard and depth gauge 20   30   50

7606 - Oxygen tanks...............................5   10   15

7607 - Navy Attack Set - life jacket, semaphore flags, hand held searchlight and binoculars, individually 5   10   15

7610 - Navy attack helmet, hand held searchlight and binoculars 15   30   40

7611 - Life jacket....................................5   10   15

7612 - Shore Patrol - jumper, neckerchief, trousers, white belt, .45 pistol, holster, nightstick, armband, sailors cap and duffel bag......35   50   75

Sears' G.I. Joe Forward Observer Set. Photo by Barry Goodman.

G.I. Joe Astronaut. C6: 30. C8: 50. C10: 70. Mint in box add 70%. Photo by Barry Goodman.

G.I. Joe Vietnam Marine Jungle Fighter. Photo by Barry Goodman.

G.I. Joe Russian. Photo by Barry Goodman.

G.I. Joe Nurse. Photo by Barry Goodman.

G.I. Joe Tan Airborne M.P., 1967. Photo by Barry Goodman.

G.I. Joe Japanese. Photo by Barry Goodman.

G.I. Joe Australian. Photo by Barry Goodman.

G.I. Joe German. Photo by Barry Goodman.

G.I. Joe 5 Star Jeep. C6: 50. C8: 80. C10: 150. Mint in Box add 70%. Photo by Barry Goodman.

	C6	C8	C10
7613 - Shore Patrol Jumper Set	15	30	40
7614 - Shore Patrol Pants	5	10	15
7615 - USN duffel bag	5	10	15
7616 - Shore Patrol w/stripe	100	150	250
7616 - Shore Patrol helmet, white belt, .45 pistol, holster and nightstick	10	25	30
7618 - .30 cal.tripod mounted machine gun and ammo box	20	30	45
7619 - Dress Parade M-1 rifle, bayonet, white cartridge belt and white billyclub	15	35	50
7620 - Deep Sea Diver Set - divers' suit, gloves, helmet, breastplate, air pump, hoses, weighted belt, weighted shoes, signal float, line, knife, scabbard and sledge hammer	20	40	65
7621 - Landing Signal Officer Set - safety striped jumpsuit, cloth helmet with headphones, goggles, binoculars, signal paddles, clipboard, pad, pencil and flare gun	30	50	100
7622 - Sea Rescue Set B - same as Sea Rescue Set A also includes life jackets	10	20	30
7623 - Deep Freeze Set - fur parka, pants, boots, snow sled, flare gun and ice pick	25	50	70
7624 - Annapolis Cadet Set - dress parade jacket, cap, pants, belt, shoes, sword, scabbard and white M-1 rifle	80	200	275
7625 - Breeches Buoy Set - buoy, pulley, slicker jacket, pants, flare gun and hand held searchlight	75	135	200
7626 - LSO helmet w/headphones, signal paddles, flare gun, clipboard, pad and pencil	25	50	75
7627 - USN Life ring	10	25	30
7628 - White sailor's cap, boots and GI Joe dogtags	15	25	35
7690 - GI Joe talking action sailor	75	150	175
8050 - Official GI Joe Sea Sled - w/GI Joe frogman	100	225	300

ACTION MARINE

	C6	C8	C10
7700 - GI Joe Action Marine	30	55	65
7701 - Communications Set - M-1 carbine, camouflage poncho, field phone, field radio, wire spool, binoculars, map and map case, individually	5	10	15
7702 - Camouflage poncho	5	10	15

	C6	C8	C10
7703 - Field radio, field phone, wire spool, map and map case	5	10	15
7704 - Flag Set - Old Glory, Army flag, Navy flag, Marine Corps flag and Air Force flag	30	60	100
7705 - Paratrooper Set - parachute pack, M-1 carbine, six grenades, knife, scabbard, belt, ammo pouch, canteen and cover, individually	5	10	15
7706 - M-1 carbine, six grenades, knife, scabbard, belt, ammo pouch, canteen and cover, individually	5	10	15
7707 - Camouflage helmet, foliage and helmet cover	10	25	30
7708 - Camouflage netting, foliage, poles and securing line	5	10	15
7709 - Parachute Pack	12.50	18.75	25
7710 - Dress Parade Set - traditional Marine "dress blues", cap and white M-1 rifle	20	40	60
7711 - Beachhead Set A - flame thrower, camouflage tent, poles, stakes, belt, ammo pouch, mess kit and utensils, individually	5	10	15
7712 - Beachhead Set B - M-1 rifle, cartridge belt, six grenades, field pack, bayonet, entrenching tool, cover, canteen and cover, individually	5	10	15
7713 - Field pack, entrenching tool and cover	10	30	40
7714 - Camouflage fatigue shirt	5	8	12
7715 - Camouflage fatigue pants	5	8	12
7716 - Mess Kit, utensils, canteen and cover	5	10	15
7717 - M-1 Rifle, bayonet, cartridge belt and six grenades	20	30	40
7718 - Flame thrower	10	15	20
7719 - Medic Set - stretcher, crutch, satchel, stethoscope, plasma bottle, IV tube, splints, bandage rolls, armbands and hospital flag, cloth bag	40	75	100
7720 crutch, stethoscope, plasma bottle, I.V. tube, splints and bandage rolls	10	25	35
7721 - Medic's helmet, satchel and two armbands	15	30	50
7722 - Fatigue cap, boots and G.I. Joe dog tags	20	25	35
7723 - G.I. bunk bed	15	25	35

G.I. Joe Polar Explorer. C6: 100. C8: 200. C10: 250. Mint in box add 70%. Photo by Barry Goodman.

	C6	C8	C10
7727 - Weapons Rack with rack, M-1 rifle, M-1 carbine, M-16 rifle and 40 mm grenade launcher	30	50	60
7731 - Tank Commander Set - leather jacket, tanker's helmet, belt, .30 cal. M-60 machine gun, tripod, ammo box, radio and tripod	75	100	150
7732 - Jungle Fighter Set - green fatigue shirt, pants, campaign hat, AR-15 rifle, belt, knife, machete, sheath, canteen, cover, flame thrower and field phone	200	350	500
7790 - G.I. Joe talking action Marine			

ACTION PILOT

	C6	C8	C10
7800 - G.I. Joe action pilot	30	55	75
7801 - Survival Set - inflatable raft, sea anchor, tow line, oar, knife, scabbard, flare gun, first aid kit and inflatable USAF life vest	50	75	100
7802 - Inflatable raft, sea anchor, tow line and oar	10	25	30
7803 - Dress Uniform - jacket, shirt, tie, pants, garrison cap, wings and captain's bars	20	40	60
7804 - Dress Jacket	10	15	20
7805 - Dress Pants	10	15	20
7806 - Dress Shirt and Cap	10	15	20
7807 - Scramble Set - gray flight suit, inflatable life vest, .45 pistol, holster, belt, clipboard, pad and pencil	25	40	75
7808 - Gray flight suit	5	10	15
7809 - Inflatable life vest, flare gun, knife, scabbard and first aid kit	10	20	30
7810 - Crash helmet w/oxygen mask	20	40	50
7811 - Parachute pack	10	15	25
7812 - Communications Set - field radio binoculars, map, map case, clipboard, pad and pencil	20	30	60

	C6	C8	C10
7813 - Marine Jungle Fighter (Vietnam)	200	300	450
7813 - A.P. Helmet Set	10	30	40
7820 - Crash Crew Set - metallic heat suit, hood, gloves, boots, tool belt and CO_2 fire extinguisher	35	65	90
7822 - Colorado Air Cadet Set - uniform, sash, cap, dress shoes, M-1 rifle, sword and scabbard	75	125	150
7823 - Fighter Pilot Set - G-suit, boots, "Mae West" life jacket, helmet, oxygen mask, flashlight and working parachute	75	200	375
7824 - Air Sea Rescue Set - three pc. orange scuba suit, mask, swim fins, air tanks, flare gun, first aid kit, rescue life ring and marker-buoy	25	60	100
7890 - G.I. Joe talking action pilot	75	200	275
7900 - G.I. Joe Action Soldier Colored (sic)	100	200	300
8020 - Official G.I. Joe Space Capsule - space suit, boots, gloves, helmet and recording of mercury control communications	80	135	260
8040 - Deluxe Crash Crew Set - fire truck, working water pump, working siren, blinking red light, fire axe, metallic heat suit, boots, gloves and hood, white stretcher	200	350	450
G.I. Jane (1965) Army Nurse	500	800	1000

"ACTION SOLDIERS OF THE WORLD"

	C6	C8	C10
8100 - German Storm Trooper - w/cartridge belt, luger pistol, holster, field pack, "Potato Masher" grenades, 9 mm Schmeisser machine gun and iron cross medal	140	225	275
8101 Japanese Imperial Soldier w/field pack, Nambu pistol, holster, cartridge belt, Arisaka rifle, bayonet and Order of the Kite medal	150	275	350
8102 - Russian Infantryman - W/D.P. light machine gun, bi-pod, field glasses, case, anti-tank grenades, ammo box and order of Lenin medal	140	225	300
8103 French Resistance Fighter - w/ Lebel revolver, shoulder holster, knife, grenades, radio set, 7.65mm Mas submachine gun and Croix de Guerre medal	140	225	275
8104 - British Commando w/gas mask,			

Left to Right: 8200, 8201, 8202, 8203, 8204, 8205. Courtesy of Sam Speers.
(The figures in this photo are not those actually sold in foreign uniforms.)

	C6	C8	C10
case, canteen, cover, sten mark 25 submachine gun and Victoria Cross medal	150	240	280
8105 - Australian Jungle Fighter - w/ grenades, flame thrower, jungle knife, entrenching tool, bush machete, sheath and Victoria Cross medal	140	225	275
8200 - German storm trooper	120	175	200
8201 - Imperial Japanese soldier	140	200	275
8202 - Russian Infantryman	120	200	225
8203 French Resistance Fighter	120	200	225
8204 - British Commando	120	200	225
8205 Australian Jungle Fighter	120	200	225
8300 - Equipment For German Storm Trooper - field pack, Luger pistol, holster, cartridge belt, 9mm Schmeisser machine gun, "Potato Masher" hand grenades and Iron Cross medal	30	60	100
8301 - Equipment For Japanese Imperial Soldier - cartridge belt, field pack, Arisaka rifle, bayonet, Nambu pistol, holster and order of Kite medal	30	60	100
8302 - Equipment For Russian Infantryman - field glasses, case, D.P. light machine gun, bi-pod, belt, ammo box, anti-tank grenades and order of Lenin medal	30	60	100

	C6	C8	C10
8303 - Equipment For French Resistance Fighter - shoulder holster, Lebel revolver, 7.65 Mas submachine gun, grenades, radio, knife and Croix de Guerre medal	15	20	30
8304 - British Commando Equipment - canteen, case, cartridge belt, gas mask, case, stern mark 2-S submachine gun and Victoria Cross medal	30	60	100
8305 - Australian Jungle Fighter Equipment - flame thrower, jungle knife, grenades, bush machete, sheath, entrenching tool and Victoria Cross medal	15	20	30

NOTE: The **Irwin Company** made the following vehicles and planes for G.I. Joe under license from Hasbro: an Armored Car, a Half Track, two motorcycles, a Duck, three airplanes, a German staff car, a Mine Sweeper and a Racing Car. The boxes are very desirable, and add 70% to the price of each toy. All sell in the following range ... 200 350 500

Mego also made a crash crew fire truck for GI Joe ... 100 250 350

Photo Boxes run $400 - $500 in Mint.

335

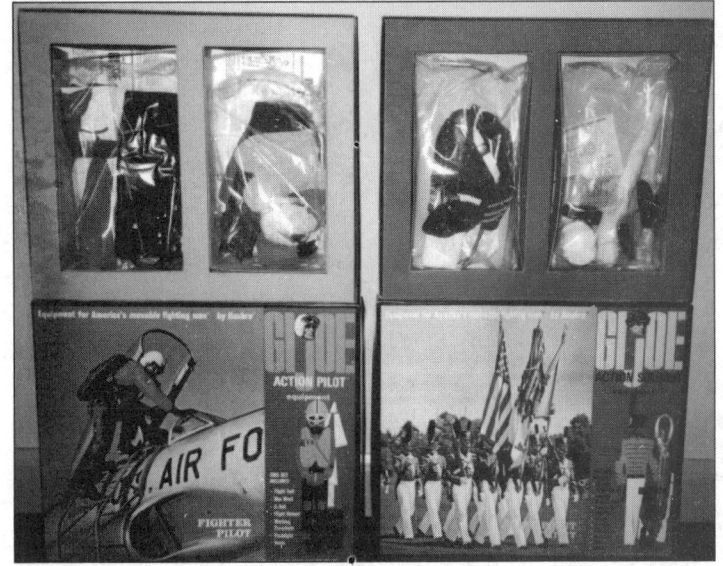

G.I. Joe Photo Boxes, worth $400 each in mint. Photo by Barry Goodman.

G.I. Joe Cadet Photo Boxes, each worth $500 in mint. Photo by Barry Goodman.

G.I. Joe Irwin German Staff Car. Photo by Barry Goodman.

G.I. Joe Irwin Amphibious Duck. Photo by Barry Goodman.

	C6	C8	C10
G.I. JOE ADVENTURERS			
Air Adventurer 20	35	45
Land Adventurer......................20	35	45
Sea Adventurer 20	35	45
Talking Man of Action 50	75	100
Man of Action, lifelike hair....................25	30	45
Talking Adventure Team Commander 35	50	65
Talking Adventure Team Commander Black 80	150	225
Talking Adventure Team Commander, lifelike hair, beard 35	50	65
Astronaut and Space Capsule Set With Equipment 80	140	200

	C6	C8	C10
Secret of the Mummy's Tomb Set with figure, vehicle, equipment 40	80	120
Adventure Team Helicopter 20	50	75
Adventure Team Training Tower 20	45	85
Adventure Team Headquarters..............25	40	60
Adventure Team Outfit, pants, flare gun 8	12	16
Adventure Team Outfit, trenchcoat, walkie-talkie......................8	12	16
Adventure Team Outfit, camouflage clothes, gun, holster 8	12	16

End G.I. Joe

	C6	C8	C10
Hasbro Charlie's Angels, Cheryl Ladd, 8" high......6	12	18
Hasbro Charlie's Angels, Farrah Fawcett-Majors, 8" high 6	12	18
Hasbro Charlie's Angels, Jaclyn Smith, 8" high......6	12	18
Hasbro Charlie's Angels, Kate Jackson, 8" high......6	12	18
Hasbro Charlie's Angels Outfits, each ...4	8	12

COLORFORMS *(List by Jim Main)*

Prices in parentheses are mint on card or in Box.

OUTER SPACE MEN

	C6	C8	C10
Colossus Rex ($150.00) 35	50	65
Cmdr. Comet ($150.00)......35	50	65
Astro-Nautilus ($150.00)......35	50	65
Xodiac ($150.00)......35	50	65
Orbitron ($150.00)......35	50	65
Electron ($150.00)......35	50	65
Alpha ($150.00)......35	50	65

	C6	C8	C10
Gabriel The Lone Ranger No. 23620, 9½" high, fully-jointed, cloth clothes 10	20	35
Gabriel Tonto No. 23621, 9½" high, fully-jointed, cloth clothes 15	25	45
Gabriel Scout No. 23626, jointed......9	13	18
Gabriel Silver plus 8-Way Action Saddle No. 27625, jointed......9	13	18
Gabriel Tonto and Scout No. 28691, cloth clothes 25	35	55

	C6	C8	C10
Gabriel The Lone Ranger and Silver No. 28675, with 8-way trick Action Saddle, cloth clothes 30	45	65
Gabriel Silver No. 31635, with removable saddle, bridle 8	12	17
Gabriel Scout No. 31636 for 3¾" Tonto, includes removable saddle and bridle ..8	12	15
Gabriel Butch Cavendish No. 31632, 3¾" high, jointed, new in 1981, with pistol..8	12	15
Gabriel Smoke No. 31637 (Butch Cavendish stallion), with removable saddle and bridle 8	12	15
Gabriel The Lone Ranger No. 31630 (Legend of the Lone Ranger), 3¾" high, jointed, new in 1981 5	10	15
Gabriel Tonto No. 31631, 3¾" high, with pistol and knife, new in 1981...5	10	15
Gabriel General George Custer No. 31633, 3¾" high, with pistol 5	10	15
Gabriel Buffalo Bill Cody No. 31634, 3¾" high, jointed, comes with carbine......5	10	15
Gabriel Figure Assortment No. 31601, 3¾" high, Lone Ranger, Tonto, Butch Cavendish, General Custer, Buffalo Bill, each individually......5	10	15
Gabriel House Assortment No. 31602, includes Silver, Scout, Smoke (for 3¾" figures), each individually 5	10	15

GALOOB *(list by Jim Main)*

Prices in parentheses are mint on card or in box.

DEFENDERS OF THE EARTH - 5½" tall

	C6	C8	C10
Flash Gordon ($15.00) 5	7	9
Garax ($25.00)......9	11	13
The Phantom ($20.00)......7	9	11
Ming ($15.00)......5	7	9
Mongor ($35.00) 10	14	18
Mandrake ($20.00) 7	9	11
Lothar ($15.00)......5	7	9
Flash's Swordship ($40.00)......15	18	21
Garax's Swordship ($40.00)......15	18	21

	C6	C8	C10
Gilbert Honey West, 12" high, 1965 40	65	90
Gilbert James Bond, 12" high 40	55	80
Gilbert (James Bond) Odd Job, 1960's......100	150	200
Gilbert James Bond Action Toy Set No. 1, 1965 - figures of 007 as scuba diver, Domino and Largo with Disco Volante's yacht, display box......30	40	60

GILBERT James Bond 3½" figures 1 - 10. Courtesy Bill Nutting.

JAMES BOND 007 SECRET AGENT TEN MOVIE CHARACTERS

	C6	C8	C10
Gilbert James Bond Action Playset No. 2 - Bond, Goldfinger, Odd Job and spin-top pool table, display box	30	40	60
Gilbert James Bond Action Toy Set No. 3 in display box, 1965, - figures of 007 on Laser Table, Goldfinger, Odd Job and Dr. No.	30	40	60
Gilbert James Bond Action Playset No. 4 - Dr. No, Bond, Domino and firespitting Dragon Tank, display box	30	40	60
Gilbert James Bond Action Playset No. 5 - Bond with Beretta, Money Penny, M, and M's secret desk, display box	30	40	60
Gilbert James Bond No. 1, 3½" high, with Beretta pistol	10	15	20
Gilbert James Bond No. 2 with rifle, 3½" tall, 1965	10	15	20
Gilbert James Bond No. 3 in Scuba Suit with Spear Gun, 3½" tall, 1965	10	15	20
Gilbert James Bond No. 4 Odd Job, 3½" tall, 1965	8	12	15

	C6	C8	C10
Gilbert James Bond No. 5 M, Bond's boss	8	12	15
Gilbert James Bond No. 6 Goldfinger	8	12	15
Gilbert James Bond No. 7 Miss Moneypenny	8	12	15
Gilbert James Bond No. 8 Largo, 3½" tall, 1965	8	12	15
Gilbert James Bond No. 9 Domino, 3½" tall, 1965	8	12	15
Gilbert James Bond No. 10 Dr. No with poison vial	8	12	15
Gilbert Man From Uncle Ilya Kurayakin, 12" high	40	60	80
Gilbert Man From Uncle Napoleon Solo	40	50	75

GILBERT MOON McDARE (*Listing by Jim Main*)

	C6	C8	C10
Moon McDare 12" figure ($125.00)	25	35	45
Space Suit outfit ($60.00)	15	20	25
Space Mutt set ($80.00)	15	30	45
Space Gun Set ($35.00)	10	14	18
Moon Explorer Set ($60.00)	15	20	25
Action Communication Set ($60.00)	15	20	25
Space Accessory Pack ($35.00)	10	14	18

HARTLAND PLASTIC ACTION FIGURES

by Gary J. Linden

Hartland Plastics, Inc. is located in southern Wisconsin and has been producing plastic figures and other plastic products since the 1950's. In 1953 The Lone Ranger, Tonto, Roy Rogers, Dale Evans and Bullet were produced. The production of these and other western figures lasted for about 10 years. The figures were molded in Acetate plastic and then painted. Most of these figures came with removable accessories, which included hats, hand guns, rifles, saddles and reins. Some of the figures had an accessory item unique to himself. Josh Randle's mares leg (rifle), Custer's Saber and Wyatt Earp's Bunt line special (long barrel revolver) to name a few. The reason for the vast price range in these western figures is that most of the common ones (C10 price of $150.00) had over 200,000 cast. The rarer figures, Col. Mackenzie for example, had only about 5,000 cast. The figures were molded in two halves, front and back for people, and left and right for the animals (horses and Bullet). A few things to keep in mind are that there were two different Lone Ranger figures. The older one, which is wearing chaps and is more of a generic figure, and the newer figure that looks more like Clayton Moore. Also there were three different Lone Ranger horses (Silver). The generic Lone Ranger's horse has a chain for reins. The newer Lone Ranger (Clayton Moore type) has both a standing horse and a rearing horse. The # 804 Sgt. Preston and the # 804 Sgt. Lance O'Rourke appear to be the same figure with a different name on the box. The #817 Jim Bowie and his horse Blaze are the same horse and the figure used for Davy Crockett and his horse Streak, the only difference being the hats. Crockett has a Coonskin cap and Bowie has a cowboy-type hat. The boxes that all these figures came in were one of three types. The box was either plain cardboard with some printing on it or some colored art work on it, and others had a full color photo on the outside. The gunfighters who had moveable arms came in either an artwork box or a box with a see-thru front. The 8" western wranglers came in a window box and the 5½" western horse and riders came on a blister card. Some of the accessory parts (hats, guns and saddles) are being reproduced today.

Hartland also produced sport figures. There were 30 different football figures, an offensive and a defensive player from each of the 14 different teams of the time and two different personage figures, Johnny Unitas being the most sought-after. Also the figures of the Redskins and the Cowboys are the most wanted out of the 28 non-personage players. There were 18 different personage baseball players produced, along with a bat boy. The rarest of the baseball figures is Dick Groat. In 1989 it was the 25TH anniversary of the baseball figures and the Hartland Company reissued all 18 players and the bat boy. These figures have a 25 in a circle on their back just below the belt.

C10 Is a figure that is mint in the box with all paper work and paper tag

C8 Is a mint figure that does not have the box or paper work or paper tag

C6 Is a figure that has been played with and shows some wear. Also a few accessory parts are missing and there is no box, paper work or paper tag

---

HARTLAND WESTERN & HISTORICAL FIGURES

(List by Gary J. Linden)

	C6	C8	C10
9½ " TALL FIGURES			
801 - Lone Ranger (old/chaps)	50	90	150
801 - The Lone Ranger (newer)	50	90	150
801P - Western Champ	50	90	150
801P - Western Champ (extra large)	50	90	150
802 - Dale Evans	50	90	150
804 - Sgt. Preston	75	140	250
804 - Sgt. Lance O'Rourke	75	140	250
805 - Tonto	50	90	150
806 - Roy Rogers	60	100	175
808 - General Robert E. Lee	50	90	150
809 - Wyatt Earp	50	90	150
812 - Brave Eagle	75	140	250
813 - Chief Thunder Cloud	50	90	150
814 - General Custer	60	100	175
815 - General George Washington	50	90	150
816 - Cochise	50	90	150
817 - Jim Bowie	75	140	250
818- Cheyenne	50	90	150
819 - Buffalo Bill	75	140	250
821 - Tom Jeffords	75	140	250
822 - Matt Dillon	50	90	150
823 - Annie Oakley	75	140	250
824 - Major Seth Adams	50	90	150
825 - Hoby Gilman	75	140	250
826 - Lucas McCain	75	140	250

	C6	C8	C10
827 - Bill Longly	100	240	400
828 - Josh Randle	120	290	480
829 - Colonel Randal Mackenzie	150	360	600
864 - Jim Hardie	50	90	150
866 - Paladin	50	90	150
? Davy Crockett	75	140	250
? Gil Favor	100	240	400
? Bret Maverick	60	100	175
? Johnny Yuma	120	290	480
? Turfking & Jockey	60	100	175
700 - Bullet	25	45	75
FAMOUS GUNFIGHTER SERIES			
709 - Marhsall Wyatt Earp	50	120	200
761 - Chris Colt	50	120	200
762 - Bret Maverick	50	120	200
763 - Clay Holister	50	120	200
764 - Jim Hardie	50	120	200
765 - Vint Bonner	75	175	300
766 - Paladin	50	120	200
767 - Dan Troop	75	175	300
768 - Johnny McKay	100	240	400
769 - Bat Masterson	65	135	225

8" WESTERN WRANGLERS (Riders Are Removable)

	C6	C8	C10
611 - Alkali Ike	35	75	125
612 - Cactus Pete	35	75	125
613 - Comanche Kid	35	75	125

5½" WESTERN HORSE & RIDERS (Hats & Riders Are Removable)

C10 Mint on blister card 50

C8 Mint, Complete of card 30

C6 Played with, off card, Missing Hat 15

Cheyenne, Gil Favor, Johnny Yuma, Wyatt Earp, Matt Dillon, The Lone Ranger, Tonto, Bret Maverick, Roy Rogers, Jim Hardie, Lucas McCain, Paladin

HARTLAND No. 805 and No. 801 Lone Ranger (newer). Courtesy Rex and Richard Gray.

HARTLAND No. 801 Lone Ranger (old chaps). Photo by Gary J. Linden.

HARTLAND No. 802 Dale Evans. Photo by Gary J. Linden.

HARTLAND No. 804 Sgt. Lance O'Rourke. Photo by Gary J. Linden.

HARTLAND No. 806 Roy Rogers. Photo by Gary J. Linden.

HARTLAND No. 809 Wyatt Earp. Photo by Gary J. Linden.

HARTLAND No. 864 Jim Hardie. Photo by Gary J. Linden.

HARTLAND No. 828 Josh Randle. Photo by Gary J. Linden.

HARTLAND No. 816 Cochise. Photo by Gary J. Linden.

HARTLAND No. 817 Jim Bowie. Photo by Gary J. Linden.

HARTLAND No. 819 Buffalo Bill. Photo by Gary J. Linden.

HARTLAND No. 821 Tom Jeffords. Photo by Gary J. Linden.

HARTLAND No. 822 Matt Dillon. Photo by Gary J. Linden.

HARTLAND No. 826 Lucas McCain. Photo by Gary J. Linden.

HARTLAND No. 769 Bat Masterson. Photo by Gary J. Linden.

HARTLAND No. 700 Bullet. Photo by Gary J. Linden.

341

HARTLAND No. 761. Photo by Gary J. Linden.

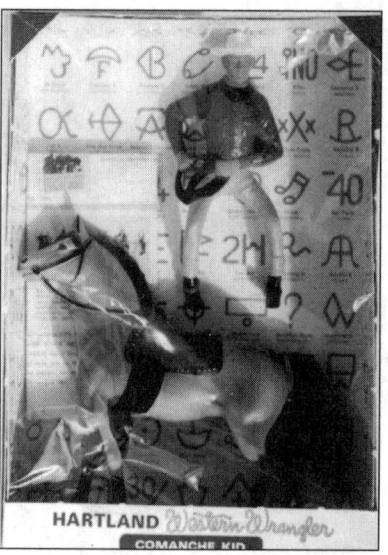

HARTLAND No. 613 Comanche Kid. Photo by Gary J. Linden.

	C6	C8	C10
Ideal Captain Action No. 3400-9 - costumed figure, Lightning Sword, scabbard, gun, gun belt, 12" high ...75		125	150
Ideal Action Boy 3420-7, new in 1967, 9" high, costumed, Panther, Space Helmet, utility belt, ray gun knife 125		200	250
Ideal Dr. Evil No. 3465-2, new in 1968, 12" high, costumed with laser gun ...125		200	250
Ideal Batgirl, 12" high, 1967 250		350	400
Ideal Mera (Aquaman's wife), 1967, 12" high 250		350	400
Ideal Supergirl, 12" high, 1967 250		350	400
Ideal Wonder Woman, 1967, 12" high .250		350	400
Ideal Aqua Lad Outfit No. 3423-1 - costume, octopus, boots, belt with sea horse knife, sea shell axe, no figure included in outfits 200		300	400
Ideal Aquaman Outfit No. 3408-2 - costume, swordfish sword, conch horns, fins, trident spear, knife with sheath, Aquaman face mask ..110		165	220
Ideal Bat Girl - helmet, cape, batarang, boots, bat gloves, halter dress for alter ego Barbara Gordon.................250		350	400
Ideal Batman Outfit No. 3402 -5 - costume, emblem , cape, boots, utility belt with 2-way radio buckle, flashlight, Batarang, laser-beam, Batrope, reel with grappling hook, hood, Batman face mask......125		165	200
Ideal Buck Rogers Outfit No. 3416-5 face mask, space belt, twin jet packs, space helmet, space gun, space light, space boots, canteen ..140		165	200

	C6	C8	C10
Ideal Captain America Outfit No. 3409-0 - uniform, belt with holster, ultrasonic pistol, laser-beam gun, boots, shield, Captain America face mask 160		225	275
Ideal Flash Gordon Outfit No. 3403-3 - silver astro-suit, space helmet, silver boots, space belt with holster and ray pistol, oxygen guidance "Zot" gun, Flash Gordon face mask 100		125	165
Ideal Green Hornet Outfit No. 3413-2 - face mask, watch message receiver, gas pistol, hornet sting, TV scanner with phone, shoulder holster, gas mask, shoes, costume .250		375	500
Ideal Lone Ranger Outfit No. 3406-6 - Wild West cowboy outfit, gun belt, two holsters, two pistols, boots with spurs, Winchester rifle, cowboy hat, Lone Ranger face mask, blue shirt version 150		200	250
Red shirt version............................200		275	350
Ideal The Phantom Outfit No. 3407-4 - costume, rifle with scope, belt, holster, pistol, knife, boots, Phantom face mask 90		135	175
Ideal Robin Outfit No. 3421-5 - 2 suction grips, Bat-a-Rang Launcher, Bat-a-Rang, 2 Bat grenades...........145		195	250
Ideal Sgt. Fury Outfit.............................125		175	225
Ideal Spiderman Outfit No. 3414-0 - spray tank with hose, utility belt, spider hook with rope and handle, mask, light, boots...........................225		275	350
Ideal Steve Canyon Outfit No. 3405-8 - uniform, 50 mission hat, parachute pack, garrison belt, holster, .45 automatic, helmet with oxygen mask, knife, boots, Steve Canyon face mask................100		135	200
Ideal Super Girl - cape, costume, boots, Krypto dog, halter dress for alter ego Linda Lee Danvers..........250		350	450
Ideal Superboy Outfit No. 3422-3 - uniform, belt, boots, cape, telepathic scrambler, interspace language translator, chem lab 200		275	350
Ideal Superman Outfit No.3401-7 - costume, super shield, belt, flying cape, boots, arm shackles, block of Kryptonite, Superman face mask, Krypto the dog..............................130		175	200

	C6	C8	C10
Ideal Tonto Outfit No. 3415-7 - face mask, gun belt, head band, pistol, knife, bow, quiver, 4 arrows, moccasins, eagle	150	225	275
Ideal Communicator Kit No.3454-6 - Solar Power Pack, Rotating Antenna dome, Beam Projectors, Secret Sound Horn	150	225	275
Ideal Directional Communicator Set No. 3454-6 - Solar Power Pack,			

	C6	C8	C10
Rotating Antenna dome, power plugs, beam projectors, Secret Sound Horn	150	225	275
Ideal Dr. Evil Gift Set No. 3466-0 - Dr. Evil, lab coat, 2 disguise masks, Reducer, Hypnotic Eye, Ionized Hypo, Laser Ray Gun, Thought Control Helmet	250	375	500
Ideal Dr. Evil Sanctuary No. 8701-5 - "space age" carrycase, storage bins, Dr. Evil figure	350	475	600

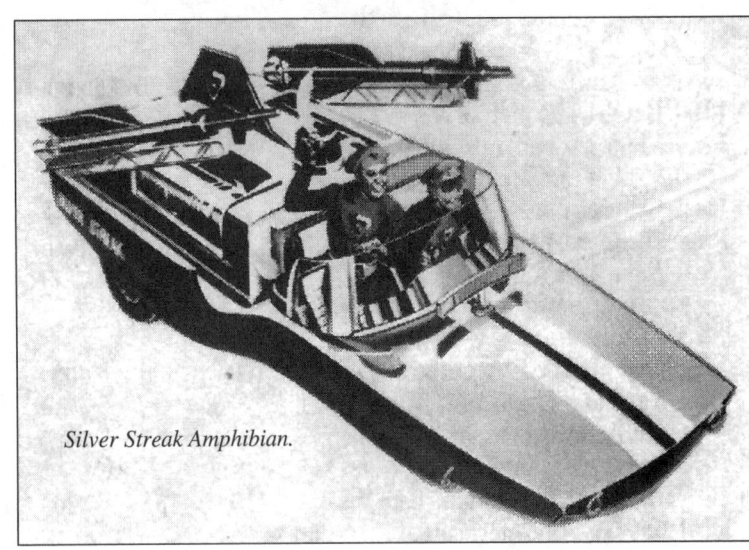

Silver Streak Amphibian.

Captain Action and Action Boy.

Top, Left to Right: Flash Gordon Outfit, Spiderman Outfit, Steve Canyon Outfit, Green Hornet Outfit, Lone Ranger Outfit, Tonto Outfit. Bottom, Left to Right: The Phantom Outfit, Batman Outfit, Captain America Outfit, Aquaman Outfit, Buck Rogers Outfit, Superman Outfit.

IDEAL Directional Communicator Set No. 3454-6 - Solar Power Pack, Rotating Antenna dome, power plugs, beam projectors, Secret Sound Horn

IDEAL Parachute Pack No. 3453-B -Parachute with Body Harness and Back Pack, Crash Helmet, jump boots

	C6	C8	C10
Ideal Jet Mortar No. 3452-0 - Mortar with Blaster Tripod, Radar Scanner, Ammo Carrier, two mortar missiles	90	135	180
Ideal Parachute Pack No. 3453-B - Parachute with Body Harness and Back Pack, Crash Helmet, jump boots	100	150	200
Ideal Power Pack No. 3455-3 - Thrust Ejector, Cosmic Boots, Cosmic Gloves, Flight Helmet	90	135	175
Ideal Silver Streak Amphibian No. 3449-6, 21¼" long	200	400	600

	C6	C8	C10
Ideal Survival Vest No. 3450-4 Utility Vest with Fishing Kit, Mirror, First Aid Kit, Folding Spade, 3 pc. Extension Claw Hook, Machete, Utility Belt with Flare Pistol and holster, Flares, Dagger, Ammo and Hatchet	175	250	325
Ideal Weapons Arsenal No. 3451-2 - Electronic Rifle, 2 Revolvers, Carbine, Automatic, 2 Grenades, Combat Knife, All - Purpose Knife, Ray Gun, Storage Rack	175	250	325

KENNER

Kenner was formed in 1947 on Kenner Street in Cincinnati by three brothers; Al, Phil and Joe Steiner. In 1967 General Mills took it over. The "Star Wars" toys have probably been its most notable success, and follow

Kenner's other action figures and toys in this listing. **Because figures that are mint on the card or in the box are so important in this category, their prices are shown in parentheses immediately following the listing.**

	C6	C8	C10
Alien, 18" high, new in 1980, "Alien" movie. Fully articulated jaws, tail moves, head glows in dark	75	150	225

Raiders of the Lost Ark (*Listing by Jim Main*): 3¾" figures:

	C6	C8	C10
Indiana Jones ($50.00)	10	15	25
Marion Ravenwood ($75.00)	20	30	40
Toht ($10.00)	4	5	6
German Mechanic ($15.00)	6	8	10
Indiana Jones in German Uniform ($30.00)	10	15	20
Belloq ($45.00)	10	20	30
Belloq (mail in figure)($15.00)	6	8	10
Cairo Swordsman ($10.00)	4	5	6
Arabian Horse ($25.00)	5	10	15
Streets of Cairo playset ($25.00)	10	12	15

	C6	C8	C10
Well of Souls playset ($35.00)	15	20	25
Map Room playset ($20.00)	5	10	15
Desert Convoy Truck ($25.00)	8	12	15

Indiana Jones 12" figure ($175.00) .....60 | 80 | 100

Six Million Dollar Man (*Listing by Jim Main*) 12" Figures:

	C6	C8	C10
Steve Austin ($50.00)	15	20	25
Bionic Woman, Jamie Summers ($50.00)	15	20	25
Oscar Goldman ($50.00)	15	20	25
Fembot ($60.00)	20	25	30
Maskatron ($60.00)	20	25	30
Bionic Bigfoot ($60.00)	20	25	30
Bionic Beauty Salon ($60.00)	20	25	30
Bionic Mission Vehicle ($45.00)	15	18	21
Mission Control Playset ($80.00)	25	35	45

	C6	C8	C10
Venus Space Probe ($75.00)................20	30	40
Transport Repair ($30.00) 8	12	16
O.S.I. Headquarters ($75.00)................20	30	40
Test Flight at 75,000 Ft. ($35.00)..........9	13	17
O.S.I. Undercover ($35.00)...................9	13	17
Mission to Mars ($35.00) 9	13	17
Critical Assignment Arms ($25.00) 7	10	12

SUPER POWERS FIGURES (*listing by Jim Main*):

	C6	C8	C10
Aquaman ($35.00) 10	15	20
Flash ($10.00) 4	5	6
Batman ($40.00) 15	20	25
Superman ($15.00)................................5	7	9
Green Lantern ($30.00)........................10	12	14
Hawkman ($40.00) 10	15	20
DeSaad (20.00)......................................6	8	10
Robin ($25.00)......................................5	10	15
Braniac ($20.00) 6	8	10
Luthor ($10.00) 4	5	6
Penguin ($30.00)..................................10	15	20
Joker ($35.00) 10	15	20
Wonder Woman ($15.00).......................5	7	9
Mr. Freeze ($25.00)...............................5	10	15
Tyr ($25.00) 5	10	15
Plastic Man ($35.00).............................10	15	20
Golden Pharoah ($75.00).......................25	35	45
Orion ($25.00)......................................12	15	18
Steppenwolf ($10.00)............................4	5	6
Clark Kent ($35.00) 10	15	20
Parademon ($20.00)...............................6	8	10

	C6	C8	C10
Mantis ($20.00).....................................6	8	10
Kalibak ($20.00)...................................6	8	10
Samurai ($75.00)..................................30	40	50
Mr. Miracle ($100.00) 35	50	65
Captain Marvel (Shazam) ($30.00).......11	13	15
Firestorm ($35.00) 12	15	18
Darkseid ($15.00) 6	7	8
Cyborg ($120.00)..................................40	60	80
Red Tornado ($25.00)...........................12	15	18
Green Arrow ($40.00)...........................10	15	25
Martian Manhunter ($25.00).................12	15	18
Dr. Fate ($20.00) 8	10	12
Cyclotron ($75.00)...............................30	40	50

Vehicles/accessories (*listing by Jim Main*):

	C6	C8	C10
Batmobile ($50.00)...............................20	25	30
Supermobile ($25.00) 10	13	16
Batcopter ($50.00) 20	25	30
Delta Probe One ($20.00) 10	12	14
Justice Jogger ($20.00) 10	12	14
Lex-Soar 7 ($20.00) 10	12	14
Kalibak Boulder Bomber ($20.00) 10	12	14
Darkseid Destroyer ($30.00).................10	15	20
Hall of Justice playset ($90.00) 30	45	60
All Terrain Trapper ....No Price Found
Super Powers Vehicle ....No Price Found

STEVE SCOUT

	C6	C8	C10
Steve Scout figure ($40.00) 10	15	20

KENNER STAR WARS ACTION FIGURES

By Whit Alexander and Neal Bates

The first set of 12 figures was introduced in 1977 and by 1984 over 80 different action figures were offered.

Over the 7 year marketing period attention given to detail and variation of accessories increased.

STAR WARS ACTION FIGURES (SW-A)

The first set of action figures all read 1977 on their legs and included SW-A1, SW-A3, SW-A4, SW-A5, SW-A6, SW-A10, SW-A11, SW-A12, SW-A15, SW-A17, SW-A18, and SW-A20. The next set read 1978 and included the 5 cantina figures (SW-A8, SW-A9, SW-A19A, SW-A19B, SW-A21), plus 4 more (SW-A13, SW-A14, SW-A15, SW-A16 and SW-A7). Bobba Fett (SW-A2) was the only figure issued in 1979.

	C6	C8	C10
SW-A1 Ben (Obi-Wan) Knobi: 3¼" high, rust with removable brown cape and retractable blue light-saber, 1977 ($80.00) 4	8	12
SW-A2 Boba Fett: 3¾" high, blue-gray with backpack and laser pistol (Weapon No. 1). Originally		

offered only through special mail order and was the only Empire Strikes Back character to be offered a year prior to the movie's release date. 1979.. ($225.00) ....4 | 8 | 12

	C6	C8	C10
offered only through special mail order... 1979.. ($225.00) 4	8	12
SW-A3 Chewbacca: 4¼" high, brown with silver bandolier and laser rifle (Weapon No. 6). 1977. ($60.00) 4	8	12
SW-A4 C-3PO: 3¾" high, metallic gold with no accessories. 1977 ($100.00)................4	8	12
SW-A5 Darth Vader: 4¼" high, black with removable black cape and retractable red light-saber. 1977. ($70.00)................4	8	12

Left to Right: SW-A15, SW-A12, SW-A1, SW-A5.

Left to Right: SW-A3, SW-A17, SW-A4, SW-A10.

Left to Right: SW-A20, SW-A11, SW-A18, SW-A6.

Left to Right: SW-A9, SW-A19B, SW-A19A, SW-A21, SW-A8.

Photos Courtesy Whit Alexander and Neal Bates.

	C6	C8	C10
SW-A6 Death Squad Commander (Star Destroyer Commander); 3¼" high, gray with black helmet and Laser pistol (Weapon No. 1). 1977. ($70.00)	4	8	12
SW-A7 Death Star Droid: 3¾" high, metallic silver with no accessories. 1978. ($70.00)	4	8	12
SW-A8 Greedo: 3¾" high, green with laser pistol (Weapon No. 2). 1978 ($40.00)	4	8	12
SW-A9 Hammerhead: 4" high, brown with blue suit and laser pistol (Weapon No. 1). 1978 ($40.00)	4	8	12
SW-A10 Han Solo: 3¾" high, white shirt with black vest and pants. Equipped with laser pistol (Weapon No. 2). 1977. ($100.00)	4	8	12
SW-A11 Jawa: 2¼" high, brown with brown cloth cape and laser rifle (Weapon No. 4) 1977. ($75.00)	3	6	10
SW-A12 Luke Skywalker: 3¾" high; white shirt with beige pants. Equipped with retractable light-saber. 1977 ($75.00)	3	6	10
SW-A13 Luke Skywalker X-Wing Pilot: 3¼" high, orange with white helmet and laser pistol (Weapon No. 2). 1978 ($25.00)	3	6	10
SW-A14 Power Droid: 2¼" high, blue TV set shape with clicking legs. No accessories. 1978. ($55.00)	2	4	8
SW-A15 Princess Leia Organa: 3½" high, white with removable white cape and laser pistol (Weapon No. 3). 1977. ($75.00)	4	8	12
SW-A16 R5-D4: 2½" high, white trash-can shape with red detail. No Accessories. 1978. ($75.00)	5	10	15
SW-A17 R2-D2: 2¼" high, white with blue detail and chrome-dome head which clicks when turned. No accessories. 1978. ($75.00)	5	10	15
SW-A18 Sand People: 3¾" high, tan with removable tan cape and Gaffic Stick (Weapon No. 5). 1977. ($75.00)	5	10	15
SW-A19A Snaggletooth: 3¾" high, blue with silver boots and laser pistol (Weapon No. 1). Offered only with Cardboard Cantina. 1978. ($65.00)	4	8	12

	C6	C8	C10

SW-A19B Snaggletooth: 2⅞" high, red
with laser pistol (Weapon No. 1).
1978. ($55.00)....................4   8   12

SW-A20A Stormtrooper: 3¾" high,
white with white helmet and laser
pistol (Weapon No. 1). 1977. ($75.00).4   8   12

SW-A21 Walrus Man: 3¾" high, blue
with orange suit and green head.
Equipped with laser pistol
(Weapon No. 1). 1978. ($45.00) 3   7   11

The Empire Strikes Back Action Figures

ESB-A1 AT-AT Commander: 3¾" high,
gray with gray hat and laser pistol
(Weapon No. 1). 1980. ($15.00) 3   6   10

ESB-A2 AT-AT Driver: 3¾" high, light
gray with white helmet and laser
pistol (Weapon No. 7). 1980. ($17.00).3   6   9

ESB-A3A Bespin Security Guard: 3⅞"
high, black man has navy uniform
and laser pistol (Weapon No. 1).
1981 ($15.00) 3   7   11

ESB-A3B Bespin Security Guard: 4"
high, white man has navy uniform
and laser pistol (Weapon No. 1).
1980 ($15.00) 3   7   11

ESB-A4 Bossk: 4" high, yellow with
olive head and laser rifle (Weapon
No. 6). 1980 ($15.00).......................3   7   11

ESB-A5 C-3PO: 4" high, metallic gold
with removable limbs and papoose.
(Acc. No. 13). 1980 ($12.00)..............3   6   10

ESB-A6 Cloud-Car Pilot: 3¾" high,
white with orange and yellow
helmet, with laser pistol (Weapon
No. 9a) and walkie-talkie (Acc.
No. 9b). 1981. ($15.00)....................3   6   10

ESB-A7 Dengar: 3⅝" high, white and
brown with backpack and head
wrap. Equipped with laser rifle
(Weapon No. 2). 1980. ($13.00) 2   4   6

ESB-A8 FX-7: 3⅜" high with head down,
silver with 9 movable arms and retract-
able head, no accessories,1980. ($20.00).2   4   8

ESB-A9 4-LOM: 3⅝" high, tan with
removable tan cape and brown
removable backpack. Equipped
with laser pistol (Weapon No. 11).
1981. ($20.00)...................................2   4   8

ESB-A10 Han Solo (Bespin outfit): 4"
high, navy vest with brown pants
and laser pistol (Weapon No. 3).
1980 ($25.00)...................................3   6   10

Left to Right: SW-A7, SW-A16, SW-A14, SW-A2, SW-A13.

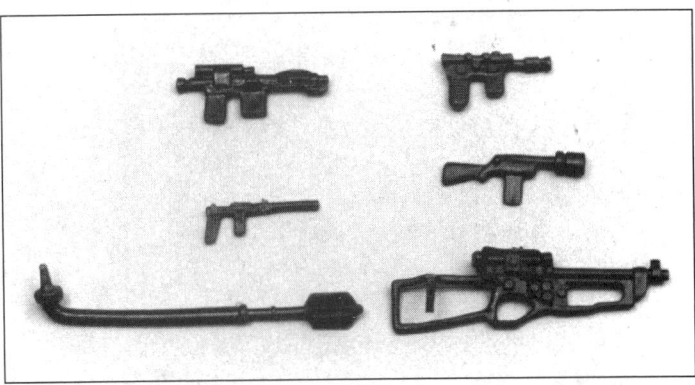

Star Wars Action Figures Weapons and Accessories. Left to Right,Top row: 1,2; Middle row: 3,4; Bottom row: 5, 6.

Photo Courtesy Whit Alexander and Neal Bates.

	C6	C8	C10

ESB-A11 Han Solo (Hoth outfit): 4"
high, blue fur-lined parka with
brown boots and laser pistol
(Weapon No. 3). 1980. ($18.00) 3   6   10

ESB-A12 IG-88: 4⅝" high, gray with
black bandolier and laser guns
(Weapons No. 1 & 16). 1980.
($18.00)...3   6   10

ESB-A13 Imperial Commander: 3⅞"
high, black hat and laser pistol
(Weapon No. 14). 1980. ($12.00) 2   4   8

ESB-A14 Imperial Stormtrooper (Hoth
Battle Gear): 3⅞" high, white with
white veil and removable white
skirt. Equipped with laser rifle
(Weapon No. 2). 1980 ($15.00) 3   5   9

ESB-A15 Imperial Tie-Fighter Pilot:
3¾" high, black with gray boots
and gloves and laser pistol
(Weapon No. 9a). 1982 ($15.00) 2   4   8

ESB-A16 Lando Calrissian: 4" high,
light blue with dark blue pants
and removable cape. Equipped
with laser pistol (Weapon No. 1).
1980 ($13.00) 2   4   8

ESB-A17 Lobot: 3⅝" high, gray-brown
with yellow sleeves and computerized

	C6	C8	C10
head band. Equipped with laser pistol (Weapon No. 1). 1980 ($15.00)	2	4	8
ESB-A18 Luke Skywalker (Bespin Fatigues): 3⅞" high, tan with brown boots. Equipped with laser pistol and light-saber (Weapons No. 3 & 5). 1980 (15.00)	3	7	11
ESB-A19 Luke Skywalker (Hoth Battle Gear): 3¾" high, white with brown vest and scarf and laser rifle (Weapon No. 17). 1981. ($25.00)	3	6	10
ESB-A20 Princess Leia Organa (Bespin Gown): 3½" high, brick red with pink cape and laser pistol (Weapon No. 4). 1980. ($30.00)	3	7	11
ESB-A21 Princess Leia Organa (Hot Outfit): 3¾" high, white with tan vest and laser pistol (Weapon No. 4). 1980 ($20.00)	3	6	10

ESB-A22 R2-D2 (With Sensorscope): 2½" high, white with blue detail. One head panel extends into radar. No accessories. Bottom

	C6	C8	C10
reads "1977" but new head was added circa 1980. ($15.00)	2	4	6
ESB-A23 Rebel Commander: 3⅞" high, white with brown scarf and laser rifle (Weapon No. 7). 1980. ($17.00)	3	6	10
ESB-A24 Rebel Soldier: 3⅞" high, white with brown vest and white hat. Equipped with laser pistol. (Weapon No. 1). 1980. ($15.00)	3	6	10
ESB-A25 2-1B: 3¾" high, blue with transparent middle and gas mask. Has medical stick. (Acc. No. 12). 1980.	3	7	11
ESB-A26 Ugnaught: 2¾" high, gray with blue apron and tool-purse (Acc. No. 8). 1980. ($25.00)	3	6	10
ESB-A27 Yoda: 2" high, brown with light green head, has cloth tan robe, removable belt, orange snake and brown stick (Acc. Nos. 10a & 10b). 1980. ($15.00)	3	6	10
ESB-A28 Zuckuss: 3¾" high, gray with blue fly-eyes and laser rifle (Weapon No. 15), 1982. ($20.00)	3	6	10

Left to Right: ESB-A21, ESB-A10, ESB-A16, ESB-A5.

Left to Right: ESB-A25, ESB-A21, ESB-A8.

Left to Right: ESB-A18, ESB-A22, ESB-A27.

Left to Right: ESB-A19, ESB-A11, ESB-A23, ESB-A24.

Photos Courtesy Whit Alexander and Neal Bates.

Left to Right: ESB-A14, ESB-A2, ESB-A15, ESB-A13, ESB-A1.

Left to Right: ESB-A17, ESB-A6, ESB-A3B, ESB-A26, ESB-A3A.

Left to Right: ESB-A7, ESB-A28, ESB-A9, ESB-A12, ESB-A4.

THE RETURN OF THE JEDI ACTION FIGURES

	C6	C8	C10
RJ-A1 Admiral Ackbar: 3⅞" high, white with tan vest and rust "lobster" head, black stick (Acc. No. 1). 1983 ($7.00)	1	2	3
RJ-A2 AT-ST Driver: 3⅞ high, light gray with dark gray helmet and laser pistol (Weapon No. 2). 1984 ($8.00)	2	3	4
RJ-A3 B-Wing Pilot: 3⅞" high, red with silver and brown helmet and laser pistol (Weapon No. 2). 1984 ($5.00)	1	2	3

	C6	C8	C10
RJ-A4 Bib Fortuna: 4⅛" high, blue with removable beige cape and removable gray chestplate. Has wrap-around horn and staff (Acc. No. 6). 1983 ($10.00)	1	2	3
RJ-A5 Biker Scout: 4" high, black with white armor and laser pistol (Weapon No. 4). 1983 ($10.00)	2	3	4
RJ-A6 Boushh: 3⅝" high, beige and brown with silver armor. Has silver and orange removable helmet and laser stick. (Weapon No. 7). 1983. ($16.00)	1	2	3
RJ-A7 Chief Chirpa: 3" high with removable brown hood and staff (Acc. No. 21). 1983 ($6.00)	1	2	3
RJ-A8 8D8: White droid with silver and brown detail. No accessories. 1983 ($10.00)	1	2	3
RJ-A9 Emperor's Royal Guard: Brick red and crimson cape and tunic with staff (Weapon No. 8). 1983 ($10.00)	2	3	4

The Empire Strikes Back Action Figures Weapons and Accessories. Top row, Left to Right: 2, 1, 3, 4, 5. Second row: 6, 7, 8, 9a, 9b. Third row: 10a, 10b, 11, 12, 13. Fourth row: 14, 15, 16. Bottom: 17. Photos Courtesy Whit Alexander and Neal Bates.

Left to Right: RJ-A28, RJ-A7, RJ-A15, RJ-A25.

Left to Right: RJ-A13A, RJ-A13B, RJ-A8, RJ-A18.

Left to Right: RJ-A3, RJ-A11, RJ-A1, RJ-A17.

Left to Right: RJ-A5, RJ-A22, RJ-A19.

Photos Courtesy Whit Alexander and Neal Bates.

	C6	C8	C10
RJ-A10 Gamorrean Guard: 3⅞" high, olive with brown garment and battle axe (Weapon No. 3). 1983 ($8.00)	1	2	3
RJ-A11 General Madine: 4" high, light gray with black boots and gloves and blue sleeves and white wand (Acc. No. 16). 1983. ($8.00)	1	2	3
RJ-A12 Han Solo (Trench Coat): 4" high, dark gray pants with light gray shirt and removable camouflage cape and laser pistol (Weapon No. 22). 1984. ($13.00)	2	3	4
RJ-A13A Klaatu: 4" high, dark green with gray shirt and silver helmet. Has animal pelt skirt and skiff stick (Weapon No. 9). 1983 ($6.00)	1	2	3
RJ-A13B Klaatu (Skiff Guard Outfit): 3⅞" high, dark green with off white garment and brown helmet with laser stick (Weapon No. 10). 1983. ($7.00)	1	2	3
RJ-A14 Lando Calrissian (Skiff Guard Disguise): 3⅞" high, brown vest with armor. Has removable brown helmet and skiff stick (Weapon No. 9). 1982. ($15.00)	1	2	3
RJ-A15 Luke Skywalker (Jedi Knight Outfit): 3⅞" high, black with removable olive cape. Has laser pistol and light-saber (Weapons No. 5a and 5b) 1983. ($15.00)	1	2	3
RJ-A16 Logray: 3⅝" high, cream and brown striped with removable black hood, medicine bag and staff (Acc. No. 18). 1983. ($8.00)	1	2	3
RJ-A17 Nien Nunb: 3⅞" high, red with navy vest, dark gray helmet and laser pistol (Weapon No. 17). 1983 ($10.00)	1	2	3
RJ-A18 Nikto: White shirt with ice-blue vest and gray pants. Has brown head wrap and laser stick (Weapon No. 11). 1983 ($8.00)	1	2	3
RJ-A19 Princess Leia Organa (Combat Poncho): 3⅝" high, gray with removable helmet and combat poncho. Has removable belt and laser pistol (Weapon No. 2). 1984 ($12.00)	1	2	3
RJ-A20 Prune Face: 3⅞" high, lime green pants with cream shirt and			

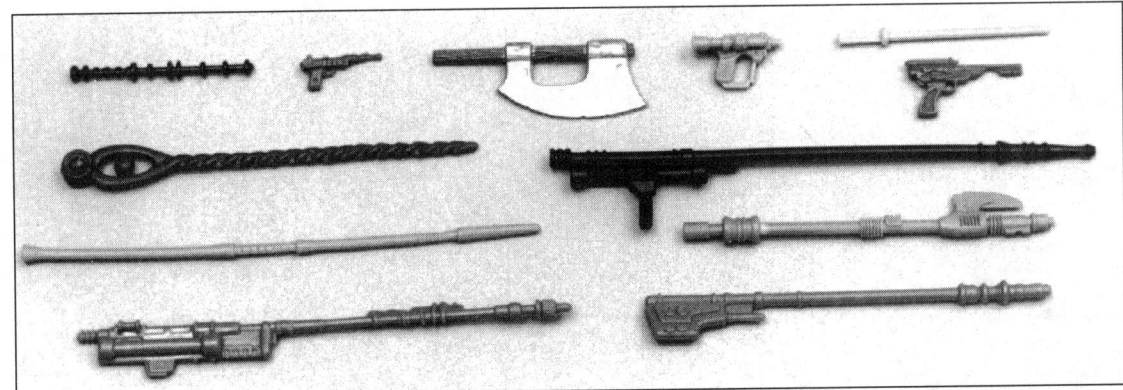

The Return of the Jedi Action Figures Weapons and Accessories, Top row, Left to Right: 1, 2, 3, 4, 5a, 5b. Second row: 6, 7. Third row: 8, 9. Bottom row: 10, 11. Photo Courtesy Whit Alexander and Neal Bates.

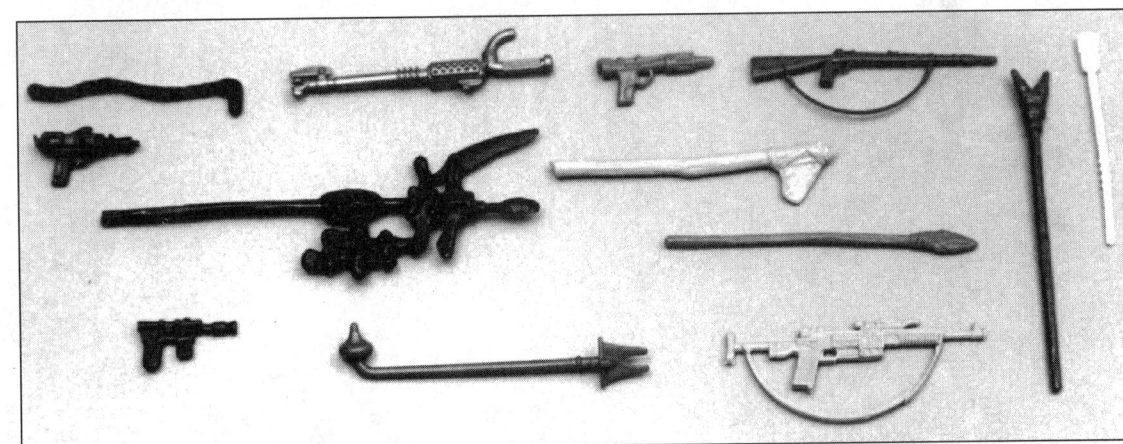

Top row, Let to Right: 12, 13, 14, 15. Second row: 17, 18, 19, 20, 21, 16. Bottom row: 22, 23, 24. Photo Courtesy Whit Alexander and Neal Bates.

	C6	C8	C10
removable tan cape. Has eyepatch and laser rifle. (Weapon No. 15) 1984 ($8.00)	1	2	3
RJ-A21 Rancor Keeper: 4" high, olive pants with no shirt. Has removable hood and stick (Acc. No. 23). 1984 ($5.00)	1	2	3
RJ-A22 Rebel Commando: 4" high, olive uniform with green helmet, brown backpack and laser rifle (Weapon No. 24). 1983 ($10.00)	1	2	3
RJ-A23 Ree-Yees: 3⅝" high, peach with three eyes and brick red garment and laser rifle. (Weapon No. 13). 1983. ($9.00)	1	2	3
RJ-A24 Squid Head: 4" high, white with white skirt, has removable belt and olive cape; head has 4 tentacles, has laser pistol. (Weapon No. 14). 1983 ($8.00)	1	2	3
RJ-A25 Teebo: 3⅞" high, light and dark gray striped. Has removable hood and horn on sling. Also has axe (Acc. No. 19) 1984 ($6.00)	1	2	3
RJ-A26 The Emperor: 4" high, dark gray with staff (Acc. No. 12). 1984 ($9.00)	1	2	3
RJ-A27 Weequay: 3⅞" high, ice blue shirt with beige pants and brown			

	C6	C8	C10
vest, gray ponytail and skiff stick (Weapon No. 9). 1983 ($10.00)	1	2	3
RJ-A28 Wickett W. Warrick: 2" high, brown with creme belly, removable hood and spear (Weapon No. 20). 1984. ($8.00)	1	2	3

VEHICLES

These vehicles are intended for use with the action figures and many are battery operated (B/O).

STAR WARS VEHICLES (SW-V)

	C6	C8	C10
SW-V1 Darth Vader Tie-Fighter (B/O), 9¾" long x 11¾" wide, dark gray with spherical cockpit and removable wing panels, red laser lights up and emits a whirring sound. 1978 ($65.00)	12	18	25
SW-V2 Imperial troop Transport: (B/O), 10¼" long x 5¼" wide, gray with red stripes, has rear and 6 side compartments, dual cockpit and rotating laser cannons and radar, 2 prisoner holsters, 6 red buttons play a variety of recordings ($55.00)	10	15	20
SW-V3 Jawa Sandcrawler: 14½" long x 5⅝" wide, rust brown with			

SW-V6, Tie-Fighter. Figure not included. Photo Courtesy Whit Alexander and Neal Bates.

SW-V7, X-Wing Fighter. Figure not included.

Photos Courtesy Whit Alexander and Neal Bates.

SW-V1, Darth Vader Tie-Fighter. Figure not included.

SW-V4, Landspeeder. Figure not included.

SW-V2, Imperial Troop Transport. Figures not included.

	C6	C8	C10
wireless remote control. 1979. ($250.00) 60		90	120
SW-V4 Landspeeder: 9½" long x 6" wide, brown with chrome grills, 3 jets and windshield, wheels can be lowered by shifter in cockpit. 1978. ($50.00) 10		15	20
SW-V5 Millenium Falcon: (B/O) 20½" long x 16½" wide, off-white with gray laser cannon. Main compartment has chessboard, laser ball, floor panel and revolving laser cannon. Emits whirring sound when side button is pressed. 1979. ($80.00) 15		22	30
SW-V6 Tie Fighter (B/O) 7⅛" long, 10¼"			

	C6	C8	C10
wide, white with spherical cockpit and removable black wing panels, red laser lights up and emits whirring sound. 1978. ($65.00) 8		12	16
SW-V7 X-Wing Fighter (B/O), 13¾" long, 11½" wide, white with red and yellow stripes and 4 laser cannons. Wings open into "X" position, red laser lights up and emits whirring sound. 1978 ($45.00) 8		12	16

SW-V5, Millenium Falcon. Figures not included.
Photo Courtesy Whit Alexander and Neal Bates.

ESB-V6, Snowspeeder. Figure not included.

ESB-V7, Twin-Pod Cloud Car. Figure not included.

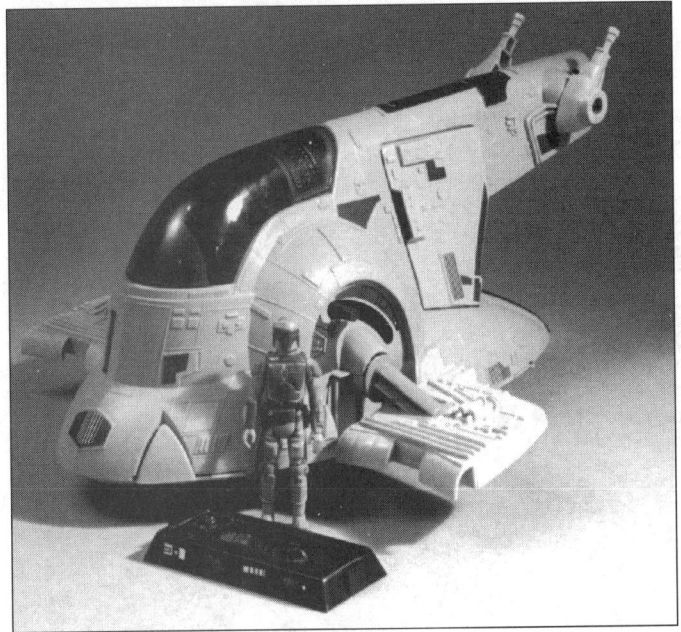

ESB-V5, Slave-1. Boba Fett not included.

Photos Courtesy Whit Alexander and Neal Bates.

ESB-V2, AT-ST (Scout Walker). Figures not included.

THE EMPIRE STRIKES BACK VEHICLES (ESB-V)

	C6	C8	C10
ESB-V1 AT-AT: (B/O), 17½" high, 22" long, light gray with black detail, 4 moveable legs and swiveling cockpit, 2 laser cannons light up and pulsate. 1981 ($75.00)............15		22	32
ESB-V2 AT-ST (Scout Walker): 11¼" high, light gray, button on back moves legs. 1982. ($45.00)............8		12	16
ESB-V3 Imperial Star Destroyer, swiveling laser cannon on bow and meditation chamber. 1981. ($75.00)............16		24	32
ESB-V4A MCL-3: light gray with tank treads and dome top. 1981. ($15.00)............4		6	8
ESB-V4B MTV-7: light gray with spring-loaded steamroller legs. 1981. ($15.00)............4		6	8
ESB-V5 Slave 1: 15" long, 12¾" wide, gray with blue windshield, 2 swiveling wing flaps, black cargo door, gray side door, revolving laser cannons on tail. Han Solo in Carbonite. 1981. ($60.00)............9		13	18
ESB-V6 Snowspeeder (B/O) 12¼" long, 12¾" wide, light gray with 2 light up laser cannons, rear harpoon gun with harpoon on string. 1980. ($40.00)............8		12	16
ESB-V7 Twin-Pod Cloud Car: 10½" wide, 8¾" long, rust orange with dual pod cockpit. 1980. ($45.00)....10		15	20

THE RETURN OF THE JEDI VEHICLES (RJ-V)

	C6	C8	C10
RJ-V1 B-Wing Fighter: light gray, cockpit on right side with fin-wing extending to the left. Circa 1985. ($50.00)............15		22	30
RJ-V1 A Battle-Damaged Imperial Tie-Fighter ($40.00)............10		15	20
RJ-V2 Ewok Combat Glider: brown with harness for one action figure and 2 stone-bombs. Circa 1984.........No Price Found			
RJ-V3 Imperial Shuttle: light gray, stationary center fin and side wings that fold up. Circa 1984. ($100.00)............20		30	40
RJ-V4 Speeder Bike: 8¾" long, light brown with black engine and detail. Bike "explodes" when pack is pressed. 1983. ($15.00)............2		3	5

	C6	C8	C10
RJ-V5 Y-Wing Fighter: light gray with twin hollow engines, 3 retractable landing skids. Circa 1984. ($50.00)............7		12	15

STAR WARS PLAYSETS (SW-P)

	C6	C8	C10
SW-P1 Action Figure Display Stand: 20" long, 5½ "wide, gray base with moving discs for 12 action figures. Front has decal with the names of the 12 original action figures. Cardboard backdrop depicts a spaceship dogfight. Available through special mail order only. 1978. ($125.00)			
SW-P2 Cardboard Cantina: 18" long, 7" high, tan base has 11 action figure pegs. Backdrop has scene from Mos Eiseley city street. Available only with Cantina figure set which included SW-A8, SW-A9, SW-A19A, and SW-A21. 1978..30		45	60
SW-P3 Collector's Case: 2 trays hold a total of 24 action figures. Case depicts scenes from Star Wars. ($35.00)			
SW-P4 Creature Cantina; 13¾" long, 7¾" wide, tan-orange base has bar and table, 2 action levers and floor button which opens the doors. Also has cardboard backdrop depicting cantina scene. 1979 ($90.00)			
SW-P5 Death Star Space Station:			

ESB-P9, Taun-Taun. Figure not included. Photo Courtesy Whit Alexander and Neal Bates.

354

	C6	C8	C10

22¼" high, gray and black, 3 floors and basement trash compactor. Compactor has foam trash and green monster. Floors have drawbridge, grappling hook swing, "exploding" laser cannon and catwalk. Main tower has elevator and 2nd and 3rd floors have cardboard surface panels. 1977. ($125.00)

SW-P6 Droid Factory: 13" x11", tan-orange base holds 38 interchangeable droid parts and crane with hook. 1979 ($100.00)..............22 33 45

SW-P7 Land of the Jawas: 13½" long, 8¼" wide. Tan base has sand cave and action lever. Escape pod fits into crater. Cardboard backdrop depicts sandcrawler and has moving elevator. 1979. ($140.00)

SW-P8 Patrol Dewback: 10½" long, green and white lizard has 4 posable limbs and trap door in back. Tail and head move together. Also has brown saddle and harness. 1979. ($20.00).............5 8 10

EMPIRE STRIKES BACK PLAYSETS (ESB-P)

ESB-P1 Cardboard Bespin Set: 9" high, 11¾" wide, cardboard base has 6 action figure pegs. Backdrop depicts Cloud City scene and has protruding Carbonite Chamber. Available only with action figures ESB-A7, ESB-A10, ESB-A17 and ESB-A26. 1980. ($15.00)

ESB-P2 Collector's Case: 2 trays hold a total of 24 action figures. Case depicts scenes from The Empire Strikes Back ($22.00)

ESB-P3 Dagobah Playset: gray with brown tree stump, 3 action levers, mud puddle and 2 storage containers. 1981. ($45.00)

ESB-P4 Darth Vader Collector Case: 14½" high, 16" wide, black with room for 31 action figures and accessories. Circa 1980. ($22.00)....4 6 8

ESB-P5 Hoth Ice Planet: 13½" long, 8¼" wide, white base has snow cave and action lever. Tank-radar sits in crater. Cardboard backdrop depicts AT-AT with moving elevator. 1981. ($105.00).............15 23 35

ESB-P6 Hoth Wampa: 6" high, white with 4 posable limbs. Circa 1981. ($15.00)........................4 6 8

ESB-P7 Imperial Attack Base: 17¼" long, 10" wide, white with revolving laser cannon and gray control room, 3 action levers make 2 part snowbridge fall, control room "explode" and action figure fall ($65.00)........................10 15 20

ESB-P8 Probot and Turret: 15½" long, 9¼" wide, white base has action lever and post for gray probot. Turret has door and revolving laser platform. 1979. ($142.00).....20 30 40

ESB-P9 Taun-Taun: 9¾" from head to tail, gray and white with brown horns, trap door in back and 4 posable limbs, brown saddle and harness. 1980. Split Belly ($25.00)..6 9 12

ESB-P10 Taun-Taun as above, 1981, Closed Belly. ($20.00) 5 7 10

RETURN OF THE JEDI PLAYSETS (RJ-P)

RJ-P1 C-3PO Collector Case: metallic gold with room for 31 action figures and accessories. Circa 1983. ($20.00)........................5 8 10

RJ-P2 Chewbacca Bandolier Strap: black, holds 10 action figures and accessories. Circa 1983. ($11.00) 2 3 4

RJ-P3 Ewok Assault Catapult: brown logs with rotating winch and 2 gray boulders. Circa 1983. ($15.00) ..3 5 7

RJ-P4 Jabba the Hutt Playset: 11" long, 5¼" wide, grayish-brown platform with 2 doors, with Jabba, Salacious Crumb and a long-armed green monster. 1983. ($32.00) 9 13 18

RJ-P5 Land of the Ewoks: 22" high, 16" long, tan platform supported by 3 trees, spit over the firering, stool, moving elevator, net and litter for carrying action figures. 1983. ($40.00)................................15 22 30

RJ-P6 Rancor Monster: 10" high, tan with 4 posable limbs. 1983. ($20.00)........................6 9 12

RJ-P7 The Jabba The Hutt Dungeon: 13" x 11", gray base, crane with hood and branding iron. Complete with action figures RJ-A13B, RJ-A18 and RJ-A8. 1983 ($30.00).......10 15 20

	C6	C8	C10
RJ-P8 Sy Snootles and the Max Rebo Band: complete with blue keyboardist and keyboard, spotted singer and microphone, pink clarinet player and microphone. Circa 1983. ($30.00) 10	15	20

LARGE FIGURES AND DOLLS

	C6	C8	C10
Ben (Obi-Wan) Knobi, 12" high, light-saber, removable cape ($200.00) 60	90	120
Boba Fett, 13¼" high, laser rifle, molded backpack ($250.00)............50	75	100
C-3PO, 12" high ($85.00) 32	48	65
Chewbacca, 18" high, stuffed ($60.00).20	30	40
Chewbacca, 15" high, with laser crossbow ($120.00) 25	38	50
Chewbacca, 8" high, furry ($80.00).......8	12	15
Darth Vader, 15" high, light-saber and removable cape ($150.00)..............40	60	80
Han Solo, 12" high, laser rifle ($450.00).100	150	225
IG-88, 15" high, laser weapons ($500.00).................................100	150	200
Jawa, 8¼" high, hooded cape and laser rifle ($140.00).......................30	50	75
Luke Skywalker, 11¾" high, lever-like arm and grappling hook ($225.00).....75	112	150
Princess Leia Organa, 11½" high, combable hair ($140.00) 30	50	75
RS-D2, 7½" high, head clicks when turned ($85.00)..............................30	45	60
R2-D2, radio controlled ($110.00)........20	32	45
Stormtrooper, 12" high, has laser rifle ($180.00).................................45	65	90

DIE CAST VEHICLES

Kenner Series 1

	C6	C8	C10
Darth Vader Tie Fighter ($65.00)...........15	25	35
X-Wing Fighter ($55.00) 13	20	30
Land Speeder ($55.00)........................13	20	35
Tie Fighter ($50.00) 12	18	25

Kenner Series II

	C6	C8	C10
Millenium Falcoln ($120.00) 35	50	70
Darth Vader's Star Ship Destroyer ($72.00).......................................20	30	40
Princess Leia's Command Ship ....*No Price Found*		
Tie Bomber ($750.00)..........................200	350	500
Y-Wing Fighter ($100.00) 30	45	60

Kenner Series III

	C6	C8	C10
Snow Speeder ($95.00) 22	35	50
Slave I Space Ship ($45.00) 10	15	25

	C6	C8	C10
Twin-Pod Cloud Car ($45.00)..............10	15	25

End Star Wars

	C6	C8	C10
LJN "V" Action Figures (TV Series)....8	12	16

MARX *(Listing by Jim Main)*

8 to 12" Figures:

	C6	C8	C10
Johnny Apollo Astronaut ($90.00) 40	50	60
Johnny and Jane Apollo Deluxe Set w/vehicles ($450.00).....................125	150	175
Stoney Smith ($80.00) 35	45	55
Sir Gordon, The Golden Knight ($80.00)...35	45	55
Bravo, The Golden Knight's Horse ($60.00)...20	25	30
Sir Stuart, The Silver Knight ($80.00)..35	45	55
Valor, The Silver Knight's Horse ($60.00)...20	25	30
Mike Hazzard, Double Agent ($250.00)...60	90	120
Girl From UNCLE (Marx British issue) ($300.00) 90	120	150

Best Of The West:

	C6	C8	C10
Johnny West ($80.00) 30	40	50
Jay West ($50.00)................................15	20	25
Janice West ($50.00)...........................15	20	25
Jane West ($60.00)..............................20	25	30
Brave Eagle ($75.00)...........................25	35	45
Jamie West ($40.00)............................15	20	25
Thundercolt ($30.00)...........................10	12	15
Thunderbolt ($40.00)...........................15	20	25
Sheriff Garret ($50.00).........................15	20	25
Sam Cobra ($75.00) 25	30	35
Pancho ($35.00) 10	12	15
Flack ($25.00) 8	10	12
Flick (($25.00) 8	10	12
Flame ($25.00) 8	10	12
Flame w/ Corral set ($50.00) 20	25	30
Jane West Set ($140.00) (w/corral and horses) 50	60	70
Johnny West Set w/horse and Jeep ($200.00)...75	90	115
Johnny West w/ Wild Mustangs set ($125.00)...45	60	75
Princess Wild Flower ($60.00) 20	25	30
Buffalo ($50.00)...................................15	20	25
Chief Cherokee ($75.00).......................25	35	45
Chief Cherokee w/ Teepee set ($150.00)...50	65	80
Circle X Ranch Playset ($225.00) 80	110	140
Commanche ($45.00)...........................15	20	25
Buckboard and Horse ($140.00)...........60	70	80

FORT APACHE FIGHTERS:	C6	C8	C10
Sgt. Zachary ($75.00)	25	35	45
General Custer ($75.00)	25	35	45

	C6	C8	C10
Capt. Maddox ($75.00)	25	35	45
Fort Apache Playset ($250.00)	90	120	150

MATTEL

Mattel was founded in 1945 by Harold Mattson and Ruth and Elliot Handler (the "Matt" in Mattson and "El" in Elliott formed the firm's name). The business, created to make picture frames, began in a Los Angeles garage, with Mattson bowing out early due to poor health. Toys were made almost from the beginning, furniture fashioned from the plastic and wood scraps left over from the frames. Its most famous toy is the Barbie doll.

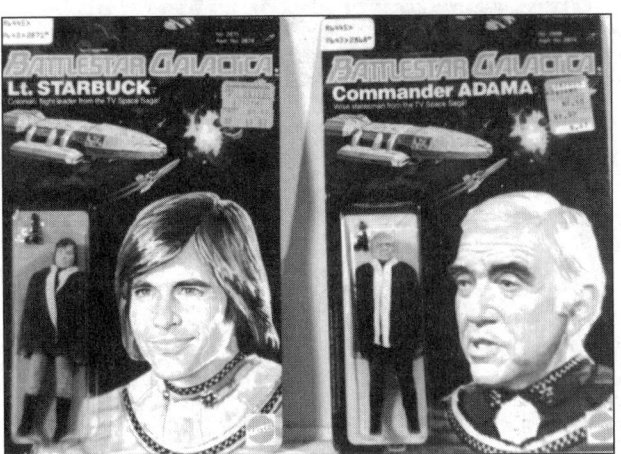

MATTEL Battlestar Galactica figures, Left to Right: Lt. Starbuck, Commander Adama. Courtesy Rex and Richard Gray.

BATTLESTAR GALACTICA *(List by Jim Main)*:	C6	C8	C10
Starbuck ($15.00)	4	5	6
Cmdr. Adama ($20.00)	8	9	10
Apollo ($15.00)	4	5	6
Baltarr ($15.00)	4	5	6
Cylon ($20.00)	8	9	10
Gold Cylon ($30.00)	10	13	16
Boray ($20.00)	8	9	10
Ovion ($30.00)	10	13	16
Daggit ($10.00)	3	4	5
Lucifer ($15.00)	4	5	6
Imperious Leader ($10.00)	3	4	6

12" Figures

	C6	C8	C10
Cylon ($40.00)	15	20	25
Colonial Warrior ($40.00)	15	20	25

BIG JIM'S P.A.C.K. *(List by Jim Main)* :	C6	C8	C10
Big Jim ($60.00)	15	25	35
Double Trouble Big Jim ($50.00)	10	20	30
Double Trouble Zorak ($50.00)	10	20	30
Torpedo Fist ($50.00)	10	20	30
Warpath ($50.00)	10	20	30
Dr. Steel ($50.00)	10	20	30
The Whip ($50.00)	10	20	30

Accessories/vehicles/outfits:	C6	C8	C10
Blitz Rig ($90.00)	30	45	60
The Howler ($35.00)	10	15	20
P.A.C.K. Dunebuggy ($30.00)	8	13	18
Lazervette ($50.00)	10	20	30
The Beast ($75.00)	20	30	40
Artic Uniform ($25.00)	10	12	14
Construction/Machine Gunner adv. ($25.00)	10	12	14
High Explosive Miner adv. ($25.00)	10	12	14
Karate outfit ($25.00)	10	12	14
Photographer/Secret Agent adv. ($25.00)	10	12	14
Policeman/SWAT adv. ($25.00)	10	12	14
Race Driver outfit ($25.00)	10	12	14
Sea Spy uniform ($25.00)	10	12	14

CLASH OF THE TITANS *(List by Jim Main)*
4" Figures :

	C6	C8	C10
Thallo ($20.00)	5	7	9
Calibos ($20.00)	5	7	9
Charon ($20.00)	5	7	9
Perseus ($20.00)	5	7	9
Pegasus ($35.00)	10	14	18
Kraken ($150.00)	45	60	75
Perseus/Pegasus set ($60.00)	15	20	25

FLASH GORDON 4" set *(List by Jim Main)*:

	C6	C8	C10
Flash Gordon ($25.00)	8	12	16
Thun ($25.00)	8	12	16
Ming ($25.00)	8	12	16
Lizard Woman ($30.00)	10	14	18
Beastman ($25.00)	8	12	16
Dr. Zarkov ($20.00)	7	9	11

MAJOR MATT MASON *(List by Jim Main)*:

	C6	C8	C10
Callisto ($200.00)	35	40	45
Captain Lazer ($150.00)	40	60	80
XRG-1 Re-Entry Glider ($225.00)	60	80	100
Talking Major Matt Mason ($180.00)	50	75	100
Talking Command Console ($150.00)	40	60	80
Space Station ($200.00)	60	90	120

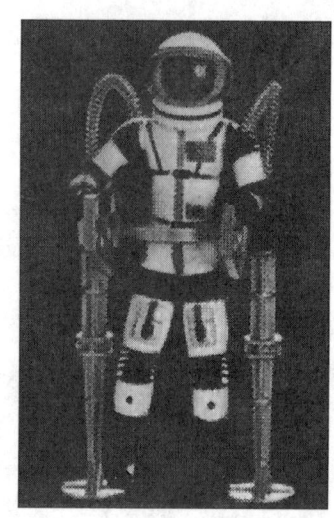

Famous spaceman with exclusive Voice Command Flight Pak. Says five things while "Flying on space cord". Removable VCF Pak may be used with all other Mattel Astronauts as well.

MATTEL Major Matt Mason in flexible space suit with jet propulsion pack and space sled.

MATTEL Major Matt Mason with moon suit.

	C6	C8	C10
Space Station/Space Crawler Deluxe Action Set ($450.00)	150	200	250
Star Seeker ($175.00)	60	90	120
Supernaut Power Limbs pak ($50.00)	15	25	30
Unitred ($75.00)	20	30	40
Unitred and Space Bubble set ($125.00)	40	60	80
Space Bubble ($50.00)	15	25	30
Astro Trac ($125.00)	40	60	80
Space Shelter Pak ($45.00)	10	15	20
Space Probe Set ($45.00)	10	15	20
Space Power Suit Pak ($60.00)	20	30	40
Doug Davis w/ Lunar Trac ($225.00)	30	45	60
Galaxy 3 playset	No Price Found		
Firebolt Space Cannon ($150.00)	40	60	80
Space Mission Team w/MMM, JL, Calisto and DD ($500.00)	100	150	200
Space Discovery Set w/DD, MMM and Calisto ($400.00)	85	125	165
Sgt. Storm w/ Cat Trac ($150.00)	40	60	80
Sgt. Storm w/ Flight Set ($200.00)	50	75	100
Gamma Ray Gard ($60.00)	20	30	40
Jeff Long w/ Lunar Trac ($225.00)	60	80	100
Lunar Base Command Set ($375.00)	100	125	150
MMM Rocketship Case ($90.00)	40	50	60
Satellite Locker ($75.00)	30	40	50
Satellite Launch pak ($50.00)	15	25	30
MMM w/ Space Sled ($175.00)	40	60	80
MMM w/ Moon Suit ($200.00)	50	70	90
MMM w/ Cat Trac ($150.00)	40	60	80
Reconojet Pak ($50.00)	15	20	25
Scorpio ($300.00)	75	100	125

PHOTO BOX Accessory Paks:

	C6	C8	C10
Supernaut Power Limbs ($175.00)	15	20	25

	C6	C8	C10
Space Shelter Pak ($175.00)	15	20	25
Gamma Ray Gard ($175.00)	15	20	25
Space Power Suit ($175.00)	15	20	25
Super Power Equipment Set ($200.00)	25	50	75

SPACE: 1999 *(list by Jim Main):*

	C6	C8	C10
Cmdr. Koenig ($30.00)	10	14	18
Dr. Russell ($25.00)	10	12	14
Prof. Bergman ($30.00)	10	14	18
Moonbase Alpha Playset ($75.00)	15	20	25
EAGLE 1 Spaceship (Not for 8" figures, but for figures w/ craft) ($150.00)	25	50	75

MARVEL SUPER HEROES SECRET WARS *(list by Jim Main):*
4 - 1/4" Figures

	C6	C8	C10
Iron Man ($20.00)	6	8	10
Captain America ($15.00)	5	6	7
Wolverine ($35.00)	12	15	18
Spiderman (Black costume) ($25.00)	10	12	14
Spiderman (Red costume) ($25.00)	10	12	14
Doctor Doom ($15.00)	5	6	7
Kang ($10.00)	5	6	7
Magneto ($15.00)	5	6	7
Baron Zemo ($25.00)	10	12	14
Daredevil ($15.00)	5	6	7
Falcon ($30.00)	10	14	18
Hobgoblin ($30.00)	10	14	18
Iceman ($40.00)	20	25	30
Constrictor ($40.00)	20	25	30
Electro ($40.00)	20	25	30

Accessories/vehicles:

	C6	C8	C10
Tower of Doom ($80.00)	30	40	50

Major MATT MASON® #6318

Mattel's most promoted man-in-space! Std. Pack: 1 Doz. Wt: 4½ Lbs.

CALLISTO® #6331

Alien with bellows-action Space Sensor. Std. Pack: 1 Doz. Wt: 4½

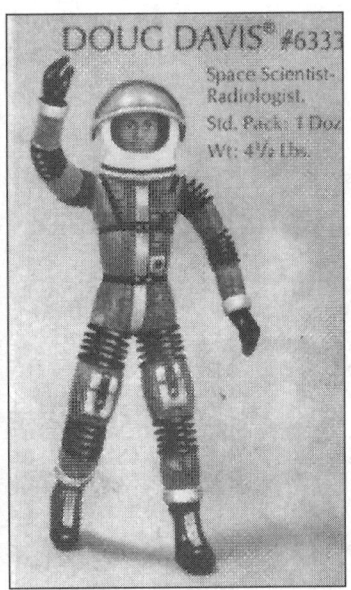

DOUG DAVIS® #6333

Space Scientist-Radiologist. Std. Pack: 1 Doz. Wt: 4½ Lbs.

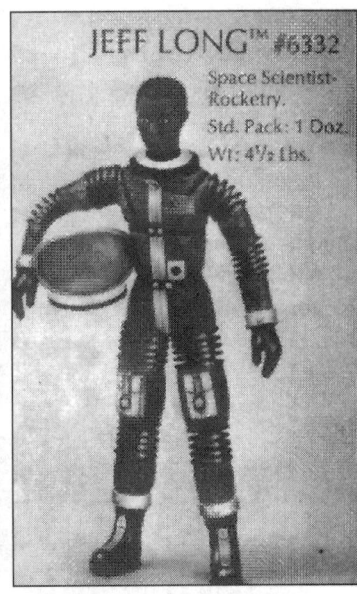

JEFF LONG™ #6332

Space Scientist-Rocketry. Std. Pack: 1 Doz. Wt: 4½ Lbs.

Major Mat Mason 6318   *Callisto 6331*   *Doug Davis 6333*   *Jeff Long 6332*

Reentry Glider 6360

Space Crawler 6304

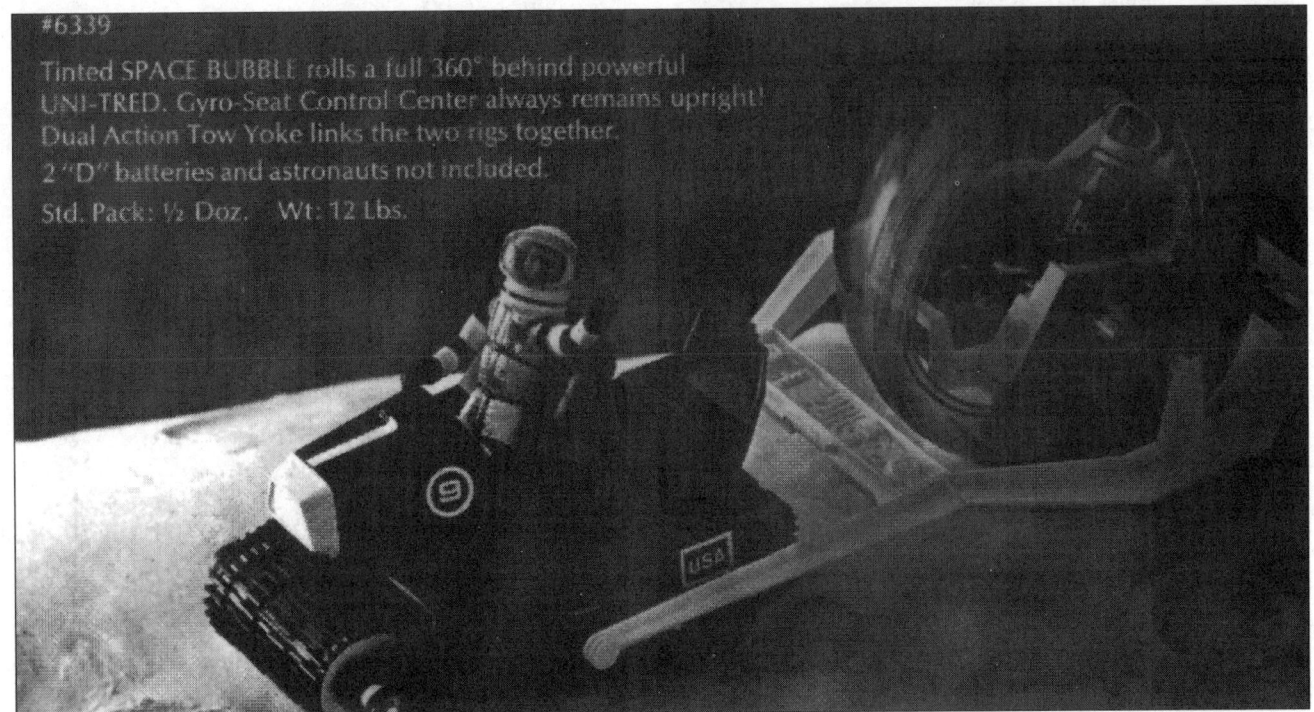

#6339
Tinted SPACE BUBBLE rolls a full 360° behind powerful UNI-TRED. Gyro-Seat Control Center always remains upright! Dual Action Tow Yoke links the two rigs together. 2 "D" batteries and astronauts not included.
Std. Pack: ½ Doz.   Wt: 12 Lbs.

	C6	C8	C10
Doom Roller ($25.00).............8	12	16
Doom Chopper ($50.00)........15	20	25
Turbo Copter ($50.00) 15	20	25
Dark Star ($40.00) 12	16	20
Star Dart ($75.00) 20	30	40
Marvel Super Heroes Machine ($80.00) ..25	40	55
Marvel Super Villains Machine ($80.00).............25	40	55
Turbo Cycle ($40.00)..............12	16	20

End Mattel

MEGO

BLACK HOLE - 12" *(List by Jim Main)*

	C6	C8	C10
Pizer ($45.00)......................15	20	25
Dr. Durant ($50.00)..............15	20	25
Captain Holland ($50.00).......15	20	25
Harry Booth ($45.00).............15	20	25
Dr. Reinhardt ($50.00)..........15	20	25
Kate McCrae ($50.00) 15	20	25

3 ¾"

	C6	C8	C10
V.I.N. cent ($20.00)................4	6	8
Pizer ($12.00)........................3	5	7
Capt. Holland ($12.00) 3	5	7
Harry Booth ($12.00)..............3	5	7
Kate McCrea ($25.00) 5	7	9
Old Bob ($40.00).................10	15	20
Humanoid ($40.00)..............10	15	20
Dr. Durant ($12.00)................3	5	7
Maximillian ($25.00).............5	7	9
Starr ($40.00).....................10	15	20
Dr. Reinhardt ($12.00) 3	5	7

BUCK ROGERS *(List by Jim Main)*
12":

	C6	C8	C10
Buck ($50.00) 15	20	25
Wilma ($60.00)....................18	23	28
Dr. Huer ($40.00).................10	15	20
Killer Kane ($45.00)..............12	14	16
Twiki ($35.00)........................8	12	15
Draco ($40.00).....................10	15	20

3¾":

	C6	C8	C10
Buck ($20.00) 6	8	10
Ardella ($12.00)......................3	5	7
Wilma ($15.00)........................5	7	9
Dr. Huer ($10.00)....................3	5	7
Tiger Man ($18.00) 5	8	11
Draco ($10.00)........................3	5	7
Killer Kane ($10.00).................3	5	7
Twiki ($12.00).........................3	5	7
Draconian Guard ($18.00)........5	8	11

	C6	C8	C10
Accessories:			
Laser Scope Fighter ($40.00)........10	16	22
Star Fighter ($45.00)..............10	17	25
Draconian Maruader ($40.00)........10	16	22
Star Fighter Command Center ($40.00)..................10	15	20

FLASH GORDON - 10" *(List by Jim Main)*

	C6	C8	C10
Flash ($60.00) 20	25	30
Dale ($60.00) 20	25	30
Dr. Zarkov ($50.00) 20	22	25
Ming ($75.00)......................25	30	35

KISS: 12" *(List by Jim Main)*

	C6	C8	C10
Paul ($125.00)......................35	40	45
Gene ($125.00).....................35	45	50
Ace ($160.00) 45	55	65
Peter ($140.00)....................40	45	50

MOONRAKER - JAMES BOND - 12" *(List by Jim Main)*

	C6	C8	C10
Bond ($125.00) 30	35	40
Holly ($125.00)....................30	35	40
Jaws ($150.00).....................40	45	50
Hugo Drax ($100.00)..............20	25	30

ONE MILLION YEARS B.C. - 8" *(List by Jim Main)*

	C6	C8	C10
Mara ($60.00) 15	20	25
Grog ($50.00) 15	20	25
Orm ($50.00) 15	20	25
Trag ($50.00)......................15	20	25

Planet of the Apes 8" figures *(List by Jim Main)*

	C6	C8	C10
Zira ($40.00) 5	10	15
Cornelius ($40.00) 5	10	15
Astronaut ($60.00) 10	15	20
Burke ($60.00) 10	15	20
Verdon ($60.00) 10	15	20
Dr. Zaius ($40.00) 5	10	15
Gen. Urko ($40.00) 5	10	15
Ursus ($40.00)........................5	10	15
Soldier Ape ($40.00)................5	10	15
Galen ($40.00) 5	10	15

	C6	C8	C10
Accessories:			
Battering Ram ($35.00) 10	15	20
Village Playset ($75.00).........15	25	35
Treehouse Playset ($75.00)....15	25	35
Fortress Playset ($75.00) 15	25	35
Forbidden Zone Trap ($60.00)......20	30	40
Catapult and Wagon ($40.00) 10	15	20
Dr. Zaius' Throne ($30.00) 8	12	16
Palamino ($30.00)...................8	12	16
Jail ($35.00) 10	15	20

Bend N' Flex figures:	C6	C8	C10
Zira ($25.00)	4	7	10
Cornelius ($25.00)	4	7	10
Soldier Ape ($25.00)	8	12	15
Astronaut ($30.00)	8	12	15
Dr. Zaius ($25.00)	4	7	10
Galen ($25.00)	4	7	10

Star Trek TV Series 8" *(List by Jim Main)*:

	C6	C8	C10
Kirk ($40.00)	10	15	20
Spock ($40.00)	10	15	20
McCoy ($60.00)	15	25	35
Scotty ($45.00)	12	18	25
Lt. Uhura ($60.00)	15	25	35
Andorian ($160.00)	40	60	80
Cheron ($140.00)	35	45	55
Mugato ($350.00)	100	150	200
Talosian ($300.00)	90	110	130
Romulan ($300.00)	90	110	130
Gorn ($175.00)	45	65	85
Neptunian ($150.00)	50	60	70
Keeper ($140.00)	50	60	70

STAR TREK THE MOTION PICTURE - 12"

	C6	C8	C10
Kirk $40.00	10	15	20
Spock $45.00	10	15	20
Decker $80.00	20	25	30
Illia $40.00	10	15	20
Klingon $60.00	15	20	25
Arcturian $75.00	20	25	30

3¾"

	C6	C8	C10
Kirk ($10.00)	3	5	7
Spock ($12.00)	3	5	7
McCoy ($15.00)	4	6	8
Decker ($10.00)	3	5	7
Scotty ($15.00)	4	6	8
Klingon ($20.00)	8	10	12
Illia ($10.00)	3	5	7
Arcturian ($25.00)	10	12	14
Zaranite ($25.00)	10	12	14
Rigellian ($30.00)	12	14	16
Betelgeusian ($30.00)	12	14	16
Megarite ($30.00)	12	14	16

SUPERHEROES *(Lists by Jim Main)*:
(Bx = Box, BP = Blister Pack):

	C6	C8	C10
Iron Man (Bx - $110.00)	25	35	45
Lizard (Bx - $175.00)	30	45	60
Kid Flash (BP - $300.00)	60	85	110
Speedy (BP - $400.00)	80	120	150
Wonder Girl (BP - $300.00)	60	85	110
Aqualad (BP - $300.00)	60	85	110

	C6	C8	C10
Aquaman (Bx - $140.00)	15	20	25
Batgirl (Bx - $300.00)	60	85	110
Batman (w/removable Mask (Bx - $325.00)	65	90	120
Batman (Bx - $125.00)	20	25	30
Batman (BP - $70.00)	20	25	30
Joker (Bx - $140.00)	25	35	40
Isis (Bx - $325.00)	20	40	60
Isis (BP - $125.00)	20	40	60
Conan (BP - $325.00)	80	120	150
Falcon (Bx - $100.00)	25	35	40
Thor (Bx - $425.00)	80	120	150
Tarzan (Bx - $75.00)	20	25	30
Supergirl (Bx - $375.00)	80	120	150
Spiderman (Bx - $90.00)	8	12	15
Spiderman (BP - $30.00)	8	12	15
Superman (Bx - $100.00)	10	15	20
Superman (BP - $65.00)	10	15	20
Catwoman (Bx - $175.00)	25	40	65
Captain America (Bx - $90.00)	20	30	40
Captain America (BP - $65.00)	20	30	40
Hulk (Bx - $60.00)	8	12	15
Hulk (BP - $35.00)	8	12	15
Mr. Fantastic (Bx - $75.00)	8	12	15
Mr. Fantastic (BP - $30.00)	8	12	15
Invisible Girl (Bx - $75.00)	8	12	15
Invisible Girl (BP - $30.00)	8	12	15
Human Torch (Bx - $75.00)	8	12	15
Human Torch (BP - $30.00)	8	12	15
Thing (Bx - $75.00)	8	12	15
Thing (BP -$30.00)	8	12	15
Riddler (Bx - $325.00)	25	45	65
Wonder Woman (Bx - $130.00)	20	40	60
Green Arrow (Bx - $175.00)	40	60	80
Penguin (Bx - $95.00)	15	25	35
Penguin (BP - $70.00)	15	25	35
Robin (Bx - $100.00)	10	15	20
Robin (BP - $60.00)	10	15	20
Robin w/removable mask ($425.00)	75	115	145

FIST FIGHTERS:

	C6	C8	C10
Robin ($225.00)	40	60	80
Batman ($250.00)	40	60	80
Joker ($300.00)	50	70	90
Riddler ($325.00)	50	70	90

ALTER EGO FIGURES:

	C6	C8	C10
Clark Kent ($325.00)	125	175	225
Peter Parker ($325.00)	125	175	225
Bruce Wayne ($325.00)	125	175	225
Dick Grayson ($325.00)	125	175	225

BENDIES:

	C6	C8	C10
Aquaman ($65.00)	15	20	25

	C6	C8	C10
Wonder Woman ($80.00) 20	25	30
Superman ($50.00) 10	15	20
Supergirl ($225.00) 60	75	90
Captain America ($60.00) 15	20	25
Batgirl ($225.00) 60	75	90
Tarzan ($50.00) 10	15	20
Penguin ($80.00) 20	25	30
Riddler ($125.00) 30	45	60
Joker ($100.00) 25	35	45
Mr. Mxyzptlk ($75.00) 20	25	30
Robin ($40.00) 8	13	18
Shazam ($50.00) 10	15	20
Spiderman ($50.00) 10	15	20
Catwoman ($175.00) 45	60	75
Batman ($90.00) 20	30	40

SUPERMAN - THE MOVIE -
12" figures

	C6	C8	C10
Superman ($60.00) 15	20	25
General Zod ($50.00) 10	15	20
Jor-El ($50.00) 10	15	20
Luthor ($50.00) 10	15	20

WONDER WOMAN:

	C6	C8	C10
Wonder Woman w/ Diana Prince outfit ($150.00) 20	35	50
Wonder Woman w/o Lynda Carter pic ($65.00) 15	20	25
Nubia ($100.00) 25	35	45
Steve Trevor ($80.00) 20	25	30
Queen Hippolite ($100.00) 25	35	45

THE WALTONS: *(List by Jim Main)*
8"

	C6	C8	C10
John boy ($35.00) 6	9	12
Granpa ($35.00) 6	9	12
Granma ($35.00) 6	9	12
Ellen ($35.00) 6	9	12

Accessories/playsets for 8" figures:

	C6	C8	C10
Wayne Foundation Playset ($600.00) ..150	225	300
Batcave Playset ($250.00) 75	90	105
Captain Americar ($150.00) 45	60	75
Green Arrowcar ($150.00) 45	60	75
Jokermobile ($125.00) 20	25	30
Batmobile ($125.00) 20	25	30
Hall of Justice Playset ($400.00) 100	150	200
Batcycle ($150.00) 25	40	55
Batcopter ($140.00) 35	45	55
Aquaman vs. the Great White Shark ($750.00) 175	250	325
Mobile Bat-Lab ($275.00) 60	80	100
Super Action SuperVator ($100.00) 30	40	50
Spider-Car ($100.00) 25	35	45

COMIC ACTION/POCKET SUPER HEROES *(List by Jim Main)*
3¾"

	C6	C8	C10
Captain America ($50.00) 10	15	20
Batman ($50.00) 10	15	20
Robin ($40.00) 8	12	15
Green Lantern ($60.00) 12	18	25
Superman ($40.00) 8	12	15
Shazam ($45.00) 10	15	20
Green Goblin ($60.00) 12	18	25
Joker ($50.00) 10	15	20
Hulk ($25.00) 8	10	12
Penguin ($35.00) 8	12	15
General Zod ($25.00) 8	10	12
Aquaman ($40.00) 8	12	15
Jor-El ($25.00) 8	10	12
Lex Luthor ($25.00) 8	10	12
Spiderman ($45.00) 10	15	20
Wonder Woman ($45.00) 10	15	20

Accessories/Playsets for above figures:

	C6	C8	C10
Batcave Playset ($150.00) 30	35	40
Fortress of Solitude Playset ($225.00)..75	90	125
Spider Car w/Spiderman and Green Goblin figures ($125.00) 20	30	40
Spider Car w/Spiderman and Hulk figures ($80.00) 20	25	30
Wonder Woman Collapsible Tower/ Invisible Plane Playset ($150.00) ...50	65	80
Invisible Plane ($60.00) 15	20	25
Batmachine ($90.00)..............................20	25	30
Batmobile ($175.00) 30	40	50
The Mangler ($90.00) 20	25	30
Batman Collapsible Bridge Playset - w/ Batman and Robin ($200.00)..........60	75	90
Batman Collapsible Bridge Playset - w/Batman, Robin, Joker and Penguin ($300.00) 90	105	120
Pressman Lone Ranger with his Horse, Silver, No. 7750 new in 1967, jointed, 40 accessories including working (cold) branding iron ....*No Price Found*
Pressman Tonto & his horse Scout No. 7751, new in 1967, jointed, 40 accessories including cold branding iron kit..............................*No Price Found*
Remco Energized Green Goblin, battery-operated, 12" 37	56	75
Remco Energized Hulk, battery-operated, 12"....................................25	37	50
Remco Energized Superman, battery-operated 37	56	75

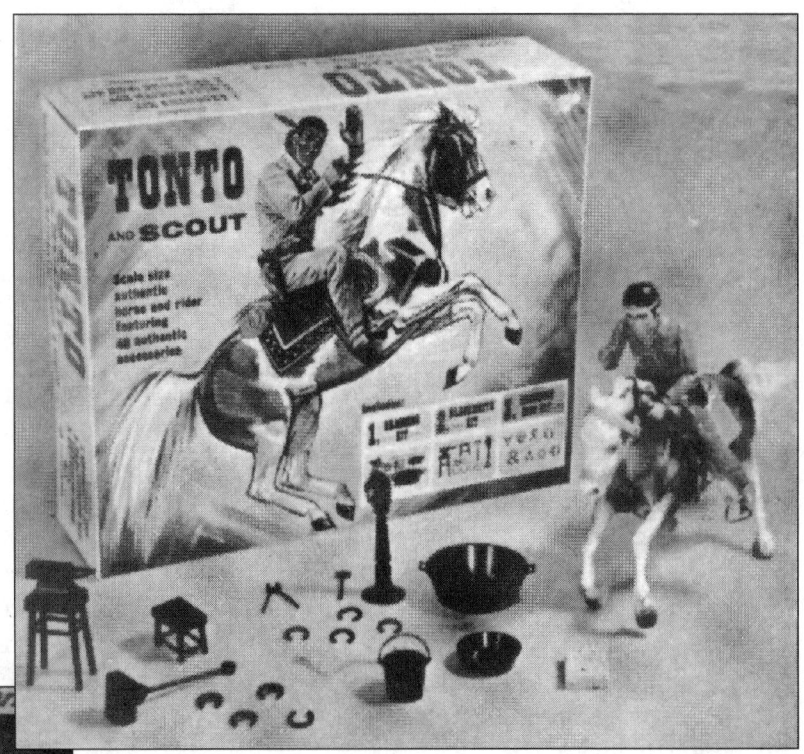

Pressman Tonto No. 7751.

Pressman Lone Ranger No. 7750.

TOPPER

	C6	C8	C10
THE TIGERS *(List by Jim Main)*			
Tex ($30.00)	10	15	20
Sarge ($30.00)	10	15	20
Big Ears ($30.00)	10	15	20
Bugle Ben ($30.00)	10	15	20
Combat Kid ($30.00)	10	15	20
Pretty Boy ($30.00)	10	15	20
Rock ($30.00)	10	15	20
Machine Gun Mike ($30.00)	10	15	20
The Tigers' Headquarters, Sears Exclusive ($100.00)	40	60	80

FIGURE KITS
by David Welch

In recent years, plastic model kits, in particular plastic figure kits, have become associated with the world of toys. Buyers of 1960s and 1970s movie, TV, and cartoon memorabilia find that figure kits fit rather nicely into their collections. The 1960s is considered the "Golden Age" for plastic kits with Aurora by far leading the way in diversity of product and current-day demand. Aurora's line-up of original and glow issue Universal Studios monsters are today's most sought-after figure kits.

CONDITION OF A KIT AND RELATION TO PRICE

Rating the condition of a figure kit can be difficult because factors such as (1) assembled parts, (2) painted parts, (3) missing pieces, (4) missing instructions, (5) box condition, and (6) country of origin drastically affect value. Mint in box [MIB] is the condition upon which the following values are based.

MIB SEALED: mint in box with box shrink wrap; most kits had factory wraps on boxes. Provided the boxes are <u>not</u> <u>damaged.</u> collectors may pay a 10-20% premium over MIB price. BEWARE of bogus re-sealing by dishonest individuals.

MIB: a complete, unused kit with an excellent box and instructions and no glue or paint on pieces. Most collectors insist that plastic "trees" that held pieces be present with pieces still attached. Again, the price listed is for a kit in <u>this</u> condition.

PARTIAL ASSEMBLY: a partially built kit with excellent box/instructions and no painting prices at 85% of MIB at best. The more assembly, the more price decreases. Old styrene glues actually "melted" pieces together. White glues (such as Elmers) do not decrease value as much as Styrene glues because they can be removed.

PARTIAL PAINTING: a complete, partially painted kit with excellent box/instruction and no gluing prices at 85% of MIB at best. Painting is not as serious as gluing because most experienced modelers know how to strip paint. Again, the more painting, the more price decreases because stripping takes time and is not always completely successful.

PARTIAL ASSEMBLY/PAINTING: together, these 2 factors can make pricing very difficult. A general guideline would be 70% of MIB with excellent box/instructions.

BUILT-UP: a fully assembled, complete kit with no box/instructions has a value of 15-45% of MIB. The more expensive the MIB kit, the more desirable the built-up. If a kit was issued several times, built-up value decreases. For example, Aurora's design of Frankenstein was issued four times (Aurora 1961, 1969, 1972, and Monogram 1983). Thus, its value is usually only 15% of MIB. Vehicles such as Batmobiles and UFOs go toward low percentages because of low visual appeal . Further, without instructions, an inexperienced person will find it virtually impossible to determine if a built-up is complete. Except for very high-priced kits, incomplete built-ups have little value.

MISSING PIECES: one missing piece from a kit gives a big decrease in value regardless of all other combined factors. Even a MIB kit missing one piece is worth only 80% at best of a truly complete MIB kit! Some collectors will not buy a kit missing a piece at all.

INSTRUCTIONS: missing instructions deduct 5-10% of MIB price. 1960s instructions sheets alone sell at $5-$10. Sheets for rare, expensive kits such as Aurora's Gigantic Frankenstein can bring over $35!

BOXES: the market for empty figure kit boxes is almost exclusive to Aurora boxes. Generally, an excellent condition box has no split corners, tape, paint, glue, punctures, severe creases, or scuffs. Excellent boxes alone have maximum value of 40% MIB price. Aforementioned box defects decrease value on MIB kits by 20% or more.

FOREIGN ISSUE: Again, this factor is an issue primarily with Aurora kits. Aurora had branches in Canada, England, and Holland which issued boxes and instructions that sometimes had wording in other languages and plastic parts in colors other than what US issues had. Ninety percent of the kits you'll ever see will not be foreign issues, but just in case, some collectors (not all) devalue MIB foreign issue kits to about 75% of US MIB prices.

A WORD ABOUT PRICING: If you're more confused about how to price a kit now than you were before, don't feel badly! Even experienced dealers have a difficult time pricing kits when faced with missing pieces, painted parts, box wear, etc. These guidelines are just that-guidelines.

It should be noted that kit values vary widely due to region of the country and local collector demand. There is strong interest in American kits, for example, in Europe and Japan. American dealers have found some of these individuals willing to pay very highly relative to U.S. collectors. So, the values listed here are conservative, mid-range prices that are indicative of what most collectors would be willing to pay. Obviously, some collectors will pay more and some will pay less.

Special thanks to Greg Roccaro of Staten Island, New York, and to Mark Karpinski of Denver, Pennsylvania, for price information. Some kit numbers and dates were taken from Science Fiction and Figure Kits by John Burns of Edmond, Oklahoma. Though not a price guide, it serves as an excellent reference regarding all known kits of this genre.

David Welch is a nationally known dealer in cartoon, comic, and TV character items. He has been collecting and/or dealing since age 13. He has contributed information for various price guides including Tomart's Disneyana (condensed edition), Tomart's Space Adventure Collectibles, and periodically Overstreet's Comic Book Price Guide. Aside from the world of collectibles, he enjoys spending time with his wife, Cynthia, and two boys, Jordan and Evan, as well as his alter-ego endeavors as a paper restorer, professional musician, and youth leader in the Church of Jesus Christ of Latter Day Saints.

AURORA
By David Welch

Regarding the Aurora monster line-up, some information may be confusing. To clarify the Frankenstein listing, for example: Frankenstein was issued first in 1961 in a long, rectangular box. The Frightening Lighting 1969 issue was the same kit with duplicate glow parts that were optional. The box was the same shape with a lightning bolt added to the art. In 1969 and 1972, the optional glow format continued and square boxes with altered artwork were introduced. The 1969 glow boxes are thicker and sturdier than the 1972 glows. In many cases, the color of

the plastic was different between the original and glow issues. The plastic kit itself will always carry the date of its original issue. The Monster Scenes and Monsters Of The Movies Frankensteins are completely different kits than the 1961, 1969, and 1972 issues.

For the Aurora line in general, dates listed may vary a year either way. It is the kit name and kit number that are most relevant. Please note, too, that different kits carried identical numbers (i.e. King Kong Glow 465 and Frankenstein's Flivver 465).

AURORA store display of its Monster Scenes, with Dr. Deadly, the Victim and Hanging Cage. Courtesy Toy Collector News. Photo by Rex Gray.

AURORA Phantom of the Opera and Napoleon Solo figure kits. Courtesy Toy Collector News. Photo by Rex Gray.

	C6	C8	C10
Addams Family House, 805, 1965			$600
Alfred E. Neumann, 802, 1965			$120
Allosaurus, 736, 1972			$50
American Astronaut, 409, 1967			$45
Ankylosourus, 744, 1974			$60
Apache Warrior, 401, 1961			$150
Aramis, K10, 1958			$75
Archies Car, 582, 1969			$50
Athos, K8, 1958			$75
Babe Ruth, 862, 1965			$200
Banana Splits Buggy, 832, 1969			$90

	C6	C8	C10
Batboat, 811			$285
Batcycle, 810, 1967			$270
Batman, 467, 1964			$200
Batman Comic Scenes, 187, 1974			$40
Batmobile, 486, 1966			$200
Batplane, 487, 1966			$200
Black Beauty, (Green Hornet) 489, 1967			$330
Black Knight, various issues			$15
Blackbeard, 463, 1965			$140
Blue Knight, various issues			$12
Bride of Frankenstein, 482, 1964			$500

AURORA Tarzan Figure Kit. Courtesy Toy Collector News. Photo by Rex Gray.

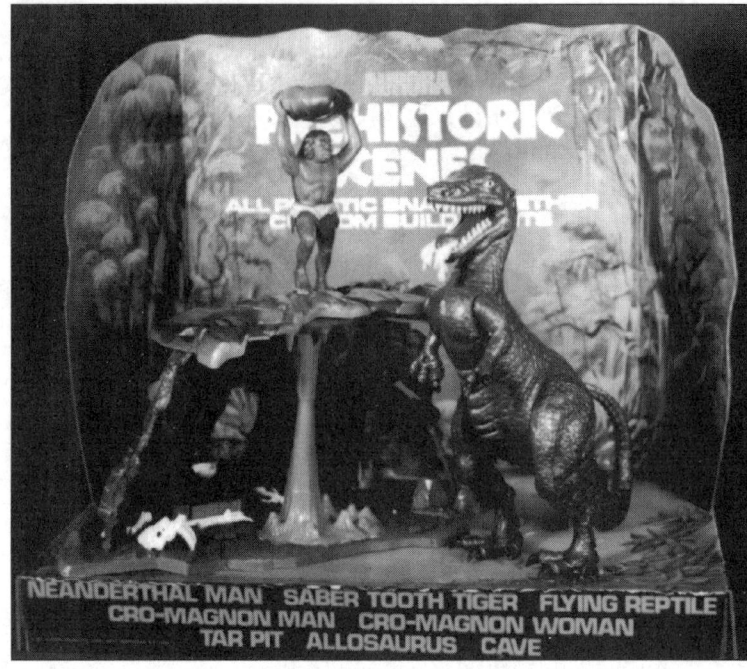

AURORA Store Display of its Prehistoric Scenes showing Cro-Magnon Man. Courtesy Toy Collector News. Photo by Rex Gray.

Aurora Godzilla's Go-Cart. Greg Roccaro Collection. Courtesy David Welch.

Aurora King Kong's Thronester. Greg Roccaro Collection. Courtesy David Welch.

Aurora Gigantic Frankenstein ("Big Frankie"). Greg Roccaro Collection. Courtesy David Welch.

	C6	C8	C10

Captain Action, 480, 1966................................$225
Captain America, 476, 1966.............................$250
Captain America Comic Scenes, 192, 1974.................$80
Captain Kidd, 464, 1965...............................$100
Cave, 732, 1972..$30
Cave Bear, 738, 1972...................................$35
Chinese Girl, 416, 1957................................$20
Chinese Mandarin, 415, 1957............................$20
Chitty Chitty Bang Bang, 828, 1968.....................$45
Confederate Raider, 402, 1959.........................$225
Crusader, K7, 1959....................................$100
Creature From the Black Lagoon, 426, 1963.............$250
Creature From the Black Lagoon, Glow, 483,
    1969/1972.......................................$90
Creature From the Black Lagoon, Monsters of the
    Movies, 654, 1975...................................$90
Cro Magnon Man, 730, 1971..............................$40
Cro Magnon Woman, 731, 1971............................$25
Customizing Monster Kit No. 1, 463, 1963..............$100
Customizing Monster Kit No. 2, 464, 1963..............$100
D'Artagnan, 410, 1966..................................$90
Dempsey vs. Firpo, 861, 1965...........................$40
Dick Tracy, 818, 1968.................................$120
Dick Tracy Space Coupe, 819, 1968......................$85
Dimetrodon, 745, 1974..................................$30
Dr. Deadly's Daughter, (The Victim), Monster
    Scenes, 632, 1971...................................$50
Dr. Deadly, Monster Scenes, 631, 1971..................$75
Dr. Jekyll, 460, 1965.................................$175
Dr. Jekyll, Glow, 482, 1969/1972.......................$60
Dr. Jekyll, Monsters of the Movies, 654, 1975..........$35
Dracula, 424, 1962....................................$180
Dracula's Dragster, 466, 1966.........................$250
Dracula, Frightening Lightening, 424/454, 1969........$240
Dracula, Glow, 454, 1969/1972..........................$60
Dracula, Monsters of the Movies, 656, 1975............$120
Dutch Boy, 413, 1957...................................$25
Dutch Girl, 414, 1957..................................$25
Flying Reptile, 734, 1974..............................$40
Flying Saucer, 256, 1975...............................$40
Flying Sub, 254, 1975..................................$40
Flying Sub, 817, 1968.................................$110
Forgotten Prisoner, 422, 1966.........................$240
Forgotten Prisoner, Frightening Lightening, 422/453, 1969..$300
Forgotten Prisoner, Glow, 453, 1969/1972..............$110
Frankenstein, 423, 1961...............................$195
Frankenstein, Frightening Lightening, 423/449, 1969...$225
Frankenstein, Glow, 449, 1969/1972.....................$60
Frankenstein, Monster Scenes 633, 1971................$110
Frankenstein, Monsters of the Movies, 651, 1975.......$120
Frankenstein's Flivver, 465, 1964.....................$240
Frog, The 451, 1966...................................$180
George Washington, 852, 1965...........................$75

Ghidrah, Monsters of the Movies, 658, 1975............$210
Giant Bird, 739, 1972..................................$30
Giant Woolly Mammoth, 743, 1972........................$60
Gigantic Frankenstein ("Big Frankie") 470,
    1964 with 3 bottles paint & brush...*price unavailable*
Gladiator, 405, 1959 with sword.......................$120
Gladiator, 406, 1959 with trident.....................$120
Godzilla, 469, 1964...................................$360
Godzilla, Glow, 466, 1969/1972........................$105
Godzilla's Go-Cart, 485, 1966...............*price unavailable*
Gold Knight on Horseback, K5,1957/475, 1965...........$150
Green Beret, 413, 1966................................$100
Gruesome Goodies, Monster Scenes, 634, 1971............$50
Guillotine, 800, 1964.................................$240
Hanging Cage, Monster Scenes, 637, 1971................$50
Hercules, 481, 1965...................................$250
Horned Dinosaur, 741, 1972.............................$35
Hulk, 421, 1966.......................................$135
Hulk, Comic Scenes 184, 1974...........................$35
Hunchback, 461, 1964..................................$180
Hunchback of Notre Dame, 481, 1969/1972................$45
Illya Kuryakin, 412, 1966.............................$105
Indian Chief, 417, 1957................................$35
Indian Squaw, 418, 1957................................$35
James Bond, 414, 1966.................................$180
Jerry West, 865, 1965..................................$90
Jesse James, 408, 1966................................$150
Jimmy Brown, 863, 1965.................................$90
John F. Kennedy, 851, 1964............................$110
Johnny Unitas, 864, 1965...............................$90
Jungle Swamp, 740, 1972................................$60
King Kong, 468, 1964..................................$450
King Kong's Thronester, 484, 1966......*price unavailable*
King Kong, Glow, 465, 1969/1972........................$80
Land of the Giants, Snake Scene, 816, 1968............$210
Land of the Giants Spaceship, 830, 1968...............$265
Lone Ranger, 808, 1967.................................$75
Lone Ranger, Comic Scenes, 188, 1974...................$35
Lost In Space, 419, 1966..............................$550
Lost in Space, 420, 1966..............................$750
Mad Barber, 455.............................*price unavailable*
Mexican Caballero, 421, 1957...........................$20
Mexican Senorita, 422, 1957............................$20
Mod Squad Woodie, 583, 1970............................$60
Moon Bus, 829, 1968 (2001: A Space Odyssey)...........$210
Mr. Hyde, Monsters of the Movies, 655, 1975............$35
Mummy, 427, 1963......................................$150
Mummy's Chariot, 459, 1965............................$300
Mummy, Frightening Lightening, 427/452, 1969..........$210
Mummy, Glow, 452, 1969/1972............................$50
Munsters Family, 804, 1965............................$550
Napoleon Solo, 411, 1966..............................$135
Neanderthal Man, 729, 1972.............................$30

	C6	C8	C10

Nutty Nose Nipper, 806, 1965................................$90
Odd Job, 415, 1966...$210
Orion, 252, 1975...$40
Pain Parlor, 635, 1971 ....$85
Pan Am Space Clipper, 148, 1968 (2001: A Space
    Odyssey)..$105
Pendulum, The, Monster Scenes, 636, 1971 ....$80
Penguin, 416, 1967...$325
Phantom of the Opera, 428, 1963.........................$150
Phantom of the Opera, 451, 1969/1972....................$55
Phantom of the Opera, Frightening Lightening,
    428/451, 1969..$210
Porthos, K9, 1958..$75
Pushmi-Pullyu, (Dr. Doolittle) 814, 1968 ....$75
Rat Patrol Diorama, 340, 1967.............................$100
Red Knight, various issues $30
Robin, 488, 1966...$45
Robin, Comic Scenes, 193, 1974 ....$45
Robot, 418, 1968 (Lost in Space)..........................$525
Rodan, Monsters of the Movies, 657, 1975 ....$180
Sabre Tooth Tiger, 722, 1972 ....$50
Scotch Lad, 419, 1957...$25
Scotch Lassie, 420, 1957......................................$25
Seaview, 707, 1966...$150
Seaview, 253, 1975...$50
Silver Knight, various issues $15
Spartacus, 405, 1965 ....$180
Spiderman, 477, 1966..$150
Spiderman, Comic Scenes, 182, 1974......................$45
Spiked Dinosaur, 742, 1972 ....$35
Spindrift, 255, 1975..$55
Steve Canyon, 404, 1966.....................................$75
Superboy, 478, 1965...$160
Superboy, Comic Scenes, 186, 1974........................$45
Superman, 562, 1963...$135
Superman, Comic Scenes, 185, 1974........................$35
Tar Pit, 735, 1971..$55
Tarzan, 820, 1967..$90
Tarzan, Comic Scenes, 181, 1974 ....$24
Tonto, 809, 1967...$80
Tonto, Comic Scenes, 183, 1974............................$20
Tyrannosaurus Rex, 746, 1974.............................$100
U.S. Infantryman, 1956..$45
U.S. Marine, 412, 1956..$45
U.S. Marshall, 408, 1959.....................................$75
U.S. Sailor, 410, 1958...$35
U.F.O., 813, 1968...$120
Undertakers Dragster, 570..................................$150
Vampire, 452, 1966...$150
Vampirella, Monster Scenes, 638, 1971 ....$90
Viking, K6, 1959..$120
Voyager, 831, 1969 (Fantastic Voyage)...................$300
Wacky Back Whacker, 807, 1965 ....$120
Willie Mays, 860, 1965 ....$110

Witch, Glow, 470, 1969/1972................................$50
Witch, 483, 1965...$180
Wolfman, 425, 1962..$165
Wolfman's Wagon, 458, 1965 ....$350
Wolfman, Frighting Lightening, 425/450, 1969.........$210
Wolfman, Glow, 450, 1969/1972............................$50
Wolfman, Monsters of the Movies, 652, 1975 ....$110
Wonder Woman, 479, 1965 ....$400
Zorro, 801, 1965...$95

ADDAR

Caesar, Planet Of The Apes, 106, 1974....................$25
Cornelius, Planet Of The Apes, 101, 1973.................$25
Cornfield Roundup, Super Scenes, 216, 1975............$18
Dr. Zaius, Planet Of The Apes, 102, 1973..................$25
Dr. Zira, Planet Of The Apes, 105, 1974...................$25
General Aldo, Planet Of The Apes, 104, 1974............$25
General Ursus, Planet Of The Apes, 103, 1974 ....$25
Jail Wagon, Super Scenes, 217, 1975......................$18
Soldier On Stallion, Planet Of The Apes, 107, 1975 ...$35
Spirit In A Bottle, Super Scenes, 227, 1975...............$25
Tree House, Super Scenes, 215, 1975 ....$25

AMT

Bigfoot, 7701..$25
Dragula, Munsters TV Car, 905, 1964 ....$165
Exploration Set, 958, 1974....................................$75
Fred Flintstones Family Sedan, 496, 1974.................$45
Fred Flintstones Rock Cruncher, 497, 1974................$45
Fred Flintstones Sports Car, 495, 1974 ....$45
Galileo 7, 959, 1974 ....$45
Klingon Cruiser, 922, 1967 ....$120
Klingon Cruiser, 952..$65
Klingon Cruiser, 971, 1979 ....$27.50
Klingon Cruiser, 6682, 1985 ....$12.50
K-7 Space Station, 955, 1975................................$40
Mr. Spock With Snake, 956, 1975...........................$60
Mr. Spock Without Snake, 973, 1979.......................$30
Munsters Koach, Munsters TV, 1964......................$175
Romulan Ship, 957, 1975......................................$45
Spaceship Set, 953, 1975......................................$60
Spaceship Set, 6677, 1984.................................$27.50
USS Enterprise With Lights, 931, 1967 ....$175
USS Enterprise Without Lights, 951, 1976.................$50
USS Enterprise, 970, 1979.................................$27.50
USS Enterprise, 6676, 1983..................................$18
USS Enterprise, 6675, 1985..................................$18
USS Enterprise Bridge, 950, 1975........................$27.50
Vulcan Shuttle, 5112, 1979 ....$24
Vulcan Shuttle, 972, 1980 ....$24
Vulcan Shuttle, 6679, 1985 ....$15

HAWK

Beach Bunny Catchin Rays, 542, 1964....................$45
Daddy The Swingin Suburbanite, 532, 1963 ....$45

	C6	C8	C10

Davey The Psycho Cyclist, 531, 1963 ....$45
Digger The Way Out Dragster, 530, 1963 ....$45
Drag Hag, 536, 1963 ....$45
Endsville Eddy, 537, 1963 ....$45
Francis The Foul, 535, 1963 ....$18
Frantic Banana Punishing Skins, 548, 1965 ....$45
Frantic Cats, 549, 1965 ....$45
Freddie Flameout, 533, 1963 ....$45
Hodad Making The Scene, 543, 1964 ....$45
Hot Dogger Hangin Ten, 541, 1964 ....$35
Hot Dogger Hangin Ten, 164, 1970, Glow $20
Huey's Hut Rod, 538, 1963 ....$30
Huey's Hut Rod, 163, 1969, Glow $18
Killer McBash, 539, 1963 ....$45
Leaky Boat Louie, 534, 1963 ....$45
Riding Tandem, 544, 1965 ....$45
Sling Rave Curvette, 637, 1964 ....$12
Steel Pluckers Havin A Bash, 547, 1965 ....$45
Totally Fab, 550, 1965 ....$45
Wade A. Minit, 636, 1964 ....$45
Wierdsville Customizing Kit, 301, 1964 ....$135
Woodie On A Surfari, 540, 1964 ....$45
Woodie On A Surfari, 165, 1970 ....$30

LINDBERG

Big Wheeler, 277, 1965 ....$75
Blurp, 280, 1964 ....$45
Creeping Crusher, 273, 1965 ....$60
Glob, 281, 1964 ....$45
Green Ghoul, 274, 1965 ....$60
Krimson Terror, 272, 1965 ....$60
Mad Maestro, 284, 1965..$135
Mad Mangler, 275, 1965 ....$60
Road Hog, 276, 1965 ....$75
Satan's Crate, 279, 1965 ....$120
Scuttle Bucket, 278, 1965...$75
Voop, 283, 1964..$45
Zopp, 282, 1964 ....$45

MONOGRAM

Dracula, 6008, 1983, re-issue of Aurora kit $25
Flip Out, Fred Flypogger, 105, 1965 ....$100
Frankenstein, 6007, Aurora re-issue...........................$25
Godzilla, 6300, 1978 Aurora re-issue $40
Mummy, 6010, 1983, Aurora re-issue.........................$25
Speed Shift, Fred Flypogger, 106, 1965 ....$100
Super Fuzz, Fred Flypogger, 104, 1965 ....$150
Superman, 6301, 1978, Aurora re-issue $15
Wolfman, 6009, 1983, Aurora re-issue $25

MPC

Alian, 1961, movie, 1979 ....$60
Barnabas Collins, TV Dark Shadows, 1550, 1969......$150
Barnabas Vampire Van, TV Dark Shadows, 1626,
    1969 ....$90
Batman, 1702, 1984, Aurora re-issue $20

	C6	C8	C10

C3PO, Star Wars, 1913, 1978-1980 ....$15
C3PO, Star Wars, 1935, 1983......................................$10
Condemned To Chains, 5003, 1973, Disney Pirates
    Of Caribbean $30
Curl's Girl, 103, 1965..$45
Curl's Girl With Hot Shot, 103, 1965..........................$45
Darth Vader, 1916, 1978/1980.....................................$20
Dead Man's Raft, 5005, 1973, Pirates Of Caribbean ..$30
Dead Men Tell No Tales, 5001, 1973, Disney Pirates
    of Caribbean $30
Escape From The Crypt, 5053, 1974, Disney
    Haunted Mansion $45
Fate Of the Mutineer, 5004, 1974,
    Disney Pirates Of Caribbean $30
Freed In The Nick Of Time, 5007, 1973, Pirates Of
    The Caribbean $30
Ghost Of America With Stroker McGurk, 104, 1964 .$110
Ghost Of The Treasure, 5006, 1973, Pirates Of
    Caribbean $30
Grave Robbers Reward, 5050, 1974, Disney
    Haunted Mansion $45
Hoist High The Jolly Roger, 5002, 1973, Pirates of
    Caribbean $30
Hot Curl, 101, 1965 ....$45
Hot Shot With Hot Dog, 103, 1965 ....$45
Incredible Hulk, 1932, 1979.......................................$20
Play It Again Sam, 5052, 1974, Disney Haunted
    Mansion...$45
Raiders Coach, Paul Revere & Raiders, 1969, 0622....$90
R2-D2, Star Wars, 1912, 1978-1980 ....$20
R2-D2, Star Wars, 1934, 1983.....................................$10
Spiderman, 1931, 1978 ....$20
Stroker McGurk And Surf Rod, 100, 1964 ....$65
Superman, 1701, 1985, Aurora re-issue $20
Tall T With Stroker McGurk, 102, 1964 ....$65
Vampire Midnight Madness, 5051, 1974, Disney
    Haunted Mansion $45
Werewolf, TV Dark Shadows, 1552, 1969..................$210
Yellow Submarine, Beatles, 617, 1968 ....$150

MULTIPLE

Automatic Baby Feeder, 955, 1965 ....$20
Back Scrubber and Hat Remover, 958, 1965 ....$20
Disappearing Lady, 1257, 1966...................................$45
Floating On Air, 1256, 1966..$45
Iron Maiden, 981, 1966...$120
Painless Tooth Extractor, 956, 1965 ....$20
Saw The Lady In Half, 1258, 1966 ....$45
Signal For Shipwrecked Sailor, 957, 1965 ....$20
Torture Chair, 980, 1966...$120
Torture Wheel, 979, 1966..$120

PYRO

The Curler, 177, 1970...$35
Der Baron, 166, 1970 ....$35
Ghost Rider, 167, 1970..$35

	C6	C8	C10
The Gladiator, 175, 1970			$35
Lil Corporal, 168, 1970			$35
Rawhide, 276, 1958			$60
Restless Gun, 277, 1958			$60
Surf's Up, 176, 1970			$40
Wyatt Earp, 278, 1958			$60

REMCO

	C6	C8	C10
Flintstones Sports Car, 450, 1961			$90
Flintstones Yacht, 451, 1961			$90
Flintstones Paddy Wagon, 452, 1961			$90

REVELL

	C6	C8	C10
Angel Fink, 1307, 1965			$90
Beatnik Bandit, 1279, 1963, Ed Roth			$50
Birthday Bird, 2051, 1960 (Dr. Seuss)			$60
Bonanza, 1931, 1966			$60
Brother Rat Fink, 1304, 1964			$25
Busby The Afghan Yak, 2006, 1959, (Dr. Seuss)			$60
Cat In The Hat, 2000, 1958 (Dr. Seuss)			$60
Cat In The Hat With Thing 1&2, 2050, 1960 (Dr. Seuss)			$75
Dragnut, 1303, 1963, Ed Roth			$35
Fink Eliminator, 1310,. 1965, Ed Roth			$120
Flash Gordon and Martian, 1450, 1965			$90

	C6	C8	C10
Flipper and Sandy, 1930, 1965			$50
Game of the Yertle, 2100, 1960 (Dr. Seuss)			$75
George Harrison, 1353, 1964			$150
Gowdy The Dowdy Grackle, 2002, 1958 (Dr. Seuss)			$60
Grickily The Gractus, 2005, 1959 (Dr. Seuss)			$60
Grickily, Busby, and Rosco, 2081, 1060 (Dr. Seuss)			$150
Horton The Elephant, 2052, 1960 (Dr. Seuss)			$75
John Lennon, 1352, 1964			$150
Mothers Worry, 1302, 1963, Ed Roth			$55
Mr. Gasser, 1301, 1963, Ed Roth			$60
Norval The Bashful Blinket, 2003, 1959 (Dr. Seuss)			$60
Outlaw, Ed Roth			$50
Paul McCartney, 1350, 1964			$110
Phantom And Witch Doctor, 1451, 1965			$90
Rat Fink, 1305, 1963			$27.50
Ringo Starr, 1351, 1964			$110
Robbin Hood Fink, 1270, 1965, Ed Roth			$175
Roscoe The Many Footed Lion, 2004, 1959 (Dr.Seuss)			$60
Scuz Fink, 1308, 1964			$185
Superfink, 1308, 1964			$185
Surfink, 1306, 1965			$60
Tingo The Stroodle, 2001, 1958 (Dr. Seuss)			$60
Tingo, Gowdy, And Norval, 2080, 1960, (Dr. Seuss)			$150
Tweedy Pie With Boss Fink, 1271, 1965 Ed Roth			$90

PEZ CANDY DISPENSERS

by David Welch

Pez candy dispensers first became available in the US around 1950. The candy itself was produced in Austria as far back as the 1930s. It wasn't until the late 1940s that the "box" or dispenser became available with the candy. The very first dispenser had no head (the aspect most of us associate with Pez), making it resemble a Bic lighter. Soon thereafter, a Spacegun, full-bodied Santa and Robot, and many more appeared. Who can forget the fun of your favorite cartoon friends tilting their heads back to give you a piece of Pez candy?!

Over the years, Pez dispensers have been manufactured in Austria, Yugoslavia, Hong Kong and USA. Dispensers are usually marked with one of these four patent numbers: (a) 2,620,061; (b) 3,410,455; (c) 3,845,882; or (d) 3,942,683. It is virtually impossible to date a dispenser with any surety, although the patent number can sometimes be a vague indicator. Neither the country of origin, patent number, nor age are necessarily tied to value. The bottom line on value is which head is on the dispenser!

Since their introduction in the US, Pez dispensers have been continuously available to present day. As of January, 1991, there are approximately 250 different Pez dispensers known. This figure excludes color variation and other minor differences occurring on individual dispensers. Only the most valuable dispensers are currently listed here. Other companies such as Totems, Yummies, and Smarties copied the dispenser-with-head concept but none have approached the universal acceptance of Pez.

CONDITION

Prices given are for excellent or better condition dispensers. Defects such as missing pieces, melt marks, scuffs, excessive dirt, and cracks decrease the value by a minimum of 20%. The condition of the cartridge that holds the candy does not affect value as much as the condition of the head. Exceptions to this rule apply in the cases of Regulars, Die-Cuts, Guns, Zorro A, Psychedelics and other dispensers in which the cartridge itself is an important part of the identity or appearance. Missing head pieces and facial melt marks can render most dispensers virtually valueless. However, the heads alone are sometimes of value on the most expensive dispensers.

Pez Gun, B. Handgun. Courtesy Barry Koester.

Pez Gun, A. Space 1950s. Courtesy Barry Koester.

	C6	C8	C10
Alpine, 1972 Olympics			125
Arithmetic			100
Astronaut			
A. White helmet			30
B. Blue helmet			30
C. Clear helmet			65
D. Clear helmet with "Cocoa Marsh" on side			65
E. Small helmet (silver or white)			70
Baseball Glove with ball			75
with home plate/bat			125
Batman with cape			75
Betsy Ross			30
Bozo			40
Bozo Die-Cut ("Bozo/Butch" on side)			60
Bride with white veil			100
Brutus (from Popeye)			75
Bullwinkle			80
Camel Whistle			10
Captain			35
Casper			45
Casper Die-Cut ("Casper" on side)			75
Chick in Egg (no hat)			35
Clown with "Pez" on hat (Peter Pez)			30

	C6	C8	C10
Cow with large nose, circular ears			70
Cowboy			85
Creature From the Black Lagoon			
A. With green cartridge/head			85
B. Darker green head/orange cartridge			70
C. Black head			70
Crocodile			25
Daniel Boone with coonskin cap			70
Doctor			18
Dog			40
Donald Duck Die-Cut (3 Duck nephews on side)			75
Dopey			85
Easter Bunny with thin/straight ears			30
Easter Bunny Die-Cut (bunny with eggs on side)			95
Football Player			25
Frankenstein			80
Giraffe			30
Green Hornet			125
Groom with black top hat and hat band			80
Gun			
A. Space 1950s			85
B. Handgun (mail-order premium)			125
C. Space 1980s			40
Indian Brave			65
Indian Chief			25
Indian Squaw			25
Joker, softhead (Batman)			30
Knight			40
Koala whistle			12
Lion's Club Lion, 1962			125
Make-A-Face (similar to Mr. Potato Head) with approximately 24 face pieces			200
Mary Poppins			90
Mickey Mouse Die-Cut ("Minnie" on side)			60
Monsters, softheads, 6 different, each			45
Olive Oyl			80
Orange			30
Panther, blue head			28
Pear with visor			165
Penguin, softhead (from Batman)			30
Peter Pan			85
Pilgrim			35
Pineapple			175
Pinocchio, (old version) has eyes looking up, feather is part of hat			35
Popeye, (old version) hat cannot be removed			30
Psychedelic Eye, hand holding eyeball			150
Psychedelic Flower, eyeball in flower			150
Regular (no heads)			
A. Personalized, has paper label on side			80
B. Witch, has picture of witch on side			175
C. Golden Glow, with gold shiny finish			60
D. US Zone Germany marking			75

Pez, Left to Right: Indian Squaw, Indian Chief, Indian Brave, Pilgrim (1976 Bicentennials). Courtesy Barry Koester.

Pez Lion's Club Lion. Courtesy Barry Koester.

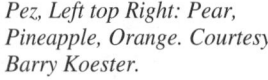

Pez, Left top Right: Pear, Pineapple, Orange. Courtesy Barry Koester.

Pez Make-A-Face. Courtesy Barry Koester.

Pez Monsters, Soft Heads, Left to Right: Spook, Air Spirit, Vamp, Zombie, Spook, Diabolic. Courtesy Barry Koester.

Pez, Left to Right: Mickey Mouse, Donald Duck, Easter Bunny, Casper, Bozo, all die cut. Courtesy Barry Koester.

Pez, Left to Right: Psychedelic Eye, Psychedelic Flower. Courtesy Barry Koester.

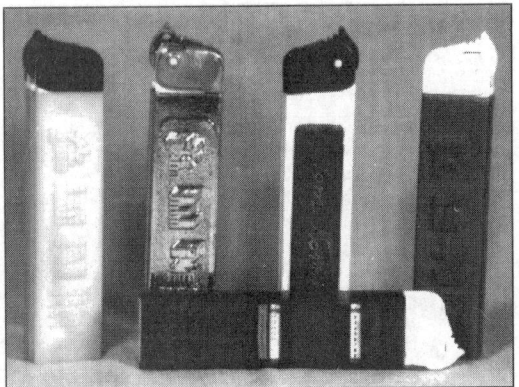

Pez, Left to Right: Regular E, C, A, E. Bottom: Arithmetic. Courtesy Barry Koester.

Pez, Left to Right: Santa Face and beard same, full body, flesh face. Courtesy Barry Koester.

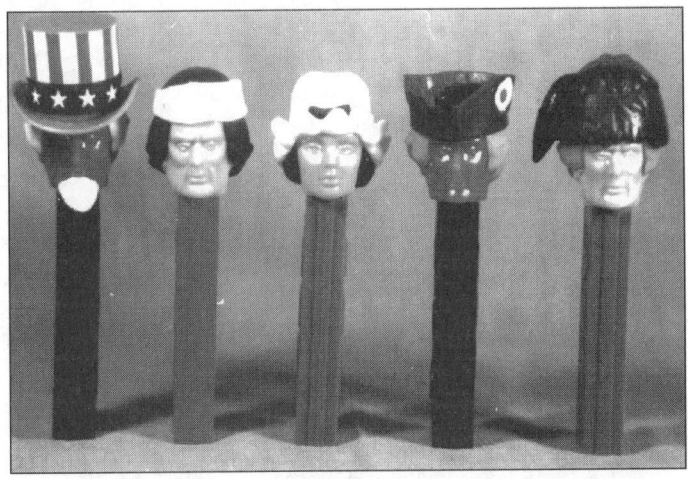

Pez, Left to Right: Uncle Sam, Wounded Soldier, Betsy Ross, Captain, Daniel Boone (1976 Bicentennials). Courtesy Barry Koester.

Pez Wolf, 1984 Olympics, Left to Right: A, C, B, Snowman with Arms. Courtesy Barry Koester.

Pez, Left to Right: Regular B. Witch, Witch, 1 piece. Courtesy Barry Koester.

Pez, Left to Right: Wolfman, Creature from Black Lagoon, Frankenstein. Courtesy Barry Koester.

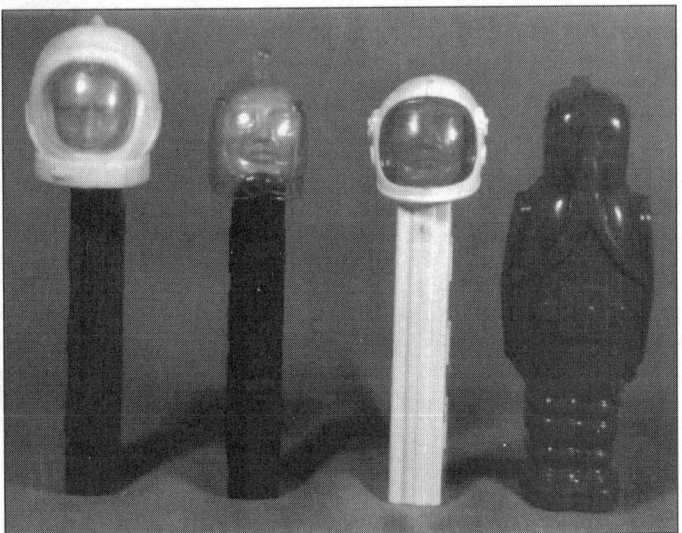

Pez Astronauts, Left to Right: A, C, E, Robot, full body. Courtesy Barry Koester.

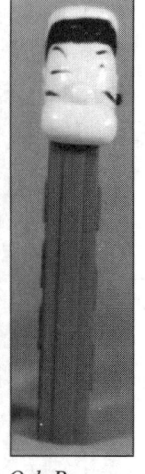

Pez, Left to Right: Brutus, Olive Oyl, Popeye.
Courtesy Barry Koester.

Pez, Left to Right: Dopey, Snow White, Peter Pan, unlisted, Tinkerbell.
Courtesy Barry Koester.

Pez, Left to Right: Groom, Bride. Courtesy
Mary Ann Kennedy.

PREMIUMS

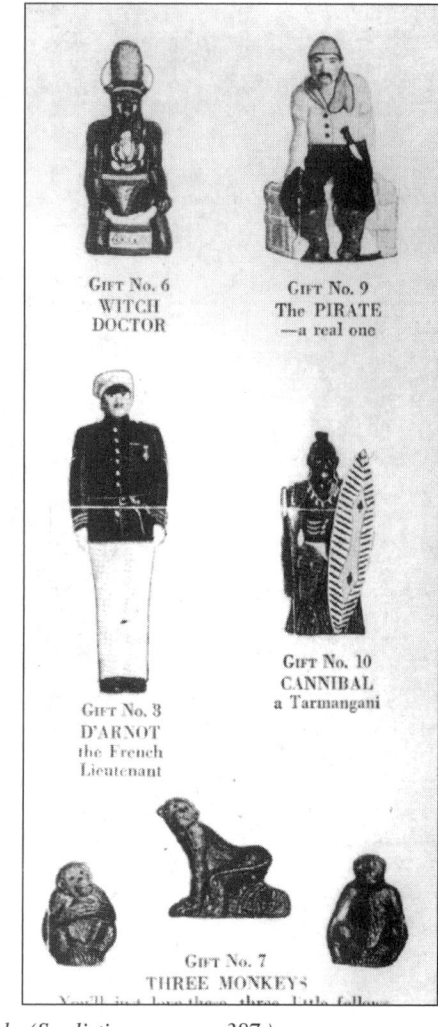

GIFT No. 1
TARZAN
with set of wa-
ter color paints,
brush and color
chart.

GIFT No. 2
KALA
the Mother Ape

GIFT No. 3
NUMA
the Lion

GIFT No. 4
JANE PORTER
the Girl

GIFT No. 5
SHEETA
the Panther

GIFT No. 6
WITCH
DOCTOR

GIFT No. 9
The PIRATE
—a real one

GIFT No. 3
D'ARNOT
the French
Lieutenant

GIFT No. 10
CANNIBAL
a Tarmangani

GIFT No. 7
THREE MONKEYS

PREMIUMS

Tom Mix Western Movie Viewer. Courtesy Jim
Harmon. (See listing on page 390.)

Tarzan Gift Statues, Foulds. (See listing on page 387.)

PREMIUMS

The average mint price of premiums was $61.34 in the last edition,
rising to $80.86 in this, an increase of 32%.

TOYS FREE AS THE AIR

By Jim Harmon

Many radio premiums were nearly as free as the wonderful radio shows that advertised them.

We did have to pay the electric bill (or our folks did) to run the radio, and to get the offered toys we did have to send in a box-top from the sponsor's product.

Sometimes it was only that, a proof of purchase (Orphan Annie and Captain Midnight were particularly generous in responding with gifts for inner labels or inner seals from Ovaltine drink mix) and other times, usually only a dime was required "to handle the cost of handling and mailing". (That's really all it did do - the cost of the premium itself came from the advertising budget.)

The lure of the premium to kids then and for grown-up kids who are now collectors is difficult to explain to those who never lived through the era themselves. The ring or badge was more than the toy itself; it was our tangible link to those magical friends on the other side of the speaker cloth.

Those voices were wonderful out there - The rumbling bass of Brace Beemer as the Lone Ranger; the slightly "country" sound of Curley Bradley as Tom Mix; Bret Morrison, whom we recognized even as children was "sophisticated" as Lamont Cranston, alias The Shadow - but they were bodiless and yes, a bit remote.

It was the premium they offered, the same as the one they were using in the story, that put us in touch with them.

There were historic precedents for radio premiums. There were pictures of famous actresses in cigarette packages around the turn of the century, and early radio personalities, such as bandleader Vincent Lopez, offered their autographed pictures. But such footnotes to history aside, radio premiums began with **Little Orphan Annie** in 1931. The plucky little waif from the Sunday comics first gave away sheet music of her theme song ("Who's that little chatterbox with the pretty auburn locks?") and her own photo, but very shortly, she offered a drinking mug that could be used to shake-up Ovaltine powder with milk to make something resembling a soda fountain milk shake. The first significant radio premium, it was the only successful one that encouraged further use of the sponsor's product.

Many different models of the shake-up mug were offered by Annie, and later by Captain Midnight (on both radio and TV). So successful were the offers, shake-up mugs are not rare or high in dollar value. (The most sought after is the orange and blue, embossed - not decaled - Midnight mug.)

It took two more years after Annie came to radio for the fledgling medium to develop its really classic adventure heroes. In 1933, there appeared the Lone Ranger, Tom Mix and Jack Armstrong. Unlike Annie, the two Westerners and the All-American Boy were still around until the 1950s, when television began driving out all radio drama. In those nearly twenty years, these shows offered hundreds of give-away toys, which inspired similar premiums on dozens of other shows.

Any small toy that could be manufactured inexpensively enough might turn up as a premium. Those concerned with the great outdoors were popular. We had compasses, pedometers, telescopes, flashlights, pocketknives, signal mirrors, portable telegraph sets.

The secret society of childhood had its emblems and tokens. So had secret decoders and secret manuals of every size and description. It is these and other **paper** items that have the greatest dollar value. They were the most easily lost or used up in the rush to adulthood. A Captain Midnight Secret Manual is worth more than the metallic decoder it accompanied.

The rarest paper item is the Lone Ranger Frontier Town offered about 1947. To complete this model of a Western village, one had to get four different envelopes by mail, then augment this by buying several packages of Cheerios to cut out the model buildings from the packs. The complete set has been known to sell for hundreds of dollars and today might bring $1,500.00, the highest dollar premium.

Perhaps the most popular single type of premium was the ring. Rings let the listener show his loyalty to the fraternity of his favorite hero, but in a less officious and more "grown-up" way than the badge (although they were also highly popular). Besides . . . the rings looked neat, and many of them could **do** things - some of them pretty incredible things.

As with radio premiums in general, the Tom Mix show (and Ralston cereal's premium manufacturer, the Robbins Company) blazed the trail with ingenious ring designs. In 1937, Tom Mix Straight Shooters could get a Signet Ring with their own initial on it. (Years later, Captain Midnight would offer a ring that would ink-stamp your initial.) By 1938, Tom had a ring that let you look in a peep-hole and see a magnified picture of himself and his horse, Tony. (Technology had progressed so much that by the fifties, Straight Arrow offered a similar ring that put your own photo, if supplied, alongside radio's great Indian hero.)

After World War II and the ease in metal rationing, Tom Mix offered a Magnet Ring (good for picking up paperclips - like the one on the stolen plans to the atomic bomb, in Tom's case). His spinning siren whistle ring was neat (but admittedly borrowed in design from Jack Armstrong's 1937 Egyptian Whistle Ring). Tom's Sliding Whistle Ring that played different musical notes (about 1948) was unique, however. His Look-Around Ring concealed an inner mirror that let you see behind you (sort of), a design rustled for a later Tennessee Jed ring.

The final Tom Mix ring looked attractive, sporting a glowing cat's-eye, but the Tiger-Eye Ring was only lightweight plastic in 1949, a far cry from the well-crafted metal rings of a decade earlier. But then, the decade was nearly over, and so was the era, fading in the light of another glowing eye in the living room.

The Shadow's own Glow-in-the-Dark Ring in 1939 had a band composed of two sculpted Shadow figures holding up a jagged blue stone - a proxy lump of his sponsor's product, Blue Coal. One of the very few Shadow premiums and the best-looking, this ring has sold for a record $650.00.

One glowing plastic ring - the identical mold - was used for several different radio shows. The band had two crocodiles holding a setting in their mouths. The oval "stone" was **green** when it was Jack Armstrong's Dragon Eye Ring in 1940. It stayed green for **Terry and the Pirates** in the mid-forties, but it was **black** for Carey Salt's Shadow ring in 1947 (not the rare Blue Coal model). The setting was **red** for Buck Rogers' Ring of Saturn in 1945. It is back to **black** in the slightly lumpy counterfeit being manufactured today, one of the handful of premiums of simple enough design to be faked for profit. The best way to authenticate these rings is by the accompanying paper instruction sheets, naming the famous character whose prize it is.

These rings, as are all radio premiums, are worth whatever you will pay to possess them. A fair average price is $60.00 with $200.00 a top price for very rare, complex and fragile items. No one who is not familiar with the whole field should pay more. Even though $200.00 or more may be easier to come by today than a dime and a box-top were in those days of yesteryear.

PREMIUM UPDATE

There has been a radical change in the prices of radio and early TV premiums (and associated toys). For nearly twenty years, there had been no appreciable rise in premium prices. In fact, premium prices had not even kept up with inflation. You could have bought a Tom Mix Magnet Ring for $35.00 in 1967 and bought the same Magnet Ring for the same $35.00 in 1987. but now there has come a radical change in premium pricing, especially for rings. The Magnet Ring generally brings $95 for a mint copy in 1991.

Part of the reason is the unnatural influence of

"investor" types who have manipulated the market, much as they had the old comic book market for years. If events follow those in the comic book market, in a few years those interested in premiums for pleasure will be priced out of the market by manipulators interested only in holding them for a time as value accrues and selling them for profit. Now, if ever, is certainly the time to buy. Premiums are becoming difficult to find in any shape.

Events in the real world are also influencing the premium market. New stores of attic collections are no longer turning up; those in existence have already surfaced. Many of the good examples of the premiums have been sold and have disappeared into collections. More and more, premiums of secondary condition - frankly poor condition at times - are being offered at mint prices. **Condition** becomes more and more critical. A very rare premium in a battered, rusted, even broken condition is virtually worthless.

Slowly, a new source of premiums is becoming evident. Older collectors are retiring from their occupations, and sadly, selling their collections for needed money. Some die, and survivors sell. These collectors and families know the value of collectibles and sell for top market value. This pattern is bound to continue, but currently very slowly.

The items connected to once well-known characters, and some still well-known today, are going up fastest. The minor and unknown character items are not being given away, but probably won't increase in adjusted dollar value. **Rings** have a great appeal to many, and are the hottest ticket in the premium market - the rare ones are going up and up. The Shadow Blue Coal Ring, Green Hornet Seal Ring, and Captain Midnight Mystic Sun God Ring will probably go over the thousand dollar mark in the next few years (although the complete Lone Ranger Frontier Town is the only premium known to have sold for over one thousand dollars at this writing).

A new development is the rising prices on the old cereal boxes associated with famous characters. Any old box of Wheaties is worth money, but an offer of a Jack Armstrong premium can raise the price from a previous twenty-five dollars to a present seventy-five. The top of this line are complete boxes of the nine Lone Ranger Frontier Town Cheerios packs (about one hundred dollars each; the cut complete backs with unassembled model buildings can go for twenty-five).

A few new authentic premiums have appeared in recent years: Boraxo offered a 20 Mule Team model in 1980 (similar to the Death Valley Days original of the '30's and '40's); Cheerios offered a Lone Ranger Deputy Kit in 1981 styled after the movie of that year but similar to earlier offers with mask, badge, etc. In 1982, Ralston began a limited Tom Mix revival with which the present author, Jim Harmon, was involved; offering a set of four

Mix Ralston cereal bowls, a wind-up wrist watch, a Straight Shooters membership kit, a Tom Mix photo, a Mix in-box miniature comic book (edited by Harmon), and a Long Play recording with three old Mix radio episodes and one 1983 episode featuring Curly Bradley and produced by Harmon. In 1987, Ovaltine resurrected their original formula in jars, and instituted new premiums of their character, Captain Midnight of the Secret Squadron, with a tee-shirt that year, with a Midnight digital watch in 1988, an arm patch in 1989 (apparently the last of the current revival). Dick Tracy premiums came with the new movie in 1990, such as the Quaker wrist radio. Already these new premiums are bringing high prices - the Mix wrist watch for over one hundred dollars - and some dealers might try to represent them as being older and more valuable than they are. But they are valuable enough.

*JIM HARMON is a writer of non-fiction (**The Great Radio Heroes**) and science fiction (including the often-anthologized "The Place Where Chicago Was") magazine editor (**Monsters of the Movies**) and writer-producer-co-star with radio's Tom Mix in the 1970s **Curley Bradley, U.S. Marshal** radio and recording series. He has written virtually every imaginable category of fiction or non-fiction, has appeared in movies, radio drama and many major TV talk shows. Harmon has produced several new radio episodes of **Tom Mix** for Ralston which have been both broadcast and offered on premium record albums. He has also edited a **Mix** mini-comic book included in specially marked boxes of Hot Ralston. His new book, **Radio Mystery and Adventure**, is due from McFarland in 1992. He lives with his wife, Barbara, a microbiologist, and daughter, Dawn, a U.C.L.A. student, in California.*

	C6	C8	C10
Admiral Television Studio Giveaway - 1953 paper punchout TV studio and characters, features Sky King, Flight to Mars, Walt Disney's Peter Pan and Three Little Pigs. 15"x16"	52	78	105
Amos & Andy Pepsodent Give-away- Amos' Wedding	38	53	75
Amos & Andy Puzzle	32	48	65
Archie Comics Club Button	3.50	5.25	7
Aunt Jemima Breakfast Club Badge, metal	10	15	20
Barney Baxter Junior Birdmen of America wings, metal, circa late 1930s	9	13.50	18
Bendix Radio - 5½" WW II military figures circa 1944. Color photos with stands. a. Lt. (jg) Navy; b. Marine 1st Lt. (dress uniform); c. Commander-Coast Guard; d. Army Air Force officer with parachute harness; e. 2nd Lt. with modern Mae West; f. Flier with flying suit; g. Capt. Army Air Force; h. Air officer with fur-lined jacket and helmet. Price per each	3	4.50	6
Betty Boop face mask - 1931 theatre premium	18	27	35
Betty Boop pin "Roxy Theatre, New York," large	10	15	20
Blondie & Dagwood Go To Leisureland, 1940, Westinghouse	7	11	14

	C6	C8	C10
Bobby Benson Code Rule 1935 cardboard decoder, Hecker H-O	47	72	95
Bobby Benson's Game Circus, 1934	37	53	75
Buck Jones Club Ring	32	48	65
Buck Jones Horseshoe Pin	32	48	65
Buck Jones Jr. Sheriff Badge	32	48	65
Buck Roger Badge, enameled	47	72	95
Buck Rogers Birthstone and initial ring	125	188	250
Buck Rogers Chief Explorer Badge	42	63	85
Buck Rogers lead figures, solid, Cocomalt, Buck, Wilma, Killer Kane, per each	7.50	11.25	15
Buck Rogers Flight Commander Whistle Badge	50	75	100
Buck Rogers Girl's charm bracelet	62	93	125
Buck Rogers Helmet	75	113	150
Buck Rogers Knife	50	75	100
Buck Rogers Morton Salt Punch-o-Bag, 1930s	25	38	50
Buck Rogers Morton Salt Spaceship (came in envelope)	60	90	120
Buck Rogers Pendant	25	38	50
Buck Rogers Pinback button, circa 1935, Whitehead and Hoag, "Buck Rogers in the 25th Century"	32	48	65
Buck Rogers Repeller Ray Ring (seal ring)	125	188	250
Buck Rogers Ring of Saturn, glows in the dark, with red stone	125	188	250
Buck Rogers Ring of Saturn Instruction Sheet	30	45	60

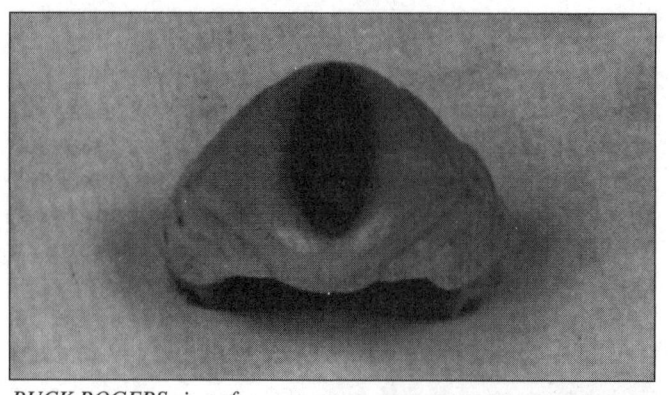

BUCK ROGERS ring of Saturn. Courtesy Jim Harmon.

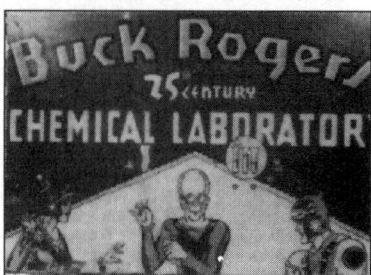

BUCK ROGERS Chemical laboratory. Courtesy HAKE'S Americana & Collectibles.

	C6	C8	C10
Buck Rogers Solar Scouts Badge, all brass color	32	48	65
Buck Rogers Solar Scouts Spaceship Commander Badge, 1936 Cream of Wheat premium	32	48	65
Buck Rogers Solar Scout Sweater Emblem	30	45	60
Buck Rogers Telescope	50	75	100
Buck Rogers items given away for Cream of Wheat green triangle (sold in stores also):			
Buck Rogers Films for projector	7.50	11.25	15
Buck Rogers Interplanetary Game	60	90	120
Buck Rogers lead figures, hollow lead, Buck, Wilma, Huer, Robot, Kane, Ardala, average price per each, Britains	150	300	400
Buck Rogers Lite Blaster Flashlight	17	26	35
Buck Rogers Movie Projector	60	90	120
Buck Rogers Printing Set (12 rubber stamps)	32	48	65
Buck Rogers Super Dreadnaught, balsa wood	32	48	65
Buck Rogers Uniform	125	188	250
Buffalo Bill Bamby Bread Horseshoe Badge, late 1930s	6	9	12
Buffalo Bill Jr. brass ring, Buffalo in relief on top, TV premium	15	22	30
Buster Brown Gang (Smilin' Ed) Ring	32	48	65
Buster Brown Gang tab pins, assorted, price per each	7.50	11.25	15
Butter-Nut Bread premium, "Sail-Me" glider with 4½" wingspan, c. 1930	6	9	12

	C6	C8	C10
Captain America Sentinel of Liberty Badge	100	150	200
Captain Franks Air Hawks Ring	32	48	65
Captain Franks Air Hawks Wings, circa late 1930s, Post's 40% Bran Flakes premium	32	48	65
Captain Gallant Medal, c. 1950 dated 1939-1945 with an animal on it	12	18	24
Captain Gallant Medal, 1950s, this one is a cross with GRI on it	12	18	24
Captain Hawk Sky Patrol Propeller Badge, circa late 1930s	22	33	45
Captain Marvel Club button	32	48	65
Captain Marvel's Magic Whistle c. 1943, American Seed Co. Has full color picture of Captain Marvel on both sides and American Seed Co. ad on the inside	25	38	50
Captain Midnight Aerial Torpedo Bomber (Airplane), 1941	57	85	115
Captain Midnight American Flag Loyalty Badge, 1940	30	45	60
Captain Midnight Flight Patrol Wings Badge, 1941	32	48	65
Captain Midnight Flight Patrol Wings Badge, 1942	32	48	65
Captain Midnight Code-O-Graph Decoder Pin, 1941, Eagle on top	62	93	125
Captain Midnight Code-O-Graph Badge, 1942, with photo of Captain Midnight	62	93	125
Captain Midnight Code-O-Graph, 1945, magnifier	55	83	110
Captain Midnight Code-O-Graph, 1946, Mirrormatic, (best looking, desirable)	75	113	150
Captain Midnight Code-O-Graph, 1947, works as a whistle	25	38	50
Captain Midnight Code-O-Graph, 1948, round, with mirror	47	70	95
Captain Midnight Code-O-Graph, 1949, Key-O-Matic (with key)	75	113	150
Captain Midnight Detect-O-Scope, 1941	36	54	72
Captain Midnight Flight Commander Commission, 1956	30	45	60
Captain Midnight Flight Commander Flying Cross, 1942	30	45	60
Captain Midnight Flight Commander Ring, 1941	87	130	175
Captain Midnight Flight Commander Signet Ring, 1957	95	145	195
Captain Midnight FLight Commander Ring, 1959	95	145	195

CAPTAIN MIDNIGHT Code-O-Graph Badge, 1942. Courtesy Jim Harmon.

CAPTAIN MIDNIGHT Medal, 1940. Courtesy Jim Harmon.

	C6	C8	C10
Captain Midnight Jumping Bean Target, 1939 15		23	30
Captain Midnight MJC-10 Plane Detector, 1942, distance-finder 55		83	110
Captain Midnight Magic Blackout Lite-Ups, 1942 27		40	54
Captain Midnight 1941 Manual for Decoder 60		90	120
Captain Midnight 1942 Manual for Decoder 120		180	240
Captain Midnight 1945 Manual for Code-O-Graph 39		60	78
Captain Midnight 1946 Manual for Code-O-Graph 47		70	95
Captain Midnight 1947 Manual for Code-O-Graph 47		70	95
Captain Midnight 1948 Manual for Code-O-Graph 47		70	95
Captain Midnight 1949 Manual for Code-O-Graph 37		53	75
Captain Midnight 1956 Manual for Decoder Badge 120		180	240
Captain Midnight 1957 Manual for Silver Dart decoder 120		180	240
Captain Midnight Marine Corps Ring, 1942 70		105	140
Captain Midnight medal, brass, pictures of cast, secret word, spinner, 1940 9		13.50	18
Captain Midnight Mystic Eye Detector Ring, 1942 72		108	145
Captain Midnight Mystic Sun God Ring, 1946 275		413	550
Captain Midnight Printing Ring, 1948 ..62		93	125
Captain Midnight Secret Squadron Decoder Badge, 1955 60		90	120

	C6	C8	C10
Captain Midnight Secret Squadron Decoder Badge, 1956 60		90	120
Captain Midnight Secret Squadron Insignia transfer, 1949 15		23	30
Captain Midnight Service Ribbon pin, 1944 32		48	65
Captain Midnight Silver Dart Decoder Badge, 1957 60		90	120
Captain Midnight Spy Scope, 1947 37		53	75
Captain Midnight Surprise Package, 1942 21		32	42
Captain Midnight 3-Way Mystic Dog Whistle, 1942 15		23	30
Captain Midnight Trick and Riddle Book, 1939 Skelly Oil Premium, 64 pages 17		25	35
Captain Midnight Weather Wings, 1940, predicts weather 30		45	60
Captain Midnight Whirlwind Whistling Ring, 1941 62		93	125
Capt. Tim Ivory Club Pin - Ivory Soap, circa 1936 ....6.50		9.75	13
Captain Video Flying Saucer Ring 47		72	95
Captain Video Rite-O-Lite 32		48	65
Captain Video Rocket Launcher and Ships, 1950s 47		72	95
Captain Video Secret Seal Ring, 1950s 60		90	120
Captain Video Space Fleet Ray Gun, 1952, TV premium - Powerhouse ...87		120	175
Captain Video X-9 Rocket Balloon, 1950s 27		40	55
Chandu the Magician Galloping Coin Trick, 1930s 27		40	55
Chandu The Magician Hindu Cones, 1930s 27		40	55
Chandu Boxed Set of Tricks 250		375	500
Charlie McCarthy Puppet Doll - 21" high, cardboard, Chase & Sanborn mailer 32		48	65
Charlie McCarthy Radio Party Game - Giveaway by Standard Brands, 1938, 21 cardboard figures 38		57	76
Cinnamon Bear (annual Christmas show, circa 1940s) Silver Star 25		38	50

	C6	C8	C10
Cisco Kid Badge, western hat on chain, 1950s	12	18	24
Cisco Kid cardboard gun, 7" long, Harvest Bread giveaway, clicker sounds when handle squeezed	10	15	20

	C6	C8	C10
Cisco Kid and Pancho face masks, 1953, price per each	17	26	35
Cisco Kid Triple S Club Kit	21	33	42
Cisco Kid Picture Ring, 1950s	39	58	78
Coco Wheats Radio Club Badge shape of microphone	15	23	30

CRACKER JACK

Cracker Jack was first introduced in 1893 by the Ruckheim brothers, F.W. and Louis, at the Chicago World's Columbian Exposition. Toys first appeared in the boxes of popcorn and peanuts in 1912 and were bought from various manufacturers. Over 10,000 different have been produced over the years. From 1912 to 1930 they included whistles, tops, yo-yos, brooches and puzzles.

From 1930 to 1940 the accent was on miniatures, such as irons, shoes, binoculars, trolley cars, trains, etc. 1940 to 1950 tended towards military items, with plastics being introduced in the late 1940s. Prices can range from $1.00 or less to $80.00. There are about thirty serious Cracker Jack collectors known in this country.

DICK TRACY Secret Service Patrol Member Pin. Courtesy Jim Harmon.

	C6	C8	C10
David Harding Counterspy, Junior Agent Badge	32	48	65
Davy Crockett goldplated ring	6	9	12
Dick Tracy Air Detective Ring	50	75	100
Dick Tracy Badge, "Capt."	40	60	80
Dick Tracy Badge, "Crime Stoppers"	9	13.50	18
Dick Tracy Badge, "Detective," picture of Tracy and Junior	15	23	30
Dick Tracy Badge, "Lt."	37	53	75
Dick Tracy Badge - Republic Pictures	37	53	75
Dick Tracy Badge - "Sgt."	30	45	60
Dick Tracy Decoder, green, 1948	22	33	45
Dick Tracy Decoder, red, 1948	22	33	45
Dick Tracy Detective Club Badge with secret money pouch in rear	37	53	75
Dick Tracy Glider Airplane, 1938	37	53	75
Dick Tracy Ring, in shape of Tracy's head	32	48	65
Dick Tracy Secret Compartment Ring	62	93	125
Dick Tracy Secret Service Patrol Member pinback, early 1940s	15	23	30
Dick Tracy Secret Service 2nd Year Member Pin	22	33	45
Dick Tracy's Secret Detective Methods & Magic Tricks, 1939 Quaker Oats, 68 pages	30	45	60
Dionne Quints "All Aboard for Shut-Eye Town" paper dolls, Palmolive Soap	12	18	24
Don Winslow Decoder Torpedo	45	68	90
Don Winslow Honor Badge	21	32	42
Don Winslow Magic Slate Secret Code Book	15	23	42
Don Winslow Ring	32	48	65
Don Winslow USN Secret Code Book, 1935, 16 page Oxydol giveaway, 7¾" x 4"	18	27	36

	C6	C8	C10
Donald Duck Punchout figure, circa late 1940s, Donald Duck Bread	10	15	20
Donald Duck Playboard, 1946, 9" high, Comics giveaway	17	25	35
Elsie The Cow, set of four figural buttons on color illustrated card, Borden 1949	5	7.50	10
Fighting Devil Dogs Ring, 1938, Republic Pictures serial ring, has bulldog head on top	40	60	80
Flash Gordon Ring, 1949 Post Toasties Corn Flakes	18	27	36
Fort Apache (Rin Tin Tin) plastic ring 1950s TV premium	9	13.50	18
Frank Buck Explorer's sun watch, post WW II (offered by Jack Armstrong)	37	53	75
Frank Buck Leopard Ring	100	150	200
G.E. Punchout Circus - 65 pieces	72	108	145
G.E. Rodeo Punchout - 65 pieces	12	18	24
G-Man Badge	2	3	4
G-Man Official Signet Ring, 1933-35, G-man radio program premium, metal	21	32	42

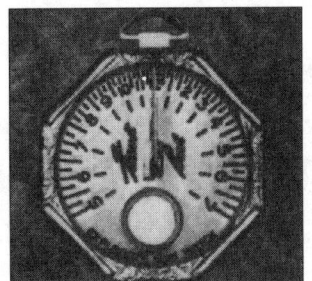

FRANK BUCK Explorer's Sun Watch. Courtesy Jim Harmon.

	C6	C8	C10
Gabby Hayes Antique Cars, 1950s, set for:	27	40	54
Gabby Hayes Quaker Cannon Ring, 1950s	50	75	100
Gabby Hayes Western Gun Collection, 6 weapons, 3 pistols, 3 rifles, solid non-working, 1950s	27	40	54
Gabby Scoops Junior Press Club Car, 1954 Crackajack Comics	3	4.50	6
Gabby Scoops 1940-41 Press Card, Crackajack Comics	3	4.50	6
Gangbusters Pin	17	25	35
Goofy Playboard, 1946, 9" high, comics giveaway	17	25	35
Green Hornet Secret Compartment Ring, hornet seal, glows in dark	225	338	450
Gun, cardboard - Giveaway from Theatorium in Lykens, Pa. Pat'd Dec. 1914 by Spots Spec. Co. Lexington, Ky. Swoop downward to produce bang. "The Bang Gun For Young America"	3	4.50	6
H.C.B. Club Kit, contains badge, etc., early Cream of Wheat	15	23	30
Hop Harrigan Para-Plane, cardboard plane from Grape Nut Flakes plus two code signal blinders. Also in tail of plane is a small parachute that drops a cardboard "water" canister	162	243	325
Hop Harrigan (unmarked) Sun Dial Ring	27	40	54
Hopalong Cassidy Bar 20 Compass ring	15	23	30
Hopalong Cassidy Face Ring	17	26	35
Hopalong Cassidy tin badge, Post Raisin Bran giveaway, circa 1950s	10	15	20
Howdy Doody Climber - cardboard, with string, Welch's Premium, 1950s	17	26	35
Howdy Doody Face Flashlight Ring, 1950s	22	33	45

	C6	C8	C10
Howdy Doody Flicker Key Chain - 3D picture of Howdy Doody flicks to Poll Parrot (Poll Parrot Shoes), 1950s	9	13.50	18
Howdy Doody Flicker Ring - Poll Parrot Premium, flicks from Howdy to Poll	10	15	20
Howdy Doody 8" Howdy Doody flexible cardboard figure - Wonder Bread	20	30	40
Howdy Doody puppet, Mars Candy, cardboard, 15" high, 1950s	30	45	60
Howdy Doody Princess dancing puppet, 13" high, joints moveable, 1950s Snickers premium	10	15	20
Howdy Doody, Princess Spring, etc. cardboard figure, 14" high	10	15	20
I Am A Spy Smasher button, 1940, Fawcett Comics	12	18	24
Indian Chief tin badge, Post Raisin Bran, circa 1950s	2.50	3.75	5
Indian Gum Chief's Head Ring - Goudey Gum card premium, 1930s, silver	3	4.50	6
Jack Armstrong Crocodile Ring, glows in the dark, green stone	75	113	150
Jack Armstrong Big 10 Football Game	45	68	90
Jack Armstrong Explorer's Telescope	17	25	35
Jack Armstrong Flashlight	15	23	30
Jack Armstrong Hike-O-Meter	22	33	45
Jack Armstrong Magic Answer Box	37	53	75
Jack Armstrong Ped-O-Meter (blue or silver models)	22	33	45
Jack Armstrong, Secret Norden Bomb Sight, circa WW II with three bombs, paper target ships	165	247	330
Jack Armstrong paper airplane models, many different, price per each	17	25	35

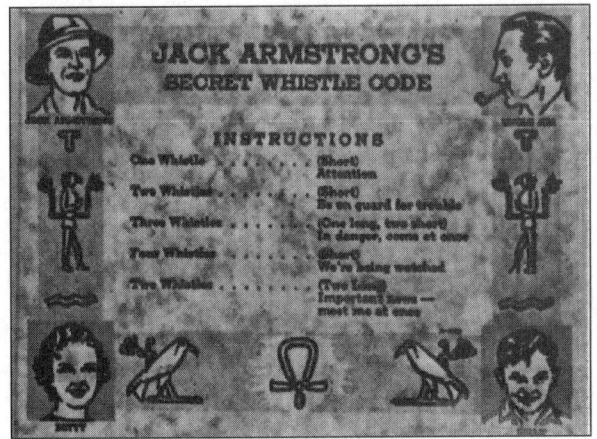

JACK ARMSTRONG Secret Whistle Code Card. Courtesy Jim Harmon.

JACK ARMSTRONG Ped-O-Meter.
Courtesy Jim Harmon.

JIMMIE ALLEN Richfield Hi-Octane Flying Cadet wings.
Courtesy Jim Harmon.

	C6	C8	C10
Reprints of above (identified as such)....5	7.50	10
Jack Armstrong Secret Whistle Code Card for Secret Egyptian Coder Siren ring..........15	23	30
Jack Armstrong Secret Egyptian Coder Siren Ring, late 1930s, Wheaties..........39	58	78
Jack Armstrong 3-D viewer, filmstrip...25	38	50
Jeff paper mask, 1933 Shell Oil 7	10.50	14
Jimmie Allen Colonial Gasoline Flying Cadet wings, late 1930s, bronze..........15	23	30
Jimmie Allen High-Speed Gasoline Flying Cadet wings, late 1930s, bronze..........20	30	40
Jimmie Allen Richfield Hi-Octane Flying Cadet wings, circa 1930s..........20	30	40
Jimmie Allen Richfield Hi-Octane Pilot's Identification Bracelet, late 1930s, all metal..........21	32	42
Jimmie Allen Skelly Oil Die-Cut Airplane cadet wings, late 1930s....15	23	30
Jimmie Allen Skelly Oil Flying Cadet Wings, late 1930s, bronze..........15	23	30
Joe E. Brown pin 8	12	16
Junior G-Man Membership kit, circa mid-1930s 21	32	42
Junior G-Men of America, late 1930s, gold-plated tin badge 15	23	30
Junior Texas Ranger Badge, 1936 premium..........15	23	30
Kellogg's Frogmen, 1950s, add baking soda and they swim underwater.......7	10.50	14
Kellogg's Krumbles - Around-the-World paper dolls. Each cutout from box contains boy and girl, 10: Italy 11: Mexico 13: France 17: Czechoslovakia. Price per each ..2	3	4

	C6	C8	C10
Kellogg's Nautilus Nuclear Submarine, 1950s..........12	18	24
Kellogg's Pep Airplane Carrier, 6½"x10" cut-out sheet with airplane carrier, 5 planes with ¾" wingspan 18	27	36
Kellogg's Pep Warplanes circa 1945, balsa wood models, price per each ...12	18	25
Kellogg's Pep Warplanes circa 1945, balsa, with Superman ad on envelope 12	18	25
Kellogg's Pep Warplanes - circa 1944, cardboard, price per each 7	11	15
"The Liberty Gun For Young America - McGrath's Big Store," 7" cardboard with photos of Charlie Chaplin 12	18	24
Little Orphan Annie Necklace, circa 1936, metal enamel figure of LOA on metal chain..........18	27	36
Little Orphan Annie pinback button, Little Orphan Annie, Member Funy Frosty's Club, mid-1930s 21	32	42
Lone Ranger, A Republic Serial - brass star badge..........47	70	95
Lone Ranger Atom Bomb Ring (very common) 33	49	66
Lone Ranger Blackout Kit, 1942, Kix cereal glow in the dark material (two pieces), glow in the dark pledge to flag, glow in the dark Lone Ranger Volunteers armband, plus instruction..........36	54	72
Lone Ranger Bond Bread Safety Club Badge, 1938 15	23	30
Lone Ranger Clicker Pistol, black, 1939 movie giveaway, Lone Ranger on one side and ruby on other, non-moveable silver cylinder 62	93	125
Lone Ranger Deputy Shield - brass with secret compartment..........32	48	65

"The Liberty Gun For Young American - McGarth's Big Store", 7" cardboard with photos of Charlie Chaplin. Courtesy HAKE'S Americana & Collectibles.

LONE RANGER Frontier Town, complete. Courtesy HAKE'S Americana & Collectibles.

LONE RANGER Secret Compartment Ring. Courtesy Jim Harmon.

	C6	C8	C10
Lone Ranger Flashlight Ring	37	53	75
Lone Ranger Frontier Town - full set	750	1125	1500
Lone Ranger Glow-in-the-dark Belt, 1941	48	72	96
Lone Ranger Hiyo Silver Pin, 1938	10	15	20
Lone Ranger Kix Air Base with cereal box cut-outs, precursor of Frontier Town - complete $275			
Lone Ranger Lucky Piece - advertises 17th anniversary 1933-50	11	16	22
Lone Ranger Mask. About the last radio premium, c. 1953 or 1954, back of black mask promotes a personal appearance by "The Lone Ranger and Silver!"	15	23	30
Lone Ranger Movie Film ring, late 1940s Cheerios premium	47	70	95
Lone Ranger Pedometer, 1943 Cheerios	15	23	30
Lone Ranger Rubber Band Gun and 6 different targets, 1938 Morton Salt giveaway, cardboard	27	41	54
Lone Ranger Secret Compartment Ring, with picture of Lone Ranger and Silver	47	70	95
Lone Ranger Silver bullet, secret compartment compass	32	48	65
Lone Ranger Silver Saddle Film ring, late 1940s, Cheerios	47	70	95
Lone Ranger Chief Scout Badge, Silvercup Bread, early 1940s premium, red, blue and gold	47	70	95
Lone Ranger Safety Scout Badge, Silvercup Bread, 1935	17	25	35
Lone Ranger Silvercup Bread Safety Patrol, metal-silver and blue	15	23	30

	C6	C8	C10
Lone Ranger Six-Shooter Ring, gun ring with plastic and metal gun attached to top. Turn wheel and flint sparks	55	83	110
Lone Ranger Victory Corps Badge, 1942, Kix Cereal	20	30	40
Lone Ranger Weather Ring - color square stone on top with litmus paper. No markings to identify as Lone Ranger	20	30	40
Magic Show Kit, 1946 General Mills	15	23	30
Magician's Book of Cigarette Tricks, 1933, Camel Cigarettes	4.50	6.75	9
Major Bowes - Home Microphone	27	40	54
Maltex Health Club - pinback button	2	3	4
Melvin Purvis Junior G-Man Corps Badge, late 1930s	15	23	30
Melvin Purvis Junior G-Man Corps Roving Operative Badge, late 1930s	15	23	30
Melvin Purvis Law and Order Ring	27	40	55
Melvin Purvis Law & Order Patrol Lieutenant's Secret Operator Badge, mid-1930s	15	23	30
Melvin Purvis Law & Order Patrol Secret Operator Badge, late 1930s	15	23	30
Melvin Purvis Secret Operator, Girl's Division	21	31	42
Mickey and Donald's Race to Treasure Island, 1939, 12"x25" Standard Oil giveaway	60	90	120
Mickey and Donald's Race to Treasure Island, 1939, map of U.S. in full color 20"x27", Calco Gasoline giveaway, with stamps	200	300	400
Mickey Mouse Club Pinback button, "Copyright 1928-30 by W.E. Disney," 1¼"	30	45	60

	C6	C8	C10
Mickey Mouse Globe Trotters Map, 28"x20", NBC Bread, 1937 225	338	450
Mickey Mouse Globe Trotters Map, 28"x22", NBC Bread, with all pictures pasted on.........................250	375	500
Mickey Mouse Globe Trotters Map, 1930s, Pevely Milk premium.........225	338	450
Mickey Mouse Official Money, 1930s Mickey Mouse Cones dollar bills Denomination is "1" (each) 9	13.50	18
Mickey Mouse Playboard, 1946, 9" high, comics giveaway....................17	26	35
Morton Salt "Bat-O-Ball," 1939, features The Shadow (cartoon).......42	63	85
My-T-Fine Grocery Store folds into an 8"x3" full color grocery store with period products on the shelves, shoppers, workers, etc. Dated 1930 21	31	42
Nabisco Finger Puppet Rings, Slim Chants, horse Humbolt, gun, hand, Prairie Mary, Tagalong Boswell, Cold Deck Charlie, Sam Spiel, price per each figure 1	1.50	2
Nabisco Santa Fe Twin Unit Diesel Train, 1956, includes engine, train, tracks, ground, background..............7	10.50	14
Nabisco Sound-Jet Glider.........................5	7.50	10
Nabisco Trailblazers of America cards, six cards make up horse-drawn van and open van, 1956................4.25	6.38	8.50
Nabisco Shredded Wheat Nabisco Flying Circus, 1948, designed by Wallace Rigby, 4"x7" cards, planes, once cut out, can glide. Series of 24. Price per each...............5	7.50	10
The Nebbs - Detroit Times series No. 27544 (comic strip) 4.50	6.75	9
New York World's Fair Children's World G-Man Badge, giveaway, 3-color brass badge 20	30	40
Newsboy Brand Soups and Vegetables Official Booster Badge, late 1930s 3.50	5.25	7
Pep Pins - Little Orphan Annie 6	9	12
Pep Pins - Flash Gordon 12	18	24
Pep Pins - Felix the Cat 3	4.50	6
Pep Pins - The Phantom 6	9	12
Pep Pins - Popeye and Olive Oyl - each...3.50	5.25	7
Pep Pins - Superman 12.50	18.75	25
Pep Pins - Others, includes Smitty, Inspector, Harold Teen, Skeezix, Corky, Pop Jenks, Goofy, Spud,		

	C6	C8	C10
Andy Gump, Gravel Gertie, Punjab, Hans, Kayo, Smilin' Jack, Dagwood, B.O. Plenty, Mr. Bailey, Shadow, Moon Mullins, Flattop, Rip Winkle, Uncle Willie, Emma, Inspector, Chief Brandon, Vitamin Flintheart, Sandy, Uncle Bim, Sundown, Lillums, Tilda, Uncle Walt, Perry Winkle, Judy, Min Gump, Wilmer, Smoky Stover, Daisy, Ma Winkle, Tess Trueheart, Herbie, Mamie, Breezie, Pat Patton, Maggie, Barney Google, Fat Stuff, Chief Brandon, Toots, Nina, etc., average 4	6	8
Pep Rings - Jack Kramer, Dennis O'Keefe, Burt Lancaster, Sitting Bull, Pocahontas, Pan American Clipper, Douglas F-3D Sky Knight, Republic XF91 Thundercepter, each 2	3	4
Pepsodent's Moving Picture Machine shows Mickey Mouse, Donald Duck, Snow White and Seven Dwarfs in color 150	225	300
Pillsbury-Farina Complete Tel-A-Phone Set, 1938, two holders, mouthpieces, ear phones and 50 feet of line 15	23	30
Pinocchio Playboard, 1946, Disney Comics sub. giveaway 17	25	35
Popeye The Sailor Man Button, ¾" copyright 1935, theatre giveaway ...10	15	20
Popsicle Movie Star coins - Aluminum coins circa early 1930s, includes Irene Dunne, Clark Gable, Marion Davies, Fredric March, Marie Dressler, Gary Cooper...4	6	8
Porcelain Enamel & Mfg. Co. 6" West Point Cadet on 3"x6" card with Pemco ad on back...................60	.90	1.25
Post Grape Nuts Flakes Playing-Filling Station, circa 1950s............2.50	3.75	5
Post Toasties 1939 Walt Disney cut-out figures on box, Mickey the Traffic Cop, two types of Pinocchio, etc. Price per each box 15	23	30
Post Toasties Corn Flakes Comic Rings 1949, Fritz, Hans, Tillie the Toiler, Toots, Casper, etc.................5	7.50	10
Post's Cereal Junior Detective Club Sergeant Badge, late 1930s.............10	15	20

Left to Right: RADIO ORPHAN ANNIE Decoder Badges, 1938 and 1939. Courtesy Jim Harmon.

RADIO ORPHAN ANNIE Decoder Badge 1936. Courtesy Jim Harmon.

	C6	C8	C10
Post's Explorer Ring, 1947, includes compass, sun watch, sunset predictor and star finder, plastic dome	21	32	42
Post Cereal Rings - 1948, Perry Winkle, Winnie Winkle, Harold Teen, Skeezix, Lillums, Herbie, Smoky Stover, etc.	5	7.50	10
Post Cereal Rings - 1948 - Dick Tracy	15	23	30
Post Grape Nuts tin rings, Little King, Phantom, Skeezix, Lillums, Harold Teen	4	6	8
Post Raisin Bran Sheriff Badge	1.25	1.88	2.50
Radio Orphan Annie - Annie and Joe Corntassel button, 1931	12	18	24
Radio Orphan Annie - Associated Membership Pin, 1934	12	18	24
Radio Orphan Annie Bandanna, 1934	21	32	42
Radio Orphan Annie Birthstone Ring, 1935	21	32	42
Radio Orphan Annie Capt. Sparks Aviation Trainer	200	300	400
Radio Orphan Annie Circus Cut-Outs, 1935	150	225	300

	C6	C8	C10
Radio Orphan Annie Code Captain Belt and Buckle, 1940	48	72	96
Radio Orphan Annie Code Captain Pin, 1939	32	48	65
Radio Orphan Annie Manual, 1934	39	60	78
Radio Orphan Annie 1935 Decoder Manual	39	60	78
Radio Orphan Annie 1936 Decoder Manual	39	60	78
Radio Orphan Annie 1937 Decoder Manual	39	60	78
Radio Orphan Annie 1938 Decoder Manual	39	60	78
Radio Orphan Annie 1939 Decoder Manual	39	60	78
Radio Orphan Annie 1940 Decoder Manual	60	90	120
Radio Orphan Annie 1942 Decoder Manual and cardboard decoder	150	225	300
Radio Orphan Annie Decoder Pin, 1935	15	23	30
Radio Orphan Annie Decoder Badge, 1936	15	23	30
Radio Orphan Annie Decoder Badge, 1937	15	23	30
Radio Orphan Annie Decoder Badge, 1938	15	23	30
Radio Orphan Annie Decoder Badge, 1939	15	23	30
Radio Orphan Annie Decoder Badge, 1940	15	23	30
Radio Orphan Annie Foreign Coins, 1937	12	18	24
Radio Orphan Annie Goofy Circus, 1939	27	40	54
Radio Orphan Annie Identification Bracelet, 1934	21	32	42
Radio Orphan Annie Identification Bracelet, 1935	21	32	42
Radio Orphan Annie Identification Tag, 1939	24	36	48
Radio Orphan Annie Magic Transfer Pictures, 1935	21	32	42
Radio Orphan Annie Magic Transfer Picture, 1937	18	27	36
Radio Orphan Annie Mask, 1933	36	54	72
Radio Orphan Annie Mystic Eye Ring, 1939	39	60	78
Radio Orphan Annie Package, 1942, includes Whirl-O-Matic Decoder, Whistle Badge, booklet, and order blanks	125	188	250
Radio Orphan Annie Pin, 1937	12	18	24

	C6	C8	C10
Radio Orphan Annie Portrait Ring, 1934, ring has head of Annie embossed on top	30	45	60
Radio Orphan Annie Premium Manual, 1937	21	31	42
Radio Orphan Annie Premium Manual, 1938	45	68	90
Radio Orphan Annie Punchouts	120	180	240
Radio Orphan Annie Ring, 1934	30	45	60
Radio Orphan Annie Ring, 1935	30	45	60
Radio Orphan Annie Roller Skates, 1938	36	54	72
Radio Orphan Annie Secret Egyptian Compass and Sundial, 1938	27	41	54
Radio Orphan Annie Secret Society Pin, 1934	18	27	36
Radio Orphan Annie Signet Ring, 1937	27	41	54
Radio Orphan Annie Silver Star Pin, 1934	18	27	36
Radio Orphan Annie Silver Star Pin, 1935	18	27	36
Radio Orphan Annie Secret Society Silver Star Ring, 1936	32	48	65
Radio Orphan Annie Silver Star Ring, 1937	32	48	65
Radio Orphan Annie Silver Star Ring, 1938	20	30	40
Radio Orphan Annie School Pin, 1939	12	18	24
Radio Orphan Annie Secret Guard Clicker, 1942	21	31	42
Radio Orphan Annie Shake-Up Game, 1931	12	18	24
Radio Orphan Annie Sun Watch, 1938	17	25	35
Radio Orphan Annie 3-Way Dog Whistle, 1940	21	32	42
Radio Orphan Annie Treasure Hunt Game, 1933	27	41	54
Radio Orphan Annie Treasure Hunt Game, 1935	27	41	54
Range Rider & Dick West button, Peter Pan bread, 1950s	6	9	12
Red Ryder Lucky Coin	4.50	6.75	9
Renfrew of the Mounted pin-back	4.50	6.75	9
Rin Tin Tin "Ball-in-the-hole" Games (sealed coin-size games of Rinty, Rip Masters, Fort Apache, etc.) each	9	13.50	18
Rin Tin Tin Ring, plastic, 1950s	9	13.50	18
Rin Tin Tin set of plastic dinosaurs (Radio-TV 1954)	39	60	78
Rin Tin Tin Wonderscope (Telescope-			

	C6	C8	C10
Microscope-Compass) Radio-TV 1954, has "Rin-Tin-Tin" on face (Same item, without name, recently, perhaps currently, on sale in stores for under $1.00)	27	41	54
Rip Masters (Rin Tin Tin) plastic rings, 1950s	6	9	12
Rocky Lane's Explorer's Sun Watch, 1951, Carnation Milk	15	23	30
Roy Rogers Branding Iron Ring	39	60	78
Roy Rogers Deputy Badge	5	7.50	10
Roy Rogers Microscope Ring, 1947, Quaker Oats	38	57	76
Roy Rogers Paint Set, 1950s	9	13.50	18
Roy Rogers Signal Badge with mirror, secret compartment and whistle	39	60	78
Roy Rogers Silver Hat Ring	18	27	36
Roy Rogers - Trigger's Lucky Horseshoe, full size, black rubber	9	13.50	18
Roy Rogers Tuck-A-Way Gun	7.50	11.25	15
Scoop Ward News of Youth Official Reporter Badge, late 1930s, Ward's Soft Bun Bread giveaway	5	7.50	10
Secret Three Badge, with manual of secret codes	6	9	12
Sgt. Preston Distance Finder	27	40	54
Sgt. Preston Firefighting Set	27	40	54
Sgt. Preston Flashlight - Signals, has two filters	22	33	45
Sgt. Preston Klondike Land Pouch	15	23	30
Sgt. Preston Klondike Movie Film Viewer	47	72	95
Sgt. Preston Pedometer	22	33	45
Sgt. Preston Police Whistle with nylon cord, brass, 1950	21	31	42
Sgt. Preston Skinning Knife	27	40	54
Sgt. Preston Totem Pole Set	50	75	100
Sgt. Preston Trail Kit, rare, (probably the most complex of all premiums)	250	375	500
Sgt. Preston Yukon Village	210	315	420
Shadow Ring, Glow in Dark, "blue coal" jewel on white ring	325	488	650
Shadow "Carey Salt" Ring (same as J. Armstrong Crocodile ring except for black stone; this ring has been counterfeited; original is smoothly circular with clean-cut design	125	188	250
Shield G-Man Club Badge, 1942, Pep Comics premium, lithographed celluloid pinback	25	38	50
Skippy S.S.S.S. Captain, pinback button, all celluloid, 1930s	9	13.50	18

SKY KING Teleblinker Ring. Courtesy Jim Harmon.

	C6	C8	C10
Skippy Compass, 1930s?	7	10	14
Sky Birds Propeller Ring, brass and silver, 1930s, Goudey Gum premium	3	4.50	6
Sky King Aztec Indian Ring	55	83	110
Sky King Detecto Microscope	25	38	50
Sky King Detecto Writer	50	75	100
Sky King Electronic Television Ring	50	75	100
Sky King Magni-Glo Ring	50	75	100
Sky King Mystery Picture Ring (picture never works)	50	75	100
Sky King Navajo Indian Ring	60	90	120
Sky King - Small plastic statues of Sky King, Penny, Sky King's horse, Sky King's plane The Songbird, Nabisco giveaways in Wheat Honey and Rice Honey, 1950s, each	12	18	24
Sky King Signal Scope	50	75	100
Sky King Stamp Kit	32	48	65
Sky King Teleblinker Ring	47	71	95
Snow White Game, Tek Toothbrush	30	45	60
Space Patrol Binoculars, circa 1950s	37	53	75
Space Patrol Diplomatic Pouch, contains money, stamps, etc.	37	53	75
Space Patrol Goggles	25	38	50
Space Patrol 1951 Jet Glow Code Belt	100	150	200
Space Patrol Ring, with secret powder compartment, circa early 1950s	100	150	200
Space Patrol Smoke Gun, 1950s	125	188	250
Space Patrol Space Helmet, circa 1950s	150	225	300
Space Patrol 1952 Space-O-Phone	75	113	150
Space Patrol Space Ship, circa 1950s	75	113	150
Speed Gibson's Flying Police Badge, Dreikorn's Bread	12.50	18.75	25
Straight Arrow Magic Cave Ring, 1949 with original art	87	113	175
Straight Arrow Magic Cave Ring, reissued 1988 with new art and customer's photos (Discontinued)	20	30	40

	C6	C8	C10
Straight Arrow Face Ring, circa early 1950s	37	53	75
Straight Arrow Puppets and props, 1949, Nabisco radio premium	25	38	50
Straight Arrow Target Game, lithographed tin target board, 10"x14" National Biscuit Company copyright on the edge	30	45	60
Straight Arrow Tom-Tom, circa early 1950s	15	23	30
Straight Arrow Wrist Bracelet with secret compartment - circa early 1950s	37	53	75
Sunbrite "Junior Nurse Corps" brass badge	5	7.50	10
Sunbrite "Junior Nurse Corps" pinback button, pictures of Dorothy Hart	4	6	8
Superman Crusader Ring	125	188	250
Superman Kellogg's Gy Rocket	42	63	84
Superman Kellogg's Silver Jet Airplane Ring, plane flies off	37	53	75
Superman Kellogg's Walkie-Talkie	38	53	75
Superman Pin, 1940s, "Read Superman Action Comics Magazine"	22	33	45
Superman Planes from Pep cereal, set of 8, 1948	30	45	60
Superman Premium Club Set - Certificate, Button and Decoder	87	113	175
Superman Tim Club Ring	175	263	350
Superman's Secret Code, circa 1939	24	36	48
Supermen of America button - 1939 version, 1⅜" pinback button	32	48	65
Tarzan Gift Statues, Foulds, 1930s, Tarzan, Jane, Kala, etc. Price per set	475	700	950
Tarzan Jungle Map and Treasure Hunt Weston Biscuit, 1933	60	90	120
Tennessee Jed Lariat	37	53	75
Tennessee Jed Look Around Ring, 1940s	30	45	60
Tennessee Jed Paper Gun, circa 1940s	21	32	42
Terry And The Pirates Glow in the Dark ring, crocodiles on sides	32	48	65
Terry And The Pirates Gold Detector ring	37	53	75
Texas Longhorn tin badge, Post Raisin Bran, circa 1950s	2.50	3.75	5
Tom Corbett Space Cadet Badge, early 1950s	25	38	50
Tom Corbett Space Cadet Belt Buckle Decoder, early 1950s	50	75	100
Tom Corbett Decoder, cardboard, 1950s	25	38	50

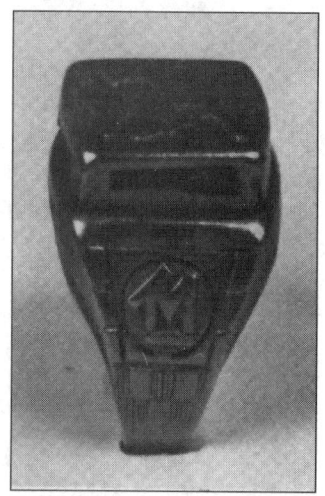

TOM MIX Look-Around Ring. Courtesy Jim Harmon.

TOM MIX Compass-Magnifying Glass, 1937. Courtesy Jim Harmon.

TOM MIX Six Shooter. Courtesy Jim Harmon.

TOM MIX Compass-Magnifying Glass, 1947. Courtesy Jim Harmon.

	C6	C8	C10
Tom Corbett Rings, Kellogg's, 1950-55, 12 different including: Space Cruiser, Rocket Scout, Space Academy, Space Suit, Space Helmet, Corbett-Space Cadet, Cadet Dress Uniform, Girl's Space Uniform, Parallo-Ray Gun, Strate-Telescope, Sound Ray Gun, per each	10	15	20
Tom Mix Airplane and Parachute	75	113	150
Tom Mix Arm Patch (TM bar on checkerboard design) 1933 - predominantly blue: 1947- predominantly red; 1983 - predominantly black (worth probably as much as older versions - only 1000 issued)	22	33	44
Tom Mix Badge - Ranch Box	32	48	65
Tom Mix Bag of Marbles	15	23	30
Tom Mix Bandanna, has TM Brand	45	68	90
Tom Mix Baseball	21	31	42
Tom Mix Baseball bat	21	31	42

	C6	C8	C10
Tom Mix Baseball cap	21	31	42
Tom Mix Belt Buckle with Secret Compartment, belt glows in the dark (offered only on cereal boxes after radio show ended)	75	113	150
Tom Mix Blowdart Game	52	78	105
Tom Mix Branding Iron, TM Brand	36	48	72
Tom Mix Bullet Flashlight	39	60	78
Tom Mix Bullet Telescope, bird-call device comes with it, approx. 4" long	21	31	42
Tom Mix Catalog of Straight Shooter Premiums, 8½"x11" b/w sheet with order form on reverse and descriptions and small pictures of premiums on the front. Includes sheepskin vest, rodeo rope, leather cuffs, wood gun, lucky spinner, etc.	15	23	30
Tom Mix Charm Bracelet with charm-steer head, gun, horseman, TM brand	47	71	95

388

TOM MIX Decoder Badge. Courtesy Jim Harmon.

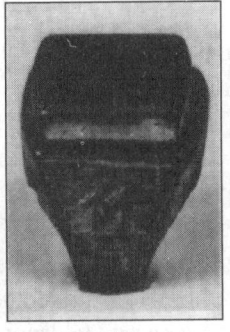

TOM MIX Magnet Ring. Courtesy Jim Harmon.

TOM MIX Brand Ring.

TOM MIX Sharpshooters Medal. Courtesy Jim Harmon.

TOM MIX Sharpshooters Medal. Courtesy Jim Harmon.

TOM MIX Mystery Picture Ring ad. Courtesy Jim Harmon.

TOM MIX Whistle Ring. Courtesy Jim Harmon.

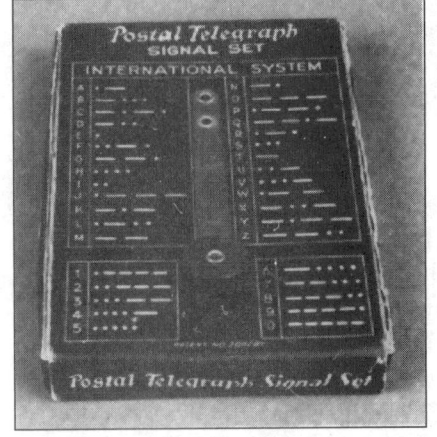

TOM MIX Postal Telegraph Set. Courtesy Jim Harmon.

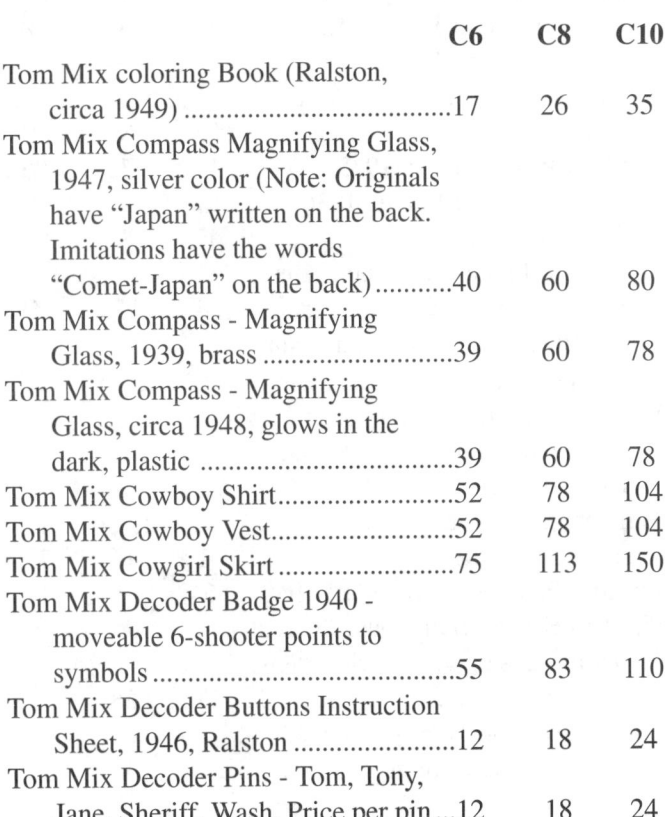

	C6	C8	C10
Tom Mix coloring Book (Ralston, circa 1949) ...17		26	35
Tom Mix Compass Magnifying Glass, 1947, silver color (Note: Originals have "Japan" written on the back. Imitations have the words "Comet-Japan" on the back) ...40		60	80
Tom Mix Compass - Magnifying Glass, 1939, brass ...39		60	78
Tom Mix Compass - Magnifying Glass, circa 1948, glows in the dark, plastic ...39		60	78
Tom Mix Cowboy Shirt ...52		78	104
Tom Mix Cowboy Vest ...52		78	104
Tom Mix Cowgirl Skirt ...75		113	150
Tom Mix Decoder Badge 1940 - moveable 6-shooter points to symbols ...55		83	110
Tom Mix Decoder Buttons Instruction Sheet, 1946, Ralston ...12		18	24
Tom Mix Decoder Pins - Tom, Tony, Jane, Sheriff, Wash. Price per pin ...12		18	24

	C6	C8	C10
Tom Mix Decoder Pin "Curley Bradley" ...18		27	36
Tom Mix Deputy Ring, 1934, chewing gum premium ...62		93	125
Tom Mix Glow-in-the-Dark Arrowhead, 1946, has compass and magnifying glass ...39		60	78
Tom Mix Gold Ore Badge ...21		31	42
Tom Mix Ore Charm, 1940, Ralston, contains genuine gold ore under plastic dome ...21		31	42

	C6	C8	C10
Tom Mix "Good Luck" Spinner	18	27	36
Tom Mix Horseshoe nail ring, 1933 (can be verified only by accompanying papers)	30	45	60
Tom Mix Identification Bracelet	27	41	54
Tom Mix Initial Ring, 1935	50	75	100
Tom Mix Look-Around Ring, circa post 1945	37	53	75
Tom Mix Lucky Wrist Band, 1936, Ralston premium, metal, TM bar brand, with leather strap and buckle	45	68	90
Tom Mix Magnet Gun and Signal Arrowhead bracelet, gun and arrowhead glow in the dark	50	75	100
Tom Mix Magnet Ring, 1945	47	72	95
Tom Mix Makeup kit (two grease-paint model, plus five grease-paint model)	150	225	300
Tom Mix 1941 Manual	36	48	72
Tom Mix 1944 Manual	41	62	82
Tom Mix 1946 Manual	33	49	66
Tom Mix Mask, cardboard	39	60	78
Tom Mix Mystery Picture Ring, 1939, with "look-in" picture of Tom Mix and Tony, viewed through one side of the ring	100	150	200
Tom Mix Parachute - 1936 Ralston premium	45	68	90
Tom Mix Periscope	39	60	78
Tom Mix Postal Telegraph Set - Blue, metal clicker, 1938	39	60	78
Tom Mix Premium Enclosures and Correspondence; Many picture postcards, letters on Straight Shooter stationery, etc. were sent out to listeners who wrote in to the radio show; these and various coupons, instruction sheets, contest entries are offered by dealers and collectors. Average value	18	27	36
Tom Mix Telegraph Set - red, uses batteries, 1940	120	180	240
Tom Mix Ralston Straight Shooters Pocket Knife, 1940	39	60	78
Tom Mix RCA TV set - shows photographs or comic strips (brown model or reddish model)	32	48	65
Tom Mix Secret Code Manual	33	48	66
Tom Mix Sharpshooters Medal, glows in the dark	37	53	75
Tom Mix Sheriff of Dobie County Siren Badge, 1946, Ralston	37	53	75

	C6	C8	C10
Tom Mix Signal Arrowhead, 1949 with magnifying glass and "whizzer" flute-type whistle, made of lucite	39	60	78
Tom Mix Signal Flashlight	39	60	78
Tom Mix Signature Ring, pre WW II	62	95	125
Tom Mix Siren Ring, 1945	48	72	95
Tom Mix Six-Shooter - wooden, barrel breaks and cartridge drum spins - 1933	62	93	125
Tom Mix Six Shooter - wooden, barrel spins, 1936	62	93	125
Tom Mix Six-Shooter - wooden, no moving parts, 1939	55	83	110
Tom Mix Spinning Rope, 1936, Ralston, hemp with wood handle	47	72	95
Tom Mix Spurs - metal, with plastic glow-in-the-dark rowels. Late	45	68	90
Tom Mix "Square and Fair" Spinner	22	33	44
Tom Mix Straight Shooters Campaign Medal, gold	32	48	65
Tom Mix Straight Shooters Campaign Medal, silver	32	48	65
Tom Mix Sundial Watch	45	68	90
Tom Mix Telephone Set	47	72	95
Tom Mix Telescope, TM brand on side	39	53	78
Tom Mix Tiger Eye Ring, 1949, Ralston	87	130	175
Tom Mix TM Brand ring, circa 1933	47	72	95
Tom Mix Tri-Color Flashlight	39	60	78
Tom Mix Western Movie Viewer - shows scenes from Tom Mix films, 1935	55	83	110
Tom Mix Whistle Ring, 1945	47	72	95
Tom Mix Wrangler Badge, 1936, Ralston	47	72	95
Toonerville Trolley cardboard village put out by Coca Cola	84	126	168
Trigger Button, ⅞", Post Grape Nut Flakes	2.50	3.75	5
Welch's Grape Juice Train, paper engine, box car, passenger car, caboose. Price for each	2	3	4
Complete Set above	9	13.50	18
Wheaties Jogometer	11	16	22
Wheaties Pedometer, circa late 1940s	6	9	12
Wild Bill Hickok Bunkhouse Set (cut-out pin-ups of Bill, Jingles, guns, ropes, etc.)	25	38	50
Wild Bill Hickok Treasure Map & Guide, 1952, Kellogg's	21	32	42

COMIC CHARACTER

(See also Movies, Battery-Operated, Premiums, Paper, Mechanical Banks, Vehicles - Tootsietoy)

Average mint price of these toys in the last edition was $336.89 and this year was $671.96, an increase of 99%.

Comic character toys are attractive to collectors as they are often colorful and eye-catching, as well as evocative of happy childhood memories. Popeye continues to be a magnet for collectors, with such as The Yellow Kid, Buck Rogers, Flash Gordon, Tarzan, Superman, Felix the Cat, Barney Google and Happy Hooligan also proving strong lures.

Alphonse, HUBLEY, two goats pulling wagon. Courtesy Kruse Auctioneers.

BARNEY GOOGLE cloth and wood doll, SHOENHUT. Courtesy Sotheby's New York.

B.O. PLENTY holding SPARKLE PLENTY. Photo by Don Hultzman.

	C6	C8	C10
Albert Alligator (Pogo) plastic, 1969, approx. 5" high ("Duz")	6	9	12
Alphonse, Hubley, in a goat-pulled cart, cast iron, 13¾" long, 7½" high, early 1900s, from comic strip team of Alphonse and Gaston, head-nodder, movable arms and hands	200	300	400
Alphonse in horse-drawn carriage, nodder toy, circa 1910, 10½" long	425	638	850
Alphonse, Hubley, mule pulling wagon, 7" long, cast iron nodder	250	375	500
Alphonse, Hubley, two goats pulling wagon, cast iron, 13¾" long, 7½" high, early 1900s, head-nodder, movable arms and hands	150	225	300
Alphonse Nodder Figure	600	900	1200

Alphonse & Gaston animated car, cast iron, auctioned in 1990 for $15,000, $7840 and $12,650.

	C6	C8	C10
Andy Gump Roadster, "348" Arcade, 7" long	2250	3375	4500
Andy Gump wooden dancing doll 9", tin legs	125	188	250
B.O. Plenty holding Sparkle Plenty, circa mid-1940s, tin wind-up, Marx	150	225	300
Baby Snookums (The Newlyweds) fabric doll, 5½" high	150	225	300
Baby Sparkle Plenty paper dolls, Saalfield No. 1510	35	52	70
Barney Google, cloth and wood, Schoenhut	*See Schoenhut*		
Barney Goggle Doll, 9" high, wood with composition head, movable arms and legs	200	300	400
Barney Google glass candy container	150	225	300
Barney Google and Sparkplug pulltoy, tin litho, Sparkplug in barn	1500	2250	3000
Barney Google and Sparkplug Scooter Race, 1920's, Nifty Toy Co., 8" long pull toy	3500	5250	7000
Barney Google riding Sparkplug, wooden	*See Schoenhut*		
Barney Google tin wind-up circa 1923	450	675	900
Barney Google and Sparkplug, tin wind-up by Nifty	1300	1950	2600
Batman Batchute, 1966	15	22	30
Batman Bat Ray, Remco, 1977	30	45	60
Batman "Batmobile-Batman Driver," 1966, Marx	75	112	150
Batman "Batmobile- Robin Driver," Marx, 4" long	75	112	150
Batman Bullhorn, 1966, Bayshore Ind, plastic	21	31	42
Batman candy container, Pez	*See Pez*		
Batman glasses, 1966	4	6	8
Batman Handpuppet, cloth body	20	30	40
Batman Handpuppet, vinyl, Ideal	22	33	44
Batman Helmet and cape, helmet fits over whole head, 1966, Ideal	40	60	80
Batman Picture Pistol, Marx, 1966	137	205	275
Batman Playset, Sears, 1966	500	750	1000

Alphonse, HUBLEY, mule pulling wagon. Courtesy Christie's East.

Alphonse & Gaston animated car, cast iron. Courtesy James S. Maxwell/Virginia Caputo. Photo by Virginia Caputo.

Andy Gump Roadster "348", ARCADE. Courtesy Christie's East.

BLONDIE, "Blondie's Jalopy". Courtesy Christie's East.

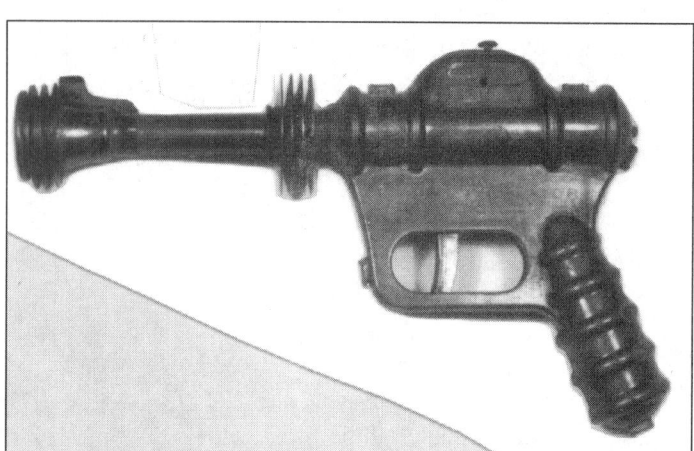

Buck Rogers Disintegrator Pistol. Courtesy James S. Maxwell/Virginia Caputo. Photo by Virginia Caputo.

Bluto (Popeye) Dippy Dumper. Courtesy Christie's East.

	C6	C8	C10
Batman Thingmaker set, 1960s	40	60	80
Batman Utility Belt, 1941, with belt-radio buckle	140	210	280
Batman Utility Belt Set, 1979, Remco	42	63	85
Beauregard (Pogo), plastic, 1969	6	9	12
Beetle Bailey vinyl figure, 3"	6	9	12
Beetle Bailey's Camp Swampy Playset, MPC	87	131	175
Billy Batson (Capt. Marvel) Magic Box	40	60	80
Blondie "Blondie's Jalopy," actually has only Alexander and Dagwood in car, other characters lithoed on chassis, 16" long	1550	2325	3100
Blondie Hingees Set, 1944	20	30	40
Blondie, 1940, Whitman 982, paper cut-outs	30	45	60
Blondie, 1947, Whitman 967, paper cut-outs	30	45	60
Bluto (Popeye) Dippy Dumper Truck, celluloid, tin, 9½"	300	450	600
Bluto on Horse Cart, celluloid and tin windup, 7½"	300	450	600
Bonnie Braids (Dick Tracy), "Bonnie Braids Doll," Marx, 1950s, wind-up, 9" long	150	225	300
Bonnie Braids Paper Dolls - Dick Tracy's daughter and wife Tess, Saalfield No 2724, 1951, cut-outs	25	38	50
Bonnie Braids Walker, Charmore Co., 1951, tin litho walker, nurse-maid pushes Bonnie, plastic	32	48	65
Boob McNutt, 9" high		See Schoenhut	
Boob McNutt tin wind-up, Strauss	500	750	1000
Boots and Her Buddies Paper Dolls, 1943, Saalfield 2460	27	41	55
Bringing Up Father, Hingees, 1944	20	30	40

	C6	C8	C10
Broom Hilda, 14" high, Knickerbocker, circa 1970	38	53	75
Brutus (Popeye) cardboard mask, 1940s	40	60	80
Buck Rogers Atomic Pistol, 1946, U-235, sparks and pops, Daisy	130	195	260
Buck Rogers Battle Cruiser, Toot-sietoy, 1937, two grooved wheels on top to run on string	125	188	250
Buck Rogers binoculars, 1950s	60	90	120
Buck Rogers Casting Set, 1930s, Junior Caster, Rapaport Bros	325	488	650
Buck Rogers Chemical Laboratory, Gropper Toys, 1937	1000	1500	2000
Buck Rogers Disintegrator pistol, 1936, Daisy	60	90	120
Buck Rogers figure, Tootsietoy, 1¾" high	38	56	75
Buck Rogers "Flash Blast" Attack Ship, Tootsietoy, 1937, two grooved wheels on top to run string, 4½" long	125	188	250
Buck Rogers Flying Saucer, 1940s	60	90	120
Buck Rogers Helmet Daisy, 1933, leather	200	300	400
Buck Rogers lead figures - these are generally new, from early casting sets. Sell for $8.00 painted.			
Buck Rogers Liquid Helium water pistol, Daisy, 1936	500	750	1000
Buck Rogers "Pop" pistol, 1930s	125	188	250
Buck Rogers Rocket Pistol, XZ-31, 1934, Daisy, 9½" long	85	128	170
Buck Rogers Rocket Police Patrol, wind-up, Marx, 1939	850	1275	1700
Buck Rogers Rocket Ship, Marx Wind-up, 12" long, 1934	450	675	900

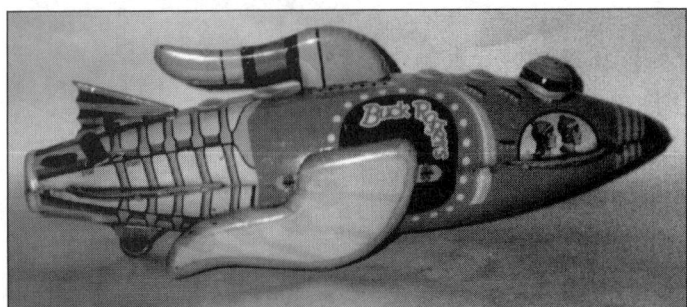

BUCK ROGERS Rocket Police Patrol. Courtesy PB Eighty-Four.

BUCK ROGERS Rocket Ship. Photo by Don Hultzman.

BUCK ROGERS Battlecruiser. Courtesy PB Eighty-Four.

Flash Attack Ship. Courtesy PB Eighty-Four.

Venus Duo Destroyer. Courtesy PB Eighty-Four.

BUCK ROGERS Atomic Pistol. Courtesy HAKE'S Americana & Collectibles.

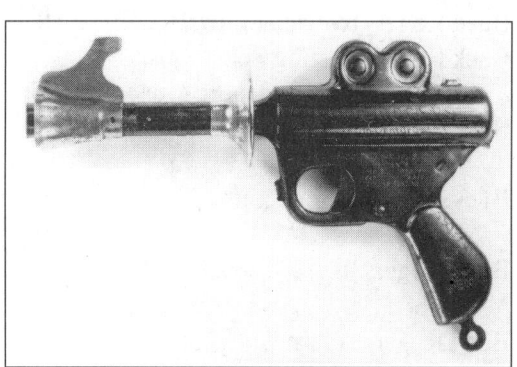

BUCK ROGERS Rocket Pistol. Courtesy HAKE'S Americana & Collectibles.

	C6	C8	C10
"Buck Rogers Rubber Band Gun," 5"x10" punchouts card, 1940	38	53	75
Buck Rogers Sonic Ray Gun, yellow plastic, uses bulb and battery	40	60	80
Buck Rogers Strato Kite, 1946	25	38	50
Buck Rogers Super-Scope, 1953, Norton-Honer Mfg. Co., 8½" long, adjustable plastic telescope	40	60	80
Buck Rogers Super Sonic Glasses (binoculars), 1953	40	60	80
Buck Rogers U-238 Atomic Pistol & Holster set, 1948	150	225	300
Buck Rogers U-238 Atomic Pistol & Holster set, with box, adventure book and coupon, 1948, Daisy	160	240	320
Buck Rogers "USN Los Angeles" Tootsietoy, 5" long dirigible	117	175	235
Buck Rogers Venus Duo Destroyer, Tootsietoy, two grooved wheels on top to run on string, 1937	125	188	250
Buck Rogers Walkie Talkie, 1950s	37	56	75
Buck Rogers "Wilma" pistol and holster set, 1930s, small version of Buck Rogers "Pop" pistol	225	338	450
Buster Brown cast iron, painted	100	150	200
Buster Brown in cart pulled by Tige, 7½" long, cast iron	310	465	620
Buster Brown & Tige paper dolls, J. Ottman Lith. Co., N.Y. Envelope, dolls, Tige, 4 suits, 4 hats, plus hat for Tige	60	90	120
Buster Brown & Tige ring, brass, 1930s	50	75	100

	C6	C8	C10
Buster Brown & Tige tin windup, circa early 1900s, streetlamp, bell	2000	3500	5000
Buster Brown Doll, 23" high, 1920s	110	165	220
Buster Brown figure, lead	6	9	12
Buster Brown, Lehmann tin windup, drives horseless carriage	1100	1650	2200
Buster Brown Rolly Dolly	*See Schoenhut*		
Buster Brown Secret Agent Periscope, circa 1950	30	45	60
Buster Brown Seesaw, Buster and Tige, 9½", German tin windup	1000	1500	2000
Buttercup (Toots & Casper) stuffed cloth doll, 18" high, jointed head, arms, legs, circa 1924	250	375	500
Buttercup, crawls, 4¼", German, cloth and composition	50	75	100
Buttercup & Spareribs, Nifty, Buttercup beats Spareribs with broom, 1920s, 7½" long	1350	2025	2700
Captain America Utility Set, Remco, 1977	10	15	20

Captain Marvel Buzz Bomb. Courtesy Continental Hobby House.

	C6	C8	C10
Captain Marvel Buzz Bomb	10	15	20
Captain Marvel Comic Hero Punch-Outs, 1942, Samuel Lowe, has Captain Marvel (2), Capt. Marvel Jr., Bulletman, Bulletgirl, Spy Smasher, Ibis, Golden Arrow (2), Minute Man, Freddy Freeman, Mr. Scarlet, Commando Yank, Pinky, Bulletdog	210	315	420
Captain Marvel Gun, movie gun with film	175	263	350
Captain Marvel Magic Flute, copyright 1946, picture of Captain Marvel on side	60	90	120

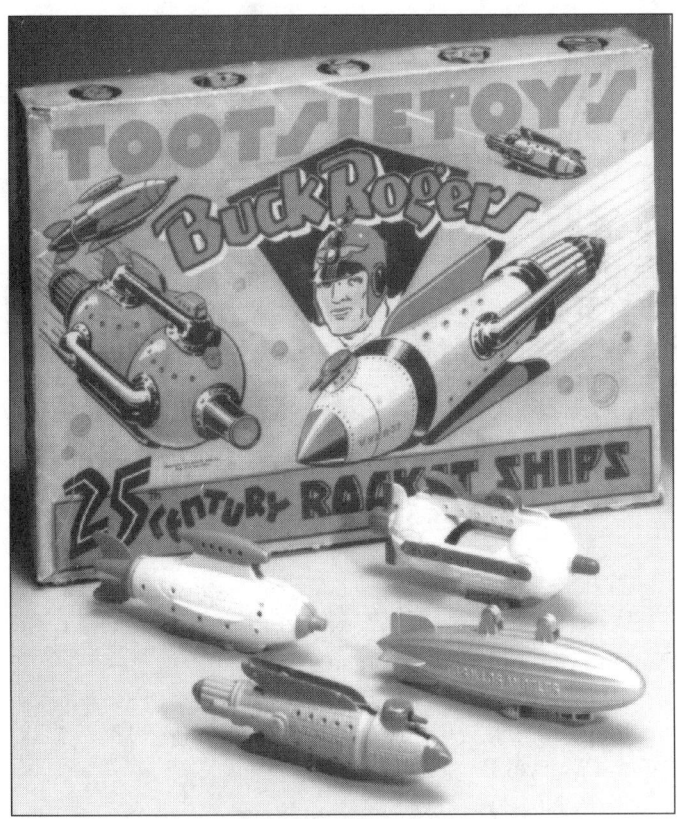

Buck Rogers Rocket Ships with box. Left to Right: Battlecruiser, Venus Duo Destroyer, Flash Attack Ship, "U.S.N. Los Angeles" (the latter listed in Aircraft). Courtesy Christie's East.

Buster Brown & Tige tin wind-up, circa early 1900s, streetlamp, bell. Courtesy Christie's East.

Buttercup & Spareribs, NIFTY. Courtesy Christie's East.

Captain Marvel Comic Hero Punch-Outs. Courtesy Bruce Bergstrom-Artman Originals.

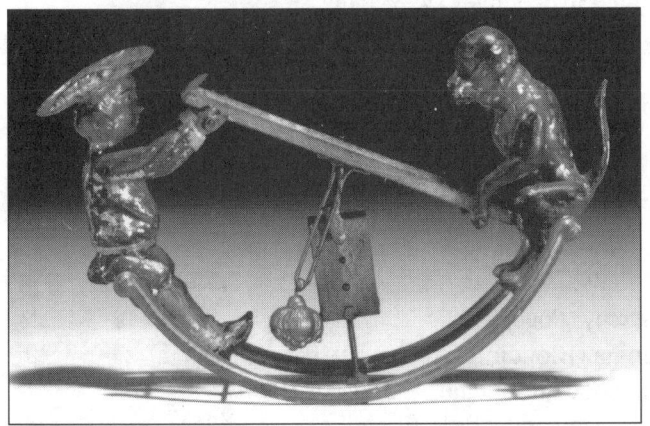

Buster Brown Seesaw, Buster and Tige. Courtesy Christie's East.

Captain Marvel Lightning Racing Cars. Courtesy Christie's East.

CHESTER GUMP Pony Cart. Courtesy PB Eighty-Four, New York.

DAISY MAE WITH LI'L ABNER IN PAPER DOLLS. Photo by Jonathan A. Newman. Courtesy Barbara and Jonathan Newman.

DICK TRACY Squad Car No.1, MARX, 11" long. Courtesy Gary Linden.

DICK TRACY Squad Car No.1, MARX, 6¾" long. Courtesy Gary Linden.

DICK TRACY Riot Car. Photo by Gary Linden.

	C6	C8	C10
Captain Marvel Lightning race car, 1948, Fawcett, tin wind-up, 4" long	75	113	150
Captain Marvel Porsche Car, Corgi, 1979, No. 262	22	33	45
Captain Marvel Toss Bag	27	41	55
Captain Marvel Jr. Ski Jump, 7"x10", circa 1946, paper, Reed & Associates, Chicago	10	15	20
Captain Marvel's Magic Picture, circa 1944, Reed	30	45	60
Captain Marvel's Magic Eyes, circa 1945, Reed	25	38	50
Captain Marvel's Rocket Raider, circa 1944-47, Reed	35	53	70
Charlie Brown composition bouncing head, 1950s, possibly first Peanuts toy	20	30	40
Chester Gump 13" high oilcloth doll, circa 1920s, Livelong Toys	100	150	200
Chester Gump Cart, Arcade, 1920s, horse, open two-wheel cart, Chester driving	338	405	675
Comic Strip Rings, 1953, King Features, Phantom, Blondie, Barney Google, etc.	11	16	22
Comics Paper Doll Cut-out Book, Saalfield, 1935, page each of Popeye, Katzenjammers, Just Kids, Blondie, Dumb Dora, Annie Rooney, Polly and Her Pals	175	263	350
Churchy (Pogo) plastic, 1969, 4½" high	7	11	15
Cookie (Blondie) Syrocco, 1940s	15	23	30
Dagwood Aeroplane, 1935, Marx "Dagwood's Solo Flight"	425	638	850

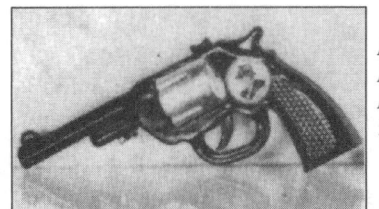

DICK TRACY Click Pistol. Courtesy PB Eighty-Four, New York.

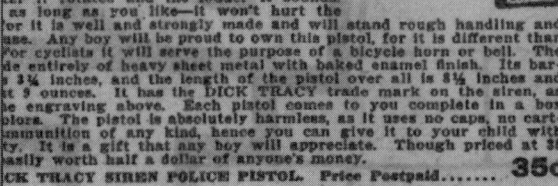

Ad for the Dick Tracy Siren Pistol by Marx, 1930s.

DICK TRACY "Police Station" with 7" long automatic siren car. Courtesy Don Hultzman. Photo by Ron Chojnacki.

	C6	C8	C10
Dagwood "Dagwood the Driver" Crazy Car, 1935, Marx, 8" long.....450	675	900
Dagwood Marionette, 15" wood body, plastic head, hands, feet, "Hazelle's," life-like hair, 1940s.....60	90	120
Daisy Mae Dogpatch Family Doll, Circa 1950s 125	188	250
Daisy Mae and Li'l Abner Paper Dolls with Mammy and Pappy Yokum, Saalfield No. 2360, 1941 45	68	90
Daisy Mae with Li'l Abner in Paper Dolls, Saalfield No. 280, 1942.....45	68	90
Daisy Mae Stringless Marionette, 1940s, National Mask & Puppet Corp 70	105	140
Dan Dunn Det. Corps Secret Operative 28 tin badge, circa 1930s.....30	45	60
Dennis the Menace, 7" high, Hall,1957.....22	33	45
Denny Dimwit (Winnie Winkle) 11" composition doll 225	338	450
Dick Tracy, 13½" high, painted composition, mouth moves 275	413	550
Dick Tracy Air Detective Wings, circa late 1930s.....20	30	40
Dick Tracy and Junior Knife with Crimestopper whistle and clue detector.....40	60	80
Dick Tracy Automatic, Hubley, with picture of Eagles 80	120	160
Dick Tracy Click Pistol, Marx No. 36...60	90	120
"Dick Tracy Copmobile", Ideal, 1963, plastic.....110	165	220

	C6	C8	C10
"Dick Tracy Crime Stoppers Lab" , 1940s, Porter Chem Co., 10"x12" box.....150	225	300
Dick Tracy Crimestoppers Set, badge, handcuffs, billy club 40	60	80
Dick Tracy detective badge with secret compartment, late 1930s, large, metal, leather pouch on back.....38	56	75
Dick Tracy Detective Fingerprint Set, 1933 35	53	70
"Dick Tracy Double Target Game", 1941, 9½" square with 8" tin gun and darts.....100	150	200
Dick Tracy Electronic Wrist Radio 52	78	105
Dick Tracy G-Man wind-up gun.....90	135	180
Dick Tracy Handpuppet, Ideal, 1961 25	38	50
Dick Tracy Hingee, paper figures, 1940s, set of six 25	38	50
Dick Tracy Inspector General badge.....70	105	140
Dick Tracy Pen-Lite, 1940s?.....30	45	60
Dick Tracy "Police Station" with 7" long automatic siren car, 1950s 400	600	800
Dick Tracy Riot Car, circa 1946, Marx, heavy tin or sheetmetal litho, 7½" long, friction motor.....140	210	280
Dick Tracy Siren Pistol, red with blue siren, circa late 1930s.....110	165	220
Dick Tracy Siren Police Whistle No. 64, Marx, tin.....40	60	80
Dick Tracy Soaky 62	93	125
Dick Tracy Space Coupe, 1966, Aurora 375	563	750

	C6	C8	C10
Dick Tracy Sparkling Pop Pistol, tin litho, Marx No. 96	80	120	160
Dick Tracy Squad Car, convertible, heavy tin or sheetmetal, 20" long, Marx, circa 1948, friction motor with siren and battery-powered flashing light, Dick Tracy and Sam Catchum in plastic	175	263	350
Dick Tracy Squad Car No. 1, Marx, 11" long, friction	175	263	350
Dick Tracy Squad Car No. 1, Marx, 6¾" long, friction	60	90	120
Dick Tracy Sub-Machine Gun, 1946, "Raider"	100	150	200
Dick Tracy Target Game, Marx, G25	40	60	80
Dick Tracy Target Game, Marx G34	50	75	100
Dick Tracy Telephone, Marx, 1967	17	26	35
Dick Tracy tin wind-up police car, 1949, 7" long	62	93	125
Dick Tracy viewer, 1940s, two films	60	90	120
Dick Tracy Jr. Click Pistol No. 78, Marx, aluminum	70	105	140
Dick Tracy's Handcuffs for Junior, circa 1946, John Henry Products No. 700	20	30	40
Dick Tracy Water Pistol, plastic, 1955	15	22	30
Dr. Pimm (Little Nemo) Rolly Dolly, 11½" high, Schoenhut	2000	3000	4000
Don Winslow Flashlight Gun	70	105	140
Ella Cinders 17" high cloth and composition, 1925	100	150	200
Elmer Fudd Handpuppet, 1950s	20	30	40

FELIX THE CAT on scooter. Courtesy Phillips New York.

	C6	C8	C10
Elmer Fudd Soaky, 10" high, 1960s	17	26	35
Favorite Funnies large size rubber print set, Dick Tracy, Orphan Annie, etc. 14 stamps, pad, booklet	42	63	85
Felix The Cat, 2" high, cast iron, 1923	60	90	120
Felix The Cat, 2" high, pot metal nodding head figure, copyright Pat Sullivan on bottom of feet	100	150	200
Felix The Cat, 2½" high, lead	60	90	120
Felix The Cat 2½" high, cast iron, with tin umbrella	200	300	400
Felix the Cat, 4" high, wooden	*See Schoenhut*		
Felix the Cat, 6" high, wood	*See Schoenhut*		

Felix the Cat "Speedy Felix" car and Felix the Cat, 2½" high, cast iron, with tin umbrella. Courtesy Christie's East.

Dr. Pimm (little Nemo) Rolly Dolly. Courtesy Christie's East.

Felix the Cat, 13" high, composition. Courtesy Christie's East.

Left to Right: Felix the Cat Walker, German, tin Wind-up, Felix the Cat Pull Toy, Felix chases mice. Courtesy Sotheby's New York.

	C6	C8	C10
Felix the Cat, 6½" rubber squeeze toy 37	56	75	
Felix the Cat, 7 - 9", wood .... *See Schoenhut*			
Felix The Cat, 9" high, 1940s, wood, jointed with rubber head 100	150	200	
Felix The Cat 12" high, wood 300	450	600	
Felix The Cat, 13" high, composition, circa 1930s 275	413	550	
Felix The Cat Doll, 15" high, stuffed, Gund, hands molded rubber, the rest cloth, circa 1950 80	120	160	
Felix The Cat, China Set 60	90	120	
Felix The Cat on fire truck, gong bell pull toy 110	165	220	
Felix The Cat on pole, Schoenhut, 9" high, wood 287	432	575	
Felix The Cat on scooter, Nifty 850	1275	1700	
Felix The Cat on tricycle, gong bell pull toy 220	330	440	
Felix The Cat Pull Car, 12" long, Borgfeldt, 1925 300	450	600	
Felix the Cat Pull Toy, Felix chases mice 400	600	800	
Felix The Cat "Speedy Felix" in car 425	638	850	
Felix The Cat Walker, German tin windup 250	375	500	
Flash Gordon aluminum pistol, 10" long, shoots blast of air using rubber diaphragm 120	180	240	
Flash Gordon Arresting Ray, Marx, 1936?, picture of Flash on handle .140	210	280	
Flash Gordon Automatic Disintegrator, Hubley 200	300	400	
Flash Gordon belt, many illos, large plastic buckle showing rocket ship in flight, 1950s 22	33	44	
Flash Gordon Click Ray Pistol, 1950s, 10" long, Marx 200	300	400	
Flash Gordon jet-propelled kite 35	52	70	
Flash Gordon playset, Tootsietoy, No. 1793, diecast, 1978 21	31	42	
Flash Gordon Playsuit, Equire Novelty, 1952 55	83	110	
Flash Gordon Radio Repeater clicker pistol, No. 58, Marx, 1950s, 10" long 450	675	900	
Flash Gordon Rocket Fighter, Marx wind-up, 12" long, 1939 240	360	480	
Flash Gordon Signal Pistol, tin litho, Marx No. 74 100	150	200	
Flash Gordon Solar commando; three plastic space men and one ship, 1950s 60	90	120	
Flash Gordon Space Cruiser, 1952 40	60	80	

FLASH GORDON Signal Pistol. Courtesy PB Eighty-Four, New York.

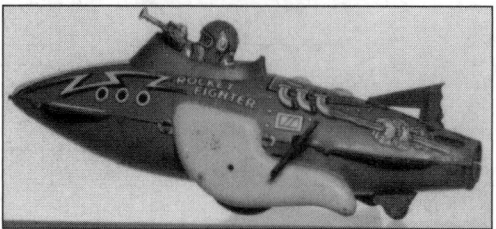

FLASH GORDON Rocket Fighter. Courtesy PB Eighty-Four, New York.

	C6	C8	C10
Flash Gordon Space Outfit, Esquire Novelty 55	83	110	
Flash Gordon Space Target, metal, standup, Alex Raymond illustration, 12x14 80	120	160	
Flash Gordon Sparkling Battle Rocket, 1969 30	45	60	
Flash Gordon Strat-O-Wagon, 9" long, Wyandotte 120	180	240	
Flash Gordon Two way telephone, Marx, circa 1940 100	150	200	
Flash Gordon water gun, plastic, 1950s 20	30	40	
Flip (Little Nemo) Bell Toy, 6½" long, cast iron 400	600	800	

Flip (little Nemo) Bell Toy. Courtesy Christie's East.

	C6	C8	C10
Flying Captain Marvel, 1944-47, Reed, 7"x10", paper 11	16	22	
Foxy Grandpa, 17" high, cloth and composition 450	675	900	
Foxy Grandpa Bell Toy, vehicle pulled by two boys, cast iron, 7" long 425	638	850	
Foxy Grandpa clockwork figure, tin, German, 8¼" high 300	450	600	

Foxy Grandpa Roly-Dolly. Courtesy Lloyd W. Ralston Auctions.

Foxy Grandpa Jack in the Box. Courtesy PB 84 New York.

Happy Hooligan Roly-Poly. Courtesy Lloyd W. Ralston Auctions.

Happy Hooligan on a ladder. Courtesy PB Eighty-Four, New York.

Happy Hooligan, 9½" high, bisque face, dressed as clown. Courtesy Christie's East.

Happy Hooligan in cart, horse pulled.

Foxy Grandpa clockwork figure. Courtesy PB 84 New York.

Happy Hooligan in Car, Hill Brass. Courtesy Christie's East.

Gloomy Gus in horse cart, Harris. Courtesy Christie's East.

Happy Hooligan Police Patrol. Courtesy James S. Maxwell/Virginia Caputo. Photo by Virginia Caputo.

*Left to **Right**: Foxy Grandpa nodder, Harris, Foxy Grandpa **Bell** Toy. Courtesy Christie's East.*

Happy Hooligan in horse-drawn wagon with Gloomy Gus, Driver. Courtesy Christie's East.

400

	C6	C8	C10
Foxy Grandpa Jack in the Box, papier mache and paper litho on wood, 1900, 4" square	160	240	320
Foxy Grandpa Nodder, papier mache, 1900 6" tall	120	180	240
Foxy Grandpa nodder, Hubley, circa 1910, cast iron, 6½", Grandpa large-headed in cart pulled by donkey	400	600	800
Foxy Grandpa nodder, Harris, cast iron, in donkey cart, 7¼" long	200	300	400
Foxy Grandpa Roly Dolly	*See Schoenhut*		
"Gasoline Alley Garage and Auto Racer," 1924, Girard, tin litho garage and "Bearcat Racer" car	300	450	600
"Gloomy Gus," (Happy Hooligan's brother), 1903, Harris Toy Co., cast iron, 5" tall	300	450	600
Gloomy Gus in goat cart, cast iron, 14" long	400	600	800
Gloomy Gus in horse cart, Harris, cast iron, 14" long	1600	2400	3200
Gloomy Gus in mule cart, Harris, cast iron	550	825	1100
Green Hornet Aurora Slot Car	125	188	250
Gremlin (Gloom) T.E. Powers, in leather clothes, 1943	20	30	40
Happy Hooligan, 9½" high, bisque face, dressed as clown	550	825	1100
Happy Hooligan Donkey Cart, circa 1925, (possibly Wilkins), 10" long	240	360	480
Happy Hooligan Hand Puppet, cast iron and cloth, 9¼"	35	52	70
Happy Hooligan in car, 5¾", circa 1903, Hill Brass, cast iron	1250	1875	2500
Happy Hooligan in cart, Kenton, early 1900s, 10¼" long, 7½" high, horse-pulled, head nods, cast iron	750	1125	1500
Happy Hooligan in cart, windup, 1930s, European	1000	1500	2000
"Happy Hooligan In Donkey Cart", 1930s, Ingap Co., 7" long	400	600	800
Happy Hooligan in Goat Cart, 7½" long, cast iron	200	300	400
Happy Hooligan in Horse Cart, Wilkins, cast iron, 17" long	1250	1875	2500
Happy Hooligan in horse-drawn wagon, with Gloomy Gus, driver, Harris, c. 1905, cast iron	1750	2650	3500
"Happy Hooligan Jigger," 1920s, Kiddee Metal Toys, 10" tall, Crank action	800	1200	1600

	C6	C8	C10
Happy Hooligan Jigger, Kiddies' Metal Toys Co., tin litho, dressed as clown, tap dances on drum, windup, 9"	650	975	1300
Happy Hooligan on a Ladder	200	300	400
Happy Hooligan on Rabbit, Candy Container, composition, 7½"	900	1350	1800
Happy Hooligan Police Patrol, Kenton, 18" long, Happy hit by cop as Gloomy Gus drives	2425	3638	4850
Happy Hooligan Roly Poly	50	75	100
Happy Hooligan walking toy, Chein wind-up, 1932, 6" high	300	450	600
Happy Hooligan, wooden	*See Schoenhut*		
Heckle, squeeze toy, 1950s	27	41	55
Henry, 9½" high rubber squeeze toy, 1950s	20	30	40
Henry and his Brother, celluloid wind-ups, Japanese, on wheels	900	1350	1800
Henry celluloid and tin wind-up, Japanese, Henry sits on elephant's trunk	1050	1575	2100
Henry "Henry and his Swan," celluloid mechanical	2150	3225	4300
Henry "Henry Eating Candy," 1950s, Linemar	300	450	600

Left to Right: Henry and his Brother, Henry's Mahout on Donkey, Henry on Trapeze. Courtesy Christie's East.

Henry celluloid and tin wind-up, Japanese, Henry sits on elephant's trunk. Courtesy Christie's East.

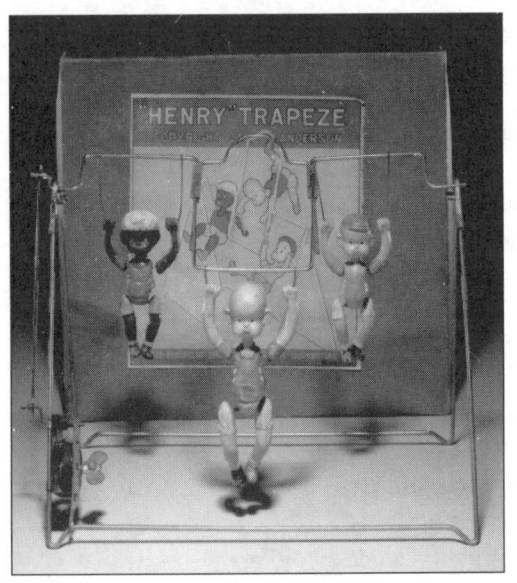

Henry Trapeze. Courtesy Christie's East.

HI-WAY HENRY. Courtesy Phillips New York.

Jeep (Popeye) wood-jointed. Courtesy Christie's East.

"Jiggs Jazz Car", NIFTY. Courtesy Christie's East.

HUMPHREYMOBILE. Courtesy Mapes Auctioneers & Appraisers.

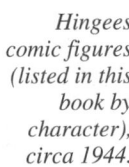

Hingees comic figures (listed in this book by character), circa 1944.

LI'L ABNER AND HIS DOGPATCH BAND, UNIQUE. Courtesy Phillips New York.

Jaymar wood-jointed toys, 5" high and shorter, Left to Right: Popeye, Olive Oyl, Wimpy, Moon Mullins, Kayo, Little Orphan Annie, Sandy. Photo by Blossom Abell.

	C6	C8	C10
Henry On Trapeze, just Henry, celluloid windup	375	500	750
Henry Trapeze, Japan, windup, part celluloid, Henry, brother and mahout	1000	1500	2000
Henry's Mahout on donkey	350	525	715
Herby, 10" oilcloth doll	20	30	40
Herman (Harvey Comics Character) "Herman Nodder," 1950s, Linemar, 4½" high - Rare	300	450	600
Hi-Way Henry, wind-up, 1920s, jalopy with man, woman, laundry above roof	3750	5625	7500
Hoppy the Flying Marvel Bunny, circa 1944-47, Reed, paper	6	9	12
Howland Owl (Pogo), 1969, plastic, 4½" high ("Duz")	6	9	12
Humphrey, 14½" high, Ideal, cloth and composition	175	263	350
Humphrey Mobile (Joe Palooka) tin wind-up, circa mid-1940s, Wyandotte, 7½" high with smokestack	350	525	700
Jane Arden, 1942, Saalfield 2408, paper dolls	30	45	60
Jean (Gasoline Alley), Livelong toys	25	38	50
Jeep (Popeye) wood-jointed, 1930s, 7¼"	400	600	800
Jeff 6" composition doll, ball joints, felt clothes	162	243	325
Jeff bendable figure, 1946	120	180	240
Jeff Stick Puppet, 12" high	40	60	80
Jiggs 3" high, hard plastic, 1960s	6	9	12
Jiggs 5" wood-jointed doll, Jaymar?	80	120	160
Jiggs 7" high, wood-jointed doll, Schoenhut	*See Schoenhut*		
"Jiggs Jazz Car," Nifty, 1920s windup, 6½" long	1100	3000	5500
Jiggs Stick Puppet, 12" high	80	120	160
Joan Palooka doll	80	120	160
Joe Palooka, 4" high, wood-jointed	35	52	70
Joe Palooka 5½" high wood-jointed doll	50	75	100
Joe Palooka Championship belt buckle, circa early 50s, heavy gold-plated brass buckle shows Palooka with hands raised in victory	40	60	80
Joe Palooka Filmatic, 12 different comic strips	50	75	100
Joe Palooka Punching Bag, circa 1950	30	60	90
Katzenjammer Kids, Hingees, 1945	16	24	32
Katzenjammer Kids, Mama spanking Kid, other Kid standing, as Sailor drives mule cart, Kenton, 1911, 12" long	1050	1575	3100

KATZENJAMMER KIDS. Mama Spanking Kid, KENTON, 1911. Courtesy Ed Hyers Antique Toys.

KRAZY KAT platform toy, NIFTY, used Felix the Cat's head as a cost-cutting measure. It also made the Felix version. Courtesy Phillips New York.

	C6	C8	C10
Katzenjammer Kids See-Saw Bell Toy, Kenton	900	1350	1800
Kayo (Moon Mullins), 5" high, Jaymar, wood jointed	50	75	100
Kayo, 9¾" oilcloth doll	60	90	120
Kayo 10" high Sun Rubber circa 1937, head swivels	200	300	400
Komic Kamera - All metal viewer circa mid-1930s, used to view 35mm film strips. With set of five film strips	80	120	160
Komic Kamera, without film strips	26	34	48
Krazy Kat Platform Toy, tin wind-up, Nifty, 1920s, 7½" long	300	450	600
Li'l Abner Dogpatch Family doll, circa 1950s	125	188	250
Li'l Abner Handpuppet, Baby Barry	35	52	70
Li'l Abner and His Dogpatch Band, 1945, Unique, wind-up	350	525	700
Li'l Abner stringless marionette, 1940s, National Mask & Puppet Corp	70	105	140

LITTLE LULU doll. Courtesy Toy Collector News.

LITTLE MARY MIXUP AND HER FRIEND PEGGY. Photo by Jonathan Newman. Courtesy Barbara and Jonathan Newman.

LITTLE ORPHAN ANNIE STOVE, 4⅜" high. Courtesy James S. Maxwell/Virginia Caputo. Photo by Virginia Caputo.

Little Orphan Annie skipping rope. Courtesy Christie's East.

Little Lulu, 14" high, Georgene Novelties. Courtesy Christie's East.

Comic strip toys of the 1920s from LIVE LONG TOYS, of 221 W. Madison Street, Chicago, Ill.. The owners seem to have been William A. Benoliel and Eileen Benoliel. The stuffed oilcloth dolls shown here are from "Gasoline Alley". From left, Baby Skeezix, Uncle Walt, Pal, Rachel the Maid, Jean the Playmate, Auntie (Phyllis) Blossom, Skeezix as a boy. Photo by Blossom Abell.

404

	C6	C8	C10
Little Beaver Archery Set, 1951............30	45	60
Little King Walker, plastic, circa 1956..40	60	80
Little King, wooden pull toy, Jay-Mar, 1938, 4" high..............80	120	160
Little Lulu 10" high felt doll 100	150	200
Little Lulu 14" high, Georgene Novelties, stuffed doll....................250	375	500
Little Lulu, 14" high, doll with mask face, 1944, M.H. Buell....................55	83	110
Little Lulu "Shape Book," 1971, Whitman No. 1970..........................10	15	20
"Little Max Speshul," (Joe Palooka), SALS metal tin windup.................3500	5250	7000
Little Mary Mixup And Her Friend Peggy, 1922, Saalfield No. 294, paper dolls.....................40	60	80
Little Nemo and Mr. Flip bell toy.........950	1425	1900
Little Orphan Annie, 5" high, Jaymar, wood jointed 50	75	100
Little Orphan Annie 9½" printed fabric doll, 1930s 60	90	120
Little Orphan Annie 16¼" oilcloth doll, circa 1920s............................150	225	300
Little Orphan Annie Hingees, 1944, Annie, Sandy, Daddy, Punjab, price per set....................60	90	120
Little Orphan Annie Skipping Rope, tin wind-up, 1930s, Marx, 5" high....338	507	675
Little Orphan Annie and Sandy, tin wind-up, Marx, 1930s, 2 pc. set, 4½" long 420	630	840
Little Orphan Annie Soaky....................14	21	28
Little Orphan Annie stove, 8" high, circa 1930s 125	188	250
Little Orphan Annie stove, 4⅜" high ...100	150	200
Little Orphan Annie Water Pistol..........70	105	140
Little Orphan Annie Junior Commandos, 1943, Saalfield No. 299..........30	45	60
Lonesome Polecat (Li'l Abner), 1950s, rubber squeak toy, Reinert 50	75	100
Lucy 7¾" high squeeze toy, 1950s........12	18	24
Lucy 8¾" high, vinyl squeeze toy, 1950s............................15	22	30
Maggie 3" hard plastic, 1960s 6	9	12
Maggie 9" high wood jointed doll.......... *See Schoenhut*		
Maggie & Jiggs, 1920s, Nifty, seated on 4-wheeled platform, 8" long 1500	2250	3000
Maggie & Jiggs tin litho squeeze toy, circa 1925, German, 8" 275	410	550
Maggie & Jiggs wind-up, Strauss, 1924, 7¼" long, German...............800	1200	1600
Mammy Yokum, Dogpatch Family doll, circa 1950s............................125	188	250

Maggie & Jiggs tin litho squeeze toy. Courtesy Christie's East.

MAGGIE & JIGGS, 1920s, NIFTY. Courtesy PB Eighty-Four, New York.

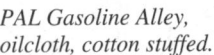

MOON MULLINS and KAYO on Hand Car. Courtesy Phillips New York.

PAL Gasoline Alley, oilcloth, cotton stuffed.

Popeye "Boom Boom Popeye". Courtesy Mapes Auctioneers & Appraisers.

405

	C6	C8	C10
Mandrake the Magician Magic Kit, 1949, Transogram 125	188	250
Mighty Mouse, rubber, 9" high, no mfr. listed 27	41	55
Mighty Mouse, 15" high, vinyl 300	450	600
Mighty Mouse Soaky 15	22	30
Moon Maid's Daughter (Dick Tracy) 16½" doll with space helmet, Ideal, 1965 90	135	180
Moon Mullins, 5" high, Jaymar, wood jointed 55	83	110
Moon Mullins and Kayo on Hand Car, 1930s, 6" long, Marx tin wind-up 375	563	750
Moon Mullins and Mamie Face Masks, 1933, each...........................20	30	40
Movie Komics, reels of film for toy viewers, circa 1940s........................14	21	28
Mrs. Blossom (Gasoline Alley) 17" high oilcloth, Livelong Toys 120	180	240
Mutt 8" high composition doll with ball joints, felt clothes....................160	240	320
Mutt bendable figure, 1946 140	210	280
Mutt Wooden Dancing Doll 40	60	80
Nancy 14" high stuffed doll, Georgene Novelties 90	135	180
Olive Oyl 11" Gund marionette 35	52	70
Olive Oyl "Ballet Dancer", Linemar tin mechanical 175	282	350
Olive Oyl Handpuppet, circa 1938, Gund..60	90	120
Olive Oyl Hingees No. 102, paper punchouts, Reed & Associates........12	18	24
Olive Oyl Mask, cardboard, 1940s........20	30	40
Olive Oyl Riding Tricycle, 4", Linemar...1400	2100	2800
Olive Oyl Rubber Squeeze Toy, 1950s..90	135	180
Olive Oyl approx. 5" high, Jaymar circa 1940s, jointed wood figure..100	150	200
Olive Oyl and Sweepea Hand Car, Marx, 1930s 240	360	480
Pal (Gasoline Alley) oilcloth doll, cotton-stuffed, 1923, Livelong Toys..90	135	180
Pappy Yokum Doll, Dogpatch Family Doll circa 1950s...........................125	188	250
Pappy Yokum Handpuppet....................20	30	40
Peanuts figures: Charlie Brown, Lucy, Linus, Schroeder, Snoopy, Avon, price per each 10	15	20
Pete (the Tramp?) 1930s composition doll, strung 130	195	260

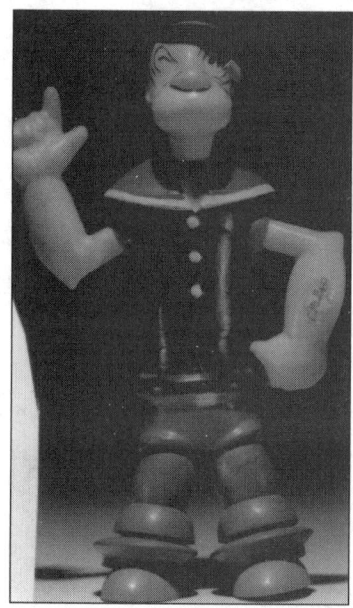
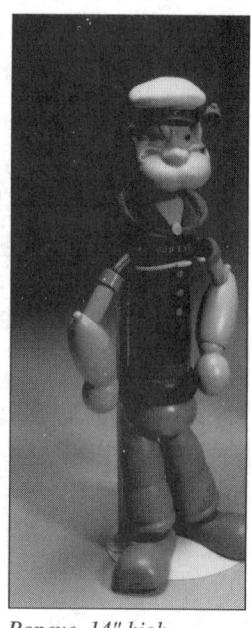

Popeye, 10½" high, wood-jointed, circa 1932. Courtesy Christie's East.

Popeye, 14" high, composition. Courtesy Christie's East.

Let to Right: Popeye & Olive Oyl jiggers, Popeye Express - MARX, overhead airplane.

POPEYE Spinach Patrol. Photo by C.B.C. Lee.

Popeye in a Barrel, celluloid wind-up walker. Courtesy Christie's East.

Popeye the Pilot. Courtesy Sotheby's New york.

406

POPEYE in a Barrel, CHEIN. Photo by Don Hultzman.

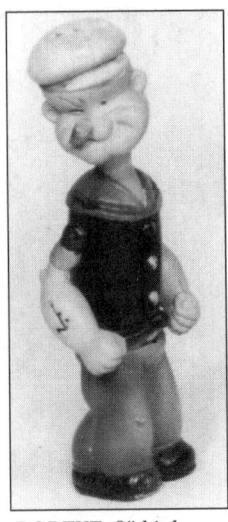

POPEYE, 8" high, celluloid, key-wind, head spins, foreign. Courtesy Phillips New York.

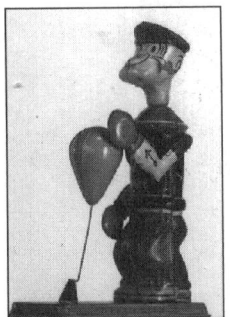

POPEYE Puncher. Courtesy Sotheby Parke Bernet.

Popeye Dippy Dumper. Courtesy Christie's East.

POPEYE "POPEYE PATROL", HUBLEY, 8½" long. Courtesy Phillips New York.

POPEYE the Pilot. Photo by Don Hultzman.

	C6	C8	C10
Pogo plastic, 1969, 4" high	6	9	12
Pogo Pogomobile	200	300	400
Popeye 3½" high, cast iron, circa 1930	100	150	200
Popeye 4" high, solid celluloid, 1930s	170	225	340
Popeye, 5" high, Jaymar, wood, jointed	75	112	150
Popeye, 6½" high, Chein tin windup walker	375	563	750
Popeye 7" high, hollow rubber, dated "1935" on back	100	150	200
Popeye, 8" high, wood body, jointed, composition head	325	488	650
Popeye, 8" high, celluloid, keywind, head spins, foreign, 1930s, Japan	300	450	600
Popeye, 9" high, celluloid wind-up, neck goes up and down, circa 1930	450	675	900
Popeye, 10¼" high, wood-jointed, circa 1932	70	105	140
Popeye, 11" high, wood jointed, circa 1935	300	450	600
Popeye 11" high, Chein, circa 1935	400	600	800
Popeye 14" high, "Cameo" hard rubber, jointed at neck, hips, shoulders	120	180	240
Popeye 14" high, composition, "Popeye 1935 King Features Syn"	410	615	820
Popeye 14" high, wood and composition, jointed arms and legs, "1935"	200	300	400
Popeye 15" high, composition, rolling up sleeve	100	150	200
Popeye, 17" high, Knickerbocker, stuffed cloth, 1930s	187	230	375
Popeye 20" high, rubber arms and head, stuffed body, Gund, circa 1950s	70	105	140
Popeye Acrobat, Marx, tin wind-up	2700	4050	5400
"Popeye and Mean Man" - Mechanical Fighters, 1950s, Linemar Co., 6" long - RARE	6000	9000	12000
"Popeye Basketball Player," Linemar tin wind-up	550	825	1100
Popeye "Bifbat" paddle toy, 1929	60	90	120
Popeye "Bo Lo Paddle," 1929	20	30	40
Popeye "Boom Boom Popeye," Fisher Price, drummer, 491	*see Fisher-Price*		
Popeye carrying parrots in cages, Marx wind-up, 1935, 7¾" high	275	413	550
Popeye "Dippy Dumper" truck, Marx	450	675	900

POPEYE Basketball Player box. Courtesy Phillips New York.

POPEYE on a Unicycle, LINEMAR. Courtesy Phillips New York.

Popeye Turnover Tank, LINEMAR. Photo by Don Hultzman.

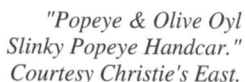

"Popeye & Olive Oyl Slinky Popeye Handcar." Courtesy Christie's East.

POPEYE Rollerskating. Courtesy PB Eighty-Four, New York.

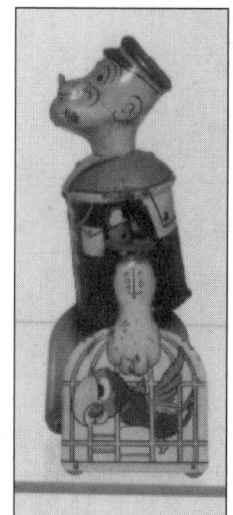

POPEYE carrying parrots in cages. Courtesy PB Eighty-Four, New York.

"Popeye The Champ", MARX. Courtesy Phillips New York.

"POPEYE EXPRESS". Photo Courtesy PB Eighty-Four.

Popeye in a Rowboat, 1935, HOGE. Courtesy Christie's East.

Popeye & Olive Oyl, Ball Toss. Courtesy Christie's East.

	C6	C8	C10
Popeye "Eccentric Plane," 1940, Marx wind-up, 8" long	450	675	900
Popeye Express - Marx, overhead airplane, 1935, flies over train	750	1125	1500
Popeye Express - Marx, Popeye pushing box with parrot, wind-up, 1935	400	600	800
Popeye Handcar, Marx, 1935, Popeye & Olive Oyl, composition, 6" long	700	1050	1400
Popeye Handpuppet	14	21	28
"Popeye Heavy Hitter," Chein, tin wind-up, 11½"	3000	4500	6000
Popeye Hingee paper figures, No. 102, Reed, 1940s, price per each	20	30	40
Popeye in a Barrel, celluloid windup walker, 5½" high, Japan	750	1125	1500
Popeye in a Barrel, Chein, 7" high	425	638	850
Popeye in a Horsecart, Marx, celluloid and tin, circa 1935, 7½"	1750	2625	3500
Popeye Jack-in-the-Box, Mattel Co., tin mechanical, Popeye pops out of spinach can	45	68	90
"Popeye Lantern Toy," 1950's, Linemar, 7½" high	250	375	500
Popeye "Popeye Jigger" (on rooftop), Marx wind-up, 9½" high	412	618	825
Popeye mask, cardboard, 1940s	30	45	60
Popeye Moving Van, tin friction, Linemar	300	450	600
Popeye One-Man Band, pole with drum and cymbals, rubber Popeye head on top, 69" high, 1950s	100	150	200
Popeye Pirate, click pistol, Marx No. 68	175	263	350
Popeye the Pilot, 1930, Marx wind-up early version, 8" long	500	750	1000
Popeye the Pilot, later version, 8" long	400	600	800
Popeye "Popeye & Olive Oyl Slinky Handcar" 1950s pulltoy, Linemar	550	825	1100
Popeye on a Tricycle, Linemar, metal and celluloid	700	1050	1400
Popeye "Popeye On A Unicycle," Linemar, 1950s, windup	600	900	1200
Popeye "Popeye Patrol," Hubley, 8½" long	2250	3375	4500
Popeye Puncher, Chein, 1930, tin and celluloid, floor bag	750	1125	1500
Popeye Puncher, Chein, overhead bag	2150	3225	4300
Popeye Pushing wheelbarrow, plastic walker, Marx, circa 1950s	40	60	80
Popeye Rollerskating, Linemar	1100	1650	2200
Popeye Roly-Poly, 3½" celluloid, Japan	100	150	200
Popeye in a Rowboat, 1935, Hoge	2850	4275	5700
Popeye rubber squeeze toy, 1950s	20	30	40
Popeye Sand Toy teeter-totter with Popeye, Sweepea, Olive Oyl, Jeep, tin litho	200	300	400
"Popeye Shadow Boxer," 1930s, Chein, 7" tall	700	1050	1400
Popeye "Smoking Popeye", battery-operated, Linemar, 8½" high	1500	2250	3000
Popeye "Sparkling Popeye," 1959, Chein Co., 5" long	500	750	1000
Popeye on Sparkplug, 1930s	*See Fisher-Price*		
Popeye "Popeye Spinning Olive Oyl in a Chair," 1950s, Linemar, 9" high	500	750	1000
Popeye "Spinach Patrol" Hubley	300	450	600
Popeye Squeeze Toy, Linemar	400	600	800
Popeye Strength Tester, Holgate, 14"	62	93	125
"Popeye" The Champ, Marx	1250	1875	2500
Popeye "Tumbling Popeye," Linemar, 5" high wind-up	450	675	900
Popeye Turnover Tank, Linemar tin wind-up, 1950s, 6" long	300	450	600
Popeye Walker, plastic, pushing cart	20	30	40
Popeye Whistle Pipe, Northwest Products of St. Louis, 3½" long, cardboard bowl with illos of Popeye characters, metal stem with whistle at base	70	105	140
"Popeye Xylophone Player," 1957, American Preschool Co., 9" long	350	375	500
Popeye Yazoo Pipe, Northwestern Productions, St. Louis, Mo, 1934	80	120	160
Popeye & Olive Oyl Ball Toss, circa 1950, 19" long, Linemar, tin wind-up	325	438	650
Popeye & Olive Oyl Jiggers (Popeye dancing on roof, Olive Oyl playing concertina), Marx	600	900	1200
Popeye & Olive Oyl Sand Toy, tin litho, T. Cohn, 8¼" high	325	488	650
Porky (Pogo) plastic, 1969	6	9	12
Porky Pig cowboy with lariat, Marx tin wind-up, 1949, 9" high	310	465	620
Porky Pig squeeze toy, Sun Rubber, approx. 6" high, hollow with squeaker, has hands behind back, circa 1940	40	60	80
Porky Pig hand puppet, 1950s, 8" high	15	22	30

Porky Pig, tin wind-up, with original box. Courtesy Wilkinson Collection, Detroit Antique Toy Museum.

	C6	C8	C10
Porky Pig Soaky, 9" high, 1960s	12	18	25
Porky Pig tin litho wind-up, 1939, 8½" high, holding umbrella, Marx	235	352	470
Porky Pig tin litho wind-up, holds umbrella, raises hat, Marx, 1939, 8"	225	338	450
Prince Valiant Castle Fort, Marx, boxed set with knights, etc.	250	375	500
Prince Valiant Shield, tin litho	30	45	60
Prince Valiant Sword and tin Scabbard, 1950s, Mattel	50	75	100
Rachel (Gasoline Alley) oilcloth doll, cotton-stuffed, 1923, Live long Toys	120	180	240
Red Ryder BB Gun No. 111, Daisy	60	90	120
"Red Ryder Cork Carbine," Daisy, plastic stock	30	45	60
Red Ryder gun and holster set, Daisy	12	18	25
Red Ryder Pop-Um shooting game, Daisy	50	75	100
Red Ryder Molding Set, 1948	40	60	80
Red Ryder Target Game, 1939	55	83	110
Roosevelt Bear on Bicycle, tin litho, 9" long, circa 1920	225	338	450
Rudy the Ostrich (Barney Google), 1924, tin, Nifty	475	713	950
Sad Sack 15½" vinyl doll, 1950	140	210	280
Sad Sack 20" high vinyl doll, cloth uniform, Sterling Doll Co., circa 1952	70	105	140
Sandy, 5" long, Jaymar, wood jointed	50	75	100
Sandy 10½" long oilcloth doll, circa 1920s, Live Long Toys	140	210	280
Sandy (Orphan Annie's dog) with suitcase in mouth, tin wind-up	350	525	700

	C6	C8	C10
Sandy (Orphan Annie) "Sandy Dog with Magic Tail," 1930s, Marx, 7" long	125	187	250
Sandy (Orphan Annie) "Sandy's Dog House" with wheeled Sandy, Marx	260	390	520
Schroeder (Peanuts) rubber squeeze toy, circa 1960	10	15	20
Secret Agent X-9 Gun and Billy Club	12	18	24
Shmoo (Li'l Abner) doll, vinyl inflatable, 15" high, 1940s	60	90	120
"Sight Seeing Auto 899", cast iron, Kenton, circa 1910, has Mama Katzenjammer, Uncle Heine, Alphonse, Gloomy Gus, Happy Hooligan, 10½" long	4500	6750	9000
Skeezix oilcloth doll, cotton-stuffed, 1924 (Baby Skeezix), Live Long Toys	100	150	200
Skeezix oilcloth doll, cotton-stuffed, 1924 (as boy) Live Long Toys	100	150	200
Skeezix Radio Toy, circa 1924, 5" high, tin litho	1000	1500	2000
Skippy Oilcloth doll, 12" high, with hat	50	75	100
Smitty 9¾" oilcloth doll	100	150	200
"Smitty On A Scooter," tin wind-up, Marx, circa 1930, 8" high	1250	1875	2500
Smokey Stover, hard plastic, 3" high, 1960s	12	18	25
Smokey Stover, Hingees, 1944	20	30	40
Snoopy Astronaut, doll, 9½" high, 1969, vinyl	7.50	11.25	15
Snoopy rubber squeeze toy, 1958	10	15	20
Snowflakes & Swipes platform toy, 7½" long, tin litho, circa 1929	1900	2750	3800
Snuffy Smith Handpuppet, cloth, with rubber head, Gund, "King Features"	30	45	60
Sparkle Plenty Paperdoll Set, 1948, Saalfield No. 5160	20	30	40
Sparkle Plenty Washing Machine, Kalon Radio Corp., litho tin, crank action, circa 1947, 13" tall	100	150	200
Sparkplug, 1920s, Schoenhut jointed wood figure	*See Schoenhut*		
"Sparkplug" (Barney Google), on wheels, 3¼" high	200	300	400
Sparkplug (Barney Google) stuffed cloth	125	188	250
Sparkplug Candy Container	75	112	150
Spiderman Handpuppet, 1967, Ideal	30	45	60
Steve Canyon Glider Bomb Truck, Ideal	90	135	180

Rudy the Ostrich. Courtesy James S. Maxwell/Virginia Caputo. Photo by Virginia Caputo.

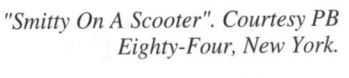

"Smitty On A Scooter". Courtesy PB Eighty-Four, New York.

Roosevelt Bear on Bicycle. Courtesy Wilkinson Collection, Detroit Antique Toy Museum.

SPARKPLUG, 1920s, SCHOENHUT. Courtesy PB Eighty-Four, New York.

Sandy (Orphan Annie) "Sandy's Dog House". Courtesy Christie's East.

Sandy with suitcase in mouth. Courtesy Christie's East.

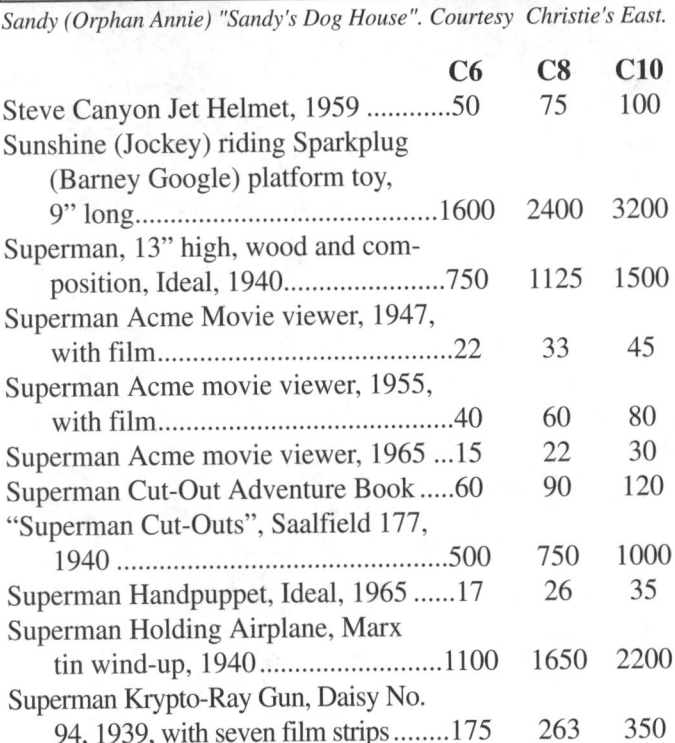

	C6	C8	C10
Steve Canyon Jet Helmet, 1959	50	75	100
Sunshine (Jockey) riding Sparkplug (Barney Google) platform toy, 9" long	1600	2400	3200
Superman, 13" high, wood and composition, Ideal, 1940	750	1125	1500
Superman Acme Movie viewer, 1947, with film	22	33	45
Superman Acme movie viewer, 1955, with film	40	60	80
Superman Acme movie viewer, 1965	15	22	30
Superman Cut-Out Adventure Book	60	90	120
"Superman Cut-Outs", Saalfield 177, 1940	500	750	1000
Superman Handpuppet, Ideal, 1965	17	26	35
Superman Holding Airplane, Marx tin wind-up, 1940	1100	1650	2200
Superman Krypto-Ray Gun, Daisy No. 94, 1939, with seven film strips	175	263	350

	C6	C8	C10
Superman Krypton Rockets, circa 1939	160	240	320
Superman Kryptonite Rock	6	9	12
"Superman Rollover Airplane," 1940s, Marx Co., 6½" long, blue version	1100	1650	2200
"Superman Rollover Airplane," 1940s, Marx Co., 6½" long, bronze-tone version	700	1050	1400
"Superman Rollover Airplane," 1940s, Marx Co., 6½" long, red version	850	1275	1700
Superman Rollover Tank, 1940s, 4" long	400	600	800
"Superman Roll Over Tank" (silver version) Marx Co., 1940s, 4" long	500	750	1000
"Superman Tank", Linemar, 12" long	*See Battery Operated*		
"Superman Tank", Linemar, 4" long	550	825	1100
Superman Water Pistol, shape of Superman flying, circa 1950s	20	30	40

DAISY Superman Krypto-Raygun Ad.

"Sight Seeing Auto 899". Courtesy Christie's East.

Toonerville Trolley, "Crackerjack" size. Courtesy Wilkinson Collection Detroit Antique Toy Museum.

Snowflake & Swipes.Courtesy Christie's East.

THIMBLE THEATRE Mystery Playhouse figures, Olive Oyl, Popeye, Wimpy. Courtesy Mapes Auctioneers & Appraisers.

"Toonerville Trolley", NIFTY tin wind-up. Courtesy PB Eighty-Four, New York.

Superman Rollover Airplanes, Left to Right: Blue, Red, Bronze-tone or Gold. Courtesy Christie's East.

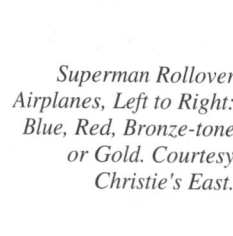

Toonerville Trolley, DENT. Photo by Don Hultzman.

Toonerville Trolley, lead, circa 1923. Courtesy PB Eighty-Four, New York.

Left to Right: Toonerville Trolley "The Powerful Katrinka", 6½" long, pushing boy in wheelbarrow; "The Powerful Katrinka", raises and lowers boy in her hand. Courtesy Sotheby's New York.

Uncle Wiggily, MARX, Crazy Car. Courtesy Sotheby's New York.

Uncle Wiggily Crazy Car, DISTLER (Germany). Courtesy Wilkinson Collection, Detroit Antique Toy Museum.

RACHEL, Gasoline Alley, oilcloth, cotton stuffed.

SKEEZIX, oilcloth, cotton stuffed.

Left to Right: Yellow Kid, 6½" high, cast iron, burlap gown, Yellow Kid in Goat Cart. Courtesy Christie's East.

Yellow Kid Ladder Toy. Some figures missing in photo. Courtesy James S. Maxwell/Virginia Caputo. Photo by Virginia Caputo.

	C6	C8	C10
Sweepea Hingees No. 102, 1944, paper punchouts, Reed	20	30	40
Sweepea Mask, cardboard, 1940s	10	15	20
Tarzan, Corgi Gift Set No. 36, figures and truck with cage trailer	40	60	80
Tarzan, mask of Akut the Ape, Northern Paper Mills, 1933	60	90	120
Tarzan, mask of Numa the Lion, paper, 1933 by Northern Paper Mills	60	90	120
Tarzan, mask of Tarzan, 1933, Northern Paper Mills, paper	70	105	140
Tarzan In The Jungle dart board game, 1935, large	130	195	260
Tarzan "Tarzan In The Jungle," 1935 battery-operated target game	140	210	280
Tarzan Thingmaker Kit, Mattel, 1966	32	48	65
Terry And The Pirates Hingees, 1944, set contains Terry, Flip Corkin, Pat Ryan, Burma, Taffy Tucker	22	33	45
Thimble Theatre Mystery Playhouse "Starring Popeye with Wimpy and Olive Oyl," copyright 1939, Harding Products, Philadelphia, 12x10x3", figures composition, with wooden "Shuffle" feet, individual figures sell for $325 in mint	1250	1875	2500
Three Flying Marvels (Captain, Jr., Mary), paper, circa 1944-47, Reed	16	24	32
Toonerville Trolley, lead, circa 1923	280	420	560
Toonerville Trolley, tin wind-up, "Copyright 1922 by Fontaine Fox," 7½" high, Skipper driving, Nifty	600	900	1200

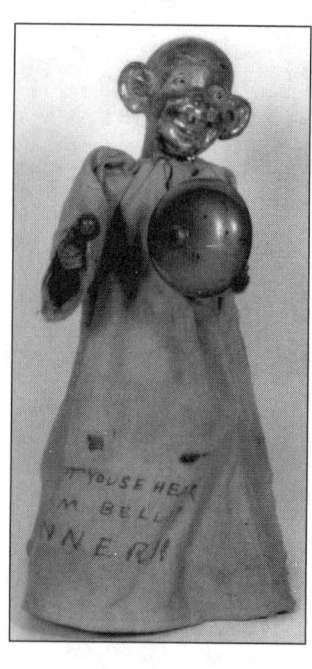

Yellow Kid Standing Bell Ringer. Courtesy James S. Maxwell/Virginia Caputo. Photo by Virginia Caputo.

WIMPY Tricyclist, LINEMAR. Courtesy Phillips New York.

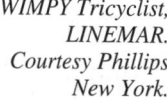

Yellow Kid Cap Bomb, 1½" high. Courtesy James S. Maxwell/Virginia Caputo. Photo by Virginia Caputo.

Yellow Kid Stuffed Doll, Arnold Print Works, 8" high.. Courtesy James S. Maxwell/Virginia Caputo. Photo by Virginia Caputo.

	C6	C8	C10
Toonerville Trolley, 1921, Strauss wind-up, RARE	800	1200	1600
Toonerville Trolley, 1⅞" high, sometimes called Crackerjack size	325	488	650
Toonerville Trolley - Dent, cast iron	600	900	1200
Toonerville Glass Candy Container, 3¼" long	500	750	1000
Toonerville Trolley, "Powerful Katrinka," 6½" long, pushing boy in wheelbarrow, tin wind-up, Lehmann, 1925	1600	2400	3200
Toonerville Trolley, "The Powerful Katrinka," raises and lowers Jimmy in her hand, tin windup, 6¾" high, Nifty, 1925	1500	2500	3000
Tweety Bird rubber squeeze toy, 1950s	15	22	30
Uncle Walt (Gasoline Alley), oilcloth, 26" high, Live Long Toys	80	120	160
Uncle Wiggily Crazy Car, Distler (Germany), circa 1922, 9½" long	1100	1650	2200
Uncle Wiggily, Marx, Crazy Car	325	490	650
Walter Lantz ink stamp character set, 12 different rubber stamps	12	18	24
Western Thrills with Billy The Kid, character from Funny Animals Comics, circa 1944-47, Reed, paper toy	12	18	24
Willie The Worm and Sammy in Car Trouble, paper toy, Fawcett Comics characters, Reed, circa 1944-47	10	15	20
Willie The Worm and Sammy Flying Machine	12	18	25
Willie The Worm and Sammy Fish-n Fun	10	15	20
Wimpy 3" hard plastic figure, 1960s	12	18	24

	C6	C8	C10
Wimpy 3⅛" high, cast iron Hubley	120	180	240
Wimpy 4" high, wood-jointed, "by K.F.S."	100	150	200
Wimpy, 5" high, Jaymar, jointed wood figure	100	150	200
Wimpy 8" high rubber squeeze toy	60	90	120
Wimpy Dippy Dumper	550	825	1100
Wimpy Handpuppet, Gund	25	38	50
Wimpy mask, cardboard, 1940s	10	15	20
Wimpy Motorcyclist, Linemar	300	450	600
Wimpy Tricyclist, Linemar	300	450	600
Wolfman Soaky	40	60	80
Woody Woodpecker Handpuppet, Mattel, 1962, "W. Lantz" rubber head, cloth body	32	48	64
Woody Woodpecker, 6½" high, rubber, "Walter Lantz"	10	15	20
Woody Woodpecker Soaky	11	16	22
Yellow Kid Cap Bomb, cast iron, 1½" high	75	112	150
Yellow Kid 6½" high, cast iron, burlap gown, movable arms	475	713	950
Yellow Kid, 8" high, Arnold Printworks, "Design copyrighted 1894 and 1896"	225	338	450
Yellow Kid in Cart, Kenton, early 1900s, 10" long, 6" high, pulled by mule, cast iron	800	1200	1600
Yellow Kid in Goat Cart, Kenton, 1890, painted cast iron, 7½" long	400	600	800
Yellow Kid Ladder Toy, 16½" high	600	900	1200
Yellow Kid papier mache and wood, 11" high, early 1900s	400	600	800
Zero (Beetle Bailey), hand puppet, Gund, 1960s, vinyl & cloth	30	45	60

MOVIES, RADIO, TELEVISION

(See also Paper, Premiums, Banks, Miscellaneous, Comic Character,
Marx Playsets, Action Figures, Figure Kits)

The average mint price in this category in the last edition was $202.47,
and in this edition averages $349.10, an increase of 72%.

AMOS &ANDY tin wind-ups, 12" high, eyes move. Courtesy Lloyd W. Ralston Auctions.

AMOS &ANDY Fresh-Air Taxi, cast iron. Courtesy Christie's East.

AMOS & ANDY Fresh-Air Taxi. Courtesy Sotheby's New York.

	C6	C8	C10
Alvin Chipmunk Soaky, 1963 10	15	20
Amos Sparkler..600	900	1200
Amos tin wind-up, 1930, Marx, 12" high 600	900	1200
Amos and Andy in car, glass, 4½" long 400	600	800
Amos and Andy wood jointed dolls, 6" high, price for pair, Jaymar 300	450	600
Amos and Andy Fresh-Air Taxi, cast iron, 6" 550	825	1100
Amos & Andy Fresh-Air Taxi, tin wind-up, Marx, 8" long, 1930s 700	1050	1400
Andy Tin Wind-Up, 12" high, Marx, 1930s..600	900	1200
Andy Panda, 14" high, Ideal, plush, 1950s...60	90	120
Babalooie, 14", rubber face...................12	18	25
Baby Huey Hand Puppet 20	30	40
Barney Rubble (Flintstones) 10" high vinyl doll, 1960 30	45	60
Bat Masterson Gun & Holster set with cane and vest, 1958, Carneli 60	90	125

	C6	C8	C10
BEANY & CECIL *(list by Brad Krewson)*			
Beany Doll (doesn't talk), 15" high, Mattel, 1960....................................30	45	60
Beany Doll, Talks, 17" high, Mattel, 1960 30	55	80
Beany Halloween Costume, Ben Cooper...25	38	55
Beany Hat with Two Propellers.............30	45	60
Beany & Cecil Colorforms set, 1961, with box 60	90	125
Beany & Cecil Getar, Cecil's eyes move, 1961, Mattel 30	45	60
Beany & Cecil Tea Set, 6 place settings, 1960, Worcester 40	60	80
Cecil Halloween Costume, Ben Cooper ...25	38	55
Cecil Disguise Kit, Mattel, 1962...........35	52	70
Cecil Doll (doesn't talk), Mattel, 24" high 42	63	84

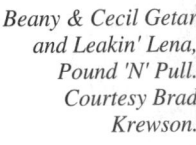

Beany & Cecil Getar and Leakin' Lena, Pound 'N' Pull. Courtesy Brad Krewson.

Beany & Cecil Leakin' Lena, plastic toy boat. Courtesy Brad Krewson.

Left to Right: Betty Boop, 12" high, jointed wood and composition, Betty Boop, 7" high, celluloid, Japanese. Courtesy Christie's East.

Beverly Hillbillies Car, IDEAL. Photo by Ron Chojnacki. Courtesy Don Hultzman.

	C6	C8	C10
Cecil Doll, talks, Mattel, 29" high, 1960	60	90	150
Cecil Hand Puppet, talks, Mattel, 1961	30	45	60
Cecil Music Box, metal, plays show's theme song, Cecil pops up, 1961, Mattel	150	225	300
Dishonest John Handpuppet, talks, Mattel, 1961	80	120	160
Leakin' Lena plastic toy boat, Irwin Toy, 1962	75	112	150
Leakin' Lena wood toy ship, Pressman, 1960s	60	90	120
Leakin' Lena Pound & Pull, wooden, Pressman, 1961	50	75	100

End Beany & Cecil

	C6	C8	C10
Beatles, Ringo, John, Paul, George, 5" vinyl figures, 1964, Remco. Price per each	50	75	100
Ben Casey Play Hospital Set, Transogram	40	60	80
Ben Hur Sword, scabbard and shield, Marx, only produced in 1959, when movie was made	120	180	240
Betty Boop, approx. 3¾" high, "1931", wood-jointed	90	135	180
Betty Boop, 7" high, celluloid, Japanese, head shakes	600	900	1200
Betty Boop, 9½" tall, 1930s, jointed	240	360	480
Betty Boop, 12" high, jointed, wood and composition, c. 1930	350	525	700

	C6	C8	C10
Betty Boop acrobat, celluloid and metal, Japanese, 1930s windup	350	550	750
Betty Boop and Bunny mechanical toy	150	225	300
Beverly Hillbillies car, Ideal, 1960s, windup	375	563	750
Bob Burns Bazooka, brass kazoo-like toy, patterned after radio-movie comic Burns' famous musical invention (the Army weapon gets its name from it) metal sliding tube, M.M. Pochapia Toys, 13" long when not extended, 1930s	20	30	40
Bobba-Louie 14" stuffed doll, vinyl head, Knickerbocker, 1959	25	38	50

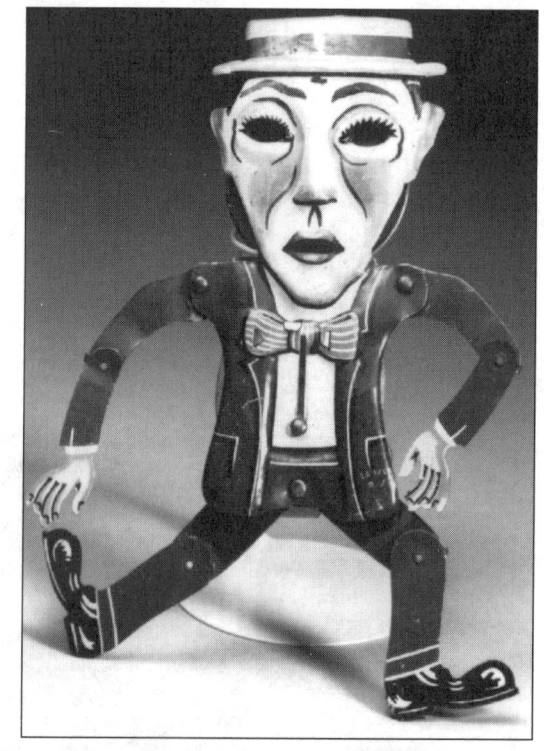

Buster Keaton Sparkler, Spanish, Courtesy Christie's East.

416

	C6	C8	C10
Bobba-Louie 18" stuffed doll, vinyl face, plush body, Knickerbocker 1959	25	38	50
"Bojangles Dances Again," tin litho and wood, 1930s, tap button on base and he dances	200	300	400
Bozo the Clown handpuppet	15	22	30
Bozo the Clown Jumpkin, Kohner, 1960	15	22	30
Bozo the Clown talking handpuppet	20	30	40
Buck Jones Rangers chaps	90	135	180
Buffalo Bill Jr. belt and buckle (TV), 1950s	25	38	50
Bugs Bunny Soaky, 10" high	15	22	30
Bugs Bunny & Porky Pig talking toy in original box, 1940s, has record that talks	100	150	200
"Bullet" (Roy Rogers' dog) stuffed doll, circa 1955	40	60	80
Bullwinkle, 14" high, stuffed, 1970, Gund	35	52	75
Bullwinkle, Terrytoons, 15" high, 1961	50	75	100
Bullwinkle Flexie, Whamo	12	18	25
Bullwinkle Soaky, 11" high	15	22	30
Buster Kenton Sparkler, Spanish, c. 1925, tin litho, 7" high, arms and legs move	1650	2475	3300
Captain Gallant Foreign Legion Holster outfit	80	120	160
Captain Kangaroo 20" talking doll, 1967	22	33	45
Captain Kangaroo badge, tin shield, 1960s	20	30	40
Casper The Friendly Ghost 11" stuffed doll, body is beanbag, 1960s	40	60	80

	C6	C8	C10
Casper The Friendly Ghost Hopper, 1950s, Linemar, 5" high	200	300	400
Casper The Friendly Ghost Turnover Tank, Linemar tin wind-up	220	330	440
Cecil Sea Serpent	*See Benny & Cecil*		
Charlie Chaplin Bell Ringer squeeze toy, German, tin litho, metal bell, 7¼"	1500	2250	3000
Charlie Chaplin Bell Toy, cast iron, circa 1912, 9¾"	300	450	600
Charlie Chaplin Bell Toy, metal, 3-wheeled, 5¼"	350	525	700
Charlie Chaplin, celluloid, 4" high	900	1350	1800
Charlie Chaplin Cymbal-Player, tin litho, squeeze action, German-made, 6¾"	700	1050	1400
Charlie Chaplin Doll, Boucher, 7½" high, steel, lead and cloth, ball-jointed, movable arms, legs and feet	250	375	500
Charlie Chaplin Doll, Louis Amberg, 14" high, circa 1915, composition and cloth	75	113	150
Charlie Chaplin driving 3-wheel vehicle, tin windup, Paya (Spain)	2100	3150	4200
Charlie Chaplin, Ferguson Novelty Co., 9" high, windup, composition, cloth and metal walker	1100	1650	2200
Charlie Chaplin flat tin litho, tips hat when string is pulled	110	165	220
Charlie Chaplin, Mark Hampton Company, 9" high, composition, "CHAS. CHAPLIN" on base	350	525	700
Charlie Chaplin, Martin, 1920, clock-work, 7" high, papier mache, lead, wire cane, cloth clothes	500	750	1000

Charlie Chaplin, Left to Right: Charlie Chaplin Cymbal-Player, Charlie Chaplin wind-up, 7" high, French, Charlie Chaplin, Mark Hampton Co., Charlie Chaplin tin litho squeeze toy, Spanish, Charlie Chaplin Wind-up Walker, Charlie Chaplin Bell Toy, metal, 3-wheeled, Charlie Chaplin, Ferguson Novelty Co..Courtesy Christie's East.

Left to Right: Charlie Chaplin Tin Wind-up with spinning cane, Charlie Chaplin Doll, Boucher, Charlie Chaplin wind-up, Boucher, Charlie Chaplin wooden whistler toy, Charlie Chaplin Bell Ringer squeeze toy, Charlie Chaplin Doll, Louis Amberg, Charlie Chaplin Bell Toy, cast iron, circa 1912, 9¾". Courtesy Christie's East.

	C6	C8	C10
Charlie Chaplin, Schuco tin wind-up, 1920s	500	750	1000
Charlie Chaplin tin litho squeeze toy, Spanish, c. 1925, 7¾" high	900	1350	1800
Charlie Chaplin tin litho windup, 7" high, walks	1300	1950	2600
Charlie Chaplin Tin Windup, 8½" high, Nifty, 1920s	1100	1650	2200
Charlie Chaplin Tin Windup with spinning cane, 6¾" high (Unique Art?)	900	1350	1800
Charlie Chaplin Tricycle Rider tin windup, c. 1930, 3½"	900	1350	1800
Charlie Chaplin windup, Boucher, metal, tin and cloth, 8¼" high	1000	1500	2000
Charlie Chaplin windup, 7" high, French, composition, tin and cloth walker	450	675	900
Charlie Chaplin Windup Walker, composition, cloth and metal, 11½" high	200	300	400
Charlie Chaplin wooden whistler toy, circa 1920, whistles "How Dry I Am", 13¼" high	1250	1875	2500
"Charlie McCarthy" written on top hat, standing erect, tin wind-up, circa 1938	250	375	500
Charlie McCarthy rubber doll, Effanbee	45	68	90
Charlie McCarthy 13" high, composition mouth moves, 1930s	200	300	400

	C6	C8	C10
Charlie McCarthy, approx. 20" high, Effanbee, mouth moves	350	525	700
Charlie McCarthy, 20" high, Effanbee, Mouth moves, in tweed jacket	425	638	850
Charlie McCarthy, 20" high, Effanbee in, summer suit, mouth moves	400	600	800
Charlie McCarthy in his Benzine Buggy, Marx	350	525	700
Charlie McCarthy Drummer Boy, 1938 Marx tin windup, 8" high	400	600	800
Charlie McCarthy Facemask, molded gauze, complete with separate monocle	50	75	100
Charlie McCarthy Handpuppet, composition head, circa 1939	110	165	225
Charlie McCarthy paper money	3	4	5
Charlie McCarthy Ventriloquist doll, composition with cloth body, ring pull in back of head to activate lower jaw, 14½" tall	600	900	1200

Left to Right: Charlie Chaplin Tricycle Rider, Charlie Chaplin driving 3-wheel vehicle. Courtesy Christie's East.

Charlie McCarthy, approx. 20" high, Effanbee, mouth moves. Courtesy Christie's East.

Charlie McCarthy, 20" high, Effanbee, mouth moves, in tweed jacket. Courtesy Christie's East.

Charlie McCarthy paper money. Courtesy Toy Collector News.

Charlie McCarthy paper money. Courtesy Rex and Richard Gray.

Charlie McCarthy in his Benzine Buggy. Courtesy PB Eighty-Four, New York.

"Charlie McCarthy and Mortimer Snerd Private Car". Courtesy Phillips New York.

Charlie McCarthy Drummer Boy. Courtesy Christie's East.

	C6	C8	C10
Charlie McCarthy Ventriloquist Doll, 18".300		450	600
Charlie McCarthy Ventriloquist Doll, 33", Puppet Maker K&S	500	750	1000
Charlie McCarthy "Charlie McCarthy and Mortimer Snerd Private Car," Marx, two heads sticking out of top of car	1300	1900	2600

	C6	C8	C10
CHIPS Motocycle, Mego	3.50	5.25	7
Cisco Kid Broomstick Horse, 1950s, "Ride 'em Cisco Kid"	35	53	70
Cisco Kid Neckerchief with nickel sombrero slide	10	15	20
Cisco Kid Western Outfit, 1950s	60	90	120
Clyde Beatty Hingees Set, 1944	20	30	40
Cowardly Lion (Wizard of Oz) molded gauze facemask	40	60	80
Dale Evans holster outfit	90	135	180
Deputy Dawg, 14" high stuffed doll, Ideal, 1961	40	60	80
Deputy Dawg Soaky	16	24	32
Dick Van Dyke doll from Chitty Chitty Bang Bang, 1967, talks, Mattel	40	60	80
Dr. Doolittle Music Box, Gee-Tar, Mattel, 1967	38	56	75
Dr. Doolittle Talking Handpuppet, 1967	35	52	70
Dragnet Crime Lab, 1955, flashlight, signal gun, badge, handcuffs, fingerprint kit, etc.	100	150	200

Flintstone Pals on Dino, Fred and Barney riders, MARX.

FROGGIE THE GREMLIN. Courtesy Toy Collector News.

*Fanny Brice
(Baby Snooks),
IDEAL.
Courtesy
Christie's East.*

	C6	C8	C10
Dragnet Police Set, gun, handcuffs, badge...24		36	48
Dragnet Los Angeles Police No. 714 badge...12		18	25
Dragnet Shoulder Holster & Pistol, 1950s...62		93	125
Dragnet talking police car, Ideal Toys, circa 1954...90		135	180
Dragnet Water Pistol, circa 1955, 714 badge emblazoned on handle...24		36	48
Dragnet Whistle, black plastic...5		8	10
Dukes of Hazzard, 4 vehicles, Ertl set...15		22	30
Ed Wynn Fire Chief, litho on wood, pull toy, Schoenhut, 12” long...*See Schoenhut*			
Fanny Brice (Baby Snooks), Ideal, composition and wire doll, 12” high...110		165	220
Farfel (Jimmy Nelson) handpuppet, Juro...85		127	170
Farmer Alfalfa (Terrytoons) circa 1950, 17½” high, stuffed body, vinyl head, hands...30		45	60
Flintstones Bam Bam 12½” high, Ideal...50		75	100
Flintstones “The Flintstones Bedrock Express Handcar,” 1962, Marx wind-up playset 22x26...240		360	480
Flintstones Choo Choo Train, Marx, “Bedrock Express,” tin wind-up, Linemar Co., 13” long, 1950s...360		540	720

	C6	C8	C10
Flintstones “Dino On Tricycle,” 1962, Linemar, 4” high...300		450	600
Flintstones “Dino the Dinosaur,” 1961, Linemar, 9” long...600		900	1200
Flintstones “Flintstone Friction Cars,” (Fred, Barney, Wilma, etc.), 1962, Linemar, 4” long, price per each...90		135	180
Flintstones “Flintstone Pals” (Barney on Dino), Linemar, 1962, 8” long, windup...200		300	400
Flintstones “Flintstone Pals” (Fred on Dino), Linemar, 1962, 8” long, windup...200		300	400
“Flintstone Flivver,” 1962, Marx, (Japan), Friction, 6¾” long...300		450	600
Flintstones “Hopping Barney Rubble,” 1962, Marx (Japan) windup, 4” high...200		300	400
Flintstones “Hopping Fred Flintstone,” Linemar, 4” high...220		330	440
Flintstones “Hopping Dino,” 1962, Linemar, 4” high...240		360	480
Flintstones Pebbles 7” jointed doll...37		56	75
“Flintstones Mechanical Shooting Gallery,” 1962, Marx, 13” long...400		600	800
Flintstones Paddy Wagon, Remco, 1961...100		150	200
Flintstones Turnover Tank, Linemar tin wind-up, 1950s, 4” long...320		480	720
Flub-A-Dub push puppet, plastic, felt, wood, 5” high...50		75	100
Flub-A-Dub (Howdy Doody) 3½” plastic figure...55		82	110
Fred Flintstone, 5¾” tall, hollow vinyl figure...22		33	44
Flying Nun Flying Toy, Rayline, 1970...45		68	90
Frankenstein Soaky...75		112	150
Froggie The Gremlin hollow rubber doll, squeeze toy, 5” high, of the Buster Brown radio with TV show, squeeze and tongue sticks out, 1950s...50		75	100

Harold Lloyd, Left to Right: Harold Lloyd Bell Toy, Harold Lloyd "Funny Face", Harold Lloyd Sparkler. Courtesy Christie's East.

Harold Lloyd Donkey Cart. Courtesy Christie's East.

	C6	C8	C10
Froggie The Gremlin, 9¼" squeeze toy 200		300	400
Froggie The Gremlin, 10¾" squeeze toy 225		375	450
Gabby (Gulliver's Travels), 10½" high, Ideal, wood-jointed 300		450	600
Gene Autry Marionette, 18" high, 1940s 140		210	280
Get Smart Spy Purse Kit, Miner Ind., 7" long 15		22	30
Gomez (Addams Family) handpuppet ..87		130	175
Green Hornet Handpuppet, Ideal...........200		300	400
Green Hornet Raft 175		263	350
Groucho Marx "Ventriloquist Play Pal," Goldberger 32		48	65
Gulliver's Travels Boat, wooden (Paramount) 110		165	220
Gulliver's Travels Drum, tin, Chein, 1939 25		38	50
Gulliver's Travels Musical Top, Chein .30		45	60
Gulliver's Travels Sandpail, tin, Chein....40		60	80
Gumby "Bendee" figure 12		18	25
Gumby Handpuppet, 1965, Lakeside 14		21	28
Gumby vinyl wind-up, dated 1966, approx. 4" high 37		56	75
Harold Lloyd Bell Toy, German, 6½" high 250		375	500
Harold Lloyd Donkey Cart, tin litho, Spanish, c. 1929, 9¼" long 2200		3300	4500
Harold Lloyd "Funny Face," Marx wind-up walker, 1929 310		465	620
Harold Lloyd Policeman, 12" high, tin wind-up 200		300	400
Harold Lloyd Sparkler, German tin litho 300		450	600

	C6	C8	C10
Henry Fonda Texas Ranger Sheriff Badge, The Deputy, 1951 40		60	80
Herman Munster Doll, Mattel 112		168	225
Herman Munster Puppet...............87		132	175
Herman Munster Talking Puppet 87		132	175
Highway Patrol "Highway Patrol Car," Broderick Crawford litho, 8" long...............100		150	200
"Highway Patrol Pistol Outfit," Halco, 1956, gun, holster, badge, handcuffs, ID, whistle, etc. 125		188	250
Hoot Gibson Cowboy Outfit, Wornova Clothes, 1935 70		105	140
Hoot Gibson lariat 40		60	80
Hoot Gibson Wornova Clothes (Squaw style), 1930s...............60		90	120
"Hopalong Cassidy Automatic Television Set," 1950s, Automatic Toy Co., 5" cube 120		180	240
Hopalong Cassidy Badge, tin with inset photo...............17		26	35
Hopalong Cassidy Binoculars, circa 1950, plastic 22		33	45
Hopalong Cassidy compass...............105		158	210
Hopalong Cassidy Cowgirl's outfit 85		128	170
Hopalong Cassidy dart board, 14"x17", stagecoach holdup and target practice, 1950, Toy Ent. 30		45	60
Hopalong Cassidy Field Glasses, 1940, metal...............55		82	110
Hopalong Cassidy Flashlight Gun, plastic, 8" long, Hoppy's name on side...........25		38	50
Hopalong Cassidy "Hop-A-Long Cassidy," 1938 Marx 9½" high (on "Range Rider" rocker base).....350		525	700

	C6	C8	C10
Hopalong Cassidy knife, circa mid-1940s, 3½" long	42	63	85
Hopalong Cassidy Photo Ring, circa late 1940s	12	18	25
"Hopalong Cassidy Picture Gun and Theater", 1939, Stephens Co., 12" long - 8" high	100	150	300
Hopalong Cassidy Rocking Horse Cowboy, Marx	350	525	700
"Hopalong Cassidy Shooting Gallery", 1950s, Automatic Toy Co., 18" long	200	300	400
Hopalong Cassidy Signet Ring, all metal, late 1940s	19	28	38
Hopalong Cassidy Spurs, leather and metal	60	90	120
Hopalong Cassidy Western Frontier set, with figures, stagecoach and buildings	220	330	440
Hopalong Cassidy woodburning set, 1950, American Toy and Furniture Co.	120	180	240
Hopalong Cassidy Zoomerang Gun, shoots paper, Tigrett Enterprises, Chicago, 1950, 9" long	80	120	160
Howdy Doody 4" high plastic push-puppet, Hohner, has NBC mike	70	105	140
Howdy Doody 6" high, wall walker doll	31	46	62
Howdy Doody 7½" high, 1950s, plastic cloth clothes, eyes close, mouth opens	30	45	60
Howdy Doody 12" high, moveable jaws, Goldberger Dolls	60	90	120
Howdy Doody 26" ventriloquist dummy	50	75	100
Howdy Doody Acrobat	200	300	400
"Howdy Doody Air-O-Doodle Circus Train," Kagran, 1950s, wind-up, 16" long	90	135	180
Howdy Doody and Bob Smith at the piano, tin wind-up, Unique	600	900	1200
Howdy Doody "Clarabelle Clown," 1950s, Linemar, squeeze action cable, 6½" high	120	180	240
Howdy Doody "Clarabelle Clown," 1950s, Linemar, 5" high, Kagran Corp., wind-up	200	300	400
Howdy Doody "Clarabelle Hurdy Gurdy," 1950s, FBA Industries, Kagran, 8" long	200	300	400
Howdy Doody, Clarabelle's horn, 1950s	50	75	100

	C6	C8	C10
Howdy Doody, Clarabelle Playsuit, Wonderland Costumes	62	93	125
Howdy Doody, Cowboy Gloves, leather, 1950s	40	60	80
Howdy Doody hand puppets, no date, no. mfr., rubber heads, cloth bodies	20	30	40
Howdy Doody Jeep, Marx windup	77	122	155
Howdy Doody Life Preserver, plastic, 1950s, show Howdy, Mr. Bluster, etc.	17	25	35
Howdy Doody Marionette, 17" high, wooden arms and legs, composition head	75	112	150
Howdy Doody Marionette, 16" high, composition head, hands and feet, handpainted features, 1950s	75	112	150
Howdy Doody Mask, rubber	12	18	24
Howdy Doody Piano, Howdy plays it	160	240	320
Howdy Doody plastic puppet toys, with levers in back of head to move mouths. Consists of Howdy, Bluster, Clarabelle, Princess, Dilly Dally, Tee-Vee Toys No. 549. Price for set	100	150	200
Howdy Doody plastic Ukulele, Emenee, 1950s	50	75	100
Howdy Doody Princess Summer-Fall Winter-Spring Puppet	45	68	90
"Howdy Doody Pumpmobile," 1950s wind-up, Nylint, 9" long	275	412	550
Howdy Doody "Pump-Mobile," Nylint, unauthorized Howdy, rides cart, 8½" long, 7" high	275	412	550
Howdy Doody "Put-In-Head," similar to Mr. Potato Head, but with Howdy characters: Howdy, Bluster, Clarabelle, Princess. Price for set	50	75	100
Howdy Doody Sand Forms, 1952, molds of Howdy, Bluster, Flub-A-Dub, Clarabelle, plus shovel	20	30	40
Howdy Doody Squeeze Toy, 7" high	40	60	80
Howdy Doody TV Set with paper filmstrips, Lego, 1950s	35	52	70
Howdy Doody tin wind-up, circa 1950, Marx, 5" high, Howdy plays banjo and moves head	200	300	400
Howdy Doody tin wind-up circa 1950, Howdy does jig and Bob Smith sits at piano, Marx, 5½" high	500	750	1000
Howdy Doody wood-jointed doll, 13" high	100	150	200
Howdy Doody wood-jointed doll, 5½" high, holding NBC mike	200	300	400

Howdy Doody Pumpmobile. Photo by Don Hultzman.

Jackie Coogan ("The Kid") tin wind-up walker.

Jackie Gleason "Away We Go" Bus. Courtesy Don Coviello.

Joe Penner tin wind-up. Courtesy Sotheby's New York.

HOOT GIBSON Cowboy outfit, WORNOVA CLOTHES, apparently new in 1935 and still on sale in 1939. Courtesy Heinz Mueller, Continental Hobby House.

Left to Right: Lone Ranger Doll, 20" high, Tonto, 20" high, both DOLLCRAFT. Courtesy Christie's East.

Harold Lloyd Bell Toy. Courtesy Sotheby's New York.

Jetsons Turnover Tank, LINEMAR. Photo by Don Hultzman.

HOWDY DOODY and BOB SMITH At The Piano. Courtesy PB Eighty-Four, New York.

JETSON EXPRESS Choo Choo Train. Photo by Don Hultzman.

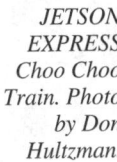

	C6	C8	C10
Huckleberry Hound, 18" stuffed doll, 1959, Knickerbocker	18	27	36
Huckleberry Hound as Fireman, rubber squeeze toy, 1960s, 9" high	17	26	35
Huckleberry Hound with top hat, rubber squeeze toy, 1960s	17	26	35
Huckleberry Hound "Huckleberry Hound Car," 1962, Marx (Japan), wind-up, 4" long	85	127	170
Huckleberry Hound "Huckleberry Hound Hopper" 1962, Linemar, 4½" high	175	263	350
"Huckleberry Hound Tricycle," 1961, Linemar, 4" high	400	600	800
Hugh O'Brian-Wyatt Earp, Dodge City Western Town, Marx, 1950s	450	675	900
1 Spy Target Set	37	56	75
J. Fred Muggs (Today Show) hand-puppet	12	18	25
Jackie Coogan glass candy container, 5" high	800	1200	1600
Jackie Coogan ("The Kid") tin wind-up walker, German, 7" high	800	1200	1600
Jackie Gleason "Away We Go" bus, 13"	450	675	900
Jackie Gleason "Story Stage Theatre," Utopia Enterprises, copyright 1955	100	150	200
James Bond, "Aston Martin," 1960s, Corgi, 4" diecast	20	30	40
James Bond "Aston Martin," 1979, Corgi, 2¾", diecast	10	15	20
James Bond, "Aston Martin", 1966, Corgi, 5¼" long	40	60	80
James Bond Aston-Martin	*See Battery-Operated*		
James Bond 007 Attache Case, 11". Code Book, rifle, which converts to pistol, bullets, Code-O-Matic, billfold with money and James Bond business cards and instructions, circa 1965	150	225	300
James Bond Camera, shoots	120	180	240
"James Bond-100 Shot Repeater Cap Pistol with Silencer," 1961, 9" long - total length - from "Goldfinger" - Lone Star Co.	170	255	340
Jerry Mahoney ventriloquist dummy	112	168	225
Jerry Lewis/Dean Martin two-sided handpuppet	52	78	105
Jetsons "Astro - the Jetsons' Dog," 1963 Marx wind-up (Japan), 5" high	138	205	275

	C6	C8	C10
Jetsons "George Jetson" 1963 Marx, (Japan) squeeze action cable, 4" high	140	210	280
Jetsons George Jetson circa 1965, Marx, tin wind-up, 4" high	225	338	450
Jetsons "Jetson Express Choo Choo Train," 1960s Marx (Japan), wind-up, 13" long	275	412	550
Jetsons Turnover Tank, Linemar tin wind-up	275	412	550
Joe Penner tin wind-up, Marx, circa 1930s, 8" high, tips hat, walks, "Wanna Buy a Duck?"	400	600	800
King Little (Gulliver's Travels), Ideal, 12" jointed composition	250	375	500
Lambchop Shari Lewis Handpuppet	16	24	32
Lone Ranger Acme Moviescope Set, 1948, includes 4 films: No. 1 Superman, No. 2 Lone Ranger, No. 3 Lone Ranger, No. 4 Lone Ranger. With pop-up box including films and viewer	37	56	75
Lone Ranger and Silver composition figure, 1938	80	120	160
Lone Ranger Chuck Wagon Lantern	75	112	150
Lone Ranger Deputy Badge, 1950s	60	90	120
Lone Ranger Doll, 20" high, 1938, very realistic composition head, hands, feet, Dollcraft	500	750	1000
Lone Ranger Flashlight	62	93	125

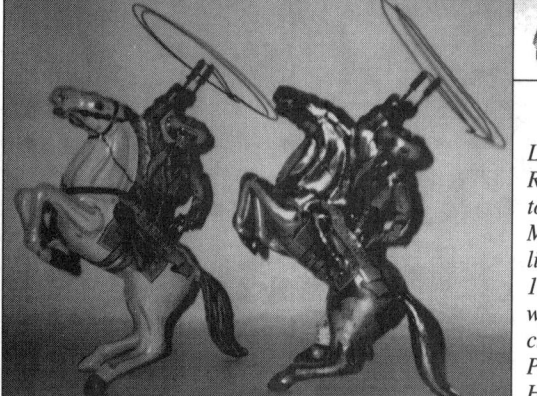

LONE RANGER, "Hiyo Silver", the Lone Ranger. Courtesy PB Eighty-Four, New York.

LONE RANGER, Left to Right: 1938 MARX wind-up, litho version, 1938 MARX wind-up, chrome version. Photo by Don Hultzman.

	C6	C8	C10
Lone Ranger Film Viewer, four films, 1953 50	75	100
Lone Ranger Harmonica, Magnus, 1950 40	60	80
Lone Ranger Hat, 1930s, official 37	56	75
Lone Ranger Hat, cowboy hat of white felt w/red trim. "Lone Ranger Hi! Yo! Silver!" inscribed, 1940s 22	33	45
Lone Ranger Official First Aid Kit with contents, 1938, tin litho 80	120	160
Lone Ranger "Official Outfit," 1939, mask, jail keys, badge, silver bullet, glow belt, Lone Ranger buckle, Lee Powell and Chief Thundercloud on belt 112	180	225
Lone Ranger "Lone Ranger Official Outfit," M.A. Henry Co., 1942 (belt, holster, guns, cuffs) 70	105	140
Lone Ranger 1938 Marx wind-up (on "Range Rider" rocker base), 10½" high 320	480	720
Lone Ranger 1938 Marx wind-up, chrome version, 8½" high from top of lariat 200	300	400
Lone Ranger 1938 Marx wind-up, litho version, 8½" high from top of lariat 125	188	250
Lone Ranger Picture Printing Set, 1939, 8 rubber stamps 50	75	100
Lone Ranger, Ranch Set, series 500, Marx Playset 300	450	600
Lone Ranger Rides Again movie viewer, 1939 60	90	120
Lone Ranger Rodeo, Marx set with metal bldgs., plastic figures, etc., 1950s, No. 9392 200	300	400
Lone Ranger Signal Siren, Flashlight, 1950's, with silver bullet secret code, United States Electric Mfg. Co. 60	90	120
Lone Ranger Silver Bullet Knife, length 3" closed 100	150	200
Lone Ranger "Stringless Marionette" handpuppet, cloth and vinyl 120	180	240
Lone Ranger Strongbox (coinbank) 50	75	100
Lone Ranger Target Game, 1938, Marx 60	90	120
Lucy (Peanuts) 1950s, vinyl squeeze doll 15	22	30
Lurch (Addams Family), Remco 65	98	130
Magilla Gorilla, Ideal, 1960s, 19" high 200	300	400

Milton Berle Car. Courtesy Mapes Auctioneers & Appraisers.

Mortimer Snerd band, MARX. Courtesy Christie's East.

Mortimer Snerd tin wind-up, MARX. Courtesy PB Eighty-Four, New York.

	C6	C8	C10
Matt Dillon, U.S. Marshall badge (Gunsmoke) 15	22	30
Men Into Space space helmet, retractable visor, space mike, etc. From series starring William Lundigan as Col. McCaulety. Made of fortiflex 100	150	200
Milton Berle Car, two large wheels, two small, Marx, 1950s, "What the Hey," etc. written on car 275	412	550
Mortimer Snerd, 13" high, Ideal, composition and wire 75	112	150
Mortimer Snerd Band, Marx, wind-up, 1935, "Hometown Band" 750	1125	1500
Mortimer Snerd, Jack In The Box, circa 1930s, 8" high 100	150	200
"Mortimer Snerd Teeth," plastic teeth and dental wax, circa 1950 15	22	30
Mortimer Snerd Tin Wind-up, Marx, circa 1939, Mortimer's hat tips as he walks 212	318	425

	C6	C8	C10
"Mortimer Snerd's Tricky Auto," 1939, Marx	325	487	650
Mr. Ed handpuppet, Mattel, 1962	17	26	35
Mr. Magoo Car, battery, tin litho...*See Battery Toys "MaGoo"*			
Mr. Magoo Doll, Ideal, 15" high	65	88	130
Mr. Magoo Handpuppet	25	38	50
Mr. Magoo Soaky, 11" high	15	22	30
Munsters, Herman *See Herman Munster*			
Munsters, Lily Munster handpuppet, 1960s	60	90	120
My Favorite Martian "Martian Magic Tricks," Gilbert, 1964, magic set	50	75	100
Oliver Hardy Doll, Dean	400	600	800
Oliver Hardy Handpuppet, Knickerbocker	20	30	40
Oliver Hardy Roly Poly, 10½" high, plastic	35	52	70
Oliver Hardy Sparkler, Isla, Spanish	1000	1500	2000
Oliver Hardy windup, Lakeside, 5" high, 1960s	20	30	40
"Oswald, Universal Pictures, Irwin Prod." 18½" wind-up, wood and cardboard body with cloth clothes, stuffed arms and head, character created by Disney, early	400	600	800
Oswald Stuffed Toy, 20⅞" high	110	165	220
Our Gang Dolls and Clubhouse, Mego	162	243	325
Pink Panther handpuppet, early, cloth body, Gund	15	22	30
Pinky Lee Pull Toy, Gong Bell	100	150	200
Pinky Lee vinyl doll. Squeeze and his head pops up, 1950	140	210	280
Poky (Gumby) "Bendee" figure	10	15	20
Poky Handpuppet, 1965, Lakeside	14	21	28
Poky "Jack In The Box", Lakeside, 1965	17	26	35
Poky vinyl windup, dated 1966, approx. 4" high	37	56	75
Quick Draw McGraw, "Animal Airplane," 1960s, Linemar, 8½" long - 9½" wingspan (Yogi Bear and Huckleberry Hound's head also used)	300	450	600
Quick Draw McGraw "Quick Draw McGraw Hopper," 1962, Linemar, 4½" high	200	300	400
Rat Patrol Giant Action Battle Set	112	168	225
Rat Patrol Jeep, Marx	150	225	300
Rifleman (TV) Ranch, Marx	450	675	900
Rin Tin Tin and Rusty Knife, 1950s	60	90	120
Rin Tin Tin - Marx Fort Apache Stockade, 1950s, No. 3628	300	450	600

Mortimer Snerd, 13" high, IDEAL. Courtesy Christie's East.

"Oswald" wind-up, wood and cardboard body with cloth clothes (1932 ad).

Oliver Hardy Sparkler, ISLA. Courtesy Christie's East.

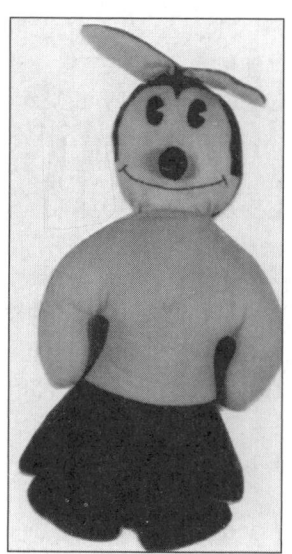

Oswald stuffed toy, 20⅞" high. Courtesy James S. Maxwell/Virginia Caputo. Photo by Virginia Caputo

	C6	C8	C10
Robin Hood Bow & Arrow Set, 1956, Richard Greene	6	9	12
Robin Hood Money Pouch, six foreign coins from Richard Greene TV series, 1953-54	20	30	40
Robin Hood Money Pouch, fifteen foreign coins, from Richard Greene TV series	20	30	40
Robin Hood Shield. Badge with embossed Robin Hood and gem stone, circa 1956	25	38	50
Rocky The Flying Squirrel Bendee figure, 1960s	40	60	80

	C6	C8	C10
Rocky The Flying Squirrel Soaky 15	22	30
Rootie Kazootie Marionette, 14" hard rubber head and hands, wooden shoes and body wearing clothes......90	135	180
Rootie Kazootie, 19", Effanbee.............62	93	125
"Roy Rogers and Bullet Hobby Horse," No. 812, 1950s, N.N. Hill Brass Co., 19" long 200	300	400
Roy Rogers bandanna, large 20	30	40
Roy Rogers Bobbin' Head doll, 6" high, 1962 90	135	180
Roy Rogers Branding Iron Set 40	60	80
Roy Rogers Double R Bar Ranch, 1950s, tin litho ranch house, Marx.....75	112	150
Roy Rogers Mineral City, town with hotel, music hall, cafe, bank, barber shop, trade goods, etc., tin ..120	180	240
Roy Rogers Nellie Belle Jeep, metal.....75	112	150
Roy Rogers pocket flashlight 37	53	75
Roy Rogers Quickshooter Hat with Secret Gun........90	135	180
Roy Rogers "Ranch Lantern," No. 90, metal, hurricane type with plastic chimney, 1950s, 7¾" tall 48	72	96
Roy Rogers Rodeo Ranch, Marx Playset.160	240	320
Roy Rogers "Roy Rogers Buckboard," 1950s, Ideal, 16" long 65	98	130
Roy Rogers "Roy Rogers Chuck Wagon," Ideal, 1950s, 13" long......90	135	180
Roy Rogers "Roy Rogers Fix-it Stage Coach," 1950s, Ideal, 13" long.......90	135	180
Roy Rogers "Roy Rogers Horse Trailer & Jeep," Ideal, 1950s, 15" long........125	188	250
Roy Rogers "Roy Rogers Stage Coach Wagon Train," wind-up, 14" long, plastic, 1950s 125	188	250
Roy Rogers Signal Flashlight................40	60	80
Roy Rogers Telescope 40	60	80
Roy Rogers and Trigger Pocket Knife ..40	60	80
Roy Rogers Wagon Train, Marx...........150	225	300
Scarecrow (Wizard of Oz) molded gauze facemask 60	90	120
Scrappy (Columbia Pictures), 14½" high, circa 1935, E.D. & T.C. Co., cloth and composition....................100	150	200
Scrappy & Margie wooden pull toy, 13½" long, he plays xylophone, she revolves......300	450	600

Sgt. Bilko Holster Set from the CBS TV series "You'll Never Get Rich," starring Phil Silvers. Photo-illustrated box contains leather holster and belt with realistic

ROY ROGERS "Stage Coach Wagon Train". Courtesy Continental Hobby House.

Roy Rogers "Roy Rogers Chuckwagon", Nellie Belle Jeep. Photo by Don Hultzman.

Scrappy (Columbia Pictures), 14½" high. Courtesy Christie's East.

Roy Rogers Signal Flashlight. Photo by Gary J. Linden.

	C6	C8	C10
Army .45 made of silvered die cast metal. Sgt.'s arm patch and Sgt. Bilko hat with Badge, Halco Brand, 1956...........100	150	200
Shadow Crimefighter Detection Belt, with pistol, handcuffs, etc., 1978, Madison Ltd. 15	22	30
Shirley Temple Playhouse 120	180	240

W.C. Fields, 19" high,
Effanbee. Courtesy
Christie's East.

Tom Corbett Space
Cadet Flashlight
with built-in signal
siren. Photo by
Gary J. Linden.

TOM CORBETT "Polaris" Rocket Ship. Photo by Don Hultzman.

"Tom Mix Circus Wild West" by Arcade. The wagon is wood.

	C6	C8	C10
Small Fry Club Kit, 1949, button, etc., Dumont TV show (may be premium)..30		45	60
"Sneak" Facemask, molded gauze (Gulliver's Travels,) 1939...............50		75	100
Soupy Sales dolls, 1965, Sunshine Doll Co...45		68	90
Stan Laurel Bendem Doll, 1960...........12		18	25
Stan Laurel Doll, Dean......................400		600	800
Stan Laurel Handpuppet, Knicker-bocker...40		60	80
Stan Laurel wind-up, Lakeside, 5" high, 1960s...................................20		30	40
Star Trek - Mr. Spock Vulcan Ears, 1976 5		7.50	10
Sylvester, 1971, 15" high, cloth 30		45	60
Tales of the Texas Rangers Deputy Badge 12		18	24
Three Stooges handpuppet, 1959, 9½" high, Moe, Curley and Larry, price per each...................................100		150	200
Tim Holt Litho Target with Dart Gun ...70		105	140
Tinman Facemask (Wizard of Oz) molded gauze 60		90	120
Tom Corbett Space Cadet, 14 different figures, Marx, 1950s. Price per set...36		54	72

	C6	C8	C10
Tom Corbett, 7 different figures, same as above, price per set......................28		42	56
Tom Corbett Cosmic Vision Space Helmet, one-way vision, plastic, early 1950s......................................110		165	225
Tom Corbett Space Cadet Molding and Coloring Set, Model Craft (All Tom Corbett toys 1950-55) 80		120	160
Tom Corbett Space Cadet Field Glasses, 3 power, Herald, 5½" long 38		56	75
Tom Corbett Space Cadet Flashlight with built-in signal siren, 7" long, metal, US Alite Corp 62		93	125
Tom Corbett Official Outfit, Yankiboy 100		150	200
Tom Corbett "Polaris" Rocket Ship, wind-up Marx, 1952, 12" long, Tom, Astro and Rogers looking out of cockpit 375		563	750
Tom Corbett Space Hat, Lee 25		38	50
Tom Corbett Space Cadet official Space Pistol, Marx No. 105 70		105	140
Tom Corbett Space Cadet Rifle, Marx, No. 0239.............................37		56	75
Tom Corbett Space Station...................200		300	400
Tom Corbett Space Cadet, 2-Way Space Phone, Zimmerman 80		120	160
Tom Corbett "Tom Corbett Space			

	C6	C8	C10
Cadet Atomic Rifle," Marx, 1950s, 24" long	100	150	200
Tom Corbett "Tom Corbett Space Cadet Official Space Pistol," 1950s, Rockhill, 9½" long	100	150	200
Tom Mix "Circus Wild West," Arcade circus wagon with driver, two horses, 14½" long, circa 1936, wagon is wood - (See Animal Drawn, Arcade "Big Six")	550	825	1100
Tom Mix metal and leather spurs, 1934 (not a premium)	150	225	300
Tom Mix on Tony, Arcor Rubber, 1930s	50	75	100
Tom Mix Rocking Horse, wooden, 1930s	225	338	450
Tom Mix Rodeorope, 1928, comes with box and instructions	100	150	200
Tonto (Lone Ranger) 20" high doll, 1938, very realistic, composition head, hands, feet, Dollcraft	500	750	1000
Topo Gigo (Ed Sullivan Show) Nodder	30	45	60
Umbriago (Jimmy Durante) hand-puppet, 1945, American Merchandise	60	90	120
W.C. Fields, 19" high, Effanbee, movable mouth	425	638	850
Wendy (Casper) Soaky, 10" high	14	21	28
Wild Bill Hickock & Jingles holster set	50	75	100
Wild Bill Hickock & Jingles TV Show, 42 piece Western Bunkhouse	22	33	45
Wild Bill Hickock Marshal Star Badge with picture of Hickock and Jingles in center	21	31	42
Wizard of Oz masks, set of five, Einson-Freeman Co., Inc., 1939, "Par-T-Mask"	200	300	400

	C6	C8	C10
Wizard of Oz, Mego, Dorothy & Toto	10	15	20
Wizard of Oz, Mego, Glinda, 8", 1972	10	15	20
Wizard of Oz, Mego, Lion, 1972	12	18	25
Wizard of Oz, Mego, Munchkins (4), per each	32	48	65
Wizard of Oz, Mego, Scarecrow, 1972, 8" high	18	27	36
Wizard of Oz, Mego, Tinman, 8" high, 1972	16	24	32
Wizard of Oz, Mego, Wicked Witch, 8", 1972	34	51	68
Wizard of Oz, Mego, Wizard, 8"	10	15	20
Wizard of Oz, Mego, Emerald City Playset	55	83	110
Wizard of Oz Munchkinland Playset	125	188	250
Yogi Bear, 7½" high, stuffed, 1973, Knickerbocker	12.50	18.75	25
Yogi Bear Friction Car, Marx, 1962	90	135	180
Yogi Bear Go-Cart, Linemar	150	225	300
Yogi Bear Handpuppet	10	15	20
Yogi Bear "Jellystone National Park" Marx Playset	350	525	700
Yogi Bear Tricky Trapeze, 1967, 5" high	15	22	30
Yogi Bear "Yogi Bear Car," 1962 Marx (Japan), 4" long	65	97	130
Yogi Bear "Yogi Bear Hopper," 1962, Linemar, 4" high wind-up	300	450	600
Yosemite Sam, Dakin Squeak Toy, 1970, 4" high	40	60	80
Wyatt Earp U.S. Marshall Badge, Lone Star	12	18	25
Wyatt Earp U.S. Marshall Badge, 20th century, 1950s, Hugh O'Brian photo	17	26	35
Wyatt Earp U.S. Marshall's Outfit, Pla-Master	37	56	75

DISNEY

(See also Paper, Premiums, Fisher-Price)

The average mint price of Disney toys in the last edition was $352.45, and in this edition it is $568.47, an increase of 61%.

Although Walt Disney was involved in animation as early as 1920, his first really notable character was Oswald the Rabbit, introduced in 1927. However, Disney did not own the rights, which eventually fell into the hands of another animator, Walter Lantz. Mickey Mouse first appeared in the 1928 short "Plane Crazy", but the third Mickey cartoon, "Steamboat Willie", seems to have been the first released, on November 18, 1928, and Mickey was a success from that point on. Minnie Mouse also appeared in the latter film, with Pluto emerging in 1930, though not called that till 1931, Goofy debuting in 1932, and Donald Duck in 1934. Mickey Mouse toys were first produced in 1930, and since then the stream of Disneyana has been unending, and apparently all of it deemed collectible.

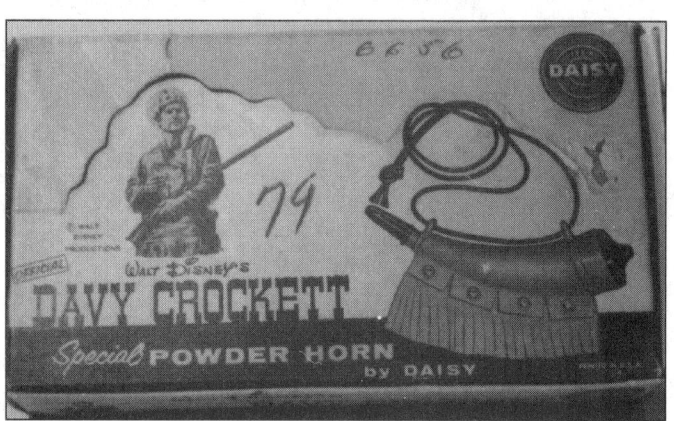

DAVY CROCKETT Powder Horn, DAISY. Courtesy Toy Collector News.

	C6	C8	C10
Babes In Toyland, tin litho wind-up Indian on rollerskates, Linemar, 1950s, 6½" tall	160	240	320
"Babes In Toyland Soldier", 1950's, Linemar, 6½" tall, tin windup	150	225	300
Babes In Toyland Wood Officer on horseback, wheeled, Jaymar	175	263	350
Babes In Toyland Wood Soldier with cannon, Jaymar	210	315	420
Bambi "Jumping Bambi", Linemar, 1950s, trigger action, 6" high	250	375	500
Bashful 1½" lead figure, Britains	40	60	80
Bashful, approx. 7" high, Ideal	125	188	250
Bashful, approx. 12" high, 1938, Ideal	80	120	160
Bashful Party Mask, 1937	20	30	40
Bashful stuffed doll	60	90	120
"Big Bad Wolf and The Three Little Pigs", 1950s, Linemar, 4 ¼" tall, 4 pc. set	750	1125	1500
Big Bad Wolf Halloween costume, 4' high	60	90	120
Big Bad Wolf celluloid pinback, 1¼"	38	53	75
Big Bad Wolf Stuffed toy in tux, with carnation, glass eyes, 20" tall	450	675	900
Captain Hook marionette, 1950s	75	112	150
"Casey Jr. Disneyland Express", loco, 3 cars, tin & plastic, Marx	62	93	125
Cinderella wind-up 4¾" high, Irwin, umbrella, spins and dances	50	75	100

	C6	C8	C10
Cinderella and Prince - Dancing, No. 7000, Irwin Co., 1950s, plastic wind-up, 5" high	62	93	135
Cleo facemask, (Pinocchio) by Gillette, 1939	10	15	20
Cleo The Goldfish (Pinocchio) Sun Rubber squeeze toy	30	45	60
Davy Crockett Auto-Magic Picture Gun	30	45	60
Davy Crockett Badge, 1950s, "Frontier Marshal"	27	41	55
Davy Crockett Coonskin Hat	16	24	32
Davy Crockett doll, 8" high, Fortune Toy, 1950s	50	75	100
Davy Crockett doll, 20" high, Gund, vinyl	48	72	95
Davy Crockett Flying Arrows, balsa wood figures to be made into flying arrows. Copyright 1955	10	15	20
Davy Crockett "Frontierland Davy Crockett Outfit", gun, coonskin hat, etc.	40	60	80
Davy Crockett hand-gun, pop-action, tin litho, 1950s	40	60	80
Davy Crockett Play Knife, 1950s	25	38	50
Davy Crockett Powder Horn, Daisy	20	30	40
Davy Crockett Prairie Wagon, 5" long	75	112	150
"Davy Crockett Wagon Train", 1950's, Marx (plastic) 14" long	140	210	280
Disney Showboat, 1960, large	62	93	125
"Disney Show Boat", 1981, Playworld Toys, plastic	4	6	8
Disneyland Concert Xylophone, Tudor, 18" long	19	29	38
Disney Ferris Wheel, circa late 1956, Chein, tin wind-up, 17" high	375	563	750
"Disneyland Happy Birthday Carousel", 1950s, Ross Co., 6" high	150	225	300
"Disneyland Jeep", 1960s, Marx, 10" long push toy	100	150	200

DISNEYLAND Roller Coaster, Chein. Courtesy Continental Hobby House.

DISNEYLAND Happy Birthday Carousel. Photo by Don Hultzman.

	C6	C8	C10
"Disneyland Melody Player". 1950s, Chein, 7" cubic	150	225	300
"Disneyland Melody Player" Extra paper rolls, different songs, 1950s, for Melody Player, each	10	15	20
Disneyland Playset, Marx	425	638	850
Disneyland Roller Coaster, Chein, 10" high, 2 tin cars, 1950s	250	375	500
Doc 1½" lead figure, Britains	60	90	120
Doc (Snow White), approx.7" high, Ideal	125	188	250
Doc, 11½" high, stuffed molded oil-cloth face, Ideal	100	150	200
Doc Party Mask, 19377	14	21	28
Donald Duck, 3½" high, celluloid walker, Japan wind-up	350	525	700
Donald Duck, 4" high tin wind-up, Linemar	275	363	550
"Donald Duck", 5" high, 1930s, long-billed celluloid, Borgfeldt (Japan)	750	1125	1500
Donald Duck, 6" high, 1930s, long billed, celluloid wind-up	450	675	900
"Donald Duck", 6" high, 1950s, Linemar squeeze action	100	150	200
"Donald Duck", 6" high, Schuco wind-up, German, "984"	350	525	700
Donald Duck, 6" high drummer, mechanical, Linemar	300	450	600
Donald Duck 6" high, Seiberling Rubber, long-billed, 1930s	230	345	460
"Donald Duck" 7" high, 1960s, Marx wind-up, hard plastic	50	75	100
Donald Duck, 9" high, composition and cloth, long billed, in Russian costume	1000	1500	2000

	C6	C8	C10
Donald Duck 10" high, Sun Rubber	100	150	200
Donald Duck 13" stuffed doll, long-billed, Knickerbocker, 1930s	150	225	300
Donald Duck, 13" high, celluloid, 1940s	135	198	270
Donald Duck, 13½" high, Gund, circa 1949	110	165	220
Donald Duck 13½" high, Character Novelty, 1940	110	165	220
Donald Duck 16" high, long bill, 1930s	80	120	160
Donald Duck Acrobat, Linemar, 1950s, 8½" high	250	375	500
"Donald Duck and His Nephews", 1950s, Marx, 11" long-plastic wind-up	220	330	440
"Donald Duck and Huey With Voice", 1950s, Linemar, 7" long (string pull toy)	500	750	1000

DISNEYLAND Ferris Wheel. Courtesy HAKE'S Americana & Collectibles.

431

Donald Duck Dipsy Car. Photo by Don Hultzman.

DONALD DUCK, 6" high, Sieberling, rubber, long-billed. Courtesy HAKE'S Americana & Collectibles.

Donald Duck and Pluto in Roadster, SUN RUBBER. Photo by David Leopard.

Donald Duck Xylophone Player. Courtesy Lloyd W. Ralston Auctions.

	C6	C8	C10
Donald Duck "Choo Choo" No. 450	*See Fisher-Price*		
"Donald Duck Climbing Fireman", 1950s Linemar, 13½'" wind-up	300	450	600
"Donald Duck Convertible", 1950s, Linemar, 5" long, tin, friction	300	450	600
Donald Duck Crawler, celluloid wind-up, 9¾" long	No Price Found		
Donald Duck Crazy Car, 1950s, Linemar, 5½" long wind-up	275	363	550
Donald Duck Delivery Tricycle, tin and plastic, 5", Marx	180	270	360
"Donald Duck Dipsy Car", 1950s, 5¼" long, Marx, tincar, (plastic Mickey or Donald)	200	300	400
"Donald Duck "Dipsy Car - Donald Duck", 1950s, Linemar wind-up, 6" long	350	525	700
"Donald Duck Disney Flivver", 1950s, Linemar, 5½" long, push-down on head	250	375	500

	C6	C8	C10
Donald Duck Doctor Kit	60	90	120
Donald Duck "Donald & His Nephew" 1950s, Linemar, pull string action, 5½" high	375	563	750
Donald Duck "Donald the Driver", 1950s Linemar friction car, 6½" long	200	300	400
Donald Duck "Donald the Drummer", 1950s, Marx wind-up, 9" tall	200	300	400
Donald Duck "Donald Race Car", celluloid wind-up, occupied Japan	225	338	450
"Donald Duck Drummer", 1950s, Linemar wind-up, 6" high walker	350	525	700
"Donald Duck Drummer", 1950s Linemar wind-up, 6" tall, rocker	200	300	400
Donald Duck Duet, small Donald, large Goofy, circa 1945, Marx tin wind-up	550	825	1100
"Donald Duck Dump Truck", 1950s, Linemar, 5" long	250	375	500

Donald Duck, 9" high, composition and cloth, long billed, in Russian costume. Courtesy Christie's East.

DONALD DUCK Climbing Fireman. Photo by Don Hultzman.

Donald Duck and his Nephews. Photo by Don Hultzman.

Donald Duck Railroad Car. Courtesy Christie's East.

Donald Duck Duet. Courtesy Mapes Auctioneers & Appraisers.

Donald Duck on Rocking Horse. Courtesy James S. Maxwell/Virginia Caputo. Photo by Virginia Caputo.

Donald Duck Rowboat, Chad Valley. Courtesy Christie's East.

	C6	C8	C10
Donald Duck Fire Chief Crazy Car, Linemar wind-up, tin litho, extremely rare	No Price Found		
"Donald Duck In His Convertible", 1950s, Linemar friction, 6" long	225	338	450
Donald Duck Jigger, 11" high, papier mache wind-up	800	1200	1600
Donald Duck Mousketeers Hat	15	22	30
Donald Duck on paddle, string-puller, long-billed	See Fisher-Price		

	C6	C8	C10
Donald Duck on Rocking Horse, Japan, celluloid tin, wind-up, 3⅜" long	3000	4500	6000
"Donald Duck on Tractor", 1950s, Marx friction, 3½" long, plastic	120	180	240
"Donald Duck on Trapeze", 1930's, Borgfeldt, 9" high-Donald 4¾" long	600	900	1200
Donald Duck pulled by Pluto, celluloid, with tin cart, Japan, 1930s, long billed	1750	2625	3500

433

	C6	C8	C10
Donald Duck pulltoy, baton-twirler, No. 400 .... *See Fisher-Price*			
Donald Duck pultoy, No. 765, plastic feet, 1950s .... *See Fisher-Price*			
Donald Duck pulltoy, 6½" long, long-billed, on platform .... *See Fisher-Price*			
Donald Duck pull toy, No. 400, 1940, 10" tall, 7½" long, wooden figure with movable arms and legs, composition head .... *See Fisher-Price*			
Donald Duck pull toy - wagon, circa 1940, No. 544 .... *See Fisher-Price*			
Donald Duck pull toy, with Xylophone, circa 1938, No. 185 .... *See Fisher-Price*			
"Donald Duck Railroad Car" with Pluto, Doghouse, 10" long, Lionel No. 1107, 1930s	500	750	1000
Donald Duck Riding Mule, long-billed celluloid wind-up, 7¾"	850	1275	1700
Donald Duck Rowboat, Chad Valley (England), wood and paper litho, 12¼" long	300	450	600
Donald Duck Rubber Boat, Sun Rubber Co., circa 1940s	40	60	80
Donald Duck Skier, Linemar	300	450	600
Donald Duck Skier, Marx, 1940s, plastic Donald	150	225	300
"Donald Duck Straight Shoooter", 1960s plastic wind-up,6½" high	125	188	250
Donald Duck Teapot, Ohio Art	30	45	60
Donald Duck Tractor, Sun Rubber	112	188	225
Donald Duck Tricycle, 3½" long, Linemar, wind-up, 1950s	300	450	600
"Donald Duck Tricycle", (with twirling parasol), 1950s, MT Co., Japan, 7½" high	200	300	400
"Donald Duck Waddler", 1930s, K Co., Japan, long bill, tin and celluloid, 3¼" high	600	900	1200
"Donald Duck Waddler", 1930s, "K" Co., 3½" tall	600	900	1200
"Donald Duck Washing Machine", 1950s, MT Co., Japan, 7½" high	400	600	800
"Donald Duck with Whirling Tail", 1950s, Linemar, tin wind-up, 5¼" high	200	300	400
"Donald Duck with Whirling Tail", 1950s, Marx plastic wind-up, 6½" high	60	90	120
Donald Duck Zylophone, Tudor, 10" long	20	30	40

	C6	C8	C10
Donald Duck and Pluto in roadster, Sun Rubber, 1930s, about 6½" long	75	112	150
Donkey (Pinocchio) rubber, Seiberling, 1940	70	105	140

DOPEY Tin Wind-up, MARX. Courtesy PB Eighty-Four, New York.

DONKEY (Pinoccho) rubber, 4" high. Courtesy HAKE'S Americana & Collectibles.

	C6	C8	C10
Dopey 1½" lead figure, Britains	40	60	80
Dopey, approx. 7" high, Ideal	125	188	250
Dopey Doll, 9" composition with velvet clothes, Knickerbocker	130	195	260
Dopey 10" rubber squeeze toy, 1950s	10	15	20
Dopey, approx. 12" high, Ideal, 1938	150	225	300
Dopey, Doc pull toy, 14" long	200	300	400
Dopey Doll, Madame Alexander, 1938	150	225	300
Dopey Hand Puppet, composition, 1938, Crown Toys, bell, buckling belt	140	210	280
Dopey Marionette, circa 1952, Peter Puppet Playthings	80	120	160
Dopey Party Mask, 1937	20	30	40

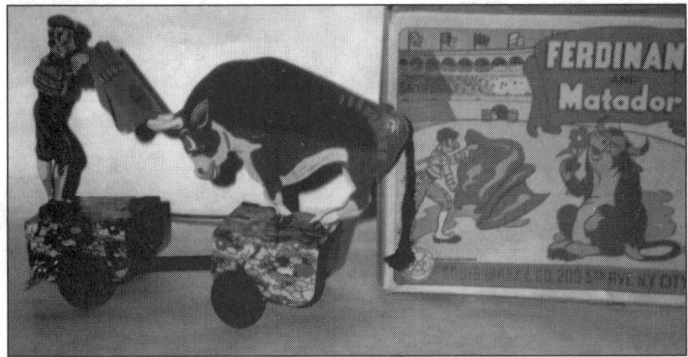

FERDINAND & MATADOR. Photo by Don Hultzman.

DUMBO Tin Windup, MARX, Dumbo flips over. Photo by Don Hultzman.

434

ELMER ELEPHANT, rubber, SEIBERLING, head moves. Courtesy HAKE'S Americana & Collectibles.

Ferdinand the Bull, Copyright 1938, MARX. Photo by Don Hultzman.

	C6	C8	C10
Dopey Soaky 7	11	15
Dopey tin wind-up, Marx, 1938..........375	563	750
Dumbo hand puppet, Gund, circa 1955, 10" 9	13	18
Dumbo tin wind-up, Marx, Dumbo flips over, 1941, 4" high 230	345	460
Elmer Elephant 5" celluloid and string figure, 1930s 120	180	240
Elmer Elephant pull toy, 1936.................*See Fisher-Price*		
Elmer Elephant, rubber, Seiberling, head moves 50	75	100
Ferdinand The Bull, Linemar...............250	375	500
Ferdinand The Bull, copyright 1938, Marx, tail whirls, body shakes, wind-up.......300	450	600
Ferdinand the Bull, handpuppet, 1938, Crown 55	82	110
Ferdinand The Bull pull toy, Hill, 8¾" long...200	300	400
Ferdinand The Bull, late 1930s, Seiberling Latex Products, hard rubber, 6" long, 3½" high 55	82	110
Ferdinand The Bull, jointed, wood, 9" 100	150	200
Ferdinand and Matador, 1938, Marx tin wind-up 800	1200	1600
"Figaro", 1950s, Linemar, tin friction toy, 3" long 60	90	120
Figaro (Pinocchio) paper mask, 1939, Gillette 10	15	20
Figaro tin wind-up, Marx, 1940, 4¾" long 150	225	300
"Flower," 1950s, Linemar, 3" long friction, tin 60	90	120
Frontierland Logs, No. 915, Halsam.....10	15	20
Gepetto facemask (Pinocchio) by Gillette 1939 10	15	20
Gepetto 5½" wood figure holding his chin, Multi Products, 1940 70	105	140
Goofy, 5¼" high tin wind-up, Linemar 210	315	420
Goofy "Goofy the Walking Gardener," Marx, tin wind-up.........................1000	1500	2000
Goofy on a unicycle, tin wind-up 5½" high 375	563	750
Goofy Soaky 8	12	16
Goofy 1930 tin figure............................400	600	800
"Goofy Tricycle", 1950s, Linemar, 4" tall 200	300	400
"Goofy With Whirling Tail", 1950s, Linemar, 5" tall.............................300	450	600
"Goofy with Whirling Tail," 1950s Marx plastic wind-up, 8" high.......100	150	200
"Goofy's Disneyland Stock Car", 1950s, Linemar, 6" long 150	225	300

Goofy "Goofy the Walking Gardener". Courtesy Christie's East.

	C6	C8	C10
"Goofy's Stock Car", Linemar, 1950s, 6" long	150	225	300
Grumpy lead figure, 1½" high, Britains	40	60	80
Grumpy, approx. 7" high, Ideal	140	210	280
Grumpy Doll, stuffed, oilcloth face, velvet pants, 11" high, 1938	80	120	160
Grumpy, 11½" high, stuffed, molded oilcloth face, Ideal	90	135	180
Grumpy, Ideal, approx, 12" high, 1938	80	120	160
Grumpy Party Mask, 1937	15	22	30
Grumpy rubber squeeze toy, 1950s	10	15	20
"Gym Toys Acrobats," 1950s Linemar, 8½" high (Mickey, Donald, Minnie, etc.) each priced at	150	225	300
Happy 1½" lead figure, Britains	30	45	60
Happy 3¼" high, Seiberling Rubber, 1938	60	90	120
Happy, approx. 7" high, Ideal	125	188	250
Happy marionette, Madam Alexander, 9½" high, 1938	110	155	220
Happy party mask, 1937	40	60	80
Happy rubber squeeze toy, 1950s	10	15	20
Happy, approx. 12" high, Ideal, 1938	110	165	220
Horace Horsecollar hand puppet, Gund, circa 1960	17	25	34
"Huey - Louie - Dewey Locomotive," 1950s, Marx friction, 3½" long, plastic	40	60	80
"Jiminy Cricket" 6" high, 1950s Linemar squeeze cable hopper	250	375	500
Jiminy Cricket, 9" high, wood jointed, Ideal, 1940	225	375	450
Jiminy Cricket, 10" high, Knickerbocker, circa 1940	238	357	475

	C6	C8	C10
Jiminy Cricket 12" approx. rubber head, wooden feet, cloth body, Gund	10	15	20
Jiminy Cricket 13" high, latex head, hands and feet, cloth body	60	90	120
Jiminy Cricket 14" high, Crown Toy, felt and cloth	150	225	300
Jimmy Crickett 15½" high, Crown Toy, felt and cloth	150	225	300
Jiminy Cricket facemask (Pinocchio) 1939 from Gillette	10	15	20
Jiminy Cricket Handpuppet, vinyl and cloth, Gund	11	16	22
Jiminy Cricket, Linemar, tin litho wind-up, 1950s, 5½" tall	240	360	480
Jiminy Cricket pushing bass fiddle, Marx walkie	15	22	30
Jiminy Cricket Soaky	14	21	28
Johnny Tremain Flintlock cap pistol, Marx	60	90	120
Jungle Book Dancing Bear, Marx plastic wind-up	80	120	160
Ludwig Von Drake, 7" rubber squeeze toy, circa 1960	25	38	50
Ludwig Von Drake, litho tin wind-up, Linemar, 1950s, 6" tall	240	360	480
Ludwig Von Drake go-cart, friction, Marx, 1961	175	263	350
Mad Hatter puppet (Alice in Wonderland)	30	45	60
Mad Hatter's Taxi, Linemar, 5" long, 1950s	250	375	500
Mickey Mouse, first toy made by Borgfeldt of NY in 1930, wooden Mickey with jointed hands, arms, legs and wire tail, leather ears. "Copyright 1928-1930 by Walter E. Disney"	550	825	1100
Mickey Mouse larger-size squeeze toy with clothes, 1950, Sun Rubber	30	45	60

JIMINY CRICKET, LINEMAR tin litho wind-up. Photo by Don Hultzman.

LUDWIG VON DRAKE litho tin windup, LINEMAR. Photo by Don Hultzman.

Mickey Mouse Tumbler, SCHUCO, atop Mickey Mouse Piano, MARKS BROS. Courtesy Christie's East.

Mickey Mouse Bank, cast iron, 9" high, French-made. Courtesy James S. Maxwell/Virginia Caputo. Photo by Virginia Caputo.

MICKEY MOUSE, 7" high, wood-jointed, early, BORGFELDT. Courtesy HAKE'S Americana & Collectibles.

Mickey Mouse, 13¾" high, stuffed. Courtesy James S. Maxwell/Virginia Caputo. Photo by Virginia Caputo.

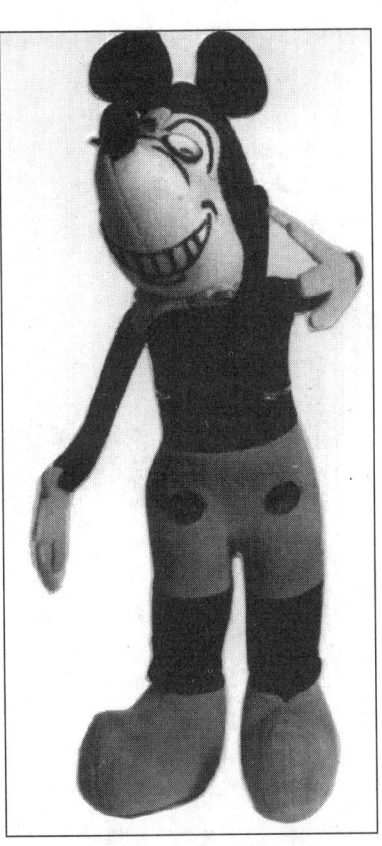

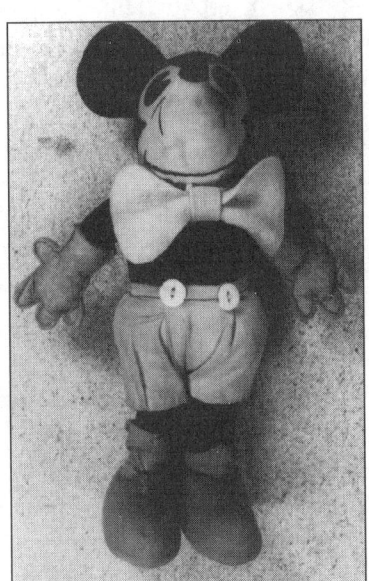

MICKEY MOUSE, 5" high wood doll, FUN-E-FLEX, leather ears. Courtesy HAKE'S Americana & Collectibles.

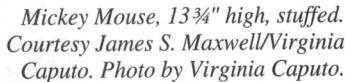

MICKEY MOUSE Boat. Courtesy Continental Hobby House.

MICKEY MOUSE, 11" high, cloth, "Walt Disney Mickey Mouse Geo. E. Borgfelt & Company, New York" on bottom of one foot. Courtesy HAKE'S Americana & Collectibles.

MICKEY MOUSE Mickey on Scooter, LINEMAR. Photo by Don Hultzman.

MICKEY'S TRACTOR, SUN RUBBER. Photo by Dave Leopard.

MICKEY MOUSE Felt Doll, STEIFF, 12" high. Courtesy Lloyd W. Ralston Auctions.

	C6	C8	C10
Mickey Mouse with red shirt and yellow pants, squeeze toy, Sun Rubber, 1950	30	45	60
Mickey Mouse, 3½" high, Seiberling Rubber, 1930s	87	135	175
Mickey Mouse 5" high wood doll, Fun-E-Flex leather ears	160	240	320
Mickey Mouse, 5½" high, vibrates, Linemar tin wind-up, 1950s	340	510	680
Mickey Mouse, 6" high, rubber, circa 1935, Seiberling	160	240	320
Mickey Mouse, 7" high, wood jointed, early Borgfeldt	390	585	780
"Mickey Mouse," 7" high, 1960s Marx wind-up, hard plastic	125	188	250
Mickey Mouse, 8" high, Sun Rubber	60	90	120
Mickey Mouse, 8" high, wooden, jointed arms and legs, circa 1933	600	900	1200
Mickey Mouse, 9½" high, "Dell," rubber	40	60	80
Mickey Mouse, 10" high, Sun Rubber, 1940s	30	45	60
Mickey Mouse, 11" high, cloth "Walt Disney Mickey Mouse Geo. E. Borgfeldt & Company New York" on bottom of one foot	400	600	800
Mickey Mouse, 12" high, 1930s, Knickerbocker	310	465	620
Mickey Mouse, 12" high felt doll, early 1930s, Steiff	640	960	1280
Mickey Mouse, 12" high, Borgfeldt	625	938	1250
Mickey Mouse, 12" high, "Cowboy Michey," Knickerbocker, 1936	650	975	1300
Mickey Mouse, 13¾" high, stuffed, early (Dean Rag?)	400	600	800
Mickey Mouse, 16" high, stuffed, 1930s	650	975	1300
Mickey Mouse, 17", rubber, Lakeside Mfg. Co.	80	120	160
Mickey Mouse, 18" high, felt, Character Co., circa 1939-40	70	105	140
Mickey Mouse, 19½" high, circa 1935, Knickerbocker, in cowboy outfit	1400	2100	2800
Mickey Mouse, 21" high, circa 1933	350	525	700
Mickey Mouse, 31" high, all felt dressed, opening in back for storing things, black jacket with yellow buttons, red pants, bells on toes of yellow shoes, 1950s	120	180	240
Mickey Mouse, 1950s, Linemar, tin friction toy, 3" long	60	90	120
Mickey Mouse, 1930s, 4" long, pie-eyed tumbler, Schuco	150	225	300
Mickey Mouse, Acrobat, clockwork trapeze, celluloid Mickey, 1930s, Japan	700	1050	1400
"Mickey Mouse Acrobat" 1950s, Linemar (Gym Toys), 9" high, Mickey 6" long	300	450	600
Mickey Mouse Airmail, rubber "Mickey's Airmail"	90	135	180
Mickey Mouse and Donald on back of alligator, Marx, 1950s, plastic walker	50	75	100
Mickey Mouse and Donald Handcar, windup, plastic, 1948, Marx	200	300	400
Mickey Mouse and Donald in fire truck, late 1930s, Sun Rubber, 6½" long	60	90	120
Mickey Mouse and Minnie Mouse Tea Set, circa 1935, 13 pieces	140	210	280
Mickey Mouse and Minnie Mouse Swing Toy, celluloid with red and green flag, 11½" tall	420	630	840
Mickey Mouse Bank, Cast iron, 9" high, France, "Depose," auctioned for $880 and $9504 in late 1990			
Mickey Mouse Banjo, 1930s, 17" long	140	210	280
Mickey Mouse Beverages felt soda jerk hat, shows Mickey from shoulders up saying "have one on me," 5"x11", circa 1930	60	90	120
Mickey Mouse Boat, 13"	150	205	300
Mickey Mouse Bubble Buster Gun, metal Mickey standing at gun sight. Cast iron, Kilgore, 6" long	140	210	280
"Mickey Mouse Bus Lines - Walt Disney Stars", Gong Bell, circa 1960, 19½" long riding toy	250	375	500
Mickey Mouse cardboard mask, circa 1935	60	90	120
Mickey Mouse, celluloid on wood hobby horse, 4½", circa 1935	1200	1800	2400
Mickey Mouse Circus, Geo. Borgfeldt 6/3785, 1931, two wood figures revolving on swinging mechanism, 11" long	450	675	900
Mickey Mouse Circus Train Set, Lionel No. 1536, Engine, tender, containing Mickey, three carriage cars, dining car, Mickey Mouse Circus, Mickey Mouse Band, composition Mickey and track	1800	2700	3600
Mickey Mouse Circus Train, Mickey shoveling tender, three Disney Circus cars, wind-up train, red, circa 1931	1200	1800	2400

Mickey Mouse, Left to Right, 18" high, 16" high, both stuffed. Courtesy Sotheby's New York.

Mickey Mouse 19½" high, circa 1935, Knickerbocker. Courtesy Christie's East.

MICKEY MOUSE "Mickey-In-The-Box". Photo PB Eighty-Four, New York.

MICKEY MOUSE Acrobat (1930s, Japan). Photo PB Eighty-Four, New York.

MICKEY MOUSE Drum, OHIO ART, 6" diameter, tin. Courtesy HAKE'S Americana & Collectibles.

"Mickey Mouse and Donald Duck Handcar". Photo by Don Hultzman.

MICKEY MOUSE "Climbing Mickey Mouse", DOLLY TOY COMPANY. Courtesy Phillips New York.

MICKEY MOUSE Circus Train Set. Photo PB Eighty-Four, New York.

Mickey Mouse, "Mickey on Scooter", 1950s, LINEMAR. Courtesy Christie's East.

"Mickey Mouse Bus Lines - Walt Disney Stars." Courtesy Wilkinson Collection, Detroit Antique Toy Museum.

Mickey Mouse, celluloid, on wood hobby horse. Courtesy Christie's East.

MICKEY MOUSE Racing Car. Photo PB Eighty-Four, New York.

Mickey Mouse Hand Car. Photo PB Eighty-Four, New York.

Mickey Mouse Circus. Photo PB Eighty-Four, New York.

Mickey Mouse Dipsy Car, MARX. Photo by Don Hultzman.

Mickey Mouse Express. Photo by Don Hultzman.

Mickey Mouse "Mickey the Magician". Courtesy Christie's East.

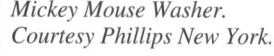

Mickey Mouse Tap Dancer, crank toy, German. Courtesy Christie's East.

Mickey Mouse Washer. Courtesy Phillips New York.

	C6	C8	C10
Mickey Mouse Clicker, tin litho, circa 1930, Mickey showing teeth while playing violin	90	135	180
Mickey Mouse, "Climbing Mickey Mouse," 1930s, Dolly Toy Co., cardboard, 8" long	250	375	500
Mickey Mouse Club Auto-Magic Picture Gun, 1946, projects films	35	52	70
Mickey Mouse Club Newsreel	30	45	60
"Mickey Mouse Dipsy Car," 1950s, 5¼" long, Marx, tin car, plastic Mickey	200	300	400
"Mickey Mouse Dipsy Car," 1950s, Linemar, 5¼" long, all tin	300	450	600
Mickey Mouse Drum, Ohio Art, 6" diameter, tin	55	82	110
Mickey Mouse Drum Set, tin and cardboard, circa 1940, Minnie watching while Mickey juggles	240	360	480
Mickey Mouse Explorer's Outfit	87	132	175
"Mickey Mouse Express," 1950s Marx, 9" diameter (Mickey in airplane)	200	300	400
Mickey Mouse Express tin litho train set, 14" long, base 21x13", Marx, 1950s	400	600	800
Mickey Mouse Hand Car, green base	600	900	1200
Mickey Mouse Hand Car, red base	700	1050	1400
"Mickey Mouse Handcar", 1930s, Lionel Co., 7" long - with Minnie, orange housing	1000	1500	2000
Mickey Mouse Hingees, 1944	30	45	60
Mickey Mouse holding flag, cast iron, 1930s	140	210	280
Mickey Mouse Jazz Drummer, finger-activated tin toy, Nifty 4¾" high	80	120	160
"Mickey Mouse Jockey", 1935, M-T Co., 4½" long - celluloid Mickey on wooden hobby horse	1200	1800	2400
Mickey Mouse Kaleidoscope, 1950s	29	44	58
Mickey Mouse Knickerbocker doll, 1935, 22" high	500	750	1000
Mickey Mouse, lead, 2½" high, 1933, Allied Toys	60	90	120
Mickey Mouse Marionette, circa 1930, 9½" high, felt body stuffed with cotton	160	240	320
Mickey Mouse Marionette, Peter Puppet Playthings Co., 1952, 14" tall	100	150	200
"Mickey Mouse Meteor Five-Car Train, Walt Disney's" tin litho, Marx, 43" long	300	450	600
Mickey Mouse "Mickey-In-The-Box," 7" high jack-in-the-box	260	390	520
Mickey Mouse On Pluto, rocks, tin wind-up, Linemar, 1950s, 6½" long	1200	1800	2400
Mickey Mouse "Mickey on Scooter," 1950s, Linemar, 4½" high, all tin, Rare	1000	1500	2000
Mickey Mouse "Mickey on Unicycle," 1950s, Linemar, 5" high	400	600	800
Mickey Mouse "Mickey Race Car," celluloid windup, occupied Japan	225	338	450
Mickey Mouse "Mickey the Driver," 1950s Marx (Japan), 6½" long friction	500	750	1000
Mickey Mouse "Mickey the Magician," Linemar, 10", battery-operated	1200	1800	2400
Mickey Mouse "Mickey the Musician - I Play the Xylophone," 1950s Marx wind-up, 10" high	325	488	650
Mickey Mouse "Mickey's Delivery," Pluto on Tricycle-Cart, tin litho wind-up, celluloid head on Pluto, Linemar, 1950s, 5½" long	450	675	900
Mickey Mouse "Mickey's Mouse-kemovers" moving van, 13" long, 1950s, Linemar	400	600	800
Mickey Mouse "Mickey's Service Truck," 1950s Marx friction, 3½" long, plastic	40	60	80
Mickey Mouse "Mickey's Tractor," Sun Rubber, 1930s, Mickey's head turns, 4½" long	60	90	120
"Mickey Mouse Motorcycle," 1950s Linemar friction, 3" long	150	225	300
"Mickey Mouse Motorcycle," 1950s, Linemar, tin friction toy, 3½" long	300	450	600
"Mickey Mouse Movie Fun Optical Toy", 1950s, Mastercraft, 7"x7"x5"	150	225	300
Mickey Mouse Movie-Jecter, 1935	90	135	180
Mickey Mouse Movie Projector No. E-18, Keystone, 1930s, 10" high	225	375	450
"Mickey Mouse Newsreel," 1950s, Mattel, 9½" high, includes 3 records and 5 films	100	150	200
Mickey Mouse on Hand Car, Japan, 8" long, basket on back	138	208	275
Mickey Mouse Organ Grinder, Minnie Mouse dancing on organ pushed by much larger Mickey, German	1200	1800	2400
Mickey Mouse piano, wooden, grand, with decal showing Mickey playing, Minnie listening, circa 1935	200	300	400

	C6	C8	C10
Mickey Mouse Piano, Marks Bros., circa 1935, 10"............1250	1875	2500
Mickey Mouse Pocket Knife, 1935 40	60	80
"Mickey Mouse Projector No. E-18" 1930s, Keystone Co. 7" long, 10" high, 9" wide 200	300	400
Mickey Mouse "Puddle Jumper," No. 310, circa 1950s.............*See Fisher-Price*		
Mickey Mouse Puppet, approx. 10" high, "Gund"..................11	16	22
Mickey Mouse Puppet, early 40s style, very large composition head, hands and feet, the rest of the body wood, cloth costume, felt ears.................175	263	350
Mickey Mouse Puppet, Pelham 24" high, rubber legs and arms, wood body 200	300	400
"Mickey Mouse Race Car," 1930s, T.M. Co., 3" long.............250	375	500
Mickey Mouse Racing Car, red lithographed tin wind-up car with Mickey at the wheel, 4" long, 1930s..250	375	500
"Mickey Mouse Rollerskater," 1950s, Linemar, 6" high.............350	525	700
Mickey Mouse Roly Poly, celluloid, early, 4" high 140	210	280
Mickey Mouse Rower, Fun-E-Flex, wooden, 10¾" 1700	2550	3400
Mickey Mouse "Running Mickey on Pluto," 1940s, M-T Co., 5½" long, celluloid, occupied Japan..........5000	7500	10,000
Mickey Mouse "Santa Car with Mickey Mouse and His Gift Pack" hand car, Lionel No. 1105, 1935 900	1350	1800
Mickey Mouse "Scooter Jockey," Mavco Co., 1950s, all plastic, 6" high wind-up.............160	240	320
Mickey Mouse Soaky.............11	16	22
Mickey Mouse Sparkler Toy, 1930s, 5½" tall, Nifty.............300	450	600
Mickey Mouse Tambourine, Noble & Cooley Co., 1936, 9" heavy paper head, Mickey juggling while Minnie watches.............310	465	620
Mickey Mouse Tap Dancer, crank toy, German, sold for $17,600 in 1990.		
Mickey Mouse Tea Service, 24 piece, tin, Chein, 1930s.............120	180	240
Mickey Mouse Tin Flute.............40	60	80
Mickey Mouse Tin Washboard set, circa 1935, complete.............80	120	160
Mickey Mouse Tool Chest, 1935, Hamilton Metal, complete.............170	255	340
Mickey Mouse on Tricycle, tin litho, wind-up, celluloid Mickey, 1940s, 3½" long 450	675	900
"Mickey Mouse Tricycle", 1950s, Linemar, 4" tall.............200	300	400
Mickey Mouse Tumbler, Schuco, 4" high.............200	300	400
Mickey Mouse Tumbling, 1947, Marks Bros., 8" high 90	135	180
Mickey Mouse Viewer, with film of "Brave Little Tailor," 1946.............60	90	120
Mickey Mouse Walker, plastic.............20	30	40
Mickey Mouse Washer, 1932 or 33 Ohio Art Co., tin litho washing machine, 7" high, two scenes with Mickey, Minnie, Pluto 100	150	200
"Mickey Mouse with Twirling Tail," 1950s Linemar, 5½" high 350	525	700
Mickey Mouse Xylophone, tin wind-up, 1930s.............275	413	550
Mickey Mouse Xylophone Player, Linemar, tin wind-up, 1950s, 6" high.............550	825	1100
Mickey Mouse Club Bow and Arrow Set, circa 1955 20	30	40
Mickey Mouse Club Snap-on Ears, plastic, 1950s.............10	15	20
"Mickey & Minnie Acrobats," 1934, Borgfeldt (Japan), 11" high 1750	2625	3500
Mickey & Minnie Barrel organ, English...112	168	225
Mickey & Minnie Mouse Car, Gong Bell, circa 1933, wood & metal, 10¾" long 1050	1575	2100
Mickey & Minnie on Elephant, celluloid, Japan, 1930s, auctioned in 1990 for $7150.		
Mickey & Minnie on Motorcycle, tin litho 4000	6000	8000
Mickey & Minnie Mouse Playland, celluloid, Japan 1800	2700	3600
Minnie Mouse, wooden, June Flex 150	225	300
Minnie Mouse 3" high, wooden, jointed, 1940s 100	150	200
Minnie Mouse, 5" high, celluloid, 1930s, "Fat head" 275	413	550
Minnie Mouse, 5½" high, wooden, 1930s.............187	286	375
Minnie Mouse, 6" high, celluloid, 1930s, string tail 425	638	850
Minnie Mouse, 7" high, Fun-E-Flex 280	420	560
"Minnie Mouse" 7" high, 1960s Marx wind-up, hard plastic 50	75	100

Mickey Mouse Rower, Fun-E-Flex. Courtesy Christie's East.

Mickey & Minnie Mouse Playland, 10¼".. Courtesy Christie's East.

Mickey & Minnie on Elephant, celluloid, Japan. Courtesy Christie's East.

Minnie Mouse carrying two suitcases. Courtesy Christie's East.

	C6	C8	C10
Minnie Mouse 10½" high, Sun Rubber, 1940s	40	60	80
Minnie Mouse, 12" high, 1930, wearing dress, high heels, undies	225	338	450
Minnie Mouse 14½" high, early cloth figure dressed in a red and white polka dot skirt, wearing composition heeled shoes	300	450	600
Minnie Mouse 16" high , cloth, early 1930s	650	975	1300
Minnie Mouse cardboard mask, circa 1935	40	60	80
Minnie Mouse Carrying Two Suitcases, tin wind-up, 6½" high, circa 1928, Spanish, auctioned for $12,100 (with replaced ears) in 1990.			
Minnie Mouse cowgirl, Knickerbocker, 18" high, 1936	470	705	940
Minnie Mouse Handpuppet, Peter Puppet Playthings, circa 1952	100	150	200
Minnie Mouse Knitter, tin litho wind-up, Linemar, 1950s, 7" high	333	500	666
Minnie Mouse Lead, 2½" high, 1933, Allied Toys	40	60	80
Minnie Mouse Marionette, circa 1930, 9½" high, felt body stuffed with cotton	230	345	460
Minnie Mouse Marionette, 13" wood and composition, 1950s	100	150	200
Minnie Mouse Puppet, Pelham, 24" high, rubber legs and arms, wood body	100	150	200

MINNIE MOUSE Knitter. Photo by Don Hultzman.

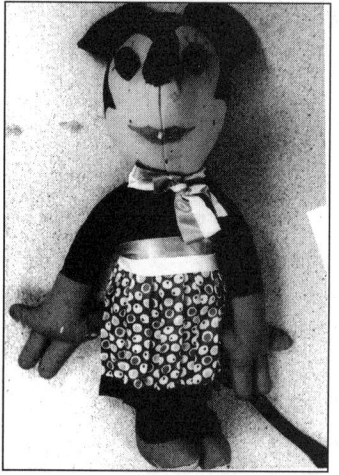
MINNIE MOUSE 16" high, cloth, early 30s. Courtesy HAKE'S Americana & Collectibles.

MICKEY MOUSE Xylophone Player, LINEMAR. Photo by Don Hultzman.

Left to Right; MINNIE MOUSE DOLL 14½" high, MICKEY MOUSE, 21" high. Photo PB Eighty-Four, New York.

	C6	C8	C10
Minnie Mouse Roly Poly, celluloid, 4"	60	90	120
Minnie Mouse Tricycle, 1950s, Linemar, 4"	200	300	400
Minnie Mouse Walker, plastic	20	30	40
Minnie Mouse Washing Machine, 1950, Precision Specialties, Inc.	100	150	200
"Mousketeer Electric TV Story Teller, T. Cohn, late 1950s, tin litho TV set and record player, records and film reels	200	300	400
Mouseketeers Hat, 50% wool, 50% rayon, by Denayaluee, 1950s	30	45	60
Mouseketeers Outfit, Western Style	138	205	275
"1001 Dalmations" set of 6 wooden nodders, 1959	125	188	250
Oswald the Rabbit, circa 1927, 6½" long celluloid crib toy	250	375	500
"Parade Roadster" Marx lithographed tin wind-up, convertible car decorated with Mickey and other characters, with Donald at the wheel, Pluto and Mickey and Minnie Mouse as passengers, 1950s, 11¼" long	300	450	600
Pecos Bill, Marx wind-up, plastic, 1950s	110	165	220
Peter Pan 9¾" high, Sun Rubber, circa 1952	24	36	48
Peter Pan Marionette, circa 1952, Peter Puppet Playthings	90	135	180
Peter Pan Tea Set, circa 1953, 23 pieces	80	120	160
Peter Pan Train Car, 1977	22	33	45
Pinocchio cloth and jointed wood figure, Kreuger	160	240	320
Pinocchio 2½" high, molded wood fiber figure, Multi Products, 1940	100	150	200
Pinocchio 5" high, molded wood fiber figure, Multi Products, 1940	150	225	300
Pinocchio, 5½" high, rubber, Seiberling	27	41	55
Pinocchio 7½" high, jointed, circa 1940, Ideal	125	188	250
Pinocchio 8" high, Ideal	275	363	550
Pinocchio 10½" high, Ideal, wood and composition	250	375	500
Pinocchio 10½" high, wood and papier mache wind-up, George Borgfeldt, 1940	350	525	700
Pinocchio 11" high, jointed, circa 1940	200	300	400
Pinocchio 12" high, Ideal jointed wood and composition	300	450	600

	C6	C8	C10
Pinocchio 19¾" high, jointed, circa 1940 400	600	800
"Pinocchio Delivery", Marx 325	488	650
Pinocchio Handpuppet, Gund, 1950s....15	22	30
Pinocchio Paper Mask, Gillette, 1939...10	15	20
Pinocchio Express, pull toy, 1940, 11" long.....................*See Fisher-Price*		
Pinocchio on Donkey, pull toy, 1940, bell-ringer ....*See Fisher-Price*		
Pinocchio Soaky.......................9	13	18
Pinocchio The Acrobat, "Watch Him Go!" tin wind-up, 1939, Marx.......300	450	600
Pinocchio tin wind-up, litho eyes, 8½" high, Marx, standing erect, circa 1940 300	450	600
Pinocchio tin wind-up, Marx, standing erect, moving eyes, 1939, 8½" high...............................400	600	800
Pinocchio, tin litho wind-up, Linemar Co., 1950s, 5½" tall 300	450	600
Pinocchio "Walking Pinocchio," Marx, plastic, 1950s 30	45	60
Pluto, 3", bendable legs, circa 1934, wooden 225	338	450
Pluto 4" long Seiberling Rubber, circa 1935 60	90	120
Pluto, 7½" long, Seiberling Rubber 50	75	100
Pluto 9" long, wood jointed 150	225	300
"Pluto", 1950s, Linemar, tin friction toy, 3" long 60	90	120
"Pluto" Marx wind-up, 1960s plastic, 4½" high 40	60	80
Pluto "Begging Rollover Pluto," 1950s, Linemar, 6½" long.......................60	90	120
Pluto Drum Major, Marx tin windup, 1940s 240	360	480
Pluto "Drum Major" Linemar, 1950s, 6½" tall, tin litho wind-up 250	375	500
Pluto hand puppet, Gund, 1950s 18	27	36
"Pluto In His Sports Car," 1950s, 4" long, friction drive, all plastic........110	165	220
Pluto, lead, 2½" high, 1933 Allied Toys...40	60	80
"Pluto Motorcycle," 1950s, Linemar, tin friction toy, 3½" long 300	450	600
Pluto "Musical Pluto," 1960s, Marx, (Dog Race Type), 8"x8" base with 2½" Pluto-plastic...................400	600	800
Pluto Mysterious Pluto, Marx 140	210	280
Pluto on Rockers, wooden, circa 1930s 130	195	260
Pluto, plastic wind-up, Marx, metal tail spins, 1950s 110	165	220

PECOS BILL, MARX windup, plastic, 1950s. Photo by Don Hultzman.

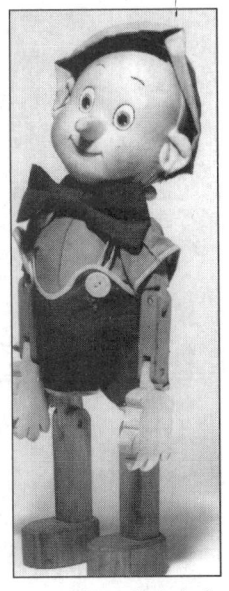

Pinocchio, cloth and jointed wood figure, KREUGER. Courtesy PB Eighty-Four, New York.

PINOCCHIO Doll, IDEAL, 8" high. Lloyd W. Ralston Auctions.

PINOCCHIO, tin litho windup, LINEMAR. Photo by Don Hultzman.

PINOCCHIO, tin windup, MARX, "Walking Pinocchio". Courtesy Ed Hyers Antique Toys.

GILLETTE, Free Pinocchio masks offer from 1940 (see Cleo, Figaro, Gepetto, Jiminy Cricket). Courtesy Rex and Richard Gray

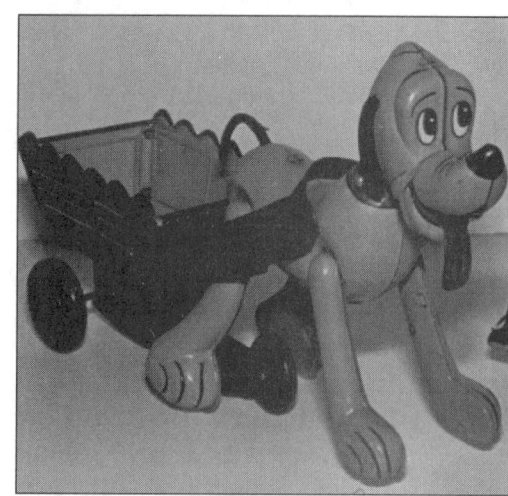

"Pluto - Pulling Cart", 1950s LINEMAR. Courtesy Ed Hyers Antique Toys.

Pluto Mysterious Pluto, MARX. Photo by Don Hultzman.

Pluto "Wise Pluto". Photo by Don Hultzman.

Pluto With Basket, 8" long. Courtesy Lloyd W. Ralston Auctions.

Pluto, plastic wind-up, MARX, metal tail spins.

PLUTO Drum Major. Photo by Don Hultzman.

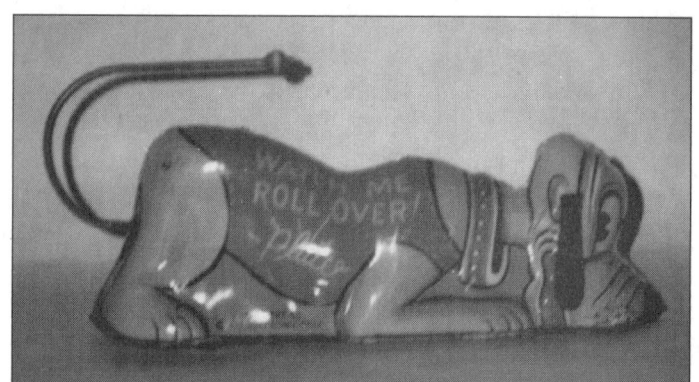

PLUTO "Watch Me Roll Over," MARX.

PLUTO "Playful Pluto & Goofy". Photo by Don Hultzman.

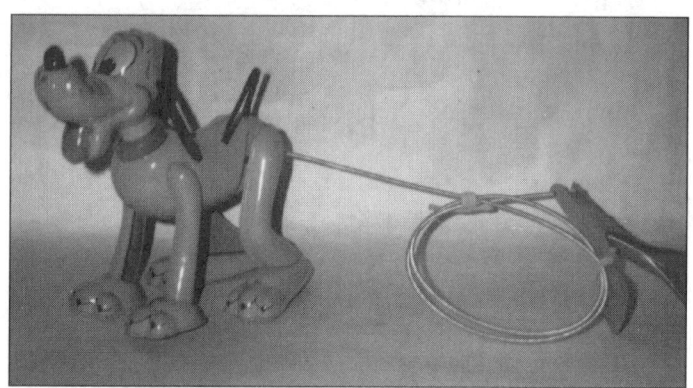

PLUTO tin litho squeeze-action with cable, LINEMAR. Photo by Don Hultzman.

	C6	C8	C10
Pluto "Playful Pluto & Goofy" 1950s Linemar, 2 piece set, windups	750	1125	1500
"Pluto - Pulling Cart," 1950s Linemar friction, 8½" long	325	488	650
Pluto, sitting position, rubber squeeze toy, 1960s	20	30	40
Pluto Soaky	10	15	20
Pluto Squeeze toy, Sun Rubber No. 11520, 1930s	45	68	90
Pluto, tin litho squeeze-action with cable, Linemar, 1950s, 4¼" tall	210	315	420
"Pluto Tricycle", 1950s, Linemar, 4" tall	200	300	400
Pluto "Watch Me Roll Over," Marx, 1939	170	255	340
Pluto, "Wise Pluto," 1939, Marx, 8" long, (like "Watch Me Roll Over")	200	300	400
Pluto With Basket paper litho on wood, 8" long	*See Fisher-Price*		
"Pluto with Whirling Tail," 1950s, Linemar wind-up, 4" high	117	176	235
Pluto, wooden, hand base, string-operated, many jointed, marionette-type, 1936	*See Fisher-Price*		
Practical Pig Doll, Gund	112	168	225
Practical Pig, tin litho windup, Linemar	263	390	520
"Professor Von Drake Go Mobile," 1950s, 6" long, Linemar windup	100	150	200
Sand Pail, 1938, Ohio Art tin litho, Mickey, Minnie and Goofy pictured	60	90	120
Seven Dwarfs, all, puppet-marionettes, Pelham	1500	2250	3000
Seven Dwarfs, all, Seiberling Rubber, 1938, 5½" high	350	525	700

	C6	C8	C10
Si-Am (Lady & Tramp) 16" high, stuffed, vinyl face, Gund, circa 1955	40	60	80
Sleeping Beauty squeeze toy, sitting with animals, 6½"	30	45	60
Sleepy 1½" lead figure, Britains	45	68	90
Sleepy, Ideal, approx. 7" high	125	188	250
Sleepy, Ideal approx. 12" high, 1938	120	180	240
Sleepy party mask, 1937	20	30	40
Sneezy, 1½" lead figure, Britains	45	68	90
Sneezy, 3¼" high, Seiberling Rubber, 1938	60	90	120
Sneezy, Ideal, approx. 7" high	125	188	250
Sneezy, Ideal, approx. 12" high, 1938	120	180	240
Sneezy Party Mask, 1937	20	30	40
Sneezy rubber squeeze toy, 1950s	10	15	20
Snow Shovel, 26" long, shows Mickey and Pluto building snowman	90	135	180
Snow White and the Seven Dwarfs lead figures by Lincoln Logs, all	500	750	1000
Snow White 2½" lead figure, Britains	45	68	90
Snow White doll, Seiberling Rubber	250	375	500
Snow White 13" high, Madame Alexander, 1938	120	180	240
Snow White, Ideal, 15" high, 1938	150	225	300
Snow White Party Mask	20	30	40
Snow White Soaky	11	16	22
Snow White Washing Machine, circa 1950, Revell Plastics, 7½" high with wringer	80	120	160
Snow White and the Seven Dwarfs Blocks, 18 blocks, in box	175	263	350
Snow White and the Seven Dwarfs, 4½" dishes, china, with cups, creamer, sugar bowl, 6" plate	210	315	420

SEVEN DWARFS, puppet-marionettes, PELHAM.

	C6	C8	C10
Snow White and the Seven Dwarfs musical top, Chein, 6½" across	80	120	160
Snow White and The Seven Dwarfs Sewing Set, Hasbro	20	30	40
Snow White Sink and Stove, Wolverine	30	45	60
Three Little Pigs clothes washer	65	98	130
"Three Little Pigs - Drummer," 1930s, 4½" tall, Schuco	110	165	220
"Three Little Pigs - Flutist", 1930s, 4½" tall, Schuco	130	195	260
Three Little Pigs Mask, 1933 Par-T-Mask	40	60	80
Three Little Pigs Sand Bucket, 3" tall	30	45	60
"Three Little Pigs - Violinist," 1930s, 4½" tall, Schuco	120	180	240
Three Little Pigs wooden pig, circa 1933, Borgfeldt, fiber arms and legs, 3¼" high	120	180	240
"Thumper", 1950s, Linemar, tin friction toy, 3" long	60	90	120
Thumper 6" friction, Marx, 1950s	100	150	200
Thumper 7" squeeze toy, Sun Rubber	30	45	60
Thumper 14" high, Gund, 1950s	38	57	76
Thumper 17" high, Gund, early 1940s	80	120	160
Timothy Mouse (Dumbo) stuffed, 17" high, Character Novelty, 1942	160	240	320
"Tramp The Dog," 1960s, Linemar friction, 4" high	90	135	180
Uncle Scrooge Handpuppet, 1960s? wearing high hat	20	30	40

	C6	C8	C10
Uncle Scrooge Limousine, "$" on back fender	110	165	220
Uncle Scrooge vinyl squeeze toy bank, 7" high, circa 1960	40	60	80
"Walt Disney Character Carousel," 1950s, Linemar Co., 7" high with 3" characters	250	375	500
"Walt Disney Character T.V. Set", 1950s, Automatic Toy Co., 5" cubic	150	225	300
Walt Disney Television Car, Marx, 1950s, 7½" long	210	315	420
"Walt Disney's Friction Delivery Wagon," 1950s, Linemar, 6" long, Mickey, Donald, Pluto, etc.	200	300	400
"Walt Disney's Friction Go-Mobile," 1960s Marx (Japan), 6" long, Mickey, Pluto, Donald, etc.	110	165	220
"Walt Disney's Mechanical Tricycle," 1950s Linemar, 4" high, Pluto, Mickey, Donald, etc.	140	210	280
"Walt Disney's Television Playhouse," Marx Playset, 39 characters	450	675	900
Wendy (Peter Pan), handpuppet	11	16	22
Wendy Marionette, 1950s	75	112	150
Witch (Snow White) party mask	20	30	40
Zorro Handpuppet	22	33	45
Zorro Flintlock Pistol, Marx	25	38	50
Zorro Playset, Marx	325	488	650
Zorro Ring, black top with Z and 'Zorro' name	22	33	45

Seven Dwarfs, all, Seiberling Rubber, 1938, 5½" high. Photo by Stan Alekna.

Snow White and the Seven Dwarfs, IDEAL, Snow White approx. 15" high, the Dwarfs 7". Courtesy Christie's East.

GUNS

(See also Premiums, Comic Character)

Average mint prices of guns in the fourth edition were $91.51 and in this edition
they average $114.32, an increase of 25%.

SOME THOUGHTS ON TOY GUN COLLECTING

By Charles W. Best

Amid all the various toys in the world, the toy gun stands out as the one type most distinctly American and native to the United States, and with good reason. From the earliest days of our history up through the late 19th century, firearms were the primary tool that enabled us to survive, settle, explore, and subdue this land. Firearms gave us our freedom in 1776 and were instrumental in preserving that freedom throughout our first hundred turbulent years. Those years, as we now know, were to become an era of "romantic" wars when boys and young men dreamed of attaining fame and glory on the battlefield or out on the Western Frontier. The War of 1812, the Mexican War, the Civil War, and numerous Indian conflicts were all fought, basically, with small arms, so it is small wonder then that when toys first began to be mass produced after the Civil War, toy guns were among the first to appear on the market. Their success was instantaneous and toy guns remained among our most popular selling toys until as recently as the 1960's.

Although toy guns were patented in the 1850's they were not manufactured in any quantity until a decade later due to the wartime shortages. These early toy guns were, for the most part, pea shooters and cork poppers and were usually made of wood with metal hardware although iron and lead types may occasionally be found among them. As you might suspect, these early examples are hard to find today and most are known only through their patent drawings. By 1870, inventors, trying to add realism to these toy guns, began using paper caps, a then new invention which had been developed just prior to the Civil War and was known as the Maynard Tape Primer. This tape primer was originally intended to detonate muzzle loading arms and closely resembled a roll of modern day paper caps. Now, for the first time, toy guns could make a loud noise yet still be relatively safe and harmless. Naturally, this spurred the demand for these new toys and designers worked overtime to create new and appealing guns. Their output was prolific and, today, the period from 1870 to 1900 is regarded as the "golden age" of the toy gun and especially the toy cap pistol, in America.

By 1880, the cast iron cap pistol had become the most popular type of toy gun by far and the various toy makers, primarily J. & E. Stevens and Ives, were competing among themselves to see who could produce the most unique and appealing designs. A glance at any collection of these early day toy pistols will show that, in those days, realism was secondary to artistic imagination. Many pistols from this period were literally covered with ornamentation and, is some cases, any resemblance to a real gun was purely coincidental. Leaf and scroll designs were the most popular but pistols can also be found with numerous other designs, including both two and three dimensional figures. Those guns with moving figures are known as "animated" pistols and even though not as rare as some, are worth much more to a collector than an ordinary-looking pistol from the same period.

Another very desirable pistol from this same era is now known as the "head" pistol and featured a head, either animal or human, which was placed at the breech end of the barrel with the mouth open to receive the cap. Over two dozen varieties of head and animated pistols are known to exist but are so much in demand that they are seldom offered for sale.

The most popular material used to make these early toy pistols was, of course, cast iron, which continued to be used heavily into the 20th century, until the demands of World War II cut off the supply. Many varieties of old toy guns were, however, made of other materials than iron. I have seen examples made from such diverse materials as paper, wood, steel, tin, lead, rubber, zinc, glass, and even wax. During the Second World War, to meet the heavy demand, toy guns were even made of molded sawdust mixed with glue. After the war a few cast iron pistols were produced and assembled, using both new and old parts, but the cost proved to be prohibitive, and makers soon turned to less expensive metals such as steel and die cast zinc. By 1950, most toy pistols were being made of the die cast material and also plastic, both of which continue to be used today.

From almost the very beginning, toy gun makers have felt the need to personalize their products and literally hundreds of different names can be found embossed on these little guns. Some examples that come to mind are: EXCELSIOR, VICTOR, AMERICAN BULLDOG, ACORN, SUN, BOOM, DARB, ACE, DAISY, COWBOY KING, POLO, TRIUMPH, TERROR, etc. Many names were used only once on one particular gun and then dropped while others have reappeared time and again on different guns over the years. This custom of naming toy guns still goes on today and a visit to any toy store will turn up names such as: COWHAND, TOP GUN JR., 007, etc. Many of these names seem to reflect current events or personalities while on others, the meaning has become obscure.

For the toy collector, or would-be collector, the collecting of toy guns and especially pistols, not only offers a large diversity of models and styles but, because of their tremendous popularity in the past, also the opportunity to find and acquire interesting and unusual examples at an affordable price. Guns from as far back as the 1920's and '30's can still be found at flea markets, garage sales, and second hand stores, often at a price that is only a fraction of what other toys from these same years will sell for.

NOTE: Measurements given, in general, are from one end of the gun to the other, rather than on a diagonal from grip to muzzle. Much of the information on manufacturers,

measurements, etc., comes from Charles W. Best's excellent book "Cast Iron Toy Pistols" (see bibliography). Dates of manufacturers can vary within five years, though most of the later dates are considerably more accurate.

CHARLES W. BEST is a leading authority on toy weapons, and has been collecting them in earnest since 1966. His collection is regarded as one of the finest and most comprehensive in existence, and has won many awards at various gun shows. In addition to writing a number of articles on the subject in such magazines as Gun Report and Antique Toy World, he is the Author of "Cast Iron Toy Pistols" (see Bibliography).

	C6	C8	C10
Ace cast iron cap pistol. Stevens, "Made in U.S.A." 5" long, 1930.....30	35	40
Ace cast iron cap pistol, 5" long, 1935..25	30	35
Acme steel cap automatic, repeater, circa 1930......10	13	18

"America" by STEVENS. Photo by Charles W. Best.

American Bulldog, 1910. Courtesy Sotheby's New York.

	C6	C8	C10
Acorn cast iron pistol 75	100	125
Admiral Dewey cast iron cap bomb.....125	150	200
Aeromatic Glider Gun, steel automatic, circa 1940, shoots balsa airplanes......10	24	32
Agitator, The, cast iron cap and torpedo shooter, 1908, John Fox, 8¼"......125	150	175
Aim To Save, circa 1909 200	235	285
Air Blaster, Wham-O, shoots burst of air, plastic......20	25	35
Air Raid Warning signal pistol......30	50	75
America cap pistol with shield, pat. 1873 150	175	200
America, 1880, Stevens, 8¾"......135	200	275
American cast iron cap pistol, Kilgore, 1940, 9⅝"......125	160	200
American Bulldog cast iron .22 cal. blank shooter, 1910, 4½" long, second trigger tips barrel to load, Kenton, handle projects outward 40	50	65

"American", by KILGORE. Photo by Charles W. Best.

Army 45. Photo by Charles W. Best.

	C6	C8	C10
American Bulldog cast iron .22 blank shooter, 1920, 4½" long, Kenton, second trigger tips barrel to load, handle curves inward 45	55	75
Army cast iron cap pistol, 1910............40	50	65
Army 45 cast iron cap automatic, Hubley 1940 "Made in U.S.A." 6⅝"..55	65	80
Army 45 diecast zinc cap automatic, Hubley, 1940, plastic grips, "Made in U.S.A." 6½" long........................35	40	55
Army pistol with revolving cylinder, tin litho, Marx no. 625 20	25	30
Army sparkling pop gun, Marx No. 197 20	25	30
Atomic Disintegrator cap pistol, Hubley..125	150	185
Auto Magic Picture Gun, projects film onto wall. 1936. comes with film and instructions, in box 50	60	75
Automatic Repeater Paper Pop Pistol No. 74, Marx, aluminum..................15	20	25
Automatic Repeater, pressed steel, 7" long, 1920s, Wyandotte No. 40.......20	25	30
Bang cast iron cap pistol, Kilgore, "Made in U.S.A.," 6" long..............25	30	35
Bang-O cast iron cap pistol, Stevens, 1938, "Made in U.S.A.," 7" long....40	50	60
Banner, blank-shooting mechanical cast iron pistol, Ives, 5" 150	175	250

Left to Right. Top: BIG BILL, PLUCK, DICK. Middle: ATOMIC DISINTEGRATOR, SURE SHOT SAFETY. Bottom: TIGER, GENE AUTRY 44. Photo Courtesy Garth's Auctions Inc.

Banner. Courtesy Sotheby's New York.

	C6	C8	C10
Bell Pistol, Wyandotte............................15	20	25
Benjamin Pump early BB gun, before 1910 75	85	150
Biff cast iron cap automatic, Kenton, 1935, "Made in U.S.A. Pat. Apld. For," 4½" 25	35	45
Biff Jr. cast iron cap automatic, Kenton 1935, "Made in U.S.A. Pat. Apld. For," 4⅛" long 25	35	45
Big Bill cast iron cap pistol, large hammer, "Made in U.S.A.," Kilgore 1935, 4⅞" 20	25	30
Big Bill cast iron cap pistol, Kilgore, 1925, 5½" long 20	25	30

"Big Horn". Photo by Charles W. Best.

	C6	C8	C10
Big Bill cast iron cap pistol, large hammer, "Made in U.S.A.," Kilgore 1930, 5¾" 20	25	30
Big Buster cast iron cap automatic, Kilgore 1915, "Patd Jul 2 1907, Made in U.S.A.," 5", two-piece trigger..70	85	125
Big Chief cast iron cap pistol, Kilgore, 1935, 6" long...................................25	30	40
Big Chief cast iron cap pistol, Kilgore, 1935, has star and "K", 6" 25	30	40
Big Chief cast iron cap pistol, early-looking, but made in 1930, 3½", Dent "Made in U.S.A." 20	25	30
Big Clip cast iron cap pistol, Stevens 1930, "Made in U.S.A.", 6¾".........30	35	40
Big Horn cast iron cap pistol, revolving cylinder, Kilgore, 1939, 8⅜" ...100	130	150
Big Injun, hammerless............................150	175	250

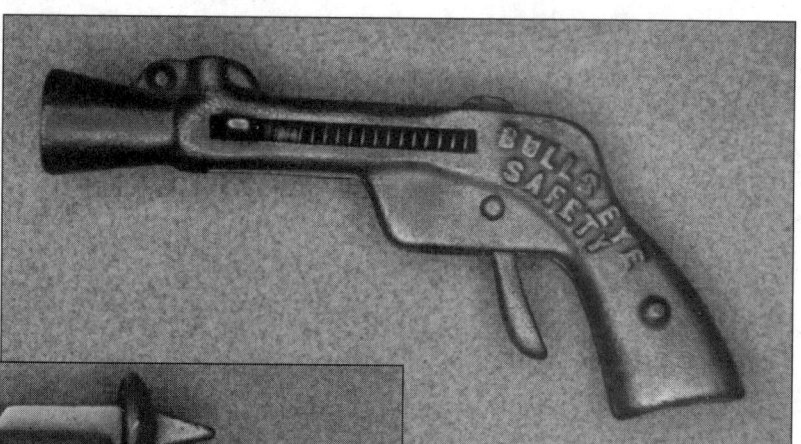

Bull's Eye Safety. Photo by Charles W. Best.

"Bigger Bang". Photo by Charles W. Best.

Border Patrol, 1940. Courtesy Sotheby's New York.

	C6	C8	C10
Big Scout, 1935 60		75	90
Big Scout, 1940 (engraved) 35		45	55
Bigger Bang large hammer cast iron cap pistol, Kilgore 1930, 6" long 30		40	50
Bill 40		50	60
Billy The Kid cast iron cap pistol, Kilgore 1930, 6¾" 85		100	135
Black Jack cast iron cap pistol, long barrel, Kenton 1930, "Pat. Sept. 11-23", 11" 125		135	165
Blaze Away Dart Pistol, Marx No. G23.....................15		20	25
Bob cast iron cap pistol, Kilgore, 1930, 5" long.....................25		30	35
Boom 150		200	275
Border Patrol cast iron cap automatic, Kilgore, 1930, 4¼" long 35		45	60
Border Patrol cast iron cap automatic, Kilgore, 1935, "Pat. Apld. For, Made in U.S.A.," 4½" long 35		45	60
Border Patrol, 1940 35		45	60
Boss cast iron mammoth cap pistol, 1925, Kenton, 6¼".....................30		35	40
Boy's Delight Pat. June 1891, cast iron cap pistol.....................150		165	200
Boy's Police Automatic 8" cardboard pop gun, circa 1940s 8		10	15
Brat cast iron cap pistol 30		40	50
Bravo 75		95	120

	C6	C8	C10
Brevet Depose 300		400	525
Bronc cast iron cap pistol, Kenton 1935, "Kenton, Made in U.S.A.," 6".....................30		35	50
Buc-A-Roo cast iron cap pistol, Kilgore 1940, 7¾" 35		50	70
Buck cast iron pistol, Hubley 1930, looks earlier, 3¼".....................25		35	45
Buck Jones Special Daisy Pump Repeater Rifle, with compass and sun dial in stock, 1937 65		75	100
Buddy, 1930.....................21		31	42
Buddy, 1935.....................21		31	42
Buffalo Bill, 1890.....................200		250	350
Buffalo Bill cast iron cap pistol, Kenton, 1925, "Pat. Sept. 11-23," 11⅜", very long barrel 100		150	185
Buffalo Bill cast iron cap pistol, Kenton 1930, "Pat Sept. 11-23," 13½", perhaps the longest-barreled cap pistol 250		350	450
Buffalo Bill cast iron cap pistol, Stevens, 1940, "Made in U.S.A.", 7¾" long 40		50	65
Bull cast iron cap pistol, Hubley, 1940, "Pat Appld. for Pat. Mch. 25, '24," 6¼" 25		30	35
Bull Dog cast iron cap pistol, Hubley, 1935, "Pat. 1,488,046," 6¼" long...25		30	40

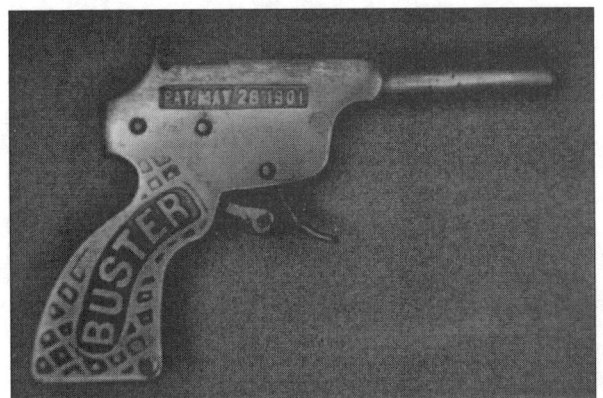

"Buster", maker unknown, 1901, 6" long.

	C6	C8	C10
Bulldozer cast iron cap pistol, six-shooter, July 1874	150	200	250
Bull's Eye cast iron cap pistol, Kenton, 1940, "Gene Autry" signature on grips, 6½"	45	60	80
Bullseye Safety cast iron pistol, flare barrel, with spring	75	100	150
Bunker Hill cast iron cap pistol, National, 1925, 5¼" long	25	35	45
Burp Gun, Mattel, 1956, 13" long, aluminum, die cast, plastic	45	55	70
"Buster," maker unknown, 1901, 6"	50	75	125
Buster cast iron cap automatic, 1910, Kilgore, 5½"	45	60	90
Butting Match mechanical pistol, cast iron	250	325	400
Cadet, 1930	24	36	48
Cal, 1925	30	45	60
Cannon - Animated Cap Pistol	250	350	450
Cap Bomb, cast iron, head shape	75	95	125
Cap Bomb, dog's head	75	95	125
Cap Pistol, cast iron, ornate, 1878	65	100	125

	C6	C8	C10
Cap Pistol, cast iron, revolving cylinder, 1887	100	145	200
Cap Pistol, cast iron, six-shot, dated 1895	100	145	185
Cast iron pistol, ornate, six shot, 1895	100	145	185
Cast iron pistol, shoots caps, embossed	20	25	30
Cast iron pistol, shoots caps, plated barrel	20	25	30
Cap pistol, steel, repeating, red, Wyandotte, 8" long	15	20	30
Captain cast iron cap automatic, Kilgore, 1940, 4¼" long	20	30	35
Cat (animated)	450	700	900
Cavalier cast iron cap automatic, Kilgore, 1935, "Pat. Appld. For, Made in U.S.A.," 4½"	30	40	50
Challenge, 1890	150	200	300
Champ Automatic, 5", die cast, Hubley	25	30	35
Chief (1900-1910)	25	30	35
Chief cast iron .22 cal. blank shooter, Kenton, 1915, 6" long, second trigger tips up barrel to load	50	60	75
Chief cast iron cap pistol, Hubley 1930, "Pat 1,488,046," 6⅛"	30	35	45
Chief cap pistol, aluminum single shot, Hubley	10	15	20
Chieftain cast iron cap pistol, National, 1920, 11" long	75	95	130
Chinese Must Go mechanical cap pistol	300	385	525
"Click Pistol" Marx No. 32	15	20	25
Click Pistol, Marx, approx. 7¾" long, pressed steel, with box	15	20	25
Click Pistol, tin litho, Marx No. 36	15	20	25

Cannon. Courtesy Sotheby's New York.

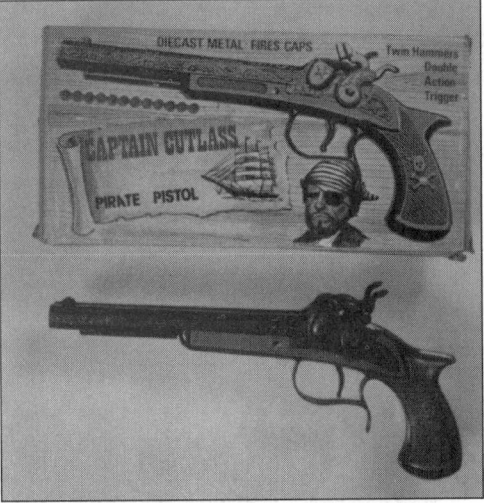

Captain Cutlass Pirate Pistol, maker unknown, possibly foreign. Copy of Pirate by HUBLEY. Diecast. Photo by Charles W. Best. No Price Found.

Clown (on barrel). Photo by Charles W. Best.

"Champ". Photo by Charles W. Best.

"Corporal". Photo by Charles W. Best.

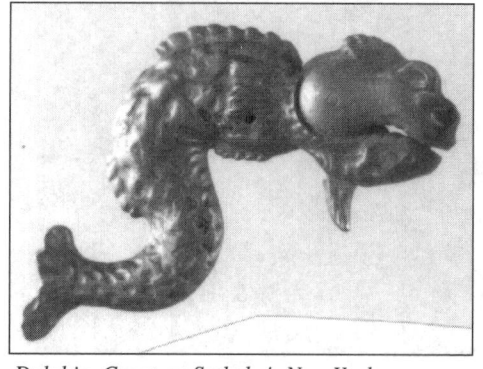

Dolphin. Courtesy Sotheby's New York.

Daniel Boone Wilderness Scout Derringer. Photo by Gary J. Linden.

"Columbia" by STEVENS, 1890. Photo by Charles W. Best.

"Dagger Derringer". Photo by Charles W. Best.

"Doughboy". Courtesy Charles D. Richards.

Daisy No. 25 BB gun. Courtesy Sotheby's New York.

Duck. Courtesy Sotheby's New York.

DAISY No. 118 Targeteer. Photo by Bill Kaufman. Courtesy Good Old Days Store.

454

	C6	C8	C10
Clicker Pistol, plain black, late 1930s, early 1940s.....................15	20	25	
Clip Jr. cast iron cap pistol, Stevens, 1935, 5¼".................25	30	35	
Clipper cast iron cap automatic, Kilgore, 1935, 4⅛".........35	45	55	
Clown and mule animated pistol..........500	600	750	
Clown (on a barrel)....................350	450	600	
Colt cast iron cap pistol, Stevens 1920, "Patented June 17, 1890, Made in U.S.A.," 5½"................35	45	60	
Colt cast iron cap pistol, Stevens, 1935, 6½".................30	35	45	
Colt .45 die cast Hubley.......................70	85	100	
Columbia 1885 cast iron cap pistol......200	250	300	
Columbia 1890 cast iron cap pistol, Stevens, 8¾"...................200	250	300	
Columbia cast iron cap pistol, pat. June 1891...................200	250	300	
Columbian Junior Early BB gun..........200	250	500	
Comet, 1885, 5½", Stevens.................135	200	300	
Comet, 1925, 7⅛", Stevens..................40	60	80	
Cop cast iron cap pistol Hubley 1930 "Pat 1,488,046" or "Pat. Mch. 25 '24," 5"...................25	30	35	
Cork-popper pistol, Wyandotte, spur trigger.......................20	25	30	
Cork-shooting rifle, Marx No. 206........25	30	35	
Corn Shooter cap pistol.....................55	65	85	
Corporal, maker unknown, 1900, 8⅞"..60	85	125	
Cowboy cast iron cap pistol, Ives, 1890, 7⅝"..............75	85	125	
Cowboy cast iron cap pistol, Stevens, 1935, "Made in U.S.A.," 3½".........20	25	30	
Cowboy cast iron cap pistol, long barrel, Stevens, 1930, "Made in U.S.A."............150	165	200	
Cowboy cast iron cap pistol, Hubley 1940 "Made in U.S.A.," 8"............45	60	75	
Cowboy King, 1940.............................65	75	90	
Coyote die cast Hubley........................30	35	45	
Crack, 1925, Stevens, 5"......................40	60	80	
Cupid, 1900, 5¼".................................60	85	125	
Dagger Derringer die cast Hubley.........35	45	60	
Daisy 1895.............................95	135	185	
Daisy 1925.............................25	35	45	
Daisy Buzz Barton Special No. 195, BB gun.......................75	100	135	
Daisy cast iron cap pistol, Pat. Apr. 1873.............................70	120	150	
Daisy cast iron cap pistol, Hubley 1935, 4⅛"................20	25	30	

	C6	C8	C10
Daisy "Daisy Mfg. Co. No. 80" water pistol, Pat. 1807839, approx. 7¼" long...................15	20	25	
Daisy Pump No. 25 BB gun (early)......35	40	60	
Daisy Defender BB gun, No. 140.........125	150	300	
Daisy early BB gun, 3rd model, with cast iron frame.....................200	235	400	
Daisy Red Ryder BB gun No. 111.....*see Comic Character*			
Daisy "Scout" No. 75 BB gun, circa 1955, plastic stock................25	30	40	
Daisy No. 7 water pistol.........................10	15	20	
Daisy No. 8 water pistol all metal, patent 1915.....................20	25	30	
Daisy No. 26 Remington.......................90	140	200	
Daisy Targeteer Air Pistol, circa 1947, 1940s..........................30	35	40	
Daisy "Daisy No. 118 Targeteer" automatic 10¼" long, target pistol..30	35	40	
Daisy No. 96.........................50	65	90	
Daisy No. 99 Champion.......................70	120	150	
Daisy air rifle, cast iron and brass, early, 31" long.....................200	250	400	
Daisy No. 155 Plymouth.......................35	60	75	
Daisy Cinematic Picture Pistol, circa mid-1940s.....................50	65	85	
Daisy Double Duty Pistol, pops and shoots water from separate barrel, very similar to Buck Rogers pistol .45	60	75	
Daisy Zooka "Pop" Pistol, similar to Buck Rogers pistol.....................50	65	95	
Dandy cast iron cap pistol, Hubley, 1935, can have variety of markings, 5¾"................30	40	50	
Daniel Boone Wilderness Scout Derringer, Marx, mint on card........25	30	40	
Darb cast iron cap pistol, Kenton 1930 "Pat. Sept. 11-23", 5½" long.....25	30	40	
Dart Pistol, Wyandotte, colorful, fancy lithographing.................15	20	25	

DRAGNET - Detective Special Reporting Revolver Cap Gun, circa 1955. Courtesy HAKE'S Americana & Collectibles.

Dude cast iron cap. Photo by Charles W. Best.

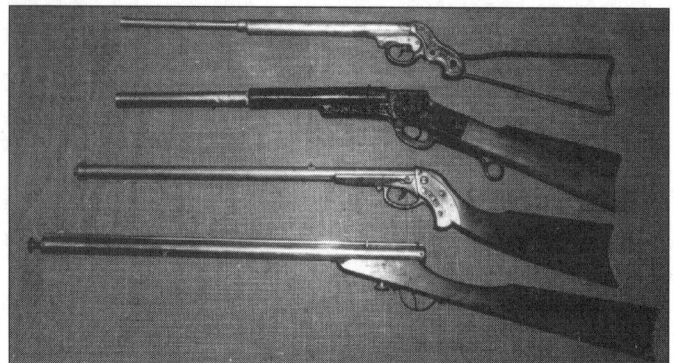

Typical B.B. Guns from the year 1900. Row 1: Daisy 3rd MODEL; Row 2: COLUMBIAN JUNIOR; Row 3: KING; Row 4: BENJAMIN (pump). Courtesy Charles W. Best.

Typical Cast Iron Cap Pistols 1900-1910. Left to Right. Top: NEMO, LAS, TIGER 1915. Middle: GO, BUSTER 1910, SCOUT 1890. Bottom: unmarked, NATIONAL, Stevens 1920, unmarked. Courtesy Charles W. Best.

	C6	C8	C10
David	40	50	75
Dead Shot	75	90	125
Defence, 1896	75	95	135
Derby cast iron cap pistol, Hubley, 1930, 7"	30	40	50
Detroit cast iron cap pistol, 1910, 6⅝" long	65	85	100
Dick cast iron cap pistol, Hubley 1930, 6"	25	30	35
Dick cast iron cap automatic, Hubley 1940, "Made in U.S.A.," 4⅛"	20	25	30

	C6	C8	C10
DIK cast iron cap pistol, Kenton 1935, "Pat. Sept. 11-23," 4¾"	25	30	35
Dixie (1888-1890)	75	95	130
Dixie cast iron cap pistol, Kenton 1935, "Made in U.S.A. Pat. Appld. For," 6¼"	35	45	60
Doc cast iron cap pistol, Kenton, 1940, "Pat. Sept. 11-23," 4½"	20	25	30
Dolphin animated cap pistol (may actually be Sea Serpent)	400	500	650
Double-barrel cast iron cap pistol, dated 1880	125	165	225
Double-barrel pop gun-rifle, Marx No. 230.50		75	100
Double-barrel cork gun rifle, Marx No. 232	50	80	125
Double-faced cap bomb, cast iron	60	75	90
Double-trigger cast iron match-shooting pistol, large, Stephens, PA 1873	125	150	200
Doughboy cast iron cap automatic, Kilgore 1920, "Made in U.S.A.," 5"	30	45	50
Dragnet Detective Special repeating revolver cap gun, circa 1955	25	30	35
Duck, animated cap pistol, cast iron, 3¾" long, 1884	2500	3000	5000
Dude cast iron cap pistol, Stevens 1887, "Pat. Mar. 22 '87," 3½"	75	125	150
Dude cast iron cap pistol, plastic grips, 1941, Kenton, 6½"	35	50	65
Eagle cast iron cap pistol, Stevens, 1895, "Pat. June 17, 1890," 7½"	100	125	150
Eagle, circa 1940	30	40	60
Echo cap pistol, six-shooter cast iron, 1881	150	250	400
Echo cast iron cap pistol, Stevens 1920, 4¼"	20	25	35
Echo cast iron cap pistol, Stevens 1930, "Made in U.S.A.", 4½"	10	15	20
Excelsior cast iron cap pistol, Stevens, 1875, "Pat'd Apr. 22, '73," 5¼"	125	150	175
Federal cast iron cap pistol, Kilgore, 1920, 5½"	25	30	35
Federal cast iron cap automatic, Kilgore 1940, 4⅞", has removable clip to hold caps	35	40	55
Federal cast iron cap pistol, Kilgore 1920, "Pat. Dec. '14; Made in U.S.A."	35	40	50
Federal - Kilgore No. 1 cast iron cap pistol, 1925, 5¼", Kilgore	20	30	40
Federal No. 2 cast iron cap pistol, Kilgore 1925, 6⅜"	65	75	100
Fido, 4", 1910	50	65	85
Firecracker pistol, filigree handle, cast iron	100	125	150

	C6	C8	C10
First No. 1, 1920, 6¾"	135	190	275
Five-barrel firecracker pistol, iron and brass, 1877	650	800	950
5-Star steel dart pistol, Wyandotte	15	20	30
Flash cast iron cap pistol, Hubley 1934, "Pat'd" 6¼"	35	50	75
Flintlock die cast Hubley	25	30	35
Flintlock Junior die cast, Hubley	15	20	25
Flintlock Midget, die cast, Hubley	10	15	20
Four Way cast iron cap pistol, Kenton 1930, "Pat. Appld. For", shoots pea or dart, rubber band and cap, all at same time	150	185	250
49-ER cast iron cap pistol, Stevens 1940, 9"	100	135	155
Fox cast iron cap pistol, Hubley 1935, 4½"	20	25	30
Frontier cast iron cap pistol, Ives, 1890, "Pat. June 21, 1887 and June 17, 1890," Dog's head atop the barrel facing hammer	200	250	325
G-Man cast iron cap automatic, Kilgore			

	C6	C8	C10
1935, 6", looks like German Luger, removable magazine holds caps	65	75	95
G-Man bakelite-framed cap automatic, Kilgore, 1940, 6"	50	65	85
G-Man clicker pistol, tin, black	25	30	35
G-Man wind-up steel spark pistol, painted finish	30	35	40
G-Man wind-up steel spark pistol, nickel finish with jewels on grip	35	40	45

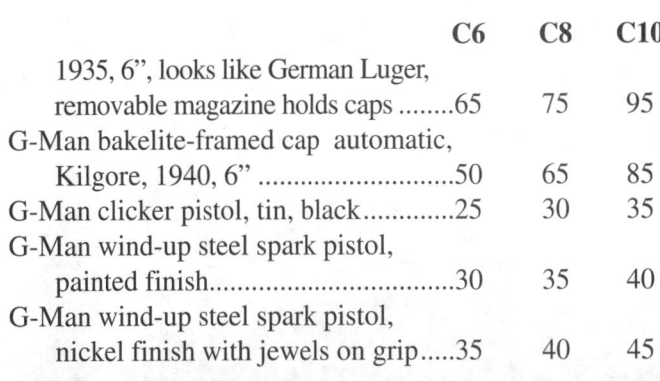

Typical Cast Iron Cap Pistols, 1920-1930. Left to Right. Top: OH BOY 1922, BUNKER HILL, BIG BILL 1925; Middle: FEDERAL 1920, RANGER 1920, NEW 50 SHOT INVINCIBLE; Bottom: IMPERIAL, MASTER 1922, NATIONAL No. 380. Courtesy Charles W. Best.

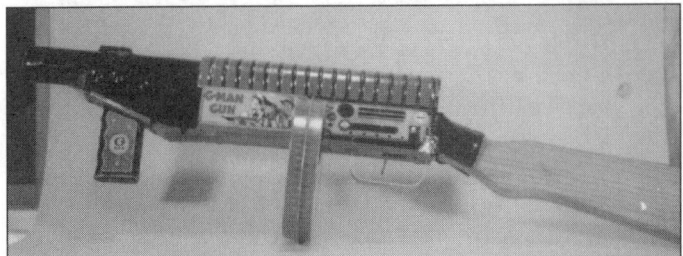

G-MAN GUN, MARX, tin litho with wood stock. Courtesy Gary Linden.

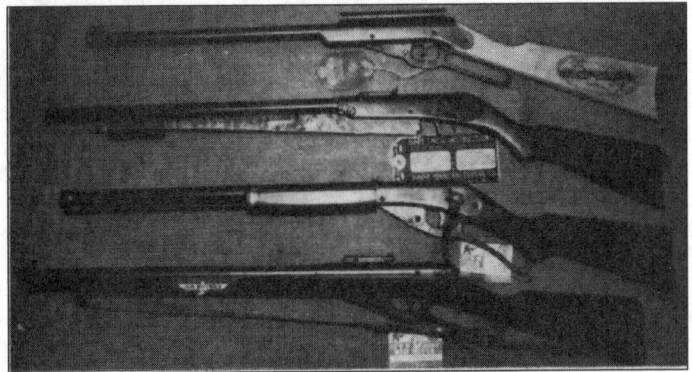

Popular Daisy B.B. Guns from the 1930s (top to bottom): Daisy BUZZ BARTON SPECIAL, No. 195; Daisy Pump No. 25; Daisy RED RYDER, NO. 111; Daisy DEFENDER, No. 140. Courtesy Charles W. Best.

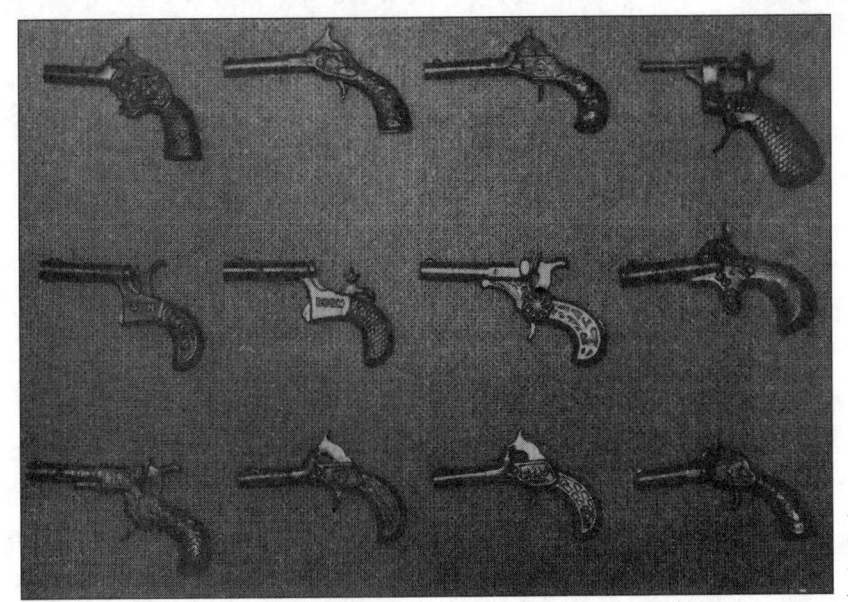

Federal - Kilgore No. 1. Courtesy Sotheby's New York.

Typical Cast Iron Cap Pistols, 1870-1880. Left to Right. Top: Unmarked, DAISY, Unmarked, SURE SHOT. Middle: SUN, BOOM, Unmarked, TIP TOP NO. 50. Bottom: KING, Unmarked, 1880, OUR ARMY FOREVER. Courtesy Charles W. Best.

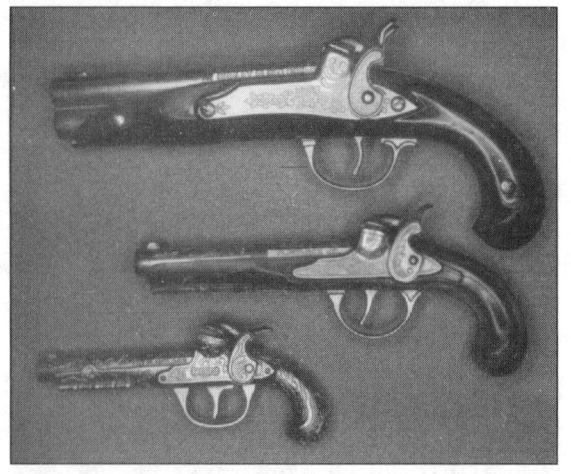

Top to Bottom: Flintlock, Flintlock Jr. Flintlock Midget. Photo by Charles W. Best.

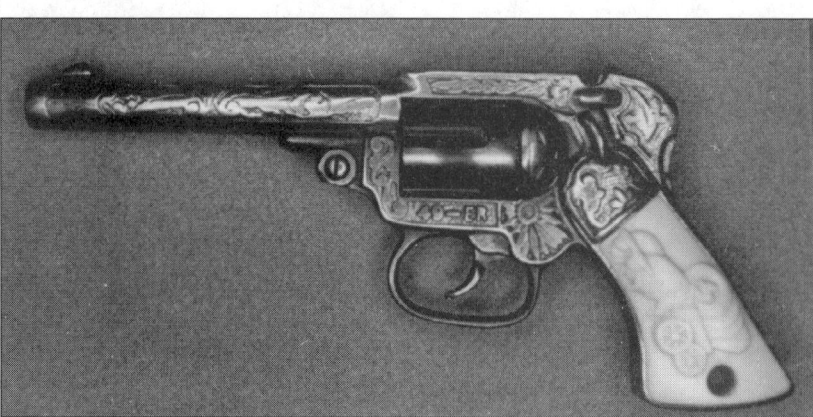

"49 - ER". Photo by Charles W. Best.

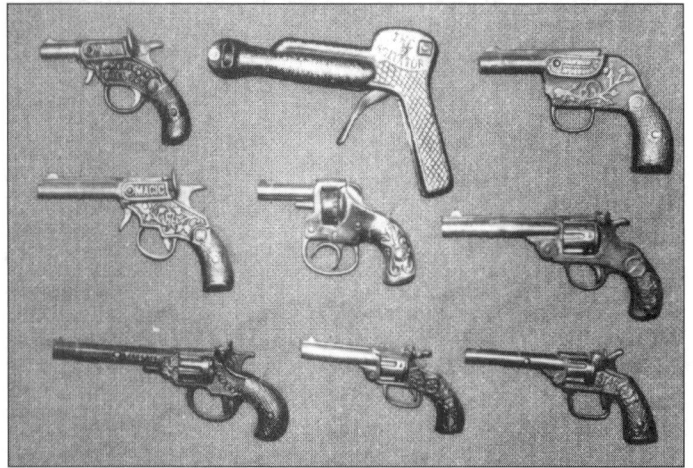

Typical Cast Iron Cap Pistols, 1900-1910. Left to Right. Top: AMERICAN BULLDOG 1920, AGITATOR, THE HANSON-LINDSBORG K.S.; Middle: MAGIC 1900, unmarked .22 blank shooter, unmarked; Bottom: COWBOY 1890, BOSS 1925, STAR 1910. Courtesy Charles W. Best.

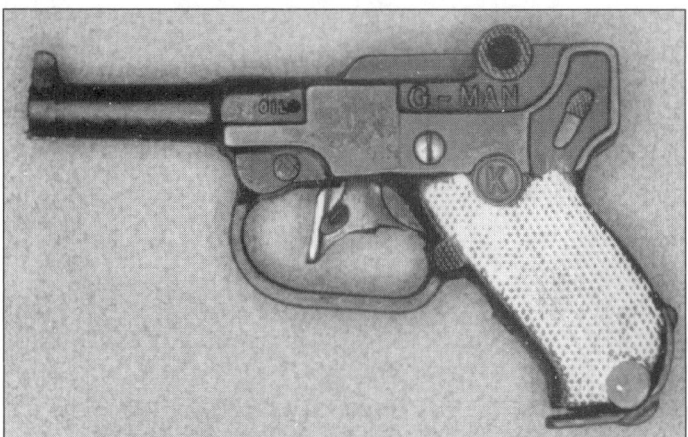

G-Man cast iron cap automatic, KILGORE, 1935.Photo by Charles W. Best.

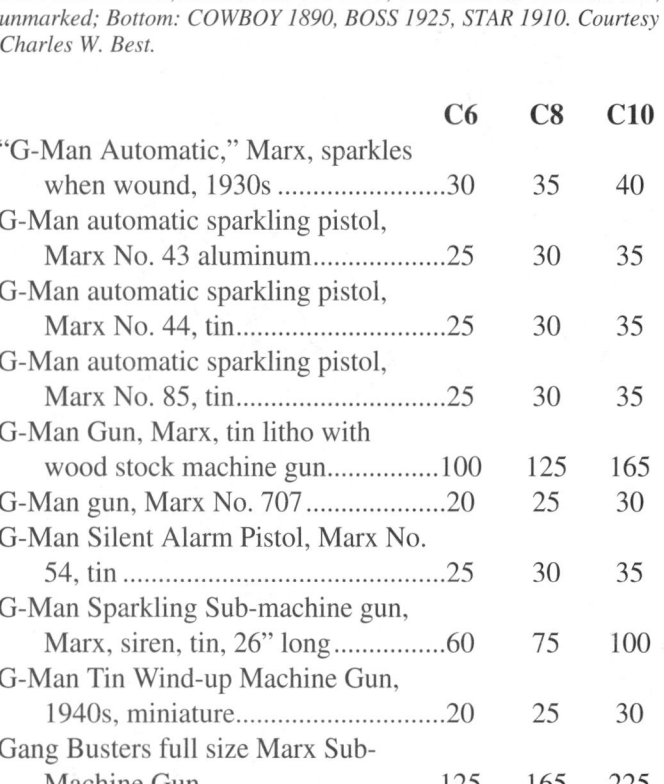

	C6	C8	C10
"G-Man Automatic," Marx, sparkles when wound, 1930s	30	35	40
G-Man automatic sparkling pistol, Marx No. 43 aluminum	25	30	35
G-Man automatic sparkling pistol, Marx No. 44, tin	25	30	35
G-Man automatic sparkling pistol, Marx No. 85, tin	25	30	35
G-Man Gun, Marx, tin litho with wood stock machine gun	100	125	165
G-Man gun, Marx No. 707	20	25	30
G-Man Silent Alarm Pistol, Marx No. 54, tin	25	30	35
G-Man Sparkling Sub-machine gun, Marx, siren, tin, 26" long	60	75	100
G-Man Tin Wind-up Machine Gun, 1940s, miniature	20	25	30
Gang Busters full size Marx Sub-Machine Gun	125	165	225

	C6	C8	C10
Gem cast iron cap pistol, Stevens, 1900, 3"	30	35	40
Gem 1925	20	30	40
Gene Autry cast iron cap pistol, Kenton 1939, 8⅜"	65	75	95
Gene Autry cast iron cap pistol, Kenton 1939, "Made in U.S.A. Pat. Appld. For," 6½"	65	75	95
Gene Autry cast iron cap pistol, Kenton 1940, "Made in U.S.A.," 6½", red grips	65	75	95
Gene Autry cast iron pistol (doesn't fire caps), Kenton, 1940, "Made in U.S.A.," 6½"	80	90	110
Gip, 1900	40	60	80
Go cast iron cap pistol, 1910, maker unknown, 6¾"	35	45	55
Go Bang	100	145	200
Guard cast iron cap pistol, Kilgore 1935, "Made in U.S.A.," 6¼"	30	35	40
H-Bar-O cast iron cap pistol, Kilgore, 1925, "Made in U.S.A.," 7½"	45	55	70
Halt	45	50	60

Gene Autry cast iron cap pistol, KENTON, 1939, 8⅜". Photo by Charles W. Best.

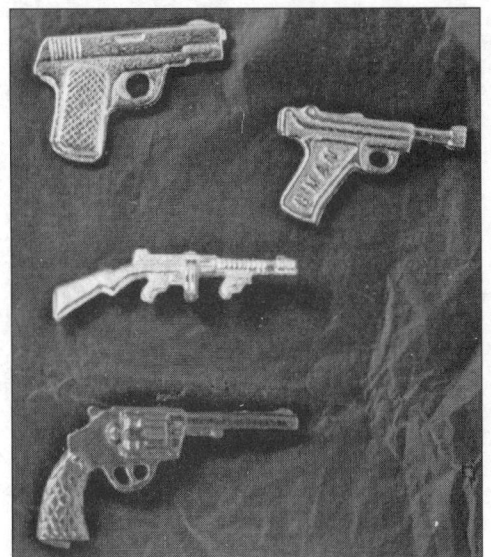

GREY IRON cast these solid cast iron weapons in the 1930s and early 1940s. John Wright casts them today. The Revolver is 2½" long. Since there may be no way of telling old castings from new, the price averages about $1 each.

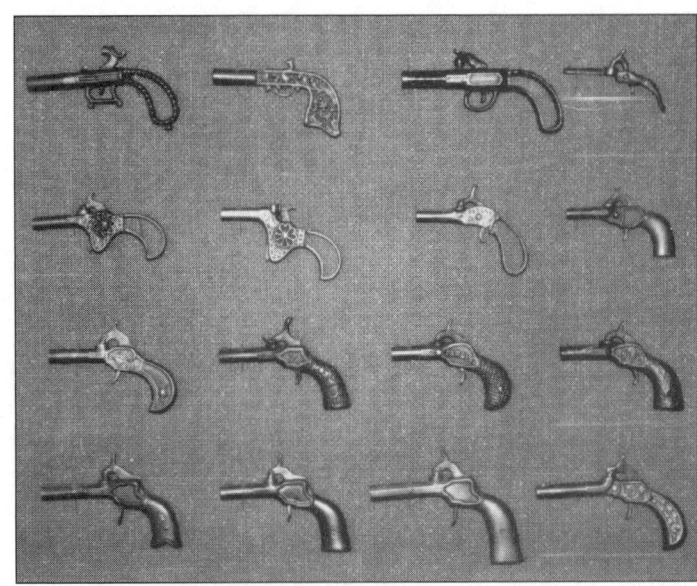

Typical Cast Iron Cap Pistols, 1870-1880. Left to Right. Row 1: Three Unmarked Firecracker Pistols, Unmarked Penny Pistol; Row 2: Unmarked, Unmarked, GO BANG, Unmarked; Row 3: Unmarked, "7", PAROLE, Unmarked; Row 4: All Unmarked. Courtesy Charles W. Best.

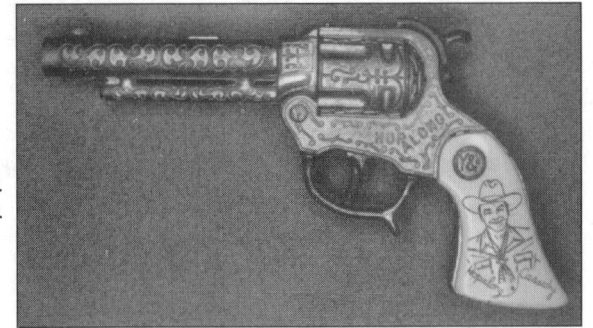

"Hopalong Cassidy". Photo by Charles W. Best.

	C6	C8	C10
Hammerless cast iron cap pistol, Stevens, 1892, "Pat. Appld. For," 7¼", four revolving triggers, hammer, concealed	150	200	285
Hanson-Lindsborg K.S. cast iron firecracker pistol, 1905, Hanson "Pat. Appld. For," 6⅜", fires firecracker	65	75	100
Hero cast iron cap pistol, Stevens, 1937, 5¼"	15	20	25
Hero, 1940	15	25	30
Hero Auto cast iron cap automatic, 1920, Stevens, 4¾"	45	50	65
Hi-Ho cast iron cap pistol, Stevens, 1940, "Made in U.S.A.," 7"	40	50	65
Hi-Ho cast iron pistol, can fire caps, Stevens, 1940, "Made in U.S.A.," 7"	40	50	65
Hi-Ho cast iron cap pistol, Kilgore, 1940, 6½"	40	50	65
Hi-Ho cast iron cap pistol, Kenton, 1940, "Pat. Sept. 11-23," 5⅛"	40	50	65
Hi-Ranger cast iron cap pistol, Stevens, 1940, 7¾"	35	45	55

	C6	C8	C10
Hopalong Cassidy 9" revolver, Wyandotte, "Hopalong" on both sides of handle	85	100	125
Hopalong Cassidy 10" Revolver with bust of Hopalong, Schmidt	135	145	165
Hub cast iron cap pistol, Hubley, 1940, 6¼"	25	30	35
Hustler cast iron pistol	55	70	115
Ibex, 1895, Stevens, 4½"	60	75	110
Ideal, tin dart-shooter	15	20	30
Imperial cast iron cap pistol, Kilgore, 1935, 5¼"	45	55	65
Indian cast iron cap pistol	60	70	90
Invincible New 50 Shot, 1930	30	35	50
Invincible cast iron cap pistol, Kilgore 1935, 5¼", "Pat. Dec. 14"	30	35	45
Jack Armstrong airplane gun, Daisy, 1936	35	45	60
Jax cast iron cap pistol, Kenton, 1930, "Pat. Sept. 11-23," 4"	20	25	30
Johnnie's Little Gun	200	250	350
Joker	135	175	225
Jumbo cast iron cap pistol, "Pat. June 17, 1890; Made in U.S.A.," 9½", Stevens 1895	125	150	250

Some classic Hubley die-cast cap pistols from the 1950s. Row 1: COLT .45, FLINTLOCK; Row 2: PIONEER, Padlock Pistol w/key, FLINTLOCK JR.; Row 3: COYOTE, FLINTLOCK MIDGET; Row 4: DAGGER DERRINGER, REMINGTON .36; Row 5: ARMY ,45 (automatic). Courtesy Charles W. Best.

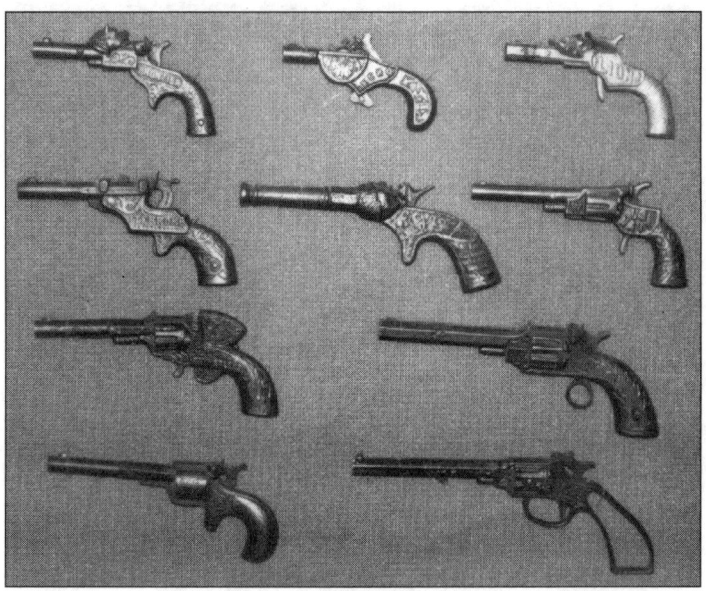

"Typical Cast Iron Cap Pistols, 1880-1890. Left to Right. Top Row: FRONTIER, ECHO, LION; Row 2: TERROR, BREVET DEPOSE, US NAVY; Row 3: HAMMERLESS, AMERICA; Row 4: Unmarked, TEXAS JACK. Courtesy Charles W. Best. Photo by Charles W. Best.

"Just Out." Courtesy Lloyd W. Ralston Auctions.

	C6	C8	C10
Jr. Police Chief, cast iron cap automatic, Kenton, 1938, "Made In U.S.A.," 3⅞"	35	40	45
Junior: Police 32 cast iron cap pistol, Hubley, 1940, "Hubley; Pat'd. 2088891," 5¼"	30	35	45
Jr. Ranger .32 cal. 1925	25	35	50
Junior Six-Shooter cast iron cap pistol, Kilgore, 1935, 5½"	30	35	50
"Just Out" cast iron animated cap pistol, 1880s	400	500	650
Kid 1930	20	30	40
Kido cast iron cap pistol, Kenton 1936, "Kenton, Made in U.S.A.," 5⅜"	25	30	35
Kilgore cast iron cap pistol, Kilgore, 1910, 5"	35	40	50
Kilgore cast iron cap pistol, Kilgore, 1912, 5¼"	35	40	50
King BB gun, early	85	125	200
King cast iron cap pistol, Pat. Aug. 1879	75	135	200
King cast iron cap pistol, Stevens, 1925, "Made in U.S.A.," 4¾"	25	30	40
King 1930	20	25	35
King Junior No. 10 cork rifle, Markham Rifle Co., "1909" 21" long	25	30	35
Kit Carson cast iron cap pistol, Kenton, 1928, "Pat. Sept. 11-23," 9"	50	65	85
Korker	135	165	225
L.F. & Co.	75	100	135
Las cast iron cap pistol	80	125	160
Lasso 'Em Bill cast iron cap gun, red			

	C6	C8	C10
rubies in handle, cylinder turns, 1930, 9"	125	145	175
Lawmaker cast iron cap pistol, Kenton, 1941, 8⅜"	60	70	90
Liberty 1875	125	175	250
Liberty, circa 1912, tin, ornate	35	40	60
Lightning Express, mechanical cap pistol, train slides forward along barrel to explode cap at end, 5", 1913, Arcade or Kenton	300	350	450
Lion, Ives, 1887, 3¾"	300	375	450
Lion, 1890, Stevens, 5¼"	200	250	300
Lion 1920	35	45	60
Lion head cast iron cap pistol, Pat. 1890, 5¼", Stevens	200	250	300
Little Bill cast iron cap pistol, Kilgore 1925, 5"	20	25	30
Little Chief Firefighter, water squirt gun	8	10	15

Invincible. Courtesy Sotheby's New York.

Top to Bottom: "Lone Eagle", "Patrol". Photo by Charles W. Best.

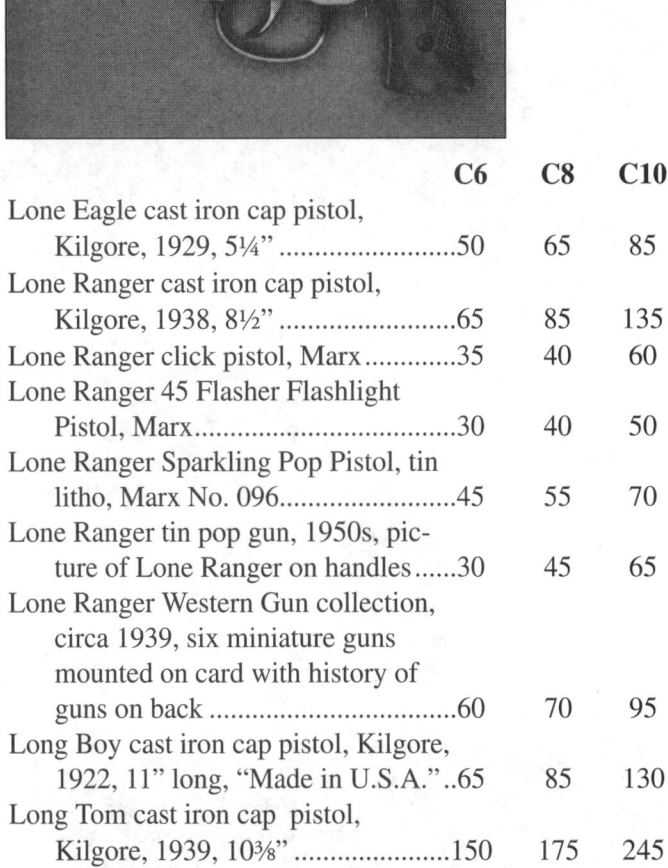

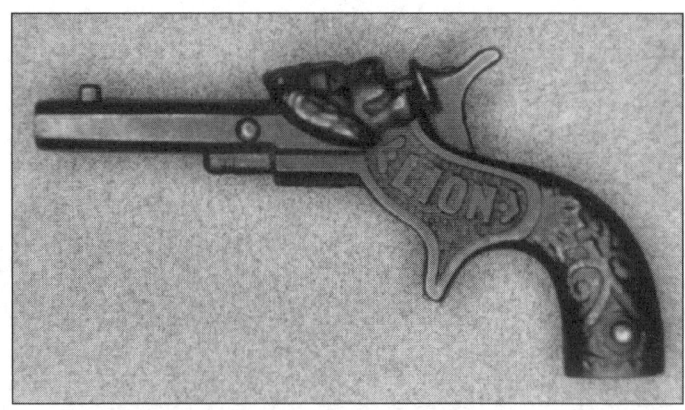

"Lion" by IVES, 1887. Photo by Charles W. Best.

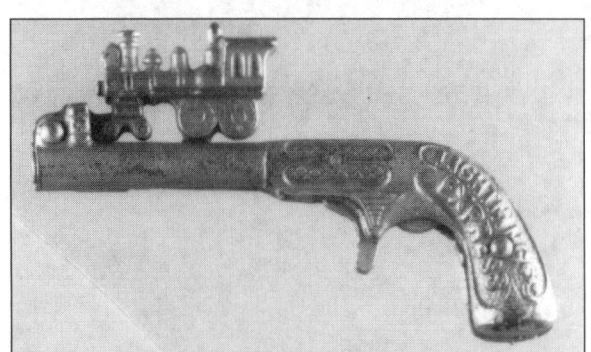

Lightning Express. Courtesy Sotheby's New York.

	C6	C8	C10
Lone Eagle cast iron cap pistol, Kilgore, 1929, 5¼"	50	65	85
Lone Ranger cast iron cap pistol, Kilgore, 1938, 8½"	65	85	135
Lone Ranger click pistol, Marx	35	40	60
Lone Ranger 45 Flasher Flashlight Pistol, Marx	30	40	50
Lone Ranger Sparkling Pop Pistol, tin litho, Marx No. 096	45	55	70
Lone Ranger tin pop gun, 1950s, picture of Lone Ranger on handles	30	45	65
Lone Ranger Western Gun collection, circa 1939, six miniature guns mounted on card with history of guns on back	60	70	95
Long Boy cast iron cap pistol, Kilgore, 1922, 11" long, "Made in U.S.A."	65	85	130
Long Tom cast iron cap pistol, Kilgore, 1939, 10⅜"	150	175	245
Look Out dog's head cast iron cap pistol	200	295	400
M&L water pistol, die-cast, rubber ball	10	15	20

	C6	C8	C10
Machine Gun, cast iron cap automatic, Kilgore, 1938, comes with crank, which when turned, fires the caps rapidly, "Ra-Ta-Ta-Tat," 5"	65	80	100
Magazine, 1892	100	150	200
Magic cast iron .22 cal. blank pistol, Kenton, 1900, "Pat'd Oct. 17 '99," 6¼" long, ornate, has second trigger to open barrel for loading	65	85	100
Major	45	55	65
Mars, 1920	40	50	75
Marx miniatures of Famous Guns: Civil War Revolver; Mare's Leg; Tommy Gun; Saddle Rifle, price for mint on card	50	75	100
Mascot cast iron cap automatic, Kilgore, 1936, 3⅞"	25	30	35
Master cast iron cap automatic, 1922, Kilgore, 4⅝"	30	35	45
Master cast iron cap automatic, Kilgore, 1930, 4⅝"	30	35	45
Mauser, The, maker unknown (English?), 1915, 6¾"	250	325	450
Me and My Buddy, animated pistol with figure, steel, Wyandotte	50	65	85
Medrick Repeater	75	100	150
Mick 1930	30	45	60
Minute Man cast iron cap rifle,			

461

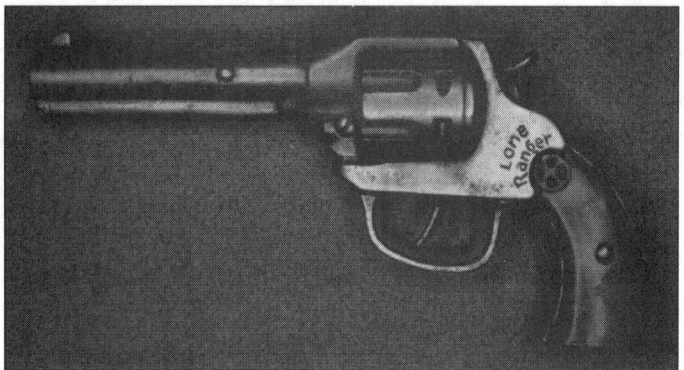

"Lone Ranger", 1940. Photo by Charles W. Best.

Typical Cast Iron Cap Pistols, 1910-1920. Left to Right. Top: HERO AUTO, REX 1914, TERROR 1915, NATIONAL 1915; Middle: KILGORE 1910, KILGORE 1912, FEDERAL 1920, NEW 50 SHOT INVINCIBLE; Bottom: NATIONAL 1911, NATIONAL 1909, BIG BUSTER. Courtesy Charles W. Best.

Typical Cast Iron Cap Pistols, 1890-1900. Left to Right. Top Row: KORKER, DEFENSE, EAGLE; Row 2: DIXIE, Cannon (animated), EAGLE; Row 3: UNMARKED (small); Row 4: AMERICAN BULLDOG, Locomotive (animated), EAGLE; Row 5: MAGIC, ZULU, LIBERTY; Row 6: Unmarked Dart Shooter, MEDRICK REPEATER, MAGAZINE; Row 7: JUMBO, CHALLENGE; Row 8: DEAD SHOT, BUFFALO BILL. Courtesy Charles W. Best.

"Officer Pistol." Photo by Charles W. Best.

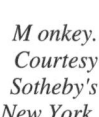 *M onkey. Courtesy Sotheby's New York.*

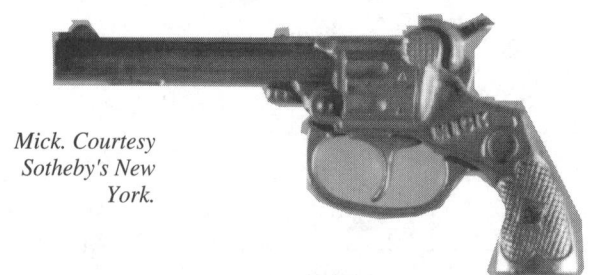 *Mick. Courtesy Sotheby's New York.*

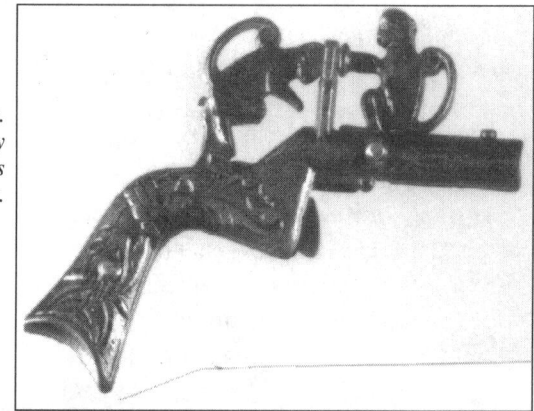

Minute Man cast iron cap rifle, KILGORE. Photo by Charles W. Best.

462

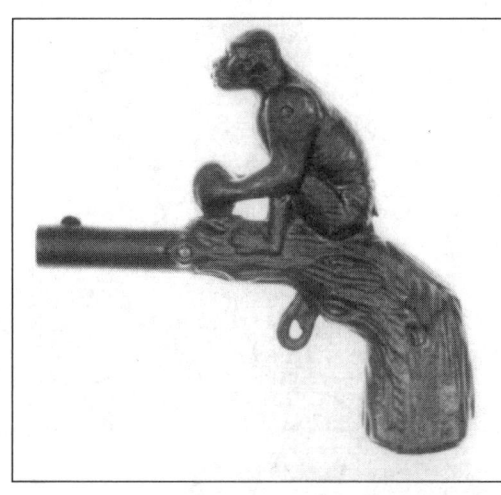

Monkey and Coconut. Photo by Charles W. Best.

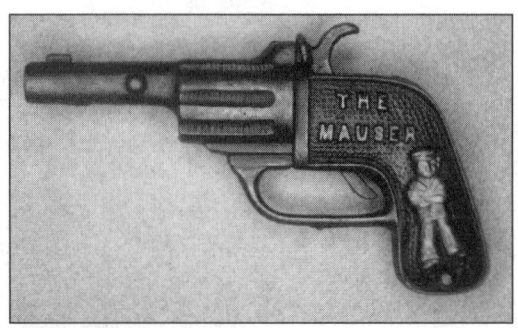

"The Mauser". Photo by Charles W. Best.

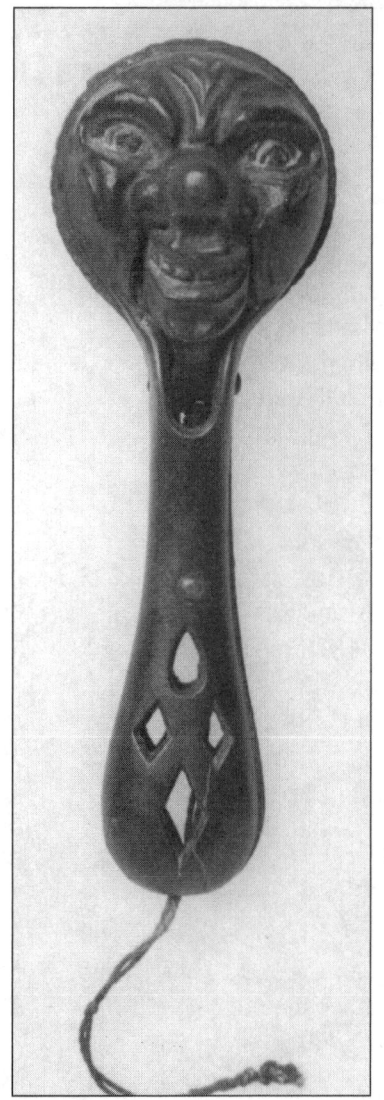

"Moonface". Photo by Charles W. Best.

	C6	C8	C10
Kilgore 1936, "Pat. Appld. For," "Made in U.S.A.," 20"	150	200	325
Model, Pat. 1890, cast iron, 5⅜"	30	40	50
Model 1900	35	55	75
Monkey and Coconut animated cap pistol, 1878, 4¼", 1882	No Price Found		
Monkeys animated cap pistol, Lockwood, 4¼", 1882	550	700	900
Moonface capshooter, Stevens, circa 1880	500	650	800
Mordt cast iron cap pistol, maker unknown, 1930, 8"	No Price Found		
Mountie cap automatic, Kilgore No. 6, diecast, 6" long	25	32	38
National, 1915	30	40	55
National cast iron cap automatic, 1915, National, 3¾"	30	35	45
National cast iron cap pistol, National, 1909, 4⅞"	30	40	60
National cast iron cap pistol, National, 1911, 5"	30	40	50
National cast iron cap pistol, Stevens, 1920, 5⅜"	25	35	45
National cast iron cap automatic, National, 1925, "Made in U.S.A.," 5¼"	25	30	35
National cast iron cap automatic, National, 1925, 4¼"	30	35	50
National No. 350, cast iron cap automatic, National, 1928, 5½"	40	50	75
National No. 380 cast iron cap pistol, 1930s, National, 7"	30	35	45
National Liquid Pistol, Parker/Stearns, 1900, 4⅞"	55	70	100
Navy, 1878	120	185	250
Navy, 1910	40	55	75
Navy, 1925	25	35	45
Navy cast iron cap pistol, Kenton 1930, "Pat. Sept. 11-23," 5½"	40	45	65
Navy double barrel cap pistol	150	175	225
Nemo cast iron cap pistol, maker unknown, 1910, 6⅝"	45	55	75
New 50 Shot Invincible cast iron cap pistol, 1930, Kilgore, 5½"	25	35	45
Nigger Head cap pistol, cast iron, Ives, 1887, 4½"	200	275	325
"No. 71 Water Pistol" (Daisy?) automatic, approx. 5½" long	15	20	30
No. 500 (like Luger) 1935	55	85	100
Novelty cast iron cap pistol, Stevens, 1885, "Pat. Appld For," 5"	150	185	225
Nu-Matic Paper pop gun, 7" long	10	15	25

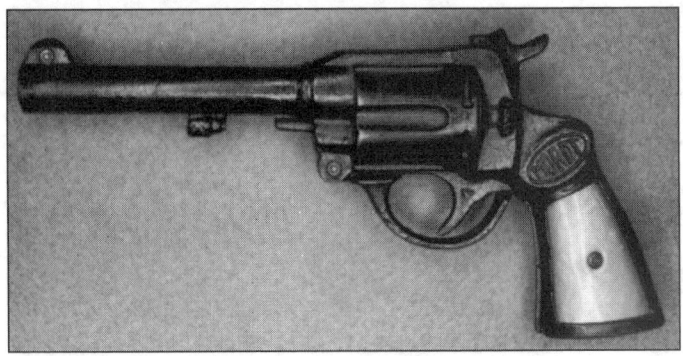

"Mordt". Photo by Charles W. Best.

National cast iron cap automatic, National, 1925, 4¼". Courtesy Sotheby's New York.

"National Liquid Pistol". Photo by Charles W. Best.

	C6	C8	C10
Officer Pistol, cast iron cap automatic, Kilgore, 1940, 6", modeled after German Luger ...65	75	100
Official Detective-Type Sub-machine Gun, Marx, No. 2146 ...35	50	65
Oh Boy automatic cap, Kilgore, 1933, "Made In U.S.A.; Pat'd. Aug. 8, 1933," works both as automatic and crank-operated rapid-fire gun, 4⅛" ...40	45	60
Oh Boy cast iron cap pistol, National, 1922, 5½" ...25	30	45
Oh Boy iron cap pistol, Kenton 1930, "Pat. Sept. 11-23," 5⅛" ...25	30	35
OK cast iron cap automatic, maker unknown, 1935, 3¾" ...35	40	45
Old Ironsides cast iron cap pistol, 10¾" ...65	85	125
101 Ranch ...95	125	175
Our Army Forever ...175	250	350
"P" ...70	80	125
P-38 steel clicker pistol, circa 1945 ...15	20	25
Padlock cap pistol, and key, Hubley, 4¼" ...75	85	100
Pal cast iron cap pistol, Kilgore, 1930, 4" ...25	30	35
Pal cast iron cap automatic, Kilgore, 1930, 4" ...30	35	40
Parole ...50	65	75
Pat cast iron cap pistol, Kenton, 1935, "Pat. Sept. 11-23," 6⅛" ...25	30	35

	C6	C8	C10
Patrol cast iron cap pistol, Hubley, 1939, "Made in U.S.A.," 6" ...35	45	55
Pawnee Bill, circa 1940 ...85	100	125
Pea Matic pea-shooting steel repeater ...15	20	25
Pea Shooter ...15	20	25
Pea shooter, pewter, highly embossed handle ...40	50	70
Peacemaker cast iron cap pistol, Stevens, 1940, "Made in U.S.A.," 8½" ...50	65	80
Peerless, 1905, 5½" ...70	85	125
Persuader cast iron cap pistol, Kenton, 1939, "Made in U.S.A." Pat. Appld. For," 6⅜" ...35	50	65
Pet, 4¼", Hubley, diecast ...5	10	15
Ping-Pong rifle ...10	15	20
Pioneer diecast Hubley ...45	50	65
Pirate cap pistol die cast zinc with cast iron hammers and trigger, Hubley 1941, two-barrel, two hammers that cock, 9⅜" ...65	85	100
"Pistol Packin' Mama," wood with cardboard sides, circa 1944, four revolving triggers, 8½" long, shoots wooden pegs ...20	25	40
Pluck cast iron cap pistol, at least four versions known, 1895 version ...75	100	125
Pluck cast iron cap pistol, Stevens, 1930, 3½", "Made in U.S.A.," early-looking ...20	25	30
Police large steel automatic cap pistol, 8" ...20	25	30
Police 1935 automatic ...40	55	70
Police bakelite-framed cap automatic, Kilgore, 1940, 5¼" ...35	40	55
Police Chief 1935 ...35	40	55
Police Chief gun and leather shoulder holster set, circa late 1940s, Wyandotte ...25	30	35

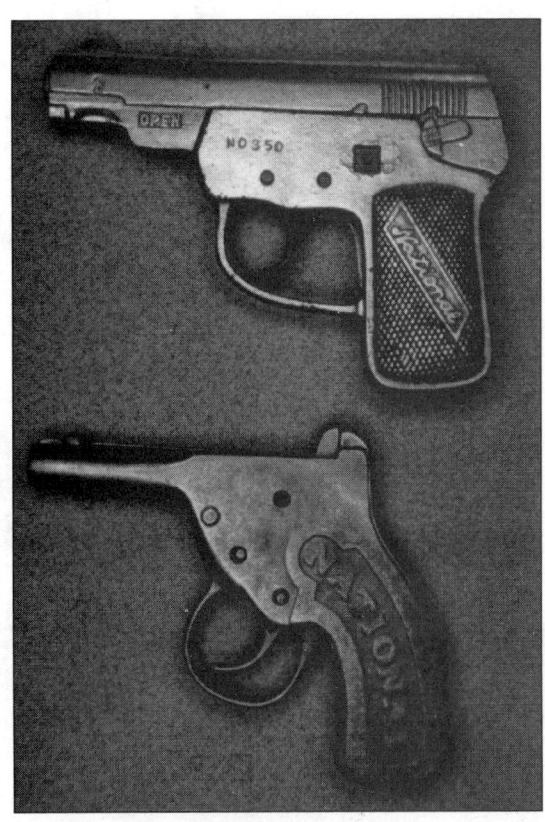

Pirate, HUBLEY, 1941. Photo by Charles W. Best.

Top to Bottom:
"National No. 350",
"National" by
NATIONAL, 1911.
Photo by Charles W.
Best.

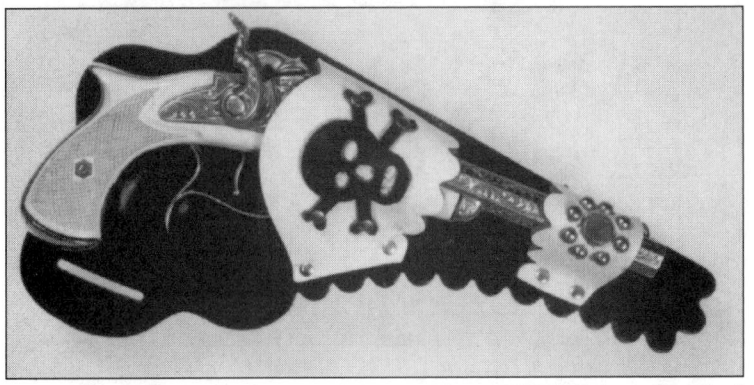

Pirate, HUBLEY, in rare original
holster. Photo by Charles W. Best.

Pirate, HUBLEY, with original box. Rare colored stock and
blue finish, probably post WWII. Photo by Charles W. Best.

Presto, with original box. Courtesy James S. Maxwell/Virginia
Caputo. Photo by Virginia Caputo.

Top: Pluck, STEVENS, 1930. Bottom: Big Chief, 1930, DENT.
Photo by Charles W. Best.

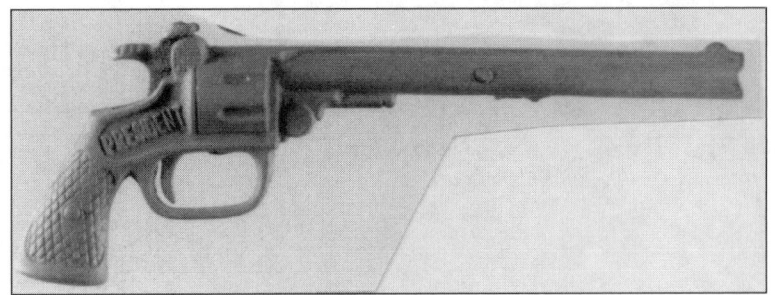

President. Courtesy Sotheby's New York.

Punch & Judy. Courtesy Sotheby's New York.

Scout cast iron cap pistol, STEVENS, 1890. Courtesy Sotheby's New York.

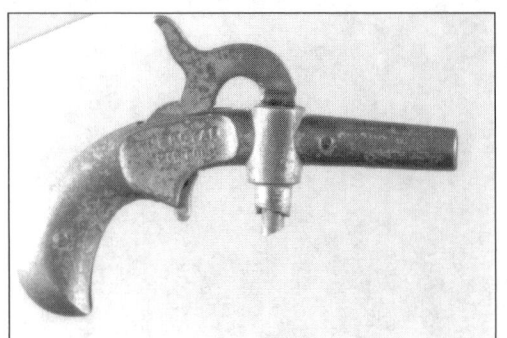

The Royal Pistol. Courtesy Sotheby's New York.

Sea Serpent. Photo by Charles Best.

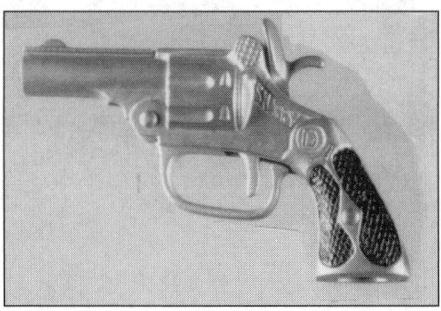

Snappy. Courtesy Sotheby's New York.

Sambo. Courtesy Sotheby's New York.

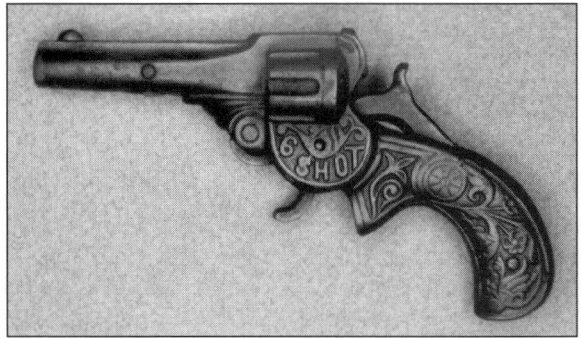

6 Shot cast iron cap pistol, STEVENS, 1895. Photo by Charles Best.

Red Ranger Steel Clicker Pistol, WYANDOTTE. Courtesy Continental Hobby House.

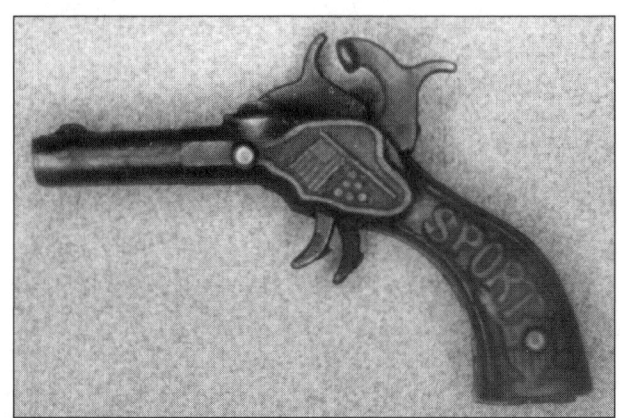

"Sport" by Ives. Photo by Charles W. Best.

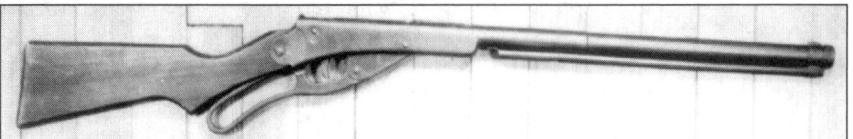

Red Ryder DAISY Air Rifle, circa 1950s. Courtesy Hake's Americana & Collectibles.

466

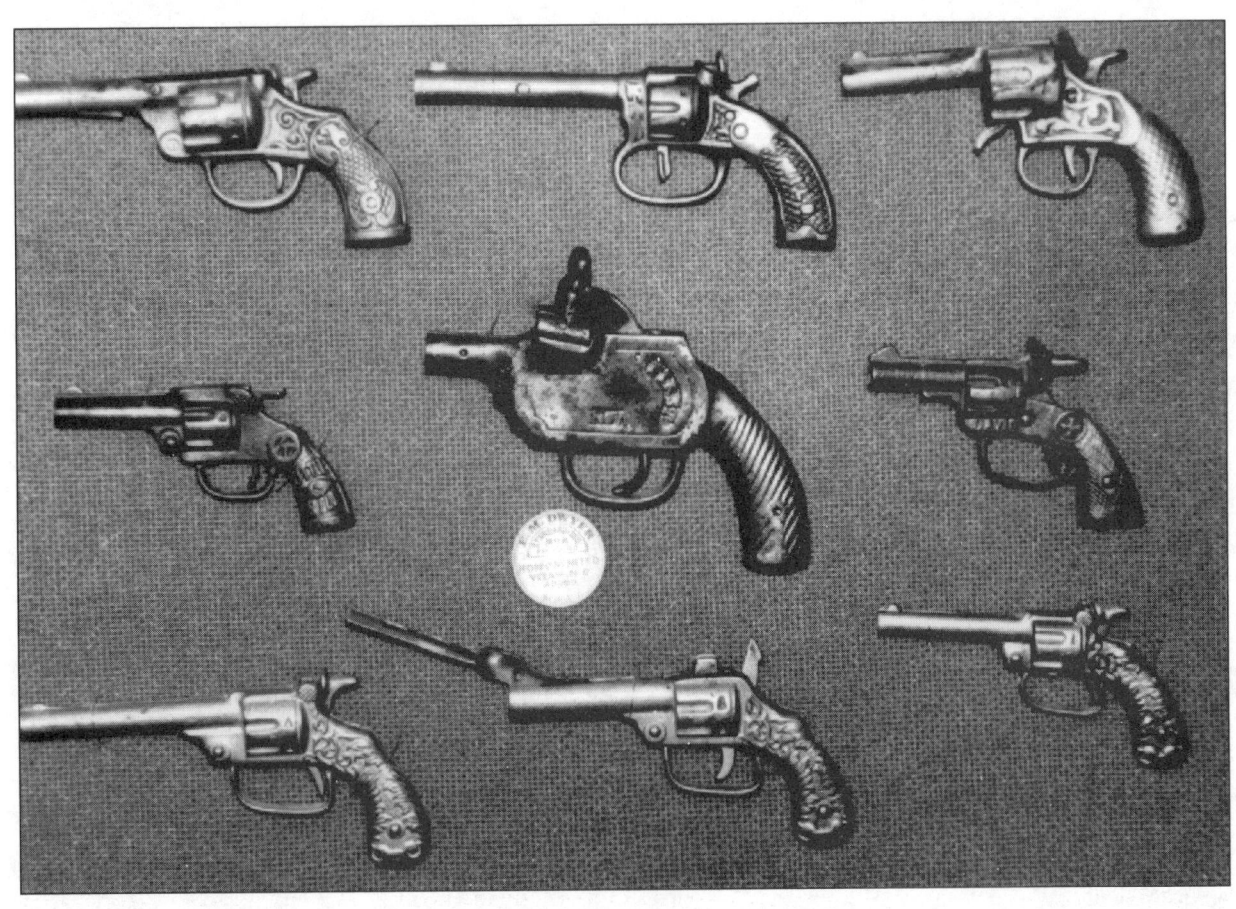

Typical Cast Iron Cap Pistols, 1910-1920. Left to Right. Top: DETROIT, WILD WEST, Unmarked; Middle: LITTLE BILL, FIRST NO. 1, DAVID; Bottom: all unmarked with the middle a disk shooter. Courtesy Charles W. Best.

	C6	C8	C10
Polo, 1878, Ives, 6"	50	60	75
Polo. later, Ives, has trigger guard	50	60	75
Pono cast iron cap pistol, Kenton 1936, "Pat. Sept. 11-23," 5⅛"	30	35	40
Powder keg cast iron cap bomb	85	110	135
Premier Safety, 1914	40	55	75
President, cast iron cap pistol, 8¾", 1925, Kilgore	60	70	100
Presto cast iron cap automatic, Kilgore, 1940, 5⅛"	30	40	50
Punch & Judy cast iron animated cap pistol, 1880, 5" "Patented," Ives, Punch explodes cap with nose, on Judy's back	400	500	700
Pup 1930	25	35	45
Ranger (1890-1900)	80	100	125
Ranger cast iron cap pistol, Kilgore, 1920, 5⅜"	30	35	40
Ranger cast iron cap pistol, Kilgore, 1939, 8½"	60	75	100
Ranger cast iron cap pistol, Kilgore, 1940, 8½", hammer protrudes more than earlier version	60	75	100
Record	10	15	20
"Red Ranger," steel clicker pistol, Wyandotte, circa 1939, 8" long, black, red "jewel"	20	25	30
"Red Ranger," steel clicker pistol, Wyandotte, 8" long, circa 1941	15	20	25

	C6	C8	C10
Red Ranger steel click pistol, Wyandotte, 7¾"	15	20	25
Red Ranger steel six shooter repeater with plastic handles, Wyandotte, revolving cylinder	25	35	45
Red Ryder Air Rifle, Daisy	*see Comic Character*		
Remington .36 die cast Hubley	35	40	55
Repeating Cap Pistol, Marx No. G375, die cast	20	25	30
Rex cast iron cap automatic, 1914, Dent, 4⅛"	30	35	45
Rex cast iron cap automatic, Kilgore, 1939, 3⅞"	30	35	40
Rex Mars Planet Patrol X-92 Gun	50	75	100
RIP, circa 1909	65	85	125
Rival 1920	50	70	100
Rob Roy, circa 1875	150	175	225
Rocket Ship Space Pistol, Late 1940s, Irwin	30	40	50
Rotor Fifty cast iron cap pistol, Kilgore, 6⅛" long, 1930	35	45	55
Roy Rogers cast iron cap pistol, 11"	300	400	500
Roy Rogers Forty Niner pistol and spurs set, 8½" long, 1940s	100	125	175
Roy Rogers Tuck Away Gun, 2½" derringer, circa early 1950s	35	40	50
Royal Pistol, The, 1878, cast iron cap mechanical pistol, fires spring-			

	C6	C8	C10
loaded top which is attached to bottom of the barrel, approx. 5", "Pat. Apr. 23 '78" 400	500	700
S&S 1880 100	150	200
Safety cast iron cap pistol, Hubley, 1924, "Pat. Mch. 25, '24," 5" 25	30	35
Safety First cast iron cap automatic, 1920, "Safe," 3⅜", maker unknown ..30	40	50
Sambo cast iron cap pistol, hammer hits head, 1887, Ives, "Pat. June 21, 1887," 4⅜" 175	260	325
Say I cast iron cap bomb 75	90	125
Scout cast iron cap pistol, Stevens, 1890, "Pat'd. June 17, 1890," 7" 50	70	95
Scout cast iron cap pistol, Stevens, 1935, "Made in U.S.A.," 6¾" 45	50	60
Scout cast iron cap pistol, Stevens, 1940, 6⅛" 45	50	60
Scout cap pistol, tin, 1914, automatic ...25	30	40
Scout Jr. cast iron cap pistol, Stevens, 1935, "Made In U.S.A.," 6" 35	40	50
Scoutmaster, 6¾", Dent 65	80	95
Sea Serpent - .... *see Dolphin*		
Senator cast iron cap pistol, Kilgore, 1925, 7" marked with star and "K" 50	60	75
1776-1876 cast iron cap pistol, Stevens, 1876, 5¼", produced for America's (100th) centennial 200	250	300
Shoo Fly cast iron cap pistol 125	150	165
Shoot The Hat cast iron mechanical cap pistol 500	700	1000
Shotgun, double-barreled, steel, wood stock, 28", both barrels break down, cock and shoot.........35	40	45
Siren Signal Pistol, Marx, 1940s, tin.....15	22	30
Siren Sparkling Airplane Pistol, tin litho, Marx No. 182 35	40	50
Siren Sparkling Pistol, tin litho, Marx No. 164 50	60	75
Six Shooter cast iron cap pistol, Kilgore, 1935, 6½" 40	50	65
Six Shooter cast iron cap pistol with plastic-type grips, Kilgore, 1935, 6½" .45	55	70
Six Shooter cast iron cap pistol, Kilgore, 1938, "Made in U.S.A." on hammer, 6½" 30	40	50
Six Shooter cast iron cap pistol, Kilgore, 1938, "Made in U.S.A." on hammer, plastic type grips,6½".....35	45	55
Six Shooter cast iron cap pistol, Kilgore, 1930, 7" 45	55	65
Six Shooter Automatic cast iron cap pistol (not an automatic), Kilgore, 1934, 6½" 40	50	65

	C6	C8	C10
6 Shot cast iron cap pistol, Stevens, 1895, "Pat'd. U.S.A., Jan. 22, 1895," 6¾" 110	150	200
Sliko cast iron cap pistol, Kenton, 1930, "Pat. Sept. 11-23," 6¼" 25	30	35
Snap, 1890 30	45	65
Snappy, 1930, Dent, 5" 45	55	70
Snappy Jack, circa 1935, English 40	55	65
Space Gun, Remco 25	38	50
Sparkling Atom Buster, die cast Marx No. 46 30	35	40
Sparkling G-Man Sub-Machine Gun, Marx No. 2308 85	100	150
Sparkling G-Man Sub-Machine Gun, Marx No. 2310 85	100	150
Sparkling Pop Gun, Marx No. 198 30	40	50
Sparkling Space Gun, Marx 45	55	75
Sparkling Sure Shot 15	20	25
Spitfire cast iron cap automatic, Stevens, 1940, "Made in U.S.A." 4⅝" 35	45	60
Sport Ives, 1875, 4" 175	225	350
Sport cast iron cap pistol, Kilgore, 1930, "Made in U.S.A.," 7½" 25	30	35
Spud Gun, tin automatic, circa 1940 15	17	20
Spud Gun No. 504, B.J. Cossman, Hollywood, Calif. die-cast 10	12	15
Spy cast iron cap pistol, Kilgore, 1936, "Made in U.S.A.," 4¼" 25	30	35
Star pot metal cap pistol, steer on handle ...5	8	10
Star, circa 1878 125	150	200
Star cast iron cap pistol, 1910, Stevens, 6¼" 35	50	65
Stephans Pat, 1873, 5" 120	180	240
Stevens Repeater cast iron cap pistol, Stevens, 1930, 6¼", "Mammoth Cap; Made in U.S.A." 35	45	60
Stevens 6 Shot, 1932, 6¼", Stevens.....35	45	60
Stevens 6-Shot Rapid Load cast iron cap pistol, 1932, Stevens, "Made in U.S.A.," 6½" 35	45	60
Streamline Siren Sparkling Pistol, tin litho, Marx No. 155 35	45	75
Sun cast iron cap pistol 125	140	175
S&W cast iron cap gun, 6" 25	30	45
Super cast iron cap pistol, Kenton 1930, "Pat. Sept. 11-23," 8¾" 35	45	60
Super Automatic Tom Gun, steel spark automatic 15	20	30
Super Nu-Matic Paper Buster Gun.........15	20	25
Sure Shot 1870-1880 165	250	365
Sure Shot cast iron cap automatic, Hubley, 1940, 4¼" 30	35	40

Top, Left to Right: "Teddy", "Chief"; Middle: "Buffalo Bill"; Bottom, Left to Right: "25 Jr", "Pal", "Army 45". Courtesy Mapes Auctioneers & Appraisers.

Texan, HUBLEY, late cast-iron model. Early models have a rampant colt instead of a star on the grips. The cylinder is diecast. Circa 1940-48. Photo by Charles Best.

STEVENS 6 Shot. Courtesy Sotheby's New York.

Texan, diecast, gold plated deluxe version, HUBLEY, circa 1950. Photo by Charles Best.

	C6	C8	C10
Target cast iron cap pistol, Hubley, 1935, "Pat. 1,488,046," 8"	50	60	80
Teddy cast iron cap pistol, Hubley 1938, 5⅝"	25	30	35
Terror 1888	250	385	500
Terror cast iron cap automatic, Dent, 1915, "Pat. Jan 16 '15," 4¼"	25	30	35
Terror 1925	25	35	50
Terror, people embossed, cast iron cap pistol, 1882	165	225	350
Texan cast iron cap pistol, Hubley 1940, "Made in U.S.A.," 9¼" long	75	85	100
Texan Jr. cast iron cap pistol, Hubley 1941, Made in U.S.A.," 8⅛"	60	70	85
Texas cast iron cap pistol, Kenton, 1936, Pat'd No. 1993916, 5¾"	35	45	55
Texas cast iron cap pistol, Kenton, 1930, "Pat. Sept. 11-23," 6⅝"	35	45	55

	C6	C8	C10
Texas Centennial, 1936, 11"	165	275	450
Texas Jack, 1886, Ives, 9⅜"	200	250	300
The Big Noise, circa 1922	50	60	75
The Forty Five cast iron cap pistol, unusual shape, National 1928, Made in U.S.A.,," 11⅛"	65	75	95
The Sheriff cast iron cap pistol, Stevens, 1940, 8½"	50	60	75
Tiger cast iron cap pistol, Stevens, 1915, 6¾"	30	40	50
Tiger cast iron cap pistol, Hubley, 1935, 6⅞"	30	35	40
Tin Tin Gun, 3x5", turn crank and it makes noise, Woodhaven Metal Stamping Co.	15	20	25
Tip Top cast iron cap pistol, 1880, Stevens, 3½"	125	150	200
Trainer	15	20	25

Typical Cast Iron Cap Pistols 1920-1930. Left to Right; Top Row: DANDY (Police .38), SIX SHOOTER; Second Row: Army .45, TEXAS CENTENNIAL 1936, G-MAN; Third Row: BULL DOG, MACHINE GUN, TARGET; Fourth Row: TEXAN JR., SIX SHOOTER; Fifth Row: LASSO 'EM BILL, LONE RANGER; Sixth Row: GENE AUTRY, AMERICAN,; Bottom: GENE AUTRY, PAWNEE BILL. Courtesy Charles W. Best.

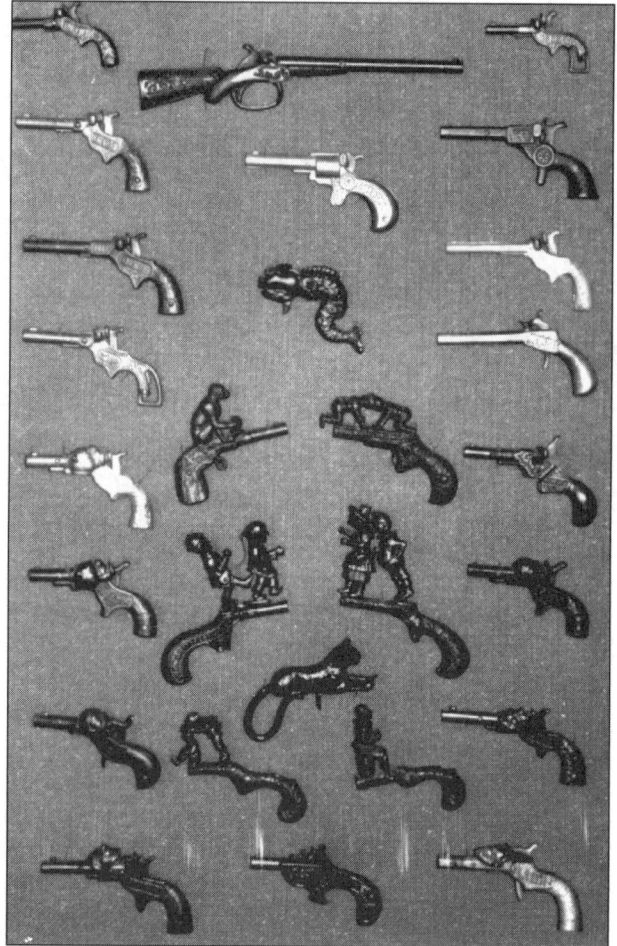

Typical Cast Iron Cap Pistols 1880-1890. Left to Right; Top Row: PLUCK, JOHNNIE'S LITTLE GUN (rifle), ACORN; Second Row: IBEX, 1776-1876, VICTOR; Third Row: DIXIE, Sea Serpent, CHIEF; Fourth Row: ZIP, VOLUNTEER; Fifth Row: LOOK OUT, Monkey with Coconut, BUTTING MATCH, NOVELTY; Sixth Row: BULL DOG, CHINESE MUST GO, PUNCH & JUDY, SAMBO; Seventh Row; Cat (animated); Eighth Row; NIGGER HEAD, SHOOT THE HAT, CLOWN (on barrel), LION; Bottom: FRONTIER, ECHO, LION. Courtesy Charles W. Best.

	C6	C8	C10
Trapper cast iron cap automatic, Kilgore, 1935, 4½", fires only single shot, but roll of caps can be carried in the grip	45	60	75
Triumph, 1878, 5⅛"	125	165	225
Trooper cast iron cap pistol, Hubley 1938, 5⅛"	35	40	45
Trooper Safety, 1925	35	50	70
Trooper Safety cast iron cap pistol, Kilgore, 1930, "Pat. Pend; Made in U.S.A.,," 10" operates either as straight cap pistol, or can be fired with crank	85	100	145
Trooper Safety cast iron cap pistol, Kilgore, 1925, 10¼"	75	90	125
25 Jr. cast iron cap automatic, Stevens, 1930, Made in U.S.A.,; Patented," 4⅛"	25	30	35

	C6	C8	C10
25-50 cast iron cap automatic, Stevens, 1928, "Pat Appld. For; Made in U.S.A.," 4½"	30	35	45
25-50, 1930	30	35	45
25-50 Cast iron cap automatic Stevens 1935, "Made in U.S.A.,; Pat. Appld. For," 4½"	20	25	30
25-50 Cast iron cap automatic, Stevens 1935, "Oil Moving Parts; Made in U.S.A. Patented" 4½"	20	30	35
25-50 Cast iron cap automatic, can be fired rapidly with crank, hole near muzzle holds removable crank, Stevens, 1935, "Oil Moving Parts; Made in U.S.A., Patented"	45	60	80
25-50 Target cast iron cap automatic with "silencer" type barrel, Stevens, 1935, "Oil Moving Parts, Made in U.S.A.; Patented"	100	130	200

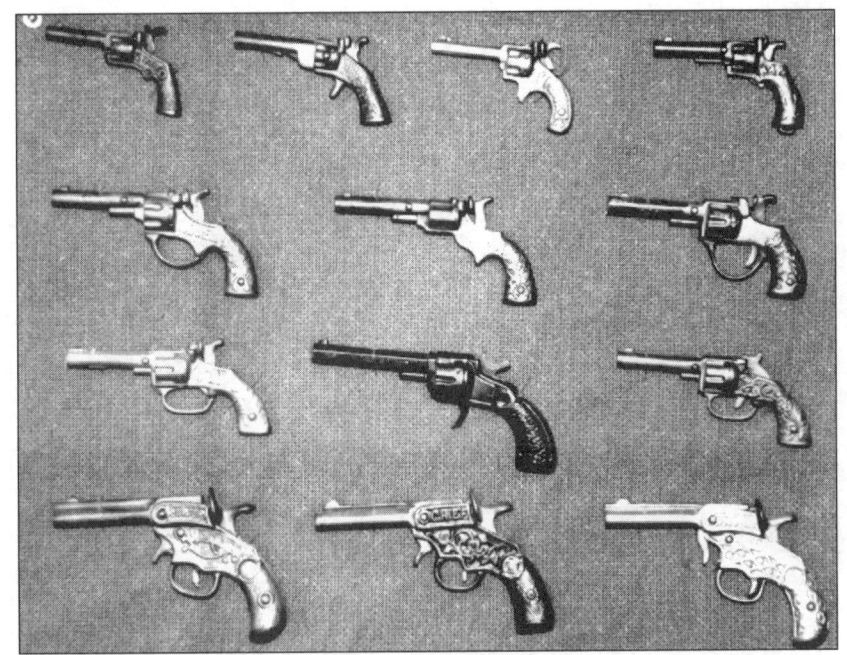

Typical Cast Iron Cap Pistols 1900-1910. Left to Right; Top Row: STAR, Unmarked, "P", SNAP; Second Row: MODEL, MODEL, Unmarked; Third Row: GIP, WILD-WEST, Unmarked; Bottom: MAJOR, CHIEF, RIVAL. Courtesy Charles W. Best.

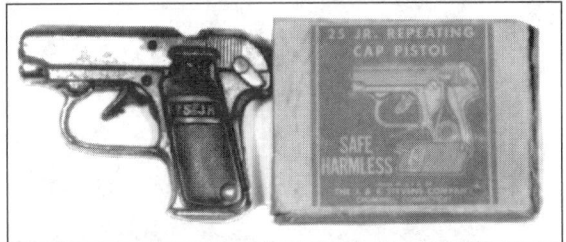

25 Jr. with original box. Courtesy James S. Maxwell/Virginia Caputo. Photo by Virginia Caputo.

25-50 Cast Iron Cap Automatic, STEVENS, 1935, "Oil Moving Parts", with original box. Courtesy James S. Maxwell/Virginia Caputo. Photo by Virginia Caputo.

Top to Bottom: "Tip Top", Unmarked, maker unknown, 1878, 3¾" long. Photo by Charles W. Best.

Top to Bottom: "Wild West", "101 Ranch", "Victor", "Rodeo". Photo by Charles W. Best.

	C6	C8	C10
Two Dogs On Bench cap shooter (only two known, the one sold, condition unknown, sold for $3400 in 1981, its last sale)			
"2 in 1" cast iron cap pistol, 9¼"	55	65	85
"2 Monkeys," 1882 cast iron animated cap pistol, 4½" maker unknown, monkey butts head against coconut held by another monkey	500	600	700
Two Time cast iron cap and rubber band pistol, 1930, Kenton, "Pat. Appld. For," 9¼"	65	75	100
Unmarked, unknown maker, 1878, 3¾"	75	90	125
Unxld Steel cap automatic, 6½", nickel plated	20	25	30

	C6	C8	C10
Urica	10	15	20
U.S.A. Liquid Pistol cast iron water pistol, Parker-Stearns, 1896, Pat'd. June 30, 1896," 4¾"	55	75	90
U.S. Navy 1885, 6½"	65	85	125
Veteran 1935	45	60	80
Victor cast iron pistol	125	150	225
Villa cast iron cap pistol, Dent, 1934, Made in U.S.A.," 4¾"	45	55	65
Volunteer cast iron cap pistol, Stevens, 1873, "Pat'd April 22, '73"	125	145	170
W on one side, S on other, cast iron cap pistol, nickel-plated, normal size barrel	20	25	30

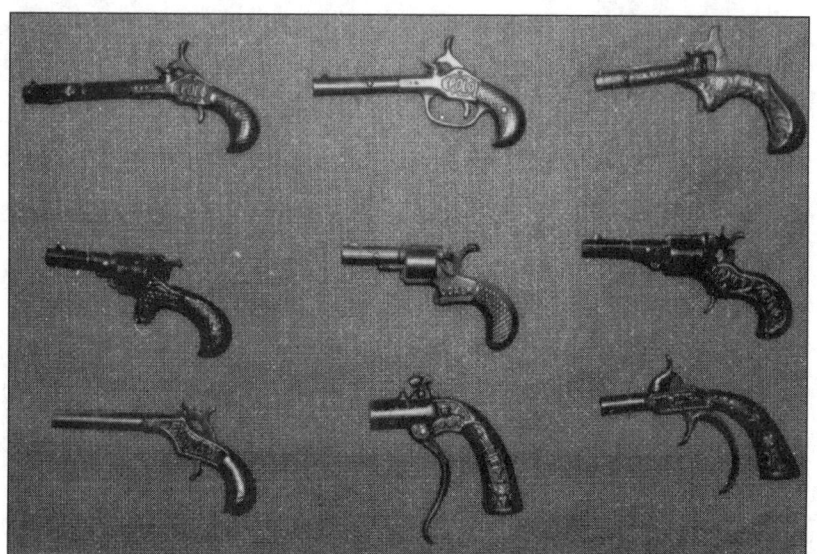

Typical Cast Iron Cap Pistols 1870-1880. Left to Right; Top Row: POLO, POLO, TRIUMPH; Second Row: BRAVO, JOKER, COMET; Bottom:EXCELSIOR, L.F.& C., STEPHANS PAT. Courtesy Charles W. Best.

Wyandotte guns, as shown in a January, 1925 ad. Courtesy Playthings Magazine.

Typical Cast Iron Cap Pistols 1920-1930. Left to Right; Top Row: PLUCK, BUCK, GEM, unmarked, unmarked; Second Row: DAISEY, BILL, VILLA; Third Row: ZIP, BILL, KING; Bottom Row: SAFETY, BULL, COP. Courtesy Charles W. Best.

	C6	C8	C10
W on one side, S on other, snub nose, single shot, cast iron nickel-plated..20		25	30
War cast iron cap pistol, Kenton, 1930, "Pat. Sept. 11-23," 4¼".........40		45	60
Warrior cast iron cap pistol, maker unknown, 1926, "Pat. Appld. For, 1926," 9".......................................75		90	135
Water Pistol, Wyandotte No. 41 10		15	20
Water Pistol, Wyandotte, unmarked 10		15	20
Western cast iron cap pistol, Kenton, 1935, "Pat. Sept. 11-23," 7"............35		45	65
Western cast iron cap pistol, Kenton, 1936, "Pat. Sept. 11-23," 7", has "jewel" over grips 40		50	75
Western cast iron cap pistol, Kenton, 1939, Made in U.S.A.," 7½"..........40		50	65
Westo cast iron cap pistol, Kenton, 1936, "Kenton," 7" 30		40	50

	C6	C8	C10
Westo cast iron pistol (doesn't fire caps), 1938, Kenton, "Kenton", 7" .35		40	50
Whoopie cast iron cap pistol, Kenton, 1932, 5⅞"...................................40		50	65
Wild West cast iron cap pistol, National, 1930, Made in U.S.A.," 6½" 45		50	60
Winner cast iron cap automatic, Hubley, 1940, 4⅜" 30		35	45
Wizard 1896 65		95	125
Woodsman cast iron cap automatic, Stevens, 1938, "Patented; Made in U.S.A.," 5¼"..................................55		75	95
Wyandotte double barrel shotgun, circa 1935, steel and wood, 25" long.......30		35	40
Wyatt Earp Gun & Holster set, Esquire Novelty 15		22	30
Xtra cast iron pistol, Kenton, 1936, "Made in U.S.A.," 5" long 25		30	35

Typical Cast Iron Cap Pistols 1890-1900. Left to Right; Top Row: Unmarked, S&S, Unmarked, Fido; Second Row: HALT, COLT, RANGER; Third Row: CUPID, NAVY, ARMY; Bottom: 6-SHOT 1895, U.S.A. LIQUID PISTOL, STAR. Courtesy Charles W. Best.

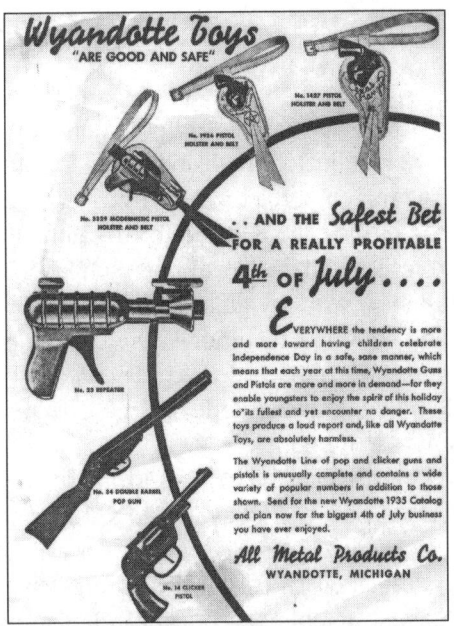

Typical Cast Iron Cap Pistols 1910-1920. Left to Right; Top Row: ECHO, CRACK, CAL; Second Row: Unmarked, Unmarked, PEERLESS; Third Row: "730". LION, LION, Unmarked Automatic; Fourth Row: PREMIER SAFETY, Unmarked, OK, PREMIER SAFETY; Bottom (small pistols): GEM, GEM. Courtesy Charles W. Best.

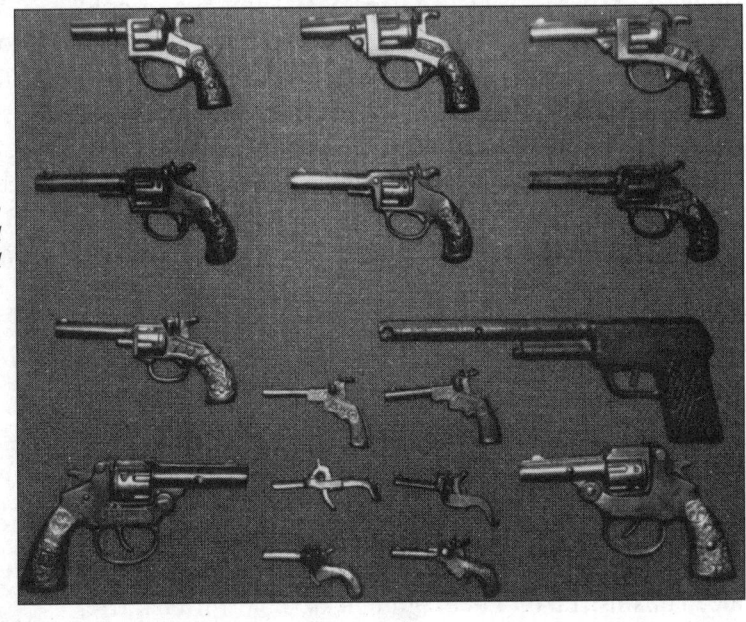

Typical Cast Iron Cap Pistols 1920-1930. Left to Right; Top Row: Unmarked, OK, Unmarked; Second Row: SAFETY FIRST, SCOUT MASTER, ARMY; Third Row: WARRIOR, Unmarked, TWO TIME; Bottom:Unmarked blank shooters. Courtesy Charles W. Best.

	C6	C8	C10
Yank cast iron cap pistol, 1880............	125	135	165
Yankee cast iron cap pistol, Stevens, 1895, 5½".....................................	125	135	165
York cast iron cap pistol, Kenton, 1930, "Pat. Sept. 11-23," 7"............	35	45	55
Young Sportsman, wood, circa 1868.....	75	100	135
Zip (1880-1890)	25	30	35
Zip cast iron cap pistol, Hubley, 1930, 5" .	25	30	35
Zip cast iron cap pistol, Hubley, 1938, 6"...	30	35	40
Zulu cast iron cap pistol, maker unknown, 1890, 6⅝", has decoration of African warrior with spear pursuing bird	150	200	300

WESTERN-STYLE TOY GUNS

by James Schleyer

In the past few years, interest in toy guns has escalated tremendously as collectors realize their charm, beauty and scarcity. America's love affair with its childhood memories has pushed the demand for toy guns far beyond what is currently available in the marketplace. Virtually every child played with toy guns, and the countless battles, gunfights, and hunting expeditions have taken a heavy toll. Many toy guns were discarded, confiscated by teachers, lost or broken due to their fragile nature. The survival rate of many guns is extremely low.

Today's collector can specialize in single manufacturers such as: Hubley, Nichols, Kenton, Kilgore, etc. They can collect various types such as: revolvers, derringers, automatics, rifles, etc. They might specialize in just pop guns, water pistols, clickers, dart guns, or cap shooters. There are niches like special finishes in gold, antique bronze, blue, black, and nickel. A few only collect guns with revolving cylinders or those that accept fake bullets. Since there are thousands of toy gun varieties, every collector should be able to find a special favorite. For many years, collectors favored the older cast iron guns and they still have quite a following. However, the die cast guns from the 1940-1965 era are currently receiving the most attention. The prices for these newer toys are skyrocketing!

The post-war era until 1965 witnessed an explosion of western movies, TV shows, comic books, radio programs, clothing, memorabilia and toy guns. The cowboy craze touches virtually every product, advertisement and person. Toy guns that resembled a Colt Peacemaker or Winchester rifle found a welcoming market. This was the period of glamorous finishes, sparkling metals, inventive mechanisms, fake bullets, gimmicks, colorful character names, imaginative plastic grips and fancy holster sets gleaming with metal studs and jewels! It was an era where Hoppy, Roy, Gene and the Lone Ranger were predominant. It's fairly obvious why so many toy gun collectors want only western or cowboy-style guns.

This section of the book will only address itself to western-styled toy guns. It primarily covers all die cast, plastic and tin guns with a special reduced section of western cast iron favorites. The listing is not intended as a price list, but rather an approximate value guide for collectors. Very few toy guns are mint; many are average and most have broken, cracked or missing parts. To simplify values, I have only listed prices for average specimens. For clarification, average condition means no broken or missing parts, it contains most of the original finish and works properly. Obviously, some guns are worth more due to their scarcity or market desirability among collectors. Rarity is not necessarily a guide to higher value.

Mint condition or new guns are worth between 35% to 50% over the value listed. Used guns in below average condition are worth about 50% less than the value listed. Original boxes in excellent condition are worth between $20 and $50. Dummy varieties of guns which cannot fire caps are worth about $15 more. A complete set of bullets for guns that accept them are worth about $15 to $25. Gold and antique bronze finishes are rarer and usually add $10 to $25.

Be aware that many die cast guns are very difficult or expensive to repair so use caution in buying damaged ones. The current vogue in western toys is fancy leather holster sets. Double holsters are more desirable than single ones. Character names and western decorations are eagerly sought after. Sets with metal studs, conchos, bullets and jewels bring higher prices directly influenced by the amount of decoration. Non-leather sets have very limited value. A highly decorated, leather, double holster set in excellent condition could be worth as much as $150 without the guns! The demand for certain models and special character guns can greatly influence the value. Locations within the country and current fads can also affect value.

Codes:	
Rep	Repeater
SS	Single Shot
Bul	Accepts Bullets
RC	Revolving Cylinder
N	Nickel
BK	Black or Dark Finish
G	Gold
AB	Antique Bronze
BE	Blue
LB	Long Barrel
CW	Civil War Style

James Schleyer is a long-time collector and appraiser who has specialized in toy guns for many years. He has authored three other collector books, written numerous articles and several newsletters on collectibles. He is the former president of the Toy Gun Purveyors (TGP), an international organization that shared knowledge and memories of toy guns, and former editor of TGP quarterly newsletter.

Diecast Western

Apache, 11¼", Lone Star - Black -
(Some R. Rogers' Sets) 35

Apache, 11¼", Lone Star - N & G 35

Gene Autry, 9", Leslie Henry - N 65

Gene Autry, 9", Leslie Henry - Gold 80

Gene Autry, 9", Leslie Henry - Antique Bronze (Rare) ...85

Gene Autry, 10½", Leslie Henry - LB(Rare) 100

Gene Autry 7½", Buzz Henry - Insert Grip - G & N 45

Gene Autry, 7½", Buzz Henry - Full Grip - G & N 45

Gene Autry, 26", Double Bar. Pop - Empress H. -
London (Rare) 100

Gene Autry, Wooden Pop Souvenir Rifle - W.
Hollywood Craft 50

Gene Autry, 27", Leslie Henry - Lever Action Rifle -
Flying A 90

Gene Autry, 10½", Leslie Henry - Pop-up Magazine -
N & G 100

Gene Autry, 11", Leslie Henry - 44 - R.C. - N, AB & G...100

Gene Autry, Some 44 guns have removable bullets
(**Rare**) 125

Big Buck, 8¼", Kilgore - SS 25

Big Chief, 8", Stevens - Indian Grips 30

Big Horn, 7¼", Kilgore - RC - Lanyard Ring on
Some 30

Billy the Kid, 8", Service Manufacturing Company -
Rep 30

Bonanza, 9", Leslie Henry 65

Bonanza, 10½", Leslie Henry - Long Barrel (Rare)......85

Bonanza, 11", Leslie Henry 44 - RC - N & B 65

Brave, 6", Nichols - SS 30

Bronco, 9¼, Kilgore - RC - Tree Eng. - Horse Grip 45

Bronco, 8½", Kilgore - RC - N, G, & BE - Horse
Eng. - Sadl. Grip 40

Buckeroo, 8", Actoy - SS 15

Buck, 6½", Kilgore - SS 20

Buck, 7¼", Kilgore - Rep 25

Buckle Gun, 3", Mattel - Remington Style Derringer ...50

Buck'n Bronc, 9½", Geo. Schmidt - Horse & Rider
Grips - N & G......................75

Buck'n Bronc, 9½", Geo. Schmidt - Metal Grips 60

Buck'n Bronc, 10½", Geo. Schmidt - LB 45

Buck'n Bronc, 10½", Geo. Schmidt - Hoppy Bust
Grips 150

Buffalo Bill, 8", Stevens 30

Buffalo Bill 45, 10½", Balantyne Mfg. Co. - RC..........85

Bunt-Line, 10½", Lone Star - Notch Bar Grip 50

Kit Carson, 8¼", Kilgore - Rep - N & G..................25

Kit Carson, 10", Kilgore - Rep - N & G..................30

Hopalong Cassidy, 9", Wyandotte - Rep - N & G 85

Hopalong Cassidy, 9¼", Geo. Schmidt - Bust Grip -
N & G......................145

Hopalong Cassidy, 10¼", Geo Schmidt - Bust Grip -
N......................150

Hopalong Cassidy, 7½", Wyandotte - SS - N & G........75

Champion, 9", Leslie Henry - Rp - N 75

Champion, 11", Kilgore - Fast Draw - Timer in Grips ..65

Cheyenne, 32", Daisy - Ricochet Lever Rifle 60

Cheyenne, 10", Hamilton - Rep......................25

Chief, 7", Hubley - SS 10

Cisco Kid, 8½", Lone Star - Rep 35

Colt Special, Nichols 35

Colt, 31", Revolving C. Rifle - Mattel (**Rare**)..............100

Colt 38, 10¾", Hubley - RC - Bullets 80

Cowboy, 12", Hubley - Dummy - RC - N, G & BK......45

Cowboy Jr., 9", Hubley - Lanyard Ring - Rep 30

Cowboy King, 9½", Stevens - Rep - Stag 30

Cowboy King, 9", Stevens - Rep - Pearl 25

Cowman, 8½" Nichols......................30

Cowpoke, Jr., 8", Lone Star - SS 20

Cowpuncher, 8⅞", Nichols - SS 25

Cowtyke, 7⅝", Nichols - Rep 30

Coyote, 8¼", Hubley - CW style - Rep 30

Davy Crockett, 9", Leslie Henry - Rep (**Rare**)............85

Davy Crockett, 10¼", Geo. Schmidt - Rep (**Rare**) 125

Davy Crockett, 8", Tin Clicker Pistol 20

Davy Crockett, 35", Daisy - Pop Lever Rifle 75

Dagger-Derringer, 7", Hubley - Pull-Out Knife 35

Deputy, 10¾", Hubley - Ribbed Barrel - Rep 35

Deputy BB, 8½", Geo. Schmidt - Small - Rep............40

Deputy Sheriff, 6¾", Kilgore RC - Rep 35

Matt Dillon 45, 11½", Halco - Break-top - RC -
Bullets 150

Dyna-Mite, 3", Nichols - Rem. Style Derringer 25

Eagle, 8", Kilgore - RC - N & G 25

Wyatt Earp, 9", Actoy - Rep......................40

Wyatt Earp, 11", Hubley - Rep......................70

Wyatt Earp, 9", L.I. Die Cast Co. - Rep......................75

Wyatt Earp, 11", Service Mfg. Go. - Rep 85

Wyatt Earp, 10½", Geo. Schmidt - Rep - N 75

Wyatt Earp, 11", Actoy Buntline Special - N & AB 65

Wyatt Earp, 13½", Lone Star - Buntline......................50

Dale Evans, 10¼", Geo. Schmidt - Jewel......................125

Dale Evans, 8½", Geo. Schmidt - Small (**Rare**) 135

Dale Evans, 7½", Buzz Henry - Insert Grip - N & G 75

Fanner 50, 10⅝", Mattel - RC - Bullets - N & BK........35

Fanner 50, 10⅝", Mattel - Non RC - N & BK - No
Bul 30

Fanner, 9", Mattel RC Shootin Shell 35

Fanner 50, 10⅝", Mattel Safari - Impala Grips - N -
AB 35

Flip, 10", Hubley - Rep......................35

Flip Spc. Rifleman, 32½, Hubley Lever Rifle..............75

41-40, Nichols - RC - Bullets 150

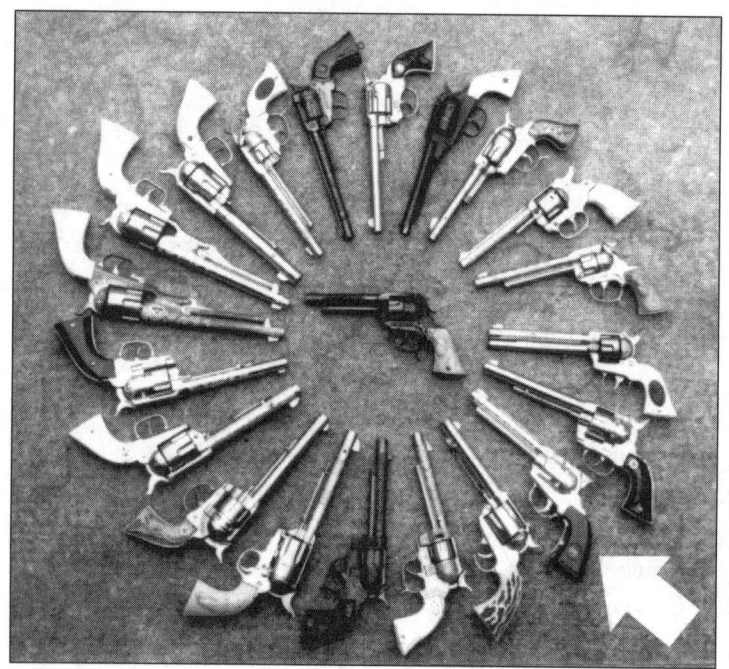

Starting with the arrow and going clockwise; Champion Fast Draw, Fanner .45, Wild Bill Hickok-44, Gene Autry-44 Antique Bronze, Marx Thundergun, Hubley Cowboy with Turquoise Grips, Nichols Stallion .45 Mark II, Hubley Ric-O-Shay .45, Hubley 44 Cal Model 1860, Hubley 45 Colt, Nichols Stallion .45, Hubley 44 Cal Model 1860, Hubley 45 Colt, Nichols Stallion .45 First Model, Leslie Henry Maverick with Long Barrel, Actoy Wyatt Earp in Antique Bronze, Hubley Wyatt Earp, Lone Star Apache in Black Finish (found in some Roy Rogers' sets), Classy Roy Rogers, Kilgore Roy Rogers, Leslie Henry Gene Autry with Long Barrel, Halco Marshal 6-7 Shot, Hubley Gold Cowboy Classic and in the center, a Leslie Henry Gene Autry in Antique Bronze.

Starting with the arrow and going clockwise; Wyandotte Hopalong cassidy in Gold, Wyandotte Red Ranger, Hubley Deputy, Hubley Remington .36 with Long Barrel, Stevens Cowboy King, Hubley Marshal, Fanner 9" Shootin' Shell, Hubley Texan Jr. in Gold, Hubley Western, Stevens Cowboy King, Kilgore Mustang, Geo. Schmidt Hopalong Cassidy in Gold, Geo. Schmidt Dale Evans with Jewel, Geo. Schmidt Roy Rogers, Geo. Schmidt Roy Rogers Engraved with Jewel, Lone Ranger Clicker with Celluloid Grips and Jewel, Geo. Schmidt Dale Evans Small Model, Leslie Henry Gene Autry and in the center a Buzz Henry Gene Autry in Gold with insert Grips and a Gene Autry with Full Grips.

	C6	C8	C10
44 Daisy, 10½", (Cap & Ball Style) like Nichols #61 (**Rare**)			100
44 Cal Model 1860, 14", Hubley - RC - (**Rare**)			85
45 Colt, 14", Hubley - CW Style - RC			70
45 Smoker, Product Eng. Company			30
45 Shootin Shell, 11¼", Mattel - RC - N (**Rare**)			200
Gabriel, 8¾", Rep			20
Gray Ghost, 9¼", Lone Star - Rep - Silver Grips			65
Grizzley, 10¼", Kilgore - RC - Rep			75
Gunfighter, 9¼", Lone Star - Rep			30
Gunsmoke, 9", Leslie Henry - Rep			50
Gunsmoke, 9", Leslie Henry - Bronze Matt Dillon Grips			65
Haig Western, 13½", Long Barrel - Plastic			35
Hide-A-Mite, 3", Canell - SS - Derringer			25
Indian Scout Rifle, 30", Mattel - Rolling Block			100
Jesse James, 9¼", Lone Star - Rep			50
Kelly's Rifle, 32", Hubley - Rep - Lever Action			35
Alan Ladd, 10¼", Geo. Schmidt - Rep (**Rare**)			150
Lasso Em Bill, 10¼", Geo Schmidt - Rep			75
Lone Rider, 8", Buzz Henry - SS - N & BK			45
Lone Ranger, 32", Marx - Winchester Lever Rifle			50
Lost Frontier, Nichols			30
Mares Laig, 14", Marx - Rifle Pistol - Rep			75
Marshal BB, 10¼", Geo. Schmidt - Rep			40
Marshal, 10", Hubley - Rep			25
Marshal, 10½", Leslie Henry/Halco - RC - Bul - N & AB			70
Marshal 6-7 Shot, 10½", LH/Halco - Extra Barrel - RC - Bul (**Rare**)			150
Maverick, 10½", Leslie Henry - Rep - Long Barrel (**Rare**)			85
Maverick, 9", Leslie Henry - Rep			50

	C6	C8	C10
Maverick 45, 11", Halco Break-top - RC - Bul (**Rare**)			150
Maverick, 10¼", Geo. Schmidt - Marshal Copper Grips (**Rare**)			130
Maverick, 8¾", Lone Star - Notch Bar Grips			40
Maverick Rifle, 26", Lever Action			30
Me & My Buddy, 8", Tin Clicker - Marx			50
Model 61, 10½", Nichols - RC - CW Style (**Rare**)			150
Mustang, 9¼", Kilgore - Rep - G & N			20
Mustang 500, 12¼", Nichols - Rep - BE & N			80
No Name 44, 11¼", Leslie Henry - RC - AB &			35
No Name, 10½", Leslie Henry - Long Barrel - Rep (**Rare**)			65
No Name 9 Leslie Henry - Rep			25
No Name, 10½", Classy - Scroll Grips - N & BK			40

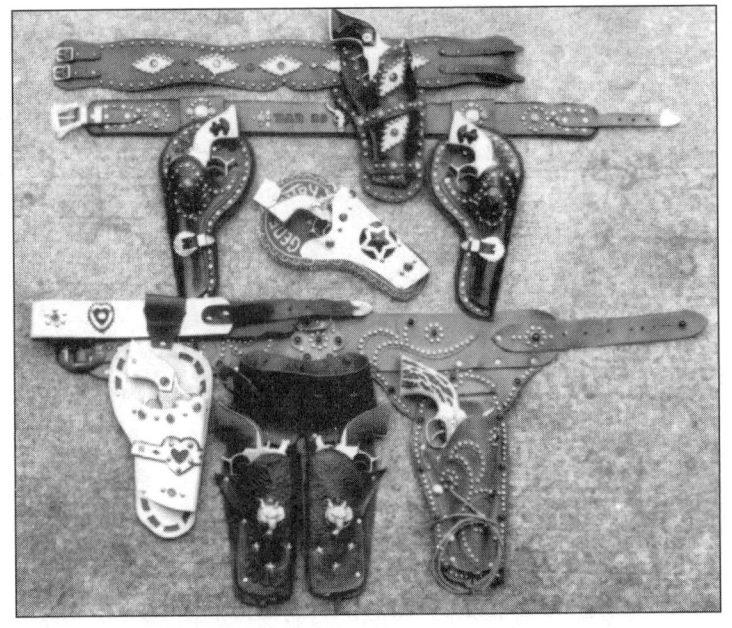

A selection of very desirable leather holster sets. Top to Bottom; Fancy set with numerous studs, jewels and painted diamonds, a double holster set marked Hopalong Cassidy and Bar 20 Ranch with jewels, studs and Hoppy busts, Gene Autry single holster with jewels and cutouts, a girl's white holster in red and white with jewels, studs and pierced hearts, a double Roy Rogers set with silver saddles, studs, jewels and stars, and a superb large holster with hundreds of studs, jewels and appliqued leather pieces. Holsters of this quality are in high demand and bring premium prices.

	C6	C8	C10
No Name, 10½", Classy - Wrap-Around Grip - BK			35
Annie Oakley, 9", Leslie Henry - Rep **(Rare)**			125
Annie Oakley, 32", Daisy Lever Pop Rifle - Gold			75
Paint, 3", Nichols (miniature) G&N			10
Paladin, 9", Leslie Henry - Rep			55
Paladin 45, 11", Halco - Break-top - RC - Bul - **(Rare)**			150
Pathfinder, 12", Geo. Schmidt - RC - Compass in Grip **(Rare)**			125
Patrol, 10¼", Geo. Schmidt - Rep			35
Pecos Kid, 9⅛", Lone Star - Rep			30
Pinto, 8½", Hubley/Halco SS			15
Pinto, 9", Gabriel - Rep			15
Pioneer, 10¼", Hubley - Black Grip with Compass - CW			.85
Pioneer, 10¼", Hubley - Rep - CW			45
Plainsman, 10½", National - RC			30
Pony, 7, Nichols - SS - Be			30
Pony Boy, 10", Actoy - Rep			20
Rancho, 6", Nichols - SS - BE			30
Ranger, 8", Lone Star - SS			20
Ranger, 9⅛", Kilgore - Rep - Cowboy on Grip			20
Red Ranger, 8", Tin Clicker			25
Red Ranger, 9", Wyandotte - Dragoon Style			65
Red Ranger, 7¾", Wyandotte - Rep			30
Lone Ranger, 8", Tin Clicker - Decal - Jewel			35
Lone Ranger, 8", Tin Clicker - Celluloid insert grips			50
Lone Ranger, 10", Actoy - Rep - N & AB			70
Lone Ranger 4 in 1, Actoy - Pistol - Rifle - Carbine - N **(Rare)**			200
Lone Ranger, 32", Marx - Winchester Lever Rifle			40
Rebel, 11¼", Lone Star - RC - Rep - N, BK & G			80
Rebel Scattergun, 21", Double Barrel Shotgun **(Rare)**			125
Remington 36, 8¼", Hubley - RC - Bul			35
Remington 36, 10", Hubley - RC - Bul - Long Barrel **(Rare)**			85

	C6	C8	C10
Restless Gun, 10", Actoy - Secret Compartment in Grip			60
Restless Gun, 9½", Actoy - Rep			40
Restless Gun 4 in 1, Actoy - Pistol - Rifle - Carbine **(Rare)**			175
Ric-O-Shay 45, 12¼", Hubley - RC - Bul			50
Ric-O-Shay, Jr., 10", Hubley - Rep			40
Range Rider, 10¼", Geo. Schmidt - Rep			35
Ruf Rider, 10½", Latco - Rep - Scroll Grips			35
Ring Rifle, 32", Hubley - Lever Rifle			50
Rin Tin Tin, 9", Actoy - Rep - N & AB			50
Rodeo, 8", Hubley - SS - Steerhead Grips			20
Rodeo, 7¼", Hubley - SS - N & BK			15
Roy Rogers, 10¼", Geo. Schmidt - Rep			100
Roy Rogers, 10½", Classy - N & G			100
Roy Rogers, 9", Geo. Schmidt - Engraved - Jewel			125
Roy Rogers, 8½", Geo. Schmidt - small frame			100
Roy Rogers, 2½", Tuck-A-Way - Derringer - N & G			35
Roy Rogers, 9", Classy - Rep - Rearing Horse Grip			75
Roy Rogers, 7½", Buzz Henry - Insert Grips - N & G			75
Roy Rogers, 9", Leslie Henry - Rep - N & G			90
Roy Rogers, 10½", Lone Star - RC - Indian Head Grips - N & G			115
Roy Rogers, 8½", Lone Star - RR & Steerhead Grips			85
Roy Rogers, 10¼", Kilgore - RC - RR & Horsehead			120
Roy Rogers, 9", Kilgore - Rep - RR & Horsehead			50
Roy Rogers, 8¼", Kilgore - Rep - RR & Horsehead			45
Roy Rogers 45, 10½", RC Balantyne Mfg. Co.			150
Roy Rogers, 24", Marx - Plastic Winchester Rifle Clicker			45
Roy Rogers, 26", Cap Shooting Winchester Rifle			55
Roy Rogers, 34", Winchester 348 Rifle - Cap Shooting			85
Scout Rifle, 32½", Hubley Winchester Lever			35
Sharps Civil War, 27", Carbine - Cap Shooting			75
Sheriff, 7½", Wyandotte - SS			20
Silver Colt, 8", Nichols Rep **(Rare)**			60
Silver Pony, 8¼", Nichols - Rep			40
Six Gun, 10½", Lone Star - RC - Bul - N & G			40
Smoky Joe, 9", Leslie Henry - N & G			35
Smoky Joe, 9", Leslie Henry - Bronze Steerhead Grip			45
Smoky Joe, 8", Hubley - Rep			20
Smoky Joe, 9", Stevens - Rep - AB - Black Grip			35
Snubnose 38, 7", Western Style - Mattel Shottin Shell - RC			75

	C6	C8	C10

Special, 11", Actoy - Rep - Long Barrel......................45

Spit-Fire, 8½", Nichols - Mini Rifle.........................30

Stallion .22, Nichols - RC - Bullets 30

Stallion .32, Nichols - RC - Bullets - G & N.............35

Stallion .38, 9½", Nichols - RC - Bullets 45

Stallion .45, 12", Nichols - 1st model - Horse Grip -
  RC - Bul - Jewell..150

Stallion .45, 12", Nichols - Mark II - RC - Bullets - N....145
  (Mark II Stallion .45 in Gold and Steel blue Rare)

Stallion .45, 12", Nichols/Kusan - Dummy Bullets - RC ..125

Stallion 300, 28½", Saddle Gun - Nichols - Lever.......115

Star, 7", Hubley - SS 10

Sure Shot, 8¼", Hubley - Rep 15

Texan, Jr., 10", Hubley - Rep - Side Opening 25

Texan, Jr., 9", Hubley - Button Release - N & G.........35

Texan, 9½", Hubley - RC - Rep - N & G.....................50

Texan .38, 10¾", Hubley - RC - Bullets.....................85

Texas, 9", Leslie Henry - Rep 35

Texas, 4", Halco - Spur Trigger Derringer 15

Texas, 6½", Hubley - All Metal.................................15

Texas Ranger, 27", Leslie Henry Lever Rifle.............35

Texas Ranger, 11¼", Leslie Henry - CW Style - RC -
  N & AB 40

Texas Ranger 44, 11¼", Leslie Henry - RC - N & AB 75

Texas Ranger, 8½", Stevens Rep - N & G..................35

Texas Smoker 77, 10", Leslie Henry 65

Thundergun, 12½", Marx - Rep - N & BK **(Rare)**........85

Top-Hand 250, 10", Nichols - Rep 45

Trail Boss, 30", Daisy - Lever Pop Rifle 35

Trigger, 8½", Stevens - Rep......................................40

2-1, 8½" & 6", Hubley (2 Barrels) Rep......................30

250 Shot, 10", Actoy - Rep.......................................25

38 Daisy, 9½", RC - Blued (Similar Nichols 38) 65

U.S. Marshal, 11¼", 44 Leslie Henry - RC - N &
  AB - Bul..55

Wagon Train, 10½", Leslie Henry - Long Barrel -
  Rep **(Rare)** 100

Wagon Train, 9", Leslie Henry - Rep 55

Wagon Train, 11¼", 44 Leslie Henry - RC - N - AB 65

Wagon Train, 11¼" +, 44 - LH - with stock & 11¼"
  Ext. Bar - RC **(Rare)**..150

Wells Fargo, 9", Actoy - Rep - N & AB 45

Wells Fargo, 11", Actoy - Rep - Long Barrel - N &
  AB 55

Western, 9", Hubley - Rep..20

Wild Bill Hickok, 9", Leslie Henry - Rep 45

Wild Bill Hickok, 11¼", 44 Leslie Henry - RC.............65
  (Can be found with cylinder for bullets)

Wild Bill Hickok, 10½", Leslie Henry Long Barrel
  (Rare) 100

Wild Bill Hickok, 10½", Leslie Henry - Pop-up
  Magazine - N - G..85

Winchester Saddle Gun, Mattel Shootin Shell 80

Winner, 8¾", Hubley - Plastic & Metal - Rep...............35

W-Dot Ranch, 8", Wyandotte Tin Clicker...................25

Young Buffalo Bill, 8", Stevens - Rep........................25

Young Buffalo Bill, 7½", Halco - LH - Rep.................25

CAST IRON WESTERN

American, 9⅜", Kilgore - RC - Rep............................125

Bango, 7", Stevens - Rep...40

Big Horn, 8⅝", Kilgore - RC - Rep............................100

Billy the Kid, 6¾", Stevens - Rep 85

Buc-A-Roo, 7¾", Kilgore - SS...................................35

Buffalo Bill, 11½", Kenton - SS................................100

Buffalo Bill, 13½", Kenton - SS - Extra Long Bar. **(Rare)**..250

Buffalo Bill, 7¾", Stevens - Rep................................40

Bulls Eye, 6½", Kenton - Rep - N & BK 75

C-Boy, 6½", Kenton - Rep (Rare)..............................95

Cowboy, 8", Hubley - Rep - N & BK 45

Cowboy, 12", Stevens - SS (Rare).............................150

Cowboy King, 9", Stevens - Rep................................65

49-ER, 9", Stevens - RC - Rep - N, G & AB................100

Gene Autry, 8⅜", Kenton - Rep - N & BK 75

Gene Autry, 8⅜", Kenton - Engraved - N & BK
  (Rare)...125

Gene Autry, 6½", Kenton - Rep - N & BK 65

Gene Autry, 6½", Kenton - Engraved - N & BK **(Rare)**...150

Lasso Em Bill, 9", Kenton - RC - Bul 90

Lasso Em Bill, 9", Kenton - RC - Bul - Jewels **(Rare)** ...150

Lawmaker, 8⅜", Kenton - Rep...................................60

Lone Ranger, 8¼", Kilgore - Rep...............................65

Long Tom, 10⅜", Kilgore - RC **(Rare)**.....................200

101 Ranch, 11½", Hubley - SS...................................145

Pawnee Bill, 7⅝", Stevens - Rep................................85

Peacemaker, 8½", Stevens - Rep - N & G...................50

Ranger, 8½", Kilgore - Engraved - Rep 85

Ranger, 8½", Kilgore - Rep.......................................60

Rodeo, 11", Hubley - SS..125

Roy Rogers, 8¼", Hubley (Similar Cowboy) Rep
  (Rare)...350

Roy Rogers, 10¼", Kilgore - RC (Similar Long Tom)
  Rep **(Rare)** 300

Six Shooter, 6½", Kilgore - RC - Rep 60

Smoky Joe, 8¼", Hubley (Similar Cowboy) Rep
  (Rare)...135

Texan, 9¼", Hubley - RC - Rep - N - BK 75

Texan, Jr., 8⅛", Hubley - Rep - N - BK 60

The Sheriff, 8½", Stevens - Rep.................................50

Western, 7¼", Kenton - SS 45

Western Boy, 7¾", Stevens - Rep...............................80

Wild West, 11½", Kenton - SS 110

AIRCRAFT

by Capt. Perry R. Eichor USAF, Ret.
(See also Tin Wind-Up, Comic Character, Premiums and Paper)

Aircraft in the last edition averaged $107.34 in mint condition, and this time
averaged $293.77, an increase of 174%

The airplane, until the last several years, was one aspect of toy collecting that attracted little interest and even less enthusiasm. Prices of toy airplanes generally reflected this lethargy.

Then, suddenly, those of us born and raised during 1920-1940 (the golden age of aviation) had the time, the inclination and the means to acquire those objects on which our fantasies were transported during childhood. The scramble began, and demand and prices have been climbing steadily ever since.

Collecting toy aircraft and memorabilia has finally come into its own. As an investment, they seem a good risk, although I find few true collectors who get any joy from acquiring only objects that are guaranteed to appreciate in value. True value lies in the ability of an object to rekindle the fires of our memories and bring to mind those halcyon days of our youth when our ambitions were great, our desire simple and our potential unlimited.

The majority of us would never fly, at least not in the pilot's seat, but the future and the unknown were not limiting factors for young minds. We had not been exposed to the harsh realities of the world, and our concepts of truth, justice, freedom and opportunity were not yet jaded. Naivete was a mantle we wore proudly, for we knew the future was ours for the taking.

Pick up a Hubley Airacuda, a Tootsietoy Army Pursuit, an ID model of a P-38, or any number of other types. Make sure no one is looking. Then, with the toy in your hand, let your inner self, the child within, take over. With toy aircraft, you need not be constrained by earthly bonds, deteriorating eyesight, shortness of breath, or any of the other myriad aches and pains that announce the onslaught of middle age.

Those interested in collecting toy aircraft can limit themselves to diecast and will choose from Tootsietoy, Hubley, Erie, Manoil, Barclay, Dinky, Mercury, S.R., Solido, Tekno, C.I.J., and a host of others. Cast iron was used by numerous companies before WWII and included Hubley, Arcade, Dent and Kilgore, to name a few. Pressed steel seemed to be dominated by Wyandotte and Marx for the smaller types, while Keystone, Kingsbury and Steelcraft, among others, produced the larger types. Tin is unlimited, ranging from the pre-war types, made by Marx, Strauss, Chein, Kingsbury, Girard, American Flyer and numerous European makes, up to the Japanese invasion of the 50's. Some of the later Japanese tin types were very accurate representations of actual aircraft, while others resembled real aircraft as much as Godzilla resembles Snow White.

Some of the nicest toy aircraft ever produced were the "Gnom" series made by Lehmann in the 1930's. These accurate small tin toys were based on two Heinkel aircraft and variations thereof. They are difficult to find and quite a nice display item.

In addition to the above, there are numerous examples of slush cast items from Barclay, Kansas Toy and Novelty, Tommy Toy, Ralstoy, etc., in addition to rubber facsimiles made by the Sun and Auburn companies. For obvious reasons, undistorted, well-preserved rubber toy aircraft are very rare.

Some excellent plastic types were produced immediately after WW II and into the 50's. Some items such as the P-38, B-25, B17 and P-40 by Renwal and the B-26 by Hubley were faithful copies, while others such as the P-39 by Ideal are so out of proportion that they lack even the symbiotic charm that often accompanies grotesqueness. Other toy manufacturers of plastic toy aircraft were Thomas, Acme, Premier, Lido, and Reliable.

Of course, if one collects toy aircraft, it follows that they must be displayed, and they really look best on the numerous toy airports depicting structures of the same time period. In addition to airfields and hangars, there were numerous ground support personnel and vehicles. As with other toys, related memorabilia begin to encroach into the aircraft collector's acquisitions.

Interest in aviation is on the rise, and the flight of the Voyager, along with numerous other record-setting craft, will have a dramatic effect on the interest in things related to flight. Consequently, prices will rise and availability will decrease out of the proportion to interest.

However, there will always be room for those of us who were excited during our youth by the sound of a rotary engine in a biplane passing overhead, doing slow rolls among cotton-ball clouds. We all still secretly yearn to fly with our youthful heros and perform daring feats of aerial combat. How many of you have a leather jacket in your closet? I rest my case.

Keep 'em Flying!

CAPT. PERRY R. EICHOR, USAF, RET. was born in Oklahoma and is currently living in South Carolina. His interest in aircraft toys was reborn when he was a young officer in the Air Force and his mother sent him several toys that had been his as a boy. Twenty-one years in the Air Force only served to deepen his interest in the subject. Today, when he is not out collecting, researching or writing about aeronautical toys, he works as a Criminal Justice Administrator as well as an appraiser and auctioneer.

American Flyer No. 560 Monoplane, "A.F. Lines Air Service", 1929. Courtesy Wilkinson Collection, Detroit Antique Toy Museum.

	C6	C8	C10
A. C. Gilbert "Erector" Biplane, with electric motor	120	180	240
Adam Bomb, circa 1946, wingspan approx. 11", wood and metal	50	100	150
Airford, small, cast iron, two-passenger, steel wheels, single engine	45	60	75
Airplane, early 1900's, single wing, prop behind tail, pilot, open fuselage	300	450	600
Airplane, wood, ride-on	75	100	150
Airport Set No. 88 T. Cohn Co., circa 1940s. Mechanical tin litho airport with early plastic planes that fly. Control tower controls for stunts, crash truck pumps water, airport bus, gasoline truck, etc.	50	75	125
American Flyer No. 560 Monoplane, "A.F. Lines Air Service", 1929, Wingspan 24"	800	1200	1600
American Flyer Spirit of America, 18" wingspan, 1928	125	175	300
American Flyer Spirit of Columbia, "555," pressed tin friction, 18" wingspan	500	750	1000
American National air mail pedal plane, 1926	3000	5000	9000
"Ancient Art Metal Co., Brooklyn N.Y." Spirit of St. Louis, lead 5⅛" wingspan, circa 1927 "Pat. No. 74042"	24	36	48
Arcade Airplane No. 361 cast iron, twin engine, 4⅞" wingspan, "United Boeing"	50	90	150
Arcade Airplane No. 3620, cast iron, tri-motor, 4" wingspan, pressed steel props	38	57	75

	C6	C8	C10
Arcade Airplane No. 3630, cast iron body, twin engine, pressed steel wing, 7" wingspan	50	90	150
Arcade Airplane, cast iron body, single engine, pressed steel wing, body resembles Corsair, red and yellow, or blue and yellow, wingspan 10", **No. 3640**	100	180	300
Arcade Monocoupe **No. 355**, cast iron, 8½" wingspan, steel wing	225	300	650
Arcade Monocoupe, cast iron, 11" wingspan, pull toy, **No. 357**	150	275	500
Arcade "The Monocoupe", 4½" long, **No. 353**	75	140	250
AA1 Auburn Rubber No. 1548 Boeing C-98 "Clipper," 8" wingspan	15	25	45
AA2 Auburn Rubber Consolidated A-11 light bomber, 4" wingspan	10	20	35
AA3 Auburn Rubber No. 586 Army Pursuit Plane, "US 1X2755" on wings, Curtiss P-37	10	15	25
AA4 Auburn Rubber Douglas DC2 Transport	20	30	45
AA5 Auburn "Jet 559"	10	15	25
Autogyro, 6" long, pressed steel, wheels turn blades via gear mechanism	21	31	42
Automatic Toy Co. Rocket and Space Ship, No. 305, friction, tin litho with rubber wheels, sparks, 9" long, 4½" wide, 3" tall, late thirties	30	50	75
Automatic Toy Co. Silver Eagle aluminum plane, 13" wingspan, wooden wheels, two-engine, 1930s	75	125	200

A.C. GILBERT "Erector" Biplane, incomplete in photo. Photo by Bill Kaufman. Courtesy Good Old Days Store.

Adam Bomb. Photo by Bill Kaufman. Courtesy Good Old Days Store.

"Ancient Art Metal Co." Lindy-type plane. Photo by Bill Kaufman.

Left to Right. Top: AA1, AA2; Bottom: AA3, AA4. Photo by Ed Poole.

American Flyer aircraft as advertised in the January, 1929 Playthings Magazine.

Auburn AA5 "JET 559". Photo by Max Heiss.

481

BARCLAY AIRCRAFT

	C6	C8	C10
BA1 307 Lindy-type plane, wingspan approx. 4⅜" long, early-mid 30s....15	20	30
BA1a 307 Monoplane, single engine 15	20	30
BA2 Transatlantic Bremen, circa 1928 .17	23	35
BA3 Monoplane, single engine, high wing, Crackajack size, one-piece, sold with Aeroplane Carrier and piggy-backed on 195 Aeroplane.....10	15	20
BA4 No. 57 Giant Zeppelin 17	23	35
BA4a Dirigible, 4⅜" long, early-mid 30s 20	30	40
BA5 610 Rocket Ship............................25	38	50

	C6	C8	C10
BA6 611 Rocket Ship.........................25	38	50
BA7 195 Aeroplane, "U.S. Army" single engine transport, 3¾" wingspan........17	23	35
BA7a 195 Aeroplane with BA3 monoplane piggy-backed on it 30	45	60
BA7b 195 Aeroplane with clip of bombs attached to it........................25	35	50
BA8 "Old 307"...................................12	18	24
BA9 Thick-winged monoplane, approximately 2½" long with oversized wheels in 1935 Butler Bros. Catalog...17	23	35
BA10 No. 52 Small Lindy-type plane....6	9	12

BARCLAY BA7. Photo by Bill Kaufman.

BARCLAY BA1, BA4a. Photo by Bill Kaufman.Courtesy Evelyn Besser.

BARCLAY (BA3) Monoplanes atop the firm's No. 372 Aeroplane Carrier. From the Barclay Catalog Book.

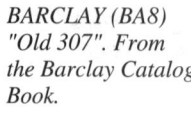

BARCLAY (BA8) "Old 307". From the Barclay Catalog Book.

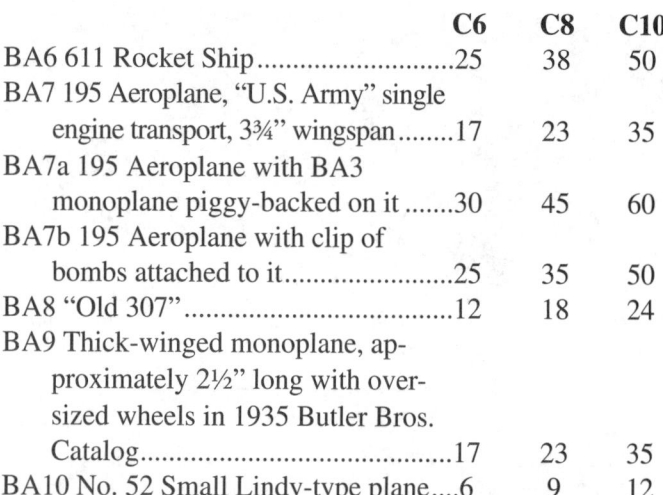

BARCLAY BA9. Courtesy Perry R. Eichor.

BARCLAY BA2. Photo by Bill Kaufman.

BARCLAY (BA4) No. 57 Giant Zeppelin. From the Barclay Catalog Book.

BARCLAY (BA5) No. 610 Rocket Ship. From the Barclay Catalog Book.

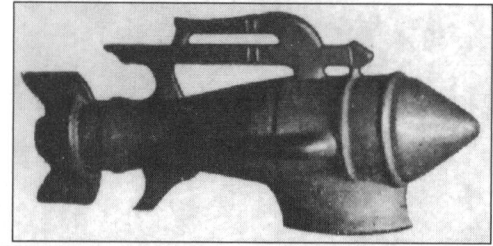

BARCLAY (BA6) No. 611 Rocket Ship. From the Barclay Catalog Book.

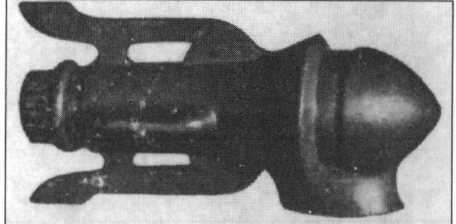

BARCLAY BA7b. Courtesy Hank Anton.

Big Bang monoplane No. 11-P. Courtesy Sotheby's New York.

BEST - see KANSAS TOY & NOVELTY

	C6	C8	C10
Big Bang Monoplane No. 11-P, 10" long, cast iron	400	650	900
Biplane, wooden, approx. 7½" wingspan, tin tail, aluminum propellor, pull plane, propeller spins	40	60	90
Boycraft "NX-130", high wing monoplane, pressed steel, 22" wingspan	300	450	600
Buddy L. No. 603 Transport Airplane (Ford), 27" wingspan, circa 1946	300	450	600
Buddy L. No. 959 Army Tank Transport Plane, 27" wingspan,			

	C6	C8	C10
two detachable tanks under wings, tanks have hum motor device, pressed steel, 1941	400	600	800
Buddy L. No. 2007 Monoplane and Catapult Hangar, 1930-31	750	1000	1500
Buddy L. No. 5000 single high wing monoplane, 1929-31	200	250	500
Buddy L. No. 5010 Triple Hangar and three planes, 1931, planes are monocoupes	750	1200	2250
"Champion" high wing monoplane, cast iron, 5" long	90	135	180

C.A.W. NOVELTY COMPANY - THE INVISIBLE COMPANY

By Fred Maxwell, Slushmold Contributing Editor and Perry Eichor,
Aircraft Contributing Editor, with the assistance of Gary Franson and The Clay Center Historical Society.

Charles A. Wood was known as the "Pioneer Birdman" in Clay Center, Kansas. Master aircraft mechanic, early pilot and aviation booster, his emphasis on aircraft in his toy line reflected his life-long love. And like aircraft, his toys have been too invisible. As a toymaker, did he fly too high?

He must have been a perfectionist, for he was a meticulous and creative moldmaker. All of his toys are crisp, high quality castings. So why have his toys and his company been overlooked by the collecting world until 1990? His was no basement hobby; his company was active from 1925 to 1940. He made 30 to 50 different toys, of which 15 or more were aircraft. He had over 60 employees and an output of about 2 million toys in his best year. Perhaps he was more doer than publicist.

In comparing his toys and others, we see that he didn't take any shortcuts: a Ford Trimotor with the landing gear and outboard motors on struts; pilots' heads showing through open cockpit windows; a most realistic model of Ben Howard's famous stunt-plane with "Mr. Mulligan" prominently embossed. All of his pieces are more models than toys; miniature souvenirs of history; replicas of famous aircraft, local airliners and mailplanes.

Although researching slush toys for 20 years, we had only heard a rumor of "a little molder in Clay Center" a few miles from the well known Kansas Toy Co. Then a few years ago Fred found a neat little monoplane with initials "C.A.W." under the tail plane. Putting the pressure on his Kansas friends, he finally found a mint collection owned by a relative of Wood, as well as a small exhibit in the local Historical Museum.

Because Wood was such an activist a brief biography

may be of interest. Born about 1891. Went to work for Longren Aircraft Mfg. Co., Topeka, Ks. in 1915. Opened the toy factory in Clay Center in 1925. Was influential in establishing a local airport in a wheat field in 1929. Received pilots license, bought a Waco F biplane, erected a Butler hangar and opened a repair service in 1930. He was active in persuading Midland Air Express and Western Air Express lines to make route stops there in 1931. This put this County Seat on the air map.

In 1938, during National Airmail Week, he flew a commemorative load (wish I had one of those First Day Covers) from Morganville to Kansas City. One mail sack was delivered to the airfield by a "Pony Express"

horseman. During the war he was an instructor at a Naval Training Center. Later, he owned a Rearwin plane, was a Piper Cub dealer, and in 1955 designed and built a monoplane dubbed "Little Monster." He continued to fly until 1976 - a grand old man of early aviation.

Note: *The accompanying (partial) sales flyer of C&H Mfg. Co. was issued about 1936. All evidence suggests C&H was a distributor, and that this sheet covered only C.A.W. toys.*

Note: *Wood's early production had metal disk wheels with painted black "tires." Later toys had rubber or plastic wheels. All aircraft had cast propellers, tapered and rounded wings except CWA.*

C.A.W. NOVELTY CO.: Back Row: CWA 1, CWA 2, CWA 8, CWA 6; Front Row: CWA 5, CWA9, CWA7. Photo by Perry Eichor.

C.A.W. NOVELTY CO.: Top Row: CWA 13, CWA 9, CWA 8; Bottom Row: CWA 11, CWA 12. Photo by Perry Eichor.

C.A.W. NOVELTY CO.: CWA 10. Courtesy Perry Eichor.

	C6	C8	C10
CWA1 Small monoplane, 2⅜" x 2⅛". High wing Lindy type, 6 cyl. radial engine, negative dihedral in wings. See #41 set.			No Price Found
CWA2 Small monoplane, 2⅝" x 2½". High wing racing type, V8 engine, closed cockpit in front of wing, 6 windows, "C A W" & "Pat, appld.for." under tailplane.	30	45	60

	C6	C8	C10
CWA2b ? Small monoplane. Similar to above, except no markings and stubbier wings. (CAW copy?)	34	51	68
CWA3 Monoplane, 3⅝" x 3½". High wing, Ford model 2 ?, V12 engine, 8 window + 2 restroom, crew of 2 in open cockpit behind wing, tail wheel.			No Price Found

C.A.W. NOVELTY CO. Left to Right: CWA 3, CWA 4, CWA 2. Photo by Fred Maxwell.

	C6	C8	C10
CWA4 Monoplane, same as above with closed cockpit ahead of wing, no crew.	10	15	20
CWA5 Small monoplane, 2¼" x 2½". Amphibian, Douglas Dolphin ?, bimotored. See #41 set.	No Price Found		
CWA6 Monoplane, 3¼" x 3⅝", larger version of CWA5	No Price Found		
CWA7 Monoplane, #12, 3⅛" x 4⅜". Ford Trimotor model 4, 7 cyl. radial engines, outboards and landing gear on struts, tail wheel	No Price Found		
CWA8 Jr. LOW WING MONOPLANE, #28, 2⅞" x 3". Lockheed or Northrop ? Cowled radial engine, 6 windows pilot in open cockpit near tail. (modern copy available, in different finish and "wire" wheels	20	40	60
CWA9 Sr. LOW WING MONOPLANE, #29, 3¾" x 4". Larger version of above, tail wheel	20	40	60
CWA10 Mr. MULLIGAN AIRPLANE, #34, 3" x 3½". High wing, "Mr. Mulligan," "NR-273Y", cowled radial engine, 2 windows, 2 doors. Circa 1936 production	40	60	80

	C6	C8	C10
CWA11 BOEING BOMBER, #36, 2⅝" x 3½". Low wing "Boeing," "NC 13361", "Made in USA", bimotored, 3 bladed props. Called a "bomber" (war was in the air), it looks like a Boeing mod. 247 airliner	20	40	60
CWA12 ARMY PURSUIT PLANE, #37, 2⅞" x 3½". Low wing "Seversky" P-37 monoplane. Under wing is Air Corps "star-in-circle", "37" and "Made in USA." Cowled radial engine	20	40	60
CWA13 Monoplane, 3½" x 3⅝". Low wing cabin or pursuit plane, cowled radial engine, forward cockpit, divided windshield, open windows w/pilot's head inside	20	40	60
CWA14 ? Large monoplane. High-wing Lindy Ryan type, but V8 engine, oversized propeller, 5 windows and door. Probably C.A.W.	No Price Found		
CWA15 Small biplane. (This from the maker's own mouth, but no description available)	No Price Found		
CWA16 THREE PIECE AIRPLANE SET, #41. Apparently 2 types, see CWA1 and CWA5, above.	No Price Found		

DENT 'Los Angeles" dirigible.

Dent "Air Express". Courtesy Wilkinson Collection - Detroit Antique Toy Museum.

	C6	C8	C10
Dayton No. 700 high wing monoplane, 13" wingspan, open cockpit and pilot, red, yellow or blue, painted disc wheels	125	250	400
Dent "Air Express," cast iron, 12" wingspread	750	1200	1500

	C6	C8	C10
Dent "Air Express", cast iron, tri-motor, 11½" wingspan	1500	2400	3000
Dent "Airline" monoplane, "?" on fuselage, cast aluminum, 12½" wingspan, stripes on rudder	700	1050	1400

DENT "Lucky Boy" Glider.

ERIE, Left to Right: E1, E2, E3. Photo by Perry R. Eichor.

ERIE, Left to Right: E4, E5. Photo by Perry R. Eichor.

	C6	C8	C10
Dent "Airline" monoplane, "X5043" cast on rudder, cast iron, 12½" wingspan	500	750	1000
Dent Ford Trimotor, cast iron, 12" wingspan, #1417 cast on rudder above "Ford"	800	1400	2000
Dent "Lindy," 12½" wingspan, cast iron	1000	1700	2400
Dent "Los Angeles" dirigible, 13" long, cast iron, circa 1925	1000	1500	2000
Dent "Los Angeles" dirigible, 8½", cast iron, circa 1925	450	675	900
Dent "Los Angeles" dirigible, 6¾", circa 1932	130	195	265
Dent "Lucky Boy" cast iron, X6043 cast on rudder, 12½" wingspan	600	1000	1400
Dent "Lucky Boy" trimotor, cast iron, 7" wingspan	500	750	1000
Dent "Lucky Boy Glider," cast iron, 6½" wingspan, high wing	225	500	750
Dent "Question Mark" trimotor, cast iron, "?" on fuselage, 12" wingspan	1200	2000	3000

	C6	C8	C10
Dent "Zep" Zeppelin, 6½" long, cast iron	150	280	375
Dent "Zep" Zeppelin, 5" long, cast iron	100	150	200
Erie E1 Single seat open cockpit Northrup Gamma	25	40	75
Erie E2 2-place open cockpit, "U.S. Army" on wings	15	25	40
Erie E3 Northrup Delta single engine passenger airliner	25	40	75
Erie E4 Boeing 247 twin engine "U.S. Army"	20	40	60
Erie E5 Boeing B-17	25	50	100
Fighter, tin circa 1940, single engine, four machine guns mounted on wing	15	22	30
"Flagship America" airplane, metal Ford Tri-Motor, pressed steel, 1930s, 25" wingspan	75	100	200
Girard High-Wing Monoplane, 10" wingspan, pressed steel	100	200	400
Girard High-Wing Monoplane, 18" wingspan, pressed steel	150	500	750
Girard Whiz Skyfighter biplane, early	85	130	170
Glass Airplane, candy container, 5" long	75	112	150
Helicopter, Army, 13" long, tin litho, friction drive, spinning prop	20	25	45

HUBLEY

	C6	C8	C10
H1 "America" cast iron, largest cast iron plane made, 17" wingspan, trimotor, open cockpit, pilot, copilot	2000	3200	7000
H2 Bell Airacuda, XFM-1, diecast, red and silver, folding landing			

	C6	C8	C10
gear, movable guns in front of twin pusher engines, 3-bladed props, new in 1941 100	150	200
H3 No. 377 "Lindy" cast iron, 3½" wingspan, single engine 25	38	75
H4 No. 431 U.S. Army Plane, diecast, 5½" wingspan, white rubber tires, enclosed in cast fairings, single engine, low wing monoplane 15	25	40
H5 No. 389 twin engine, cast iron, 5⅝" wingspan, painted and nickle plate, "TAT NC 431" 25	50	75
H6 Twin engine, 3⅜" wingspan, silver and red or green 15	30	45
H7 No. 430 jet, diecast, single engine, folding wings, retractable landing gear, 6" wingspan, cast cockpit, red and silver or blue and silver 12	20	40
H8 "U.S.N. 3-B-4" diecast, twin engine, 5⅛" wingspan, twin vertical stabilizer, retractable landing gear 12	20	30
H9 "Lindy," cast iron, 10" wingspan ... 500	900	1200
H10 "Lindy," cast iron, 10" wingspan, prop turns via gear attached to wheel 750	1200	2000
H11 "Lindy" cast iron, with "Spirit of St. Louis" decals, ratchet drive action noisemaker, has wing struts .. 1200	2500	3250
H12 "Bremen," aluminum, 6½" wingspan .. 250	500	750
H13 "Bremen," cast iron, 6½" wingspan 200	500	750
H13A "Bremen," cast iron," 7" wingspan 500	800	1300
H14 "Bremen," cast iron, 10" wingspan, "Junkers Bremen" on fuselage, open cockpit with 2 pilots, prop turned by wheels 1000	5000	8000
H15 "America," cast iron, single engine, 17" wingspan, wire spring drive, with 2 pilots in open cockpit 2000	5000	10,000
H16 "Friendship," cast iron seaplane, "Fokker" embossed on fuselage, 13" wingspan 1500	2500	5000
H17 "U.S. Army" diecast, 8" wingspan, low wing single engine monoplane, folding wheels, silver and red (early versions had red wood hubs with white rubber tires, later had large black rubber tires - cast cockpit may have openings or be cast or solid), introduced in 1939 20	30	50

HUBLEY H1.

HUBLEY H2.. Photo by Perry R. Eichor.

HUBLEY, Left; H3 and Right; H5. Photo by Perry R. Eichor.

HUBLEY H9. Photo by Perry R. Eichor.

487

Hubley planes, as shown in the December, 1929 Butler Bros. Catalog.

HUBLEY H17 cockpit variations. Photo by Perry Eichor.

HUBLEY, Left to Right: H7, H20, H22. Photo by Perry R. Eichor.

	C6	C8	C10
H18 "U.S. Army," plastic, like above, folding wheels, 6" wingspan, "U.S. Army" embossed on horizontal stabilizer	10	20	30
H19 No. 326 Attack Bomber, plastic, retractable landing gear Martin B-26 Marauder copy, 7⅞" wingspan	20	30	60
H20 P-39, diecast and tin, "U.S. Army" imprinted on rear horizon stabilizers, tin wings are 5½"	15	20	35
H21 No. 495 on wings, diecast, 11½" wingspan, single engine, folding wings, retractable landing gear, sliding plastic cockpit (numerous versions, and later packaged as "American Eagle" or "Flying Circus"):			
Early - red & silver, 4-bladed prop, no airscoop on top of engine cowl	38	60	100
Mid - two tone blue, red cowl, large airscoop atop engine cowl, 4-bladed prop	25	38	50
Late - orange & yellow, large airscoop, either 4 or 2-bladed prop	15	22	30
H22 No. 433 Piper Club, red 7⅞" wingspan, also in olive drab L-4 version	10	20	30

	C6	C8	C10
H23 P-40, diecast, 8" wingspan, early version was silver & red with 3-bladed prop, later version orange & yellow with 2-bladed prop	18	30	45
H24 P-38, diecast, red & silver, 12⅝" wingspan, retractable landing gear, later versions are yellow & green camouflage	30	60	100
H25 No. 467 diecast, 8⅝" wingspan, folding wings, retractable landing gear, plastic cockpit, resembles Brewster Buffalo, red & silver with 4-bladed prop in early version, later version was green & yellow with 2-blade prop	15	22	45
H26 No. 751 folding delta wing jet, diecast, 6⅛" wingspan, retractable landing gear, red & silver plastic cockpit	12	20	40
H27 No. 427 Crusader, diecast, 5⅛" wingspan, twin engine, twin boom, "TAT NC-31"	15	25	50
H28 No. 303 cast iron, 5" wingspan, low wing single engine monoplane, nickel plate wings & prop with various colored body	25	40	75
H29 No. 305 cast iron, 3¾" wingspan, low wing single engine monoplane, nickel plate wings & prop	15	30	40

	C6	C8	C10
H30 No. 304 Giro plane, cast iron with nickel plate rotor, prop & engine 40		60	100
H31 302 DO-X, cast iron, 4" wingspan, 6 engine, high wing seaplane 50		75	125
H32 DO-X, cast iron, 5" wingspan, larger version of above 70		100	200
H33 Hellcat, 9¼" wingspan, plastic 10		15	20

	C6	C8	C10
H34 "Lindy" Glider, cast iron, 6¼" long 300		500	850
H35 Helicopter 55		82	110
H36 "Question Mark" Trimotor, 12½" wingspan..........1200		2200	3500
H37 Lockheed Sirius, "Lindy NR-211," 9" long 1200		2200	3500
H38 "Air Ford" cast iron, 2 open cockpits, 4" long 100		150	200

HUBLEY H19. Photo by Perry R. Eichor.

HUBLEY H24, two variations. Photo by Perry R. Eichor.

HUBLEY H21, early and later versions. Photo by Perry R. Eichor.

HUBLEY, Left to Right: H25, H23. Photo by Perry R. Eichor.

HUBLEY H27. Photo by Perry R. Eichor.

HUBLEY, Left to Right: H33, H18.. Photo by Perry R. Eichor.

HUBLEY H34. Courtesy Sotheby's New York.

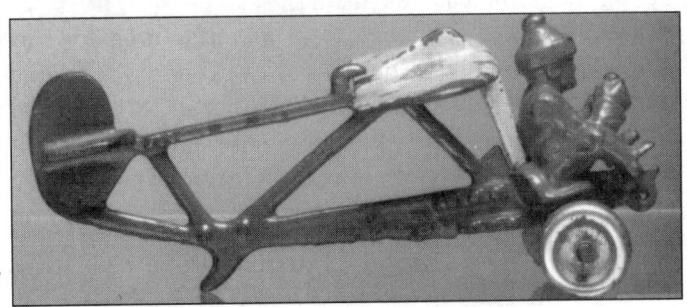

H31 Hubley DO-X.

HUBLEY, Left to Right: H28, H29, H8, H4. Photo by Perry R. Eichor.

I.D. PLANES

by Richard L. MacNary

The popularly called "black I.D. planes" were manufactured during World War II primarily as training aids initially for the U.S. Navy and then U.S. Army. The WW II airplanes covered in this section were all made in 1/72 scale (1" = 6'), all were colored black, and usually marked on the bottom in raised lettering with (1) the country of ownership/design (U.S., British, German, etc.), (2) the aircraft type (P-38, Spitfire, FW189, etc.), and date of model issue (7-42, 8-42, 5-42, etc.).

While the program reportedly started the day after Pearl Harbor, the earliest marking on any of the known models is 5-42. (The dates so marked on the planes are dates of model issue or copyright, not the date that the actual plane became operational.)

Some of the early WW II attempts at manufacturing these identification aircraft used materials such as reinforced plaster (too lumpy), paper-mache (too little detail), a hard rubber-like material (too pliable for long sections like wings), Wood's metal and even cast iron (too heavy for shipping and perhaps needed elsewhere).

The vast majority of these I-D aircraft were molded by the Cruver Company of Chicago. The master molds were made by either the Comet Engraving Company or H&H Specialty Company, also both of Chicago. A few models were produced (molded) by Design Center and Leominster as noted in the listing.

While these airplanes were manufactured for our Armed Forces, Polk's Hobbies of New York did sell some domestically under the Aristo-Craft name. Most of the surviving WW II types, though, were probably midnight requisitioned by pilot or gunner trainees. The quantity produced during the War was staggering. *Flying* magazine

of February, 1944 states that Cruver had manufactured over 2,000,000 model aircraft since the spring of 1941 (sic - they meant spring of 1942). Not many remain today.

The following listing of WW II model planes was taken from the most complete compilation known; it may not be totally inclusive nor may all of these planes have been made in quantity. The best story of all types of I.D. aircraft made from different materials and in different scales as well as those of the later Korean War vintage was well covered by Robert C. Mikesh in his excellent article in the May/June 1984 issue of *Fine Scale Modeler* magazine.

You will note in the guide that not much distinction is made between the values for similar size models. There is just not enough buying and selling nor large enough collections to accurately determine which plane is more rare than another. They could all be equally hard to find today.

As to grading, C10 is just that - no scuffs, no warpage, no "prune-skin," no repainting or, in other words, a brand new 45-year-old airplane. C8 covers models that are very nice; planes should be complete with wheels or floats if on originally; free of serious defects like "prune-skin" or missing parts, and not repainted (restored maybe). The C6 grade covers everything else and likely includes the majority of those models still in existence.

A special thanks is due to master modeler Ray ".43 Magnum" Wheeler of Lilburn, GA for his help in identifying some of the more obscure types listed.

Comments and especially documented corrections are always welcome.

As previously reported in O'Brien's **Guide to Electric Trains**, *RICHARD MACNARY had his first childhood outside of Chicago during WW II. While his wife and two children say he really never left his first, his second childhood has spanned the last 23 years while serving as the Atlanta District Manager for the Ohio Brass Company, the premier manufacturer of high voltage electrical equipment.*

Dick's own WW II I.D. aircraft were the punch-out, three dimensional, black pressboard planes. These were sent back from the ETO by the Army son of his father's insurance partner. These cardboard models lasted about as long as his Built-Rite No. 25 forts in the damp Northern Indiana soil!

Punchout replacement aircraft along with some 8 dozen of the listed plastic WW II I.D. models are now hangered in Lilburn, GA, the home of MacNary Field (Deactivated), U.S. Army Air Corps.

WW II IDENTIFICATION MODELS
1/72 SCALE
(Black I.D. Airplanes)

Each model is identified by type and date marked.

UNITED STATES	C6	C8	C10
A-20 Havoc, 6-42	25	37	50
A-24 Dauntless, SBD - 3, 7-42	15	22	30
A-26 Invader, 2-44	25	37	50
A-29 Hudson (PBO-16), none	25	37	50
A-30 Baltimore, 2-43	25	37	50
A-31 Vengeance, 7-42	15	22	30
A-31 Vengeance, 7-44	15	22	30
A-35 Vengeance, 4-44	15	22	30
AT17 Bobcat*, 7-43	25	37	50
B-17 Flying Fortress, 7-42	50	75	100
B-24 Liberator, 7-42	50	75	100
B-25 Mitchell, 7-42	25	37	50
B-26 Marauder, 10-42	25	37	50
B-26 Marauder, none	25	37	50
B-29 Super Fortress, 3-44	50	75	100
B-29 Super Fortress, 9-44	50	75	100
B-29 Super Fortress, none	50	75	100
B-32 Dominator, 12-44	50	75	100
C-46 Commando, 3-43	25	37	50
C-47 Skytrain 3-43	25	37	50
C-47 Skytrain**, 5-43	25	37	50
C-54 Skymaster, 3-43	50	75	100

	C6	C8	C10
C60A Lodestar, 3-43	25	37	50
C69 Constellation, 4-44	50	75	100
C78 Bobcat, 6-44	25	37	50
C87 Liberator, 3-44	50	75	100
CG-4A Waco Glider, 6-43	15	22	30
F4F-4 Wildcat, 5-43	15	22	30
F4U-1 Corsair, 3-43	15	22	30
F6F Hellcat, 4-43	15	22	30
GH-1 Nightingale*, 5-43	25	37	50
J2F-4 Duck, 12-42	30	45	60
JRF OA-09 Goose*, 7-43	30	45	60
JRS-1 (S43), 11-42	30	45	60
JR2S-1 (S44) Excalibur, 11-44	60	90	120
L-1 Vigilant, 3-43	25	37	50
L-2 Grasshopper, 7-44	25	37	50
L-4 Grasshopper, 2-43	25	37	50
L-5 Sentinel, 1-44	25	37	50
OS2U (on floats)*, 2-43	25	37	50
OS2U (on wheels)*, 2-43	25	37	50

* - molded by Design Center
** - molded by Leominster
All other molded by Cruver

ID PLANE, U.S. B-29 Super Fortress, 9/44. MacNary Collection. Courtesy RLM.

ID PLANE, U.S. P-38 Lightning. MacNary Collection. Courtesy RLM.

491

ID PLANE/JR2S1 (S44) Excalibur. MacNary Collection. Courtesy RLM.

ID PLANE, British, Left to Right: Spitfire 9B (10/44), Spitfire 8/42. MacNary Collection. Courtesy RLM.

	C6	C8	C10
OS2U-1 (on floats), 7-43	25	37	50
PBM - 3 Mariner, 6-43	30	45	60
PBY-5 Catalina, 5-43	30	45	60
PB2Y-3 Coronado, 4-43	60	90	120
PV-1 (B-39) Ventura, 5-43	25	37	50
PV-2 Harpoon, 5-43	25	37	50
P-38 Lightning, 7-42	25	37	50
P-39 Airacobra, 6-42	15	22	30
P-40 Warhawk, 9-42	15	22	30
P-40 Warhawk, 4-44	15	22	30
P-43 Lancer, 5-43	15	22	30
P-47 Thunderbolt, 9-42	15	22	30
P-47 (D) Thunderbolt, 2-44	15	22	30
P-47 (N) Thunderbolt, 4-45	15	22	30
P-47 Thunderbolt*, none	15	22	30
P-51 Mustang 6-42	15	22	30
P-51D Mustang 4-45	15	22	30
P-61 Black Widow, 2-44	25	37	50
P-63 King Cobra, 5-44	15	22	30
P-80 Shooting Star, 4-45	15	22	30
SB2A-2 Buccaneer, 5-43	15	22	30
SB2C-1 Helldiver, 3-43	15	22	30
SB2C-2 Helldiver, 2-45	15	22	30
SB2C-2 Helldiver, (floats)*, 3-43	25	37	50
SB2C-2 Helldiver, (wheels)*, 3-43	25	37	50
SB2U-3 Vindicator, 6-43	15	22	30
SNJ-2 Texan, 7-42	15	22	30
SNJ-3 Texan, 7-42	15	22	30
S03C-1 Seagull (floats), 3-43	25	37	50
S03C-2 Seagull (wheels), 3-43	25	37	50
SR-10B Reliant 10-42	25	37	50
TBD-1 Devastator, 5-43	15	22	30
TBF Avenger, 7-43	15	22	30

BRITISH

	C6	C8	C10
Albacore, 8-42	30	45	60
Albemarle, 9-44	25	37	50
Barracuda, 2-43	15	22	30
Beaufighter 1, 9-42	25	37	50
Beaufighter 2, 9-42	25	37	50
Beaufighter 6, 5-44	25	37	50
Beaufort, 9-42	25	37	50
Beaufort, none	25	37	50

	C6	C8	C10
Blenheim IV, 8-42	25	37	50
Boomerang (Aust.)*, none	15	22	30
Botha, 8-42	25	37	50
Defiant, 8-42	15	22	30
Firefly, 2-43	15	22	30
Fulmar, 8-42	15	22	30
Halifax, 9-42	50	75	100
Hampden, 8-42	25	37	50
Hastings, none	50	75	100
Horsa, 9-44	25	37	50
Hotspur, 6-43	15	22	30
Hurricane, 8-43	15	22	30
Lancaster, 4-43	50	75	100
Lerwick, 9-42	30	45	60
Lysander, 7-43	25	37	50
Manchester, 8-42	25	37	50
Maryland, 2-43	25	37	50
Mosquito, 3-43	25	37	50
Roc, 8-42	15	22	30
Skua, 8-42	15	22	30
Spitfire, 8-42	15	22	30
Spitfire, 1-44	15	22	30
Spitfire 9A, 10-44	15	22	30
Spitfire 9B, 10-44	15	22	30
Spitfire 22, 7-45	15	22	30
Stirling, 5-42	50	75	100
Sunderland, 9-42	60	90	120
Swordfish, 9-42	30	45	60
Tempest 2, 3-45	15	22	30
Tempest 5, 10-44	15	22	30
Typhoon, 6-43	15	22	30
Walrus, 4-44	25	37	50
Wellington 2, 9-42	25	37	50
Wellington 3, 9-42	25	37	50
Whirlwind, 8-43	25	37	50
Whitley, 9-42	25	37	50
York, 9-44	50	75	100

GERMAN

	C6	C8	C10
Arado Ar196, 12-43	25	37	50
Blohm & Voss BV138, 5-44	50	75	100
Blohm & Voss HA139, 11-42	60	90	120
Blogm & Voss BV222, 2-44	60	90	120

ID Plane, German. Focke Wulf FW189, with box. MacNary Collection, Courtesy RLM.

	C6	C8	C10
DFS 230, 8-43	15	22	30
Dornier DO 172, 9-42	25	37	50
Dornier DO 215, 9-42	25	37	50
Dornier DO 217E, 8-42	25	37	50
Fi 156 Storch, none	25	37	50
Focke Wulf FW 187, 8-42	25	37	50
Focke Wulf FW 189, 5-42	25	37	50
Focke Wulf FW 190, 7-42	15	22	30
Focke Wulf FW 190, 12-42	15	22	30
Focke Wulf 200, 3-44	50	75	100
Focke Wulf FW 200K, 9-42	50	75	100
Gotha Go 242, 7-42	25	37	50
Heinkel He 111, 9-42	25	37	50
Heinkel He 112, 7-42	15	22	30
Heinkel He 113, 5-42	15	22	30
Heinkel He 113, 9-42	15	22	30
Heinkel He 115K, 9-42	30	45	60
Henschel Hs 126, 10-42	25	37	50
Henschel Hs 129, 8-44	25	37	50
Junkers Ju 52, 8-42	50	75	100
Junkers Ju 86K, 9-42	25	37	50
Junkers Ju 87B, 8-42	15	22	25
Junkers Ju 88, 9-42	25	37	50
Junkers Ju 90, 9-42	50	75	100
Junkers Ju 188, 7-44	25	37	50
Messers. Me 109E, 7-42	15	22	30
Messers. Me 109F, 7-42	15	22	30
Messers. Me 110, 8-42	25	37	50
Messers. Me 210, 7-43	25	37	50

* - Molded by Design Center
** - Molded by Leominster
All others molded by Cruver

ITALIAN

	C6	C8	C10
Cantiere Z.506B, 9-42	50	75	100
Cantiere Z.1007, 9-42	30	45	60
Caproni CA.133, 9-42	50	75	100
Fiat BR.20, 6-42	25	37	50
Fiat CR. 42, 9-42	30	45	60
Fiat CR. 42, 1-43	30	45	60

	C6	C8	C10
Fiat G.50, 8-42	15	22	30
Macchi C.200, 8-42	15	22	30
Macchi MC, 202, 3-43	15	22	30
Piaggio P.32 BIS, 9-42	15	37	50
Reggiane Rc. 2000, 9-42	15	22	30
Reggiane Re. 2001, 3-43	15	22	30
Savoia Marchetti 79, 9-42	30	45	60
Savoia Marchetti 81, 9-42	50	75	100
Savoia Marchetti 82 9-42	30	45	60
Savoia Marchetti 84, 4-43	30	45	60

JAPANESE

	C6	C8	C10
(Adam) Naka. 97, 11-42	25	37	50
(Ann) Mitsu. T-98, 7-42	25	37	50
(Babs) Mitsu. T-97, 6-42	25	37	50
Betty (G4M1), 9-43	25	37	50
Betty (G4M2), 4-45	25	37	50
(Claude) Mitsu. T-96, 6-42	25	37	50
(Dave) Naka. T-95-NOB, 7-42	25	37	50
Dinah (Ki46), 8-44	25	37	50
Emily (H8K2), 3-45	25	37	50
Francis (P1Y), 3-45	25	37	50
Frank (Ki84), 5-45	15	22	30
George (NIKI-J), 5-45	15	22	30
Hamp (T-00, Zeke 32), 7-43	15	22	30
Helen (Ki49), -44	25	37	50
(Ida) Mitsu. T-98 ALB, 6-42	25	37	50
Irving (J1N1), *5-45	25	37	50
Jack (J2M1), 12-44	15	22	30
Jake (E13A), 9-44	25	37	50
Jill (B6N)*, 5-45	15	22	30
Judy (D4Y), 3-45	15	22	30
(Kate) Naka. T-97, 6-42	15	22	30
Lily (Ki48), 9-43	25	37	50
(Mary) T-97 ALB, 6-42	25	37	50
(Mavis) Kawa.,, 11-42	60	90	120
Myrt (C6N), 3-45	15	22	30
(Nate) "97" Fighter, 9-42	25	37	50
(Nell) Mitsu. T-96, 6-42	25	37	50
Nell (G3M), 1-44	25	37	50

	C6	C8	C10
Nick (Ki45), 8-44	25	37	50
Oscar T-01 (Ki43), 9-43	15	22	30
Paul 14, Exp*, 12-44	25	37	50
Pete (F1M2), 6-43	30	45	60
Rufe (A6M2-N), 8-43	25	37	50
(Sally) Mitsu. T-97, 6-42	25	37	50
(Sonia) Mitsu. T-99, 7-42	15	22	30
Tojo (Ki44), 6-44	15	22	30
Tojo (Ki44), 3-45	15	22	30
Tony (Ki61), 7-44	15	22	30
Tony (Ki61), 4-45	15	22	30
(Topsy) Mitsu. MC-20, 10-42	25	37	50
(Val) Aichi T-99, 6-42	25	37	50
Val T-99 MK2, 8-43	25	37	50
(Zeke) Mitsu. 00, 9-42	15	22	30
Zeke 52 (A6M5)*, 12-44	15	22	30

NOTE: Japanese abbreviations used above:
Kawa. - Kawanishi   Mitsu. - Mitsubishi   Naka. - Nakajima

	C6	C8	C10
NETHERLANDS			
Fokker T8W, 11-42	30	45	60
RUSSIAN			
DB-3F, 9-42	25	37	50
DB- 3F, 4-44	25	37	50
I-16, none	15	22	30
IL-2, 9-42	15	22	30
IL-2, 12-43	15	22	30
MiG-3, 8-42	15	22	30
I-18 (MiG-3), 2-43	15	22	30
MiG-3, 2-44	15	22	30
Pe-2, 9-42	15	22	30
SB-3, 11-43	15	22	30
TB-7*, 4-44	15	22	30

End ID

	C6	C8	C10
Ideal Globemaster	30	45	60
Irwin Helicopter, 15" long, friction, circa 1950	30	45	60

KANSAS TOY & NOVELTY COMPANY

By Fred Maxwell, Slushmold Contributing Editor and Perry Eichor, Aircraft Contributing Editor, with the assistance of Bob Condray and Lorene Sorell

To Aviation the 1920-1940 period was decisive - an Era of ferment and growth. It was a time of barnstorming, excitement and record-breaking, including the conquering of the oceans and Lindbergh's impact on our consciousness. Kansas played a large part in the development of airmail and airlines with its manufacturing centers at Topeka and Wichita (Beach, Boeing, Cessna, Laird, Stearman and others). To Kansans this must have been a source of civic pride and we might have expected the toy industry to reflect it. Some did, but even Lindy's Flight of the Decade was poorly represented. Tootsietoy had a recognizable replica but called it Aero Dawn. The closest KT&N came to it was #32, probably already in production in 1927, with Army Air Corps insignia; (Years later Best Toy reproduced it with the name "Combat Airplane").

Kansas Toy barely got the fever, settling for a few basic designs, yet they must have been aware of diversity in cast-iron toys and Tootsietoy and other slushmolders. KT&N #6 and its versions of mailplanes are reminiscent of the Stout-Ford predecessors of the famous "Tin Goose". #45 and #47 are probably Fokkers; although of foreign origin, these fine aircraft were more prominent in building US aviation than most of us remember. These and #56 glider are not easy to rationalize; Best Toy later named #47 a "Seaplane" - with its engine on its prow? OK for kids but good for a chuckle from adult collectors.

Listed below are the aircraft said to have been made by KT&N from 1924 to circa 1931, using metal disk or wire wheels. Reproductions from Best Toy and Ralstoy will be found with later wheels. KTA4, below, has not been positively identified; it could have been made by others or been a sample.

KANSAS TOY Aircraft: KTA2, KTA1. Photo courtesy of Perry Eichor.

KANSAS TOY (later BEST)
KANSAS TOY Seaplane. Drawing by Deb Eccles.
KANSAS TOY "Glider". Drawing by Deb Eccles.

KANSAS TOY Aircraft: KTA3, unnumbered version "U.S. Mail" on both sides. Photo by Perry Eichor.

KANSAS TOY Aircraft: KTA6, KTA5. Photo Courtesy of Perry Eichor.

	C6	C8	C10
KTA1 Cabin plane, "6", 3¾" x 3". High wing with flaring positive dihedral, Army Air Corps star-in-circle insignia, 6 cyl. radial engine, pilot head in open cockpit, 8 oval windows, cast prop., lacquer finish. Also unnumbered version with large tin propeller	14	21	28
KTA2 Cabin plane, no #, 3⅝ x 3". Similar to above, Air Service dot-in-circle insignia. V-8 engine, cast propeller	14	21	28
KTA3 Large cabin plane, "24". 5⅝ " x 4⅜". High wing, larger "U.S. Mail" version of above, dot-in-2-circles insignia, V-8 engine, cast propeller, white disk wheels with painted black "tires." Also an unnumbered version	No Price Found		
KTA4 ? Large cabin plane, no#, about 5". Lindy type, high negative dihedral wing w/large stars, 6 cylinder radial engine, wheels w/black "tires." Kansas Toy?	No Price Found		
KTA5 Small cabin plane, "32", 2⅜ x 2⅛". High, positive dihedral wing, Air Corps star insignia, 6 cyl., radial engine, 6 oval windows, 3 metal "wire" wheels, large tin or cast propeller.	6	8	12
KTA6 Small cabin plane, no#, 2⅜" x 2⅛". Similar to above, w/o "windows" and diff. rudder., or wingtip	6	8	12
KTA7 Zeppelin, "44", 4¼". Front and rear cabins, 3 tail planes, mooring loop on nose, rear axle			

	C6	C8	C10
through rear cabin (unusual design)	No Price Found		
KTA8 Airliner, "45", 2½" x 2½". Fokker ?, high, oval, corrugated wing and tail, 9 circular cabin windows, 9 rectangular flight-deck windows, 6 cylinder radial engine, large tin propeller	No Price Found		
KTA9 Airliner, "KTN 47", 3⅝" x 3½". Fokker, similar to #45. Sometimes called a "seaplane." Why?	No Price Found		
KTA10 Airliner, "KTN 47", 4" X ?". Larger version of above	No Price Found		
KTA 11 Glider, "56", 2⅝" x 2⅜". High oval wing w/"GLIDER", pilot in front, flat lattice fuselage	No Price Found		

NOTE: Best Toys later reproductions will have "Made in U.S.A." embossed; and may have small white rubber wheels.

	C6	C8	C10
Jet, USAF, 5" wingspan, friction-powered, tin litho	15	20	35
Katz Toys "The Pathfinder," tri-motor monoplane, 22" wing-span	350	525	700
Katz Toys "The Red Arrow" No. 137 single engine mono-plane, pull toy	300	450	600

KATZ TOYS "The Red Arrow" No. 137. Photo by Perry Eichor.

KENTON "Air Mail", wingspan approx. 8". Courtesy Chic Gast.

KEYSTONE Riding plane, 28" wingspan, No. 293 "Ride 'Em" Fighter. Courtesy Bob Black, Jr.

KEYSTONE Mail Plane, 27" long. Photo by Calvin L. Chaussee.

KINGSBURY 'Trans Atlantic" Monoplane. Courtesy Lloyd W. Ralston Auctions.

KILGORE Sea Gull, approx. 9" wingspan. Courtesy Chic Gast.

	C6	C8	C10
KD-1 Mak-a-plane - 4" long, mechanical, all metal with rubber wheels, 1940s	40	50	70
Kenton "Air Mail," wingspan approx. 8"	100	150	250
Kenton "Pony Blimp," 6" long, cast iron	125	188	250
Keystone "Airmail" plane, pressed steel, "NX-265," 24" wingspan	900	1350	1800
Keystone "Airmail" "NC-263	500	750	1000
Keystone riding plane, seat over tail, steering bar over cabin, single wing, high, one engine, 23½" long	175	250	450
Keystone riding plane, 28" wingspan, No. 293, "Ride Em" fighter	150	250	450
Kilgore "Bullet," open cockpit monoplane, 4" long, cast iron	112	168	225
Kilgore Ford Trimotor cast iron, 13½" wingspan, "TAT"	2000	3000	4500
Kilgore Hiwing Monocoupe, 5½"	125	188	250
Kilgore High Wing monoplane, 3½" long	50	75	100
Kilgore "N4", open cockpit mono-plane, 4" long, cast iron	112	168	225
Kilgore, Seagull, high wing, pusher prop, 8¼" wingspan	300	500	750
Kilgore Seagull, like above, but 4" wingspan	250	375	500
Kilgore "TAT No. 401" twin engine passenger monoplane, 4½" long	150	250	325
Kilgore "Travel Air Mystery," double open cockpits, cast iron, 6" long	250	400	550
Kingsbury Monoplane, high wing, trimotor, 15" wingspan, clock-work	200	300	500
Kingsbury Tin Goose, tri-engine, 21" wingspan, 1930s	600	900	1500
Kingsbury "Trans Atlantic" monoplane, painted pressed steel wind-up, 1930, 11" long	200	300	450
Kingsbury "U.S. Airmail" biplane, 15" long, steel windup	200	500	900

LINCOLN WHITE METAL AIRCRAFT

LWA1 Airplane, 3¼" x 4½". Tri-motored, Fokker F-11 ?, tapered high wings with wings symbol embossed, 7 cylinder radial

	C6	C8	C10

engines, outboards mounted on landing gear struts, tin propellers, metal wheels, no windows 25   40   75

LWA2 Airplane, 2½" x 2½". Tri-motored, similar to above but outboard engines mounted in wings, unrealistic window patterns, metal wheels 20   30   55

LWA?3 Airplane, c.4½" x 3". Streamlined, swallow-shaped, pilot, cowled radial engine, tin, propeller. It would be called "Batplane" today 40   60   75

LWA?4 Airplane, c.3" x 2½". Smaller version of above 30   45   55

"Lindy" cast iron, nickel prop and wheels, 3½" wingspan 40   60   75

Lindy type Plane, lead, 2¼" wingspan .10   20   30

Lionel No. 55 Airplane and Pylon 300   450   600

Luscombe Airplane, 4" long 30   45   60

Manoil No. 517, Lockheed F90 20   30   40

Manoil No. 518 Navion 20   30   40

Manoil No. 519 Bonanza B-35 20   30   40

Manoil No. 520 Ercoupe 20   30   40

Marx American Airlines Flagship..105   158   210

Marx "Army Bomber" No. 1025, tri-motor, 26" wingspan, circa 1935 75   150   250

Marx Bomber, 14¾" wingspan, 4 engines, drops wooden bombs..75   120   170

Marx Bomber, 18" wingspan, tin litho, sparkling mechanism, camouflaged, four-engine 60   90   120

Marx Crop Duster Plane 20   40   60

Marx Curtiss Transport, 9½" wingspan, khaki, pressed steel 60   90   120

Marx DC-3 Transport, 10" wingspan, pressed steel, circa 1939 80   120   175

Marx DC-4 type, four-motor passenger, circa, 1930s, pressed steel 40   75   100

Marx DC-6 transport plane, plastic...75   120   150

Marx Friction-powered 4-motor transport with whirling propellors, tin litho...60   90   120

Marx Futuristic Airport........................225   338   450

Marx Gyroplane ....No Price Found

Marx Hangar, tin litho, circa 1941 50   75   100

Marx "Little Lindy Aeroplane," 1930s, friction, 6" wingspan 100   150   200

LINCOLN White Metal: LWA1, LWA2. Photo by Perry Eichor.

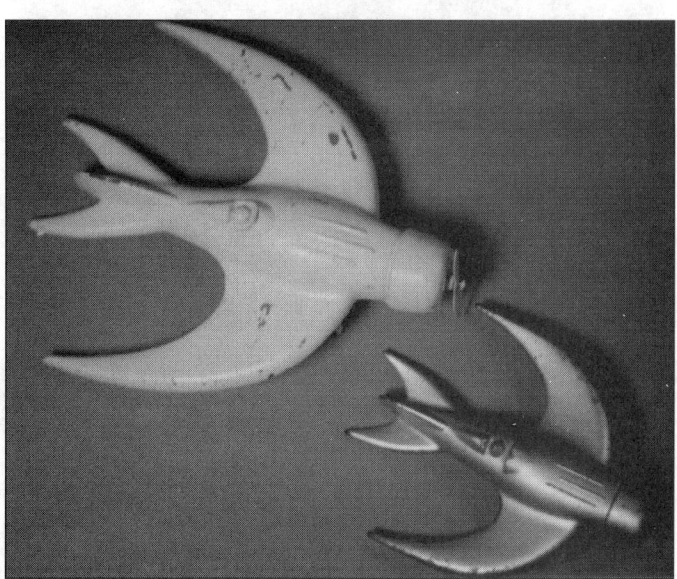

Though there is no hard evidence as yet, these two "Batplanes" have been attributed to Lincoln White Metal. Left to Right: LWA?3, LWA?4.

MARX Pan American 4-motor, 1940, 27" wingspan. Courtesy Lloyd W. Ralston Auctions.

MANOIL Airplanes, Left to Right: 517, 518, 519, 520. Courtesy Peter and Marjorie Ruben.

MARX Bomber, 14¾" wingspan, 4 engine, drops wooden bombs. Photo by Perry R. Eichor.

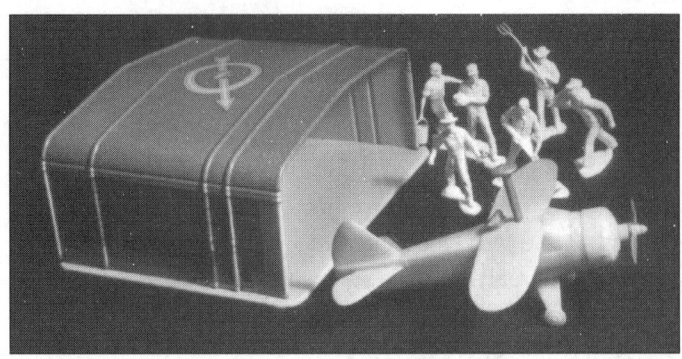

MARX Crop Duster Plane. Photo by Perry R. Eichor.

MARX DC-6 Transport Plane, plastic. Photo by Perry R. Eichor.

MARX Hangar, tin litho, circa 1941. Photo by James Apthorpe.

MARX P-35, 13½" wingspan. Photo by Perry R. Eichor.

MARX P35 - type 2-engine bomber. Photo by Bob West.

MARX Pan American Super 7 Clipper, 17½" wingspan, also as American Airlines. Photo by Perry R. Eichor.

MARX, Left to Right: Trimotor Biplane, 9½" wingspan, Gyroplane. Photo by Perry R. Eichor.

CONSTRUCTION AIRPLANES

"Spirit of St. Louis" All-Metal Construction Airplanes

Bigger and better than ever before! Units made of heavy bright rustproof steel, wood landing wheels. Practically all types of planes can be constructed, including 3-motor type in both monoplane and biplane models ("Spirit of St. Louis," "Ryan," "Fokker," "Columbia," etc.). Each set in colored "Spirit of St. Louis" box with instructions.

1F2960—8½ in. long, 11½ in. wing spread, builds over 18 models. ⅓ doz. sets in box... **Doz sets $7.75**

1F2881—10½ in. long, 14½ in. wing spread, builds over 25 models. ⅓ doz. sets in box. **Doz sets $11.00**

1F2882—10½ in. long, 14½ in. wing spread, builds over 100 models. 1 set in box... **Set $1.90**

1F2896—16½ in. long, 11½ in. wing spread, builds over 252 models, will build 2 planes at one time. Aviation Engineering book written by a famous aviator included. 1 set in box. **Set $3.00**

"METALCRAFT" AIRPLANES

ACTUALLY FLIES. Put together with nuts and bolts....easily assembled....adjustable to fly various distances.

1F2969—"Zeppelin," 18 in. long, set up, 4 in. diam., heavy yellow metal body, red trim, 100 parts bolt construction, 3 gondolas, 2 with revolving propellers, easily assembled, each in box with instructions, will build over 8 different dirigibles. ⅓ doz. sets in pkg... **Doz $7.85**

1F3021—(Mfrs 965) Dismantled, ready to be assembled. **Doz $8.00**

1F2701—(Mfrs 966) (Same as 1F3021) Assembled, ready to fl (except attaching wings). **Doz $11.70**

1F2785—"Zeppelin," 18 in. long, set up, realistic gray enameled, rustproof silvered trimmings, builds Zeppelins and Dirigibles, set consists 45 major parts and 140 nuts and bolts, each in attractive three color display box. ⅓ doz. in pkg. **Doz $11.5...**

1F2757—"Zeppelin" 18 in. long set up, realistic gray enameled, rustproof silvered trimmings, builds "Graf Zeppelin," "Los Angeles" and all other famous ships, set consists 90 major parts and hundreds nuts and bolts, each in attractive three color display box, 1 in pkg. **Each $3.25**

METAL CAST No. 66 Aeroplane. Photo by Norbert Schachter.

Metalcraft Aircraft Construction Sets, as shown in a December, 1929 Butler Bros. Catalog.

	C6	C8	C10
Marx Mainstream Airport, circa 1930s	110	165	220
Marx P35, 13½" wingspan, pressed steel, with and without wheel skirts	60	90	120
Marx P35-type 2-engine bomber, 15⅞" wingspan	70	105	140
Marx Pan American 4-motor, propellor-driven, also as PAA, 27" wingspan, 1940, pressed steel	50	75	120
Marx Pan American Super 7 clipper, 17½" wingspan, also as American Airlines	150	225	300
Marx "Pioneer Air Express," 25½" wingspan, tin litho, high wing monoplane	75	100	200
Marx "Sky Cruiser" two-motored Transport Plane with siren and whirling propellors, Stratoliner 700, 18" wingspan, rubber wheels, 1940s	45	75	100
Marx "Skycruiser Stratoliner 700," 4 engine	45	75	100
Marx sparkling Rocket Fighter No. 1425, tin litho	37	56	75
Marx Trimotor Biplane, 9½" wingspan	No Price Found		
Marx TWA Mail Plane	90	135	180
Marx Universal Airport with two metal planes	55	90	150
Metal Cast No. 43 twin engine bomber, B-25?, 5¼" wingspan	10	15	20
Metal Cast No. 66 Aeroplane, approx. 4½" wingspan, 2-engine,			

METALCRAFT Spirit of St. Louis, 9" long. Courtesy Mapes Auctioneers & Appraisers.

	C6	C8	C10
circa 1940s, lead (some marked "Fred Greene")	5	7.50	10
Metal Cast No. 321, Aeroplane, 3¼" long, "U. S. 256," Air Corps star insignia	10	15	20
Metalcraft Build-A-Zep, builds 21 different 18" zeppelins	152	225	400
Metalcraft Northrup Alpha Monoplane, wingspan approx. 17", "PURE the Pure Oil Company"	300	750	1500
Metalcraft Riding Rocket, 24" long	35	53	100
Metalcraft Spirit of St. Louis, 9" long, came as kit	150	225	300
Ohio Art "Sea Patrol Plane," 9" long, pontoons, moves on water, early 40s wind-up	45	68	90
Ohio Art Seaplane "Hot Job" tin litho, checkerboard wings, spinning propeller, 10" wingspan, 3½" long, 1950s	20	30	40

RALSTOY? RAA5. Photo by Perry Eichor.

RALSTOY: RAA4, RAA2, RAA3. Photo by Perry Eichor.

	C6	C8	C10
P-38 glass candy container	50	75	100
Passenger Plane, high-wing, four-engine, approx. 9" wingspan, three wooden wheels	9	13	18
Pedal Car, Biplane, 2-motor, 54" long	500	900	1800
Pedal Car, Pursuit Plane	400	600	800

RALSTOY AIRCRAFT

By Perry Eichor, Aircraft Contributing Editor, and Fred Maxwell, Slushmold Contributing Editor

Ralstoy issued new aircraft and reproduced popular Kansas Toy numbers issued during the 1920s. The late 1930s toys reflected the growing awareness of the war in Europe.

	C6	C8	C10
RAA1 Small cabin plane "32", 2½" x 2¼". "Ralstoy," wings positive dihedral. (See Kansas KTA5)	6	8	12
RAA2 Cabin Plane, "NC414," 3⅜" x 3⅜". "Ralstoy" midwing, V12 engine, tin propellor	20	30	40
RAA3, Cabin Plane, 3⅝" x 3½". High wing, cowled radial engine, 2 doors, 6 windows. "Ralstoy," "Made in USA."	20	30	40
RAA4 Pursuit plane, "P40," 3" x 3¼" Curtiss "U.S. Army" midwing, Air Corps star-in-circle insignia, V 12 engine, 2 machine guns, 3 bladed propellor. "Made in USA," "Ralstoy" in diamond.	20	30	40

	C6	C8	C10
RAA5 ? Cabin Plane, 3" x 3¾". Slim midwing, cowled radial engine, pilot, tin propellor. Underside is "Scout," "Made in USA." Ralstoy?	20	30	40
RAA6 ? Large cabin plane. Lindy type, high wing, 6 cylinder radial engine, metal wheels. Ralstoy?	20	30	40
Renwal B-17, small	5	10	20
Renwal B-17, 9¼" wingspan, plastic, circa 1944	15	30	40
Renwal B-25, 6¾" wingspan, plastic circa 1944	12	25	30
Renwal B-29, No. 29	12	25	30
Renwal C54 Transport, large, plastic	10	15	25
Renwal P38, plastic	10	25	40
Renwal P40, plastic	10	15	20
Renwal P47, plastic	15	20	30
Renwal PB2Y Flying Boat	15	20	30

RENWAL; Left to Right, Top: B-17 No. 777, P-38; Middle: B-25 No. 25, B-29 No. 29, C54 Transport; Bottom: B-17 (small) No. 17, P-40. Photo by Perry R. Eichor.

Top Left: Savoye Blimp. Top Right: What may have been the version sold by Tommy Toy. Bottom: Savoye Monoplane. Photo by Fred Maxwell.

Schieble Ford Trimotor, 26¼" wingspan, No. 30. Courtesy Wilkinson Collection - Detroit Antique Toy Museum.

STEELCRAFT Monoplane, early. Photo by Calvin L. Chaussee.

SUN RUBBER, Left to Right: No. 12009, Pursuit Ship, No. 12010. Courtesy Ed Poole.

STEELCRAFT "NX130 U.S. Mail Plane", one engine. Photo by Calvin L. Chaussee.

STEELCRAFT "Pan American World Airways Clipper". Photo by Calvin L. Chaussee.

	C6	C8	C10
Savoye Blimp, 4" long, "U.S.N."	20	30	40
Savoye Monoplane, 3" long	20	30	40
Schieble Ford Tri motor, 29½" long, steel	200	400	800
"Sky Cruiser" tin litho, 18" wingspan, 2-motor transport, engines turn with friction mechanism	40	75	100
"Spirit of America" pull toy aeroplane, 14" long, steel and litho	12	18	24
Spirit of St. Louis glass candy container, 4⅜" long	150	225	300
Steelcraft "Akron" blimp pull toy, 25" long	75	112	150

	C6	C8	C10
Steelcraft "Army Scout Plane" single engine, 22½" wingspan, high wing monoplane, 1920s	100	200	400
Steelcraft "Army Scout Plane" trimotor, single high wing, 1920s	200	300	550
Steelcraft Army Scout Plane, green and orange, 23" wingspan	100	200	400
Steelcraft "Graf Zeppelin," 30½" pressed steel pull toy	100	150	250
Steelcraft Graf Zeppelin, 32" long pull toy	125	225	350
Steelcraft Lockheed Sirius pull toy, 21½" wingspan	300	500	750

	C6	C8	C10
Steelcraft Monoplane, 2 open cockpits, 1930s, 16" wingspan 250	375	500
Steelcraft No. 79 pedal plane, high wing monoplane, 32" wingspan, 48" long............700	1250	3000
Steelcraft NX107, "Little Jim," 23" wingspan 200	400	600
Steelcraft NX130, blue eagles on wings, 23" wingspan............200	400	600
Steelcraft "NX130 U.S. Mail Plane," one engine 200	400	600
Steelcraft NX131, Tri-Motor, U.S. Mail plane, pull toy, 26½" wingspan 200	400	750
Steelcraft Pedal Plane "Pursuit," 1940 1000	1700	2500
Strauss "Chicago" Dirigible, 10" tin litho............125	188	250
Strauss "Flying Airship" (boxtop description) aluminum windup......275	363	550
Strauss Graf Zeppelin, 16" long 240	360	480
Sun Rubber "Pursuit Ship," "25-P75," circa 1940-41, 4¼" wingspan.........12	18	25
Sun Rubber No. **12008 Racing Plane**, circa 1947, also called "Scout," both same plane as "Pursuit Ship"............12	18	25
Sun Rubber No. **12009 Transport,** 4" long............15	22	30
Sun Rubber No. 12010 Dual-Control Plane, 4½" long............20	30	40
Theodore Hahn Aeroplane No. 187, lead alloy, 1920s 10	15	20
Thomas Toys Defiant, 4" long, plastic............6	9	12
Thomas Toys F-80 Jet Action Rocket Launcher 10	15	20
Thomas Toys Warhawk, 4" long, plastic............6	9	12
Tommy Toy Dirigible, "USN" slush lead, 1930s 15	22	40
Tootsietoy 106 Lockheed Sirius, tin low wing 20	25	30
Tootsietoy 107 Bellanca, high tin wing monoplane............25	30	40
Tootsietoy 119 Northrup Alpha "U.S. Army" pursuit 15	20	25
Tootsietoy 125 Lockheed Electra, twin engine............10	15	20
Tootsietoy 717 DC-2, "TWA"............20	25	35
Tootsietoy 718 Waco, "U.S. Navy," C model Biplane 25	35	50
Tootsietoy No. #. Waco "Dive Bomber" model Biplane 40	60	75
Tootsietoy 719 Crusader, twin boom, twin engine............25	35	45
Tootsietoy 720 "Fly-N-Giro" Autogyro, small version............25	40	75
Tootsietoy 721 "Curtis P-40" Pursuit....50	80	125
Tootsietoy DC-4 "Super Mainliner" 20	30	40
Tootsietoy 722 Military DC-4, "Army Transport" 30	45	60
Tootsietoy 4482 Bleriot, 67mm long............20	30	40
Tootsietoy 4491 Bleriot, 25 mm long............15	20	25
Tootsietoy 4649 Ford Trimotor, tin wing 25	40	75
Tootsietoy 4650 Biplane, Jenny type............30	50	70
Tootsietoy 4659 Auto-Gyro, tin wing, large version............25	45	65
Tootsietoy 4660 AC Aero-Dawn, high wing monoplane, tin wing 15	25	35
Tootsietoy Aero-Dawn, seaplane version............20	30	45
Tootsietoy 4675 Wings, Biplane, tin wing............25	35	45
Tootsietoy Wings, seaplane version......30	40	50
Tootsietoy P-38............20	30	40
Tootsietoy P-39, tin wing, two-bladed prop 30	50	80
Tootsietoy S-58, Sikorsky Helicopter............20	30	40
Tootsietoy Lockheed 749 Constellation, "PAA N88846" 30	45	60
Tootsietoy Boeing 377 Stratocruiser "PAA N102SV" 30	45	60
Tootsietoy Corvair CV-240 twin engine...20	30	40
Tootsietoy "Piper Cub," low wing monoplane............5	10	15
Tootsietoy Navion 5	10	15
Tootsietoy Beechcraft Bonanza 5	10	15
Tootsietoy P-80 "Shooting Star" Jet 10	15	20
Tootsietoy F7V-3 "Cutlass" Jet............10	15	20
Tootsietoy "F-86 Sabre" Jet, 2-piece casting............20	25	30
Tootsietoy "F-86 Sabre" Jet, 1-piece casting 5	10	15
Tootsietoy F9F-2 Panther Jet, 2-piece casting............25	30	35
Tootsietoy F9F-2 Panther Jet, 1-piece casting............5	10	15
Tootsietoy F4D Douglas Skyray............5	10	15
Tootsietoy "Delta," 2-piece casting 20	25	30

THOMAS TOYS F-80 Jet Action Rocket Launcher. Courtesy Islyn Thomas.

Theodore Hahn Aeroplane.

TOMMY TOY "U.S.N." Dirigible. Photo by Bill Kaufman. Courtesy Charles E. Weldon, Jr.

THOMAS TOYS, Left to Right: Warhawk, Defiant, plastic, 4" long.

TOOTSIETOY, Left to Right; Top: P-39, 720; Bottom: Sikorsky S-43, 721, 722. Photo by Perry Eichor.

TOOTSIETOY, Left to Right; Top: 4649 Tri-Motor Plane, 4660 Aero-Dawn, 4650 Biplane, 4675 Wings, High-Wing Floatplane. Middle: 4659 Autogyro, 718 Waco Bomber, 719 Crusader. Bottom: 119 Army Plane, 125 Lockheed Electra, 717 TWA Douglas Airliner, DC4 Super Mainliner. Photo by Ed Poole.

TOOTSIETOY DC4 "Super Mainliner", three versions. Photo by Perry R. Eichor.

TOOTSIETOY "U.S.N. Los Angeles" dirigible, also sold as part of Buck Rogers set, 1937. Photo by Ed Poole.

WYANDOTTE high wing passenger monoplane, No. 2 Lockheed Vega. Photo courtesy Dick and Nancy Dice.

503

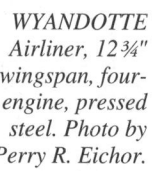

Vindex Fokker, cast iron. Photo by Perry R. Eichor.

WYANDOTTE Airliner, 12¾" wingspan, four-engine, pressed steel. Photo by Perry R. Eichor.

WYANDOTTE Crusader, two variations. Photo by Perry R. Eichor.

WYANDOTTE, Left to Right: Airacuda, Airliner, circa WW II, two engine. Photo by Perry R. Eichor.

	C6	C8	C10
Tootsietoy "F-94 Starfire" Jet	10	15	20
Tootsietoy Boeing 707	10	15	20
Tootsietoy, Sikorsky S:43	20	30	40
Tootsietoy "Tootsietoy Airport," hangar and two planes	300	450	600
Tootsietoy U.S. Moon Rocket, 3 types, all have 2 wheels to run on string, mid-1960s replicas of original Buck Rogers spaceships (see Comic Character)	40	75	100
Tootsietoy "U.S.N. Los Angeles" dirigible, two grooved wheels on top to run on string (also was sold as part of Buck Rogers set)	37	56	75
Turner High Wing Monoplane, 18½" wingspan, one engine, 1930s	400	600	800
Turner High Wing Monoplane, 22½" wingspan, pressed steel	400	600	800
United Electric "Spirit of St. Louis" go around tower, 2 planes, electrical, pressed steel	800	1200	1600
"U.S." high wing monoplane, single engine, 8" wingspan, open ironwork body, spool wheel works prop	200	300	400
Vindex Fokker, cast iron	100	400	800
Watrous single engine biplane, pressed steel bell toy, 8¼" wingspan, circa 1915	162	244	325

	C6	C8	C10
Williams, A.C. UX83, cast iron, 3¼" wingspan	30	45	60
Williams, A. C. "UX-99" cast iron, wingspan approx. 4½"	80	120	160
Williams, A. C. "UX-166", Lindy-type plane, wingspan approx. 5¾", cast iron, nickeled engine and wheels	40	60	80
Wyandotte Airacuda, 8½" wingspan, pressed steel, twin vertical stabilizers, twin pusher engines, blue or red	20	40	65
Wyandotte Airliner, 12¾" wingspan, 4 engine, pressed steel	50	75	100
Wyandotte Airliner, circa WWII, two engine, wooden wheels	55	82	110
Wyandotte American Airlines Flagship plane, 28" wingspan	44	66	80
Wyandotte Bomber, Army, pressed steel, two-engine	90	135	180
Wyandotte China Clipper, 13" wingspan, No. 207	60	90	150
Wyandotte City Airport, American Airlines, two hangars, control tower, etc., lights up	100	150	250
Wyandotte Crusader, 9¾" wingspan	20	30	40
Wyandotte Gyrocopter, 12½"			

WYANDOTTE China Clipper. Courtesy Wilkinson Collection - Detroit Antique Toy Museum.

WYANDOTTE Gyrocopter, 12½" wingspan. Photo by Perry R. Eichor.

WYANDOTTE Stratocruiser, 13" wingspan. Photo by Perry R. Eichor.

ZEPPELIN, "Graf Zeppelin", A.C. Williams, 5¼" long, cast iron (1932 ad).

WYANDOTTE "Rocket Racer #319" Rocket Ship, from an August, 1935 ad in Toys and Novelties magazine.

	C6	C8	C10
wingspan, twin engine passenger plane, circa 1930s	60	90	120
Wyandotte High Wing Passenger monoplane, No. 2 Lockheed Vega, single engine, bullet nose, 18" wingspan	50	75	150
Wyandotte Military Air Transport, 13" wingspan	25	38	50
Wyandotte Mystery Plane No. 101, twin engine, wings trail backward, 4½" wingspan	70	105	140
Wyandotte Rocket Racer No. 319, rocket ship sold in 1935	50	75	100
Wyandotte Stratocruiser, 13" wingspan	37	56	75
Zeppelin, cast iron, approx.. 3" long	40	60	80
Zeppelin, "Akron," Marx, 28" long, 1930s	100	140	250
Zeppelin, "EPL 1," Lehmann, No. 651	300	450	600
Zeppelin "EPL 2," Lehmann, No. 652, 1907	225	375	450
Zeppelin, "Graf Zeppelin," 16" long, aluminum, Strauss	175	263	350

	C6	C8	C10
Zeppelin, "Graf Zeppelin," A. C. Williams, 8" long, cast iron	75	112	150
Zeppelin, "Graf Zeppelin," A. C. Williams, 5½" long, cast iron	50	75	125
Zeppelin, "Graf Zeppelin," A. C. Williams, 5" long, cast iron	50	75	125
Zeppelin "Los Angeles," cast iron, 12" long	300	500	1200
Zeppelin, pull-toy "Little Giant"	50	80	125
Zeppelin pull-toy, "Macon"	50	80	125
Zeppelin "Pony DE107," cast iron, 5½" long	50	80	125
Zeppelin "U.S. Akron," potmetal, circa 1932, 6" long	25	38	50
Zeppelin "ZEP," cast iron, 4" long	40	80	150
Zeppelin, "Goodyear" decals, 25" long, hatch opens	125	188	250
Zeppelin, 6" long, silver, pull toy, circa 1920-30s, cast iron	60	90	120
Zeppelin, metal, 25" long	42	64	85
Zeppelin, metal, 26½" long	45	68	90
Zeppelin, metal, 27½" long	50	75	100

SCHOENHUT

By Blossom Abell with Jim and Patsy Carlson

The A. Schoenhut Company had a long history of toy manufacturing. Many items were produced, including animals, figures, moving pictures, Palmer Cox Brownies, children's musical instruments, and dolls. This section covers some of the items in the Humpty Dumpty Circus.

A brief chronological history of the A. Schoenhut Company follows:

- 1872   -Produced the first toy pianos
- 1903   -Began producing Humpty Dumpty Circus items
           -Began producing glass eyed animals, molded/two part head personnel
- 1909/11 -Produced Teddy Roosevelt figures
- 1910   -Produced bisque head ring master, lady circus rider, lion tamer, lady/gent acrobats
- 1918   - Produced painted eyed animals, wooden head personnel
- 1923   -Began producing reduced size circus
- 1927   -Produced miniature set (donkey, elephant, clown)
- 1935   -Company closed
- 1950   -Nelson Delavan purchased manufacturing rights and produced several figures and animals.

This history is not all inclusive, but should help the collector identify age for some animals/figures.

The Humpty Dumpty items covered in this section span the years of 1903 to 1935. Glass eyed animals and carved face personnel along with other rare examples are priced higher than painted eye animals and pressed head figures produced later. Delavan items are generally priced lower than reduced size figures.

In the past few years, popularity from toy collectors and folk art collectors have driven prices upward. Particular interest in Teddy Roosevelt's "Adventures in Africa" series produced from 1909 to 1911 have led the price increase.

This price list should serve as a guideline for the collector. Several points deserve additional comment. Those comments are:

- Condition determines price (See photo of four horses for examples of condition C2 to C8).
- Mint condition Schoenhut toys are virtually non-

existent. Mint condition means the toy was never played with. Toys found in this condition demand higher prices. Boxes increase value, and mint with the box commands a sizable premium.
- Glass eyed animals, early figures with plaster faces, and rare animals demand high prices also.
- It is acceptable to include rare figures and rare animals of lesser condition in a collection.
- Bisque headed figures and molded/two part head figures usually are priced higher than carved face figures.
- Condition on the majority of animals and figures found today is between C4 and C8.
- Skillful restoration can increase value. Anyone selling an animal or figure with restored sections should indicate where restoration has occurred.
- Prices in this guide have not been established for every style of animal and figure.

Additional information on Schoenhut figures or Schoenhut dolls can be obtained by joining the Schoenhut Collectors Club. For membership application, please contact: Barbara Black, Schoenhut Club Secretary, 5865 N. River Forest Drive, Glendale, WI 53209.

About the Authors. *Blossom Abell has been involved in collecting Schoenhut circus toys for over 20 years. Jim and Patsy Carlson began collecting folk art, discovered Schoenhut several years ago and are active collectors.*

SCHOENHUT Cloth Circus Tent, 34" high, with performers and animals. Courtesy Wilkinson Collection, Detroit Antique Toy Museum.

SCHOENHUTS, Left to Right: Glass-eyed Horse, missing leather belly strap, (C8 plus), GE Horse, very worn paint and missing platform and belly strap, (C4), GE Horse, kid repainted, chipped wood and missing all attachable parts, (C2); foreground, GE Horse, good paint, missing attachable parts. Photo by Blossom Abell.

Prices below for Painted Eye animals most frequently seen, usually the later models. Not all animals have been included.

Painted Eye Only	C6	C8	C10	Total Range*
Alligator	250	325	450	250 - 750
Brown Bear	250	325	400	250 - 900
Brown Bear, Reduced	200	325	450	250 - 450
Buffalo	300	390	550	300 - 1,200
Buffalo, Reduced	250	325	450	250 - 450
Bulldog	375	490	700	375 - 1,500
Burro	250	325	450	250 - 550
Camel, Arabian, 1 hump	275	360	500	275 - 525
Camel, Bactrian, 2 hump	875	1,200	1,750	875 - 1,750
Camel, Bactrian, Reduced	190	275	375	190 - 425
Cat, 1 piece head	700	910	1,300	550 - 2,200
Cow	250	340	450	250 - 750
Deer	440	575	800	440 - 1,100
Donkey	55	70	85	55 - 250
Donkey, Reduced	35	45	55	35 - 55
Elephant	100	125	175	100 - 300
Elephant, Reduced	60	75	105	60 - 105
Gazelle	750	1,000	1,500	750 - 2,200
Giraffe	225	260	500	225 - 600
Giraffe, Reduced	250	325	450	250 - 450
Goose	300	390	550	275 - 550
Gorilla	1,300	1,500	1,800	1,300-2,000
Hippopotamus	250	350	450	250 - 1,100
Hippopotamus, Reduced	300	390	550	300 - 550
Horse, Brown	125	150	190	125 - 275
Horse, Brown, Reduced	100	125	175	100 - 175
Horse, White	150	180	225	150 - 300
Horse, White, Reduced	100	125	175	100 - 175

Painted Eye Only	C6	C8	C10	Total Range*
Hyena	1,200	1,440	1,800	1,200-2,500
Kangaroo	600	720	900	600 - 2,450
Leopard	300	390	550	300 - 750
Leopard, Reduced	250	300	375	250 - 375
Lion	350	425	525	350 - 1,800
Lion, Reduced	250	300	375	250 - 375
Monkey, Blk Face	300	390	400	300 - 400
Monkey, White Face	430	540	675	450 - 675
Ostrich	275	325	400	275 - 850
Ostrich, Reduced	350	390	550	350 - 550
Pig	250	325	400	250 - 900
Pig, Reduced	400	475	550	400 - 600
Polar Bear	600	800	900	600 - 1,400
Poodle	125	150	185	100 - 800
Poodle, Reduced	375	425	600	375 - 600
Rhinoceros	375	450	575	375 - 1,000
Rhinoceros, Reduced	300	360	450	300 - 450
Sea Lion	500	625	770	500 - 1,000
Sheep	300	360	450	300 - 600
Tiger	300	360	450	300 - 850
Tiger, Reduced	250	300	375	250 - 375
Wolf	800	1,000	1,300	800 - 3,000
Zebra	350	400	570	350 - 1,000
Zebra, Reduced	450	525	650	450 - 650
Zebu	1,400	1,600	1,800	1,400-2,600

* - Total Range has been determined by showing the price for the least expensive animal/figure (C6) to the most wanted animal/figure (C10).

** - The definition "rare" means not enough examples have been sold to determine prices.

SCHOENHUT, Left to Right: Hobo (C8) 2part head; Chinaman Acrobat (C6) 2 part head, replaced felt on jacket. Collection/Photo Blossom Abell.

SCHOENHUT, Left to Right: Lady Rider, Reduced (C8); Lady Rider Bisque Head (C8); Lady Rider, 2 part Head (C7) Replaced skirt. Collection/Photo Blossom Abell.

SCHOENHUT, Left to Right: Lion, (C10) GE cloth mane; Monkey, (C8) white face. Collection/Photo Blossom Abell.

SCHOENHUT, Left to Right: Ostrich (C9+) GE; Ostrich (C9+) PE. Collection/Photo Blossom Abell.

SCHOENHUT, Left to Right: Camel (C9), reduced; Camel (C9), GE Arabian, 1 hump; Camel (C9) GE Bactrian, 2 hump. Collection/Photo Blossom Abell.

SCHOENHUT, Left to Right: Buffalo (C6) GE, cloth mane, mane worn; Buffalo (C9+) GE, carved mane. Collection/Photo Blossom Abell.

SCHOENHUT, Left to Right: Clown (C7) wood hat/leather ears; Clown (C7) cloth hat over wood cone; Poodle (C8) reduced; Clown (C7) molded ears, all clowns reduced. Collection/Photo Blossom Abell.

508

SCHOENHUT, Left to Right: Clown (C7) plaster face, 2part head, sunburst suit; Clown (C7) wood head; Clown (C7) wood head.. Collection/Photo Blossom Abell.

SCHOENHUT Piano, 16¾" long, 16 keys, circa 1915, sold for $450 in 1985. Courtesy Wilkinson Collection, Detroit Antique Toy Museum.

Prices below for wooden/pressed headed figures. Not all figures have been included.

Total range includes wooden/pressed 1 part heads, Bisque heads, and plaster face 2 part heads.

Wooden/Pressed Head Only

	C6	C8	C10	Total Range*
Chinaman Acrobat	350	450	600	350 - 1,000
Clown	65	85	120	65 - 230
Clown, Reduced	75	95	150	75 - 150
Gent Acrobat	Rare**	(Wooden head)		.350 - 1,000
Hobo	250	325	450	250 - 1,000
Hobo, Reduced	300	360	450	300 - 450
Lady Acrobat	250	325	450	250 - 600
Lady Rider	200	240	300	200 - 1,000
Lady Rider, Reduced	125	175	225	125 - 225
Lion Tamer	200	240	300	200 - 1,000
Negro Dude	350	480	600	350 - 2,400

SCHOENHUT, Left to Right: Giraffe (C9) PE, carved head; Giraffe (C9) GE. Collection/Photo Blossom Abell.

An early SCHOENHUT piano. Courtesy Continental Hobby House, Sheboygan, Wisconsin.

Wooden/Pressed Head Only

	C6	C8	C10	Total Range*
Negro Dude, Reduced	350	450	550	350 - 550
Ring Master	250	325	450	250 - 1,000
Ring Master, Reduced	150	175	225	150 - 250

** - The Definition of "rare" means not enough examples have been sold to determine prices.
Not all accessories have been included

Prices below for Accessory Items, full-size unless otherwise marked.

Description	Accessories		
	C6	C8	C10
Ball	40	60	90
Ball, Reduced	30	40	50
Barrel	6	8	12
Bottle (With Label)	Rare**		
Chair	8	12	15

SCHOENHUT, *Negro Dude (C8), possibly the African Chief. Courtesy Mapes Auctioneers & Appraisers.*

SCHOENHUT, *Left to Right: Pig (C9) reduced, fancy face; Pig (C8) GE, one piece head/neck; Pig (C6) ball joint head, body restoration. Collection/Photo Blossom Abell.*

SCHOENHUT, *Left to Right: Tiger (C9) reduced; Tiger (C6) PE; Tiger (C10) PE (early). Collection/Photo Blossom Abell.*

Description	Accessories		
	C6	C8	C10
Flexible Cage	275	400	550
Goblet	8	12	15
Hoop	45	60	75
Horizontal Bar	Rare**		
Ladder	10	15	20
Parade Wagons	Rare**		
Pedestal, Tall	20	30	50
Pedestal, Short	20	30	50
Table	20	30	40
Tent, 25" x 16" (Small)	400	650	1,000
Tent, 24" x 36" (Large)	1,200	2,000	3,000
Tent, Litho with Panels	5,000	9,000	12,000
Tub	15	20	25
Weights, 50/100/200 lb	Rare**		
Whip, 5.5" shaft	45	65	85
Whip, 4.5" shaft	30	45	60

Prices below for Teddy Roosevelt's Adventures in Africa. Glass eye (GE) animals shown correspond to some of the animals represented in Schoenhut catalogue sets. Teddy Roosevelt accessories have not been included.

Teddy Roosevelt's Adventures in Africa

	Total Range	
Teddy Roosevelt	1,200	- 2,400
Photographer	1,400	- 2,900
African Native	500	- 1,400
African Drummer	500	- 2,800
Arab Chief	1,800	- 3,400
Doctor	1,800	- 3,400
Naturalist	1,400	- 2,900

SCHOENHUT, *Left to Right: Polar Bear (C8) PE; (foreground) Polar Bear (C7) PE; 12" Wild Animal Cage Wagon (C8); Polar Bear (C7) GE; Lion Tamer (C9) 1 part head. Collection/Photo Blossom Abell.*

Animals for Teddy's Adventures in Africa

	Total Range
Alligator, GE	450 - 750
Camel, Arabian, GE	875 - 1,750
Deer, GE	600 - 1,100
Elephant, GE	150 - 225
Gazelle, GE	1,400 - 2,200
Giraffe, GE	325 - 600
Gorilla, Carved Ear	1,300 - 2,000
Hippopotamus, GE	800 - 1,100
Lion, Carved Mane, GE	900 - 1,800
Rhinoceros, GE	800 - 1,000
Zebra, GE	750 - 1,000
Zebu, GE	1,700 - 2,600

SCHOENHUT, Left to Right: Leopard (C8) GE; Leopard (C9) reduced; Leopard (C7) PE, worn paint on face. Collection/Photo Blossom Abell.

Prices below for a small number of the Miscellaneous items produced by the A. Schoenhut Company

Description	Miscellaneous		
	C6	C8	C10
Milk Wagon w/Driver & Horse	2,000	3,600	6,000
RailRoad Station, Lge	300	400	500
Doll House, Small	175	250	350
Doll House, Medium	225	300	400
Doll House, Large	400	600	800
Golfer, Girl	225	325	425
Golfer, Man	200	300	400
Pianos	*No information available*		

* -Total Range has been determined by showing the price for the least condition animal/figure (C6) to (C10).

** - The definition of "rare" means not enough examples have been sold to determine prices.

SCHOENHUT: A portion of Teddy Roosevelt's Adventures in Africa.. Photo by Blossom Abell.

SCHOENHUT golfer in skirt. Photo Courtesy PB84.

SCHOENHUT Golfer Man. Courtesy Sotheby's New York.

Prices below for a small number of Comic Characters produced by the A. Schoenhut Company.

Description	Comic Characters		
	C6	C8	C10
Felix, 4"	135	160	175
Felix, 6"	400	600	800
Felix, 8"	200	300	400
Speedy Felix	200	300	400
Maggie/Jiggs, Complete			
With Rolling Pin/Bucket	900	1,100	1,300
Boob McNutt	1,000	1,400	1,800
Happy Hooligan	1,000	1,400	1,800

Description	Comic Characters		
	C6	C8	C10
Koko the Clown	Rare**		
Bonzo	Rare		
Barney Google and			
SparkPlug	600	800	1,200
Max and Moritz	1,500	1,800	2,000
Rolly Dolly			
Foxy Grandpa, Large	400	600	900
Santa, Large	900	1,500	2,500
Santa, Medium	600	900	1,500
Dutch Girl, Medium	225	300	400

SCHOENHUT Felix the Cat, all three sizes. Photo by Blossom Abell.

SCHOENHUT, Left to Right: Barney Google, 7" high, Sparkplug, Barney Google (older model), 7¾" high. Photo by Blossom Abell.

SHIPS

(See also Tin Wind-Up, Paper)

Mint prices in this category averaged $784.94 in the last edition, and in
this edition averaged $1032.80, an increase of 32%.

AUBURN RUBBER Battleship and Submarine. Photo by Ed Poole.

	C6	C8	C10
"Adirondack" Sidewheeler, cast iron, approx. 13" long	500	750	1000
Admiral Dewey's Flagship from the White Fleet, wood and paper, 6" long	100	150	200
Admiral Dewey Flagship paper litho on wood, 30" long, c. 1900	300	450	600
Aircraft Carrier "65" tin litho, large, circa 1950s	50	75	100
Althof-Bergmann "America," painted tin sidewheeler, c. 1874, 20" long	7000	11000	18000
Arcade "Showboat," cast iron, approx. 10¾" long, 1929	500	750	1000
Argo Aircraft Carrier, 36" long, steel, with 3 6" jet planes which fire rockets, shells or drop bombs	75	113	150
"Automatic Submarine," remote-controlled, tin litho	40	60	80
Atwood Motors, California "Amazon Side-Wheeler," plastic and metal, circa 1950s	200	300	400
Auburn Rubber Battleship, 8¼" long, circa 1940, No. 1582	10	15	20

	C6	C8	C10
Auburn Rubber Dreadnaught, 9⅛" long, new in 1941	10	18	25
Auburn Rubber Freighter, 9¼" long, new in 1941	8	12	15
Auburn Rubber Submarine, 6½" long, circa 1941	8	12	15
Authenticast French warships, including Richelieu, Algiers, Fantasque and others, each	30	45	60
Authenticast German Warships, scale models including Narvik, Galster and others, each	30	45	60
Authenticast Japanese Warships, including Fuso, Kaga, Mogani and others, each	30	45	60
Authenticast U. S. scale model warships, World War II including: Iowa, Enterprise, Sims and Farragut and submarine Sarge, each	30	45	60
B-LO submarine, metal, pat. no. 1318048	75	112.50	150
"Baby" cast iron racing boat, circa 1930, wheeled, 4½" long, Hubley?	60	90	120
Barclay 372 Aeroplane Carrier	25	37.50	50
Barclay 373 Battleship	27	40	55
Battleship "Admiral" paper litho, 1890, 20" long	600	900	1200
Battleship, cast iron, 14½" long	300	450	600
Battleship, glass, approx. 3" long, candy container	60	90	120
Battleship, Hillclimber, 15" long, pressed steel	200	300	400
Battleship Oregon, 25" long, paper litho and wood	700	1050	1400
Battleship "Rover" paper litho and wood, 20" long	600	900	1200
Battleship, Tin Friction, 9½" long, circa 1920s	200	300	400

ARCADE "Showboat", 1929.

AUBURN freighter (damaged).

"Baby" cast iron racing boat. Photo by Bill Kaufman. Courtesy Good Old Days Store.

Battleship "Admiral", 1890, 20" long. Courtesy Lloyd W. Ralston Auctions.

Top: BARCLAY 372 Aeroplane Carrier; Bottom: BARCLAY 373 Battleship. Photos by Ed Poole.

BLISS Battleship New York, 36" long. Courtesy Lloyd W. Ralston Auctions.

Boat, tin friction, 13" long, two smokestacks, four lifeboats. Courtesy PB 84 New York (probably D.P. CLark or Schieble, circa 1908-1924).

	C6	C8	C10
"Big Bang Battleship," 8¼" long	125	187.50	250
Big Bang Gunboat, 8" long, cast iron, early	125	187.50	250
Bliss "Battleship New York" paper litho and stained wood, 1890, 36"x22"	450	675	900
Bliss "Conqueror"	900	1350	1800
Bliss "Marguerite" sailing schooner, 22" long	350	525	700
Bliss? "Union" ferry, sidewheel, c. 1900, 24" long	225	375	450
Boat, Hot Air, tin with driver, 9" long	100	150	200
Boat, pull motor, metal	100	150	200
Boat, tin friction, lithographed	100	150	200
Boat, tin friction, painted, early	100	150	200
Boat, tin friction, painted, early	150	225	300
Boat, tin friction, 13" long, two smokestacks, four lifeboats	90	135	180
Boucher "Gee Whiz" speedboat, painted sheetmetal, heavy			

	C6	C8	C10
clockwork motor, bronze propellor, 25" long	550	825	1100
Bradley "Columbia" side paddlewheeler, paper litho on wood, 24" long, c. 1890	400	600	800
Buckman "Pike" steam launch	2500	3800	5500
Buckman twin sidewheeler steamboat, 11" long, "patented May 7, 1872," steam engine	2000	3500	5000
Buddy L "49 LST," 12" long	32	48	65
Buddy L No. 3000 Tugboat, 1929-30	5000	8000	12500
"C.C. JR." Brass-mounted Wood Boat, wind-up motor concealed within the rudder controlled from the wheel in the circular cockpit with a start-stop lever, 14½" long	90	135	180
Canoe, wood, 6" long	15	22	30
Cohn Naval Base #888 Playset	225	375	450
"Columbia" riverboat, 1890, paper litho, tin litho, wood, working walking beam, 2' long	650	975	1300

BUDDY L '"49 LST". Photo by Ed Poole.

BUDDY L No. 3000 Tugboat. Photo Courtesy Thomas W. Sefton.

"Columbia" riverboat, 1890, 2' long. Courtesy Lloyd W. Ralston Auctions.

FALLOWS "Jumbo" riverboat, 14" long. Courtesy Lloyd W. Ralston Auctions.

BUCKMAN twin sidewheeler steamboat, 11" long. Courtesy Wilkinson Collection, Detroit Antique Toy Museum.

FLEISCHMANN Ocean Liner, 1930, 20½" long. Courtesy Lloyd W. Ralston Auctions.

GEORGE BROWN "Atlantic" sidewheel riverboat, 14" long. Courtesy Lloyd W. Ralston Auctions.

	C6	C8	C10
Cruiser, glass, approx. 3" long, candy container	50	75	100
Dayton Battleship, 16" long, friction, circa 1920	200	300	400
Dent Adirondack, 15" long, cast iron	600	900	1200
Dent Battleship New York, circa 1900, 21", largest cast iron boat made	2000	3000	4000
Destroyer, on wheels, 12" long, cast iron	1000	1500	2000
Fallows "Constitution" sidewheeler, 10" long	2000	3000	4000
Fallows "Jumbo" riverboat, side-wheel, painted tin, 1880, 14" long, mechanical walking beam	1000	1500	2000
Fallows "Volunteer IXL," 16" long	1800	2700	3600

	C6	C8	C10
"Ferry Go" twin paddlewheel ferry boat pull toy, tin litho, 14" long	125	185	250
Fleischmann Battleship	2000	3000	4000
Fleischmann Ocean Liner, 1930, painted tin clockwork, working, 20½" long	700	1350	1800
Fleischmann Oil Tanker	750	1125	1500
George Brown "Atlantic" sidewheel riverboat, painted and stenciled tin, 14" long	2250	3375	4500
Gunboat, tin friction, large wheel rises above deck, circa early 1920s, smokestack	300	450	600
Gunboat, tin friction, rocks back and forth on wheels, 10" long	250	375	500
Gunboat, 19" long, friction	400	600	800
Gunboat, two guns, 2 small stacks, 2 stories above deck, wheeled, friction, 1920s or earlier	300	450	600
Hill Climber pressed steel battleship, 18" long	300	450	600

Hill-Climber pressed steel Battleship. Courtesy Mapes Auctioneers.

KEYSTONE Action Submarine. Courtesy Jack Matthews.

HUBLEY "Sea Horse". Courtesy Ed Hyers Antique Toys.

IDEAL Pirate Ship (missing pirate flag).

IDEAL Varsity Racing Scull, 8 rowers, coxswain. Courtesy Wilkinson Collection, Detroit Antique Toy Museum.

IVES, U.S. Merchant Marine, painted pressed tin clockwork.

"Kearsage" gunboat. Courtesy PB 84 New York.

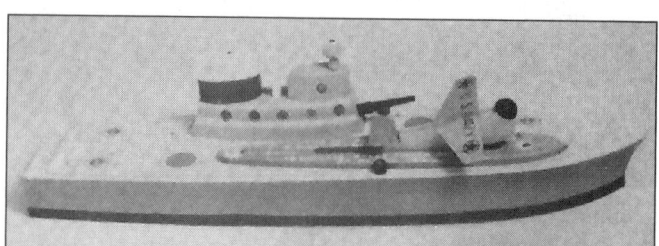

KEYSTONE Aircraft Carrier, wooden, 12" long. Courtesy Mapes Auctioneers & Appraisers.

Aircraft Carrier "Libertania" (see Liberty Playthings). Courtesy Mapes Auctioneers & Appraisers.

MANOIL Submarine. Courtesy K. Warren Mitchell

	C6	C8	C10
Hubley "Penn Yan" motorboat, 15" long, 5 people, very rare, unauthorized by Penn Yan, which stopped Hubley's production	2250	3375	4500
Hubley "Sea Horse" cast iron motorboat	1750	2625	3500
Hubley "Static" speedboat, cast iron	2000	3000	4000
Ideal Destroyer, 15" long, plastic	125	188	250
Ideal Pirate Ship, plastic, with 6 pirates, new in 1953	100	150	200
Ideal Pumping Fire Boat with siren, 1955, plastic	58	88	115
Ideal Slo Motion VI, 13" long windup motorboat	60	90	120
Ideal Varsity Racing Scull, 8 rowers, coxswain, 1890, 14" long, cast iron, oars move	2000	3000	4000
Ives "Miss Liberty" speedboat, 13½" long, steam-powered	750	1125	1500
Ives Ocean Liner, 13½" long	1000	1500	2000
Ives U. S. Merchant Marine Boat, painted pressed tin clockwork	1100	1650	2200
Ives "Vim" speedboat, 10½" long	650	975	1300
Ives "Vixen" speedboat, 12" long	650	975	1300
"Johnson's Sea Horse" cast iron speedboat with figure, 10½" long	1,750	2,625	3,500
"Kearsage" gunboat, 13¾" long, cast iron	1000	1500	2000
Keystone Action Submarine	50	75	100

	C6	C8	C10
Keystone Aircraft Carrier, wooden, 12" long	50	75	100
Keystone Battleship, wooden, approx. 2' long with guns, airplanes take off from a spring on deck of ship	130	195	260
Keystone Battleship, under 2' length, early 1940s	55	83	110
Keystone Ferryboat, wooden, circa 1930s, two wood cars, two wood trucks, 14" long	40	60	80
Keystone fishing boat, wooden, 12" long, circa 1940s	35	52	70
Keystone Racing Sailboat, wood	30	45	60
Kingsbury Boat, 10" long	100	150	200

LIBERTY PLAYTHINGS

Liberty Playthings was in business in the late 1920s and early 1930s in Niagara Falls, New York. All its toys, which were made of wood and metal, seem to have borne names with some variations of the word "Liberty," and all seem to have been sea-connected. Those advertised in 1929 were: No. 2 Tug and Scow; No. 5 Freighter; No. 6 Airplane Carrier; No. 7 Fire Boat; No. 8 Destroyer; No. 22 Seaplane. The carrier, which in the ad was called "Liberator" sold for $10. The "Libertania" aircraft carrier seems to be the same ship, or a slight variation.

	C6	C8	C10
Liberty Playthings "Libertania" Aircraft Carrier, wood and tin litho with lead planes, 27¾" long	60	90	120
Life Boat, steel, 11" long by 5¼" wide, simple design, circa late 1930s	20	30	40
Lionel Craft No. 43 wind-up speedboat	340	510	680
Lionel Craft No. 44 wind-up speed boat	350	525	700
Manoil No. 79 Submarine, lead alloy	12	18	25
Marx "Caribbean" friction Luxury Liner, sparkling, 15" long, 3½" tall	85	127	170

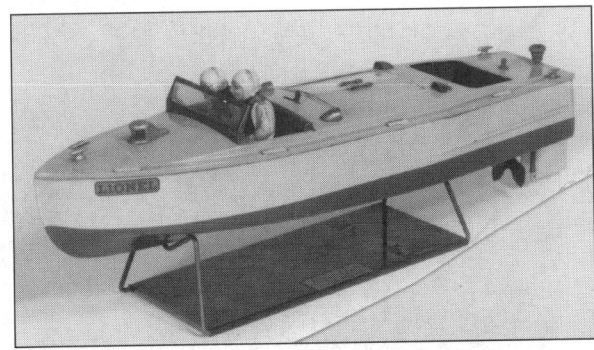

LIONEL No. 43 wind-up speedboat. Courtesy Phillips New York.

LIONEL No. 44 wind-up speedboat. Courtesy Sotheby's New York.

517

	C6	C8	C10
Marx Mosquito Fleet Putt Putt Boat......80	120	160	
Multiple Products Pirate Ship, plastic with pirates..................60	90	125	
"New York" warship, metal, 17", circa 1899..................500	750	1000	
Ohio Battleship, friction, 16" long, painted pressed steel 140	210	280	

ORKIN

ORKIN, of Cambridge, Massachusetts, was founded by Samuel Orkin about the end of World War One. His metal ships were modeled after the real thing. They were big, ranging from about 15 to 35", but relatively inexpensive.

	C6	C8	C10
Orkin Battleship B2, 36" long, pressed steel 3000	5000	8000	

ORKIN CRAFT was owned by the president of the Waterman Pen Company, with manufacturing done by Calwis Industries Ltd. of Beverly Hills, California. The pleasure boats sold by the firm were too expensive for the era (the price was in the $15-20 range), which is probably why it failed about 1935 or 1936. All the boats were motor-driven. Some were all metal, and some had wood decks.

	C6	C8	C10
Orkin Craft speedboat, clockwork, 29" long 1000	1500	2100	
"Priscilla" Side-Wheeler Approx. 10" long, Dent or Wilkins, cast iron 500	750	1000	
PT107 30	45	60	
"Pull For The Shore," W. S. Reed, litho paper on wood..................3500	8000	12000	
Pull Toy boat by Hustilar Toy Corp., Sterling Ill., wood with some metal parts, oarsmen row in unison..................75	112	150	
"Puritan" Sidewheeler, cast iron approx. 10½" long..................480	720	960	
Reed "Pilgrim" River Boat, 28½" long, paper litho 1000	1500	2000	

	C6	C8	C10
Reed "River Queen" Side-Wheeler, 25" long, litho on wood, c. 1895 1000	1500	2000	
Remco "Big Caesar" Roman warship, 29" long, with figures 175	263	350	
Remco "Fighting Lady" battleship No. 710, 31" long..................85	127	170	
Remco Gallant Gladiator Roman Warship, 17" long, plastic..............60	90	120	
Remco "Mighty Matilda" aircraft carrier, plastic, 35" long, complete with all accessories 75	113	150	
Remco Showboat Theater 38	53	75	
Renwal Drawbridge Set, bridge, 12 cars and boats..................63	95	125	
Renwal "Panama Canal," circa 1957, No. 273, 29x11" 55	82	110	
Renwal Viking Ship No. 245, 17" long, sold in 1955..........................82	123	165	
Row Boat with four men and oars, cast iron, mechanical, 9" long.......1250	1875	2500	
Row Boat, tin rubber band driver, 9" long with man rowing 40	60	80	
Schiebel Battleship, circa 1927, unpowered..................1000	1500	2000	
Schiebel Battleship, wood stacks and large wood guns and turrets, friction motor, circa 1920 1250	1875	2500	
Schoenhut Submarine and Dreadnought Naval War Toy, Pat. 4/6/15, torpedo explodes ship 100	150	200	
Scull, 9-man crew, U.S. Hardware, 14" long, wheeled 1600	2400	3200	
Shore Patrol, battery operated, tin boat, 9" long..................10	15	20	
Showboat, cast iron, 11" long..............1000	1500	2000	
Side-Wheeler Boat, "The Star," tin, height with stand, 21", length 14½"..................3500	5200	7000	
Side-Wheeler, cast iron, approx. 5½" long 125	187	250	
Side-Wheeler, cast iron, 8" long..........150	225	300	
Side-Wheeler, cast iron, 10½" long 150	225	300	

ORKIN Battleship B2. Courtesy Sotheby's New York.

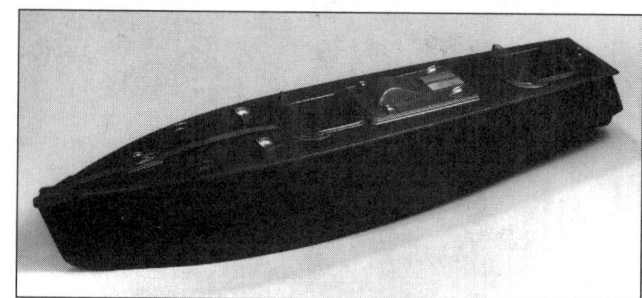

ORKIN Craft Speedboat, clockwork, 29" long. Courtesy Mapes Auctioneers & Appraisers.

REED 'River Queen'. Courtesy Wilkinson Collection, Detroit Antique Toy Museum.

RENWAL 'Panama Canal', circa 1957. Courtesy Islyn Thomas.

RENWAL Viking Ship No. 245, sold in 1955. Courtesy Islyn Thomas.

"Speed Boat", A.C. Williams, 4" long, cast iron. (1932 ad)

Speedboat on cradle, 1930, 25" long. Courtesy Lloyd W. Ralston Auctions.

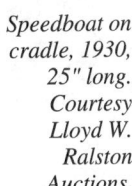

SIDE WHEELER BOAT, tin, "The Star", 21" high with stand, 14½" long.

Tillicum Battle Fleet No. 115. Courtesy John D. (Jack) Matthews.

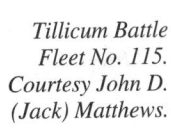

Tillicum National Defense Set, Milton Bradley. Courtesy John D. (Jack) Matthews.

519

Tillicum Convoy Set, Milton Bradley. Courtesy John D. (Jack) Matthews.

THOMAS TOYS No. 480 Racing Hydroplane, Plastic wind-up. Courtesy Islyn Thomas.

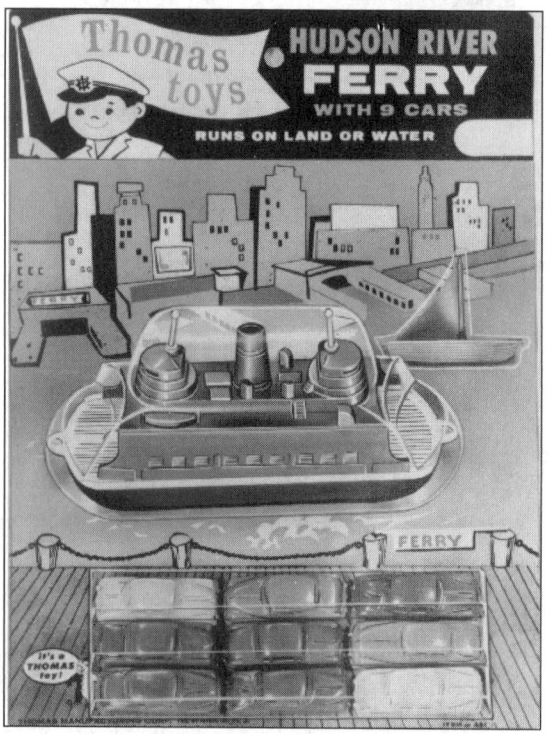

THOMAS TOYS No. 481 Ferry Boat with 9 Cars and Sailboat. Courtesy Islyn Thomas.

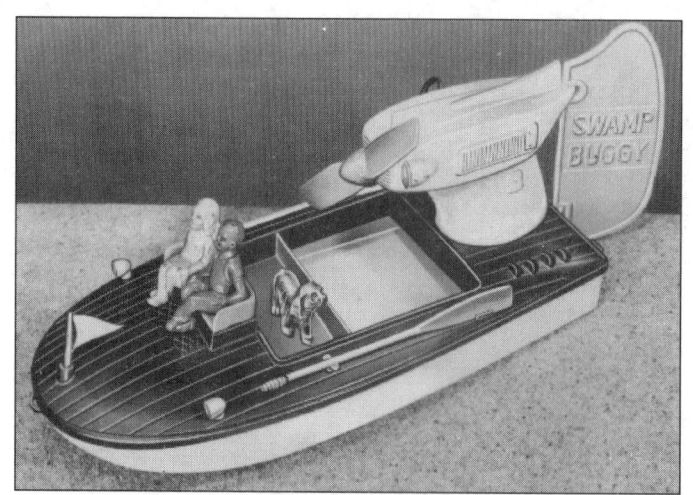

THOMAS TOYS No. 487 Swamp Buggy, motorized. Courtesy Islyn Thomas.

THOMAS TOYS, Top, Left to Right: Queen Mary, Battleship. Bottom, Left to Right: Aircraft Carrier, Freighter. All 5½" long, plastic.

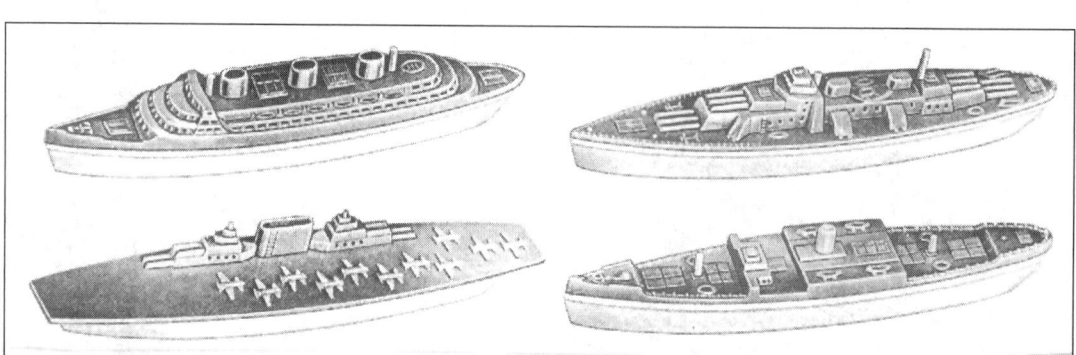

	C6	C8	C10		C6	C8	C10
Side-Wheeler, tin clockwork, 11" long .90		135	180	"Speed Boat", 4¾" long, A. C. Williams, cast iron with rider 120		180	240
"Sinking Battleship," Walbert Mfg., rubber band torpedo strikes die on ship and sinks it 250		375	500	"Speed Boat", 4" long, A. C. Williams, cast iron 45		68	90
"Speed Boat", 5¼" long, A. C. Williams, cast iron 60		90	120	"Speed Boat, Kansas Toy & Novelty "52", 2¾" long, lead alloy, driver ....No Price Found			

	C6	C8	C10
Speed Boat, wood, rubber-band propelled......40	60	80
SS United States, tin friction, 6½" long 50	75	100
Steam Boat "Memphis" Kansas Toy & Novelty "53", 2⅞" long, lead alloy, metal disc wheels ......No Price Found		
Steam Boat, tin, self-propelled, 17" long 150	225	300
Steamer, lithographed paper on wood, 39" long, 22½" high......450	675	900
Steamship, alcohol burner, ca. 1885, 19" long......200	300	400
Sterling 56" scale model, all wood and metal Battleship Missouri, radio control, with three electric motors......350	525	700
Submarine, "575," tin litho, remote-controlled, circa 1960 40	60	80
Submarine, glass......225	338	450
Submarine, steel, 6" long 40	60	80
Texaco Tanker 80	120	160
Thomas Toys Aircraft Carrier, 5½" long, plastic......3	4.50	6
Thomas Toys Battleship, 5½" long, plastic......3	4.50	6
Thomas Toys Freighter, 5½" long, plastic......3	4.50	6
Thomas Toys Queen Mary, 5½" long, plastic......3	4.50	6
Thomas Toys No. 480 Racing Hydroplane, plastic 16	20	25
Thomas Toys No. 481 Ferry Boat with sailboat, 9 cars, plastic 10	15	20
Thomas Toys No. 487 Swamp Buggy, motorized, plastic......10	15	20
Tillicum Battle Fleet No. 115, Milton Bradley, circa late 1920s......31	46	62
Tillicum Convoy Set, Milton Bradley, 1940s, 2 destroyers, 3 freight boats, 3 ocean liners, 2 patrol boats, painted wood, destroyers 5½" long, others about 4½" long...350	525	700
Tillicum National Defense Set, Milton Bradley......40	60	80

TOOTSIETOY

(Compiled by Ed Poole)

	C6	C8	C10
1034 Battleship, 6" long, 1939 on, U.S.S. New York......9	14	18
1035 Cruiser, 5½" long, 1939 on, U.S.S. Portland......8	12	16
1036 Carrier, 6" long, 1939 on, Aeroplane Carrier Saratoga 9	14	18
1037 Transport, 6" long, 1939 on......6	9	12
1038 Freighter, 6" long, 1940 on......6	9	12
1039 Tanker, 6" long, 1940 on 6	9	12
127 Destroyer, 4" long, 1939 7	11	14
128 Submarine, 4" long, 1939 on......7	11	14
129 Tender, 4" long, 1940 on 6	9	12
130 Yacht, 4" long, 1940 on......6	9	12

TOOTSIETOY MIDGET SERIES

	C6	C8	C10
Battleship 2.50	3.75	5
Destroyer......2.50	3.75	5
Carrier......2.50	3.75	5
Cruiser......2.50	3.75	5
Tug (Probably Not Tootsie) 2.50	3.75	5
Submarine 2.50	3.75	5
Turbo Boat, pressed, tin, 10½" long......40	60	80
U.S. Naval Base,Superior......60	90	120
U. S. Hardware Rowers, circa 1890, 8-man crew and coxswain, cast iron, large wheels, 14½" long 2000	3200	4500
U. S. Hardware Rowers, circa 1890, 4-man crew and coxswain, cast iron, large wheels 1250	1875	2500
"U.S.S. Maine", paper litho on wood, Reed?......600	900	1200
"U.S.S. Narwahl" submarine, lead, mfr. unknown, 1930s, 7½" long.....20	30	40
"U.S.S. New Mexico" battleship, lead, manufacturer unknown, 1930s......20	30	40
"U.S. Submarine," 13" long, painted wood, fires torpedo for target set 20	30	40
U.S. Wasp, Carrier 27" long, wood storage under deck for planes 50	75	100

WANNATOYS

WANNATOYS were manufactured by Dillon-Beck Manufacturing Company of Irvington, New Jersey from 1941 on. They were plastic.

	C6	C8	C10
Wannatoys Cruiser......3	4.50	6
Wannatoys Freighter......3	4.50	6
Wannatoys Submarine 3	4.50	6
Weeden "Dewey" Steamboat, 15½" long, circa 1900......500	750	1000
Weeden Launch, steam-driven, 18" long.350	525	700
Weeden Steamboat, live steam, 15" long......300	450	600
Wilkins Battleship, cast iron......1500	2250	3000
Wilkins "City of New York" riverboat, 15" long......750	1125	1500
Wilkins Riverboat, 5¾" long......140	210	280

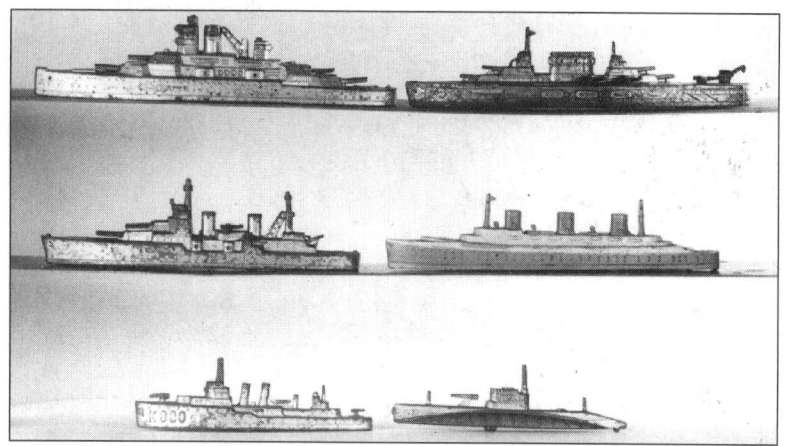

TOOTSIETOY, Left to Right; Top: 1034 Battleship, 1036 Carrier. Middle: 1035 Cruiser, 1037 Liner. Bottom: 127 Destroyer, 128 Submarine. Photo by Ed Poole.

TOOTSIETOY, Left top Right; Top: 1037 Transport, 1039 Tanker. Bottom: 129 Tender, 130 Yacht. Photo by Ed Poole.

WOLVERINE Diving Submarine. Courtesy Mapes Auctioneers & Appraisers.

Steamship, alcohol burner, circa 1885, 19" long. Courtesy Mapes Auctioneers & Appraisers.

U.S. HARDWARE Rowers, circa 1890. Courtesy Ed Hyers Antique Toys.

WEEDEN Launch, steam-driven, 18" long. Courtesy Heinz Mueller, Continental Hobby House.

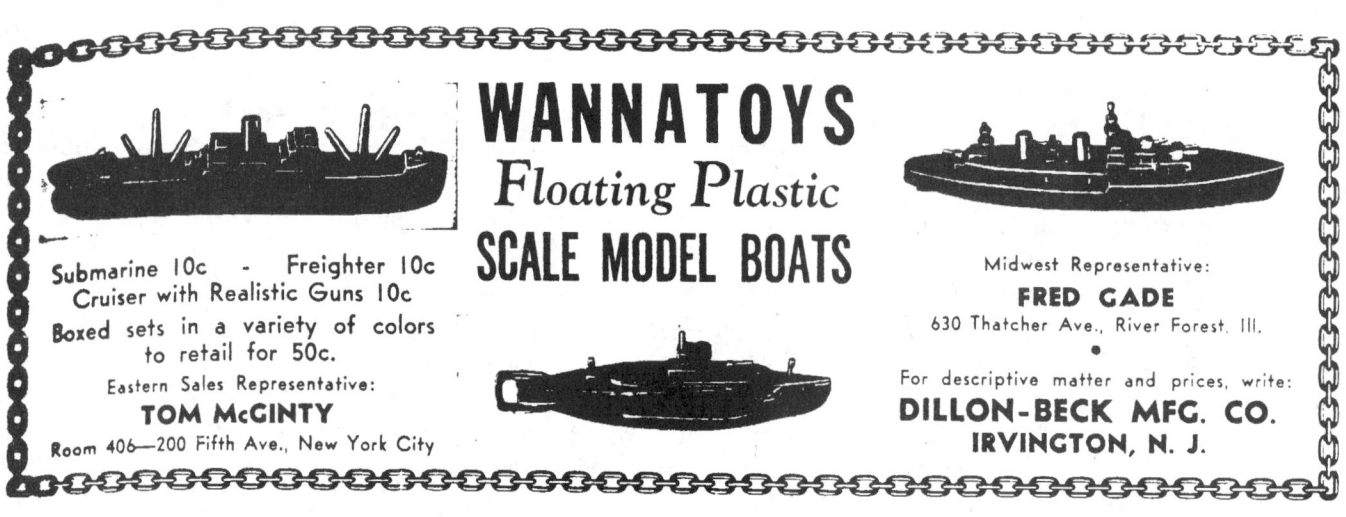
WANNATOYS (Dillion-Beck) plastic ships, advertised in the July, 1941 Playthings. Plastic Toys, Inc. copied the submarine a few years later.

	C6	C8	C10
Wilkins Riverboat, 7½" long, circa 1910, cast iron	300	450	600
Wilkins Riverboat, 10½" long, cast iron	450	675	900
Wilkins Rowers, circa 1890, 4-man crew and coxswain in 10" long, big-wheeled boat, cast iron	1250	1875	2500
Wolverine Diving Submarine, 13" long	110	165	220
Wolverine Ocean Liner	125	188	250
Wolverine "Sandy Andy Ferry," tin litho, 13½" long	75	112.50	150

	C6	C8	C10
Wolverine Sandy Andy "Ferrygo," 11" long, tin and wood	150	225	300
Wyandotte Pocket Battleship, 7" long, tin litho, wheeled	60	90	120
Wyandotte, "S.S. America," 7" long, moves on metal wheels, 1930s	50	75	100
Wyandotte, "Sand-o'Land," 10" long, tin litho sandtoy, wood wheels, 1940s	40	60	80
Yacht-type ship, 28" long with spring-wind motor, either Ives or Bing	2000	3000	4000

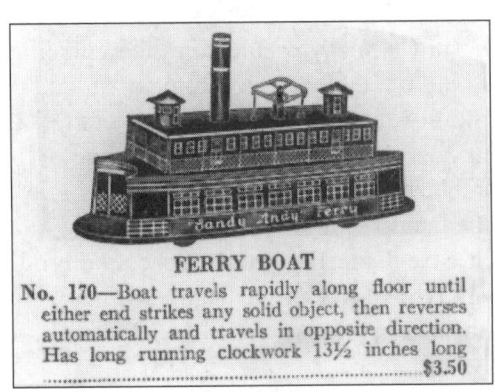

FERRY BOAT

No. 170—Boat travels rapidly along floor until either end strikes any solid object, then reverses automatically and travels in opposite direction. Has long running clockwork 13½ inches long $3.50

WOLVERINE "Sandy Andy" Ferry.

Top to Bottom: "U.S.S. New Mexico, U.S.S. Narwahl". Courtesy Hank Anton.

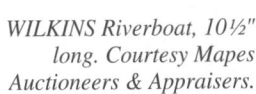

WILKINS Riverboat, 10½" long. Courtesy Mapes Auctioneers & Appraisers.

FISHER-PRICE TOYS

by John Murray

Fisher-Price toys in the last edition averaged $183.38 in mint condition and this year averaged $322.19, an increase of 76%.

On October 1, 1930, in East Aurora, New York, the Fisher-Price Toy Company began operation. Uniquely located on a small side street in a small town atmosphere, it would grow and eventually be considered one of the major manufacturers of toys.

Herman Fisher and Irving Price shared their names in developing a name for their new company. Herman Fisher, a past employee of the FairChild Company, a manufacturer of games, and Irving Price, who had sound experience with the Woolworth Company, would form the guidelines by which they would run their new company.

The first manufacturing facility was located on Church Street in East Aurora, New York. To date it still exists, but was sold by Fisher-Price in the 1970s due to lack of use for the facility.

The Church Street facility would be considered a small area for any type of manufacturing today, but would serve as the main and only facility for Fisher-Price toys for the first twenty years.

The most important factor in constructing this new company was to create a work force that could contribute their efforts towards a smooth, profitable venture. Among the most important employees would be Helen M. Schelle and Margaret Evans Price.

Helen M. Schelle was the first secretary and treasurer of Fisher-Price toys. She developed her skills in the retail management field through a business in which she operated, the Walker Toy Shop, in Binghamton, New York, Given the opportunity to manage the early company's activities, Helen proved to be a great asset to the advancement of Fisher-Price toys.

Margaret Evans Price was the company's first artist and designer for their new line of toys. She developed her early skills as a writer and illustrator for Rand McNally and Harper & Brothers, and by creating children's art for Strecher Lithography Company of Rochester, New York. Many of Margaret Evans Price's art work can still be found on early post cards, valentines, and children's books. These early paper collectibles are most often marked "M.E.P."

Margaret created the early art work for the reproduction of color lithography for the toys. She was also talented in drawing, produced designs for early toys, and contributed in the development of her concepts to Fisher-Price's early line of toys. The Roycroft printers contributed their skills to produce the sales catalogs that prospective retailers would use to choose the toys that they would market.

The most important early development for the company was the forming of the labor force that would generate their efforts towards building the new toy line that would be sold to the public in 1931. The initial work force that first year was approximately 25 employees. As typical of any small town like East Aurora, most employees were neighbors, friends, and relatives, who contributed to a work force that took great pride in the product that they made, since many of the operations were done by hand labor.

Many of the early operations, such as band sawing, drilling, nailing, and painting were shared by these early employees. Quality control would be created by one employee checking the other and making any corrections immediately.

As Fisher-Price began toymaking, numbers were assigned to each toy. This number system started at Number 5 and went up into the thousands. To add to the confusion for collectors today, many of the numbers have been used more than once on various toys.

With the abundance of pine and its ease of workability, this was the main wood used in construction of Fisher-Price toys. During the 30s, another material was used, a heavy cardboard, in which brass eyelets were inserted to prevent wear from spinning axles.

Creating action from child power was of great importance. The use of bellows was common to produce sound, and, as time passed, the introduction of bells was added to create sound and action.

Because of the immense amount of time required to assemble various toys, cottage-type industries were set up by employees, families, and residents of East Aurora. Toys such as the Pop-up Kritter were completely hand assembled in area homes. Because of the large demand, this would prove to be a quick and efficient method of assembly.

As the demand for Fisher-Price toys consistently rose, they began to use the skills of a freelance designer, Edward Savage, a mechanical engineer from the University of Minnesota. He crated some of Fisher-Price's most successful toys. In his home in Rochester, New York, Savage created such toys as the Pop-up Kritters, Snoopy Sniffer, and many of the wind-up toys. The most popular of the toys that he created was the Snoopy Sniffer, which was produced from the 30s to the 80s, in four different versions.

After well over a decade of positive growth for Fisher-Price toys in the 30s and 40s, Fisher-Price would meet a major challenge of limited production.

With the United States entering World War II, Fisher-Price, like many companies, served its patriotic duty in a quite different type of manufacturing

Because of the type of manufacturing that Fisher-Price was set up for, the ability to create and produce wood products set the basis for essential goods needed for war production. Ship fenders, first aid kits, cots, bomb crates, and glider ailerons were among the items produced from 1943 - 1946.

During this time of near non-existent toy manufacturing, very limited toy production continued on a material-availability basis. These toys were made from scraps of wood, with bells and some metal parts painted instead of plated. Toys made during this time sometimes used parts from similar toys, leaving odd and sometimes unusual variations.

As the World War came to an end, normal production began to resume. Well into the 50s, Ponderosa Pine, with a proven durability, was the main source of material in Fisher-Price toys. As wood became more difficult to obtain, the experimentation with plastics as a new material began. The first toy to use this new material successfully was the Busy Bee. Because of the ease of molding, durability, and bright colors, plastic was more prevalent in toys of the 50s.

In 1951, Fisher-Price moved to its new manufacturing facility on Girard Avenue in East Aurora, New York. The Girard Avenue facility handled most operations well into the late 50s. In 1957, Tri Mold of Kenmore, New York, a plastics manufacturer, became a subsidiary of Fisher-Price and their main molding facility.

As the demand for plastics became greater and greater, a new molding facility was built in Holland, New York. This was completed in July 1962. The Holland plant produced many of the plastic parts used in the construction of a more plastic-dominated toy line.

As the 60's advanced, plastic would eventually take over as the main material used to produce toys.

In 1969, the Quaker Oats Company acquired Fisher-Price toys. Three years prior to this acquisition, Herman Fisher resigned as president of the company, and was chairman of the board until the Quaker Oats acquisition. Since Fisher-Price was taken over by Quaker Oats, a plant in Medina, New York, was built, and numerous plants and facilities both nationally and internationally were created.

Considered one of the oldest and largest manufacturers of toys, Fisher-Price has its main offices at the Girard Avenue address in East Aurora, New York.

CONDITION

There are many factors that may contribute to values of Fisher-Price toys. The most important factor to consider is the paper lithography. Most Fisher-Price toys found have what I call "edge wear." Edge wear may be considered as wear only around the outer corners of edge of the toy. Most toys found with edge wear may also be called normal-wear toys. Any toys with this type of wear most often fall in a value class of good/very good. When determining the condition of a toy, other areas of importance to the litho would be the amount of soil on the litho, and the extent to which it has faded and/or lost its color. These areas may be considered as less important, unless there is more than slight soiling or discoloration. When a Fisher-Price toy has advanced conditions of wear, soiling, or missing litho, the toy would be considered as less than good condition, and therefore, a value of less than good (poor) would be placed on it.

The next area that is of importance with regard to condition of the toy in determining value would be paint and originality. Toys with slight paint wear on wheels, bases, and handles would fall into the good/very good condition category, unless however, there is litho damage as stated above. Any parts missing also affect the value of the toy, especially lithography parts, such as arms, legs, and heads. These are especially important, since once the litho is gone, there is no means of replacement. Also lessening the value of a toy would be missing wheels and axles.

A toy which is mint is one that has absolutely no wear or damage on a complete basis. (Litho, paint, wheels, etc. in mint condition). These toys will reflect the highest of values. Boxes for older Fisher-Price toys may add up to 20% more for a mint toy, depending upon the condition of the box. Boxes from toys from the 1930s would be of the most value because of age, and are most often missing. Always consider condition of the box towards a value of a toy.

The last area that seems to have led the way demanding higher prices would be comic characters and the use of other company's names on Fisher-Price toys. Most often toys of this nature have much higher values placed on them than other Fisher-Price toys, due to the fact that there are many Disney, Popeye, and other comic-area collectors.

Because a toy may be a Disney, Popeye, or comic figure does not necessarily mean that it may be a rarer toy. There are many other Fisher-Price toys that are much rarer, since rarity is based on the amount of toys produced over a given period of time, and the amount still in existence.

Also, many toys that had accessories or figures that were often misplaced will bring higher values. Often these accessories and/or figures are difficult to locate separately from the toy itself. If a toy is found mint in the box with accessories, this most certainly will demand higher pricing. The prices reflected in this guide for Fisher-Price toys were established by taking an average of toys seen at toy shows, flea markets, dealers, and collectors.

JOHN J. MURRAY was born, raised, and educated in the Buffalo, New York, area. He presently resides in Eden, a suburb of Buffalo, with his wife Mary and daughter Amanda.

John, known to many as Jack, began his career in the printing industry and after serving in the Armed Forces, began his over 15-year career with Fisher-Price in the Research and Development Art Production Department. He is responsible for creating new color development and decoration for photo and TV models.

John pioneered the first documentation of Fisher-Price in Collecting Toys, volume 4 & 5, and has since completed the most extensive book on Fisher-Price. It is entitled, FISHER-PRICE, 1931-1963, HISTORICAL, RARITY, VALUE GUIDE, by John J. Murray and Bruce R. Fox. The book is available from John by writing to him at Box 29, Eden, NY 14057. The cost is $24.95 plus $3.00 shipping.

In addition, John serves as Chairman of Toyfest in East Aurora, NY, which has become one of the largest antique toy gatherings in the U.S.

777 SQUEAKY THE CLOWN. Photo by Ross MacKearnin. Courtesy John Murray.

770 DOC & DOPEY DWARFS.
Photo by Ross MacKearnin. Courtesy John Murray.

777 TEDDY ZILO.
Photo by Ross MacKearnin. Courtesy John Murray.

	C6	C8	C10
7 Looky Fire Truck	85	125	170
8 Bouncy Racer	40	60	80
10 Bunny Cart	85	125	170
11 Ducky Cart	85	125	170
16 Ducky Cart	85	125	170
28 Bunny Egg Cart	85	125	170
50 Baby Chick Tandem Cart	85	125	170
100 Musical Sweeper	175	225	350
120 Cackling Hen (white)	40	60	80
123 Cackling Hen (red)	35	60	70
123 Roller Chimes (with push stick)	85	125	170
125 Uncle Timmy Turtle (with glasses) (see picture)	85	125	170

	C6	C8	C10
131 Toy Wagon	225	325	450
132 Dr. Doodle	85	125	170
137 Pony Chime	40	60	80
138 Pony Chime	30	40	50
139 Tuggy Turtle	85	125	160
140 Katy Kackler (see picture)	85	120	150
145 Musical Elephant (with original ears) (see picture)	285	325	450
150 Timmy Turtle	85	125	170
151 Happy Hippo	85	125	170
155 Moo-oo Cow	85	125	170
156 F/P Circus Wagon (see picture)	400	500	700
161 Looky Chug-Chug (with tender)	200	250	350
164 Mother Goose	45	55	70

765 TALKING DONALD DUCK.
Photo by Ross MacKearnin. Courtesy John Murray.

491 BOOM BOOM POPEYE. *Photo by Ross MacKearnin. Courtesy John Murray.*

480 LEO THE DRUMMER. *Photo by Ross MacKearnin. Courtesy John Murray.*

494 PLUCKY PINOCCHIO. *Photo by Ross MacKearnin. Courtesy John Murray.*

	C6	C8	C10
166 Bucky Burro	225	275	350
168 F/P Chug Chug (with 2 cars)	55	70	80
168 Snorky Fire Engine (with all figures)	85	125	170
169 Snorky Fire Engine (with all figures)	85	125	170
170 American Airlines Flagship (with original propellors)	600	900	1200
175 Gold Star Stage Coach (with baggage-two) (see picture)	225	325	450
177 Donald Duck Xylophone (see picture)	225	325	450
180 Snoopy Sniffer (see picture)	95	150	195
185 Donald Duck Xylophone	400	600	800

	C6	C8	C10
190 Molly Moo-Moo	225	275	325
191 Golden Gulch Express	85	125	170
192 Playland Express	85	125	170
195 Teddy Bear Parade	600	900	1200
200 Winky Blinky Fire Truck	85	125	170
210 Pluto the Pup	350	475	600
211 Walt Disney's Elmer the Elephant	350	475	600
215 Streamliner Express	600	900	1200
220 Looky Chug-Chug (see picture)	95	125	170
225 Musical Sweeper	85	125	170
230 Musical Sweeper	85	125	170
234 Nifty Station Wagon (with roof and four figures) see pictures	225	325	450

757 HUMPTY DUMPTY. Photo by Ross MacKearnin. Courtesy John Murray.

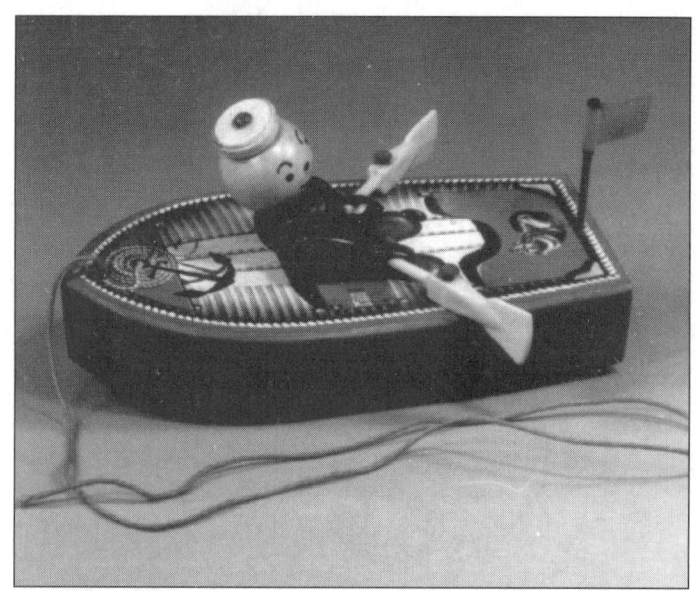

730 RACING ROWBOAT. Photo by Ross MacKearnin. Courtesy John Murray.

703 POPEYE THE SAILOR. Photo by Ross MacKearnin. Courtesy John Murray.

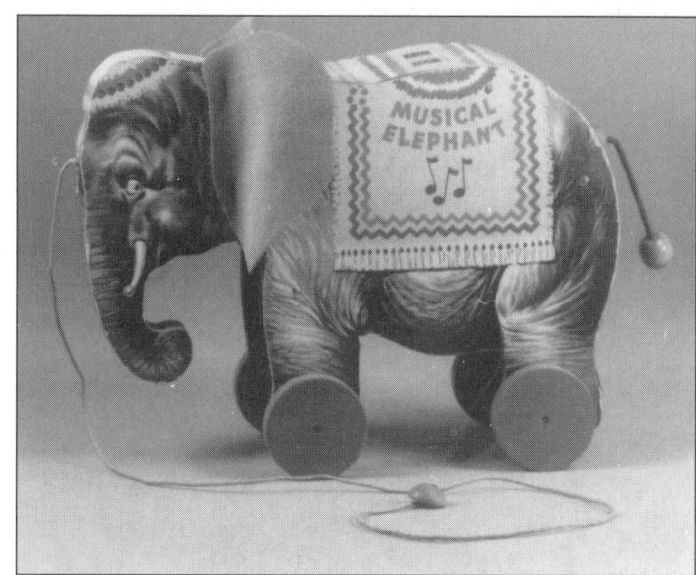

145 MUSICAL ELEPHANT.Photo by Ross MacKearnin. Courtesy John Murray.

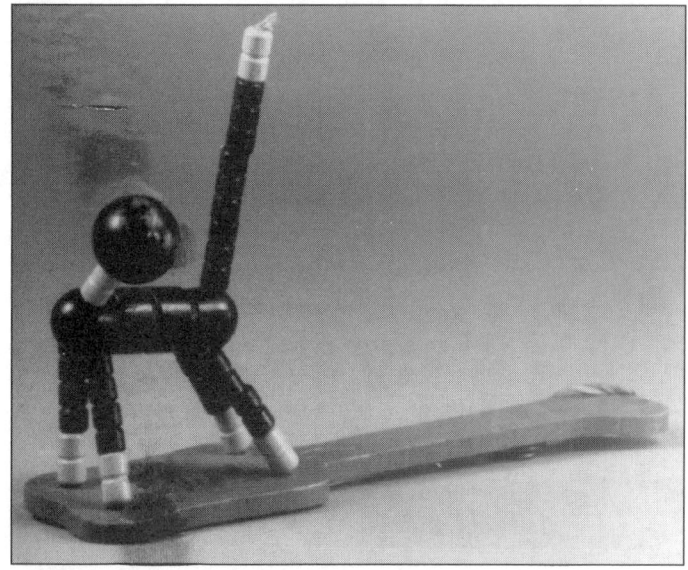

400 TAILSPIN TABBY. Photo by Ross MacKearnin. Courtesy John Murray

156 FISHER PRICE CIRCUS WAGON. Photo by Ross MacKearnin. Courtesy John Murray.

	C6	C8	C10
237 Riding Horse (with original tail) ...600	900	1200
301 Bunny Basket Cart..........................40	60	80
302 Chick Basket Cart..........................40	60	80
303 Bunny Basket Cart..........................85	125	170
305 Walking Duck Cart 45	60	90
307 Bouncing Bunny Cart......................45	60	90
310 Mickey Mouse Puddle Jumper 90	135	180
314 Queen Buzzy Bee (see picture) 40	50	80
325 Buzzy Bee......................................40	50	80
333 Butch the Pup.................................85	125	170
350 Go'n Back Mule (with original		
ears) 600	900	1200
400 Donald Duck Drum Major 225	325	450
400 Tailspin Tabby (original pull		
loops) (see picture) 90	135	180
401 Bunny Cart 200	300	400
406 Bunny & Cart 45	60	90
407 Chick & Cart 45	60	90
410 Stoopy Storky (with original		
cardboard feet)................................225	325	450
415 Lop-Ear Looie (see picture) 275	375	475
415 Super-Jet (see picture) 175	225	275
432 Mickey Mouse Choo-Choo		
early version) 600	900	1200
433 Dizzy Donkey (see picture)............85	125	170
434 Ferdinand the Bull (see picture) 600	900	1200
440 Goofy Gertie..................................225	325	450
440 Pluto Pop-Up..................................90	125	165
444 Puffy Engine...................................60	80	120
444 Fuzzy Fido (see picture) 225	325	450
445 Hot Dog Wagon (see picture)........225	325	450
445 Nosey Pup (see picture)..................50	75	100
450 Donald Choo-Choo..........................225	325	450
450 Jolly Jumper 85	125	170
454 Donald Duck Drummer (see		
picture)..225	325	450
455 Tailspin Tabby 85	125	170
462 Barky Dog 85	125	170
472 Peter Bunny Cart 225	275	375
472 Jingle Giraffe 175	225	275
473 Merry Mutt 85	125	170
476 Mickey Mouse Drummer 225	235	450
476 Cookie Pig......................................40	50	60
477 Dr. Doodle 225	300	450
478 Pudgy Pig.......................................40	50	60
479 Donald Duck & Nephews		
(with 2 nephews) 375	475	575
480 Leo The Drummer (see picture) 225	280	375
485 Mickey Mouse Choo-Choo		
(see picture)......................................85	125	170
487 Bunny Cart 225	325	450
488 Popeye Spinach Eater...................600	900	1200
491 Boom-Boom Popeye (see picture)....600	900	1200
494 Plucky Pinocchio (see picture)......400	600	800

415 LOP-EAR-LOOIE. Photo by Ross MacKearnin. Courtesy John Murray.

177 DONALD DUCK XYLOPHONE. Photo by Ross MacKearnin. Courtesy John Murray.

415 SUPER JET. Photo by Ross MacKearnin. Courtesy John Murray.

445 NOSEY PUP. *Photo by Ross MacKearnin. Courtesy John Murray.*

454 DONALD DUCK DRUMMER. *Photo by Ross MacKearnin. Courtesy John Murray.*

485 MICKEY MOUSE CHOO CHOO. *Photo by Ross MacKearnin, Courtesy John Murray.*

678 KRISS KRICKET. *Photo by Ross MacKearnin. Courtesy John Murray.*

472 PETER BUNNY CART. *Photo by Ross MacKearnin. Courtesy John Murray.*

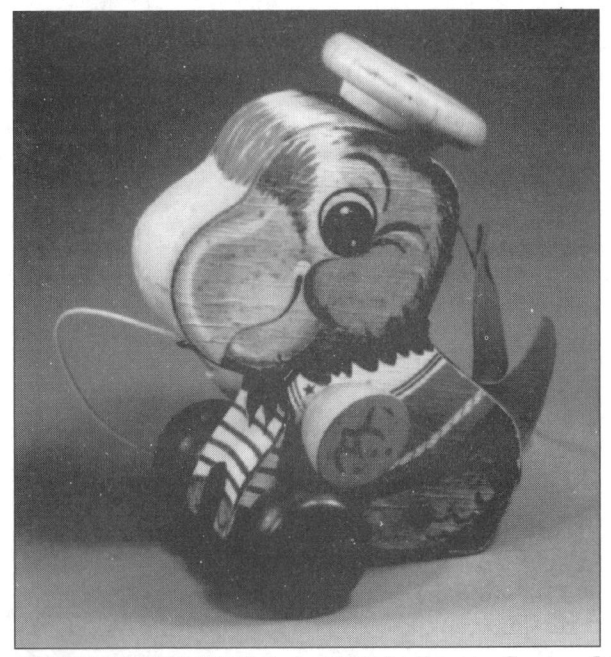

698 TALKY PARROT. *Photo by Ross MacKearnin. Courtesy John Murray.*

166 BUCKY BURRO. *Photo by Ross MacKearnin. Courtesy John Murray.*

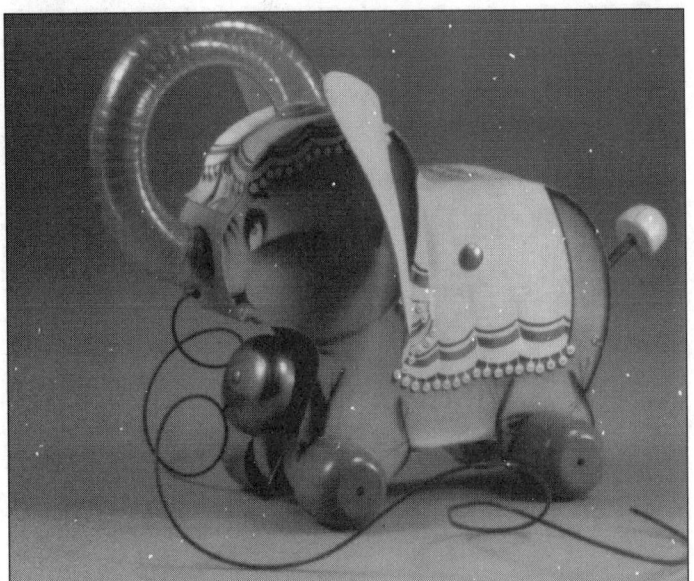

735 JUGGLING JUMBO. *Photo by Ross MacKearnin. Courtesy John Murray.*

434 FERDINAND THE BULL. *Photo by Ross MacKearnin. Courtesy John Murray.*

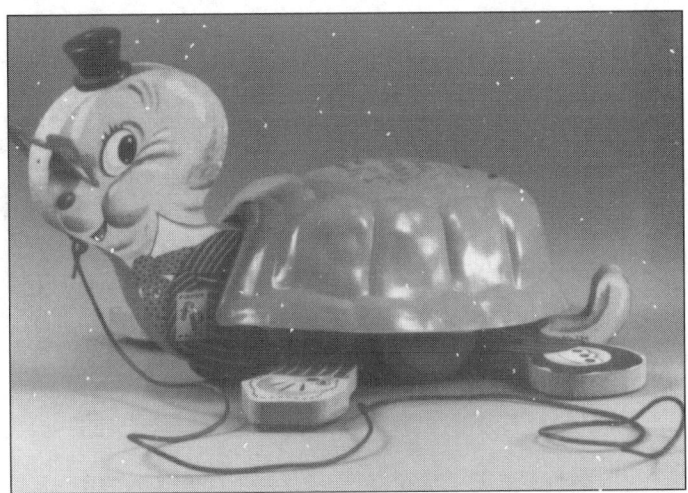

125 UNCLE TIMMY TURTLE. *Photo by Ross MacKearnin. Courtesy John Murray.*

314 QUEEN BUZZY BEE. *Photo by Ross MacKearnin. Courtesy John Murray.*

733 FISHER PRICE GENERAL HAULING. *Photo by Ross MacKearnin. Courtesy John Murray.*

531

7 LOOKY FIRE TRUCK. Photo by Ross MacKearnin. Courtesy John Murray.

450 DONALD DUCK CHOO CHOO. Photo by Ross MacKearnin. Courtesy John Murray.

479 DONALD DUCK & NEPHEWS. Photo by Ross MacKearnin. Courtesy John Murray.

	C6	C8	C10
495 Sleepy Sue	45	55	65
498 Happy Helicopter	225	275	325
508 Bunny Bell Drummer	85	125	160
533 Thumper Bunny	425	575	800
544 Donald Duck Cart	225	325	425
600 Tailspin Tabby Pop-up	200	275	325
610 Tailspin Tabby	85	125	160
616 Chuggy Pop-Up	85	125	170
617 Whistling Engine	85	125	160
621 Suzie Seal (ball)	40	50	60
623 Suzie Seal (umbrella)	40	50	60
625 Playful Puppy	45	55	65
626 Playful Puppy	45	55	65
634 Tiny Teddy	50	60	85
635 Tiny Teddy	50	55	65
636 Tiny Teddy	40	50	60
640 Wiggily Woofer	60	80	100
642 Smokie Engine	20	35	45

	C6	C8	C10
653 Allie Gator	85	95	125
654 Tawny Tiger	85	95	125
656 Bossy Bell	35	45	55
658 Lady Bug	45	55	65
662 Merry Mousewife	40	55	65
674 Sports Car	85	125	150
678 Kriss Kricket (see picture)	85	95	150
686 Perky Pot	85	110	140
695 Pinky Pig	60	80	100
698 Talky Parrot	85	95	150
703 Popeye the Sailor (see picture)	600	900	1200
707 Fido Zilo	85	95	150
712 Teddy Tooter	225	275	400
720 Pinocchio Express	600	800	1100
721 Peter Bunny Engine	225	300	375
728 Buddy Bullfrog	80	100	120
730 Racing Rowboat (see picture)	175	250	325
733 Fisher-Price General Hauling	200	300	400

745 ELSIE'S DAIRY TRUCK. Photo by Ross MacKearnin. Courtesy John Murray.

765 DANDY DOBBIN. Photo by Ross MacKearnin. Courtesy John Murray.

445 HOT DOG WAGON. Photo by Ross MacKearnin. Courtesy John Murray.

444 FUZZY FIDO. Photo by Ross MacKearnin. Courtesy John Murray.

	C6	C8	C10
733 Mickey Mouse Safety Patrol	250	375	500
735 Juggling Jumbo (see picture)	175	225	275
738 Dumbo Circus Racer (original arms)	600	900	1200
738 Shaggy Zilo	80	125	160
739 Poodle Zilo	80	125	160
742 Dashing Dobbin	325	450	625
745 Elsie's Dairy Truck with 2 milk bottles-deduct $25.00 for each missing bottle (see picture)	400	575	700
750 Hot Dog Wagon	400	600	800
750 Space Blazer	300	400	500
752 Teddy Xylophone	175	250	350
755 Jumbo Rollo	175	225	375
757 Humpty-Dumpty (see picture)	200	300	400
758 Pony Chime	175	250	350
765 Dandy Dobbin (see picture)	200	275	400
770 Doc & Dopey Dwarfs (see picture)	600	900	1200
775 Gabby Goofies	40	50	60

	C6	C8	C10
776 Gabby Goofies	40	50	60
777 Teddy Bear Zilo	80	125	160
777 Squeaky the Clown (see picture)	175	225	375
785 Blackie Drummer	500	600	1000
794 Big Bill Pelican (with cardboard fish-add $20.00)	55	75	100
795 Musical Duck	80	125	160
798 Chatter Monk	85	125	160
799 Quacky Family	40	60	80
810 Timber Toter	50	75	100
875 Looky Push Car (with steering wheel push stick)	60	80	130
900 Big Performing Circus (with all accessories)	225	350	475
926 Cement Mixer	225	300	450
983 Safety School Bus (with all figures)	175	275	400
984 Safety School Bus (with all figures)	170	275	400
999 Huffy Puffy Train (with 4 cars)	90	130	160

175 GOLD STAR STAGE COACH. Photo by Ross MacKearnin. Courtesy John Murray.

220 LOOKY, CHUG, CHUG. Photo by Ross MacKearnin. Courtesy John Murray.

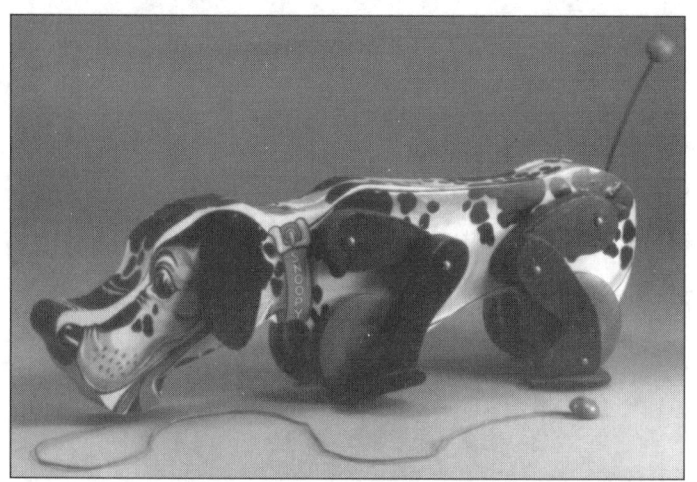

180 SNOOPY SNIFFER. Photo by Ross MacKearnin. Courtesy John Murray.

234 NIFTY STATION WAGON. Photo by Ross MacKearnin. Courtesy John Murray.

140 KATY KACKLER. Photo by Ross MacKearnin. Courtesy John Murray.

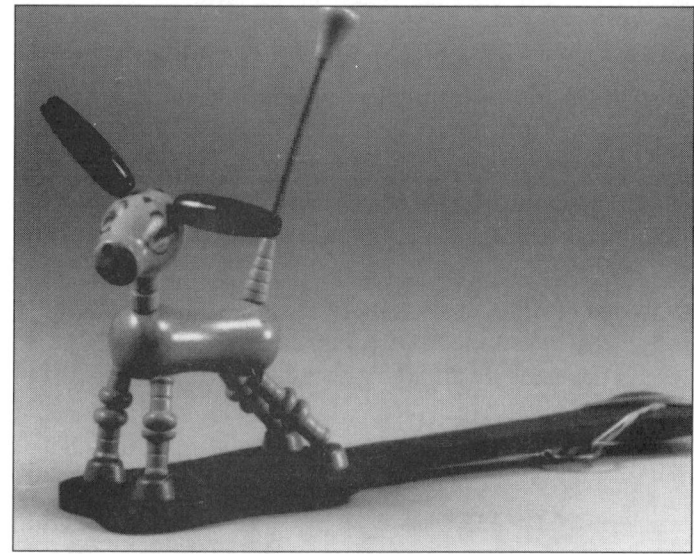

433. DIZZY DONKEY. Photo by Ross MacKearnin. Courtesy John Murray.

MISCELLANEOUS

Average mint price in this category in the last edition was $430.96, and in
this edition it is $580, and increase of 35%.

A.C. GILBERT

Alfred Carlton Gilbert, Jr. (1884-1961) began as a schoolboy magician who turned to producing magic kits under the name of Mysto Manufacturing Company. In 1916 his father bought out A.C.'s partner, and the firm became known as A.C. Gilbert Company, located on Erector Square in New Haven, Connecticut. The company produced non-toys as well as its various toy sets. Upon Gilbert's death, his son, Alfred Carlton Gilbert III took over, but died four years later. Since his death, the company has passed through several hands, with many of its items still being manufactured today, including what is probably its most famous product, the Erector Set.

A.C. GILBERT Erector Set No.10181 Action Helicopter Set. Courtesy Continental Hobby House.

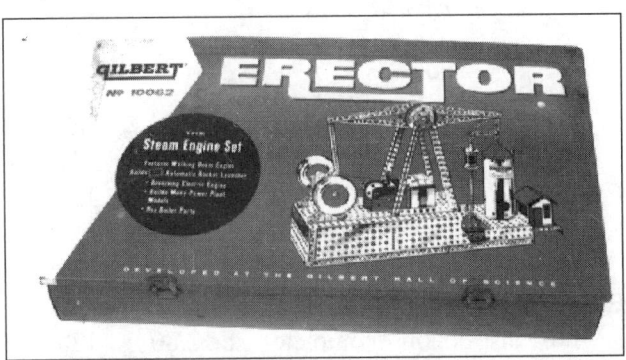

A.C. GILBERT Erector Set No.10062 Steam Engine Set. Courtesy Continental Hobby House.

A.C. GILBERT Mystro Erector Set No.2. Courtesy Continental Hobby House.

A.C. GILBERT Mysto Erector Sets Nos.1, 1A, 2A, 3A. Courtesy Continental Hobby House.

A.C. GILBERT

	C6	C8	C10
Atomic Energy Lab	750	1125	1500
Big Boy Tool Chest No. 6, with tools	20	30	40
No. 12052 Chemistry Experiment Lab, in three-piece metal box, complete	30	45	60
"Electric Eye" early photoelectric toy, 1935, in metal box with original instruction booklet, complete	20	30	40
Erector Motor, early, 2½" x 2" x 3"	10	15	20
Erector Set No. 1, complete	125	188	250
Erector Set No. 2, Junior, copyright 1949, complete	20	30	40
Erector Set No. 2, 1919, "Patented Jan. 16th 1917, Patented May 6th 1918" includes box, complete	45	68	90
Erector Set No. 2½, instructions and complete	12	18	24
Erector Set No. 3	20	30	40
Erector Set No. 4, 1919, price includes box, instructions, complete	40	60	80
Erector Set No. 4, 1929, includes box, instructions, complete	40	60	80
Erector Set No. 4, 1930, instructions, complete	130	195	260
Erector Set No. 4, 1940, instruction, complete	170	255	340
Erector Set No. 4½, copyright 1938	45	68	90
Erector Set No. 4½, 1954	12	18	25
Erector Set No. 6½, Electric engine	45	68	90
Erector Set No 6½, 1954	21	31	42
Erector Set No. 7, builds steam shovel, price includes wood box, complete	170	255	340

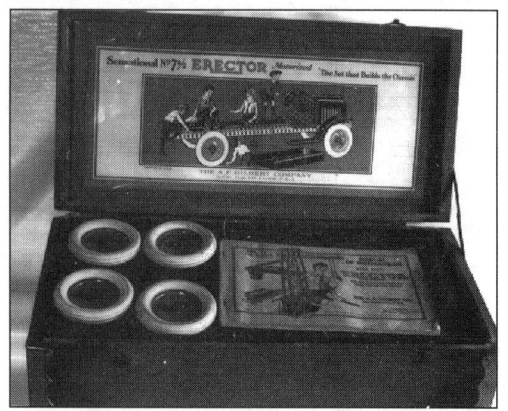

A.C. GILBERT Erector Set No. 7½, makes truck. Courtesy Continental Hobby House.

A.C. GILBERT Erector Set No. 8½,. Courtesy Continental Hobby House.

A.C. GILBERT Erector Set No. 10052 Rocket Launcher. Courtesy Continental Hobby House.

	C6	C8	C10
Erector Set No. 7½, Engineers Set, early 1950s	50	75	100
Erector Set No. 7½, makes truck, complete	100	150	200
Erector Set No., 8½, instructions, complete, motorized	95	142	190
Erector Set No. 9, price includes wood box, instructions, complete	80	120	160
Erector Set No. 10, giant deluxe set, includes box approx. 30x30" makes zeppelin (fabric included), Hudson and Tender, White Truck etc. complete	1000	1500	2000
Erector Set No. 10½, Merry-Go-Round	75	112	150
Erector Set No. 49, remote control	25	38	50
Erector Set No. 217, makes train engine and tender, price includes wood box, complete	80	120	160
Erector Set "The New Erector World's Greatest Toy, Copy. 1928," "A.C. Gilbert Co., New Haven, Conn. USA," complete set with box and directions	120	180	240
Erector How To Make 'Em Book, 1938, tells how to make various projects with Erector Set	6	9	12
Erector Hudson Locomotive	900	1350	1800
Erector Set Manual of Instructions for Set Number 4, 1928, illustrated	4	6	8
Erector, very large set, comes with big white truck, trains, crane, instructions, complete	100	150	200
Erector Set No. 10042 Radar Scope Set	17	26	35
Erector Set No. 10052, Rocket Launcher Set	31	47	62
Erector Set No. 10062 Steam Engine Set	17	26	35
Erector Set No. 10083, Amusement Park	150	225	300
Erector Set No. 10093, Master Builder	150	225	300
Erector Set No. 10181, Action Helicopter	45	68	90

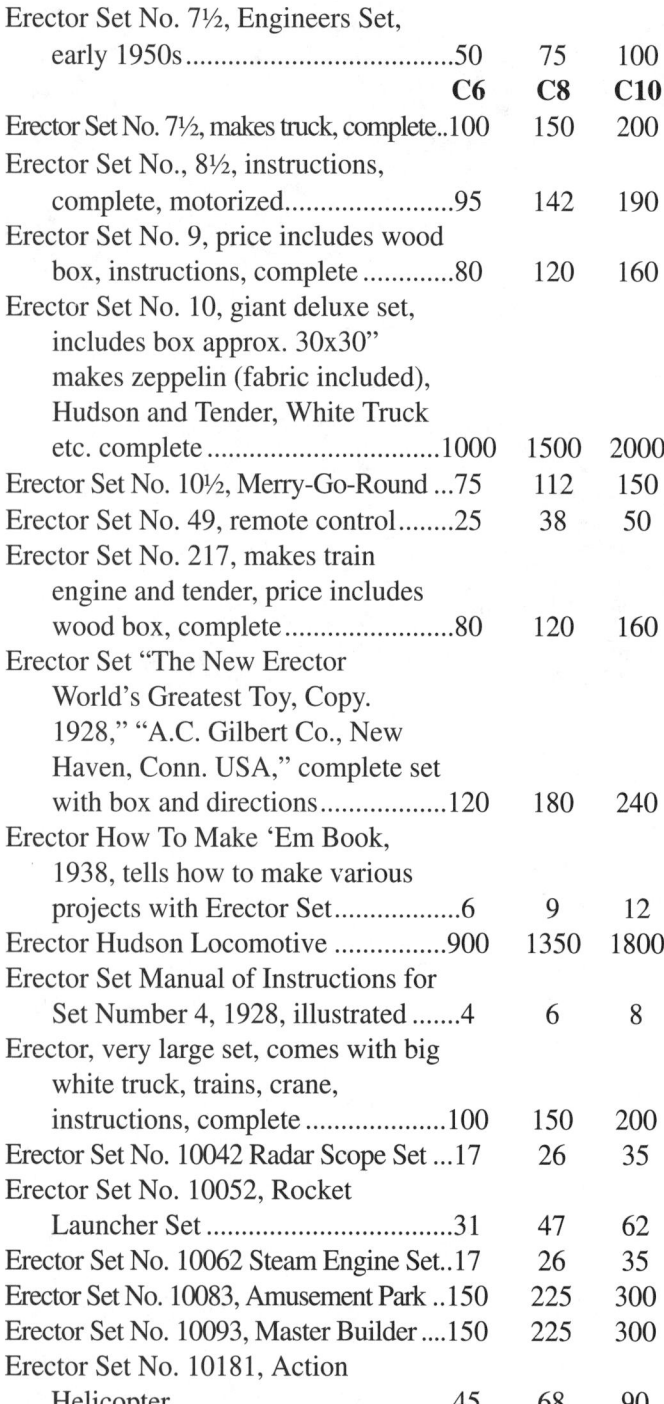

A.C. GILBERT Erector Sets, as shown in a December, 1929 Butler Bros. catalog.

	C6	C8	C10
Erector Set No. 10621 "5 in 1"	17	26	35
Microscope Set No. 6, circa 1938 with Polaroid Jr. microscope, original manual, vials, test tube and other equipment	37	56	75
Mysto Erector Set No. 1, 1A, 2A, 3A Price per each	60	90	120

	C6	C8	C10
Telegraph Outfit and instructions 10	15	20
Trumodel Set No. 77, 1929, instructions, complete 60	90	120
Wood Tool Box and Tools, complete 20	30	40

End GILBERT

	C6	C8	C10
"Acrobatic Monkey" John Henry Prod., 1950s, 10" long push toy 60	90	120
Air Raid Warden Junior Kit, felt hat, arm band, gas mask, whistle, window sign, forms and street-plan sheets, stethoscope, book of instructions, WW II era, rare 100	150	200
All-Nu Horse, not made to have rider ...15	22	30
Alligator, cast iron, 9" 20	30	40
Alligator, cast iron, two-part, 9" long....30	45	60
American Badge ring, circa 1930s or 1940s, heavy metal, may have been premium 20	30	40
American Logs - similar to Lincoln Logs, circa WW II, price includes box, instructions..........30	45	60
American Toy Co. Dancing Black Women, two 600	900	1200
Animate Toy Co. "Baby Haymaker," 1916 tin push toy playset 100	150	200
"Anti-Aircraft Rapid-Fire Machine Gun," cast iron, on wheels 50	75	100
Arcade Bathroom Set, 3-piece, cast iron tub, stool, sink 30	45	60
Arcade cast iron highway sign, "Men Working Ahead" 15	22	30
Arcade cast iron highway sign, "Road Closed"..........15	22	30
Arcade "Don't Park Here" cast iron sign, 4½" high..........15	22	30
Arcade "Don't Park Here" sign, painted cast iron, 1920, 5" tall 15	22	30
Arcade Garage..........300	450	650
Arcade Gas Pump, 6" 35	52	70
Arcade Grand Piano and bench, 3" 80	120	160
"Arcade Service" gas station, No. 900, 1941 400	600	800
Arcade "Stop" sign, cast iron 15	22	30
Arcade tools, cast iron, No. 779N, small, nickel finish, screwdriver, hammer, monkey wrench, pipe wrench, crescent wrench and S wrench, came in set of 6, 1938. Price per each..................4	6	8
Arcade Weapons, cast iron, No. 778N, small, nickel finish, cutlass, pistol, automatic, aerial bomb, tommy gun, airplane, came in set of six, 1938. Price per each 10	15	20

	C6	C8	C10
Arcade Pump and Tub 60	90	120
Arcade Windmill, cast iron, 15¼", high 125	188	250
Arkitoy Play Lumber by G.B. Lewis Co., 1926, No. 3 20	30	40
Artascope, optical toy, circa 1920, pressed steel, spin base with multi-colors, see thru mirrors 60	90	120
Auburn Rubber Calf, circa 1937 7	11	15
Auburn Rubber Chicken, circa 1937 4	6	8
Auburn Rubber Collie, circa 1937 7	11	15
Auburn Rubber Colt, circa 1937 7	11	15
Auburn Rubber Cow, circa 1937 7	11	15
Auburn Rubber Duck, circa 1937..........4	6	8
Auburn Rubber Fence Section, circa 1937 4	6	8
Auburn Rubber Horse, circa 1937..........7	11	15
Auburn Rubber Pig, circa 1937 5	8	10
Auburn Rubber Piglet, circa 1937 4	6	8
Automatic Toy Co., "Rocket Space Ship No. 305," 1930s, 8½" long, tin, friction, sparks 80	120	160

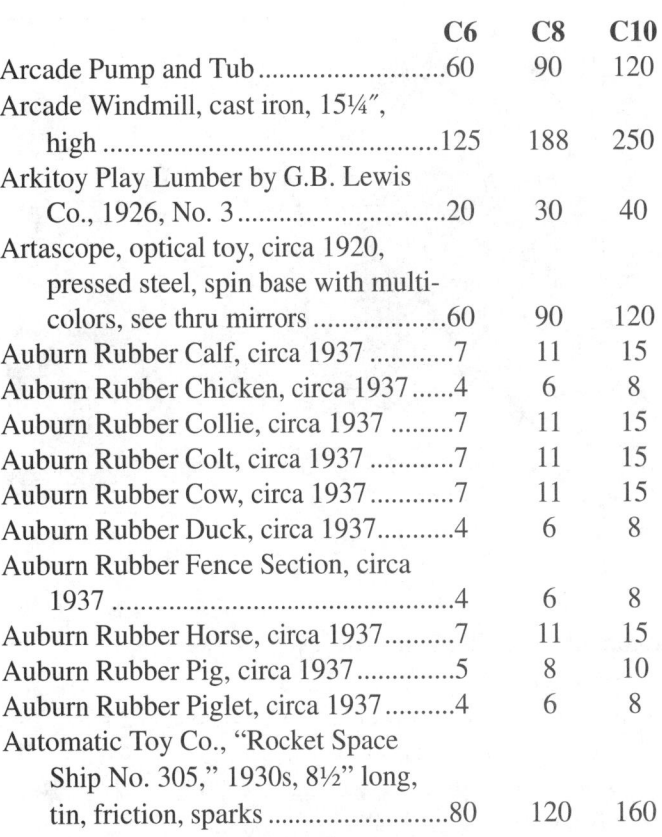

ARCADE "Don't Park Here" sign, 1920, 5" high. Courtesy Lloyd W. Ralston Auctions.

ARCADE Cast Iron Highway Signs. Courtesy Lloyd W. Ralston Auctions.

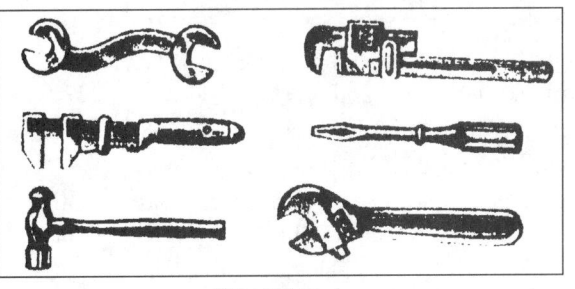

ARCADE Tools.

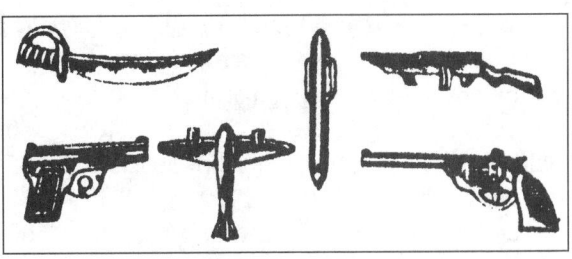

ARCADE Weapons.

ARCADE Garage. Photo by Virginia Caputo. Courtesy James S. Maxwell/Virginia Caputo.

ARCADE Pump and Tub. Courtesy Mapes Auctioneers.

ARCADE signs and tools; "Men Working Ahead", "Road Closed", "Slow". Courtesy Continental Hobby House.

	C6	C8	C10
Automatic Toy Co., "Space Rocket Ship No. 306," 1930's, 8½" long, tin friction, sparks, siren 150	225	300
B& R Co. — "Bossy The Moo Cow," 1930's, 11" long 80	120	160
Baby Buggy, cast iron, 4¼" high 25	37	50
Baby Carriage, tin, with folding cloth top, 7¾" long 40	60	80
Badge, "Dick Steel News Service: 20	30	40
Badge, G-Man, lead.........5	7	10
Badge, Jet Ranger.........6	9	12
Badge, Junior Counter Spy Agent with picture, No. 161731 10	15	20
Badge, "Junior Detective," heavy six-pointed star badge with copper in-set, nickel badge.........10	15	20
Badge, Junior G-Man, circa late 1930s, brass, shield-shaped, eagle on top...10	15	20
Badge, Junior Secret Agent, metal 12	18	24
Badge, "The Purple Mask" detective badge.........10	15	20
Badge, "Sheriff," six-pointed star, black oval insert and work :Oklahoma," nickeled metal 18	27	36
Badge, Wyatt Earp Marshall, six-pointed 20	30	40
Baggage Cart, cast iron, 5" high.........36	54	72

BALDWIN

Baldwin was located in Brooklyn, New York at 361 State Street. Its material was pressed steel.

	C6	C8	C10
Baldwin Chicken on nest, marbles for eggs, 5" long.........40	60	80
Baldwin Kingpin, spring action bowling ..30	45	60
Baldwin "Little Red Hen," 1930s, crank action, 5" long.........40	60	80

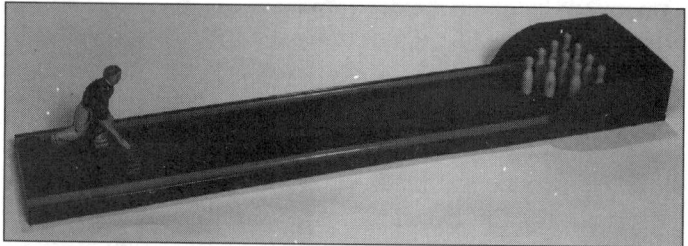

BALDWIN Kingpin, spring action. Courtesy Scott Smiles. Photo by Mike Adams.

	C6	C8	C10
Barbed Wire (Army), 8" long, for toy soldiers.........12	18	25
Barbed Wire, mesh, for toy soldiers......12	18	25
Barclay Searchlight, swivels on base, 3".........20	30	40
Barclay No. 209 Work Horse.........5.00	7.50	10.00
Barclay No. 210 Horse 5.00	7.50	10.00
Barclay No. 211 Grazing Horse.........5.00	7.50	10.00
Barclay No. 212 Standing Cow 5.00	7.50	10.00
Barclay No. 213 Grazing Cow 5.00	7.50	10.00
Barclay No. 214 Lying Cow 5.00	7.50	10.00
Barclay No. 215 Bull 5.00	7.50	10.00
Barclay No. 216? Grazing Sheep 5.00	7.50	10.00
Barclay No. 217 Standing Sheep.......5.00	7.50	10.00
Barclay No. 218 Resting Sheep.........5.00	7.50	10.00

BARCLAY, Left to Right; Top: 209, 210, 213, 214. Bottom: 215, 217, 218, 219, 220, 216?.

538

Bell Toy, Horse, FALLOWS, tin. Courtesy Lloyd W. Ralston Auctions.

BEAUT MFG. CO. Wagon. Courtesy George Buhler. Photo by Bill Kaufman.

Bell Toy, Clown & Pig, 1900. Courtesy Lloyd W. Ralston Auctions.

Bell Toy, Billy Goat, GONG BELL No. 51. Courtesy Lloyd W. Ralston Auctions.

Bell Toy, "Are You A Buffalo". Courtesy James S. Maxwell/Virginia Caputo. Photo by Virginia Caputo.

Bell Toy, Goat, FALLOWS. Courtesy Lloyd W. Ralston Auctions.

Bell Toy, Hunter and Rabbit, N.N. HILL. Courtesy Lloyd W. Ralston Auctions.

Bell Toy, Cat and Dog, Gong Bell. Courtesy James S. Maxwell/Virginia Caputo. Photo by Virginia Caputo.

	C6	C8	C10
Barclay No. 219 Ram	5.00	7.50	10.00
Barclay No. 220 Pig	5.00	7.50	10.00
Barclay Mess Table, two benches (wooden)	20	30	40
Beaut Mfg. Co. Wagon No. 50	6	9	12
Bell Toy, Acrobats holding bells, Gong Bell No. 54	1400	2100	2800
Bell Toy, Alligator ridden by Black Boy, 5½" long, N.N. Hill, 1910, cast iron	1250	1875	2500
Bell Toy, Alligator Snapping at teasing boy, cast iron, 9¼" long	1300	1950	2600
Bell Toy, Althof Bergmann, tin "Chime & Design Patd. May 19th 1874," 3 soldiers, one with flag, two with rifles	1600	2400	3200

	C6	C8	C10
Bell Toy, "Are You a Buffalo," Gong Bell	800	1200	1600
Bell Toy, bear, iron, bounces in air	400	600	800
Bell Toy, bear on tricycle, 4" long	150	225	300
Bell Toy, , Billy Goat, Gong Bell, No. 51, cast iron, goat mechanically butts bell, 7½" long, 1900	750	1125	1500
Bell Toy, bird and bell, tin and iron, 6" long	600	900	1200
Bell Toy, Boy and Goat, Althof Bergmann, tin 9" long	600	900	1200
Bell Toy, Boy Scouts, iron, rest pressed steel, heart-shaped tin wheels, 13½" long	750	1125	1500
Bell Toy, Boys Eating Bananas, cast iron	700	1050	1400

Bell Toy, alligator ridden by black boy. Courtesy Ed Hyers Antique Toys.

Pull Toy, Sheep, tin, circa 1890. Photo courtesy PB Eighty-Four.

Bell Toy, Goat, tin, circa 1890. Photo courtesy PB Eighty-Four.

Bell Toy, "Oriental Clown & Poodle". Courtesy Lloyd W. Ralston Auctions.

	C6	C8	C10
Bell Toy, Cat and Dog, Gong Bell	1500	2250	3000
Bell Toy, Cinderella Chariot, 9¼" long	400	600	800
Bell Toy, Clown	250	375	500
Bell Toy, Clown and Pig, 1900, painted cast iron, 6¼" long	750	1125	1500
Bell Toy, Clown bell-ringers riding back to back on a mule	1000	1500	2000
Bell Toy, Clown and black man on see-saw, circa 1905, 6½" long, six colors, Watrous, cast iron	600	900	1200
Bell Toy, Comic Characters, two, pressed steel and iron, 3 bells, pierced heart wheels	700	1125	1400
Bell Toy, "Daisy," Gong Bell, 9" long	725	1088	1450
Bell Toy, "Ding Dong Bell, Pussy's Not In The Well," cast iron c. 1880, 9½" long, Gong Bell Co.	600	900	1200
Bell Toy, Dog on Platform	400	600	800
Bell Toy, Dog on Platform (Fallows)	400	6500	9000
Bell Toy, Elephant on Platform, Fallows 6¾" long	300	450	600

	C6	C8	C10
Bell Toy, Elephant with bell in trunk, N.N. Hill, circa 1905	700	1050	1400
Bell Toy, "Eskimo & Bear," pressed steel body, iron figures	750	1125	1500
Bell Toy, Francis, Field & Francis, Clown rotates, hits bell, 6" long	300	450	600
Bell Toy, Goat, Fallows, 1880, painted tin, 14" long x 14" tall	1100	1650	2200
Bell Toy, Goat, Lamb and Girl on Platform, George Brown, tin, 11" long, early	750	1125	1500
Bell Toy, Goat, tin, circa 1890, small woman at left leg of goat, 7½" high, either Althof Bergmann or Ives	500	750	1000
Bell Toy, "Hello Hello Telephone Chimes" with monkey, Gong Bell	2000	3000	4000
Bell Toy, Horse, Fallows	450	675	900
Bell Toy, Horse, 9¼" long, tin	200	300	400
Bell Toy, Horse on Rocker	700	1050	1400
Bell Toy, Horse, tin, pulling heart-shaped wheel	200	300	400
Bell Toy, Ives, 9½" long, white horse pulling heart-shaped wheels, circa 1896	1000	1500	2000
Bell Toy, horse and rider, 9" long, heart-shaped wheels, tin	750	1125	1500
Bell Toy, Hunter and Rabbit, N.N. Hill, 1900, cast iron rabbit pops out	750	1125	1500

Bell Toy, "Daisy". Courtesy Sotheby's New York.

Bell Toy, FRANCIS, FIELD & FRANCIS, Clown rotates. Courtesy Sotheby's New York.

Bell Toy, "Ding Dong Bell, Pussy's Not In The Well". Courtesy Sotheby's New York.

Bell Toy, "Hello, Hello Telephone Chimes". Courtesy James S. Maxwell/Virginia Caputo. Photo by Virginia Caputo.

Bell Toy, Elephant on Platform, FALLOWS, 6¾" long. Courtesy Wilkinson Collection, Detroit Antique Toy Mueum.

Bell Toy, "Landing of Columbus". Courtesy Sotheby's New York.

Bell Toy, Jonah & Whale, Hill. Courtesy James S. Maxwell/Virginia Caputo. Photo by Virginia Caputo.

541

Bell Toy, Monkey and Horse, Gong Bell. Photo by Virginia Caputo. Courtesy James S. Maxwell/Virginia Caputo.

Bell Toy, Liberty Bell Centennial. Courtesy Sotheby's New York.

Bell Toy, Monkey and Coconut, N,N, Hill. Courtesy Ed Hyers Antique Toys.

Bell Toy, Jack and Jill on seesaw, WATROUS. Courtesy Ed Hyers Antique Toys.

Bell Toy, Clown and Pig, Gong Bell. Courtesy Ed Hyers Antique Toys.

Bell Toy, Monkey in Wheeled Chariot. Photo by Virginia Caputo. Courtesy James S. Maxwell/Virginia Caputo.

Bell Toy, "Poodle Dog Bell Ringer", with Clown. Photo by Virginia Caputo. Courtesy James S. Maxwell/Virginia Caputo.

Bell Toy, Trick Pony, GONG BELL CO., 1893. Photo courtesy PB Eighty-Four.

Bell Toy, Trick Elephant, Gong Bell. Photo by Virginia Caputo. Courtesy James S. Maxwell/Virginia Caputo.

Bell Toy, Uncle Sam and the Don. Uncle Sam's bell is missing in photo. Photo by Virginia Caputo. Courtesy James S. Maxwell/Virginia Caputo.

Bell Toy, Monkey Riding Elephant, Fallows.

	C6	C8	C10
Bell Toy, Jack and Jill on seesaw, 7½" long, cast iron and tin, Watrous	500	750	1000
Bell Toy, Jockey on Horse, early, 7½" long	200	300	400
Bell Toy, Jonah & Whale, Hill	650	975	1300
Bell Toy, "Landing of Columbus," 7" long	250	375	500
Bell Toy, Liberty Bell Centennial, Gong Bell Co., 8" long	800	1200	1600
Bell Toy, Monkey and Coconut, N.N. Hill, 6" long "Monkey Mobile"	350	525	700
Bell Toy, "Monkey and Dog," heart wheels, 7" long, cast iron and tin	500	750	1000
Bell Toy, Monkey and Horse, Gong Bell, cast iron and tin, "No. 23"	1500	2250	3000
Bell Toy, Monkey in wheeled chariot (Gong Bell?)	2000	3000	4000

	C6	C8	C10
Bell Toy, Monkey on a Log, cast iron, Gong Bell Mfg. Co., circa 1900.....750		1125	1500
Bell Toy, Monkey on Tricycle, J&E Stevens, 8" high, cast iron 750		1125	1500
Bell Toy, Monkey Riding Elephant, Fallows, 10" long, tin, clockwork.....1400		2100	2800
Bell Toy, Mule kicks bell, No. 42.........600		900	1200
Bell Toy, nursery rhymes on drums, one horse 600		900	1200
Bell Toy, "Oriental Clown & Poodle," No. 44, painted cast iron, 1900, cloth in hoop, 13" long, poodle jumps through hoop and back.......1250		1875	2500
Bell Toy, "Poodle Dog Bell Ringer" with Clown, Gong Bell 900		1350	1800
Bell Toy, Rough Rider, Watrous, 6½" long 90		135	180
Bell Toy, Soldier & Sailor 550		825	1100
Bell Toy, Stevens, "Evening News Baby Quieter," 1890s cast iron, 8" long, man reading paper to baby...2000		3000	4000
Bell Toy, "Teddy Roosevelt" 90		135	180
Bell Toy, Trick Elephant, Gong Bell, 7¾" long.........800		1200	1600
Bell Toy, Trick Pony, Gong Bell Co., 1893, "39," cast iron, 5¼" high 400		600	800
Bell Toy, Uncle Sam and The Don, Gong Bell.........2250		3375	4500
Bell Toy, Victory a shell-form chariot, cast iron, mounted with bell and eagle 1500		2250	3000
Bell Toy, Watermelon, N.N. Hill Brass Co., circa 1905, 8½" long 600		900	1200
Bell Toy, Wild Mule Jack, cast iron 750		1125	1500
Big Boy (Restaurants) vinyl doll............9		14	18
Bilt-E-Z Skyscraper Building Blocks, Scott Manufacturing, Chicago, circa 1925.........90		135	180
Bliss Brooklyn Bridge, 1880s, 4' long x 11" tall, paper litho and stained wood, mechanical 600		900	1200

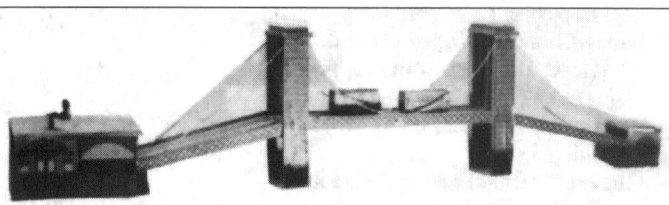

BLISS Brooklyn Bridge. Courtesy Lloyd W. Ralston Auctions.

	C6	C8	C10
Bliss Church building blocks, circa 1900, 8¾" high, litho on wood.........500		750	1000

	C6	C8	C10
Blocks, Auburn Rubber building bricks, 1940s.........25		38	50
Blocks, The Brownie, by McLoughlin Bros., 1891, 20 litho blocks...........375		563	750
Blocks, Chautauqua Architectural Building No. 510, circa 1920s........75		112	150
Block, Crandall's "Building Blocks" No. 3, pat. 1867.........50		85	160
Block, Halsam American Plastic Bricks.........22		33	45
Blocks, Halsam American Blocks, Wood, 1939, No. 60...........55		82	110
Blocks, Halsam Logs, Senior Size ¾", No. 815.........15		22	30
Blocks Leecraft Circus Blocks, 12 wooden blocks, painted with lion, tiger, letters and numbers, contained in wooden pull-toy cage, 1930s .35		52	70
Blocks, Lincoln Logs, Set No. 1A, John Wright, pat. 1920, complete............10		15	20
Blocks, Lincoln Logs set 1C, post WW II 35		52	70
Blocks, Lincoln Logs set 2-L 21		31	42
Blocks, Lincoln Logs set S-C.................7		11	15
Blocks, Lincoln Logs, Set No. 29, early ...60		90	120
Blocks, Lincoln Logs, 1923 10		15	20
Blocks, Lincoln Logs, 1930 12		18	25
Blocks, Lincoln Logs, 1947 12		18	25
Blocks, Lincoln Timbers, pre WW II, with box, complete.........30		45	60

BLISS Church building blocks, circa 1900. Courtesy Wilkinson Collection, Detroit Antique Toy Museum.

Blocks, RICHTER'S ANCHOR BLOCKS No. 7. Courtesy Continental Hobby House.

Bones Player. Courtesy Lloyd W. Ralston Auctions.

Boy on Velocipede. Courtesy Sotheby's New York.

Boy on Velocipede, STEVENS & BROWN. Courtesy Phillips New York.

	C6	C8	C10
Blocks, Richter's Anchor Blocks No. 7....60		90	120
Blocks, Richter's Anchor Blocks, No. 12.........................250		375	500
Blocks, "Stabuilt Blocks," The Embossing Co., 1916, 20x12"..............42		63	85
Blocks, "Union Building Blocks" No. 7, early 75		112	150
Blocks, set of six puzzle blocks depicting The Three Bears, Old Mother Hubbard,, Little Bo-Peep, Puss in Boots, Jack the Giant Killer and Red Riding Hood. Copyright 1892....35		52	70
Blocks, nested, 6, paper litho on cardboard, picturing children and animals, 1920, Cramer Publishing Co. 20		30	40
Blocks, 16, embossed, wooden, 1¾" square, red and blue, alphabet and pictures, 7½" square box, Dutch scene on cover, The Embossing Company's Toy Blocks, USA, price includes box 20		30	40

	C6	C8	C10
Blocks, 64, wooden, 1¼" square, very colorful, letters and numbers on sides, box 6" square, price includes box 22		33	45
Bones Player, Secor, 1880, cloth-dressed, cast iron, wood and tin figure with hair, painted pot metal-head, clockwork mechanism in body 1250		1875	2500
Boo Berry, vinyl squeeze toy 22		33	45
Boxers, Black, mechanical wind-up with Ives clockwork mechanism...1000		1500	2000
Boy climbing windmill, tin, weight driven, 16" high, 1900s..................100		150	200

	C6	C8	C10
Boy on Sled friction toy, rear wheels have spokes	240	360	480
Boy on Tricycle, boy celluloid, trike tin, wind-up	180	270	360
Boy on Velocipede, papier mache, cloth and cast iron, wind up, Stevens & Brown, or Althorp & Bergmann, circa 1870-1880, 10¾" long	500	750	1000
Boy Scout Five-In-One Mystery Hidden Compass	30	45	60
Bradley's Interchangeable Combination Circus in wooden box with label. Patented May 30, 1882. Contains 35 3"x5¼" interchangeable panels which make up a changeable 15¾"x9" circus scene	400	600	800
Brownies, Brownie Glass Candy Container	500	750	1000
Buddy L. tool chests, 1927-28, four different, per each, includes tools	125	187	250
Buffalo Toys "Mother Duck," 1930s wind-up (figure 8s), 9" long	60	90	120

BUFFALO TOYS Mother Duck. Photo by Don Hultzman.

	C6	C8	C10
Bulldog, kid-covered wind-up, walks and turns head, 7½" long, German, rare	200	300	400
Cackling Hen, cardboard, drum, 2¼"x3½", with brown plaster chicken standing on top of drum, metal side handle activates cackling, dated 1936 (also Rooster)	20	30	40
Candy Container, tin, shaped like cannon, candy comes out barrel when crank is turned, "West Bros. Co. Grapeville, PA.," 7½" long	45	68	90
Candy Container shaped like a desk phone, glass base with cast pewter mouthpiece and wooden receiver, paper labels "lines busy," 4¼" high	10	15	20

	C6	C8	C10
Cannon, "Admiral Dewey," cast iron, c. 1890s, 11" long	200	300	400
Cannon, Arcade howitzer, 4" long, c. 1941	20	30	40
Cannon, Auburn Rubber (Aubrubr) Fieldpiece, 75 mm, 7" long	17	25	34
Cannon, Auburn Rubber Howitzer, 155 mm, 7" long	17	25	34
Cannon, Baldwin, No. 890, 16" long, wood and metal	20	30	40
Cannon, Barclay, barrel elevated, 2½" long	6	9	12
Cannon, Barclay, circa 1931 (may be first Barclay cannon, from 1924)	25	38	50

Cannon, BARCLAY, circa 1931 (may be Barclay's earliest, from 1924). Courtesy Ed Poole.

BARCLAY, Left to Right; Top: Cannon, spring-firing, spoked wheels, 4" long, Cannon, barrel elevated, Cannon, spoked wheels, 3" long, Cannon, 7¾" long. Bottom: Coast Defense Rifle, Mortar, heavy, Searchlight. Photo by Ed Poole.

	C6	C8	C10
Cannon, Barclay Coast Defense Rifle, 4½" long, 5-man	45	68	90
Cannon, Barclay, Howitzer, 4 wheels, loop hitch horizontal, 3" long	12	18	25
Cannon, Barclay Howitzer, 4 wheels, loop hitch vertical, 3" long	12	18	25
Cannon, Barclay Mortar, heavy, swivels on base, 3" long	20	30	40
Cannon, Barclay, 4" long, Post WW II, very large wheels	15	22	30
Cannon, Barclay, silver, black rubber wheels, 7¾" long	24	36	48
Cannon, Barclay, spoked wheels, 3" long	6	9	12

Cannon, "Big Bang", approx. 23" long. Photo by Bill Kaufman. Courtesy Good Old Days Store.

	C6	C8	C10
Cannon, Barclay, spring-firing, spoked wheels, 4" long	25	38	50
Cannon, Big Bang, 8½" long	20	30	40
Cannon, Big Bang, 9" long	20	30	40
Cannon, Big Bang, 12" long	30	45	60
Cannon, Big Bang, 13"	30	45	60
Cannon, Big Bang. 16" long	20	30	40
Cannon, Big Bang, No. 10, 18" long	15	22	30
Cannon, Big Bang, 23" long	40	60	80
Cannon, Big Bang, 24" long	37	56	75
Cannon, Big Parade, cast iron	25	38	50
Cannon, "Boy Ranger," fires marbles, cast iron	125	188	250
Cannon, "Boy Scout Machine Gun," 19" with 8¼" wheels	40	60	80
Cannon, C.A.W. Novelty Co., with limber, 6", lead, 2-piece, 1930s	No Price Found		
Cannon, cast iron, 5" long	10	15	20
Cannon, cast iron on wood base, 5½" long	10	15	20
Cannon, cast iron, 6" long	15	22	30
Cannon, cast iron, 6½" long	18	27	36
Cannon, cast iron, 7" long, early	30	45	60
Cannon, cast iron, 7" long, pat. 1894	30	45	60
Cannon, cast iron, 8" long, unusual design	30	45	60
Cannon, cast iron, 9" long, Pat. 1888	40	60	80
Cannon, cast iron with turned barrel, "Hotchkiss," 9½" long	30	45	60
Cannon, cast iron, 10" long, black	32	48	64
Cannon, cast iron, 11" long	40	60	80
Cannon, cast iron, 12" long, Ives?, works on black powder	60	90	120
Cannon, cast iron, 14" long	50	75	100
Cannon, cast iron, 14" long, on 4-wheel platform	100	150	200
Cannon, cast iron, 15½"	30	45	60
Cannon, cast iron, 15½", "Young America," "Rapid Fire Gun"	130	195	260
Cannon, Coast Defense Gun, 5" long, camouflaged, litho tin	30	45	60

	C6	C8	C10
Cannon, "Dainty" cast iron, on wood base, 10" long	175	263	350
Cannon, David Carlin mortar, circa WW I, 15" long, cast iron	60	90	120
Cannon, die cast, approx. 5½" long, old type shoots	10	15	20
Cannon, "Disappearing Coast Defense Gun," Thomas & Skinner, Indianapolis, 15" wood and steel, fires	40	60	80
Cannon, field, World War I, cast iron, 15¾"	32	48	65
Cannon, firecracker, cast iron, 4" long, "Pat. Apr. 23 1895"	40	60	80
Cannon, Grey Iron, 4½" long	12	18	25
Cannon, Howitzer, circa 1930, double-barreled, 9" long, wood-handled firing lever	15	22	30
Cannon, howitzer type, die cast, shoots, approx. 5" long, spring mechanism, pre WW II	12	18	25
Cannon, Ives, muzzle-loader, 1900, cast iron, 2 wheels	150	225	300
Cannon, Ives, cast iron, brass barrel	50	75	100
Cannon, Ives, red wheels, brass cannon, 7" long	125	188	250
Cannon, Kansas Toy "23", 3¼" long, lead	10	15	20
Cannon, Kansas Toy "34", 2¼" long, lead	10	15	20
Cannon, Kenton, Firecracker type	40	60	80
Cannon, Kilgore, 2" cast iron firecracker mortar, rubber cannon ball	40	60	80
Cannon, Kilgore, 4½" cast iron firecracker cannon, rubber cannon ball	50	75	100
Cannon, Manoil 19 Metal Action Cannon, early version, "USA"	25	38	50
Cannon, Manoil 69, metal spoked wheels, early	7	11	15
Cannon, Manoil 69, metal spoked wheels, marked "M" left side, early 2nd version	7	11	15
Cannon, Manoil 69, solid wood wheels	9	13	18
Cannon, Manoil 69, solid wood wheels, variant	9	13	18
Cannon, Manoil, "Metal Action Cannon" No. 200, later version of 19, "Made in USA"	7	11	15
Cannon, Marx, 21" long, litho tin, shoots wooden balls	100	150	200

Cannon, MARX, Howitzer Cannon, 12" long, plastic, c. 1960s.
Photo by Bill Holt.

Cannon, MARX Anti-Aircraft Gun. Courtesy Joe and Sharon Freed.

Cannon, THEODORE HAHN
No. 189.

Cannon, MARX. 21" long, litho tin, shoots wooden balls. Courtesy
Charles D. Richards.

	C6	C8	C10
Cannon, Marx Anti-Aircraft Gun, No. 617 40	60	80	
Cannon, Marx "Atomic Long Range Cannon," 25" long 35	52	70	
Cannon, Marx Howitzer Cannon, 12" long, plastic, circa 1960s..........15	22	30	
Cannon, Marx "Shell Shooting Long Tom Field Cannon, " 1950s, 14" long, plastic..........40	60	80	
Cannon, Marx Twin Pom-Pom anti-aircraft cannon 50	75	100	
Cannon, "Phoenix," 8" long, brass barrel with touch hole 100	150	200	
Cannon, Premier, large thick barrel, large wheels, cast iron.........20	30	40	
Cannon, pressed steel base, 9½" 15	22	30	
Cannon, Ralstoy No. 23 8	12	16	
Cannon, Ralstoy No. 34 8	12	16	
Cannon, Ralstoy 3¾" long 8	12	16	
Cannon, Ranger Jr. cast iron, 10" long.125	188	250	
Cannon, rapid fire, cast iron, embossed eagle 200	300	400	
Cannon, "Remember The Maine," W.S. Hawkes Foundry, Dayton, Ohio, 13" long, circa 1900.........120	180	240	
Cannon, sheetmetal, shoots small marbles, 14" long, blue with red wheels 30	45	60	
Cannon, Theodore Hahn, No. 189, 1920s, lead alloy ....No Price Found			

	C6	C8	C10
Cannon, tin, pull lever for corks, 14" wood wheels 20	30	40	
Cannon, tin, striped spring-loaded barrel with lever 20	30	40	
Cannon, tin, two-wheel, 7¼", 4" high, circa 1915.........30	45	60	
Cannon, tinplate, 7" long, spring action, 1950s, Japan.........20	30	40	
Cannon, Tootsietoy, approx, 3¾" long, pre WW II, shoots.........10	15	20	
Cannon, Tootsietoy, 40 MM AA gun, pre WW II 10	15	20	
Cannon, Tootsietoy, 155 MM gun, pre WW II 20	30	40	
Cannon, Tootsietoy, 155 MM self-propelled howitzer, 1950s.........20	30	40	
Cannon, Tootsietoy, 1930s, approx. 5½" long, shoots 30	45	60	
Cannon, Wyandotte, shoots marbles, 14" 40	60	80	
Canoe, Kansas Toy and Novelty, slush lead, "50", two paddling Indians "Rain-In-The-Face" and "Chief Big Foot," 4 wheels, 3½" long ....No Price Found			

Carousel, ALTHOF BERGMANN, 1870. Courtesy LLoyd W. Ralston Auctions.

	C6	C8	C10
Carousel, Althof Bergmann, 1870, painted tin, wood base, cloth canopy, 20" tall, clockwork, bisque head doll, wood body, tin arms, turns, cranks and gives motion	1500	2250	3000
Carpet Sweeper, miniature Bissell	12	18	24
Cat, cardboard, standing on piece of wood, circa 1900	3	4	6
Catalog: Aldens Xmas 1946	45	68	90
Catalog: Arcade 1931	125	188	250
Catalog: Auburn Rubber, pre WW II	50	75	100
Catalog: Baltimore Price Reducer, 1928, illustrated with toys, games, etc.	15	22	30
Catalog: Barclay, pre-WW II	200	300	400
Catalog: Bilt E-Z, 1924	5.00	7.50	10.00
Catalog: Butler Bros. 1889, tin toys, squeak toys, etc.	30	45	60
Catalog: Butler Bros. 1891, illustrated with mechanical banks, toys, dolls etc	30	45	60
Catalog: Butler Bros., Nov. 1899	40	60	80
Catalog: Butler Bros., Xmas 1930	35	52	70
Catalog: Carpenter, Francis, 1880s	900	1350	1800
Catalog: Daisy, 1975	22	33	45
Catalog: Dent Hardware Co., 1900, 40 pages	40	60	80
Catalog: Dent Hardware Co., 1905	30	45	60
Catalog: Dent Hardware, circa 1910	15	22	30
Catalog: Dent Hardware Co., Fullerton, Pa., undated	30	45	60
Catalog: Dent Hardware Co., Fullerton, Pa., iron toys, 1930	32	48	65
Catalog: "Dunham," Buckley & Co., New York, 1895, toys, etc.	40	60	80
Catalog: Ehrich Bros. New York, 1892, illus. of banks, toys, dolls, etc.	40	60	80
Catalog: Erector Set, 1938, 38 pp.	15	22	30
Catalog: Eureka Trick & Novelty Co., circa 1875, 32 pages	20	30	40

	C6	C8	C10
Catalog: A.J. Fisher, N.Y. 1877, illustrating cap pistols, etc.	18	27	36
Catalog: Gendron, 1927	600	900	1200
Catalog: Gong Bell, 1912	85	128	170
Catalog: Hasbro, 1975	27	41	55
Catalog: Hubley, 1974	22	33	45
Catalog: Ives, Blakeslee & Williams, two-sided broadside, circa 1890, 18x24"	70	105	140
Catalog: Ives Yachts, Ships and Shipping circa 1915, 24 pages	50	75	100
Catalog: Illustrated brochure of cap pistols and animated cap pistols by Ives and Williams	20	30	40
Catalog: Kenton Hardware Co., No. 16, 1920s, 112 pages	80	120	160
Catalog: Kenton Hardware Co., 1934, illus. in color	100	150	200
Catalog: Kilgore 1977-78	22	33	45
Catalog: Kingsbury Toys, Motor Driven, 1936, 16 pages	60	90	120
Catalog: Knapp Electric Toys No. 35	10	15	20
Catalog: Manoil, circa 1935-1939	100	150	200
Catalog: Matchbox, 1966	5	7.50	10
Catalog: Matchbox, 1968	4	6	8
Catalog: Matchbox, 1969	3	4.50	6
Catalog: Matchbox, 1970	2.50	3.75	5
Catalog: "McCadden & Bros." Philadelphia, illustrated iron and tin toys, banks, mechanical toys, dolls, games, etc.	50	75	100
Catalog: Mickey Mouse Merchandise Catalog, 1935, by Kay Kamen Co., 80 pages, hundred of illustrations of Mickey Mouse items	300	450	600
Catalog: Montgomery Ward, 1935 Xmas	150	225	300
Catalog: Montgomery Ward, 1955, each	45	68	90
Catalog: Montgomery Ward, 1941-1955, each	45	68	90
Catalog: Montgomery Ward, 1959	32	48	65
Catalog: Montgomery Ward, 1961	35	52	70
Catalog: Montgomery Ward, 1962	37	56	75
Catalog: Montgomery Ward, 1966	50	75	100
Catalog: Montgomery Ward, 1968	40	60	80
Catalog: Montgomery Ward, 1969	30	45	60
Catalog: Montgomery Ward, 1970	30	45	60
Catalog: Montgomery Ward, Xmas 1976	40	60	80
Catalog: Montgomery Ward, 1977	37	56	75
Catalog: Nicol & Co, 1895, illustrating banks, etc.	10	15	20
Catalog: Penney's Xmas 1964,65 each	.62	93	125
Catalog: Penney's Xmas 1971-75, each	20	30	40
Catalog: Popsicle Pete Radio News and Premium catalog, early	40	60	80

	C6	C8	C10
Catalog: Popsicle Pete's 1949 four-page gift list	10	15	20
Catalog: Schoenhut, 1903	100	150	200
Catalog: Schoenhut 1918	80	120	160
Catalog: Schoenhut Circus, 1928	100	150	200
Catalog: Schoenhut Humpty Dumpty Circus Toys (other toys as well), circa 1915, many illustrations	100	165	220
Catalog: Sears, 1943, 1945, 1946, 1948, 1949, 1951, 1952, 1955, each	45	68	90
Catalog: Sears, 1956, 1959, 1967, each	50	75	100
Catalog: Sears, 1961-65, each	60	90	120
Catalog: Sears, 1968-70, each	32	48	65
Catalog: Sears, 1971-75, each	20	30	40
Catalog: Selchow & Righter, 1894-5, games and toys, illustrated trains, boats, bell toys, mechanical banks, etc.	120	180	240
Catalog: Selchow & Righter, 1908-1909, 108 pages	80	120	160
Catalog: Selchow & Righter, 1921	32	48	65
Catalog: Smith-Miller (Smitty) 1954	40	60	80
Catalog: State, Adams & Dearborn Sts., Chicago, illustrated	10	15	20
Catalog: Carl P. Stern, illustrating cap pistols, etc.	15	22	30
Catalog: J.E. Stevens Co., 1906, illustrations of iron toys and mechanical banks	40	60	80
Catalog: J.E. Stevens Co., No. 51, Export	40	60	80
Catalog: Structo Toys, 1931, 8 pages	10	15	20
Catalog: Supplee-Biddle of Philadelphia, 1930, 174 pages, many toys	90	135	180
Catalog: Thorsen & Cassady, 1894, guns, etc.	20	30	40
Catalog: Tom Mix 1936 Premium Catalog	30	45	60
Catalog: A.C. Williams Co., Ohio, illustrating still banks, cast iron toys, airplanes, etc.	100	150	200
Catalog, Walt Disney Character Merchandise, 1930s	250	375	500
Catalog: Walt Disney Character Merchandise 1940-41	250	375	500
Catalog: Woolworth's Christmas Catalogs, pre WW II	30	45	60
Catalog: Woolworth's Christmas 1951	30	45	60
Cathedral Music Box, tin litho, of organ pipes and cherubs, plays loud or soft according to speed of			

Catalog: SMITH-MILLER (Smitty), 1954. Photo by Bill Kaufman. Courtesy Ray Funk.

	C6	C8	C10
cranking, 5x5x7" no markings, German	100	150	200
Charlie Tuna rubber squeeze toy	20	30	40
Chein "Busy Mike," sand seesaw, 7½" high, 1940s	90	135	180
Chein Cathedral Organ	70	105	140
Chein Drum, 6"x3½"	17	26	35
Chein Easter Egg with chicken on top, opens up to hold candy, circa 1938, tin, 5½"	15	22	30
Chein Sand Pail, 7" diameter, circa early 1940s	22	33	45
Chein "Sand Loader"	75	112	150
Chein Sand-Toy, monkey bends and twists, 7" high	20	30	40
Chein Windmill sand toy, tin litho, 8" high	15	22	30
Chemcraft No. 5 Chemistry Set, wooden box	37	56	75
Chemcraft No. 418 Master Deluxe Laboratory, wooden box	175	263	350
Chemcraft Beginners Chemistry Set No. 602 by Porter, 1956	12	18	25
Chicago Printing Press, No. 15, complete	20	30	40
Children's Telephone (set of two), 1920	10	15	20
Chimes Bell-Ringer with Elephant, 7" long	40	60	80
Climbing Monkey brings coconuts down from palm tree, tin, 18" high, "Monkey Shines, Emporium Specialists"	60	90	120
Clown, balancing, copper, clown holding arched balancing pole weighted at both ends with lead balls, standing on one leg on small round platform on stationary metal ladder 6½" high. Move clown in any direction and he won't fall off platform	50	75	100

CHEIN "Busy Mike" sand seesaw. Courtesy Calvin L. Chaussee

Clown, balancing on pedestal, painted wood, circa 1920, 15" high Courtesy Mapes Auctioneers & Appraisers

	C6	C8	C10
Clown, balancing on pedestal, painted wood, circa 1920, 15" high	100	150	200
Clown, clockwork, early, cloth suit, 9½" high, German	300	450	600
Clown, wind-up, papier mache and cardboard, 43" high	90	135	180
Coffee Grinder, cast iron, 4" high	40	60	80
Cohn T. Inc. - "Superior Space Port No. 75", 1950s, 17" long, playset includes: space drome, space cannon and plastic accessories	350	525	700
"Consul," the educated monkey, tin hand toy, monkey automatically adds, subtracts, multiplies and divides, 5½"x6", dated June 27, 1916	40	60	80
Cot, Army, canvas with steel frame, circa early 1940s	8	12	17
Count Chocula, rubber squeeze toy	22	33	45

COURTLAND TOYS
(Numerical Order)
List by Joe and Sharon Freed

	C6	C8	C10
800 Zylo-P-ano. 13¼" long, 5½" wide, 1946 retail - 79¢; 1947 retail - 69¢	35	65	100
1000 Walt Reach Toys G-Man Pocket Siren Signal, 3½" long, 2⅜" wide, 1¾" high	20	25	35
1050 Courtland Walt Reach Toys Halloween Pocket Siren Signal, 3½" long, 2⅜" wide, 1¾" high	30	40	55
1060 Courtland Walt Reach Toys New Years Pocket Siren Signal, 3½" long, 2⅜" wide, 1¾" high	20	25	35
9000 Mechanical 3 pc. Train set, 24" long, 2¼" wide, 3¼" high	65	800	100
9050 Fire Department with automatic garage door. 7¾" x 10⅛"x6¾", found to have a non-powered fire chief car with the Courtland Toy Co., Phila. Pa., markings, it is quite possible that some of the 9050 garages were also manufactured in Philadelphia	25	35	45
9075 Private Garage with automatic door, 7¾"x10⅛"x6¾". Since the non-powered car which accompanies this garage is found with Courtland Toy Co., Phila. Pa. markings, it is quite possible that some of the 9075 garages were also manufactured in Philadelphia	15	25	35

COURTLAND 9050 Fire Department. Courtesy Joe and Sharon Freed.

Cozzone Construction Set #500. Courtesy Lawrence Giancola.

COZZONE

(from information developed by Larry Giancola)

The Cozzone Corporation was founded by John A. Cozzone during the 1930s. The company made fishing reels, and during WWII components for incendiary bombs, etc. Located at 18 Nuttman Street in Newark, NJ, the firm decided to diversify after the war, and spent a great deal of money developing a construction set. Although a number of different sets were pictured in the firm's catalog, only the No. 500 was actually produced. Production seems to have been in the 1948-1950 period. A crayoned price of $12.99 on a surviving set suggests the very high price for the time is why relatively few sets were sold. John Cozzone died in 1968 and his son Tom took over, changing the name to Tomrette Corp. However, toymaking by the family seems to have begun and ended with the construction set.

	C6	C8	C10
Cozzone No. 500 Construction Set, machined metal parts, electric motor, in box	200	300	400
Crackle (Kellogg's Rice Krispies) hand-puppet	7	11	15
Crackle (Kellogg's Rice Krispies) squeeze toy, 8½"	10	15	20

CRANDALL

At 16, Charles M. Crandall took over his family's woodworking business after the death in 1849 of his father. Crandall made croquet sets after the Civil War. They were packed in thin wooden boxes that had tongue-and-groove corners. When his boys were ill, he took home a bag of the grooved scraps. The buildings they made with them inspired "Crandall Building Blocks". The success of the interlocking blocks led to production of "Acrobats", with grooved parts. Crandall, who died in 1905, produced toys into the turn of the century.

CRANDALL; "Crandall's District School". Courtesy Wilkinson Collection, Detroit Antique Toy Museum.

	C6	C8	C10
Crandall "Crandall's District School," circa 1875	412	618	825
Crandall "John Gilpin's Ride"	200	300	400
Crandall, Man in Cap on Donkey, wheeled pull toy	275	413	550
Crandall Masquerade Blocks	320	528	976
Crandall Menagerie	500	800	1200
Creepy Crawler Maker Pak No. 2, Mattel	40	60	80
Cupboard, cast iron, open work has diamond and heart pattern, two doors and one drawer	40	60	80
Dancers, black, Automatic Toy Works, New York City, 1870, on box, clockwork, carved wood and jesso bodies, clothes, 6¼"w x 10¼"t	600	900	1200

Dancers, black, AUTOMATIC TOY WORKS, 1870. Courtesy Lloyd W. Ralston Auctions

	C6	C8	C10
"Davy Crockett Alamo Express Fix-It Stage Coach," 1950s, Ideal, 13" long push toy	62	93	125
Davy Crockett Indian Target set by Keystone Wood Company. David Crockett rifle, all wood and hard-			

	C6	C8	C10

board litho set that pre-dates Davy popularity of the 50s, made about 1949. Wood stagecoach and horses, wood covered wagon and horses, Indians, bear, etc 40 60 80

Doctor's Set, Transogram, 1948, Little Country Doctor, full doctor set, chest and bag...................................32 48 65

Do-Do Toy Co. - "Do-Do Clown", 1930's, 5½" long, squeeze toy 70 105 140

Doepke No. W-11 Freddie Fireplug, wooden, comes apart....................No Price Found

Dragon, lead alloy, 2⅝" long, Kansas Toy, circa 1920s, early 1930s......No Price Found

Drum, Indian motif, tin litho, 11¾" diameter 175 263 350

Ferris Wheel, "DRGM", 11H" high. First bought in 1895. Courtesy Calvin L. Chaussee.

Drum, Indian Motif, tin litho, 11¾" diameter. Courtesy James S. Maxwell/Virginia Caputo. Photo by Virginia Caputo.

Drum, metal body, litho, red white and blue design, varnished wooden hoops, leather "ears," sheepskin head and fiber bottom, with wooden drumsticks, circa 1910 ......20 30 40

Drum, about 1920, circus decor, tin litho .40 60 80

Drum, 13" diameter, metal with drumsticks..10 15 20

Drum, 13" diameter, wooden, with harness 10 15 20

Duncan Yoyo, 1960s 6 9 12

Electric Stove, works, 1930s 42 63 85

Emenee Accordion 25 38 50

Fallows Elephant on Rocker, 8" long, tin, circa 475 712 950

Ferris Wheel, "DRGM," 11½" high, four figures, tin, 1895 ....1400 2100 2800

Flagpole, wooden, with flag that raises and lowers, approx. 8" high 10 15 20

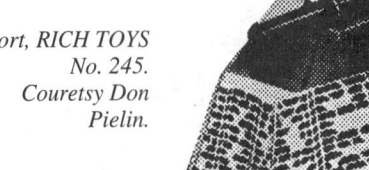

Fort, RICH TOYS No. 245. Couretsy Don Pielin.

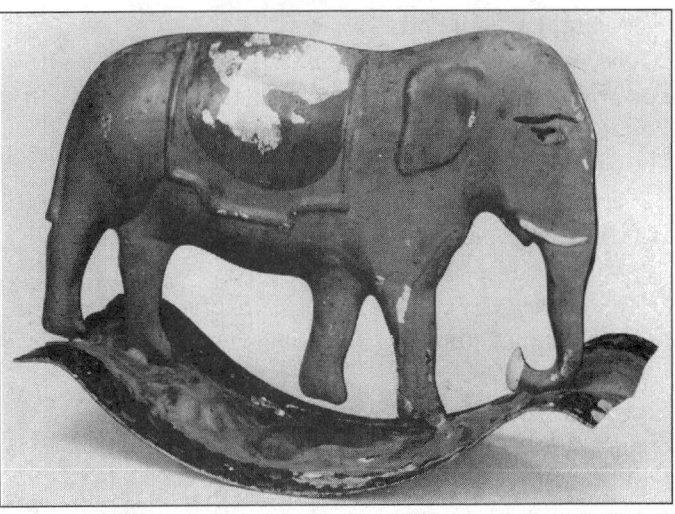

FALLOWS, Elephant on Rocker. Courtesy Wilkinson Collection, Detroit Antique Toy Museum.

	C6	C8	C10

Flying Propeller Ring, heavy metal, circa 1930s-40s, could have been a premium 10 15 20

Fort, Keystone No. 523 U.S. Coast Defense Fort...................................35 50 70

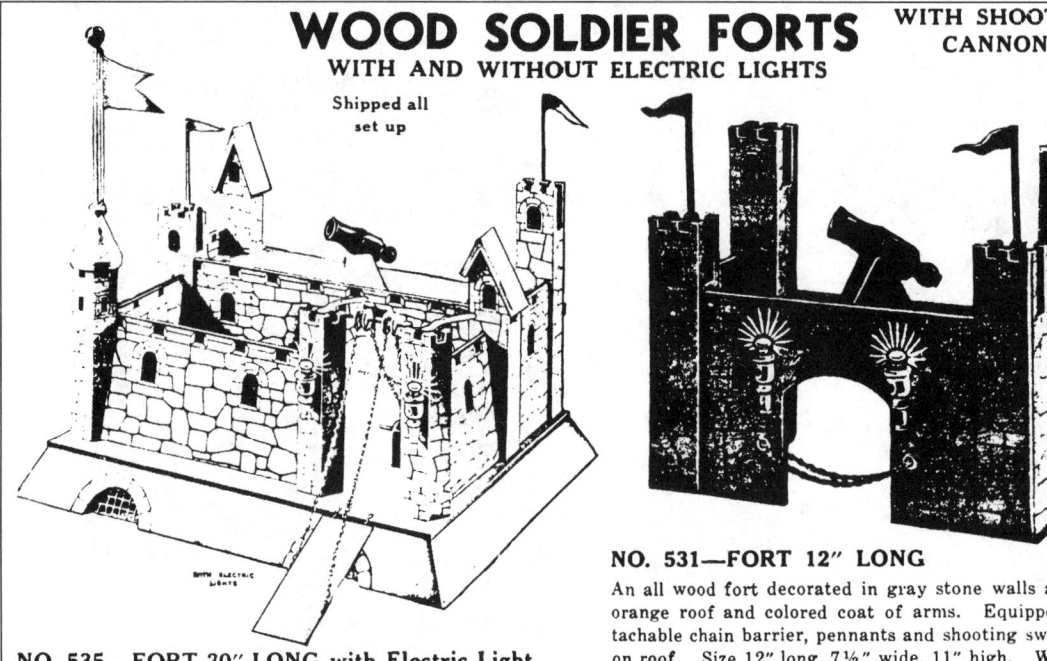

WOOD SOLDIER FORTS
WITH SHOOTING CANNONS
WITH AND WITHOUT ELECTRIC LIGHTS

Shipped all set up

Forts by KEYSTONE, showing No. 535 and 533. Original catalog illustration courtesy Ron Fink.

NO. 535—FORT 20″ LONG with Electric Light
An all wood fort mounted on wood base, decorated in gray stone walls and towers, green base, orange roof and colored turrets tops and shield. Equipped with draw-bridge, winch, swivel shooting cannon, pennants, movable flag, fire step in court yard, moat gratings and electric entrance lamps connected to batteries and operated by switch in tower tops. Size: 20″ long, 17″ wide and 19″ high. Weight when packed in Mullen-test carton 12 lbs. No battery furnished.

NO. 531—FORT 12″ LONG
An all wood fort decorated in gray stone walls and towers, orange roof and colored coat of arms. Equipped with detachable chain barrier, pennants and shooting swivel cannon on roof. Size 12″ long, 7½″ wide, 11″ high. Weight when packed for shipment 4 lbs.

NO. 533—FORT with Electric Light
Same as No. 531 with **electric entrance lamps** connected to battery and operated by switch on the roof. Weight when packed in Mullen-test carton 5 lbs. No battery furnished.

KEYSTONE MFG. CO., BOSTON, MASS.   New York Showroom, 200 Fifth Avenue

	C6	C8	C10
Fort, Keystone No. 525 U.S. Coast Defense Fort, with accessories, circa 1942	40	55	80
Fort, Keystone No. 527 U.S. Coast Guard Defense Fort, with accessories, circa 1942	40	70	100
Fort, Keystone No. 531, 12″ long	40	60	85
Fort, Keystone No. 533, same as 531, but two electric lights at entrance	50	75	100
Fort, Keystone No. 535, 20″ long, with two electric lights at entrance	60	90	120
Fort, Keystone Exploding Fort with Shooting Tank	46	69	92
Fort, Rich Toys No. 245 Siege Gun with Stone Fort	25	40	75
Fort, Rich Toys No. 246 Siege Gun with Stone Fort, two guns	30	50	80
Fort, Rich Toys No. 247 Siege Gun with stone fort, three guns	40	60	80
Fort, Rich Toys No. 260, 26¾″ long	35	50	75
Fort, Rich Toys No. 261, 26½″ long	50	75	100
Fort, Rich Toys No. 262, 27″ long	100	200	300
Fort, Rich Toys No. 263, 29″ long	275	363	550
Frankenberry vinyl squeeze toy	20	30	40
Froggie, rubber squeeze toy, Rempel, 1940s	12	18	24

	C6	C8	C10
Fruit Brute, rubber squeeze toy	22	33	45
Gibbs Service Station No. 81, 1930s	350	525	700
Girard "Knife Sharpener," crank action, 8″ high, 1930s	60	90	120
Glass Candy Container, shaped like Biplane	500	750	1000
Glass Candy Container shaped like dog	100	150	200
Glass Candy Container, Dolly's milk bottle	4	6	8
Glass Candy Container, shaped like rabbit, Victory Glass	50	75	100
Glass Candy Container, shaped like train engine, 3″ long	20	30	40
Glass Candy Container shaped like a train lantern, 3½″ high	20	30	40
Glass Candy Container, Stop and Go, glass, etc. traffic signal	100	150	200
Glass Candy Container, shaped like a train lantern, tin top and base, "Victory Glass Inc.", 3½″ high	20	30	40
Glass Candy Container, shaped like Zeppelin	100	150	200
Grandfather's Clock, tin, has weights that make hands rotate and pendulum swing, but is not a working clock, transfer decorated, 8¾″ high	40	60	80

KEYSTONE U. S. COAST DEFENSE FORTS

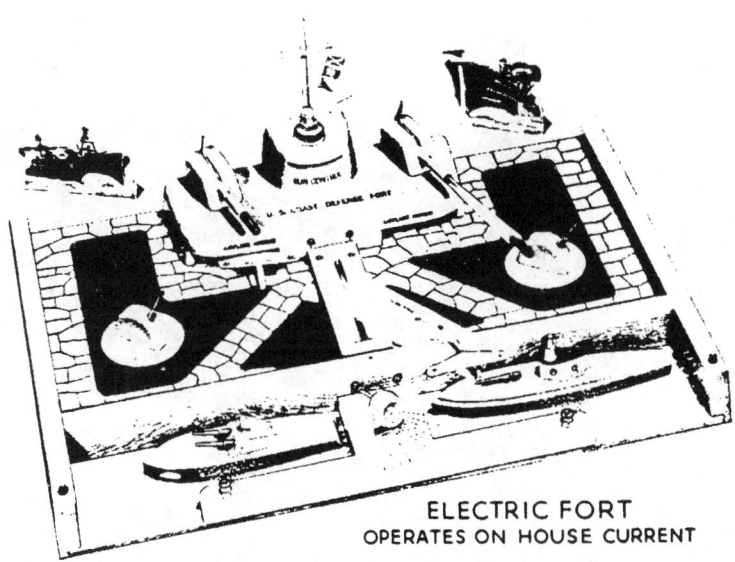

ELECTRIC FORT
OPERATES ON HOUSE CURRENT

- *Planes That Fly!*
- *Swivel Guns That Shoot!*
- *Electric Flashing Signals!*
- *Electric Searchlight!*
- *Electric Pier Lights!*
- *Turret Guns That Turn!*
- *Two Boats That Float!*
- *Two Airplane Hangars!*
- *Soldier Housing in Rear!*
- *Played From Front or Back With or Without Soldiers!*

No. 527 — U. S. COAST DEFENSE FORT

Two Flying Planes operated with catapult. *Pier and signal lights work off regular house current A.C.* Target and patrol ships and shells furnished for shooting cannons. Made of wood and fibre board. No assembling. Finished in gray, tan, green base and blue trim. Each boxed in shipping carton. Weight 175 lbs. per dozen. Size 24 x 17.

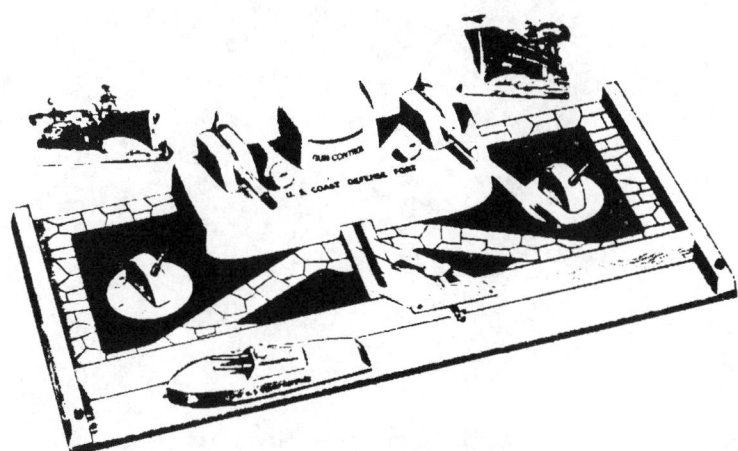

- *Plane That Flies!*
- *Swivel Guns That Shoot!*
- *Turret Guns That Turn!*
- *Boat That Floats!*
- *Soldier Housing in Rear!*
- *Battleship Target for Cannons!*
- *Play From Front or Rear With or Without Soldiers!*

No. 525 — U. S. COAST DEFENSE FORT

One Flying Plane operated with catapult. Target and scout ship and shells furnished for shooting cannons. Made of wood and fibre board. No assembling. Size 24 x 12. Finished in gray, tan, green and blue trim. Each in shipping carton. Weight 65 lbs. per dozen.

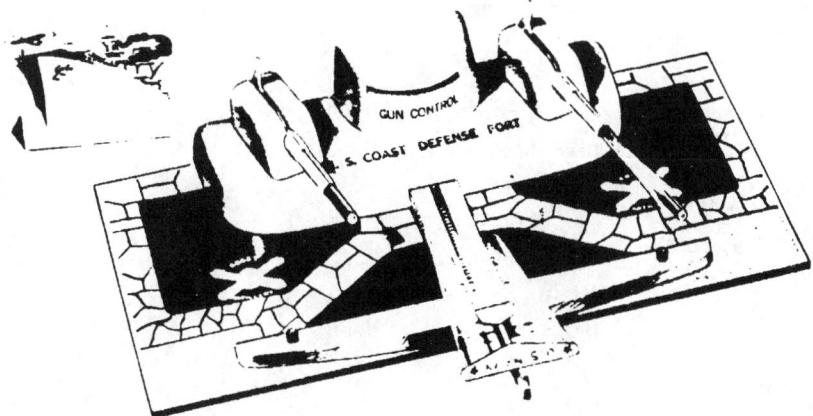

- *Plane That Flies!*
- *Swivel Guns That Shoot!*
- *Soldier Housing in Rear!*
- *Battleship Target for Cannons!*
- *Played From Front or Rear With or Without Soldiers!*

No. 523
U. S. COAST DEFENSE FORT

All wood and fibre board fort 16" x 8". Equipped with flying plane and catapult, ship target and shells for swivel shooting guns. All assembled each in a carton. Colors same as other models. Weight 30 lbs. per dozen.

KEYSTONE MFG. CO., BOSTON, MASS.
NEW YORK SHOW ROOM, 200 FIFTH AVENUE

Fort, RICH TOYS No. 260. Courtesy Ron Fink.

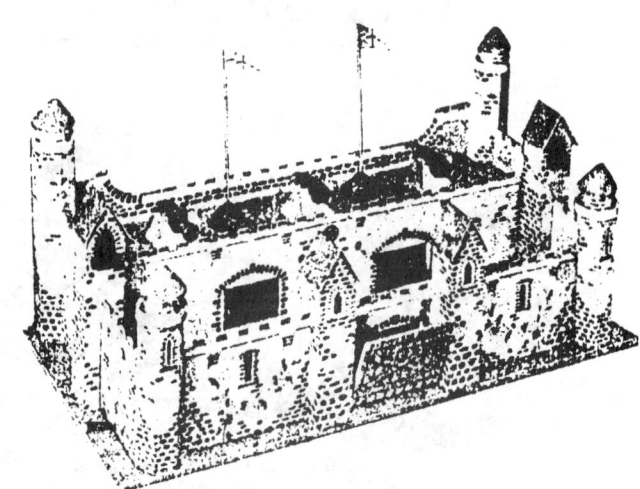

Fort, RICH TOYS NO. 262. Courtesy Ron Fink

Fort, RICH TOYS No. 261. Courtesy Ron Fink

Fort, RICH TOYS No. 263. Courtesy Ron Fink

GREY IRON Clever Clowns.

	C6	C8	C10
Grey Iron Automatic Cap Machine Gun, 9" long	75	112	150
Grey Iron Clever Clowns Trapeze Set	150	225	300
Grey Iron, Clever Clowns largest set	500	750	1000
Grocery Store, tin, 14", scales, cash register, wrapping paper, order pad and pencil, "Little Toy Town Grocery Store," shelves with small boxes of products	100	150	200
Grocery Store, wood, "Pet's Grocery Store"	400	600	800

	C6	C8	C10
H.K. Electric Engine, patented 1908, uses D.C. current	50	75	100
Handwashing Machine with wringer	10	15	20
Hasbro Mr. Potato Head No. 2000	31	46	62
Hasbro, "Mr. Potato Head," 1950s, plastic car and boat trailer, plus all the parts to create different faces	50	75	100
Hasbro Mrs. Potato Head with car	6	9	12
Hobby Horse, "Black Beauty," wooden, 34" long	25	37	50
Horse, American painted tin, 1870, 4½" long	175	263	350
Horse in Hoop, George Brown, early	400	600	800
Horse, sheet metal, with cast iron jointed legs, full form, 10¾" long, 11" high	200	300	400
Horse Race, circular track within rectangular box, circa 1900, lever-activated	100	150	200

Horse, American painted tin, 1870, 4½" long. Courtesy Lloyd W. Ralston

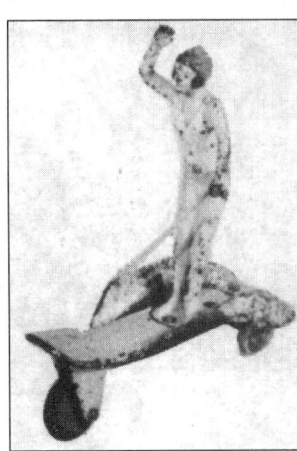

HUBLEY Jantzen Surf Girl. Photo Courtesy Lloyd W. Ralston.

Horses in Hoops, ALTHOF BERGMANN. Courtesy Lloyd W. Ralston Actions

HUBLEY Grasshopper, 1929.

1F3083 — Grasshopper, 9¼ in., green enameled body & legs, brown shaded, black eyes & mouth, green wire feelers, red enameled wheels, rubber tires, life-like action, ratchet produces cricket noise, cord, bead grip. ⅙ doz. in box.

HUBLEY Ferris Wheel, early.

HUBLEY Monkey Riding Tricycle. Courtesy James S. Maxwell/Virginia Caputo. Photo by Virginia Caputo.

HASBRO "Mr. Potato Head", early.

Glass Candy Containers, as seen in a December, 1929, BUTLER BROS. Catalog.

	C6	C8	C10
Horses in Hoops, Althof Bergmann, American painted tin, 1880, 4½" diameter	800	1200	1600
Hubley Ferris Wheel, early, cast iron, brass and tin, clockwork, 17" high	1750	2625	3500
Hubley grasshopper pull toy, cast iron	400	600	800
Hubley Jantzen Beach Patrol, 8" long, circa 1932, man on surfboard riding through waves	750	1125	1500
Hubley Jantzen Surf Girl, 8" long, 1932, girl surf-board rider, cast iron	1000	1500	2000
Hubley Jumbo the Elephant, on wheels	25	37	50
Hubley Marathon Rider (bicyclist) cast iron	300	450	600
Hubley Monkey Riding Tricycle, cast iron, aluminum, 6¼" long	800	1300	1750
Hubley Old Dutch Cleanser Woman, cast iron	750	1125	1500
Hurdy-Gurdy, turn crank and play tune, shows animal playing cello	30	45	60
Ice Box, "Alaska" cast iron, has glass cube of ice in top, 5" high	30	45	60

IVES Preacher. Courtesy Sotheby's New York.

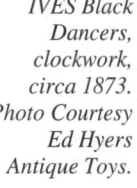

IVES Black Dancers, clockwork, circa 1873. Photo Courtesy Ed Hyers Antique Toys.

IVES, BLAKESLEY & WILLIAMS Mule Dancers. Courtesy Lloyd W. Ralston Auctions

IVES Strukt-iron set, 1915. Courtesy Lloyd W. Ralston Auctions

IVES Mechanical Bear. Courtesy PB Eighty-Four, New York

	C6	C8	C10
Ideal "Mr. Machine," first version, can be taken apart and put together, 18" high	175	263	350
Ideal "Mr. Machine" 1972 version, whistles, 17½" high	32	48	65
Ideal "Mr. Machine" 1977 version	17	26	35
Iron and Trivet, cast iron	20	30	40
Iron, tin, 5" high	7.50	11.25	15.00
Iron, tin, 3½" high	10	15	20
Irwin "Round-Up Tex the Whirling Cowboy," plastic wind-up, 1950s, 10" high	40	60	80
Ives Acrobat, 10½" high overall, hand over hand	2000	3000	4000
Ives Automatic Toy Boxers, circa 1876, 11" high	5000	7500	10,000
Ives Automatic Dancer Circus Rider, standing on horse, 15" high,			

	C6	C8	C10
auctioned in 1991 in excellent to near mint condition for $38,500.			
Ives "Autoperipateticos" walking doll	700	1050	1400
Ives Barrel Walkers, circa 1890, wood and paper litho balance toy, acrobat, ballerina, monkey	200	300	400
Ives Black Dancers circa 1873	2400	3600	4800
Ives Black Dancers, clockwork, circa 1880, 11" high	750	1125	1500
Ives Black Mechanical Walking Man, circa 1875, 9½" high	1400	2100	2800
Ives Boy on Rocking Horse, circa 1874, wood and tin, 8½" high, auctioned in 1991 in excellent condition for $57,200			

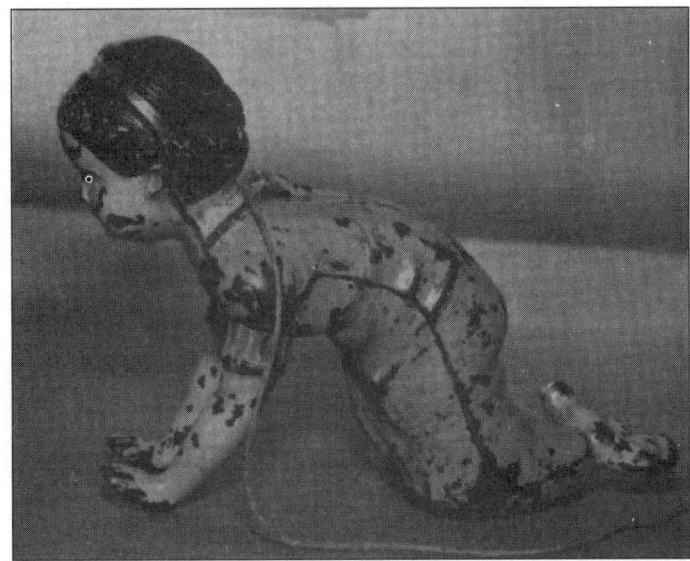

IVES "Crawling Baby," 1893. Courtesy Ed Hyers Antique Toys.

IVES General Grant, Smoking. Courtesy Sotheby's New York.

IVES Crawling Baby, circa 1871. Courtesy Phillips New York.

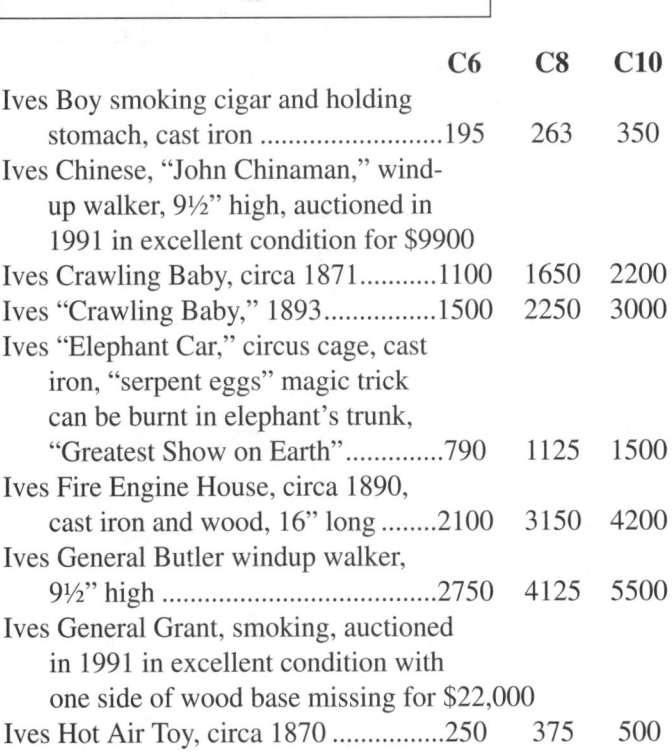

	C6	C8	C10
Ives Boy smoking cigar and holding stomach, cast iron	195	263	350
Ives Chinese, "John Chinaman," wind-up walker, 9½" high, auctioned in 1991 in excellent condition for $9900			
Ives Crawling Baby, circa 1871	1100	1650	2200
Ives "Crawling Baby," 1893	1500	2250	3000
Ives "Elephant Car," circus cage, cast iron, "serpent eggs" magic trick can be burnt in elephant's trunk, "Greatest Show on Earth"	790	1125	1500
Ives Fire Engine House, circa 1890, cast iron and wood, 16" long	2100	3150	4200
Ives General Butler windup walker, 9½" high	2750	4125	5500
Ives General Grant, smoking, auctioned in 1991 in excellent condition with one side of wood base missing for $22,000			
Ives Hot Air Toy, circa 1870	250	375	500

Uncle Tom Walking Toy, IVES? Circa 1875. Courtesy Phillips New York.

Uncle Tom Walking Toy, IVES? Variation. Courtesy Phillips New York.

	C6	C8	C10
Ives Jackass windup walker, 9½" high, auctioned in 1991 in very good condition, missing one hand, for $22,000			

Jones Animals. Left to Right, Top: J50, J51, J52; Bottom: J53, J54, J55, J56.

Jones Animals. Left to Right, Top: J42, J43, J44, J45; Bottom: J46, J47, J48, J49.

"Kid Flyer".
Courtesy PB 84 NY.

Jones Pillbox.

	C6	C8	C10
Ives Judge, clockwork, circa 1880	1500	2300	3500
Ives Juggler, clockwork, early	1000	1500	2000
Ives Mechanical Bear, patent 1872	600	900	1200
Ives Mechanical Performing Monkey, 5½" high, No. 49-10	2250	3375	4500
Ives Old Woman in a Shoe, 9" long, pull toy	3000	4500	6000
Ives Platform Horse, 9½" long pulltoy	1400	2100	2800
Ives Preacher, clockwork, 10½" high, auctioned in December, 1990 for$2750			
Ives Rower, 13" long, "Pat. Feb. 9", "U.S. Grant" auctioned in 1991 in excellent condition for $7150.			
Ives Rower, 13" long, 2 drive wheels protrude from bottom, wheel attached to rudder, auctioned in 1991 in very good to excellent condition, lacking tin hands for $8250			
Ives See-Saw, 18" long, auctioned in 1991 in excellent condition with one upper leg replaced for $13,200			
Ives Scottish Jigger	1250	1875	2500
Ives Struktiron set, 1915	100	150	200
Ives Struktiron, 1916, nonmotorized, with box	75	112	150
Ives Walking Elephant, "pat. 1873," cast iron, 3½" long, walks down incline, moving legs and trunk	225	337	450

	C6	C8	C10
Ives Walking Horse, 10" long, circa 1890s	No Price Found		
Ives Zouave windup walker, 10½" high	1500	2250	3000
Ives, Blakesley & Williams, 1890, Mule Dancers, mechanical revolving, paper litho, painted tin, wooden box, clockwork, 8" tall	1600	2400	3200
Jane Francis "Gulf Truck Service" Station	500	750	1000
"Jolly Jungleers," Milton Bradley, 1932, derringer type pistol shoots over animal targets	40	60	80
Jones Animals, hollow lead, average price each	5	8	11
Jones Pillbox, lead alloy	37	56	75
Jumping Jack, composition and wood	70	105	140
Junior WAC set, Hassenfeld Bros., hats, gas mask, bandages, etc	40	60	80
Junior G-Man Whistle	20	30	40
Kaleidoscope "C. Bush, Prov. R.I. 1874," wood, brass & glass, 14" high	220	330	440
Kaleidoscope, Stevens, 1950s	10	15	20
Kangaroo, cast iron, 6¼" long, "Jumps"	125	187	250
Kenner Easy Bake oven, 1960s	10	15	20
Kenner Give A Show Projector, 112 slides	22	33	45
Kenton Baggage Cart, 6"	30	45	60
Kenton Drag Wagon, lithographed paper on sides, driver, 15½" long	200	300	400
Kenton Egyptian Toys - Rhino, Lion, Elephant, offered at $175 each, condition unspecified			
Kenton Elephant - "Land-on Roosevelt 1936"	80	120	160

	C6	C8	C10
Kenton Stove, cast iron, marked "Oak" on door	30	45	60
Kenton Stove, with warming shelves and stove plates, high back for smokestack, "Royal" on door and shelves, 10" high	40	60	80
Keystone "Keystone Fire Department"	90	135	180
Keystone Radiopticon, 1920s	75	112	150
Keystone Service Station	130	195	260
"Kid Flyer" boy on scooter, tin litho, string-wound, 8½" long	300	450	600
Kingsbury Fire Station, No. 8, clockwork bell and door, 9"x10"x13"	150	225	300
"Knockout Target Shooting Gallery," lithographed tin with rifle, many targets	40	60	80
Ladder for fire trucks, cast iron	3.00	4.50	6.00
Ladders, stamped steel, from Hubley and Arcade trucks	10	15	20
Lawnmower, Arcade, circa 1920, iron and wood	20	30	40
Lehmann "Climbing Monkey"	80	120	160
Lehmann "Tom Tom" spiral drive top No. 677, 1920	125	188	250
Lehmann "Toy-Kadi," 1920s friction	500	750	1000
"Lindstrom's Little Show," cardboard and wood theatre with seven show strips	250	375	500
Lion in Hoop, tin 6¼" high	200	300	400
Lionel Science Kit, circa 1960	20	30	40
Machine Gun, Grey Iron, rapid fire, 9" long, cast iron, 1930s	125	188	250
Machine Gun, wood and steel, gravity fed, wooden bullets	35	52	70
Magic Lantern	55	82	110
Magic Lantern, Keystone, "Radio-ptocin"	40	60	80
Magic Lantern Projector, tin, embossed deer on door and side, 8" long	60	90	120
Man on Bicycle, animated, tin, high wheel bike, bell on top of bicycle, 10½" high	360	540	720
Manoil Target, lead, either "4-5-6" or "7-8-9", "1-2-3" doesn't appear to exist, except in a version produced by collectors Ed Poole and Ron Eccles. Manoil's order number for the targets, without specifying which, was 76	45	68	90
Marky Maypo rubber squeeze toy, 1960s	23	35	46

Manoil Targets, "4 5 6", "7 8 9". Photo by Don Pielin.

MARX "Honeymoon Garage". Photo by James Apthorpe.

	C6	C8	C10
Marx Air-Sea Power bombing set	375	563	750
Marx "Allstate Terminal & Warehouse," Sears, 1960s, 23x15x2"	150	225	300
Marx Army and Navy Mechanical Target No. G169	20	30	40
Marx Army Code Sender, 9½" Morse key and phone, pressed steel	10	15	20
Marx Ballerina, 6" high, operated by sawtooth bar, pulled through, 1930s	85	128	170
Marx Bear Cyclist, metal, lever action	100	150	200
Marx "Brightelite Filling Station"	225	338	450
Marx Bust 'Em Target Game No. G38	20	30	40
Marx Cat with Ball, cable-operated, tin litho	40	60	80
Marx "Champion Skater" ballet dancer, pull spinning rod out of motor, place skater in upright position and she spins	100	150	200
Marx "Climbing Fireman," tin and plastic	80	120	160
Marx Co. A Barracks, tin litho building, 6x8x12"	20	30	40

MARX Mechanical Gorilla, with box. Courtesy James S. Maxwell/Virginia Caputo. Photo by Virginia Caputo.

MARX Cat with Ball, cable operated. Courtesy Mapes Auctioneers & Appraisers.

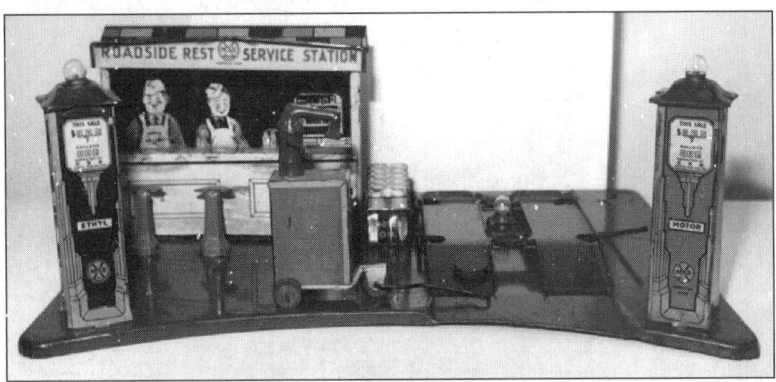

MARX Roadside Rest. Courtesy Thomas G. Nefos, Federal Shipping Network.

MARX Ballerina. Courtesy Scott Smiles. Photo by Mike Adams.

MARX "Pretty Maid Washing Machine". Photo by Bill Kaufman Courtesy Good Old Days Store.

MARX Sunny Side Service Station. Photo by Ron Chojnacki. Courtesy Don Hultzman.

MARX "Climbing Fireman", tin and plastic. Courtesy Mapes Auctioneers & Appraisers.

MARBLES

Marbles are known to date back as far as ancient Rome,
when they were made of clay. Marbles are divided into types, such as "Indian Swirls,"
"Clambroth," "Lutz Type Swirls," etc. Size numbers range from 000, which equals ½ inch to 8,
which equals 1⅛ inch. There are estimated to be 8-10,000 current collectors of marbles,
about 600 of whom belong to the Marble Collectors' Society of America
(see Leading Collectors and Dealers).
A 1991 list from Stanley A. Block of the Society shows some of the following prices:

Large Latticino Swirl, size 2½" $200
Large Divided Core Swirl, size 1⅞" $175
Sulphide, 2¼", little girl crawling,
    figure has hairline heat fracture,
    near mint $850

Sulphide, 1¾", Number Eight in pink
    glass, near mint $300
Large solid core Swirl, size 2⅜", unusual
    four lobed solid core $200

	C6	C8	C10
Marx Colonial Doll House No. 4052 ...100	150	200	
Marx "Colonial Service Station," 1960s, 27" long, 15" wide, 4" high ...90	135	180	
Marx Deluxe Dial Typewriter, 1930s 20	30	40	
Marx Dial Typewriter No. 1000A, 1930s ...30	45	60	
Marx Dishwasher K54, circa 1950s 20	30	40	
Marx Doll House No. 4021 ...20	30	40	
Marx Doll House No. 4030 ...30	45	60	
Marx "Electric Lighted Filling Station," tin litho, 1930s, 10x13½" long, see "Sunnyside Service Station"			
Marx "General Alarm Fire House," 1940s, 17" long, 11" wide, 3" high ...187	280	375	
Marx Gobbling Goose, plastic windup, 9" long ...70	105	140	
Marx Headquarters, tin litho, U.S. Army Training Center, 5x8x11" ...20	30	40	
Marx "Hometown Drug Store," "F.W. Woolworth," tin litho, 5x2x3½" ...120	180	240	
Marx "Hometown Favorite Store," "F.W. Woolworth," tin litho, 5x2x3½" ...120	180	240	
Marx "Hometown Favorite Store," "S.S. Kresge Co.," tin litho ...100	150	200	
Marx "Hometown Grocery Store," tin litho, 1930s, 5x2½x3½" ...60	90	120	
Marx "Hometown Meat Market," tin litho, 1930s ...60	90	120	
Marx "Hometown Movie Theatre," tin litho, 1930s ...62	93	125	
Marx "Hometown Police Station" ...60	90	120	
Marx "Hometown Savings Bank," tin litho building, 1930s, 5x2½x3½" ...60	90	120	
Marx "Honeymoon Cottage Village," 1930s tin litho, 17" long by 11" wide ...37	56	75	
Marx "Honeymoon Garage," 1930s, tin litho, 6½"x7"x3" ...20	30	40	
Marx "Ice Skater," 1930s, 5½" high, sawtooth bar operates it ...90	135	180	
Marx Junior Dial Typewriter No. 2109, circa 1930s ...20	30	40	
Marx Kitchen Sink K47, circa 1950s 10	15	20	
Marx King Arthur sword and shield, tin litho ...25	38	50	
Marx "Knockout Champs," celluloid, 1930s ...300	450	600	
Marx "Loop the Loop" 1930s gravity toy, track 12" long, car 1½" long ...50	75	100	
Marx "Magic Garage and Car", 1950s, garage 10" long, car 7" long, wind-up ...85	112	170	
Marx Mechanical Gorilla ...100	150	200	
Marx Newlywed Library, tin litho, 1930s, 5x2½x3½" long ...75	112	150	
Marx Pathe News Movie Camera, tin litho ...200	300	400	
Marx Practice Target Ranger, 1950s, 11" long ...30	45	60	
Marx "Pretty Maid Washing Machine," circa 1930s, 4½" high ...50	75	100	
Marx Refrigerator, K42, circa 1950s 20	30	40	
Marx Rex Mars Planet Patrol 45 Cal. machine-gun, tin and plastic, winds up, 22" long ...55	82	110	
Marx "Rex Mars Space Target Game," 1950s, 14" long ...100	150	200	
Marx Roadside Rest, four pumps, car, garage, 1930 ...200	300	400	
Marx Searchlight, tin litho, 3½" high 20	30	40	
Marx Son of Garloo plastic and tin windup ...105	158	210	

	C6	C8	C10
Marx Stove K39, circa 1950s 20	30	40
Marx "Sunnyside Service Station," 1930s, complete 400	600	800
Marx "Super Service" center...............175	263	350
Marx Swinging Arm Target Game No. G52 and Gun...........................40	60	80
Marx Swinging Arm Target Game No. G55 and Gun 40	60	80
Marx Suburban Colonial Dollhouse, metal...60	90	120
Marx Trixo Monkey string climber.......35	52	70
Marx Tunnel, tin litho, 8"x10"x7" depicts farm scene, rolling hills, houses...10	15	20
Marx Typewriter No. 1110, metal and plastic, circa 1950s-1960s...............10	15	20
Marx "Universal Gas Service Station," 1940s, 6½" high, base 12" long.....100	150	200
Marx Walkers, plastic, jungle animals with riders, 1970s, each 4	8	12
Mattel "Farmer In The Dell," tin, crank, 7" high, 1951.........................70	105	140
Mattel - "Four & 20 Blackbirds," 1950s, 9" diameter, crank action - musical toy.....................................70	105	140
Mattel Jack in the Music Box, 1961......10	15	20
Mattel Mad Scientist Dissect - An Alien..6	9	12
Mattel Mad Scientist Monster Lab 10	15	20
Mattel Mad Scientist Operating Room 5	8	10
Mattel Music Box Carousel..................75	112	150
Mattel Thingmaker Creepy Crawlers Pak, 1960s.....................................35	52	70
Mattel Thingmaker Fang 'n Claw Kit, 1967 20	30	40
Mattel Thingmaker People Makers Pak 30	45	60
Mattel Thingmaker Slitherees Kit, 1967 20	30	40
Mattel Vacuform with molds.................30	45	60
Meat Grinder with clamp, die cast.......5.00	7.50	10.00
Meccano Set 0 10	15	20
Meccano Set 1 12	18	25
Meccano Set 1A 10	15	20
Meccano Set 1X 75	112	150
Meccano Set 2 25	37	50
Meccano Set 2A 10	15	20
Meccano Set 3 10	15	20
Meccano Set 3A 10	15	20
Meccano Set 4 50	75	100
Meccano Set 4A 25	37	50
Meccano Engineering Erector Set.........10	15	20

MATTEL "Farmer In The Dell", tin, crank, 7" high. Courtesy Calvin L. Chaussee

NOAH'S ARK. Courtesy Continental Hobby House.

PARKER BROS. Toy Town Garage. Courtesy Lloyd W. Ralston Auctions.

	C6	C8	C10
Meccano Microscope Set, 1933 10	15	20
Merry-Go-Round, wind-up, lithographed paper and wood, with four bisque figures riding four fur-skinned papier mache horses......................600	900	1200
Merry-Go-Round, wood and lithographed paper Jenny musical wind-up with five horse-form seats...200	300	400

	C6	C8	C10
Microphone, Ward toy......40	60	80
Mr. Machine......	*See Ideal*	
Mr. Potato Head......	*See Hasbro*	
Monkey, mechanical, in red pants, red-checked shirt, squeeze metal lever attached to 34" spiral wire and monkey jumps alongside you, hitting cymbals, 10" high......50	75	100
Monkey, stuffed, red felt cap and jacket, glass eyes, moveable arms and legs, move his tail and head moves from side to side, and up and down, circa 1910, 9½" high.....60	90	120
Mound of Earth, tin litho, 4" long (for toy soldiers)......12	18	25
Mound of Rocks, tin litho (for toy soldiers)......12	18	25
Movie-Jector, hand crank......40	60	80
Movie Projector, "Flip Movies," turn crank and flip cards from "Midgette" movies, with film, circa early 1930s......56	84	112
"Movie Projector Gun," film only, 1937, Box 1 contains Chaplin, Gasoline Alley, Babe Ruth, Buffalo Bill, Harold Teen; Box 2 contains Dick Tracy, Terry & Pirates, Smitty, Orphan Annie, Winnie Winkle; box 3 contains Clyde Beatty, Gumps, Little Joe, Tiny Tim, Buffalo Bill; Box 4 contains Gasoline Alley, Chaplin, Tracy, Lone Ranger, Harold Teen. Price per box......10	15	20
Movie Projector, "Uncle Sam," hand cranks, circa 1930s......100	150	200
Music Box, tin, shaped like coffee grinder, 3" high, German......80	120	160
Myrioptican, optical toy, Milton Bradley.100	150	200
Mysto Erector Set No. 1......75	112	150
Mysto Erector Set No. 1A......50	75	100
Mysto Erector Set No. 2, circa 1915....50	75	100
Mysto Erector Set No. 2A......50	75	100
Mysto Erector Set No. 3A......50	75	100
Noah's Ark, 6½" long, wooden, 12 animals, Noah......50	75	100
Noah's Ark, 11" long, 27 animals......75	112	150
Noah's Ark, Bliss, 13¼" long, 10 animals, wooden......150	225	300
Noah's Ark, cardboard, with animals, 14" long......20	30	40
Noah's Ark, Converse, 14" long, carved wooden animals......60	90	120

	C6	C8	C10
Noah's Ark, Pyro, plastic, with animals....20	30	40
Noah's Ark with wooden village blocks......20	30	40
Noah's Ark, wood litho, 10" long with animals......30	45	60
Noise Maker, tin, shaped like old-fashioned phone mouthpiece, 2¼" high......6	9	12
Nutty Mads figures, Marx, 1963 issue, vinyl, each......11	16	22

OHIO ART

Ohio Art was started in October, 1908 by a dentist, H.S. Winzeler. Originally its intent was to make metal picture frames (thus its name), but in 1917 the firm bought C.E. Carter (Erie Toy Plant) and began producing metal toys, including a climbing monkey on a string for Ferdinand Strauss. Winzeler later sold the plant to Louis Marx, but continued making tin toys, while Marx, according to Ohio Art history, used the former Carter plant as the foundation of his own company. Ohio Art is still making toys in Bryan Ohio.

	C6	C8	C10
Ohio Art Barrel Organ, musical, 5½" tall......40	60	80
Ohio Art Beach Toy Water Pumper, circa 1939, 8½" high, signed Elaine Ends Hileman"......27	41	55
Ohio Art Children's Tea Set, tin, 14 pieces, 1950s......10	15	20
Ohio Art Drum, 6"x4" + 2 sticks......20	30	40
Ohio Art "Fido's Musical Dog House," 1960s, 8" high......40	60	80
Ohio Art "Mini Farm Set," 1960s playset, 12" long, 5" high......80	120	160
Ohio Art "Realistic Farm Set" No. 197 1960s playset, 16" long, 7" high......80	120	160
Ohio Art Sandpail, 1940s, tin litho......7	11	15
Ohio Art Shooting Gallery, key wind-circus......40	60	80
Ohio Art Sunnyfield Farms Barn and Silo set with animals, tin litho, 1950s......80	120	160
Ohio Art Toyland Band, drums, bass and snare, cymbals, triangle and sticks, 7½" high......20	30	40
Ohio Art Washtub, tin litho, wood and metal scrubboard, 1940s......16	24	32
Ohio Art Watering Can, tin litho, 1940s....7	11	15
"Old Kentucky Home" wood litho action toy, six dancers, singer-musicians, moved by hand crank, 15½" long......366	549	732

	C6	C8	C10
Organ Grinder, monkey, 6" wooden, push bottom, squeaks and dances, Kohner Bros.	20	30	40
Paddle Wheel and Tower on base, tin, 14" high	20	30	40
"Paris Coaster," wood-wheeled cart	30	45	60
Parker Bros., 1910, Toy Town Garage, 3 litho tin penny cars, paper litho garage	600	900	1200
Parker Bros. "Toy Town Grocery Store"	220	330	440
Phonograph, toy, Genola, cranks, with sound horn	100	150	200

	C6	C8	C10
Phonograph, toy, Nerona, cranks, sound comes from horn connected to needle, early	100	150	200
Pig and Piglet in cage, wood, cloth and lithographed paper, spring-loaded squeak toy	50	75	100
Pillsbury Poppin' Fresh, 5" high	8	12	16
Pillsbury Poppin' Fresh, 10" high	10	15	20
Pillsbury Poppie Fresh, 5" high	8	12	16
Plarola Corporation Organ, tin lithographed, with six organ rolls	300	450	600

PLASTICVILLE

(from information developed by Mark Schulz)

Plasticville Buildings and accessories were produced by Bachmann Bros., which dates back to 1833. In its early history Bachmann produced ivory cane handles and combs. In 1907 the firm purchased the second injection molding machine made, and began making eyeglass frames. After World War II, the growth in the toy train market led Bachmann to create plastic picket fences to enclose toy train platforms. This evolved into building kits, the first of which was the Log Cabin. Production continued into the late 1960s, with HO and N scale by then the main emphasis. In recent years, Bachmann has reintroduced some of the old O/S scale buildings. During its heyday the Plasticville line boasted over 100 items. C8 and C10 include box. All prices assume that no glue has been used.

PLASTICVILLE Barnyard Animal Set. Photo by Gary Linden.

PLASTICVILLE Billboard. Photo by Gary Linden.

PLASTICVILLE Barn. Photo by Gary Linden.

PLASTICVILLE Birdbath, French Section, Trellis. Photo by Gary Linden.

PLASTICVILLE Cape Cod House. Photo by Gary Linden.

PLASTICVILLE Fence and Gate. Photo by Gary Linden.

PLASTICVILLE Fire House Kit. Photo by Gary Linden.

PLASTICVILLE Frosty Bar. Photo by Gary Linden.

PLASTICVILLE Diner. Photo by Gary Linden.

PLASTICVILLE Diner Kit Box. Photo by Gary Linden.

PLASTICVILLE 5 & 10. Photo by Gary Linden.

PLASTICVILLE Hobo Shacks. Photo by Gary Linden.

	C6	C8	C10
Airport Admin Bldg.	10	15	20
Airport Hangar	8	11	15
Apartment House	30	38	45
Apartment Add-a-Floor	10	15	20
Autumn Trees	25	35	50
Bank	10	20	28
Barn	4	6	8
Barbecue	1	2	2
Barnyard Animal Set (18)	4	6	8

PLASTICVILLE House Under Construction. Photo by Gary Linden.

PLASTICVILLE Mobile Home. Photo by Gary Linden.

PLASTICVILLE Outhouse, Telephone Booth, Well, Barbecue, Pump. Photo by Gary Linden.

PLASTICVILLE Police Dept. O scale. Photo by Gary Linden.

PLASTICVILLE Log Cabin, Rustic Fence & Tree. Photo by Gary Linden.

PLASTICVILLE Plasticville Citizens. Photo by Gary Linden.

PLASTICVILLE Police Dept. Kit, HO scale box. Photo by Gary Linden.

PLASTICVILLE Police Dept. Kit box, O scale. Photo by Gary Linden.

PLASTICVILLE Supermarket, large. Photo by Gary Linden.

PLASTICVILLE Supermarket Box, small size. Photo by Gary Linden.

PLASTICVILLE Railroad Signal Bridge. Photo by Gary Linden.

PLASTICVILLE Trailer. Photo by Gary Linden.

PLASTICVILLE Street Accessories Unit. Photo by Gary Linden.

PLASTICVILLE Street Accessories Unit box. Photo by Gary Linden.

	C6	C8	C10
Billboard	25	.50	1.00
Birdbath, Fence Section, Trellis	6	10	14
Bungalow	10	15	20
Cape Cod House Kit	2	4	6
Cathedral	12	16	20
Cattle Loading Pen	8	11	15
Church/Parish Church	4	6	8
Coaling Station	8	10	12
Colonial Church	8	12	15

	C6	C8	C10
Colonial Mansion	8	14	18
Corner Store	10	15	20
Country Church	3	4	6
Covered Bridge	4	6	8
Dairy Barn	5	8	10
Diner Kit	4	6	8

PLASTICVILLE Supermarket, small. Photo by Gary Linden.

PLASTICVILLE Suburban Station. Photo by Gary Linden.

PLASTICVILLE Trees and Fern. Photo by Gary Linden.

PLASTICVILLE Trees. Photo by Gary Linden.

PLASTICVILLE Switch Tower. Photo by Gary Linden.

PLASTICVILLE Water Tank. Photo by Gary Linden.

	C6	C8	C10
Factory	15	20	25
Fence and Gate (12 pcs.)	1	2	3
Fire House Kit	4	6	8
5 & 10	8	9	10
Frosty Bar	12	15	18
Gas Station, small	4	6	8
Greenhouse	18	23	28
Hobo Shacks (two bldgs.)	30	37	42
Hospital (w/furniture)	8	12	16
House Under Construction	15	20	25
Log Cabin Rustic Fence & Tree	2	4	6
Mobile Home	15	20	30
Motel	5	7	9
New England Ranch House	5	8	10
Outhouse	2	4	5
Pharmacy/Hardware	8	9	10
Plasticville Citizens (24 or 16)	2	4	5
Police Dept., HO scale	8	11	15

	C6	C8	C10
Police Dept, O scale	8	11	15
Post Office	6	8	10
Pump	1	2	2
Raiload Signal Bridge	4	6	8
Railroad Work Car	4	6	8
Ranch House	5	8	10
Roadside Stand	8	11	15
Schoolhouse	5	8	10
Split Level House	6	8	10
Street Accessories Unit (15 pcs.)	8	15	20
Suburban Station	3	4	6
Supermarket, large	8	10	12
Supermarket, small	4	6	8
Switch Tower (Railroad)	1	2	3
Telephone Booth	2	5	8
Town Hall	10	15	20
Trailer	15	20	30
TV Station	6	9	12
Union Station	7	10	14
Water Tank (Railroad)	3	5	7
Well	2	4	5
Windmill	14	18	22
Roadrace Accessories			
Grandstand	15	20	25
Officials' Stand	8	11	15
Pit Stop	15	20	25
Sitting People	10	15	20

End Plasticville

	C6	C8	C10
"Play Store Register," tin and brass, Durable Toy and Novelty Co., 4" high	18	27	36
Pop (Kellogg's Rice Krispies) squeeze toy, 8½" high	10	15	20
Pop (Kellogg's Rice Krispies) hand puppet	7	11	15
Pull Toy, Camel on Platform, tin, Althof-Bergmann	600	900	1200
Pull Toy, Clown on Elephant, Kenton, 1911	400	600	800
Pull Toy, Elephant, hide-covered with bisque head, native	150	225	300
Pull Toy, Elephant, tin, 4½" long, 1870, nothing on back	140	210	280
Pull Toy, Elephant, tin, with blanket, iron wheels, 4½" long	60	90	120
Pull Toy, elephant with saddle, tin. Iron wheels, 4½" high	75	112	150
Pull Toy, Elephant, tin, 9" long, early	850	1275	1700
Pull Toy, Elephant with howdah, cast iron	600	900	1200
Pull Toy, Elephants, two, on platform, tin, 12" long	300	450	600
Pull Toy, Gibbs, jockeys on horses, 10" long, wood and paper litho	750	1125	1500
Pull Toy, Goat, 9½" long, tin, early	150	225	300
Pull Toy, four race horses and riders, tin with cast iron wheels, 8¼" long	400	600	800
Pull Toy, horse, galloping, tin, 7" long	75	112	150
Pull Toy, horse, tin, 8½" long, Harwood, circa 1876	2500	3750	5000
Pull Toy, horse, 13¼" high, leather reins, metal stirrups, felt saddle, circa 1880	125	187	250
Pull Toy, horse and animated figure with composition head and tin arms playing drum and cymbal.			

	C6	C8	C10
Horse is tin, wheels, wooden platform, 13½" long	500	750	1000
Pull Toy, horse and cart with chicken-shaped sides, iron wheels, tin, 5¼" long	125	187	250
Pull Toy, horse and covered delivery wagon, tin, 5¼" long	150	225	300
Pull Toy, horse and polo player on horse's back, tin, 4¼" long	75	112	150
Pull Toy, horse and rider, tin, iron wheels, 4½" long	80	120	160
Pull Toy, horse and rider, tin, iron wheels, 11" long	150	225	300
Pull Toy, horse (white) and water wagon, tin, 6¾" long	250	375	500
Pull Toy, horse (dark) and water wagon, tin, 7¼" long	150	225	300
Pull Toy, horse and wagon, tin, 9¼" long	150	225	300
Pull Toy, horse on platform, George Brown, 1880, American painted tin, 6½" long	250	375	500
Pull Toy, horsewoman riding side-saddle on pony, cast iron	225	337	450
Pull Toy, jockey on dog, 10¼" long, tin, early, Ives	1000	1500	2000
Pull Toy, jockey on goat, Ives, 9½" long	3500	5200	7000
Pull Toy, Jonah & Whale, cast iron	400	600	800
Pull Toy, Jockey on Horse, 9" long, tin, hair tail	600	900	1200
Pull Toy, Jumbo Elephant on wheels, Gibbs, 10" long	200	300	400
Pull Toy, Rider on Horse, tin, 10" long	500	750	1000
Pull Toy, rooster, tin, 3¼" long	400	600	800
Pull Toy, rooster on platform, 1890 painted tin, 4¾" long	100	150	200

Pull Toy, Jumbo Elephant (wheels missing), GIBBS. Courtesy Continental Hobby House.

Pull Toy, Elephant tin 4½" long, 1870, nothing on back. Courtesy Lloyd W. Ralston Auctions

Pull Toy, horse on platform, 6½" long. Courtesy Lloyd W. Ralston Auctions

Pull Toy, Rooster on Platform. Courtesy Lloyd W. Ralston Auctions

Pull Toy, Rider on Horse, tin, 10" long. Courtesy Sotheby's New York.

Pull Toy, Swan Chariot. Courtesy James S. Maxwell/Virginia Caputo. Photo by Virginia Caputo.

Pull Toy, Two Frogs, 7¼" long, painted tin, FALLOWS, 1898. Courtesy James S. Maxwell/Virginia Caputo. Photo by Virginia Caputo.

Push Toy, Horse and Rider, WILKINS. Courtesy Wilkinson Collection, Detroit Antique Toy Museum.

	C6	C8	C10
Pull Toy, sheep, tin, 6¼" high, circa 1890	150	225	300
Pull Toy, Swan Chariot	6000	9000	12000
Pull Toy, three bears by Toycraft	30	45	60
Pull Toy, Two Frogs, 7½" long, painted tin, Fallows, 1898	900	1350	1800
Pump, tin, with round trough, transfer of puppies, 7" high	15	22	30
Punch and Judy Puppet Theatre with 6 puppets: Punch, Judy, Devil, Princess, Sailor, Workman	400	600	800
Push Toy, butterfly that flaps its wings	40	60	80
Push Toy, clown on log, bell toy, cast iron	500	750	1000

	C6	C8	C10
Push Toy, horse and rider, Wilkins, 29" long, circa 1910, cast iron and wood	375	563	750
Push Toy, large running horses, tin, cast iron wheels, 14" high by 14½", horses' size	500	750	1000
Push Toy, horse, wooden, walks	40	60	80
Q.R.S. Playasax, uses paper rolls, Devry Corp., 12" long	87	131	175
Quake rag doll, 1960s, 12" high	20	30	40
Quisp rag doll, 1960s, 11" high	20	30	40
Rabbit, moves ears, small	110	165	220
Rabbits, two, mashing ingredients in small bowl, tin, animated by squeezing, 6" high	15	22	30

	C6	C8	C10
Ranger Steel "Drive Safely" set 112	168	225
Ranger Steel Co. "Gas Station - Auto Laundry," 1940s, 3x5x13", long 150	225	300
Refrigerator, cast iron, Hubley, 7" high, "GE" 150	225	300
Remco B-52 Ball Turret 37	56	75
Remco Johnny Reb Cannon 55	82	110
Remco Movieland Drive-In Theatre 40	60	80
Renwal Drawbridge, plastic, 2 plastic autos, 2 boats, cardboard river scene, 27" long, early 50s 125	187	250
Renwal Globe Trotter Set No. 305-150, 4 boats, 3 cars, train, jet plane..............................19	28	38
Renwal "Visible Dog, The"...................30	45	60
Renwal "Visible Man, The" 30	45	60
Renwal "Visible Woman, The" 30	45	60
Ripley's Believe It or Not Disk-O-Knowledge, round piece of cardboard with another piece attached on top, turn to reveal questions and answers, 1932, 9½" diameter ...10	15	20
"Rocket Ring," with futuristic rocket on top of ring, whistles, 1930s........30	45	60
Rocking Horse, hand carved, all wood, 1890s..............................425	638	850
Rocking Horse, "Shoo Fly" 100	150	200
Rocking Toy, tin, girl on horse, 3¾" long, German - Penny Toy 220	330	440
Rolmonica, harmonica that plays rolls of tunes, "Blow, crank and play," with three songs, 1930s...................80	120	160
Roly Poly, Boy on Horse, circa 1900 ...140	210	280
Roly Poly Clown, circa 1900, 10" high, papier mache.......................120	180	240
Roly Poly Clown, circa 1900, 13" high 140	210	280
Sand Toy Set, Chick Art Co., 1942, includes tin litho frog, sailboat, shovel and round sieve...................36	54	78

	C6	C8	C10
Sandbags, variously marked, for toy soldiers............................3	4.50	6
Sand Pail, tin litho, circa 1940 15	22	30
Scales, cast iron, tin tray and four brass weights, 5¾" long................26	39	52
Scales, cast iron, "Dayton," 3½" high...40	60	80
Secor Banjo Player, black man, early, auctioned in 1991 for $18,000		
Secor Bones Player, black man, early windup, auctioned in 1991 for $22,000		
Seiberling Latex Prod. Panda, rubber squeak toy 60	90	120
Sewing Machine, 6" high, circa 1920 ...85	127	170
Shooting Gallery Chickens, cast iron, 10¼" long...75	112	150
Signal Jr. R-70 Twin Wireless Practice Set, two beginner's sending keys, and one advanced key, circa 1920 ..30	45	60
Simplex Typewriter No. 300, tin 14	21	28
Slinky, 1947, with box...........................17	26	35
Snap (Kellogg's Rice Krispies) squeeze toy, 8½" high...................................10	15	20
Snap (Kellogg's Rice Krispies) hand puppet...7	11	15
Steam Engine, Big Giant Brass boiler Upright, 11¼" 80	120	200
Steam Engine, Doll & Co. upright, cast iron base, 11¼".........................90	150	220
Steam Engine, Empire Horizontal, twin boiler and twin fly.................140	210	280
Steam Engine, Empire, mounted on base board with transmission, concrete mixer, table saw, grinding wheel..160	240	320

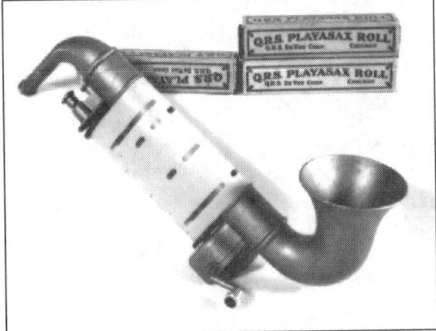

Q.R.S. Playasax, with music rolls. Courtesy Continental Hobby House.

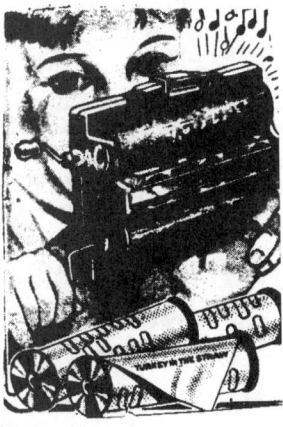

Rolmonica

Sewing Machine, 6" high, circa 1920. Photo by Bill Kaufman. Courtesy Good Old Days Store

Steam Engine, WEEDEN No. 49. Courtesy Heinz Mueller Continental Hobby House.

Stove, "Eagle," cast iron, 11½" high. Courtesy Mapes Auctioneers and Appraisers.

	C6	C8	C10
Steam Engine, Empire vertical boiler, stationary, Metal Ware Corp., pat. Jan. 25, 1921 140	210	280
Steam Engine, Huber, 8" 150	225	300
Steam Engine, Weeden No. 49 with dual flywheels, cast iron base 200	300	400
Steam Engine, Weeden, No. 42, 12" high 80	120	160
Steam Engine, Weeden No. 902, base 7¼"x9" 70	105	140
Steam Engine, Weeden dual flywheel, base 10", 11½" high 150	225	300
Steam Engine, Weeden, Early cast iron, deluxe model with cast iron boiler front, mounted on wood base inside wooden case, 1880 model 125	200	300
Steam Engine, Weeden Electric Steam Engine, 3½"x7¼" base 30	45	60
Steam Engine, Weeden, horizontal, 4" cast flywheel, mechanism on top of boiler............120	180	240
Steam Engine, Weeden, horizontal, 6" boiler, stationary 70	105	140
Steam Engine, Weeden, upright steam engine, 9½"x7" cast iron base, cast iron mechanism............70	105	140
Steam Engine, Weeden Upright Steam Engine on wooden base, 10" tall 45	67	90
Steam Engine, Weeden, Upright, early tin, 11"............60	90	120

	C6	C8	C10
Steam Engine, Weeden, Upright, early 11¼"............50	75	100
Steam Engine, Weeden, Upright, boiler only. Flywheel assembly mounted on base. Base is 8"x4" 100	150	200
Steam Engine, Wooden Dual Flywheel steam engine, base 10"x7"x11½" 150	225	300
Stitchwell Sewing Machine, child's floor model, circa 1920s 80	120	160
Stove, cast iron, "American"............100	150	200
Stove, "Daisy," cast white metal, 4¼"high .15	22	30
Stove, "Eagle," cast iron, 4¼" high.......50	75	100
Stove, "Eagle," cast iron, 11½" high....100	150	200
Stove, "Eagle," cast iron, 13½" high....125	187	250
Stove, cast iron, 13"x11½" high............75	112	150
Stove, cast iron, Ark, 4"x5" 25	37	50
Stove, electric, one burner, two ovens, chrome-finished steel, porcelain on oven doors, 16" wide, 14" tall 75	112	150
Stove, "Lancaster," "Eagle," on door and shelf, 10¾", cast iron 60	90	120
Stove, wood-burning cast iron, "The Queen" 45	67	90
Stove, Roper, Arcade gas burner, cast iron, 6" high 100	150	200
Stove, wood-burning cast iron, "The Triumph Range"............100	150	200
Stove, tin, with four plate covers, four pans and one skillet, 5" high..........150	225	300

	C6	C8	C10
Stretcher for 3" toy soldiers, pre-WW II	8	12	16
Structo Erector Set, 1910	50	75	100
Structo No. 3	70	105	140
Sulky, cast iron, single casting	30	45	60
Swing, animated, cast iron and pressed steel, for doll, with eagle, wheel	600	900	1200
Swinging Clown, tin, base marked "C.D. Kenny Co.," 4¼" high	120	180	240
"The Symmetroscope," wood and tin type of kaleidoscope, 6¼" high, F.P. Irving, Troy, N.Y.	60	90	120
Tea Kettle, cast iron, 3¼" long	30	45	60
Teeter-Totter, Gibbs Toys, 14½" high, when inverted, two children work their way down, tin, 1910	275	513	550
Tent, Army, two pole, two flags on top, approx. 5" long	7.50	11.25	15.00
Tent, "Bat. A," two flags	14	21	28
Tent, canvas, white, 9" long	7.50	11.25	15.00
Tent, Army, "Field Hangar, U.S. Aviation Corp. Squadron 1," two flags atop tent, approx. 9" long	11	16	22
Tent, Army, "U.S. Battery B. Coast Artillery," two poles, two flags on top	14	21	28
Tent "Guard Tent Co. A" 4¼" high	5.00	7.50	10.00
Tent, "Inf. Co. C"	9	13	18
Tent, "Medical Unit"	12	18	24
Tent, "Mess Hall," wood base	12	18	25
Tent "Sail-Me" Co., 6 with box, c. 1931, paper	40	60	80
Tent, "U.S. Infantry Co. A," 4½" high, two flags on top	11	16	22

	C6	C8	C10
Tent "U.S. Infantry Co. B"	6	9	12
Tent, paper, 5" high, "State Camp Co. A"	1.50	2.25	3.00
Tent, No. 76, small pup, white with cardboard base, center support	4	6	8
Tin dog with boy rider, 13½" long, on wheeled platform	600	900	1200
Tinker Toys, round box, 12" high, 1940s	12	18	24
Tinker Toys, Electric ET-1	30	45	60
Tinker Toys No. 104	12	18	25
Toledo Scales, 4x4", cast iron	25	37	50
"Tom Thumb" cash register, metal, 6½"x7½"x8¼" by Western Stamping Co.	18	27	36
Tools, Grey Iron, 1933, price per set	15	22	30
Tool Set, Greycraft (Grey Iron) 1940, cast iron, steel and wood	12	18	25
Tootsietoy Bathroom set	80	120	160
Tootsietoy Bedroom set	50	75	100
Tootsietoy Dining Room set	60	90	120

TOOTSIETOY, Bathroom Set. Courtesy Continental Hobby House.

TOOTSIETOY, Dining Room Set. Courtesy Continental Hobby House.

	C6	C8	C10
Tootsietoy furniture, six chairs, moveable bar, two side tables and a dining table	50	75	100
Tootsietoy living room set, two chairs, lamp, gramophone, sofa secretaire, table	50	75	100
Tootsietoy metal kitchen and bathroom furniture, sink, bathtub, toilet, stove, table and cupboard	45	67	90
Tootsietoy Music Room, set	110	165	220
Top, Carnival Whistling Top, tin litho circus decor, spring-wound, 4" diameter, Lupor, 1930s	30	45	60
Top, gyro style, 1918	16	24	32
Top, wooden, circa 1940	4	6	8
Transworld Airlines, Jr. Pilot Wings	10	15	20
Tricycle, iron, Kilgore, 2¾"	60	90	120

Teeter-Totter, GIBBS. Courtesy Garth's Auctions Inc.

"Uncle Sam's Cash Store Register". Courtesy James S. Maxwell/Virginia Caputo. Photo by Virginia Caputo.

Whirligig of Life. Courtesy Lloyd W. Ralston Auctions.

Water Tank Wagon, 1910. Courtesy Lloyd W. Ralston Auctions'

	C6	C8	C10
Trix Rabbit, rubber squeeze toy 17		26	35
Turner Firehouse, 12x15x21", heavy sheet metal 200		300	400
Turner Garage, heavy sheet metal, one window on each side, divided into four panes 100		150	200
The Twister, 12" high, in black cloth pants and red stripe shirt with porkpie hat, reminiscent of outfits worn at the Peppermint Lounge where the Twist was born. Stands on a 7" sq. platform, 3½" high, inscribed "Let's Twist!", which is exactly what he does, early 60s 90		135	180
"Uncle Sam's Cash Store Register," Durable Toy and Novelty, 5" high, steel..........14		21	28
Waffle Iron, cast iron, Wagner...............25		37	50
Wagon, Champion Express Coaster, 8" with handle...................................95		112	150
Wagon, "Express" wood spoke wheels 250		375	500
Wagon, Express Flyer, cast iron 125		187.50	250
Wagon "Kiddie Kart" c. 1925. H.I. White, 20" long 50		75	100
Wagon "Pony Express," 38" long.........100		150	200
Wagon, wood, for child, 1900 75		112	150
Walking Horse, metal and papier mache wind-up, early 8¼"..............400		600	800
Washing Machine, 1900, salesman's sample 100		150	200
Washing Machine, tin, works, circa 1940, seashore scene on side 32		48	65
Water Tank Wagon, 1910, painted pressed steel, 26" long 250		375	500
"Western Union" telegraph key, battery powered, code printed on front..........22		33	44

	C6	C8	C10
Wheelbarrow, cast iron, 4½", 1930.......25		37	50
Wheelbarrow, cast iron, approx. 5½"....30		40	60
Wheelbarrow, cast iron, 6½" long.........35		52	70
Wheelbarrow, cast iron, 7" long, with tools, 1915....................................50		75	100
Wheelbarrow, 9" long...........................25		37	50
Whirligig of Life, McLoughlin, 1870s, illusion of motion.........................600		900	1200
Wilkins Fire House No. 8, tin, 18½" long 600		900	1200
Wilkins Horse and Jockey, 1900, 10", cast iron, wheeled pull toy 600		900	1200
Windmill, metal, with pumping apparatus 75		112	150

WOLVERINE

Wolverine, of Pittsburgh, Pa., was founded in 1903 by B.F. Bain. The company got its name from Bain's Michigan hometown. In later years Wolverine became a subsidiary of Spang Industries, and in 1970 moved to Boonville, Arkansas. The "Sandy Andy," in all its variations, was probably Wolverine's most successful and famous toy. The firm's name is now Today's Kids.

	C6	C8	C10
Wolverine-"Adding Machine No. 39", 1940s, 7" long 40		60	80
Wolverine Auto Magic Sand Loader, 1947, 11" high...............................160		240	320
Wolverine "Automatic Coal Loader," 1940s, 10" high 55		83	110

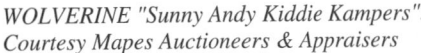
*WOLVERINE "Sunny Andy Kiddie Kampers".
Courtesy Mapes Auctioneers & Appraisers*

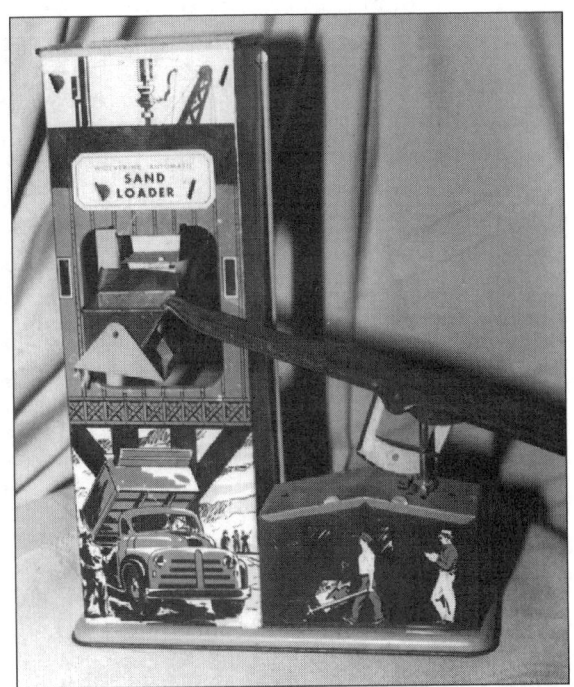

WOLVERINE Automatic Coal Loader. Photo by Don Hultzman.

*WOLVERINE Automatic Sand Loader, 1947. Courtesy
Calvin L. Chaussee.*

*WOLVERINE Captain Sandy Andy 63C. Photo by Ron Chojnacki.
Courtesy Don Hultzman.*

*WOLVERINE "General Grocery". Photo by Ron Chojnacki. Courtesy
Don Hultzman.*

	C6	C8	C10
Wolverine "Automatic Sand Crane," tin	112	168	225
Wolverine Bizzy Andy, 11" high sand toy, pat. 1914, steel and tin	80	120	160
Wolverine, Bizzy Andy Trip Hammer, 1917	60	90	120
Wolverine "Captain Sandy Andy" No. 63C sand toy, 1930s, 13" high	90	135	180
Wolverine "Dumping Sandy," 1916, 12" high	80	120	160

	C6	C8	C10
Wolverine Farm Wagon, 10" long, plastic windup	40	60	80
Wolverine - "General Grocery", 1930s, 20¼" opened and 10¼" closed. Includes 10¼" tin counter, scale, phone, paper dispenser and groceries	200	300	400
Wolverine Merry Masons 16" high sand toy	40	60	80
Wolverine "Music Box No. 38, 1930s, 6" high (crank action)	30	45	60

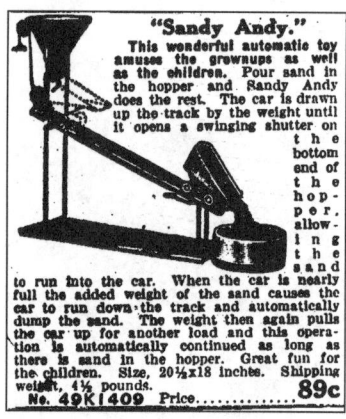
WOLVERINE Sandy Andy.

WOLVERINE "The Corner Grocer. Photo by Ron Chojnacki. Courtesy Don Hultzman.

	C6	C8	C10
Wolverine Organ, tin, turn crank to make organ-like sounds	120	180	240
Wolverine "Post Office" with cardboard accessories	125	188	250
Wolverine "Sandy Andy No. 60 Automatic Sand Toy," Patented 1909 and 1911	80	120	160
Wolverine "Sandy Andy Full Back," 1920s	120	180	240
Wolverine "Shell" Service Station with 3 vehicles	175	263	350
Wolverine "Ski Jumper," 1940s, 18" long, catapult action	47	71	95
Wolverine "Skyscraper Elevator," 1915, 24" high with "2000 lbs." counterweight	150	225	300
Wolverine - "State Capital Quiz No. 43", 1940s, 7" long	40	60	80
Wolverine - "Streamline Railway No. 129", 17" long - pull toy	210	315	420
Wolverine "Sunny Andy" Cable Car Set No. 53, 12" high, circa 1920-30s	80	120	160
Wolverine - "Sunny Andy Fun Fair - No. 65", 1930s, 14" long. Action toy gravity activated by steel balls	150	225	300
Wolverine Sunny Andy "Kiddie Kampers," action toy, 5⅝ by 3½", color litho, three boy scouts and two girl scouts in backdrop camp setting; boys chop and saw wood and girls signal with flags, marbles drop down chute, circa 1929	200	300	400

WOLVERINE sand and other toys, as shown in a December, 1929 Butler Bros. Catalog.

	C6	C8	C10
Wolverine - "Sunny Andy Rabbit Chase", 1930s, 9½" diameter	150	225	300
Wolverine Sandy Andy sand loader, 1912	62	93	125
Wolverine "Texaco Service Station," 1960s, 25x15"	90	135	180
Wolverine - "The Corner Grocer No. 182", 1930s, 31" long - opened; 15¾" - closed. Includes 16" tin counter, scale, phone, paper dispenser and groceries	400	600	800

	C6	C8	C10
"Wonder Clown," No. 110, 1950s, Nesco Co. 5¾" high - spinning top action	80	120	160
Wood Cage with horse, when gate is opened horse pops out and whinnies	125	187	250
Wood Cage, mechanical, rooster flies out when door is open	50	75	100
Wooden Music Maker, "Auto Phone Co. H.B. Horton's Ithaca, N.Y.," 9½" high, uses player rolls	100	150	200
Wyandotte Black Sambo target game, tin, has gun	60	90	120
Wyandotte "Carnival," with ferris wheel, carousel and airplane ride, metal	220	330	440
Wyandotte hen, chubby, tin, lays egg when body pressed down, 8½" long, with eight eggs	60	90	120

	C6	C8	C10
Wyandotte "Musical" push top, circa 1939	30	45	60
Wyandotte "Posse" Shooting Gallery, 14" wide, wind-up gallery	75	112	150
Wyandotte "Shooting Gallery," 1930s, wind-up, 14" long, 11" high	100	150	200
"Zoetrope," wood and cardboard, illusion of motion game, Milton Bradley	300	450	600
"Zulu Blow Gun," copyright 1925, 2' long, 4 arrows, target, instructions, etc. mfd. Battle Creek, Michigan	50	75	100
"Zulu Blow Gun" same as above, different coloring and target, no instruction sheet	45	68	90

WYANDOTTE "Carnival". Courtesy Joe and Sharon Freed

WYANDOTTE "Musical" Push Top. Photo by Bill Kaufman. Courtesy Good Old Days Store.

WYANDOTTE "Posse" Shooting Gallery. Photo by Bill Kaufman. Courtesy Good Old Days Store.

Zoetrope. Photo Courtesy Milton Bradley.

TOY MUSEUMS AND MUSEUMS THAT FEATURE TOYS

AUBURN-CORD-DUSENBERG MUSEUM
Auburn, Indiana 46706
*(Auburn toys and Cord and
Dusenberg automobiles)*

MUSEUM OF THE CITY OF NEW YORK
5th Avenue and 103rd Street
New York, NY

SMITHSONIAN
Washington, DC

DAISY GUN MUSEUM
U.S. 71 South
Rogers, Arkansas
*(The world's most complete collection of
air rifles, dating from the 18th century)*

NASHVILLE TOY MUSEUM
(Next to Opryland USA)
2613 McGavok Pike
Nashville, Tennessee
*(Cover Photo: Ship, Animal-Drawn, Tin Aircraft
and Tank)*

MARGARET WOODBURY STRONG MUSEUM
One Manhattan Square
Rochester, New York, 14607

LAWRENCE SCRIPPS WILKINSON COLLECTION
c/o Detroit Antique Toy Museum
6325 West Jefferson
Detroit, Michigan 48209
(383) 843-9775
(Available only for traveling exhibitions)

TOY TRAIN MUSEUM
Paradise Lane
Strasburg, Pennsylvania

THE STERLING COLLECTION
Stone Castle
804 North Third Street
Bardstown, Kentucky

BAUER TOY MUSEUM (Donald A. Bauer)
233 E. Main
Fredericksburg, Texas
(512) 997-9394

MUSEUM OF CHILDHOOD
8 Broad Street
Greensport, New York

ISLIP TOWN MUSEUM
Montauk Highway
Oakdale, New York

SAN FRANCISCO INTERNATIONAL TOY MUSEUM
2801 Leavenworth St.
San Francisco, CA

SULLIVAN-JOHNSON MUSEUM
(Kenton Toys exhibit)
223 North Main Street
Kenton, Ohio

WASHINGTON DOLL'S HOUSE & TOY MUSEUM
5236 44th Street, NW
Washington, DC 20015

THE TOY MUSEUM
42 Bridge St. Row
Chester, Cheshire
England

THE LONDON TOY & MODEL MUSEUM
23 Craven Hill
London, England

TOY AND SOLDIERS MUSEUM
1100 Cherry St.
Vicksburg, Mississippi

ANTIQUE TOY MUSEUM
Exit 230, I-44
P.O. Box 175
Stanton, Missouri 63079
(314) 927-5555

REMEMBER WHEN TOY MUSEUM
Box 226A
Canton, Missouri 63435
(314) 288-3995 or 288-3176

BIBLIOGRAPHY AND RECOMMENDED PUBLICATIONS

Antique Toy World - Monthly, $25 for one year subscription, payable to Dale Kelley, PO Box 34509, Chicago, IL 60634

U.S. Toy Collector (Vehicles Only) - Monthly, $18 per year, 231 S. Grove St., Missoula, MT 59801

Cast Iron Toy Guns and Capshooters. Heavily illustrated book by Samuel H. Logan and Charles W. Best. $55 from Sam Logan, 1200 Harvard Drive, Davis, CA 95616

The Inside Collector - 9 issues yearly, $30, P.O. Box 98, Elmont NY 11003

Collectors' Showcase - Monthly. $39.90 for one year subscription, Sports Magazines of America, 7130 S. Lewis, Suite 210, Tulsa, OK 74136

Fisher-Price 1931-1963 (1991 edition) Books Americana, $24.95

Jim Harmon's Nostalgia Catalogue by Jim Harmon, Tarcher/Hawthorn

Old Toy Soldier Newsletter, $18 for one-year subscription (bimonthly), payable to Steve Sommers, 209 North Lombard, Oak Park, IL 60302

Toy Soldier Review, $12 for one-year subscription (quarterly), Vintage Castings Inc., 127-74th Street, North Bergen, NJ 07047

Regiments of All Nations (Postwar Britains) available at $20 from Joe Wallis, PO Box 2294, Washington, DC 20013

Toy Shop, monthly newspaper of toy ads, free copy on one-time basis; 700 E. State Street - Sample Copy Department, Iola, WI 54990

Plastic Figure & Playset Collector, bimonthly, $18 a year, Specialty Publishing Company, PO Box 1355, LaCrosse, WI 54602-1355

The Toy Farmer (Farm Toys only) $15 for 12 issues, RR 2 Box 5 - Sub. Dept., LaMoure, ND 58458

Arcade Toys by Al Aune, 1990, published by Robert F. Mannella, 4441 Shari Ann Lane, Brooklyn Park, MN 55443

The Barclay Catalog Book - Early Barclay catalogs, drawings, photos, etc. $16 from Richard O'Brien, 135 Stephensburg Rd., RD 2, Port Murray, NJ 07865

The Second Catalog Book - Reprints of catalogs by Manoil, Barclay, Warren, All-Nu, Authenticast, Beton, Grey Iron. $16 from Richard O'Brien, 135 Stephensburg Rd. RD 2, Port Murray, NJ 07865

The Story of American Toys by Richard O'Brien, 1990, Abbeville Press, $49.95

AUCTIONEERS

These are established firms experienced in disposing of large collections of toys by auction.

SOTHEBY'S
1334 York Avenue
New York, NY 10021
(212) 606-7000

PHILIPS NEW YORK
406 E. 79th St.
New York, NY 10021

CHRISTIE'S EAST
219 East 67th Street
New York, NY 10021
(212) 606-0400

MAPES AUCTIONEERS & APPRAISERS
1600 Vestal Parkway West
Vestal, NY 13850
(607) 754-9193

HAKE'S AMERICANA & COLLECTIBLES
Sample catalog $3.00
P.O. Box 1444N
York, Pennsylvania 17405
(717) 848-1333

LLOYD W. RALSTON
173 Post Road
Fairfield, Connecticut 06430
(203) 255-1233

CONTINENTAL AUCTIONS (Mail)
P.O. Box 193
Sheboygan, Wisconsin 53082

SMITH HOUSE (Mail)
P.O. Box 336
Eliot, Maine 09903
(207) 439-4614

RICHARD OPFER AUCTIONEERING, INC.
1919 Greenspring Drive
Timonium, MD 21093

REX & KATHY BARRETT (Mail)
P.O. Box 254
Medinah, Illinois 60157

NOEL BARRETT ANTIQUES & AUCTIONS
P.O. Box 1001-T
Carversville, PA 18913

TED MAURER
1003 Brookwood Dr.
Pottstown, Pennsylvania 19646
(215) 323-1573 or 367-5024

DEBBIE & MARTY KRIM'S NEW ENGLAND
AUCTION GALLERY (Mail)
Box 2273-T
West Peabody, MA 01960
(508) 535-3140

BUTTERFIELD & BUTTERFIELD
1244 Sutter Street
San Francisco, CA 94109
(415) 861-7500

MID-HUDSON AUCTION GALLERIES
One Idlewild Avenue
Croton-On-Hudson, NY 12520

JEFF BUB
1658 Barbara Drive
Brunswick, Ohio 44212
(216) 225-1110

SOME LEADING COLLECTORS AND DEALERS

(It is suggested that, when writing to any of the following, you enclose a stamped, self-addressed envelope.)

JIM HARMON
Radio premiums and tapes, comic books and strips
634 S. Orchard Dr.
Burbank, CA 91506

BARBARA & JONATHAN NEWMAN
Paper toys, old and new
The Paper Soldier
8 McIntosh Lane
Clifton Park, NY 12065

CHARLES W. BEST
Old toy pistols, etc.
6288 South Pontiac
Englewood, CO

BIZARRE BAZAAR
Quality collectible toys
Place des Antiquaires
125 East 57th Street
New York, NY 10022
(212) 688-1830

JOHN MURRAY
Fisher-Price
Box 29
Eden, NY 14057

HANK ANTON
Toy Soldier Information System Service (free)
92 Swain Avenue
Meriden, CT 06450
(203) 237-5356

JOE WALLIS
Britains Soldiers
P.O. Box 2294
Washington, DC 20013

ED HYERS
Dealer in Antique toys
P.O. Box 18448
Asheville, NC 28814

EDWARD K. POOLE
Toy soldiers, 1/36 scale ID vehicles and
old wooden military vehicle kits
926 Terrace Mt. Drive
Austin, TX 78746

DON PIELIN
Toy Soldiers
1009 Kenilworth
Wheeling, IL 60090

PERRY R. EICHOR
Aircraft toys and literature
703 North Almond Dr.
Simpsonville, SC 29681

JOE & SHARON FREED
Vehicles
6209 Sandy Forks Rd.
Raleigh, NC 27609

JAMES S. MAXWELL - VIRGINIA CAPUTO
Old toys, all types, buy and sell
Box 367
Lampeter, PA 17537

SECOND CHILDHOOD
Antique Toys
283 Bleecker Street
New York, NY

THE SOLDIER SHOP
Britains, other Soldiers
1222 Madison Avenue
New York, NY 10128
(212) 535-6788

GARY J. LINDEN
Marx and other plastic toys
P.O. Box 5243
River Forest, IL 60305

MEMORABLE THINGS
American and foreign toy soldiers,
vehicles, etc.
P.O. Box 10505
Towson, MD 21204
(Shop address: 31 W. Allegheny Ave., Towson MD, 2nd
floor)

BILL BERTOIA
Mechanical banks, antique toys
2413 Madison Avenue
Vineland, NJ 08360
(609) 692-4092

RICHARD MacNARY
Marx Trains, Coca-Cola vehicles,
wood, cardboard, paper toys,
soldiers
4727 Alpine Drive
Lilburn GA 30247

ECCLES BROTHERS
Toy Soldiers, Comic Figures and
vehicles from original molds
Catalog $3.00
R.R. 1, Box 253-D
Burlington, IA 52601

BILL LANGO
Barclay vehicles, animals and soldiers
from original and new molds - Send
for flyer
127 74th Street
North Bergen, NJ 07047

K. WARREN MITCHELL
Soldiers of all types, Regular lists at
no charge
1008 Forward Pass
Pataskala, OH 43062

STEVE BALKIN
Toy Soldiers including Warren
BURLINGTON ANTIQUE TOYS
1082 Madison Avenue
New York, NY 10028

STEVE LEONARD
Antique Mechanical Toys, etc.
Box 127T
Albertson, L.I., NY 11507
(516) 742-0979

HERMAN & FLORENCE LOTSTEIN
Trains, toys and books on toys
Cook's Antique Flea Market
Rt. 29,
Lambertville, NJ

BLOSSOM ABELL
Schoenhut toys, including repairs
420 LaFox River Drive
Algonquin, IL 60102

BOB LOWE'S TOONERVILLE JUNCTION
Classic American and European Toys
7 E. Church Street
Bethlehem, PA 18018
(215) 691-6736

LONDON BRIDGE COLLECTOR'S TOYS
Britains Soldiers, etc. and Britains replacement parts
East Penn Plaza, 1325 Chestnut Street
Emmaus, PA 18049
(215) 967-6887

RON SMITH
Tin plate cars & planes, plastic promotional cars
33005 Arlesford
Solon, OH 44139

BUDDY K TOYS
Buddy L Toys, etc.
RD 9 Box 322, Bingen Road
Bethlehem, PA 18015

MARBLE COLLECTORS SOCIETY OF AMERICA
P.O. Box 222
Trumble, CT 06611

EXCALIBUR HOBBIES LTD.
Toy Soldiers, all types
63 Exchange Street
Malden, MA 02148-5523
(617) 322-2959

BRAD KREWSON
Beany & Cecil toys
588 Lindford Drive
Bay Village, OH 44140

DON HULTZMAN
Tin wind-up and battery-operated, also repairs,
restorations
5026 Sleepy Hollow Road
Medina, OH 44256
(Front and back cover toys: Mickey on Pluto & Popeye)

SCOTT SMILES
Tin wind-ups, etc.
848 S. Atlantic Dr., E.
Lantana, FL 33462

CONTINENTAL HOBBY HOUSE
Toys and Trains, Regular catalogs
P.O. Box 193
Sheboygan, WI 53082

FRED THOMPSON
New designs of Smitty vehicles
Smith-Miller Inc.
P.O. Box 139
Canoga Park, CA 91305

REX MILLER
Premiums
Route 1, Box 457-D
East Prairie, MO 63845

JOHN D. (JACK) MATTHEWS
World War II toys, etc.
1255 23rd Street NW
Washington, DC 20037

DUTKINS' COLLECTABLES
Tin Toys, soldiers, etc.
1019 W. Route 70
Cherry Hill, NJ 08002
(609) 428-9559

DANNY FUCHS
Superman toys, games, etc.
209-80 18th Avenue
Bayside, NY 11360

DAVID M. LEOPARD
Old toy cars and trucks
2507 Feather Run Trail
West Columbia, SC 29169-4915

DARROW'S FUN ANTIQUES
Old toys of all types
309 E. 61st Street
New York, NY 10021
(212) 838-0730

FRED MAXWELL - COLLECTOR-RESEARCHER
Slush mold cars, planes, novelties, literature, toys
4722 No. 33 Street
Arlington, VA 22207

CHARLES FRANCIS WILDING
Secretary, Capitol Miniature Auto Collectors Club
10207 Greenacres Dr.
Silver Springs, MD 20903

FERDINAND ZEGEL
Antique toys, postwar, Corgi, Dinky
P.O. Box 589
Ft. Belvoir, VA 22060

FRED & MARGARET WILHELM
Disney, Popeye, Comic, Barclay, Manoil soldiers
W & F Collectibles
Box 2054
Leucadia, CA 92024

BARRY GOODMAN
G.I. Joes, Barbies, Robots, all 1950s-60s character toys
P.O. Box 218
Woodbury, NY 11797
(516) 338-2701 FAX: (516) 681-3612

CLASSIC TOYS
New and old toys; military, vehicles, zoo, etc.
69 Thompson St.
New York, NY 10012

PHIL SAVINO
Mail Auctions in various toy categories - send SSAE
Rt. 2, Box 76
Micanopy, FL 32667

TONY AND JACKI GRECCO
Toy soldiers and related items
P.O. Box 3490
Poughkeepsie, NY 12603
(914) 462-8829

JIM MAIN
Action Figures/toys, old and new
P.O. Box 623
New Milford, CT 06776

DAVID WELCH
Pez, Cereal Boxes, Model Kits, TV, Disney, Premiums
P.O. Box 714, 2308 Clay Street
Murphysboro, IL 62966
(618) 687-2282

CALVIN L. CHAUSSEE
Antique Toy Buyer - Any Quantity
1530 Kenland Court
Colorado Springs, CO 80915
(719) 597-4000

THOMAS G. NEFOS
FEDERAL SHIPPING NETWORK
Investment quality transportation toys
P.O. Box 707
Brigantine, NJ 08203-0707

JIM & PATSY CARLSON
Schoenhut Collectors
7939 Caberfae Trail
Clarkston, MI 48348

LARRY BRUCH
Old Toys Wanted & For Sale
P.O. Box 25
Mountaintop, PA 18707
(717) 678-7395

CARL LOBEL
Toys of all eras
Box 74A
Warren, VT 05674
(802) 496-4025

RAY FUNK
Toys, Bicycles
P.O. Box 5019
Upland, CA 91785

CHARLIE BRESLOW
Toys of all Types
971 Canton Drive
Toms River, NJ 08753
(908) 286-7618

NEW ERA TOYS
Restorations Service for
pressed steel toys, pedal cars
P.O. Box 10
Lambertville, NJ 08530
(609) 397-2113

MARK SUOZZI
Antique Penny Banks & Toys
Box 102
Ashfield, MA 01330
(413) 628-3241

RONALD L. SIMKOFF
Holgate Toys
5171 Mayfield Rd.
Lyndhurst, OH 44124
(216) 461-2660

BILL HELLIE
ALL AMERICAN TOY COMPANY
American Toy Company parts and
limited editions; buy, sell, restore antique toys
P.O. Box 4266
Salem, OR 97302

A. (GUS) HANSEN
Mignot, Dimestore, Britains, etc.
4645 Lilac Avenue
Glenview, IL 60025

James Schleyer
Toy Guns
Box 243-C
Burke, VA 22015

COLLECTING TOY TRAINS
Identification and Value Guide

by Richard O'Brien

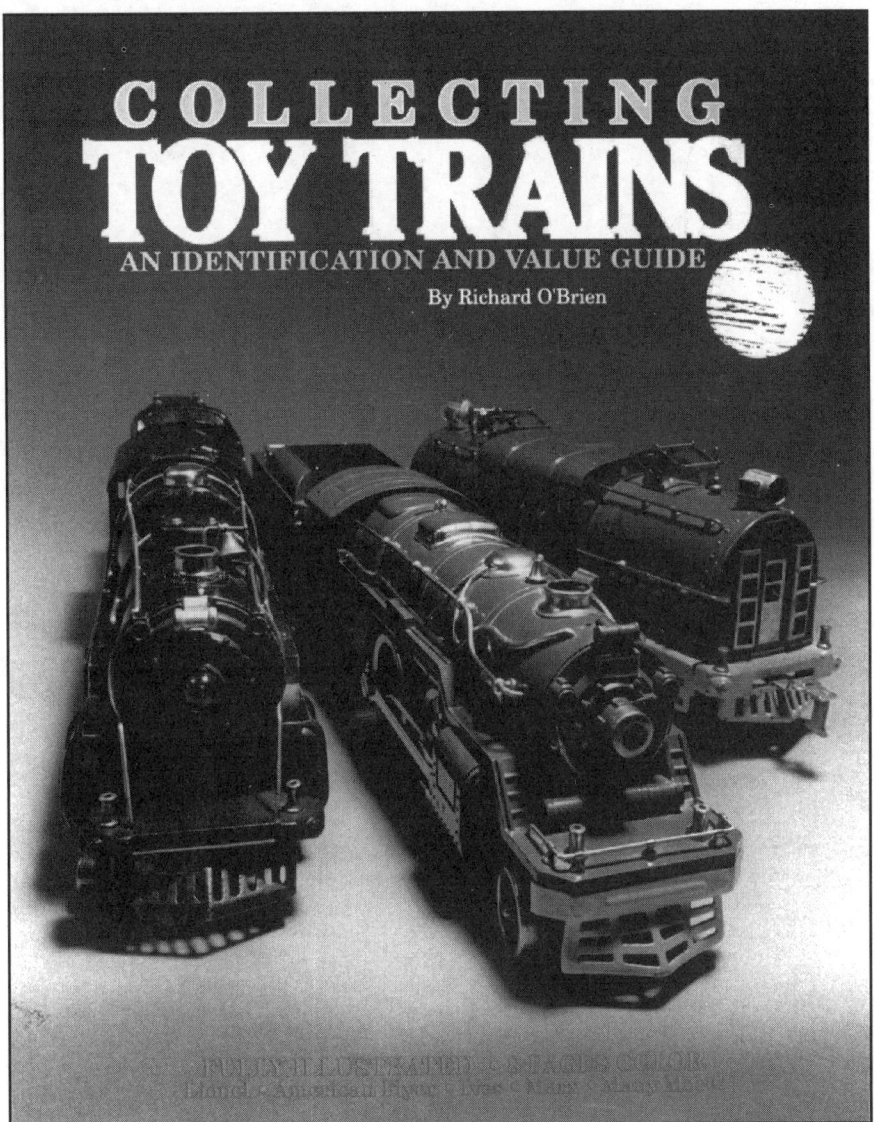

$22.95

This 3rd edition has added hundreds of new photos and listings.
LIONEL, MARX, AMERICAN FLYER, IVES, BUDDY L, plus others.
This guide includes engines, cars and accessories with descriptions, prices and photos.
Richard O'Brien (Collecting Toys No. 6) has had the aid of the top train collectors
from across the country.
Now in large format (8½" x 11"), 352 pages, 8 in color, softcover.

ISBN 0-89689-084-8

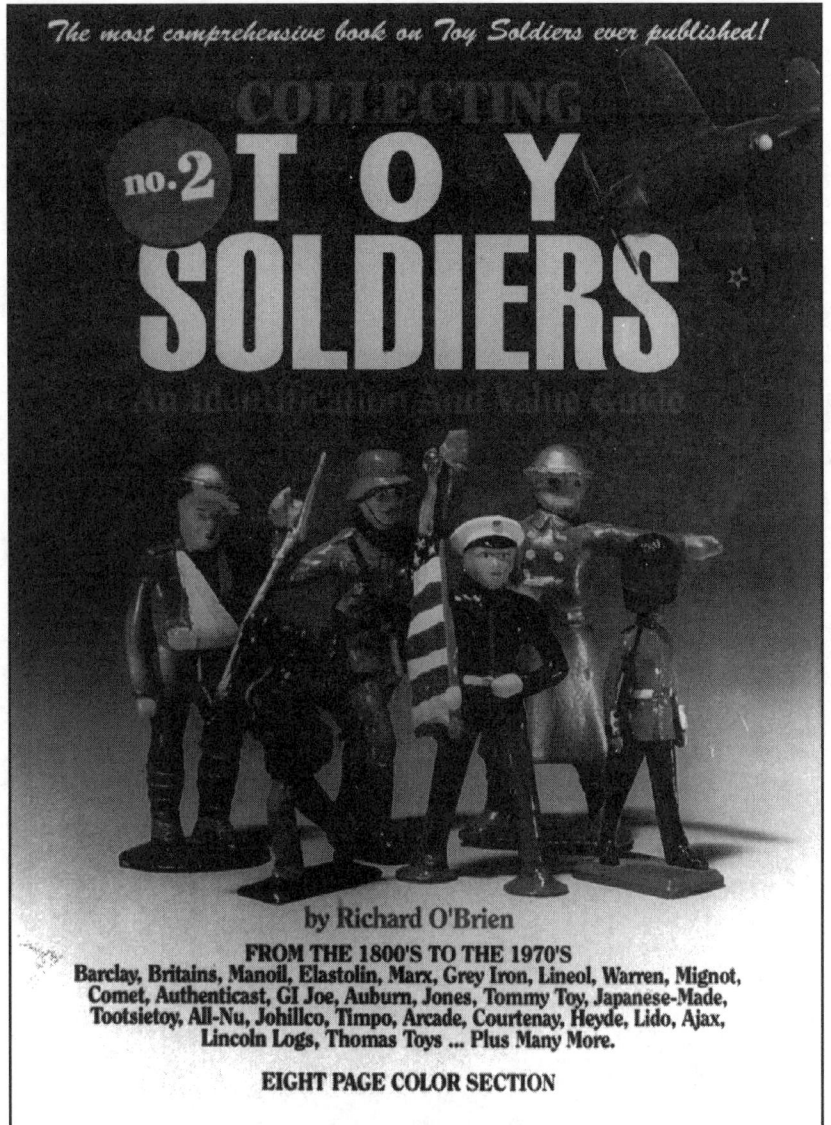